OFFICIAL BASEBALL GUIDE for 1977

•

PUBLISHER
C. C. JOHNSON SPINK

EDITORS
JOE MARCIN
CHRIS ROEWE
LARRY WIGGE
LARRY VICKREY

•

PUBLISHED BY
The Sporting News
1212 North Lindbergh Boulevard
St. Louis, Missouri 63166

Copyright © 1977
The Sporting News Publishing Company
a Times Mirror company

ISBN 0-89204-019-X

Directory of Organized Baseball

MAJOR LEAGUES

COMMISSIONER—Bowie K. Kuhn

SECRETARY-TREASURER—Alexander H. Hadden

HEADQUARTERS—75 Rockefeller Plaza
New York, N. Y. 10019

Telephone—586-7400 (area code 212)

Teletype—710-581-4279

EXECUTIVE COUNCIL—Bowie K. Kuhn, Commissioner; Leland S. MacPhail, Jr., President of American League; Charles S. Feeney, President of National League; John E. Fetzer and Edmund D. Fitzgerald, representatives of American League, and Walter F. O'Malley and John J. McHale, representatives of National League.

ADMINISTRATIVE OFFICER—John Johnson

SPECIAL ASSISTANT TO THE COMMISSIONER—Joseph L. Reichler

DIRECTOR OF INFORMATION—Robert A. Wirz

DIRECTOR OF BROADCASTING—David L. Meister

CONTROLLER—Donald C. Marr, Jr.

CO-ORDINATOR OF INTER-AMERICAN BASEBALL—Roberto Maduro

DIRECTOR OF SECURITY—Henry A. Fitzgibbon

NATIONAL ASSOCIATION REPRESENTATIVES—Robert R. Bragan, President of the National Association, and members of National Association Executive Committee.

NATIONAL ASSOCIATION
OF PROFESSIONAL BASEBALL LEAGUES

PRESIDENT-TREASURER—Robert R. Bragan

VICE-PRESIDENT—P. Patrick McKernan

ASSISTANT TO PRESIDENT—John P. Dittrich

ADMINISTRATOR OF ASSOCIATION TRANSACTIONS—Don Avery

SECRETARY TO PRESIDENT—Celia Perez

FIELD REPRESENTATIVES—Robert L. Freitas, Jim Mills

HEADQUARTERS—225 Fourth Street South, P. O. Box A
St. Petersburg, Fla. 33731

Telephone—813-822-6937

Teletype—810-863-0361

EXECUTIVE COMMITTEE—P. Patrick McKernan, Chairman, President of the Eastern League, Roy Jackson, President of the International and Pacific Coast Leagues, John H. Moss, President of the Western Carolinas League.

TABLE OF CONTENTS

For Complete Index See Pages 559 & 560

ON THE COVER: Top left, Randy Jones, San Diego—THE SPORTING NEWS N.L. Pitcher of the Year, 1976; top right, Jim Palmer, Baltimore—THE SPORTING NEWS A.L. Pitcher of the Year, 1976; bottom left, George Foster, Cincinnati—THE SPORTING NEWS N.L. Player of the Year, 1976; bottom right, Thurman Munson, New York—THE SPORTING NEWS A.L. Player of the Year, 1976.

CHARLES S. FEENEY
President of the National League

NATIONAL LEAGUE

Including

Club Directories

Club Reviews of 1976 Season

Club Day-By-Day Scores

N. L. Team Pictures

1976 League Leaders

1976 Official N. L. Averages

All-Time N. L. Player Performance Tables

National League

Organized 1876

CHARLES S. FEENEY
President

WARREN C. GILES
President Emeritus

JOHN J. McHALE
Vice-President

FRED G. FLEIG
Secretary-Treasurer

BLAKE CULLEN
Director of Public Relations

LOUIS H. KREMS
Business Manager

Headquarters—1 Rockefeller Plaza, New York, N. Y. 10019

Telephone—582-4213 (area code 212)

UMPIRES—Nick Colosi, Jerry Crawford, Jerry Dale, David Davidson, Robert Engel, Bruce Froemming, H. Douglas Harvey, John Kibler, John McSherry, Ed Montague, Andy Olsen, Paul Pryor, Frank Pulli, Jim Quick, Laurence (Dutch) Rennert, Paul Runge, Dick Stello, Ed Sudol, Terry Tata, Ed Vargo, Harry Wendelstedt, Lee Weyer, Art Williams, William G. Williams.

OFFICIAL STATISTICIANS—Elias Sports Bureau, Inc., 500 5th Ave., Suite 2114, New York, N. Y. 10036. Telephone (212) 869-1530.

Players cannot be transferred from one major league club to another after June 15 to the close of the championship season except through regular waiver channels.

WAIVER PRICE, $20,000. Interleague waivers, $20,000, except for selected players and draft-excluded players.

ATLANTA BRAVES

Chairman of the Board—William C. Bartholomay

President—R. E. (Ted) Turner III
Director of Player Personnel—Bill Lucas
Vice-President, Player Development—Hank Aaron
Secretary—Phyllis Collins
Minor League Administrator—Paul Snyder
Manager of Broadcast Sales—Wayne Long
Director of Broadcasting—Ernie Johnson
Controller—Charles Sanders
Chief Accountant—Michael Warren
Ticket Distribution Manager—Lamar Vernon
Director of Public Relations, Promotions and Ticket Sales—
Bob Hope
Publicity Manager—Randy Donaldson
Ticket Sales Manager—Kris Krebs
Group Sales Manager—John Marshall
Director of Stadium Operations—Joe Shirley
Manager—Dave Bristol
Club Physician—Dr. David T. Watson
Executive Offices—P. O. Box 4064, Atlanta, Ga. 30302
Telephone—522-7630 (area code 404)

SCOUTS—Sam Berry, Ted Cabrall, Pedro Gonzales, Phil Holmes, Burney R. (Dickey) Martin, Tom Morgan, Pat Nugent, Bob Turzilli, William R. Wight, H. F. (Red) Wooten, Wesley Westrum.

PARK LOCATION—Atlanta-Fulton County Stadium, on Capitol Avenue at the junction of Interstate Highways 20, 75 and 85.

Seating capacity—51,556

FIELD DIMENSIONS—Home plate to left field at foul line, 330 feet; to center field, 402 feet; to right field at foul line, 330 feet.

CHICAGO CUBS

President—Philip K. Wrigley

Executive Vice President & Treasurer—Wm. J. Hagenah, Jr.
Vice President-Baseball Operations—Robert D. Kennedy
Honorary Vice President—Charles Grimm
Secretary & Director of Park Operations—E. R. Saltwell
Assistant Director of Park Operations—Chas. S. Feeney, Jr.
Chief Accounting Officer—Joseph Kirchen
Director of Player Development—John Cox
Director of Scouting—Vedie Himsl
Traveling Secretary—Dennis Beyreuther
Assistant Traveling Secretary—G. A. Settergren
Home Secretary—Howard Roberts
Manager of Information & Services—Buck Peden
Statistician—Jim Davidovich
Director of Group Sales—Ernie Banks
Director of Group Services—Dave Lamont
Director of Ticket Services—Jerome Foran
Grounds Superintendent—Roy Bogren
Manager—Herman Franks
Club Physician—Dr. Jacob Suker
Executive Offices—Wrigley Field, N. Clark and Addison Streets,
Chicago, Ill. 60613
Telephone—281-5050 (area code 312)

SCOUTS—Jack Bloomfield, William Capps, Frank DeMoss, Walt Dixon, Ruben Gomez, Eugene Handley, Herman Hannah, Bob Hartsfield, John Hennessy, Roy Johnson, Robert D. Kennedy, Jr., Eddie Lyons, Joe Mathes, John (Buck) O'Neil, Evo Pusich, Harrison Wickel, H. D. (Rube) Wilson, Pedrin Zorilla.

PARK LOCATION—Wrigley Field, Addison Street, N. Clark Street, Waveland Avenue and Sheffield Avenue.

Seating capacity—37,741

FIELD DIMENSIONS—Home plate to left field at foul line, 355 feet; to center field, 400 feet; to right field at foul line, 353 feet.

CINCINNATI REDS

Chairman of the Board—Louis Nippert
President & Chief Executive Officer—Robert L. Howsam
Executive Vice-President & General Manager—Richard Wagner
Vice-President—William J. Williams
Treasurer—James R. Williams
Secretary—Andrew Hopple
Assistant Secretary—Henry Hobson, Jr.
Director of Player Personnel—Sheldon Bender
Business Manager—Dale Stoeber
Director of Publicity—Jim Ferguson
Director of Promotion and Sales—Roger Ruhl
Special Assignment Scout—Ray Shore
Director of Scouting—Joe Bowen
Controller—D. L. Porco
Traveling Secretary—Paul Campbell
Director of Stadium Operations—Tom Jackson
Director of Publications—Bob Rathgeber
Director of Speakers' Bureau—Gordy Coleman
Director of Broadcasting—Jim Winters
Director of Ticket Department—Craig Dissinger
Director of Group Sales—Dan Hunter
Director of Season Tickets—Ann Mansfield
Director of Advertising—Fred Khammar, Jr.
Manager—George (Sparky) Anderson
Club Physician—Dr. George Ballou
Executive Offices—100 Riverfront Stadium, Cincinnati, O. 45202
Telephone—421-4510 (area code 513)

SCOUTS—Larry Barton, Sr., Larry Barton, Jr., Gene Bennett, Porter Blinn, Joe Campise, Joseph Caputo, Bill Clark, Larry D'Amato, Reno De-Benedetti, Larry Doughty, Elmer Gray, Edwin Howsam, Chester Montgomery, Tony Robello, Neil Summers, Fred Uhlman, George Zuraw.

PARK LOCATION—Riverfront Stadium, downtown Cincinnati, bounded by Second Street to Ohio River and from Walnut Street to Broadway.

Seating capacity—51,963

FIELD DIMENSIONS—Home plate to left field at foul line, 330 feet; to center field, 404 feet; to right field at foul line, 330 feet.

HOUSTON ASTROS

ASTRODOMAIN CORPORATION

Directors—George V. Brown III, Warren A. Genee, Martin J. Kelly,
T. H. Neyland, Gary Wendt
President—T. H. Neyland
Executive Vice-President & Chief Operating Officer—
Martin J. Kelly
Financial Vice-President & Treasurer—David L. Murphy

HOUSTON SPORTS ASSOCIATION, INC.

President & General Manager—Talbot M. Smith
Vice-President, Marketing, Sales, Broadcasting—Dean Borba
Vice-President—Earl Allen
Assistant to the General Manager—John W. Mullen
Director of Minor League Clubs & Scouting—Lynwood Stallings
Assistant Director of Minor League Clubs & Scouting—
William J. Wood
Coordinator of Minor League Instruction—Cliff Davis
Traveling Secretary—Arthur V. Perkins
Director of Public Relations and Publicity—Donald Davidson
Assistant to the Director of Public Relations—Paul Darst
Director of Promotions—James C. "Slick" Johnson
Comptroller—Adam Richards
Director of Broadcasting—Art Elliott
Director of Broadcast Sales—Hugh Pickett
Ticket Manager—Ralph Stolarski
Director of Season and Group Sales—M. M. "Buddy" Hancken
Manager—Bill Virdon
Club Physicians—Drs. Harold J. Brelsford, Hatch Cummings

ASTRODOME-ASTROHALL STADIUM CORPORATION

Executive Vice-President—Jimmie D. Fore
Director, Event Coordination—Gerard J. Tollett
Vice-President Stadium Operations—Tom Martin
Stadium Engineering and Maintenance—James R. Garner
Director of Customer Service and Security—Don Collins
Executive Offices—Astrodome, P. O. Box 288
Houston, Tex. 77001
Telephone—748-4500 (area code 713)
Teletype—910 881-1740

SCOUTS—Jim Beauchamp, Harry Craft, Paul Florence, Stan Holl-
mig, Walt Matthews, Tony Pacheco, Earl Rapp, Billy Smith.

PARK LOCATION—Astrodome, Kirby and Interstate Loop 610

Seating capacity—45,000

FIELD DIMENSIONS—Home plate to left field at foul line, 340 feet; to
center field, 406 feet; to right field at foul line, 340 feet.

LOS ANGELES DODGERS

BOARD OF DIRECTORS

Walter F. O'Malley Chairman of the Board; Peter O'Malley, President; Harry M. Bardt, Treasurer; Roland Seidler, Jr., Secretary; Sylvan Oestreicher, Robert L. Gordon.

H. C. McClellan—Director Emeritus

President—Peter O'Malley

Vice-President, Player Personnel—Al Campanis

Vice-President, Minor League Operations—William P. Schweppe

Vice-President, Marketing—Merritt Willey

Vice-President, Public Relations and Promotions—Fred Claire

Special Consultant—Walter Alston

Controller and Assistant Treasurer—Ken Hasemann

Assistant Secretary—Irene Tanji

Director, Advertising, Novelties and Souvenirs—Danny Goodman

Director, Dodgertown—Charles Blaney

Director, Stadium Operations—Bob Smith

Director, Ticket Operations—Walter Nash

Director, Stadium Club and Transportation—Bob Schenz

Director, Dodger Network—David Van de Walker

Director, Scouting—Ben Wade

Director, Publicity—Steve Brener

Director, Community Relations—Don Newcombe

Director, Group Sales—Barry Stockhamer

Director, Speakers' Bureau—Bill Shumard

Executive Pilot, Dodger 720-B Fan Jet—Captain Lewis G. Carlisle

Administrative Assistant—Ike Ikuhara

Traveling Secretary—Lee Scott

Auditor—Michael Strange

Manager—Tom Lasorda

Club Physicians—Dr. Frank Jobe, Dr. Robert Woods

Executive Offices—Dodger Stadium, 1000 Elysian Park Avenue, Los Angeles, Calif. 90012.

Telephone—224-1500 (area code 213)

SCOUTS—Rafael Avila, Boyd Bartley, Bill Brenzel, Jim Garland, Dick Hager, Dennis Haren, Gail Henley, Goldie Holt, Tony John, Dale Jones, John Keenan, Marty Keough, Ron King, Ed Liberatore, Dick McLaughlin, Dale McReynolds, Tommy Mixon, Lew Morton, Greg Mulleavy, John O'Neil, Regie Otero, Bill Pleis, Ed Roebuck, Rudy Rufer, Jerry Stephenson, Corito Varona, Guy Wellman, Bert Wells.

PARK LOCATION—Dodger Stadium, 1000 Elysian Park Avenue.

Seating capacity—56,000

FIELD DIMENSIONS—Home plate to left field at foul line, 330 feet; to center field, 395 feet; to right field at foul line, 330 feet.

MONTREAL EXPOS

Board of Directors—Charles R. Bronfman, Lorne C. Webster, John J. McHale, Sydney Maislin, Paul Beaudry, Hugh Hallward, Charlemagne Beaudry, E. Leo Kolber, Melvin W. Griffin, Louis R. Desmarais

Chairman of the Board—Charles R. Bronfman

President and Chief Executive Officer—John J. McHale

Vice-President & Secretary-Treasurer—Harry Renaud

Honorary Treasurer—Arnold Ludwick

Vice-President, Baseball-General Manager—Charles Fox

Executive Assistant—Kevin McHale

Vice-President, Player Development—James Fanning

Director of Scouting—Danny Menendez

Co-ordinator of Canadian Scouting—Bill MacKenzie

Scouting Assistant—Dick Rock

Director of Public Relations—Larry Chiasson

Traveling Secretary—Rodger Brulotte

Controller—Gerry Trudeau

Director of Sales—Robert Armand

Manager, Group Sales & Speakers' Bureau—Roger Savard

Manager, Tickets—Lucien Geoffrion

Manager, Game Services—Ronald Piche

Public Relations Assistants—Monique Giroux, Richard Griffin

Manager—Dick Williams

Club Physician—Dr. Robert Brodrick

Mailing Address—P. O. Box 500, Station R, Montreal,

Quebec H1V 3P2 Canada

Telephone—253-3434 (area code 514)

SCOUTS (special assignment)—Ed Lopat, Carroll (Whitey) Lockman; (regular)—Bill Adair, Terry Boyle, Harry Bright, Bob Guess, Al Harper, Mercer Harris, John (Red) Murff, Herb Newberry, Bob Oldis, Jack Paepke, Harry Postove; (Canadian)—Wayne Norton, Andre Pratte.

PARK LOCATION—Olympic Stadium, Montreal, Quebec H2R 2W1 Canada.

Seating capacity—60,000

FIELD DIMENSIONS—Home plate to left field at foul line, 330 feet; to center field, 400 feet; to right field at foul line, 330.

NEW YORK METS

Chairman of the Board—M. Donald Grant

President—Mrs. Vincent de Roulet
Executive Vice-President-Treasurer—G. Herbert Walker, Jr.
Vice-President-Business Manager—James K. Thomson
Secretary—John W. Payson
Assistant Secretary—Robert M. Riggs
Assistant Secretary and Assistant Treasurer—Francis M. Ellis
Directors—Mrs. Vincent de Roulet, M. Donald Grant, G. Herbert
Walker, Jr., John W. Payson, Frederick K. Trask, James K. Thomson,
Joseph A. McDonald.

General Manager—Joseph A. McDonald
Director of Minor League Operations—Pete Gebrian
Director of Player Development—Nelson Burbrink
Special Consultant—Robert B. Scheffing
Controller—William Murray
Ticket Manager—Bob Mandt
Director of Public Relations—Arthur Richman
Promotion Director—Lauren Matthews
Traveling Secretary—Lou Niss
Manager—Joe Frazier
Club Physician—Dr. James C. Parkes II
Executive Offices—William A. Shea Stadium, Roosevelt
Avenue and 126th Street, Flushing, N. Y. 11368
Telephone—672-2000 (area code 212)

SCOUTS—Bob Bishop, Wayne Britton, Ed Charles, Jocko Collins,
Nino Escalera, Jim Hughes, Roger Jongewaard, Hank Kelly, Buddy Kerr,
Buddy Lewis, Dave Madison, Hershel Martin, Walter Millies, Harry
Minor, Julian Morgan, Roy Partee, Warren (Sheriff) Robinson, Marvin
Scott, Paul Tretiak, Ollie Vanek, Len Zanke.

PARK LOCATION—William A. Shea Stadium, Roosevelt Avenue and
126th Street, Flushing, N. Y. 11368.

Ticket Information—672-3000 (area code 212)

Seating capacity—55,300

FIELD DIMENSIONS—Home plate to left field at foul line, 341 feet; to
center field, 410 feet; to right field at foul line, 341 feet.

PHILADELPHIA PHILLIES

Chairman of Board—R. R. M. (Bob) Carpenter, Jr.
President—R. R. M. (Ruly) Carpenter III
Executive Vice-President—William Y. Giles
Vice-President-Director of Player Personnel—Paul Owens
Vice-President-Director of Finance— George F. H. Harrison
Secretary-Treasurer—G. Theodore Harrison
Director of Minor Leagues and Scouting— G. Dallas Green
Administrative Assistant—Keith Carpenter
Director of Sales—David P. Montgomery
Director of Publicity and Public Relations—Larry Shenk
Ticket Manager—Raymond B. Krise
Director of Advertising—Thomas T. Hudson
Director of Promotions—Frank H. Sullivan
Director of Stadium Operations—Patrick J. Cassidy
Traveling Secretary—Eddie Ferenz
Director of Group Sales—Richard Deats
Director of Season Ticket Sales—Ray Krise, Jr.
Assistant Director of Minor Leagues— Howie Bedell
Administrator, Scouting—Jack Pastore
Executive Secretary, Minor Leagues— William V. Gargano
Assistant Director of Stadium Operations —Andrew J. Clarke
Assistant Director of Publicity and Public Relations—
Chris Wheeler
Public Relations Assistant-Director of Radio Network—
Dennis Lehman

National Scouting Supervisor—Brandy Davis
Manager—Danny Ozark
Club Physician—Dr. Phillip Marone
Executive Offices—Philadelphia Veterans Stadium, Broad
Street and Pattison Avenue, Philadelphia, Pa. 19148
Telephone—463-6000 (area code 215)

Scouts—Herb Anderson, Hugh Alexander, Ruben Amaro, Edward Bockman, George Bradley, Brandy Davis, Paul Duval, Doug Gassaway, Gordon Goldsberry, Fred Goodman, Carl Greene, Bill Harper, Wilbur Johnson, John Jorgensen, Lou Kahn, Bill Kelso, Wes Livengood, Anthony Lucadello, Larry Maxie, Gary Nickels, Tom Oliver, Scott Reid, Joe Reilly, Ernie Schuerman, A. C. Swails, Dick Teed, Elmer Valo, Carlton Willey, Don Williams.

PARK LOCATION—Philadelphia Veterans Stadium, Broad Street and Pattison Avenue.

Seating capacity—58,651

FIELD DIMENSIONS—Home plate to left field at foul line, 330 feet; to center field, 408 feet; to right field at foul line, 330 feet.

PITTSBURGH PIRATES

President—Daniel M. Galbreath
Chairman of the Board—John W. Galbreath
Vice-President and Secretary—Thomas P. Johnson
Vice-President—Harry L. "Bing" Crosby
Vice-President-Business Administration, Treasurer—
Joseph M. O'Toole
Vice-President-Player Personnel—Harding Peterson
Assistant to the Vice-Presidents—Milt Graff
Director of Publicity and Public Relations—
William J. Guilfoile
Assistant Director of Publicity and Public Relations—
Joseph Safety
Director of Minor League Clubs and Scouting—Murray Cook
Assistant Director of Minor League Clubs and Scouting—
Branch B. Rickey III
Assistant Farm Director—William G. Turner
Assistant Director of Scouting—Jon Neiderer
Director of Marketing and Promotions—Edward A. Routzong
Director of Season and Group Sales—Jack H. Berger
Assistant Director of Season and Group Sales—Steve Greenberg
Director of Advertising Sales—Olin J. DePolo
Assistant Treasurer/Secretary and Controller—Douglas G. McCormick
Assistant Controller—Kenneth C. Curcio
Ticket Manager—Richard C. Holland
Manager—Chuck Tanner
Traveling Secretary—Charles Muse
Club Physician—Dr. Joseph Finegold
Executive Offices—Three Rivers Stadium, 600 Stadium Circle,
Pittsburgh, Pa. 15212
Telephone—323-1000 (area code 412)

Special Assignment Scouts—Gene Baker, Jim Maxwell, Joe L. Brown, George Detore, Jerry Gardner, Lenny Yochim, Howie Haak, Bill Lentini.

Scouting Assistants—Bud Baurle, Carman Beatrice, Calvin Biron, Willie Bojos, Paul Bordi, Bill Bryan, Joe Buccolo, Nash Carmichael, F. "Kid" Carr, Bill Cayavec, Frank Coimbre, Cecil Cole, Dick Coury, Pablo Cruz, Bill Darden, Bob Dawson, Pal Eldridge, Ed Farnum, Ben Fiore, Jim Frail, Pete Grasso, Fred Hannum, Jack Heimbucher, Herbert Hess, Merrill Hess, Leroy Hill, Bud Hoff, Myron Hunt, Bob Johnson, Joe Lacko, Julio Martinez, Luis Mayoral, Andy Moynihan, Tom Myers, Steve Oleschuk, Dutch Overton, Elmo Plaskett, Harold Ray, George Schmidt, Jesse Smith, Lloyd Sorrells, Cloy Sikes, Tom Urich, Tom Venditelli, Bill White.

PARK LOCATION—Three Rivers Stadium, 600 Stadium Circle.

Seating capacity—50,235

FIELD DIMENSIONS—Home plate to left field at foul line, 335 feet; to center field, 400 feet; to right field at foul line, 335 feet.

ST. LOUIS CARDINALS

Chairman of the Board, President and Chief Executive Officer–
August A. Busch, Jr.

Vice-President–August A. Busch, III
Vice-President–Fred L. Kuhlmann
Vice-President–Margaret M. Snyder
Secretary and Treasurer–John L. Hayward
Controller–Bob Dilliard
Assistant Secretary–Richard Schwartz
Assistant Treasurer–H. F. Suellentrop
Executive Vice-President & General Manager–V. P. (Bing) Devine
Executive Vice-President, Business Affairs–Joe McShane
Senior Vice-President–Stan Musial
Vice-President-Public Relations–Jim Toomey
Traveling Secretary–Lee Thomas
Director of Player Development & Scouting–Jim Bayens
Ticket Director–Mike Bertani
Director of Promotions–Ken Daust
Director of Sales–Joe Cunningham
Assistant Director of Public Relations–Marty Hendin
Manager–Vern Rapp
Club Physician–Dr. Stan London
Executive Offices–Busch Memorial Stadium, 250 Stadium
Plaza, St. Louis, Mo. 63102
Telephone–421-3060 (area code 314)

SCOUTS–Dave Bartosch, James Belz, Red Brown, Bus Campbell, Eddie Collins, Walker Cress, Roberto Diaz, Tom DuFour, Angel Figueroa, Robert Folkins, Phil Gagliano, Denny Galehouse, Ray Goodman, Don Hennelly, Bob Holmes, Byron Humphrey, James Johnston, Earl Jones, Thornton Lee, Phil Mazzeo, Fred McAlister, Jr., Tom McCormick, Virgil Melvin, Carlos Negron, Jerry Oswald, Charles (Chase) Riddle, William Sayles, George Silvey, Danny Simons, John Tatum, Chuck Taylor, Charles (Tim) Thompson, Harry Walker.

PARK LOCATION–Busch Memorial Stadium, Broadway, Walnut Street, Stadium Plaza and Spruce Street.

Seating capacity–50,100

FIELD DIMENSIONS–Home plate to left field at foul line, 330 feet; to center field, 414 feet; to right field at foul line, 330 feet.

SAN DIEGO PADRES

BOARD OF DIRECTORS

Ray A. Kroc, Chairman and Treasurer; Joan Kroc, E. J. Bavasi, Donald G. Lubin, Dr. Robert K. Kerlan.

President—E. J. Bavasi
Vice-President and Secretary—Donald G. Lubin
Assistant Secretary—Robert N. Grant
Vice-President, Player Personnel—Bob Fontaine
Minor League Administrator—Mike Port
Administrative Assistant—Bob Bavasi
Director of Business Operations—Elten Schiller
Director of Public Relations—Mike Ryan
Director of Promotions—Jim Wiegel
Director of Group Sales—Tom Mulcahy
Director of Season Ticket Sales—Andy Strasberg
Controller—Jan Willis
Traveling Secretary and Trainer—John Mattei
Manager—John McNamara
Club Physician—Dr. Paul Bauer
Executive Offices—P. O. Box 2000, San Diego, Calif. 92120
Telephone—283-4494 (area code 714)

SCOUTS—Ken Bracey, Cliff Ditto, Bobby Fontaine, Warren Hacker, Andy Harred, Al Heist, Billy Herman, Mark Just, Don Lee, Gus Lombardo, Jim Marshall, Jim McLaughlin, Richard Schlenker.

PARK LOCATION—San Diego Stadium, 9449 Friars Road.
Seating capacity—48,460

FIELD DIMENSIONS—Home plate to left field at foul line, 330 feet; to center field, 410 feet; to right field at foul line, 330 feet.

SAN FRANCISCO GIANTS

Co-Chairmen—Bob Lurie, Bud Herseth
General Manager—H. B. "Spec" Richardson
Baseball Consultant—Jerry Donovan
Director of Scouting and Minor League Operations—
Jack Schwarz
Director of Player Development—Carl Hubbell
Traveling Secretary—Frank Bergonzi
Ticket Manager—Arthur Schulze
Director of Marketing—Pat Gallagher
Director of Publicity—Stu Smith
Assist. Director of Publicity—Ralph Nelson
Speakers Bureau—Joe Orengo
Controller—John Wagner
Director of Stadium Operations—Don Foreman
Stadium Club Manager—Morty Miller
Manager—Joe Altobelli
Executive Offices—Candlestick Park, San Francisco, Calif. 94124
Telephone—(415) 467-8000

SCOUTS—John D. (Dutch) Anderson, Morris A. (Dutch) Deutsch, Frank (Chick) Genovese, George M. Genovese, Joseph W. Henderson, Richard G. (Richie) Klaus, Jim Lyke, Horacio Martinez, Edward F. (Eddie) Montague, Hugh Poland, Jack Shafer, Hank Sauer (also batting instructor), Junior E. (Gene) Thompson, Richard (Dick) Wilson. Grady E. Hatton (major leagues).

PARK LOCATION—Candlestick Point, Bayshore Freeway.

Seating capacity—58,000

FIELD DIMENSIONS—Home plate to left field at foul line, 335 feet; to center field, 410 feet; to right field at foul line, 335 feet.

Cincinnati Reds' first baseman Tony Perez (with hat in hand) gets a roaring welcome as he is introduced during World Series victory celebration after team returned from New York. More than 35,000 people attended the welcome rally and parade.

WEST DIVISION
Reds Capture Second Straight Title
By EARL LAWSON

Not since the 1950s when the Dodgers won five pennants has any club dominated the National League the way the Cincinnati Reds of the 1970s have.

During the past seven years the Reds have won five division titles, four pennants and two World Championships.

The first of those two World Championships came in 1975 when the Reds beat the Boston Red Sox in a seven-game series that will be remembered as one of the most thrilling in the game's history.

And when the Reds beat the New York Yankees four straight games to win the 1976 Series they became the first National League club to win back-to-back World Championships since the Giants of 1921 and '22.

You get an idea of just how much talent the Reds of 1976 possessed when it's noted that five members of the club—catcher Johnny Bench, second baseman Joe Morgan, shortstop Dave Concepcion, third baseman Pete Rose and outfielder George Foster—were voted starting berths on the National League All-Star team by the nation's baseball fans.

Reds' manager Sparky Anderson added two more Red players—first baseman Tony Perez and right fielder Ken Griffey—when he completed the N. L. squad.

Foster was named the most valuable player in the All-Star game at Philadelphia. He hit a homer and drove in three runs.

A tip-off to just how talented the Reds have been is the fact that a member of the club has won the league's Most Valuable Player Award five of the past seven years.

Bench, an All-Star catcher and Gold Glove winner since his rookie season of 1968, won the MVP award in 1970.

And the Reds' catcher repeated in 1972. Rose was voted the award in 1973, the same year he captured his third National League batting title.

In 1975 the MVP award went to Morgan, who has been the game's No. 1 offensive player the past three years.

When Morgan repeated in 1976 as the league's MVP he became the second player in National League history to accomplish the feat. The first was Ernie Banks of the Chicago Cubs, who won the MVP award in 1958 and '59.

The loop's MVP award which went to Morgan was just one of many honors heaped upon members of a Reds' team rated the best in the club's history . . . a club which swept three straight games from the Philadelphia Phils in the playoffs to win the N. L. pennant and then went on to topple the Yankees four in a row.

Foster, who batted .306, led the Reds with 29 homers and the league with 121 RBIs, was voted The Sporting News' National League Player of the Year in a poll conducted among the loop's players.

And Rawly Eastwick, pitching only his second full season in the majors, was named The Sporting News' Fireman of the Year after compiling an 11-5 won-lost record, accompanied by a 2.08 earned-run average and 26 saves.

And, too, Bench, Concepcion, Morgan, and center fielder Cesar Geronimo

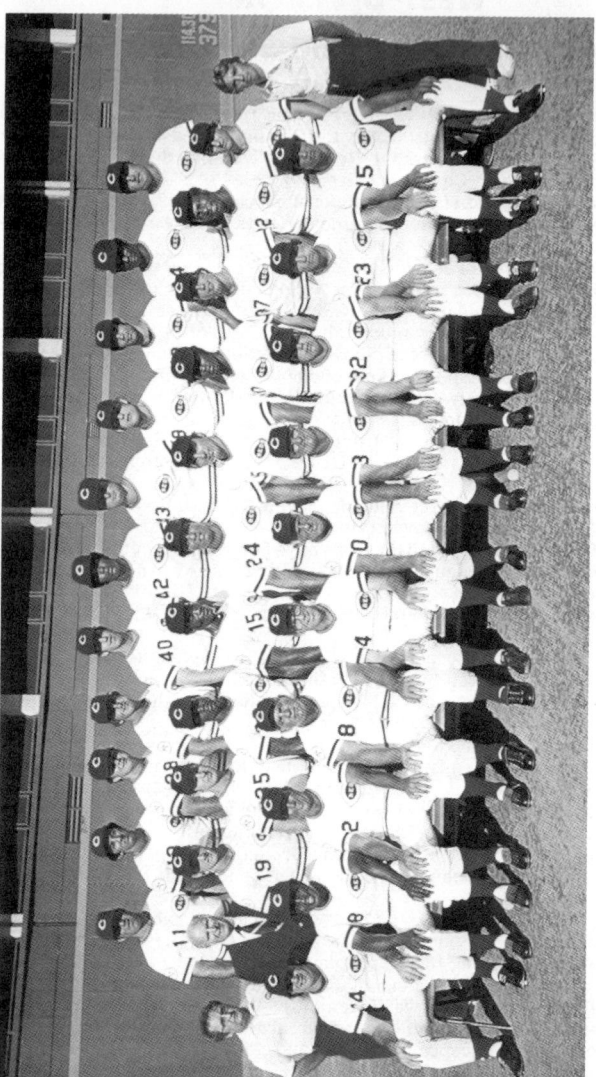

CINCINNATI REDS—1976

Front row—Rose, Morgan, Nixon, coach; Kluszewski, coach; Anderson, manager; Scherger, coach; Norman, Flynn, Sarmiento. Second row—B. Stowe, equipment manager; Campbell, traveling secretary; Youngblood, Gullett, Armbrister, Foster, Perez, Bench, Griffey, McEnaney, Driessen, M. Stowe, batboy; Starr, trainer. Third row—Bailey, Concepcion, Nolan, Plummer, Zachry, Alcala, Billingham, Eastwick, Geronimo, Borbon, Lum.

repeated as winners of Gold Gloves in recognition of their outstanding defensive play and selection to THE SPORTING NEWS All-Star fielding team.

Pat Zachry, a 6-5, 175-pound righthander from Waco, Tex., polled 11 of 24 votes to tie the San Diego Padres' ace relief pitcher Butch Metzger for rookie of the year honors after compiling a regular season 14-7 won and lost record with a 2.74 ERA.

The Reds, in making a runaway race of the West Division, finished the season with five regulars—Rose, Morgan, Foster, Geronimo and Ken Griffey—boasting .300-plus averages.

Griffey, playing only his second full season in the majors, wound up the year with a .336 batting mark, losing the league's batting title to the Chicago Cubs' Bill Madlock on the final day of the season.

As a team the Reds batted .280, the club's top mark in 46 years. And, in doing so, they amassed 857 runs, a club record.

The 210 bases the Reds stole in 1976 marked the club's top total since 1914.

There wasn't a 20-game winner on the Reds' pitching staff. But seven of the hurlers won 10 or more games, and that's a first for a National League club.

Gary Nolan, a 15-game winner, was tops on the staff. In notching those 15 victories, Nolan became the 13th pitcher in the club's history to reach 100 victories.

Rose, in scoring 130 runs and rapping out 42 doubles in 1976, became the first player in National League history to lead the loop in these two categories three straight years.

Pete's 215 hits, also tops in the league, boosted his lifetime total within 238 of the coveted 3,000-mark.

Eight times now Rose has collected 200 or more hits in a season, one short of a major league record held by the immortal Ty Cobb.

Perez added to the honors collected by Red players when he retained his title as the top run-producer among active players. The veteran Red first baseman topped the 90 mark in RBIs for the 10th straight year when he drove home three runs against the Atlanta Braves on the final day of the season.

For the Reds, 1976 was both an artistic and a tremendous financial success. While topping the 2,000,000 attendance mark for the fourth straight year, the 1976 edition of the Big Red Machine led the majors by luring 2,629,708 fans through the turnstiles.

SCORES OF CINCINNATI REDS' 1976 GAMES

APRIL			Winner	Loser	MAY			Winner	Loser
8—Houston	W	11-5	Nolan	Richard	1—Montreal	W	6-1	Gullett	Carrithers
10—Houston	W	13-7	Billingham	Dierker	2—Montreal	W	4-8z	Stanhouse	Darcy
11—Houston	W	9-3	Darcy	Niekro	4—At N. Y.	L	3-5	Seaver	Norman
13—At Atl.	W	6-1	Norman	Torrealba	5—At N. Y.	W	2-0‡	Eastwick	Hall
15—At Atl.	L	5-10	Niekro	Billingham	6—At N. Y.	L	2-4	Swan	Gullett
16—S. Fran.	L	7-14	Barr	Darcy	7—At Chi.	W	3-1	Billingham	Frailing
17—S. Fran.	W	11-0	Norman	Halicki	8—At Chi.	W	14-4	Alcala	R. Reuschel
18—S. Fran.	L	1-5	Montefusco	Nolan	9—At Chi.	W	14-2	Zachry	Burris
20—S. Diego	L	5-7	Metzger	McEnaney	11—Pitts.	W	6-0	Nolan	Kison
21—S. Diego	W	5-4	Norman	Wehrmeister	12—Pitts.	L	3-6	Rooker	Gullett
23—At Mon.	L	4-5	Stanhouse	Billingham	14—N. York	W	5-1	Billingham	Lolich
24—At Mon.	W	6-4‡	Eastwick	Carrithers	15—N. York	W	2-0	Alcala	Seaver
25—At Mon.	W	7-0	Gullett	Renko	16—N. York	L	5-7	Matlack	Nolan
26—At Phila.	L	9-10	McGraw	Eastwick	16—N. York	W	8-1	Gullett	Swan
27—At Phila.	W	7-3	Billingham	Underwood	17—At L. A.	W	5-3	Zachry	Sutton
28—At Phila.	L	6-7	Lonborg	Darcy	18—At L. A.	L	0-5	Rhoden	Billingham
30—Montreal	W	7-2	Nolan	Warthen	19—At S. F.	W	5-4	Alcala	Montefusco
		Won 10, Lost 7			20—At S. F.	L	5-6	Heaverlo	McEnaney

MAY

			Winner	Loser
21—At S. D.	L	2-4	Jones	Nolan
22—At S. D.	W	3-2	Zachry	Foster
23—At S. D.	W	11-0	Billingham	Strom
25—Atlanta	W	10-4	Alcala	Morton
26—Atlanta	L	3-4	Leon	Eastwick
28—Los Ang.	W	9-0	Zachry	Sutton
29—Los Ang.	W	6-5	Eastwick	Marshall
30—Los Ang.	L	5-6	Hough	Eastwick
30—Los Ang.	W	7-2	Alcala	Hooton
31—At Hous.	W	4-2	Darcy	Richard

Won 18, Lost 10

JUNE

1—At Hous.	L	1-2	Andujar	Zachry
2—At Hous.	W	8-7	McEnaney	Forsch
3—At Hous.	L	3-5	Dierker	Alcala
4—At St. L.	W	11-2	Nolan	McGlothen
5—At St. L.	W	5-1	Gullett	Denny
6—At St. L.	W	13-2	Zachry	Falcone
7—At Pitts.	L	4-5	Moose	McEnaney
8—At Pitts.	W	10-5	Alcala	Rooker
9—At Pitts.	W	6-1	Nolan	Reuss
10—At Pitts.	W	6-1	Gullett	Medich
11—St. Louis	W	8-7	Eastwick	Hrabosky
12—St. Louis	L	4-5	Falcone	Billingham
13—St. Louis	W	4-0	Norman	Curtis
13—St. Louis	L	9-12	Forsch	Alcala
14—Chicago	W	3-2	Nolan	Zamora
15—Chicago	W	6-4	Gullett	Knowles
16—Chicago	L	3-5*	Bonham	Zachry
18—At Phila.	L	5-6	Lonborg	Billingham
19—At Phila.	W	4-3	Nolan	Reed
20—At Phila.	L	1-6	Kaat	Gullett
21—Los Ang.	W	3-1	Zachry	Rau
22—Los Ang.	W	6-0	Norman	Sutton
23—Phila.	L	2-4	Reed	Borbon
24—Phila.	L	4-5	Kaat	Nolan
25—At Hous.	W	8-6	Borbon	Griffin
26—At Hous.	L	0-3	Andujar	Zachry
27—At Hous.	W	4-2	Norman	Richard
28—At S. D.	W	7-3	Alcala	Foster
29—At S. D.	W	12-5x	Zachry	Spillner
30—At S. D.	L	1-3	Jones	Billingham

Won 18, Lost 12

JULY

2—Houston	L	8-10x	Pentz	Hinton
2—Houston	L	2-3	Andujar	Norman
3—Houston	W	9-8	Borbon	Niekro
4—Houston	W	7-2	Nolan	Dierker
5—At Mon.	W	11-2	Billingham	Lang
6—At Mon.	W	10-7	Eastwick	Kirby
7—At Mon.	W	4-3	Hinton	Rogers
9—Pitts.	W	12-11†	Eastwick	Demery
9—Pitts.	W	2-1	Norman	Medich
10—Pitts.	L	1-7	Candelaria	Billingham
11—Pitts.	L	5-8	Tekulve	Borbon
15—Montreal	L	3-4	Rogers	McEnaney
16—Montreal	W	4-3†	Eastwick	Murray
17—Montreal	W	4-1	Alcala	Fryman
18—At Pitts.	W	9-8	Billingham	Medich
19—At Pitts.	W	4-2	Zachry	Rooker
20—N. York	L	1-2	Koosman	Nolan
21—N. York	W	4-0	Norman	Matlack
23—At Atl.	W	3-1	Alcala	Niekro
24—At Atl.	L	4-5	Marshall	Hinton
24—At Atl.	W	6-3	Gullett	LaCorte
25—At Atl.	W	7-6	Nolan	Dal Canton
26—S. Fran.	W	9-3	Norman	Montefusco
27—S. Fran.	L	4-9	Barr	Billingham
28—S. Fran.	L	0-7	D'Acquisto	Alcala
29—S. Diego	W	9-3	Zachry	Freisleben

JULY

			Winner	Loser
30—S. Diego	W	13-8	Sarmiento	Spillner
30—S. Diego	W	4-2	Nolan	Folkers
31—S. Diego	W	12-1	Norman	Strom

Won 20, Lost 9

AUGUST

1—S. Diego	W	5-4	Alcala	Jones
2—At S. F.	W	5-1	McEnaney	D'Acquisto
3—At S. F.	W	9-0	Billingham	Caldwell
4—At S. F.	L	1-4	Montefusco	Nolan
5—At L. A.	W	3-2	Norman	Sutton
6—At L. A.	W	7-4	Eastwick	Rhoden
7—At L. A.	W	4-1	Zachry	John
8—At L. A.	W	3-2	Billingham	Hooton
10—At Chi.	L	3-6	Burris	Nolan
11—At Chi.	W	13-10†	Zachry	Knowles
12—At Chi.	W	8-3	Sarmiento	Sutter
13—At N. Y.	W	7-3	Billingham	Lolich
14—At N. Y.	L	1-2	Espinosa	Zachry
15—At N. Y.	L	0-1	Koosman	Nolan
16—Atlanta	L	3-4	Morton	Norman
17—Atlanta	L	2-3	Devine	Sarmiento
18—Atlanta	W	4-1	Billingham	Ruthven
19—Atlanta	W	3-2‡	Borbon	Devine
20—Chicago	W	4-3	Nolan	Burris
21—Chicago	L	2-3	R. Reuschel	Norman
22—Chicago	W	4-3	Sarmiento	Coleman
23—St. Louis	L	5-9	Denny	Billingham
24—St. Louis	L	1-4	Falcone	Zachry
26—Phila.	L	4-5§	McGraw	Eastwick
27—Phila.	W	4-1	Norman	Underwood
28—Phila.	W	8-7	Eastwick	McGraw
29—Phila.	W	6-5y	Alcala	Kaat
30—At St. L.	L	1-7	Denny	McEnaney
31—At St. L.	W	6-5	Borbon	Falcone

Won 18, Lost 11

SEPTEMBER

1—At St. L.	L	0-1‡	Hrabosky	Eastwick
3—At Atl.	W	10-5	Eastwick	Devine
4—At Atl.	W	5-1	Zachry	LaCorte
5—At Atl.	W	6-4	Sarmiento	Ruthven
6—Houston	W	9-8	Sarmiento	Richard
7—Houston	L	5-10	Sambito	Borbon
8—At Hous.	W	3-0	Nolan	McLaughlin
9—At Hous.	W	4-3‡	Eastwick	Forsch
10—At S. F.	W	4-1	Gullett	Knepper
11—At S. F.	W	8-5	Henderson	Lavelle
12—At S. F.	L	1-3	Barr	Norman
12—At S. F.	W	9-8‡	Henderson	Toms
14—Los Ang.	L	0-9	John	Nolan
15—Los Ang.	W	4-3	Zachry	Downing
16—Los Ang.	W	4-2	Gullett	Rau
17—S. Fran.	L	2-4	Barr	Billingham
18—S. Fran.	L	0-5	Lavelle	Norman
19—S. Fran.	W	5-2	Nolan	Montefusco
21—S. Diego	W	9-1	Zachry	Johnson
22—S. Diego	W	4-3	Gullett	Strom
24—At L. A.	L	6-7	Hough	McEnaney
25—At L. A.	W	4-3	Nolan	Sosa
26—At L. A.	L	1-2	Rau	Zachry
27—At S. D.	L	3-5	Griffin	Alcala
28—At S. D.	W	5-4	Billingham	Sawyer
29—At S. D.	L	1-6	Strom	Norman

Won 16, Lost 10

OCTOBER

1—Atlanta	W	5-2	Nolan	Ruthven
2—Atlanta	L	0-3	Niekro	Zachry
3—Atlanta	W	11-1	Gullett	LaCorte

Won 2, Lost 1

* 7 innings.   † 10 innings.   ‡ 11 innings.   § 13 innings.   x 14 innings.   y 15 innings   z 16 innings.

Bridesmaid Dodgers Bid Alston Farewell

By GORDON VERRELL

In what was to be Walter Alston's final season as the club's manager, ending a storied 23-year career, the Dodgers made remarkable strides.

They slashed Cincinnati's huge winning margin of 1975 exactly in half.

Unfortunately, since the Reds won by 20 games in 1975, that still leaves the Dodgers 10 more games to make up in 1977.

Even so, their 92-70 won-lost record ranked fourth in the major leagues, behind only Cincinnati, Philadelphia and the New York Yankees.

In view of the fact the Dodgers lost one of their top pitchers, Andy Messersmith, who won a series of court decisions and gained his free agent status, it's a considerable achievement.

The season started ominously enough when the Dodgers' home opener was rained out. That ended a streak of 737 consecutive home games without a washout and was only the second-ever rainout at Dodger Stadium.

Worse yet, the Dodgers lost their first five games.

They rebounded from their dismal opening to win 23 games in 27 starts, the club's best run since the Brooklyn Dodgers opened the 1955 season with a 25-4 record. During their streak, the Dodgers won 12 straight and spent much of the month of May in or tied for first place.

The Dodgers fell off, though, and never seriously threatened again, going down for the count formally the first week in August when the Reds swept a four-game series, leaving Los Angeles staggering 13 games out of first place.

Just to rub it in, the day after the fourth straight loss to the Reds they suffered the humiliation of being no-hit, by the Pirates' John Candelaria, on August 9.

"I don't think we were quite as good as that hot streak in April and May," said the 65-year-old Alston, "but I do know we were better than we showed later."

Part of the Dodgers' woes during the season was their inability to play well in their own division, especially against Cincinnati, San Diego and San Francisco. The Dodges wound up 42-48 against West Division rivals, including 5-13 against the Reds, 6-12 against the Padres and 8-10 against the Giants.

By contrast, Los Angeles won 50 of 72 starts against the East.

The Dodgers' pitching, despite losing Messersmith, who won 14, 20 and 19 games in his three seasons with Los Angeles, finished with a 3.02 staff ERA, second only in the majors to the New York Mets.

The major reasons were Don Sutton's stunning turnabout from a so-so summer to his first 20-win season; the remarkable comeback of Tommy John who closed at 10-10 with a 3.09 ERA after missing 1½ years; the emergence of righthander Rick Rhoden who won his first nine decisions and ended the season with a 12-3 record, and the consistency of lefthander Doug Rau who posted career highs in wins (16) and ERA (2.57), barely losing the N. L. earned-run average title the final day of the season.

For Sutton, the 31-year-old ace of the staff, there were two seasons in one.

Struggling early in the season, Sutton was still 7-8 with a 4.65 ERA in early July. Yet, he won 14 of his final 16 decisions and ended with 21 victories.

In the bullpen, Charlie Hough supplanted controversial reliever Mike

LOS ANGELES DODGERS—1976

Front row—Rodriguez, Sizemore, Smith, Baker, Basgall, coach; Adams, coach; Alston, manager; Gilliam, coach; Lasorda, coach; Buckner, Mota, Cruz. Second row—Buhler, trainer; Woods, team physician; Jobe, team physician; Yeager, Lacy, Auerbach, Cey, Russell, Lopes, Goodson, Garvey, Walker, batting instructor; Scott, traveling secretary; Homel, assistant trainer. Third row—Downing, Walton, Wall, Sosa, Sutton, Rhoden, Rau, Hough, John, Cresse, batting practice catcher. In front—Scully, Henley and Wetton, batboys.

Marshall, dispatched to Atlanta in June. The knuckleballing Hough appeared in 77 games, winning 12 of 20 decisions and recording 18 saves, six more saves than he managed in all of his first six seasons in the majors.

Offensively, the Dodgers offered little in the way of scoring punch. In fact, their run production of 608 was 249 less than what Cincinnati scored.

The winter trade for Atlanta's Dusty Baker flopped, although it started out well enough. He homered his first time to the plate as a Dodger. But he didn't homer again for two months and ended the season with only four round-trippers.

Baker, Reggie Smith, Bill Russell and Bill Buckner all reported for post-season surgery to repair various injuries.

Smith, like Baker, played all season with injuries after coming to the Dodgers from St. Louis on June 15. He was batting only .218 when the Dodgers got him and, though he batted .280 in 65 games with Los Angeles, he ended the season at only .253. Of his 10 Dodger homers, five were against his former club, the Cardinals, whom the Dodgers whipped 10 out of 12 times.

Steve Garvey remained consistent, leading the club in hitting with a .317 mark, sixth best in the league, while putting together his third successive 200-hit season. He's the first Dodger to collect 200 or more hits three straight seasons.

Garvey, along with Ron Cey, shared the club lead in RBIs with 80.

One reason neither approached the 100-RBI plateau was the slow start of leadoff hitter Dave Lopes, who missed the first five weeks of the season as well as most of spring training because of a muscle injury.

When he did get on base he was dynamite. He still led the league in stolen bases, with 63, his second straight stolen base championship.

A week before the close of the season, Alston announced that he was stepping down and two days later third base coach Tom Lasorda was elevated to the post of manager.

Alston closed his long career with 2,042 victories and 1,615 losses, only the sixth man to hit the 2,000-win circle.

"I just wish," he said, "that I could have used a few of those wins this season and we might have caught the Reds."

As for Lasorda, only the second man to manage the club since it was shifted to Southern California in 1958, he was anxious to get rollin'.

SCORES OF LOS ANGELES DODGERS' 1976 GAMES

APRIL			Winner	Loser	MAY			Winner	Loser
9—At S. F.	L	2-4	Montefusco	Sutton	1—St. Louis	W	4-3*	Marshall	Hrabosky
11—At S. F.	L	4-6	Moffitt	Marshall	2—St. Louis	W	3-1	Rau	McGlothen
13—S. Diego	L	5-8	Strom	Hooton	4—At Chi.	W	9-6	Hooton	R. Reuschel
14—S. Diego	L	1-3	Jones	Sutton	5—At Chi.	W	14-12	Sutton	Burris
16—At Atl.	L	1-3	Ruthven	John	7—At Phila.	W	10-8	Hough	Reed
17—At Atl.	W	5-1	Rau	Morton	8—At Phila.	L	4-6	Garber	John
18—At Atl.	L	6-7	Sosa	Hooton	9—At Phila.	L	3-10	Lonborg	Rau
19—At Hous.	L	3-8	Dierker	Sutton	10—At St. L.	W	4-3	Marshall	Rasmussen
20—At Hous.	W	6-3	Rhoden	Niekro	11—At St. L.	W	4-0	Sutton	Curtis
21—At Hous.	L	0-1z	Barlow	Wall	12—At St. L.	W	6-3	Marshall	Rasmussen
22—At Hous.	W	7-2	Rau	Andujar	14—At Pitts.	W	3-2	Hough	Candelaria
23—Chicago	L	3-4†	P. Reuschel	Downing	15—At Pitts.	L	2-4	Medich	Rau
24—Chicago	W	2-1	Sutton	Bonham	16—At Pitts.	W	6-0	Hooton	Reuss
25—Chicago	W	5-4*	Hough	Garman	17—Cinn.	L	3-5	Zachry	Sutton
26—Pitts.	W	7-1	John	Medich	18—Cinn.	W	5-0	Rhoden	Billingham
27—Pitts.	W	5-3	Rau	Kison	19—Atlanta	W	4-1	John	Ruthven
28—Pitts.	W	2-1	Hooton	Reuss	20—Atlanta	W	3-2	Hough	Sosa
29—St. Louis	W	4-0	Sutton	Falcone	21—Houston	W	2-1	Hooton	Richard
30—St. Louis	W	5-1	Rhoden	Curtis	22—Houston	W	6-5§	Hough	Siebert
			Won 10, Lost 9		23—Houston	W	6-5*	Wall	Siebert

MAY

			Winner	Loser
24—At S. D.	L	0-2	Freisleben	John
25—At S. D.	L	2-5	Jones	Hooton
26—At S. D.	W	8-0	Rau	Reynolds
28—At Cinn.	L	0-9	Zachry	Sutton
29—At Cinn.	L	5-6	Eastwick	Marshall
30—At Cinn.	W	6-5	Hough	Eastwick
30—At Cinn.	L	2-7	Alcala	Hooton
31—S. Fran.	L	1-7‡	Moffitt	Marshall

Won 18, Lost 10

JUNE

			Winner	Loser
1—S. Fran.	L	0-6	Halicki	Sutton
2—S. Fran.	W	11-3	Rhoden	Montefusco
3—S. Fran.	W	3-2*	Hough	Lavelle
4—N. York	L	0-11	Seaver	Hooton
5—N. York	L	1-3	Matlack	Rau
6—N. York	W	10-3	Sutton	Koosman
7—Phila.	L	6-8	Reed	Hough
8—Phila.	L	2-14	Christenson	John
9—Phila.	W	3-2	Hooton	Lonborg
10—Phila.	L	6-10‡	McGraw	Wall
11—Montreal	W	7-4	Sutton	Kirby
12—Montreal	W	4-3	Rhoden	Warthen
13—Montreal	W	6-3	John	Fryman
15—At N. Y.	L	1-2	Matlack	Hooton
16—At N. Y.	W	4-1	Rau	Koosman
17—At N. Y.	L	0-1x	Lockwood	Hough
18—At Mon.	W	6-5	Marshall	Murray
19—At Mon.	L	1-2	Stanhouse	Hough
20—At Mon.	L	4-5	Carrithers	Hooton
21—At Cinn.	L	1-3	Zachry	Rau
22—At Cinn.	L	0-6	Norman	Sutton
23—At Hous.	W	1-0	Rhoden	Richard
24—At Hous.	W	5-1	John	Dierker
25—S. Fran.	L	0-1	Halicki	Hooton
26—S. Fran.	L	2-4	Moffitt	Rau
27—S. Fran.	W	12-8	Sutton	Caldwell
28—Atlanta	W	5-2	Rhoden	Ruthven
29—Atlanta	W	2-1	John	Moret
30—Atlanta	L	3-8	Niekro	Hooton

Won 14, Lost 15

JULY

			Winner	Loser
1—At S. D.	L	3-5	Strom	Rau
2—At S. D.	L	3-6	Foster	Sutton
3—S. Diego	W	3-1	Rhoden	Freisleben
4—S. Diego	L	2-5	Jones	John
5—At Phila.	W	6-0	Hooton	Lonborg
6—At Phila.	W	5-1	Rau	Christenson
7—At Phila.	W	6-5	Sutton	Reed
9—At St. L.	L	3-4	Greif	Sosa
10—At St. L.	L	3-6	Falcone	John
11—At St. L.	W	9-6	Sutton	Forsch
15—Chicago	W	5-2	Rau	R. Reuschel
16—Chicago	W	4-1	Sutton	Renko
17—Chicago	W	5-4	Rhoden	Stone
18—Phila.	L	1-2	Reed	Hough
19—Phila.	L	3-5	Garber	Rau
20—St. Louis	W	3-2	Rau	McGlothen
21—St. Louis	W	7-6*	Hough	Hrabosky
22—S. Diego	L	4-5†	Metzger	Sosa
23—S. Diego	W	5-0	John	Strom
24—At S. D.	L	5-6	Metzger	Sosa
25—At S. D.	L	1-0	Rau	Freisleben
26—At Atl.	W	6-2	Sutton	Morton
28—At Atl.	L	2-7	Niekro	John
30—At S. F.	L	3-5	Williams	Hooton
31—At S. F.	L	3-6‡	Montefusco	Rau

Won 13, Lost 12

AUGUST

			Winner	Loser
1—At S. F.	W	4-1	Sutton	Barr
1—At S. F.	W	4-3*	Hough	Heaverlo
2—Houston	W	5-4†	Sosa	Pentz
3—Houston	W	2-0	Hooton	Larson
4—Houston	L	0-1	Richard	Rau
5—Cinn.	L	2-3	Norman	Sutton
6—Cinn.	L	4-7	Eastwick	Rhoden
7—Cinn.	L	1-4	Zachry	John
8—Cinn.	L	2-3	Billingham	Hooton
9—At Pitts.	L	0-2	Candelaria	Rau
10—At Pitts.	W	5-1	Sutton	Reuss
11—At Pitts.	W	2-0	Rhoden	Demery
13—At Chi.	L	2-3y	Coleman	Hough
13—At Chi.	W	8-7	Downing	Knowles
14—At Chi.	L	0-2	Burris	Rau
15—At Chi.	W	3-2	Sutton	Bonham
17—N. York	W	4-3	Rhoden	Matlack
18—N. York	W	3-2	Hough	Seaver
19—N. York	W	6-5	Hough	Apodaca
20—Pitts.	W	8-1	Rau	Kison
21—Pitts.	W	5-1	Sutton	Moose
22—Pitts.	L	1-6	Demery	Rhoden
23—Montreal	W	6-3	John	Stanhouse
24—Montreal	W	6-0	Hooton	Carrithers
25—Montreal	W	3-1	Rau	Rogers
27—At N. Y.	W	5-2	Sutton	Koosman
28—At N. Y.	L	1-2	Matlack	Rhoden
29—At N. Y.	W	2-1	John	Seaver
31—At Mon.	W	5-1	Rau	Fryman

Won 19, Lost 10

SEPTEMBER

			Winner	Loser
2—At Mon.	W	2-1	Sutton	Rogers
2—At Mon.	W	5-3	Sosa	Dunning
3—At Hous.	W	4-3	Hooton	Dierker
4—At Hous.	L	2-5	Andujar	John
5—At Hous.	W	4-0	Rau	Larson
6—At S. D.	W	4-1	Sutton	Jones
7—At S. D.	L	2-4	Freisleben	Hooton
8—S. Fran.	L	0-1†	Halicki	Hough
9—S. Fran.	L	2-4	Montefusco	John
12—Atlanta	L	2-3*	Devine	Hough
12—Atlanta	W	2-0	Sutton	Moret
13—Atlanta	L	1-5	LaCorte	Hooton
13—Atlanta	W	4-3	Rhoden	Leon
14—At Cinn.	W	9-0	John	Nolan
15—At Cinn.	L	3-4	Zachry	Downing
16—At Cinn.	L	2-4	Gullett	Rau
17—At Atl.	L	0-1‡	Devine	Hough
17—At Atl.	W	11-7	Hooton	Moret
18—At Atl.	L	2-5	Easterly	Lewallyn
19—At Atl.	W	8-1	John	Ruthven
21—At S. F.	W	3-2	Rau	Moffitt
22—At S. F.	W	3-1	Sutton	Knepper
23—At S. F.	W	4-1	Hooton	Montefusco
24—Cinn.	W	7-6	Hough	McEnaney
25—Cinn.	L	3-4	Nolan	Sosa
26—Cinn.	W	2-1	Rau	Zachry
27—Houston	W	2-0	Sutton	Larson
28—Houston	L	0-1	Richard	Hooton
29—Houston	W	1-0	Wall	Sambito

Won 17, Lost 12

OCTOBER

			Winner	Loser
1—S. Diego	W	8-1	Lewallyn	Owchinko
2—S. Diego	L	1-4	Griffin	Sutton
3—S. Diego	L	2-3	Sawyer	Rau

Won 1, Lost 2

* 10 innings. † 11 innings. ‡ 12 innings. § 13 innings. x 14 innings. y 15 innings. z 16 innings.

Young Hurlers Initiate Astros' Upswing

By HARRY SHATTUCK

The summer of '76 didn't provide the best season in Houston's 15-year major league history. But, considering the remarkable progress made, it may rank as the most satisfying.

The Astros barely missed reaching the .500 mark, compiling an 80-82 record. When compared to the previous year's 64-97 disaster, it's no wonder folks in the Houston area are optimistic about the future.

The satisfaction with 1976 goes beyond the improvement in games won, even beyond the unexpected jump from sixth to third place in the National League West Division.

General Manager Tal Smith and Manager Bill Virdon had stressed back in the spring that they would emphasize youth, that they would not sacrifice the future in an effort to discover instant success. Smith and Virdon held true on their pledge—and the youngsters added to rather than detracted from the summer effort.

Rookie pitchers won 29 games and were so impressive that after mid-July only two non-rookies—Larry Dierker and James Rodney Richard—started a game. First-year hurlers opened all but eight contests in September.

So it was not surprising, after the season and after the trading away of Dierker to St. Louis, that Smith listed seven candidates for starting jobs in 1977 and six owned one year or less of experience.

Among that number were Joaquin Andujar, who won nine games, pitched four shutouts and beat world champion Cincinnati three times; Dan Larson, a five-time winner who gave only 81 hits in 92 innings and merited a 3.03 earned-run average; Bo McLaughlin, a four-time victor whose ERA was 2.85; Joe Sambito, a three-time winner with a 3.57 ERA; Mark Lemongello, 3-1 with a 2.79 ERA, and Floyd Bannister, THE SPORTING NEWS collegiate player of the year, who was undefeated with three minor league teams in six weeks in the Houston system.

If the ERAs seem impressive but the victory totals low, consider that none of that group began the year in the starting rotation. Andujar got his first start two months into the season; Larson, McLaughlin and Sambito were promoted following the All-Star Game and Lemongello spent just three weeks as an Astro.

Indeed, the veteran of Houston's pitching staff now—and the seventh man Smith listed as top starting candidates for next year—is James Rodney Richard. And "old man" Richard is a sprightly 26.

Richard finally matured into a consistent pitcher in 1976, becoming only the second 20-game winner ever for the Orange (Dierker did it in 1969) when he defeated San Francisco on the season's final afternoon. Richard had a 2.75 ERA, worked 291 innings and struck out 214.

There is no question pitching was the highlight of Houston's 1976 season, especially considering that it was the team's downfall during the 1975 ordeal and that Smith and Virdon were not at all sure at season's beginning who would be throwing the ball regularly.

Dierker threw the ball July 9 and he threw it with better results that evening in the Astrodome than did any other Houston pitcher all year. The right-

HOUSTON ASTROS—1976

Front row—Johnson, DaVanon, Jutze, Wright, coach; Lillis, coach; Virdon, manager; Jones, coach; Pacheco, coach; Gross, Watson. Second row—Perkins, traveling secretary; Andrews, Howe, Boswell, Milbourne, Metzger, Howard, Cruz, Cedeno, Cosgrove, Roberts, Lake, equipment manager; Ewell, trainer. Third row—McIntosh, Pentz, Hardy, Griffin, Andujar, Richard, Barlow, Dierker, Forsch, Rondon, Niekro. In front—Walker, batboy.

hander, senior member of the club with 13 years' service at his departure, pitched a no-hitter against the Montreal Expos. Dierker had flirted with no-hitters four previous times, once surviving 8⅔ innings before giving a safety.

When Houston pitchers needed relief, Ken Forsch was so dependable that he was the only bullpen regular named to the N.L. All-Star team. Forsch saved 19 games, even though he missed more than a month with injuries.

Offensively, Houston had its positive spots, too.

Bob Watson remained one of baseball's best and most unsung players, batting .313, hitting 16 home runs and driving in 102 runs.

Cesar Cedeno batted .297, led the Astros with 18 homers, drove in 83 runs, set a personal and team record with 58 stolen bases and won a fifth straight Gold Glove for his center fielding.

The surprises in Houston's lineup were Jose Cruz and Enos Cabell. Cruz, ticketed for part-time duty, earned a starter's job by hitting .303, stealing 28 bases and learning consistency both offensively and defensively. Cabell, charged with the challenging responsibility of replacing Doug Rader at third base, fielded in the tradition of Houston's departed Red Rooster, batted a steady .273 and was a genuine team leader.

Roger Metzger continued his superb defense at shortstop, Ken Boswell set a club mark with 20 pinch hits, Jerry DaVanon batted .290 as a utilityman and catcher Ed Herrmann came from California in June to aid considerably in developing the young pitching staff.

A final bit of good news came as the season ended. The Astros, operated by creditors all year and obviously hurting financially, were purchased by General Electric Credit Corp. and Ford Motor Co. Credit Corp.

And so a year that began with Houston's spring training field in Cocoa, Fla., condemned and unrepaired because of a lack of funds, ended with great hopes that the Astro fortunes were on the upswing.

SCORES OF HOUSTON ASTROS' 1976 GAMES

APRIL		Winner	Loser		MAY			Winner	Loser
8—At Cinn.	L	5-11	Nolan	Richard	9—At St. L.	W	10-5	Dierker	Denny
10—At Cinn.	L	7-13	Billingham	Dierker	11—Montreal	W	5-3	Griffin	Kirby
11—At Cinn.	L	3-9	Darcy	Niekro	12—Montreal	L	2-7	Fryman	Richard
12—S. Fran.	W	5-0	Richard	Halicki	14—Phila.	L	1-5	Christenson	Cosgrove
13—S. Fran.	W	2-1	Barlow	Montefusco	15—Phila.	L	1-2	Lonborg	Dierker
14—S. Fran.	W	5-3	Dierker	Caldwell	16—Phila.	L	2-12	Carlton	Griffin
16—S. Diego	W	4-1	Niekro	Wehrmeister	17—Atlanta	L	2-3	Messersmith	Richard
17—S. Diego	W	5-4	Richard	Spillner	17—Atlanta	W	3-2	Forsch	Dal Canton
18—S. Diego	W	4-2	Griffin	Strom	18—Atlanta	L	2-3*	Sosa	Barlow
18—S. Diego	L	5-11	Jones	Andujar	19—At S. D.	W	9-4	Griffin	Spillner
19—Los Ang.	W	8-3	Dierker	Sutton	20—At S. D.	W	5-4	Niekro	Wehrmeister
20—Los Ang.	L	3-6	Rhoden	Niekro	21—At L. A.	L	1-2	Hooton	Richard
21—Los Ang.	W	1-0x	Barlow	Wall	22—At L. A.	L	5-6‡	Hough	Siebert
22—Los Ang.	L	2-7	Rau	Andujar	23—At L. A.	L	5-6*	Wall	Siebert
23—N. York	W	3-1	Cosgrove	Koosman	24—At S. F.	L	1-5	Dressler	Cosgrove
24—N. York	L	1-7	Seaver	Dierker	25—At S. F.	L	6-7	Heaverlo	Forsch
25—N. York	L	2-4	Sanders	Niekro	26—At S. F.	L	4-11	Barr	Dierker
28—At Mon.	W	6-4	Richard	Fryman	29—At Atl.	W	4-3	J. Niekro	P. Niekro
28—At Mon.	L	7-8	Carrithers	Barlow	30—At Atl.	W	5-2	Griffin	Messersmith
29—At Mon.	W	3-1	Dierker	Murray	30—At Atl.	W	16-5	Rondon	Moret
30—At N. Y.	L	1-3	Matlack	Niekro	31—Cinn.	L	2-4	Darcy	Richard
		Won 11, Lost 10					Won 10, Lost 17		

MAY					JUNE				
2—At N. Y.	W	5-4	Richard	Apodaca	1—Cinn.	W	2-1	Andujar	Zachry
2—At N. Y.	L	4-7	Koosman	Rondon	2—Cinn.	L	7-8	McEnaney	Forsch
4—At Phila.	L	0-5	Lonborg	Dierker	3—Cinn.	W	5-3	Dierker	Alcala
5—At Phila.	L	3-6	Reed	Niekro	4—Chicago	W	1-0	Cosgrove	R. Reuschel
7—At St. L.	W	3-1	Richard	Forsch	5—Chicago	W	4-3	Richard	Zamora
8—At St. L.	L	1-5	McGlothen	Cosgrove	6—Chicago	W	2-0	Andujar	Bonham

JUNE			Winner	Loser
6—Chicago	W	5-1	Rondon	Fraling
7—St. Louis	L	6-7	Curtis	Niekro
8—St. Louis	W	2-0	Dierker	Forsch
9—St. Louis	W	5-2	Richard	McGlothen
11—At Chi.	L	3-8	Bonham	Cosgrove
12—At Chi.	L	4-7	R. Reuschel	Andujar
13—At Chi.	L	3-8	Burris	Dierker
14—Pitts.	L	1-2	Reuss	Richard
16—Pitts.	L	3-6	Medich	Andujar
18—At Pitts.	L	3-7	Candelaria	Dierker
20—At Pitts.	W	9-4	Griffin	Moose
21—At Atl.	L	9-11	Sosa	Pentz
22—At Atl.	W	9-7	Pentz	LaCorte
23—Los Ang.	L	0-1	Rhoden	Richard
24—Los Ang.	L	1-5	John	Dierker
25—Cinn.	L	6-8	Borbon	Griffin
26—Cinn.	W	3-0	Andujar	Zachry
27—Cinn.	L	2-4	Norman	Richard
28—At S. F.	W	8-2	Cosgrove	Dressler
29—At S. F.	W	4-3	Dierker	Barr
30—At S. F.	L	2-10	Halicki	Rondon
			Won 13, Lost 14	

JULY				
2—At Cinn.	W	10-8§	Pentz	Hinton
2—At Cinn.	W	3-2	Andujar	Norman
3—At Cinn.	L	8-9	Borbon	Niekro
4—At Cinn.	L	2-7	Nolan	Dierker
5—N. York	W	7-3	Niekro	Apodaca
6—N. York	W	1-0*	Richard	Lockwood
7—N. York	L	4-12	Koosman	Andujar
8—Montreal	W	7-6	Forsch	Dunning
9—Montreal	W	6-0	Dierker	Stanhouse
10—Montreal	W	4-2	Richard	Kirby
11—Montreal	W	1-0	Andujar	Rogers
15—At N. Y.	L	1-3	Koosman	Richard
16—At N. Y.	W	4-3	Dierker	Matlack
17—At N. Y.	W	1-0	Andujar	Seaver
18—At Mon.	W	7-6*	Forsch	Murray
18—At Mon.	W	14-11	Larson	Dunning
19—At Mon.	W	3-1	Richard	Rogers
20—At Pitts.	L	3-5	Candelaria	Griffin
20—At Pitts.	W	4-3	Forsch	Giusti
21—At Pitts.	L	1-5	Reuss	Dierker
21—At Pitts.	L	1-4	Demery	Andujar
23—S. Fran.	L	0-3	Barr	Richard
24—S. Fran.	W	5-4‡	Pentz	Heaverlo
24—S. Fran.	L	1-0	D'Acquisto	Larson
25—S. Fran.	W	1-0*	McLaughlin	Halicki
26—S. Diego	W	7-0	Dierker	Spillner
27—S. Diego	W	4-1	Richard	Johnson
28—S. Diego	L	1-2*	Jones	Andujar
30—Atlanta	L	2-3	Messersmith	Larson
31—Atlanta	W	2-1	Richard	Ruthven
31—Atlanta	W	9-6	Sambito	Dal Canton
			Won 20, Lost 11	

AUGUST				
1—Atlanta	W	6-0	Dierker	Niekro
2—At L. A.	L	4-5†	Sosa	Pentz
3—At L. A.	L	0-2	Hooton	Larson

AUGUST			Winner	Loser
4—At L. A.	W	1-0	Richard	Rau
5—At S. D.	L	3-4	Freisleben	McLaughlin
6—At S. D.	L	3-9	Griffin	Dierker
7—At S. D.	L	2-3	Sawyer	Andujar
8—At S. D.	L	3-4	Metzger	Richard
9—At St. L.	W	13-4	Larson	Forsch
10—At St. L.	L	1-8	McGlothen	McLaughlin
11—At St. L.	W	8-1	Dierker	Denny
13—Pitts.	L	5-8	Tekulve	Niekro
14—Pitts.	L	4-5	Giusti	Pentz
15—Pitts.	L	0-3	Medich	Larson
15—Pitts.	L	6-8	Reuss	Sambito
16—Chicago	L	3-5	Sutter	Dierker
17—Chicago	W	8-1	Richard	Stone
19—At Phila.	L	1-7	Carlton	Andujar
20—At Phila.	W	8-3	Larson	Twitchell
21—At Phila.	W	4-4	Kaat	Richard
22—At Phila.	L	1-5	Underwood	Dierker
24—At Chi.	W	4-3	Andujar	Renko
25—At Chi.	L	1-5	Burris	Larson
26—At Chi.	W	5-3	Richard	R. Reuschel
27—St. Louis	W	2-1	McLaughlin	Rasmussen
28—St. Louis	W	4-3	Dierker	Forsch
29—St. Louis	W	6-0	Sambito	McGlothen
30—Phila.	W	3-1	Larson	Christenson
31—Phila.	W	3-2	Richard	McGraw
			Won 13, Lost 16	

SEPTEMBER				
1—Phila.	W	1-0	McLaughlin	Kaat
3—Los Ang.	L	3-4	Hooton	Dierker
4—Los Ang.	W	5-2	Andujar	John
5—Los Ang.	L	0-4	Rau	Larson
6—At Cinn.	L	8-9	Sarmiento	Richard
7—At Cinn.	W	10-5	Sambito	Borbon
8—Cinn.	L	0-3	Nolan	McLaughlin
9—Cinn.	L	3-4†	Eastwick	Forsch
11—At S. D.	L	1-4	Jones	Dierker
11—At S. D.	W	2-1	Richard	Sawyer
14—At Atl.	W	4-3	Lemongello	Ruthven
14—At Atl.	L	2-5	Autry	McLaughlin
15—At Atl.	W	4-3	Larson	Camp
16—At Atl.	L	3-5	Niekro	Andujar
18—S. Diego	L	1-4	Freisleben	Richard
19—S. Diego	W	3-2	Lemongello	Jones
19—S. Diego	W	3-2y	McLaughlin	Metzger
21—Atlanta	L	2-6	Niekro	Larson
22—Atlanta	W	5-2	Andujar	LaCorte
24—At S. F.	W	14-5	Richard	Riccelli
25—At S. F.	L	0-10	Barr	McLaughlin
26—At S. F.	L	1-5	Lavelle	Lemongello
27—At L. A.	L	0-2	Sutton	Larson
28—At L. A.	W	1-0	Richard	Hooton
29—At L. A.	L	0-1	Wall	Sambito
			Won 11, Lost 14	

OCTOBER				
1—S. Fran.	W	5-4	Lemongello	Barr
2—S. Fran.	W	10-1	Richard	Dressler
			Won 2, Lost 0	

* 10 innings. † 11 innings. ‡ 13 innings. § 14 innings. x 16 innings. y Part of September 10 doubleheader at San Diego transferred to Houston.

San Francisco's Giants Finish Fourth

By ART SPANDER

For much of the winter, it seemed the Giants were going to Canada. For much of the summer, a lot of the fans in San Francisco were wishing they had. A couple of guys named Robert Lurie and Bud Herseth saved the franchise for Northern California just about the time it seemed certain to move to Toronto. But once the season actually began, it turned out no one could save the Giants.

No, San Francisco did not finish last in the National League West, although it tried its hardest. The Giants gained the basement April 28 and didn't get out until September 5, eventually gaining a measure of respectability by ending up in fourth. But that distinction and a no-hit, no-run game by pitcher John (The Count) Montefusco September 29, as the days dwindled down to an unprecious few, were about the only things worth recalling around Candlestick Park in 1976. Along with the emergence of rookie Larry Herndon.

The rest of the memories were, in a word, bad. There was that disastrous period from the end of April to the end of May when the Giants lost 22 out of 27 games; there was the constant grumbling in the clubhouse, and demands to be sent elsewhere—a request that was fulfilled for Willie Montanez; there were the errors and errors and errors, eventually a league high 186 of them; and there was the blowup between Montefusco and manager Bill Rigney which managed to deteriorate even further a hopeless situation.

Former owner Horace Stoneham did his best to sell the Giants to interests in Toronto, but a sympathetic judge, a determined new San Francisco mayor —George Moscone—and the financial benevolence of Lurie and Herseth kept the team in the Bay Area. Lurie's next order of business was to name his old friend Rigney to take over the managerial job the Giants relieved him of 16 years earlier.

When San Francisco opened with a couple of wins over the Dodgers before good-sized crowds at Candlestick Park, it looked like the renaissance was on. And when, with a 7-5 record two weeks into the season, the Giants were tied for first place, people even started talking about a pennant. That, it turned out, was an idea whose time had not come.

San Francisco then started going downhill faster than Jean-Claude Killy. They made four errors in some games, five in others. They failed to score— going 35⅓ innings without a run at one stretch—and failed to show any spirit. Bobby Murcer thought it was too cold. Ditto for Montanez. Derrel Thomas didn't sign his contract until August. Gary Matthews didn't sign at all, and after the season ended up with Atlanta in the free agent re-entry draft.

Montanez eventually was dispatched to the Braves in early June for Darrell Evans and Marty Perez, which stopped some of the complaining in the locker room—but not all.

Every time you picked up a newspaper, the Giants were ending another losing streak.

The disappointment and frustration were emphasized when, on August 22, Rigney removed Montefusco from a game after the pitcher had given up a home run. Although San Francisco eventually won, The Count was livid. He called the manager a loser and demanded he be fired. Montefusco, after being fined $500, refused to communicate with Rigney—until John pitched the no-hitter the final week of the season. By that time, however, Rigney, insisting he had lost his enthusiasm for the game, announced his retirement.

One guy who didn't lose any enthusiasm was Herndon. After beginning the season in the minors, he was inserted into the lineup in May and started to make running catches and clutch hits like a gentleman who had preceded

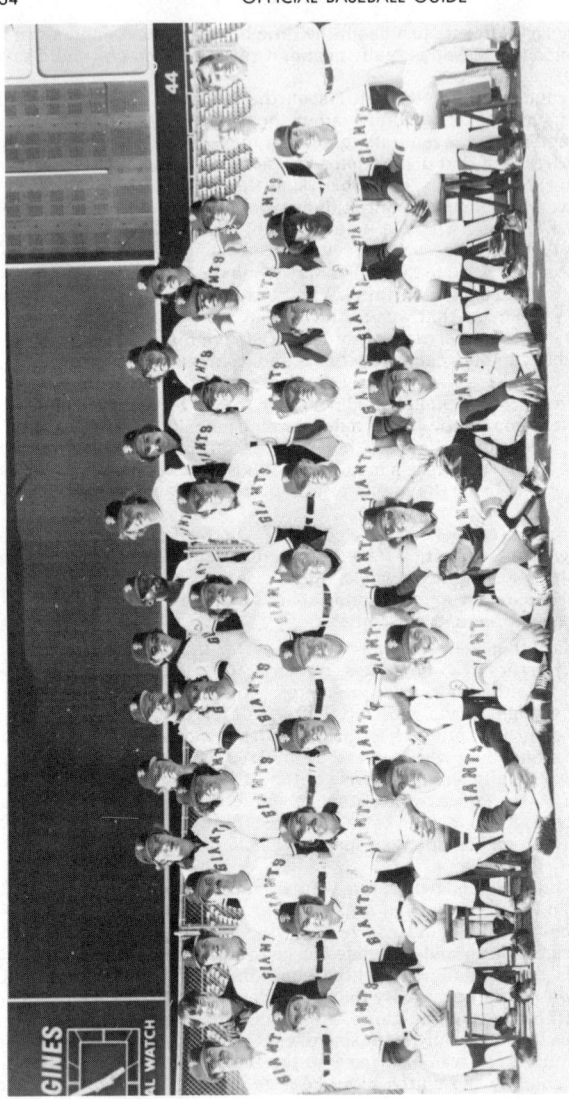

SAN FRANCISCO GIANTS—1976

Front row—Sadek, Montefusco, Ontiveros, Funk, coach; Winkles, coach; Rigney, manager; Davenport, coach; Rodgers, coach; Thomasson, Matthews, Adams. Second row—D'Acquisto, Murphy, assistant equipment manager; Hill, Rader, Williams, Barr, Caldwell, Moffitt, Perez, Thomas, Murcer, Logan, equipment manager; Liscio, trainer. Third row—Speier, Arnold, Heaverlo, Lavelle, Herndon, Halicki, Dressler, Evans, Reitz. In front—Batboys Quinlin, Dougherty, Peterson, Dudum.

him in center field by a few years, Willie Mays. For a while, Herndon was batting .400, and seemingly throwing someone out at the plate in every game. Larry eventually finished hitting .288, which was high on the Giants and good enough to win THE SPORTING NEWS National League Rookie Player of the Year award.

The Giants named minor league manager Joe Altobelli to succeed Rigney for 1977. Everybody knows the team won't be going to Toronto this time, but no one knows where it may go in the pennant race.

SCORES OF SAN FRANCISCO GIANTS' 1976 GAMES

APRIL			Winner	Loser
9—Los Ang.	W	4-2	Montefusco	Sutton
11—Los Ang.	W	6-4	Moffitt	Marshall
12—At Hous.	L	0-5	Richard	Halicki
13—At Hous.	L	1-2	Barlow	Montefusco
14—At Hous.	L	3-5	Dierker	Caldwell
16—At Cinn.	W	14-7	Barr	Darcy
17—At Cinn.	L	0-11	Norman	Halicki
18—At Cinn.	W	5-1	Montefusco	Nolan
20—At Atl.	W	12-11†	Halicki	Sosa
21—At Atl.	L	0-3	Ruthven	Barr
23—Pitts.	W	7-3	Montefusco	Reuss
24—Pitts.	W	3-1	Halicki	Rooker
25—Pitts.	L	0-3	Candelaria	Caldwell
26—St. Louis	L	7-15	Wallace	Moffitt
27—St. Louis	L	1-7	McGlothen	D'Acquisto
28—St. Louis	L	2-4z	Proly	Caldwell
30—Chicago	L	2-5	R. Reuschel	Halicki
		Won 7, Lost 10		
MAY				
1—Chicago	W	3-1	Lavelle	Schultz
2—Chicago	L	5-6y	Frailing	Lavelle
2—Chicago	L	5-6‡	Knowles	Minton
4—At Pitts.	L	5-6	Reuss	Caldwell
5—At Pitts.	L	1-6	Kison	Halicki
6—At Pitts.	L	0-3	Rooker	Barr
8—At Mon.	L	5-7	Fryman	D'Acquisto
9—At Mon.	W	4-2	Montefusco	Warthen
9—At Mon.	L	0-8	Rogers	Minton
11—At Chi.	L	0-4	Zamora	Halicki
12—At Chi.	L	0-1‡	Garman	Moffitt
13—At Chi.	W	9-5	Moffitt	Sutter
14—At St. L.	L	1-3	McGlothen	Montefusco
15—At St. L.	W	2-0†	Lavelle	Hrabosky
16—At St. L.	L	3-9	Falcone	Halicki
17—S. Diego	L	2-12	Jones	Barr
18—S. Diego	L	6-7‡	Metzger	Moffitt
19—Cinn.	L	4-5	Alcala	Montefusco
20—Cinn.	W	6-5	Heaverlo	McEnaney
21—Atlanta	L	0-8	Messersmith	Dressler
22—Atlanta	L	2-3	Moret	Barr
23—Atlanta	L	2-9	Ruthven	Halicki
23—Atlanta	W	1-0†	Montefusco	Leon
24—Houston	W	5-1	Dressler	Cosgrove
25—Houston	W	7-6	Heaverlo	Forsch
26—Houston	W	11-4	Barr	Dierker
27—At S. D.	L	1-3	Strom	Halicki
28—At S. D.	W	5-0	Montefusco	Foster
29—At S. D.	L	0-4	Freisleben	Dressler
30—At S. D.	L	3-4†	Jones	Lavelle
31—At L. A.	W	7-1§	Moffitt	Marshall
		Won 11 Lost 20		
JUNE				
1—At L. A.	W	6-0	Halicki	Sutton
2—At L. A.	L	3-11	Rhoden	Montefusco
3—At L. A.	L	2-3†	Hough	Lavelle
4—Phila.	W	5-1	Barr	Lonborg
5—Phila.	W	4-2	Halicki	Carlton
6—Phila.	L	3-9	Kaat	Montefusco
8—Montreal	L	4-9	Fryman	Dressler

JUNE			Winner	Loser
9—Montreal	W	6-2	Barr	Stanhouse
10—Montreal	L	5-6	Carrithers	Halicki
11—N. York	W	5-0	Montefusco	Koosman
12—N. York	L	1-3	Swan	D'Acquisto
13—N. York	L	2-4	Lolich	Dressler
13—N. York	L	1-4	Seaver	Barr
15—At Phila.	L	2-10	Carlton	Halicki
16—At Phila.	L	1-6	Kaat	Montefusco
17—At Phila.	L	2-3	Garber	Lavelle
18—At N. Y.	L	2-3	Seaver	Dressler
19—At N. Y.	L	5-0	Barr	Lolich
20—At N. Y.	W	9-2	Halicki	Matlack
21—At S. D.	L	3-6	Freisleben	Montefusco
22—At S. D.	L	2-4	Jones	D'Acquisto
23—S. Diego	W	7-6	Heaverlo	Strom
23—S. Diego	W	8-7	Barr	Tomlin
24—S. Diego	W	8-5	Williams	Reynolds
25—At L. A.	W	1-0	Halicki	Hooton
26—At L. A.	W	4-2	Moffitt	Rau
27—At L. A.	L	8-12	Sutton	Caldwell
28—Houston	L	2-8	Cosgrove	Dressler
29—Houston	L	3-4	Dierker	Barr
30—Houston	W	10-2	Halicki	Rondon
		Won 13, Lost 17		
JULY				
2—Atlanta	L	2-7	Messersmith	Montefusco
3—Atlanta	L	0-4	Ruthven	D'Acquisto
4—Atlanta	W	3-2	Dressler	LaCorte
5—At St. L.	W	6-4	Lavelle	Rasmussen
6—At St. L.	L	7-13	Forsch	Halicki
7—At St. L.	W	3-2	Lavelle	McGlothen
9—At Chi.	L	3-5	Sutter	Dressler
10—At Chi.	L	6-8	Knowles	Moffitt
11—At Chi.	W	2-0	Halicki	Stone
15—Phila.	L	3-5	Carlton	Caldwell
16—Phila.	L	1-0	Halicki	Kaat
17—Phila.	W	4-1	Montefusco	Underwood
18—St. Louis	W	5-4	Barr	Falcone
18—St. Louis	L	4-5†	Wallace	Heaverlo
19—St. Louis	W	5-3	D'Acquisto	Forsch
20—Chicago	L	2-3	R. Reuschel	Halicki
21—Chicago	W	2-1	Montefusco	Sutter
23—At Hous.	W	3-0	Barr	Richard
24—At Hous.	L	4-5x	Pentz	Heaverlo
24—At Hous.	W	4-0	D'Acquisto	Larson
25—At Hous.	L	0-1†	McLaughlin	Halicki
26—At Cinn.	L	3-9	Norman	Montefusco
27—At Cinn.	W	9-4	Barr	Billingham
28—At Cinn.	W	7-0	D'Acquisto	Alcala
30—Los Ang.	W	5-3	Williams	Hooton
31—Los Ang.	W	6-3	Montefusco	Rau
		Won 15, Lost 11		
AUGUST				
1—Los Ang.	L	1-4	Sutton	Barr
1—Los Ang.	L	3-4†	Hough	Heaverlo
2—Cinn.	L	1-5	McEnaney	D'Acquisto
3—Cinn.	L	0-9	Billingham	Caldwell
4—Cinn.	W	4-1	Montefusco	Nolan
5—At Atl.	W	2-1	Barr	Niekro

AUGUST			Winner	Loser
6—At Atl.	L	0-7	Morton	Dressler
7—At Atl.	L	3-4	Marshall	Moffitt
8—At Atl.	L	1-2	Ruthven	Lavelle
8—At Atl.	W	4-1	Montefusco	LaCorte
9—At Mon.	L	1-2	Stanhouse	Barr
10—At Mon.	L	2-3	Carrithers	Heaverlo
11—At Mon.	L	3-9	Fryman	D'Acquisto
13—At Phila.	W	3-0	Montefusco	Kaat
14—At Phila.	L	2-13	Carlton	Barr
15—At Phila.	W	9-5	Moffitt	Garber
17—Pitts.	W	7-6	Lavelle	Moose
18—Pitts.	L	1-12*	Rooker	Montefusco
19—Pitts.	L	0-1	Candelaria	Barr
20—Montreal	W	6-3	Halicki	Carrithers
21—Montreal	W	5-4z	Dressler	Lang
22—Montreal	W	4-3	Lavelle	Taylor
24—N. York	L	0-4	Seaver	Barr
25—N. York	W	7-1	Halicki	Espinosa
27—At Pitts.	L	2-5	Demery	Montefusco
28—At Pitts.	L	1-7	Rooker	D'Acquisto
29—At Pitts.	L	2-3‡	Candelaria	Moffitt
31—At N. Y.	L	2-6	Lockwood	Halicki
			Won 10, Lost 18	

SEPTEMBER				
1—At N. Y.	L	0-1	Koosman	Montefusco
2—At N. Y.	W	10-7	Caldwell	Matlack
3—S. Diego	W	7-3	Barr	Jones
4—S. Diego	W	4-3	Lavelle	Griffin
5—S. Diego	W	5-0	Montefusco	Strom

SEPTEMBER			Winner	Loser
5—S. Diego	L	1-6	Sawyer	Dressler
6—Atlanta	W	4-3	Lavelle	Dal Canton
7—Atlanta	W	6-3	Barr	Niekro
8—At L. A.	W	1-0†	Halicki	Hough
9—At L. A.	W	4-2	Montefusco	John
10—Cinn.	L	1-4	Gullett	Knepper
11—Cinn.	L	5-6	Henderson	Lavelle
12—Cinn.	W	3-1	Barr	Norman
12—Cinn.	L	8-9‡	Henderson	Toms
13—At S. D.	W	3-2†	Heaverlo	Freisleben
14—At S. D.	W	7-6	Moffitt	Metzger
15—At S. D.	W	2-1	Riccelli	Jones
17—At Cinn.	W	4-2	Barr	Billingham
18—At Cinn.	W	5-0	Lavelle	Norman
19—At Cinn.	L	2-5	Nolan	Montefusco
21—Los Ang.	L	2-3	Rau	Moffitt
22—Los Ang.	L	1-3	Sutton	Knepper
23—Los Ang.	L	1-4	Hooton	Montefusco
24—Houston	L	5-14	Richard	Riccelli
25—Houston	W	10-0	Barr	McLaughlin
26—Houston	W	5-1	Lavelle	Lemongello
28—At Atl.	W	4-1	Knepper	LaCorte
29—At Atl.	W	9-0	Montefusco	Easterly
			Won 18, Lost 10	

OCTOBER				
1—At Hous.	L	4-5	Lemongello	Barr
2—At Hous.	L	1-10	Richard	Dressler
			Won 0, Lost 2	

* 6½ innings.   † 10 innings.   ‡ 11 innings.   § 12 innings.   x 13 innings.   y 14 innings.   z 16 innings.

Padres Gain Most Victories Ever

By PHIL COLLIER

Although they set an eight-year club record for most victories (73) and established a home attendance record (1,458,478) for the third year in a row, the 1976 season was somewhat disappointing for the San Diego Padres.

For half a season, manager John McNamara's team was one of the big surprises in the National League. Down the stretch, the Padres slumped miserably and finished fifth in the West Division, one notch lower than in 1975.

The decline resulted from a familiar problem, lack of hitting. The Padres finished 11th and next-to-last in the league in both runs scored (570) and homers (64). They were shut out 23 times, the most in the majors.

For a while, though, the Padres held their own at the plate. On June 22, they defeated San Francisco and moved into second place, only five games behind streaking Cincinnati.

The collapse began without warning after a 5-2 victory at Los Angeles on July 4. At that point, the third-place Padres trailed the Dodgers by half a game and the Reds by six.

It was the first leg of a trip that seemed to demoralize the San Diego team. From Los Angeles, the Padres went to Chicago to lose three straight games, all via shutouts.

After salvaging the series finale there, the Padres went to Philadelphia to lose by scores of 4-3, 5-0, 4-2 and 3-0. As they limped home for the All-Star break, their lead over fourth-place Houston had been reduced to a half game.

The Padres didn't relinquish third place for keeps until August 27. They gave up fourth place on September 15 and were pressed the rest of the way to ward off last-place Atlanta.

"Some of the older players ran out of gas, there were injuries and we just stopped hitting," said McNamara after a slump that appeared to place his job in jeopardy. However, he was rehired for a fourth term at the end of the season.

It isn't difficult to pinpoint the reasons for the general decline.

Dave Winfield, the 25-year-old right fielder and cleanup hitter, led the club with a mere 13 homers and only two of those came after June 18.

After batting .291 and driving in 53 runs by the All-Star break, Winfield averaged .267 the rest of the way and contributed only 16 more RBIs. He missed most of the last month of the season with a leg injury.

Willie Davis, the 36-year-old center fielder, batted .283 the first half and .246 the second. He packed for Japan following the season.

Tito Fuentes, a disgruntled second baseman who was playing out his option, averaged .276 the first half and .248 the second.

Doug Rader, the 32-year-old third baseman, batted .262 the first half, slumped badly in July and August, then rebounded in September after responding to treatment for the gout.

Shortstop Enzo Hernandez, who was averaging .300 in mid-June, tailed off the rest of the way to finish at .256.

Willie McCovey, the 38-year-old first baseman who also was playing out his option, had the poorest season of his career (.203 average, seven homers) while dividing time with Mike Ivie at first base.

Ivie, 24, came on to lead the team with a .291 average and 70 RBIs but contributed only seven homers, a distressingly low total for a major league first baseman batting in the middle of the lineup.

Lack of run support caused a breakdown in San Diego's pitching staff.

Lefthander Randy Jones (22-14), who was to become the N.L.'s Cy Young Award winner, was 16-3 at the All-Star break. His record the rest of the way (6-11) was deceptive because seven of those losses were by one run and he was shut out three times in the second half.

The Padres averaged only .232 as a team behind Jones in the first half and were even more feeble (.211) behind him the rest of the way.

Brent Strom (12-16), another lefthander, also suffered. He was 8-9 the first half and 4-7 the second.

Righthander Dave Freisleben (10-13) rolled up six victories in his first seven decisions (by June 21) then lost eight in a row.

By September, Hernandez and Fuentes had been replaced by the rookie double play combination of shortstop Bill Almon and Mike Champion. Rookie left fielder Jerry Turner, who had troubles in mid-season while replacing injured John Grubb, went on a September spree that raised his final average almost 50 points, to .267.

Because of injuries to righthanders Dan Spillner and Alan Foster, the Padres labored much of the season with only eight or nine able-bodied pitchers.

The staff was overworked until the front office made the mid-season acquisitions of righthanders Rick Sawyer (Syracuse) and Tom Griffin (Houston). Sawyer was 5-3 with the Padres and Griffin was 4-3 after leaving the Astros.

The team set a record with 42 victories at home but it was only 19-29 in one-run games and only 17-32 against lefthanded pitchers.

SAN DIEGO PADRES—1976

Front row—Peralta, equipment manager; Kendall, Hernandez, Foster, Jones, Craig, coach; Amalfitano, coach; McNamara, manager; Wietelmann, coach; Sisler, coach; Freisleben, Ivie. Second row—Dent, assistant trainer; Fuentes, Rader, Turner, Strom, Sawyer, Melendez, Folkers, W. Davis, Johnson, Rettenmund, Mattei, trainer and traveling secretary. Third row—Torres, Grubb, R. Davis, Griffin, Winfield, Tomlin, Metzger, Kubiak. Absent—Spillner.

Following the season, the Padres signed free agents Gene Tenace and Rollie Fingers from Oakland.

Fingers is expected to share the bullpen chores with Butch Metzger, THE SPORTING NEWS N. L. Rookie Pitcher of the Year in 1976.

Metzger was 11-4 in '76, with a 2.93 ERA and 16 saves.

SCORES OF SAN DIEGO PADRES' 1976 GAMES

	W/L	Score	Winner	Loser
APRIL				
9—Atlanta	W	8-2	Jones	Morton
10—Atlanta	L	0-3	Niekro	Spillner
11—Atlanta	L	2-4	Ruthven	Greif
13—At L.A.	W	8-5	Strom	Hooton
14—At L.A.	W	3-1	Jones	Sutton
16—At Hous.	L	1-4	Niekro	Wehrmeister
17—At Hous.	L	4-5	Richard	Spillner
18—At Hous.	L	2-4	Griffin	Strom
18—At Hous.	W	11-5	Jones	Andujar
20—At Cinn.	W	7-5	Metzger	McEnaney
21—At Cinn.	L	4-5	Norman	Wehrmeister
23—St. Louis	W	5-1	Jones	Denny
24—St. Louis	W	4-3	Metzger	Rasmussen
25—St. Louis	L	1-3	Curtis	Spillner
26—Chicago	W	6-2	Greif	R. Reuschel
27—Chicago	L	2-4	Burris	Wehrmeister
28—Chicago	L	5-8	Bonham	Jones
29—Chicago	W	9-5	Metzger	Garman
30—Pitts.	L	3-4	Rooker	Spillner
Won 9, Lost 10				
MAY				
1—Pitts.	L	6-10	Candelaria	Greif
2—Pitts.	W	4-2	Jones	Medich
5—At Mon.	W	6-4	Strom	Rogers
6—At Mon.	W	4-1	Spillner	Kirby
7—At N.Y.	L	2-6	Koosman	Jones
8—At N.Y.	L	2-7	Lolich	Folkers
9—At N.Y.	W	4-0	Strom	Seaver
11—At Phila.	L	1-9	Carlton	Spillner
12—At Phila.	W	4-0	Jones	Kaat
14—At Chi.	W	7-4	Strom	P. Reuschel
16—At Chi.	L	5-6	R. Reuschel	Greif
17—At S.F.	W	12-2	Jones	Barr
18—At S.F.	W	7-6†	Metzger	Moffitt
19—Houston	L	4-9	Griffin	Spillner
20—Houston	L	4-5	Niekro	Wehrmeister
21—Cinn.	W	4-2	Jones	Nolan
22—Cinn.	L	2-3	Zachry	Foster
23—Cinn.	L	0-11	Billingham	Strom
24—Los Ang.	W	2-0	Freisleben	John
25—Los Ang.	W	5-2	Jones	Hooton
26—Los Ang.	L	0-8	Rau	Reynolds
27—S. Fran.	W	3-1	Strom	Halicki
28—S. Fran.	L	0-5	Montefusco	Foster
29—S. Fran.	W	4-0	Freisleben	Dressler
30—S. Fran.	W	4-3*	Jones	Lavelle
31—At Atl.	W	10-7	Folkers	Leon
Won 15, Lost 11				
JUNE				
1—At Atl.	L	1-9	Moret	Strom
4—At Pitts.	L	2-7	Reuss	Freisleben
5—At Pitts.	W	11-9§	Freisleben	Hernandez
6—At Pitts.	W	6-1	Strom	Candelaria
7—N. York	W	5-1	Foster	Swan
8—N. York	W	3-0	Freisleben	Lolich
9—N. York	W	3-0	Jones	Seaver
10—N. York	L	0-6	Matlack	Strom
11—Phila.	L	2-4	Kaat	Foster
12—Phila.	L	2-3§	Underwood	Reynolds
13—Phila.	W	5-0	Jones	Lonborg
13—Phila.	W	4-3	Folkers	Christenson
14—Montreal	L	0-3	Stanhouse	Strom
15—Montreal	W	2-1	Foster	Carrithers
16—Montreal	W	6-2	Freisleben	Warthen
JUNE				
18—At St.L.	L	4-7	Falcone	Jones
19—At St.L.	L	0-1	Curtis	Strom
20—At St.L.	W	5-4	Spillner	Greif
21—S. Fran.	W	6-3	Freisleben	Montefusco
22—S. Fran.	W	4-2	Jones	D'Acquisto
23—At S.F.	L	6-7	Heaverlo	Strom
23—At S.F.	L	7-8	Barr	Tomlin
24—At S.F.	L	5-8	Williams	Reynolds
25—Atlanta	L	1-4	Moret	Freisleben
26—Atlanta	W	9-7	Metzger	Marshall
26—Atlanta	L	3-7	Niekro	Spillner
27—Atlanta	W	3-2	Strom	Messersmith
28—Cinn.	L	3-7	Alcala	Foster
29—Cinn.	W	5-12‡	Zachry	Spillner
30—Cinn.	W	3-1	Jones	Billingham
Won 15, Lost 15				
JULY				
1—Los Ang.	W	5-3	Strom	Rau
2—Los Ang.	W	6-3	Foster	Sutton
3—At L.A.	L	1-3	Rhoden	Freisleben
4—At L.A.	W	5-2	Jones	John
5—At Chi.	L	0-1	Renko	Strom
6—At Chi.	L	0-4	Stone	Foster
7—At Chi.	L	0-10	R. Reuschel	Freisleben
8—At Chi.	W	6-3	Jones	Bonham
9—At Phila.	L	3-4	Underwood	Strom
10—At Phila.	L	0-5	Carlton	Foster
10—At Phila.	L	2-4	Lonborg	Spillner
11—At Phila.	L	0-3	Kaat	Freisleben
15—St. Louis	L	1-2	Forsch	Strom
16—St. Louis	L	2-4	McGlothen	Jones
17—St. Louis	L	1-7	Denny	Freisleben
18—Chicago	W	2-1	Metzger	Burris
19—Chicago	W	3-2	Strom	Bonham
20—Phila.	W	3-0	Jones	Carlton
21—Phila.	L	1-5	Kaat	Freisleben
22—At L.A.	W	5-4†	Metzger	Sosa
23—At L.A.	L	0-5	John	Strom
24—Los Ang.	W	6-5	Metzger	Sosa
25—Los Ang.	L	0-1	Rau	Freisleben
26—At Hous.	L	0-7	Dierker	Spillner
27—At Hous.	L	1-4	Richard	Johnson
28—At Hous.	W	2-1*	Jones	Andujar
29—At Cinn.	L	3-9	Zachry	Foster
30—At Cinn.	L	8-13	Sarmiento	Spillner
30—At Cinn.	L	2-4	Nolan	Folkers
31—At Cinn.	L	1-12	Norman	Strom
Won 10, Lost 20				
AUGUST				
1—At Cinn.	L	4-5	Alcala	Jones
2—At Atl.	W	7-3	Metzger	Devine
2—At Atl.	W	7-0	Sawyer	LaCorte
3—At Atl.	L	3-7	Messersmith	Folkers
4—At Atl.	L	0-1	Ruthven	Jones
5—Houston	W	4-3	Freisleben	McLaughlin
6—Houston	W	9-3	Griffin	Dierker
7—Houston	W	3-2	Sawyer	Andujar
8—Houston	W	4-3	Metzger	Richard
10—At N.Y.	L	4-5	Koosman	Jones
11—At N.Y.	L	1-2	Matlack	Griffin
12—At N.Y.	W	3-0	Sawyer	Seaver
13—At Mon.	L	0-6	Rogers	Freisleben
13—At Mon.	W	4-3	Strom	Dunning
14—At Mon.	W	7-2	Jones	Stanhouse

AUGUST			Winner	Loser
15—At Mon.	W	6-1	Griffin	Carrithers
16—At St.L.	W	11-7	Freisleben	Greif
17—At St.L.	L	4-9	Denny	Strom
18—At St.L.	L	4-5	Falcone	Jones
21—N. York	L	1-7	Koosman	Griffin
22—N. York	L	0-1	Matlack	Jones
23—Pitts.	W	5-4	Johnson	Rooker
24—Pitts.	W	7-3	Strom	Candelaria
25—Pitts.	L	0-3	Kison	Freisleben
27—Montreal	W	2-0	Jones	Fryman
28—Montreal	L	4-7	Murray	Metzger
29—Montreal	L	0-3	Rogers	Sawyer
31—At Pitts.	L	0-3	Reuss	Jones
			Won 14, Lost 14	

SEPTEMBER				
1—At Pitts.	L	1-4	Kison	Strom
2—At Pitts.	L	0-5	Demery	Freisleben
3—At S.F.	L	3-7	Barr	Jones
4—At S.F.	L	3-4	Lavelle	Griffin
5—At S.F.	L	0-5	Montefusco	Strom
5—At S.F.	W	6-1	Sawyer	Dressler
6—Los Ang.	L	1-4	Sutton	Jones
7—Los Ang.	W	4-2	Freisleben	Hooton
8—Atlanta	L	1-3*	Leon	Johnson

SEPTEMBER			Winner	Loser
9—Atlanta	W	4-3	Metzger	Beard
11—Houston	W	4-1	Jones	Dierker
11—Houston	L	1-2	Richard	Sawyer
13—S. Fran.	L	2-3*	Heaverlo	Freisleben
14—S. Fran.	L	6-7	Moffitt	Metzger
15—S. Fran.	L	1-2	Riccelli	Jones
18—At Hous.	W	4-1	Freisleben	Richard
19—At Hous.	L	2-3	Lemongello	Jones
19—At Hous.	L	2-3x	McLaughlin	Metzger
21—At Cinn.	L	1-9	Zachry	Johnson
22—At Cinn.	L	3-4	Gullett	Strom
24—At Atl.	W	6-4	Jones	Devine
25—At Atl.	L	8-11	Ruthven	Owchinko
26—At Atl.	L	4-10	Devine	Metzger
27—Cinn.	W	5-3	Griffin	Alcala
28—Cinn.	L	4-5	Billingham	Sawyer
29—Cinn.	W	6-1	Strom	Norman
			Won 8, Lost 18	

OCTOBER				
1—At L.A.	L	1-8	Lewallyn	Owchinko
2—At L.A.	W	4-1	Giffin	Sutton
3—At L.A.	W	3-2	Sawyer	Rau
			Won 2, Lost 1	

* 10 innings. † 11 innings. ‡ 14 innings. § 15 innings. x Part of September 10 doubleheader at San Diego transferred to Houston.

Turner, Braves' Ratings Hit Bottom

By WAYNE MINSHEW

It was a season which began with new players, a new atmosphere enhanced by different ownership and, certainly, new hope. But, in the end, the Braves' finish was new only in that they dropped still another notch in the National League West standings, from fifth to sixth.

Yet, while a 70-92 record marked the first cellar finish in the club's Atlanta history, nobody could say it was a dull season. If the new owner of the Braves, communications executive-yachtsman Robert E. "Ted" Turner, wasn't making news by signing free agent Andy Messersmith, which he did on April 10 to the astonishment of the baseball world, he was racing motorized bathtubs or nose-pushing baseballs while fulfilling his vow "not to be just another boy on the block."

On the field, Messersmith, nicknamed "Channel 17" after Turner's local television ownership, broke even in 22 decisions but was hampered by injuries which created a controversy when he skipped the All-Star Game. He also was given no rest by the media who quizzed him at every stop about his beating baseball's time-honored reserve system.

Still, the veteran righthander was one of the Braves' few pluses. So was righthander Dick Ruthven, who won 14 games early, although he faltered near the end of the season and wound up with 17 losses. And, as has happened for most of the 11 years the Braves have been here, old pro Phil Niekro emerged as the leading Brave pitcher with 17 wins against 11 defeats. Included was a one-hitter against the powerful Reds, October 2.

The most notable deed of the year, however, was turned in by an outfielder, Rowland Office, who put together a 29-game hitting streak which lasted from May 23 until June 24, when he was stopped by the Expos' Don Stanhouse.

However, in mid-July Office suffered a knee injury while diving for a fly ball in a game at Pittsburgh and was virtually through for the year. He played in only 99 games, batting .281.

The Braves also lost to injuries for varying times outfielder Ken Henderson, catcher Biff Pocoroba, relief pitchers Mike Marshall (two wins, six saves in 24 games at Atlanta) and Max Leon and Messersmith. At one time or another during the campaign, no fewer than seven Brave players had to use crutches to remain ambulatory.

A fellow who got around rather well, however, was first baseman Willie Montanez. Obtained in a trade with the Giants for Darrell Evans and Marty Perez, Montanez batted .321 for the Braves and .317 overall.

Again, though, the Braves' minuses outweighed the pluses. After an 8-5 start and a share of the West Division lead, the Braves proceeded to lose 13 straight games. Too-often sloppy defense, a pitching staff too shallow to be consistently good and an offensive attack lacking punch helped to dump the Braves into last place in the West on September 5 and left them there for the remainder of the season.

Still, attendance climbed from an all-time Atlanta low of 534,672 to 818,179, including two standing-room-only turnouts of better than 50,000 for games during the season.

The surge in attendance was attributed to local ownership, with Turner purchasing the club "on nothing down and easy payments" which amounted to $10 million. The dynamic, sailing-champion television-station owner convulsed crowds by jumping out of his seat and onto the field to shake hands with home run hitters and by sweeping bases during the course of a game.

And while the Braves finished in the cellar, Turner rewarded his manager, Bristol, with a two-year contract at the end of the season.

Slugger Jeff Burroughs, the American League MVP in 1974, became a Brave during the winter meetings. Atlanta surrendered pitchers Carl Morton, Adrian Devine and Roger Moret and outfielders Dave May and Henderson to the Texas Rangers, with $250,000.

Outfielder Gary Matthews, who hit .279 with 20 homers and 84 RBIs at San Francisco in '76, was signed as a free agent to add some punch to the Braves' lineup.

However, the repercussions of this signing were to cost Turner dearly.

Commissioner Bowie Kuhn fined the Braves $10,000 and the loss of their first-round pick in the January free-agent draft for tampering charges.

Another charge of tampering was levied by Matthews' former San Francisco employers, after Atlanta had inked Matthews to a multi-year pact. This time the Braves lost their first-round free-agent choice in June and Commissioner Kuhn suspended Turner, prohibiting him from taking part in Braves' activities for one year.

SCORES OF ATLANTA BRAVES' 1976 GAMES

APRIL			Winner	Loser	APRIL			Winner	Loser
9—At S.D.	L	2-8	Jones	Morton	21—S. Fran.	W	3-0	Ruthven	Barr
10—At S.D.	W	3-0	Niekro	Spillner	23—At Phila.	W	6-5	Dal Canton	McGraw
11—At S.D.	W	4-2	Ruthven	Greif	24—At Phila.	L	5-10	Reed	Sosa
13—Cinn.	L	1-6	Norman	Torrealba	25—At Phila.	W	3-2	Niekro	Christenson
15—Cinn.	W	10-5	Niekro	Billingham	26—At N.Y.	L	1-3	Lolich	Ruthven
16—Los Ang.	W	3-1	Ruthven	John	27—At N.Y.	L	5-6	Hall	Torrealba
17—Los Ang.	L	1-5	Rau	Morton	28—At N.Y.	L	0-3	Swan	Messersmith
18—Los Ang.	W	7-6	Sosa	Hooton	29—At N.Y.	L	0-2	Seaver	Niekro
20—S. Fran.	L	11-12*	Halicki	Sosa				Won 8, Lost 9	

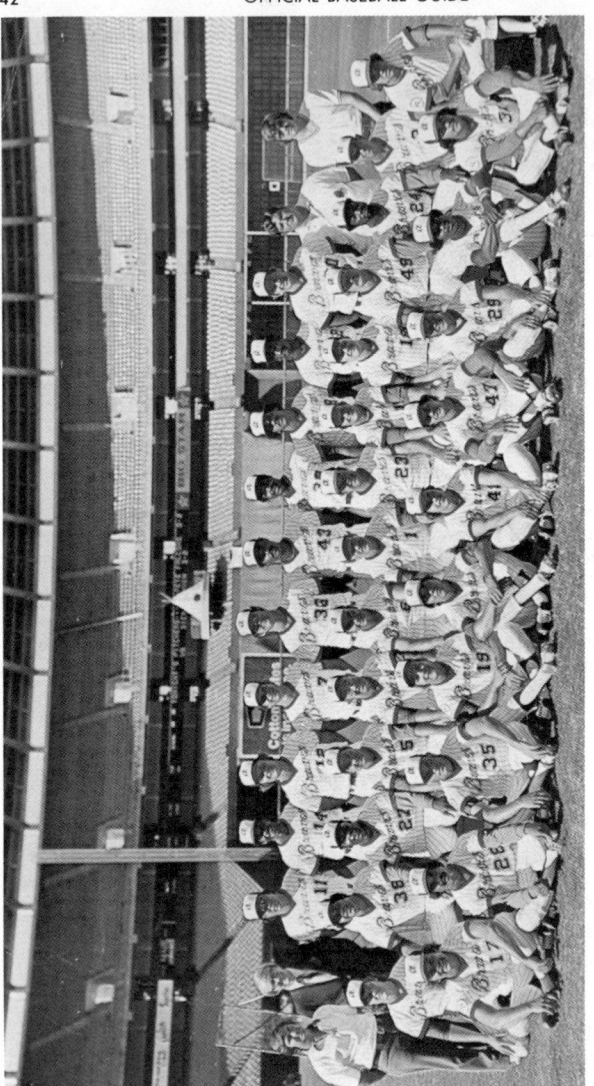

ATLANTA BRAVES—1976

Front row—Messersmith, Torrealba, Niekro, Gilbreath, Perez, Pocoroba, Capra, Correll, Royster, Leon. Second row—Rary, batboy; Sosa, May, Haas, coach; Benson, coach; Cannizzaro, coach; Bristol, manager; Starrette, coach; Chaney, Crowley, Morton, Wynn, Appling, instructor; Stensland, batboy. Third row—Acree, equipment manager; Van Wieren, traveling secretary; Evans, Moret, Paciorek, Henderson, Devine, Gaston, Williams, Quintana, Office, Dal Canton, Pursley, trainer; Holland, assistant equipment manager.

MAY

Date		Score	Winner	Loser
1—Phila.	L	0-3	Christenson	Ruthven
1—Phila.	L	2-4	Carlton	Morton
2—Phila.	L	2-8	Kaat	Messersmith
4—St. Louis	L	7-8‡	Rasmussen	Devine
5—St. Louis	L	0-4	Falcone	Ruthven
6—St. Louis	L	4-5	Curtis	Morton
7—At Pitts.	L	1-3	Candelaria	Messersmith
8—At Pitts.	L	3-5	Medich	Niekro
9—At Pitts.	L	2-5	Reuss	Ruthven
11—N. York	W	8-7	Sosa	Apodaca
12—N. York	L	3-6	Koosman	Messersmith
15—Montreal	W	3-1	Ruthven	Rogers
15—Montreal	L	1-6	Warthen	Niekro
16—Montreal	L	4-5	Scherman	Sosa
17—At Hous.	W	3-2	Messersmith	Richard
17—At Hous.	L	2-3	Forsch	Dal Canton
18—At Hous.	W	3-2*	Sosa	Barlow
19—At L.A.	L	1-4	John	Ruthven
20—At L.A.	L	2-3	Hough	Sosa
21—At S.F.	W	8-0	Messersmith	Dressler
22—At S.F.	W	3-2	Moret	Barr
23—At S.F.	W	9-2	Ruthven	Halicki
23—At S.F.	L	0-1*	Montefusco	Leon
25—At Cinn.	L	4-10	Alcala	Morton
26—At Cinn.	W	4-3	Leon	Eastwick
29—Houston	W	3-4	J. Niekro	P. Niekro
30—Houston	L	2-5	Griffin	Messersmith
30—Houston	L	5-16	Rondon	Moret
31—S. Diego	L	7-10	Folkers	Leon

Won 8, Lost 21

JUNE

Date		Score	Winner	Loser
1—S. Diego	W	9-1	Moret	Strom
4—At Mon.	W	2-0	Messersmith	Carrithers
5—At Mon.	W	8-0	Ruthven	Kirby
6—At Mon.	W	14-8	Devine	Dunning
8—At Chi.	W	7-3	Niekro	Burris
9—At Chi.	W	2-0	Messersmith	Coleman
10—At Chi.	L	6-7	Renko	Ruthven
11—Pitts.	L	2-6	Candelaria	Moret
12—Pitts.	L	2-4†	Moose	Devine
13—Pitts.	L	5-6	Demery	Leon
14—At St.L.	W	5-2	Messersmith	McGlothen
15—At St.L.	W	5-4	Ruthven	Rasmussen
16—At St.L.	L	3-4	Hrabosky	Beard
18—Chicago	L	4-6	R. Reuschel	Morton
19—Chicago	W	9-3	Messersmith	Burris
19—Chicago	W	12-5	Niekro	Coleman
20—Chicago	W	5-0	Ruthven	Renko
21—Houston	W	11-9	Sosa	Pentz
22—Houston	W	7-9	Pentz	LaCorte
23—Montreal	W	5-2	Messersmith	Dunning
23—Montreal	W	3-0	Niekro	Fryman
24—Montreal	W	2-1	Ruthven	Stanhouse
25—At S.D.	W	4-1	Moret	Freisleben
26—At S.D.	L	7-9	Metzger	Marshall
26—At S.D.	W	7-3	Niekro	Spillner
27—At S.D.	L	2-3	Strom	Messersmith
28—At L.A.	L	2-5	Rhoden	Ruthven
29—At L.A.	L	1-2	John	Moret
30—At L.A.	W	8-3	Niekro	Hooton

Won 18, Lost 11

JULY

Date		Score	Winner	Loser
2—At S.F.	W	7-2	Messersmith	Montefusco
3—At S.F.	W	4-0	Ruthven	D'Acquisto
4—At S.F.	L	2-3	Dressler	LaCorte
5—Pitts.	W	8-6	Dal Canton	Hernandez
6—Pitts.	W	4-2	Messersmith	Rooker
7—Pitts.	L	7-9	Reuss	Ruthven
8—N. York	L	2-5	Seaver	LaCorte
9—N. York	W	5-3	Niekro	Espinosa
10—N. York	L	2-4	Lockwood	Messersmith
11—N. York	W	9-8	Dal Canton	Apodaca
15—At Pitts.	L	1-13	Candelaria	Niekro

JULY

Date		Score	Winner	Loser
16—At Pitts.	L	2-7	Reuss	Messersmith
17—At Pitts.	W	10-2	Ruthven	Kison
18—At N.Y.	L	0-2	Lolich	Morton
19—At N.Y.	W	4-2	Niekro	Swan
20—At Mon.	L	3-4	Carrithers	Messersmith
21—At Mon.	L	3-4	Murray	Dal Canton
22—At Mon.	W	7-1	Morton	Fryman
23—Cinn.	L	1-3	Alcala	Niekro
24—Cinn.	W	5-4	Marshall	Hinton
24—Cinn.	L	3-6	Gullett	LaCorte
25—Cinn.	L	6-7	Nolan	Dal Canton
26—Los Ang.	L	2-6	Sutton	Morton
28—Los Ang.	W	7-2	Niekro	John
30—At Hous.	W	3-2	Messersmith	Larson
31—At Hous.	L	1-2	Richard	Ruthven
31—At Hous.	L	6-9	Sambito	Dal Canton

Won 12, Lost 15

AUGUST

Date		Score	Winner	Loser
1—At Hous.	L	0-6	Dierker	Niekro
2—S. Diego	L	3-7	Metzger	Devine
2—S. Diego	L	0-7	Sawyer	LaCorte
3—S. Diego	W	7-3	Messersmith	Folkers
4—S. Diego	W	1-0	Ruthven	Jones
5—S. Fran.	L	1-2	Barr	Niekro
6—S. Fran.	W	7-0	Morton	Dressler
7—S. Fran.	W	4-3	Marshall	Moffitt
8—S. Fran.	W	2-1	Ruthven	Lavelle
8—S. Fran.	L	1-4	Montefusco	LaCorte
10—At Phila.	W	2-1	Niekro	Christenson
11—At Phila.	L	1-4	Underwood	Morton
12—At Phila.	W	4-3	LaCorte	Lonborg
13—St. Louis	L	0-8	Falcone	Ruthven
14—St. Louis	L	0-4	Rasmussen	Messersmith
15—St. Louis	W	3-2	Niekro	Forsch
16—At Cinn.	W	4-3	Morton	Norman
17—At Cinn.	W	3-2	Devine	Sarmiento
18—At Cinn.	L	1-4	Billingham	Ruthven
19—At Cinn.	L	2-3†	Borbon	Devine
20—At St.L.	L	4-6	Rasmussen	Niekro
21—At St.L.	W	6-2	Morton	Forsch
22—At St.L.	L	0-8	McGlothen	LaCorte
23—Phila.	L	2-4	Lonborg	Ruthven
24—Phila.	L	3-14	Carlton	Messersmith
25—Phila.	W	5-1	Niekro	Christenson
27—At Chi.	L	4-9	Bonham	LaCorte
28—At Chi.	L	2-5	Renko	Ruthven
29—At Chi.	L	2-3	Burris	Niekro
31—Chicago	W	5-3	LaCorte	R. Reuschel

Won 13, Lost 17

SEPTEMBER

Date		Score	Winner	Loser
1—Chicago	L	5-7§	Knowles	Capra
3—Cinn.	L	5-10	Eastwick	Devine
4—Cinn.	L	1-5	Zachry	LaCorte
5—Cinn.	L	4-6	Sarmiento	Ruthven
6—At S.F.	L	3-4	Lavelle	Dal Canton
7—At S.F.	L	3-6	Barr	Niekro
8—At S.D.	W	3-1*	Leon	Johnson
9—At S.D.	L	3-4	Metzger	Beard
12—At L.A.	W	3-2*	Devine	Hough
12—At L.A.	L	0-2	Sutton	Moret
13—At L.A.	W	5-1	LaCorte	Hooton
13—At L.A.	L	3-4	Rhoden	Leon
14—Houston	L	3-4	Lemongello	Ruthven
14—Houston	W	4-3	Autry	McLaughlin
15—Houston	L	3-4	Larson	Camp
16—Houston	W	5-3	Niekro	Andujar
17—Los Ang.	L	1-0†	Devine	Hough
17—Los Ang.	L	7-11	Hooton	Moret
18—Los Ang.	W	5-2	Easterly	Lewallyn
19—Los Ang.	L	1-8	John	Ruthven
21—At Hous.	W	6-2	Niekro	Larson
22—At Hous.	L	2-5	Andujar	LaCorte
24—S. Diego	L	4-6	Jones	Devine

SEPTEMBER				Winner	Loser	OCTOBER			Winner	Loser
25—S. Diego	W	11-8		Ruthven	Owchinko	1—At Cinn.	L	2-5	Nolan	Ruthven
26—S. Diego	W	10-4		Devine	Metzger	2—At Cinn.	W	3-0	Niekro	Zachry
28—S. Fran.	L	1-4		Knepper	LaCorte	3—At Cinn.	L	1-11	Gullett	LaCorte
29—S. Fran.	L	0-9		Montefusco	Easterly			Won 1, Lost 2		
		Won 10, Lost 17								

* 10 innings.   † 11 innings.   ‡ 12 innings.   § 14 innings.

EAST DIVISION

Phils Raise Flag in Bicentennial Year

By RAY KELLY

The Liberty Bell chimed in Philadelphia for the nation's 200th birthday in 1976 and the city's favorite baseball team, the Phillies, won the National League East Division title.

In some respects it was the greatest year in the Phillies' history. With a 101-61 record, Danny Ozark's legions drew captivating attention from their followers. A record 2,480,150 fans turned out to see the Phils, more than 500,000 than ever before.

The Phils finished nine lengths ahead of the Pittsburgh Pirates in the East Division. Their 101 victories represented a difference of nine successes from the 1964 previous club high water mark of 92 wins.

The 1964 failure—when Philadelphia lost 10 straight down the stretch to squander a 6½ game lead—was a mental roadblock for the 1976 Phillies. However, the 1964 season's second-place finish was just a miserable memory overcome by Ozark's very real champions.

The overriding disappointment, of course, was felt in losing three straight games to the Cincinnati Reds in the National League Championship Series.

However, the season produced more than enough glory to spread around.

Ozark was named THE SPORTING NEWS Major League Manager of the Year in a poll of fellow big league managers.

Mike Schmidt paced the majors in home runs with 38 for his third consecutive big league homer title.

Center fielder Garry Maddox had a marvelous season at bat and in the field. Hitting .330, Maddox wound up third for the batting championship, nine points behind Chicago's Bill Madlock and six points in arrears to Cincinnati's Ken Griffey. Garry also won his second Gold Glove, as a member of THE SPORTING NEWS All-Star fielding team.

Schmidt and catcher Bob Boone also secured positions on the All-Star fielding squad.

Jay Johnstone was plucked from the role of a platoon player to rather regular duty and responded with a .318 average. He was the Phils' brightest player in the playoff loss to Cincinnati, sporting a .778 average with seven hits in nine at-bats.

Greg Luzinski completed the season with a .304 mark and 21 homers and 95 RBIs. Dave Cash (.284), who became a free agent and signed with Montreal after the season, and Larry Bowa (.248) each struggled a little at the plate (they both hit over .300 in 1975). But their defensive work up the middle remained air tight.

Steve Carlton was the bellwether of the pitching staff. He had a 20-7 won-lost record with a 3.13 ERA. Jim Lonborg captured his first eight decisions and racked up an 18-10 slate.

Starter-reliever Ron Reed proved perhaps the most pleasant surprise of the 1976 season. He appeared in 59 games and totaled eight victories and 14 saves. Reed and his bullpen cohorts, Gene Garber (nine wins, 11 saves) and Tug McGraw (seven wins, 11 saves), combined for 24 victories and 36 saves.

There was an interval in late August and early September when the Phillies went into a drastic swoon.

They lost eight games in a row, rallied, but lost five outings to the onrushing Pirates in September. The margin dropped to three games on September 17.

Then the Phillies proceeded to take charge, rolling to 13 victories in their final 16 contests and completing the season with a nine-game bulge over Pittsburgh.

Ironically, after clinching the championship in the first game of a doubleheader at Montreal September 26, the Phillies put a damper on their own celebration.

Controversial slugger Richie Allen remained in the dugout during the twinbill intermission. When the second game started he and some of his teammates (Cash, Ollie Brown, Maddox and Schmidt) went into the clubhouse and stayed there sympathizing with a disgruntled Allen.

Allen was unhappy when the Phillies did not put Tony Taylor's name among those eligible for postseason play. He claimed that he wouldn't play in the Championship Series unless Taylor was also eligible.

Afterwards, when the Phillies went on to St. Louis to complete their road trip, Allen hopped into a plane and went back to Philadelphia.

On and off the disabled list during the season, Allen hit .268 with 15 homers and 49 RBIs. He became a free agent following the season and did not figure to be in the Phillies' plans for 1977.

Mike Schmidt provided the single most excitement by a Phillie in 1976. On April 17, he knocked out four home runs and a single in an 18-16 victory at Chicago.

SCORES OF PHILADELPHIA PHILLIES' 1976 GAMES

APRIL			Winner	Loser	MAY			Winner	Loser
10—Pitts.	L	4-5x	Demery	McGraw	2—At Atl.	W	8-2	Kaat	Messersmith
11—Pitts.	L	3-8	Kison	Carlton	4—Houston	W	5-0	Lonborg	Dierker
14—At Mon.	W	8-2	Lonborg	Rogers	5—Houston	W	6-3	Reed	Niekro
15—At Mon.	L	5-8	Fryman	Kaat	7—Los Ang.	L	8-10	Hough	Reed
17—At Chi.	W	18-16§	McGraw	Knowles	8—Los Ang.	W	6-4	Garber	John
18—At Chi.	W	8-5	Christenson	Burris	9—Los Ang.	W	10-3	Lonborg	Rau
20—At Pitts.	W	5-1	Kaat	Candelaria	11—S. Diego	W	9-1	Carlton	Spillner
21—At Pitts.	W	3-0	Underwood	Medich	12—S. Diego	L	0-4	Jones	Kaat
23—Atlanta	L	5-6	Dal Canton	McGraw	14—At Hous.	W	5-1	Christenson	Cosgrove
24—Atlanta	W	10-5	Reed	Sosa	15—At Hous.	W	2-1	Lonborg	Dierker
25—Atlanta	L	2-3	Niekro	Christenson	16—At Hous.	W	12-2	Carlton	Griffin
26—Cinn.	W	10-9	McGraw	Eastwick	19—At N. Y.	W	2-1	Christenson	Lolich
27—Cinn.	L	3-7	Billingham	Underwood	20—At N. Y.	W	5-3	Lonborg	Seaver
28—Cinn.	W	7-6	Lonborg	Darcy	21—St. Louis	W	2-1	Carlton	Falcone
			Won 8, Lost 6		22—St. Louis	L	6-7	Hrabosky	McGraw
					23—St. Louis	W	3-2x	McGraw	Hrabosky
MAY					24—N. York	W	7-1	Christenson	Lolich
1—At Atl.	W	3-0	Christenson	Ruthven	25—N. York	W	8-4	Lonborg	Seaver
1—At Atl.	W	4-2	Carlton	Morton	26—N. York	W	5-0	Carlton	Matlack

PHILADELPHIA PHILLIES—1976

Front row—K. Bush, Sr., equipment manager; Tolan, Oates, Taylor, Wine, coach; Ozark, manager; Beringer, coach; Rippelmeyer, coach; Cash, Bowa, McGraw. Second row—Ferenz, traveling secretary; Schmidt, Martin, Hutton, Harmon, Brown, Allen, Boone, Luzinski, Garber, Cera, assistant equipment manager. Third row—Maddox, Schueler, Reed, Twitchell, Lonborg, Carlton, Kaat, Christenson, Johnstone, McCarver, Underwood. In front—Cooper, assistant trainer; K. Bush, Jr., batboy; Anderson, ballboy; Seger, trainer. Missing—DeMars, coach.

MAY

				Winner	Loser
27	N. York	L	2-5	Koosman	Garber
28	Montreal	W	10-3	Reed	Stanhouse
29	Montreal	W	6-1	Christenson	Carrithers
30	Montreal	W	7-1	Lonborg	Kirby
31	Chicago	L	5-7	R. Reuschel	Carlton
31	Chicago	W	4-1	Kaat	Garman

Won 22, Lost 5

JUNE

				Winner	Loser
1	Chicago	W	6-1*	Reed	Renko
2	At St. L.	W	4-1	Underwood	Curtis
3	At St. L.	L	1-7	Forsch	Christenson
4	At S. F.	L	1-5	Barr	Lonborg
5	At S. F.	L	2-4	Halicki	Carlton
6	At S. F.	W	9-3	Kaat	Montefusco
7	At L. A.	W	8-6	Reed	Hough
8	At L. A.	W	14-2	Christenson	John
9	At L. A.	L	2-3	Hooton	Lonborg
10	At L. A.	W	10-6y	McGraw	Wall
11	At S. D.	W	4-2	Kaat	Foster
12	At S. D.	W	3-2a	Underwood	Reynolds
13	At S. D.	L	0-5	Jones	Lonborg
13	At S. D.	L	3-4	Folkers	Christenson
15	S. Fran.	W	10-2	Carlton	Halicki
16	S. Fran.	W	6-1	Kaat	Montefusco
17	S. Fran.	W	3-2	Garber	Lavelle
18	Cinn.	W	6-5	Lonborg	Billingham
19	Cinn.	L	3-4	Nolan	Reed
20	Cinn.	W	6-1	Kaat	Gullett
21	Montreal	W	8-3	Underwood	Warthen
22	Montreal	L	3-8	Kirby	Lonborg
23	At Cinn.	W	4-2	Reed	Borbon
24	At Cinn.	W	5-4	Kaat	Nolan
25	St. Louis	W	12-4	Christenson	Curtis
26	St. Louis	L	2-3§	Hrabosky	McGraw
27	St. Louis	W	6-2	Lonborg	McGlothen
28	At Mon.	W	6-2	Carlton	Rogers
29	At Mon.	W	2-1	Garber	Murray

Won 20, Lost 9

JULY

				Winner	Loser
2	At Pitts.	L	9-10§	Hernandez	Garber
3	At Pitts.	W	3-2	McGraw	Moose
4	At Pitts.	W	10-5	Carlton	Demery
4	At Pitts.	L	1-7	Kison	Kaat
5	Los Ang.	L	0-6	Hooton	Lonborg
6	Los Ang.	L	1-5	Rau	Christenson
7	Los Ang.	L	5-6	Sutton	Reed
9	S. Diego	W	4-3	Underwood	Strom
10	S. Diego	W	5-0	Carlton	Foster
10	S. Diego	W	4-2	Lonborg	Spillner
11	S. Diego	W	3-0	Kaat	Freisleben
15	At S. F.	W	5-3	Carlton	Caldwell
16	At S. F.	L	0-1	Halicki	Kaat
17	At S. F.	L	1-4	Montefusco	Underwood
18	At L. A.	W	2-1	Reed	Hough
19	At L. A.	W	5-3	Garber	Hooton
20	At S. D.	L	0-3	Jones	Carlton
21	At S. D.	W	5-1	Kaat	Freisleben
22	Pitts.	W	3-0	Underwood	Kison
23	Pitts.	W	11-1	Lonborg	Medich
24	Pitts.	L	5-8	Rooker	Christenson
24	Pitts.	W	7-1	Carlton	Moose
25	Pitts.	W	13-7	Reed	Giusti
26	N. York	W	4-1	Christenson	Matlack
27	N. York	L	1-4	Myrick	Underwood
28	Chicago	L	2-5x	Sutter	Reed
29	Chicago	W	3-2x	Garber	Knowles
30	At N. Y.	L	2-3	Koosman	Kaat
31	At N. Y.	W	2-1	Christenson	Matlack

Won 17, Lost 12

AUGUST

				Winner	Loser
1	At N. Y.	W	7-6x	Garber	Lockwood
1	At N. Y.	W	2-0	Twitchell	Espinosa
2	At Chi.	L	2-4	Bonham	Lonborg
3	At Chi.	L	0-4	R. Reuschel	Kaat
3	At Chi.	W	8-5	Carlton	Stone
4	At Chi.	W	7-5	Garber	Coleman
5	At St. L.	W	5-2‡	Twitchell	McGlothen
6	At St. L.	L	2-6	Denny	Lonborg
7	At St. L.	L	1-4	Falcone	Kaat
8	At St. L.	W	3-2	Carlton	Greif
10	Atlanta	L	1-2	Niekro	Christenson
11	Atlanta	W	4-1	Underwood	Morton
12	Atlanta	L	3-4	LaCorte	Lonborg
13	S. Fran.	L	0-3	Montefusco	Kaat
14	S. Fran.	W	13-2	Carlton	Barr
15	S. Fran.	L	5-9	Moffitt	Garber
17	Montreal	W	11-3	Underwood	Rogers
18	Montreal	W	5-4	Lonborg	Stanhouse
19	Houston	W	7-1	Carlton	Andujar
20	Houston	L	3-8	Larson	Twitchell
21	Houston	W	7-4	Kaat	Richard
22	Houston	W	5-1	Underwood	Dierker
23	At Atl.	W	4-2	Lonborg	Ruthven
24	At Atl.	W	14-3	Carlton	Messersmith
25	At Atl.	L	1-5	Niekro	Christenson
26	At Cinn.	W	5-4z	McGraw	Eastwick
27	At Cinn.	L	1-4	Norman	Underwood
28	At Cinn.	L	7-8	Eastwick	McGraw
29	At Cinn.	W	5-6a	Alcala	Kaat
30	At Hous.	L	1-3	Larson	Christenson
31	At Hous.	L	2-3	Richard	McGraw

Won 16, Lost 15

SEPTEMBER

				Winner	Loser
1	At Hous.	L	0-1	McLaughlin	Kaat
3	At N. Y.	L	0-1	Seaver	Carlton
4	At N. Y.	L	3-7	Espinosa	Lonborg
5	At N. Y.	W	3-1	Christenson	Lolich
6	At Pitts.	L	2-6	Kison	Kaat
6	At Pitts.	L	1-5	Demery	Underwood
8	At Pitts.	L	6-7	Rooker	Carlton
9	Chicago	W	4-2	Lonborg	Bonham
10	Chicago	L	2-3	R. Reuschel	Kaat
11	Chicago	L	1-4y	Sutter	Reed
12	Chicago	W	8-0	Christenson	Renko
13	Montreal	W	7-2	Carlton	Blair
14	Montreal	W	3-2	Lonborg	Fryman
15	Pitts.	L	2-7	Candelaria	Kaat
16	Pitts.	L	6-7	Tekulve	Reed
17	At Chi.	L	3-4y	Sutter	Reed
18	At Chi.	W	4-1	Carlton	R. Reuschel
19	At Chi.	L	0-1	Burris	Lonborg
21	St. Louis	W	5-1	Underwood	Denny
22	St. Louis	W	9-4	Garber	Walker
23	St. Louis	L	7-3	Carlton	Rasmussen
24	At Mon.	W	9-3	Christenson	Rogers
24	At Mon.	L	2-3	Stanhouse	Kaat
25	At Mon.	W	6-5	Twitchell	Fryman
26	At Mon.	W	4-1	Lonborg	Warthen
26	At Mon.	W	2-1†	Schueler	Blair
27	At St. L.	W	9-1	Kaat	Falcone
28	At St. L.	L	3-5	Rasmussen	Carlton
29	At St. L.	W	6-5	McGraw	Curtis

Won 15, Lost 14

OCTOBER

				Winner	Loser
1	N. York	W	2-1	Garber	Koosman
2	N. York	W	7-4	Lonborg	Matlack
3	N. York	W	2-1	Carlton	Swan

Won 3, Lost 0

---

* 6 innings.   † 7 innings.   ‡ 8 innings.   § 10 innings.   x 11 innings.   y 12 innings.   z 13 innings.   a 15 innings.

Era Ends in Pittsburgh Baseball

By CHARLEY FEENEY

Danny Murtaugh managed the Pittsburgh Pirates to 92 victories in 1976, equalling their National League East Division championship total of 1975. The Pirates, however, finished second, nine game behind the Philadelphia Phillies.

Just two months after Murtaugh announced his retirement, he died of a stroke. The smiling Irishman was 59 years old. He had managed Pittsburgh to world championships in 1960 and again in 1971.

Murtaugh's resignation came four days after his longtime friend Joe Brown resigned as general manager of the Pirates.

Off-season tragedy also struck relief pitcher Bob Moose, who died in an automobile accident, October 9, his 29th birthday.

Murtaugh and Brown had formed a successful combination in Pittsburgh baseball. The era was now over.

The 1976 season brought some drastic changes in the Pirates' scheme. Once, the most feared hitters' team in baseball, the Bucs changed their style.

They stole more bases (130) than they hit home runs (110). It was the first time since 1958 and only the second time since the 1920s that a Pirate team stole more than 100 bases.

Frank Taveras emerged as one of the game's outstanding base thieves. He stole 58 bases and was caught only 11 times.

While Taveras improved on the attack, there were many deficiencies that dropped the Pirates well behind the Phillies in July.

The defense, as in past years, failed to properly support the pitchers. The hitting was streaky.

Willie Stargell, moving up in years and with an early season personal problem, finished at .257 with 20 homers and 65 RBIs.

Stargell's wife, Dolores, came near death because of a blood clot near her brain in May. No doubt, her condition worried the Pirates' captain.

In mid-July, Murtaugh pin-pointed one major disappointment. "The starting pitchers," he said, "aren't doing the job we expected them to do."

About a month later, those same starting pitchers began to put things together. Only one change was made in the rotation. Larry Demery, a young righthander, replaced George (Doc) Medich, obtained from the Yankees in December, 1975, and a flop in the first three months of the season.

John Candelaria, who hurled a no-hit, no-run game against the Dodgers on August 9 in Pittsburgh, became the club's most effective pitcher. Bruce Kison, Jim Rooker and Jerry Reuss won consistently and so did Demery.

The result was a near-comeback. Trailing the Phillies by 15 and one-half games on August 25, the Pirates rolled to 15 victories in 17 games. They continued a torrid pace and, on September 17, after beating the Mets, the Pirates were within three games of first place.

The greatest comeback in baseball history was in the works. So it seemed. Then it happened. The Pirates cooled off. The Mets beat them three in a row and less than a week later, the Pirates' big push ended in failure.

Individually, it was a team of ups and downs. Dave Parker, who finished at

.313 with 90 RBIs, missed more than a month of the season when he injured his knee in May.

Rennie Stennett, expected to be a strength at second base, played poorly in the field until mid-July. Taveras, the shortstop, had some brilliant fielding spurts, but near the close of the season, he became erratic again. He made 35 errors in 141 games.

Richie Hebner spent the first half of the season fighting a slump, a carry-over from the 1975 season. Hebner finished strongly, but his .249 mark was 30 points below his lifetime average.

Richie Zisk doesn't do too many things impressively in left field and his bat is almost taken for granted. He finished with a .289 BA and 89 RBIs, second to Parker on the club.

In center field, there was Al Oliver. In 1976, there were two Al Olivers. There was the Al Oliver, who in July, led the league in hitting and was a threat to win the National League batting crown.

By August, Oliver was a sick man. An inner ear infection caused balance problems. He finished at .323, but he missed 41 games—that's more time than he missed in the previous three seasons.

Behind the plate, Manny Sanguillen started the season in his regular role as No. 1 catcher. In August, Duffy Dyer began to share the catching with Sanguillen who eventually was forced out because of an injury to his collarbone.

When the season ended, the players voted for a most valuable player. The man who won the award was probably the best non-regular in the big leagues last season.

The name is Bill Robinson, formerly of the Braves and the Yankees and the Phillies. This was Robinson's second year with the Pirates. He figured to be a No. 4 outfielder—a fill-in.

He was a Super Sub. He played all three outfield positions and, for awhile, he took the third base job away from Hebner. He also subbed at first base for Stargell.

In 122 games, he batted .303, hit 21 homers (tying Zisk for the club lead) and drove in 64 runs.

The relief corps was effective, only the names changed. Dave Giusti, once the No. 1 man in the pen, became just another reliever.

Two men replaced Giusti. For the first two months of the season, Bob Moose was the No. 1 fireman. He didn't allow an earned run going into June 1.

From July 1 through the rest of the season, Kent Tekulve, a stringbean righthander, assumed the role as No. 1 man in the pen.

Ramon Hernandez, once the lefthanded ace, was shipped to the Cubs on waivers in early September.

Candelaria, in his first full season, blossomed as a star. He became the first Pirate to pitch a no-hit, no-run game in Pittsburgh. Back on September 20, 1907, Nicholas Maddox of the Pirates beat Brooklyn at old Exposition Field on a no-hitter, but he allowed a run, winning, 2-1.

Candelaria, only 22, became the club ace. He led with 16 wins, shutouts (4), strikeouts (138) and total innings (220).

PITTSBURGH PIRATES—1976

Front row—J. Hallahan, equipment manager; Hernandez, Oliver, Skinner, coach; Pagan, coach; Murtaugh, manager; Osborn, coach; Leppert, coach; Dyer, Helms, Bartirome, trainer. Second row—Graff, traveling secretary; Tekulve, Ott, Mendoza, Taveras, Zisk, Rooker, Moose, Kirkpatrick, Giusti, Sanguillen, Finegold, team physician. Third row—Kison, Robinson, Candelaria, Stargell, Parker, Reuss, Medich, Demery, Robertson, Hebner. In front—G. Hallahan, batboy.

Rooker won 15 games and Reuss and Kison each won 14. It was a personal high for Kison, a World Series hero in 1971.

Demery, who worked short and long relief before he moved into the rotation, won 10 games. Medich won eight.

Chuck Tanner obtained in a trade from Oakland for Sanguillen, is the new manager, Harding Peterson the new G. M. A whole new regime is replacing a winning combination. The end of an era.

SCORES OF PITTSBURGH PIRATES' 1976 GAMES

APRIL			Winner	Loser
10–At Phila.	W	5-4‡	Demery	McGraw
11–At Phila.	W	8-3	Kison	Carlton
13–St. Louis	W	14-4	Reuss	Falcone
15–St. Louis	W	9-3	Rooker	McGlothen
16–N. York	W	3-1	Medich	Lolich
17–N. York	L	1-17	Koosman	Kison
18–N. York	W	7-5	Reuss	Swan
20–Phila.	L	1-5	Kaat	Candelaria
21–Phila.	L	0-3	Underwood	Medich
23–At S.F.	L	3-7	Montefusco	Reuss
24–At S.F.	L	1-3	Halicki	Rooker
25–At S.F.	L	3-5	Candelaria	Caldwell
26–At L.A.	L	1-7	John	Medich
27–At L.A.	L	1-4	Rau	Kison
28–At L.A.	L	1-2	Hooton	Reuss
30–At S.D.	W	4-3	Rooker	Spillner
		Won 8, Lost 8		
MAY				
1–At S.D.	W	10-6	Candelaria	Greif
2–At S.D.	L	2-4	Jones	Medich
4–S. Fran.	W	6-5	Reuss	Caldwell
5–S. Fran.	W	6-1	Kison	Halicki
6–S. Fran.	W	3-0	Rooker	Barr
7–Atlanta	W	3-1	Candelaria	Messersmith
8–Atlanta	W	5-3	Medich	Niekro
9–Atlanta	W	5-2	Reuss	Ruthven
11–At Cin.	L	0-6	Nolan	Kison
12–At Cin.	W	6-3	Rooker	Gullett
14–Los Ang.	L	2-3	Hough	Candelaria
15–Los Ang.	W	4-2	Medich	Rau
16–Los Ang.	L	0-6	Hooton	Reuss
17–At St.L.	W	2-1	Kison	Curtis
18–At St.L.	W	4-1	Rooker	Hrabosky
19–At St.L.	W	7-6	Hernandez	Rasmussen
20–At St.L.	L	1-4	Denny	Medich
21–Chicago	L	4-5	R. Reuschel	Demery
22–Chicago	W	4-3z	Moose	P. Reuschel
23–Chicago	L	5-6	Zamora	Tekulve
23–Chicago	W	9-1	Reuss	Garman
24–Montreal	L	2-4	Fryman	Candelaria
25–Montreal	L	3-6‡	Granger	Moose
26–Montreal	W	6-3	Demery	Warthen
29–At Chi.	L	1-4	Bonham	Kison
30–At Chi.	W	4-2	Rooker	Burris
31–At N.Y.	L	2-13	Matlack	Reuss
31–At N.Y.	W	2-1	Medich	Apodaca
		Won 17, Lost 11		
JUNE				
1–At N.Y.	W	3-2	Candelaria	Koosman
2–At Mon.	W	4-2	Kison	Fryman
3–At Mon.	L	1-7	Stanhouse	Rooker
4–S. Diego	W	7-2	Reuss	Freisleben
5–S. Diego	L	9-11y	Freisleben	Hernandez
6–S. Diego	L	1-6	Strom	Candelaria
7–Cinn.	W	5-4	Moose	McEnaney
8–Cinn.	L	5-10	Alcala	Rooker
9–Cinn.	L	1-6	Nolan	Reuss
10–Cinn.	L	1-6	Gullett	Medich
11–At Atl.	W	6-2	Candelaria	Moret
12–At Atl.	W	4-2‡	Moose	Devine
13–At Atl.	W	6-5	Demery	Leon

JUNE			Winner	Loser
14–At Hous.	W	2-1	Reuss	Richard
16–At Hous.	W	6-3	Medich	Andujar
18–Houston	W	7-3	Candelaria	Richard
20–Houston	L	4-9	Griffin	Moose
22–At Chi.	W	10-7	Demery	Knowles
23–At Chi.	L	5-6	Zamora	Moose
24–At Chi.	L	1-2x	Zamora	Langford
25–At Mon.	W	9-2	Kison	Carrithers
26–At Mon.	W	7-6	Demery	Murray
27–At Mon.	L	3-4	Fryman	Medich
28–Chicago	W	9-2	Rooker	Coleman
29–Chicago	W	10-1	Candelaria	Renko
30–Chicago	W	7-5	Kison	Bonham
		Won 16, Lost 10		
JULY				
2–Phila.	W	10-9†	Hernandez	Garber
3–Phila.	L	2-3	McGraw	Moose
4–Phila.	L	5-10	Carlton	Demery
4–Phila.	W	7-1	Kison	Kaat
5–At Atl.	L	6-8	Dal Canton	Hernandez
6–At Atl.	L	2-4	Messersmith	Rooker
7–At Atl.	W	9-7	Reuss	Ruthven
9–At Cinn.	L	11-12†	Candelaria	Demery
9–At Cinn.	L	1-2	Norman	Medich
10–At Cinn.	W	7-1	Candelaria	Billingham
11–At Cinn.	W	8-5	Tekulve	Borbon
15–Atlanta	W	13-1	Candelaria	Niekro
16–Atlanta	W	7-2	Reuss	Messersmith
17–Atlanta	L	2-10	Ruthven	Kison
18–Cinn.	L	8-9	Billingham	Medich
19–Cinn.	L	2-4	Zachry	Rooker
20–Houston	W	9-5	Candelaria	Griffin
20–Houston	L	3-4	Forsch	Giusti
21–Houston	W	5-1	Reuss	Dierker
21–Houston	W	4-1	Demery	Andujar
22–At Phila.	L	0-3	Underwood	Kison
23–At Phila.	L	1-11	Lonborg	Medich
24–At Phila.	W	8-5	Rooker	Christenson
24–At Phila.	L	1-7	Carlton	Moose
25–At Phila.	L	7-13	Reed	Giusti
27–At St.L.	W	3-1	Kison	Falcone
28–At N.Y.	W	1-0x	Giusti	Sanders
29–At N.Y.	W	2-1†	Tekulve	Lockwood
30–Montreal	W	4-3x	Tekulve	Kerrigan
31–Montreal	L	6-7	Murray	Moose
		Won 15, Lost 15		
AUGUST				
1–Montreal	L	0-2	Rogers	Kison
2–St. Louis	L	0-4	Falcone	Medich
3–St. Louis	W	2-1	Rooker	Greif
3–St. Louis	L	2-4	Hrabosky	Giusti
4–St. Louis	W	2-1§	Giusti	Wallace
5–N. York	L	4-7	Matlack	Reuss
7–N. York	W	12-3	Kison	Seaver
7–N. York	L	2-4	Espinosa	Medich
8–N. York	L	4-7	Lolich	Rooker
9–Los Ang.	W	2-0	Candelaria	Rau
10–Los Ang.	L	1-5	Sutton	Reuss
11–Los Ang.	L	0-2	Rhoden	Demery
13–At Hous.	W	8-5	Tekulve	Niekro
14–At Hous.	W	5-4	Giusti	Pentz

AUGUST			Winner	Loser
15—At Hous.	W	8-6	Medich	Larson
15—At Hous.	W	3-0	Reuss	Sambito
17—At S.F.	L	6-7	Lavelle	Moose
18—At S.F.	W	12-1*	Rooker	Montefusco
19—At S.F.	W	1-0	Candelaria	Barr
20—At L.A.	L	1-8	Rau	Kison
21—At L.A.	L	1-5	Sutton	Moose
22—At L.A.	W	6-1	Demery	Rhoden
23—At S.D.	L	4-5	Johnson	Rooker
24—At S.D.	L	3-7	Strom	Candelaria
25—At S.D.	W	3-0	Kison	Freisleben
27—S. Fran.	W	5-2	Demery	Montefusco
28—S. Fran.	W	7-1	Rooker	D'Acquisto
29—S. Fran.	W	3-2‡	Candelaria	Moffitt
31—S. Diego	W	3-0	Reuss	Jones
			Won 16, Lost 13	

SEPTEMBER				
1—S. Diego	W	4-1	Kison	Strom
2—S. Diego	W	5-0	Demery	Freisleben
3—At Mon.	W	9-7	Rooker	Stanhouse
3—At Mon.	W	7-2	Candelaria	Carrithers
4—At Mon.	W	5-3	Giusti	Murray
5—At Mon.	L	0-1	Fryman	Reuss
6—Phila.	W	6-2	Kison	Kaat
6—Phila.	W	5-1	Demery	Underwood
8—Phila.	W	6-1	Rooker	Carlton
10—Montreal	L	2-4	Fryman	Candelaria

SEPTEMBER			Winner	Loser
11—Montreal	W	4-3	Reuss	Rogers
12—Montreal	W	6-1	Kison	Stanhouse
13—N. York	W	0-5	Seaver	Demery
14—N. York	L	3-4	Lockwood	Rooker
15—At Phila.	W	7-2	Candelaria	Kaat
16—At Phila.	W	7-6	Tekulve	Reed
17—At N.Y.	W	4-1	Medich	Matlack
18—At N.Y.	L	2-6	Seaver	Demery
19—At N.Y.	L	6-7	Espinosa	Giusti
20—At N.Y.	L	4-5	Apodaca	Tekulve
21—At Chi.	W	4-3	Kison	Renko
21—At Chi.	L	1-2x	P. Reuschel	Moose
22—At Chi.	L	3-4	Coleman	Tekulve
23—At Chi.	W	5-4†	Giusti	Knowles
24—At St.L.	L	6-10	Forsch	Candelaria
24—At St.L.	W	11-1	Rooker	Curtis
25—At St.L.	L	0-3	McGlothen	Reuss
26—At St.L.	L	2-5	Denny	Kison
28—Chicago	W	5-1	Medich	R. Reuschel
29—Chicago	L	0-1	Renko	Demery
			Won 17, Lost 13	

OCTOBER				
2—St. Louis	W	8-0	Candelaria	McGlothen
3—St. Louis	W	1-0	Rooker	Denny
3—St. Louis	W	1-0	Reuss	Falcone
			Won 3, Lost 0	

* 6½ innings.   † 10 innings.   ‡ 11 innings.   § 12 innings.   x 13 innings.   y 15 innings.   z 16 innings.

Missing Ingredients Spell End for Mets

By JACK LANG

Whether the season ended for the Mets on a college basketball court in Virginia in February or in Joe McDonald's office in St. Petersburg in March or in left field in Shea Stadium on the night of July 19, no one will ever know for sure. But certainly all these dates added up to prevent the Mets from making any serious run at the Philadelphia Phillies, who waltzed off with the National League's East Division championship.

The Mets, 86-76, like to think that at least the incidents of February and July did mitigate against their chances of catching the front-running Phils and they may be right.

For without Mike Vail . . . without Tom Seaver having another 20-win season . . . and without the potent home run bat of Dave Kingman for a full season . . . the Mets were destined for their fifth third-place finish in the last seven seasons.

What hurt most is difficult to say. Certainly Vail's dislocated ankle suffered while playing basketball at Old Dominion College one Sunday afternoon in February had an effect on the Mets' chances.

During the winter, the Mets had unloaded Rusty Staub, their best hitter, and designated Vail as his right field replacement. They were overjoyed with Mike's .302 hitting the final 38 games of the 1975 season and were certain they had a future star on their hands.

But Vail's injury kept him out of the lineup until the middle of June and when he was able to play again it was hardly with the same authority he had shown at the plate the previous year. Mike managed to hit only .217.

As with all other clubs, spring training got off to a late start for the Mets because of the players' strike. However, Tom Seaver and several of his Mets' pitching teammates did not let any grass grow under their feet. Under Seaver's supervision, an ersatz spring training camp was set up at Eckerd College in St. Petersburg and it proved to be a tremendous help to the Mets in getting off to a good start.

Every morning, Seaver's Mets and players from the Cardinals and Pirates would work out on the Eckerd College diamond and that early conditioning did much for people like Seaver, Jon Matlack, Jerry Koosman, Skip Lockwood and Mickey Lolich. When the camps finally opened, all the Mets' pitchers were ready and when the official league play began, that early conditioning helped the Mets to jump off to a 13-7 start in April.

As late as April 30th, the Mets held a two-game lead in the National League East and on May 13 they were still tied for first place. But the following day they dropped out and never were serious contenders again.

Besides the players' strike, which created considerable acrimony between the players and the owners, Seaver had his own personal problems with the Mets' front office. His desire for a long-term contract with security resulted in a long bitter struggle and a so-called war of words between Tom and General Manager Joe McDonald.

McDonald even went to great lengths to unload Seaver and, in fact, had a deal all set with the Dodgers that would have sent the three-time Cy Young Award winner to Los Angeles in exchange for Don Sutton and an unnamed outfielder. On Sunday, March 28, McDonald conferred in Vero Beach with Larue Harcourt, Sutton's agent, and virtually consummated the deal.

But one reporter with the Mets caught wind of the proposed trade and broke the story. Such a furor followed, the Mets did not dare trade Tom Terrific away. Seaver himself, infuriated with the shabby treatment he was getting from the sophomore general manager, walked into McDonald's St. Petersburg office one day and demanded: "There's the phone, pick it up and trade me if that's what you want."

The Mets, of course, did not trade Seaver and one week later he signed the most lucrative contract any pitcher ever received. It was for three years at a base salary of $225,000 with all sorts of bonuses for games won beyond 19. It was not until mid-season that the "performance" contract, one of the first of its kind in baseball, was approved by the league.

But Seaver did not have the kind of season that the contract called for. He won only 14 games, his lowest total ever in a healthy season, but he did lead the league in strikeouts with 235. It was the fifth time he has led in that department and the ninth time in his career he went over 200, a major league record.

The Mets started the season under the leadership of Joe Frazier, a long-time minor league manager. Frazier became the sixth man to manage the Mets and the third in six years.

While the Mets' players did not exactly go into ecstacies over their new pilot and some found him bush league in many ways, they nevertheless accepted him. There was more of a settling influence later in the season when Frazier's contract was renewed for another year.

Perhaps the biggest blow the Mets suffered all season came on the night of July 19 when Dave Kingman, diving for a ball in left field, tore the ligaments in his thumb and was lost to the team for the next six weeks. At the time, Kong was leading the majors with 32 home runs and had already knocked in 69 runs for the Mets. He was seven days ahead of the home run pace set by Hack Wil-

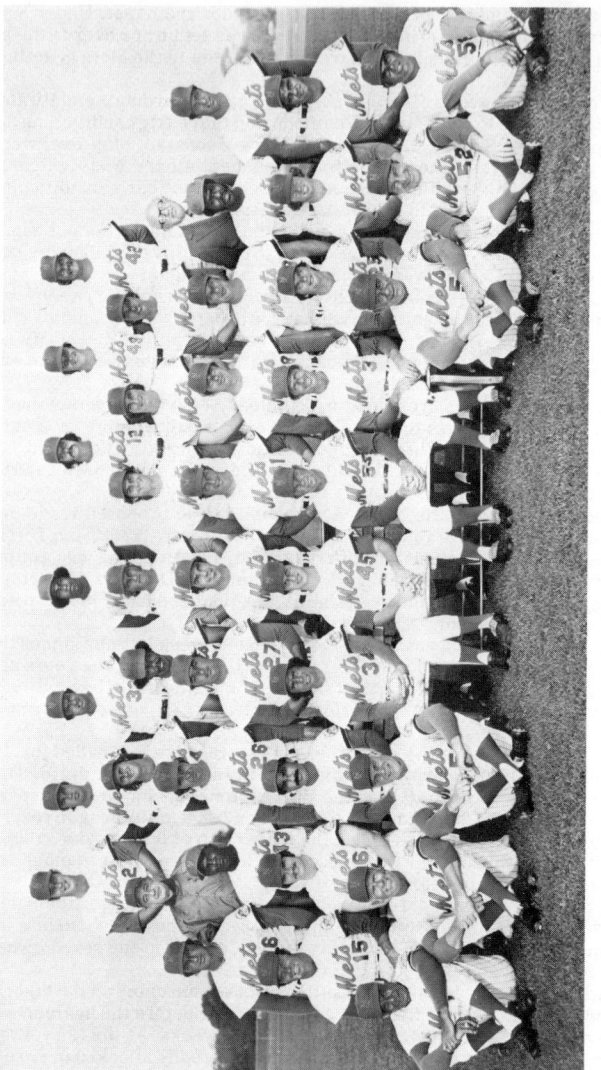

NEW YORK METS—1976

Front row—Coaches Cavarretta, McMillan, Yost, Walker, Pignatano, Connors. Second row—Grote, Vail, Millan, Apodaca, R. Baldwin, Frazier, manager; Harrelson, Unser, Garrett, Torre. Third row—Koosman, Perry, Kingman, Swan, Kranepool, Seaver, Lockwood, Lolich, Hall, Matlack. Fourth row—McKenna, trainer; Boisclair, B. Baldwin, Trapp, Phillips, Tate, Webb, Niss, traveling secretary. Fourth row—Staiger, Stearns, Sanders, Espinosa, Heidemann, Grose, Hodges.

son when the former Cub set the National League record with 56 homers in 1930.

When Kingman finally did return to the lineup on August 27, he played in great pain. He hit only five home runs the rest of the year but narrowly missed being the home run champ of the majors when Philadelphia's Mike Schmidt edged him by one.

Still, playing in only 123 games, Kingman led the Mets with 86 RBIs and they had to believe later that his absence cost them at least second place if not a shot at the Phils.

The 2.94 earned-run average that the Mets' pitchers turned in was the best in baseball as were the 1,025 strikeouts. No other staff allowed less than three earned runs per game or struck out more than one thousand batters.

While Seaver did not have his usual good year, two others did. Jerry Koosman won 21 games, reaching the magic 20 circle for the first time in his career. And Jon Matlack achieved a personal high of 17 victories.

Mickey Lolich, in his first year in the National League, was a bit of a disappointment with an 8-13 record. Skip Lockwood won 10 games in relief and stopped many opposition uprisings, recording 19 saves.

Despite the loss of Vail and Kingman and the mid-season deal that sent center fielder Del Unser to Montreal, the Mets really were hurt badly in the infield when Bud Harrelson was unable to play his usual good game at shortstop. Coming off a knee operation, Harrelson was unable to cover the ground his pitchers require if they are to be successful.

The Mets also were hurt in one other area. They drew only 1,468,754 paying customers. While that's respectable for most clubs, it was their lowest ever in Shea Stadium and a drop of almost 300,000 over the previous year.

SCORES OF NEW YORK METS' 1976 GAMES

APRIL			Winner	Loser	MAY			Winner	Loser
9—Montreal	W	3-2	Seaver	Rogers	14—At Cinn.	L	1-5	Billingham	Lolich
10—Montreal	W	1-0	Matlack	Fryman	15—At Cinn.	L	0-2	Alcala	Seaver
11—Montreal	L	6-7	Scherman	Lolich	16—At Cinn.	W	7-5	Matlack	Nolan
13—At Chi.	L	4-5	Garman	Lockwood	16—At Cinn.	L	1-8	Gullett	Swan
14—At Chi.	L	5-6	Schultz	Webb	19—Phila.	L	1-2	Christenson	Lolich
15—At Chi.	W	10-8	Lockwood	Dettore	20—Phila.	L	3-5	Lonborg	Seaver
16—At Pitts.	L	1-3	Medich	Lolich	21—At Mon.	W	4-3	Lockwood	Murray
17—At Pitts.	W	17-1	Koosman	Kison	22—At Mon.	W	4-1	Koosman	Scherman
18—At Pitts.	L	5-7	Reuss	Swan	23—At Mon.	L	4-5	Lang	Swan
19—At St.L.	W	4-3y	Apodaca	Wallace	24—At Phila.	L	1-7	Christenson	Lolich
20—At St.L.	W	8-0	Matlack	McGlothen	25—At Phila.	L	4-8	Lonborg	Seaver
21—At St.L.	L	4-7	Rasmussen	Lolich	26—At Phila.	L	0-5	Carlton	Matlack
23—At Hous.	L	1-3	Cosgrove	Koosman	27—At Phila.	W	5-2	Koosman	Garber
24—At Hous.	W	7-1	Seaver	Dierker	28—St. Louis	L	0-6	Curtis	Swan
25—At Hous.	W	4-2	Sanders	Niekro	29—St. Louis	L	2-3†	Hrabosky	Sanders
26—Atlanta	W	3-1	Lolich	Ruthven	30—St. Louis	L	5-6‡	Hrabosky	Lockwood
27—Atlanta	W	6-5	Hall	Torrealba	31—Pitts.	W	13-2	Matlack	Reuss
28—Atlanta	W	3-0	Swan	Messersmith	31—Pitts.	L	1-2	Medich	Apodaca
29—Atlanta	W	2-0	Seaver	Niekro			**Won 11, Lost 17**		
30—Houston	W	3-1	Matlack	Niekro					
		Won 13, Lost 7			JUNE				
					1—Pitts.	L	2-3	Candelaria	Koosman
MAY					2—Chicago	L	3-5	Bonham	Swan
2—Houston	L	4-5	Richard	Apodaca	3—Chicago	L	1-2	Burris	Lolich
2—Houston	W	7-4	Koosman	Rondon	4—At L.A.	W	11-0	Seaver	Hooton
4—Cinn.	W	5-3	Seaver	Norman	5—At L.A.	W	3-1	Matlack	Rau
5—Cinn.	L	0-2‡	Eastwick	Hall	6—At L.A.	L	3-10	Sutton	Koosman
6—Cinn.	W	4-2	Swan	Gullett	7—At S.D.	L	1-5	Foster	Swan
7—S. Diego	W	6-2	Koosman	Jones	8—At S.D.	L	0-3	Freisleben	Lolich
8—S. Diego	W	7-2	Lolich	Folkers	9—At S.D.	L	0-3	Jones	Seaver
9—S. Diego	L	0-4	Strom	Seaver	10—At S.D.	W	6-0	Matlack	Strom
11—At Atl.	L	7-8	Sosa	Apodaca	11—At S.F.	L	0-5	Montefusco	Koosman
12—At Atl.	W	6-3	Koosman	Messersmith	12—At S.F.	W	3-1	Swan	D'Acquisto

JUNE			Winner	Loser
13—At S.F.	W	4-2	Lolich	Dressler
13—At S.F.	W	4-1	Seaver	Barr
15—Los Ang.	W	2-1	Matlack	Hooton
16—Los Ang.	L	1-4	Rau	Koosman
17—Los Ang.	W	1-0x	Lockwood	Hough
18—S. Fran.	W	3-2	Seaver	Dressler
19—S. Fran.	L	0-5	Barr	Lolich
20—S. Fran.	L	2-9	Halicki	Matlack
21—At St.L.	L	2-7	McGlothen	Koosman
22—At St.L.	L	0-3	Denny	Swan
23—At St.L.	W	5-4	Seaver	Falcone
25—At Chi.	W	7-4	Matlack	Burris
26—At Chi.	W	10-2	Koosman	Bonham
27—At Chi.	W	13-3	Swan	R. Reuschel
28—St. Louis	W	5-4	Lockwood	Greif
29—St. Louis	W	2-0	Lolich	Falcone
			Won 15, Lost 13	

JULY				
1—St. Louis	W	13-0	Matlack	Forsch
2—Chicago	W	2-1	Koosman	Coleman
3—Chicago	W	3-2†	Lockwood	R. Reuschel
4—Chicago	W	9-4	Swan	Bonham
4—Chicago	L	2-4	Burris	Lolich
5—At Hous.	L	3-7	Niekro	Apodaca
6—At Hous.	L	0-1†	Richard	Lockwood
7—At Hous.	W	12-4	Koosman	Andujar
8—At Atl.	W	5-2	Seaver	LaCorte
9—At Atl.	L	3-5	Niekro	Espinosa
10—At Atl.	W	4-2	Lockwood	Messersmith
11—At Atl.	L	8-9	Dal Canton	Apodaca
15—Houston	W	3-1	Koosman	Richard
16—Houston	L	3-4	Dierker	Matlack
17—Houston	L	0-1	Andujar	Seaver
18—Atlanta	W	2-0	Lolich	Morton
19—Atlanta	L	2-4	Niekro	Swan
20—At Cinn.	W	2-1	Koosman	Nolan
21—At Cinn.	L	0-4	Norman	Matlack
23—At Mon.	L	2-3‡	Murray	Lockwood
24—At Mon.	W	10-4	Lolich	Kirby
25—At Mon.	L	1-2	Carrithers	Koosman
26—At Phila.	L	1-4	Christenson	Matlack
27—At Phila.	W	4-1	Myrick	Underwood
28—Pitts.	L	0-1§	Giusti	Sanders
29—Pitts.	L	1-2†	Tekulve	Lockwood
30—Phila.	W	3-2	Koosman	Kaat
31—Phila.	L	1-2	Christenson	Matlack
			Won 13, Lost 15	

AUGUST				
1—Phila.	L	6-7‡	Garber	Lockwood
1—Phila.	L	0-2	Twitchell	Espinosa
2—Montreal	L	4-5	Taylor	Lockwood
3—Montreal	W	9-8	Apodaca	Kerrigan
4—Montreal	W	4-0	Koosman	Carrithers
5—At Pitts.	W	7-4	Matlack	Reuss
7—At Pitts.	L	3-12	Kison	Seaver

AUGUST			Winner	Loser
7—At Pitts.	W	4-2	Espinosa	Medich
8—At Pitts.	W	7-4	Lolich	Rooker
10—S. Diego	W	5-4	Koosman	Jones
11—S. Diego	W	2-1	Matlack	Griffin
12—S. Diego	L	0-3	Sawyer	Seaver
13—Cinn.	L	3-7	Billingham	Lolich
14—Cinn.	W	2-1	Espinosa	Zachry
15—Cinn.	W	1-0	Koosman	Nolan
17—At L.A.	L	3-4	Rhoden	Matlack
18—At L.A.	L	2-3	Hough	Seaver
19—At L.A.	L	5-6	Hough	Apodaca
21—At S.D.	W	7-1	Koosman	Griffin
22—At S.D.	W	1-0	Matlack	Jones
24—At S.F.	W	4-0	Seaver	Barr
25—At S.F.	L	1-7	Halicki	Espinosa
27—Los Ang.	L	2-5	Sutton	Koosman
28—Los Ang.	W	2-1	Matlack	Rhoden
29—Los Ang.	L	1-2	John	Seaver
31—S. Fran.	W	6-2	Lockwood	Halicki
			Won 14, Lost 12	

SEPTEMBER				
1—S. Fran.	W	1-0	Koosman	Montefusco
2—S. Fran.	L	7-10	Caldwell	Matlack
3—Phila.	W	1-0	Seaver	Carlton
4—Phila.	W	7-3	Espinosa	Lonborg
5—Phila.	L	1-3	Christenson	Lolich
6—At Chi.	W	7-4	Koosman	Stone
7—At Chi.	W	11-0	Matlack	Burris
8—At Chi.	W	11-5	Seaver	Renko
10—At St.L.	W	4-3	Lolich	Denny
11—At St.L.	W	4-1	Koosman	Falcone
12—At St.L.	L	5-6	Capilla	Apodaca
13—At Pitts.	W	5-0	Seaver	Demery
14—At Pitts.	W	4-3	Lockwood	Rooker
15—St. Louis	L	0-7	Denny	Lolich
15—St. Louis	L	1-4	Curtis	Espinosa
16—St. Louis	W	4-1	Koosman	Falcone
17—Pitts.	L	1-4	Medich	Matlack
18—Pitts.	L	6-2	Seaver	Demery
19—Pitts.	W	7-6	Espinosa	Giusti
20—Pitts.	W	5-4	Apodaca	Tekulve
21—At Mon.	L	0-4	Warthen	Koosman
22—At Mon.	W	4-2	Matlack	Landreth
24—Chicago	W	4-3	Lockwood	Coleman
25—Chicago	W	5-2	Swan	Renko
26—Chicago	W	2-1	Koosman	Bonham
27—Montreal	W	10-3*	Matlack	Landreth
28—Montreal	W	5-4	Lockwood	Kerrigan
28—Montreal	L	2-4z	Hannahs	Myrick
29—Montreal	L	2-7	Rogers	Seaver
			Won 20, Lost 9	

OCTOBER				
1—At Phila.	L	1-2	Garber	Koosman
2—At Phila.	L	4-7	Lonborg	Matlack
3—At Phila.	L	1-2	Carlton	Swan
			Won 0, Lost 3	

*7½ innings. †10 innings. ‡11 innings. §13 innings. x14 innings. y17 innings. zSeptember 23 game at Montreal transferred to New York.

Cubs: Attendance Record to Treadmill

By JEROME HOLTZMAN

The Cubs made what could be described as minor progress in 1976, mostly the result of a strong second-half. They finished fourth in the National League East, an improvement from the previous season when they tied Montreal for last place.

The North Siders had a home gate of 1,026,217, the ninth successive year they reached the million mark, and also had the league's batting champion in third baseman Bill Madlock who retained his title with a .339 average. Outfielder-first baseman Rick Monday, though batting leadoff, was third in home runs with 32, the only other Cub hitter among the league leaders.

The Cubs were under the general managership of E. R. (Salty) Saltwell, a longtime organization man formerly in charge of concessions, and began with great expectations: a record home opener crowd of 44,818, obviously hungry for championship baseball, witnessed a 5-4 win over the Mets.

The Cubs were on the usual treadmill thereafter. They never again had a home gate in excess of 30,000, and on May 4, only 23 games into the season, tumbled below the .500 level and out of the first division, never to return.

The problem early was ineffective pitching, from both starters and relievers. Rookie Bruce Sutter, recalled from the minors on May 8, helped patch the bullpen which was in constant action. There were only four complete-pitched games in the first 76, and one was a seven-inning struggle stopped by rain. The Cubs' worst skid began on June 19 and extended through the first game of a July 4 doubleheader, a 15-game stretch in which they lost 13 of 15 games, including nine in a row, a slump that prompted owner Philip K. Wrigley to describe his players as "clowns."

The 81-year old Wrigley, suffering from ailments of old age, was largely confined to his exurban retreat where he often watched the games on television. He subsequently expressed some satisfaction when the Cubs began performing with considerably more enthusiasm and vigor. The turnabout occurred immediately after Manager Jim Marshall squelched some isolated player grumbling publicly voiced by outfielder Jerry Morales who said Marshall was "gutless." Morales retreated from this position and from July 20, to the season's end, a span of 73 games, the Cubs were 39-34, five games over .500.

The pitching was remarkably effective during this surge and was led by Ray Burris who, for the second year in a row, topped the club in victories with 15. Ineffective early, Burris won 11 of his last 13 decisions and had a 2.64 earned-run average for his last 17 starts, which included nine complete games and four shutouts. He was 6-1 in August, the only month in which the Cubs had a winning record, and had a sequence of 25 consecutive scoreless innings, tying for the league high in this department.

Rick Reuschel, with a 14-12 record, was the only other starter with more than nine victories and led the staff with 146 strikeouts. Bill Bonham was next in starts with 31 and third in victories with nine. Steve Renko, acquired in a June trade, won eight games. Rookie Sutter, the ace of the bullpen, earned 10 saves and six victories. The team earned-run average was 3.93, the first time in four years it was below 4.00 but, nonetheless, ranked 11th in the league.

All three members of the so-called "M Squad"—Bill Madlock, Rick Monday and Jerry Morales—reached career highs in home runs. Monday hit 32, Morales 16 and Madlock 15.

Madlock led in runs batted in with 84 and became the first Cub since the legendary Cap Anson of the 1880s to lead the league in batting two years in a row. Madlock won the title with an impressive 4-for-4 performance in the final game which enabled him to overtake Cincinnati's Ken Griffey.

Jose Cardenal, disabled at the finish, batted .299 and had the distinction of being the only major league player to knock out six hits in one game.

The Cubs were definitely improved in the field and were charged with 140

CHICAGO CUBS—1976

Top row—Bonham, Kelleher, Morales, Summers. Second row—Burris, Knowles, P. Reuschel, Swisher. Third row—Cardenal, LaCock, R. Reuschel, Sutter. Fourth row—Frailing, Madlock, Rosello, Trillo. Fifth row—Marshall, manager; Bloomfield, coach; Dunlop, coach; Garman, Mitterwald, Schultz, Wallis. Bottom row—Grissom, coach; Saul, coach; Adams, Hundley, Monday, Stone, Zamora.

errors, the lowest team total since 1972. Manny Trillo emerged as one of the best fielding second basemen in the league. He committed only 17 errors, 12 less than the previous year. To tighten the defense, Monday was moved to first base late in the season, yielding his center field position to Joe Wallis who did well in the field and batted .254.

SCORES OF CHICAGO CUBS' 1976 GAMES

APRIL			Winner	Loser
9–At St. L.	L	0-5	McGlothen	Burris
10–At St. L.	W	4-3	Bonham	Rasmussen
11–At St. L.	W	8-5	Knowles	Curtis
13–N. York	W	5-4	Garman	Lockwood
14–N. York	W	6-5	Schultz	Webb
15–N. York	L	8-10	Lockwood	Dettore
17–Phila.	L	16-18‡	McGraw	Knowles
18–Phila.	L	5-8	Christenson	Burris
19–Montreal	L	3-4	Rogers	Bonham
21–Montreal	L	6-12c	Fryman	Zahn
22–Montreal	W	5-4§	Zamora	Murray
23–At L. A.	W	4-3§	P. Reuschel	Downing
24–At L. A.	L	1-2	Sutton	Bonham
25–At L. A.	L	4-5‡	Hough	Garman
26–At S. D.	W	2-6	Greif	R. Reuschel
27–At S. D.	W	4-2	Burris	Wehrmeister
28–At S. D.	W	8-5	Bonham	Jones
29–At S. D.	L	5-9	Metzger	Garman
30–At S. F.	W	5-2	R. Reuschel	Halicki
		Won 9, Lost 10		
MAY				
1–At S. F.	L	1-3	Lavelle	Schultz
2–At S. F.	W	6-5z	Frailing	Lavelle
2–At S. F.	W	6-5§	Knowles	Minton
4–Los Ang.	L	6-9	Hooton	R. Reuschel
5–Los Ang.	L	12-14	Sutton	Burris
7–Cinn.	L	1-3	Billingham	Frailing
8–Cinn.	L	4-14	Alcala	R. Reuschel
9–Cinn.	L	2-14	Zachry	Burris
11–S. Fran.	W	4-0	Zamora	Halicki
12–S. Fran.	L	1-0§	Garman	Moffitt
13–S. Fran.	L	5-9	Moffitt	Sutter
14–S. Diego	L	4-7	Strom	P. Reuschel
16–S. Diego	W	6-5	R. Reuschel	Greif
20–At Mon.	L	0-3	Fryman	Burris
21–At Pitts.	W	5-4	R. Reuschel	Demery
22–At Pitts.	L	3-4b	Moose	P. Reuschel
23–At Pitts.	W	6-5	Zamora	Tekulve
23–At Pitts.	L	1-9	Reuss	Garman
25–St. Louis	L	2-5	McGlothen	Burris
26–St. Louis	W	4-2	R. Reuschel	Denny
27–St. Louis	W	2-1	Renko	Falcone
29–Pitts.	W	4-1	Bonham	Kison
30–Pitts.	L	2-4	Rooker	Burris
31–At Phila.	W	7-5	R. Reuschel	Carlton
31–At Phila.	L	1-4	Kaat	Garman
		Won 11, Lost 14		
JUNE				
1–At Phila.	L	1-6*	Reed	Renko
2–At N. Y.	W	5-3	Bonham	Swan
3–At N. Y.	W	2-1	Burris	Lolich
4–At Hous.	L	0-1	Cosgrove	R. Reuschel
5–At Hous.	L	3-4	Richard	Zamora
6–At Hous.	L	0-2	Andujar	Bonham
6–At Hous.	L	1-5	Rondon	Frailing
8–Atlanta	L	3-7	Niekro	Burris
9–Atlanta	L	0-2	Messersmith	Coleman
10–Atlanta	W	7-6	Renko	Ruthven
11–Houston	W	8-3	Bonham	Cosgrove
12–Houston	W	5-2	R. Reuschel	Andujar
13–Houston	W	8-3	Burris	Dierker
14–At Cinn.	L	2-3	Nolan	Zamora
15–At Cinn.	L	4-6	Gullett	Knowles
16–At Cinn.	W	5-3†	Bonham	Zachry

JUNE			Winner	Loser
18–At Atl.	W	6-4	R. Reuschel	Morton
19–At Atl.	L	3-9	Messersmith	Burris
19–At Atl.	L	5-12	Niekro	Coleman
20–At Atl.	L	0-5	Ruthven	Renko
22–Pitts.	L	7-10	Demery	Knowles
23–Pitts.	W	6-5	Zamora	Moose
24–Pitts.	W	2-1y	Zamora	Langford
25–N. York	L	4-7	Matlack	Burris
26–N. York	L	2-10	Koosman	Bonham
27–N. York	L	3-13	Swan	R. Reuschel
28–At Pitts.	L	2-9	Rooker	Coleman
29–At Pitts.	L	1-10	Candelaria	Renko
30–At Pitts.	L	5-7	Kison	Bonham
		Won 10, Lost 19		
JULY				
2–At N. Y.	L	1-2	Koosman	Coleman
3–At N. Y.	L	2-3‡	Lockwood	R. Reuschel
4–At N. Y.	L	4-9	Swan	Bonham
4–At N. Y.	W	4-2	Burris	Lolich
5–S. Diego	W	1-0	Renko	Strom
6–S. Diego	W	4-0	Stone	Foster
7–S. Diego	W	10-0	R. Reuschel	Freisleben
8–S. Diego	L	3-6	Jones	Bonham
9–S. Fran.	W	5-3	Sutter	Dressler
10–S. Fran.	W	8-6	Knowles	Moffitt
11–S. Fran.	L	0-2	Halicki	Stone
15–At L. A.	L	2-5	Rau	R. Reuschel
16–At L. A.	L	1-4	Sutton	Renko
17–At L. A.	L	4-5	Rhoden	Stone
18–At S. D.	L	1-2	Metzger	Burris
19–At S. D.	L	2-3	Strom	Bonham
20–At S. F.	W	3-2	R. Reuschel	Halicki
21–At S. F.	L	1-2	Montefusco	Sutter
22–At St. L.	W	8-4	Stone	Falcone
23–At St. L.	W	4-3	Burris	Rasmussen
24–At St. L.	L	3-12	Forsch	Bonham
25–At St. L.	L	3-4	McGlothen	R. Reuschel
26–Montreal	L	1-2	Stanhouse	Stone
26–Montreal	L	1-3	Dunning	Renko
27–Montreal	W	5-0	Burris	Rogers
28–At Phila.	W	5-2§	Sutter	Reed
29–At Phila.	L	2-3§	Garber	Knowles
30–St. Louis	W	7-6	P. Reuschel	Forsch
31–St. Louis	W	6-2	Renko	McGlothen
		Won 13, Lost 16		
AUGUST				
1–St. Louis	W	2-1‡	Burris	Denny
2–Phila.	W	4-2	Bonham	Lonborg
3–Phila.	W	4-0	R. Reuschel	Kaat
3–Phila	L	5-8	Carlton	Stone
4–Phila.	L	5-7	Garber	Coleman
5–At Mon.	W	4-3	Burris	Stanhouse
6–At Mon.	W	6-5y	P. Reuschel	Taylor
6–At Mon.	W	1-0	Stone	Kerrigan
7–At Mon.	W	4-3§	Knowles	Kerrigan
7–At Mon.	L	2-7	Dunning	Zamora
8–At Mon.	W	7-1	Renko	Lang
10–Cinn.	W	6-3	Burris	Nolan
11–Cinn.	L	10-13‡	Zachry	Knowles
12–Cinn.	L	3-8	Sarmiento	Sutter
13–Los Ang.	W	3-2a	Coleman	Hough
13–Los Ang.	L	7-8	Downing	Knowles
14–Los Ang.	W	2-0	Burris	Rau
15–Los Ang.	L	2-3	Sutton	Bonham

AUGUST			Winner	Loser	SEPTEMBER			Winner	Loser
16—At Hous.	W	5-3	Sutter	Dierker	12—At Phila.	L	0-8	Christenson	Renko
17—At Hous.	L	1-8	Richard	Stone	13—At St. L.	L	3-4	Forsch	Bonham
20—At Cinn.	L	3-4	Nolan	Burris	14—At St. L.	W	6-3	R. Reuschel	McGlothen
21—At Cinn.	W	3-2	R. Reuschel	Norman	15—At Mon.	W	2-0	Burris	Rogers
22—At Cinn.	L	3-4	Sarmiento	Coleman	16—At Mon.	L	3-4	Landreth	Renko
24—Houston	W	3-4	Andujar	Renko	17—Phila.	W	4-3x	Sutter	Reed
25—Houston	W	5-1	Burris	Larson	18—Phila.	L	1-4	Carlton	R. Reuschel
26—Houston	L	3-5	Richard	R. Reuschel	19—Phila.	L	1-0	Burris	Lonborg
27—Atlanta	W	9-4	Bonham	LaCorte	21—Pitts.	L	3-4	Kison	Renko
28—Atlanta	W	5-2	Renko	Ruthven	21—Pitts.	W	2-1y	P. Reuschel	Moose
29—Atlanta	W	3-2	Burris	Niekro	22—Pitts.	W	4-3	Coleman	Tekulve
31—At Atl.	L	3-5	LaCorte	R. Reuschel	23—Pitts.	L	4-5‡	Giusti	Knowles
		Won 17, Lost 13			24—At N. Y.	L	3-4	Lockwood	Coleman
					25—At N. Y.	L	2-5	Swan	Renko
SEPTEMBER					26—At N. Y.	L	1-2	Koosman	Bonham
1—At Atl.	W	7-5z	Knowles	Capra	28—At Pitts.	L	1-5	Medich	R. Reuschel
3—St. Louis	W	8-5	Sutter	Solomon	29—At Pitts.	W	1-0	Renko	Demery
4—St. Louis	W	5-1	Renko	McGlothen			**Won 12, Lost 15**		
5—St. Louis	L	0-1§	Hrabosky	Coleman					
6—N. York	L	4-7	Koosman	Stone					
7—N. York	L	0-11	Matlack	Burris	**OCTOBER**				
8—N. York	L	5-11	Seaver	Renko	1—Montreal	W	3-1	Bonham	Stanhouse
9—At Phila.	L	2-4	Lonborg	Bonham	2—Montreal	W	3-1	Burris	Warthen
10—At Phila.	W	3-2	R. Reuschel	Kaat	3—Montreal	W	8-2	R. Reuschel	Fryman
11—At Phila.	W	4-1x	Sutter	Reed			**Won 3, Lost 0**		

* 6 innings. † 7 innings. ‡ 10 innings. § 11 innings. x 12 innings. y 13 innings. z 14 innings. a 15 innings. b 16 innings. c Suspended game, completed April 22.

Cards Fumble, Stumble to Fifth

By NEAL RUSSO

Just about everything conceivable went wrong with the Cardinals in 1976. The Redbirds picked a heckuva time to fall flat on their faces. In the Bicentennial year, they should have been inspired by the fact that the first Cardinal pennant ever—and the first Redbird world championship—came exactly half a century earlier.

Instead, the Cardinals, in their twelfth and last year under Red Schoendienst as manager, wound up a dismal fifth in their division. Their won-lost percentage of .444 (72 victories and 90 losses) was their next to worst since a .422 mark in 1924. The 1955 Cardinals finished at .442.

There was a distinct lack of timely hitting as the Cards finished a horrible 21-37 in one-run decisions. Just a year earlier they were the National League's No. 1 club in one-run verdicts.

What with a spacious home park where the ball doesn't carry, nobody expects the Cardinals to lead in home runs. But they finished dead last with 63 four-baggers. The 63 total was the club's lowest since the early 1940s.

The '76 Cardinals actually ranked fourth in the N.L. in runs with 629, but they spaced their runs poorly. And only four clubs yielded more runs.

Their erratic defense combined with spotty starting pitching, mediocre relief duty and injuries doomed the Cardinals early.

The mound crew went into the season with high expectations. There were good arms, and most of them were young arms. But who would have imagined that Bob Forsch, the club's leading hurler in 1975, wouldn't pocket a complete game until the season was almost over, and would wind up with just two route-going jobs?

John Denny, who deserved better than an 11-9 record, had the league's best earned-run mark, just 2.52, but Lynn McGlothen was so-so with a 13-15 record. There was Forsch with 8-10, John Curtis with 6-11 and Harry (now Eric) Rasmussen, 6-12 as a combination reliever-starter. Newcomer Pete Falcone experienced more than his share of hard luck as he checked in with a 12-16 record, but an impressive 3.23 ERA.

Al Hrabosky, the super bellwether in the bullpen the previous two years, had plenty of trouble as he limped in with an 8-6 mark and 13 saves. Bill Greif, obtained from the Padres in hopes of shoring up the righthanded side of the pen, started off rather well, but he closed out on the losing side. He was 1-5 as a Redbird with six saves.

Injuries were to plague the Cardinals almost from the start of the season. Mike Tyson, who had just been shifted back to second base, his primary position, with Don Kessinger available for shortstop, was knocked out of action in the second game of the season.

Tyson, who had turned in a solid .266 mark the previous season, also missed numerous games because of a finger injury. So he had only 245 official at-bats, and hit a solid .286. He was missed both on offense and defense.

Bake McBride had only 272 official at-bats—and he finished at .335. Reggie Smith had his injuries, too, and batted only .218 before he was dispatched to the Dodgers in mid-June.

Ted Simmons had, for him, somewhat of an off season. He hit .291 and drove in just 75 runs. Heity Cruz, continuing the tough transition from an outfielder to a third baseman, hit only .228, but he whacked 13 homers and collected 71 RBIs.

Lou Brock showed he was hardly ready for the ash-heap as he batted .301 and swiped 56 bases in 75 tries to close within 27 of Ty Cobb's modern career stolen base mark of 892. Brock climbed to 865 steals at age 37.

After a miserable start, first baseman Keith Hernandez sizzled and closed with .289, giving great promise for '77.

The Cardinals, whose 174 errors were topped only by the Giants, had one consolation from the horrible season in which they beat out only the hapless Expos in their division. By lagging so far behind so early, they were able to expedite their youth movement.

For instance, hot shortstop prospect Garry Templeton was able to get into 53 games. He batted an impressive .291, even though his professional experience was considerably limited and he was still learning how to switch-hit.

Templeton made 24 errors, but he made more than his share of outstanding plays in the field and was rated almost a sure-bet top notcher.

With the trade of Smith, Jerry Mumphrey got a king-sized cram course in the outfield. Mumphrey, another of the many Cardinal swift switch-hitters, hit only .258. He covered much ground and swiped 22 bases.

Willie Crawford, who was dealt to the Giants after the season, was a big help to the sagging offense. The ex-Dodger logged in with a .304 mark. He hit nine homers.

The Cardinals finished 37-44 at home and 35-46 on the road. They managed to battle the West Division clubs rather well (34-38) but folded against the East (38-52). The Birds were 6-12 against the Phillies, Pirates and Cubs, just 2-10 against the Dodgers and 3-9 against the Astros.

It seems hard to believe that the Birds' longest losing streak was only five games. But then their longest winning skein was a mere four games.

Falcone's five-game winning string in August was the longest for a St.

ST. LOUIS CARDINALS—1976

Front row—Anderson, Cruz, Rasmussen, Simmons, Smith, Guerrero, McGlothen, Forsch, Kessinger. Second row—Brock, Tyson, Fairly, Torres, Milliken, coach; Gomez, coach; Schoendienst, manager; Lewis, coach; Koenig, coach; Tamargo, Alvarado, Melendez, Yarkeman, equipment manager. Third row—Bauman, trainer; McBride, Parker, Harris, Easler, Allen, Hernandez, Chant, Potter, Proly, Reynolds, Wallace, Rudolph. Fourth row—Crawford, Hrabosky, Richard, Camper, Nordhagen, Denny, Curtis, Waterbury, Staniland, Falcone, Mumphrey, Gieselmann, trainer.

Louis pitcher. On the other side of the coin, Rasmussen lost seven in a row, going winless between May 10 and July 28.

And here's a significant point: the Cardinals left 1,172 men on base. Only the Reds, who could afford to, stranded more in the N.L.

SCORES OF ST. LOUIS CARDINALS' 1976 GAMES

APRIL			Winner	Loser
9—Chicago	W	5-0	McGlothen	Burris
10—Chicago	L	3-4	Bonham	Rasmussen
11—Chicago	L	5-8	Knowles	Curtis
13—At Pitts.	L	4-14	Reuss	Falcone
15—At Pitts.	L	3-9	Rooker	McGlothen
17—Montreal	W	4-3†	Rasmussen	Scherman
18—Montreal	W	2-1	Denny	Warthen
19—N. York	L	3-4y	Apodaca	Wallace
20—N. York	L	0-8	Matlack	McGlothen
21—N. York	W	7-4	Rasmussen	Lolich
23—At S.D.	L	1-5	Jones	Denny
24—At S.D.	L	3-4	Metzger	Rasmussen
25—At S.D.	W	3-1	Curtis	Spillner
26—At S.F.	W	15-7	Wallace	Minton
27—At S.F.	W	7-1	McGlothen	D'Acquisto
28—At S.F.	W	4-2x	Proly	Caldwell
29—At L.A.	L	0-4	Sutton	Falcone
30—At L.A.	L	1-5	Rhoden	Curtis
		Won 8, Lost 10		
MAY				
1—At L.A.	L	3-4†	Marshall	Hrabosky
2—At L.A.	L	1-3	Rau	McGlothen
4—At Atl.	W	8-7§	Rasmussen	Devine
5—At Atl.	W	4-0	Falcone	Ruthven
6—At Atl.	W	5-4	Curtis	Morton
7—Houston	L	1-3	Richard	Forsch
8—Houston	W	5-1	McGlothen	Cosgrove
9—Houston	L	5-10	Dierker	Denny
10—Los Ang.	L	3-4	Marshall	Rasmussen
11—Los Ang.	L	0-4	Sutton	Curtis
12—Los Ang.	L	3-6	Marshall	Rasmussen
14—S. Fran.	W	3-1	McGlothen	Montefusco
15—S. Fran.	L	0-2‡	Lavelle	Hrabosky
16—S. Fran.	W	9-3	Falcone	Halicki
17—Pitts.	L	1-2	Kison	Curtis
18—Pitts.	L	1-4	Rooker	Hrabosky
19—Pitts.	L	6-7	Hernandez	Rasmussen
20—Pitts.	W	4-1	Denny	Medich
21—At Phila.	L	1-2	Carlton	Falcone
22—At Phila.	W	7-6	Hrabosky	McGraw
23—At Phila.	L	2-3‡	McGraw	Hrabosky
25—At Chi.	W	5-2	McGlothen	Burris
26—At Chi.	L	2-4	R. Reuschel	Denny
27—At Chi.	L	1-2	Renko	Falcone
28—At N.Y.	W	6-0	Curtis	Swan
29—At N.Y.	W	3-2†	Hrabosky	Sanders
30—At N.Y.	L	6-5‡	Hrabosky	Lockwood
		Won 12, Lost 15		
JUNE				
1—At Mon.	W	6-2	Falcone	Warthen
2—Phila.	L	1-4	Underwood	Curtis
3—Phila.	W	7-1	Forsch	Christenson
4—Cinn.	L	2-11	Nolan	McGlothen
5—Cinn.	L	1-5	Gullett	Denny
6—Cinn.	L	2-13	Zachry	Falcone
7—At Hous.	W	7-6	Curtis	Niekro
8—At Hous.	L	0-2	Dierker	Forsch
9—At Hous.	L	2-5	Richard	McGlothen
11—At Cinn.	L	7-8	Eastwick	Hrabosky
12—At Cinn.	W	5-4	Falcone	Billingham
13—At Cinn.	L	0-4	Norman	Curtis
13—At Cinn.	W	12-9	Forsch	Alcala
14—Atlanta	L	2-5	Messersmith	McGlothen
15—Atlanta	L	4-5	Ruthven	Rasmussen
16—Atlanta	W	4-3	Hrabosky	Beard

JUNE			Winner	Loser
18—S. Diego	W	7-4	Falcone	Jones
19—S. Diego	W	1-0	Curtis	Strom
20—S. Diego	L	4-5	Spillner	Greif
21—N. York	W	7-2	McGlothen	Koosman
22—N. York	W	3-0	Denny	Swan
23—N. York	L	4-5	Seaver	Falcone
25—At Phila.	L	4-12	Christenson	Curtis
26—At Phila.	W	3-2†	Hrabosky	McGraw
27—At Phila.	L	2-6	Lonborg	McGlothen
28—At N.Y.	L	4-5	Lockwood	Greif
29—At N.Y.	L	0-2	Lolich	Falcone
		Won 11, Lost 16		
JULY				
1—At N.Y.	L	0-13	Matlack	Forsch
2—Montreal	W	3-0	McGlothen	Fryman
3—Montreal	W	9-0	Denny	Rogers
4—Montreal	L	3-4	Stanhouse	Falcone
5—S. Fran.	L	4-6	Lavelle	Rasmussen
6—S. Fran.	W	13-7	Forsch	Halicki
7—S. Fran.	L	2-3	Lavelle	McGlothen
9—Los Ang.	W	4-3	Greif	Sosa
10—Los Ang.	W	6-3	Falcone	John
11—Los Ang.	L	6-9	Sutton	Forsch
15—At S.D.	W	2-1	Forsch	Strom
16—At S.D.	W	4-2	McGlothen	Jones
17—At S.D.	W	7-1	Denny	Freisleben
18—At S.F.	L	4-5	Barr	Falcone
18—At S.F.	W	5-4†	Wallace	Heaverlo
19—At S.F.	L	3-5	D'Acquisto	Forsch
20—At L.A.	L	2-3	Rau	McGlothen
21—At L.A.	L	6-7†	Hough	Hrabosky
22—Chicago	L	4-8	Stone	Falcone
23—Chicago	L	3-4	Burris	Rasmussen
24—Chicago	W	12-3	Forsch	Bonham
25—Chicago	W	4-3	McGlothen	R. Reuschel
27—Pitts.	L	1-3	Kison	Falcone
28—Montreal	L	0-3	Fryman	Rasmussen
30—At Chi.	L	6-7	P. Reuschel	Forsch
31—At Chi.	L	2-6	Renko	McGlothen
		Won 11, Lost 15		
AUGUST				
1—At Chi.	L	1-2†	Burris	Denny
2—At Pitts.	W	4-0	Falcone	Medich
3—At Pitts.	L	1-2	Rooker	Greif
3—At Pitts.	W	4-2	Hrabosky	Giusti
4—At Pitts.	L	1-2§	Giusti	Wallace
5—Phila.	L	2-5*	Twitchell	McGlothen
6—Phila.	W	6-2	Denny	Lonborg
7—Phila.	W	4-1	Falcone	Kaat
8—Phila.	L	2-3	Carlton	Greif
9—Houston	L	4-13	Larson	Forsch
10—Houston	W	8-1	McGlothen	McLaughlin
11—Houston	L	1-8	Dierker	Denny
13—At Atl.	W	8-0	Falcone	Ruthven
14—At Atl.	W	4-0	Rasmussen	Messersmith
15—At Atl.	L	2-3	Niekro	Forsch
16—S. Diego	L	7-11	Freisleben	Greif
17—S. Diego	W	9-4	Denny	Strom
18—S. Diego	W	5-4	Falcone	Jones
20—Atlanta	W	6-4	Rasmussen	Niekro
21—Atlanta	L	2-6	Morton	Forsch
22—Atlanta	W	8-0	McGlothen	LaCorte
23—At Cinn.	W	9-5	Denny	Billingham
24—At Cinn.	W	4-1	Falcone	Zachry
27—At Hous.	L	1-2	McLaughlin	Rasmussen

AUGUST			Winner	Loser		SEPTEMBER			Winner	Loser
28—At Hous.	L	3-4	Dierker	Forsch		15—At N.Y.	W	4-1	Curtis	Espinosa
29—At Hous.	L	0-6	Sambito	McGlothen		16—At N.Y.	L	1-4	Koosman	Falcone
30—Cinn.	W	7-1	Denny	McEnaney		17—At Mon.	L	5-9	Hannahs	Rasmussen
31—Cinn.	L	5-6	Borbon	Falcone		18—At Mon.	W	4-1	Forsch	Stanhouse
			Won 14, Lost 14			18—At Mon.	W	7-4	Solomon	Keener
						19—At Mon.	W	9-7	Walker	Kerrigan
SEPTEMBER						19—At Mon.	L	0-1	Fryman	LaGrow
1—Cinn.	W	1-0‡	Hrabosky	Eastwick		21—At Phila.	L	1-5	Underwood	Denny
3—At Chi.	L	5-8	Sutter	Solomon		22—At Phila.	L	4-9	Garber	Walker
4—At Chi.	L	1-5	Renko	McGlothen		23—At Phila.	L	3-7	Carlton	Rasmussen
5—At Chi.	L	1-0‡	Hrabosky	Coleman		24—Pitts.	W	10-6	Forsch	Candelaria
6—At Mon.	W	3-1	Falcone	Rogers		24—Pitts.	L	1-11	Rooker	Curtis
6—At Mon.	L	2-3	Taylor	Curtis		25—Pitts.	W	3-0	McGlothen	Reuss
7—At Mon.	W	7-4	Wallace	Taylor		26—Pitts.	W	5-2	Denny	Kison
8—Montreal	L	5-7	Kerrigan	Curtis		27—Phila.	L	1-9	Kaat	Falcone
8—Montreal	L	7-8	Kerrigan	Walker		28—Phila.	W	5-3	Rasmussen	Carlton
9—Montreal	W	6-1	McGlothen	Carrithers		29—Phila.	L	5-6	McGraw	Curtis
10—N. York	L	3-4	Lolich	Denny					**Won 16, Lost 17**	
11—N. York	L	1-4	Koosman	Falcone						
12—N. York	W	6-5	Capilla	Apodaca		**OCTOBER**				
13—Chicago	W	4-3	Forsch	Bonham		2—At Pitts.	L	0-8	Candelaria	McGlothen
14—Chicago	L	3-6	R. Reuschel	McGlothen		3—At Pitts.	L	0-1	Rooker	Denny
15—At N.Y.	W	7-0	Denny	Lolich		3—At Pitts.	L	0-1	Reuss	Falcone
									Won 0, Lost 3	

* 8 innings. † 10 innings. ‡ 11 innings. § 12 innings. x 16 innings. y 17 innings.

Last-Place Expos Slide at Gate

By IAN MacDONALD

So far as the Montreal Expos were concerned the best thing about the 1976 season was that it mercifully came to a close.

Sure they lost at the end but that's the way it started as well. There was one stretch when the Expos lost 38 of 50 starts.

It was not a year that anyone connected with the team will want to remember.

The overall 55-107 record was the worst in baseball for the year. It was the Expos' sorriest performance by far since they went 52-110 in their 1969 inaugural season.

The disaster of the campaign goes even further than that. In 1975, the Expos drew less than a million fans for the first time when they attracted 908,292.

This past season the total attendance was 646,704.

For the first time in their eight years of operation, the Expos lost money. For the first time they changed managers in midstream.

Some excuses can be given but the major problem was that they were a bad team.

The injuries to ace righthander Steve Rogers, super star prospect Gary Carter and Andre Thornton hurt dearly.

Rogers was placed on the disabled list May 26 after breaking a bone in his right hand in a freak accident.

Carter, runner-up for National League rookie of the year honors the season before, broke his thumb in an outfield collision with teammate Pepe Mangual on June 6. Mangual suffered a mild concussion but missed only a few games.

Less than a week later, Thornton, who had been secured from the Chicago Cubs to supply some righthanded power and responded by hitting home runs in his first two games as an Expo, suffered a fractured finger.

Rogers was out for a month, Carter missed 40 games and at that was rushed back too quickly, his hand still tender. Thornton missed three weeks.

When Rogers was hurt the Expos were 16-19. By the time Carter returned, they were 28-57 and putting a firm lock on the National League East's basement.

It was a trying season from the start. After launching a youth movement in 1975, the Expos fired the man who had been their only manager, Gene Mauch, at the end of the season.

It wasn't long into the '76 season under rookie manager Karl Kuehl that the Expos realized Mauch had indeed worked miracles in winning 75 games with basically the same team the year before.

Fiery shortstop Tim Foli tried to help Kuehl. In fact, he interfered quite openly at times. When Foli attempted to overrule an intentional walk ordered by Kuehl during a game in Philadelphia, the youthful skipper felt he had to put his foot down.

The following morning the two had a meeting. Kuehl suggested that if Foli wanted to manage, space could be found on the bench. Foli thought Kuehl was kidding.

When he wasn't in the lineup the next night, Foli exploded. He explained to the press how Kuehl was not competent to manage the club and then in a showdown clubhouse meeting told Kuehl a lot of other things in very colorful language in front of all of the players.

Shattered, Kuehl kept Foli on the bench until ordered otherwise by top management. There never was a fine imposed.

Many of the players confided later that the late May action in Philadelphia spelled the end for Kuehl. The players in many cases, unwittingly lost respect.

In early September, Kuehl was fired. Scout Charlie Fox took over. The Expos were 43-84 under the direction of the 38-year old Kuehl. They were 12-23 with Fox as manager.

There can't be too many highlights with a team that wins 55 games during an entire major league schedule, but a few were;

Jose Morales set major league records for most at-bats as a pinch-hitter (78); most hits as a pinch-hitter (25). His 24 runs batted in as a pinch-hitter were just one shy of the major league record. He also led the Expos in game-winning hits with seven.

Woodie Fryman kept his arthritic left arm together enough to lead the team in wins with 13 and gain recognition as the Expos' player of the year.

Foli set personal highs in hits—144; doubles—a club record 36; home runs—six; and RBIs 54. His 18 errors were the fewest he has had with Montreal and his fielding average of .975 was his best ever.

Young Ellis Valentine, playing both center field and right after a July 16 recall from Denver, batted .279 and finished the season with 14 consecutive steals. And he hit .329 with runners in scoring position.

Dick Williams was hired to manage the Expos in 1977 and Dave Cash was signed away from the East Division champion Philadelphia Phillies.

Anticipation over use of the Olympic Stadium appeared to be the best news for Montreal fans. The Expos have often been burdened with many doubleheaders each season. The domed facility should remedy that problem.

MONTREAL EXPOS—1976

Front row—Mackanin, Unser, Foli, Rivera, Morales, Doby, coach; Bearnarth, coach; Fox, manager; Adair, coach; Piche, coach; Virgil, coach; Rogers, Frias, Jorgensen, Garrett. Second row—Belanger, trainer; Trubiano, ballboy; Plamondon, batboy; Scanlon, Scott, Dunning, Carter, Stanhouse, Fryman, Taylor, Thornton, Landreth, Warthen, Cromartie, White, Atkinson, Rock, traveling secretary. Third row—Keener, Foote, Kirby, Hannahs, Dawson, Lang, Valentine, Kerrigan, Murray, Blair, Williams, Roenicke, Parrish, Carrithers, Freed.

SCORES OF MONTREAL EXPOS' 1976 GAMES

APRIL

Date		Score	Winner	Loser
9—At N.Y.	L	2-3	Seaver	Rogers
10—At N.Y.	L	0-1	Matlack	Fryman
11—At N.Y.	W	7-6	Scherman	Lolich
14—Phila.	L	2-8	Lonborg	Rogers
15—Phila.	W	8-5	Fryman	Kaat
17—At St.L.	L	3-4‡	Rasmussen	Scherman
18—At St.L.	L	1-2	Denny	Warthen
19—At Chi.	W	4-3	Rogers	Bonham
21—At Chi.	W	12-6z	Fryman	Zahn
22—At Chi.	L	4-5§	Zamora	Murray
23—Cinn.	W	5-4	Stanhouse	Billingham
24—Cinn.	L	4-6§	Eastwick	Carrithers
25—Cinn.	L	0-7	Gullett	Renko
28—Houston	L	4-6	Richard	Fryman
28—Houston	W	8-7	Carrithers	Barlow
29—Houston	L	1-3	Dierker	Murray
30—At Cinn.	L	2-7	Nolan	Warthen

Won 6, Lost 11

MAY

Date		Score	Winner	Loser
1—At Cinn.	L	1-6	Gullett	Carrithers
2—At Cinn.	W	8-4y	Stanhouse	Darcy
5—S. Diego	L	4-6	Strom	Rogers
6—S. Diego	L	1-4	Spillner	Kirby
8—S. Fran.	W	7-5	Fryman	D'Acquisto
9—S. Fran.	L	2-4	Montefusco	Warthen
9—S. Fran.	W	8-0	Rogers	Minton
11—At Hous.	L	3-5	Griffin	Kirby
12—At Hous.	W	7-2	Fryman	Richard
15—At Atl.	L	1-3	Ruthven	Rogers
15—At Atl.	W	6-1	Warthen	Niekro
16—At Atl.	W	5-4	Scherman	Sosa
20—Chicago	W	3-0	Fryman	Burris
21—N. York	L	3-4	Lockwood	Murray
22—N. York	L	1-4	Koosman	Scherman
23—N. York	W	5-4	Lang	Swan
24—At Pitts.	W	4-2	Fryman	Candelaria
25—At Pitts.	W	6-3§	Granger	Moose
26—At Pitts.	L	3-6	Demery	Warthen
28—At Phila.	L	3-10	Reed	Stanhouse
29—At Phila.	L	1-6	Christenson	Carrithers
30—At Phila.	L	1-7	Lonborg	Kirby

Won 10, Lost 12

JUNE

Date		Score	Winner	Loser
1—St. Louis	L	2-6	Falcone	Warthen
2—Pitts.	L	2-4	Kison	Fryman
3—Pitts.	W	7-1	Stanhouse	Rooker
4—Atlanta	L	0-2	Messersmith	Carrithers
5—Atlanta	L	0-8	Ruthven	Kirby
6—Atlanta	L	8-14	Devine	Dunning
8—At S.F.	W	9-4	Fryman	Dressler
9—At S.F.	L	2-6	Barr	Stanhouse
10—At S.F.	W	6-5	Carrithers	Halicki
11—At L.A.	L	4-7	Sutton	Kirby
12—At L.A.	L	3-4	Rhoden	Warthen
13—At L.A.	L	3-6	John	Fryman
14—At S.D.	W	3-0	Stanhouse	Strom
15—At S.D.	L	1-2	Foster	Carrithers
16—At S.D.	L	2-6	Freisleben	Warthen
18—Los Ang.	L	5-6	Marshall	Murray
19—Los Ang.	W	2-1	Stanhouse	Hough
20—Los Ang.	W	5-4	Carrithers	Hooton
21—At Phila.	L	3-8	Underwood	Warthen
22—At Phila.	W	8-3	Kirby	Lonborg
23—At Atl.	L	2-5	Messersmith	Dunning
23—At Atl.	L	0-3	Niekro	Fryman
24—At Atl.	L	1-2	Ruthven	Stanhouse
25—Pitts.	L	2-9	Kison	Carrithers
26—Pitts.	L	6-7	Demery	Murray
27—Pitts.	W	4-3	Fryman	Medich
28—Phila.	L	2-6	Carlton	Rogers
29—Phila.	L	1-2	Garber	Murray

Won 8, Lost 20

JULY

Date		Score	Winner	Loser
2—At St.L.	L	0-3	McGlothen	Fryman
3—At St.L.	L	0-9	Denny	Rogers
4—At St.L.	W	4-3	Stanhouse	Falcone
5—Cinn.	L	2-11	Billingham	Lang
6—Cinn.	L	7-10	Eastwick	Kirby
7—Cinn.	L	3-4	Hinton	Rogers
8—At Hous.	L	6-7	Forsch	Dunning
9—At Hous.	L	0-6	Dierker	Stanhouse
10—At Hous.	L	2-4	Richard	Kirby
11—At Hous.	L	0-1	Andujar	Rogers
15—At Cinn.	W	4-3	Rogers	McEnaney
16—At Cinn.	L	3-4‡	Eastwick	Murray
17—At Cinn.	L	1-4	Alcala	Fryman
18—Houston	L	6-7‡	Forsch	Murray
18—Houston	L	1-14	Larson	Dunning
19—Houston	L	1-3	Richard	Rogers
20—Atlanta	W	4-3	Carrithers	Messersmith
21—Atlanta	W	4-3	Murray	Dal Canton
22—Atlanta	L	1-7	Morton	Fryman
23—N. York	W	3-2§	Murray	Lockwood
24—N. York	L	4-10	Lolich	Kirby
25—N. York	W	2-1	Carrithers	Koosman
26—At Chi.	W	2-1	Stanhouse	Stone
26—At Chi.	W	3-1	Dunning	Renko
27—At Chi.	L	0-5	Burris	Rogers
28—At St.L.	W	3-0	Fryman	Rasmussen
30—At Pitts.	L	3-4x	Tekulve	Kerrigan
31—At Pitts.	W	7-6	Murray	Moose

Won 10, Lost 18

AUGUST

Date		Score	Winner	Loser
1—At Pitts.	W	2-0	Rogers	Kison
2—At N.Y.	W	5-4	Taylor	Lockwood
3—At N.Y.	L	8-9	Apodaca	Kerrigan
4—At N.Y.	L	0-4	Koosman	Carrithers
5—Chicago	L	3-4	Burris	Stanhouse
6—Chicago	L	5-6x	P. Reuschel	Taylor
6—Chicago	L	0-1	Stone	Kerrigan
7—Chicago	L	3-4§	Knowles	Kerrigan
7—Chicago	W	7-2	Dunning	Zamora
8—Chicago	L	1-7	Renko	Lang
9—S. Fran.	W	2-1	Stanhouse	Barr
10—S. Fran.	L	3-2	Carrithers	Heaverlo
11—S. Fran.	W	9-3	Fryman	Freisleben
13—S. Diego	W	6-0	Rogers	Dunning
13—S. Diego	L	3-4	Strom	Dunning
14—S. Diego	L	2-7	Jones	Stanhouse
15—S. Diego	L	1-6	Griffin	Carrithers
17—At Phila.	L	3-11	Underwood	Rogers
18—At Phila.	L	4-5	Lonborg	Stanhouse
20—At S.F.	L	3-6	Halicki	Carrithers
21—At S.F.	L	4-5y	Dressler	Lang
22—At S.F.	L	3-4	Lavelle	Taylor
23—At L.A.	L	3-6	John	Stanhouse
24—At L.A.	L	0-6	Hooton	Carrithers
25—At L.A.	L	1-3	Rau	Rogers
27—At S.D.	L	0-2	Jones	Fryman
28—At S.D.	W	7-4	Murray	Metzger
29—At S.D.	W	3-0	Rogers	Sawyer
31—Los Ang.	L	1-5	Rau	Fryman

Won 9, Lost 20

SEPTEMBER

Date		Score	Winner	Loser
2—Los Ang.	L	1-2	Sutton	Rogers
2—Los Ang.	L	3-5	Sosa	Dunning
3—Pitts.	L	7-9	Rooker	Stanhouse
3—Pitts.	L	2-7	Candelaria	Carrithers
4—Pitts.	L	3-5	Giusti	Murray
5—Pitts.	W	1-0	Fryman	Reuss
6—St. Louis	L	1-3	Falcone	Rogers
6—St. Louis	L	3-2	Taylor	Curtis
7—St. Louis	L	4-7	Wallace	Taylor
8—At St.L.	W	7-5	Kerrigan	Curtis
8—At St.L.	W	8-7	Kerrigan	Walker

SEPTEMBER			Winner	Loser
9—At St.L.	L	1-6	McGlothen	Carrithers
10—At Pitts.	W	4-2	Fryman	Candelaria
11—At Pitts.	L	3-4	Reuss	Rogers
12—At Pitts.	L	1-6	Kison	Stanhouse
13—At Phila.	L	2-7	Carlton	Blair
14—At Phila.	L	2-3	Lonborg	Fryman
15—Chicago	L	0-2	Burris	Rogers
16—Chicago	W	4-3	Landreth	Renko
17—St. Louis	W	9-5	Hannahs	Rasmussen
18—St. Louis	L	1-4	Forsch	Stanhouse
18—St. Louis	L	4-7	Solomon	Keener
19—St. Louis	L	7-9	Walker	Kerrigan
19—St. Louis	W	1-0	Fryman	LaGrow
21—N. York	W	4-0	Warthen	Koosman
22—N. York	L	2-4	Matlack	Landreth
24—Phila.	L	3-9	Christenson	Rogers

SEPTEMBER			Winner	Loser
24—Phila.	W	3-2	Stanhouse	Kaat
25—Phila.	L	5-6	Twitchell	Fryman
26—Phila.	L	1-4	Lonborg	Warthen
26—Phila.	L	1-2*	Schueler	Blair
27—At N.Y.	L	3-10†	Matlack	Landreth
28—At N.Y.	L	4-5	Lockwood	Kerrigan
28—At N.Y.	W	4-2a	Hannahs	Myrick
29—At N.Y.	W	7-2	Rogers	Seaver
Won 12, Lost 23				

OCTOBER				
1—At Chi.	L	1-3	Bonham	Stanhouse
2—At Chi.	L	1-3	Burris	Warthen
3—At Chi.	L	2-8	R. Reuschel	Fryman
Won 0, Lost 3				

* 7 innings. † 7½ innings. ‡ 10 innings. § 11 innings. x 13 innings. y 16 innings. z Suspended game, completed April 22. a September 23 game at Montreal transferred to New York.

BILL MADLOCK
• CUBS •
BATTING CHAMPION (.339)

DAVE LOPES
• DODGERS •
STOLEN BASES (63)

MIKE SCHMIDT
• PHILLIES •
HOMERS (38)

1976 NATIONAL LEAGUE LEADERS

TOM SEAVER
• METS •
STRIKEOUTS (235)

RANDY JONES
• PADRES •
WINS (22)
GAMES STARTED (40)
COMPLETE GAMES (25)
INNINGS (315)

STEVE CARLTON
• PHILLIES •
WINNING PCT. (.741)

National League Averages for 1976

CHAMPIONSHIP WINNERS IN PREVIOUS YEARS

1876—Chicago .788	1910—Chicago .675	1944—St. Louis .682
1877—Boston .646	1911—New York .647	1945—Chicago .636
1878—Boston .683	1912—New York .682	1946—St. Louis* .628
1879—Providence .705	1913—New York .664	1947—Brooklyn .610
1880—Chicago .798	1914—Boston .614	1948—Boston .595
1881—Chicago .667	1915—Philadelphia .592	1949—Brooklyn .630
1882—Chicago .655	1916—Brooklyn .610	1950—Philadelphia .591
1883—Boston .643	1917—New York .636	1951—New York† .624
1884—Providence .750	1918—Chicago .651	1952—Brooklyn .627
1885—Chicago .777	1919—Cincinnati .686	1953—Brooklyn .682
1886—Chicago .726	1920—Brooklyn .604	1954—New York .630
1887—Detroit .637	1921—New York .614	1955—Brooklyn .641
1888—New York .641	1922—New York .604	1956—Brooklyn .604
1889—New York .659	1923—New York .621	1957—Milwaukee .617
1890—Brooklyn .667	1924—New York .608	1958—Milwaukee .597
1891—Boston .630	1925—Pittsburgh .621	1959—Los Angeles‡ .564
1892—Boston .680	1926—St. Louis .578	1960—Pittsburgh .617
1893—Boston .662	1927—Pittsburgh .610	1961—Cincinnati .604
1894—Baltimore .695	1928—St. Louis .617	1962—San Francisco§ .624
1895—Baltimore .669	1929—Chicago .645	1963—Los Angeles .611
1896—Baltimore .698	1930—St. Louis .597	1964—St. Louis .574
1897—Boston .705	1931—St. Louis .656	1965—Los Angeles .599
1898—Boston .685	1932—Chicago .584	1966—Los Angeles .586
1899—Brooklyn .677	1933—New York .599	1967—St. Louis .627
1900—Brooklyn .603	1934—St. Louis .621	1968—St. Louis .599
1901—Pittsburgh .647	1935—Chicago .649	1969—New York (East)a .617
1902—Pittsburgh .741	1936—New York .597	1970—Cincinnati (West)b .630
1903—Pittsburgh .650	1937—New York .625	1971—Pittsburgh (East)c .599
1904—New York .693	1938—Chicago .586	1972—Cincinnati (West)b .617
1905—New York .686	1939—Cincinnati .630	1973—New York (East)d .509
1906—Chicago .763	1940—Cincinnati .654	1974—Los Angeles (West)b .630
1907—Chicago .704	1941—Brooklyn .649	1975—Cincinnati (West)b .667
1908—Chicago .643	1942—St. Louis .688	
1909—Pittsburgh .724	1943—St. Louis .682	

*Defeated Brooklyn, two games to none, in playoff for pennant. †Defeated Brooklyn, two games to one, in playoff for pennant. ‡Defeated Milwaukee, two games to none, in playoff for pennant. §Defeated Los Angeles, two games to one, in playoff for pennant. aDefeated Atlanta (West) in Championship Series. bDefeated Pittsburgh (East) in Championship Series. cDefeated San Francisco (West) in Championship Series. dDefeated Cincinnati (West)in Championship Series.

STANDING OF CLUBS AT CLOSE OF SEASON

EAST DIVISION

Club	Phil.	Pitt.	N.Y.	Chi.	St.L.	Mon.	Atl.	Cin.	Hou.	L.A.	S.D.	S.F.	W.	L.	Pct.	G.B.
Philadelphia	....	8	13	10	12	15	7	7	8	7	8	6	101	61	.623	......
Pittsburgh	10	....	8	10	12	10	9	4	10	3	7	9	92	70	.568	9
New York	5	10	....	13	9	10	8	6	6	5	7	9	86	76	.531	15
Chicago	8	8	5	....	12	11	6	3	5	3	6	8	75	87	.463	26
St. Louis	6	6	9	6	....	11	6	3	2	8	7	12	72	90	.444	29
Montreal	3	8	8	7	7	....	4	3	2	2	4	7	55	107	.340	46

WEST DIVISION

Club	Cin.	L.A.	Hou.	S.F.	S.D.	Atl.	Chi.	Mon.	N.Y.	Phil.	Pitt.	St.L.	W.	L.	Pct.	G.B.
Cincinnati	....	13	12	9	13	12	9	9	6	5	8	6	102	60	.630	......
Los Angeles	5	....	13	8	6	10	9	10	7	5	9	10	92	70	.568	10
Houston	6	5	....	10	10	11	7	10	6	4	2	9	80	82	.494	22
San Francisco	9	10	8	....	10	9	4	5	5	6	3	5	74	88	.457	28
San Diego	5	12	8	8	....	8	6	8	5	4	5	4	73	89	.451	29
Atlanta	6	8	7	9	10	....	6	8	4	5	3	4	70	92	.432	32

CHAMPIONSHIP SERIES—Cincinnati defeated Philadelphia, three games to none.

RECORD AT HOME

EAST DIVISION

Club	Phil.	Pitt.	N.Y.	Chi.	St.L.	Mon.	Cin.	L.A.	Hou.	S.D.	S.F.	Atl.	W.	L.	Pct.
Philadelphia	.....	4-5	7-2	5-4	7-2	8-1	4-2	2-4	5-1	5-1	4-2	2-4	53	28	.654
Pittsburgh	5-4	.....	3-6	6-3	7-2	4-5	1-5	2-4	4-2	4-2	6-0	5-1	47	34	.580
New York	3-6	4-5	.....	6-3	4-5	6-4	4-2	3-3	3-3	4-2	3-3	5-1	45	37	.549
Chicago	4-5	5-4	2-7	.....	7-2	5-4	1-5	2-4	4-2	4-2	4-2	4-2	42	39	.519
St. Louis	4-5	4-5	4-5	4-5	.....	5-4	2-4	2-4	2-4	4-2	3-3	3-3	37	44	.457
Montreal	2-7	3-6	4-4	3-6	3-6	.....	1-5	2-4	1-5	1-5	5-1	2-4	27	53	.338

WEST DIVISION

Club	Cin.	L.A.	Hou.	S.D.	S.F.	Atl.	Phil.	Pitt.	N.Y.	Chi.	St.L.	Mon.	W.	L.	Pct.
Cincinnati	.....	7-2	6-3	8-1	3-6	5-4	3-3	3-3	4-2	4-2	2-4	4-2	49	32	.605
Los Angeles	3-6	.....	7-2	3-6	3-6	6-3	1-5	5-1	4-2	5-1	6-0	6-0	49	32	.605
Houston	3-6	3-6	.....	7-3	7-2	5-4	3-3	0-6	3-3	5-1	5-1	5-1	46	36	.561
San Diego	4-5	6-3	5-3	.....	5-4	4-5	3-3	3-3	3-3	4-2	2-4	3-3	42	38	.525
San Francisco	3-6	4-5	6-3	6-3	.....	4-5	4-2	3-3	2-4	2-4	4-2	4-2	40	41	.494
Atlanta	2-7	5-4	3-6	5-4	4-5	.....	1-5	2-4	3-3	4-2	1-5	4-2	34	47	.420

RECORD ABROAD

EAST DIVISION

Club	Phil.	Pitt.	N.Y.	St.L.	Chi.	Mon.	Cin.	L.A.	Atl.	Hou.	S.F.	S.D.	W.	L.	Pct.
Philadelphia	.....	4-5	6-3	5-4	5-4	7-2	3-3	5-1	5-1	3-3	2-4	3-3	48	33	.593
Pittsburgh	5-4	.....	5-4	4-5	4-5	6-3	3-3	1-5	4-2	6-0	3-3	3-3	45	36	.556
New York	2-7	6-3	.....	5-4	7-2	4-4	2-4	2-4	3-3	3-3	4-2	3-3	41	39	.513
St. Louis	2-7	2-7	5-4	.....	2-7	6-3	4-2	0-6	5-1	1-5	4-2	2-4	35	46	.432
Chicago	4-5	3-6	3-6	4-5	.....	2-4	0-6	2-4	1-5	2-4	3-3	2-4	33	48	.407
Montreal	1-8	5-4	4-6	4-5	4-5	.....	2-4	0-6	2-4	1-5	2-4	3-3	28	54	.341

WEST DIVISION

Club	Cin.	L.A.	Atl.	Hou.	S.F.	S.D.	Phil.	Pitt.	N.Y.	St.L.	Chi.	Mon.	W.	L.	Pct.
Cincinnati	.....	6-3	7-2	6-3	6-3	5-4	2-4	5-1	2-4	4-2	5-1	5-1	53	28	.654
Los Angeles	2-7	.....	4-5	6-3	5-4	3-6	4-2	4-2	3-3	4-2	4-2	4-2	36	45	.444
Atlanta	4-5	3-6	.....	4-5	5-4	5-4	4-2	1-5	1-5	3-3	2-4	4-2	34	46	.425
Houston	3-6	2-7	6-3	.....	3-6	3-5	1-5	2-4	3-3	4-2	2-4	1-5	34	47	.420
San Francisco	6-3	6-3	5-4	2-7	.....	4-5	2-4	0-6	3-3	3-3	2-4	4-2	31	51	.378
San Diego	1-8	6-3	4-5	3-7	3-6	.....	1-5	2-4	2-4	2-4	2-4	5-1			

SHUTOUT GAMES

Club	Hous.	Cinn.	L.A.	Chi.	Pitt.	St.L.	S.F.	N.Y.	Atl.	Phil.	Mont.	S.D.	W.	L.	Pct.
Houston	...	1	3	2	0	2	2	2	1	1	2	1	17	11	.607
Cincinnati	1	...	2	0	1	1	2	3	0	0	1	1	12	8	.600
Los Angeles	5	2	...	0	2	2	0	0	1	1	2	3	17	14	.548
Chicago	0	0	1	...	1	0	2	0	0	2	3	3	12	10	.545
Pittsburgh	1	0	1	0	...	3	3	1	0	0	0	3	12	11	.522
St. Louis	0	1	0	2	2	...	0	3	4	0	2	1	15	14	.517
San Francisco	3	2	1	0	1		...	2	2	2	0	2	18	17	.514
New York	0	1	2	1	1	3	2	...	3	1	2	2	18	18	.500
Atlanta	0	1	1	2	0	0	4	0	...	0	3	2	13	13	.500
Philadelphia	1	0	0	1	2	0	0	2	1	...	0	2	9	10	.474
Montreal	0	0	0	1	2	2	1	1	0	0	...	3	10	15	.400
San Diego	0	0	1	0	0	0	1	4	1	3	1	...	11	23	.324

OFFICIAL NATIONAL LEAGUE BATTING AVERAGES

Compiled by Elias Sports Bureau, New York, N.Y.

CLUB BATTING

Club	Pct.	G.	AB.	R.	OR.	H.	TB.	2B.	3B.	HR.	RBI.	SH.	SF.	SB.	CS.	LOB.
Cinci'ti ..	.280	162	5702	857	633	1599	2419	271	63	141	802	67	60	210	57	1328
Phil'hia ..	.272	162	5528	770	557	1505	2184	259	45	110	708	59	67	127	70	1148
Pittsb'gh	.267	162	5604	708	630	1499	2190	249	56	110	660	61	50	130	45	1101
St. Louis	.260	162	5516	629	671	1432	1978	243	57	63	584	86	45	123	55	1172
Houston	.256	162	5464	625	657	1401	1894	195	50	66	571	57	39	150	57	1153
Chicago..	.251	162	5519	611	728	1386	1965	216	24	105	559	75	41	74	74	1105
Los Ang.	.251	162	5472	608	543	1371	1912	200	34	91	561	91	47	144	55	1138
S. Diego	.247	162	5369	570	662	1327	1809	216	37	64	528	125	42	92	46	1145
N. York..	.246	162	5415	615	538	1334	1906	198	34	102	560	92	33	66	58	1182
S. Fran.	.246	162	5452	595	686	1340	1880	211	37	85	552	80	48	88	55	1129
Atlanta ..	.245	162	5345	620	700	1309	1785	170	30	82	586	107	47	74	61	1151
Montreal	.235	162	5428	531	734	1275	1845	224	32	94	507	75	40	86	44	1070
Totals	.255		65814	7739	7739	16778	23767	2652	499	1113	7178	975	559	1364	677	13822

INDIVIDUAL BATTING

(Top Fifteen Qualifiers for Batting Championship—502 or More Plate Appearances)

°Bats lefthanded.   †Switch-hitter.

Player and Club	Pct.	G.	AB.	R.	H.	TB.	2B.	3B.	HR.	RBI.	SH.	SF.	SB.	CS.
Madlock, Bill, Chicago	.339	142	514	68	174	257	36	1	15	84	3	4	15	11
Griffey, G. Kenneth, Cincinnati°	.336	148	562	111	189	253	28	9	6	74	0	3	34	11
Maddox, Garry, Philadelphia	.330	146	531	75	175	242	37	6	6	68	0	9	29	12
Rose, Peter, Cincinnati†	.323	162	665	130	215	299	42	6	10	63	0	2	9	5
Morgan, Joe, Cincinnati°	.320	141	472	113	151	272	30	5	27	111	0	12	60	9
Garvey, Steven, Los Angeles	.317	162	631	85	200	284	37	4	13	80	5	9	19	8
Montanez, Guillermo, S.F.-Atl.°	.317	163	650	79	206	272	29	2	11	84	1	3	2	5
Parker, David, Pittsburgh°	.313	138	537	82	168	255	28	10	13	90	0	4	19	7
Watson, Robert, Houston	.313	157	585	76	183	268	31	3	16	102	2	9	3	3
Geronimo, Cesar, Cincinnati°	.307	149	486	59	149	201	24	11	2	49	2	5	22	5
Foster, George, Cincinnati.............	.306	144	562	86	172	298	21	9	29	121	0	9	17	3
Luzinski, Gregory, Philadelphia	.304	149	533	74	162	255	28	1	21	95	0	11	1	2
Brock, Louis, St. Louis°	.301	133	498	73	150	196	24	5	4	67	4	6	56	19
Buckner, William, Los Angeles°	.301	154	642	76	193	250	28	4	7	60	6	5	28	9
Cardenal, Jose, Chicago	.299	136	521	64	156	209	25	2	.8	47	3	3	23	14

DEPARTMENTAL LEADERS: G—Montanez, 163; AB—Cash, 666; R—Rose, 130; H—Rose, 215;
TB—Schmidt, 306; 2B—Rose, 42; 3B—Cash, 12; HR—Schmidt, 38; RBI—G. Foster, 121; SH—Gilbreath, 20;
SF—Morgan, 12; SB—Lopes, 63; CS—Brock, 19.

(All Players—Listed Alphabetically)

Player and Club	Pct.	G.	AB.	R.	H.	TB.	2B.	3B.	HR.	RBI.	SH.	SF.	SB.	CS.
Adams, Glenn, San Francisco°	.243	69	74	2	18	22	4	0	0	3	0	0	1	0
Adams, R. Michael, Chicago	.138	25	29	1	4	6	2	0	0	2	0	0	0	0
Alcala, Santo, Cincinnati	.140	30	43	5	6	7	1	0	0	2	5	0	0	0
Alexander, Gary, San Francisco	.178	23	73	12	13	22	1	1	2	7	0	1	1	0
Allen, Richard, Philadelphia	.268	85	298	52	80	143	16	1	15	49	1	3	11	4
Almon, William, San Diego	.246	14	57	6	14	20	3	0	1	6	1	0	3	1
Alvarado, Luis, St. Louis..............	.286	16	42	5	12	13	1	0	0	3	0	0	0	0
Anderson, Michael A., St. Louis	.291	86	199	17	58	71	8	1	1	12	1	3	1	1
Andrews, Fred, Philadelphia	.667	4	6	1	4	4	0	0	0	0	0	0	1	1
Andrews, Robert, Houston	.256	109	410	42	105	123	8	5	0	23	5	0	7	3
Andujar, Joaquin, Houston	.140	28	57	4	8	9	1	0	0	1	2	0	0	0
Apodaca, Robert, New York	.125	43	16	0	2	3	1	0	0	1	0	0	0	0
Armas, Antonio, Pittsburgh	.333	4	6	0	2	2	0	0	0	1	0	0	0	0
Armbrister, Edison, Cincinnati.......	.295	73	78	20	23	36	3	2	2	7	5	1	7	3
Arnold, Christopher, San Francisco..	.217	60	69	4	15	17	0	1	0	5	0	1	0	0
Ashford, Thomas, San Diego	.600	4	5	0	3	4	1	0	0	0	0	0	2	0
Asselstine, Brian, Atlanta°	.212	11	33	2	7	10	0	0	1	3	1	1	0	0
Atkinson, William, Montreal°	.000	4	0	0	0	0	0	0	0	0	0	0	0	0
Auerbach, Frederick, Los Angeles	.128	36	47	7	6	6	0	0	0	1	0	0	0	1
Autry, Albert, Atlanta	.000	1	2	0	0	0	0	0	0	0	0	0	0	0
Ayala, Benigno, New York	.115	22	26	2	3	6	0	0	1	2	0	0	0	1
Bailey, Robert, Cincinnati	.298	69	124	17	37	63	6	1	6	23	0	1	0	0

Player and Club	Pct.	G.	AB.	R.	H.	TB.	2B.	3B.	HR.	RBI.	SH.	SF.	SB.	CS.
Bair, C. Douglas, Pittsburgh	.000	4	0	0	0	0	0	0	0	0	0	0	0	0
Baker, Johnnie, Los Angeles	.242	112	384	36	93	118	13	0	4	39	1	4	2	4
Baldwin, Rick, New York°	.333	11	3	0	1	1	0	0	0	0	0	0	0	0
Baldwin, Robert, New York°	.273	9	22	4	6	12	1	1	1	5	0	1	0	0
Barlow, Michael, Houston°	.000	16	3	0	0	0	0	0	0	0	0	0	0	0
Barr, James, San Francisco	.162	41	74	3	12	18	2	2	0	9	12	1	2	0
Beard, Michael, Atlanta°	.000	30	1	0	0	0	0	0	0	0	0	0	0	0
Belloir, Robert, Atlanta	.200	30	60	5	12	14	2	0	0	4	4	0	0	0
Bench, Johnny, Cincinnati	.234	135	465	62	109	183	24	1	16	74	0	4	13	2
Biittner, Lawrence, Mtl.-Chi.°	.237	89	224	23	53	69	14	1	0	18	2	0	0	2
Billingham, John, Cincinnati	.237	34	59	4	14	17	3	0	0	4	8	0	0	0
Blackwell, Timothy, Philadelphia†	.250	4	8	0	2	2	0	0	0	1	0	0	0	0
Blair, Dennis, Montreal	.000	5	4	0	0	0	0	0	0	0	0	0	0	0
Boisclair, Bruce, New York°	.287	110	286	42	82	107	13	3	2	13	6	0	9	5
Bonham, William, Chicago	.200	32	65	6	13	17	4	0	0	2	7	0	0	0
Boone, Robert, Philadelphia	.271	121	361	40	98	132	18	2	4	54	4	7	2	5
Borbon, Pedro, Cincinnati	.222	69	18	2	4	4	0	0	0	2	0	0	3	0
Bosetti, Richard, Philadelphia	.278	13	18	6	5	6	1	0	0	0	1	0	3	0
Boswell, Kenneth, Houston°	.262	91	126	12	33	43	8	1	0	18	1	2	1	0
Bowa, Lawrence, Philadelphia†	.248	156	624	71	155	188	15	9	0	49	11	5	30	8
Brock, Louis, St. Louis°	.301	133	498	73	150	196	24	5	4	67	4	6	56	19
Brown, Leon, New York	.214	64	70	11	15	18	3	0	0	2	0	0	2	4
Brown, Ollie, Philadelphia	.254	92	209	30	53	80	10	1	5	30	1	4	2	1
Buckner, William, Los Angeles°	.301	154	642	76	193	250	28	4	7	60	6	5	28	9
Burke, Glenn, Los Angeles	.239	25	46	9	11	13	2	0	0	5	1	0	3	2
Burris, B. Ray, Chicago	.111	39	81	4	9	9	0	0	0	1	8	1	0	0
Cabell, Enos, Houston	.273	144	586	85	160	193	13	7	2	43	3	2	35	8
Caldwell, R. Michael, San Fran.	.158	50	19	1	3	4	1	0	0	1	0	0	0	0
Camp, Rick, Atlanta	.000	5	2	0	0	0	0	0	0	0	0	0	0	0
Candelaria, John, Pittsburgh°	.184	32	76	5	14	18	2	1	0	5	5	0	0	0
Capilla, Douglas, St. Louis°	.000	7	0	0	0	0	0	0	0	0	0	0	0	0
Capra, Lee, Atlanta	.000	5	0	0	0	0	0	0	0	0	0	0	0	0
Cardenal, Jose, Chicago	.299	136	512	64	156	209	25	2	8	47	3	3	23	14
Carlton, Steven, Philadelphia°	.217	35	92	5	20	21	1	0	0	6	7	0	0	0
Carrithers, Donald, Montreal	.108	35	37	1	4	6	0	1	0	3	0	0	0	0
Carter, Gary, Montreal	.219	91	311	31	68	96	8	1	6	38	2	3	0	2
Cash, David, Philadelphia	.284	160	666	92	189	230	14	12	1	56	1	4	10	12
Cedeno, Cesar, Houston	.297	150	575	89	171	261	26	5	18	83	0	4	58	15
Cey, Ronald, Los Angeles	.277	145	502	69	139	232	18	3	23	80	2	4	0	4
Champion, R. Michael, San Diego°	.237	11	38	4	9	14	2	0	1	2	1	0	0	0
Chaney, Darrel, Atlanta†	.252	153	496	42	125	164	20	8	1	50	8	5	5	7
Chant, Charles, St. Louis	.143	15	14	0	2	2	0	0	0	0	0	0	0	0
Chiles, Richard, Houston°	.500	5	4	1	2	3	1	0	0	0	0	0	0	0
Christenson, Larry, Philadelphia	.196	32	51	5	10	20	4	0	2	9	6	0	0	0
Clarey, Douglas, St. Louis	.500	9	4	2	1	4	0	0	1	2	0	0	0	0
Clark, Jack, San Francisco	.225	26	102	14	23	39	6	2	2	10	3	2	6	2
Colbert, Nathan, Montreal	.200	14	40	5	8	16	2	0	2	6	0	0	3	1
Coleman, Joseph, Chicago	.154	39	13	0	2	2	0	0	0	0	0	0	0	0
Concepcion, David, Cincinnati	.281	152	576	74	162	231	28	7	9	69	4	6	21	10
Correll, Victor, Atlanta	.225	69	200	26	45	70	6	2	5	16	2	0	0	1
Cosgrove, Michael, Houston°	.087	22	23	1	2	2	0	0	0	1	5	0	0	0
Cox, James, Montreal	.172	13	29	2	5	7	0	1	0	2	0	0	0	0
Crawford, Willie, St. Louis°	.304	120	392	49	119	173	17	5	9	50	2	6	2	1
Cromartie, Warren, Montreal°	.210	33	81	8	17	18	1	0	0	2	0	0	1	2
Crosby, Kenneth, Chicago	.500	7	2	0	1	1	0	0	0	0	0	0	0	0
Crowley, Terrence, Atlanta°	.000	7	6	0	0	0	0	0	0	1	0	1	0	0
Cruz, Hector, St. Louis	.228	151	526	54	120	178	17	1	13	71	4	3	1	0
Cruz, Henry, Los Angeles°	.182	49	88	8	16	32	2	1	4	14	1	0	0	2
Cruz, Jose, Houston°	.303	133	439	49	133	176	21	5	4	61	2	2	28	11
Curtis, John, St. Louis°	.200	38	35	3	7	10	1	1	0	0	5	0	0	0
D'Acquisto, John, San Francisco	.269	28	26	1	7	8	1	0	0	2	4	0	0	0
Dal Canton, J. Bruce, Atlanta°	.222	42	9	2	2	2	0	0	0	0	1	0	0	0
Darcy, Patrick, Cincinnati°	.182	11	11	1	2	2	0	0	0	0	1	0	0	0
DaVanon, F. Gerald, Houston	.290	61	107	19	31	43	3	3	1	20	0	1	0	2
Davis, Robert, San Diego	.205	51	83	7	17	19	0	1	0	5	0	2	0	0
Davis, William, San Diego°	.268	141	493	61	132	185	18	10	5	46	3	5	14	2
Dawson, Andre, Montreal	.235	24	85	9	20	26	4	1	0	7	2	0	1	2
DeJesus, Ivan, Los Angeles	.171	22	41	4	7	11	2	1	0	2	2	0	0	1
Demery, Lawrence, Pittsburgh	.125	40	40	0	5	5	0	0	0	1	4	1	0	0

Player and Club	Pct.	G.	AB.	R.	H.	TB.	2B.	3B.	HR.	RBI.	SH.	SF.	SB.	CS.
Denny, John, St. Louis	.224	30	67	3	15	17	2	0	0	4	7	0	1	0
Dettore, Thomas, Chicago°	.000	4	0	0	0	0	0	0	0	0	0	0	0	0
Devine, P. Adrian, Atlanta	.000	48	14	0	0	0	0	0	0	0	2	0	0	0
Dierker, Lawrence, Houston	.141	28	64	3	9	12	0	0	1	4	3	2	0	0
Dilone, Miguel, Pittsburgh†	.235	16	17	7	4	4	0	0	0	0	0	0	5	1
Downing, Alphonso, Los Angeles	.000	17	6	0	0	0	0	0	0	0	0	0	0	0
Dressler, Robert, San Francisco	.129	25	31	2	4	4	0	0	0	1	2	0	0	0
Driessen, Daniel, Cincinnati°	.247	98	219	32	54	88	11	1	7	44	0	6	14	1
Dunning, Steven, Montreal	.133	32	15	0	2	2	0	0	0	0	3	0	0	0
Dupree, Michael, San Diego	1.000	12	1	1	1	1	0	0	0	0	0	0	0	0
Dwyer, James, Mtl-NY°	.181	61	105	9	19	24	3	1	0	5	0	1	0	0
Dyer, Don, Pittsburgh	.223	69	184	12	41	58	8	0	3	9	3	1	0	0
Easterly, James, Atlanta†	.111	4	9	0	1	1	0	0	0	0	0	0	0	0
Eastwick, Rawlins, Cincinnati	.000	71	17	0	0	0	0	0	0	0	2	0	0	0
Eden, E. Michael, Atlanta†	.000	5	8	0	0	0	0	0	0	1	0	0	0	0
Espinosa, Arnulfo, New York	.000	12	9	1	0	0	0	0	0	0	1	0	0	0
Evans, Darrell, Atl-SF°	.205	136	396	53	81	125	9	1	11	46	1	2	9	1
Fairly, Ronald, St. Louis°	.264	73	110	13	29	33	4	0	0	21	1	2	0	0
Falcone, Peter, St. Louis°	.129	32	62	3	8	9	1	0	0	2	12	0	0	0
Ferguson, Joseph, LA-StL	.211	125	374	46	79	132	15	4	10	39	4	2	6	2
Flynn, R. Douglas, Cincinnati	.283	93	219	20	62	74	5	2	1	20	4	2	2	0
Foli, Timothy, Montreal	.264	149	546	41	144	200	36	1	6	54	2	8	6	5
Folkers, Richard, San Diego°	.000	33	4	0	0	0	0	0	0	0	1	0	0	0
Foote, Barry, Montreal	.234	105	350	32	82	119	12	2	7	27	0	0	2	1
Forsch, Kenneth, Houston	.091	52	11	0	1	1	0	0	0	1	2	0	0	0
Forsch, Robert, St. Louis	.177	35	62	6	11	16	2	0	1	5	9	0	0	0
Foster, Alan, San Diego	.056	29	18	1	1	1	0	0	0	0	3	0	0	0
Foster, George, Cincinnati	.306	144	562	86	172	298	21	9	29	121	0	9	17	3
Foster, Leonard, New York	.203	24	59	11	12	17	2	0	1	15	0	0	3	0
Frailing, Kenneth, Chicago°	.000	6	3	0	0	0	0	0	0	0	1	0	0	0
Freed, Roger, Montreal	.200	8	15	0	3	4	1	0	0	1	0	0	0	0
Freisleben, David, San Diego	.189	34	37	3	7	9	0	1	0	2	9	0	0	0
Frias, Jesus, Montreal	.248	76	113	7	28	33	5	0	0	8	3	1	1	1
Frisella, Daniel, St. Louis°	.000	18	1	0	0	0	0	0	0	0	0	0	0	0
Fryman, Woodrow, Montreal	.109	34	64	1	7	8	1	0	0	2	11	0	0	0
Fuentes, Rigoberto, San Diego†	.263	135	520	48	137	161	18	0	2	36	16	4	5	3
Garber, H. Eugene, Philadelphia	.286	59	7	0	2	2	0	0	0	0	3	0	0	0
Garman, Michael, Chicago	.000	47	7	0	0	0	0	0	0	0	0	0	0	0
Garrett, R. Wayne, NY-Mtl°	.231	139	428	51	99	133	12	2	6	37	2	0	9	7
Garvey, Steven, Los Angeles	.317	162	631	85	200	284	37	4	13	80	5	9	19	8
Gaston, Clarence, Atlanta	.291	69	134	15	39	55	4	0	4	25	0	0	1	0
Geronimo, Cesar, Cincinnati°	.307	149	486	59	149	201	24	11	2	49	2	5	22	5
Gilbreath, Rodney, Atlanta	.251	116	383	57	96	126	11	8	1	32	20	3	7	7
Giusti, David, Pittsburgh	.000	44	4	0	0	0	0	0	0	0	0	0	0	0
Goodson, J. Edward, Los Angeles°	.229	83	118	8	27	40	4	0	3	17	0	2	0	0
Granger, Wayne, Montreal	.000	27	3	0	0	0	0	0	0	0	2	0	0	0
Greif, William, SD-StL†	.000	52	12	0	0	0	0	0	0	0	0	0	0	0
Griffey, G. Kenneth, Cincinnati°	.336	148	562	111	189	253	28	9	6	74	0	3	34	11
Griffin, Thomas, Hou-SD	.065	32	31	2	2	2	0	0	0	4	0	0	0	0
Gross, Gregory, Houston°	.286	128	426	52	122	140	12	3	0	27	5	6	2	6
Grote, Gerald, New York	.272	101	323	30	88	118	14	2	4	28	3	1	1	2
Grubb, John, San Diego°	.284	109	384	54	109	148	22	1	5	27	6	2	1	2
Gullett, Donald, Cincinnati	.182	25	44	2	8	8	0	0	0	3	6	0	0	0
Hale, John, Los Angeles°	.154	44	91	4	14	18	2	1	0	8	2	1	4	1
Halicki, Edward, San Francisco	.170	32	53	3	9	9	0	0	0	3	7	0	1	0
Hall, Tom, New York°	.000	5	0	0	0	0	0	0	0	0	0	0	0	0
Hanna, Preston, Atlanta	.000	5	1	0	0	0	0	0	0	0	0	0	0	0
Hannahs, Gerald, Montreal°	.375	3	8	1	3	3	0	0	0	0	0	0	0	0
Hardy, H. Lawrence, Houston	.000	15	2	0	0	0	0	0	0	0	0	0	0	0
Harmon, Terry, Philadelphia	.295	42	61	12	18	24	4	1	0	6	2	0	3	0
Harrelson, Derrel, New York†	.234	118	359	34	84	107	12	4	1	26	8	0	9	3
Harris, Victor, St. Louis†	.228	97	259	21	59	80	12	3	1	19	6	0	1	2
Heaverlo, David, San Francisco	.333	61	3	0	1	1	0	0	0	0	1	0	0	0
Hebner, Richard, Pittsburgh°	.249	132	434	60	108	159	21	3	8	51	4	4	1	3
Heidemann, Jack, New York	.083	5	12	0	1	1	0	0	0	0	1	0	0	0
Helms, Tommy, Pittsburgh	.276	62	87	10	24	34	5	1	1	13	2	2	0	0
Henderson, Joseph, Cincinnati°	.000	4	0	0	0	0	0	0	0	0	0	0	0	0
Henderson, Kenneth, Atlanta†	.262	133	435	52	114	172	19	0	13	61	2	5	5	7
Hernandez, Enzo, San Diego	.256	113	340	31	87	109	13	3	1	24	16	1	12	7

Player and Club	Pct.	G.	AB.	R.	H.	TB.	2B.	3B.	HR.	RBI.	SH.	SF.	SB.	CS.
Hernandez, Keith, St. Louis°	.289	129	374	54	108	160	21	5	7	46	2	0	4	2
Hernandez, Ramon, Pitt-Chi†	.000	39	3	0	0	0	0	0	0	0	0	0	0	0
Herndon, Larry, San Francisco°	.288	115	337	42	97	120	11	3	2	23	3	0	12	10
Herrmann, Edward, Houston°	.204	79	265	14	54	71	8	0	3	25	3	2	0	0
Hill, Marc, San Francisco	.183	54	131	11	24	38	5	0	3	15	2	2	0	1
Hinton, Richard, Cincinnati°	.000	12	1	0	0	0	0	0	0	0	0	0	0	0
Hodges, Ronald, New York°	.226	56	155	21	35	53	6	0	4	24	1	1	2	0
Hooton, Burt, Los Angeles	.097	33	62	2	6	7	1	0	0	4	13	2	0	0
Hosley, Timothy, Chicago	.000	1	1	0	0	0	0	0	0	0	0	0	0	0
Hough, Charles, Los Angeles	.286	77	21	1	6	8	2	0	0	4	0	0	0	0
Howard, Wilbur, Houston†	.220	94	191	26	42	56	7	2	1	18	1	2	7	5
Howe, Arthur, Houston	.138	21	29	0	4	5	1	0	0	0	0	0	0	0
Hrabosky, Alan, St. Louis	.000	68	7	0	0	0	0	0	0	0	3	0	0	0
Hundley, C. Randolph, Chicago	.167	13	18	3	3	5	2	0	0	1	0	1	0	0
Hutton, Thomas, Philadelphia°	.202	95	124	15	25	35	5	1	1	13	1	1	1	2
Ivie, Michael, San Diego	.291	140	405	51	118	168	19	5	7	70	2	4	6	6
Javier, I. Alfredo, Houston	.208	8	24	1	5	5	0	0	0	0	0	0	0	0
John, Thomas, Los Angeles	.109	31	64	3	7	8	1	0	0	3	10	0	0	0
Johnson, Clifford, Houston	.226	108	318	36	72	127	21	2	10	49	0	0	0	0
Johnson, Jerry, San Diego	.000	24	3	0	0	0	0	0	0	0	0	0	0	0
Johnson, L. Doby, Montreal	.154	6	13	0	2	3	1	0	0	0	1	0	0	0
Johnstone, John, Philadelphia°	.318	129	440	62	140	201	38	4	5	53	1	7	5	5
Jones, Randall, San Diego	.058	40	103	6	6	6	0	0	0	2	15	0	0	0
Jorgensen, Michael, Montreal°	.254	125	343	36	87	118	13	0	6	23	1	3	7	1
Joshua, Von, San Francisco°	.263	42	156	13	41	50	5	2	0	2	1	1	1	3
Jutze, Alfred, Houston	.152	42	92	7	14	22	2	3	0	6	0	1	0	0
Kaat, James, Philadelphia°	.177	42	79	4	14	22	3	1	1	8	1	1	0	0
Keener, Joseph, Montreal	.000	2	1	0	0	0	0	0	0	0	1	0	0	0
Kelleher, Michael, Chicago	.228	124	337	28	77	91	12	1	0	22	7	2	0	4
Kendall, Fred, San Diego	.246	146	456	30	112	135	17	0	2	39	5	5	1	1
Kerrigan, Joseph, Montreal	.000	38	2	0	0	0	0	0	0	0	0	0	0	0
Kessinger, Donald, St. Louis†	.239	145	502	55	120	157	22	6	1	40	9	4	3	0
Kingman, David, New York	.238	123	474	70	113	240	14	1	37	86	0	3	7	4
Kirby, Clayton, Montreal†	.056	22	18	1	1	2	1	0	0	3	6	0	0	0
Kirkpatrick, Edgar, Pittsburgh°	.233	83	146	14	34	43	9	0	0	16	0	3	1	0
Kison, Bruce, Pittsburgh	.203	31	59	4	12	18	2	2	0	3	8	0	0	0
Kleven, Jay, New York	.200	2	5	0	1	1	0	0	0	2	0	0	0	0
Knepper, Robert, San Francisco°	.111	4	9	0	1	1	0	0	0	1	0	0	0	0
Knowles, Darold, Chicago°	.143	58	7	0	1	1	0	0	0	0	2	0	0	0
Koosman, Jerry, New York	.215	34	79	5	17	19	2	0	0	6	13	0	0	0
Kranepool, Edward, New York°	.292	123	415	47	121	170	17	1	10	49	2	3	1	0
Krukow, Michael, Chicago	.000	2	1	0	0	0	0	0	0	0	0	0	0	0
Kubiak, Theodore, San Diego†	.236	96	212	16	50	59	5	2	0	26	5	2	0	3
LaCock, R. Pierre, Chicago°	.221	106	244	34	54	91	9	2	8	28	2	1	1	4
LaCorte, Frank, Atlanta	.091	21	33	1	3	3	0	0	0	1	3	0	0	0
Lacy, Leondaus, Atl-LA	.269	103	338	42	91	117	11	3	3	34	4	2	3	4
LaGrow, Lerrin, St. Louis	.000	8	5	0	0	0	0	0	0	0	0	0	0	0
Landreth, Larry, Montreal	.000	3	3	0	0	0	0	0	0	0	0	0	0	0
Lang, Robert, Montreal	.167	29	6	0	1	1	0	0	0	1	2	0	0	0
Langford, J. Rick, Pittsburgh	.200	12	5	1	1	2	1	0	0	0	0	0	0	0
Larson, Daniel, Houston	.290	14	31	5	9	12	1	1	0	6	2	0	0	0
Lavelle, Gary, San Francisco†	.077	65	13	0	1	1	0	0	0	1	2	0	0	0
Lee, Leron, Los Angeles°	.133	23	45	1	6	8	0	1	0	2	0	0	0	0
LeMaster, Johnnie, San Francisco	.210	43	100	9	21	28	3	2	0	9	2	1	2	0
Lemongello, Mark, Houston°	.000	4	8	0	0	0	0	0	0	0	1	0	0	0
Leon, Maximino, Atlanta	.000	30	2	0	0	0	0	0	0	0	0	0	0	0
Lerch, Randy, Philadelphia°	1.000	1	1	1	1	2	1	0	0	0	0	0	0	0
Lewallyn, Dennis, Los Angeles	.000	4	5	0	0	0	0	0	0	0	0	0	0	0
Locklear, Gene, San Diego°	.224	43	67	9	15	18	3	0	0	8	2	1	0	0
Lockwood, Claude, New York	.333	56	18	2	6	7	1	0	0	2	3	0	0	1
Lolich, Michael, New York	.130	31	54	5	7	7	0	0	0	1	11	0	0	0
Lonborg, James, Philadelphia	.164	33	67	5	11	12	1	0	0	4	6	0	0	0
Lopes, David, Los Angeles	.241	117	427	72	103	146	17	7	4	20	2	2	63	10
Lum, Michael, Cincinnati°	.228	84	136	15	31	47	5	1	3	20	1	4	0	1
Luzinski, Gregory, Philadelphia	.304	149	533	74	162	255	28	1	21	95	0	11	1	2
Lyttle, James, Mtl-LA°	.248	65	153	9	38	50	7	1	1	13	1	0	0	1
Mackanin, Peter, Montreal	.224	114	380	36	85	128	15	2	8	33	3	1	6	2
Maddox, Garry, Philadelphia	.330	146	531	75	175	242	37	6	6	68	0	9	29	12
Madlock, Bill, Chicago	.339	142	514	68	174	257	36	1	15	84	3	4	15	11

Player and Club	Pct.	G.	AB.	R.	H.	TB.	2B.	3B.	HR.	RBI.	SH.	SF.	SB.	CS.
Mangual, Jose, Mtl-NY	.237	107	317	49	75	107	14	3	4	25	5	1	24	10
Marshall, Michael, LA-Atl	.091	54	11	1	1	1	0	0	0	1	1	1	0	0
Martin, Jerry, Philadelphia	.248	130	121	30	30	43	7	0	2	15	0	1	3	2
Matlack, Jonathan, New York°	.193	35	88	10	17	18	1	0	0	9	7	0	0	0
Matthews, Gary, San Francisco	.279	156	587	79	164	260	28	4	20	84	2	6	12	5
May, David, Atlanta°	.215	105	214	27	46	66	5	3	3	23	0	2	5	1
Mazzilli, Lee, New York†	.195	24	77	9	15	23	2	0	2	7	0	1	5	4
McBride, Arnold, St. Louis	.335	72	272	40	91	121	13	4	3	24	1	2	10	5
McCarver, J. Timothy, Phila°	.277	90	155	26	43	67	11	2	3	29	1	2	2	1
McCovey, Willie, San Diego°	.203	71	202	20	41	71	9	0	7	36	0	0	0	0
McEnaney, William, Cincinnati°	.167	55	6	0	1	1	0	0	0	0	1	0	0	0
McGlothen, Lynn, St. Louis°	.211	33	71	3	15	18	3	0	0	11	7	2	0	0
McGraw, Frank, Philadelphia	.143	58	7	1	1	2	1	0	0	0	0	0	0	0
McLaughlin, Michael, Houston	.000	17	19	0	0	0	0	0	0	0	2	0	0	0
Medich, George, Pittsburgh	.096	29	52	3	5	5	0	0	0	1	8	0	0	0
Mejias, Samuel, St. Louis	.143	18	21	1	3	4	1	0	0	0	0	0	2	0
Melendez, Luis, StL-SD	.224	92	143	15	32	37	5	0	0	5	0	1	1	1
Mendoza, Mario, Pittsburgh	.185	50	92	6	17	22	5	0	0	12	0	1	0	1
Messersmith, John, Atlanta	.179	29	67	3	12	13	1	0	0	10	6	0	0	0
Metzger, Clarence, San Diego	.000	77	8	1	0	0	0	0	0	0	2	0	0	0
Metzger, Roger, Houston†	.210	152	481	37	101	130	13	8	0	29	8	2	1	1
Milbourne, Lawrence, Houston†	.248	59	145	22	36	40	4	0	0	7	1	0	6	1
Millan, Felix, New York	.282	139	531	55	150	182	25	2	1	35	6	2	2	4
Miller, C. Bruce, San Francisco	.160	12	25	1	4	5	1	0	0	2	0	0	0	0
Milner, John, New York°	.271	127	443	56	120	198	25	4	15	78	0	3	0	7
Minton, Gregory, San Francisco†	.200	11	5	0	1	1	0	0	0	0	0	0	0	0
Mitterwald, George, Chicago	.215	101	303	19	65	87	7	0	5	28	0	6	1	2
Moffitt, Randall, San Francisco	.143	58	14	1	2	2	0	0	0	1	0	0	0	0
Monday, Robert, Chicago°	.272	137	534	107	145	271	20	5	32	77	2	3	5	9
Montanez, Guillermo, SF-Atl°	.317	163	650	74	206	272	29	2	11	84	1	3	2	5
Montefusco, John, San Francisco	.103	38	78	3	8	9	1	0	0	3	6	1	0	0
Moore, Alvin, Atlanta	.269	20	26	1	7	8	1	0	0	2	1	0	0	0
Moose, Robert, Pittsburgh	.250	53	12	2	3	8	0	1	1	2	0	0	0	0
Morales, Jose, Montreal	.316	104	158	12	50	73	11	0	4	37	0	2	0	0
Morales, Julio, Chicago	.274	140	537	66	147	212	17	0	16	67	1	4	3	8
Moreno, Omar, Pittsburgh	.270	48	122	24	33	45	4	1	2	12	1	1	15	5
Moret, Rogelio, Atlanta†	.130	27	23	3	3	3	0	0	0	1	2	1	0	0
Morgan, Joe, Cincinnati°	.320	141	472	113	151	272	30	5	27	111	0	12	60	9
Morton, Carl, Atlanta	.178	27	45	2	8	8	0	0	0	6	5	2	1	0
Mota, Manuel, Los Angeles	.288	50	52	1	15	18	3	0	0	13	0	1	0	0
Mumphrey, Jerry, St. Louis†	.258	112	384	51	99	127	15	5	1	26	2	3	22	6
Murcer, Bobby, San Francisco	.259	147	533	73	138	231	20	2	23	90	0	3	12	7
Murphy, Dale, Atlanta	.262	19	65	3	17	23	6	0	0	9	0	0	0	0
Murray, Dale, Montreal	.000	81	8	0	0	0	0	0	0	0	3	0	0	0
Myrick, Robert, New York°	.000	21	3	0	0	0	0	0	0	1	0	0	0	0
Nahorodny, William, Philadelphia	.200	3	5	0	1	2	1	0	0	0	0	0	0	0
Niekro, Joseph, Houston	.185	36	27	1	5	10	2	0	1	1	4	0	0	0
Niekro, Philip, Atlanta	.191	38	94	5	18	24	3	0	1	12	9	1	0	1
Nolan, Gary, Cincinnati	.101	34	79	1	8	8	0	0	0	3	6	0	0	0
Norman, Fredie, Cincinnati†	.140	33	50	1	7	7	0	0	0	1	7	1	0	0
Oates, Johnny, Philadelphia°	.253	37	99	10	25	27	2	0	0	8	0	0	0	1
Office, Rowland, Atlanta°	.281	99	359	51	101	132	17	1	4	34	5	4	2	8
Oliver, Albert, Pittsburgh°	.323	121	443	62	143	211	22	5	12	61	1	6	6	2
Ontiveros, Steven, San Francisco†	.176	59	74	8	13	16	3	0	0	5	0	1	0	0
Ott, N. Edward, Pittsburgh°	.308	27	39	2	12	14	2	0	0	5	0	1	0	0
Owchinko, Robert, San Diego°	.000	2	1	0	0	0	0	0	0	0	1	0	0	0
Paciorek, Thomas, Atlanta	.290	111	324	39	94	124	10	4	4	36	2	2	2	3
Parker, David, Pittsburgh°	.313	138	537	82	168	255	28	10	13	90	0	4	19	7
Parrish, Larry, Montreal	.232	154	543	65	126	197	28	5	11	61	1	6	2	6
Pasley, Kevin, Los Angeles	.231	23	52	4	12	14	2	0	0	2	1	0	0	0
Pentz, Eugene, Houston	.200	40	5	1	1	1	0	0	0	0	0	0	0	0
Perez, Atanasio, Cincinnati	.260	139	527	77	137	238	32	6	19	91	0	4	10	5
Perez, Martin, Atl-SF	.257	124	428	49	110	138	17	1	3	32	14	4	3	4
Phillips, Michael, New York°	.256	87	262	30	67	95	4	6	4	29	3	5	2	2
Plummer, William, Cincinnati	.248	56	153	16	38	58	6	1	4	19	1	0	0	2
Pocoroba, Biff, Atlanta†	.241	54	174	16	42	49	7	0	0	14	1	2	1	0
Potter, Michael, St. Louis	.000	9	16	0	0	0	0	0	0	0	0	0	0	0
Proly, Michael, St. Louis	.000	14	0	0	0	0	0	0	0	0	0	0	0	0
Putman, Eddy, Chicago°	.429	5	7	0	3	3	0	0	0	0	0	0	0	0

Player and Club	Pct.	G.	AB.	R.	H.	TB.	2B.	3B.	HR.	RBI.	SH.	SF.	SB.	CS.
Rader, David, San Francisco*	.263	88	255	25	67	85	15	0	1	22	1	1	2	0
Rader, Douglas, San Diego	.257	139	471	45	121	178	22	4	9	55	5	6	3	4
Rasmussen, Harold, St. Louis	.105	43	38	0	4	5	1	0	0	2	4	0	0	0
Rau, Douglas, Los Angeles*	.150	34	60	5	9	9	0	0	0	2	8	1	0	0
Reed, Ronald, Philadelphia	.167	59	24	2	4	5	1	0	0	2	2	0	0	0
Reitz, Kenneth, San Francisco	.267	155	577	40	154	192	21	1	5	66	3	9	5	4
Renko, Steven, Mtl-Chi	.107	34	56	3	6	6	0	0	0	1	4	0	0	0
Rettenmund, Mervin, San Diego	.229	86	140	16	32	45	7	0	2	11	3	0	4	1
Reuschel, Paul, Chicago	.154	50	13	0	2	2	0	0	0	1	0	1	0	0
Reuschel, Ricky, Chicago	.229	38	83	9	19	23	4	0	0	6	7	0	0	0
Reuss, Jerry, Pittsburgh*	.242	31	66	7	16	19	1	1	0	8	3	0	0	0
Reynolds, G. Craig, Pittsburgh*	.250	7	4	1	1	4	0	0	1	1	0	0	0	0
Reynolds, Kenneth, San Diego*	.000	19	5	0	0	0	0	0	0	0	0	0	0	0
Rhoden, Richard, Los Angeles	.308	27	65	6	20	26	3	0	1	9	7	0	0	0
Riccelli, Frank, San Francisco*	.167	4	6	0	1	1	0	0	0	0	0	0	0	0
Richard, James, Houston	.140	39	100	6	14	21	1	0	2	9	1	2	0	0
Richard, Lee, St. Louis	.176	66	91	12	16	24	4	2	0	5	2	0	1	0
Rivera, Jesus, Montreal	.276	68	185	22	51	76	11	4	2	19	1	0	1	0
Roberts, Leon, Houston	.289	87	235	31	68	104	11	2	7	33	1	2	1	0
Robertson, Robert, Pittsburgh	.217	61	129	10	28	41	5	1	2	25	0	2	0	1
Robinson, Craig, SF-Atl	.267	30	30	8	8	9	1	0	0	5	1	1	0	1
Robinson, William, Pittsburgh	.303	122	393	55	119	210	22	3	21	64	3	3	2	4
Robles, Sergio, Los Angeles	.000	6	3	0	0	0	0	0	0	0	0	0	0	0
Rockett, Patrick, Atlanta	.200	4	5	0	1	1	0	0	0	0	0	0	0	0
Rodriguez, Eliseo, Los Angeles	.212	36	66	10	14	14	0	0	0	9	0	2	0	0
Roenicke, Gary, Montreal	.222	29	90	9	20	31	3	1	2	5	0	1	0	0
Rogers, Stephen, Montreal	.149	35	74	2	11	11	0	0	0	4	6	0	1	0
Rondon, Gilbert, Houston	.286	19	14	1	4	4	0	0	0	1	2	0	0	0
Rooker, James, Pittsburgh	.216	33	74	9	16	23	2	1	1	6	5	1	0	0
Rose, Peter, Cincinnati†	.323	162	665	130	215	299	42	6	10	63	0	2	9	5
Rosello, David, Chicago	.242	91	227	27	55	65	5	1	1	11	1	1	1	2
Royster, Jeron, Atlanta	.248	149	533	65	132	162	13	1	5	45	14	5	24	13
Rudolph, Kenneth, St. Louis	.160	27	50	1	8	11	3	0	0	5	0	0	0	0
Russell, William, Los Angeles	.274	149	554	53	152	190	17	3	5	65	6	6	15	5
Ruthven, Richard, Atlanta	.171	37	76	6	13	14	1	0	0	5	9	0	0	1
Sadek, Michael, S. F.	.204	55	93	8	19	21	2	0	0	7	4	0	0	0
Sambito, Joseph, Houston*	.222	20	9	1	2	2	0	0	0	1	0	0	0	0
Sanders, Kenneth, New York	.000	31	2	0	0	0	0	0	0	0	0	0	0	0
Sanguillen, Manuel, Pittsburgh	.290	114	389	52	113	147	16	6	2	36	3	4	2	4
Sarmiento, Manuel, Cincinnati	.000	22	7	0	0	0	0	0	0	0	0	0	0	0
Sawyer, Richard, San Diego	.208	13	24	2	5	5	0	0	0	2	5	0	0	0
Scanlon, J. Patrick, Montreal*	.185	11	27	2	5	9	1	0	1	2	1	0	0	0
Scherman, Frederick, Montreal*	.250	31	4	0	1	1	0	0	0	0	1	0	0	0
Schmidt, Michael, Philadelphia	.262	160	584	112	153	306	31	4	38	107	3	7	14	9
Schueler, Ronald, Philadelphia	.000	35	2	0	0	0	0	0	0	1	1	0	0	0
Schultz, C. Budd, Chicago	.000	29	4	0	0	0	0	0	0	0	0	0	0	0
Scott, Rodney, Montreal	.400	7	10	3	4	4	0	0	0	0	0	0	2	0
Seaver, G. Thomas, New York	.085	35	82	5	7	7	0	0	0	3	9	0	0	0
Siebert, Paul, Houston*	.000	19	2	0	0	0	0	0	0	0	0	0	0	0
Simmons, Ted, St. Louis†	.291	150	546	60	159	215	35	3	5	75	0	6	0	7
Simpson, Joe, Los Angeles*	.133	23	30	2	4	5	1	0	0	0	0	0	0	1
Sizemore, Ted, Los Angeles	.241	84	266	18	64	74	8	1	0	18	10	1	2	3
Smith, C. Reginald, StL-LA†	.253	112	395	55	100	179	15	5	18	49	0	1	3	2
Solomon, Eddie, St. Louis	.400	26	5	0	2	3	1	0	0	4	0	0	0	0
Sosa, Elias, Atl-LA	.143	45	7	0	1	1	0	0	0	0	1	0	0	0
Sosa, Jose, Houston	.000	9	0	0	0	0	0	0	0	0	0	0	0	0
Speier, Chris, San Francisco	.226	145	495	51	112	147	18	4	3	40	6	7	2	2
Sperring, Robert, Chicago	.258	43	93	8	24	27	3	0	0	7	4	1	0	2
Spillner, Daniel, San Diego	.040	33	25	2	1	1	0	0	0	0	4	0	0	0
Staiger, Roy, New York	.220	95	304	23	67	83	8	1	2	26	1	4	3	3
Stanhouse, Donald, Montreal	.212	34	52	7	11	13	2	0	0	3	4	0	0	0
Stargell, Wilver, Pittsburgh*	.257	117	428	54	110	196	20	3	20	65	0	4	2	0
Stearns, John, New York	.262	32	103	13	27	39	6	0	2	10	0	1	1	2
Stennett, Renaldo, Pittsburgh	.257	157	654	59	168	223	31	9	2	60	4	4	18	6
Stone, Steven, Chicago	.143	17	21	1	3	3	0	0	0	1	0	0	0	0
Strom, Brent, San Diego	.063	38	63	4	4	6	0	1	0	1	10	1	0	0
Summers, John, Chicago*	.206	83	126	11	26	37	2	0	3	13	1	1	1	0
Sutcliffe, Richard, Los Angeles*	.000	1	1	0	0	0	0	0	0	0	0	0	0	0
Sutter, H. Bruce, Chicago	.000	52	8	0	0	0	0	0	0	0	0	0	0	0

Player and Club	Pct.	G.	AB.	R.	H.	TB.	2B.	3B.	HR.	RBI.	SH.	SF.	SB.	CS.
Sutton, Donald, Los Angeles	.083	35	84	2	7	8	1	0	0	3	9	0	0	0
Swan, Craig, New York	.103	23	39	3	4	4	0	0	0	1	6	0	0	0
Swisher, Steven, Chicago	.236	109	377	25	89	123	13	3	5	42	7	5	2	1
Tabb, Jerry, Chicago°	.292	11	24	2	7	7	0	0	0	0	0	0	0	0
Tamargo, John, St. Louis†	.300	10	10	2	3	3	0	0	0	1	0	1	0	0
Taveras, Alejandro, Houston	.217	14	46	3	10	10	0	0	0	2	0	0	1	2
Taveras, Franklin, Pittsburgh	.258	144	519	76	134	154	8	6	0	24	6	0	58	11
Taylor, Antonio, Philadelphia	.261	26	23	2	6	7	1	0	0	3	1	0	0	0
Taylor, Charles G., Montreal	.000	31	3	0	0	0	0	0	0	0	0	0	0	0
Tekulve, Kenton, Pittsburgh	.000	64	9	0	0	0	0	0	0	0	1	0	0	0
Templeton, Garry, St. Louis†	.291	53	213	32	62	77	8	2	1	17	2	2	11	7
Thomas, Derrel, San Francisco†	.232	81	272	38	63	82	5	4	2	19	6	2	10	11
Thomasson, Gary, San Francisco°	.259	103	328	45	85	139	20	5	8	38	0	2	8	3
Thornton, Andre, Chi-Mtl	.194	96	268	28	52	100	11	2	11	38	1	4	4	1
Tolan, Robert, Philadelphia°	.261	110	272	32	71	93	7	0	5	35	2	5	10	5
Tomlin, David, San Diego°	.000	49	8	2	0	0	0	0	0	0	1	0	0	0
Toms, Thomas, San Francisco	.000	7	0	0	0	0	0	0	0	0	0	0	0	0
Torre, Joseph, New York	.306	114	310	36	95	126	10	3	5	31	2	2	1	3
Torrealba, Pablo, Atlanta°	.000	36	4	0	0	0	0	0	0	0	0	0	0	0
Torres, Hector, San Diego	.195	74	215	8	42	60	6	0	4	15	3	0	2	1
Trillo, J. Manuel (Marcano) Chi	.239	158	582	42	139	181	24	3	4	59	7	4	17	6
Turner, John, San Diego°	.267	105	281	41	75	116	16	5	5	37	4	3	12	6
Twitchell, Wayne, Philadelphia	.167	26	6	1	1	2	1	0	0	0	0	0	0	0
Tyrone, O. Wayne, Chicago	.228	30	57	3	13	17	1	0	1	8	1	0	0	0
Tyson, Michael, St. Louis	.286	76	245	26	70	109	12	9	3	28	0	3	3	1
Underwood, Thomas, Philadelphia°	.109	34	46	2	5	5	0	0	0	5	3	0	0	0
Unser, Delbert, NY-Mtl°	.228	146	496	57	113	176	19	4	12	40	11	6	7	7
Vail, Michael, New York	.217	53	143	8	31	38	5	1	0	9	0	3	0	1
Valentine, Ellis, Montreal	.279	94	305	36	85	125	15	2	7	39	2	4	14	1
Valentine, Robert, San Diego	.367	15	49	3	18	22	4	0	0	4	2	0	0	1
Varney, Richard, Atlanta	.100	5	10	0	1	1	0	0	0	0	0	0	0	0
Vukovich, John, Philadelphia	.125	4	8	2	1	4	0	0	1	2	0	0	0	0
Walker, R. Thomas, St. Louis	.400	10	5	0	2	2	0	0	0	0	0	0	0	0
Wall, Stanley, Los Angeles°	.000	31	4	0	0	0	0	0	0	0	0	0	0	0
Wallace, Michael, St. Louis°	.333	49	3	1	1	1	0	0	0	0	0	0	0	0
Wallis, H. Joseph, Chicago°	.254	121	338	51	86	122	11	5	5	21	4	1	3	9
Walton, Daniel, Los Angeles†	.133	18	15	0	2	2	0	0	0	2	0	1	0	0
Warthen, Daniel, Montreal†	.000	23	27	0	0	0	0	0	0	0	1	0	0	0
Waterbury, Steven, St. Louis	.000	5	0	0	0	0	0	0	0	0	0	0	0	0
Watson, Robert, Houston	.313	157	585	76	183	268	31	3	16	102	2	9	3	3
Webb, Henry, New York	.000	8	1	1	0	0	0	0	0	0	0	0	0	0
Wehrmeister, David, San Diego°	.000	7	6	0	0	0	0	0	0	0	0	0	0	0
Werner, Donald, Cincinnati	.500	3	4	0	2	3	1	0	0	1	0	0	0	0
White, Jerome, Montreal†	.245	114	278	32	68	87	11	1	2	21	2	0	15	7
Williams, Charles, San Francisco	.125	48	8	1	1	1	0	0	0	0	0	0	0	0
Williams, Earl, Atl-Mtl	.225	122	374	35	84	152	13	2	17	55	2	5	0	0
Winfield, David, San Diego	.283	137	492	81	139	212	26	4	13	69	2	5	26	7
Wynn, James, Atlanta	.207	148	449	75	93	165	19	1	17	66	0	8	16	6
Yeager, Stephen, Los Angeles	.214	117	359	42	77	127	11	3	11	35	1	2	3	1
Youngblood, Joel, Cincinnati	.193	55	57	8	11	14	1	1	0	1	0	0	1	0
Zachry, Patrick, Cincinnati	.113	38	62	1	7	7	0	0	0	2	12	0	0	0
Zahn, Geoffrey, Chicago°	.000	3	3	0	0	0	0	0	0	0	0	0	0	0
Zamora, Oscar, Chicago	.000	40	9	0	0	0	0	0	0	0	0	0	0	0
Zisk, Richard, Pittsburgh	.289	155	581	91	168	270	35	2	21	89	0	8	1	0

AWARDED FIRST BASE ON INTERFERENCE—Garrett, Mont. 3 (Hodges, Mitterwald, Swisher); Torres, S.D. 2 (C. Johnson, Sanguillen); Andrews, Hous. (Sanguillen); Carlton, Phila. (C. Johnson); Kessinger, St.L. (Hill); Kubiak, S.D. (C. Johnson); Phillips, N.Y. (Pocoroba); Richard, Hous. (Swisher); Thornton, Mont. (Hodges).

PLAYERS WITH TWO OR MORE CLUBS
(Alphabetically Arranged With Player's First Club on Top)

Player and Club	Pct.	G.	AB.	R.	H.	TB.	2B.	3B.	HR.	RBI.	SH.	SF.	Tot. BB.	Int. BB.	HP.	SO.	SB.	CS.	GI DP.
Biittner, Mtl	.188	11	32	2	6	7	1	0	0	1	0	0	0	0	0	3	0	0	2
Biittner, Chi	.245	78	192	21	47	62	13	1	0	17	2	0	10	3	1	6	0	2	4
Dwyer, Mtl	.185	50	92	7	17	22	3	1	0	5	0	1	11	1	0	10	0	0	3
Dwyer, NY	.154	11	13	2	2	2	0	0	0	0	0	0	2	1	0	1	0	0	0
Evans, Atl	.173	44	139	11	24	27	0	0	1	10	0	0	30	0	0	33	3	0	3
Evans, SF	.222	92	257	42	57	98	9	1	10	36	1	2	42	4	0	38	6	1	2
Ferguson, LA	.222	54	185	24	41	66	7	0	6	18	2	0	25	1	1	41	2	0	3
Ferguson, StL	.201	71	189	22	38	66	8	4	4	21	2	2	32	3	1	40	4	2	6
Garrett, NY	.223	80	251	36	56	78	8	1	4	26	1	0	52	5	1	26	7	5	5
Garrett, Mtl	.243	59	177	15	43	55	4	1	2	11	1	0	30	7	0	20	2	2	1
Greif, SD	.000	5	8	0	0	0	0	0	0	0	0	0	0	0	0	3	0	0	0
Greif, StL	.000	47	4	0	0	0	0	0	0	0	0	0	2	0	0	2	0	0	0
Griffin, Hou	.000	20	5	0	0	0	0	0	0	0	1	0	1	0	0	2	0	0	0
Griffin, SD	.077	12	26	2	2	2	0	0	0	0	3	0	0	0	0	7	0	0	0
Hernandez, Pitt	.000	37	3	0	0	0	0	0	0	0	0	0	0	0	0	1	0	0	0
Hernandez, Chi	.000	2	0	0	0	0	0	0	0	0	0	0	0	0	0	0	0	0	0
Lacy, Atl	.272	50	180	25	49	66	4	2	3	20	3	0	6	1	1	12	2	2	5
Lacy, LA	.266	53	158	17	42	51	7	1	0	14	1	2	16	2	0	13	1	2	7
Lyttle, Mtl	.271	42	85	6	23	32	4	1	1	8	1	0	7	1	0	13	0	0	2
Lyttle, LA	.221	23	68	3	15	18	3	0	0	5	0	0	8	4	0	12	0	1	0
Mangual, Mtl	.260	66	215	34	56	76	9	1	3	16	2	1	50	2	2	49	17	7	0
Mangual, NY	.186	41	102	15	19	31	5	2	1	9	3	0	10	0	0	32	7	3	0
Marshall, LA	.000	30	5	1	0	0	0	0	0	1	0	1	3	0	0	2	0	0	0
Marshall, Atl	.167	24	6	0	1	1	0	0	0	0	1	0	1	0	0	1	0	0	0
Melendez, StL	.125	20	24	0	3	3	0	0	0	0	0	0	0	0	0	3	0	0	3
Melendez, SD	.244	72	119	15	29	34	5	0	0	5	0	1	3	1	0	12	1	1	3
Montanez, SF	.309	60	230	22	71	96	15	2	2	20	1	2	15	5	1	15	2	1	10
Montanez, Atl	.321	103	420	52	135	176	14	0	9	64	0	1	21	6	0	32	0	4	16
Perez, Atl	.250	31	96	12	24	31	4	0	1	6	4	1	8	0	0	9	0	0	6
Perez, SF	.259	93	332	37	86	107	13	1	2	26	10	3	30	0	0	28	3	4	2
Renko, Mtl	.333	5	3	0	1	1	0	0	0	0	0	0	0	0	0	1	0	0	0
Renko, Chi	.094	29	53	3	5	5	0	0	0	1	4	0	0	0	0	16	0	0	3
Robinson, SF	.308	15	13	4	4	5	1	0	0	2	1	0	3	0	0	4	0	1	0
Robinson, Atl	.235	15	17	4	4	4	0	0	0	3	0	1	5	0	0	2	0	0	0
Smith, StL	.218	47	170	20	37	70	7	1	8	23	0	0	14	2	1	28	1	2	4
Smith, LA	.280	65	225	35	63	109	8	4	10	26	0	1	18	4	1	42	2	0	4
Sosa, Atl	.143	21 *	7	0	1	1	0	0	0	0	0	0	0	0	0	0	0	0	0
Sosa, LA	.000	24	0	0	0	0	0	0	0	0	1	0	0	0	0	0	0	0	0
Thornton, Chi	.200	27	85	8	17	29	6	0	2	14	0	1	20	1	2	14	2	0	0
Thornton, Mtl	.191	69	183	20	35	71	5	2	9	24	1	3	28	0	3	32	2	1	1
Unser, NY	.228	77	276	28	63	95	13	2	5	25	5	3	18	1	1	40	4	4	4
Unser, Mtl	.227	69	220	29	50	81	6	2	7	15	6	3	11	0	0	44	3	3	3
Williams, Atl	.212	61	184	18	39	69	3	0	9	26	2	2	19	2	1	33	0	0	8
Williams, Mtl	.237	61	190	17	45	83	10	2	8	29	0	3	14	2	0	32	0	0	8

OFFICIAL MISCELLANEOUS NATIONAL LEAGUE BATTING RECORDS

CLUB MISCELLANEOUS BATTING RECORDS

Club	Slg. Pct.	G.	Tot. BB.	Int. BB.	HP.	SO.	GIDP.	ShO.
Cincinnati	.424	162	681	63	28	902	103	8
Philadelphia	.395	162	542	55	40	793	119	10
Pittsburgh	.391	162	433	56	29	807	131	11
St. Louis	.359	162	512	69	22	860	127	14
Chicago	.356	162	490	66	30	834	126	10
New York	.352	162	561	53	28	797	127	18
Los Angeles	.349	162	486	71	29	744	129	14
Houston	.347	162	530	54	21	719	127	11
San Francisco	.345	162	518	52	25	778	122	17
Montreal	.340	162	433	43	16	841	107	15
San Diego	.337	162	488	57	23	716	119	23
Atlanta	.334	162	589	46	19	811	131	13
Totals	.361		6263	685	310	9602	1468	164

INDIVIDUAL MISCELLANEOUS BATTING RECORDS
(Top Fifteen Qualifiers for Slugging Championship—502 or More Plate Appearances)

Player—Club	Slg. Pct.	Tot. BB.	Int. BB.	HP.	SO.	GI DP.		Player—Club	Slg. Pct.	Tot. BB.	Int. BB.	HP.	SO.	GI DP.
Morgan, Cin	.576	114	8	1	41	2		Cey, LA	.462	89	13	3	74	11
Foster, Cin	.530	52	4	4	89	11		Watson, Hou	.458	62	10	4	64	12
Schmidt, Phila	.524	100	8	11	149	7		Maddox, Phila	.456	42	8	4	59	10
Monday, Chia	.507	60	8	2	125	7		Cedeno, Hou	.454	55	7	1	51	16
Kingman, NY	.506	28	4	5	135	11		Perez, Cin	.452	50	9	5	88	10
Madlock, Chi	.500	56	15	11	27	21		Griffey, Cin	.450	62	0	1	65	3
Luzinski, Phila	.478	50	2	11	107	11		Garvey, LA	.450	50	11	1	69	20
Parker, Pitt	.475	30	6	2	80	16		Rose, Cin	.450	86	7	6	54	17
Zisk, Pitt	.465	52	3	0	96	20								

DEPARTMENTAL LEADERS: Tot. BB—Wynn, 127; Int. BB—Simmons, 19; HP—Luzinski, Madlock, Schmidt, 11; SO—Schmidt, 149; GIDP—Montanez, 26.

(All Players—Listed Alphabetically)

Player—Club	Slg. Pct.	Tot. BB.	Int. BB.	HP.	SO.	GI DP.		Player—Club	Slg. Pct.	Tot. BB.	Int. BB.	HP.	SO.	GI DP.
Adams, SF	.297	1	0	0	12	4		Beard, Atl	.000	0	0	0	1	0
Adams, Chi	.207	8	0	1	7	0		Belloir, Atl	.233	5	1	0	7	0
Alcala, Cin	.163	2	0	0	26	0		Bench, Cin	.394	81	6	2	95	9
Alexander, SF	.301	10	1	0	16	1		Biittner, Mtl-Chi	.308	10	3	1	9	6
Allen, Phila	.480	37	2	0	63	13		Billingham, Cin	.288	3	0	0	12	1
Almon, SD	.351	2	0	0	9	0		Blackwell, Phila	.250	0	0	0	1	0
Alvarado, StL	.310	3	1	0	6	0		Blair, Mtl	.000	0	0	0	2	1
Anderson, StL	.357	26	4	1	30	5		Boisclair, NY	.374	28	5	0	55	3
Andrews, Phila	.667	2	0	1	0	0		Bonham, Chi	.262	2	0	0	15	1
Andrews, Hou	.300	33	1	0	27	16		Boone, Phil	.366	45	14	1	44	10
Andujar, Hou	.158	2	0	0	29	0		Borbon, Cin	.222	0	0	0	4	0
Apodaca, NY	.188	1	0	0	3	2		Bosetti, Phila	.333	1	0	0	3	1
Armas, Pitt	.333	0	0	0	2	0		Boswell, Hou	.341	8	2	0	8	8
Armbrister, Cin	.462	6	0	0	22	0		Bowa, Phila	.301	32	3	0	31	11
Arnold, SF	.246	6	1	0	16	4		Brock, StL	.394	35	7	1	75	19
Ashford, SD	.800	1	0	0	0	0		Brown, NY	.257	4	0	0	4	3
Asselstine, Atl	.303	1	0	0	2	0		Brown, Phila	.383	33	5	0	33	1
Atkinson, Mtl	.000	0	0	0	0	0		Buckner, LA	.389	26	6	1	26	8
Auerbach, LA	.128	6	0	0	6	3		Burke, LA	.283	3	0	1	8	1
Autry, Atl	.000	0	0	0	1	0		Burris, Chi	.111	1	0	0	28	1
Ayala, NY	.231	2	0	0	6	0		Cabell, Hou	.329	29	1	2	79	13
Bailey, Cin	.508	16	1	0	26	7		Caldwell, SF	.211	0	0	0	4	0
Bair, Pitt	.000	0	0	0	0	0		Camp, Atl	.000	0	0	0	1	0
Baker, LA	.307	31	3	1	54	15		Candelaria, Pitt	.237	7	0	0	17	4
Ri. Baldwin, NY	.333	0	0	0	2	0		Capilla, StL	.000	0	0	0	0	0
Ro. Baldwin, NY	.545	1	0	0	2	0		Capra, Atl	.000	0	0	0	0	0
Barlow, Hou	.000	0	0	0	1	1		Cardenal, Chi	.401	32	0	1	39	5
Barr, SF	.243	4	0	1	21	0		Carlton, Phila	.228	1	0	2	24	1

Player—Club	Slg. Pct.	Tot. BB.	Int. BB.	HP.	SO.	GI DP.
Carrithers, Mtl	.162	0	0	0	13	1
Carter, Mtl	.309	30	2	1	43	7
Cash, Phila	.345	54	3	2	13	16
Cedeno, Hou	.454	55	9	1	51	16
Cey, LA	.462	89	13	3	74	11
Champion, SD	.368	1	0	0	3	1
Chaney, Atl	.331	54	7	1	92	9
Chant, StL	.143	0	0	0	4	0
Chiles, Hou	.750	0	0	0	0	0
Christenson, Phila	.392	3	0	0	28	0
Clarey, StL	1.000	0	0	0	1	0
Clark, SF	.382	8	0	0	18	0
Colbert, Mtl	.400	9	1	0	16	0
Coleman, Chi	.154	0	0	0	4	0
Concepcion, Cin	.401	49	11	1	68	11
Correll, Atl	.350	21	5	1	37	7
Cosgrove, Hou	.087	2	0	0	6	0
Cox, Mtl	.241	2	0	0	2	1
Crawford, StL	.441	37	6	1	53	10
Cromartie, Mtl	.222	1	0	0	5	2
Crosby, Chi	.500	0	0	0	0	0
Crowley, Atl	.000	0	0	0	0	0
Cruz, StL	.338	42	7	2	119	13
Cruz, LA	.364	9	3	0	11	1
Cruz, Hou	.401	53	5	0	46	6
Curtis, StL	.286	2	0	0	13	1
D'Acquisto, SF	.308	1	0	0	11	1
DalCanton, Atl	.222	1	0	0	2	0
Darcy, Cin	.182	2	0	0	3	0
DaVanon, Hou	.402	21	1	1	12	2
R. Davis, SD	.229	5	1	0	13	0
W. Davis, SD	.375	19	2	2	34	6
Dawson, Mtl	.306	5	1	0	13	0
DeJesus, LA	.268	4	0	0	9	2
Demery, Pitt	.125	2	0	0	16	0
Denny, StL	.254	1	0	0	27	0
Dettore, Chi	.000	0	0	0	0	0
Devine, Atl	.000	0	0	0	3	0
Dierker, Hou	.188	0	0	0	20	1
Dilone, Pitt	.235	0	0	0	0	0
Downing, LA	.000	0	0	0	4	0
Dressler, SF	.129	0	0	1	14	0
Driessen, Cin	.402	43	2	0	32	11
Dunning, Mtl	.133	2	0	0	7	0
Dupree, SD	1.000	0	0	0	0	0
Dwyer, Mtl.-NY	.229	13	2	0	11	3
Dyer, Pitt	.315	29	10	3	35	3
Easterly, Atl	.111	0	0	0	2	0
Eastwick, Cin	.000	0	0	0	10	0
Eden, Atl	.000	0	0	0	0	1
Espinosa, NY	.000	1	0	0	3	0
Evans, Atl-SF	.316	72	4	0	71	5
Fairly, StL	.300	23	3	0	12	5
Falcone, StL	.145	1	0	1	23	1
Ferguson, LA-StL	.353	57	4	2	81	9
Flynn, Cin	.338	10	1	0	24	3
Foli, Mtl	.366	16	1	0	33	15
Folkers, SD	.000	0	0	0	1	0
Foote, Mtl	.340	17	3	1	32	8
Forsch, Hou	.091	1	0	0	3	1
Forsch, StL	.258	1	0	0	17	3
Foster, SD	.056	3	0	0	6	0
Foster, Cin	.530	52	4	4	89	11
Foster, NY	.288	8	1	0	5	0
Frailing, Chi	.000	0	0	0	0	0
Freed, Mtl	.267	0	0	0	3	0
Freisleben, SD	.243	2	0	0	8	0
Frias, Mtl	.292	4	3	0	14	2
Frisella, StL	.000	0	0	0	0	0
Fryman, Mtl	.125	1	0	0	17	0
Fuentes, SD	.310	18	0	1	38	12
Garber, Phila	.286	2	0	0	3	0
Garman, Chi	.000	0	0	0	4	0
Garrett, NY-Mtl	.311	82	12	1	46	6
Garvey, LA	.450	50	11	1	69	20
Gaston, Atl	.410	13	1	0	21	6
Geronimo, Cin	.414	56	13	6	95	6
Gilbreath, Atl	.329	42	1	4	36	9
Giusti, Pitt	.000	1	0	0	0	0
Goodson, LA	.339	8	2	0	19	7
Granger, Mtl	.000	0	0	0	1	0
Greif, SD-StL	.000	2	0	0	5	0
Griffey, Cin	.450	62	0	1	65	3
Griffin, Hou-SD	.065	1	0	0	9	0
Gross, Hou	.329	64	3	0	39	8
Grote, NY	.365	38	4	1	19	15
Grubb, SD	.385	65	10	4	53	5
Gullett, Cin	.182	1	0	0	7	2
Hale, LA	.198	16	1	2	14	0
Halicki, SF	.170	6	0	0	23	1
Hall, NY	.000	0	0	0	0	0
Hanna, Atl	.000	0	0	0	0	0
Hannahs, Mtl	.375	0	0	0	3	0
Hardy, Hou	.000	0	0	0	0	0
Harmon, Phila	.393	3	0	0	10	1
Harrelson, NY	.298	63	5	2	56	1
Harris, StL	.309	16	0	1	55	6
Heaverlo, SF	.333	0	0	0	1	0
Hebner, Pitt	.366	47	2	4	39	5
Heidemann, NY	.083	0	0	0	0	0
Helms, Pitt	.391	10	0	1	5	0
Henderson, Cin	.000	0	0	0	0	0
Henderson, Atl	.395	62	7	1	68	12
Hernandez, SD	.321	32	4	0	16	5
Hernandez, StL	.428	49	5	3	53	8
Hernandez, Pitt-Chi	.000	0	0	0	1	0
Herndon, SF	.356	23	0	2	45	4
Herrmann, Hou	.268	22	2	4	40	6
Hill, SF	.290	10	2	1	19	3
Hinton, Cin	.000	0	0	0	0	0
Hodges, NY	.342	27	2	0	16	4
Hooton, LA	.113	3	0	1	28	0
Hosley, Chi	.000	0	0	0	0	0
Hough, LA	.381	0	0	0	5	0
Howard, Hou	.293	7	1	0	28	5
Howe, Hou	.172	6	1	0	6	1
Hrabosky, StL	.000	2	0	1	4	0
Hundley, Chi	.278	1	0	0	4	0
Hutton, Phila	.282	27	0	0	11	4
Ivie, SD	.415	30	8	5	41	10
Javier, Hou	.208	2	1	0	5	1
John, LA	.125	2	0	0	10	4
Johnson, Hou	.399	62	6	4	59	9
Johnson, SD	.000	0	0	0	2	0
Johnson, Mtl	.231	0	0	0	2	0
Johnstone, Phila	.457	41	5	2	39	9
Jones, SD	.058	5	0	0	39	0
Jorgensen, Mtl	.344	52	9	0	48	5
Joshua, SF	.321	4	2	0	20	3
Jutze, Hou	.239	4	0	0	16	2
Kaat, Phila	.278	2	0	0	24	0
Keener, Mtl	.000	0	0	0	1	0
Kelleher, Chi	.270	15	3	2	32	8
Kendall, SD	.296	36	4	3	42	20
Kerrigan, Mtl	.000	0	0	0	0	0
Kessinger, StL	.313	61	5	1	51	13

Player—Club	Slg. Pct.	Tot. BB.	Int. BB.	HP.	SO.	GI DP.
Kingman, NY	.506	28	4	5	135	11
Kirby, Mtl.	.111	1	0	0	5	0
Kirkpatrick, Pitt	.295	14	2	0	15	3
Kison, Pitt	.305	5	0	0	20	1
Kleven, NY	.200	0	0	0	1	1
Knepper, SF	.111	0	0	0	3	0
Knowles, Chi.	.143	3	0	0	0	0
Koosman, NY	.241	2	0	0	34	1
Kranepool, NY	.410	35	4	0	38	10
Krukow, Chi	.000	0	0	0	0	0
Kubiak, SD	.278	25	2	0	28	9
LaCock, Chi	.373	42	6	1	37	5
LaCorte, Atl	.091	0	0	0	15	0
Lacy, Atl-LA	.346	22	3	1	25	12
LaGrow, StL	.000	0	0	0	3	0
Landreth, Mtl	.000	0	0	0	2	0
Lang, Mtl	.167	0	0	0	3	0
Langford, Pitt	.400	0	0	0	2	0
Larson, Hou	.387	1	0	0	3	0
Lavelle, SF	.077	0	0	0	3	0
Lee, LA	.178	2	1	0	9	1
LeMaster, SF	.280	2	0	0	21	2
Lemongello, Hou	.000	1	0	0	3	0
Leon, Atl	.000	0	0	0	0	0
Lerch, Phil	2.000	0	0	0	0	0
Lewallyn, LA	.000	0	0	0	5	0
Locklear, SD	.269	4	1	0	15	0
Lockwood, NY	.389	2	0	0	3	0
Lolich, NY	.130	5	0	1	25	2
Lonborg, Phila	.179	6	0	0	20	2
Lopes, LA.	.342	56	1	4	49	8
Lum, Cin	.346	22	1	1	24	2
Luzinski, Phila	.478	50	2	11	107	11
Lyttle, Mtl-LA	.327	15	5	0	25	2
Mackanin, Mtl	.337	15	1	2	66	10
Maddox, Phila	.456	42	8	4	59	10
Madlock, Chi	.500	56	15	11	27	21
Mangual, Mtl-NY	.338	60	2	2	81	0
Marshall, LA-Atl	.091	4	0	0	3	0
Martin, Phila	.355	70	0	0	28	5
Matlack, NY	.205	8	0	1	35	3
Matthews, SF	.443	75	3	1	94	8
May, Atl	.308	26	3	1	31	4
Mazzilli, NY	.299	14	0	1	10	0
McBride, StL	.445	18	0	6	28	2
McCarver, Phila	.432	35	2	1	14	1
McCovey, SD	.351	21	7	1	39	4
McEnaney, Cin	.167	2	0	0	4	0
McGlothen, StL	.254	1	0	0	15	0
McGraw, Phila	.286	0	0	0	2	0
McLaughlin, Hou	.000	2	0	0	7	0
Medich, Pitt	.096	4	0	0	21	2
Mejias, StL	.190	2	1	0	2	2
Melendez, StL-SD	.259	3	1	0	15	6
Mendoza, Pitt	.239	4	1	0	15	3
Messersmith, Atl	.194	4	0	0	19	1
Metzger, SD	.000	2	0	0	2	0
Metzger, Hou	.270	52	10	0	63	11
Milbourne, Hou	.276	14	0	1	10	3
Millan, NY	.343	41	5	7	19	15
Miller, SF	.200	2	1	0	5	0
Milner, NY	.447	65	1	0	53	12
Minton, SF	.200	0	0	0	2	0
Mitterwald, Chi	.287	16	2	0	63	9
Moffitt, SF	.143	0	0	0	5	0
Monday, Chi	.507	60	8	2	125	7
Montanez, SF-Atl	.418	36	11	1	47	26
Montefusco, SF	.115	5	0	1	42	1
Moore, Atl	.308	4	0	1	4	0
Moose, Pitt	.667	0	0	0	0	1
Morales, Mtl	.462	3	3	2	20	5
Morales, Chi	.395	41	7	0	49	20
Moreno, Pitt.	.369	16	0	1	24	0
Moret, Atl	.130	0	0	0	8	0
Morgan, Cin	.576	114	8	1	41	2
Morton, Atl	.178	2	0	0	15	0
Mota, LA	.346	7	3	0	5	1
Mumphrey, StL.	.331	37	0	1	53	2
Murcer, SF	.433	84	10	4	78	11
Murphy, Atl	.354	7	0	0	9	0
Murray, Mtl	.000	0	0	0	4	0
Myrick, NY	.000	0	0	0	2	0
Nahorodny, Phila	.400	0	0	0	0	0
Niekro, Hou	.370	1	0	0	8	0
Niekro, Atl	.255	0	0	1	8	3
Nolan, Cin	.101	3	0	0	33	0
Norman, Cin	.140	1	0	0	9	0
Oates, Phila	.273	8	0	0	12	5
Office, Atl	.368	37	3	2	49	4
Oliver, Pitt	.476	26	7	5	29	13
Ontiveros, SF	.216	6	0	1	11	2
Ott, Pitt	.359	3	1	0	5	0
Owchinko, SD	.000	0	0	0	0	0
Paciorek, Atl	.383	19	2	3	57	8
Parker, Pitt	.475	30	6	2	80	16
Parrish, Mtl	.363	41	2	2	91	13
Pasley, LA	.269	3	1	0	7	0
Pentz, Hou	.200	1	0	0	1	0
Perez, Cin.	.452	50	9	5	88	10
Perez, Atl-SF	.322	38	0	0	37	8
Phillips, NY	.363	25	8	0	29	2
Plummer, Cinn	.379	14	0	0	36	7
Pocoroba, Atl	.282	19	2	0	12	8
Potter, StL	.000	1	0	0	6	0
Proly, StL	.000	0	0	0	0	0
Putman, Chi	.429	0	0	0	0	2
Rader, SF	.333	27	8	0	21	12
Rader, SD	.378	55	3	3	102	12
Rasmussen, StL	.132	2	0	0	15	1
Rau, LA	.150	7	0	0	15	4
Reed, Phila	.208	0	0	0	3	0
Reitz, StL	.333	24	5	1	48	24
Renko, Mtl-Chi	.107	0	0	0	17	3
Rettenmund, SD	.321	29	0	0	23	3
P. Reuschel, Chi	.154	1	0	0	4	0
R. Reuschel, Chi	.277	6	0	1	16	2
Reuss, Pitt	.288	9	0	0	22	0
Reynolds, Pitt	1.000	0	0	0	0	0
Reynolds, SD	.000	0	0	0	0	0
Rhoden, LA	.400	1	0	0	12	1
Riccelli, SF	.167	0	0	0	3	0
Richard, Hou	.210	0	0	1	33	0
Richard, StL	.264	4	1	0	9	4
Rivera, Mtl	.411	13	1	0	32	5
Roberts, Hou	.443	19	1	3	43	2
Robertson, Pitt	.318	16	0	0	23	1
Robinson, SF-Atl	.300	8	0	0	6	0
Robinson, Pitt	.534	16	1	1	73	14
Robles, LA	.000	0	0	0	2	0
Rockett, StL	.200	0	0	0	1	0
Rodriguez, LA.	.212	19	2	3	12	1
Roenicke, Mtl	.344	4	0	1	18	1
Rogers, Mtl	.149	1	0	0	24	1
Rondon, Hou	.286	0	0	0	4	1
Rooker, Pitt	.311	1	0	0	31	1
Rose, Cin	.450	86	7	6	54	17

Player—Club	Slg. Pct.	Tot. BB.	Int. BB.	HP.	SO.	GI DP.
Rosello, Chi	.286	41	8	1	33	4
Royster, Atl	.304	52	4	1	53	11
Rudolph, StL	.220	1	0	0	7	2
Russell, LA	.343	21	9	3	46	14
Ruthven, Atl	.184	3	0	1	21	1
Sadek, SF	.226	11	2	1	10	2
Sambito, Hou	.222	3	0	0	2	0
Sanders, NY	.000	0	0	0	0	0
Sanguillen, Pitt.	.378	28	14	2	18	14
Sarmiento, Cin	.000	0	0	0	1	0
Sawyer, SD	.208	2	0	0	2	0
Scanlon, Mtl.	.333	2	0	0	5	1
Scherman, Mtl	.250	0	0	0	0	0
Schmidt, Phila	.524	100	8	11	149	7
Schueler, Phila	.000	0	0	0	2	0
Schultz, Chi	.000	0	0	0	0	0
Scott, Mtl.	.400	1	0	0	1	0
Seaver, NY	.085	9	0	0	26	1
Siebert, Hou	.000	0	0	0	0	0
Simmons, StL	.394	73	19	0	35	9
Simpson, LA	.167	1	0	0	6	0
Sizemore, LA	.278	15	1	0	22	5
Smith, StL-LA	.453	32	6	2	70	8
Solomon, StL	.600	0	0	0	3	0
Sosa, Atl-LA	.143	0	0	0	0	0
Sosa, Hou	.000	0	0	0	0	0
Speier, SF	.297	60	1	4	52	16
Sperring, Chi	.290	9	0	0	25	2
Spillner, SD	.040	3	0	0	8	1
Staiger, NY	.273	25	6	1	35	8
Stanhouse, Mtl	.250	5	0	0	13	0
Stargell, Pitt	.458	50	6	5	101	4
Stearns, NY	.379	1	0	1	11	4
Stennett, Pitt	.341	19	2	1	32	15
Stone, Chi	.143	0	0	0	9	0
Strom, SD	.095	5	0	0	18	1
Summers, Chi	.294	13	1	1	31	3
Sutcliffe, LA	.000	0	0	0	1	0
Sutter, Chi	.000	1	0	0	6	0
Sutton, LA	.095	6	0	0	19	3
Swan, NY	.103	3	0	1	17	0
Swisher, Chi	.326	20	3	2	82	11
Tabb, Chi	.292	3	0	0	2	0
Tamargo, StL	.300	3	0	0	1	0
Taveras, Hou	.217	2	0	0	1	2
Taveras, Pitt	.297	44	1	4	79	11
Taylor, Phila	.304	1	0	1	7	0
Taylor, NY	.000	0	0	0	1	0
Tekulve, Pitt	.000	0	0	0	6	0
Templeton, StL	.362	7	0	1	33	1
Thomas, SF	.301	29	0	4	26	5
Thomasson, SF	.424	30	7	1	45	4
Thornton, Chi-Mtl.	.373	48	1	5	46	1
Tolan, Phila	.342	7	3	4	39	8
Tomlin, SD	.000	1	0	0	2	0
Toms, SF	.000	0	0	0	0	0
Torre, NY	.406	21	1	5	35	16
Torrealba, Atl.	.000	0	0	0	0	0
Torres, SD	.279	16	3	1	31	8
Trillo, Chi	.311	53	4	3	70	17
Turner, SD	.413	32	3	0	38	3
Twitchell, Phila.	.333	0	0	0	4	0
Tyrone, Chi	.298	3	2	0	21	0
Tyson, StL	.445	16	5	0	34	6
Underwood, Phila	.109	3	0	0	18	3
Unser, NY-Mtl	.355	29	2	1	84	7
Vail, NY	.266	6	0	0	19	4
Valentine, Mtl.	.410	30	0	0	51	5
Valentine, SD	.449	6	0	0	2	2
Varney, Atl	.100	0	0	0	2	1
Vukovich, Phila.	.500	0	0	0	2	0
Walker, StL	.400	0	0	0	0	0
Wall, LA.	.000	0	0	0	1	0
Wallace, StL	.333	0	0	0	1	0
Wallis, Chi	.361	33	3	1	62	1
Walton, LA	.133	1	0	0	2	0
Warthen, Mtl	.000	0	0	0	13	0
Waterbury, StL.	.000	0	0	0	0	0
Watson, Hou	.458	62	10	4	64	12
Webb, NY	.000	1	0	0	0	0
Wehrmeister, SD	.000	0	0	0	1	0
Werner, Cin	.750	1	0	0	1	0
White, Mtl	.313	27	2	2	31	4
Williams, SF	.125	0	0	1	4	0
Williams, Atl-Mtl	.406	33	4	1	65	16
Winfield, SD	.431	65	8	3	78	14
Wynn, Atl	.367	127	1	0	111	7
Yeager, LA	.354	30	3	7	84	5
Youngblood, Cin	.246	2	0	1	8	1
Zachry, Cin.	.113	3	0	0	25	0
Zahn, Chi	.000	0	0	0	3	0
Zamora, Chi	.000	0	0	0	3	0
Zisk, Pitt	.465	52	3	0	96	20

OFFICIAL NATIONAL LEAGUE FIELDING AVERAGES

CLUB FIELDING

Club	Pct.	G.	PO.	A.	E.	TC.	DP.	TP.	PB.
Cincinnati	.984	162	4413	1678	102	6193	157	0	6
Philadelphia	.981	162	4377	1671	115	6163	148	0	6
Los Angeles	.980	162	4412	1833	128	6373	154	0	14
New York	.979	162	4347	1683	131	6161	116	0	8
Chicago	.978	162	4414	1854	140	6408	145	0	11
San Diego	.978	162	4297	1901	141	6339	148	0	9
Houston	.978	162	4333	1800	140	6273	155	0	32
Montreal	.976	162	4320	1956	155	6431	179	0	11
Pittsburgh	.975	162	4399	1878	163	6440	142	0	13
Atlanta	.973	162	4314	1820	167	6301	151	0	38
St. Louis	.973	162	4361	1840	174	6375	163	0	16
San Francisco	.971	162	4385	1940	186	6511	153	1	15
Totals	.977		52372	21854	1742	75968	1811	1	179

INDIVIDUAL FIELDING

*Throws lefthanded.

FIRST BASEMEN

Leader—Club	Pct.	G.	PO.	A.	E.	DP.
GARVEY, LA	.998	162	1583	67	3	138

(Listed Alphabetically)

Player—Club	Pct.	G.	PO.	A.	E.	DP.
Allen, Phila	.989	85	671	44	8	71
Anderson, StL	.970	5	30	2	1	3
Arnold, SF	1.000	1	5	0	0	2
Bench, Cin	.000	1	0	0	0	0
Biittner, Chi°	.985	33	232	33	4	20
Boone, Phila	.943	4	30	3	2	0
Buckner, LA°	.000	1	0	0	0	0
Cabell, Hou	1.000	3	3	0	0	0
Colbert, Mtl	.969	6	58	4	2	2
Driessen, Cin	.997	40	291	21	1	33
Evans, 36 Atl-83 SF	.992	119	966	91	9	78
Fairly, StL°	.995	27	174	21	1	19
Foote, Mtl	1.000	1	11	0	0	0
Foster, Cin	.000	1	0	0	0	0
Freed, Mtl	1.000	3	24	1	0	1
Garvey, LA	.998	162	1583	67	3	138
Gaston, Atl	1.000	2	16	1	0	2
Goodson, LA	1.000	3	7	0	0	0
Grubb, SD	1.000	9	64	3	0	7
Hernandez, StL°	.990	110	862	107	10	87
Hill, SF	1.000	1	1	0	0	0
Hutton, Phila°	1.000	72	292	28	0	25
Ivie, SD	.995	135	1020	70	5	89
Johnson, Hou	1.000	16	117	1	0	8
Johnstone, Phila	.906	6	27	2	3	1
Jorgensen, Mtl°	.989	81	599	57	7	59
Kingman, NY	1.000	16	91	8	0	11
Kirkpatrick, Pitt	.990	25	190	15	2	15
Kranepool, NY°	.996	86	675	33	3	48
Kubiak, SD	1.000	1	1	0	0	0
LaCock, Chi°	.975	54	435	30	12	47
Martin, Phila	1.000	1	7	0	0	2
McCarver, Phila	1.000	2	11	0	0	0
McCovey, SD°	.991	51	420	44	4	39
Milner, NY°	1.000	12	44	2	0	4
Mitterwald, Chi	.995	25	192	10	1	11
Monday, Chi°	.991	32	309	22	3	17
Montanez, 58 SF-103 Atl°	.987	161	1569	107	22	141
Morales, Mtl	.977	21	109	19	3	9
Oliver, Pitt°	1.000	3	26	0	0	5
Ontiveros, SF	.867	4	12	1	2	1
Paciorek, Atl	1.000	12	101	6	0	8
Perez, Cin	.996	136	1158	73	5	110
Putman, Chi	1.000	1	12	0	0	0
Robertson, Pitt	.996	29	257	17	1	28
Robinson, Pitt	1.000	3	22	0	0	4
Scanlon, StL	1.000	1	7	0	0	0
Simmons, StL	.988	30	219	21	3	21
Smith, StL	.986	17	128	10	2	16
Speier, SF	1.000	1	4	1	0	0
Stargell, Pitt°	.988	111	1037	53	13	76
Summers, Chi	1.000	10	69	4	0	10
Tabb, Chi	1.000	6	52	2	0	4
Thomasson, SF°	.980	39	322	18	7	28
Thornton, 25 Chi-43 Mtl	.991	68	528	45	5	60
Tolan, Phila°	.992	50	354	13	3	36
Torre, NY	.989	78	590	49	7	40
Tyrone, Chi	1.000	5	30	3	0	6
Valentine, SD	1.000	4	37	4	0	1
Vukovich, Phila	1.000	1	5	0	0	0
Watson, Hou	.990	155	1395	96	15	126
Williams, 17 Atl-47 Mtl	.986	64	497	49	8	46

TRIPLE PLAY: Evans.

SECOND BASEMEN

Leader—Club	Pct.	G.	PO.	A.	E.	DP.
CASH, Phila	.988	158	407	424	10	118

(Listed Alphabetically)

Player—Club	Pct.	G.	PO.	A.	E.	DP.
Adams, Chi	1.000	1	1	1	0	0
Alvarado, StL	.936	16	22	22	3	3
Andrews, Phila	1.000	4	7	3	0	1
Andrews, Hou	.977	107	228	354	14	66
Arnold, SF	1.000	8	7	25	0	2
Auerbach, LA	.973	7	16	20	1	4
Belloir, Atl	.957	5	13	9	1	3
Boswell, Hou	1.000	3	1	0	0	0
Cash, Phila	.988	158	407	424	10	118
Champion, SD	.940	11	23	24	3	2
Chaney, Atl	1.000	1	0	1	0	0
Clarey, StL	1.000	7	3	1	0	0
Cox, Mtl	.958	11	24	22	2	6
DaVanon, Hou	.980	17	30	67	2	7
Eden, Atl	1.000	2	2	5	0	1
Flynn, Cin	.988	55	68	90	2	21
Foster, NY	1.000	3	3	5	0	0
Frias, Mtl	.957	35	26	41	3	11
Fuentes, SD	.971	127	339	387	22	91
Garrett, 10 NY-54 Mtl	.985	64	146	175	5	35
Gilbreath, Atl	.975	104	239	311	14	76
Goodson, LA	.000	1	0	0	0	0
Harmon, Phila	.958	13	10	13	1	2
Harris, StL	.945	37	91	97	11	21
Heidemann, NY	1.000	1	3	2	0	2
Helms, Pitt	1.000	11	22	19	0	4
Howard, Hou	.889	2	2	6	1	1
Howe, Hou	1.000	2	1	7	0	2
Kelleher, Chi	.957	5	8	14	1	4
Kessinger, StL	.958	31	53	85	6	21
Kubiak, SD	.992	25	56	61	1	16
Lacy, 44 Atl-2 LA	.970	46	93	103	6	25
Lopes, LA	.964	100	218	266	18	56
Mackanin, Mtl	.965	100	201	289	18	60
Mendoza, Pitt	.000	1	0	0	0	0
Metzger, Hou	1.000	2	5	6	0	0
Milbourne, Hou	.965	32	67	106	6	19
Millan, NY	.977	136	311	315	15	68
Miller, SF	.920	8	8	15	2	3
Moore, Atl	1.000	1	1	2	0	0
Morgan, Cin	.981	133	342	335	13	85

SECOND BASEMEN—Continued

Player—Club	Pct.	G.	PO.	A.	E.	DP.
Perez,						
18 Atl-89 SF	.978	107	227	317	12	61
Phillips, NY	.989	19	44	48	1	9
Reynolds, Pitt.	.000	1	0	0	0	0
Richard, StL	.975	26	59	59	3	14
Robinson,						
7 SF-5 Atl	.952	12	11	29	2	4
Rosello, Chi	1.000	1	1	0	0	0
Scott, Mtl	1.000	6	2	3	0	1
Sizemore, LA	.986	71	168	191	5	51

Player—Club	Pct.	G.	PO.	A.	E.	DP.
Speier, SF	1.000	7	8	18	0	2
Sperring, Chi	1.000	4	7	6	0	0
Stennett, Pitt	.981	157	430	502	18	111
Taveras, Hou	.923	7	15	21	3	2
Taylor, Phila	.000	2	0	0	0	0
Thomas, SD	.964	69	160	212	14	52
Torres, SD	1.000	3	5	3	0	1
Trillo, Chi	.981	156	349	527	17	103
Tyson, StL	.971	74	158	237	12	54
Youngblood, Cin	.000	1	0	0	0	0

THIRD BASEMEN

Leader—Club	Pct.	G.	PO.	A.	E.	DP.
ROSE, Cin	.969	159	115	293	13	25

(Listed Alphabetically)

Player—Club	Pct.	G.	PO.	A.	E.	DP.
Adams, Chi	1.000	3	0	1	0	0
Arnold, SF	.833	4	2	3	1	0
Ashford, SD	1.000	1	1	2	0	0
Auerbach, LA	.714	8	2	3	2	1
Bailey, Cin	.889	10	4	12	2	1
Belloir, Atl	.947	10	3	15	1	0
Boswell, Hou	.933	16	7	21	2	4
Cabell, Hou	.958	143	128	263	17	24
Cey, LA	.965	144	111	334	16	22
Chaney, Atl	1.000	1	0	1	0	0
Cruz, StL	.934	148	100	270	26	19
DaVanon, Hou	.900	9	3	6	1	1
DeJesus, LA	1.000	7	2	8	0	0
Evans,						
7 Atl-5 SF	.969	12	12	19	1	2
Flynn, Cin	1.000	23	5	8	0	1
Foli, Mtl	1.000	1	2	1	0	0
Foote, Mtl	1.000	2	0	2	0	0
Foster, NY	.920	9	6	17	2	1
Frias, Mtl	.667	4	1	3	2	1
Garrett,						
64 NY-2 Mtl	.949	66	48	138	10	12
Gilbreath, Atl	.750	7	6	3	3	1
Goodson, LA	.833	16	8	27	7	2
Grubb, SD	.667	3	1	1	1	0
Harmon, Phila	1.000	5	2	4	0	0
Harris, StL	.857	12	1	5	1	0
Hebner, Pitt	.953	126	87	236	16	16
Helms, Pitt	.921	22	8	27	3	4
Howe, Hou	.938	8	6	9	1	1
Ivie, SD	1.000	2	1	1	0	1
Kelleher, Chi	.943	22	12	21	2	1
Kessinger, StL	1.000	2	1	0	0	0

Player—Club	Pct.	G.	PO.	A.	E.	DP.
Kirkpatrick, Pitt	.333	1	0	1	2	0
Kubiak, SD	.971	27	20	47	2	5
Lacy, 1 Atl-3 LA	.909	4	3	7	1	3
Mackanin, Mtl	.950	8	2	17	1	4
Madlock, Chi	.961	136	107	234	14	21
Mendoza, Pitt	1.000	2	0	2	0	0
Miller, SF	1.000	2	1	1	0	0
Moore, Atl	.929	6	5	8	1	1
Ontiveros, SF	1.000	7	4	6	0	1
Paciorek, Atl	.500	1	0	1	1	0
Parrish, Mtl	.945	153	122	310	25	35
Perez, Atl	1.000	2	0	2	0	0
Phillips, NY	.957	10	4	18	1	1
Rader, SD	.955	137	109	318	20	22
Reitz, SF	.959	155	140	303	19	32
Richard, StL	.000	1	0	0	0	0
Robinson,						
2 SF-1 Atl	.800	3	0	4	1	0
Robinson, Pitt	.909	37	24	46	7	5
Rose, Cin	.969	159	115	293	13	25
Royster, SF	.963	148	156	306	18	35
Scanlon, Mtl	.842	7	4	12	3	0
Schmidt, Phila	.961	160	139	377	21	29
Simmons, StL	.571	2	3	1	3	0
Sizemore, LA	.500	3	2	0	2	0
Smith,						
13 StL-1 LA	1.000	14	15	30	0	2
Speier, SF	.889	5	4	4	1	2
Sperring, Chi	.955	20	10	11	1	1
Staiger, NY	.967	93	55	209	9	18
Taylor, Phila	1.000	1	0	1	0	1
Thomas, SF	1.000	1	0	1	0	0
Torre, NY	1.000	4	3	3	0	2
Torres, SD	1.000	4	3	5	0	0
Tyrone, Chi	1.000	5	5	7	0	0
Vukovich, Phila	1.000	4	1	2	0	0
Youngblood, Cin	.750	6	1	2	1	1

SHORTSTOPS

Leader—Club	Pct.	G.	PO.	A.	E.	DP.
METZGER, Hou	.986	150	253	462	10	93

(Listed Alphabetically)

Player—Club	Pct.	G.	PO.	A.	E.	DP.
Almon, S.D.	.962	14	23	52	3	8
Andrews, Hou	1.000	3	0	2	0	0
Arnold, S.F.	1.000	1	0	1	0	0
Auerbach, L.A.	.943	12	23	27	3	8
Belloir, Atl	.929	12	9	17	2	5
Bowa, Phil	.975	156	180	492	17	90
Chaney, Atl	.950	151	243	466	37	88

Player—Club	Pct.	G.	PO.	A.	E.	DP.
Concepcion, Cin	.968	150	304	506	27	93
DaVanon, Hou	.911	17	20	21	4	8
DeJesus, L.A.	.950	13	18	39	3	7
Flynn, Cin	.978	20	34	54	2	11
Foli, Mtl	.975	146	247	469	18	102
Foster, N.Y.	1.000	7	9	20	0	1
Frias, Mtl	.955	35	54	72	6	16
Garrett, N.Y.	1.000	1	1	1	0	1
Gilbreath, Atl	.000	1	0	0	0	0
Harmon, Phila	.960	19	16	32	2	4
Harrelson, N.Y.	.962	117	183	330	20	44

SHORTSTOPS—Continued

Player—Club	Pct.	G.	PO.	A.	E.	DP.
Harris, St.L.	.000	1	0	0	0	0
Heidemann, N.Y.	1.000	3	2	5	0	1
Helms, Pitt.	.000	1	0	0	0	0
Hernandez, S.D.	.964	101	132	344	18	64
Kelleher, Chi	.980	101	147	289	9	52
Kessinger, St.L.	.969	113	212	350	18	84
Kubiak, S.D.	.667	6	0	2	1	0
LeMaster, S.F.	.937	31	54	109	11	17
Mackanin, Mtl	1.000	3	0	1	0	0
Mendoza, Pitt	.967	45	42	103	5	19
Metzger, Hou	.986	150	253	462	10	93
Perez, 17Atl-5 S.F.	.971	22	29	38	2	10
Phillips, N.Y.	.955	53	67	125	9	16
Reitz, S.F.	1.000	1	1	1	0	1
Reynolds, Pitt.	.889	4	2	6	1	1
Richard, St.L.	.857	12	12	12	4	4
Robinson, 1 SF-2 Atl	.667	3	1	3	2	0
Rockett, Atl	1.000	2	0	1	0	0
Rosello, Chi	.966	86	128	217	12	45
Royster, Atl	.857	2	2	4	1	0
Russell, L.A.	.963	149	251	476	28	90
Scott, Mtl	1.000	3	4	5	0	1
Speier, S.F.	.974	135	225	441	18	81
Sperring, Chi	1.000	15	11	23	0	4
Staiger, N.Y.	.000	1	0	0	0	0
Stennett, Pitt	.857	4	2	4	1	0
Taveras, Hou	1.000	7	11	23	0	2
Taveras, Pitt	.952	141	210	481	35	74
Templeton, St.L.	.922	53	111	172	24	41
Thomas, S.F.	.667	1	0	2	1	0
Torres, S.D.	.949	63	64	160	12	29
Trillo, Chi	1.000	1	1	0	0	0

TRIPLE PLAY: Speier.

OUTFIELDERS

Leader—Club	Pct.	G.	PO.	A.	E.	DP.
FOSTER, Cin	.994	142	322	9	2	3

(Listed Alphabetically)

Player—Club	Pct.	G.	PO.	A.	E.	DP.
Adams, S.F.	1.000	6	3	0	0	0
Adams, Chi.	1.000	4	3	0	0	0
Anderson, St.L.	.982	58	106	5	2	1
Armas, Pitt	1.000	2	3	0	0	0
Armbrister, Cin.	.972	32	31	4	1	1
Asselstine, Atl	1.000	9	19	0	0	0
Ayala, N.Y.	.889	7	7	1	1	0
Bailey, Cin	.974	31	35	2	1	1
Baker, L.A.	.996	106	254	3	1	1
Ro. Baldwin, N.Y.°	.929	5	12	1	1	1
Bench, L.A.	.667	5	4	0	2	0
Biittner, 7 Mtl-24 Chi°	.981	31	51	2	1	0
Boisclair, N.Y.°	.981	87	156	3	3	1
Bosetti, Phil	1.000	6	9	1	0	0
Boswell, Hou	.000	1	0	0	0	0
Brock, St.L.°	.983	123	221	6	4	0
Brown, N.Y.	1.000	43	46	3	0	1
Brown, Phil	.949	75	105	7	6	2
Buckner, L.A.°	.985	153	315	7	5	0
Burke, L.A.	.971	20	33	0	1	0
Cardenal, Chi	.981	128	246	10	5	1
Carter, Mtl	1.000	36	53	6	0	1
Cedeno, Hou	.980	146	377	11	8	5
Chant, St.L.	1.000	14	15	1	0	0
Chiles, Hou°	1.000	1	1	0	0	0
Clark, S.F.	.987	26	71	3	1	1
Colbert, Mtl	1.000	7	8	2	0	1
Crawford, St.L.°	.982	107	209	6	4	1
Cromartie, Mtl°	.943	20	32	1	2	0
Cruz, L.A.°	.976	23	39	1	1	1
Cruz, Hou°	.972	125	265	10	8	4
W. Davis, S.D.°	.992	128	349	6	3	2
Dawson, Mtl.	.969	24	61	1	2	1
Dilone, Pitt.	1.000	3	11	0	0	0
Driessen, Cin	.962	20	23	2	1	0
Dwyer, 19 Mtl-2 N.Y.°	.972	21	35	0	1	0
Ferguson, 39 L.A.-14 St.L.	.952	53	97	2	5	0
Foster, Cin	.994	142	322	9	2	3
Freed, Mtl	1.000	1	1	0	0	0
Frias, Mtl.	.000	1	0	0	0	0
Gaston, Atl	.977	28	42	1	1	0
Geronimo, Cin°	.985	146	386	4	6	2
Goodson, L.A.	1.000	2	2	0	0	0
Griffey, Cin°	.979	144	270	10	6	2
Gross, Hou°	.978	115	208	13	5	4
Grote, N.Y.	1.000	2	5	0	0	0
Grubb, S.D.	.974	98	183	3	5	0
Hale, L.A.	.983	37	55	3	1	0
Harris, St.L.	.976	35	81	1	2	0
Henderson, Atl	.987	122	219	3	3	0
Herndon, S.F.	.967	110	226	8	8	4
Howard, Hou	.961	63	96	2	4	1
Hutton, Phil°	1.000	1	2	0	0	0
Javier, Hou	1.000	7	7	0	0	0
Johnson, Hou	.975	20	39	0	1	0
Johnstone, Phil.	.982	122	266	8	5	1
Jorgensen, Mtl°	.981	41	52	1	1	0
Joshua, S.F.°	.948	35	70	3	4	1
Kingman, N.Y.	.959	111	202	10	9	0
Kirkpatrick, Pitt	1.000	9	15	1	0	0
Kranepool, N.Y.°	1.000	31	46	2	0	0
LaCock, Chi°	.957	19	19	3	1	0
Lacy, 5 Atl-37 LA	.980	42	97	1	2	0
Lee, L.A.	1.000	10	12	0	0	0
Locklear, S.D.	.952	11	20	0	1	0
Lopes, L.A.	.974	19	36	2	1	0
Lum, Cin°	1.000	38	48	0	0	0
Luzinski, Phil	.964	144	204	8	8	0
Lyttle, 29 Mtl-18 LA	.990	47	87	8	1	4
Mackanin, Mtl	.000	1	0	0	0	0
Maddox, Phil	.989	144	441	10	5	0
Mangual, 62 Mtl-38 NY	.973	100	210	5	6	2
Martin, Phil	.975	110	78	0	2	0
Matthews, S.F.	.975	156	265	8	7	0
May, Atl.	.972	60	98	5	3	1
Mazzilli, N.Y.	.983	23	55	2	1	2
McBride, St.L.	.981	66	201	5	4	0
Mejias, St.L.	1.000	17	19	1	0	0
Melendez, 8 Stl-60 SD	.990	68	99	0	1	0

OUTFIELDERS—Continued

Player—Club	Pct.	G.	PO.	A.	E.	DP.
Milner, N.Y.°	.985	112	195	7	3	2
Monday, Chi°	.993	103	278	4	2	0
Moore, Atl	1.000	1	1	0	0	0
Morales, Chi	.983	136	273	12	5	6
Moreno, Pitt°	.960	42	93	3	4	1
Mota, L.A.	1.000	6	11	1	0	0
Mumphrey, St.L.	.993	94	261	6	2	1
Murcer, S.F.	.961	146	282	11	12	2
Office, Atl°	.986	92	204	3	3	2
Oliver, Pitt°	.984	106	301	4	5	0
Ontiveros, S.F.	1.000	7	2	1	0	0
Paciorek, Atl	.983	84	115	3	2	0
Parker, Pitt	.956	134	294	12	14	0
Potter, St.L.	1.000	4	9	0	0	0
Rettenmund, S.D.	.977	43	79	6	2	1
Rivera, Atl	.950	56	89	7	5	3
Roberts, Hou	.980	60	99	1	2	0
Robinson, Pitt	.993	78	140	7	1	2
Roenicke, Mtl	.955	25	39	3	2	0
Rose, Cin	.000	1	0	0	0	0
Simmons, St.L.	1.000	7	11	0	0	0
Simpson, L.A.°	1.000	20	24	0	0	0

Player—Club	Pct.	G.	PO.	A.	E.	DP.
Smith,						
16 StL-58 LA	.989	74	171	8	2	2
Sperring, Chi	1.000	3	8	0	0	0
Summers, Chi	.964	26	26	1	1	0
Thomas, S.F.	1.000	2	3	0	0	0
Thomasson, S.F.°	.959	54	114	2	5	0
Thornton, Mtl	.938	11	14	1	1	0
Tolan, Phil°	.955	35	41	1	2	0
Turner, S.D.°	.960	74	115	6	5	0
Tyrone, Chi	1.000	7	4	0	0	0
Unser,						
77 NY-65 Mtl°	.990	142	288	10	3	2
Vail, N.Y.	.941	35	63	1	4	0
Valentine, Mtl	.972	88	162	12	5	4
Valentine, S.D.	1.000	10	18	2	0	1
Wallis, Chi	.976	90	193	11	5	3
White, Mtl	.982	92	157	4	3	0
Winfield, S.D.	.982	134	304	15	6	4
Wynn, Atl	.971	138	287	17	9	2
Youngblood, Cin	.938	9	14	1	1	1
Zisk, Pitt	.987	152	300	11	4	2

CATCHERS

Leader—Club	Pct.	G.	PO.	A.	E.	DP.	PB.
BENCH, Cin	.997	128	651	60	2	11	5

(Listed Alphabetically)

Player—Club	Pct.	G.	PO.	A.	E.	DP.	PB.
Alexander, S.F.	.964	23	92	16	4	0	3
Bench, Cin	.997	128	651	60	2	11	5
Blackwell, Phil.	1.000	4	17	0	0	0	0
Boone, Phil	.993	108	557	36	4	5	5
Carter, Mtl	.994	60	311	36	2	7	3
Correll, S.D.	.981	65	319	36	7	1	11
R. Davis, S.D.	.965	47	120	19	5	1	3
Dyer, Pitt	.994	58	279	37	2	4	4
Ferguson,							
17 LA-48 StL	.975	65	312	42	9	8	9
Foote, Mtl	.989	96	476	59	6	13	6
Grote, N.Y.	.993	95	617	49	5	6	3
Herrmann, Hou	.987	79	412	37	6	5	10
Hill, S.F.	.995	49	185	24	1	3	1
Hodges, N.Y.	.976	52	262	18	7	0	4
Hundley, Chi	.923	9	22	2	2	0	0
Ivie, S.D.	.846	2	11	0	2	0	0
Johnson, Hou	.977	66	312	34	8	2	12
Johnson, Mtl	1.000	5	22	2	0	0	0
Jutze, Hou	.986	42	125	21	2	5	10
Kendall, S.D.	.994	146	582	54	4	6	6
Kleven, N.Y.	1.000	2	10	0	0	0	0
McCarver, Phil.	1.000	41	254	9	0	1	1
Mitterwald, Chi	.981	64	320	40	7	2	3

Player—Club	Pct.	G.	PO.	A.	E.	DP.	PB.
Morales, Mtl	1.000	12	28	2	0	0	1
Murphy, Atl	.974	19	100	13	3	0	9
Nahorodny, Phil.	1.000	2	7	0	0	0	0
Oates, Phil.	.994	33	155	15	1	1	0
Ott, Pitt.	1.000	8	20	6	0	1	1
Pasley, L.A.	.971	23	86	15	3	0	1
Plummer, Cin	.977	54	235	21	6	1	1
Pocoroba, Atl	.978	54	273	39	7	5	10
Putman, S.D.	1.000	3	4	0	0	0	0
Rader, S.F.	.984	81	349	32	6	4	8
Robles, L.A.	1.000	6	9	0	0	0	2
Rodriguez, L.A.	.986	33	128	17	2	2	3
Rudolph, St. L.	.940	14	61	2	4	1	0
Sadek, S.F.	.985	51	191	11	3	0	3
Sanguillen, Pitt	.978	111	518	52	13	7	8
Simmons, St.L.	.993	113	493	66	4	4	9
Sizemore, L.A.	1.000	2	8	0	0	0	0
Stearns, N.Y.	.987	30	200	20	3	2	1
Summers, Chi	.000	1	0	0	0	0	0
Swisher, N.Y.	.983	107	574	49	11	6	8
Tamargo, St.L.	1.000	1	4	0	0	0	0
Varney, Atl	1.000	5	9	3	0	1	3
Werner, Cin	1.000	3	7	2	0	0	0
Williams,							
38 Atl-13 Mtl	.996	51	218	15	1	4	6
Yeager, L.A.	.985	115	522	77	9	9	6
Youngblood, Cin	.000	1	0	0	0	0	0

PITCHERS

Leader—Club	Pct.	G.	PO.	A.	E.	DP.
JONES, SD°	1.000	40	31	81	0	12

(Listed Alphabetically)

Player—Club	Pct.	G.	PO.	A.	E.	DP.
Alcala, Cin	.962	30	8	17	1	0
Andjuar, Hou	.923	28	12	24	3	1
Apodaca, NY	1.000	43	8	17	0	1
Atkinson, Mtl	1.000	4	0	1	0	0
Autry, Atl	.000	1	0	0	0	0
Bair, Pitt	1.000	4	1	0	0	0
Ri. Baldwin, NY	1.000	11	1	4	0	0
Barlow, Hou	1.000	16	0	7	0	0

Player—Club	Pct.	G.	PO.	A.	E.	DP.
Barr, SF	.951	37	22	56	4	0
Beard, Atl°	1.000	30	3	9	0	1
Billingham, Cin	.972	34	10	25	1	1
Blair, Mtl	1.000	5	1	2	0	0
Bonham, Chi	.930	32	8	32	3	2
Borbon, Cin	1.000	69	6	18	0	0
Burris, Chi	.919	37	15	42	5	3
Caldwell, SF°	.968	50	8	22	1	2
Camp, Atl	.889	5	3	5	1	0
Candelaria, Pitt°	1.000	32	3	31	0	2
Capilla, StL°	1.000	7	1	1	0	0
Capra, Atl	1.000	5	0	3	0	0
Carlton, Phila°	1.000	35	4	19	0	2

PITCHERS—Continued

Player—Club	Pct.	G.	PO.	A.	E.	DP.
Carrithers, Mtl	.973	34	13	23	1	5
Christenson, Phila.	.885	32	9	14	3	1
Coleman, Chi	.947	39	6	12	1	0
Cosgrove, Hou.°	1.000	22	2	14	0	2
Crosby, Chi.	1.000	7	1	2	0	0
Curtis, StL°	1.000	37	7	22	0	1
D'Acquisto, SF	.917	28	5	17	2	0
Dal Canton, Atl	.913	42	4	17	2	0
Darcy, Cin	.857	11	1	5	1	0
Demery, Pitt.	.938	36	9	21	2	2
Denny, StL	.935	30	24	34	4	3
Dettore, Chi	1.000	4	2	0	0	0
Devine, Atl	.917	48	3	8	1	0
Dierker, Hou	.946	28	17	18	2	2
Downing, LA°	1.000	17	0	9	0	1
Dressler, SF	.889	25	13	19	4	1
Dunning, Mtl	.913	32	8	13	2	0
Dupree, SD	1.000	12	1	4	0	0
Easterly, Atl°	1.000	4	1	4	0	0
Eastwick, Cin	1.000	71	3	9	0	0
Espinosa, NY	1.000	12	0	3	0	0
Falcone, NY	1.000	32	3	14	0	0
Folkers, SD°	1.000	33	4	8	0	0
Forsch, Hou	1.000	52	4	17	0	0
Forsch, StL	.929	33	24	28	4	2
Foster, SD	1.000	26	9	9	0	1
Frailing, Chi°	1.000	6	1	3	0	0
Frisella, StL	1.000	18	2	3	0	0
Freisleben, SD	.961	34	16	33	2	2
Fryman, Mtl°	1.000	34	9	30	0	2
Garber, Phila	.964	59	13	14	1	0
Garman, Chi	1.000	47	3	14	0	1
Giusti, Pitt	.938	40	4	11	1	0
Granger, Mtl	.857	27	1	5	1	0
Greif, 5 SD-47 StL	1.000	52	6	9	0	0
Griffin, 20 Hou-11 SD	.880	31	6	16	3	1
Gullett, Cin°	1.000	23	4	20	0	1
Halicki, SF	.884	32	16	22	5	3
Hall, NY°	1.000	5	0	2	0	0
Hanna, Atl	1.000	5	1	0	0	0
Hannahs, Mtl°	1.000	3	0	2	0	0
Hardy, Hou	1.000	15	0	4	0	1
Heaverlo, SF	.917	61	7	15	2	1
Henderson, Cin	1.000	4	1	2	0	0
Hernandez, 37 Pitt-2 Chi°	.778	39	0	7	2	1
Hinton, Cin.°	.667	12	0	2	1	0
Hooton, LA	1.000	33	6	31	0	0
Hough, LA	.962	77	3	22	1	0
Hrabosky, StL°	.933	68	1	13	1	1
John, LA°	.973	31	3	33	1	2
Johnson, SD	.875	24	4	3	1	0
Jones, SD°	1.000	40	31	81	0	12
Kaat, Phila°	.949	38	18	19	2	3
Keener, Mtl	1.000	2	0	1	0	0
Kerrigan, Mtl	.941	38	7	9	1	2
Kirby, Mtl	1.000	22	1	9	0	1
Kison, Pitt	.959	31	16	31	2	2
Koosman, NY°	.936	34	5	39	3	1
Knepper, SD°	1.000	4	1	4	0	1
Knowles, Chi°	.929	58	3	23	2	2
Krukow, Chi	.000	2	0	0	0	0
LaCorte, Atl	.864	19	5	14	3	0
LaGrow, StL	1.000	8	1	4	0	0
Landreth, Mtl	1.000	3	0	1	0	0
Lang, Mtl	.941	29	6	10	1	1
Langford, Pitt	1.000	12	2	4	0	1
Larson, Hou	1.000	13	7	13	0	2
Lavelle, SF°	.800	65	5	11	4	0
Lemongello, Hou	1.000	4	1	9	0	0
Leon, Atl	1.000	30	1	3	0	0
Lerch, Phila°	.000	1	0	0	0	0
Lewallyn, LA	1.000	4	0	5	0	0
Lockwood, NY	.867	56	2	11	2	1
Lolich, NY°	.857	31	9	27	6	1
Lonborg, Phila	1.000	33	21	16	0	0
Marshall, 30 LA-24 Atl	1.000	54	7	24	0	1
Matlack, NY°	.978	35	10	35	1	0
McEnaney, Cin°	.850	55	4	13	3	1
McGlothen, StL	1.000	33	20	18	0	3
McGraw, Phila°	.800	58	4	12	4	0
McLaughlin, Hou	1.000	17	10	10	0	2
Medich, Pitt	.955	29	6	36	2	2
Messersmith, Atl.	.904	29	14	33	5	2
Metzger, SD	.957	77	5	17	1	0
Minton, SF	.778	10	3	4	2	0
Moffitt, SF	.889	58	11	13	3	0
Montefusco, SF	.917	37	12	21	3	0
Moose, Pitt	.895	53	3	14	2	0
Moret, Atl°	1.000	27	0	13	0	1
Morton, Atl	.978	26	18	26	1	1
Murray, Mtl	.979	81	8	38	1	3
Myrick, NY°	1.000	21	0	7	0	1
Niekro, Hou	.880	36	9	13	3	1
Niekro, Atl	.968	38	19	41	2	2
Nolan, Cin	1.000	34	9	22	0	0
Norman, Cin°	1.000	33	4	14	0	0
Owchinko, SD°	1.000	2	0	1	0	0
Pentz, Hou	1.000	40	3	12	0	2
Proly, StL	1.000	14	3	3	0	0
Rasmussen, StL	.980	43	15	34	1	2
Rau, LA°	.978	34	5	39	1	1
Reed, Phila	.909	59	7	13	2	1
Renko, 5 Mtl-28 Chi	.963	33	9	17	1	1
P. Reuschel, Chi	.958	50	4	19	1	2
R. Reuschel, Chi	.950	38	23	53	4	0
Reuss, Pitt°	.944	31	8	26	2	2
Reynolds, SD°	.833	19	2	3	1	0
Rhoden, LA	.967	27	9	20	1	0
Riccelli, SF°	1.000	4	0	1	0	1
Richard, Hou	.853	39	19	39	10	2
Rogers, Mtl	.962	33	26	50	3	3
Rondon, Hou	1.000	19	5	4	0	0
Rooker, Pitt°	.949	30	8	29	2	1
Ruthven, Atl	.984	36	18	44	1	2
Sambito, Hou°	1.000	20	4	10	0	1
Sanders, NY	1.000	31	8	8	0	0
Sarmiento, Cin	1.000	22	2	2	0	0
Sawyer, SD	1.000	13	3	12	0	0
Scherman, Mtl°	1.000	31	2	4	0	0
Schueler, Phila	.875	35	2	5	1	0
Schultz, Chi°	1.000	29	5	4	0	0
Seaver, NY	.981	35	12	41	1	3
Siebert, Hou°	.800	19	3	1	1	0
Solomon, StL	.929	26	2	11	1	1
Sosa, 21 Atl-24 LA	.846	45	1	10	2	0
Sosa, Hou	1.000	9	2	5	0	0

PITCHERS—Continued

Player—Club	Pct.	G.	PO.	A.	E.	DP.	Player—Club	Pct.	G.	PO.	A.	E.	DP.
Spillner, SD	.903	32	7	21	3	3	Twitchell, Phila	.909	26	1	9	1	1
Stanhouse, Mtl	.983	34	24	33	1	4	Underwood, Phila*	.952	33	3	17	1	1
Stone, Chi	.900	17	3	6	1	1	Walker, StL	1.000	10	1	0	0	0
Strom, SD*	.938	36	13	32	3	3	Wall, LA*	1.000	31	0	6	0	1
Sutcliffe, LA	.000	1	0	0	0	0	Wallace, StL*	.929	49	1	12	1	2
Sutter, Chi	.938	52	6	9	1	1	Warthen, Mtl.*	1.000	23	3	13	0	0
Sutton, LA	.973	35	5	31	1	2	Waterbury, StL	1.000	5	1	0	0	0
Swan, NY	.920	23	6	17	2	0	Webb, NY	1.000	8	0	3	0	0
Taylor, Mtl	1.000	31	2	5	0	1	Wehrmeister, SD	1.000	7	1	4	0	1
Tekulve, Pitt	.968	64	6	24	1	0	Williams, SF	.870	48	1	19	3	2
Tomlin, SD*	.935	49	8	21	2	1	Zachry, Cin	.971	38	13	20	1	2
Toms, SF	1.000	7	1	1	0	0	Zahn, Chi*	.750	3	0	3	1	0
Torrealba, Atl*	1.000	36	1	13	0	2	Zamora, Chi	.800	40	1	7	2	0

OFFICIAL NATIONAL LEAGUE PITCHING AVERAGES

Compiled by Elias Sports Bureau, New York, N.Y.

CLUB PITCHING

Club	ERA	G	CG	Sv	ShO	IP	H	BFP	R	ER	HR	SH	SF	Tot. BB	Int. BB	HB	SO	WP	Bk.
New York	2.94	162	53	25	18	1449	1248	5908	538	473	97	76	36	419	56	23	1025	43	12
Los Angeles	3.02	162	47	28	17	1470⅔	1330	6085	543	493	97	84	42	479	31	23	747	32	3
Philadelphia	3.08	162	34	44	9	1459	1377	6024	557	499	98	59	40	397	43	19	918	38	6
Pittsburgh	3.36	162	34	45	12	1466⅓	1402	6146	630	548	95	71	52	491	70	18	762	26	7
Cincinnati	3.51	162	33	45	11	1471	1436	6191	633	573	100	71	44	491	56	21	790	43	9
San Francisco	3.53	162	33	31	12	1461⅓	1464	6264	686	573	89	80	48	518	55	25	746	47	7
Houston	3.56	162	42	29	17	1444⅓	1349	6213	657	571	82	80	48	581	43	25	780	57	9
St. Louis	3.60	162	35	26	15	1453⅔	1416	6212	671	582	82	79	55	581	56	20	731	61	12
San Diego	3.65	162	47	15	11	1432⅓	1368	6087	662	581	87	72	45	543	57	40	652	48	8
Atlanta	3.86	162	33	27	13	1438	1435	6232	700	617	86	90	45	564	83	28	818	60	17
Chicago	3.93	162	27	33	12	1471⅓	1511	6289	728	643	123	90	50	490	57	40	850	38	16
Montreal	3.99	162	26	21	10	1440	1442	6282	734	639	89	106	55	659	75	43	783	63	11
Totals	3.50		449	362	164	17457⅓	16778	73933	7739	6792	1113	975	559	6263	685	310	9602	556	116

(BFP totals includes 12 batsmen awarded first base because of interference or obstruction.)

Note—Totals for earned runs for several clubs do not agree with the composite totals for all pitchers of each respective club due to instances in which provisions of Section 10.18 (i) of the Scoring Rules were applied. The following differences are to be noted: Chicago pitchers add to 644; Montreal, 640; New York, 474; Philadelphia, 502; Pittsburgh, 549; St. Louis, 583.

PITCHERS' RECORDS

(Top Fifteen Qualifiers for Earned-Run Average Leadership—162 or More Innings)

*Throws lefthanded.

Pitcher and Club	ERA	W	L	Pct.	G	GS	CG	ShO	Sv	GF	IP	H	BFP	R	ER	HR	SH	SF	Tot. BB	Int. BB	HB	SO	WP	Bk.
Denny, John, St. Louis	2.52	11	9	.550	30	30	8	3	0	0	207	189	861	71	58	11	8	1	74	3	8	74	5	0
Rau, Douglas, Los Angeles*	2.57	14	11	.571	32	32	8	3	0	0	231	221	950	69	66	18	15	2	69	1	1	98	2	1
Seaver, G. Thomas, New York	2.59	14	11	.560	35	34	13	5	0	0	271	211	1079	83	78	14	17	4	77	9	7	235	12	0
Koosman, Jerry, New York	2.70	21	10	.677	34	34	17	3	0	0	247	205	994	83	74	19	6	6	66	1	4	200	5	0
Zachry, Patrick, Cincinnati	2.74	14	7	.667	38	28	6	1	0	2	204	174	842	70	62	7	9	6	83	4	2	143	3	1
Jones, Randall, San Diego*	2.74	22	14	.611	40	40	25	5	0	0	315	274	1251	109	96	14	13	5	50	4	4	93	0	1
Richard, James, Houston	2.75	20	15	.571	39	36	14	6	0	0	291	221	1218	105	89	11	14	4	151	8	4	214	13	1
Montefusco, John, San Francisco	2.85	16	14	.533	37	37	11	6	0	0	253	224	1045	104	80	18	9	7	60	7	7	172	3	3
Barr, James, San Francisco	2.89	15	12	.556	37	28	8	3	0	0	252	260	1056	104	81	17	5	7	53	1	2	75	3	1
Matlack, Jonathan, New York*	2.95	17	10	.630	35	35	16	6	0	0	262	236	1054	94	86	18	12	4	74	5	5	153	13	3
Rhoden, Richard, Los Angeles	2.98	12	3	.800	29	17	4	2	1	4	181	165	744	66	60	14	5	7	53	2	2	77	10	1
Messersmith, John, Atlanta	3.04	11	11	.500	28	28	12	1	0	1	207	166	847	83	70	14	15	6	74	5	1	135	10	0
Sutton, Donald, Los Angeles	3.06	21	10	.677	35	34	15	4	0	0	268	231	1093	91	91	22	10	6	82	6	6	161	2	1
Kison, Bruce, Pittsburgh	3.08	14	9	.609	31	29	9	1	1	1	193	180	800	83	66	10	8	6	52	6	3	98	1	1
Lonborg, James, Philadelphia	3.08	18	10	.643	33	32	8	1	1	1	222	210	916	85	76	18	10	6	50	4	5	118	2	1

DEPARTMENTAL LEADERS: W—Jones, 22; L—Rogers, 22; 28, SH—Burris, 18; SF—R. Reuschel, 13; Tot.BB—Richard, 151; int.BB—Metz-
Pct.—Carlton, .741; G—Murray, 81; GS—Jones, 40; CG—Jones, 25; GF—Metzger, ger, 14; HB—Fryman, 9; SO—Seaver, 235; WP—P. Niekro, 14; Bk—Andujar,
62; Sv—Eastwick, 26; ShO.—Matlack, Montefusco, 6; IP—Jones, 315; H—Jones, Ruthven, 5.
274; BFP—Jones, 1251; R—R. Reuschel, 117; ER—Ruthven, 112; HR—Nolan,

(All Pitchers—Listed Alphabetically)

Pitcher and Club	ERA	W.	L.	Pct.	G.	GS.	CG.	GF.	Sv.	ShO.	IP.	H.	BFP.	R.	ER.	HR.	SH.	SF.	Tot.BB.	Int.BB.	HB.	SO.	WP.	Bk.
Alcala, Santo, Cincinnati	4.70	11	4	.733	30	21	3	3	0	0	132	131	583	72	69	12	6	4	69	8	3	67	3	2
Andujar, Joaquin, Houston	3.61	9	10	.474	28	25	5	1	0	1	172	163	729	74	69	4	4	7	75	2	1	59	5	5
Apodaca, Robert, New York	2.80	3	7	.300	43	0	0	30	9	0	90	90	364	34	28	4	10	2	29	12	0	45	4	4
Atkinson, William, Montreal	0.00	0	0	.000	4	0	0	1	0	0	5	3	21	0	0	0	0	0	5	0	0	3	0	0
Autry, Albert, Atlanta	5.40	0	0	1.000	4	1	0	1	0	0	5	5	28	3	3	2	0	0	3	1	0	4	0	1
Bair, C. Douglas, Pittsburgh	6.00	0	0	.000	4	0	0	1	0	0	6	4	28	4	4	0	0	0	5	0	1	3	0	0
Baldwin, Rick, New York	4.50	0	0	.000	16	0	0	7	0	0	23	27	89	13	11	3	5	1	10	3	0	11	0	0
Barlow, Michael, Houston	2.35	2	2	.500	37	0	0	8	1	0	23	27	107	13	6	1	7	1	14	3	0	11	1	1
Barr, James, San Francisco	2.89	15	12	.556	37	37	8	0	0	1	252	260	1056	104	81	19	7	7	60	3	4	75	1	0
Beard, Michael, Atlanta*	4.24	0	2	.000	34	0	0	7	0	0	34	38	150	18	17	7	1	0	14	3	2	13	0	2
Billingham, John, Cincinnati	4.32	12	10	.545	34	29	5	1	0	0	177	190	762	96	85	17	9	10	62	5	2	76	1	0
Blair, Dennis, Montreal	3.94	2	2	.500	32	5	1	11	0	0	38	40	167	21	17	1	1	0	14	0	2	9	1	2
Bonham, William, Chicago	4.27	9	13	.409	31	31	3	0	0	0	187	215	879	102	93	21	12	11	96	2	5	110	9	0
Borbon, Pedro, Cincinnati	3.35	4	4	.500	69	0	0	26	8	0	121	135	515	49	45	8	12	0	31	11	1	55	1	0
Burris, B. Ray, Chicago	3.11	15	13	.536	37	36	10	0	0	2	249	251	1053	102	86	22	18	8	70	5	5	112	0	0
Caldwell, R. Michael, San Fran*	4.88	0	7	.000	69	0	0	19	2	0	107	145	480	58	58	5	13	5	30	2	0	7	1	0
Camp, Rick, Atlanta	6.55	1	1	.571	5	0	0	2	0	0	11	13	46	9	5	0	0	0	6	0	0	55	0	0
Candelaria, John, Pittsburgh*	3.15	16	7	.696	35	31	11	1	0	2	220	173	881	88	77	22	13	8	60	4	2	138	8	1
Capilla, Douglas, St. Louis*	5.63	0	1	.000	5	0	0	2	0	0	11	8	37	9	5	0	1	0	6	2	1	4	0	0
Capra, Lee, Atlanta	9.00	0	0	1.000	5	0	0	2	0	0	4	8	44	5	5	0	1	1	6	0	1	2	0	0
Carlton, Steven, Philadelphia*	3.13	20	7	.741	35	35	13	0	0	2	253	224	1031	94	88	19	9	7	72	2	4	195	8	0
Carrithers, Donald, Montreal	4.44	4	12	.333	42	19	3	10	0	0	140	142	642	84	69	7	8	4	78	13	1	71	4	1
Christenson, Larry, Philadelphia	3.67	13	8	.619	36	29	4	1	0	1	169	199	727	77	69	11	10	5	42	1	7	54	1	0
Coleman, Joseph, Chicago	4.10	3	5	.200	30	4	0	16	2	0	79	72	339	39	36	5	9	3	35	3	1	34	0	0
Cosgrove, Michael, Houston*	5.50	3	4	.429	22	16	0	1	0	0	90	106	425	63	55	6	7	3	58	10	8	66	8	0
Crosby, Kenneth, Chicago	12.00	0	0	.000	5	0	0	1	0	0	12	11	64	16	16	3	3	1	6	2	0	3	0	1
Curtis, John, St. Louis*	3.13	6	11	.353	37	15	3	10	1	0	134	139	579	94	67	11	7	9	65	8	1	52	3	0
D'Acquisto, John, San Francisco	4.50	9	8	.529	28	19	1	5	0	0	106	93	503	48	63	5	9	5	102	8	1	71	10	3
Dal Canton, J. Bruce, Atlanta	5.35	3	5	.375	42	4	1	16	1	0	73	93	328	41	35	5	6	2	42	8	8	36	3	0
Darcy, Patrick, Cincinnati	3.58	3	5	.400	17	4	1	2	0	0	39	41	173	27	27	8	11	4	22	3	3	15	0	0
Demery, Lawrence, Pittsburgh	6.23	10	7	.588	36	15	4	7	0	0	145	123	604	71	58	5	9	11	58	2	3	72	5	2
Denny, John, St. Louis	3.17	11	9	.550	30	30	8	0	0	0	207	189	861	81	58	18	9	9	74	8	3	74	4	0
Dettore, Thomas, Chicago	2.52	0	5	.000	32	7	0	7	0	0	73	73	319	30	30	8	6	0	33	3	0	5	0	0
Devine, P. Adrian, Atlanta	10.29	6	3	.455	11	0	0	24	2	0	47	43	196	26	26	9	4	4	26	7	7	48	2	0
Dierker, Lawrence, Houston	3.21	3	14	.481	28	28	7	0	0	1	188	171	790	85	72	7	11	4	72	6	6	72	12	0
Downing, Alphonso, Los Angeles*	3.69	13	7	.650	28	17	1	6	0	0	47	43	196	21	20	9	5	5	18	4	4	30	1	2
Dressler, Robert, San Francisco	3.83	3	3	.333	13	8	0	2	0	0	108	98	480	53	53	8	8	1	35	1	0	30	1	2
Dunning, Steven, Montreal	4.42	3	10	.231	31	19	0	7	0	0	91	93	390	50	42	3	11	4	33	3	0	72	1	1
Dupree, Michael, San Diego	4.15	2	6	.250	32	7	0	0	0	0	16	18	71	12	12	4	5	1	13	0	0	5	1	0
Easterly, James, Atlanta*	9.00	0	1	.500	7	0	0	7	0	0	22	23	96	12	12	3	1	1	13	1	0	11	2	0
Eastwick, Rawlins, Cincinnati	2.08	11	5	.688	71	0	0	59	26	0	108	98	439	30	25	6	6	2	27	2	2	70	1	0

Pitcher and Club	W.	L.	Pct.	ERA.	G.	GS.	CG.	GF.	Sv.	ShO.	IP.	H.	BFP.	R.	ER.	HR.	SH.	SF.	Tot. BB.	Int. BB.	HB.	SO.	WP.	Bk.
Espinosa, Arnulfo, New York	4	4	.500	3.64	12	5	0	5	0	0	42	41	175	21	17	3	4	3	13	3	1	30	1	0
Falcone, Peter, St. Louis*	12	16	.429	3.23	32	32	0	0	0	2	212	173	893	87	76	12	8	8	93	3	1	138	9	1
Folkers, Richard, San Diego*	2	3	.400	5.25	33	2	0	6	0	0	60	67	273	39	35	10	6	2	25	5	2	49	2	0
Forsch, Kenneth, Houston	4	3	.571	2.15	32	0	0	19	9	0	92	76	372	29	22	5	9	4	26	7	2	49	1	2
Forsch, Robert, St. Louis	8	10	.444	3.94	33	32	8	0	0	1	194	209	844	112	85	17	6	6	71	8	4	76	4	0
Foster, Alan, San Diego	3	6	.333	3.21	26	11	0	4	1	1	87	75	360	36	31	5	4	4	35	2	2	22	0	0
Frailing, Kenneth, Chicago*	1	2	.333	2.37	6	3	0	1	0	0	19	20	79	9	5	0	0	1	7	1	0	10	0	0
Freisleben, David, San Diego	10	13	.435	3.51	34	24	6	5	0	1	172	163	736	73	67	10	10	5	66	7	1	81	7	1
Frisella, Daniel, St. Louis	1	1	.500	3.91	18	0	0	10	1	0	23	23	99	11	10	1	0	0	13	1	0	11	0	0
Fryman, Woodrow, Montreal*	13	13	.500	3.38	34	32	11	0	0	0	216	218	933	89	81	14	11	6	76	1	1	123	3	1
Garber, H. Eugene, Philadelphia	9	3	.750	2.81	59	0	0	33	11	0	93	93	384	33	29	7	6	2	30	8	0	92	2	0
Garman, Michael, Chicago	4	4	.500	4.97	47	0	0	21	6	0	76	79	339	42	42	7	4	1	31	9	0	37	1	0
Giusti, David, Pittsburgh	2	2	.500	4.34	40	0	0	22	6	0	58	59	257	31	28	3	6	1	28	9	0	24	2	0
Granger, Wayne, Montreal	2	4	.333	3.66	52	0	0	27	2	0	32	29	143	15	13	3	2	2	16	4	0	16	0	0
Greif, William, San Diego-St. Louis	2	8	.200	5.26	31	5	2	7	0	0	77	87	348	48	45	8	6	1	37	5	1	37	3	0
Griffin, Thomas, Houston-San Diego	11	6	.647	4.10	32	13	6	8	0	0	112	100	505	56	51	8	6	5	45	7	0	69	3	0
Gullett, Donald, Cincinnati*	11	3	.786	3.00	23	20	6	0	0	1	126	105	529	48	42	10	3	0	48	6	1	64	1	1
Halicki, Edward, San Francisco	3	12	.200	3.63	32	31	10	0	0	1	186	171	770	86	75	10	9	5	61	7	2	130	0	1
Hall, Tom, New York*	1	1	.500	5.40	12	0	0	2	0	0	8	11	37	5	5	0	0	0	4	0	0	8	1	0
Hanna, Preston, Atlanta	0	0	.000	4.50	3	3	0	0	0	0	20	20	90	14	10	2	0	0	12	0	0	10	0	0
Hannahs, Gerald, Montreal*	1	0	1.000	6.75	3	3	0	0	0	0	22	35	106	19	17	2	2	1	10	0	0	8	0	0
Hardy, H. Lawrence, Houston	0	4	.000	6.95	15	0	0	15	0	0	35	44	155	30	27	5	7	0	16	3	0	18	1	1
Heaverlo, David, San Francisco	4	4	.500	4.44	61	0	0	31	0	0	75	84	322	45	37	1	0	0	16	5	0	41	0	0
Henderson, Joseph, Cincinnati	0	2	.000	0.00	3	0	0	2	0	0	11	9	48	1	0	0	0	0	8	0	0	1	0	0
Hernandez, Ramon, Pitts.-Chicago*	2	2	.500	3.40	39	1	0	17	0	0	45	44	191	15	17	2	1	3	16	3	1	60	1	0
Hinton, Richard, Cincinnati*	1	0	1.000	7.50	12	0	0	5	0	0	18	30	92	15	15	1	0	0	11	1	1	8	0	0
Hooton, Burt, Los Angeles	11	15	.423	3.25	33	33	8	0	0	2	227	202	925	93	82	16	6	5	65	3	5	116	8	0
Hough, Charles, Los Angeles	12	8	.600	2.20	77	0	0	55	18	0	143	103	600	43	35	6	3	0	77	9	0	81	7	0
Hrabosky, Alan, St. Louis*	8	6	.571	3.32	68	0	0	45	13	0	95	93	407	43	35	7	8	3	39	4	3	77	3	0
John, Thomas, Los Angeles*	10	10	.500	3.09	31	31	8	0	0	4	207	207	868	76	71	15	7	5	61	5	4	91	7	0
Johnson, Jerry, San Diego	0	2	.000	5.31	40	0	0	17	0	0	39	39	179	25	23	5	0	6	23	5	0	27	3	0
Jones, Randall, San Diego	22	14	.611	2.74	40	40	25	0	0	5	315	274	1251	109	96	15	5	7	50	2	2	93	6	0
Kaat, James, Philadelphia*	12	14	.462	3.47	38	35	17	0	0	0	228	241	958	95	88	21	9	4	32	7	7	83	7	0
Keener, Joseph, Montreal	0	2	.000	11.25	3	0	0	0	0	0	4	6	27	5	5	2	0	0	4	0	0	5	0	0
Kerrigan, Joseph, Montreal	3	8	.273	3.79	22	9	0	17	0	0	57	63	244	28	24	5	9	0	23	4	2	22	2	0
Kirby, Clayton, Montreal	1	2	.333	5.70	31	15	6	0	0	0	79	81	370	55	50	10	9	0	61	3	1	51	5	1
Kison, Bruce, Pittsburgh	14	9	.609	3.08	34	31	6	0	0	1	193	180	800	76	66	9	10	6	52	7	2	98	7	1
Knepper, Robert, San Francisco*	1	2	.333	3.24	4	3	0	0	0	0	25	26	104	13	9	0	3	0	12	2	0	26	0	0
Knowles, Darold, Chicago*	1	2	.333	2.88	58	0	0	28	0	0	72	61	310	26	23	4	0	0	26	7	2	39	3	0
Koosman, Jerry, New York*	21	10	.677	2.70	34	34	17	0	0	2	247	205	1010	81	74	19	5	6	66	2	6	200	3	1
Krukow, Michael, Chicago	3	0	1.000	4.71	8	3	0	2	0	0	24	21	99	15	13	3	0	0	14	0	0	9	0	1
LaCorte, Frank, Atlanta	0	3	.000	9.00	19	0	0	0	0	0	11	20	60	15	11	2	1	0	10	0	1	10	1	1
LaGrow, Lerrin, St. Louis	1	2	.333	1.50	8	0	0	0	0	0	24	13	100	5	4	0	0	2	3	0	0	7	0	0
Landreth, Larry, Montreal	1	1	.500	4.09	11	9	1	0	0	0	53	56	244	30	24	4	6	3	34	0	1	30	1	1
Lang, Robert, Montreal	0	2	.000	4.21	29	0	0	0	0	0	62	56	275	32	29	3	3	1	34	2	3	30	0	1
Langford, J. Rick, Pittsburgh	1	0	1.000	6.26	12	2	0	5	0	0	23	27	105	17	16	2	1	0	14	0	2	8	0	1

Pitcher and Club	ERA.	W.	L.	Pct.	G.	GS.	CG.	GF.	Sv.	ShO.	IP.	H.	BFP.	R.	ER.	HR.	SH.	SF.	Tot. BB.	Int. BB.	HB.	SO.	WP.	Bk.
Larson, Daniel, Houston	3.03	5	8	.385	13	13	1	0	0	0	92	81	379	40	31	6	1	1	28	2	1	42	7	1
Lavelle, Gary, San Francisco°	2.70	10	6	.625	65	0	0	40	12	0	110	102	478	37	33	6	6	6	52	10	2	71	1	2
Lemongello, Mark, Houston	2.79	9	14	.391	30	30	9	0	0	1	229	221	922	102	71	11	5	3	49	3	2	96	7	0
Leon, Maximino, Atlanta	2.75	3	4	.333	30	0	0	15	9	0	36	26	156	12	11	2	5	5	15	2	1	9	0	0
Lerch, Randy, Philadelphia*	3.00	10	7	.588	56	26	5	1	0	2	32	62	122	31	14	4	4	2	34	0	0	108	11	0
Lewallyn, Dennis, Los Angeles	2.12	0	1	.000	4	0	0	1	0	0	3	3	12	5	4	0	0	0	0	0	0	0	0	0
Lockwood, Claude, New York	2.68	1	7	.588	63	0	0	44	19	0	17	12	67	5	5	1	0	1	6	0	0	4	1	1
Lolich, Michael, New York*	3.22	8	13	.381	33	30	5	0	0	2	193	184	797	85	69	14	11	4	52	4	2	120	4	2
Lonborg, James, Philadelphia	3.08	18	10	.643	33	32	8	0	0	2	222	210	916	85	76	18	13	3	50	2	1	118	4	1
Marshall, Michael, Los Ang.-Atlanta	4.00	6	10	.600	35	0	0	20	7	0	99	99	430	44	44	6	8	8	39	2	2	56	1	0
Matlack, Jonathan, New York*	2.95	7	10	.630	35	35	16	0	0	6	262	236	1054	94	86	18	12	6	57	5	5	153	1	3
McEnaney, William, Cincinnati*	4.88	3	9	.250	68	0	0	39	11	0	72	67	333	36	39	10	10	7	23	10	3	28	6	1
McGlothen, Lynn, St. Louis	2.51	7	6	.464	33	31	10	1	0	4	205	209	868	96	89	10	7	5	68	1	0	106	3	0
McGraw, Frank, Philadelphia*	2.85	7	5	.538	58	0	0	31	9	0	97	81	408	34	27	6	8	6	42	9	2	76	5	1
McLaughlin, Michael, Houston	3.52	1	5	.444	11	0	0	6	1	0	17	11	305	8	7	0	2	0	17	1	0	32	5	1
Medich, George, Pittsburgh	3.04	11	11	.421	29	26	3	0	0	3	179	193	759	80	70	14	4	7	48	4	0	86	1	0
Messersmith, John, Atlanta	2.93	11	11	.500	29	28	12	0	0	3	207	166	847	70	67	14	6	4	74	7	3	135	3	0
Metzger, Clarence, San Diego	4.85	11	4	.733	77	0	0	62	16	0	123	119	528	74	40	4	11	8	52	14	1	89	8	0
Minton, Gregory, San Francisco	2.27	1	1	.500	58	0	0	31	0	0	26	32	117	12	18	4	11	5	12	4	1	50	8	1
Moffitt, Randall, San Francisco	2.85	5	9	.357	53	0	0	26	11	0	103	92	437	36	40	4	17	4	35	8	5	55	3	1
Montefusco, John, San Francisco	3.68	16	14	.533	36	36	11	0	0	6	253	232	1045	116	86	17	6	8	74	7	1	172	2	0
Moose, Robert, Pittsburgh	5.03	3	9	.250	26	12	3	5	2	0	88	100	388	71	84	8	11	6	32	8	1	38	0	0
Moret, Rogelio, Atlanta	3.04	3	5	.375	56	2	2	0	1	0	77	100	335	47	39	4	6	4	27	7	2	43	6	1
Morton, Carl, Atlanta	3.27	4	9	.308	33	24	8	0	0	3	147	172	679	73	42	11	8	4	45	12	1	35	6	4
Murray, Dale, Montreal	3.27	1	1	.500	26	0	0	0	0	0	113	100	479	49	44	5	14	5	37	4	1	30	6	1
Myrick, Robert, New York*	3.36	4	9	.308	36	3	0	55	13	0	107	108	126	52	44	3	3	5	13	1	1	77	1	0
Niekro, Joseph, Houston	3.29	13	9	.500	44	37	7	0	0	5	249	260	515	117	89	18	11	7	56	3	7	173	9	0
Niekro, Philip, Atlanta	3.46	16	8	.500	43	37	10	0	0	4	247	249	1078	117	99	18	14	8	101	7	5	113	8	1
Nolan, Gary, Cincinnati	3.10	4	7	.607	34	24	8	0	0	4	118	153	1157	67	62	9	3	3	31	3	1	126	0	1
Norman, Fredie, Cincinnati*	2.95	14	6	.625	38	34	8	0	0	1	239	179	953	79	71	10	12	5	70	5	1	36	7	0
Owchinko, Robert, San Diego°	3.71	9	12	.632	33	33	4	0	0	3	180	153	745	71	62	14	4	1	31	1	3	98	4	0
Pentz, Eugene, Houston	18.00	0	2	.000	14	0	0	9	0	0	4	11	27	26	8	2	0	0	6	1	2	4	0	0
Proly, Michael, St. Louis	3.54	3	3	.500	43	14	1	11	1	0	64	62	279	27	21	5	1	5	54	6	1	76	4	2
Rasmussen, Harold, St. Louis	2.57	11	12	.333	34	32	11	0	0	3	231	221	950	94	78	14	17	10	69	7	6	98	13	0
Rau, Douglas, Los Angeles*	2.46	14	8	.571	31	28	8	0	0	2	128	88	499	39	35	12	5	3	32	4	1	96	7	0
Reed, Ronald, Philadelphia	3.99	8	12	.533	50	0	0	25	15	0	176	179	742	87	78	16	5	3	49	8	7	116	2	2
Renko, Steve, Montreal-Chicago	4.55	8	12	.400	38	37	9	0	0	1	87	94	377	94	42	12	13	4	33	4	1	55	7	0
Reuschel, Paul, Chicago	3.46	4	12	.667	37	0	0	17	7	0	209	209	1078	117	100	16	12	4	64	10	2	146	10	1
Reuschel, Ricky, Chicago	3.53	14	12	.538	39	31	8	0	0	4	209	180	880	98	86	17	13	4	51	3	4	108	18	0
Reuss, Jerry, Pittsburgh*	2.98	14	8	.609	33	37	11	0	0	3	209	209	880	94	88	14	17	8	53	10	1	177	7	0
Reynolds, Kenneth, San Diego°	6.47	3	2	.000	19	19	2	0	0	0	32	38	155	27	23	7	2	1	29	2	1	78	1	0
Rhoden, Richard, Los Angeles	2.98	12	10	.800	31	26	6	0	0	3	181	165	744	66	66	6	9	4	53	4	4	78	13	1
Riccelli, Frank, San Francisco°	5.63	1	3	.500	27	0	0	3	1	0	16	16	68	10	10	2	1	2	24	0	0	18	0	0
Richard, James, Houston	2.75	18	12	.571	39	39	14	0	0	3	291	221	1218	105	89	14	13	4	151	9	4	214	2	2
Rogers, Stephen, Montreal	3.21	17	16	.292	33	33	17	0	0	1	230	212	944	93	82	10	17	5	69	7	0	150	9	2
Rondon, Gilbert, Houston	5.67	2	2	.500	19	0	0	3	0	0	54	70	264	37	34	6	5	1	39	0	0	20	0	0

Pitcher and Club	ERA	W.	L.	Pct.	G.	GS.	CG.	GF.	Sv.	ShO.	IP.	H.	BFP	R.	ER.	HR.	SH.	SF.	Tot. BB.	Int. BB.	HB.	SO.	WP.	Bk.
Rooker, James, Pittsburgh*	3.35	15	8	.652	30	29	10	1	0	1	199	201	851	83	74	12	4	9	72	5	8	92	7	1
Ruthven, Richard, Atlanta	4.20	14	17	.452	36	36	6	0	0	1	240	255	1042	112	112	14	12	6	90	8	6	142	4	5
Sambito, Joseph, Houston*	3.57	3	2	.600	53	0	0	18	8	0	53	39	207	21	21	4	5	2	12	4	1	26	0	1
Sanders, Kenneth, New York	2.87	1	2	.333	21	0	0	6	0	0	47	36	188	16	15	2	4	1	12	4	1	16	2	0
Sarmiento, Manuel, Cincinnati	2.05	5	1	.833	22	11	0	0	0	2	82	84	354	24	18	3	3	8	38	8	3	20	3	1
Sawyer, Richard, San Diego	2.52	5	3	.625	10	0	0	8	0	0	44	42	177	14	12	2	1	3	14	2	1	33	0	3
Scherman, Frederick, Montreal*	4.95	2	2	.500	35	0	0	14	0	0	40	37	181	25	22	5	4	2	16	3	2	18	3	1
Schueler, Ronald, Philadelphia	2.88	1	1	.500	29	0	0	12	0	0	50	44	203	22	16	4	1	2	14	1	3	43	0	3
Schultz, C. Budd, Chicago*	6.00	0	0	.000	19	0	0	7	0	0	24	29	116	18	16	3	4	3	9	1	1	15	0	0
Seaver, G. Thomas, New York	2.59	14	11	.560	35	34	13	0	0	5	271	211	1079	103	78	14	7	9	77	9	1	235	1	0
Siebert, Paul, Houston*	3.12	0	2	.000	26	0	0	6	0	0	26	29	124	10	9	2	0	1	18	7	1	10	1	2
Solomon, Eddie, St. Louis	4.86	1	2	.333	45	2	0	24	0	0	37	45	170	20	20	5	2	2	16	1	1	19	1	0
Sosa, Elias, Atlanta-Los Angeles	4.43	2	8	.200	32	0	0	13	0	0	69	71	302	42	34	4	4	6	25	6	3	52	0	0
Sosa, Jose, Houston	6.75	1	2	.333	17	0	0	5	0	0	12	16	60	9	9	3	4	1	6	2	0	7	2	0
Spillner, Daniel, San Diego	5.05	2	11	.154	36	24	4	5	0	1	113	120	483	70	63	11	9	6	55	6	4	79	4	0
Stanhouse, Donald, Montreal	3.77	9	12	.429	52	26	8	8	0	0	182	182	804	84	77	11	11	10	92	10	8	57	2	0
Stone, Steven, Chicago	4.08	3	6	.333	35	15	4	1	0	2	75	70	312	36	34	7	7	3	21	1	4	79	0	0
Strom, Brent, San Diego*	3.28	12	8	.600	31	33	8	0	0	4	211	188	878	100	77	15	10	6	73	8	3	103	13	0
Sutcliffe, Richard, Los Angeles	0.00	0	2	.000	2	0	0	0	0	0	5	5	17	0	0	0	0	0	1	0	0	3	0	0
Sutter, H. Bruce, Chicago	2.71	6	3	.667	52	0	0	28	10	0	83	63	332	27	25	5	3	2	26	6	1	73	3	0
Sutton, Donald, Los Angeles	3.06	21	10	.677	35	35	15	0	0	4	268	231	1093	98	91	22	7	6	82	6	3	161	0	0
Swan, Craig, New York	3.55	6	9	.400	38	22	3	0	0	1	132	129	568	64	52	11	5	3	44	3	6	89	4	3
Taylor, Charles, Montreal	2.45	2	3	.400	26	0	0	13	0	0	40	38	158	20	15	3	5	1	13	1	1	14	2	0
Tekulve, Kenton, Pittsburgh	2.84	5	3	.625	64	0	0	33	9	0	103	91	409	30	28	1	1	2	25	6	3	68	0	0
Tomlin, David, San Diego*	2.84	2	1	.667	49	0	0	14	0	0	73	62	290	24	23	4	5	5	20	7	2	43	4	0
Toms, Thomas, San Francisco	6.00	0	2	.000	10	1	0	3	0	0	9	13	39	9	6	0	0	0	1	0	0	3	2	0
Torrealba, Pablo, Atlanta*	3.57	1	2	.333	36	0	0	18	0	0	53	55	241	25	21	3	5	7	22	3	7	33	0	0
Twitchell, Wayne, Philadelphia	1.74	0	1	.000	26	7	3	2	0	2	62	55	254	18	12	2	3	0	18	1	1	67	6	0
Underwood, Thomas, Philadelphia*	3.52	10	5	.667	33	25	3	2	0	1	156	154	666	63	61	9	6	3	63	7	3	94	4	3
Walker, R. Thomas, St. Louis	4.05	2	2	.500	10	3	0	2	0	0	50	22	211	24	22	5	3	1	3	0	0	27	0	0
Wall, Stanley, Los Angeles*	3.60	2	2	.500	49	0	0	15	1	0	20	20	87	10	8	3	5	1	15	3	1	11	0	1
Wallace, Michael, St. Louis*	4.09	3	2	.600	49	0	0	13	0	0	66	66	295	34	30	8	2	6	39	2	2	40	6	0
Warthen, Daniel, Montreal*	5.30	2	10	.167	16	16	3	0	0	0	90	76	405	59	53	6	8	3	66	6	1	67	0	0
Waterbury, Steven, St. Louis	6.00	0	1	.000	5	0	0	1	0	0	16	17	74	12	10	2	0	0	3	0	0	4	1	0
Webb, Henry, New York	4.50	0	1	.000	8	0	0	3	0	0	17	27	88	9	8	4	0	1	11	2	0	7	0	0
Wehrmeister, David, San Diego	7.58	0	2	.000	48	4	0	13	0	0	19	27	90	17	16	4	0	0	9	0	1	10	2	1
Williams, Charles, San Francisco	2.96	2	0	1.000	38	8	1	15	0	0	85	80	365	33	28	8	9	2	39	3	2	34	1	0
Zachry, Patrick, Cincinnati	2.74	14	7	.667	40	28	6	2	0	1	204	170	842	70	62	8	6	4	83	4	3	143	5	3
Zahn, Geoffrey, Chicago*	11.25	0	1	.000	8	6	0	0	0	0	16	43	70	20	20	0	1	0	4	2	0	7	1	1
Zamora, Oscar, Chicago*	5.24	5	3	.625	40	0	0	13	0	0	55	70	248	34	32	8	6	2	17	1	1	27	1	1

NOTE—Following pitchers combined to pitch shutout games: Atlanta (3)—Niekro and Torrealba; Ruthven and Messersmith, LaCorte and Devine; Chicago (4)—Frailing and Zamora, R. Reuschel and Garman, Renko and Coleman, Stone and Sutter; Cincinnati (4)—Nolan and Eastwick 2, Gullett and Darcy, Norman and McEnaney; Houston (2)—Richard, Hardy and Forsch, Richard, Forsch and Barlow; Los Angeles (1)—Sutcliffe, Wall and Hough; Montreal (2)—Fryman and Murray 2; New York (1)—Swan and Lockwood; Philadelphia (5)—Underwood and McGraw, Christenson, Underwood and McGraw, Underwood and Reed, Twitchell and Schueler, Christenson and McGraw; Pittsburgh (2)—Rooker and Demery, Medich and Giusti; St. Louis (4)—Falcone, Proly and Hrabosky, Curtis and Greif, Rasmussen and Hrabosky, Denny, Greif and Hrabosky; San Francisco (5)—Halicki and Lavelle 2, Caldwell and Lavelle, D'Acquisto and Caldwell, D'Acquisto and Lavelle.

PITCHERS WITH TWO OR MORE CLUBS
(Alphabetically Arranged With Pitcher's First Club on Top)

Pitcher and Club	ERA	W.	L.	Pct.	G.	GS.	CG.	GF.	Sv.	ShO.	IP.	H.	BFP.	R.	ER.	HR.	SH.	SF.	Tot. BB.	Int. BB.	HB.	SO.	WP.	Bk.
Greif, San Diego	8.06	1	3	.250	5	5	0	0	0	0	22⅓	27	104	20	20	2	1	1	11	2	0	5	1	0
Greif, St. Louis	4.12	1	5	.167	47	0	0	21	6	0	54⅔	60	244	28	25	5	4	5	26	5	2	32	6	0
Griffin, Houston	6.05	5	3	.625	20	2	2	2	0	0	41⅔	44	201	29	28	4	2	3	37	2	1	33	3	0
Griffin, San Diego	2.94	4	3	.571	11	11	2	0	0	0	70⅓	56	304	27	23	0	7	2	42	1	1	36	6	0
Hernandez, Pittsburgh	3.56	2	2	.500	37	0	0	17	3	0	43	42	184	17	17	3	3	4	16	5	1	17	2	1
Hernandez, Chicago	0.00	0	0	.000	2	0	0	0	0	0	1⅔	2	7	0	0	0	1	0	0	0	0	1	0	0
Marshall, Los Angeles	4.45	4	3	.571	30	0	0	23	8	0	62⅔	64	273	33	31	2	8	2	25	5	1	39	1	0
Marshall, Atlanta	3.19	2	1	.333	24	0	0	21	6	0	36⅔	35	157	15	13	4	5	2	14	2	1	17	3	0
Renko, Montreal	5.54	0	1	1.000	5	1	0	1	0	0	13	15	56	8	8	2	1	0	3	0	0	4	0	0
Renko, Chicago	3.86	8	11	.421	28	27	4	0	0	1	163⅓	164	686	79	70	12	6	1	43	8	0	112	1	0
E. Sosa, Atlanta	5.35	4	4	.500	21	0	0	10	3	0	35⅓	41	161	26	21	3	2	2	13	2	1	32	1	0
E. Sosa, Los Angeles	3.48	2	4	.333	24	0	0	14	1	0	33⅔	30	141	16	13	0	3	2	12	4	0	20	0	0

1976 N.L. Pitching Against Each Club

ATLANTA—70-92

Pitcher	Chi. W–L	Cin. W–L	Hou. W–L	L.A. W–L	Mont. W–L	N.Y. W–L	Phila. W–L	Pitts. W–L	St.L. W–L	S.D. W–L	S.F. W–L	Totals W–L
Autry	0–0	0–0	1–0	0–0	0–0	0–0	0–0	0–0	0–0	0–0	0–0	1– 0
Beard	0–0	0–0	0–0	0–0	0–0	0–0	0–0	0–0	0–1	0–0	0–1	0– 2
Camp	0–0	0–0	0–1	0–0	0–0	0–0	0–0	0–0	0–0	0–0	0–0	0– 1
Capra	0–1	0–0	0–0	0–0	0–0	0–0	0–0	0–0	0–0	0–0	0–0	0– 1
Dal Canton	0–0	0–0	0–2	0–0	0–1	1–0	1–0	1–0	0–0	0–0	0–1	3– 5
Devine	0–0	1–2	0–0	2–0	1–0	0–0	0–0	0–1	0–1	1–2	0–0	5– 6
Easterly	0–0	0–0	0–0	1–0	0–0	0–0	0–0	0–0	0–0	0–0	0–1	1– 1
LaCorte	1–1	0–3	0–2	1–0	0–0	0–1	1–0	0–0	0–1	0–3	0–1	3–12
Leon	0–0	0–1	0–0	0–1	0–0	0–0	0–0	0–1	0–0	1–1	1–0	2– 4
Marshall	0–0	1–0	0–0	0–0	0–0	0–0	0–0	0–0	0–0	1–0	0–1	2– 1
Messersmith	2–0	0–0	2–1	0–0	2–1	0–3	0–2	1–2	1–1	1–1	2–0	11–11
Moret	0–0	0–0	0–1	0–3	0–0	0–0	0–0	0–1	0–0	2–0	1–0	3– 5
Morton	0–1	1–1	0–0	0–2	1–0	0–1	0–2	0–0	1–1	0–0	1–0	4– 9
Niekro	2–1	2–1	2–2	2–0	1–1	2–1	3–0	0–2	1–1	2–0	0–2	17–11
Ruthven	1–2	0–3	0–2	1–3	3–0	0–1	0–2	1–2	3–0	4–0	1–2	14–17
Sosa	0–0	0–0	2–0	1–1	0–0	1–0	0–1	0–1	0–0	0–0	0–1	4– 4
Torrealba	0–0	0–1	0–0	0–0	0–0	0–0	0–1	0–0	0–0	0–0	0–0	0– 2
Totals	6–6	6–12	7–11	8–10	8–4	4–8	5–7	3–9	4–8	10–8	9–9	70–92

No Decisions: Hanna.

CHICAGO—75-87

Pitcher	Atl. W–L	Cin. W–L	Hou. W–L	L.A. W–L	Mont. W–L	N.Y. W–L	Phila. W–L	Pitts. W–L	St.L. W–L	S.D. W–L	S.F. W–L	Totals W–L
Bonham	1–0	1–0	1–1	0–2	1–1	1–3	1–1	1–1	1–2	1–2	0–0	9–13
Burris	1–2	1–2	2–0	1–1	4–1	2–2	1–1	0–1	2–2	1–1	0–0	15–13
Coleman	0–2	0–1	0–0	1–0	0–0	0–2	0–1	1–1	0–1	0–0	0–0	2– 8
Dettore	0–0	0–0	0–0	0–0	0–0	0–1	0–0	0–0	0–0	0–0	0–0	0– 1
Frailing	0–0	0–1	0–1	0–0	0–0	0–0	0–0	0–0	0–0	1–0	0–0	1– 2
Garman	0–0	0–0	0–0	0–1	0–0	1–0	0–1	0–1	0–0	0–1	1–0	2– 4
Knowles	1–0	0–0	0–0	0–1	1–0	0–0	0–2	0–2	1–0	2–0	0–0	5– 7
Renko	2–1	0–0	0–1	0–1	1–2	0–0	0–2	1–2	3–0	1–0	0–0	8–11
P. Reuschel	0–0	0–0	0–0	1–0	1–0	0–0	0–0	1–1	1–0	0–1	0–0	4– 2
R. Reuschel	1–1	1–1	1–2	0–2	1–0	0–0	3–1	1–1	2–1	2–1	2–0	14–12
Schultz	0–0	0–0	0–0	0–0	0–0	1–0	0–0	0–0	0–0	0–0	0–1	1– 1
Stone	0–0	0–0	0–1	0–1	1–1	0–1	0–1	0–0	1–0	1–0	0–1	3– 6
Sutter	0–0	0–1	1–0	0–0	0–0	0–0	3–0	0–0	1–0	0–0	1–2	6– 3
Zahn	0–0	0–0	0–0	0–0	0–0	0–1	0–0	0–0	0–0	0–0	0–0	0– 1
Zamora	0–0	0–1	0–0	1–0	1–1	0–0	0–0	3–0	0–0	0–0	1–0	5– 3
Totals	6–6	3–9	5–7	3–9	11–7	5–13	8–10	8–10	12–6	6–6	8–4	75–87

No Decisions: Crosby, Hernandez, Krukow.

CINCINNATI—102-60

Pitcher	Atl. W–L	Chi. W–L	Hou. W–L	L.A. W–L	Mont. W–L	N.Y. W–L	Phila. W–L	Pitts. W–L	St.L. W–L	S.D. W–L	S.F. W–L	Totals W–L
Alcala	2–0	1–0	0–1	1–0	1–0	1–0	1–0	1–0	0–1	2–1	1–1	11– 4
Billingham	1–1	0–0	1–0	1–1	1–1	2–0	1–1	1–1	0–2	2–1	1–2	12–10
Borbon	1–0	0–0	2–1	0–0	0–0	0–0	0–1	0–1	1–0	0–0	0–0	4– 3
Darcy	0–0	0–0	2–0	0–0	0–1	0–0	0–1	0–0	0–0	0–0	0–1	2– 3
Eastwick	1–1	0–0	1–0	2–1	3–0	1–0	1–2	1–0	1–1	0–0	0–0	11– 5
Gullett	2–0	1–0	0–0	1–0	2–0	1–1	1–1	1–1	1–0	1–0	0–0	11– 3
Henderson	0–0	0–0	0–0	0–0	0–0	0–0	0–0	0–0	0–0	2–0	0–0	2– 0
Hinton	0–1	0–0	0–1	0–0	1–0	0–0	0–0	0–0	0–0	0–0	0–0	1– 2
McEnaney	0–0	0–0	1–0	0–1	0–1	0–0	0–0	0–1	0–1	0–1	1–1	2– 6
Nolan	2–0	2–1	1–0	3–1	1–0	0–3	1–1	2–0	1–0	1–1	1–2	15– 9
Norman	1–1	0–1	1–1	2–0	0–0	1–1	1–0	1–0	1–0	2–2	2–1	12– 7
Sarmiento	1–1	2–0	1–0	0–0	0–0	0–0	0–0	0–0	0–0	0–0	1–0	5– 1
Zachry	1–1	2–1	0–2	5–1	0–0	0–1	0–0	1–0	1–1	4–0	0–0	14– 7
Totals	12–6	9–3	12–6	13–5	9–3	6–6	5–7	8–4	6–6	13–5	9–9	102–60

No Decisions: None.

HOUSTON—80-82

Pitcher	Atl. W–L	Chi. W–L	Cin. W–L	L.A. W–L	Mont. W–L	N.Y. W–L	Phila. W–L	Pitts. W–L	St.L. W–L	S.D. W–L	S.F. W–L	Totals W–L
Andujar	1–1	2–1	3–0	1–1	1–0	1–1	0–1	0–2	0–0	0–3	0–0	9–10
Barlow	0–1	0–0	0–0	0–1	0–1	0–0	0–0	0–0	0–0	0–0	1–0	2–2
Cosgrove	0–0	1–1	0–0	0–0	0–0	1–0	0–1	0–0	0–1	0–0	1–1	3–4
Dierker	1–0	0–2	1–2	1–2	2–0	1–1	0–3	0–1	4–0	1–2	2–1	13–14
Forsch	1–0	0–0	0–2	0–0	2–0	0–0	0–0	1–0	0–0	0–0	0–1	4–3
Griffin	1–0	0–0	0–1	0–0	1–0	0–0	0–1	1–1	0–0	2–0	0–0	5–3
Larson	1–2	0–1	0–0	0–3	1–0	0–0	2–0	0–1	1–0	0–0	0–1	5–8
Lemongello	1–0	0–0	0–0	0–0	0–0	0–0	0–0	0–0	0–0	1–0	1–1	3–1
McLaughlin	0–1	0–0	0–1	0–0	0–0	0–0	1–0	0–0	1–1	1–1	1–1	4–5
Niekro	1–0	0–0	0–2	0–1	1–0	0–0	1–2	0–1	0–1	2–0	0–0	4–8
Pentz	1–1	0–0	1–0	0–1	0–0	0–0	0–0	0–0	0–1	0–0	1–0	3–3
Richard	1–1	3–0	0–4	2–2	3–1	2–1	1–1	0–2	2–0	3–2	3–1	20–15
Rondon	1–0	1–0	0–0	0–0	0–0	0–1	0–0	0–0	0–0	0–0	0–1	2–2
Sambito	1–0	0–0	1–0	0–1	0–0	0–0	0–0	0–1	1–0	0–0	0–0	3–2
Siebert	0–0	0–0	0–0	0–2	0–0	0–0	0–0	0–0	0–0	0–0	0–0	0–2
Totals	11–7	7–5	6–12	5–13	10–2	6–6	4–8	2–10	9–3	10–8	10–8	80–82

No Decisions: Hardy, Sosa.

LOS ANGELES—92-70

Pitcher	Atl. W–L	Chi. W–L	Cin. W–L	Hou. W–L	Mont. W–L	N.Y. W–L	Phila. W–L	Pitts. W–L	St.L. W–L	S.D. W–L	S.F. W–L	Totals W–L
Downing	0–0	1–1	0–1	0–0	0–0	0–0	0–0	0–0	0–0	0–0	0–0	1–2
Hooton	1–3	1–0	0–2	3–1	1–1	0–2	2–1	2–0	0–0	0–3	1–2	11–15
Hough	1–2	1–1	2–0	1–0	0–1	2–1	1–2	1–0	1–0	0–0	2–1	12–8
John	3–2	0–0	1–1	1–1	2–0	1–0	0–2	1–0	0–1	1–2	0–1	10–10
Lewallyn	0–1	0–0	0–0	0–0	0–0	0–0	0–0	0–0	0–0	1–0	0–0	1–1
Marshall	0–0	0–0	0–1	0–0	1–0	0–0	0–0	0–0	3–0	0–0	0–2	4–3
Rau	1–0	1–1	1–2	2–1	2–0	1–1	1–1	2–2	2–0	2–2	1–2	16–12
Rhoden	2–0	1–0	1–1	2–0	1–0	1–1	0–0	1–1	1–0	1–0	1–0	12–3
Sosa	0–0	0–0	0–1	1–0	1–0	0–0	0–0	0–0	0–1	0–2	0–0	2–4
Sutton	2–0	4–0	0–4	1–1	2–0	2–0	1–0	2–0	3–0	1–3	3–2	21–10
Wall	0–0	0–0	0–0	2–1	0–0	0–0	0–1	0–0	0–0	0–0	0–0	2–2
Totals	10–8	9–3	5–13	13–5	10–2	7–5	5–7	9–3	10–2	6–12	8–10	92–70

No Decisions: Sutcliffe.

MONTREAL—55-107

Pitcher	Atl. W–L	Chi. W–L	Cin. W–L	Hou. W–L	L.A. W–L	N.Y. W–L	Phila. W–L	Pitts. W–L	St.L. W–L	S.D. W–L	S.F. W–L	Totals W–L
Blair	0–0	0–0	0–0	0–0	0–0	0–0	0–2	0–0	0–0	0–0	0–0	0–2
Carrithers	1–1	0–0	0–2	1–0	1–1	1–1	0–1	0–2	0–1	0–2	2–1	6–12
Dunning	0–2	2–0	0–0	0–2	0–1	0–0	0–0	0–0	0–0	0–1	0–0	2–6
Fryman	0–2	2–1	0–1	1–1	0–2	0–1	1–2	4–1	2–1	0–1	3–0	13–13
Granger	0–0	0–0	0–0	0–0	0–0	0–0	0–0	1–0	0–0	0–0	0–0	1–0
Hannahs	0–0	0–0	0–0	0–0	0–0	1–0	0–0	0–0	1–0	0–0	0–0	2–0
Keener	0–0	0–0	0–0	0–0	0–0	0–0	0–0	0–0	0–1	0–0	0–0	0–1
Kerrigan	0–0	0–2	0–0	0–0	0–0	0–2	0–0	0–1	2–1	0–0	0–0	2–6
Kirby	0–1	0–0	0–1	0–2	0–1	0–1	1–1	0–0	0–0	0–1	0–0	1–8
Landreth	0–0	1–0	0–0	0–0	0–0	0–2	0–0	0–0	0–0	0–0	0–0	1–2
Lang	0–0	0–1	0–0	0–0	0–0	1–0	0–0	0–0	0–0	0–0	0–1	1–3
Murray	1–0	0–1	0–0	0–2	0–1	1–1	0–1	1–2	0–0	1–0	0–0	4–9
Renko	0–0	0–0	0–1	0–0	0–0	0–0	0–0	0–0	0–0	0–0	0–0	0–1
Rogers	0–1	1–2	1–1	0–2	0–2	1–1	0–4	1–1	0–2	2–1	1–0	7–17
Scherman	1–0	0–0	0–0	0–0	0–0	1–1	0–0	0–0	0–1	0–0	0–0	2–2
Stanhouse	0–1	1–2	2–0	0–1	1–1	0–0	1–2	1–2	1–1	1–1	1–1	9–12
Taylor	0–0	0–1	0–0	0–0	0–0	1–0	0–0	0–0	1–1	0–0	0–1	2–3
Warthen	1–0	0–1	0–1	0–0	0–1	1–0	0–2	0–1	0–2	0–1	0–1	2–10
Totals	4–8	7–11	3–9	2–10	2–10	8–10	3–15	8–10	7–11	4–8	7–5	55–107

No Decisions: Atkinson.

NEW YORK—86-76

Pitcher	Atl. W–L	Chi. W–L	Cin. W–L	Hou. W–L	L.A. W–L	Mont. W–L	Phila. W–L	Pitts. W–L	St.L. W–L	S.D. W–L	S.F. W–L	Totals W–L
Apodaca	0–2	0–0	0–0	0–2	0–1	1–0	0–0	1–1	1–1	0–0	0–0	3– 7
Espinosa	0–1	0–0	1–0	0–0	0–0	0–0	1–1	2–0	0–1	0–0	0–1	4– 4
Hall	1–0	0–0	0–1	0–0	0–0	0–0	0–0	0–0	0–0	0–0	0–0	1– 1
Koosman	1–0	4–0	2–0	3–1	0–3	2–2	2–1	1–1	2–1	3–0	1–1	21–10
Lockwood	1–0	3–1	0–0	0–1	1–0	2–2	0–1	1–1	1–1	0–0	1–0	10– 7
Lolich	2–0	0–2	0–2	0–0	0–0	1–1	0–3	1–1	2–2	1–1	1–1	8–13
Matlack	0–0	2–0	1–1	1–1	3–1	3–0	0–4	2–1	2–0	3–0	0–2	17–10
Myrick	0–0	0–0	0–0	0–0	0–0	0–1	1–0	0–0	0–0	0–0	0–0	1– 1
Sanders	0–0	0–0	0–0	1–0	0–0	0–0	0–0	0–0	0–1	0–0	0–0	1– 2
Seaver	2–0	1–0	1–1	1–1	1–2	1–1	1–2	2–1	1–0	0–3	3–0	14–11
Swan	1–1	3–1	1–1	0–0	0–0	0–1	0–1	0–1	0–2	0–1	1–0	6– 9
Webb	0–0	0–1	0–0	0–0	0–0	0–0	0–0	0–0	0–0	0–0	0–0	0– 1
Totals	8–4	13–5	6–6	6–6	5–7	10–8	5–13	10–8	9–9	7–5	7–5	86–76

No Decisions: Ri. Baldwin.

PHILADELPHIA—101-61

Pitcher	Atl. W–L	Chi. W–L	Cin. W–L	Hou. W–L	L.A. W–L	Mont. W–L	N.Y. W–L	Pitts. W–L	St.L. W–L	S.D. W–L	S.F. W–L	Totals W–L
Carlton	2–0	2–1	0–0	2–0	0–0	2–0	2–1	2–2	3–1	2–1	3–1	20– 7
Christenson	1–3	2–0	0–0	1–1	1–1	2–0	5–0	0–1	1–1	0–1	0–0	13– 8
Garber	0–0	2–0	0–0	0–0	2–0	1–0	2–1	0–1	1–0	0–0	1–1	9– 3
Kaat	1–0	1–2	2–1	1–1	0–0	0–2	0–1	1–3	1–1	3–1	2–2	12–14
Lonborg	1–1	1–2	2–0	2–0	1–2	5–1	3–1	1–0	1–1	1–1	0–1	18–10
McGraw	0–1	1–0	2–1	0–1	1–0	0–0	0–0	1–1	2–2	0–0	0–0	7– 6
Reed	1–0	1–3	1–1	1–0	2–2	1–0	0–0	1–1	0–0	0–0	0–0	8– 7
Schueler	0–0	0–0	0–0	0–0	0–0	1–0	1–0	0–0	0–0	0–0	0–0	1– 0
Twitchell	0–0	0–0	0–0	0–1	0–0	1–0	1–0	0–0	1–0	0–0	0–0	3– 1
Underwood	1–0	0–0	0–2	1–0	0–0	2–0	0–1	2–1	2–0	2–0	0–1	10– 5
Totals	7–5	10–8	7–5	8–4	7–5	15–3	13–5	8–10	12–6	8–4	6–6	101–61

No Decisions: Lerch.

PITTSBURGH—92-70

Pitcher	Atl. W–L	Chi. W–L	Cin. W–L	Hou. W–L	L.A. W–L	Mont. W–L	N.Y. W–L	Phila. W–L	St.L. W–L	S.D. W–L	S.F. W–L	Totals W–L
Candelaria	3–0	1–0	1–0	2–0	1–1	1–2	1–0	1–1	1–1	1–2	3–0	16– 7
Demery	1–0	1–2	0–1	1–0	1–1	2–0	0–2	2–1	0–0	1–0	1–0	10– 7
Giusti	0–0	1–0	0–0	1–1	0–0	1–0	1–1	0–1	1–1	0–0	0–0	5– 4
Hernandez	0–1	0–0	0–0	0–0	0–0	0–0	0–0	1–0	1–0	0–1	0–0	2– 2
Kison	0–1	2–1	0–1	0–0	0–2	3–1	1–1	3–1	2–1	2–0	1–0	14– 9
Langford	0–0	0–1	0–0	0–0	0–0	0–0	0–0	0–0	0–0	0–0	0–0	0– 1
Medich	1–0	1–0	0–3	2–0	1–1	0–1	3–1	0–2	0–2	0–1	0–0	8–11
Moose	1–0	1–2	1–0	0–1	0–1	0–2	0–0	0–2	0–0	0–0	0–1	3– 9
Reuss	3–0	1–0	0–1	3–0	1–1	1–2	1–2	0–0	2–1	2–0	1–1	14– 9
Rooker	0–1	2–0	1–2	0–0	0–0	1–1	0–2	2–0	5–0	1–1	3–1	15– 8
Tekulve	0–0	0–2	1–0	1–0	0–0	1–0	1–1	1–0	0–0	0–0	0–0	5– 3
Totals	9–3	10–8	4–8	10–2	3–9	10–8	8–10	10–8	12–6	7–5	9–3	92–70

No Decisions: Bair.

ST. LOUIS—72-90

Pitcher	Atl. W–L	Chi. W–L	Cin. W–L	Hou. W–L	L.A. W–L	Mont. W–L	N.Y. W–L	Phila. W–L	Pitts. W–L	S.D. W–L	S.F. W–L	Totals W–L
Capilla	0–0	0–0	0–0	0–0	0–0	0–0	1–0	0–0	0–0	0–0	0–0	1– 0
Curtis	1–0	0–1	0–1	1–0	0–2	0–2	2–0	0–3	0–2	2–0	0–0	6–11
Denny	0–0	0–2	2–1	0–2	0–0	2–0	2–1	1–1	2–1	2–1	0–0	11– 9
Falcone	2–0	0–2	2–2	0–0	1–1	2–1	0–4	1–2	1–3	2–0	1–1	12–16
Forsch	0–2	2–1	1–0	0–4	0–1	1–0	0–1	1–0	1–0	1–0	1–1	8–10
Greif	0–0	0–0	0–0	0–0	1–0	0–0	0–1	0–1	0–1	0–2	0–0	1– 5
Hrabosky	1–0	1–0	1–1	0–0	0–2	0–0	2–0	2–1	1–1	0–0	0–1	8– 6
LaGrow	0–0	0–0	0–0	0–0	0–0	0–1	0–0	0–0	0–0	0–0	0–0	0– 1
McGlothen	1–1	3–3	0–1	2–2	0–2	2–0	1–1	0–2	1–2	1–0	2–1	13–15
Proly	0–0	0–0	0–0	0–0	0–0	0–0	1–0	0–0	0–0	0–0	0–0	1– 0
Rasmussen	3–1	0–2	0–0	0–1	0–2	1–2	1–0	1–1	0–1	0–1	0–1	6–12
Solomon	0–0	0–1	0–0	0–0	0–0	0–0	1–0	0–1	0–0	0–0	0–0	1– 1
Walker	0–0	0–0	0–0	0–0	0–0	1–1	0–0	0–1	0–0	0–0	0–0	1– 2
Wallace	0–0	0–0	0–0	0–0	0–0	0–0	1–0	0–1	0–1	0–0	2–0	3– 2
Totals	8–4	6–12	6–6	3–9	2–10	11–7	9–9	6–12	6–12	8–4	7–5	72–90

No Decisions: Frisella, Waterbury.

SAN DIEGO—73-89

Pitcher	Atl. W–L	Chi. W–L	Cin. W–L	Hou. W–L	L.A. W–L	Mont. W–L	N.Y. W–L	Phila. W–L	Pitts. W–L	St.L. W–L	S.F. W–L	Totals W–L
Folkers	1–1	0–0	0–1	0–0	0–0	0–0	0–1	1–0	0–0	0–0	0–0	2– 3
Foster	0–0	0–1	0–2	0–0	1–0	1–0	1–0	0–2	0–0	0–0	0–1	3– 6
Freisleben	0–1	0–1	0–1	2–0	2–2	1–1	1–0	0–2	1–3	1–1	2–1	10–13
Greif	0–1	1–1	0–0	0–0	0–0	0–0	0–0	0–0	0–1	0–0	0–0	1– 3
Griffin	0–0	0–0	1–0	1–0	1–0	1–0	0–2	0–0	0–0	0–0	0–1	4– 3
Johnson	0–1	0–0	0–1	0–1	0–0	0–0	0–0	0–0	1–0	0–0	0–0	1– 3
Jones	2–1	1–1	2–1	3–1	3–1	2–0	1–3	3–0	1–1	1–3	3–2	22–14
Metzger	3–1	2–0	1–0	1–1	2–0	0–1	0–0	0–0	0–0	1–0	1–1	11– 4
Owchinko	0–1	0–0	0–0	0–0	0–1	0–0	0–0	0–0	0–0	0–0	0–0	0– 2
Reynolds	0–0	0–0	0–0	0–0	0–1	0–0	0–0	0–1	0–0	0–0	0–1	0– 3
Sawyer	1–0	0–0	0–1	1–1	1–0	0–1	1–0	0–0	0–0	0–0	1–0	5– 3
Spillner	0–2	0–0	0–2	0–3	0–0	1–0	0–0	0–2	0–1	1–1	0–0	2–11
Strom	1–1	2–1	1–3	0–1	2–1	2–1	1–1	0–1	2–1	0–3	1–2	12–16
Tomlin	0–0	0–0	0–0	0–0	0–0	0–0	0–0	0–0	0–0	0–0	0–1	0– 1
Wehrmeister	0–0	0–1	0–1	0–2	0–0	0–0	0–0	0–0	0–0	0–0	0–0	0– 4
Totals	8–10	6–6	5–13	8–10	12–6	8–4	5–7	4–8	5–7	4–8	8–10	73–89

No Decisions: Dupree.

SAN FRANCISCO—74-88

Pitcher	Atl. W–L	Chi. W–L	Cin. W–L	Hou. W–L	L.A. W–L	Mont. W–L	N.Y. W–L	Phila. W–L	Pitts. W–L	St.L. W–L	S.D. W–L	Totals W–L
Barr	2–2	0–0	0–1	0–1	0–1	1–1	1–2	1–1	0–2	1–0	2–1	15–12
Caldwell	0–0	0–0	0–1	0–1	0–1	0–0	1–0	0–1	0–2	0–1	0–0	1– 7
D'Acquisto	0–1	0–0	1–1	1–0	0–0	0–2	0–1	0–0	0–1	1–1	0–1	3– 8
Dressler	1–2	0–1	0–0	1–2	0–0	1–1	0–2	0–0	0–0	0–0	0–2	3–10
Halicki	1–1	1–3	0–1	1–2	3–0	1–1	2–1	2–1	1–1	0–2	0–1	12–14
Heaverlo	0–0	0–0	1–0	1–1	0–1	0–1	0–0	0–0	0–0	0–1	2–0	4– 4
Knepper	1–0	0–0	0–1	0–0	0–1	0–0	0–0	0–0	0–0	0–0	0–0	1– 2
Lavelle	1–1	1–1	1–1	1–0	0–1	1–0	0–0	0–1	1–0	3–0	1–1	10– 6
Minton	0–0	0–1	0–0	0–0	0–0	0–1	0–0	0–0	0–0	0–1	0–0	0– 3
Moffitt	0–1	1–2	0–0	0–0	3–1	0–0	0–0	1–0	0–1	0–0	1–1	6– 6
Montefusco	3–1	1–0	2–3	0–1	3–2	1–0	1–1	2–2	1–2	0–1	2–1	16–14
Riccelli	0–0	0–0	0–0	0–1	0–0	0–0	0–0	0–0	0–0	0–0	1–0	1– 1
Toms	0–0	0–0	0–1	0–0	0–0	0–0	0–0	0–0	0–0	0–0	0–0	0– 1
Williams	0–0	0–0	0–0	0–0	1–0	0–0	0–0	0–0	0–0	0–0	1–0	2– 0
Totals	9–9	4–8	9–9	8–10	10–8	5–7	5–7	6–6	3–9	5–7	10–8	74–88

No Decisions: None.

NATIONAL LEAGUE

PENNANT WINNERS

Year—Club	Manager	W.	L.	Pct.	°G.A.
1900—Brooklyn	Edward (Ned) Hanlon	82	54	.603	4½
1901—Pittsburgh	Frederick Clarke	90	49	.647	7½
1902—Pittsburgh	Frederick Clarke	103	36	.741	27½
1903—Pittsburgh	Frederick Clarke	91	49	.650	6½
1904—New York	John McGraw	106	47	.693	13
1905—New York	John McGraw	105	48	.686	9
1906—Chicago	Frank Chance	116	36	.763	20
1907—Chicago	Frank Chance	107	45	.704	17
1908—Chicago	Frank Chance	99	55	.643	1
1909—Pittsburgh	Frederick Clarke	110	42	.724	6½
1910—Chicago	Frank Chance	104	50	.675	13
1911—New York	John McGraw	99	54	.647	7½
1912—New York	John McGraw	103	48	.682	10
1913—New York	John McGraw	101	51	.664	12½
1914—Boston	George Stallings	94	59	.614	10½
1915—Philadelphia	Patrick Moran	90	62	.592	7
1916—Brooklyn	Wilbert Robinson	94	60	.610	2½
1917—New York	John McGraw	98	56	.636	10
1918—Chicago	Fred Mitchell	84	45	.651	10½
1919—Cincinnati	Patrick Moran	96	44	.686	9
1920—Brooklyn	Wilbert Robinson	93	61	.604	7
1921—New York	John McGraw	94	59	.614	4
1922—New York	John McGraw	93	61	.604	7
1923—New York	John McGraw	95	58	.621	4½
1924—New York	John McGraw	93	60	.608	1½
1925—Pittsburgh	William McKechnie	95	58	.621	8½
1926—St. Louis	Rogers Hornsby	89	65	.578	2
1927—Pittsburgh	Owen (Donie) Bush	94	60	.610	1½
1928—St. Louis	William McKechnie	95	59	.617	2
1929—Chicago	Joseph McCarthy	98	54	.645	10½
1930—St. Louis	Charles (Gabby) Street	92	62	.597	2
1931—St. Louis	Charles (Gabby) Street	101	53	.656	13
1932—Chicago	Charles Grimm	90	64	.584	4
1933—New York	William Terry	91	61	.599	5
1934—St. Louis	Frank Frisch	95	58	.621	2
1935—Chicago	Charles Grimm	100	54	.649	4
1936—New York	William Terry	92	62	.597	5
1937—New York	William Terry	95	57	.625	3
1938—Chicago	Charles (Gabby) Hartnett	89	63	.586	2
1939—Cincinnati	William McKechnie	97	57	.630	4½
1940—Cincinnati	William McKechnie	100	53	.654	12
1941—Brooklyn	Leo Durocher	100	54	.649	2½
1942—St. Louis	William Southworth	106	48	.688	2
1943—St. Louis	William Southworth	105	49	.682	18
1944—St. Louis	William Southworth	105	49	.682	14½
1945—Chicago	Charles Grimm	98	56	.636	3
1946—St. Louis†	Edwin Dyer	98	58	.628	2
1947—Brooklyn	Burton Shotton	94	60	.610	5
1948—Boston	William Southworth	91	62	.595	6½
1949—Brooklyn	Burton Shotton	97	57	.630	1
1950—Philadelphia	Edwin Sawyer	91	63	.591	2
1951—New York‡	Leo Durocher	98	59	.624	1
1952—Brooklyn	Charles Dressen	96	57	.627	4½
1953—Brooklyn	Charles Dressen	105	49	.682	13
1954—New York	Leo Durocher	97	57	.630	5
1955—Brooklyn	Walter Alston	98	55	.641	13½
1956—Brooklyn	Walter Alston	93	61	.604	1
1957—Milwaukee	Fred Haney	95	59	.617	8
1958—Milwaukee	Fred Haney	92	62	.597	8
1959—Los Angeles§	Walter Alston	88	68	.564	2

PENNANT WINNERS—Continued

Year Club	Manager	W.	L.	Pct.	°G.A.
1960—Pittsburgh	Daniel Murtaugh	95	59	.617	7
1961—Cincinnati	Frederick Hutchinson	93	61	.604	4
1962—San Francisco x	Alvin Dark	103	62	.624	1
1963—Los Angeles	Walter Alston	99	63	.611	6
1964—St. Louis	John Keane	93	69	.574	1
1965—Los Angeles	Walter Alston	97	65	.599	2
1966—Los Angeles	Walter Alston	95	67	.586	1½
1967—St. Louis	Albert (Red) Schoendienst	101	60	.627	10½
1968—St. Louis	Albert (Red) Schoendienst	97	65	.599	9
1969—New York (E)°°	Gilbert Hodges	100	62	.617	8
1970—Cincinnati (W)°°	George (Sparky) Anderson	102	60	.630	14½
1971—Pittsburgh (E)°°	Daniel Murtaugh	97	65	.599	7
1972—Cincinnati (W)°°	George (Sparky) Anderson	95	59	.617	10½
1973—New York (E)°°	Lawrence (Yogi) Berra	82	79	.509	1½
1974—Los Angeles (W)°°	Walter Alston	102	60	.630	4
1975—Cincinnati (W)°°	George (Sparky) Anderson	108	54	.667	20
1976—Cincinnati (W)°°	George (Sparky) Anderson	102	60	.630	10

*Games ahead of second-place club. †Defeated Brooklyn, two games to none, in playoff for pennant. ‡Defeated Brooklyn, two games to one, in playoff for pennant. §Defeated Milwaukee, two games to none, in playoff for pennant. xDefeated Los Angeles, two games to one, in playoff for pennant. °°Won Championship Series.

YEARLY FINISHES

Year	Atl.	Chi.	Cin.	Hou.	L.A.	N.Y.	Phil.	Pitt.	St.L.	S.F.
1900	°4	x5	7	....	†1	....	3	2	x5	‡8
1901	°5	6	8	....	†3	....	2	1	4	‡7
1902	°3	5	4	....	†2	....	7	1	6	‡8
1903	°6	3	4	....	†5	....	7	1	8	‡2
1904	°7	2	3	....	†6	....	8	4	5	‡1
1905	°7	3	5	....	†8	....	4	2	6	‡1
1906	°8	1	6	....	†5	....	4	3	7	‡2
1907	°7	1	6	....	†5	....	3	2	8	‡4
1908	°6	1	5	....	†7	....	4	x2	8	x‡2
1909	°8	2	4	....	†6	....	5	1	7	‡3
1910	°8	1	5	....	†6	....	4	3	7	‡2
1911	°8	2	6	....	†7	....	4	3	5	‡1
1912	°8	3	4	....	†7	....	5	2	6	‡1
1913	°5	3	7	....	†6	....	2	4	8	‡1
1914	°1	4	8	....	†5	....	6	7	3	‡2
1915	°2	4	7	....	†3	....	1	5	6	‡8
1916	°3	5	x7	....	†1	....	2	6	x7	‡4
1917	°6	5	4	....	†7	....	2	8	3	‡1
1918	°7	1	3	....	†5	....	6	4	8	‡2
1919	°6	3	1	....	†5	....	8	4	7	‡2
1920	°7	x5	3	....	†1	....	8	4	x5	‡2
1921	°4	7	6	....	†5	....	8	2	3	‡1
1922	°8	5	2	....	†6	....	7	x3	x3	‡1
1923	°7	4	2	....	†6	....	8	3	5	‡1
1924	°8	5	4	....	†2	....	7	3	6	‡1
1925	°5	8	3	....	x†6	....	x6	1	4	‡2
1926	°7	4	2	....	†6	....	8	3	1	‡5
1927	°7	4	5	....	†6	....	8	1	2	‡3
1928	°7	3	5	....	†6	....	8	4	1	‡2
1929	°8	1	7	....	†6	....	5	2	4	‡3
1930	°6	2	7	....	†4	....	8	5	1	‡3
1931	°7	3	8	....	†4	....	6	5	1	‡2
1932	°5	1	8	....	†3	....	4	2	x6	x‡6
1933	°4	3	8	....	†6	....	7	2	5	‡1
1934	°4	3	8	....	†6	....	7	5	1	‡2
1935	°8	1	6	....	†5	....	7	4	2	‡3
1936	°6	x2	5	....	†7	....	8	4	x2	‡1
1937	°5	2	8	....	†6	....	7	3	4	‡1
1938	°5	1	4	....	†7	....	8	2	6	‡3
1939	°7	4	1	....	†3	....	8	6	2	‡5

YEARLY FINISHES—Continued

Year	Atl.	Chi.	Cin.	Hous.	L.A.	N.Y.	Phil.	Pitt.	St.L.	S.F.
1940	*7	5	1	....	†2	....	8	4	3	‡6
1941	*7	6	3	....	†1	....	8	4	2	‡5
1942	*7	6	4	....	†2	....	8	5	1	‡3
1943	*6	5	2	....	†3	....	7	4	1	‡8
1944	*6	4	3	....	†7	....	8	2	1	‡5
1945	*6	1	7	....	†3	....	8	4	2	‡5
1946	*4	3	6	....	†2	....	5	7	1	‡8
1947	*3	6	5	....	†1	....	x7	x7	2	‡4
1948	*1	8	7	....	†3	....	6	4	2	‡5
1949	*4	8	7	....	†1	....	3	6	2	‡5
1950	*4	7	6	....	†2	....	1	8	5	‡3
1951	*4	8	6	....	†2	....	5	7	3	‡1
1952	*7	5	6	....	†1	....	4	8	3	‡2
1953	*2	7	6	....	†1	....	x3	8	x3	‡5
1954	*3	7	5	....	†2	....	4	8	6	‡1
1955	*2	6	5	....	†1	....	4	8	7	‡3
1956	*2	8	3	....	†1	....	5	7	4	‡6
1957	*1	x7	4	....	†3	....	5	x7	2	‡6
1958	*1	x5	4	....	7	....	8	2	x5	3
1959	*2	x5	x5	....	1	....	8	4	7	3
1960	*2	7	6	....	4	....	8	1	3	5
1961	*4	7	1	....	2	....	8	6	5	3
1962	*5	9	3	8	2	10	7	4	6	1
1963	*6	7	5	9	1	10	4	8	2	3
1964	*5	8	x2	9	x6	10	x2	x6	1	4
1965	*5	8	4	9	1	10	6	3	7	2
1966	5	10	7	8	1	9	4	3	6	2
1967	7	3	4	9	8	10	5	6	1	2
1968	5	3	4	10	x7	9	x7	6	1	2

	EAST DIVISION						WEST DIVISION				
Year	Chi.	Mon.	N.Y.	Phila.	Pitt.	St.L.	Atl.	Cin.	Hous.	L.A.	S.D.	S.F.
1969	2	6	1	5	3	4	1	3	5	4	6	2
1970	2	6	3	5	1	4	5	1	4	2	6	3
1971	x3	5	x3	6	1	2	3	x4	x4	2	6	1
1972	2	5	3	6	1	4	4	1	2	3	6	5
1973	5	4	1	6	3	2	5	1	4	2	6	3
1974	6	4	5	3	1	2	3	2	4	1	6	5
1975	x5	x5	x3	2	1	x3	5	1	6	2	4	3
1976	4	6	3	1	2	5	6	1	3	2	5	4

*Record of predecessor Boston (1900-1952) and Milwaukee (1953-1965) clubs; †Brooklyn club; ‡New York Giants. xTied for position.

LEADING BATSMEN

Year Player and Club	G.	AB.	R.	H.	TB.	2B.	3B.	HR.	RBI.	B.A.
1900—John (Honus) Wagner, Pittsburgh	134	528	107	201	302	45	22	4	....	.381
1901—Jesse Burkett, St. Louis	142	597	139	228	313	21	17	10	....	.382
1902—Clarence Beaumont, Pittsburgh	131	544	101	194	227	21	6	0	....	.357
1903—John (Honus) Wagner, Pittsburgh	129	512	97	182	265	30	19	5	....	.355
1904—John (Honus) Wagner, Pittsburgh	132	490	97	171	255	44	14	4	....	.349
1905—J. Bentley Seymour, Cincinnati	149	581	95	219	325	40	21	8	....	.377
1906—John (Honus) Wagner, Pittsburgh	140	516	103	175	237	38	9	2	....	.339
1907—John (Honus) Wagner, Pittsburgh	142	515	98	180	264	38	14	6	91	.350
1908—John (Honus) Wagner, Pittsburgh	151	568	100	201	308	39	19	10	106	.354
1909—John (Honus) Wagner, Pittsburgh	137	495	92	168	242	39	10	5	102	.339
1910—Sherwood Magee, Philadelphia	154	519	110	172	263	39	17	6	116	.331
1911—John (Honus) Wagner, Pittsburgh	130	473	87	158	240	23	16	9	108	.334
1912—Henry Zimmerman, Chicago	145	557	95	207	318	41	14	14	98	.372
1913—Jacob Daubert, Brooklyn	139	508	76	178	215	17	7	2	46	.350
1914—Jacob Daubert, Brooklyn	126	474	89	156	205	17	7	6	44	.329
1915—Lawrence Doyle, New York	150	591	86	189	261	40	10	4	68	.320
1916—Harold Chase, Cincinnati	142	542	66	184	249	29	12	4	84	.339
1917—Edd Roush, Cincinnati	136	522	82	178	237	19	14	4	62	.341

LEADING BATSMEN—Continued

Year	Player and Club	G.	AB.	R.	H.	TB.	2B.	3B.	HR.	RBI.	B.A.
1918	Zachariah Wheat, Brooklyn	105	409	39	137	158	15	3	0	48	.335
1919	Edd Roush, Cincinnati	133	504	73	162	216	19	13	3	69	.321
1920	Rogers Hornsby, St. Louis	149	589	96	218	329	44	20	9	94	.370
1921	Rogers Hornsby, St. Louis	154	592	131	235	378	44	18	21	126	.397
1922	Rogers Hornsby, St. Louis	154	623	141	250	450	46	14	42	152	.401
1923	Rogers Hornsby, St. Louis	107	424	89	163	266	32	10	17	83	.384
1924	Rogers Hornsby, St. Louis	143	536	121	227	373	43	14	25	94	.424
1925	Rogers Hornsby, St. Louis	138	504	133	203	381	41	10	39	143	.403
1926	Eugene Hargrave, Cincinnati	105	326	42	115	171	22	8	6	62	.353
1927	Paul Waner, Pittsburgh	155	623	113	237	338	40	17	9	131	.380
1928	Rogers Hornsby, Boston	140	486	99	188	307	42	7	21	94	.387
1929	Frank O'Doul, Philadelphia	154	638	152	254	397	35	6	32	122	.398
1930	William Terry, New York	154	633	139	254	392	39	15	23	129	.401
1931	Chas. (Chick) Hafey, St. Louis	122	450	94	157	256	35	8	16	95	.349
1932	Frank O'Doul, Brooklyn	148	595	120	219	330	32	8	21	90	.368
1933	Charles Klein, Philadelphia	152	606	101	223	365	44	7	28	120	.368
1934	Paul Waner, Pittsburgh	146	599	122	217	323	32	16	14	90	.362
1935	J. Floyd (Arky) Vaughan, Pittsburgh	137	499	108	192	303	34	10	19	99	.385
1936	Paul Waner, Pittsburgh	148	585	107	218	304	53	9	5	94	.373
1937	Joseph Medwick, St. Louis	156	633	111	237	406	56	10	31	154	.374
1938	Ernest Lombardi, Cincinnati	129	489	60	167	256	30	1	19	95	.342
1939	John Mize, St. Louis	153	564	104	197	353	44	14	28	108	.349
1940	Debs Garms, Pittsburgh	103	358	76	127	179	23	7	5	57	.355
1941	Harold (Pete) Reiser, Brooklyn	137	536	117	184	299	39	17	14	76	.343
1942	Ernest Lombardi, Boston	105	309	32	102	149	14	0	11	46	.330
1943	Stanley Musial, St. Louis	157	617	108	220	347	48	20	13	81	.357
1944	Fred (Dixie) Walker, Brooklyn	147	535	77	191	283	37	8	13	91	.357
1945	Philip Cavarretta, Chicago	132	498	94	177	249	34	10	6	97	.355
1946	Stanley Musial, St. Louis	156	624	124	228	366	50	20	16	103	.365
1947	Harry Walker, St. Louis-Phila.	140	513	81	186	250	29	16	1	41	.363
1948	Stanley Musial, St. Louis	155	611	135	230	429	46	18	39	131	.376
1949	Jack Robinson, Brooklyn	156	593	122	203	313	38	12	16	124	.342
1950	Stanley Musial, St. Louis	146	555	105	192	331	41	7	28	109	.346
1951	Stanley Musial, St. Louis	152	578	124	205	355	30	12	32	108	.355
1952	Stanley Musial, St. Louis	154	578	105	194	311	42	6	21	91	.336
1953	Carl Furillo, Brooklyn	132	479	82	165	278	38	6	21	92	.344
1954	Willie Mays, New York	151	565	119	195	377	33	13	41	110	.345
1955	Richie Ashburn, Philadelphia	140	533	91	180	239	32	9	3	42	.338
1956	Henry Aaron, Milwaukee	153	609	106	200	340	34	14	26	92	.328
1957	Stanley Musial, St. Louis	134	502	82	176	307	38	3	29	102	.351
1958	Richie Ashburn, Philadelphia	152	615	98	215	271	24	13	2	33	.350
1959	Henry Aaron, Milwaukee	154	629	116	223	400	46	7	39	123	.355
1960	Richard Groat, Pittsburgh	138	573	85	186	226	26	4	2	50	.325
1961	Roberto Clemente, Pittsburgh	146	572	100	201	320	30	10	23	89	.351
1962	H. Thomas Davis, Los Angeles	163	665	120	230	356	27	9	27	153	.346
1963	H. Thomas Davis, Los Angeles	146	556	69	181	254	19	3	16	88	.326
1964	Roberto Clemente, Pittsburgh	155	622	95	211	301	40	7	12	87	.339
1965	Roberto Clemente, Pittsburgh	152	589	91	194	273	21	14	10	65	.329
1966	Mateo Alou, Pittsburgh	141	535	86	183	225	18	9	2	27	.342
1967	Roberto Clemente, Pittsburgh	147	585	103	209	324	26	10	23	110	.357
1968	Peter Rose, Cincinnati	149	626	94	210	294	42	6	10	49	.335
1969	Peter Rose, Cincinnati	156	627	120	218	321	33	11	16	82	.348
1970	Ricardo Carty, Atlanta	136	478	84	175	279	23	3	25	101	.366
1971	Joseph Torre, St. Louis	161	634	97	230	352	34	8	24	137	.363
1972	Billy L. Williams, Chicago	150	574	95	191	348	34	6	37	122	.333
1973	Peter Rose, Cincinnati	160	680	115	230	297	36	8	5	64	.338
1974	Ralph Garr, Atlanta	143	606	87	214	305	24	17	11	54	.353
1975	Bill Madlock, Chicago	130	514	77	182	246	29	7	7	64	.354
1976	Bill Madlock, Chicago	142	514	68	174	257	36	1	15	84	.339

LEADERS IN RUNS SCORED

Year	Player and Club	Runs	Year	Player and Club	Runs
1900	Roy Thomas, Philadelphia	131	1903	Clarence Beaumont, Pittsburgh	137
1901	Jesse Burkett, St. Louis	139	1904	George Browne, New York	99
1902	John (Honus) Wagner, Pittsburgh	105	1905	Michael Donlin, New York	124

LEADERS IN RUNS SCORED—Continued

Year	Player and Club	Runs
1906—	John (Honus) Wagner, Pittsburgh	103
	Frank Chance, Chicago	103
1907—	W. Porter Shannon, New York	104
1908—	Frederick Tenney, New York	101
1909—	Thomas Leach, Pittsburgh	126
1910—	Sherwood Magee, Philadelphia	110
1911—	James Sheckard, Chicago	121
1912—	Robert Bescher, Cincinnati	120
1913—	Thomas Leach, Chicago	99
	Max Carey, Pittsburgh	99
1914—	George Burns, New York	100
1915—	Cliff. (Gavvy) Cravath, Philadelphia	89
1916—	George Burns, New York	105
1917—	George Burns, New York	103
1918—	Henry Groh, Cincinnati	88
1919—	George Burns, New York	86
1920—	George Burns, New York	115
1921—	Rogers Hornsby, St. Louis	131
1922—	Rogers Hornsby, St. Louis	141
1923—	Ross Youngs, New York	121
1924—	Frank Frisch, New York	121
	Rogers Hornsby, St. Louis	121
1925—	Hazen (Kiki) Cuyler, Pittsburgh	144
1926—	Hazen (Kiki) Cuyler, Pittsburgh	113
1927—	Lloyd Waner, Pittsburgh	133
	Rogers Hornsby, New York	133
1928—	Paul Waner, Pittsburgh	142
1929—	Rogers Hornsby, Chicago	156
1930—	Charles (Chuck) Klein, Philadelphia	158
1931—	Terry, New York-Klein, Philadelphia	121
1932—	Charles (Chuck) Klein, Philadelphia	152
1933—	John (Pepper) Martin, St. Louis	122
1934—	Paul Waner, Pittsburgh	122
1935—	August Galan, Chicago	133
1936—	J. Floyd (Arky) Vaughan, Pittsburgh	122
1937—	Joseph Medwick, St. Louis	111
1938—	Melvin Ott, New York	116
1939—	William Werber, Cincinnati	115
1940—	J. Floyd (Arky) Vaughan, Pittsburgh	113

Year	Player and Club	Runs
1941—	Harold (Pete) Reiser, Brooklyn	117
1942—	Melvin Ott, New York	118
1943—	J. Floyd (Arky) Vaughan, Brooklyn	112
1944—	William Nicholson, Chicago	116
1945—	Edward Stanky, Brooklyn	128
1946—	Stanley Musial, St. Louis	124
1947—	John Mize, New York	137
1948—	Stanley Musial, St. Louis	135
1949—	Harold (Pee Wee) Reese, Brooklyn	132
1950—	C. Earl Torgeson, Boston	120
1951—	Musial, St. Louis-Kiner, Pittsburgh	124
1952—	Musial, St. Louis-Hemus, St. Louis	105
1953—	Edwin (Duke) Snider, Brooklyn	132
1954—	Musial, St. Louis-Snider, Brooklyn	120
1955—	Edwin (Duke) Snider, Brooklyn	126
1956—	Frank Robinson, Cincinnati	122
1957—	Henry Aaron, Milwaukee	118
1958—	Willie Mays, San Francisco	121
1959—	Vada Pinson, Cincinnati	131
1960—	William Bruton, Milwaukee	112
1961—	Willie Mays, San Francisco	129
1962—	Frank Robinson, Cincinnati	134
1963—	Henry Aaron, Milwaukee	121
1964—	Richard Allen, Philadelphia	125
1965—	Tommy Harper, Cincinnati	126
1966—	Felipe Alou, Atlanta	122
1967—	Henry Aaron, Atlanta	113
	Louis Brock, St. Louis	113
1968—	Glenn Beckert, Chicago	98
1969—	Bobby Bonds, San Francisco	120
	Peter Rose, Cincinnati	120
1970—	Billy Williams, Chicago	137
1971—	Louis Brock, St. Louis	126
1972—	Joe Morgan, Cincinnati	122
1973—	Bobby Bonds, San Francisco	131
1974—	Peter Rose, Cincinnati	110
1975—	Peter Rose, Cincinnati	112
1976—	Peter Rose, Cincinnati	130

LEADERS IN HITS

Year	Player and Club	Hits
1900—	William Keeler, Brooklyn	208
1901—	Jesse Burkett, St. Louis	228
1902—	Clarence Beaumont, Pittsburgh	194
1903—	Clarence Beaumont, Pittsburgh	209
1904—	Clarence Beaumont, Pittsburgh	185
1905—	J. Bentley Seymour, Cincinnati	219
1906—	Harry Steinfeldt, Chicago	176
1907—	Clarence Beaumont, Boston	187
1908—	John (Honus) Wagner, Pittsburgh	201
1909—	Lawrence Doyle, New York	172
1910—	John (Honus) Wagner, Pittsburgh	178
	Robert Byrne, Pittsburgh	178
1911—	Roy Miller, Boston	192
1912—	Henry Zimmerman, Chicago	207
1913—	Cliff. (Gavvy) Cravath, Philadelphia	179
1914—	Sherwood Magee, Philadelphia	171
1915—	Lawrence Doyle, New York	189
1916—	Harold Chase, Cincinnati	184
1917—	Henry Groh, Cincinnati	182
1918—	Charles Hollocher, Chicago	161
1919—	Ivy Olson, Brooklyn	164

Year	Player and Club	Hits
1920—	Rogers Hornsby, St. Louis	218
1921—	Rogers Hornsby, St. Louis	235
1922—	Rogers Hornsby, St. Louis	250
1923—	Frank Frisch, New York	223
1924—	Rogers Hornsby, St. Louis	227
1925—	James Bottomley, St. Louis	227
1926—	Edward Brown, Boston	201
1927—	Paul Waner, Pittsburgh	237
1928—	Fred Lindstrom, New York	231
1929—	Frank O'Doul, Philadelphia	254
1930—	William Terry, New York	254
1931—	Lloyd Waner, Pittsburgh	214
1932—	Charles Klein, Philadelphia	226
1933—	Charles Klein, Philadelphia	223
1934—	Paul Waner, Pittsburgh	217
1935—	William Herman, Chicago	227
1936—	Joseph Medwick, St. Louis	223
1937—	Joseph Medwick, St. Louis	237
1938—	Frank McCormick, Cincinnati	209
1939—	Frank McCormick, Cincinnati	209
1940—	Stanley Hack, Chicago	191

LEADERS IN HITS—Continued

Year	Player and Club	Hits
	Frank McCormick, Cincinnati	191
1941—	Stanley Hack, Chicago	186
1942—	Enos Slaughter, St. Louis	188
1943—	Stanley Musial, St. Louis	220
1944—	Musial, St. Louis-Cavarretta, Chicago	197
1945—	Thomas Holmes, Boston	224
1946—	Stanley Musial, St. Louis	228
1947—	Thomas Holmes, Boston	191
1948—	Stanley Musial, St. Louis	230
1949—	Stanley Musial, St. Louis	207
1950—	Edwin (Duke) Snider, Brooklyn	199
1951—	Richie Ashburn, Philadelphia	221
1952—	Stanley Musial, St. Louis	194
1953—	Richie Ashburn, Philadelphia	205
1954—	Donald Mueller, New York	212
1955—	Theodore Kluszewski, Cincinnati	192
1956—	Henry Aaron, Milwaukee	200
1957—	Al (Red) Schoendienst, N.Y.-Mil.	200
1958—	Richie Ashburn, Philadelphia	215
1959—	Henry Aaron, Milwaukee	223

Year	Player and Club	Hits
1960—	Willie Mays, San Francisco	190
1961—	Vada Pinson, Cincinnati	208
1962—	H. Thomas Davis, Los Angeles	230
1963—	Vada Pinson, Cincinnati	204
1964—	Clemente, Pittsburgh-Flood, St. Louis	211
1965—	Peter Rose, Cincinnati	209
1966—	Felipe Alou, Atlanta	218
1967—	Roberto Clemente, Pittsburgh	209
1968—	Felipe Alou, Atlanta	210
	Peter Rose, Cincinnati	210
1969—	Mateo Alou, Pittsburgh	231
1970—	Peter Rose, Cincinnati	205
	Billy Williams, Chicago	205
1971—	Joseph Torre, St. Louis	230
1972—	Peter Rose, Cincinnati	198
1973—	Peter Rose, Cincinnati	230
1974—	Ralph Garr, Atlanta	214
1975—	David Cash, Philadelphia	213
1976—	Peter Rose, Cincinnati	215

ONE-BASE HIT LEADERS

Year	Player and Club	1B.
1900—	William H. Keeler, Brooklyn	179
1901—	Jesse C. Burkett, St. Louis	180
1902—	Clarence H. Beaumont, Pittsburgh	167
1903—	Clarence H. Beaumont, Pittsburgh	166
1904—	Clarence H. Beaumont, Pittsburgh	158
1905—	Michael J. Donlin, New York	162
1906—	Miller J. Huggins, Cincinnati	141
	William P. Shannon, St. Louis-NY	141
1907—	Clarence H. Beaumont, Pittsburgh	150
1908—	Michael J. Donlin, New York	153
1909—	Edward L. Grant, Philadelphia	147
1910—	Edward L. Grant, Philadelphia	134
1911—	Jacob E. Daubert, Brooklyn	146
	Roy O. Miller, Boston	146
1912—	William J. Sweeney, Boston	159
1913—	Jacob E. Daubert, Brooklyn	152
1914—	Beals Becker, Philadelphia	128
1915—	Lawrence J. Doyle, New York	135
1916—	David A. Robertson, New York	142
1917—	Benjamin M. Kauff, New York	141
	Edd J. Roush, Cincinnati	141
1918—	Charles J. Hollocher, Chicago	130
1919—	Ivan M. Olson, Brooklyn	140
1920—	Milton J. Stock, St. Louis	170
1921—	Carson L. Bigbee, Pittsburgh	161
1922—	Carson L. Bigbee, Pittsburgh	166
1923—	Frank F. Frisch, New York	169
1924—	Zachariah Wheat, Brooklyn	149
1925—	Milton J. Stock, Brooklyn	164
1926—	Edward W. Brown, Boston	160
1927—	Lloyd J. Waner, Pittsburgh	198
1928—	Lloyd J. Waner, Pittsburgh	180
1929—	Frank J. O'Doul, Philadelphia	181
	Lloyd J. Waner, Pittsburgh	181
1930—	William H. Terry, New York	177
1931—	Lloyd J. Waner, Pittsburgh	172
1932—	Frank J. O'Doul, Brooklyn	158
1933—	Charles P. Fullis, Philadelphia	162
1934—	William H. Terry, New York	169
1935—	Forrest D. Jensen, Pittsburgh	160
1936—	Joseph G. Moore, New York	160
1937—	Paul G. Waner, Pittsburgh	178

Year	Player and Club	1B.
1938—	Frank A. McCormick, Cincinnati	160
1939—	John A. Hassett, Boston	162
1940—	Burgess U. Whitehead, New York	141
1941—	Stanley C. Hack, Chicago	141
1942—	Enos B. Slaughter, St. Louis	127
1943—	Nicholas J. Witek, New York	172
1944—	Philip J. Cavarretta, Chicago	142
1945—	Stanley C. Hack, Chicago	155
1946—	Stanley F. Musial, St. Louis	142
1947—	Thomas F. Holmes, Boston	146
1948—	Stanley A. Rojek, Pittsburgh	150
1949—	Albert F. Schoendienst, St. Louis	160
1950—	Edward S. Waitkus, Philadelphia	143
1951—	Richie Ashburn, Philadelphia	181
1952—	Robert H. Adams, Cincinnati	145
1953—	Richie Ashburn, Philadelphia	169
1954—	Donald F. Mueller, New York	165
1955—	Donald F. Mueller, New York	152
1956—	John E. Temole, Cincinnati	157
1957—	Richie Ashburn, Philadelphia	152
1958—	Richie Ashburn, Philadelphia	176
1959—	Don L. Blasingame, St. Louis	144
1960—	Richard M. Groat, Pittsburgh	154
1961—	Vada E. Pinson, Cincinnati	150
	Maurice M. Wills, Los Angeles	150
1962—	Maurice M. Wills, Los Angeles	179
1963—	Curtis C. Flood, St. Louis	152
1964—	Curtis C. Flood, St. Louis	178
1965—	Maurice M. Wills, Los Angeles	165
1966—	Roland T. Jackson, Houston	160
1967—	Maurice M. Wills, Pittsburgh	162
1968—	Curtis C. Flood, St. Louis	160
1969—	Mateo R. Alou, Pittsburgh	183
1970—	Mateo R. Alou, Pittsburgh	171
1971—	Ralph A. Garr, Atlanta	180
1972—	Louis C. Brock, St. Louis	156
1973—	Peter E. Rose, Cincinnati	181
1974—	David Cash, Philadelphia	167
1975—	David Cash, Philadelphia	166
1976—	Guillermo Montanez, San Fran.-Atl.	164

TWO-BASE HIT LEADERS

Year Player and Club	2B.
1900— John (Honus) Wagner, Pittsburgh	45
1901— Wagner, Pitts-Beckley, Cinn	39
1902— John (Honus) Wagner, Pittsburgh	33
1903— Clarke, Pittsburgh-Mertes, New York- Steinfeldt, Cincinnati	32
1904— John (Honus) Wagner, Pittsburgh	44
1905— J. Bentley Seymour, Cincinnati	40
1906— John (Honus) Wagner, Pittsburgh	38
1907— John (Honus) Wagner, Pittsburgh	38
1908— John (Honus) Wagner, Pittsburgh	39
1909— John (Honus) Wagner, Pittsburgh	39
1910— Robert Byrne, Pittsburgh	43
1911— Edward Konetchy, St. Louis	38
1912— Henry Zimmerman, Chicago	41
1913— J. Carlisle Smith, Brooklyn	40
1914— Sherwood Magee, Philadelphia	39
1915— Lawrence Doyle, New York	40
1916— O. Albert Niehoff, Philadelphia	42
1917— Henry Groh, Cincinnati	39
1918— Henry Groh, Cincinnati	28
1919— Ross Youngs, New York	31
1920— Rogers Hornsby, St. Louis	44
1921— Rogers Hornsby, St. Louis	44
1922— Rogers Hornsby, St. Louis	46
1923— Edd Roush, Cincinnati	41
1924— Rogers Hornsby, St. Louis	43
1925— James Bottomley, St. Louis	44
1926— James Bottomley, St. Louis	40
1927— J. Riggs Stephenson, Chicago	46
1928— Paul Waner, Pittsburgh	50
1929— John Frederick, Brooklyn	52
1930— Charles Klein, Philadelphia	59
1931— Earl (Sparky) Adams, St. Louis	46
1932— Paul Waner, Pittsburgh	62
1933— Charles Klein, Philadelphia	44
1934— Cuyler, Chicago-Allen, Philadelphia	42
1935— William Herman, Chicago	57
1936— Joseph Medwick, St. Louis	64
1937— Joseph Medwick, St. Louis	56
1938— Joseph Medwick, St. Louis	47

Year Player and Club	2B.
1939— Enos Slaughter, St. Louis	52
1940— Frank McCormick, Cincinnati	44
1941— Reiser, Brooklyn-Mize, St. Louis	39
1942— Martin Marion, St. Louis	38
1943— Stanley Musial, St. Louis	48
1944— Stanley Musial, St. Louis	51
1945— Thomas Holmes, Boston	47
1946— Stanley Musial, St. Louis	50
1947— Edward Miller, Cincinnati	38
1948— Stanley Musial, St. Louis	46
1949— Stanley Musial, St. Louis	41
1950— Al (Red) Schoendienst, St. Louis	43
1951— Alvin Dark, New York	41
1952— Stanley Musial, St. Louis	42
1953— Stanley Musial, St. Louis	53
1954— Stanley Musial, St. Louis	41
1955— Logan, Milwaukee-Aaron, Milwaukee	37
1956— Henry Aaron, Milwaukee	34
1957— Donald Hoak, Cincinnati	39
1958— Orlando Cepeda, San Francisco	38
1959— Vada Pinson, Cincinnati	47
1960— Vada Pinson, Cincinnati	37
1961— Henry Aaron, Milwaukee	39
1962— Frank Robinson, Cincinnati	51
1963— Richard Groat, St. Louis	43
1964— A. Lee Maye, Milwaukee	44
1965— Henry Aaron, Milwaukee	40
1966— John Callison, Philadelphia	40
1967— Daniel Staub, Houston	44
1968— Louis Brock, St. Louis	46
1969— Mateo Alou, Pittsburgh	41
1970— M. Wesley Parker, Los Angeles	47
1971— Cesar Cedeno, Houston	40
1972— Cesar Cedeno, Houston	39
Guillermo Montanez, Philadelphia	39
1973— Wilver Stargell, Pittsburgh	43
1974— Peter Rose, Cincinnati	45
1975— Peter Rose, Cincinnati	47
1976— Peter Rose, Cincinnati	42

THREE-BASE HIT LEADERS

Year Player and Club	3B.
1900— John (Honus) Wagner, Pittsburgh	22
1901— James Sheckard, Brooklyn	21
1902— Samuel Crawford, Cincinnati	23
1903— John (Honus) Wagner, Pittsburgh	19
1904— Harry Lumley, Brooklyn	18
1905— J. Bentley Seymour, Cincinnati	21
1906— Clarke, Pittsburgh-Schulte, Chicago	13
1907— Ganzel, Cincinnati-Alperman, Brooklyn	16
1908— John (Honus) Wagner, Pittsburgh	19
1909— Michael Mitchell, Cincinnati	17
1910— Michael Mitchell, Cincinnati	18
1911— Lawrence Doyle, New York	25
1912— John (Chief) Wilson, Pittsburgh	36
1913— Victor Saier, Chicago	21
1914— Max Carey, Pittsburgh	17
1915— Thomas Long, St. Louis	25
1916— William Hinchman, Pittsburgh	16
1917— Rogers Hornsby, St. Louis	17
1918— Jacob Daubert, Brooklyn	15
1919— Hi Myers, Brooklyn-Southworth, Pitt.	14
1920— Henry (Hi) Myers, Brooklyn	22

Year Player and Club	3B.
1921— Hornsby, St. Louis-Powell, Boston	18
1922— Jacob Daubert, Cincinnati	22
1923— Carey, Pittsburgh-Traynor, Pittsburgh	19
1924— Edd Roush, Cincinnati	21
1925— Hazen (Kiki) Cuyler, Pittsburgh	26
1926— Paul Waner, Pittsburgh	22
1927— Paul Waner, Pittsburgh	17
1928— James Bottomley, St. Louis	20
1929— Lloyd Waner, Pittsburgh	20
1930— Adam Comorosky, Pittsburgh	23
1931— William Terry, New York	20
1932— Floyd (Babe) Herman, Cincinnati	19
1933— J. Floyd (Arky) Vaughan, Pittsburgh	19
1934— Joseph Medwick, St. Louis	18
1935— Ival Goodman, Cincinnati	18
1936— Ival Goodman, Cincinnati	14
1937— J. Floyd (Arky) Vaughan, Pittsburgh	17
1938— John Mize, St. Louis	16
1939— William Herman, Chicago	18
1940— J. Floyd (Arky) Vaughan, Pittsburgh	15
1941— Harold (Pete) Reiser, Brooklyn	17

THREE-BASE HIT LEADERS—Continued

Year	Player and Club	3B.
1942—	Enos Slaughter, St. Louis	17
1943—	Stanley Musial, St. Louis	20
1944—	John Barrett, Pittsburgh	19
1945—	Luis Olmo, Brooklyn	13
1946—	Stanley Musial, St. Louis	20
1947—	Harry Walker, St. Louis-Philadelphia	16
1948—	Stanley Musial, St. Louis	18
1949—	Musial, St. Louis-Slaughter, St. Louis	13
1950—	Richie Ashburn, Philadelphia	14
1951—	Musial, St. Louis-Bell, Pittsburgh	12
1952—	Robert Thomson, New York	14
1953—	James Gilliam, Brooklyn	17
1954—	Willie Mays, New York	13
1955—	Mays, New York-Long, Pittsburgh	13
1956—	William Bruton, Milwaukee	15
1957—	Willie Mays, New York	20
1958—	Richie Ashburn, Philadelphia	13
1959—	Moon, Los Angeles-Neal, Los Angeles	11
1960—	William Bruton, Milwaukee	13

Year	Player and Club	3B
1961—	George Altman, Chicago	12
1962—	Callison, Philadelphia-Virdon, Pitt.	10
	W. Davis, Wills, Los Angeles	10
1963—	Vada Pinson, Cincinnati	14
1964—	Allen, Philadelphia-Santo, Chicago	13
1965—	John Callison, Philadelphia	16
1966—	J. Timothy McCarver, St. Louis	13
1967—	Vada Pinson, Cincinnati	13
1968—	Louis Brock, St. Louis	14
1969—	Roberto Clemente, Pittsburgh	12
1970—	William Davis, Los Angeles	16
1971—	Joe Morgan, Houston	11
	Roger Metzger, Houston	11
1972—	Lawrence Bowa, Philadelphia	13
1973—	Roger Metzger, Houston	14
1974—	Ralph Garr, Atlanta	17
1975—	Ralph Garr, Atlanta	11
1976—	David Cash, Philadelphia	12

HOME RUN LEADERS

Year	Player and Club	HR.
1900—	Herman Long, Boston	12
1901—	Samuel Crawford, Cincinnati	16
1902—	Thomas Leach, Pittsburgh	6
1903—	James Sheckard, Brooklyn	9
1904—	Harry Lumley, Brooklyn	9
1905—	Fred Odwell, Cincinnati	9
1906—	Timothy Jordan, Brooklyn	12
1907—	David Brain, Boston	10
1908—	Timothy Jordan, Brooklyn	12
1909—	John (Red) Murray, New York	7
1910—	Fred Beck, Bos.-F. Schulte, Chi.	10
1911—	Frank Schulte, Chicago	21
1912—	Henry Zimmerman, Chicago	14
1913—	Cliff. (Gavvy) Cravath, Philadelphia	19
1914—	Cliff. (Gavvy) Cravath, Philadelphia	19
1915—	Cliff. (Gavvy) Cravath, Philadelphia	24
1916—	Robertson, New York-Williams, Chi.	12
1917—	Robertson, New York-Cravath, Phila.	12
1918—	Cliff. (Gavvy) Cravath, Philadelphia	8
1919—	Cliff. (Gavvy) Cravath, Philadelphia	12
1920—	Fred (Cy) Williams, Philadelphia	15
1921—	George Kelly, New York	23
1922—	Rogers Hornsby, St. Louis	42
1923—	Fred (Cy) Williams, Philadelphia	41
1924—	Jacques Fournier, Brooklyn	27
1925—	Rogers Hornsby, St. Louis	39
1926—	Lewis (Hack) Wilson, Chicago	21
1927—	Wilson, Chicago-Williams, Philadelphia	30
1928—	Wilson, Chicago-Bottomley, St. Louis	31
1929—	Charles Klein, Philadelphia	43
1930—	Lewis (Hack) Wilson, Chicago	56
1931—	Charles Klein, Philadelphia	31
1932—	Klein, Philadelphia-Ott, New York	38
1933—	Charles Klein, Philadelphia	28
1934—	Collins, St. Louis-Ott, New York	35
1935—	Walter Berger, Boston	34
1936—	Melvin Ott, New York	33
1937—	Ott, New York-Medwick, St. Louis	31
1938—	Melvin Ott, New York	36

Year	Player and Club	HR.
1939—	John Mize, St. Louis	28
1940—	John Mize, St. Louis	43
1941—	Adolph Camilli, Brooklyn	34
1942—	Melvin Ott, New York	30
1943—	William Nicholson, Chicago	29
1944—	William Nicholson, Chicago	33
1945—	Thomas Holmes, Boston	28
1946—	Ralph Kiner, Pittsburgh	23
1947—	Kiner, Pittsburgh-Mize, New York	51
1948—	Kiner, Pittsburgh-Mize, New York	40
1949—	Ralph Kiner, Pittsburgh	54
1950—	Ralph Kiner, Pittsburgh	47
1951—	Ralph Kiner, Pittsburgh	42
1952—	Kiner, Pittsburgh-Sauer, Chicago	37
1953—	Edwin Mathews, Milwaukee	47
1954—	Theodore Kluszewski, Cincinnati	49
1955—	Willie Mays, New York	51
1956—	Edwin (Duke) Snider, Brooklyn	43
1957—	Henry Aaron, Milwaukee	44
1958—	Ernest Banks, Chicago	47
1959—	Edwin Mathews, Milwaukee	46
1960—	Ernest Banks, Chicago	41
1961—	Orlando Cepeda, San Francisco	46
1962—	Willie Mays, San Francisco	49
1963—	H. Aaron, Milw.-McCovey, San Fran.	44
1964—	Willie Mays, San Francisco	47
1965—	Willie Mays, San Francisco	52
1966—	Henry Aaron, Atlanta	44
1967—	Henry Aaron, Atlanta	39
1968—	Willie McCovey, San Francisco	36
1969—	Willie McCovey, San Francisco	45
1970—	Johnny Bench, Cincinnati	45
1971—	Wilver Stargell, Pittsburgh	48
1972—	Johnny Bench, Cincinnati	40
1973—	Wilver Stargell, Pittsburgh	44
1974—	Michael Schmidt, Philadelphia	36
1975—	Michael Schmidt, Philadelphia	38
1976—	Michael Schmidt, Philadelphia	38

LEADERS IN TOTAL BASES

Year	Player and Club	T.B.
1900—	John (Honus) Wagner, Pittsburgh	302
	Elmer Flick, Philadelphia	302
1901—	Jesse Burkett, St. Louis	314
1902—	Samuel Crawford, Cincinnati	256
1903—	Clarence Beaumont, Pittsburgh	272
1904—	John (Honus) Wagner, Pittsburgh	255
1905—	J. Bentley Seymour, Cincinnati	325
1906—	John (Honus) Wagner, Pittsburgh	237
1907—	John (Honus) Wagner, Pittsburgh	264
1908—	John (Honus) Wagner, Pittsburgh	308
1909—	John (Honus) Wagner, Pittsburgh	242
1910—	Sherwood Magee, Philadelphia	263
1911—	Frank Schulte, Chicago	308
1912—	Henry Zimmerman, Chicago	318
1913—	Cliff (Gavvy) Cravath, Philadelphia	298
1914—	Sherwood Magee, Philadelphia	277
1915—	Cliff (Gavvy) Cravath, Philadelphia	266
1916—	Zachariah Wheat, Brooklyn	262
1917—	Rogers Hornsby, St. Louis	253
1918—	Charles Hollocher, Chicago	202
1919—	Henry (Hi) Myers, Brooklyn	223
1920—	Rogers Hornsby, St. Louis	329
1921—	Rogers Hornsby, St. Louis	378
1922—	Rogers Hornsby, St. Louis	450
1923—	Frank Frisch, New York	311
1924—	Rogers Hornsby, St. Louis	373
1925—	Rogers Hornsby, St. Louis	381
1926—	James Bottomley, St. Louis	305
1927—	Paul Waner, Pittsburgh	338
1928—	James Bottomley, St. Louis	362
1929—	Rogers Hornsby, Chicago	409
1930—	Charles Klein, Philadelphia	445
1931—	Charles Klein, Philadelphia	347
1932—	Charles Klein, Philadelphia	420
1933—	Charles Klein, Philadelphia	365
1934—	James (Rip) Collins, St. Louis	369
1935—	Joseph Medwick, St. Louis	365
1936—	Joseph Medwick, St. Louis	367
1937—	Joseph Medwick, St. Louis	406
1938—	John Mize, St. Louis	326
1939—	John Mize, St. Louis	353
1940—	John Mize, St. Louis	368
1941—	Harold (Pete) Reiser, Brooklyn	299
1942—	Enos Slaughter, St. Louis	292
1943—	Stanley Musial, St. Louis	347
1944—	William Nicholson, Chicago	317
1945—	Thomas Holmes, Boston	367
1946—	Stanley Musial, St. Louis	366
1947—	Ralph Kiner, Pittsburgh	361
1948—	Stanley Musial, St. Louis	429
1949—	Stanley Musial, St. Louis	382
1950—	Edwin (Duke) Snider, Brooklyn	343
1951—	Stanley Musial, St. Louis	355
1952—	Stanley Musial, St. Louis	311
1953—	Edwin (Duke) Snider, Brooklyn	370
1954—	Edwin (Duke) Snider, Brooklyn	378
1955—	Willie Mays, New York	382
1956—	Henry Aaron, Milwaukee	340
1957—	Henry Aaron, Milwaukee	369
1958—	Ernest Banks, Chicago	379
1959—	Henry Aaron, Milwaukee	400
1960—	Henry Aaron, Milwaukee	334
1961—	Henry Aaron, Milwaukee	358
1962—	Willie Mays, San Francisco	382
1963—	Henry Aaron, Milwaukee	370
1964—	Richard Allen, Philadelphia	352
1965—	Willie Mays, San Francisco	360
1966—	Felipe Alou, Atlanta	355
1967—	Henry Aaron, Atlanta	344
1968—	Billy Williams, Chicago	321
1969—	Henry Aaron, Atlanta	332
1970—	Billy Williams, Chicago	373
1971—	Joseph Torre, St. Louis	352
1972—	Billy Williams, Chicago	348
1973—	Bobby Bonds, San Francisco	341
1974—	Johnny Bench, Cincinnati	315
1975—	Gregory Luzinski, Philadelphia	322
1976—	Michael Schmidt, Philadelphia	306

RUNS BATTED IN LEADERS

Year	Player and Club	RBI
1907—	John (Honus) Wagner, Pittsburgh	91
1908—	John (Honus) Wagner, Pittsburgh	106
1909—	John (Honus) Wagner, Pittsburgh	102
1910—	Sherwood Magee, Philadelphia	116
1911—	Frank Schulte, Chicago	121
1912—	Henry Zimmerman, Chicago	98
1913—	Cliff (Gavvy) Cravath, Philadelphia	118
1914—	Sherwood Magee, Philadelphia	101
1915—	Cliff (Gavvy) Cravath, Philadelphia	118
1916—	Harold Chase, Cincinnati	84
1917—	Henry Zimmerman, New York	100
1918—	Frederick Merkle, Chicago	71
1919—	Henry (Hi) Myers, Brooklyn	72
1920—	George Kelly, New York	94
	Rogers Hornsby, St. Louis	94
1921—	Rogers Hornsby, St. Louis	126
1922—	Rogers Hornsby, St. Louis	152
1923—	Emil Meusel, New York	125
1924—	George Kelly, New York	136
1925—	Rogers Hornsby, St. Louis	143
1926—	James Bottomley, St. Louis	120
1927—	Paul Waner, Pittsburgh	131
1928—	James Bottomley, St. Louis	136
1929—	Lewis (Hack) Wilson, Chicago	159
1930—	Lewis (Hack) Wilson, Chicago	190
1931—	Charles Klein, Philadelphia	121
1932—	Frank (Don) Hurst, Philadelphia	143
1933—	Charles Klein, Philadelphia	120
1934—	Melvin Ott, New York	135
1935—	Walter Berger, Boston	130
1936—	Joseph Medwick, St. Louis	138
1937—	Joseph Medwick, St. Louis	154
1938—	Joseph Medwick, St. Louis	122
1939—	Frank McCormick, Cincinnati	128
1940—	John Mize, St. Louis	137
1941—	Adolph Camilli, Brooklyn	120
1942—	John Mize, New York	110
1943—	William Nicholson, Chicago	128
1944—	William Nicholson, Chicago	122
1945—	Fred (Dixie) Walker, Brooklyn	124
1946—	Enos Slaughter, St. Louis	130
1947—	John Mize, New York	138
1948—	Stanley Musial, St. Louis	131
1949—	Ralph Kiner, Pittsburgh	127

RUNS BATTED IN LEADERS—Continued

Year	Player and Club	RBI.
1950—	Delmer Ennis, Philadelphia	126
1951—	Monford Irvin, New York	121
1952—	Henry Sauer, Chicago	121
1953—	Roy Campanella, Brooklyn	142
1954—	Theodore Kluszewski, Cincinnati	141
1955—	Edwin (Duke) Snider, Brooklyn	136
1956—	Stanley Musial, St. Louis	109
1957—	Henry Aaron, Milwaukee	132
1958—	Ernest Banks, Chicago	129
1959—	Ernest Banks, Chicago	143
1960—	Henry Aaron, Milwaukee	126
1961—	Orlando Cepeda, San Francisco	142
1962—	H. Thomas Davis, Los Angeles	153
1963—	Henry Aaron, Milwaukee	130
1964—	Kenton Boyer, St. Louis	119
1965—	Deron Johnson, Cincinnati	130
1966—	Henry Aaron, Atlanta	127
1967—	Orlando Cepeda, St. Louis	111
1968—	Willie McCovey, San Francisco	105
1969—	Willie McCovey, San Francisco	126
1970—	Johnny Bench, Cincinnati	148
1971—	Joseph Torre, St. Louis	137
1972—	Johnny Bench, Cincinnati	125
1973—	Wilver Stargell, Pittsburgh	119
1974—	Johnny Bench, Cincinnati	129
1975—	Gregory Luzinski, Philadelphia	120
1976—	George Foster, Cincinnati	121

Note—Runs batted in not compiled prior to 1907; officially adopted in 1920.

BATTERS LEADING IN BASES ON BALLS

Year	Player and Club	BB.
1910—	Miller Huggins, St. Louis	116
1911—	James Sheckard, Chicago	147
1912—	James Sheckard, Chicago	122
1913—	Robert Bescher, Cincinnati	94
1914—	Miller Huggins, St. Louis	105
1915—	Cliff. (Gavvy) Cravath, Philadelphia	86
1916—	Henry Groh, Cincinnati	84
1917—	George Burns, New York	75
1918—	Max Carey, Pittsburgh	62
1919—	George Burns, New York	82
1920—	George Burns, New York	76
1921—	George Burns, New York	80
1922—	Max Carey, Pittsburgh	80
1923—	George Burns, New York	101
1924—	Rogers Hornsby, St. Louis	89
1925—	Jacques Fournier, Brooklyn	86
1926—	Lewis (Hack) Wilson, Chicago	69
1927—	Rogers Hornsby, New York	86
1928—	Rogers Hornsby, Boston	107
1929—	Melvin Ott, New York	113
1930—	Lewis (Hack) Wilson, Chicago	105
1931—	Melvin Ott, New York	80
1932—	Melvin Ott, New York	100
1933—	Melvin Ott, New York	75
1934—	J. Floyd (Arky) Vaughan, Pittsburgh	94
1935—	J. Floyd (Arky) Vaughan, Pittsburgh	97
1936—	J. Floyd (Arky) Vaughan, Pittsburgh	118
1937—	Melvin Ott, New York	102
1938—	Adolph Camilli, Brooklyn	119
1939—	Adolph Camilli, Brooklyn	110
1940—	Elburt Fletcher, Pittsburgh	119
1941—	Elburt Fletcher, Pittsburgh	118
1942—	Melvin Ott, New York	109
1943—	August Galan, Brooklyn	103
1944—	August Galan, Brooklyn	101
1945—	Edward Stanky, Brooklyn	148
1946—	Edward Stanky, Brooklyn	137
1947—	Henry Greenberg, Pittsburgh	104
	Harold (Pee Wee) Reese, Brooklyn	104
1948—	Robert Elliott, Boston	131
1949—	Ralph Kiner, Pittsburgh	117
1950—	Edward Stanky, New York	144
1951—	Ralph Kiner, Pittsburgh	137
1952—	Ralph Kiner, Pittsburgh	110
1953—	Stanley Musial, St. Louis	105
1954—	Richie Ashburn, Philadelphia	125
1955—	Edwin Mathews, Milwaukee	109
1956—	Edwin (Duke) Snider, Brooklyn	99
1957—	Richie Ashburn, Philadelphia	94
	John Temple, Cincinnati	94
1958—	Richie Ashburn, Philadelphia	97
1959—	James Gilliam, Los Angeles	96
1960—	Richie Ashburn, Chicago	116
1961—	Edwin Mathews, Milwaukee	93
1962—	Edwin Mathews, Milwaukee	101
1963—	Edwin Mathews, Milwaukee	124
1964—	Ronald Santo, Chicago	86
1965—	Joe Morgan, Houston	97
1966—	Ronald Santo, Chicago	95
1967—	Ronald Santo, Chicago	96
1968—	Ronald Santo, Chicago	96
1969—	James Wynn, Houston	148
1970—	Willie McCovey, San Francisco	137
1971—	Willie Mays, San Francisco	112
1972—	Joe Morgan, Cincinnati	115
1973—	Darrell Evans, Atlanta	124
1974—	Darrell Evans, Atlanta	126
1975—	Joe Morgan, Cincinnati	132
1976—	James Wynn, Atlanta	127

Note—Bases on balls not included in batting records in National League prior to 1910.

BATTERS LEADING IN STRiKEOUTS

Year	Player and Club	SO.	Year	Player and Club	SO.
1910—	John Hummell, Brooklyn	81	1943—	Vincent DiMaggio, Pittsburgh	126
1911—	Robert Coulson, Brooklyn	78	1944—	Vincent DiMaggio, Pittsburgh	83
	Robert Bescher, Cincinnati	78	1945—	Vincent DiMaggio, Philadelphia	91
1912—	Edward McDonald, Boston	91	1946—	Ralph Kiner, Pittsburgh	109
1913—	George Burns, New York	74	1947—	William Nicholson, Chicago	83
1914—	Frederick Merkle, New York	80	1948—	Henry Sauer, Cincinnati	85
1915—	H. Douglas Baird, Pittsburgh	88	1949—	Edwin (Duke) Snider, Brooklyn	92
1916—	Cliff. (Gavvy) Cravath, Philadelphia	89	1950—	Roy Smalley, Chicago	114
1917—	Fred Williams, Chicago	78	1951—	Gilbert Hodges, Brooklyn	99
1918—	Ross Youngs, New York	49	1952—	Edwin Mathews, Boston	115
	George Paskert, Chicago	49	1953—	Stephen Bilko, St. Louis	125
1919—	Raymond Powell, Boston	79	1954—	Edwin (Duke) Snider, Brooklyn	96
1920—	George Kelly, New York	92	1955—	Walter Post, Cincinnati	102
1921—	Raymond Powell, Boston	85	1956—	Walter Post, Cincinnati	124
1922—	Frank Parkinson, Philadelphia	93	1957—	Edwin (Duke) Snider, Brooklyn	104
1923—	George Grantham, Chicago	92	1958—	Harry Anderson, Philadelphia	95
1924—	George Grantham, Chicago	63	1959—	Walter Post, Philadelphia	101
1925—	Chas. (Gabby) Hartnett, Chicago	77	1960—	J. Francisco Herrera, Philadelphia	136
1926—	Bernard Friberg, Philadelphia	77	1961—	Richard Stuart, Pittsburgh	121
1927—	Lewis (Hack) Wilson, Chicago	70	1962—	Kenneth Hubbs, Chicago	129
1928—	Lewis (Hack) Wilson, Chicago	94	1963—	Donn Clendenon, Pittsburgh	136
1929—	Lewis (Hack) Wilson, Chicago	83	1964—	Richard Allen, Philadelphia	138
1930—	Lewis (Hack) Wilson, Chicago	84	1965—	Richard Allen, Philadelphia	150
1931—	H. Nicholas Cullop, Cincinnati	86	1966—	Byron Browne, Chicago	143
1932—	Lewis (Hack) Wilson, Brooklyn	85	1967—	James Wynn, Houston	137
1933—	Walter Berger, Boston	77	1968—	Donn Clendenon, Pittsburgh	163
1934—	Adolph Camilli, Chicago-Philadelphia	94	1969—	Bobby Bonds, San Francisco	187
1935—	Adolph Camilli, Philadelphia	113	1970—	Bobby Bonds, San Francisco	189
1936—	Wilbur Brubaker, Pittsburgh	96	1971—	Wilver Stargell, Pittsburgh	154
1937—	Vincent DiMaggio, Boston	111	1972—	Lee May, Houston	145
1938—	Vincent DiMaggio, Boston	134	1973—	Bobby Bonds, San Francisco	148
1939—	Adolph Camilli, Brooklyn	107	1974—	Michael Schmidt, Philadelphia	138
1940—	Chester Ross, Boston	128	1975—	Michael Schmidt, Philadelphia	180
1941—	Adolph Camilli, Brooklyn	115	1976—	Michael Schmidt, Philadelphia	149
1942—	Vincent DiMaggio, Pittsburgh	87			

Note—Strikeouts not included in batting records in National League prior to 1910.

LEADING BASE STEALERS

Year	Player and Club	SB.	Year	Player and Club	SB.
1900—	James Barrett, Cincinnati	46	1924—	Max Carey, Pittsburgh	49
1901—	John (Honus) Wagner, Pittsburgh	48	1925—	Max Carey, Pittsburgh	46
1902—	John (Honus) Wagner, Pittsburgh	43	1926—	Hazen (Kiki) Cuyler, Pittsburgh	35
1903—	Sheckard, Brooklyn-Chance, Chicago	67	1927—	Frank Frisch, St. Louis	48
1904—	John (Honus) Wagner, Pittsburgh	58	1928—	Hazen (Kiki) Cuyler, Chicago	37
1905—	Maloney, Chicago-Devlin, New York	59	1929—	Hazen (Kiki) Cuyler, Chicago	43
1906—	Frank Chance, Chicago	57	1930—	Hazen (Kiki) Cuyler, Chicago	37
1907—	John (Honus) Wagner, Pittsburgh	61	1931—	Frank Frisch, St. Louis	28
1908—	John (Honus) Wagner, Pittsburgh	53	1932—	Charles Klein, Philadelphia	20
1909—	Robert Bescher, Cincinnati	54	1933—	John (Pepper) Martin, St. Louis	26
1910—	Robert Bescher, Cincinnati	70	1934—	John (Pepper) Martin, St. Louis	23
1911—	Robert Bescher, Cincinnati	80	1935—	August Galan, Chicago	22
1912—	Robert Bescher, Cincinnati	67	1936—	John (Pepper) Martin, St. Louis	23
1913—	Max Carey, Pittsburgh	61	1937—	August Galan, Chicago	23
1914—	George Burns, New York	62	1938—	Stanley Hack, Chicago	16
1915—	Max Carey, Pittsburgh	36	1939—	Hack, Chicago-Handley, Pittsburgh	17
1916—	Max Carey, Pittsburgh	63	1940—	Linus Frey, Cincinnati	22
1917—	Max Carey, Pittsburgh	46	1941—	Daniel Murtaugh, Philadelphia	18
1918—	Max Carey, Pittsburgh	58	1942—	Harold (Pete) Reiser, Brooklyn	20
1919—	George Burns, New York	40	1943—	J. Floyd (Arky) Vaughan, Brooklyn	20
1920—	Max Carey, Pittsburgh	52	1944—	John Barrett, Pittsburgh	28
1921—	Frank Frisch, New York	49	1945—	Al. (Red) Schoendienst, St. Louis	26
1922—	Max Carey, Pittsburgh	51	1946—	Harold (Pete) Reiser, Brooklyn	34
1923—	Max Carey, Pittsburgh	51	1947—	Jack Robinson, Brooklyn	29

LEADING BASE STEALERS—Continued

Year	Player and Club	SB.
1948—	Richie Ashburn, Philadelphia	32
1949—	Jack Robinson, Brooklyn	37
1950—	Samuel Jethroe, Boston	35
1951—	Samuel Jethroe, Boston	35
1952—	Harold (Pee Wee) Reese, Brooklyn	30
1953—	William Bruton, Milwaukee	26
1954—	William Bruton, Milwaukee	34
1955—	William Bruton, Milwaukee	35
1956—	Willie Mays, New York	40
1957—	Willie Mays, New York	38
1958—	Willie Mays, San Francisco	31
1959—	Willie Mays, San Francisco	27
1960—	Maurice Wills, Los Angeles	50
1961—	Maurice Wills, Los Angeles	35
1962—	Maurice Wills, Los Angeles	104
1963—	Maurice Wills, Los Angeles	40
1964—	Maurice Wills, Los Angeles	53
1965—	Maurice Wills, Los Angeles	94
1966—	Louis Brock, St. Louis	74
1967—	Louis Brock, St. Louis	52
1968—	Louis Brock, St. Louis	62
1969—	Louis Brock, St. Louis	53
1970—	Robert Tolan, Cincinnati	57
1971—	Louis Brock, St. Louis	64
1972—	Louis Brock, St. Louis	63
1973—	Louis Brock, St. Louis	70
1974—	Louis Brock, St. Louis	118
1975—	David Lopes, Los Angeles	77
1976—	David Lopes, Los Angeles	63

SLUGGING LEADERS

Year	Player and Club	Slug. Avg.
1900—	John (Honus) Wagner, Pittsburgh	.572
1901—	James Sheckard, Brooklyn	.536
1902—	John (Honus) Wagner, Pittsburgh	.467
1903—	Fred Clarke, Pittsburgh	.532
1904—	John (Honus) Wagner, Pittsburgh	.520
1905—	J. Bentley Seymour, Cincinnati	.559
1906—	Harry Lumley, Brooklyn	.477
1907—	John (Honus) Wagner, Pittsburgh	.513
1908—	John (Honus) Wagner, Pittsburgh	.542
1909—	John (Honus) Wagner, Pittsburgh	.489
1910—	Sherwood Magee, Philadelphia	.507
1911—	Frank Schulte, Chicago	.534
1912—	Henry Zimmerman, Chicago	.571
1913—	Cliff. (Gavvy) Cravath, Philadelphia	.568
1914—	Sherwood Magee, Philadelphia	.501
1915—	Cliff. (Gavvy) Cravath, Philadelphia	.510
1916—	Zachariah Wheat, Brooklyn	.461
1917—	Rogers Hornsby, St. Louis	.484
1918—	Edd Roush, Cincinnati	.455
1919—	Henry (Hi) Myers, Brooklyn	.436
1920—	Rogers Hornsby, St. Louis	.559
1921—	Rogers Hornsby, St. Louis	.659
1922—	Rogers Hornsby, St. Louis	.722
1923—	Rogers Hornsby, St. Louis	.627
1924—	Rogers Hornsby, St. Louis	.696
1925—	Rogers Hornsby, St. Louis	.756
1926—	Fred Williams, Philadelphia	.569
1927—	Charles Hafey, St. Louis	.590
1928—	Rogers Hornsby, Boston	.632
1929—	Rogers Hornsby, Chicago	.679
1930—	Lewis (Hack) Wilson, Chicago	.723
1931—	Charles Klein, Philadelphia	.584
1932—	Charles Klein, Philadelphia	.646
1933—	Charles Klein, Philadelphia	.602
1934—	James (Rip) Collins, St. Louis	.615
1935—	J. Floyd (Arky) Vaughan, Pittsburgh	.607
1936—	Melvin Ott, New York	.588
1937—	Joseph Medwick, St. Louis	.641
1938—	John Mize, St. Louis	.614
1939—	John Mize, St. Louis	.626
1940—	John Mize, St. Louis	.636
1941—	Harold (Pete) Reiser, Brooklyn	.558
1942—	John Mize, New York	.521
1943—	Stanley Musial, St. Louis	.562
1944—	Stanley Musial, St. Louis	.549
1945—	Tommy Holmes, Boston	.577
1946—	Stanley Musial, St. Louis	.587
1947—	Ralph Kiner, Pittsburgh	.639
1948—	Stanley Musial, St. Louis	.702
1949—	Ralph Kiner, Pittsburgh	.658
1950—	Stanley Musial, St. Louis	.596
1951—	Ralph Kiner, Pittsburgh	.627
1952—	Stanley Musial, St. Louis	.538
1953—	Edwin (Duke) Snider, Brooklyn	.6271
1954—	Willie Mays, New York	.667
1955—	Willie Mays, New York	.659
1956—	Edwin (Duke) Snider, Brooklyn	.598
1957—	Willie Mays, New York	.626
1958—	Ernest Banks, Chicago	.614
1959—	Henry Aaron, Milwaukee	.636
1960—	Frank Robinson, Cincinnati	.595
1961—	Frank Robinson, Cincinnati	.611
1962—	Frank Robinson, Cincinnati	.624
1963—	Henry Aaron, Milwaukee	.586
1964—	Willie Mays, San Francisco	.607
1965—	Willie Mays, San Francisco	.645
1966—	Richard Allen, Philadelphia	.632
1967—	Henry Aaron, Atlanta	.573
1968—	Willie McCovey, San Francisco	.545
1969—	Willie McCovey, San Francisco	.656
1970—	Willie McCovey, San Francisco	.612
1971—	Henry Aaron, Atlanta	.669
1972—	Billy Williams, Chicago	.606
1973—	Wilver Stargell, Pittsburgh	.646
1974—	Michael Schmidt, Philadelphia	.546
1975—	David Parker, Pittsburgh	.541
1976—	Joe Morgan, Cincinnati	.576

LEADING PITCHERS IN WINNING PERCENTAGE

(15 OR MORE VICTORIES)

Year	Pitcher	Club	Won	Lost	Pct.
1900	Joseph McGinnity	Brooklyn	29	9	.763
1901	John Chesbro	Pittsburgh	21	9	.700
1902	John Chesbro	Pittsburgh	28	6	.824
1903	Samuel Leever	Pittsburgh	25	7	.781
1904	Joseph McGinnity	New York	35	8	.814
1905	Samuel Leever	Pittsburgh	20	5	.800
1906	Edward Reulbach	Chicago	19	4	.826
1907	Edward Reulbach	Chicago	17	4	.810
1908	Edward Reulbach	Chicago	24	7	.774
1909	Christy Mathewson	New York	25	6	.806
	Howard Camnitz	Pittsburgh	25	6	.806
1910	Leonard Cole	Chicago	20	4	.833
1911	Richard (Rube) Marquard	New York	24	7	.774
1912	Claude Hendrix	Pittsburgh	24	9	.727
1913	Albert Humphries	Chicago	16	4	.800
1914	Williams James	Boston	26	7	.788
1915	Grover Alexander	Philadelphia	31	10	.756
1916	Thomas Hughes	Boston	16	3	.842
1917	Ferdinand Schupp	New York	21	7	.750
1918	Claude Hendrix	Chicago	20	7	.741
1919	Walter Ruether	Cincinnati	19	6	.760
1920	Burleigh Grimes	Brooklyn	23	11	.676
1921	William L. Doak	St. Louis	15	6	.714
1922	Peter Donohue	Cincinnati	18	9	.667
1923	Adolfo Luque	Cincinnati	27	8	.771
1924	Emil Yde	Pittsburgh	16	3	.842
1925	William Sherdel	St. Louis	15	6	.714
1926	Ray Kremer	Pittsburgh	20	6	.769
1927	Lawrence Benton	Boston-New York	17	7	.708
1928	Lawrence Benton	New York	25	9	.735
1929	Charles Root	Chicago	19	6	.760
1930	Fred Fitzsimmons	New York	19	7	.731
1931	Paul Derringer	St. Louis	18	8	.692
1932	Lonnie Warneke	Chicago	22	6	.786
1933	Benjamin Cantwell	Boston	20	10	.667
1934	Jerome (Dizzy) Dean	St. Louis	30	7	.811
1935	William Lee	Chicago	20	6	.769
1936	Carl Hubbell	New York	26	6	.813
1937	Carl Hubbell	New York	22	8	.733
1938	William Lee	Chicago	22	9	.710
1939	Paul Derringer	Cincinnati	25	7	.781
1940	Fred Fitzsimmons	Brooklyn	16	2	.889
1941	Elmer Riddle	Cincinnati	19	4	.826
1942	Lawrence French	Brooklyn	15	4	.789
1943	Morton Cooper	St. Louis	21	8	.724
1944	Theodore Wilks	St. Louis	17	4	.810
1945	Harry Breechen	St. Louis	15	4	.789
1946	Murry Dickson	St. Louis	15	6	.714
1947	Lawrence Jansen	New York	21	5	.808
1948	Harry Brecheen	St. Louis	20	7	.741
1949	Elwin (Preacher) Roe	Brooklyn	15	6	.714
1950	Salvatore Maglie	New York	18	4	.818
1951	Elwin (Preacher) Roe	Brooklyn	22	3	.880
1952	J. Hoyt Wilhelm	New York	15	3	.833
1953	Carl Erskine	Brooklyn	20	6	.769
1954	John Antonelli	New York	21	7	.750
1955	Donald Newcombe	Brooklyn	20	5	.800
1956	Donald Newcombe	Brooklyn	27	7	.794
1957	Robert Buhl	Milwaukee	18	7	.720
1958	Warren E. Spahn	Milwaukee	22	11	.667
	S. Lewis Burdette	Milwaukee	20	10	.667
1959	ElRoy Face	Pittsburgh	18	1	.947
1960	Ernest Broglio	St. Louis	21	9	.700
1961	John Podres	Los Angeles	18	5	.783

LEADING PITCHERS IN WINNING PERCENTAGE—Continued

(15 or MORE VICTORIES)

Year	Pitcher	Club	Won	Lost	Pct.
1962—Robert Purkey		Cincinnati	23	5	.821
1963—Ronald Perranoski		Los Angeles	16	3	.842
1964—Sanford Koufax		Los Angeles	19	5	.792
1965—Sanford Koufax		Los Angeles	26	8	.765
1966—Juan Marichal		San Francisco	25	6	.806
1967—Richard Hughes		St. Louis	16	6	.727
1968—Stephen R. Blass		Pittsburgh	18	6	.750
1969—G. Thomas Seaver		New York	25	7	.781
1970—Robert Gibson		St. Louis	23	7	.767
1971—Donald E. Gullett		Cincinnati	16	6	.727
1972—Gary L. Nolan		Cincinnati	15	5	.750
1973—Thomas E. John		Los Angeles	16	7	.696
1974—John (Andy) Messersmith		Los Angeles	20	6	.769
1975—Donald E. Gullett		Cincinnati	15	4	.789
1976—Steven N. Carlton		Philadelphia	20	7	.741

LEADING PITCHERS—EARNED-RUN AVERAGE

(Based on Ten Complete Games Through 1950, Then 154 Innings Until N. L. Expanded in 1962, When It Became 162 Innings)

Year Pitcher and Club	G.	IP.	ERA.	Year Pitcher and Club	G.	IP.	ERA.
1912—Tesreau, New York	36	243	1.96	1945—Borowy, Chicago	15	122	2.14
1913—Mathewson, New York	40	306	2.06	1946—Pollet, St. Louis	40	266	2.10
1914—Doak, St. Louis	36	256	1.72	1947—Spahn, Boston	40	290	2.33
1915—Alexander, Philadelphia	49	376	1.22	1948—Brecheen, St. Louis	33	233	2.24
1916—Alexander, Philadelphia	48	390	1.55	1949—Koslo, New York	38	212	2.50
1917—Alexander, Philadelphia	45	388	1.83	1950—Hearn, St. Louis-New York	22	134	2.49
1918—Vaughn, Chicago	35	290	1.74	1951—Nichols, Boston	33	156	2.88
1919—Alexander, Chicago	30	235	1.72	1952—Wilhelm, New York	71	159	2.43
1920—Alexander, Chicago	46	363	1.91	1953—Spahn, Milwaukee	35	266	2.10
1921—Doak, St. Louis	32	209	2.58	1954—Antonelli, New York	39	259	2.29
1922—Ryan, New York	46	192	3.00	1955—Friend, Pittsburgh	44	200	2.84
1923—Luque, Cincinnati	41	322	1.93	1956—Burdette, Milwaukee	39	256	2.71
1924—Vance, Brooklyn	35	309	2.16	1957—Podres, Brooklyn	31	196	2.66
1925—Luque, Cincinnati	36	291	2.63	1958—Miller, San Francisco	41	182	2.47
1926—Kremer, Pittsburgh	37	231	2.61	1959—S. Jones, San Francisco	50	271	2.82
1927—Kremer, Pittsburgh	35	226	2.47	1960—McCormick, San Francisco	40	253	2.70
1928—Vance, Brooklyn	38	280	2.09	1961—Spahn, Milwaukee	38	263	3.01
1929—Walker, New York	29	178	3.08	1962—Koufax, Los Angeles	28	184	2.54
1930—Vance, Brooklyn	35	259	2.61	1963—Koufax, Los Angeles	40	311	1.88
1931—Walker, New York	37	239	2.26	1964—Koufax, Los Angeles	29	223	1.74
1932—Warneke, Chicago	35	277	2.37	1965—Koufax, Los Angeles	43	336	2.04
1933—Hubbell, New York	45	309	1.66	1966—Koufax, Los Angeles	41	323	1.73
1934—Hubbell, New York	49	313	2.30	1967—P. Niekro, Atlanta	46	207	1.87
1935—Blanton, Pittsburgh	35	254	2.59	1968—Gibson, St. Louis	34	305	1.12
1936—Hubbell, New York	42	304	2.31	1969—Marichal, San Francisco	37	300	2.10
1937—Turner, Boston	33	257	2.38	1970—Seaver, New York	37	291	2.81
1938—W. Lee, Chicago	44	291	2.66	1971—Seaver, New York	36	286	1.76
1939—Walters, Cincinnati	39	319	2.29	1972—Carlton, Philadelphia	41	346	1.98
1940—Walters, Cincinnati	36	305	2.48	1973—Seaver, New York	36	290	2.08
1941—E. Riddle, Cincinnati	33	217	2.24	1974—Capra, Atlanta	39	217	2.28
1942—M. Cooper, St. Louis	37	279	1.77	1975—Jones, San Diego	37	285	2.24
1943—Pollet, St. Louis	16	118	1.75	1976—Denny, St. Louis	30	207	2.52
1944—Heusser, Cincinnati	30	193	2.38				

Note—Earned-run records not tabulated in National League prior to 1912.

STRIKEOUT LEADERS—PITCHING

Year	Pitcher and Club	SO.
1900	George (Rube) Waddell, Pittsburgh	133
1901	Frank (Noodles) Hahn, Cincinnati	233
1902	Victor Willis, Boston	226
1903	Christopher Mathewson, New York	267
1904	Christopher Mathewson, New York	212
1905	Christopher Mathewson, New York	206
1906	Frederick Beebe, Chicago-St. Louis	171
1907	Christopher Mathewson, New York	178
1908	Christopher Mathewson, New York	259
1909	Orval Overall, Chicago	205
1910	Christopher Mathewson, New York	190
1911	Richard (Rube) Marquard, New York	237
1912	Grover Alexander, Philadelphia	195
1913	Thomas Seaton, Philadelphia	168
1914	Grover Alexander, Philadelphia	214
1915	Grover Alexander, Philadelphia	241
1916	Grover Alexander, Philadelphia	167
1917	Grover Alexander, Philadelphia	200
1918	James (Hippo) Vaughn, Chicago	148
1919	James (Hippo) Vaughn, Chicago	141
1920	Grover Alexander, Chicago	173
1921	Burleigh Grimes, Brooklyn	136
1922	Arthur (Dazzy) Vance, Brooklyn	134
1923	Arthur (Dazzy) Vance, Brooklyn	197
1924	Arthur (Dazzy) Vance, Brooklyn	262
1925	Arthur (Dazzy) Vance, Brooklyn	221
1926	Arthur (Dazzy) Vance, Brooklyn	140
1927	Arthur (Dazzy) Vance, Brooklyn	184
1928	Arthur (Dazzy) Vance, Brooklyn	200
1929	Perce (Pat) Malone, Chicago	166
1930	William Hallahan, St. Louis	177
1931	William Hallahan, St. Louis	159
1932	Jerome (Dizzy) Dean, St. Louis	191
1933	Jerome (Dizzy) Dean, St. Louis	199
1934	Jerome (Dizzy) Dean, St. Louis	195
1935	Jerome (Dizzy) Dean, St. Louis	182
1936	Van Lingle Mungo, Brooklyn	238
1937	Carl Hubbell, New York	159
1938	Claiborne Bryant, Chicago	135
1939	Claude Passeau, Philadelphia-Chicago	137
	William (Bucky) Walters, Cincinnati	137
1940	W. Kirby Higbe, Philadelphia	137
1941	John Vander Meer, Cincinnati	202
1942	John Vander Meer, Cincinnati	186
1943	John Vander Meer, Cincinnati	174
1944	William Voiselle, New York	161
1945	Elwin (Preacher) Roe, Pittsburgh	148
1946	John Schmitz, Chicago	135
1947	Ewell Blackwell, Cincinnati	193
1948	Harry Brecheen, St. Louis	149
1949	Warren Spahn, Boston	151
1950	Warren Spahn, Boston	191
1951	Warren Spahn, Boston	164
	Donald Newcombe, Brooklyn	164
1952	Warren Spahn, Boston	183
1953	Robin Roberts, Philadelphia	198
1954	Robin Roberts, Philadelphia	185
1955	Samuel Jones, Chicago	198
1956	Samuel Jones, Chicago	176
1957	John Sanford, Philadelphia	188
1958	Samuel Jones, St. Louis	225
1959	Donald Drysdale, Los Angeles	242
1960	Donald Drysdale, Los Angeles	246
1961	Sanford Koufax, Los Angeles	269
1962	Donald Drysdale, Los Angeles	232
1963	Sanford Koufax, Los Angeles	306
1964	Robert Veale, Pittsburgh	250
1965	Sanford Koufax, Los Angeles	382
1966	Sanford Koufax, Los Angeles	317
1967	James Bunning, Philadelphia	253
1968	Robert Gibson, St. Louis	268
1969	Ferguson Jenkins, Chicago	273
1970	G. Thomas Seaver, New York	283
1971	G. Thomas Seaver, New York	289
1972	Steven Carlton, Philadelphia	310
1973	G. Thomas Seaver, New York	251
1974	Steven Carlton, Philadelphia	240
1975	G. Thomas Seaver, New York	243
1976	G. Thomas Seaver, New York	235

SHUTOUT LEADERS

Year	Pitcher and Club	ShO.
1900	Clark C. Griffith, Chicago	4
	Frank G. Hahn, Cincinnati	4
	Charles A. Nichols, Boston	4
	Denton T. Young, St. Louis	4
1901	John D. Chesbro, Pittsburgh	6
	Albert L. Orth, Philadelphia	6
	Victor G. Willis, Boston	6
1902	John D. Chesbro, Pittsburgh	8
	Christopher Mathewson, New York	8
1903	Samuel W. Leever, Pittsburgh	7
1904	Joseph J. McGinnity, New York	9
1905	Christopher Mathewson, New York	9
1906	Mordecai P. Brown, Chicago	9
1907	Orval Overall, Chicago	9
	Christopher Mathewson, New York	9
1908	Christopher Mathewson, New York	12
1909	Orval Overall, Chicago	9
1910	Earl L. Moore, Philadelphia	7
1911	Charles B. Adams, Pittsburgh	7
	Grover C. Alexander, Philadelphia	7
1912	George N. Rucker, Brooklyn	6
1913	Grover C. Alexander, Philadelphia	9
1914	Charles M. Tesreau, New York	8
1915	Grover C. Alexander, Philadelphia	12
1916	Grover C. Alexander, Philadelphia	16
1917	Grover C. Alexander, Philadelphia	8
1918	George A. Tyler, Chicago	8
	James L. Vaughn, Chicago	8
1919	Grover C. Alexander, Chicago	9
1920	Charles B. Adams, Pittsburgh	8
1921	Grover C. Alexander, Chicago	3
	Philip B. Douglas, New York	3
	Dana Filligim, Boston	3
	Adolph Luque, Cincinnati	3
	Clarence E. Mitchell, Brooklyn	3
	John D. Morrison, Pittsburgh	3
	Joseph C. Oeschger, Boston	3
	Jesse L. Haines, St. Louis	3
1922	Arthur C. Vance, Brooklyn	6
1923	Adolfo Luque, Cincinnati	6
1924	Jesse L. Barnes, Boston	4
	A. Wilbur Cooper, Pittsburgh	4
	Remy P. Kremer, Pittsburgh	4
	Eppa Rixey, Cincinnati	4

SHUTOUT LEADERS—Continued

Year	Pitcher and Club	ShO.
	Allen S. Sothoron, St. Louis	4
	Emil O. Yde, Pittsburgh	4
1925—	Harold G. Carlson, Philadelphia	4
	Adolfo Luque, Cincinnati	4
	Arthur C. Vance, Brooklyn	4
1926—	Peter J. Donohue, Cincinnati	5
1927—	Jesse J. Haines, St. Louis	6
1928—	John F. Blake, Chicago	4
	Burleigh A. Grimes, Pittsburgh	4
	Charles F. Lucas, Cincinnati	4
	Douglas L. McWeeney, Brooklyn	4
	Arthur C. Vance, Brooklyn	4
1929—	Perce L. Malone, Chicago	5
1930—	Charles H. Root, Chicago	4
	Arthur C. Vance, Brooklyn	4
1931—	William H. Walker, New York	6
1932—	Lonnie Warneke, Chicago	4
	Jerome H. Dean, St. Louis	4
	Stephen A. Swetonic, Pittsburgh	4
1933—	Carl O. Hubbell, New York	10
1934—	Jerome H. Dean, St. Louis	7
1935—	Darrell E. Blanton, Pittsburgh	4
	Freddie L. Fitzsimmons, New York	4
	Lawrence H. French, Chicago	4
	Van L. Mungo, Brooklyn	4
	James D. Weaver, Pittsburgh	4
1936—	Darrell E. Blanton, Pittsburgh	4
	James O. Carleton, Chicago	4
	Lawrence H. French, Chicago	4
	William C. Lee, Chicago	4
	Alfred J. Smith, New York	4
	Williams H. Walters, Philadelphia	4
	Lonnie Warneke, Chicago	4
1937—	Louis H. Fette, Boston	5
	Lee T. Grissom, Cincinnati	5
	James R. Turner, Boston	5
1938—	William C. Lee, Chicago	9
1939—	Louis H. Fette, Boston	6
1940—	William L. Lohrman, New York	5
	Manuel L. Salvo, Boston	5
	J. Whitlow Wyatt, Brooklyn	5
1941—	J. Whitlow Wyatt, Brooklyn	7
1942—	Morton C. Cooper, St. Louis	10
1943—	Hiram G. Bithorn, Chicago	7
1944—	Morton C. Cooper, St. Louis	7
1945—	Claude W. Passeau, Chicago	5
1946—	Ewell Blackwell, Cincinnati	6
1947—	Warren E. Spahn, Boston	7
1948—	Harry D. Brecheen, St. Louis	7
1949—	Kenneth A. Heintzelman, Philadelphia	5
	Donald Newcombe, Brooklyn	5
	Howard J. Pollet, St. Louis	5
	Kenneth D. Raffensberger, Cincinnati	5

Year	Pitcher and Club	ShO.
1950—	James T. Hearn, New York	5
	Lawrence J. Jansen, New York	5
	Salvatore A. Maglie, New York	5
	Robin E. Roberts, Philadelphia	5
1951—	Warren E. Spahn, Boston	7
1952—	Salvatore A. Maglie, New York	7
	Ken D. Raffensberger, Cincinnati	7
	Curtis T. Simmons, Philadelphia	7
1953—	Harvey Haddix, St. Louis	6
1954—	John A. Antonelli, New York	6
1955—	Joseph H. Nuxhall, Cincinnati	5
1956—	John A. Antonelli, New York	6
	S. Lewis Burdette, Milwaukee	6
1957—	John L. Podres, Brooklyn	6
1958—	Carlton F. Willey, Milwaukee	4
1959—	John A. Antonelli, San Francisco	4
	Robert R. Buhl, Milwaukee	4
	S. Lewis Burdette, Milwaukee	4
	Roger L. Craig, Los Angeles	4
	Donald S. Drysdale, Los Angeles	4
	Sam Jones, San Francisco	4
	Warren E. Spahn, Milwaukee	4
1960—	John S. Sanford, San Francisco	6
1961—	Joseph R. Jay, Cincinnati	4
	Warren E. Spahn, Milwaukee	4
1962—	Robert B. Friend, Pittsburgh	5
	Robert Gibson, St. Louis	5
1963—	Sanford Koufax, Los Angeles	11
1964—	Sanford Koufax, Los Angeles	7
1965—	Juan A. Marichal, San Francisco	10
1966—	James P. Bunning, Philadelphia	5
	Robert Gibson, St. Louis	5
	Lawrence C. Jackson, Philadelphia	5
	Larry E. Jaster, St. Louis	5
	Sanford Koufax, Los Angeles	5
	James W. Maloney, Cincinnati	5
1967—	James P. Bunning, Philadelphia	6
1968—	Robert Gibson, St. Louis	13
1969—	Juan A. Marichal, San Francisco	8
1970—	Gaylord J. Perry, San Francisco	5
1971—	Stephen R. Blass, Pittsburgh	5
	Alphonso E. Downing, Los Angeles	5
	Robert Gibson, St. Louis	5
	Milton J. Pappas, Chicago	5
1972—	Donald H. Sutton, Los Angeles	9
1973—	John E. Billingham, Cincinnati	7
1974—	Jonathan T. Matlack, New York	7
1975—	John A. Messersmith, Los Angeles	7
1976—	Jonathan T. Matlack, New York	6
	John J. Montefusco, San Francisco	6

PRE-1900 PENNANT WINNERS

Year	Club	Manager	W.	L.	Pct.	Year	Club	Manager	W.	L.	Pct.
1876—Chicago		Albert Spalding	52	14	.788	1888—New York		James Mutrie	84	47	.641
1877—Boston		Harry Wright	31	17	.646	1889—New York		James Mutrie	83	43	.659
1878—Boston		Harry Wright	41	19	.683	1890—Brooklyn		Wm. McGunnigle	86	43	.667
1879—Providence		George Wright	55	23	.705	1891—Boston		Frank Selee	87	51	.630
1880—Chicago		Adrian Anson	67	17	.798	1892—Boston		Frank Selee	102	48	.680
1881—Chicago		Adrian Anson	56	28	.667	1893—Boston		Frank Selee	86	44	.662
1882—Chicago		Adrian Anson	55	29	.655	1894—Baltimore		Edward Hanlon	89	39	.695
1883—Boston		John Morrill	63	35	.643	1895—Baltimore		Edward Hanlon	87	43	.669
1884—Providence		Frank Bancroft	84	28	.750	1896—Baltimore		Edward Hanlon	90	39	.698
1885—Chicago		Adrian Anson	87	25	.777	1897—Boston		Frank Selee	93	39	.705
1886—Chicago		Adrian Anson	90	34	.726	1898—Boston		Frank Selee	102	47	.685
1887—Detroit		Wm. Watkins	79	45	.637	1899—Brooklyn		Edward Hanlon	88	42	.677

PRE-1900 YEARLY FINISHES

*Tied for position

Year	Bos.	Bkn.	Chi.	Cin.	N.Y.	Phil.	Pitt.	St.L.	Balt.	Buf.	Clev.
1876	4	....	1	8	6	7	....	3	....	....	....
1877	1	....	5	....	....	....	....	4	....	....	....
1878	1	....	4	2	....	....	....	....	....	....	....
1879	2	....	*3	5	....	....	....	....	....	*3	6
1880	6	....	1	8	....	....	....	....	....	7	3
1881	6	....	1	....	....	....	....	....	....	3	7
1882	*3	....	1	....	....	....	....	....	....	*3	5
1883	1	....	2	....	6	8	....	....	....	5	4
1884	2	....	*4	....	*4	6	....	....	....	3	7
1885	5	....	1	....	2	3	....	8	....	7	....
1886	5	....	1	....	3	4	....	6	....	....	....
1887	5	....	3	....	4	2	6	....	....	....	....
1888	4	....	2	....	1	3	6	....	....	....	....
1889	2	....	3	....	1	4	5	....	....	....	6
1890	5	1	2	4	6	3	8	....	....	....	7
1891	1	6	2	7	3	4	8	....	....	....	5
1892	1	3	7	5	8	4	6	11	12	....	2
1893	1	*6	9	*6	5	4	2	10	8	....	3
1894	3	5	8	10	2	4	7	9	1	....	6
1895	*5	*5	4	8	9	3	7	11	1	....	2
1896	4	*9	5	3	7	8	6	11	1	....	2
1897	1	*6	9	4	3	10	8	12	2	....	5
1898	1	10	4	3	7	6	8	12	2	....	5
1899	2	1	8	6	10	3	7	5	4	....	12

Year	Det.	Hart.	Ind.	K.C.	Lou.	Mil.	Prov.	Syr.	Troy	Wash.	Wor.
1876	....	2	....	....	5	....	....	....	....	....	....
1877	....	3	....	....	2	....	....	....	....	....	....
1878	....	....	5	....	....	6	3	....	....	....	....
1879	....	....	....	....	....	....	1	8	7	....	....
1880	....	....	....	....	....	....	2	....	4	....	5
1881	4	....	....	....	....	....	2	....	5	....	8
1882	6	....	....	....	....	....	2	....	7	....	8
1883	7	....	....	....	....	....	3	....	....	....	....
1884	8	....	....	....	....	....	1	....	....	....	....
1885	6	....	....	....	....	....	4	....	....	....	....
1886	2	....	....	7	....	....	....	....	....	8	....
1887	1	....	8	....	....	....	....	....	....	7	....
1888	5	....	7	....	....	....	....	....	....	8	....
1889	....	....	7	....	....	....	....	....	....	8	....
1890	....	....	....	....	....	....	....	....	....	....	....
1891	....	....	....	....	....	....	....	....	....	....	....
1892	....	....	....	....	9	....	....	....	....	10	....
1893	....	....	....	....	11	....	....	....	....	12	....
1894	....	....	....	....	12	....	....	....	....	11	....
1895	....	....	....	....	12	....	....	....	....	10	....
1896	....	....	....	....	12	....	....	....	....	*9	....
1897	....	....	....	....	11	....	....	....	....	*6	....
1898	....	....	....	....	9	....	....	....	....	11	....
1899	....	....	....	....	9	....	....	....	....	11	....

PRE-1900 LEADERS

LEADING BATSMEN

Year	Player and Club	G.	H.	Pct.	Year	Player and Club	G.	H.	Pct.
1876	Barnes, Chicago	66	138	.404	1889	Brouthers, Boston	126	181	.373
1877	White, Boston	48	82	.385	1890	Glasscock, New York	124	172	.336
1878	Dalrymple, Milwaukee	60	95	.356	1891	Hamilton, Philadelphia	133	179	.338
1879	Anson, Chicago	49	90	.407	1892	Brouthers, Brooklyn	152	197	.335
1880	Gore, Chicago	75	114	.365		Childs, Cleveland	144	185	.335
1881	Anson, Chicago	84	137	.399	1893	Duffy, Boston	131	203	.378
1882	Brouthers, Buffalo	84	129	.367	1894	Duffy, Boston	124	236	.438
1883	Brouthers, Buffalo	97	156	.371	1895	Burkett, Cleveland	132	235	.423
1884	O'Rourke, Buffalo	104	157	.350	1896	Burkett, Cleveland	133	240	.410
1885	Connor, New York	110	169	.371	1897	Keeler, Baltimore	128	243	.432
1886	Kelly, Chicago	118	175	.388	1898	Keeler, Baltimore	128	214	.379
1887	Anson, Chicago	122	*224	.421	1899	Delahanty, Philadelphia	145	234	.408
1888	Anson, Chicago	134	177	.343					

*Bases on balls counted as hits.

TWO-BASE HIT LEADERS

Year	Player and Club	2B.	Year	Player and Club	2B.
1876	Roscoe Barnes, Chicago	23	1888	James Ryan, Chicago	37
1877	Adrian (Cap) Anson, Chicago	20	1889	John Glasscock, Indianapolis	39
1878	Lewis Brown, Providence	18	1890	Samuel Thompson, Philadelphia	38
1879	Charles Eden, Cleveland	31	1891	Michael Griffin, Brooklyn	36
1880	Fred Dunlap, Cleveland	27	1892	Brouthers, Bkn.-Delahanty, Phil	33
1881	Michael (King) Kelly, Chicago	28	1893	Oliver (Pat) Tebeau, Cleveland	35
1882	Michael (King) Kelly, Chicago	36	1894	Hugh Duffy, Boston	50
1883	Edward Williamson, Chicago	50	1895	Edward Delahanty, Philadelphia	47
1884	Paul Hines, Providence	34	1896	Edward Delahanty, Philadelphia	42
1885	Adrian (Cap) Anson, Chicago	35	1897	Jacob Stenzel, Baltimore	40
1886	Dennis (Dan) Brouthers, Detroit	41	1898	Napoleon Lajoie, Philadelphia	40
1887	Dennis (Dan) Brouthers, Detroit	35	1899	Edward Delahanty, Philadelphia	56

THREE-BASE HIT LEADERS

Year	Player and Club	3B.	Year	Player and Club	3B.
1876	George Hall, Athletics	12	1888	R. Connor, N.Y.-R. Johnson, Bos	17
1877	Brown, Bos.-McVey, Chi.-White, Bos	9	1889	Connor, N.Y.-Fogarty, Ph.-Wilmot, W.	17
1878	Thomas York, Providence	9	1890	John McPhee, Cincinnati	25
1879	L. Dickerson, Cin.-M. Kelly, Cin	14	1891	Jacob Beckley, Pittsburgh	20
1880	Harry Stovey, Worcester	14	1892	Dennis (Dan) Brouthers, Brooklyn	20
1881	John Rowe, Buffalo	11	1893	Perry Werden, St. Louis	33
1882	Roger Connor, Troy	17	1894	Henry Reitz, Baltimore	29
1883	Dennis (Dan) Brouthers, Buffalo	17	1895	A. Selbach, Wash.-S. Thompson, Phil	22
1884	William (Buck) Ewing, New York	18	1896	McCreery, Lou.-G. Van Haltren, N.Y.	21
1885	R. Connor, N.Y.-J. O'Rourke, N.Y.	15	1897	Harry Davis, Pittsburgh	28
1886	Roger Connor, New York	19	1898	John Anderson, Bkn.-Wash.	19
1887	Samuel Thompson, Detroit	23	1899	James Williams, Pittsburgh	27

HOME RUN LEADERS

Year	Player and Club	HR.	Year	Player and Club	HR.
1876	George Hall, Athletics	5	1888	Roger Connor, New York	14
1877	George Shaffer, Louisville	3	1889	Samuel Thompson, Philadelphia	20
1878	Paul Hines, Providence	4	1890	T. Burns, Bkn.-M. Tiernan, N.Y.	13
1879	Charles Jones, Boston	9	1891	H. Stovey, Bos.-M. Tiernan, N.Y.	16
1880	J. O'Rourke, Bos.-H. Stovey, Wor.	6	1892	James Holliday, Cincinnati	13
1881	Dennis (Dan) Brouthers, Buffalo	8	1893	Edward Delahanty, Philadelphia	19
1882	George Wood, Detroit	7	1894	H. Duffy, Boston-R. Lowe, Boston	18
1883	William (Buck) Ewing, New York	10	1895	William Joyce, Washington	17
1884	Edward Williamson, Chicago	27	1896	Delahanty, Phil.-S. Thompson, Phil	13
1885	Abner Dalrymple, Chicago	11	1897	Napoleon Lajoie, Philadelphia	10
1886	Harding Richardson, Detroit	11	1896	James Collins, Boston	14
1887	R. Connor, N.Y.-T. O'Brien, Wash	17	1899	John (Buck) Freeman, Washington	25

PRE-1900 LEADERS—Continued

STOLEN BASE LEADERS

Year	Player and Club	SB.
1886—	George Andrews, Philadelphia	56
1887—	John M. Ward, New York	111
1888—	William (Dummy) Hoy, Washington	82
1889—	James Fogarty, Philadelphia	99
1890—	William Hamilton, Philadelphia	102
1891—	William Hamilton, Philadelphia	115
1892—	John M. Ward, Brooklyn	94
1893—	John M. Ward, New York	72
1894—	William Hamilton, Philadelphia	99
1895—	William Hamilton, Philadelphia	95
1896—	William Lange, Chicago	100
1897—	William Lange, Chicago	83
1898—	Frederick Clarke, Louisville	66
1899—	James Sheckard, Baltimore	78

LEADING PITCHERS IN WINNING PERCENTAGE

(15 OR MORE VICTORIES)

Year	Pitcher and Club	W.	L.	Pct.
1876—	Albert Spalding, Chicago	47	13	.783
1877—	Thomas Bond, Boston	31	17	.646
1878—	Thomas Bond, Boston	40	19	.678
1879—	Jom M. Ward, Providence	44	18	.710
1880—	Fred Goldsmith, Chicago	22	3	.880
1881—	Chas. Radbourn, Providence	25	11	.694
1882—	Lawrence Corcoran, Chicago	27	13	.675
1883—	James McCormick, Cleveland	27	13	.675
1884—	Chas. Radbourn, Providence	60	12	.833
1885—	Michael Welch, New York	44	11	.800
1886—	John Flynn, Chicago	24	6	.800
1887—	Charles Getzein, Detroit	29	13	.690
1888—	Timothy Keefe, New York	35	12	.745
1889—	John Clarkson, Boston	49	19	.721
1890—	Thomas Lovett, Brooklyn	32	11	.744
1891—	John Ewing, New York	22	8	.733
1892—	Denton (Cy) Young, Cleve.	36	11	.766
1893—	Frank Killen, Pittsburgh	34	10	.773
1894—	Jouett Meekin, New York	34	9	.791
1895—	William Hoffer, Baltimore	30	7	.811
1896—	William Hoffer, Baltimore	26	7	.788
1897—	Amos Rusie, New York	29	8	.784
1898—	Edward Lewis, Boston	25	8	.758
1899—	James Hughes, Brooklyn	28	6	.824

AMERICAN LEAGUE

Including

Club Directories

Club Reviews of 1976 Season

Club-Day-By-Day Scores

A. L. Team Pictures

1976 League Leaders

1976 Official A. L. Averages

All-Time A. L. Player Performance Tables

LELAND S. MacPhail, JR.
President of the American League

American League

Organized 1900

LELAND S. MacPHAIL, Jr.
President

JOSEPH E. CRONIN
Chairman

CALVIN R. GRIFFITH
Vice-President

ROBERT F. HOLBROOK
Secretary

ROBERT O. FISHEL
Assistant to the President

DONALD C. MARR, Jr.
Controller

DICK BUTLER
Supervisor of Umpires

JEANNE COLLINS
Manager, Waiver & Records Department

RICHARD E. WHITE
Assistant Public Relations Director

TESS BASTA, PAT FREEMAN, PHYLLIS MERHIGE
Staff

Headquarters—280 Park Avenue, New York, N. Y. 10017

Telephone—682-7000 (area code 212)

UMPIRES—Lawrence Barnett, Nicholas Bremigan, Joseph Brinkman, Nestor Chylak, Alan Clark, Terry Cooney, Bill Deegan, Donald Denkinger, Louis DiMuro, James Evans, Dale Ford, Arthur Frantz, Rich Garcia, Russell Goetz, William Haller, Gregory Kosc, William Kunkel, Ronald Luciano, George Maloney, Larry McCoy, James McKean, Jerome Neudecker, David Phillips, Martin Springstead.

OFFICIAL STATISTICIANS—Sports Information Center, 1776 Heritage Drive, No. Quincy, Mass. 02171.

Players cannot be transferred from one major league club to another after June 15 to close of the championship season except through regular waiver channels.

WAIVER PRICE, $20,000. Interleague waivers, $20,000, except for selected players and draft-excluded players.

NOTE: Four new umpires to be named at end of spring training.

BALTIMORE ORIOLES

Chairman of the Board—Jerold C. Hoffberger

Chairman of Executive Committee and Treasurer—Zanvyl Krieger
Executive Vice-President-General Manager—Henry J. Peters
Vice-President for Business Affairs—Jack Dunn, III
Vice-President-Secretary—Joseph P. Hamper, Jr.
Vice-President—J. Frank Cashen
Public Relations Director—Robert W. Brown
Traveling Secretary—Philip E. Itzoe
Director of Business Affairs—Alan E. Harazin
Special Assistant to the General Manager—James J. Russo
Coordinator of Player Development and Scouting—
James M. McLaughlin
Director of Player Development—Clyde Kluttz
Director of Scouting—Thomas A. Giordano
Sales Manager—Don B. Shaver
Ticket Manager—Walter R. Freeman, Jr.
Assistant Ticket Manager—Joseph B. Codd
Assistant Public Relations Director—Allen McC. Barrett, Jr.
Consultant-President, Oriole Foundation—Herbert E. Armstrong
Manager—Earl S. Weaver
Club Physician—Dr. Leonard Wallenstein
Executive Offices—Memorial Stadium, Baltimore, Md. 21218
Telephone—243-9800 (area code 301)

SCOUTS—Jack Baker, Fred Benham, Julio Blanco-Herrera, Dick Bowie, Joe Bowman, Ray Crone, Joe DeLucca, Albert Elliott, Myron Hayworth, Edward Lewis, Frank McGowan, Don McShane, Lamar North, Jack Sanford, John Stokoe, George Thompson, Ramon Vargas, Bill Werle.

PARK LOCATION—Memorial Stadium, 33rd Street, Ellerslie Avenue, 36th Street and Ednor Road.

Seating capacity—52,137

FIELD DIMENSIONS—Home plate to left field at foul line, 309 feet; to center field, 405 feet; to right field at foul line, 309 feet.

BOSTON RED SOX

President—Mrs. Thomas A. Yawkey

Executive Vice-President-General Manager—Richard H. O'Connell
Assistant General Manager—John W. Claiborne
Vice-President, Administration—Gene Kirby
Vice-President, Player Personnel—Haywood C. Sullivan
Treasurer—John L. Harrington
Secretary—Joseph LaCour
Director, Minor League Clubs—Edward F. Kenney
Traveling Secretary—John J. Rogers
Director of Public Relations—William C. Crowley
Statistician-Assistant Director of Public Relations—
Richard L. Bresciani
Manager—Donald W. Zimmer
Club Physician—Dr. Thomas M. Tierney
Executive Offices—24 Jersey Street, Boston, Mass. 02215
Telephone—267-9440 (area code 617)

SCOUTS—Milton Bolling, Ray Boone, Mace Brown, George Digby, Howard (Danny) Doyle, Bill Enos, Earl Johnson, Eddie Kasko, Charles Koney, Wilfred (Lefty) Lefebvre, Don Lenhardt, Tommy McDonald, Felix Maldonado, Frank Malzone, Sam Mele, Ramon Naranjo, Willie Paffen, Edward Scott, Matt Sczesny, Joe Stephenson, Larry Thomas, Charlie Wagner.

PARK LOCATION—Fenway Park, Jersey Street, Lansdowne Street and Ipswich Street.

Seating capacity—33,513

FIELD DIMENSIONS—Home plate to left field at foul line, 315 feet; to center field, 420 feet; to right field at foul line, 302 feet; average right field distance, 382 feet.

CALIFORNIA ANGELS

BOARD OF DIRECTORS

Gene Autry, Chairman of the Board; Harry Dalton, Arthur E. Patterson, Walton S. Reid, Forrest Shumway, A. Ray Smith, Clair L. Stout.

President—Arthur E. (Red) Patterson
Executive Vice-President-General Manager—Harry Dalton
Vice-President, Treasurer—Francis X. Leary
Consultant—Fred Haney
Assistant to President, Public Relations—Tom Seeberg
Stadium Operations Director—Dick Foster
Scouting Director—Walter Shannon
Minor League Director—Tom Sommers
Promotions, Media Advertising Director—George Lederer
Ticket Manager—Carl Gordon
Traveling Secretary and Trainer—Freddie Frederico
Group Sales Director—Lynn Kirchmann
Publications Director—Mel Franks
Speakers' Bureau Director—Leslie Wilson
Scorebook Advertising Director—Tim Reilly
Administrative Asst., Minor Leagues—Chuck Franklin
Film Coordinator, Special Statistics—George Goodale
Manager—Norm Sherry
Club Physician—Dr. Jules Rasinski
Executive Offices—Anaheim Stadium, 2000 State College Blvd.,
Anaheim, Calif. 92806
Telephone—634-2000 (area code 714)

SCOUTS—Special Assignments: Al Hollingsworth, Frank Lane, Del Rice, Ray Scarborough. Supervisors: Al Kubski, Nick Kamzic, Walter Youse. Staff: Greg Bock, Gib Bodet, Loyd Christopher, Lou Cohenour, John Herbold, Larry Himes, Gene Kerns, Joe McIlvaine, Johnny Neun, George Noga, Carlos Pieve, Red Smith, Sam Suplizio, Red Whitsett.

PARK LOCATION—Anaheim Stadium, 2000 State College Boulevard.

Seating capacity—43,250

FIELD DIMENSIONS—Home plate to left field at foul line, 333 feet; to center field, 404 feet; to right field at foul line, 333 feet.

CHICAGO WHITE SOX

Chairman of the Board—Wm. O. DeWitt

President—Bill Veeck
Vice-President—Roland Hemond
Treasurer—Leo Breen
Secretary—Newton P. Frye, Jr.
Business Manager—Rudie Schaffer
Assistant Business Manager—Mike Veeck
Director of Public Relations—Don Unferth
Traveling Secretary—Glen Rosenbaum
Farm Director—C. V. Davis
Assistant Farm Director—Charlie Evranian
General Sales Manager for TV—Marshall Black
Manager—Bob Lemon
Club Physicians—Drs. Edwin Feldman, William Meltzer,
and Sid J. Shafer
Executive Offices—Comiskey Park, Dan Ryan at 35th Street,
Chicago, Ill. 60616
Telephone—924-1000 (area code 312)

SCOUTS—Carl Ackerman, Bruce Andrew, Loren Babe, Joe Begani, Al Brown, Sam Hairston, Bennie Huffman, Gary Johnson, Bill Kimball, Leo Labossiere, Dario Lodigiani, Al Lynch, Mel Preibisch, George Sobek, Steve Vrablik, Walter Widmayer.

PARK LOCATION—Comiskey Park, Dan Ryan at 35th Street, Chicago, Ill. 60616.

Seating capacity—44,492

FIELD DIMENSIONS—Home plate to left field at foul line, 352 feet; to center field, 440 feet; to right field at foul line, 352 feet.

CLEVELAND INDIANS

President—Ted Bonda

Vice-President & Treasurer—Dudley S. Blossom, III
Vice-President & General Manager—Phillip D. Seghi
Vice-President of Operations—Carl Fazio, Jr.
Vice-President—Bruce Fine
Director of Scouting & Minor League Operations—Bob Quinn
Traveling Secretary—Mike Seghi
Director of Stadium Operations—Dan Zerbey
Public Relations Director—Randy Adamack
Promotions Director—Jackie York
Group Sales Director—Rich Rollins
Director of Season Ticket Sales—Joe Bick
Accountant—Art Pease
Director of Community Affairs—Jim Grant
Minor League Administration—Paul O'Dea
Farm Club Administration—Joe Pavia
Sales Representative—Jim Slattery
Group Sales Assistant—Tony Saranita
Sales & Marketing—Carl Hoerig
Special Assignment Scout—Dan Carnevale
Manager—Frank Robinson
Club Physician—Dr. Walter Lewin
Executive offices—Cleveland Stadium, Cleveland, Ohio 44114
Telephone—861-1200 (area code 216)

SCOUTS: Willie Calvino, Dan Carnevale, Jack Cassini, Merrill Combs, Red Gaskill, Leon Hamilton, Paul O'Dea, Bob Shupala.

PARK LOCATION—Cleveland Stadium, Boudreau Blvd.

Seating capacity—76,713

FIELD DIMENSIONS—Home plate to left field at foul line, 320 feet; to center field, 400 feet; to right field foul line, 320 feet.

DETROIT TIGERS

Owner—John E. Fetzer

Executive Vice-President-General Manager—James A. Campbell
Consultant—Richard B. (Rick) Ferrell
Secretary-Treasurer—Alex Callam
Director of Public Relations—Hal Middlesworth
Director of Player Development—Walter A. (Hoot) Evers
Director of Player Procurement—William R. Lajoie
Coordinator of Scouting—Edward G. Katalinas
Director of Ticket Sales—William H. Willis
Director of Stadium Operations—Ralph Snyder
Business Manager—William E. Haase
Traveling Secretary—Vince Desmond
Assistant Director of Public Relations—Bill A. Brown
Assistant Director Public Relations, Special Events—Lew Matlin
Assistant Director of Player Development—Dave Miller
Assistant Director Stadium Operations, Administration—
George Minnis
Assistant Directors Stadium Operations, Grounds & Maintenance—
Mike Fenell and Frank Feneck
Manager—Ralph Houk
Club Physician—Dr. Clarence Livingood
Executive Offices—Tiger Stadium, Detroit, Mich. 48216
Telephone—962-4000 (area code 313)

SCOUTS—Wayne Blackburn, Gates Brown, James Miller, William Schudlich, Frank Skaff, Jack Tighe, Richard Wiencek.

PARK LOCATION—Tiger Stadium, Michigan Avenue, Cochrane Avenue, Kaline Drive and Trumbull Avenue.

Seating capacity—54,226.

FIELD DIMENSIONS—Home plate to left field at foul line, 340 feet; to center field, 440 feet; to right field at foul line, 325 feet.

KANSAS CITY ROYALS

BOARD OF DIRECTORS—Joe Burke, William Deramus III, Charles Hughes, Ewing Kauffman, Mrs. Ewing Kauffman, Earl Smith.

President—Ewing Kauffman

Executive Vice-President and General Manager—Joe Burke

Vice-President for Operations—Spencer "Herk" Robinson

Vice-President and Legal Counsel—Phil Koury

Controller—Dale Rohr

Director of Scouting and Player Development—John Schuerholz

Director of Public Relations—Dean Vogelaar

Director of Promotions and Assistant Public Relations Director—Bryan Burns

Traveling Secretary—Bill Beck

Advertising, Group Sales—Bruce Carnahan

Ticket Manager—Al Marcum

Director of Advance Ticket Sales—Joe Grigoli

Assistant Farm Director—Dick Balderson

Manager—Whitey Herzog

Club Physician—Dr. Paul Meyer

Executive Offices—Royals Stadium, Harry S. Truman Sports Complex

Mailing Address—P. O. Box 1969, Kansas City, Mo. 64141

Telephone—921-8000 (area code 816)

SCOUTS—Gary Blaylock, Al Diez, Tom Ferrick, Bill Fischer, Rosey Gilhousen, Art Lilly, Art Stewart.

PARK LOCATION—Royals Stadium, Harry S. Truman Sports Complex.

Seating capacity—40,762

FIELD DIMENSIONS—Home plate to left field at foul line, 330 feet; to center field, 410 feet; to right field at foul line, 330 feet.

MILWAUKEE BREWERS

President, Chief Executive Officer—Allen H. (Bud) Selig

Chairman of the Board—Edmund B. Fitzgerald
DIRECTORS—Edmund B. Fitzgerald, Allan H. Selig, Everett
G. Smith, Roswell N. Stearns, Carlton P. Wilson.
Secretary—Bernard S. Kubale
Vice-President, Director of Baseball Operations—James S. Baumer
Vice-President, Administration—Thomas J. Ferguson
Vice-President, Stadium & Broadcast Operations—Gabe Paul, Jr.
Vice-President, Marketing & Director of Public Relations—
Richard Hackett
Treasurer, Controller, Assistant Secretary—Richard R. Hoffmann
Farm Director & Administrator of Scouting—Anthony C. Siegle
Director of Scouting—Dee Fondy
Director of Player Development—Al J. Widmar
Director of Information & Services—Tom Skibosh
Assistant Director of Stadium Operations—Jack Hutchinson
Advance and Group Sales—Steve Comte
Manager—Alex Grammas
Club Physician—Dr. Gary N. Guten
Executive Offices—Milwaukee Brewers Baseball Club, Inc.,
Milwaukee County Stadium, Milwaukee, Wis. 53214
Telephone—933-9000 (area code 414)

SCOUTS— Dick Bogard, Felix Delgado, Roland LeBlanc, Eddie Mathews, Roberto Pena, Anton A. Roig.

PARK LOCATION—Milwaukee County Stadium, S. 44th Street off Bluemound Road.

Seating capacity—54,187

FIELD DIMENSIONS—Home plate to left field at foul line, 320 feet; to center field, 402 feet; to right field at foul line, 315 feet.

MINNESOTA TWINS

Chairman of Board, President—Calvin R. Griffith

Vice-President-Assistant Treasurer—Mrs. Thelma Griffith Haynes
Vice-President, Secretary, Treasurer—Clark Griffith
Vice-President—Bruce G. Haynes
Director—H. Gabriel Murphy
Director—Eugene V. Young
Director—Wheelock Whitney
Vice-President—William S. Robertson
Vice-President—James K. Robertson
Vice-President-Farm Director—George Brophy
Vice-President-Traveling Secretary—Howard T. Fox, Jr.
Assistant Farm Director—Jim Rantz
Controller—Jack Alexander
Director of Public Relations—Tom Mee
Director of Sales—Don Cassidy
Stadium Superintendent—Richard Ericson
Manager—Gene Mauch
Club Physicians—Dr. Leonard J. Michienzi and Dr. Harvey O'Phelan
Executive Offices—Metropolitan Stadium, 8001 Cedar Avenue,
Bloomington, Minn. 55420
Telephone—854-4040 (area code 612)

SCOUTS—Floyd Baker, Zinn Beck, Otto Bluege, Edward Dunn, Jesse Flores, Jesse Flores, Jr., Angelo Giuliani, Lee Irwin, William Messmann, Marvin Olson, Carlos Pascual, Spencer (Red) Robbins, Stanley Rogers, Walter Via.

PARK LOCATION—Metropolitan Stadium, 8001 Cedar Avenue, Bloomington, Minn. 55420.

Seating capacity—45,919

FIELD DIMENSIONS—Home plate to left field at foul line, 343 feet; to center field, 402 feet; to right field at foul line, 330 feet.

NEW YORK YANKEES

Principal Owner—George M. Steinbrenner III

Limited Partners—Harold Bowman, Michael Burke, Lester Crown, John Z. DeLorean, Thomas Evans, Michael Friedman, Harvey Leighton, Daniel McCarthy, John J. McMullen, Harry Nederlander, Robert Nederlander, Francis J. "Steve" O'Neill, William J. O'Neill, Gabe Paul, Albert Rosen, Edward Rosenthal, Marvin Warner, Charlotte Witkind.

President—Gabe Paul
Vice-President—Cedric Tallis
Administrative Vice-President—Eugene J. McHale
Vice-President, Secretary—Bruce Poston
Controller—David Weidler
Administrative Assistant—Bill Kane
Administrative Assistant—Gene Michael
Director, Minor League Operations—Jack Butterfield
Assistant Director, Minor League Operations—Barbara Tammero
Stadium Manager—Patrick Kelly
Director of Marketing and Broadcast—Barry M. Landers
Assistant Director of Marketing—Peter Gill
Assistant Director of Broadcast—Pam Boucher
Director of Publicity—Mickey Morabito
Assistant Director of Publicity—Larry Wahl
Traveling Secretary—Gerry Murphy
Ticket Director—Michael Rendine
Assistant Ticket Director—Jerry Waring
Director, Customer Services—Jim Naples
Assistant Director of Accounting—Steven Sabbagh
Director, Yankee Alumni Association—Jim Ogle
Director Emeritus, Speakers' Bureau—Jackie Ferrell
Manager—Billy Martin
Club Physician—Dr. Edward Crane
Executive Offices—Yankee Stadium, Bronx, N. Y. 10451
Telephone—293-4300 (area code 212)

SCOUTS—Howard Cassady, Al Cuccinello, Whitey Ford, Tom Greenwade, Epy Guerrero, Roy Hamey, Clyde King, Donald Lindeberg, Wayne Morgan, Bob Nieman, Frank O'Rourke, Herb Raybourn, Grover Resinger, Jax Robertson, Birdie Tebbetts, Jerry Walker, Jack Warner, Dave Yoakum.

PARK LOCATION—Yankee Stadium, E. 161st St. and River Ave., Bronx, N. Y. 10451.

Ticket Information—293-6000 (area code 212)

Seating capacity—57,145

FIELD DIMENSIONS—Home plate to left field at foul line, 312 feet; to center field, 417 feet; to right field at foul line, 310 feet.

OAKLAND A's

President—Charles O. Finley

Secretary and Treasurer—Charles O. Finley, Jr.
Controller—Chuck Cottonaro
Minor League Administrator—Norm Koselke
Director of Public Relations and Promotions—Carl Finley
Traveling Secretary and Public Relations—Ed Munson
Minor League Department—Bobby Hofman
Ticket Manager—Lorraine Paulus
Manager—Jack McKeon
Club Physician—Dr. Charles Hudson
Executive Offices—Oakland-Alameda County Coliseum, Oakland,
Calif. 94621
Telephone—762-3100 (area code 415)

SCOUTS—Jim Guinn, Phil Pote, Fred J. Shaffer, Caesar Sinibaldi.

PARK LOCATION—Oakland-Alameda County Coliseum, Nimitz
Freeway and Hegenberger Road.

Seating capacity—49,649

FIELD DIMENSIONS—Home plate to left field at foul line, 330 feet; to center field, 400 feet; to right field at foul line, 330 feet.

SEATTLE MARINERS

Managing General Partners—Danny Kaye and Lester M. Smith

General Partners—Stanley Golub, Walter Schoenfeld,
James Stillwell, James Walsh
Executive Director-General Manager—Richard Vertlieb
Director of Baseball Operations—James "Lou" Gorman
Director of Public Relations—Hal Childs
Director of Minor Leagues & Scouting—Mel Didier
Director of Sales & Marketing—Kip Horsburgh
Director of Group Sales—Jeff Odenwald
Director of Promotions—Bill Harris
Director, Ticket Services—Bill Maley
Administrative Aide—Charlene Yoritsune
Traveling Secretary—Bob Vrooman
Controller—Bill McKenzie
Accounting Manager—Gary Halperin
Assistant Director, Public Relations—David Szen
Assistant Director, Ticket Services—Tom Berg
Assistant Director, Minor Leagues and Scouting—Steve Schryver
Manager—Darrell Johnson
Club Physician—Dr. Ernie Burgess
Executive Offices—P. O. Box 4100, Seattle, Washington 98104
Telephone—628-3555 (area code 206)
SCOUTS—Edward "Bill" Hallauer, Bob Harrison, Willie Harris, Bill Jurges, Bill Kearns, Jerry Krause, Gatin "Tom" Laspina, Jeff Malinoff, Willie Moore, Steve Ray, George Staller, Ed Stevens, Rip Tutor.

PARK LOCATION—Kingdome, King County Stadium, 201 South King Street, Seattle, Washington

Seating capacity—59,059

FIELD DIMENSIONS—Home plate to left field at foul line, 316 feet; to center field, 405 feet; to right field at foul line, 316 feet.

TEXAS RANGERS

Chairman of the Board—Bradford G. Corbett

Executive Vice-President—Eddie Robinson
Vice-President—Amon G. Carter, Jr.
Vice-President-Treasurer—Raymond D. Nasher
Vice-President-Secretary—William H. Seay
General Manager—Daniel F. O'Brien
Farm Director—Hal Keller
Assistant Farm Director—Joseph Klein
Assistant Treasurer-Business Affairs—Charles F. Wangner
Traveling Secretary-News Media Director—Burton S. Hawkins
Marketing Director, Promotions Director—Dan McDonald
Stadium Operations Director—John L. Welaj
Special Assignments—Dick Gernert
Ticket Manager—Mary Ann Bosher
Equipment and Clubhouse Manager—Joseph Macko
Manager—Frank Lucchesi
Club Physician—Dr. B. J. Mycoskie
Executive Offices—Arlington Stadium, P. O. Box 1111, 1500 Copeland Road, Arlington, Tex. 76010
Telephone—265-9101 (area code 817)

SCOUTS—Harley Anderson, Lee Ballanfant, Joseph Branzell, Paddy Cottrell, Joseph Lewis, Joseph Marchese, Don Nichols.

PARK LOCATION—Arlington Stadium, 1500 Copeland Road, Arlington, Tex.

Seating capacity—35,698

FIELD DIMENSIONS—Home plate to left field at foul line, 330 feet; to center field, 400 feet; to right field at foul line, 330 feet.

TORONTO BLUE JAYS

DIRECTORS:—N. E. Hardy, D. A. Lewis, D. J. McDougall, J. P. Robarts, R. Howard Webster.

Chairman of the Board—R. Howard Webster

Executive Vice-President & General Manager—Peter Bavasi

Vice-President, Administration—Paul Beeston

Vice-President, Player Personnel—Pat Gillick

Vice-President, Marketing—Ron Millichamp

Director, Public Relations—Howard Starkman

Director, Operations—Terry Barthelmas

Administrator, Player Personnel—Elliott Wahle

Director, Team Travel—Mike Cannon

Director, Sales—Bob Hewitson

Director, Ticket Operations—George Holm

Director, Canadian Scouting—Bob Prentice

Manager, Promotions—Peter Durso

Assistant Director, Public Relations—Joe Bodolai

Season & Group Sales Administrator—Joanne Devine

Controller—Gary Gould

Assistant Director of Operations—Millie Tancrajter

Manager—Ray Hartsfield

Team Physicians—Dr. Robert Galway, Dr. Bruce Edey

Executive Offices—Exhibition Stadium, Exhibition Place, Toronto, Ontario

Telephone—595-0077 (area code 416)

SCOUTS—Robert Engle, Ric Fleury, Al LaMacchia, Duane Larson, Bobby Mattick, John McLaren, Brian McRobie, John Osborne, Jim Ridley, William Slack.

PARK LOCATION—Exhibition Stadium on the grounds of Exhibition Place. Entrances to Exhibition Place via Lakeshore Boulevard, Queen Elizabeth Way Highway and Dufferin and Bathurst Streets.

Seating capacity—40,000

FIELD DIMENSIONS—Home plate to left field at foul line, 330 feet; to center field, 400 feet; to right field at foul line, 330 feet.

NEW YORK YANKEES—1976

Front row—Hendricks, Locklear, Stanley, Michael, coach; Howard, coach; Martin, manager; Lemon, coach; Howser, coach; Berra, coach; Alomar, Munson, Guidry, White, Randolph. Second row—Monahan, trainer; Blomberg, Velez, Piniella, Tidrow, Healy, Alexander, Chambliss, Ellis, Mason, Sheehy, equipment manager. Third row—Jackson, Figueroa, Maddox, Holtzman, Hunter, Ellis, Nettles, Lyle, Kane, traveling secretary. In front—Garris, D'Ambrosio and Vines, batboys. Absent—Gamble, Rivers.

EAST DIVISION
Yankees on Top Once Again
By PHIL PEPE

It was one of those magic moments, one of those once-in-a-lifetime moments, and the image of it will be indelibly imprinted in the minds of the thousands who witnessed it . . .

. . . Chris Chambliss has swung and the sound of his bat meeting the ball has reverberated throughout the huge, renovated Yankee Stadium with a resounding crack. For an instant, Chambliss has remained transfixed at home plate watching the flight of the ball and you can see the power in those tremendous thighs and the bat has whipped around behind his back as he still has not uncoiled from the lusty swing.

Quickly, your eyes refocus and catch a glimpse of the ball as it soars into the night, disappearing from sight. Now, back to Chambliss. He has thrown his arms, both of them, straight up into the air in celebration and he is dancing, practically skipping, around the bases.

You are conscious of a mighty sustained roar from the crowd, a pulsating, demanding roar, a kind of letting loose of more than a decade of frustration and disappointment. Now the field is awash with humanity, hundreds of youngsters blocking Chambliss' path around the bases, clutching at him, at the turf, at the bases, at anything, as if trying to grab a piece of history.

The Yankees have won the American League pennant; they have won for the first time in 12 years, and they have done it in the most dramatic fashion imaginable—a leadoff home run on the first pitch of the last of the ninth inning in the fifth playoff game.

If you are a Yankee fan, it would be wise to forget what happened from that moment on, to put aside all the unpleasantness of the World Series.

But not really, because that unpleasantness is reality, and it gives the Yankees something to work for, something to look forward to, something to hope for.

"The playoffs were our World Series," pitcher Dick Tidrow wisely observed. "Their (the Cincinnati Reds) World Series was the World Series."

In a sense, the World Series was an anti-climax for the Yankees, sort of coming to the top of a mountain, panting and gasping and flushed with success, and then finding there is still another mountain to climb.

The Yankees climbed their first mountain in the playoffs. And like a baby must learn to walk one step at a time, the Yankees have merely taken the first step.

"Disappointed?" Yankee owner George Steinbrenner repeated the question. "I'm not disappointed. I'm high. I'm higher than I've been all year, except for the moment when Chris hit the home run. Why should I be down? A pennant is going to be flying over Yankee Stadium for the first time in 12 years."

It had, indeed, been a great year for the Yankees despite the World Series debacle. A brand new Stadium, attendance over two million for the first time since 1950, a runaway pennant, outstanding individual performances by Thurman Munson (the Yankees' first MVP since 1963), Graig Nettles (their first home run champion since 1961), Mickey Rivers, Chris Chambliss, Roy White (league leader in runs scored) and 19-game winner Ed Figueroa. And there was vindication that the much criticized Bobby Bonds for Rivers and Figueroa trade was a success.

"Remember three years ago when our group bought the club from CBS?" Steinbrenner said. "I said at the time it would take three years to build this team back to where it once was. Nobody believed it, but here we are. Do you know how hard it is to build a business in three years?

"A lot of teams who were ahead of us then are behind us now. I'm very proud of what we've done here. But we're not finished. We're not yet where we want to be. I'm not ready to say to the city of New York, 'This is my finished product.' We don't have the team we want. Not yet. But we're working at it and we're going to get the team we want. It's a big jump just to play in the World Series and I'm grateful we were able to do it for the people of New York."

The view from Billy Martin's eyes was a little different. He is a hard loser and it was going to take him some time to get over the disappointment of the World Series.

"People say it was a great year, but how can it be a great year when you lose four straight?" Billy wanted to know.

There was, of course, no answer. Not really. But, then, he didn't expect one.

"If you have pride," he continued, "you just don't turn it off that quickly, do you? They beat us and they're a good club. Let them take the bows, they deserve it.

"But we're going to be there next year," Martin said. "And next year, we're going to go all the way."

They may do just that. A big step was taken in December when free agents Reggie Jackson and Don Gullett signed with the A.L. champions.

SCORES OF NEW YORK YANKEES' 1976 GAMES

APRIL			Winner	Loser		MAY			Winner	Loser
8—At Milw.	L	0-5	Slaton	Hunter		15—Balt.	W	7-3	Figueroa	Cuellar
10—At Milw.	W	9-7	Lyle	Murphy		16—Balt.	L	0-7	Holtzman	Ellis
12—At Balt.	W	3-0	Hunter	Grimsley		18—At Cleve.	W	11-6a	Lyle	Kern
13—At Balt.	W	7-1	Ellis	Palmer		19—At Cleve.	W	3-2	May	Hood
15—Minn.	W	11-4	Tidrow	Albury		20—Boston	L	2-8	Cleveland	Figueroa
17—Minn.	W	10-0	Figueroa	Hughes		21—Boston	W	6-5x	Lyle	Willoughby
18—Minn.	L	4-5	Blyleven	Hunter		22—Boston	W	1-0§	Hunter	House
20—Chicago	W	5-4	Martinez	Johnson		23—Boston	L	6-7	Cleveland	Lyle
21—Chicago	W	10-7	May	Hamilton		24—Milw.	W	5-2	Figueroa	Colborn
23—Kan. C.	L	2-3	Splittorff	Hunter		25—Milw.	L	1-1	Travers	Ellis
24—Kan. C.	W	9-8§	Lyle	Pattin		26—Cleve.	W	4-3	Hunter	Hood
27—At Texas	W	1-0	Ellis	Perry		27—Cleve.	L	3-5	Bibby	May
30—At K. C.	W	5-3	Hunter	Splittorff		28—At Det.	W	9-5	Figueroa	Ruhle
			Won 10, Lost 3			29—At Det.	L	1-4	Roberts	Ellis
						30 At Det.	W	4-0	May	Laxton
						31—At Bos.	W	8-3	Hunter	Jenkins
MAY									**Won 16, Lost 12**	
1—At K. C.	L	1-4	Busby	Figueroa						
2—At K. C.	L	1-2§	Bird	Lyle		**JUNE**				
4—At Calif.	W	2-1	Ellis	Tanana		2—At Bos.	W	7-2	Figueroa	Pole
5—At Calif.	W	10-4	Hunter	Ryan		3—At Bos.	L	2-8	Tiant	Ellis
6—At Calif.	W	4-2	Figueroa	Ross		4—Oakland	L	4-6§	Todd	Lyle
7—At Oak.	W	14-4	May	Blue		5—Oakland	L	6-7	Fingers	Lyle
8—At Oak.	W	8-4	Tidrow	Todd		6—Oakland	L	2-3	Blue	Figueroa
9—At Oak.	L	3-4x	Lindblad	Hunter		6—Oakland	W	5-2	Pagan	Lindblad
11—Detroit	L	3-4	Grilli	Figueroa		8—Calif.	W	4-2	Ellis	Ross
12—Detroit	W	7-6	Bird	Bare		9—Calif.	W	4-3	Hunter	Kirkwood
13—Detroit	L	2-3	Ruhle	May		10—Calif.	L	0-2	Tanana	May
14—Balt.	L	2-6	Grimsley	Hunter						

JUNE

Date		Score	Winner	Loser
11—Texas	W	7-5	Martinez	Blyleven
12—Texas	L	1-2	Briles	Pagan
13—Texas	L	1-7	Umbarger	Hunter
15—At Minn.	W	4-2	Ellis	Redfern
16—At Minn.	W	9-4	Figueroa	Singer
17—At Chi.	W	5-4	Hunter	Forster
18—At Chi.	W	3-2y	Jackson	Hamilton
19—At Chi.	W	4-3	Alexander	Gossage
20—At Chi.	W	6-3	Ellis	Brett
21—Cleve.	W	6-0	Figueroa	Eckersley
22—Cleve.	L	2-3	Waits	Hunter
23—Cleve.	L	1-4	Hood	Holtzman
24—Cleve.	W	6-5	Lyle	LaRoche
25—Milw.	W	1-0	Ellis	Travers
26—Milw.	W	6-3	Figueroa	Slaton
27—Milw.	W	6-2	Hunter	Augustine
27—Milw.	W	10-2	Tidrow	Broberg
28—At Det.	L	1-5	Fidrych	Holtzman
29—At Det.	L	5-7	Lemanczyk	Lyle

Won 17, Lost 11

JULY

Date		Score	Winner	Loser
1—At Cleve.	L	2-3	Dobson	Figueroa
2—At Cleve.	W	7-1	Hunter	Waits
3—At Cleve.	W	7-3	Holtzman	Hood
4—At Cleve.	W	4-3	Ellis	Brown
5—Kan. C.	L	1-2	Splittorff	Alexander
6—Kan. C.	L	1-3	Bird	Figueroa
6—Kan. C.	W	7-4	Lyle	Busby
7—Kan. C.	L	1-2	Littell	Hunter
8—Chicago	W	6-0	Holtzman	Gossage
9—Chicago	W	2-1	Ellis	Forster
10—Chicago	L	1-4	Brett	Alexander
11—Chicago	W	5-0	Figueroa	Johnson
15—At Texas	W	7-6	Figueroa	Perry
15—At Texas	W	6-4‡	Hunter	Hoerner
16—At Texas	W	3-0	Holtzman	Blyleven
17—At Texas	W	7-5	Ellis	Barr
18—At Texas	W	2-3x	Hargan	Lyle
19—At Chi.	W	3-2	Figueroa	Hamilton
20—At Chi.	W	14-9†	York	Vuckovich
21—Oakland	W	10-1	Hunter	Norris
22—Oakland	L	5-6	Fingers	Tidrow
23—Boston	W	9-1	Alexander	Lee
24—Boston	W	4-1	Figueroa	Jones
25—Boston	W	6-5	Tidrow	House
26—At Balt.	L	1-3	Grimsley	Hunter
27—At Balt.	L	1-4	Palmer	Ellis
28—At Balt.	L	3-4	F. Martinez	Alexander
30—At Bos.	W	6-4	Figueroa	Tiant
31—At Bos.	L	2-4	Jenkins	Holtzman
31—At Bos.	L	4-6	Cleveland	Hunter

Won 18, Lost 12

AUGUST

Date		Score	Winner	Loser
1—At Bos.	L	4-5	Lee	Tidrow
2—Detroit	W	1-0	Alexander	Roberts
3—Detroit	W	4-3	Jackson	Fidrych
4—At Milw.	L	3-4	Travers	Hunter
4—At Milw.	W	7-2	Holtzman	Slaton
5—At Milw.	L	3-9*	Frisella	Ellis
7—Balt.	L	4-7	May	Alexander
8—Balt.	L	5-8	Grimsley	Hunter
9—At K. C.	L	2-8	Leonard	Holtzman
10—At K. C.	W	2-1§	Ellis	Mingori
11—At K. C.	W	5-3	Alexander	Bird
12—At Minn.	W	12-5	Hunter	Luebber
13—At Minn.	W	9-3	Figueroa	Bane
14—At Minn.	W	5-4	Holtzman	Goltz
15—At Minn.	L	8-9	Hughes	Lyle
16—Texas	W	5-1	Hunter	Perry
17—Texas	W	2-1	Alexander	Boggs
18—Texas	W	8-6	Lyle	Hargan
20—Calif.	L	3-5	Kirkwood	Figueroa
21—Calif.	L	3-4‡	Scott	Tidrow
22—Calif.	L	8-11§	Monge	Lyle
23—Minn.	W	9-4	Holtzman	Singer
24—Minn.	W	5-4	Alexander	Bane
25—Minn.	W	5-4b	Jackson	Burgmeier
27—At Calif.	W	5-0z	Jackson	Monge
28—At Calif.	W	8-1	Ellis	Ryan
29—At Calif.	L	4-5§	Scott	Tidrow
30—At Oak.	W	5-2	Figueroa	Norris
31—At Oak.	W	2-1	Alexander	Bahnsen

Won 18, Lost 11

SEPTEMBER

Date		Score	Winner	Loser
1—At Oak.	L	0-5	Blue	Hunter
3—At Balt.	W	3-1	Ellis	Garland
4—At Balt.	W	4-2	Holtzman	Palmer
4—At Balt.	L	2-6	May	Figueroa
5—At Balt.	L	3-5	Grimsley	Hunter
6—Boston	W	6-5	Alexander	Jones
7—Boston	W	4-2	Ellis	Tiant
8—Milw.	W	8-0	Figueroa	Augustine
9—Milw.	W	4-2	Holtzman	Travers
10—Milw.	W	6-4	Hunter	Slaton
11—Detroit	L	5-6	Roberts	Alexander
12—Detroit	L	0-6	Fidrych	Ellis
12—Detroit	W	3-1	Figueroa	Glynn
13—Detroit	L	1-3	Crawford	Holtzman
14—At Cleve.	W	8-2	Jackson	Dobson
15—At Cleve.	W	2-0	Alexander	Waits
17—At Milw.	W	5-3§	Figueroa	Kobel
18—At Milw.	W	5-3	Ellis	Travers
19—At Milw.	W	2-1*	Hunter	Slaton
20—At Milw.	L	2-4	Beare	Holtzman
21—Balt.	L	8-11‡	F. Martinez	Tidrow
22—Balt.	L	0-2	Palmer	Ellis
22—Balt.	L	2-5	May	Figueroa
23—Balt.	L	1-2	Flanagan	Hunter
24—At Det.	L	0-3	Roberts	Holtzman
24—At Det.	W	8-0	Jackson	Crawford
25—At Det.	W	10-6	Alexander	Glynn
28—At Bos.	L	5-7	Kreuger	Figueroa
29—At Bos.	W	9-6	Hunter	Tiant

Won 16, Lost 13

OCTOBER

Date		Score	Winner	Loser
2—Cleve.	W	6-5	Ellis	Thomas
2—Cleve.	W	4-3c	Holtzman	Buskey

Won 2, Lost 0

* 6 innings. † 8 innings. ‡ 10 innings. § 11 innings. x 12 innings. y 14 innings. z 15 innings. a 16 innings. b 19 innings. c May 17 game at Cleveland transferred to New York.

Slow Start Dooms Orioles' Pennant Quest

By JIM HENNEMAN

For the Baltimore Orioles, 1976 was the most turbulent season in the organization's 23-year history.

And it may well have marked the end of an era.

A disastrous start, which has been an annual occurrence the last five years, drove the Orioles out of contention immediately. This time they lagged so far back that their traditional late surge hardly mattered.

Manager Earl Weaver's club managed to finish second in the East Division, but they were hardly in sight of the Yankees, who were runaway winners.

Still, what happened to the Orioles during the season was mild compared to what took place later.

They lost Reggie Jackson (Yankees), Bobby Grich (Angels) and Wayne Garland (Indians) through the re-entry draft and were left with a skeleton crew to face the uncertainties of the future.

Suddenly, a team that had ranked among the pre-season favorites for the last 17 years was reduced to just another member of the pack.

Since 1960, the Orioles have won with more consistency than any team in baseball, but now they will be forced to struggle to maintain respectability unless they can produce a solid crop of rookies who can blossom overnight.

"It could be a lot better," said General Manager Hank Peters in a classic understatement while trying to remain optimistic, "but it's not as bad as some people think. We'll be all right."

That's what the Orioles thought last April 2 when they combined with the Oakland Athletics to complete the first of two blockbuster trades. While giving up outfielder Don Baylor and pitchers Mike Torrez and Paul Mitchell, they landed Jackson and southpaw hurler Ken Holtzman.

The deal was made to provide long-needed lefthanded power and give Weaver's lineup better balance.

The situation, however, turned chaotic almost immediately as Jackson refused to report while trying to negotiate the $3 million-plus contract he eventually got from the Yankees. It wasn't until a month after the deal that Jackson showed up, and then he struggled for another five weeks while going through a second spring training period.

After reporting, Jackson's presence stirred almost as much controversy as his absence. While nine other unsigned Orioles, including Holtzman, were playing at a 20 percent cut in pay, Jackson was lured to Baltimore by a $60,000 increase over his 1975 salary of $140,000. Peters was kept busy defending himself against "double standard" charges, with Holtzman the most outspoken critic, and the club floundered on the playing field as Jackson played his way into shape and Grich and Lee May suffered early season injuries.

Eventually, all the pay cuts were restored, but not until after Peters swung another mammoth trade—this one with the Yankees. Convinced that he would never be able to meet Holtzman's demands, Peters worked out a deal with Kansas City, only to have it fall through when the lefthander couldn't come to terms with the Royals either.

Two days later, on June 15, Holtzman was sent to the Yankees, along with Doyle Alexander, likewise involved in a contract hassle, Grant Jackson, Elrod Hendricks and minor leaguer Jimmy Freeman. In return the Orioles secured pitchers Rudy May, Tippy Martinez and Dave Pagan, catcher Rick Dempsey and Scott McGregor, a lefthanded pitching prospect.

May settled into the starting rotation and completed the best year of his career with a 15-10 record, Martinez became the Orioles' most effective reliever and Dempsey eventually surfaced with a regular job. Pagan had a good start but then encountered control problems, was generally ineffective and wound up going to Seattle in the expansion draft. McGregor finished strong at Rochester, leading the International League in shutouts, and is considered a strong candidate to claim a spot in Weaver's starting rotation in 1977.

By the time the Orioles got their roster set, the pieces started to fall in place. From the All-Star break on they played even with the Yankees, compiling a 48-32 record, but by that time they were already 10½ games back, and they never did get seriously into the race.

The closest they came to the Yankees, a team they beat 13 times in 18 tries, over the second half of the season was September 24, when they reduced the deficit to seven games. The next day they were eliminated—the earliest a Baltimore team had been removed from contention since 1968.

There were the usual number of individual highlights along the way. Jim Palmer won THE SPORTING NEWS "Pitcher of the Year" and the Cy Young awards for the third time in the last four seasons while posting a 22-13 record, with a 2.51 earned-run average, and leading the league in wins, starts (40), and innings pitched (315).

Lee May, cited as the club's Most Valuable Player, led the American League with 109 runs batted in and tied for fourth with 25 home runs as he continued to be one of the game's steadiest, if least spectacular, run producers.

Ken Singleton led the club in hitting for the second straight year, overcoming a horrible start to finish with a .278 mark. The switch-hitting outfielder also hit 13 home runs and totaled 70 RBIs.

Mark Belanger finally achieved All-Star recognition after enjoying one of the best years of his remarkable career. He finished with a .270 batting average and turned in another flawless job defensively.

Garland, only 2-5 in 1975, emerged from the bullpen in June and went on to record a 20-7 season—sufficient reason for the Indians to break the bank with a reported 10-year contract.

Despite his late start, Jackson had a productive season, finishing with 27 homers, 91 RBIs, 28 stolen bases, a .277 batting average and a league-leading slugging percentage of .502.

Palmer, Grich, Belanger and Jackson were named to the American League All-Star team by THE SPORTING NEWS, and the first three were also honored with "Gold Gloves," signifying their defensive excellence.

And despite the lack of a competitive pennant race, the club attracted a satisfactory total of 1,058,609 spectators.

Now comes the real test.

SCORES OF BALTIMORE ORIOLES' 1976 GAMES

APRIL			Winner	Loser	APRIL			Winner	Loser
9—Boston	W	1-0	Palmer	Jenkins	30—Oakland	L	1-11	Torrez	Palmer
10—Boston	W	5-1	Holtzman	House			**Won 6, Lost 9**		
11—Boston	L	2-6	Tiant	Cuellar					
12—N. York	L	0-3	Hunter	Grimsley	MAY				
13—N. York	L	1-7	Ellis	Palmer	2—Oakland	L	2-6	Blue	Grimsley
17—At Oak.	W	6-1	Palmer	Torrez	2—Oakland	W	4-3	Garland	Abbott
18—At Oak.	L	1-28†	Fingers	Miller	4—Chicago	L	1-3	Wood	Holtzman
19—At Calif.	L	4-9	Tanana	Cuellar	5—Chicago	W	2-0	Palmer	Gossage
20—At Calif.	L	0-5	Ryan	Alexander	7—Kan. C.	W	4-3	Garland	Pattin
21—At Calif.	W	5-1	Palmer	Kirkwood	8—Kan. C.	L	3-6	Leonard	Holtzman
24—At Minn.	L	1-2y	Campbell	Jackson	9—Kan. C.	L	4-7	Littell	Palmer
25—At Minn.	L	2-7	Burgmeier	Palmer	11—At Milw.	W	5-2	Cuellar	Colborn
27—Calif.	W	3-2†	Jackson	Drago	12—At Milw.	W	8-6	Alexander	Augustine
28—Calif.	W	4-2	Holtzman	Ross	13—At Milw.	W	5-3	Palmer	Travers

BALTIMORE ORIOLES—1976

Front row—Cuellar, Miller, Frey, coach; Hunter, coach; Weaver, manager; Bamberger, coach; Ripken, coach; Grimsley, Bumbry. Second row—Reid, equipment manager; Harper, DeCinces, Singleton, Belanger, Dempsey, Robinson, Holdsworth, Martinez, Crowley, Jackson, Salvon, trainer. Third row—L. May, Mora, Garland, Nordbrook, Grich, Muser, Pagan, R. May, Duncan, Blair. Inset—Palmer. In front—Cashen, batboy.

MAY			Winner	Loser
14–At N. Y.	W	6-2	Grimsley	Hunter
15–At N. Y.	L	3-7	Figueroa	Cuellar
16–At N. Y.	W	7-0	Holtzman	Ellis
17–Milw.	W	4-3	Miller	Rodriguez
19–Milw.	W	5-3	Cuellar	Colborn
21–Detroit	W	8-5	Alexander	Bare
22–Detroit	W	8-4	Garland	Crawford
23–Detroit	L	6-10	Hiller	Miller
24–Cleve.	L	0-4	Eckersley	Cuellar
25–Cleve.	L	1-3	Dobson	Palmer
26–At Det.	W	6-0	Alexander	Laxton
26–At Det.	L	2-6	Bare	Grimsley
27–At Det.	W	4-3	Holtzman	Coleman
28–At Bos.	W	4-1	Garland	Cleveland
29–At Bos.	W	7-2	Palmer	Tiant
30–At Bos.	L	1-3	Wise	Alexander
31–At Cleve.	L	1-4	Kern	Holtzman
31–At Cleve.	L	3-4	Dobson	Cuellar
		Won 16, Lost 12		

JUNE				
2–At Cleve.	W	2-0y	Garland	Buskey
4–Minn.	L	6-8†	Campbell	Flanagan
5–Minn.	W	5-1	Holtzman	Decker
6–Minn.	L	2-3	Singer	Palmer
6–Minn.	L	6-11	Hughes	Cuellar
7–Texas	L	4-6	Umbarger	Grimsley
8–Texas	L	3-6	Peterson	Alexander
9–Texas	L	1-4	Perry	Holtzman
10–At K. C.	L	0-7	Splittorff	Palmer
11–At K. C.	L	0-4	Bird	Cuellar
12–At K. C.	L	6-7	Busby	Alexander
13–At K. C.	L	4-8	Leonard	Flanagan
15–At Chi.	W	4-0	Palmer	Gossage
16–At Chi.	W	10-2	Cuellar	Barrios
17–At Texas	W	4-1	Garland	Briles
18–At Texas	W	9-4	May	Umbarger
19–At Texas	W	8-4	Palmer	Foucault
20–At Texas	W	2-0	Cuellar	Perry
21–Boston	W	2-0	Garland	Tiant
22–Boston	L	5-6z	Cleveland	Pagan
23–Boston	W	3-2†	Palmer	Willoughby
25–Cleve.	L	5-6	Thomas	Pagan
26–Cleve.	W	2-1	Garland	Eckersley
27–Cleve.	L	3-6	Dobson	May
27–Cleve.	W	6-2	Grimsley	Waits
28–At Bos.	L	8-12	Jenkins	Flanagan
29–At Bos.	L	0-2	Wise	Cuellar
30–At Bos.	L	4-6	Willoughby	Garland
		Won 12, Lost 16		

JULY				
1–Detroit	L	0-2	Roberts	May
2–Detroit	W	2-1	Palmer	Ruhle
3–At Det.	L	0-4	Fidrych	Cuellar
4–At Det.	W	7-4	Garland	Hiller
5–At Oak.	L	1-4	Torrez	May
6–At Oak.	L	0-2	Blue	Palmer
7–At Oak.	L	3-5	P. Mitchell	Cuellar
8–At Oak.	W	9-6	Garland	Lindblad
9–At Calif.	W	4-3	May	Tanana
10–At Calif.	W	5-2	Palmer	Ross
11–At Calif.	W	3-1	Pagan	Ryan
15–Calif.	W	4-0	Palmer	Ross
16–Calif.	W	5-4	Garland	Ryan
17–Calif.	L	3-7	Tanana	May
18–Calif.	L	6-8	Drago	Cuellar
19–At K. C.	W	4-3	Palmer	Leonard
20–At K. C.	W	10-3	Garland	Bird
21–At Texas	W	6-4§	F. Martinez	Hoerner
22–At Texas	W	4-3	Holdsworth	Perry
23–Milw.	W	3-4x	Slaton	F. Martinez
24–Milw.	L	1-4	Rodriguez	Cuellar
24–Milw.	L	0-5	Augustine	Garland
25–Milw.	L	1-3	Travers	Pagan
26–N. York	W	3-1	Grimsley	Hunter

JULY			Winner	Loser
27–N. York	W	4-1	Palmer	Ellis
28–N. York	W	4-3	F. Martinez	Alexander
29–At Det.	W	1-0	May	Fidrych
30–At Det.	W	7-3	Grimsley	Ruhle
31–Detroit	L	4-5	Lemanczyk	Palmer
		Won 17, Lost 12		

AUGUST				
1–Detroit	W	4-3	Holdsworth	Hiller
2–At Milw.	L	1-7	Colborn	May
3–At Milw.	L	2-4	Rodriguez	Grimsley
4–At Cleve.	L	0-3	Waits	Palmer
5–At Cleve.	W	6-2	Garland	Bibby
7–At N. Y.	W	7-4	May	Alexander
8–At N. Y.	W	8-5	Grimsley	Hunter
10–Minn.	W	2-0	Palmer	Goltz
11–Minn.	L	0-2	Singer	Garland
13–Chicago	L	2-5	Gossage	May
14–Chicago	W	8-6	Palmer	Forster
14–Chicago	W	6-5	Miller	Brett
15–Chicago	W	3-0	Garland	Barrios
16–At Minn.	W	8-4	Grimsley	Luebber
17–At Minn.	W	10-3	May	Johnson
18–At Minn.	L	1-5	Goltz	Palmer
19–At Minn.	L	4-5	Singer	Pagan
20–At Chi.	W	6-4	Garland	Barrios
21–At Chi.	L	10-11§	Hamilton	Cuellar
22–At Chi.	W	6-2	Palmer	Kravec
22–At Chi.	L	3-7	Vuckovich	Grimsley
23–Oakland	L	0-3	Blue	Flanagan
24–Oakland	L	4-5	Bahnsen	Garland
25–Oakland	W	9-4	May	P. Mitchell
27–Texas	W	3-0	Palmer	Perry
28–Texas	W	6-4	Holdsworth	Hargan
29–Texas	L	0-11	Umbarger	Garland
30–Kan. C.	W	3-2	May	Hassler
31–Kan. C.	W	4-3	Palmer	Pattin
		Won 17, Lost 12		

SEPTEMBER				
1–Kan. C.	W	7-1	Flanagan	Bird
3–N. York	L	1-3	Ellis	Garland
4–N. York	L	2-4	Holtzman	Palmer
4–N. York	W	6-2	May	Figueroa
5–N. York	W	5-3	Grimsley	Hunter
6–At Det.	L	4-5	Roberts	Miller
7–At Det.	W	5-3	Garland	Fidrych
8–Cleve.	W	3-1	Palmer	Eckersley
9–Cleve.	L	3-4	Dobson	May
10–Cleve.	W	4-3	Grimsley	Waits
11–At Milw.	W	5-1	Garland	Rodriguez
11–At Milw.	W	3-2	Flanagan	Colborn
12–At Milw.	W	3-1	Palmer	Augustine
13–At Milw.	W	5-3†	Holdsworth	Castro
14–Detroit	W	9-7	J. Martinez	Hiller
15–Detroit	W	1-0*	Garland	Roberts
18–At Cleve.	L	1-5	Thomas	Palmer
18–At Cleve.	W	3-2	May	Bibby
19–At Cleve.	L	4-5	Dobson	Garland
19–At Cleve.	L	2-3x	Kern	Miller
21–At N. Y.	W	11-8†	F. Martinez	Tidrow
22–At N. Y.	W	2-0	Palmer	Ellis
22–At N. Y.	W	5-2	May	Figueroa
23–At N. Y.	W	2-1	Flanagan	Hunter
24–Boston	W	3-0	Garland	Wise
25–Boston	L	0-1	Tiant	Grimsley
26–Boston	L	3-8	Cleveland	J. Martinez
28–Milw.	W	7-5‡	Garland	Rodriguez
28–Milw.	W	7-3	May	Colborn
29–Milw.	L	3-6	Augustine	McGregor
		Won 20, Lost 10		

OCTOBER				
1–At Bos.	L	4-7	Wise	Holdsworth
2–At Bos.	L	0-1	Cleveland	J. Martinez
3–At Bos.	L	2-3z	Willoughby	Flanagan
		Won 0, Lost 3		

* 6 innings. † 10 innings. ‡ 11 innings. § 12 innings. x 13 innings. y 14 innings. z 15 innings.

BOSTON RED SOX—1976

Front row—Rice, Fisk, Petrocelli; Pesky, coach; Williams, coach; Johnson, manager; Bryant, coach; Zimmer, coach; Cooper, Burleson, Lynn. Second row—Moss, trainer; Doyle, Miller, Darwin, Montgomery, Evans, Griffin, Dillard, Heise, Merchant, Orlando, equipment manager; Cerrone, equipment manager. Third row—House, Cleveland, Murphy, Wise, Willoughby, Jones, Jenkins, Pole, Tiant. Insets—Yastrzemski, Lee, Hobson. In front—Krall and Naticchioni, batboys.

Red Sox Draw Well, Play Poorly

By LARRY WHITESIDE

Don Zimmer said it best. His Red Sox, defending American League champions, had rallied to win 15 of the last 18 games and finish in third place by winning on the final day of the season. But clearly, there was no joy in Fenway Park.

"I know we're better than we've played this year," said Zimmer, the man who took over when Boston's hopes for 1976 reached rock bottom. "The whole world knows it. We had the team that everybody figured would win it. But we simply didn't do it."

The Red Sox had an outstanding year at the gate, drawing 1,895,846 fans, second highest in their history. The brand new electronic scoreboard in center field proved to be the most efficient and least controversial item in Fenway Park and helped pick up many a dull moment with statistical fact and fantasy.

But 1976 will be forever remembered in Boston as the year that never was. Where the dreams of a second straight pennant and a return to the magic of 1975 never materialized. A year shattered early by contract squabbles and a 10-game losing streak in May that suddenly made it a major adventure just to catch the front-running Yankees. A year of tragedy, not only because the club barely finished above .500 (83-79), but because Tom Yawkey, Boston's proud owner, died quietly on July 9 and never realized his dream of seeing a world championship flag fly over Fenway Park.

A year of frustration. Frustration for last year's Most Valuable Player Fred Lynn, who suffered from something far more serious than the sophomore jinx, and whose .314 average is no true barometer of his disappointing season. A disappointing year for catcher Carlton Fisk, who along with Lynn and Burleson staged a holdout of almost half a season as the first free agents in the club's history before signing. More than any other factor, the long drawn out contract hassle by the trio will be cited as a major cause of the disunity that overtook the club in 1976 and was not fully under control until the latter stages of Zimmer's tenure. Zimmer, the short squatty third base coach for half a season, took over when the Sox fired Darrell Johnson, the manager of the year in 1975. His 42-34 finishing record and the improved play of his club justified his sudden hiring after only a two-week trial period.

The promise of a great season was there. Four possible 20-game winners in Rick Wise, Luis Tiant, Bill Lee and Fergie Jenkins, all proven veterans. But only Tiant (21-12) lived up to his promise and won 11 of his last 13 decisions in earning Cy Young consideration. Wise (14-11) suffered from a midseason slump. Jenkins (12-11) was inconsistent and/or unlucky all year, and finally departed with a month to go, suffering from a torn right Achilles tendon. Lee (5-7) was nearly trampled to death in a fight in early May in Yankee Stadium, and injured his left arm. He came back in mid-July but was only a competitive shell of the pitcher who won 17 games in 1975.

Zimmer did manage to revive the talents of Reggie Cleveland (10-9), but the flop of rookies Rick Kreuger and Rick Jones left the Red Sox wondering about lefthanders for 1977. Relief pitcher Tom House, acquired for Roger Moret, pitched only 44 innings and was ineffective.

The Red Sox still thought they had a chance at the All-Star break, when they were 40-40 and in second place, 9½ games behind the Yankees. But they lost five of the first six after that, a development that led to Johnson's firing on July 19, and dropped 10 games under .500 (42-52) before winning 41 of the last 68 games, including a 21-11 record from September 1 through the end of the season.

The individual stars were few, but none seemed to outshine 37-year-old Carl Yastrzemski, who clubbed 21 home runs and batted in 100 runs for the fourth time in his career (102) and the most since 1970. Burleson's strong finish (71-217, .327) after he signed earned him praise by Zimmer as "my toughest hitter" down the stretch. Cecil Cooper had career highs of 451 at-bats, 127 hits and 78 RBIs. And while Jim Rice's .282 finish didn't match his rookie season for the Red Sox, he did finish the year with an 18-game hitting streak, led the club in home runs (25) and was second in RBIs (85).

The boys of 1975 have been forced into manhood and many of them won't be around in 1977 for various reasons. Forget about 1976 and the Red Sox. It was the season that never was.

SCORES OF BOSTON RED SOX' 1976 GAMES

APRIL			Winner	Loser
9—At Balt.	L	0-1	Palmer	Jenkins
10—At Balt.	L	1-5	Holtzman	House
11—At Balt.	W	6-2	Tiant	Cuellar
13—Cleve.	W	7-4	Cleveland	Dobson
14—Cleve.	L	5-6	Hood	Jenkins
15—Chicago	L	4-8	Johnson	Wise
17—Chicago	W	7-1	Tiant	Gossage
18—Chicago	L	4-10	Wood	Lee
19—Minn.	W	2-0	Jenkins	Decker
20—Minn.	W	12-3	Wise	Goltz
23—At Chi.	W	9-2	Tiant	Wood
29—At Texas	L	1-6	Briles	Lee
30—At Texas	L	5-6	Umbarger	Jenkins
			Won 6, Lost 7	
MAY				
1—At Texas	L	1-7	Singer	Wise
2—At Texas	L	3-6	Perry	Tiant
4—Kan. C.	L	5-7	Fitzmorris	Lee
5—Kan. C	L	4-8	Splittorff	Jenkins
8—Texas	W	5-6	Hargan	Pole
8—Texas	L	4-12	Umbarger	Tiant
9—Texas	L	5-6	Foucault	Willoughby
11—At Cleve.	L	3-4	Dobson	Jenkins
12—At Cleve.	W	6-4§	House	LaRoche
13—At Cleve.	W	7-5	Tiant	Kern
14—Milw.	W	2-1	Pole	Broberg
15—Milw.	W	9-4	Jenkins	Rodriguez
16—Milw.	L	5-11	Slaton	Wise
17—At Det.	W	7-0	Tiant	Coleman
18—At Det.	W	5-3	Willoughby	Crawford
19—At Det.	W	9-2	Jenkins	Roberts
20—At N. Y.	W	8-2	Cleveland	Figueroa
21—At N. Y.	L	5-6§	Lyle	Willoughby
22—At N. Y.	L	0-1‡	Hunter	House
23—At N. Y.	W	7-6	Cleveland	Lyle
24—Detroit	W	3-0	Wise	Roberts
25—Detroit	W	2-0	Tiant	Fidrych
26—At Milw.	L	2-6	Slaton	Pole
27—At Milw.	W	2-1	Jenkins	Broberg
28—Balt.	L	1-4	Garland	Cleveland
29—Balt.	L	2-7	Palmer	Tiant
30—Balt.	W	3-1	Wise	Alexander
31—N. York	L	3-8	Hunter	Jenkins
			Won 13, Lost 15	
JUNE				
2—N. York	L	2-7	Figueroa	Pole
3—N. York	W	8-2	Tiant	Ellis

JUNE			Winner	Loser
4—Calif.	L	4-5†	Scott	Willoughby
5—Calif.	W	4-3	Jenkins	Tanana
6—Calif.	W	4-1	Pole	Ryan
8—Oakland	L	5-6	Todd	Cleveland
9—Oakland	W	6-4	Wise	Torrez
10—Oakland	L	5-8	Todd	Murphy
11—At Minn.	L	4-10	Burgmeier	Pole
12—At Minn.	W	5-2	Tiant	Goltz
13—At Minn.	W	10-2	Jones	Hughes
14—At Minn.	W	5-0	Wise	Decker
15—At Oak.	L	2-3	Lindblad	Jenkins
16—At Oak.	L	1-4	P. Mitchell	Tiant
17—At Oak.	W	8-3	Pole	Torrez
18—At Calif.	W	3-1	Murphy	Hassler
19—At Calif.	L	3-5	Ryan	Wise
20—At Calif.	W	4-3‡	Murphy	Drago
21—At Balt.	L	0-2	Garland	Tiant
22—At Balt.	W	6-5x	Cleveland	Pagan
23—At Balt.	L	2-3†	Palmer	Willoughby
24—Detroit	L	3-6	Fidrych	Wise
25—Detroit	L	2-6	Hiller	Jenkins
26—Detroit	W	2-1	Tiant	Roberts
27—Detroit	L	2-4‡	Grilli	Murphy
28—Balt.	W	12-8	Jenkins	Flanagan
29—Balt.	W	2-0	Wise	Cuellar
30—Balt.	W	6-4	Willoughby	Garland
			Won 15, Lost 13	
JULY				
1—At Milw.	L	5-6†	Frisella	Cleveland
2—At Milw.	W	3-0	Pole	Augustine
3—At Milw.	L	2-6	Colborn	Cleveland
4—At Milw.	W	3-1	Wise	Broberg
5—Chicago	W	11-2	Tiant	Jefferson
6—Chicago	W	4-0	Jenkins	Brett
7—Chicago	L	3-6†	Johnson	Willoughby
8—Minn.	W	8-4	Jones	Goltz
9—Minn.	L	6-8	Campbell	Wise
10—Minn.	L	2-4	Bane	Tiant
11—Minn.	W	6-4	Jenkins	Singer
15—At K. C.	L	5-12	Leonard	Pole
15—At K. C.	W	2-1	Jones	Bird
16—At K. C.	L	1-5	Splittorff	Murphy
16—At K. C.	L	1-2	Fitzmorris	Wise
17—At K. C.	L	1-2	Littell	Tiant
18—At K. C.	L	3-6	Pattin	Cleveland
19—At Texas	L	3-4‡	Bacsik	Willoughby
20—At Texas	W	4-2	Jones	Briles
21—At Minn.	L	1-5	Goltz	Wise

JULY			Winner	Loser
22–At Minn.	L	1-5	Redfern	Tiant
23–At N. Y.	L	1-9	Alexander	Lee
24–At N. Y.	L	1-4	Figueroa	Jones
25–At N. Y.	L	5-6	Tidrow	House
26–Cleve.	L	4-9	Buskey	Tiant
27–Cleve.	W	8-7	Jenkins	Bibby
28–Cleve.	W	6-7	Kern	Willoughby
29–Cleve.	W	6-4	Wise	Dobson
30–N. York	L	4-6	Figueroa	Tiant
31–N. York	W	4-2	Jenkins	Holtzman
31–N. York	W	6-4	Cleveland	Hunter
			Won 12, Lost 19	

AUGUST				
1–N. York	W	5-4	Lee	Tidrow
2–At Cleve.	W	3-1	Wise	Dobson
3–At Cleve.	L	0-1†	Eckersley	Murphy
4–At Det.	W	4-1	Jenkins	Ruhle
5–At Det.	W	5-4	Cleveland	Lemanczyk
6–Milw.	W	2-1	Murphy	Colborn
7–Milw.	W	3-0	Tiant	Rodriguez
10–At Calif.	L	4-5	Ross	Jenkins
11–At Calif.	L	0-6	Tanana	Wise
12–At Calif.	W	2-1†	Tiant	Ryan
13–At Oak.	L	0-2	Norris	Cleveland
14–At Oak.	L	3-7	Blue	Jenkins
15–At Oak.	L	7-8	Bahnsen	Willoughby
16–At Chi.	W	12-5	Tiant	Johnson
17–At Chi.	L	1-2	Carroll	Murphy
17–At Chi.	W	11-7	Pole	Odom
18–At Chi.	L	2-4	Gossage	Jenkins
19–At Chi.	L	2-4	Brett	Wise
20–Oakland	W	2-1	Tiant	Fingers
21–Oakland	W	5-2	Cleveland	Bosman
22–Oakland	L	6-7‡	Fingers	Willoughby
23–Calif.	W	7-3	Lee	Ryan
24–Calif.	L	5-6	Hartzell	Willoughby
25–Calif.	W	8-2	Tiant	Kirkwood
26–Kan. C.	L	6-7x	Bruno	Willoughby
27–Kan. C.	W	9-4	Jenkins	Bird
28–Kan. C.	L	3-8	Fitzmorris	Lee
29–Kan. C.	W	15-6	Wise	Leonard

AUGUST			Winner	Loser
30–Texas	W	11-3	Tiant	Blyleven
31–Texas	L	3-8	Briles	Cleveland
			Won 16, Lost 14	

SEPTEMBER				
1–Texas	W	3-0	Murphy	Perry
3–At Cleve.	W	5-3	Tiant	Brown
4–At Cleve.	W	7-6	Wise	Eckersley
4–At Cleve.	L	0-4	Dobson	Lee
5–At Cleve.	L	3-6	Waits	Cleveland
6–At N. Y.	L	5-6	Alexander	Jones
7–At N. Y.	L	2-4	Ellis	Tiant
8–Detroit	W	4-3	Lee	Lemanczyk
9–Detroit	W	5-0	Wise	Ruhle
10–Detroit	L	0-1*	Bare	Cleveland
11–Cleve.	L	5-6	Bibby	Jones
12–Cleve.	W	11-3	Tiant	Thomas
13–Cleve.	L	3-8	Eckersley	Lee
14–At Milw.	L	2-3†	Frisella	Willoughby
15–At Milw.	W	2-1	Cleveland	Beare
16–At Milw.	W	4-3	Kreuger	Castro
17–At Det.	W	8-3	Tiant	Fidrych
18–At Det.	W	5-4	Lee	Ruhle
19–At Det.	W	6-1	Wise	Roberts
20–At Det.	W	12-6	Jones	Glynn
21–Milw.	W	7-1	Tiant	Haas
21–Milw.	L	1-3	Colborn	Kreuger
22–Milw.	W	6-3	Pole	Augustine
23–Milw.	W	10-3	Lee	Travers
24–At Balt.	L	0-3	Garland	Wise
25–At Balt.	L	1-0	Tiant	Grimsley
26–At Balt.	W	8-3	Cleveland	J. D. Martinez
28–N. York	W	7-5	Kreuger	Figueroa
29–N. York	L	6-9	Hunter	Tiant
			Won 18, Lost 11	

OCTOBER				
1–Balt.	W	7-4	Wise	Holdsworth
2–Balt.	W	1-0	Cleveland	J. D. Martinez
3–Balt.	W	3-2x	Willoughby	Flanagan
			Won 3, Lost 0	

* 5 innings.   † 10 innings.   ‡ 11 innings.   § 12 innings.   x 15 innings.

Indians Again Finish Fourth

By RUSSELL SCHNEIDER

The Indians continued to make progress in 1976, though, to be sure, it wasn't as positive–or as rapid–as had been hoped.

For the first time since 1968 the Indians won more games than they lost, finishing with an 81-78 record, but third place slipped out of their grasp on the final day of the season, and they wound up fourth in the American League's East Division for the third straight season.

In a way, Mother Nature could be held partially responsible because the Tribe was rained out of a re-scheduled doubleheader in New York on the final day.

Meanwhile, in Boston, the Red Sox beat the Orioles, 3-2, in 15 innings to climb a half-game ahead of the Indians, who could have withstood the challenge if they'd been able to play (and win) that afore-mentioned twin-bill.

As it was, that doubleheader in New York meant the Indians "lost" three games to inclement weather (they also were washed out of a game against Milwaukee), just as was the case in 1975 when they were fourth with a 79-80 mark, 15½ lengths behind the division champion Red Sox.

CLEVELAND INDIANS—1976

Front row—Buynak, equipment manager; Bell, Tomlinson, batboy; Torborg, coach; Colavito, coach; M. Seghi, traveling secretary; Robinson, manager. Bonda, club president; P. Seghi, general manager; Garcia, coach; Haddix, coach; Warfield, trainer. Second row—Blanks, Ashby, Pruitt, Lowenstein, Hendrick, Thomas, LaRoche, Manning, Hood, Kuiper, Duffy, Gonzalez. Third row—Waits, Brown, Fosse, Smith, Spikes, Powell, Kern, Bibby, Eckersley, Dobson, Carty, Buskey.

At least in 1976 the Indians were in the race for half the season, seriously contending for the division title until the ultimate champs, the Yankees, came to town on July 1 for a four-game series that had the fans in a genuine state of frenzy for the first time in years.

At the time the Indians were cruising along in second place with a 36-33 record, seven games behind the Yankees.

The excitement reached a fever pitch when Pat Dobson raised his record to 10-5, beating the Yankees, 3-2, in the opener of that series which was to draw almost 200,000 paying customers. The victory reduced the Indians' deficit to six games—but they were destined to get no closer.

The Yankees won the next three games of that crucial series, 7-1, 7-3, and 4-3, and that, as it turned out, was the beginning of the end for the Indians.

They immediately embarked upon a trip to the west coast, going on to lose five of six games to fall into a tie for fourth place with a 38-41 record, 11 games behind the Yankees at the All-Star break, all hopes for a pennant virtually gone once again.

They regrouped and played a little better in the second half, winning 43 and losing 37, but by then it was much too late as the Yankees never were seriously challenged.

Attendance-wise, the Indians played at home to 948,776 fans, but the total was well below the break-even point of 1.3 million and the club lost a reported $500,000, as it did in 1975.

However, proving Cleveland fans will support a winner (even a contender), the Indians and Yankees attracted major league baseball's top two crowds of 1976 (playoffs and World Series included) when 64,529 and 61,380 fans turned out for the games of July 3 and 4.

On the field, the Indians had only one player who made the All-Star team, relief pitcher Dave LaRoche (who didn't get into the game), but several others blossomed, giving hope for better things in 1977, when Frank Robinson will be back for his third term as manager. He was rehired the day after the 1976 season ended.

Center fielder Rick Manning (.292) and second baseman Duane Kuiper (.263), playing their first full seasons in the major leagues, established themselves, as did Jim Kern (10-7, 15 saves, 2.36 earned-run average) after he was switched to the relief corps, where he complemented the veteran southpaw LaRoche (1-4, 21 saves, 2.25 ERA) to give the Indians one of the best bullpens in baseball.

Others who distinguished themselves offensively were Rico Carty, Ray Fosse, Buddy Bell, Larvell Blanks, and George Hendrick, while starting pitchers Dennis Eckersley, Jim Bibby, and Dobson compiled good records even though each suffered his share of problems at one time or another.

Carty, the 36-year-old designated hitter who is enjoying a renaissance in his major league career that began in 1963, led the team with a .310 average, eighth best in the league. Carty cracked 13 homers and also paced the Indians with 83 RBIs.

Fosse, a prime candidate for the "Comeback of the Year" award, regained his regular catcher's job at mid-season and went on to hit .301 while doing a splendid job of handling the Tribe's pitchers.

Bell, who was one of only three American Leaguers to play every game in 1976 (Robin Yount of the Milwaukee Brewers and Rusty Staub of the Detroit Tigers were the others), compiled a .281 average, his best in five major league seasons, and played a solid third base.

Blanks, alternating between shortstop and second base after being acquired in December, 1975, from the Atlanta Braves (by way of the Chicago White Sox), was a major contributor with both his bat and glove. Blanks hit .280.

Hendrick led the Indians with 25 homers and drove in 81 runs, hitting .265.

Dobson finished as the Tribe's biggest winner (16-12) though he managed to capture only six decisions while losing seven after that climactic game against the Yankees on July 1.

Just the opposite were Bibby and Eckersley, both of whom shook off wretched performances in the first half to wind up respectably. Bibby was 13-7 (3.20 ERA), while Eckersley was 13-12 (3.44), striking out an even 200 batters in 199 innings.

On the negative side, however, were Boog Powell (.215, nine homers, 33 RBIs), who was the Indians' offensive leader the year before, and Charlie Spikes (.237, three homers, 31 RBIs), who also was expected to hit more, much more.

Robinson, a player-manager again—but not to be in 1977—appeared in 36 games, mostly as a pinch-hitter, batting .224 (15-for-67) and delivering three homers and 10 RBIs. Those 15 hits gave him a career total of 2,943, for 16th place among baseball's all-time leaders, and 586 homers, fourth behind Hank Aaron, Babe Ruth, and Willie Mays.

What's more, the record will show that Robinson played in 2,808 games (only seven men appeared in more), and that he became on August 14 only the 11th batter to log 10,000 major league at-bats.

As it turned out, the final hit in Robinson's splendid, 21-year playing career was a run-scoring pinch single on September 18 at home against the Orioles' southpaw Rudy May.

SCORES OF CLEVELAND INDIANS' 1976 GAMES

APRIL			Winner	Loser	MAY			Winner	Loser
10—Detroit	L	1-3	Coleman	Eckersley	15—At Det.	L	1-2	Fidrych	Dobson
13—At Bos.	L	4-7	Cleveland	Dobson	16—At Det.	W	4-0	Brown	Bare
14—At Bos.	W	6-5	Hood	Jenkins	18—N. York	L	6-11z	Lyle	Kern
16—At K. C.	L	3-5	Mingori	Peterson	19—N. York	L	2-3	May	Hood
17—At K. C.	L	3-5*	Fitzmorris	Eckersley	21—Milw.	L	3-4	Travers	Dobson
18—At K. C.	W	6-0	Dobson	Busby	22—Milw.	L	5-6	Slaton	Bibby
20—Texas	W	9-1	Bibby	Perry	23—Milw.	W	2-1	Brown	Broberg
23—Oakland	W	3-0	Eckersley	Blue	23—Milw.	W	8-5	Kern	Sprague
24—Oakland	L	7-8	Fingers	Buskey	24—At Balt.	W	4-0	Eckersley	Cuellar
25—Oakland	L	1-9	Torrez	Dobson	25—At Balt.	L	3-1	Dobson	Palmer
27—At Minn.	W	7-5	Brown	Goltz	26—At N. Y.	L	3-4	Hunter	Hood
28—At Minn.	W	9-0	Eckersley	Blyleven	27—At N. Y.	W	5-3	Bibby	May
30—Calif.	W	5-2	Kern	Drago	29—At Milw.	W	6-0‡	Brown	Colborn
		Won 7, Lost 6			30—At Milw.	L	4-5	Travers	Eckersley
					31—Balt.	W	4-1	Kern	Holtzman
MAY					31—Balt.	W	4-3	Dobson	Cuellar
1—Calif.	L	1-6	Ryan	Dobson			**Won 14, Lost 15**		
2—Calif.	W	12-3	Brown	Hassler					
2—Calif.	L	4-5	Brewer	Hood	JUNE				
3—At Oak.	W	5-4†	Buskey	Fingers	2—Balt.	L	0-2y	Garland	Buskey
4—At Oak.	L	4-8	Torrez	Peterson	4—At Chi.	L	1-4	Gossage	Eckersley
5—At Oak.	W	3-1	Dobson	Fingers	5—At Chi.	L	5-3‡	Kern	Carroll
7—At Calif.	L	4-5	Drago	Brown	6—At Chi.	L	2-3	Vuckovich	Brown
8—At Calif.	L	3-4x	Brewer	Buskey	6—At Chi.	L	0-5	Brett	Hood
9—At Calif.	L	2-3	Tanana	Peterson	7—Minn.	L	2-7	Goltz	Waits
11—Boston	W	4-3	Dobson	Jenkins	8—Minn.	L	1-3	Campbell	Eckersley
12—Boston	L	4-6§	House	LaRoche	9—Minn.	W	4-1	Dobson	Decker
13—Boston	L	5-7	Tiant	Kern	11—Chicago	W	5-4x	Kern	Forster
14—At Det.	W	6-3	Buskey	Coleman	12—Chicago	W	3-0	Waits	Vuckovich

JUNE			Winner	Loser
13—Chicago	W	8-5	Dobson	Johnson
13—Chicago	W	9-7	Kern	Carroll
15—At Texas	L	2-3	Perry	Bibby
16—At Texas	W	9-4	Brown	Blyleven
18—Kan. C.	L	3-5	Leonard	Thomas
19—Kan. C.	W	3-0	Dobson	Fitzmorris
20—Kan. C.	W	11-8	Bibby	Littell
21—At N. Y.	L	0-6	Figueroa	Eckersley
22—At N. Y.	W	3-2	Waits	Hunter
23—At N. Y.	W	4-1	Hood	Holtzman
24—At N. Y.	L	5-6	Lyle	LaRoche
25—At Balt.	W	6-5	Thomas	Pagan
26—At Balt.	L	1-2	Garland	Eckersley
27—At Balt.	W	6-3	Dobson	May
27—At Balt.	L	2-6	Grimsley	Waits
28—Milw.	W	5-3	Bibby	Colborn
29—Milw.	W	4-1	Brown	Travers
		Won 15, Lost 12		
JULY				
1—N. York	W	3-2	Dobson	Figueroa
2—N. York	L	1-7	Hunter	Waits
3—N. York	L	3-7	Holtzman	Hood
4—N. York	L	3-4	Ellis	Brown
5—At Calif.	L	1-8	Ross	Dobson
6—At Calif.	W	7-3	Eckersley	Monge
7—At Calif.	L	0-2	Ryan	Waits
9—At Oak.	L	1-2	Torrez	Brown
10—At Oak.	L	3-7	Fingers	Dobson
11—At Oak.	L	3-9	P. Mitchell	Eckersley
15—At Minn.	L	2-5	Bane	Brown
16—At Minn.	W	7-6	Dobson	Singer
17—At Minn.	W	4-0	Waits	Redfern
18—At Minn.	W	6-1	Thomas	Hughes
19—Oakland	W	3-2	Bibby	Blue
19—Oakland	L	3-10	Bosman	Brown
20—Oakland	L	4-7	Fingers	LaRoche
21—Calif.	W	6-2	Waits	Ryan
22—Calif.	W	7-5	Eckersley	Tanana
23—Detroit	W	9-4	Bibby	Roberts
24—Detroit	L	4-5	Hiller	Kern
25—Detroit	L	1-9	Ruhle	Dobson
25—Detroit	L	4-5	Lemanczyk	Waits
26—At Bos.	W	9-4	Buskey	Tiant
27—At Bos.	L	7-8	Jenkins	Bibby
28—At Bos.	W	7-6	Kern	Willoughby
29—At Bos.	L	4-6	Wise	Dobson
30—At Milw.	W	7-2†	Eckersley	Rodriguez
31—At Milw.	W	2-0	Bibby	Travers
31—At Milw.	L	5-6§	Castro	Kern
		Won 13, Lost 17		
AUGUST				
1—At Milw.	W	4-3‡	Hood	Castro
2—Boston	L	1-3	Wise	Dobson
3—Boston	W	1-0‡	Eckersley	Murphy
4—Balt.	W	3-0	Waits	Palmer
5—Balt.	L	2-6	Garland	Bibby
6—At Det.	L	1-3	Roberts	Brown
7—At Det.	L	1-6	Fidrych	Dobson
8—At Det.	L	1-2	Hiller	Eckersley

AUGUST			Winner	Loser
8—At Det.	L	5-15	Grilli	Kern
9—Chicago	W	4-2	Bibby	Brett
11—Chicago	W	4-3‡	Kern	Barrios
12—Texas	W	5-4	LaRoche	Terpko
13—Texas	L	1-2	Umbarger	Eckersley
14—Texas	L	3-4‡	Foucault	Kern
15—Texas	W	6-4	Thomas	Blyleven
15—Texas	W	3-0	Bibby	Hargan
16—At K. C.	L	1-6	Pattin	Brown
17—At K. C.	L	3-4‡	Littell	LaRoche
18—At K. C.	W	4-1	Eckersley	Fitzmorris
19—At Texas	W	7-5	Buskey	Skok
20—At Texas	L	0-3	Blyleven	Bibby
21—At Texas	L	3-5	Perry	Brown
22—At Texas	W	3-1	Dobson	Boggs
23—Kan. C.	W	4-3	Eckersley	Mingori
24—Kan. C.	W	2-1	Waits	Leonard
25—Kan. C.	L	1-2	Hassler	Kern
27—Minn.	W	7-3	Brown	Goltz
28—Minn.	W	4-3a	Buskey	Hughes
29—Minn.	W	7-4	Eckersley	Bane
31—At Chi.	W	4-2‡	Kern	Hamilton
		Won 17, Lost 13		
SEPTEMBER				
1—At Chi.	W	3-0	Bibby	Kravec
3—Boston	L	3-5	Tiant	Brown
4—Boston	L	6-7	Wise	Eckersley
4—Boston	W	4-0	Dobson	Lee
5—Boston	W	6-3	Waits	Cleveland
6—At Milw.	L	2-3	Castro	Thomas
6—At Milw.	W	3-2	Bibby	Rodriguez
7—At Milw.	L	4-17	Beare	Brown
8—At Balt.	L	1-3	Palmer	Eckersley
9—At Balt.	W	4-3	Dobson	May
10—At Balt.	L	3-4	Grimsley	Waits
11—At Bos.	W	6-5	Bibby	Jones
12—At Bos.	L	3-11	Tiant	Thomas
13—At Bos.	W	8-3	Eckersley	Lee
14—N. York	L	2-8	Jackson	Dobson
15—N. York	L	0-2	Alexander	Waits
18—Balt.	W	5-1	Thomas	Palmer
18—Balt.	L	2-3	May	Bibby
19—Balt.	W	5-4	Dobson	Garland
19—Balt.	W	3-2x	Kern	Miller
21—At Det.	L	3-5	Fidrych	Waits
22—At Det.	W	3-0	Bibby	Bare
24—Milw.	W	2-0	Eckersley	Slaton
25—Milw.	W	3-1	Dobson	Beare
28—Detroit	L	0-4	Fidrych	Bibby
28—Detroit	W	6-1	Eckersley	Roberts
29—Detroit	W	3-2	Brown	Crawford
30—Detroit	L	4-6	Glynn	Waits
		Won 15, Lost 13		
OCTOBER				
2—At N. Y.	L	5-6	Ellis	Thomas
2—At N. Y.	L	3-4b	Holtzman	Buskey
		Won 0, Lost 2		

* 5 innings. † 7½ innings. ‡ 10 innings. § 12 innings. x 13 innings. y 14 innings. z 16 innings. a 17 innings. b May 17 game at Cleveland transferred to New York.

Fidrych Brightens Tiger Picture

By JIM HAWKINS

Long after the other events of the 1976 season are forgotten, the memory of Mark Fidrych's fantastic first fling will live on.

No doubt about it: 1976 was the Year of the Bird.

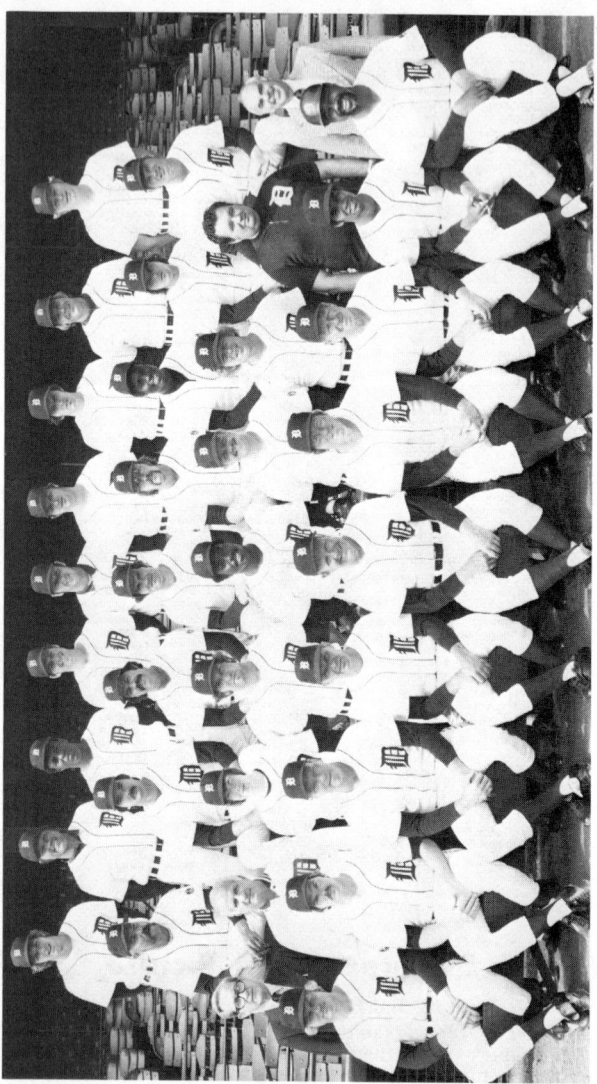

DETROIT TIGERS—1976

Front row—Meyer, Scrivener, Hegan, coach; Tracewski, coach; Houk, manager; Gladding, coach; Schultz, coach; Manuel, Horton. Second row—Livingood, team physician; Behm, trainer; Lennon, batboy; Wockenfuss, LeFlore, May, Sutherland, Hand, equipment manager; Desmond, traveling secretary. Third row—Hiller, Bare, Rodriguez, Laxton, Taylor, Oglivie, Veryzer, Ruhle. Fourth row—Fidrych, Freehan, Johnson, Crawford, Coleman, Roberts, Grilli, Stanley, Staub.

In the history of baseball, no other rookie pitcher—possibly no other player—so completely captivated the attention of the whole country the way the Tigers' flakey, free-spirited 22-year-old phenom did.

An anonymous non-roster pitcher in spring training, relegated to the bench for the first five weeks of the season, The Bird soon became the word—not only at Tiger Stadium, but everywhere the Tigers played.

Deprived of those early-season starts because Manager Ralph Houk didn't believe he was ready, Fidrych nevertheless finished with a 19-9 record and his earned-run average of 2.34 was unequalled by any other starting pitcher.

But what was even more amazing was the fact that The Bird personally drew 899,969 fans in his 29 starts—including 605,677 at home. And he put more than half of those people in the park by himself.

No team in either league improved as much as the Tigers did in '76, as they added 17 victories to their record that ranked as the worst in the major leagues the year before.

Even so, they finished fifth in the East—which gives you a good idea of how far they had to go.

And one could only wonder what the summer would have been like if it hadn't been for The Bird.

There were other bright spots, to be sure.

Ron LeFlore proved himself to be one of the most improved players in the league as he started the season with a stirring 30-game hitting streak and went on to bat .316 and steal 58 bases before he was sidelined with a ruptured tendon in September.

Rusty Staub, acquired from the New York Mets in exchange for Mickey Lolich, quickly established himself as the Tigers' most reliable RBI man, driving in 96 runs while hitting .299 as the rightfielder and occasional designated hitter.

Rookie Jason Thompson laid claim to first base after he was summoned from Evansville in April, smacking 17 homers—the most by a Tiger rookie since Rudy York hit 35 in 1937.

And if the Tigers hadn't been beset by serious injuries at key positions, they probably would have climbed higher than they did in the standings.

Milt May, whom they were counting on as their No. 1 catcher, only went to bat 25 times before he ran into a fence in Oakland and fractured his ankle April 20.

Then Willie Horton, off to an outstanding start, injured his foot and was forced out of the lineup and onto the disabled list. When he returned, Willie just wasn't the same.

Later in the season, the Tigers lost the entire left side of their infield when first Tom Veryzer and then Aurelio Rodriguez were injured sliding into second base.

Both players were placed in casts. And while their replacements, short-stop Mark Wagner and third baseman Phil Mankowski, both played well, it wasn't the same as having Veryzer and Rodriguez on duty every day.

Then, too, the Tigers lost Steve Kemp, last year's No. 1 draft pick, who had torn up the American Association, and had already been called up to Detroit, when he, too, injured his knee sliding into second at Evansville.

Finally, LeFlore, the Tigers' best base stealer since Ty Cobb, was carried off the field, taking much of the life out of the Tiger offense and depriving Houk of valuable depth in the outfield.

Although Dave Roberts, acquired from Houston last December, replaced Lolich as the leading lefthander on the starting staff with 16 wins, while losing 17, and Fidrych enjoyed an incredible season, it was obvious the Tigers still lacked the pitching it takes to be a legitimate contender.

John Hiller was again all alone in the bullpen whenever a game was on the line, as the remarkable reliever rebounded from an arm injury by winning a dozen games and saving 13 others.

But the Tigers' biggest problem was at second base where Gary Sutherland, Pedro Garcia and Jerry Manuel were all tried and rejected.

Unfortunately, The Bird couldn't do everything.

SCORES OF DETROIT TIGERS' 1976 GAMES

APRIL

Date		Score	Winner	Loser
10—At Cleve.	W	3-1	Coleman	Eckersley
13—Milw.	L	0-1	Slaton	Hiller
16—At Calif.	L	5-6x	Brewer	Grilli
17—At Calif.	W	2-0	Roberts	Ross
18—At Calif.	W	6-2	Bare	Hassler
19—At Oak.	L	5-6§	Todd	Hiller
20—At Oak.	L	5-6	Lindblad	Crawford
21—At Oak.	W	7-3	Roberts	Torrez
23—Texas	W	7-6	Hiller	Barr
24—Texas	L	4-5	Foucault	Hiller
27—Oakland	W	10-2	Coleman	Blue
28—Oakland	W	8-1	Roberts	Norris
30—At Chi.	L	4-8	Forster	Bare
			Won 7, Lost 6	

MAY

Date		Score	Winner	Loser
1—At Chi.	W	10-1	Ruhle	Johnson
4—Minn.	L	4-5§	Albury	Laxton
5—Minn.	L	2-8	Blyleven	Roberts
7—Chicago	W	5-0	Bare	Forster
8—Chicago	W	7-1	Ruhle	Johnson
9—Chicago	L	2-4	Wood	Coleman
11—At N.Y.	W	4-3	Grilli	Figueroa
12—At N.Y.	L	6-7	Ellis	Bare
13—At N.Y.	W	3-2	Ruhle	May
14—Cleve.	L	3-6	Buskey	Coleman
15—Cleve.	W	2-1	Fidrych	Dobson
16—Cleve.	L	0-4	Brown	Bare
17—Boston	L	0-7	Tiant	Coleman
18—Boston	L	3-5	Willoughby	Crawford
19—Boston	L	2-9	Jenkins	Roberts
21—At Balt.	L	5-8	Alexander	Bare
22—At Balt.	L	4-8	Garland	Crawford
23—At Balt.	W	10-6	Hiller	Miller
24—At Bos.	L	0-3	Wise	Roberts
25—At Bos.	L	0-2	Tiant	Fidrych
26—Balt.	L	0-6	Alexander	Laxton
26—Balt.	W	6-2	Bare	Grimsley
27—Balt.	L	3-4	Holtzman	Coleman
28—N. York	L	5-9	Figueroa	Ruhle
29—N. York	W	4-1	Roberts	Ellis
30—N. York	L	0-4	May	Laxton
31—Milw.	W	5-4x	Fidrych	Sprague
			Won 10, Lost 17	

JUNE

Date		Score	Winner	Loser
1—Milw.	W	8-7	Hiller	Rodriguez
1—Milw.	W	6-5	Hiller	Rodriguez
2—Milw.	W	6-4	Ruhle	Colborn
3—Milw.	L	2-6	Travers	Roberts
4—At Texas	L	4-5	Perry	Laxton
5—At Texas	W	3-2x	Fidrych	Blyleven
6—At Texas	L	6-16	Briles	Coleman
7—At K. C.	L	0-10	Busby	Ruhle
8—At K. C.	W	3-1	Roberts	Leonard
9—At K. C.	L	3-6	Fitzmorris	Bare
11—Calif.	W	4-3	Fidrych	Hartzell
12—Calif.	W	10-4	Ruhle	Ross
13—Calif.	L	7-10	Kirkwood	Roberts
14—Kan. C.	L	2-5	Fitzmorris	MacCormack
15—Kan. C.	L	7-21	Splittorff	Lemanczyk
16—Kan. C.	W	4-3	Fidrych	Pattin
17—At Minn.	L	0-4*	Goltz	Ruhle
18—At Minn.	W	4-2	Roberts	Hughes
19—At Minn.	L	4-6	Redfern	MacCormack
20—At Minn.	W	7-3	Fidrych	Singer
21—At Milw.	W	3-2x	Hiller	Slaton
22—At Milw.	L	10-4	Roberts	Augustine
23—At Milw.	L	5-9	Colborn	MacCormack
24—At Bos.	W	6-3	Fidrych	Wise
25—At Bos.	W	6-2	Hiller	Jenkins
26—At Bos.	L	1-2	Tiant	Roberts
27—At Bos.	W	4-2x	Grilli	Murphy
28—N. York	W	5-1	Fidrych	Holtzman
29—N. York	W	7-5	Lemanczyk	Lyle
			Won 17, Lost 12	

JULY

Date		Score	Winner	Loser
1—At Balt.	W	2-0	Roberts	May
2—At Balt.	L	1-2	Palmer	Ruhle
3—Balt.	W	4-0	Fidrych	Cuellar
4—Balt.	L	4-7	Garland	Hiller
5—At Texas	L	6-8	Terpko	Roberts
6—At Texas	L	2-3	Barr	Ruhle
7—At Texas	W	2-1	Hiller	Blyleven
9—Kan. C.	L	0-1	Leonard	Fidrych
10—Kan. C.	L	1-7	Fitzmorris	Roberts
11—Kan. C.	W	6-5y	Hiller	Mingori
15—Oakland	W	3-2x	Roberts	Blue
16—Oakland	W	1-0x	Fidrych	Fingers
17—Oakland	L	0-3	Norris	Ruhle
18—Oakland	L	1-10	P. Mitchell	MacCormack
19—At Minn.	L	5-6	Campbell	Roberts
20—At Minn.	W	8-3	Fidrych	Singer
21—At Chi.	L	1-4	Knapp	Ruhle
21—At Chi.	L	0-3	Johnson	Lemanczyk
22—At Chi.	L	3-9	Odom	MacCormack
22—At Chi.	W	5-1	Bare	Gossage
23—At Cleve.	L	4-9	Bibby	Roberts
24—At Cleve.	W	5-4	Hiller	Kern
25—At Cleve.	W	9-1	Ruhle	Dobson
25—At Cleve.	W	5-4	Lemanczyk	Waits
26—At Milw.	W	4-3z	Hiller	Frisella
27—At Milw.	L	4-6	Slaton	Bare
28—At Milw.	W	1-0	Roberts	Augustine
29—Balt.	L	0-1	May	Fidrych
30—Balt.	L	3-7	Grimsley	Ruhle
31—At Balt.	W	5-4	Lemanczyk	Palmer
			Won 14, Lost 16	

AUGUST			Winner	Loser
1—At Balt.	L	3-4	Holdsworth	Hiller
2—At N. Y.	L	0-1	Alexander	Roberts
3—At N. Y.	L	3-4	Jackson	Fidrych
4—Boston	L	1-4	Jenkins	Ruhle
5—Boston	L	4-5	Cleveland	Lemanczyk
6—Cleve.	W	3-1	Roberts	Brown
7—Cleve.	W	6-1	Fidrych	Dobson
8—Cleve.	W	2-1	Hiller	Eckersley
8—Cleve.	W	15-5	Grilli	Kern
9—Texas	L	1-8	Briles	Lemanczyk
10—Texas	W	7-5	Lemanczyk	Terpko
10—Texas	L	0-3	Hargan	Crawford
11—Texas	W	4-3	Fidrych	Perry
13—At K. C.	W	3-2	Ruhle	Fitzmorris
14—At K. C.	L	3-15	Leonard	Lemanczyk
15—At K. C.	L	3-7	Hassler	Roberts
17—Calif.	W	3-2	Fidrych	Tanana
18—Calif.	L	4-5x	Ryan	Hiller
19—Calif.	W	4-3	Bare	Hartzell
20—Minn.	W	3-2	Roberts	Bane
20—Minn.	L	5-8	Burgmeier	Laxton
21—Minn.	L	3-7§	Hughes	Fidrych
22—Minn.	L	4-6y	Campbell	Hiller
23—Chicago	W	5-4	Bare	Gossage
24—Chicago	L	7-12	Hamilton	Crawford
25—Chicago	W	3-1	Fidrych	Johnson
27—At Oak.	W	8-1	Ruhle	Abbott
28—At Oak.	L	2-5	Blue	Roberts
29—At Oak.	L	1-2y	Fingers	Fidrych
30—At Calif.	L	1-2	Hartzell	Crawford
31—At Calif.	L	3-6	Ryan	Ruhle
Won 13, Lost 18				

SEPTEMBER			Winner	Loser
1—At Calif.	L	1-4	Tanana	Roberts
3—Milw.	L	2-11	Augustine	Fidrych
4—Milw.	W	4-0	Ruhle	Travers
5—Milw.	L	6-8	Sadecki	Bare
6—Balt.	W	5-4	Roberts	Miller
7—Balt.	L	3-5	Garland	Fidrych
8—At Bos.	L	3-4	Lee	Lemanczyk
9—At Bos.	L	0-5	Wise	Ruhle
10—At Bos.	W	1-0*	Bare	Cleveland
11—At N. Y.	W	6-5	Roberts	Alexander
12—At N. Y.	W	6-0	Fidrych	Ellis
12—At N. Y.	L	1-3	Figueroa	Glynn
13—At N. Y.	W	3-1	Crawford	Holtzman
14—At Balt.	L	7-9	J. Martinez	Hiller
15—At Balt.	L	0-1†	Garland	Roberts
17—Boston	L	3-8	Tiant	Fidrych
18—Boston	L	4-5	Lee	Ruhle
19—Boston	L	1-6	Wise	Roberts
20—Boston	L	6-12	Jones	Glynn
21—Cleve.	W	5-3	Fidrych	Waits
22—Cleve.	L	0-3	Bibby	Bare
24—N. York	W	3-0	Roberts	Holtzman
24—N. York	L	0-8	Jackson	Crawford
25—N. York	L	6-10	Alexander	Glynn
28—At Cleve.	W	4-0	Fidrych	Bibby
28—At Cleve.	L	1-6	Eckersley	Roberts
29—At Cleve.	L	2-3	Brown	Crawford
30—At Cleve.	W	6-4	Glynn	Waits
Won 10, Lost 18				

OCTOBER			Winner	Loser
1—At Milw.	W	5-0	Hiller	Travers
2—At Milw.	W	4-1	Fidrych	Slaton
3—At Milw.	W	5-2	Roberts	Beare
Won 3, Lost 0				

* 5 innings.   † 6 innings.   ‡ 8½ innings.   § 10 innings.   x 11 innings.   y 12 innings.   z 13 innings.

No Joy in Brewtown

By LOU CHAPMAN

For Brewer officials and especially the long-suffering fans, 1976 was like watching a re-run of a film entitled "The Year That Was Rotten."

The Brewers had a new manager and coaches, but the same sad cast of characters, and there was that same, gloomy finale as the year before. Actually, the ending was even more tragic. This time they finished dead last in the American League's East Division, instead of fifth as in 1975.

General Manager Jim Baumer said the club needed "motivating" and that he expected Manager Alex Grammas to provide that key intangible. Del Crandall, the deposed manager, didn't do it.

If the Brewers were motivated, it had to be in a reverse direction, since they were able to win only 66 games—two fewer than in the 1975 disaster.

Grammas did manage to get the Brewers' locks shorn to a respectable length and had them cut off mutton chops and other facial adornments.

He did lead them to a 10-5 record in the early going and allowed cautiously that "things were going so good, it scares me."

It scared him, all right, gave him nightmares as the club went into a tailspin that would have made World War I stunt pilots envious. Only thing was they never really pulled out of that power dive.

Oh, they managed to play .500 ball or better in July and August, but September was a memorable month to forget. It's no wonder that Brewer brass were all harmonizing on a new theme song after 1976's lost chord.

MILWAUKEE BREWERS—1976

Front row—Broberg, McLish, coach; Bragan, coach; Smith, coach; Grammas, manager; Kuenn, coach; Lezcano, Castro, Rosario, Rodriguez. Second row—Ferguson, traveling secretary; Travers, Hegan, Frisella, Sadecki, Colborn, Yount, Johnson, Augustine, Sharp, Napholz, clubhouse man; Ksicinski, clubhouse man. Third row—Rayer, trainer; G. Thomas, Slaton, Moore, Aaron, Money, Austin, Scott, Joshua, Carbo, Sutherland, Sullivan, equipment manager. In front—Winter and Sires, batboys.

"There'll Be Some Changes Made," ran the chorus and President Bud Selig emphasized, "We've decided that if we're going to lose, we're going to lose with a club that at least gives 100 per cent. We're not going to lose with a club that can't rise above difficulty. We're going to change all that."

Yes, but change was supposed to have taken place in the spring of 1976. Baumer spoke of motivation and Grammas supposedly was to remove all the scars of the year before when the Crandall-Pedro Garcia affair cut the ball club down the middle.

Garcia was Grammas' second baseman and morale was high as the club left Sun City, Ariz., for the real thing. It wasn't too long, though, before Garcia was on his way to the Detroit Tigers (in exchange for Gary Sutherland) and, maybe, just maybe, a lot of people in Milwaukee thought, Crandall had been right all the time.

There were some hopeful signs, nevertheless, and for a period—brief as it turned out—Grammas even spoke of the possibility of finishing second, as the teams up front couldn't seem to get untracked. But, as George Scott says, in dusting off an antique cliche, cream always comes to the top—or in the Brewers' case, water seeks its own level. In their case, it turned out to be down deep—rock bottom.

Speaking of Scott, he was the one fitted for culprit's horns by Baumer—along with catcher Darrell Porter. They were responsible for a great deal of the power failure. Scott had tied for the American League homer crown with Reggie Jackson the year before, yet here he was having a miserable year. Porter was a big fat out most of the time and his catching also left plenty to be desired.

Scott, at one time relegated to the seventh spot in the batting order by Grammas, declaimed his extreme unhappiness and spoke in terms of being sick of playing in Milwaukee. He later recanted, claiming he never said it. But there was disenchantment at season's end—the Brewers with him as well as he with the Brewers.

Both Scott and Porter were traded in December. Scott and Bernie Carbo went to Boston for first baseman Cecil Cooper, and Porter and Jim Colborn were dealt to Kansas City for outfielder Jim Wohlford, infielder Jamie Quirk and a player to be named later.

The brightest spot in the gloomy picture was the performance of the pitching staff, headed by youngsters like Bill Travers and Jerry Augustine. There was also Bill Castro and Dan Frisella in the bullpen and rookies like Gary Beare and Bryan Haas up from the Spokane farm gave portents of a better future on the mound.

Other memorable moments came from a 42-year-old man whose accomplishments were in the past. Henry Aaron, all-time home run king and the Brewers' designated hitter, played out the final year of his illustrious career. The "old man" never seemed to run out of thrills for his admiring Milwaukee public.

There was that nostalgic September night when baseball's greats like Willie Mays and Mickey Mantle joined the guy in the bleachers to honor Aaron. It was Henry Aaron Night and even Jack Ford, son of the President, showed up. The format was patterned after an old TV favorite "This Is Your Life" and Henry's parents, children and wife, Billye, all played key roles in the sentimental scene.

Then, finally, came the last day of the year. Henry's farewell again lit up an otherwise dismal scene as the Brewers predictably lost to the Detroit Tigers. Aaron wound up as he started—with a hit in his final time at bat. It was a little dubious—an infield hit bobbled by the Tiger shortstop, but it supplied a fine note—if not a high one—for Aaron's swan song.

At that, Henry was a little ticked off privately when Grammas pulled him from his last game. Down deep apparently Aaron would have liked to have ended it with a home run. That would have had the final dramatic impact. It also would have enabled him to rid himself of one final vestige of the ghost of Babe Ruth.

Aaron finished in a tie with Ruth for runs scored—2,174. And the guy who beat out the Babe in all-time homers conceded at the finish, "I would have loved to have another run. I felt maybe I could swing again. After it was all over, there was nothing really going through my head except that I needed one more run to pass Babe Ruth."

Now that Henry's gone, what do the Brewers do for an encore? The least they could do for their long-suffering fans is not have another chorus of "When Things Were Rotten." It's getting to be like a broken record.

SCORES OF MILWAUKEE BREWERS' 1976 GAMES

Date		Score	Winner	Loser
APRIL				
8–N. York	W	5-0	Slaton	Hunter
10–N. York	L	7-9	Lyle	Murphy
13–At Det.	W	1-0	Slaton	Hiller
16–At Texas	W	3-1	Colborn	Umbarger
18–At Texas	L	4-1	Singer	Slaton
18–At Texas	W	4-1	Travers	Briles
20–Kan. C.	W	5-4	Broberg	Leonard
22–Kan. C.	L	1-2	Bird	Colborn
23–Calif.	W	4-2	Slaton	Ross
26–Calif.	W	1-0	Colborn	Tanana
28–At Chi.	W	4-1	Travers	Wood
29–At Chi.	W	8-5	Rodriguez	Carroll
Won 9, Lost 3				
MAY				
1–At Minn.	L	5-9	Campbell	Broberg
4–Texas	L	4-7	Briles	Colborn
7–Minn.	W	4-3	Slaton	Hughes
8–Minn.	L	2-13	Decker	Travers
9–Minn.	L	4-6	Campbell	Rodriguez
11–Balt.	L	2-5	Cuellar	Colborn
12–Balt.	L	6-8	Alexander	Augustine
13–Balt.	L	3-5	Palmer	Travers
14–At Bos.	L	1-2	Pole	Broberg
15–At Bos.	L	4-9	Jenkins	Rodriguez
16–At Bos.	W	11-5	Slaton	Wise
17–At Balt.	L	3-4	Miller	Rodriguez
19–At Balt.	L	3-5	Cuellar	Colborn
21–At Cleve.	W	4-3	Travers	Dobson
22–At Cleve.	W	6-5	Slaton	Bibby
23–At Cleve.	L	1-2	Brown	Broberg
23–At Cleve.	L	5-8	Kern	Sprague
24–At N. Y.	L	2-5	Figueroa	Colborn
25–At N. Y.	W	1-0	Travers	Ellis
26–Boston	W	6-2	Slaton	Pole
27–Boston	L	1-2	Jenkins	Broberg
29–Cleve.	L	0-6‡	Brown	Colborn
30–Cleve.	W	5-4	Travers	Eckersley
31–At Det.	L	4-5§	Fidrych	Sprague
Won 7, Lost 17				
JUNE				
1–At Det.	L	7-8	Hiller	Rodriguez
1–At Det.	L	5-6	Hiller	Rodriguez
2–At Det.	L	4-6	Ruhle	Colborn
3–At Det.	W	6-2	Travers	Roberts
JUNE				
4–At K. C.	L	3-4‡	Leonard	Slaton
5–At K. C.	L	4-5	Fitzmorris	Broberg
5–At K. C.	L	2-7	Splittorff	Champion
6–At K. C.	W	4-3z	Augustine	Pattin
8–Chicago	W	2-0	Travers	Johnson
9–Chicago	L	2-4	Gossage	Slaton
10–Chicago	L	5-12	Barrios	Augustine
11–Oakland	W	4-2	Colborn	Blue
12–Oakland	L	1-2	P. Mitchell	Travers
13–Oakland	W	5-4	Slaton	Torrez
14–Calif.	W	8-2	Augustine	Tanana
15–At Calif.	L	0-1	Ryan	Colborn
16–At Calif.	W	9-0	Travers	Monge
17–At Calif.	L	0-2	Ross	Slaton
18–At Oak.	W	3-2	Castro	Todd
19–At Oak.	L	4-7	Abbott	Colborn
20–At Oak.	L	5-7	Bahnsen	Travers
21–Detroit	L	2-3§	Hiller	Slaton
22–Detroit	L	4-10	Roberts	Augustine
23–Detroit	W	9-5	Colborn	MacCormack
25–At N. Y.	L	0-1	Ellis	Travers
26–At N. Y.	L	3-6	Figueroa	Slaton
27–At N. Y.	L	2-6	Hunter	Augustine
27–At N. Y.	L	2-10	Tidrow	Broberg
28–At Cleve.	L	3-5	Bibby	Colborn
29–At Cleve.	L	1-4	Brown	Travers
Won 9, Lost 21				
JULY				
1–Boston	W	6-5‡	Frisella	Cleveland
2–Boston	L	0-3	Pole	Augustine
3–Boston	W	6-2	Colborn	Cleveland
4–Boston	L	1-3	Wise	Broberg
5–Minn.	W	3-2	Travers	Bane
6–Minn.	L	6-2	Slaton	Hughes
7–Minn.	L	2-8	Singer	Augustine
8–Texas	W	5-2	Frisella	Hoerner
9–Texas	W	7-2	Rodriguez	Umbarger
10–Texas	W	3-2	Travers	Perry
11–Texas	W	6-3	Slaton	Blyleven
11–Texas	W	5-4‡	Castro	Foucault
15–At Chi.	L	3-5‡	Brett	Slaton
16–At Chi.	L	2-5	Johnson	Augustine
17–At Chi.	W	9-2	Colborn	Gossage

JULY			Winner	Loser
18—At Chi.	L	3-13	Barrios	Travers
19—Calif.	L	2-4	Hartzell	Rodriguez
19—Calif.	L	1-6	Kirkwood	Slaton
20—Calif.	W	6-2	Augustine	Ross
21—At K. C.	W	5-0	Travers	Fitzmorris
22—At K. C.	L	1-3	Splittorff	Colborn
23—At Balt.	W	4-3y	Slaton	F. Martinez
24—At Balt.	W	4-1	Rodriguez	Cuellar
24—At Balt.	W	5-0	Augustine	Garland
25—At Balt.	W	3-1	Travers	Pagan
26—Detroit	L	4-3y	Hiller	Frisella
27—Detroit	W	6-4	Slaton	Bare
28—Detroit	L	0-1	Roberts	Augustine
30—Cleve.	L	2-7†	Eckersley	Rodriguez
31—Cleve.	L	0-2	Bibby	Travers
31—Cleve.	W	6-5x	Castro	Kern
Won 18, Lost 13				
AUGUST				
1—Cleve.	L	3-4‡	Hood	Castro
2—Balt.	W	7-1	Colborn	May
3—Balt.	W	4-2	Rodriguez	Grimsley
4—N. York	W	4-3	Travers	Hunter
4—N. York	L	2-7	Holtzman	Slaton
5—N. York	W	9-3*	Frisella	Ellis
6—At Bos.	L	1-2	Murphy	Colborn
7—At Bos.	L	0-3	Tiant	Rodriguez
10—At Oak.	L	1-2	Blue	Slaton
11—At Oak.	L	5-8	Torrez	Travers
12—At Oak.	L	3-4	Fingers	Castro
13—At Calif.	W	2-0	Augustine	Hartzell
14—At Calif.	W	4-3	Sadecki	Overy
15—At Calif.	W	5-3	Travers	Ross
16—Oakland	W	4-3	Frisella	Fingers
17—Oakland	L	4-5	Lindblad	Rodriguez
18—Oakland	W	3-1	Slaton	Blue
19—Kan. C.	W	6-4	Augustine	Leonard
20—Kan. C.	L	0-3	Hassler	Travers
21—Kan. C.	L	2-6	Pattin	Colborn
22—Kan. C.	L	4-7	Bird	Frisella
23—At Texas	W	6-2	Rodriguez	Umbarger
24—At Texas	W	1-0‡	Augustine	Foucault
25—At Texas	W	5-1	Travers	Blyleven
27—Chicago	L	2-5	Kravec	Slaton
28—Chicago	W	10-8	Colborn	Gossage

AUGUST			Winner	Loser
29—Chicago	L	0-2	Brett	Rodriguez
30—At Minn.	L	3-10	Burgmeier	Augustine
31—At Minn.	L	0-4	Goltz	Travers
31—At Minn.	W	6-3	Slaton	Campbell
Won 15, Lost 15				
SEPTEMBER				
1—At Minn.	L	2-3x	Campbell	Castro
2—At Minn.	L	4-8	Johnson	Castro
3—At Det.	W	11-2	Augustine	Fidrych
4—At Det.	L	0-4	Ruhle	Travers
5—At Det.	W	8-6	Sadecki	Bare
6—Cleve.	W	3-2	Castro	Thomas
6—Cleve.	L	2-3	Bibby	Rodriguez
7—Cleve.	W	17-4	Beare	Brown
8—At N. Y.	L	0-8	Figueroa	Augustine
9—At N. Y.	L	2-4	Holtzman	Travers
10—At N. Y.	L	4-6	Hunter	Slaton
11—Balt.	L	1-5	Garland	Rodriguez
11—Balt.	L	2-3	Flanagan	Colborn
12—Balt.	L	1-3	Palmer	Augustine
13—Balt.	L	3-5‡	Holdsworth	Castro
14—Boston	W	3-2‡	Frisella	Willoughby
15—Boston	L	1-2	Cleveland	Beare
16—Boston	L	3-4	Kreuger	Castro
17—N. York	L	3-5§	Figueroa	Kobel
18—N. York	L	3-5	Ellis	Travers
19—N. York	L	1-2*	Hunter	Slaton
20—N. York	W	4-2	Beare	Holtzman
21—At Bos.	L	1-7	Tiant	Haas
21—At Bos.	W	3-1	Colborn	Kreuger
22—At Bos.	L	3-6	Pole	Augustine
23—At Bos.	L	3-10	Lee	Travers
24—At Cleve.	L	0-2	Eckersley	Slaton
25—At Cleve.	L	1-3	Dobson	Beare
28—At Balt.	L	5-7§	Garland	Rodriguez
28—At Balt.	L	3-7	May	Colborn
29—At Balt.	W	6-3	Augustine	McGregor
Won 8, Lost 23				
OCTOBER				
1—Detroit	L	0-5	Hiller	Travers
2—Detroit	L	1-4	Fidrych	Slaton
3—Detroit	L	2-5	Roberts	Beare
Won 0, Lost 3				

* 6 innings.　† 7½ innings.　‡ 10 innings.　§ 11 innings.　x 12 innings.　y 13 innings.　z 14 innings.

WEST DIVISION

Royals Are Best in West

By JOE McGUFF

Kansas City is identified with steaks and agriculture and for many years the city also had a national reputation for producing bumbling baseball teams. But no more. Gradually the Royals have changed Kansas City's baseball image and in 1976 they made the big breakthrough by winning the championship of the American League West.

The Royals held off Oakland in an exciting stretch duel that included a spying controversy, fights and a beaning. When the Royals finally clinched the title, Cookie Rojas and Fred Patek celebrated by jumping into the water display at Royals Stadium.

Area baseball fans felt like joining them, considering that they had waited 22 years for their first title of any kind.

KANSAS CITY ROYALS—1976

Front row—Rojas, Mingori, D. Nelson, Hiller, coach; Boros, coach; Herzog, manager; Cisco, coach; Lau, coach; Patek, Stinson. Second row—Dudley, trainer; Solaita, Quirk, Brett, Hall, Martinez, Bird, Gura, Wohlford, Poquette, Zych, equipment manager. Third row—Cowens, Fitzmorris, Otis, Mayberry, Littell, McRae, Busby, White, Wathan, Leonard, Splittorff. In front—Rawdon, batboy; Stiegler, ballboy. Missing—Pattin, Hassler.

The Royals met the heavily-favored Yankees in the American League Championship Series and carried New York down to the ninth inning of the fifth and final game before Chris Chambliss won it with a home run. The playoff series turned out to be far more exciting than the World Series, which Cincinnati swept in four games.

The Royals' season featured a dramatic duel for the American League batting championship between teammates George Brett and Hal McRae. Their race went down to the ninth inning of the final game of the season and ended in a controversy over a misplayed fly ball.

McRae came into the final game with an average of .33078. Brett's average was .33073 and Rod Carew of the Twins, the team playing the Royals in the last game, had an average of .32945.

Carew dropped out of contention during the game. When Brett came to bat in the ninth he needed a hit to stay alive. He hit a routine fly to left, but Steve Brye of the Twins pulled up short and when the ball landed on the synthetic turf it bounced over his head for an inside-the-park home run.

McRae followed Brett to the plate and grounded to short, thereby losing out to his teammate. His final average was .3320 to Brett's .3333. After he crossed first base, McRae made two obscene gestures toward the Twins' bench and he had to be restrained when Gene Mauch, the Minnesota manager, came on the field.

In the dressing room he said, "I know they let the ball drop." He expressed the opinion that racial prejudice was involved.

A brief investigation by the American League was conducted, but the league office concluded that Brye was guilty of nothing more than a human error.

Brye said he was playing too deep and did not see the ball well.

The season began on a disturbing note for the Royals when Steve Busby was sidelined with shoulder trouble in spring training and had to be placed on the disabled list. He later made 13 appearances, but his problem did not improve and he underwent shoulder surgery that put him out for the rest of the year.

Despite the loss of Busby, the Royals built up an early lead in the race and as late as August 28 they held what appeared to be a secure nine-game lead over the A's. Then came a collapse that almost cost the Royals their berth in the playoff.

Through the final 36 days of the season they won only 12 games and lost 22. They finished the season by losing seven of their last eight games and in their last 11 starts they scored 20 runs to their opponents' 45.

The Royals were saved by their big lead, a crucial shutout by Larry Gura and some help from, appropriately enough, the Angels.

The Royals' low point of the season came on the night of September 28 in Oakland. A seventh-inning home run by Sal Bando beat them 1-0, and reduced their lead to two and one-half games. The Royals had lost four straight and seemed ready to take their place alongside the 1964 Phillies, who blew a big lead in the closing days of the season.

On the following night Al Fitzmorris was scheduled to pitch, but he had suffered an ankle injury and Whitey Herzog was forced to turn to Gura, a lefthander who was acquired from the Yankees early in the season and who had pitched sparingly.

Had the Royals lost to the A's they probably would not have recovered, but Gura saved them by pitching a shutout and holding the A's to four singles. The Royals won, 4-0.

The offensive star was Amos Otis, who doubled in one run and homered. Otis had been beaned the week before by Oakland's Stan Bahnsen in a game in Kansas City and when he first returned to the lineup he hit so poorly that he was benched for a few days.

The Royals finally clinched the division title two days later when California defeated Oakland. Technically the Royals backed in, although Gura's shutout victory decided the race.

The playoff series with the Yankees opened in Kansas City and the fans were not sure which Kansas City team they were going to see, the Royals of the April-August period or the ineffectual Royals of September and early October.

When the Royals lost the opener to the Yankees, 4-1, there was reason to believe the playoff would be brief. Two of the runs crossed in the first inning when Brett committed two throwing errors. The Royals also lost Otis in the first inning. He hit the bag wrong at first base and suffered a severely jammed and sprained ankle. He did not play again in the Championship Series.

The Royals kept their hopes alive by winning the second game, 7-3. They stole three bases and this time it was the Yankees who stumbled, committing five errors. The decisive element in the game was the relief work of Paul Splittorff, who held the Yanks scoreless on four hits for five and two-thirds innings.

Splittorff was out through most of the last two months of the regular season after suffering a finger injury.

The Royals lost the opening game in Yankee Stadium, 5-3, after taking a 3-0 lead in the first and found themselves one game away from elimination.

"They always say that we win the big game when we have to so now we'll find out," Herzog observed.

And win the Royals did. Billy Martin, the Yankee manager, made a controversial move by bringing Jim Hunter back with three days of rest and the Royals hammered him for five runs in the first four innings on their way to a 7-4 victory that sent the series down to a fifth and deciding game.

The Yankees appeared to be on their way to a somewhat routine victory after seven innings, leading the Royals by a score of 6-3, but in the eighth Brett hit a three-run homer. In the ninth the Royals had runners on first and second with two out, but the threat ended on a controversial play at second.

Al Cowens was forced, but the Royals claimed that umpire Joe Brinkman missed the call and television replays appeared to bear them out. Had Cowens been safe the Royals would have had the bases loaded with Brett coming up.

In the last of the ninth Chris Chambliss hit Mark Littell's first pitch for a home run. Fans rushed on the field. They stole third base, Chambliss was knocked down and he touched home plate only after coming back from the clubhouse with a police escort.

In many respects the Royals were an unusual team. They hit only 65 home runs and had only four homers from August 30 through the end of the season. Only California had fewer homers than the Royals in the A.L.

Kansas City did not have a 20-game winner, Otis was the leading home run hitter with 18, no one drove in 100 runs and other than Brett's batting title none of the players won any major awards. Yet the Royals had an excellent season and came so close to reaching the World Series.

SCORES OF KANSAS CITY ROYALS' 1976 GAMES

APRIL

Date		Score	Winner	Loser
9—At Chi.	L	0-4	Wood	Splittorff
13—Calif.	W	7-4	Fitzmorris	Hassler
14—Calif.	L	6-7	Monge	Pattin
15—Calif.	L	1-5	Ryan	Splittorff
16—Cleve.	W	5-3	Mingori	Peterson
17—Cleve.	W	5-3*	Fitzmorris	Eckersley
18—Cleve.	L	0-6	Dobson	Busby
20—At Milw.	L	4-5	Broberg	Leonard
22—At Milw.	W	2-1	Bird	Colborn
23—At N.Y.	W	3-2	Splittorff	Hunter
24—At N.Y.	L	8-9x	Lyle	Pattin
30—N. York	L	3-5	Hunter	Splittorff

Won 5, Lost 7

MAY

Date		Score	Winner	Loser
1—N. York	W	4-1	Busby	Figueroa
2—N. York	W	2-1x	Bird	Lyle
4—At Bos.	W	7-5	Fitzmorris	Lee
5—At Bos.	W	8-4	Splittorff	Jenkins
7—At Balt.	L	3-4	Garland	Pattin
8—At Balt.	W	6-3	Leonard	Holtzman
9—At Balt.	W	7-4	Littell	Palmer
10—Minn.	L	4-5‡	Burgmeier	Pattin
11—Minn.	W	6-3	Bird	Luebber
12—Minn.	W	17-5	Pattin	Decker
13—Chicago	W	13-2	Leonard	Johnson
14—Chicago	W	7-1	Fitzmorris	Vuckovich
15—Chicago	W	2-1y	Littell	Gossage
16—Chicago	L	3-4	Carroll	Bird
17—Texas	W	8-7y	Hall	Foucault
18—Texas	W	3-1	Fitzmorris	Umbarger
19—Oakland	W	5-2	Splittorff	Torrez
20—Oakland	W	8-4	Bird	P. Mitchell
21—At Minn.	W	5-1	Leonard	Hughes
22—At Minn.	L	3-5	Goltz	Fitzmorris
23—At Minn.	L	1-3	Blyleven	Splittorff
24—At Texas	W	14-11	Mingori	Barr
26—At Texas	W	14-2	Leonard	Perry
26—At Texas	L	4-5§	Foucault	Pattin
27—At Texas	L	4-6	Singer	Splittorff
28—At Calif.	W	3-0	Bird	Ryan
29—At Calif.	L	2-3	Monge	Littell
29—At Calif.	L	2-7	Ross	Fitzmorris
30—At Calif.	W	3-2z	Mingori	Drago
31—At Oak.	L	1-10	Torrez	Splittorff

Won 20, Lost 10

JUNE

Date		Score	Winner	Loser
1—At Oak.	W	5-2	Bird	Bahnsen
2—At Oak.	W	4-3y	Littell	Fingers
4—Milw.	W	4-3‡	Leonard	Slaton
5—Milw.	W	5-4	Fitzmorris	Broberg
5—Milw.	W	7-2	Splittorff	Champion
6—Milw.	L	3-4z	Augustine	Pattin
7—Detroit	W	10-0	Busby	Ruhle
8—Detroit	L	1-3	Roberts	Leonard
9—Detroit	W	6-3	Fitzmorris	Bare
10—Balt.	W	7-0	Splittorff	Palmer
11—Balt.	W	4-0	Bird	Cuellar
12—Balt.	W	7-6	Busby	Alexander
13—Balt.	W	8-4	Leonard	Flanagan
14—At Det.	W	5-2	Fitzmorris	MacCormack
15—At Det.	W	21-7†	Splittorff	Lemanczyk
16—At Det.	L	3-4	Fidrych	Pattin
18—At Cleve.	W	5-3	Leonard	Thomas
19—At Cleve.	L	0-3	Dobson	Fitzmorris
20—At Cleve.	L	8-11	Bibby	Littell
21—Chicago	L	1-2x	Hamilton	Hall
22—Chicago	L	8-14	Jefferson	Busby
23—At Texas	L	5-7	Foucault	Leonard

JUNE

Date		Score	Winner	Loser
24—At Texas	L	2-5	Hargan	Fitzmorris
25—Calif.	W	6-3	Splittorff	Ross
26—Calif.	W	3-0	Pattin	Ryan
27—Calif.	W	5-4x	Bird	Drago
28—At Minn.	L	3-4	Campbell	Littell
29—At Minn.	W	1-0‡	Fitzmorris	Goltz
30—At Minn.	W	4-2	Splittorff	Bane

Won 19, Lost 10

JULY

Date		Score	Winner	Loser
1—Oakland	L	2-5	Fingers	Pattin
2—Oakland	W	8-5	Littell	Blue
3—Oakland	W	7-5	Leonard	Todd
4—Oakland	L	0-6	Norris	Fitzmorris
5—At N.Y.	W	2-1	Splittorff	Alexander
6—At N.Y.	W	3-1	Bird	Figueroa
6—At N.Y.	L	4-7	Lyle	Busby
7—At N.Y.	W	2-1	Littell	Hunter
9—At Det.	W	1-0	Leonard	Fidrych
10—At Det.	W	7-1	Fitzmorris	Roberts
11—At Det.	L	5-6y	Hiller	Mingori
15—Boston	W	12-5	Leonard	Pole
15—Boston	L	1-2	Jones	Bird
16—Boston	W	5-1	Splittorff	Murphy
16—Boston	W	2-1	Fitzmorris	Wise
17—Boston	W	2-1	Littell	Tiant
18—Boston	W	6-3	Pattin	Cleveland
19—Balt.	L	3-4	Palmer	Leonard
20—Balt.	L	3-10	Garland	Bird
21—Milw.	L	0-5	Travers	Fitzmorris
22—Milw.	W	3-1	Splittorff	Colborn
23—At Oak.	L	0-2	Blue	Pattin
24—At Oak.	W	6-5	Leonard	Todd
25—At Oak.	L	2-9	Abbott	Bird
26—At Calif.	W	4-0	Fitzmorris	Ryan
27—At Calif.	L	1-2	Tanana	Splittorff
28—At Calif.	W	3-2a	Gura	Kirkwood
30—Texas	W	2-1	Leonard	Briles
31—Texas	L	2-4	Blyleven	Fitzmorris

Won 17, Lost 12

AUGUST

Date		Score	Winner	Loser
1—Texas	L	4-8	Perry	Hassler
3—Minn.	W	7-1	Pattin	Bane
4—Minn.	W	4-2	Fitzmorris	Goltz
5—Minn.	W	6-4	Leonard	Singer
6—At Chi.	W	9-2	Hassler	Johnson
6—At Chi.	W	8-3	Bird	Gossage
7—At Chi.	L	3-5	Barrios	Mingori
8—At Chi.	L	2-5	Forster	Pattin
8—At Chi.	W	7-1	Fitzmorris	Jefferson
9—N. York	W	8-2	Leonard	Holtzman
10—N. York	L	1-2x	Ellis	Mingori
11—N. York	L	3-5	Alexander	Bird
13—Detroit	L	2-3	Ruhle	Fitzmorris
14—Detroit	W	15-3	Leonard	Lemanczyk
15—Detroit	W	7-3	Hassler	Roberts
16—Cleve.	W	6-1	Pattin	Brown
17—Cleve.	W	4-3‡	Littell	LaRoche
18—Cleve.	L	1-4	Eckersley	Fitzmorris
19—At Milw.	L	4-6	Augustine	Leonard
20—At Milw.	W	3-0	Hassler	Travers
21—At Milw.	W	6-2	Pattin	Colborn
22—At Milw.	W	7-4	Bird	Frisella
23—At Cleve.	L	3-4	Eckersley	Mingori
24—At Cleve.	L	1-2	Waits	Leonard
25—At Cleve.	W	2-1	Hassler	Kern
26—At Bos.	W	7-6a	Bruno	Willoughby
27—At Bos.	L	4-9	Jenkins	Bird
28—At Bos.	W	8-3	Fitzmorris	Lee
29—At Bos.	L	6-15	Wise	Leonard

AUGUST			Winner	Loser
30—At Balt.	L	2-3	May	Hassler
31—At Balt.	L	3-4	Palmer	Pattin
	Won 17, Lost 14			
SEPTEMBER				
1—At Balt.	L	1-7	Flanagan	Bird
3—Texas	L	1-4	Boggs	Fitzmorris
4—Texas	W	7-0	Leonard	Umbarger
5—Texas	L	1-3	Blyleven	Hassler
6—Texas	L	4-5	Hargan	Bird
7—Calif.	L	1-2	Kirkwood	Pattin
8—Calif.	L	0-2	Drago	Fitzmorris
9—Calif.	W	6-5‡	Mingori	Overy
10—At Minn.	L	3-18	Hughes	Hassler
11—At Minn.	W	8-6	Littell	Campbell
12—At Minn.	W	16-6	Pattin	Redfern
13—At Chi.	L	3-4	Knapp	Leonard
13—At Chi.	L	4-5	Brett	Mingori
14—At Chi.	W	2-1	Hassler	Forster
15—At Calif.	L	1-2	Ryan	Bird

SEPTEMBER			Winner	Loser
16—At Calif.	W	2-0	Pattin	Tanana
17—Chicago	W	3-2	Leonard	Gossage
18—Chicago	W	6-5	Gura	Brett
19—Chicago	W	6-5	Mingori	Forster
21—Oakland	W	3-1	Bird	Bahnsen
22—Oakland	L	1-11	Blue	Pattin
23—Oakland	L	1-8	Torrez	Leonard
24—At Texas	W	2-1z	Gura	Foucault
25—At Texas	L	0-1	Blyleven	Hassler
26—At Texas	L	1-3	Briles	Bird
27—At Oak.	L	3-8	Blue	Leonard
28—At Oak.	L	0-1	Torrez	Pattin
29—At Oak.	W	4-0	Gura	P. Mitchell
	Won 12, Lost 16			
OCTOBER				
1—Minn.	L	3-4	Campbell	Littell
2—Minn.	L	2-3	Singer	Hassler
3—Minn.	L	3-5	Hughes	Splittorff
	Won 0, Lost 3			

* 5 innings. † 8½ innings. ‡ 10 innings. § Suspended game, completed May 27 (10 innings). x 11 innings. y 12 innings. z 14 innings. a 15 innings.

A's Out of Playoffs First Time Since 1970

By RON BERGMAN

For turmoil and news impact, no previous A's season could top 1976, and that's quite a statement in itself. It was different in only one respect—the A's didn't win their division championship for the first time since 1970 after five straight titles. That they came in second, only two and one-half games behind the Royals, was, taking all into account, a considerable accomplishment.

Every one of the stunning events was connected to owner Charlie Finley's inability to bring most of his star players to contract terms. For openers, he traded two unsigned players, slugger Reggie Jackson and pitcher Ken Holtzman, to Baltimore one week before the season began for outfielder Don Baylor and pitchers Mike Torrez and Paul Mitchell.

Losing Jackson, who'd shared the home run title the previous season, forced Chuck Tanner, in his first and only year as A's manager, to convert to a running game. By the end of the season, the A's had stolen 341 bases, an American League record and second only in modern major league history to the 347 stolen by the 1911 New York Giants.

Running at every opportunity also had its drawbacks. Gene Tenace, for instance, severely strained his left knee trying to steal second on April 20 when the A's were three runs behind. He didn't return to action until May 27, but more critically, couldn't work behind the bat again until July 23. During this period the A's lost two games when home plate was left unguarded during rundowns.

Joe Rudi was the next to fall on the basepaths. His left leg went into a cast after he stole second on May 24 with the A's leading by four runs. After working himself back into shape, Rudi returned to the lineup and had been playing for five days when the most bizarre event of the season took place on June 15.

Finley found himself on trading deadline day with seven stars unsigned. They were eligible to play out their options and become free agents at the end of the season with no compensation for the A's. The owner decided to take drastic action at the last moment.

He signed Vida Blue in the afternoon of June 15 to a four-year contract and surprised the pitcher early that evening by selling him to the Yankees for $1.5 million. At the same time, Rudi and reliever Rollie Fingers were sold, unsigned, to the Red Sox for $1 million apiece.

Rudi and Fingers didn't have far to go because the Red Sox were in Oakland to begin a three-game series. Their new team didn't use them on June 15, thereby avoiding an awkward situation. For Commissioner Bowie Kuhn ordered the three sales suspended the next day pending a hearing on June 18 in New York. Following the hearing, Kuhn voided the sales "in the best interests of baseball," and the three players returned to the A's.

Finley filed a $10 million damage suit against the commissioner and baseball, and refused to allow the three players to compete for his team. The A's limped along short-handed until the remaining players threatened to strike on June 27 unless Finley relented. Minutes before game time, Finley gave in.

The A's won six, lost five during the three players' absence. More importantly, Blue, who'd been scheduled to pitch on June 15, missed four starts and didn't win again until July 6. That, and the fact that Rudi needed some time to get back in the groove, severely crippled the A's title chances.

Still, they crept to within four and one-half games of the collapsing Royals going into a three-game series between the two clubs in Oakland at the end of September. The A's won the first two games but seldom-used southpaw Larry Gura shut them out, 4-0, with a four-hitter in the final contest on September 29. Two days later, the A's were mathematically eliminated by losing, 2-0, to the Angels.

Some individual accomplishments were obscured by the off-field activities. Center fielder Bill North led the majors with 75 stolen bases and paced the club with a .276 batting average.

Third baseman Sal Bando finished tied for second in the league with 27 homers and also stole his career high of 20 bases. Tenace hit 22 homers, giving him four straight seasons with at least that many home runs. Shortstop Campy Campaneris stole 54 bases at the age of 34 and second baseman Phil Garner's 74 RBIs were exceptional for batting eighth or ninth most of the year.

Blue posted an 18-13 record and his 2.36 earned-run average was the second best in the league. Torrez finished at 16-12 with a 2.50 ERA, fourth best in the league.

Baylor didn't live up to expectations, perhaps because of injuries that included a broken bone in his left hand suffered in the first game. Paul Mitchell had to be farmed out at one point and couldn't pitch much down the stretch because of tendinitis in his shoulder. Nevertheless, he won nine games while losing seven.

The A's 36-44 road record was their worst since moving to Oakland in 1968 and the players insisted that Finley's reliance on commercial flights which forced them to travel many times on game days was responsible.

Tanner didn't want to return and Finley accommodated by trading him to the Pirates for $100,000 and catcher Manny Sanguillen. Six players—Fingers, Tenace, Bando, Campaneris, Rudi and Baylor—became free agents and signed with other teams. Designated hitter Billy Williams was unconditionally released after the season.

The A's drew 780,593 at home in 79 dates, a decrease of 294,925 from the previous year.

OAKLAND A's—1976

Front row—Alexander, Rudi, Lintz. Second row—Campaneris, Garner, Bando, Monchak, coach; Tanner, manager; Stock, coach; Lonnett, coach; Newman, Sandt, North. Third row—Romo, trainer; Bank, traveling secretary; Blue, Norris, Todd, Gross, McMullen, Mitchell, Williams, Bahnsen, Ciensczyk, equipment manager. Fourth row—Bosman, Washington, Abbott, Fingers, Torrez, Tenace, Haney, Baylor, Lindblad.

SCORES OF OAKLAND ATHLETICS' 1976 GAMES

APRIL			Winner	Loser
9—At Calif.	W	5-2	Torrez	Tanana
10—At Calif.	W	6-2	Blue	Ryan
11—At Calif.	W	10-7	Bahnsen	Kirkwood
12—At Texas	L	1-5	Briles	P. Mitchell
13—At Texas	L	1-3	Barr	Torrez
14—At Texas	L	2-4	Perry	Blue
17—Balt.	L	1-6	Palmer	Torrez
18—Balt.	W	2-1‡	Fingers	Miller
19—Detroit	W	6-5*	Todd	Hiller
20—Detroit	W	6-5	Lindblad	Crawford
21—Detroit	L	3-7	Roberts	Torrez
23—At Cleve.	L	0-3	Eckersley	Blue
24—At Cleve.	W	8-7	Fingers	Buskey
25—At Cleve.	W	9-1	Torrez	Dobson
27—At Det.	L	2-10	Coleman	Blue
28—At Det.	L	1-8	Roberts	Norris
30—At Balt.	W	11-1	Torrez	Palmer

Won 9, Lost 8

MAY				
2—At Balt.	W	6-2	Blue	Grimsley
2—At Balt.	L	3-4	Garland	Abbott
3—Cleve.	L	4-5*	Buskey	Fingers
4—Cleve.	W	8-4	Torrez	Peterson
5—Cleve.	L	1-3	Dobson	Fingers
7—N. York	L	4-14	May	Blue
8—N. York	L	4-8	Tidrow	Todd
9—N. York	W	4-3‡	Lindblad	Hunter
10—Calif.	W	6-3	P. Mitchell	Ryan
11—Calif.	W	6-4	Todd	Drago
14—Texas	L	3-4*	Perry	Fingers
15—Texas	L	4-6‡	Foucault	Todd
16—Texas	W	3-2	Blue	Barr
17—At Minn.	L	4-5†	Campbell	Todd
18—At Minn.	L	3-4†	Goltz	Todd
19—At K. C.	L	2-5	Splittorff	Torrez
20—At K. C.	L	4-8	Bird	P. Mitchell
21—At Chi.	L	0-6	Brett	Blue
22—At Chi.	L	2-7	Jefferson	Norris
23—At Chi.	L	1-3	Carroll	Torrez
23—At Chi.	L	3-4	Johnson	Bahnsen
24—Minn.	W	12-7	Todd	Campbell
25—Minn.	W	6-1	Blue	Hughes
26—Minn.	L	1-6	Goltz	P. Mitchell
27—Minn.	W	5-3	Torrez	Blyleven
28—Chicago	W	11-0	Bahnsen	Johnson
29—Chicago	W	2-0	Blue	Forster
30—Chicago	L	3-4‡	Carroll	Fingers
31—Kan. C.	W	10-1	Torrez	Splittorff

Won 12, Lost 17

JUNE				
1—Kan. C.	L	2-5	Bird	Bahnsen
2—Kan. C.	L	3-4‡	Littell	Fingers
4—At N. Y.	W	6-4†	Todd	Lyle
5—At N. Y.	W	7-6	Fingers	Lyle
6—At N. Y.	W	3-2	Blue	Figueroa
6—At N. Y.	L	2-5	Pagan	Lindblad
8—At Bos.	W	6-5	Todd	Cleveland
9—At Bos.	L	4-6	Wise	Torrez
10—At Bos.	W	8-5	Todd	Murphy
11—At Milw.	L	2-4	Colborn	Blue
12—At Milw.	W	2-1	P. Mitchell	Travers
13—At Milw.	L	4-5	Slaton	Torrez
15—Boston	W	3-2	Lindblad	Jenkins
16—Boston	W	4-1	P. Mitchell	Tiant
17—Boston	L	3-8	Pole	Torrez
18—Milw.	L	2-3	Castro	Todd
19—Milw.	W	7-4	Abbott	Colborn
20—Milw.	W	7-5	Bahnsen	Travers
21—Texas	W	0-1*	Blyleven	P. Mitchell
22—Texas	W	5-2	Bosman	Briles
23—At Calif.	W	8-2	Norris	Hassler
24—At Calif.	L	1-2	Monge	Abbott

JUNE			Winner	Loser
25—Minn.	W	5-2	Lindblad	Goltz
26—Minn.	L	3-11	Hughes	P. Mitchell
27—Minn.	W	5-3	Bosman	Redfern
28—At Texas	L	2-3†	Foucault	Todd
29—At Texas	W	8-3	Bahnsen	Barr
30—At Texas	L	2-3	Perry	Torrez

Won 15, Lost 13

JULY				
1—At K. C.	W	5-2	Fingers	Pattin
2—At K. C.	L	5-8	Littell	Blue
3—At K. C.	L	5-7	Leonard	Todd
4—At K. C.	W	6-0	Norris	Fitzmorris
5—Balt.	W	4-1	Torrez	May
6—Balt.	W	2-0	Blue	Palmer
7—Balt.	W	5-3	P. Mitchell	Cuellar
8—Balt.	L	6-9	Garland	Lindblad
9—Cleve.	W	2-1	Torrez	Brown
10—Cleve.	W	7-3	Fingers	Dobson
11—Cleve.	W	9-3	P. Mitchell	Eckersley
15—At Det.	L	2-3†	Roberts	Blue
16—At Det.	L	0-1†	Fidrych	Fingers
17—At Det.	W	3-2	Norris	Ruhle
18—At Det.	W	10-1	P. Mitchell	MacCormack
19—At Cleve.	L	2-3	Bibby	Blue
19—At Cleve.	W	10-3	Bosman	Brown
20—At Cleve.	W	7-4	Fingers	LaRoche
21—At N. Y.	L	1-10	Hunter	Norris
22—At N. Y.	W	6-5	Fingers	Tidrow
23—Kan. C.	W	2-0	Blue	Pattin
24—Kan. C.	L	5-6	Leonard	Todd
25—Kan. C.	W	9-2	Abbott	Bird
26—Chicago	W	3-1	P. Mitchell	Johnson
27—Chicago	W	1-0	Blue	Gossage
28—Chicago	L	1-2	Odom	Lindblad
30—At Minn.	L	7-8	Burgmeier	Fingers
31—At Minn.	L	5-6	Goltz	Bahnsen

Won 17, Lost 11

AUGUST				
1—At Minn.	L	7-8‡	Campbell	Lindblad
1—At Minn.	L	2-6	Johnson	Abbott
2—At Minn.	L	0-3	Luebber	Torrez
3—At Chi.	W	7-3	Bosman	Odom
4—At Chi.	W	5-0	P. Mitchell	Brett
6—Calif.	L	1-2	Tanana	Blue
7—Calif.	W	9-1	Torrez	Kirkwood
8—Calif.	W	9-3	Bahnsen	Monge
8—Calif.	L	13-8	Lindblad	Ryan
10—Milw.	W	2-1	Blue	Slaton
11—Milw.	W	8-5	Torrez	Travers
12—Milw.	W	4-3	Fingers	Castro
13—Boston	W	2-0	Norris	Cleveland
14—Boston	W	7-3	Blue	Jenkins
15—Boston	W	8-7	Bahnsen	Willoughby
16—At Milw.	L	3-4	Frisella	Fingers
17—At Milw.	W	5-4	Lindblad	Rodriguez
18—At Milw.	L	1-3	Slaton	Blue
20—At Bos.	L	1-2	Tiant	Fingers
21—At Bos.	L	2-5	Cleveland	Bosman
22—At Bos.	W	7-6‡	Fingers	Willoughby
23—At Balt.	W	3-0	Blue	Flanagan
24—At Balt.	W	5-4	Bahnsen	Garland
25—At Balt.	L	4-9	May	P. Mitchell
27—Detroit	L	1-8	Ruhle	Abbott
28—Detroit	W	5-2	Blue	Roberts
29—Detroit	W	2-1‡	Fingers	Fidrych
30—N. York	L	2-5	Figueroa	Norris
31—N. York	L	1-2	Alexander	Bahnsen

Won 17, Lost 12

SEPTEMBER				
1—N. York	W	5-0	Blue	Hunter
3—At Calif.	W	3-0	Torrez	Ross

SEPTEMBER			Winner	Loser
4—At Calif.	L	1-5	Hartzell	Norris
5—At Calif.	L	2-3	Ryan	Bahnsen
6—At Calif.	W	2-1†	Fingers	Verhoeven
7—Chicago	W	4-0	Torrez	Forster
8—Chicago	L	5-6	Knapp	Fingers
9—Chicago	W	2-1	Todd	Brett
10—At Texas	L	4-5*	Bacsik	Blue
11—At Texas	W	1-0	Torrez	Briles
12—At Texas	W	9-6	Bahnsen	Perry
14—At Minn.	W	4-2	Blue	Luebber
14—At Minn.	L	3-4	Goltz	Lindblad
15—Minn.	W	5-2	Torrez	Hughes
16—Minn.	L	0-4	Singer	Bahnsen
17—Texas	L	1-0	Torrez	Bosman
18—Texas	W	3-2	Blue	Boggs
19—Texas	L	1-9	Umbarger	Torres

SEPTEMBER			Winner	Loser
19—Texas	W	13-3	P. Mitchell	Hargan
21—At K. C.	L	1-3	Bird	Bahnsen
22—At K. C.	W	11-1	Blue	Pattin
23—At K. C.	W	8-1	Torrez	Leonard
24—At Chi.	L	2-4	Barrios	Fingers
25—At Chi.	W	7-4	Fingers	Gossage
27—Kan. C.	W	8-3	Blue	Leonard
28—Kan. C.	W	1-0	Torrez	Pattin
29—Kan. C.	L	0-4	Gura	P. Mitchell
	Won 16, Lost 11			
OCTOBER				
1—Calif.	L	0-2‡	Tanana	Blue
2—Calif.	W	9-8§	Fingers	Verhoeven
3—Calif.	L	0-1	Ryan	Torrez
	Won 1, Lost 2			

* 10 innings.   † 11 innings.   ‡ 12 innings.   § 14 innings.

Twins Change Tactics Under Mauch

By BOB FOWLER

For four consecutive seasons the Twins rallied to finish with a respectable record in the American League West. And each following winter, club officials spent their cold, snowy evenings telling fans, "We'll win next year."

Of course, each year the Twins left their fans with broken hearts. And 1976 was no exception.

The Twins started the season with a new manager, Gene Mauch, and the party line was that he would improve the entire club. In many respects, he did just that, but it wasn't enough to prevent another third-place finish.

Yes, the Twins were also-rans again. This time they finished five games out of first place with an 85-77 record—their best record since 1970 when they last won a division title.

So the publicity continued during the off-season as club officials enthusiastically told Minnesotans to buy tickets because "it's going to be heaven in '77."

Frankly, they finally may be correct. Based on their 1976 performance, the Twins are very close to being contenders instead of pretenders.

Here are some of the accomplishments of the club in the Bicentennial Year:

The Twins regained their No. 1 ranking in team batting with a club-record .274 average. They also led the league in runs with 743.

Individually, designated hitter Steve Braun proved to be a Pete Rose-type leadoff man with a .288 average and second-year center fielder Lyman Bostock finished fourth in the batting race with a .323 mark.

But Rod Carew, who had won five batting titles, including four in a row, lost his bid for another title on the last day of the season. The man who moved to first base for the first time in his 10-year career compiled a .331 mark, trailing Kansas City's George Brett (.333) and Hal McRae (.332) by the smallest of margins.

Yet Carew had one of his best seasons ever under his sixth manager. He set a club record with 49 stolen bases and also set a record for attempts with 71.

He collected 200 hits for the third time in his career while leading the team in doubles (29) and triples (12) and finishing second in RBIs (90).

What was amazing about 1976 was how the Twins scored their runs. They hit only 81 home runs—a club record for futility—and set new highs in stolen bases (146) and sacrifice bunts (93).

So Mauch changed the club from a power-hitting group to one that got a lot of singles, moved runners into scoring position with stolen bases or bunts and drove in runs with more singles.

There were some other exceptional individual performances offensively.

Catcher Butch Wynegar hit .260 with 69 RBIs and a team-leading 79 walks while winning THE SPORTING NEWS award as the league's Rookie Player of the Year.

Another rookie, second baseman Bobby Randall, hit .267 and was the team's best-ever at making the double play pivot, being the key man in helping establish a team record with 181 twin killings.

Left fielder Larry Hisle led the team with 96 RBIs and right fielder Dan Ford hit a club-high 20 homers and added 86 RBIs. Incidentally, Hisle, Carew and Ford's RBI totals marked the first time in Twins' history that the team had three over the 85 total.

By now you may be asking yourself, "Why didn't this team win the division championship?"

Well, its glowing offense was tarnished by an erratic defense and pitching staff.

For example, the Twins made 171 errors, missing a club record by only three. Its pitching staff ranked 10th in the league with a 3.69 ERA, but would have ranked even lower had it not been for so many of the runs it allowed being unearned.

On June 1 the staff—indeed the team—changed a great deal when Calvin Griffith traded pitcher Bert Blyleven and shortstop Danny Thompson to Texas for pitcher Bill Singer, shortstop Roy Smalley, third baseman Mike Cubbage, minor league pitching prospect Jim Gideon and $250,000. Blyleven had been Minnesota's standout pitcher since 1970, but refused to sign his contract and Griffith elected wisely to trade him rather than lose him as a free agent and receive nothing in return.

So some of the staff's low totals—29 complete games, 11 shutouts and a record-low 762 strikeouts—were understandable.

Singer had a 9-9 record with the Twins, Dave Goltz a 14-14 mark, Jim Hughes a 9-14 showing and rookie Pete Redfern an 8-8 record.

The difference between a winning and losing season was relief pitcher Bill Campbell, who was the league's top fireman with a 17-5 record and 20 saves in a club record 78 appearances.

But Campbell played the entire season without signing a contract. Thus, he and third baseman Eric Soderholm, who missed the entire campaign with knee problems, became free agents at season's end.

Campbell became the first of the free agents to sign, inking a multi-year pact with the Boston Red Sox two days after the "re-entry draft" was held. His departure means that the Twins must have pitching help to make a serious bid for the division title in 1977.

If that help materializes, home attendance at Metropolitan Stadium might climb over the one million mark for the first time since 1970, too. Minnesotans have proved they don't support teams that keep making promises and don't fulfill them.

MINNESOTA TWINS—1976

Front row—Gomez, Burgmeier, Wynegar, Oliva, McMahon, coach; Mauch, manager; Zimmerman, coach: Thompson, Brye, Albury, Braun. Second row—Jarzyna, clubhouse man; Wiesner, clubhouse man; Bostock, Terrell, Decker, Hisle, McKay, Carew, Martin, trainer; Crump, equipment manager. Third row—Borgmann, Ford, Hughes, Blyleven, Goltz, Roof, Campbell, Kusick, Luebber, Pazik, Randall. In front—Doyle, Dolan and Westcott, batboys.

SCORES OF MINNESOTA TWINS' 1976 GAMES

APRIL

Date				Winner	Loser
9—At Texas	L	1-2§		Perry	Campbell
10—At Texas	L	1-4		Umbarger	Decker
11—At Texas	W	4-3		Campbell	Terpko
13—Chicago	L	1-4		Gossage	Blyleven
14—Chicago	W	6-2		Decker	Wood
15—At N. Y.	L	4-11		Tidrow	Albury
17—At N. Y.	L	0-10		Figueroa	Hughes
18—At N. Y.	W	5-4		Blyleven	Hunter
19—At Bos.	L	0-2		Jenkins	Decker
20—At Bos.	L	3-12		Wise	Goltz
24—Balt.	W	2-1y		Campbell	Jackson
25—Balt.	W	7-2		Burgmeier	Palmer
27—Cleve.	L	5-7		Brown	Goltz
28—Cleve.	L	0-9		Eckersley	Blyleven

Won 5, Lost 9

MAY

Date				Winner	Loser
1—Milw.	W	9-5		Campbell	Broberg
4—At Det.	W	5-4‡		Albury	Laxton
5—At Det.	W	8-2		Blyleven	Roberts
7—At Milw.	L	3-4		Slaton	Hughes
8—At Milw.	W	13-2		Decker	Travers
9—At Milw.	W	6-4		Campbell	Rodriguez
10—At K. C.	W	5-4‡		Burgmeier	Pattin
11—At K. C.	L	3-6		Bird	Luebber
12—At K. C.	L	5-17		Pattin	Decker
14—At Calif.	W	6-4		Goltz	Hartzell
15—At Calif.	W	5-2		Blyleven	Ross
15—At Calif.	W	15-5		Redfern	Monge
16—At Calif.	L	1-5		Kirkwood	Hughes
17—Oakland	W	5-4§		Campbell	Todd
18—Oakland	W	4-3§		Goltz	Todd
19—At Chi.	L	1-4		Vuckovich	Blyleven
20—At Chi.	L	2-3		Gossage	Redfern
21—Kan. C.	L	1-5		Leonard	Hughes
22—Kan. C.	W	5-3		Goltz	Fitzmorris
23—Kan. C.	W	3-1		Blyleven	Splittorff
24—At Oak.	L	7-12		Todd	Campbell
25—At Oak.	L	1-6		Blue	Hughes
26—At Oak.	W	6-1		Goltz	P. Mitchell
27—At Oak.	L	3-5		Torrez	Blyleven
28—Texas	L	0-4		Umbarger	Luebber
29—Texas	W	5-1		Hughes	Hargan
30—Texas	W	3-2		Goltz	Foucault
31—Calif.	L	2-3		Tanana	Blyleven

Won 16, Lost 12

JUNE

Date				Winner	Loser
1—Calif.	L	4-6		Ryan	Redfern
2—Calif.	L	2-5		Ross	Hughes
4—At Balt.	W	8-6‡		Campbell	Flanagan
5—At Balt.	L	1-5		Holtzman	Decker
6—At Balt.	W	3-2		Singer	Palmer
6—At Balt.	W	11-6		Hughes	Cuellar
7—At Cleve.	W	7-2		Goltz	Waits
8—At Cleve.	W	3-1		Campbell	Eckersley
9—At Cleve.	L	1-4		Dobson	Decker
11—Boston	W	10-4		Burgmeier	Pole
12—Boston	L	2-5		Tiant	Goltz
13—Boston	L	2-10		Jones	Hughes
14—Boston	L	0-5		Wise	Decker
15—N. York	L	2-4		Ellis	Redfern
16—N. York	L	4-9		Figueroa	Singer
17—Detroit	W	4-0*		Goltz	Ruhle
18—Detroit	L	2-4		Roberts	Hughes
19—Detroit	W	6-4		Redfern	MacCormack
20—Detroit	L	3-7		Fidrych	Singer
21—At Calif.	L	1-2‡		Ross	Goltz
22—At Calif.	W	10-6		Hughes	Kirkwood
23—Chicago	L	3-4		Johnson	Decker
23—Chicago	L	5-9		Vuckovich	Redfern
24—Chicago	W	4-2		Singer	Gossage
25—At Oak.	L	2-5		Lindblad	Goltz
26—At Oak.	W	11-3		Hughes	P. Mitchell
27—At Oak.	L	3-5		Bosman	Redfern
28—Kan. C.	W	4-3		Campbell	Littell
29—Kan. C.	L	0-1‡		Fitzmorris	Goltz
30—Kan. C.	L	2-4		Splittorff	Bane

Won 12, Lost 18

JULY

Date				Winner	Loser
2—Calif.	W	6-5		Albury	Hassler
3—Calif.	W	2-0		Singer	Ryan
4—Calif.	L	3-5		Tanana	Goltz
4—Calif.	W	9-5		Campbell	Drago
5—At Milw.	L	2-3		Travers	Bane
6—At Milw.	L	2-6		Slaton	Hughes
7—At Milw.	W	8-2		Singer	Augustine
8—At Bos.	W	6-4		Jones	Goltz
9—At Bos.	W	8-6		Campbell	Wise
10—At Bos.	W	4-2		Bane	Tiant
11—At Bos.	L	4-6		Jenkins	Singer
15—Cleve.	W	5-2		Bane	Brown
16—Cleve.	L	6-7		Dobson	Singer
17—Cleve.	L	0-4		Waits	Redfern
18—Cleve.	L	1-6		Thomas	Hughes
19—Detroit	W	6-5		Campbell	Roberts
20—Detroit	L	3-8		Fidrych	Singer
21—Boston	W	5-1		Goltz	Wise
22—Boston	W	5-1		Redfern	Tiant
23—At Chi.	W	6-2		Burgmeier	Barrios
24—At Chi.	W	17-2		Bane	Jefferson
25—At Chi.	W	13-8		Albury	Forster
25—At Chi.	L	4-7		Brett	Singer
26—Texas	L	0-3		Blyleven	Goltz
28—Texas	W	8-5		Hughes	Hargan
28—Texas	W	8-0		Luebber	Barr
29—Texas	W	2-1		Bane	Umbarger
30—Oakland	W	8-7		Burgmeier	Fingers
31—Oakland	W	6-5		Goltz	Bahnsen

Won 18, Lost 11

AUGUST

Date				Winner	Loser
1—Oakland	W	8-7x		Campbell	Lindblad
1—Oakland	W	6-2		Johnson	Abbott
2—Oakland	W	3-0		Luebber	Torrez
3—At K. C.	L	1-7		Pattin	Bane
4—At K. C.	L	2-4		Fitzmorris	Goltz
5—At K. C.	L	4-6		Leonard	Singer
6—At Texas	L	0-6		Perry	Redfern
7—At Texas	W	3-1		Luebber	Boggs
8—At Texas	L	4-5		Terpko	Campbell
10—At Balt.	L	0-2		Palmer	Goltz
11—At Balt.	W	2-0		Singer	Garland
12—N. York	L	5-12		Hunter	Luebber
13—N. York	L	3-9		Figueroa	Bane
14—N. York	L	4-5		Holtzman	Goltz
15—N. York	W	9-8		Hughes	Lyle
16—Balt.	L	4-8		Grimsley	Luebber
17—Balt.	L	3-10		May	Johnson
18—Balt.	W	5-1		Goltz	Palmer
19—Balt.	W	5-4		Singer	Pagan
20—At Det.	L	2-3		Roberts	Bane
20—At Det.	L	8-5		Burgmeier	Laxton
21—At Det.	W	7-3‡		Hughes	Fidrych
22—At Det.	W	6-4x		Campbell	Hiller
23—At N. Y.	L	4-9		Holtzman	Singer
24—At N. Y.	L	4-5		Alexander	Bane
25—At N. Y.	L	4-5a		Jackson	Burgmeier
27—At Cleve.	L	3-7		Brown	Goltz
28—At Cleve.	L	3-4z		Buskey	Hughes
29—At Cleve.	L	4-7		Eckersley	Bane
30—Milw.	W	10-3		Burgmeier	Augustine
31—Milw.	W	4-0		Goltz	Travers
31—Milw.	L	3-6		Slaton	Campbell

Won 13, Lost 19

SEPTEMBER			Winner	Loser	SEPTEMBER			Winner	Loser
1 – Milw.	W	3-2x	Campbell	Castro	17 – At Calif.	W	11-2	Redfern	Kirkwood
2 – Milw.	W	8-4	Johnson	Castro	18 – At Calif.	L	0-6	Ross	Goltz
3 – Chicago	W	11-1	Redfern	Gossage	19 – At Calif.	W	7-5	Campbell	Monge
4 – Chicago	L	0-4	Brett	Hughes	21 – At Chi.	W	13-6	Burgmeier	Kravec
5 – Chicago	W	18-1	T. Johnson	C. B. Johnson	22 – At Chi.	W	6-3	Singer	Johnson
6 – Chicago	W	3-2	Campbell	Barrios	23 – At Chi.	W	3-0	Redfern	Brett
7 – At Texas	W	1-0	Redfern	Perry	25 – Calif.	W	6-0	Goltz	Ryan
8 – At Texas	W	3-1†	Luebber	Boggs	26 – Calif.	L	1-4	Tanana	Hughes
9 – At Texas	W	6-0	Goltz	Umbarger	28 – Texas	L	0-7	Perry	Singer
10 – Kan. C.	W	18-3	Hughes	Hassler	29 – Texas	W	9-1	Redfern	Boggs
11 – Kan. C.	L	6-8	Littell	Campbell				**Won 18, Lost 8**	
12 – Kan. C.	L	6-16	Pattin	Redfern					
14 – Oakland	L	2-4	Blue	Luebber	**OCTOBER**				
14 – Oakland	W	4-3	Goltz	Lindblad	1 – At K. C.	W	4-3	Campbell	Littell
15 – At Oak.	L	2-5	Torrez	Hughes	2 – At K. C.	W	3-2	Singer	Hassler
16 – At Oak.	W	4-0	Singer	Bahnsen	3 – At K. C.	W	5-3	Hughes	Splittorff
								Won 3, Lost 0	

* 5 innings. † 7½ innings. ‡ 10 innings. § 11 innings. x 12 innings. y 14 innings. z 17 innings. a 19 innings.

Sherry Revives Staggering Angels

By DICK MILLER

Like a bottle of fine wine allowed to age gracefully out of sight, the Angels finally realized something good out of two years spent in the darkness of the American League West cellar.

It took a revolution on a bus ride and an unexpectedly strong comeback from surgery by Nolan Ryan, but the Angels showed strong signs of progress in 1976 in advancing to fourth place in the American League West.

The season began with a revolt against manager Dick Williams and ended with a love-in with his successor, Norm Sherry.

The Angels compiled a 37-29 record after Sherry's promotion from the coaching ranks to tie Texas for fourth place. Sherry's winning percentage of .561 was five points better than the season mark of the division-winning Kansas City Royals. Sherry was rewarded with a one-year contract for 1977.

A pennant winner at Boston and Oakland, Williams was never able to get the Angels out of the cellar in his nearly two years at the helm. He was fired the morning of July 23 after an incident on the team bus with Bill Melton which came close to a physical revolt by about half a dozen players.

Melton, the former American League home run champion who had a dismal season with a .208 batting average, six home runs and 42 RBIs, was suspended for three days.

The Angels might have advanced further in the standings if it hadn't been for an injury to outfielder Bobby Bonds, who was involved in a controversial off-season trade with the Yankees that sent outfielder Mickey Rivers and pitcher Ed Figueroa to New York.

Bonds injured the middle finger on his right hand in a freak accident during an exhibition game with the Dodgers on April 3. The outfielder never had full use of the hand and finally underwent surgery on August 9 to repair the chip fracture. Bonds still led the club with 10 home runs and 54 runs batted in while stealing 30 bases in his 99-game season.

Pluses? There were a number.

At the age of 23 Frank Tanana continued to mature into one of the game's best pitchers. An early season arm injury which cost him three turns and forced a switch to a five-man pitching rotation cost the lefthander a chance to win 20 games for the first time.

He finished with a 19-10 record, a 2.44 earned-run average and finished second to Ryan with 261 strikeouts after leading the majors in 1975.

Although he didn't throw his annual no-hitter, Ryan became the first pitcher in major league history to strike out 300 batters in a season four times by fanning 327.

A 6-1 record in September-October included a pair of two-hitters, four three-hitters and three shutouts to make The Express a 17-game winner. He led American League pitchers with seven shutouts.

Another plus was the emergence of Paul Hartzell, who might have been the league's Rookie Pitcher of the Year in any other season than the Year of the Bird, Mark Fidrych of Detroit. Less than six months out of Lehigh University, Hartzell emerged from the bullpen in mid-season to compile a 7-2 record as a starter. His overall ERA of 2.77 was seventh best in the league.

The search for a shortstop continued. Orlando Ramirez opened the season as the regular, but was sent to the minors after being hurt in a freak accident while sitting in the dugout at Detroit.

Dave Chalk was shifted over from third base in mid-season and did an adequate job defensively. But his batting suffered and Chalk finished the season with a .217 average and no home runs.

Mike Miley, the former No. 1 draft choice, was given a shot the final month of the season and his batting average also was disappointing: .184. Mike was killed in an auto crash near Baton Rouge, La., January 6, 1977.

Elsewhere in the lineup, there was new-found stability. Second baseman Jerry Remy became a team leader in his second year and was voted the Owners Trophy by his teammates and most valuable player by the Angels' Booster Club.

Three mid-season acquisitions also lent helping hands to the driving finish. Infielder Mario Guerrero, purchased as defensive insurance from the Cardinals' Tulsa farm club, was an offensive surprise with a .284 batting average, best on the squad.

Catcher Terry Humphrey, also acquired because of his defensive reputation, took the job away from Andy Etchebarren by batting nearly .300 in July and August.

Tony Solaita picked up the power slack in Bonds' absence by hitting nine home runs after his arrival on July 14. The powerful Samoan was acquired on waivers from Kansas City.

The Angels picked up three solid players in the re-entry draft, signing outfielders Joe Rudi and Don Baylor of Oakland and second baseman Bobby Grich of Baltimore.

SCORES OF CALIFORNIA ANGELS' 1976 GAMES

APRIL			Winner	Loser	APRIL			Winner	Loser
9—Oakland	L	2-5	Torrez	Tanana	26—At Milw.	L	0-1	Colborn	Tanana
10—Oakland	L	2-6	Blue	Ryan	27—At Balt.	L	2-3†	Jackson	Drago
11—Oakland	L	7-10	Bahnsen	Kirkwood	28—At Balt.	L	2-4	Holtzman	Ross
13—At K. C.	L	4-7	Fitzmorris	Hassler	30—At Cleve.	L	2-5	Kern	Drago
14—At K. C.	W	7-6	Monge	Pattin			**Won 5, Lost 12**		
15—At K. C.	W	5-1	Ryan	Splittorff					
16—Detroit	W	6-5‡	Brewer	Grilli	**MAY**				
17—Detroit	L	0-2	Roberts	Ross	1—At Cleve.	W	6-1	Ryan	Dobson
18—Detroit	L	2-6	Bare	Hassler	2—At Cleve.	L	3-12	Brown	Hassler
19—Balt.	W	9-4	Tanana	Cuellar	2—At Cleve.	W	5-4	Brewer	Hood
20—Balt.	W	5-0	Ryan	Alexander	4—N. York	L	1-2	Ellis	Tanana
21—Balt.	L	1-5	Palmer	Kirkwood	5—N. York	L	4-10	Hunter	Ryan
23—At Milw.	L	2-4	Slaton	Ross	6—N. York	L	2-4	Figueroa	Ross

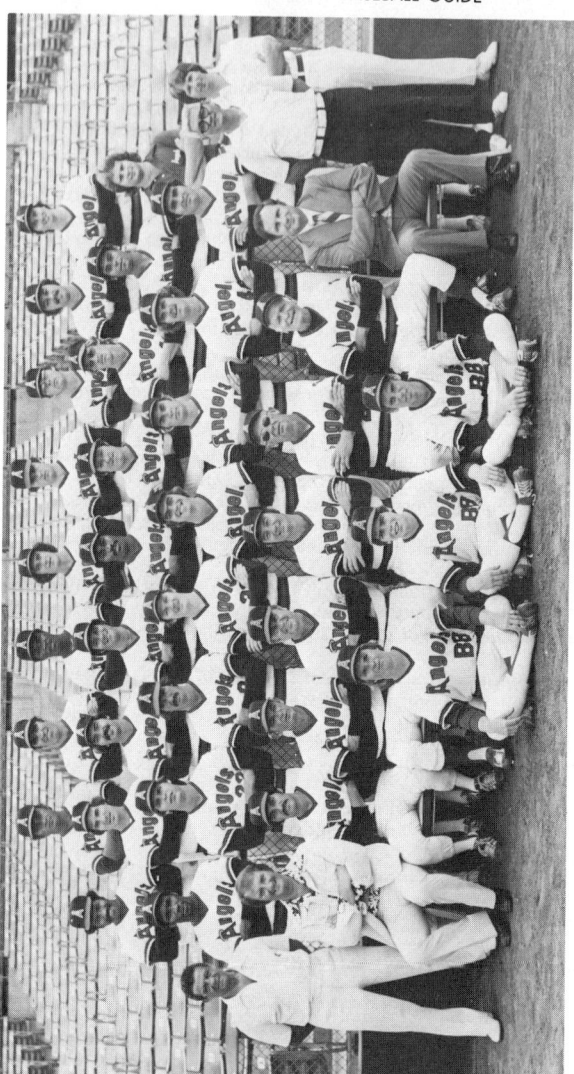

CALIFORNIA ANGELS—1976

Front row—Rasinski, team physician; Guerrero, Clear, coach; Muffett, coach; Sherry, manager; Hoscheit, coach; Reese, coach; Triggs, team physician Second row—Frederico, trainer & traveling secretary; Bonds, Bochte, Humphrey, Kirkwood, Tanana, Hartzell, Verhoeven, Monge, Shishido, equipment manager; Swart, assistant trainer. Third row—Davis, Briggs, Drago, Melton, Jackson, Ross, Jones, Torres, Schneider, clubhouse manager. Fourth row—Solaita, Etchebarren, Stanton, Scott, Ryan, Collins, Remy, Chalk. In front—Ulich, ballboy; Buzbee, ballboy; Zavat, batboy.

MAY

Date		Score	Winner	Loser
7–Cleve.	W	5-4	Drago	Brown
8–Cleve.	W	4-3x	Brewer	Buskey
9–Cleve.	W	3-2	Tanana	Peterson
10–At Oak.	L	3-6	P. Mitchell	Ryan
11–At Oak.	L	4-6	Todd	Drago
12–Texas	L	0-1	Singer	Kirkwood
13–Texas	W	7-5	Tanana	Umbarger
14–Minn.	L	4-6	Goltz	Hartzell
15–Minn.	L	2-5	Blyleven	Ross
15–Minn.	L	5-15	Redfern	Monge
16–Minn.	W	5-1	Kirkwood	Hughes
17–At Chi.	W	10-5	Tanana	Jefferson
18–At Chi.	L	0-5	Johnson	Ryan
20–At Texas	W	6-3	Ross	Perry
21–At Texas	L	2-5	Briles	Kirkwood
22–At Texas	W	5-1	Tanana	Singer
23–At Texas	L	0-9*	Umbarger	Ryan
24–Chicago	L	3-5	Vuckovich	Brewer
25–Chicago	L	1-7	Gossage	Ross
26–Chicago	L	0-1‡	Brett	Kirkwood
27–Chicago	W	5-3	Tanana	Barrios
28–Kan. C.	L	0-3	Bird	Ryan
29–Kan. C.	W	3-2	Monge	Littell
29–Kan. C.	W	7-2	Ross	Fitzmorris
30–Kan. C.	L	2-3y	Mingori	Drago
31–At Minn.	W	3-2	Tanana	Blyleven
Won 14, Lost 18				

JUNE

Date		Score	Winner	Loser
1–At Minn.	W	6-4	Ryan	Redfern
2–At Minn.	W	5-2	Ross	Hughes
4–At Bos.	W	5-4†	Scott	Willoughby
5–At Bos.	L	3-4	Jenkins	Tanana
6–At Bos.	L	1-4	Pole	Ryan
8–At N.Y.	L	2-4	Ellis	Ross
9–At N.Y.	L	3-4	Hunter	Kirkwood
10–At N.Y.	W	2-0	Tanana	May
11–At Det.	L	3-4	Fidrych	Hartzell
12–At Det.	L	4-10	Ruhle	Ross
13–At Det.	W	10-7	Kirkwood	Roberts
14–At Milw.	L	2-8	Augustine	Tanana
15–Milw.	W	1-0	Ryan	Colborn
16–Milw.	L	0-9	Travers	Monge
17–Milw.	W	2-0	Ross	Slaton
18–Boston	L	1-3	Murphy	Hassler
19–Boston	W	5-3	Ryan	Wise
20–Boston	W	3-4‡	Murphy	Drago
21–Minn.	W	2-1†	Ross	Goltz
22–Minn.	L	6-10	Hughes	Kirkwood
23–Oakland	L	2-8	Norris	Hassler
24–Oakland	W	2-1	Monge	Abbott
25–At K.C.	L	3-6	Splittorff	Ross
26–At K.C.	L	0-3	Pattin	Ryan
27–At K.C.	L	4-5†	Bird	Drago
29–At Chi.	W	4-1	Tanana	Barrios
30–At Chi.	W	2-1†	Drago	Carroll
Won 12, Lost 15				

JULY

Date		Score	Winner	Loser
1–At Chi.	W	2-1	Monge	Brett
2–At Minn.	L	5-6	Albury	Hassler
3–At Minn.	L	0-2	Singer	Ryan
4–At Minn.	W	5-3	Tanana	Goltz
4–At Minn.	L	5-9	Campbell	Drago
5–Cleve.	W	8-1	Ross	Dobson
6–Cleve.	L	3-7	Eckersley	Monge
7–Cleve.	W	2-0	Ryan	Waits
9–Balt.	L	3-4	May	Tanana
10–Balt.	L	2-5	Palmer	Ross
11–Balt.	L	1-3	Pagan	Ryan
15–At Balt.	L	0-4	Palmer	Ross
16–At Balt.	L	4-5	Garland	Ryan
17–At Balt.	W	7-3	Tanana	May
18–At Balt.	W	8-6	Drago	Cuellar
19–At Milw.	W	4-2	Hartzell	Rodriguez
19–At Milw.	W	6-1	Kirkwood	Slaton
20–At Milw.	L	2-6	Augustine	Ross
21–At Cleve	L	2-6	Waits	Ryan
22–At Cleve.	L	5-7	Eckersley	Tanana
24–Texas	W	8-0	Hartzell	Umbarger
24–Texas	W	4-3	Kirkwood	Boggs
25–Texas	W	7-3‡	Drago	Foucault
26–Kan. C.	L	0-4	Fitzmorris	Ryan
27–Kan. C.	W	2-1	Tanana	Splittorff
28–Kan. C.	L	2-3z	Gura	Kirkwood
30–Chicago	W	3-0	Ryan	Brett
31–Chicago	W	3-2‡	Drago	Forster
Won 14, Lost 14				

AUGUST

Date		Score	Winner	Loser
1–Chicago	L	1-2	Gossage	Tanana
3–At Texas	W	4-0	Hartzell	Umbarger
4–At Texas	W	9-6	Ryan	Briles
5–At Texas	L	0-1	Blyleven	Ross
6–At Oak.	W	2-1	Tanana	Blue
7–At Oak.	L	1-9	Torrez	Kirkwood
8–At Oak.	L	3-9	Bahnsen	Monge
8–At Oak.	W	8-13	Lindblad	Ryan
10–Boston	W	5-4	Ross	Jenkins
11–Boston	W	6-0	Tanana	Wise
12–Boston	L	1-2†	Tiant	Ryan
13–Milw.	L	0-2	Augustine	Hartzell
14–Milw.	L	3-4	Sadecki	Overy
15–Milw.	L	3-5	Travers	Ross
17–At Det.	L	2-3	Fidrych	Tanana
18–At Det.	W	5-4‡	Ryan	Hiller
19–At Det.	L	3-4	Bare	Hartzell
20–At N. Y.	W	5-3	Kirkwood	Figueroa
21–At N. Y.	W	4-3†	Scott	Tidrow
22–At N. Y.	W	11-8‡	Monge	Lyle
23–At Bos.	L	3-7	Lee	Ryan
24–At Bos.	W	6-5	Hartzell	Willoughby
25–At Bos.	L	2-8	Tiant	Kirkwood
27–N. York	W	0-5z	Jackson	Monge
28–N. York	L	1-8	Ellis	Ryan
29–N. York	W	5-4‡	Scott	Tidrow
30–Detroit	W	2-1	Hartzell	Crawford
31–Detroit	W	6-3	Ryan	Ruhle
Won 13, Lost 15				

SEPTEMBER

Date		Score	Winner	Loser
1–Detroit	W	4-1	Tanana	Roberts
3–Oakland	L	0-3	Torrez	Ross
4–Oakland	W	5-1	Hartzell	Norris
5–Oakland	W	3-2	Ryan	Bahnsen
6–Oakland	L	1-2‡	Fingers	Verhoeven
7–At K. C.	W	2-1	Kirkwood	Pattin
8–At K. C.	W	2-0	Drago	Fitzmorris
9–At K. C.	W	5-6†	Mingori	Overy
10–At Chi.	W	3-2	Ryan	Johnson
11–At Chi.	W	7-3	Tanana	Kravec
12–At Chi.	L	1-2†	Gossage	Monge
12–At Chi.	L	1-5	Barrios	Kirkwood
13–At Texas	W	6-2y	Drago	Bacsik
14–At Texas	W	6-4	Hartzell	Hargan
15–Kan. C.	W	2-1	Ryan	Bird
16–Kan. C.	L	0-2	Pattin	Tanana
17–Minn.	L	2-11	Redfern	Kirkwood
18–Minn.	W	6-0	Ross	Goltz
19–Minn.	L	5-7	Campbell	Monge
20–Texas	W	1-0	Ryan	Blyleven
21–Texas	W	2-1	Tanana	Hoerner
22–Texas	L	1-2	Perry	Ross
23–Texas	L	5-6	Hargan	Drago
25–At Minn.	L	0-6	Goltz	Ryan
26–At Minn.	W	4-1	Tanana	Hughes
29–Chicago	W	3-0	Ryan	Brett
30–Chicago	W	7-3	Monge	Monroe
Won 16, Lost 11				

OCTOBER

Date		Score	Winner	Loser
1–At Oak.	W	2-0§	Tanana	Blue
2–At Oak.	L	8-9y	Fingers	Verhoeven
3–At Oak.	W	1-0	Ryan	Torrez
Won 2, Lost 1				

* 5 innings. † 10 innings. ‡ 11 innings. § 12 innings. x 13 innings. y 14 innings. z 15 innings.

Bat Failures Grease Ranger Slide

By MERLE HERYFORD

The Texas Rangers of 1976, confidently predicting great things, failed to solve an age-old problem: how to win without runs. It was as simple as that as they skidded to a tie for fourth place with California, and had to work hard to make it.

Strong favorites to make a real run at the American League West Division title, the Rangers, who had slumped from second to third a year earlier, appeared to have an excellent chance.

For two months they put it all together under manager Frank Lucchesi, who replaced deposed Billy Martin late in '75. By mid-May they were in first place, and, for example, already had won the season series from the defending league champion Boston Red Sox.

If you have to pick a date for their almost unbelievable demise, make it July 7. They had a 44-32 record and trailed Kansas City by three games. But that night, in their own park, they fell, 2-1, to Detroit, and the skids were greased.

They followed that with five losses in four days at Milwaukee and came home to lose four more to the Yankees.

Ten straight defeats, and that was only the beginning. They lost 44 of their next 63 games as no one seemed capable of stopping the slide. No hits, no runs, no victories for the team which could do nothing wrong early.

Surprisingly, the hitting, which had been taken for granted, dwindled to nothing, and pitching, which had been suspect, particularly the starters, kept the club respectable—but not without effort.

Gaylord Perry once went 30 consecutive innings without a run of support, losing four games, and Bert Blyleven, who was obtained in a June trade with Minnesota, was accorded only three runs in 38 innings. He broke even, 2-2, on the strength of back-to-back, 10-inning, 1-0 shutouts over Oakland and Chicago.

Perry, despite a shaky defense and inadequate support, finished 15-14, his fewest victories in nine seasons, and Blyleven, who never got untracked with the Rangers, was 13-16 but with a 2.87 ERA.

The pitcher who probably suffered most, however, was Nelson Briles, who was obtained from Kansas City in a winter trade. The 33-year-old veteran was perhaps most consistent of the starters, and his record, 11-9, was deceptive. He could easily have won 16 or 17 and been a leading candidate for the Comeback of the Year award.

Young southpaw Jim Umbarger, in his second major league season, was brilliant and ineffective by turns, finishing 10-12, and 20-year-old Tommy Boggs, elevated in the stretch, proved he was ready for topflight competition, despite a 1-7 record which gave him sufficient grounds to sue for non-support.

What suddenly went wrong?

No one had an answer.

One semi-popular theory was that the Rangers disrupted a winning combination and gave up too much for Blyleven (infielder Mike Cubbage, second baseman-shortstop Roy Smalley, young pitching prospect Jim Gideon and righthander Bill Singer, who was making a successful comeback after two years of arm miseries).

Another was that Lucchesi didn't wield a big enough stick. Although the manager refused to admit it, it was obvious that several of his players let him down, and Lucchesi is on record that the "nice guy" days are over.

Those were the intangibles, but the inescapable facts were that the men expected to swing the productive bats didn't, at least not enough. Particularly after John Ellis fractured a leg and was out for the year. He'd been the biggest clutch-hitter.

Jeff Burroughs, having his second straight, for him, sub-par year, hit only .237, driving in 86 runs, which, as the year before, were infrequently delivered in the clutch.

Handicapped by a bad ankle, shortstop Toby Harrah slumped from a brilliant .293 in 1975 to .260, drove in 26 fewer runs and showed signs of regression afield. Finally, in the closing days, he and Lucchesi agreed to his move to third base, which had been projected two years earlier, and the search for a shortstop began.

Mike Hargrove, coming off .323 and .303 seasons, still led the regulars at bat, but at .287, and Len Randle, whose toboggan started a year earlier, wound up at .224, a drop of 78 percentage points in two years.

The experiment, successful in the 1975 stretch, of putting Roy Howell at third and Tom Grieve at designated hitter, provided mixed results.

Howell neither hit nor fielded consistently, and Grieve, though he led the club with 20 homers (two more than Burroughs) was, as always, a streak hitter whose streaks grew less frequent.

Bright spot was Gene Clines, who had been obtained over the winter. He hit .276 after being over .300 much of the way and provided what spark there was in the middle and final months.

Late in the year, owner Brad Corbett, who had been active in all front-office decisions, hired Eddie Robinson from Atlanta and installed him as executive vice-president. Corbett said he was "retiring" except for a few decisions which involved finances and certain players.

The Rangers made the biggest deal of the winter meetings, trading Burroughs to Atlanta for five players and an estimated $250,000.

The club also convinced the City of Arlington that stadium renovation and enlargement was a necessity, and seating will be increased to 42,000 in a two-year program.

SCORES OF TEXAS RANGERS' 1976 GAMES

APRIL			Winner	Loser	MAY			Winner	Loser
9—Minn.	W	2-1x	Perry	Campbell	1—Boston	W	7-1	Singer	Wise
10—Minn.	W	4-1	Umbarger	Decker	2—Boston	W	6-3	Perry	Tiant
11—Minn.	L	3-4	Campbell	Terpko	4—At Milw.	W	7-4	Briles	Colborn
12—Oakland	W	5-1	Briles	P. Mitchell	8—At Bos.	W	6-5	Hargan	Pole
13—Oakland	W	3-1	Barr	Torrez	8—At Bos.	W	12-4	Umbarger	Tiant
14—Oakland	W	4-2	Perry	Blue	9—At Bos.	W	6-5	Foucault	Willoughby
16—Milw.	L	1-3	Colborn	Umbarger	10—Chicago	L	6-7x	Hamilton	Hargan
18—Milw.	W	7-4	Singer	Slaton	11—Chicago	W	6-5	Terpko	Hamilton
18—Milw.	L	1-4	Travers	Briles	12—At Calif.	W	1-0	Singer	Kirkwood
20—At Cleve.	L	1-9	Bibby	Perry	13—At Calif.	L	5-7	Tanana	Umbarger
23—At Det.	L	6-7	Hiller	Barr	14—At Oak.	W	4-3‡	Perry	Fingers
24—At Det.	W	5-4	Foucault	Hiller	15—At Oak.	W	6-4y	Foucault	Todd
27—N. York	L	0-1	Ellis	Perry	16—At Oak.	L	2-3	Blue	Barr
29—Boston	W	6-1	Briles	Lee	17—At K.C.	L	7-8y	Hall	Foucault
30—Boston	W	6-5	Umbarger	Jenkins	18—At K.C.	L	1-3	Fitzmorris	Umbarger
			Won 9, Lost 6		20—Calif.	L	3-6	Ross	Perry

TEXAS RANGERS—1976

Front row—Yates, batboy; Beniquez, Pryor, Thompson, Moates, Randle, Robinson, ballboy. Second row—Briles, Peterson, Hoerner, Moore, coach; Lucchesi, manager; Corrales, coach; Sundberg, Hargrove, Harrah. Third row—Zeigler, trainer; Fregosi, Blyleven, Gernert, coach; Hudson, coach; Burroughs, Grieve, Fahey, Foucault. Fourth row—Clines, Terpko, Perry, Umbarger, Barr, Hargan, Howell, Macko, equipment manager.

MAY			Winner	Loser
21–Calif.	W	5-2	Briles	Kirkwood
22–Calif.	L	1-5	Tanana	Singer
23–Calif.	W	9-0*	Umbarger	Ryan
24–Kan. C.	L	11-14	Mingori	Barr
26–Kan. C.	L	2-14	Leonard	Perry
26–Kan. C.	W	5-4§	Foucault	Pattin
27–Kan. C.	W	6-4	Singer	Splittorff
28–At Minn.	W	4-0	Umbarger	Luebber
29–At Minn.	L	1-5	Hughes	Hargan
30–At Minn.	L	3-4	Goltz	Foucault
31–At Chi.	L	4-9	Vuckovich	Briles
		Won 15, Lost 12		

JUNE				
1–At Chi.	W	6-5b	Foucault	Jefferson
2–At Chi.	L	0-1x	Hamilton	Umbarger
4–Detroit	W	14-3	Perry	Laxton
5–Detroit	L	2-3x	Fidrych	Blyleven
6–Detroit	W	16-6	Briles	Coleman
7–At Balt.	W	6-4	Umbarger	Grimsley
8–At Balt.	W	6-3	Peterson	Alexander
9–At Balt.	W	4-1	Perry	Holtzman
11–At N.Y.	L	5-7	Martinez	Blyleven
12–At N.Y.	W	2-1	Briles	Pagan
13–At N.Y.	W	7-1	Umbarger	Hunter
15–Cleve.	W	3-2	Perry	Bibby
16–Cleve.	L	4-9	Brown	Blyleven
17–Balt.	L	1-4	Garland	Briles
18–Balt.	L	4-9	May	Umbarger
19–Balt.	L	4-8	Palmer	Foucault
20–Balt.	L	0-2	Cuellar	Perry
21–At Oak.	W	1-0‡	Blyleven	P. Mitchell
22–At Oak.	L	2-5	Bosman	Briles
23–Kan. C.	W	7-5	Foucault	Leonard
24–Kan. C.	W	5-2	Hargan	Fitzmorris
25–Chicago	W	8-4	Perry	Hamilton
25–Chicago	L	9-14	Vuckovich	Foucault
26–Chicago	W	1-0‡	Blyleven	Brett
27–Chicago	L	2-6	Johnson	Briles
28–Oakland	L	3-2x	Foucault	Todd
29–Oakland	L	3-8	Bahnsen	Barr
30–Oakland	L	3-2	Perry	Torrez
		Won 16, Lost 12		

JULY				
2–At Chi.	L	0-1	Johnson	Blyleven
3–At Chi.	W	3-0	Briles	Forster
4–At Chi.	L	6-7y	Hamilton	Bacsik
4–At Chi.	L	3-2	Hargan	Knapp
5–Detroit	W	8-6	Terpko	Roberts
6–Detroit	W	3-2	Barr	Ruhle
7–Detroit	L	1-2	Hiller	Blyleven
8–At Milw.	L	4-5z	Frisella	Hoerner
9–At Milw.	L	2-7	Rodriguez	Umbarger
10–At Milw.	L	1-3	Travers	Perry
11–At Milw.	L	3-6	Slaton	Blyleven
11–At Milw.	L	4-5‡	Castro	Foucault
15–N. York	L	6-7	Figueroa	Perry
15–N. York	L	4-6‡	Hunter	Hoerner
16–N. York	L	0-3	Holtzman	Blyleven
17–N. York	L	5-7	Ellis	Barr
18–N. York	W	3-2y	Hargan	Lyle
19–Boston	W	4-3x	Bacsik	Willoughby
20–Boston	L	2-4	Jones	Briles
21–Balt.	L	4-6y	F. Martinez	Hoerner
22–Balt.	L	3-4	Holdsworth	Perry
24–At Calif.	L	0-8	Hartzell	Umbarger
24–At Calif.	L	3-4	Kirkwood	Boggs
25–At Calif.	L	3-7x	Drago	Foucault
26–At Minn.	W	3-0	Blyleven	Goltz
28–At Minn.	L	5-8	Hughes	Hargan
28–At Minn.	L	0-8	Luebber	Barr
29–At Minn.	L	1-2	Bane	Umbarger

JULY			Winner	Loser
30–At K.C.	L	1-2	Leonard	Briles
31–At K.C.	W	4-2	Blyleven	Fitzmorris
		Won 8, Lost 22		

AUGUST				
1–At K.C.	W	8-4	Perry	Hassler
3–Calif.	L	0-4	Hartzell	Umbarger
4–Calif.	L	6-9	Ryan	Briles
5–Calif.	W	1-0	Blyleven	Ross
6–Minn.	W	6-0	Perry	Redfern
7–Minn.	L	1-3	Luebber	Boggs
8–Minn.	W	5-4	Terpko	Campbell
9–At Det.	W	8-1	Briles	Lemanczyk
10–At Det.	L	5-7	Lemanczyk	Terpko
10–At Det.	W	3-0	Hargan	Crawford
11–At Det.	L	3-4	Fidrych	Perry
12–At Cleve.	L	4-5	LaRoche	Terpko
13–At Cleve.	W	2-1	Umbarger	Eckersley
14–At Cleve.	W	4-3‡	Foucault	Kern
15–At Cleve.	L	4-6	Thomas	Blyleven
15–At Cleve.	L	0-3	Bibby	Hargan
16–At N.Y.	L	1-5	Hunter	Perry
17–At N.Y.	L	1-2	Alexander	Boggs
18–At N.Y.	L	6-8	Lyle	Hargan
19–Cleve.	L	5-7	Buskey	Skok
20–Cleve.	W	3-0	Blyleven	Bibby
21–Cleve.	W	5-3	Perry	Brown
22–Cleve.	L	1-3	Dobson	Boggs
23–Milw.	L	2-6	Rodriguez	Umbarger
24–Milw.	L	0-1‡	Augustine	Foucault
25–Milw.	L	1-5	Travers	Blyleven
27–At Balt.	L	0-3	Palmer	Perry
28–At Balt.	L	4-6	Holdsworth	Hargan
29–At Balt.	W	11-0	Umbarger	Garland
30–At Bos.	L	3-11	Tiant	Blyleven
31–At Bos.	W	8-3	Briles	Cleveland
		Won 12, Lost 19		

SEPTEMBER				
1–At Bos.	L	0-3	Murphy	Perry
3–At K.C.	W	4-1	Boggs	Fitzmorris
4–At K.C.	L	0-7	Leonard	Umbarger
5–At K.C.	W	3-1	Blyleven	Hassler
6–At K.C.	W	5-4	Hargan	Bird
7–Minn.	L	0-1	Redfern	Perry
8–Minn.	L	1-3†	Luebber	Boggs
9–Minn.	L	0-6	Goltz	Umbarger
10–Oakland	W	5-4‡	Bacsik	Blue
11–Oakland	L	0-1	Torrez	Briles
12–Oakland	L	6-9	Bahnsen	Perry
13–Calif.	L	2-6a	Drago	Bacsik
14–Calif.	L	4-6	Hartzell	Hargan
15–At Chi.	W	4-3	Blyleven	Johnson
16–At Chi.	W	5-4	Briles	Kravec
17–At Oak.	W	4-3	Perry	Bosman
18–At Oak.	L	2-3	Blue	Boggs
19–At Oak.	W	9-1	Umbarger	Torrez
19–At Oak.	L	3-13	P. Mitchell	Hargan
20–At Calif.	L	0-1	Ryan	Blyleven
21–At Calif.	L	1-2	Tanana	Hoerner
22–At Calif.	W	2-1	Perry	Ross
23–At Calif.	W	6-5	Hargan	Drago
24–Kan. C.	L	1-2a	Gura	Foucault
25–Kan. C.	L	1-0	Blyleven	Hassler
26–Kan. C.	W	3-1	Briles	Bird
28–At Minn.	W	7-0	Perry	Singer
29–At Minn.	L	1-9	Redfern	Boggs
		Won 13, Lost 15		

OCTOBER				
1–Chicago	W	11-8	Hargan	Barrios
2–Chicago	W	5-4‡	Bacsik	Vuckovich
3–Chicago	W	3-0	Barker	Gossage
		Won 3, Lost 0		

* 5 innings. † 7½ innings. ‡ 10 innings. § Suspended game, completed May 27 (10 innings). x 11 innings. y 12 innings. z 13 innings. a 14 innings. b 16 innings.

Sox Disappoint On Field and at Gate

By RICHARD DOZER

Only once in the last 26 years did the White Sox finish with a poorer record than they did in the 1976 season when a nine-game losing streak at the end shot them down to 64-97 and a distant last in the American League West.

The disappointment went far deeper than the numbers for Bill Veeck, president of the club and the moving force behind keeping Chicago baseball for the American League. It was Veeck who came up with the required cash at the 11th hour the previous winter in Hollywood, Fla., and went on an immediate trading spree aimed at remodeling the club with speed and defense.

But the defense was poor, especially from a porous outfield charged with covering wide open spaces in Comiskey Park, where the center field fence was torn out to leave a depth of 440 feet to the back wall, along with the previously cavernous dimensions on the lines and in the alleys.

"If we can't hit the ball out of the park, the opponent won't either," promised Veeck, who was right on that score. There weren't many home runs, to be sure, but the White Sox suffered most from that. Jorge Orta and Jim Spencer led the club with 14 apiece, and there was only one righthanded hitter on the club who hit as many as five. The latter was Kevin Bell, who played barely half the season.

But the shortage of power was calculable. Pitching was supposed to make up the difference. It didn't, although a part of it was no fault of the ball club. Wilbur Wood, usually good for up to 300 innings of workmanship, suffered a fractured kneecap May 9 and was lost for the season. Clay Carroll, a high-priced reliever, was disabled July 4 with a broken bone in his pitching hand and although he came back, he was of little value the rest of the way. Manager Paul Richards was left to suffer with a club he thought in the spring was a whole lot better—one that won 10 in a row in May!

Carroll and Wood together represented nearly a quarter of a million dollars in salary—a bitter pill for Veeck's 40 investors to swallow in a season they'd intended to be respectable and one wherein they'd surely draw more than a million customers. Instead, losing two early Sunday sellouts to the weather, they had to settle for just under 915,000—much of it papered by promotions that ranged from belly dancers to farm animal giveaways; from ethnic nights to an invasion of the field by fans with musical instruments billed as "the world's largest band."

But whether Veeck was trying to bolster a weak product with promotions or merely diverting attention from his sad ball club, there was no getting away from the day-to-day failure. The White Sox were shut out 21 times while their own pitchers turned in only 10 whitewash jobs. They had an edge on only one team (Milwaukee 7-5), and their only .300-hitting regular was Ralph Garr, who was nevertheless a disappointment. He batted in only 36 runs, refused to walk, and played a very unsteady right field.

Bucky Dent batted a disappointing .246 but played excellent shortstop.

Orta, embarrassed at both third base and in left field, was bothered by his failures when he batted. At his best as a designated hitter, he hit .274. Chet Lemon, the only other player close to being a regular, was hampered by a sore foot much of the way and hit only .246. Arm and elbow troubles plagued Brian

Downing, and Jim Essian thus got more time behind the plate, the two catchers batting .256 and .246, respectively.

Ken Brett surfaced as the most dependable pitcher but wasn't even on the club until he was acquired in a trade which sent Carlos May to the Yankees, May 18.

Brett finished 10-12, best of the flock of sub-.500 White Sox starters. Rich Gossage was 9-17, Bart Johnson 9-16 and Terry Forster 2-12 with a continuation of shoulder miseries.

Dave Hamilton, given the relief burden, led with 10 saves and six wins. Pete Vuckovich was the only hurler with the club all season who had a winning (7-4) record, though Wood was 4-3 and Chris Knapp, the prime rookie prospect, was 3-1 with some late-season brilliance. Francisco Barrios and Ken Kravec also offered some promise for the future, and without some winter additions to the club, youth is indeed about all the club has. A trade of questionable worth was made December 10 when Forster and Gossage were dealt to Pittsburgh for outfielder Richie Zisk and pitcher Silvio Martinez.

Bell, Lemon, Lamar Johnson and Alan Bannister figured as the basis for whatever optimism Veeck can generate.

SCORES OF CHICAGO WHITE SOX' 1976 GAMES

APRIL				Winner	Loser
9—Kan. C.	W	4-0		Wood	Splittorff
13—At Minn.	W	4-1		Gossage	Blyleven
14—At Minn.	L	2-6		Decker	Wood
15—At Bos.	W	8-4		Johnson	Wise
17—At Bos.	L	1-7		Tiant	Gossage
18—At Bos.	W	10-4		Wood	Lee
20—At N. Y.	L	4-5		Martinez	Johnson
21—At N. Y.	L	7-10		May	Hamilton
23—Boston	L	2-9		Tiant	Wood
28—Milw.	L	1-4		Travers	Wood
29—Milw.	L	5-8		Rodriguez	Carroll
30—Detroit	W	8-4		Forster	Bare
		Won 5, Lost 7			

MAY					
1—Detroit	L	1-10		Ruhle	Johnson
4—At Balt.	W	3-1		Wood	Holtzman
5—At Balt.	L	0-2		Palmer	Gossage
7—At Det.	L	0-5		Bare	Forster
8—At Det.	L	1-7		Ruhle	Johnson
9—At Det.	W	4-2		Wood	Coleman
10—At Texas	W	7-6‡		Hamilton	Hargan
11—At Texas	L	5-6		Terpko	Hamilton
13—At K. C.	L	2-13		Leonard	Johnson
14—At K. C.	L	1-7		Fitzmorris	Vuckovich
15—At K. C.	L	1-2§		Littell	Gossage
16—At K. C.	W	4-3		Carroll	Bird
17—Calif.	L	5-10		Tanana	Jefferson
18—Calif.	W	5-0		Johnson	Ryan
19—Minn.	W	4-1		Vuckovich	Blyleven
20—Minn.	W	3-2		Gossage	Redfern
21—Oakland	W	6-0		Brett	Blue
22—Oakland	W	7-2		Jefferson	Norris
23—Oakland	W	3-1		Carroll	Torrez
23—Oakland	W	4-3		Johnson	Bahnsen
24—At Calif.	W	5-3		Vuckovich	Brewer
25—At Calif.	W	7-1		Gossage	Ross
26—At Calif.	W	1-0‡		Brett	Kirkwood
27—At Calif.	L	3-5		Tanana	Barrios
28—At Oak.	L	0-11		Bahnsen	Johnson
29—At Oak.	L	0-2		Blue	Forster
30—At Oak.	W	4-3§		Carroll	Fingers
31—Texas	W	9-4		Vuckovich	Briles
		Won 16, Lost 12			

JUNE				Winner	Loser
1—Texas	L.	5-6z		Foucault	Jefferson
2—Texas	W	1-0‡		Hamilton	Umbarger
4—Cleve.	W	4-1		Gossage	Eckersley
5—Cleve.	L	3-5†		Kern	Carroll
6—Cleve.	W	3-2		Vuckovich	Brown
6—Cleve.	W	5-0		Brett	Hood
8—At Milw.	L	0-2		Travers	Johnson
9—At Milw.	W	4-2		Gossage	Slaton
10—At Milw.	W	12-5		Barrios	Augustine
11—At Cleve.	L	4-5x		Kern	Forster
12—At Cleve.	L	0-3		Waits	Vuckovich
13—At Cleve.	L	5-8		Dobson	Johnson
13—At Cleve.	L	7-9		Kern	Carroll
15—Balt.	L	0-4		Palmer	Gossage
16—Balt.	L	2-10		Cuellar	Barrios
17—N. York	L	4-5		Hunter	Forster
18—N. York	L	2-3y		Jackson	Hamilton
19—N. York	L	3-4		Alexander	Gossage
20—N. York	L	3-6		Ellis	Brett
21—At K. C.	L	2-1‡		Hamilton	Hall
22—At K. C.	W	14-8		Jefferson	Busby
23—At Minn.	L	4-3		Johnson	Decker
23—At Minn.	W	9-5		Vuckovich	Redfern
24—At Minn.	L	2-4		Singer	Gossage
25—At Texas	L	4-8		Perry	Hamilton
25—At Texas	W	14-9		Vuckovich	Foucault
26—At Texas	L	0-1†		Blyleven	Brett
27—At Texas	W	6-2		Johnson	Briles
29—Calif.	L	1-4		Tanana	Barrios
30—Calif.	L	1-2†		Drago	Carroll
		Won 12, Lost 18			

JULY					
1—Calif.	L	1-2		Monge	Brett
2—Texas	W	1-0		Johnson	Blyleven
3—Texas	L	0-3		Briles	Forster
4—Texas	W	7-6§		Hamilton	Bacsik
4—Texas	L	2-3		Hargan	Knapp
5—At Bos.	L	2-11		Tiant	Jefferson
6—At Bos.	L	0-4		Jenkins	Brett
7—At Bos.	W	6-3†		Johnson	Willoughby
8—At N. Y.	L	0-6		Holtzman	Gossage
9—At N. Y.	L	1-2		Ellis	Forster
10—At N. Y.	W	4-1		Brett	Alexander

CHICAGO WHITE SOX—1976

Front row—Brohamer, Stein, Hairston, Downing, Kravec, Bannister, Lemon. Second row—L. Johnson, Odom, Busby, coach; Mahoney, coach; Richards, manager; Minoso, coach; Silvestri, coach; Dent, Carroll. Third row—Saad, trainer; Licklider, equipment manager; Hamilton, Bell, Gossage, Brett, Essian, Rosenbaum, traveling secretary. Fourth row—Forster, Garr, Vuckovich, B. Johnson, Jefferson, Spencer, Barrios, Orta, Kelly.

JULY			Winner	Loser
11 – At N. Y.	L	0-5	Figueroa	Johnson
15 – Milw.	W	5-3†	Brett	Slaton
16 – Milw.	W	5-2	Johnson	Augustine
17 – Milw.	L	2-9	Colborn	Gossage
18 – Milw.	W	13-3	Barrios	Travers
19 – N. York	L	2-3	Figueroa	Hamilton
20 – N. York	L	9-14*	York	Vuckovich
21 – Detroit	W	4-1	Knapp	Ruhle
21 – Detroit	W	3-0	Johnson	Lemanczyk
22 – Detroit	W	9-3	Odom	MacCormack
22 – Detroit	L	1-5	Bare	Gossage
23 – Minn.	L	2-6	Burgmeier	Barrios
24 – Minn.	L	2-17	Bane	Jefferson
25 – Minn.	L	8-13	Albury	Forster
25 – Minn.	W	7-4	Brett	Singer
26 – At Oak.	L	1-3	P. Mitchell	Johnson
27 – At Oak.	L	0-1	Blue	Gossage
28 – At Oak.	W	2-1	Odom	Lindblad
30 – At Calif.	L	0-3	Ryan	Brett
31 – At Calif.	L	2-3‡	Drago	Forster
		Won 12, Lost 19		

AUGUST				
1 – At Calif.	W	2-1	Gossage	Tanana
3 – Oakland	L	3-7	Bosman	Odom
4 – Oakland	L	0-5	P. Mitchell	Brett
6 – Kan. C.	L	2-9	Hassler	Johnson
6 – Kan. C.	L	3-8	Bird	Gossage
7 – Kan. C.	W	5-3	Barrios	Mingori
8 – Kan. C.	W	5-2	Forster	Pattin
8 – Kan. C.	L	1-7	Fitzmorris	Jefferson
9 – At Cleve.	L	2-4	Bibby	Brett
11 – At Cleve.	L	3-4†	Kern	Barrios
13 – At Balt.	W	5-2	Gossage	May
14 – At Balt.	L	6-8	Palmer	Forster
14 – At Balt.	L	5-6	Miller	Brett
15 – At Balt.	L	0-3	Garland	Barrios
16 – Boston	L	5-12	Tiant	Johnson
17 – Boston	W	2-1	Carroll	Murphy
17 – Boston	L	7-11	Pole	Odom
18 – Boston	W	4-2	Gossage	Jenkins
19 – Boston	W	4-2	Brett	Wise
20 – Balt.	L	4-6	Garland	Barrios
21 – Balt.	W	11-10§	Hamilton	Cuellar
22 – Balt.	L	2-6	Palmer	Kravec

AUGUST			Winner	Loser
22 – Balt.	W	7-3	Vuckovich	Grimsley
23 – At Det.	L	4-5	Bare	Gossage
24 – At Det.	W	12-7	Hamilton	Crawford
25 – At Det.	L	1-3	Fidrych	Johnson
27 – At Milw.	W	5-2	Kravec	Slaton
28 – At Milw.	L	8-10	Colborn	Gossage
29 – At Milw.	W	2-0	Brett	Rodriguez
31 – Cleve.	L	2-4†	Kern	Hamilton
		Won 12, Lost 18		

SEPTEMBER				
1 – Cleve.	L	0-3	Bibby	Kravec
3 – At Minn.	L	1-11	Redfern	Gossage
4 – At Minn.	W	4-0	Brett	Hughes
5 – At Minn.	L	1-18	T. Johnson	C.B. Johnson
6 – At Minn.	L	2-3	Campbell	Barrios
7 – At Oak.	L	0-4	Torrez	Forster
8 – At Oak.	W	6-5	Knapp	Fingers
9 – At Oak.	L	1-2	Todd	Brett
10 – Calif.	L	2-3	Ryan	Johnson
11 – Calif.	L	3-7	Tanana	Kravec
12 – Calif.	W	2-1†	Gossage	Monge
12 – Calif.	W	5-1	Barrios	Kirkwood
13 – Kan. C	W	4-3	Knapp	Leonard
13 – Kan. C	W	5-4	Brett	Mingori
14 – Kan. C.	L	1-2	Hassler	Forster
15 – Texas	L	3-4	Blyleven	Johnson
16 – Texas	L	4-5	Briles	Kravec
17 – At K. C.	L	2-3	Leonard	Gossage
18 – At K. C.	L	5-6	Gura	Brett
19 – At K. C.	L	5-6	Mingori	Forster
21 – Minn.	L	6-13	Burgmeier	Kravec
22 – Minn.	L	3-6	Singer	Johnson
23 – Minn.	L	0-3	Redfern	Brett
24 – Oakland	W	4-2	Barrios	Fingers
25 – Oakland	L	4-7	Fingers	Gossage
29 – At Calif.	L	0-3	Ryan	Brett
30 – At Calif.	L	3-7	Monge	Monroe
		Won 7, Lost 20		

OCTOBER				
1 – At Texas	L	8-11	Hargan	Barrios
2 – At Texas	L	4-5†	Bacsik	Vuckovich
3 – At Texas	L	0-3	Barker	Gossage
		Won 0, Lost 3		

* 8 innings.   † 10 innings.   ‡ 11 innings.   § 12 innings.   x 13 innings.   y 14 innings.   z 16 innings.

Seattle, Toronto Join A.L. Fraternity

By LARRY WIGGE

For the third time since 1960 the American League expanded by two teams, with the addition of the Seattle Mariners and Toronto Blue Jays.

On November 5, Seattle General Manager Lou Gorman and Peter Bavasi, G. M. of Toronto, filled their rosters with 30 players, five from each of the 12 other A. L. clubs. The clubs each doled out $5.25 million, $175,000 per player, for the right to select from organizational lists after 15 players were frozen.

Outfielder Ruppert Jones was the first selection of the draft. Seattle chose the 21-year-old Kansas City Royals' chattel. The lefthanded batter hit .262 with 19 homers and 73 RBIs for Omaha (American Association) in 1976. He played in 28 games for the Royals at the end of the season, batting .216.

Toronto opted for 25-year-old shortstop Bob Bailor from the Baltimore Orioles' organization. Disabled by an arm injury in '76, Bailor, a righthanded hitter, batted .311 in 36 games at Rochester (International) and hit .333 in a nine-game stint with the Orioles.

An alphabetical roster by position with a notation from which club the players were selected follows:

SEATTLE MARINERS

PITCHERS (16)

Glenn Abbott, Oakland
Steve Barr, Texas
Pete Broberg, Milwaukee
Steve Burke, Boston
Joe Erardi, Milwaukee
Bob Galasso, Baltimore
Alan Griffin, Oakland
Grant Jackson, New York
Rick Jones, Boston
Bill Laxton, Detroit
Frank MacCormack, Detroit
Dave Pagan, Baltimore
Dick Pole, Boston
Roy Thomas, Chicago
Stan Thomas, Cleveland
Gary Wheelock, California

CATCHERS (1)

Bob Stinson, Kansas City

INFIELDERS (7)

Juan Bernhardt, New York
Steve Braun, Minnesota
Julio Cruz, California
Joe Lis, Cleveland
Tom McMillan, Cleveland
Dan Meyer, Detroit
Bill Stein, Chicago

OUTFIELDERS (6)

Dave Collins, California
Luis Delgado, Boston
Ruppert Jones, Kansas City
Carlos Lopez, California
Tommy Smith, Cleveland
Lee Stanton, California

TORONTO BLUE JAYS

PITCHERS (16)

Larry Anderson, Milwaukee
Jeff Byrd, Texas
Tom Bruno, Kansas City
Jim Clancy, Texas
Mike Darr, Baltimore
Dennis DeBarr, Detroit
Claude Edge, Milwaukee
Al Fitzmorris, Kansas City
Ted Garvin, Minnesota
Steve Hargan, Texas
Jesse Jefferson, Chicago
Leon Hooten, Oakland
Dave Lemanczyk, Detroit
Bill Singer, Minnesota
Pete Vuckovich, Chicago
Mike Willis, Baltimore

CATCHERS (1)

Ernie Whitt, Boston

INFIELDERS (8)

Doug Ault, Texas
Bob Bailor, Baltimore
Rico Carty, Cleveland
Garth Iorg, New York
Jim Mason, New York
Dave McKay, Minnesota
Steve Staggs, Kansas City
Mike Weathers, Oakland

OUTFIELDERS (5)

Steve Bowling, Milwaukee
Sam Ewing, Chicago
Otto Velez, New York
Al Woods, Minnesota
Gary Woods, Oakland

GRAIG NETTLES
• YANKEES •
HOMERS (32)

GEORGE BRETT
• ROYALS •
HITS (215)
BATTING CHAMPION (.333)
TRIPLES (14)
TOTAL BASES (298)

BILL NORTH
• A's •
STOLEN BASES (75)

1976 AMERICAN LEAGUE LEADERS

NOLAN RYAN
• ANGELS •
STRIKEOUTS (327)
SHUTOUTS (7)

MARK FIDRYCH
• TIGERS •
ERA (2.34)
COMPLETE GAMES (24)

JIM PALMER
• ORIOLES •
WINS (22)
GAMES STARTED (40)
INNINGS (315)

American League Averages for 1976

CHAMPIONSHIP WINNERS IN PREVIOUS YEARS

1900—Chicago* .607	1926—New York .591	1952—New York .617
1901—Chicago .610	1927—New York .714	1953—New York .656
1902—Philadelphia .610	1928—New York .656	1954—Cleveland .721
1903—Boston .659	1929—Philadelphia .693	1955—New York .623
1904—Boston .617	1930—Philadelphia .662	1956—New York .630
1905—Philadelphia .622	1931—Philadelphia .704	1957—New York .636
1906—Chicago .616	1932—New York .695	1958—New York .597
1907—Detroit .613	1933—Washington .651	1959—Chicago .610
1908—Detroit .588	1934—Detroit .656	1960—New York .630
1909—Detroit .645	1935—Detroit .616	1961—New York .673
1910—Philadelphia .680	1936—New York .667	1962—New York .593
1911—Philadelphia .669	1937—New York .662	1963—New York .646
1912—Boston .691	1938—New York .651	1964—New York .611
1913—Philadelphia .627	1939—New York .702	1965—Minnesota .630
1914—Philadelphia .651	1940—Detroit .584	1966—Baltimore .606
1915—Boston .669	1941—New York .656	1967—Boston .568
1916—Boston .591	1942—New York .669	1968—Detroit .636
1917—Chicago .649	1943—New York .636	1969—Baltimore (East)‡ .673
1918—Boston .595	1944—St. Louis .578	1970—Baltimore (East)‡ .667
1919—Chicago .629	1945—Detroit .575	1971—Baltimore (East)§ .639
1920—Cleveland .636	1946—Boston .675	1972—Oakland (West)a .600
1921—New York .641	1947—New York .630	1973—Oakland (West)b .580
1922—New York .610	1948—Cleveland† .626	1974—Oakland (West)b .556
1923—New York .645	1949—New York .630	1975—Boston (East)c .594
1924—Washington .597	1950—New York .636	
1925—Washington .636	1951—New York .636	

*Not recognized as major league in 1900. †Defeated Boston in one-game playoff for pennant. ‡Defeated Minnesota (West) in Championship Series. §Defeated Oakland (West) in Championship Series. aDefeated Detroit (East) in Championship Series. bDefeated Baltimore (East) in Championship Series. cDefeated Oakland (West) in Championship Series.

STANDING OF CLUBS AT CLOSE OF SEASON

EAST DIVISION

Club	N.Y.	Balt.	Bos.	Clev.	Det.	Mil.	Cal.	Chi.	K.C.	Minn.	Oak.	Tex.	W.	L.	Pct.	G.B.
New York		5	11	12	8	13	7	11	5	10	6	9	97	62	.610	....
Baltimore	13	....	7	7	12	11	8	8	6	4	4	8	88	74	.543	10½
Boston	7	11	....	9	14	12	7	6	3	7	4	3	83	79	.512	15½
Cleveland	4	11	9	....	6	11	5	9	6	9	4	7	81	78	.509	16
Detroit	9	6	4	12	....	12	6	6	4	4	6	5	74	87	.460	24
Milwaukee	5	7	6	6	6	....	8	5	4	4	5	10	66	95	.410	32

WEST DIVISION

Club	K.C.	Oak.	Minn.	Cal.	Tex.	Chi.	Balt.	Bos.	Clev.	Det.	Mil.	N.Y.	W.	L.	Pct.	G.B.
Kansas City		9	10	10	7	10	6	9	6	8	8	7	90	72	.556	....
Oakland	9	....	7	12	7	9	8	8	6	7	6	76	87	74	.540	2½
Minnesota	8	11	....	10	11	11	8	5	3	8	8	2	85	77	.525	5
California	8	6	8	....	12	11	4	5	7	6	4	5	76	86	.469	14
Texas	11	11	7	6	....	11	4	9	5	7	2	3	76	86	.469	14
Chicago	8	8	7	7	7	....	4	6	3	6	7	1	64	97	.398	25½

CANCELED GAMES—Oakland at Chicago; Milwaukee at Cleveland; New York at Detroit; Cleveland at New York (2).

CHAMPIONSHIP SERIES—New York defeated Kansas City, three game to two.

RECORD AT HOME

EAST DIVISION

Club	Bos.	N.Y.	Clev.	Balt.	Det.	Mil.	Oak.	K.C.	Minn.	Tex.	Cal.	Chi.	W.	L.	Pct.
Boston	....	5-4	4-5	7-2	5-4	7-2	3-3	2-4	4-2	2-4	4-2	3-3	46	35	.568
New York	7-2	....	5-3	1-8	4-5	8-1	2-4	2-4	5-1	4-2	2-4	5-1	45	35	.563
Cleveland	4-5	1-7	....	6-3	3-6	6-2	2-4	4-2	4-2	4-2	4-2	6-0	44	35	.557
Baltimore	5-4	5-4	4-5	....	6-3	4-5	2-4	4-2	2-4	2-4	4-2	4-2	42	39	.519
Detroit	0-9	4-4	6-3	3-6	....	5-4	2-4	2-4	1-5	3-3	4-2	4-2	36	44	.450
Milwaukee	4-5	4-5	4-5	2-7	2-7	....	4-2	2-4	3-3	5-1	4-2	2-4	36	45	.444

WEST DIVISION

Club	Oak.	K.C.	Minn.	Tex.	Cal.	Chi.	Bos.	N.Y.	Clev.	Balt.	Det.	Mil.	W.	L.	Pct.
Oakland	....	5-4	6-3	4-5	6-3	6-3	1-5	2-4	4-2	4-2	4-2	5-1	51	30	.630
Kansas City	5-4	....	5-4	4-5	5-4	6-3	5-1	3-3	4-2	4-2	4-2	4-2	49	32	.605
Minnesota	8-1	4-5	....	6-3	4-5	5-4	3-3	1-5	1-5	4-2	3-3	5-1	44	37	.543
Texas	6-3	6-3	4-5	....	3-6	6-3	5-1	1-5	3-3	0-6	4-2	1-5	39	42	.481
California	3-6	4-5	3-6	6-3	....	5-4	3-3	1-5	5-1	2-4	4-2	2-4	38	43	.469
Chicago	5-3	5-4	3-6	4-5	3-6	....	3-3	0-6	3-3	2-4	4-2	3-3	35	45	.438

RECORD ABROAD

EAST DIVISION

Club	N.Y.	Balt.	Det.	Clev.	Bos.	Mil.	K.C.	Minn.	Cal.	Tex.	Oak.	Chi.	W.	L.	Pct.
New York	....	4-5	4-4	7-1	4-5	5-4	3-3	5-1	5-1	5-1	4-2	6-0	52	27	.658
Baltimore	8-1	....	6-3	3-6	2-7	7-2	2-4	2-4	4-2	6-0	2-4	4-2	46	35	.568
Detroit	5-4	3-6	....	6-3	4-5	7-2	2-4	3-3	2-4	2-4	2-4	2-4	38	43	.469
Cleveland	3-5	5-4	3-6	....	5-4	5-4	2-4	5-1	1-5	3-3	2-4	3-3	37	43	.463
Boston	2-7	4-5	9-0	5-4	....	5-4	1-5	3-3	3-3	1-5	1-5	3-3	37	44	.457
Milwaukee	1-8	5-4	4-5	2-6	2-7	....	2-4	1-5	4-2	5-1	1-5	3-3	30	50	.375

WEST DIVISION

Club	K.C.	Minn.	Cal.	Tex.	Oak.	Chi.	N.Y.	Balt.	Det.	Clev.	Bos.	Mil.	W.	L.	Pct.
Kansas City	....	5-4	5-4	3-6	4-5	4-5	4-2	2-4	2-4	4-2	4-2	4-2	41	40	.506
Minnesota	4-5	....	6-3	5-4	3-6	6-3	1-5	4-2	5-1	2-4	2-4	3-3	41	40	.506
California	4-5	5-4	....	6-3	3-6	6-3	4-2	2-4	2-4	2-4	2-4	2-4	38	43	.469
Texas	5-4	3-6	3-6	....	5-4	5-4	2-4	4-2	3-3	2-4	4-2	1-5	37	44	.457
Oakland	4-5	1-8	6-3	3-6	....	3-5	4-2	4-2	2-4	4-2	3-3	2-4	36	44	.450
Chicago	3-6	4-5	4-5	3-6	3-6	....	1-5	2-4	2-4	0-6	3-3	4-2	29	52	.358

SHUTOUT GAMES

Club	Clev.	N.Y.	Oak.	Bos.	K.C.	Balt.	Tex.	Minn.	Calif.	Milw.	Det.	Chi.	W.	L.	Pct.
Cleveland	....	0	1	2	2	2	1	2	0	3	2	2	17	7	.708
New York	2	....	0	1	0	1	2	1	1	2	3	2	15	8	.652
Oakland	0	1	....	1	3	2	1	0	1	0	1	5	15	9	.625
Boston	0	0	0	....	0	3	1	2	0	2	4	1	13	9	.591
Kansas City	0	0	1	0	....	2	1	1	4	1	2	0	12	9	.571
Baltimore	1	2	0	3	0	....	2	1	1	0	3	3	16	16	.500
Texas	1	0	1	0	1	1	....	4	3	0	1	3	15	17	.465
Minnesota	0	0	2	0	0	1	3	....	2	1	1	1	11	13	.458
California	1	1	2	1	1	1	3	1	....	2	0	2	15	18	.455
Milwaukee	0	2	0	0	1	1	1	0	3	....	1	1	10	15	.400
Detroit	1	2	1	1	0	2	0	0	1	3	....	1	12	19	.387
Chicago	1	0	1	0	1	0	2	1	2	1	1	....	10	21	.323

OFFICIAL AMERICAN LEAGUE BATTING AVERAGES

Compiled by Sports Information Center, No. Quincy, Mass.

CLUB BATTING

Club	Pct.	G.	AB.	R.	OR.	H.	TB.	2B.	3B.	HR.	RBI.	SH.	SF.	SB.	CS.	LOB.
Minn.	.274	162	5574	743	704	1526	2093	222	51	81	691	93	49	146	75	1199
N. York..	.269	159	5555	730	575	1496	2159	231	36	120	682	50	46	163	65	1107
Kan. C ...	.269	162	5540	713	611	1490	2058	259	57	65	656	71	71	218	106	1094
Cleve. ...	.263	159	5412	615	615	1423	1943	189	38	85	567	67	60	75	69	1117
Boston ..	.263	162	5511	716	660	1448	2213	257	53	134	664	55	59	95	70	1081
Detroit ..	.257	161	5441	609	709	1401	1987	207	38	101	566	46	50	107	59	1095
Chicago..	.255	161	5532	586	745	1410	1930	209	46	73	538	79	55	120	53	1199
Texas ...	.250	162	5555	616	652	1390	1895	213	26	80	574	72	45	87	45	1215
Oakland ..	.246	161	5353	686	598	1319	1932	208	33	113	625	58	58	341	123	1067
Milw.	.246	161	5396	570	655	1326	1836	170	38	88	536	78	48	62	61	1135
Balt.	.243	162	5457	619	598	1326	1952	213	28	119	576	57	35	150	61	1080
Calif.	.235	162	5385	550	631	1265	1710	210	23	63	511	92	48	126	80	1105
Totals	.256		65711	7753	7753	16820	23708	2588	467	1122	7186	818	624	1690	867	13494

INDIVIDUAL BATTING

(Top Fifteen Qualifiers for Batting Championship—502 or More Plate Appearances)

*Bats lefthanded. †Switch-hitter.

Player and Club	Pct.	G.	AB.	R.	H.	TB.	2B.	3B.	HR.	RBI.	SH.	SF.	SB.	CS.
Brett, George, Kansas City*	.333	159	645	94	215	298	34	14	7	67	2	8	21	11
McRae, Harold, Kansas City	.332	149	527	75	175	243	34	5	8	73	2	8	22	12
Carew, Rodney, Minnesota*	.331	156	605	97	200	280	29	12	9	90	8	6	49	22
Bostock, Lyman, Minnesota*	.323	128	474	75	153	204	21	9	4	60	3	6	12	6
LeFlore, Ronald, Detroit	.316	135	544	93	172	223	23	8	4	39	5	1	58	20
Lynn, Fredric, Boston*	.314	132	507	76	159	237	32	8	10	65	0	10	14	9
Rivers, John, New York*	.312	137	590	95	184	255	31	8	8	67	2	5	43	7
Carty, Ricardo, Cleveland	.310	152	552	67	171	244	34	0	13	83	0	9	1	1
Munson, Thurman, New York	.302	152	616	79	186	266	27	1	17	105	1	10	14	11
Garr, Ralph, Chicago*	.300	136	527	63	158	204	22	6	4	36	8	4	14	5
Staub, Daniel, Detroit*	.299	161	589	73	176	255	28	3	15	96	0	11	3	1
Chambliss, C. Christopher, N.Y.*	.293	156	641	79	188	283	32	6	17	96	1	3	1	0
Manning, Richard, Cleveland*	.292	138	552	73	161	217	24	7	6	43	7	6	16	10
Burleson, Richard, Boston	.291	152	540	75	157	207	27	1	7	42	8	3	14	9
Hargrove, D. Michael, Texas*	.287	151	541	80	155	208	30	1	7	58	4	6	2	3

DEPARTMENTAL LEADERS: G—Mayberry, Staub, Yount, 161; AB—G. Brett, 645; R—R. White, 104; H—G. Brett, 215; TB—G. Brett, 298; 2B—Otis, 40; 3B—G. Brett, 14; HR—Nettles, 32; RBI—L. May, 109; SH—Smalley, 25; SF—Mayberry, 12; SB—North, 75; CS—North, 29.

EXPLANATION OF ABBREVIATION TERMS

G—Games Played. AB—At Bats. R—Runs. H—Hits. TB—Total Bases. 2B—Two-Base Hits. 3B—Three-Base Hits. HR—Home Runs. RBI—Runs Batted In. SH—Sacrifice Hits. SF—Sacrifice Flies. SB—Stolen Bases. CS—Caught Stealing. BB—Bases on Balls. IBB—Intentional Bases on Balls. HP—Hit by Pitcher. SO—Strikeouts. Pct.—Percentage. GIDP—Grounded Into Double Plays. Slg.Pct.—Slugging Percentage. OR—Opponents' Runs. LOB—Left on Bases. PO—Putouts. A—Assists. E—Errors. TC—Total Chances. DP—Double Plays. TP—Triple Plays. PB—Passed Balls. G—Games Pitched. GS—Games Started. CG—Complete Games. GF—Games Finished in Relief. ShO—Shutouts. W—Games Won. L—Games Lost. IP—Innings Pitched. BFP—Total Batters Facing Pitcher. ER—Earned Runs. HB—Hit Batsmen. WP—Wild Pitches. Bk—Balks. ERA—Earned-Run Average. Sv—Saves.

(All Players—Listed Alphabetically)

Player and Club	Pct.	G.	AB.	R.	H.	TB.	2B.	3B.	HR.	RBI.	SH.	SF.	SB.	CS.
Aaron, Henry, Milwaukee	.229	85	271	22	62	100	8	0	10	35	0	2	0	1
Alexander, Matthew, Oakland†	.033	30	16	1	1	1	0	0	0	0	0	0	20	7
Alomar, Santos, New York†	.239	67	163	20	39	46	4	0	1	10	2	0	12	7
Alvarez, Jesus M. Orlando, Calif.	.167	15	42	4	7	14	1	0	2	8	0	0	0	0
Ashby, Alan, Cleveland†	.239	89	247	26	59	78	5	1	4	32	6	3	0	2
Ault, Douglas, Texas	.300	9	20	0	6	7	1	0	0	0	0	0	0	0
Bailor, Robert, Baltimore	.333	9	6	2	2	4	0	1	0	0	1	0	0	1
Baker, Jack, Boston	.130	12	23	1	3	6	0	0	1	2	0	1	0	0
Bando, Salvatore, Oakland	.240	158	550	75	132	235	18	2	27	84	7	3	20	6
Bannister, Alan, Chicago	.248	73	145	19	36	46	6	2	0	8	4	1	12	4
Baylor, Donald, Oakland	.247	157	595	85	147	219	25	1	15	68	1	11	52	12
Belanger, Mark, Baltimore	.270	153	522	66	141	170	22	2	1	40	11	3	27	17
Bell, David, Cleveland	.281	159	604	75	170	221	26	2	7	60	5	6	3	8
Bell, Kevin, Chicago	.248	68	230	24	57	91	7	6	5	20	6	3	2	1
Beniquez, Juan, Texas	.255	145	478	49	122	144	14	4	0	33	5	1	17	6
Bernhardt, Juan, New York	.190	10	21	1	4	5	1	0	0	1	0	0	0	0
Bevacqua, Kurt, Milwaukee	.143	12	7	3	1	1	0	0	0	0	0	0	0	0
Blair, Paul, Baltimore	.197	145	375	29	74	99	16	0	3	16	13	1	15	6
Blanks, Larvell, Cleveland	.280	104	328	45	92	129	8	7	5	41	9	4	1	2
Blomberg, Ronald, New York°	.000	1	2	0	0	0	0	0	0	0	0	0	0	0
Bochte, Bruce, California°	.258	146	466	53	120	145	17	1	2	49	6	5	4	5
Bonds, Bobby, California	.265	99	378	48	100	146	10	3	10	54	0	5	30	15
Borgmann, Glenn, Minnesota	.246	24	65	10	16	22	3	0	1	6	1	0	1	1
Bostock, Lyman, Minnesota°	.323	128	474	75	153	204	21	9	4	60	3	6	12	6
Bowling, Stephen, Milwaukee	.167	14	42	4	7	9	2	0	0	2	0	0	0	0
Bradford, Charles, Chicago	.219	55	160	20	35	56	5	2	4	14	2	0	6	0
Braun, Stephen, Milwaukee	.288	122	417	73	120	147	12	3	3	61	2	4	12	4
Brett, George, Kansas City°	.333	159	645	94	215	298	34	14	7	67	2	8	21	11
Brett, Kenneth, 2 N.Y.-33 Chi.°	.083	35	12	0	1	1	0	0	0	0	0	0	0	0
Briggs, Daniel, California°	.214	77	248	19	53	73	13	2	1	14	2	2	0	3
Brohamer, John, Chicago°	.251	119	354	33	89	126	12	2	7	40	6	8	1	3
Brye, Stephen, Minnesota	.264	87	258	33	68	85	11	0	2	23	4	4	1	2
Bumbry, Alonza, Baltimore°	.251	133	450	71	113	169	15	7	9	36	2	3	42	10
Burleson, Richard, Boston	.291	152	540	75	157	207	27	1	7	42	8	3	14	9
Burroughs, Jeffrey, Texas	.237	158	604	71	143	223	22	2	18	86	2	4	0	0
Campaneris, Dagoberto, Oakland	.256	149	536	67	137	156	14	1	1	52	18	11	54	12
Carbo, Bernardo, 17 Bos.-69 Mil.°	.235	86	238	25	56	82	11	0	5	21	3	0	2	2
Carew, Rodney, Minnesota°	.331	156	605	97	200	280	29	12	9	90	8	6	49	22
Carty, Ricardo, Cleveland	.310	152	552	67	171	244	34	0	13	83	0	9	1	1
Cerone, Richard, Cleveland	.125	7	16	1	2	2	0	0	0	1	0	0	0	0
Chalk, David, California	.217	142	438	39	95	111	14	1	0	33	12	3	0	0
Chambliss, C. Christopher, N.Y.°	.293	156	641	79	188	283	32	6	17	96	1	3	1	0
Clines, Eugene, Texas	.276	116	446	52	123	141	12	3	0	38	10	4	11	9
Coggins, Richard, 7 N.Y.-32 Chi.°	.160	39	100	5	16	18	2	0	0	6	2	0	4	1
Colbert, Nathan, Oakland	.000	2	5	0	0	0	0	0	0	0	0	0	0	0
Collins, David, California†	.263	99	365	45	96	122	12	1	4	28	7	1	32	19
Cooper, Cecil, Boston°	.282	123	451	66	127	206	22	6	15	78	9	6	7	1
Cowens, Alfred, Kansas City	.265	152	581	71	154	198	23	6	3	59	2	4	23	16
Crosby, Edward, Cleveland°	.500	2	2	0	1	1	0	0	0	0	0	0	0	0
Crowley, Terrence, Baltimore°	.246	33	61	5	15	16	1	0	0	5	0	0	1	0
Cubbage, Michael, 14 Tx-104 Min°	.257	118	374	42	96	134	19	5	3	49	3	2	1	1
Dade, L. Paul, California	.111	13	9	2	1	1	0	0	0	1	0	0	0	0
Darwin, A. Bobby, 25 Mil.-43 Bos.	.207	68	179	15	37	63	8	3	4	18	1	0	1	0
Dauer, Richard, Baltimore	.103	11	39	0	4	4	0	0	0	3	0	1	0	0
Davis, H. Thomas, 72 Cal.-8 K.C.	.265	80	238	17	63	77	5	0	3	26	0	2	0	1
DeCinces, Douglas, Baltimore	.234	129	440	36	103	157	17	2	11	42	3	1	8	4
Dempsey, J. Rikard, 21 NY-59 Bal.	.194	80	216	12	42	44	2	0	0	12	4	0	1	1
Dent, Russell, Chicago	.246	158	562	44	138	170	18	4	2	52	17	2	3	5
Dillard, Stephen, Boston	.275	57	167	22	46	63	14	0	1	15	2	1	6	4
Dineen, Kerry, New York°	.286	4	7	0	2	2	0	0	0	1	0	0	1	1
Downing, Brian, Chicago	.256	104	317	38	81	104	14	0	3	30	4	3	7	3
Doyle, R. Dennis, Boston°	.250	117	432	51	108	133	15	5	0	26	5	2	8	5
Duffy, Frank, Cleveland	.212	133	392	38	83	104	11	2	2	30	12	2	10	0
Duncan, David, Baltimore	.204	93	284	20	58	77	7	0	4	17	4	0	0	0
Easler, Michael, California°	.241	21	54	6	13	16	1	1	0	4	1	2	1	1
Ellis, John, Texas	.419	11	31	4	13	18	2	0	1	8	0	0	0	0
Enright, George, Chicago	.000	2	1	0	0	0	0	0	0	0	0	0	0	0

Player and Club	Pct.	G.	AB.	R.	H.	TB.	2B.	3B.	HR.	RBI.	SH.	SF.	SB.	CS.
Essian, James, Chicago	.246	78	199	20	49	56	7	0	0	21	5	1	2	1
Etchebarren, Andrew, California	.227	103	247	15	56	67	9	1	0	21	6	0	0	2
Evans, Dwight, Boston	.242	146	501	61	121	216	34	5	17	62	3	4	6	7
Ewing, Samuel, Chicago°	.220	19	41	3	9	13	2	1	0	2	0	0	0	0
Fahey, William, Texas°	.250	38	80	12	20	25	2	0	1	9	2	0	1	0
Fairly, Ronald, Oakland°	.239	15	46	9	11	21	1	0	3	10	0	0	0	0
Fisk, Carlton, Boston	.255	134	487	76	124	202	17	5	17	58	3	5	12	5
Ford, Darnell, Minnesota	.267	145	514	87	137	235	24	7	20	86	5	6	17	6
Fosse, Raymond, Cleveland	.301	90	276	26	83	100	9	1	2	30	3	1	1	2
Freehan, William, Detroit	.270	71	237	22	64	91	10	1	5	27	1	4	0	0
Fregosi, James, Texas	.233	58	133	17	31	44	7	0	2	12	2	2	2	0
Gamble, Oscar, New York°	.232	110	340	43	79	145	13	1	17	57	2	0	5	3
Gantner, James, Milwaukee°	.246	26	69	6	17	18	1	0	0	7	3	0	1	0
Garcia, Alfonso, Baltimore	.219	11	32	2	7	13	1	1	1	4	0	0	2	1
Garcia, Pedro, 41 Mil-77 Det	.204	118	333	33	68	103	17	3	4	29	6	4	4	5
Garner, Philip, Oakland	.261	159	555	54	145	222	29	12	8	74	6	4	35	13
Garr, Ralph, Chicago°	.300	136	527	63	158	204	22	6	4	36	8	4	14	5
Garrett, H. Adrian, California°	.125	29	48	4	6	9	3	0	0	3	0	1	0	0
Gomez, Luis, Minnesota	.193	38	57	5	11	12	1	0	0	3	2	0	1	0
Gonzalez, Orlando, Cleveland°	.250	28	68	5	17	19	2	0	0	4	2	0	1	2
Grich, Robert, Baltimore	.266	144	518	93	138	216	31	4	13	54	7	1	14	6
Grieve, Thomas, Texas	.255	149	546	57	139	228	23	3	20	81	8	7	4	1
Griffin, Alfredo, Cleveland†	.250	12	4	0	1	1	0	0	0	0	0	0	0	1
Griffin, Douglas, Boston	.189	49	127	14	24	26	2	0	0	4	4	0	2	1
Gross, Wayne, Oakland°	.222	10	18	0	4	4	0	0	0	1	0	0	0	0
Guerrero, Mario, California	.284	83	268	24	76	91	12	0	1	18	5	5	0	0
Hairston, Jerry, Chicago†	.227	44	119	20	27	33	2	2	0	10	2	2	1	1
Hampton, Isaac, California†	.000	3	2	0	0	0	0	0	0	0	0	0	0	0
Haney, W. Larry, Oakland	.226	88	177	12	40	42	2	0	0	13	3	2	0	1
Hansen, Robert, Milwaukee°	.164	24	61	4	10	11	1	0	0	4	0	0	0	0
Hargrove, D. Michael, Texas°	.287	151	541	80	155	208	30	1	7	58	4	6	2	3
Harper, Tommy, Baltimore	.234	46	77	8	18	26	5	0	1	7	0	1	4	3
Harrah, Colbert, Texas	.260	155	584	64	152	220	21	1	15	67	5	5	8	5
Healy, Francis, 8 KC-46 NY	.243	54	144	12	35	38	3	0	0	10	0	0	5	1
Hegan, J. Michael, Milwaukee°	.248	80	218	30	54	79	4	3	5	31	1	3	0	0
Heidemann, Jack, Milwaukee	.219	69	146	11	32	39	1	0	2	10	9	1	1	3
Heise, Robert, Boston	.268	32	56	5	15	17	2	0	0	5	3	0	0	1
Hendrick, George, Cleveland	.265	149	551	72	146	247	20	3	25	81	1	8	4	4
Hendricks, Elrod, 28 Bal-26 NY°	.174	54	132	8	23	37	2	0	4	9	0	1	0	1
Herrmann, Edward, California°	.174	29	46	5	8	17	3	0	2	8	2	1	0	0
Hiller, John, Detroit	.000	56	1	0	0	0	0	0	0	0	0	0	0	0
Hisle, Larry, Minnesota	.272	155	581	81	158	229	19	5	14	96	11	9	31	18
Hobson, Clell, Boston	.234	76	269	34	63	104	7	5	8	34	5	3	0	1
Holt, James, Oakland°	.286	4	7	0	2	4	2	0	0	2	0	0	0	1
Hopkins, Donald, Oakland°	.000	3	0	0	0	0	0	0	0	0	0	0	0	0
Horton, Willie, Detroit	.262	114	401	40	105	164	17	0	14	56	0	4	0	0
Hosley, Timothy, Oakland	.164	37	55	4	9	14	2	0	1	4	0	0	0	0
Howard, Douglas, Cleveland	.211	39	90	7	19	23	4	0	0	13	2	3	1	1
Howell, Roy, Texas°	.253	140	491	55	124	180	28	2	8	53	5	4	1	0
Humphrey, Terral, California	.245	71	196	17	48	61	10	0	1	19	4	2	0	1
Hunter, James, New York	.000	36	1	0	0	0	0	0	0	0	0	0	0	0
Jackson, Reginald, Baltimore°	.277	134	498	84	138	250	27	2	27	91	0	2	28	7
Jackson, Ronnie, California	.227	127	410	44	93	141	18	3	8	40	4	3	5	4
Johnson, Alexander, Detroit	.268	125	429	41	115	152	15	2	6	45	1	6	14	10
Johnson, Deron, Boston	.132	15	38	3	5	8	1	1	0	0	0	0	0	0
Johnson, Lamar, Chicago	.320	82	222	29	71	96	11	1	4	33	1	4	2	1
Johnson, Timothy, Milwaukee°	.275	105	273	25	75	85	4	3	0	14	12	0	4	1
Jones, Cleon, Chicago	.200	12	40	2	8	9	1	0	0	3	1	0	0	0
Jones, Robert O., California°	.211	78	166	22	35	59	6	0	6	17	4	2	3	0
Jones, Ruppert, Kansas City°	.216	28	51	9	11	17	1	1	1	7	0	0	0	2
Joshua, Von, Milwaukee°	.267	107	423	44	113	151	13	5	5	28	5	3	8	10
Kelly, H. Patrick, Chicago°	.254	107	311	42	79	120	20	3	5	34	2	5	15	7
Kimm, Bruce, Detroit	.263	63	152	13	40	51	8	0	1	6	7	0	4	3
Klutts, Gene, New York	.000	2	3	0	0	0	0	0	0	0	0	0	0	0
Kuiper, Duane, Cleveland°	.263	135	506	47	133	158	13	6	0	37	14	4	10	17
Kusick, Craig, Minnesota	.259	109	266	33	69	115	13	0	11	36	1	3	5	1
Kusnyer, Arthur, Milwaukee	.118	15	34	2	4	5	1	0	0	3	1	0	1	0
Lahoud, Joseph, 42 Cal-38 Tex°	.200	80	185	18	37	49	7	1	1	9	1	0	1	0
Lane, Marvin, Detroit	.188	18	48	3	9	10	1	0	0	5	0	1	0	0

Player and Club	Pct.	G.	AB.	R.	H.	TB.	2B.	3B.	HR.	RBI.	SH.	SF.	SB.	CS.
Lee, William, Boston*	.000	26	0	1	0	0	0	0	0	0	0	0	0	0
LeFlore, Ronald, Detroit	.316	135	544	93	172	223	23	8	4	39	5	1	58	20
Lemon, Chester, Chicago	.246	132	451	46	111	148	15	5	4	38	7	4	13	7
Lezcano, Sixto, Milwaukee	.285	145	513	53	146	196	19	5	7	56	8	6	14	10
Lintz, Larry, Oakland†	.000	68	1	21	0	0	0	0	0	0	1	0	31	11
Lis, Joseph, Cleveland	.314	20	51	4	16	23	1	0	2	7	0	1	0	0
Littell, Mark, Kansas City*	.000	60	1	0	0	0	0	0	0	0	0	0	0	0
Locklear, Gene, New York*	.219	13	32	2	7	8	1	0	0	1	0	0	0	0
Lopez, Carlos, California	.000	9	10	1	0	0	0	0	0	0	0	0	2	0
Lowenstein, John, Cleveland*	.205	93	229	33	47	65	8	2	2	14	3	0	11	8
Lynn, Fredric, Boston*	.314	132	507	76	159	237	32	8	10	65	0	10	14	9
MacCormack, Frank, Detroit	.000	9	3	0	0	0	0	0	0	0	0	0	0	0
Maddox, Elliott, New York	.217	18	46	4	10	12	2	0	0	3	0	1	0	1
Mangual, Angel, Oakland	.167	8	12	0	2	3	1	0	0	1	0	0	0	1
Mankowski, Philip, Detroit*	.271	24	85	9	23	30	2	1	1	4	0	1	0	0
Manning, Richard, Cleveland*	.292	138	552	73	161	217	24	7	6	43	7	6	16	10
Manuel, Jerry, Detroit†	.140	54	43	4	6	7	1	0	0	2	2	0	1	0
Martinez, John, Kansas City	.228	95	267	24	61	95	13	3	5	34	9	3	0	0
Mason, James, New York*	.180	93	217	17	39	51	7	1	1	14	7	3	0	0
May, Carlos, 20 Chi-87 NY*	.259	107	351	45	91	117	13	2	3	43	1	5	5	1
May, Lee, Baltimore	.258	148	530	61	137	237	17	4	25	109	2	7	4	1
May, Milton, Detroit*	.280	6	25	2	7	8	1	0	0	1	0	0	0	0
Mayberry, John, Kansas City*	.232	161	594	76	138	203	22	2	13	95	0	12	3	2
McCovey, Willie, Oakland*	.208	11	24	0	5	5	0	0	0	0	0	0	0	0
McKay, David, Minnesota	.203	45	138	8	28	30	2	0	0	8	4	0	1	2
McMullen, Kenneth, Oakland	.220	98	186	20	41	66	6	2	5	23	1	1	1	1
McRae, Harold, Kansas City	.332	149	527	75	175	243	34	5	8	73	2	8	22	12
Melton, William, California	.208	118	341	31	71	112	17	3	6	42	2	3	2	0
Merchant, J. Anderson, Boston*	.000	2	2	0	0	0	0	0	0	0	0	0	0	0
Meyer, Daniel, Detroit*	.252	105	294	37	74	96	8	4	2	16	3	1	10	0
Miley, Michael, California†	.184	14	38	4	7	9	2	0	0	4	1	1	1	0
Miller, Richard, Boston*	.283	105	269	40	76	97	15	3	0	27	7	3	11	10
Minoso, Orestes, Chicago	.125	3	8	0	1	1	0	0	0	0	0	0	0	0
Moates, David, Texas*	.241	85	137	21	33	42	7	1	0	13	3	2	6	3
Money, Donald, Milwaukee	.267	117	439	51	117	179	18	4	12	62	6	6	6	5
Montgomery, Robert, Boston	.247	31	93	10	23	37	3	1	3	13	0	1	0	1
Moore, Charles, Milwaukee	.191	87	241	33	46	70	7	4	3	16	3	2	1	2
Mora, Andres, Baltimore	.218	73	220	18	48	77	11	0	6	25	2	3	1	0
Munson, Thurman, New York	.302	152	616	79	186	266	27	1	17	105	1	10	14	11
Murray, Larry, New York†	.100	8	10	2	1	1	0	0	0	2	0	0	2	0
Muser, Anthony, Baltimore*	.227	136	326	25	74	86	7	1	1	30	4	5	1	1
Nelson, David, Kansas City	.235	78	153	24	36	47	4	2	1	17	3	1	15	5
Nettles, Graig, New York*	.254	158	583	88	148	277	29	2	32	93	2	5	11	6
Newman, Jeffrey, Oakland	.195	43	77	5	15	19	4	0	0	4	5	0	0	0
Nordbrook, Timothy, 27 Bal-5 Cal	.167	32	30	5	5	5	0	0	0	1	0	1	0	0
Nordhagen, Wayne, Chicago	.189	22	53	6	10	12	2	0	0	5	1	3	0	0
North, William, Oakland†	.276	154	590	91	163	199	20	5	2	31	6	4	75	29
Nyman, Nyls, Chicago*	.133	8	15	2	2	3	1	0	0	1	0	0	1	0
Oglivie, Benjamin, Detroit*	.285	115	305	36	87	150	12	3	15	47	2	4	9	4
Oliva, Pedro (Tony), Minnesota*	.211	67	123	3	26	32	3	0	1	16	0	1	0	0
Orta, Jorge, Chicago*	.274	158	636	74	174	261	29	8	14	72	1	8	24	8
Otis, Amos, Kansas City	.279	153	592	93	165	263	40	2	18	86	5	8	26	7
Pape, Kenneth, Texas	.217	21	23	7	5	9	1	0	1	4	2	0	0	1
Patek, Freddie, Kansas City	.241	144	432	58	104	132	19	3	1	43	13	6	51	15
Petrocelli, Americo, Boston	.213	85	240	17	51	69	7	1	3	24	2	3	0	5
Piniella, Louis, New York	.281	100	327	36	92	129	16	6	3	38	3	1	0	1
Pole, Richard, Boston	.000	31	1	0	0	0	0	0	0	0	0	0	0	0
Poquette, Thomas, Kansas City*	.302	104	344	43	104	148	18	10	2	34	2	2	6	5
Porter, Darrell, Milwaukee*	.208	119	389	43	81	112	14	1	5	32	3	5	2	0
Powell, John, Cleveland*	.215	95	293	29	63	99	9	0	9	33	2	7	1	1
Pruitt, Ronald, Cleveland	.267	47	86	7	23	26	1	1	0	5	0	2	2	3
Pryor, Gregory, Texas	.375	5	8	2	3	3	0	0	0	1	1	0	0	0
Quirk, James, Kansas City*	.246	64	114	11	28	37	6	0	1	15	0	3	0	0
Ramirez, Orlando, California	.200	30	70	3	14	15	1	0	0	5	7	0	3	2
Randall, Robert, Minnesota	.267	153	475	55	127	156	18	4	1	34	17	3	3	5
Randle, Leonard, Texas†	.224	142	539	53	121	147	11	6	1	51	6	4	30	15
Randolph, William, New York	.267	125	430	59	115	141	15	4	1	40	6	3	37	12
Remy, Gerald, California*	.263	143	502	64	132	152	14	3	0	28	13	4	35	16
Rice, James, Boston	.282	153	581	75	164	280	25	8	25	85	2	9	8	5

Player and Club	Pct.	G.	AB.	R.	H.	TB.	2B.	3B.	HR.	RBI.	SH.	SF.	SB.	CS.
Rivers, John, New York*	.312	137	590	95	184	255	31	8	8	67	2	5	43	7
Robinson, Brooks, Baltimore	.211	71	218	16	46	67	8	2	3	11	3	2	0	0
Robinson, Frank, Cleveland	.224	36	67	5	15	24	0	0	3	10	0	1	0	0
Rodriguez, Aurelio, Detroit	.240	128	480	40	115	156	13	2	8	50	9	5	0	4
Rojas, Octavio, Kansas City	.242	63	132	11	32	38	6	0	0	16	2	3	2	0
Roof, Phillip, 18 Minn-4 Chi	.200	22	55	1	11	14	3	0	0	16	2	3	2	0
Rosario, Angel, Milwaukee†	.189	15	37	4	7	10	0	0	1	5	0	0	1	3
Rudi, Joseph, Oakland	.270	130	500	54	135	212	32	3	13	94	3	10	6	1
Sandt, Thomas, Oakland	.209	41	67	6	14	15	1	0	0	3	1	0	0	0
Scott, George, Milwaukee	.274	156	606	73	166	251	21	5	18	77	0	7	0	1
Scott, Ralph, California*	.000	35	0	1	0	0	0	0	0	0	0	0	0	0
Scrivener, Wayne, Detroit	.221	80	222	28	49	64	7	1	2	16	3	0	1	0
Sharp, William, Milwaukee*	.244	78	180	16	44	48	4	0	0	11	4	0	1	3
Shopay, Thomas, Baltimore*	.200	14	20	4	4	4	0	0	0	1	0	0	1	0
Singleton, Kenneth, Baltimore†	.278	154	544	62	151	219	25	2	13	70	2	5	2	2
Smalley, Roy, 41 Tex-103 Minn†	.259	144	513	61	133	166	18	3	3	44	25	2	2	4
Smith, Billy E., California†	.375	13	8	0	3	3	0	0	0	0	1	0	0	0
Smith, Tommy A., Cleveland*	.256	55	164	17	42	53	3	1	2	12	0	1	8	0
Solaita, Tolia, 31 KC-63 Calif*	.261	94	283	29	74	114	13	0	9	42	1	5	1	1
Spencer, James, Chicago*	.253	150	518	53	131	190	13	2	14	70	4	7	6	4
Spikes, L. Charles, Cleveland	.237	101	334	34	79	109	11	5	3	31	1	2	5	6
Stanley, Frederick, New York	.238	110	260	32	62	71	2	2	1	20	11	0	1	0
Stanley, Mitchell, Detroit	.257	84	214	34	55	86	17	1	4	29	0	1	2	0
Stanton, Leroy, California	.190	93	231	12	44	65	13	1	2	25	5	3	2	6
Staub, Daniel, Detroit*	.299	161	589	73	176	255	28	3	15	96	0	11	3	1
Stein, William, Chicago	.268	117	392	32	105	136	15	2	4	36	6	0	4	2
Stillman, Royle, Baltimore*	.091	20	22	0	2	2	0	0	0	1	0	0	0	0
Stinson, G. Robert, Kansas City†	.263	79	209	26	55	70	7	1	2	25	6	2	3	1
Sundberg, James, Texas	.228	140	448	33	102	139	24	2	3	34	9	2	0	0
Sutherland, Gary, 42 Det-59 Mil	.211	101	232	19	49	63	7	2	1	15	3	4	0	3
Tenace, F. Gene, Oakland	.249	128	417	64	104	191	19	1	22	66	1	5	5	4
Terrell, Jerry, Minnesota	.246	89	171	29	42	47	3	1	0	8	4	1	11	2
Thomas, Danny, Milwaukee	.276	32	105	13	29	48	5	1	4	15	0	0	1	2
Thomas, J. Gorman, Milwaukee	.198	99	227	27	45	82	9	2	8	36	5	3	2	3
Thompson, Danny, 34 Minn-64 Tex	.222	98	320	21	71	81	7	0	1	19	6	3	3	3
Thompson, Jason, Detroit*	.218	123	412	45	90	155	12	1	17	54	1	4	2	4
Tiant, Luis, Boston	.000	38	1	0	0	0	0	0	0	0	0	0	0	0
Torres, Rosendo, California†	.205	120	264	37	54	94	16	3	6	27	8	1	4	4
Tovar, Cesar, 29 Oak-13 NY	.167	42	84	3	14	15	1	0	0	6	2	0	1	3
Varney, Richard, Chicago	.244	14	41	5	10	21	2	0	3	5	0	0	0	0
Velez, Otoniel, New York	.266	49	94	11	25	37	6	0	2	10	0	0	0	0
Veryzer, Thomas, Detroit	.234	97	354	31	83	98	8	2	1	25	6	3	1	4
Wagner, Mark, Detroit	.261	39	115	9	30	38	2	3	0	12	3	0	0	2
Waits, Richard, Cleveland*	.000	36	0	4	0	0	0	0	0	0	0	0	0	1
Walling, Dennis, Oakland*	.273	3	11	1	3	3	0	0	0	0	0	0	0	0
Washington, Claudell, Oakland*	.257	134	490	65	126	173	20	6	5	53	3	4	37	20
Wathan, John, Kansas City	.286	27	42	5	12	13	1	0	0	5	1	0	0	2
White, Frank, Kansas City	.229	152	446	39	102	137	17	6	2	46	18	3	20	11
White, Roy, New York†	.286	156	626	104	179	256	29	3	14	65	10	9	31	13
Whitfield, Terry, New York*	.000	1	0	0	0	0	0	0	0	0	0	0	0	0
Whitt, Ernest, Boston*	.222	8	18	4	4	9	2	0	1	3	0	0	0	0
Williams, Billy, Oakland*	.211	120	351	36	74	119	12	0	11	41	1	3	4	2
Willoughby, James, Boston	.000	54	1	0	0	0	0	0	0	0	0	0	0	0
Wilson, Willie, Kansas City	.167	12	6	0	1	1	0	0	0	0	0	0	2	1
Wockenfuss, Johnny, Detroit	.222	60	144	18	32	52	7	2	3	10	1	0	0	3
Wohlford, James, Kansas City	.249	107	293	47	73	90	10	2	1	24	6	5	22	16
Woods, Gary, Oakland	.125	6	8	0	1	1	0	0	0	0	0	0	0	0
Wynegar, Harold, Minnesota†	.260	149	534	58	139	194	21	2	10	69	4	3	0	0
Yancy, Hugh, Chicago	.100	3	10	0	1	2	1	0	0	0	0	0	0	0
Yastrzemski, Carl, Boston*	.267	155	546	71	146	236	23	2	21	102	1	8	5	6
Yount, Robin, Milwaukee	.252	161	638	59	161	192	19	3	2	54	8	6	16	11

The following pitchers had no plate appearances primarily because of use of designated hitters; they are listed alphabetically by club with number of games, including pinch-running appearances, in parentheses:

BALTIMORE—Cuellar, Miguel (26); Flanagan, Michael K. (20); Garland, Wayne (38); Grimsley, Ross (28); Holdsworth, Fredrick (16); Martinez, J. Dennis (4); Martinez, Felix (39—includes 11 with New York); May, Rudolph (35—includes 11 with New York); McGregor, Scott (3); Miller, Dyar (49); Pagan, David (27—includes 7 with New York); Palmer, James (40).

BOSTON—Cleveland, Reginald (41); House, Thomas (36); Jenkins, Ferguson (30); Jones, T. Fredrick (24); Kreuger, Richard (8); Murphy, Thomas (52—includes 15 with Milwaukee); Wise, Richard (34).

CALIFORNIA—Brewer, James (13); Drago, Richard (43); Dunning, Steven (4); Hartzell, Paul (37); Kirkwood, Donald (28); Monge, Isidro (32); Overy, H. Michael (5); Ross, Gary (34); Ryan, L. Nolan (39); Tanana, Frank (35); Verhoeven, John (21); Wheelock, Gary (2).

CHICAGO—Barrios, Francisco (35); Carroll, Clay (29); Forster, Terry (29); Gossage, Richard (31); Hamilton, David (45); Jefferson, Jesse (19); Johnson, C. Barth (32); Knapp, R. Christian (11); Kravec, Kenneth (9); Kucek, John (2); Monroe, Lawrence (8); Odom, Johnny (8); Otten, James (2); Vuckovich, Peter (33); Wood, Wilbur (7).

CLEVELAND—Bibby, James (34); Brown, Jackie (32); Buskey, Thomas (39); Dobson, Patrick (35); Eckersley, Dennis (36); Hood, Donald (34); Kern, James (50); LaRoche, David (61); Parker, Harry (3); Raich, Eric (1); Thomas, Stanley (37).

DETROIT—Bare, Raymond (30); Coleman, Joseph (12); Crawford, James (32); Fidrych, Mark (31); Glynn, Edward (5); Grilli, Stephen (36); Laxton, William (26); Lemanczyk, David (20); Roberts, David A. (36); Ruhle, Vernon (32).

KANSAS CITY—Bird, J. Douglas (39); Bruno, Thomas (12); Busby, Steven (13); Cram, Gerald (4); Fitzmorris, Alan (37); Gura, Lawrence (20); Hall, Thomas (33); Hassler, Andrew (33—includes 14 with California); Leonard, Dennis (35); McClure, Robert (19); Mingori, Stephen (55); Nelson, Roger (3); Pattin, Martin (44); Sanders, Kenneth (3); Splittorff, Paul (26).

MILWAUKEE—Augustine, Gerald (39); Austin, Rick (3); Beare, Gary (6); Broberg, Peter (20); Castro, William (39); Champion, B. Billy (10); Colborn, James (32); Frisella, Daniel (32); Haas, Bryan (5); Hausman, Thomas (3); Kobel, Kevin (3); Rodriguez, Eduardo (45); Sadecki, Raymond (39—includes 3 with Kansas City); Slaton, James (38); Sprague, Edward (3); Travers, William (34).

MINNESOTA—Albury, Victor (23); Bane, Edward (18); Burgmeier, Thomas (57); Campbell, William (78); Decker, George (13); Goltz, David (37); Hughes, James (37); Johnson, Thomas R. (18); Luebber, Stephen (38); Pazik, Michael (5); Redfern, Peter (23); Singer, William (36—includes 10 with Texas).

NEW YORK—Alexander, Doyle (30—includes 11 with Baltimore); Ellis, Dock (32); Figueroa, Eduardo (34); Guidry, Ronald (7); Holtzman, Kenneth (34—includes 13 with Baltimore); Jackson, Grant (34—includes 13 with Baltimore); Lyle, Albert (64); Tidrow, Richard (47); York, James (3).

OAKLAND—Abbott, W. Glenn (19); Bahnsen, Stanley (35); Batton, Christopher (2); Blue, Vida (37); Bosman, Richard (27); Fingers, Roland (70); Lindblad, Paul (65); Mitchell, Craig (1); Mitchell, Paul (26); Norris, Michael (24); Todd, James (49); Torrez, Michael (39).

TEXAS—Bacsik, Michael (23); Barker, Leonard (2); Barr, Steven (20); Blyleven, Rikalbert (36—includes 12 with Minnesota); Boggs, Thomas (13); Briles, Nelson (32); Foucault, Steven (46); Hargan, Steven (35); Hoerner, Joseph (41); Perry, Gaylord (32); Perzanowski, Stanley (5); Peterson, Fred (13—includes 9 with Cleveland); Skok, Craig (9); Terpko, Jeffrey (32); Umbarger, James (30).

AWARDED FIRST BASE ON INTERFERENCE: Lahoud, Calif. 3 (Ashby, Downing, Fisk); Chambliss, N.Y. (Wockenfuss); Hegan, Milw. (Fisk); Hendrick, Cleve. (Wockenfuss); Patek, K.C. (Downing); Rudi, Oak. (Essian); Smalley, Tex. (Garrett); Stinson, K.C. (Essian); Torres, Calif. (Hendricks).

PLAYERS WITH TWO OR MORE CLUBS
(Alphabetically Arranged With Player's First Club on Top)

Player and Club	Pct.	G.	AB.	R.	H.	TB.	2B.	3B.	HR.	RBI.	SH.	SF.	Tot. BB.	Int. BB.	HP.	SO.	SB.	CS.	GI DP.
K. Brett, N.Y.	.000	2	0	0	0	0	0	0	0	0	0	0	0	0	0	0	0	0	0
K. Brett, Chi.	.083	33	12	0	1	1	0	0	0	0	0	0	0	0	0	1	0	0	1
Carbo, Bos.	.236	17	55	5	13	23	4	0	2	6	0	0	8	1	0	17	1	0	0
Carbo, Milw.	.235	69	183	20	43	59	7	0	3	15	3	0	33	3	0	55	1	2	5
Coggins, N.Y.	.250	7	4	1	1	1	0	0	0	1	0	0	0	0	0	1	1	0	0
Coggins, Chi.	.156	32	96	4	15	17	2	0	0	5	2	0	6	0	0	15	3	1	1
Cubbage, Tex.	.219	14	32	2	7	7	0	0	0	0	0	0	7	0	0	7	0	0	1
Cubbage, Minn.	.260	104	342	40	89	127	19	5	3	49	3	2	42	3	3	37	1	1	10
Darwin, Milw.	.247	25	73	6	18	26	3	1	1	5	0	0	6	1	2	16	0	0	2
Darwin, Bos.	.179	43	106	9	19	37	5	2	3	13	1	0	2	0	3	35	1	0	2
Davis, Calif.	.265	72	219	16	58	72	5	0	3	26	0	2	15	3	1	18	0	1	12
Davis, K.C.	.263	8	19	1	5	5	0	0	0	0	0	0	1	0	0	0	0	0	1
Dempsey, N.Y.	.119	21	42	1	5	5	0	0	0	2	1	0	5	0	0	4	0	0	0
Dempsey, Balt.	.213	59	174	11	37	39	2	0	0	10	3	0	13	0	2	17	1	1	2
P. Garcia, Milw.	.217	41	106	12	23	35	7	1	1	9	4	1	4	0	2	23	2	2	1
P. Garcia, Det.	.198	77	227	21	45	68	10	2	3	20	2	3	9	0	4	40	2	3	3
Healy, K.C.	.125	8	24	2	3	3	0	0	0	1	0	0	4	0	0	10	2	0	1
Healy, N.Y.	.267	46	120	10	32	35	3	0	0	9	0	0	9	0	0	17	3	1	3

Player and Club	Pct.	G.	AB.	R.	H.	TB.	2B.	3B.	HR.	RBI.	SH.	SF.	Tot. BB.	Int. BB.	HP.	SO.	SB.	CS.	GI DP.
Hendricks, Balt.	.139	28	79	2	11	15	1	0	1	4	0	0	7	1	0	13	0	1	0
Hendricks, N.Y.	.226	26	53	6	12	22	1	0	3	5	0	1	3	0	0	10	0	0	1
Lahoud, Calif.	.177	42	96	8	17	21	4	0	0	4	0	0	18	2	2	17	0	0	3
Lahoud, Tex.	.225	38	89	10	20	28	3	1	1	5	1	0	10	1	0	16	1	0	3
C. May, Chi.	.175	20	63	7	11	13	2	0	0	3	0	0	9	0	0	5	4	0	0
C. May, N.Y.	.278	87	288	38	80	104	11	2	3	40	1	5	34	2	5	32	1	1	6
Nordbrook, Balt.	.227	27	22	4	5	5	0	0	0	0	0	0	3	0	0	5	0	0	1
Nordbrook, Calif.	.000	5	8	1	0	0	0	0	0	0	1	0	1	0	0	3	1	0	0
Roof, Minn.	.217	18	46	1	10	13	3	0	0	4	0	0	2	0	0	6	0	0	1
Roof, Chi.	.111	4	9	0	1	1	0	0	0	0	0	0	0	0	0	3	0	0	1
Smalley, Tex.	.225	41	129	15	29	34	2	0	1	8	3	2	29	3	0	27	2	0	4
Smalley, Minn.	.271	103	384	46	104	132	16	3	2	36	22	0	47	1	2	79	0	4	7
Solaita, K.C.	.235	31	68	4	16	20	4	0	0	9	0	3	6	0	0	17	0	0	0
Solaita, Calif.	.270	63	215	25	58	94	9	0	9	33	1	2	34	3	0	44	1	1	4
Sutherland, Det.	.205	42	117	10	24	33	5	2	0	6	0	1	7	0	0	12	0	1	5
Sutherland, Milw.	.217	59	115	9	25	30	2	0	1	9	3	3	8	2	1	7	0	2	7
D. Thompson, Minn.	.234	34	124	9	29	33	4	0	0	6	2	1	3	0	1	8	1	1	1
D. Thompson, Tex.	.214	64	196	12	42	48	3	0	1	13	4	2	13	0	1	19	2	2	5
Tovar, Oak.	.178	29	45	1	8	8	0	0	0	4	1	0	4	0	2	4	1	2	0
Tovar, N.Y.	.154	13	39	2	6	7	1	0	0	2	1	0	4	1	1	3	0	1	0

OFFICIAL MISCELLANEOUS AMERICAN LEAGUE BATTING RECORDS

CLUB MISCELLANEOUS BATTING RECORDS

Club	Slg. Pct.	G.	Tot. BB.	Int. BB.	HP.	SO.	GIDP.	ShO.
Boston	.402	162	500	35	29	832	127	9
New York	.389	159	470	36	35	616	94	8
Minnesota	.375	162	550	39	41	714	121	13
Kansas City	.371	162	484	36	31	650	103	9
Detroit	.365	161	450	35	31	730	157	19
Oakland	.361	161	592	45	45	818	91	9
Cleveland	.359	159	479	42	11	631	143	7
Baltimore	.358	162	519	34	23	883	119	16
Chicago	.349	161	471	43	34	739	104	21
Texas	.341	162	568	46	29	809	141	17
Milwaukee	.340	161	511	30	23	909	112	15
California	.318	162	534	50	42	812	130	18
Totals	.361		6128	471	374	9143	1442	161

INDIVIDUAL MISCELLANEOUS BATTING RECORDS

(Top Fifteen Qualifiers for Slugging Championship—502 or More Plate Appearances)

Player—Club	Slg. Pct.	Tot. BB.	Int. BB.	HP.	SO.	GI DP.	Player—Club	Slg. Pct.	Tot. BB.	Int. BB.	HP.	SO.	GI DP.
R. Jackson, Balt.	.502	54	7	4	108	17	Ford, Minn.	.457	36	2	10	118	12
Rice, Bos.	.482	28	2	4	123	18	Hendrick, Cleve.	.448	51	6	0	82	16
Nettles, N.Y.	.475	62	6	4	94	8	L. May, Balt.	.447	41	8	3	104	11
Lynn, Bos.	.467	48	2	1	67	9	Otis, K.C.	.444	55	7	5	100	13
Carew, Minn.	.463	67	14	1	52	12	Carty, Cleve.	.442	69	9	0	45	18
Brett, K.C.	.462	49	4	1	36	8	Chambliss, N.Y.	.441	27	1	3	80	11
McRae, K.C.	.461	64	7	8	43	13	Staub, Det.	.433	83	11	7	49	23
Tenace, Oak.	.458	81	2	4	91	7							

DEPARTMENTAL LEADERS: Tot.BB—Hargrove, 97; Int.BB—Spencer, 19; HP—Baylor, 20; SO—Rice, 123; GIDP—Staub, 23.

(All Players—Listed Alphabetically)

Player—Club	Slg. Pct.	Tot. BB	Int. BB	HP	SO	GI DP
Aaron, Milw.	.369	35	1	0	38	8
Alexander, Oak.	.033	0	0	0	5	0
Alomar, N.Y.	.282	13	0	0	12	2
Alvarez, Calif.	.333	0	0	0	3	0
Ashby, Cleve.	.316	27	4	0	49	6
Ault, Tex.	.350	1	0	0	3	0
Bailor, Balt.	.667	0	0	0	0	0
Baker, Bos.	.261	1	0	0	5	1
Bando, Oak.	.427	76	1	4	74	7
Bannister, Chi.	.317	14	1	1	21	0
Baylor, Oak.	.368	58	4	20	72	11
Belanger, Balt.	.326	51	0	2	64	6
Bell, Cleve.	.366	44	3	2	49	12
Bell, Chi.	.396	18	0	1	56	3
Beniquez, Tex.	.301	39	1	3	56	10
Bernhardt, N.Y.	.238	0	0	0	4	0
Bevacqua, Milw.	.143	0	0	0	0	0
Blair, Balt.	.264	22	2	2	49	14
Blanks, Cleve.	.393	30	0	0	31	15
Blomberg, N.Y.	.000	0	0	0	0	0
Bochte, Calif.	.311	64	11	2	53	12
Bonds, Calif.	.386	41	6	3	90	7
Borgmann, Minn.	.338	19	0	0	7	2
Bostock, Minn.	.430	33	5	1	37	15
Bowling, Milw.	.214	2	0	0	5	0
Bradford, Chi.	.350	19	2	2	37	0
Braun, Minn.	.353	67	2	1	43	5
G. Brett, K.C.	.462	49	4	1	36	8
K. Brett, N.Y.-Chi.	.083	0	0	0	1	1
Briggs, Calif.	.294	13	3	1	47	7
Brohamer, Chi.	.356	44	9	3	28	9
Brye, Minn.	.329	13	0	0	31	7
Bumbry, Balt.	.376	43	2	1	76	7
Burleson, Bos.	.383	60	2	5	37	15
Burroughs, Tex.	.369	69	4	2	93	22
Campaneris, Oak.	.291	63	0	3	80	4
Carbo, Bos.-Milw.	.345	41	4	0	72	5
Carew, Minn.	.463	67	14	1	52	12
Carty, Cleve.	.442	67	9	0	45	18
Cerone, Cleve.	.125	0	0	0	2	0
Chalk, Calif.	.253	49	3	10	62	16
Chambliss, N.Y.	.441	27	1	3	80	11
Clines, Tex.	.316	16	0	4	52	17
Coggins, N.Y.-Chi.	.180	6	0	0	16	1
Colbert, Oak.	.000	1	1	0	3	0
Collins, Calif.	.334	40	2	0	55	2
Cooper, Bos.	.457	16	6	1	62	3
Cowens, K.C.	.341	26	0	3	50	9
Crosby, Cleve.	.500	0	0	0	0	0
Crowley, Balt.	.262	7	1	1	11	1
Cubbage, Tex.-Minn.	.358	49	3	3	44	11
Dade, Calif.	.111	3	0	0	3	1
Darwin, Milw.-Bos.	.352	8	1	5	51	4
Dauer, Balt.	.103	1	0	1	3	0
Davis, Calif.-K.C.	.324	16	3	1	18	13
DeCinces, Balt.	.357	29	1	2	68	11
Dempsey, N.Y.-Balt.	.204	18	0	2	21	2
Dent, Chi.	.302	43	3	2	45	10
Dillard, Bos.	.377	17	1	0	20	7
Dineen, N.Y.	.286	1	0	0	2	0
Downing, Chi.	.328	40	0	1	55	2
Doyle, Bos.	.308	22	0	0	39	9
Duffy, Cleve.	.265	29	2	2	50	13
Duncan, Balt.	.271	25	0	1	56	8
Easler, Calif.	.296	2	1	0	11	1
Ellis, Tex.	.581	0	0	0	4	1

Player—Club	Slg. Pct.	Tot. BB	Int. BB	HP	SO	GI DP
Enright, Chi.	.000	0	0	0	0	0
Essian, Chi.	.281	23	0	1	28	6
Etchebarren, Calif.	.271	24	0	4	37	9
Evans, Bos.	.431	57	4	6	92	11
Ewing, Chi.	.317	2	0	0	8	0
Fahey, Tex.	.313	11	0	1	6	2
Fairly, Oak.	.457	9	3	0	12	1
Fisk, Bos.	.415	56	3	6	71	11
Ford, Minn.	.457	36	2	10	118	12
Fosse, Cleve.	.362	20	1	0	20	8
Freehan, Det.	.384	12	0	1	27	4
Fregosi, Tex.	.331	23	1	0	33	4
Gamble, N.Y.	.426	38	4	4	38	4
Gantner, Milw.	.261	6	0	1	11	1
Garcia, Balt.	.406	0	0	0	4	0
Garcia, Minn.-Det.	.309	13	0	6	63	4
Garner, Oak.	.400	36	1	2	71	11
Garr, Chi.	.387	17	2	2	41	6
Garrett, Calif.	.188	5	0	0	16	2
Gomez, Minn.	.211	3	0	0	3	3
Gonzalez, Cleve.	.279	5	0	0	7	2
Grich, Balt.	.417	86	1	3	99	8
Grieve, Tex.	.418	35	5	4	119	18
Griffin, Cleve.	.250	0	0	0	2	0
Griffin, Bos.	.205	9	0	1	14	4
Gross, Oak.	.222	2	0	0	1	0
Guerrero, Calif.	.340	7	2	3	12	6
Hairston, Chi	.277	24	0	0	19	0
Hampton, Calif	.000	0	0	0	0	0
Haney, Oak.	.237	13	0	1	26	5
Hansen, Mil	.180	6	0	0	8	1
Hargrove, Tex	.384	97	13	6	64	5
Harper, Balt.	.338	10	0	0	16	1
Harrah, Tex.	.377	91	5	3	59	17
Healy, KC-NY	.264	13	0	0	27	4
Hegan, Mil	.362	25	1	1	54	4
Heidemann, Mil	.267	7	0	0	24	2
Heise, Bos.	.304	1	0	1	2	1
Hendrick, Cleve.	.448	51	6	0	82	16
Hendricks, Balt-NY	.280	10	1	0	23	1
Herrmann, Calif	.370	7	2	0	8	0
Hiller, Det	.000	0	0	0	0	0
Hisle, Minn	.394	56	4	4	93	11
Holt, Oak	.571	1	0	0	2	0
Hopkins, Oak	.000	0	0	0	0	0
Hobson, Bos	.387	15	1	0	62	8
Horton, Det	.409	49	7	2	63	16
Hosley, Oak	.255	8	0	0	12	1
Howard, Cleve	.256	3	2	1	13	3
Howell, Tex	.367	30	8	1	106	12
Humphrey, Calif	.311	13	0	5	30	7
Hunter, NY	.000	0	0	0	0	0
Jackson, Balt	.502	54	7	4	108	17
Jackson, Calif.	.344	30	1	7	58	10
Johnson, Det	.354	19	1	2	49	15
Johnson, Bos	.211	5	1	0	11	2
Johnson, Chi.	.432	19	1	2	37	11
Johnson, Mil	.311	19	0	2	32	7
Jones, Chi	.225	5	0	1	5	1
Jones, Calif	.355	14	3	1	30	5
Jones, KC	.333	3	0	0	16	0
Joshua, Mil	.357	18	3	0	58	5
Kelly, Chi	.386	45	1	3	45	8
Kimm, Det	.336	15	0	0	20	2
Klutts, NY	.000	0	0	0	1	0
Kuiper, Cleve	.312	30	2	1	42	13

Player—Club	Slg. Pct.	Tot. BB	Int. BB	HP	SO	GI DP.
Kusick, Minn	.432	35	0	1	44	3
Kusnyer, Mil	.147	1	1	1	5	0
Lahoud, Cal-Tex	.265	28	3	2	33	6
Lane, Det	.208	6	0	0	11	1
Lee, Bos	.000	0	0	0	0	0
LeFlore, Det	.410	51	2	2	111	12
Lemon, Chi	.328	28	0	7	65	9
Lezcano, Mil	.382	51	2	2	112	7
Lintz, Oak	.000	2	0	0	0	0
Lis, Cleve	.451	8	0	0	8	0
Littell, KC	.000	0	0	0	1	0
Locklear, NY	.250	2	0	0	7	0
Lopez, Calif	.000	2	0	0	3	0
Lowenstein, Clev	.284	25	3	0	35	4
Lynn, Bos	.467	48	2	1	67	9
MacCormack, Det	.000	0	0	0	2	0
Maddox, NY	.261	4	1	0	3	2
Mangual, Oak	.250	0	0	0	1	0
Mankowski, Det	.353	4	0	0	8	3
Manning, Cleve	.393	41	1	0	75	11
Manuel, Det	.163	3	0	1	9	1
Martinez, KC	.356	16	1	0	45	2
Mason, NY	.235	9	0	0	37	4
C. May, Chi-NY	.333	43	2	5	37	6
L. May, Balt	.447	41	8	3	104	11
May, Det	.320	0	0	0	1	0
Mayberry, KC	.342	82	7	2	73	12
McCovey, Oak	.208	3	1	0	4	0
McKay, Minn	.217	9	0	4	27	6
McMullen, Oak	.355	22	3	1	33	4
McRae, KC	.461	64	7	8	43	13
Melton, Calif	.328	44	2	2	53	5
Merchant, Bos	.000	0	0	0	2	0
Meyer, Det	.327	17	0	0	22	10
Miley, Calif	.237	4	1	0	8	1
Miller, Bos	.361	34	2	0	47	4
Minoso, Chi	.125	0	0	0	2	0
Moates, Tex	.307	11	2	0	18	0
Money, Mil	.408	47	2	0	50	11
Montgomery, Bos	.398	5	1	0	20	1
Moore, Mil	.290	43	0	1	45	4
Mora, Balt	.350	13	0	0	49	4
Munson, NY	.432	29	6	9	38	17
Murray, NY	.100	1	0	0	2	0
Muser, Balt	.264	21	4	0	34	9
D. Nelson, KC	.307	14	0	0	26	1
Nettles, NY	.475	62	6	4	94	8
Newman, Det	.247	4	0	0	12	0
Nordbrook, Bal-Cal	.167	4	0	0	8	1
Nordhagen, Chi	.226	4	0	0	12	1
North, Oak	.337	73	3	2	95	8
Nyman, Chi	.200	0	0	0	3	0
Oglivie, Det	.492	11	3	3	44	11
Oliva, Minn	.260	2	1	2	13	2
Orta, Chi	.410	38	2	5	77	15
Otis, KC	.444	55	7	5	100	13
Pape, Tex	.391	3	1	2	2	1
Patek, KC	.306	50	5	2	63	6
Petrocelli, Bos	.288	34	3	0	36	9
Piniella, NY	.394	18	8	2	34	4
Pole, Cleve	.000	0	0	0	0	0
Poquette, KC	.430	29	3	4	31	9
Porter, Mil	.288	51	3	1	61	4
Powell, Cleve	.338	41	3	0	43	10
Pruitt, Cleve	.302	16	1	0	8	1
Pryor, Tex	.375	0	0	0	1	0
Quirk, KC	.325	2	0	0	22	5
Ramirez, Calif	.214	6	0	0	11	2
Randall, Minn	.328	28	0	8	38	6
Randle, Tex	.273	46	2	2	63	4
Randolph, NY	.328	58	5	3	39	10
Remy, Calif	.303	38	1	0	43	5
Rice, Bos	.482	28	2	4	123	18
Rivers, NY	.432	13	0	3	51	3
Robinson, Balt	.307	8	0	1	24	5
Robinson, Cleve	.358	11	0	0	12	3
Rodriguez, Det	.325	19	3	1	61	19
Rojas, KC	.288	8	0	0	15	5
Roof, Minn-Chi	.255	2	0	0	9	2
Rosario, Mil	.270	3	0	0	8	0
Rudi, Oak	.424	41	10	3	71	14
Sandt, Oak	.224	7	0	0	9	1
Scott, Calif.	.000	0	0	0	0	0
Scott, Mil	.414	53	6	5	118	19
Scrivener, Det	.288	19	0	0	34	2
Sharp, Mil	.267	10	0	1	15	3
Shopay, Balt	.200	3	0	0	3	0
Singleton, Balt	.403	79	6	0	76	14
Smalley, Tex-Minn	.324	76	4	2	106	11
Smith, Calif	.375	0	0	0	2	0
Smith, Cleve	.323	8	2	0	8	4
Solaita, KC-Cal	.403	40	3	0	61	4
Spencer, Chi	.367	49	19	1	52	10
Spikes, Cleve	.326	23	3	5	50	4
Stanley, NY	.273	34	0	1	29	5
Stanley, Det	.402	14	1	0	19	7
Stanton, Calif	.281	24	1	1	57	9
Staub, Det	.433	83	11	7	49	23
Stein, Chi	.347	22	3	2	67	8
Stillman, Bal	.091	3	1	0	4	0
Stinson, KC	.335	25	2	1	29	5
Sundberg, Tex	.310	37	0	0	61	15
Sutherland, Det-Mil	.272	15	2	1	19	12
Tenace, Oak	.458	81	2	4	91	7
Terrell, Minn	.275	9	0	1	15	4
D. Thomas, Mil	.457	14	1	2	28	1
J. G. Thomas, Mil.	.361	31	1	1	67	7
Thompson, Minn-Tex	.253	16	0	2	27	6
Thompson, Det	.376	68	6	1	72	8
Tiant, Bos	.000	0	0	0	1	0
Torres, Calif	.356	36	3	0	39	4
Tovar, Oak-NY	.179	8	1	3	7	0
Varney, Chi	.512	2	0	0	9	2
Velez, NY	.394	23	1	0	26	1
Veryzer, Det	.277	21	1	6	44	11
Wagner, Det	.330	6	0	0	18	1
Waits, Cleve	.000	0	0	0	0	0
Walling, Oak	.273	0	0	0	3	0
Washington, Oak	.353	30	1	3	90	13
Wathan, KC	.310	2	0	1	5	1
White, KC	.307	19	0	3	42	4
White, NY	.409	83	1	0	52	13
Whitfield, NY	.000	0	0	0	0	0
Whitt, Bos	.500	2	0	0	2	0
Williams, Oak	.339	58	15	0	44	4
Willoughby, Bos	.000	0	0	0	0	0
Wilson, Bos	.167	0	0	0	2	0
Wockenfuss, Det	.361	17	0	1	14	3
Wohlford, Oak	.307	29	0	1	24	8
Woods, Calif	.125	0	0	0	3	0
Wynegar, Minn	.363	79	7	2	63	14
Yancy, Chi	.200	0	0	0	3	0
Yastrzemski, Bos	.432	80	6	1	67	12
Yount, Mil	.301	38	3	0	69	13

OFFICIAL AMERICAN LEAGUE DESIGNATED HITTING

CLUB DESIGNATED HITTING

Club	Pct.	AB.	R.	H.	TB.	2B.	3B.	HR.	RBI.	SH.	SF.	BB.	HP.	SO.	SB.	CS.	GI DP.
Cleveland	.307	603	78	185	265	32	0	16	90	0	11	70	0	62	1	7	19
Kansas City	.286	605	88	173	246	34	6	9	79	3	8	62	8	76	18	11	17
Detroit	.271	602	65	163	240	26	0	17	88	0	7	63	4	86	5	3	22
Minnesota	.268	631	93	169	232	25	1	12	90	1	7	69	4	91	11	5	8
Chicago	.265	626	82	166	239	29	7	10	71	3	8	61	5	87	18	7	16
New York	.255	612	68	156	213	23	5	8	73	4	4	59	6	70	2	3	11
Baltimore	.254	614	62	156	240	22	4	18	85	3	4	65	4	111	13	5	9
California	.251	618	66	155	226	29	3	12	77	6	6	58	3	93	11	7	17
Texas	.241	626	61	151	212	16	3	13	68	9	4	46	3	134	3	0	16
Boston	.236	624	71	147	257	32	9	20	89	7	8	37	5	134	4	4	13
Oakland	.228	574	74	131	195	20	1	14	66	3	7	83	3	88	36	15	7
Milwaukee	.217	599	60	130	186	16	2	12	64	5	5	66	1	108	1	4	14
Totals	.257	7334	868	1882	2751	304	41	161	940	44	79	739	46	1140	123	71	169

INDIVIDUAL DESIGNATED HITTING
(Listed According to Number of Official Times at Bat)

Player and Club	Pct.	G.	AB.	R.	H.	TB.	2B.	3B.	HR.	RBI.	SH.	SF.	BB.	HP.	SO.	SB.	CS.	GI DP.
Carty, Clev	.317	137	508	63	161	231	31	0	13	78	0	9	57	0	43	1	1	17
McRae, KC	.329	117	417	65	137	197	29	5	7	62	2	6	50	8	37	15	8	11
Horton, Det	.263	105	395	39	104	160	17	0	13	55	0	4	46	2	61	0	0	16
Grieve, Tex	.247	96	369	37	91	134	12	2	9	49	5	4	15	3	88	1	0	9
Williams, Oak	.208	106	342	36	71	115	11	0	11	40	1	3	54	0	43	4	2	3
C. May, Chi-NY	.256	81	289	37	74	98	11	2	3	34	1	3	35	4	32	3	0	4
Aaron, Milw	.229	74	262	22	60	98	8	0	10	33	0	2	32	0	37	0	1	8
Braun, Minn	.280	71	254	44	71	87	8	1	2	39	0	3	41	1	30	6	3	5
Davis, Cal-KC	.251	57	215	17	54	68	5	0	3	19	0	1	15	0	17	0	1	13
Kusick, Minn	.269	79	212	29	57	94	10	0	9	29	1	2	23	1	35	4	1	0
Kelly, Chi	.256	63	211	32	54	81	9	3	4	24	2	4	32	3	28	12	5	8
Rice, Bos	.264	54	201	19	53	87	9	2	7	29	1	5	7	3	42	2	2	6
Cooper, Bos	.245	53	200	26	49	90	12	4	7	30	4	2	4	0	29	1	1	1
L. May, Balt	.270	52	196	25	53	89	8	2	8	39	0	0	16	3	39	1	0	4
Melton, Calif	.207	51	169	17	35	60	9	2	4	26	1	2	25	2	27	1	0	3
Hegan, Milw	.245	40	139	18	34	47	3	2	2	15	1	2	11	1	32	0	0	3
Piniella, NY	.254	38	138	11	35	55	8	3	2	17	2	1	8	0	15	0	1	3
Staub, Det	.295	36	129	18	38	50	6	0	2	25	0	3	16	2	18	2	0	3
Orta, Chi	.305	31	128	17	39	59	7	2	3	25	0	3	7	0	15	4	2	1
Carbo, Bos-Milw	.203	39	128	14	26	37	5	0	2	9	1	0	18	0	47	1	2	2
Mora, Balt	.172	34	116	6	20	27	4	0	1	10	0	2	3	0	22	1	0	2
L. Johnson, Chi	.273	35	110	13	30	43	5	1	2	11	1	1	4	2	19	0	0	7
Collins, Calif	.290	22	93	11	27	36	6	0	1	5	1	0	3	0	20	8	4	0
Oliva, Minn	.217	32	92	2	20	22	2	0	0	12	0	1	0	1	11	0	0	2
Munson, NY	.270	21	89	13	24	36	3	0	3	18	0	0	1	1	9	1	0	3
Baylor, Oak	.289	23	83	12	24	30	3	0	1	9	0	3	5	1	13	5	2	0
Lahoud, Cal-Tex	.250	25	80	8	20	28	3	1	1	6	1	0	11	0	14	1	0	2
Harper, Balt	.214	27	70	5	15	23	5	0	1	7	0	1	8	0	15	3	3	1
Solaita, KC-Cal	.243	21	70	7	17	26	3	0	2	9	0	0	10	0	17	0	0	0
Johnson, Det	.250	19	68	4	17	23	3	0	1	6	0	0	1	0	5	3	3	3
Singleton, Balt	.297	19	64	7	19	27	2	0	2	7	0	0	15	0	7	0	0	0
Quirk, KC	.234	19	64	6	15	21	3	0	1	7	0	1	0	0	12	0	0	3
Darwin, Mil-Bos	.172	17	58	4	10	21	3	1	2	10	1	0	2	1	20	0	0	1
Hansen, Milw	.167	14	54	4	9	10	1	0	0	3	0	0	3	0	6	0	0	0
Wynegar, Minn	.250	15	52	7	13	17	4	0	0	5	0	1	5	0	14	0	0	0
Easler, Calif	.224	16	49	5	11	12	1	0	0	4	1	2	2	0	9	1	0	1
Robinson, Clev	.229	18	48	5	11	20	0	0	3	5	0	0	8	0	9	0	0	2
McMullen, Oak	.239	23	46	6	11	18	2	1	1	4	0	0	9	0	8	0	0	1
Crowley, Balt	.244	17	41	4	10	11	1	0	0	3	0	0	7	1	7	0	0	0
Fregosi, Tex	.220	18	41	3	9	14	2	0	1	5	1	0	10	0	11	0	0	1
R. Jackson, Balt	.459	11	37	6	17	33	1	0	5	11	0	0	6	0	9	4	1	2
Downing, Chi	.243	11	37	3	9	11	2	0	0	4	0	0	3	0	5	0	0	0
Clines, Tex	.278	10	36	3	10	10	0	0	0	3	1	0	2	0	3	0	0	1
Tovar, Oak-NY	.114	14	35	2	4	4	0	0	0	1	0	1	0	4	2	4	0	2
Ewing, Chi	.176	12	34	2	6	8	2	0	0	1	0	0	2	0	7	0	0	0

Player and Club	Pct.	G.	AB.	R.	H.	TB.	2B.	3B.	HR.	RBI.	SH.	SF.	BB.	HP.	SO.	SB.	CS.	GI DP.
Bumbry, Balt	.273	10	33	7	9	14	0	1	1	3	1	1	4	0	7	4	1	0
Healy, KC-NY	.273	10	33	2	9	9	0	0	0	3	0	0	3	0	7	1	1	0
Muser, Balt	.233	10	30	0	7	8	1	0	0	5	0	0	2	0	0	0	0	0
North, Oak	.400	8	30	6	12	13	1	0	0	6	1	1	7	0	5	6	2	1
Yastrzemski, Bos	.231	10	26	2	6	9	0	0	1	7	0	0	6	1	4	0	0	1
Money, Milw	.154	10	26	0	4	5	1	0	0	6	1	0	4	0	1	0	0	0
Cubbage, Tex-Minn..	.192	8	26	2	5	5	0	0	0	0	0	0	2	0	5	0	0	2
Johnson, Bos	.200	9	25	3	5	8	1	1	0	0	0	0	4	0	7	0	0	1
Howell, Tex	.160	8	25	4	4	7	0	0	1	1	0	0	2	0	8	0	0	1
Jackson, Calif	.391	6	23	3	9	12	3	0	0	3	1	0	0	0	2	0	1	1
Guerrero, Calif	.182	7	22	0	4	5	1	0	0	2	0	1	1	1	1	0	0	0
Rojas, KC	.091	9	22	2	2	2	0	0	0	1	1	1	2	0	2	0	0	2
McCovey, Oak	.182	9	22	0	4	4	0	0	0	0	0	0	3	0	3	0	0	0
Alomar, NY	.200	9	20	4	4	5	1	0	0	2	0	0	4	0	1	0	0	0
Garr, Chi	.421	6	19	1	8	11	0	0	1	1	0	0	0	0	3	0	0	0
Locklear, NY	.263	6	19	1	5	6	1	0	0	1	0	0	2	0	4	0	0	0
D. Nelson, KC	.222	22	18	5	4	9	0	1	1	3	0	0	4	0	5	3	2	0
Lynn, Bos	.118	5	17	3	2	4	0	1	0	1	0	0	2	0	3	0	0	2
Nordhagen, Chi	.250	6	16	6	4	5	1	0	0	0	0	0	4	0	2	0	0	0
Sutherland, Det-Mil	.250	8	16	1	4	4	0	0	0	0	2	0	2	0	0	0	0	1
Washington, Oak	.375	6	16	2	6	10	1	0	1	4	0	0	1	1	2	3	2	1
Harrah, Tex	.313	4	16	1	5	6	1	0	0	1	0	0	0	0	1	0	0	1
Dillard, Bos	.267	7	15	2	4	6	2	0	0	1	0	0	0	0	2	0	0	0
Lowenstein, Clev	.400	11	15	4	6	7	1	0	0	4	0	0	2	0	2	0	1	0
Hargrove, Tex	.214	5	14	0	3	3	0	0	0	1	0	0	3	0	1	0	0	0
Garrett, Calif	.083	4	12	1	1	2	1	0	0	1	0	0	2	0	6	0	0	0
Jones, Chi	.455	3	11	1	5	6	1	0	0	2	0	0	2	0	1	0	0	0
Mayberry, KC	.000	2	11	0	0	0	0	0	0	0	0	0	4	0	5	0	0	0
Petrocelli, Bos	.100	4	10	1	1	2	1	0	0	0	0	0	3	0	5	0	0	0
Sharp, Milw	.300	7	10	1	3	4	1	0	0	2	0	0	0	0	1	0	0	0
Ault, Tex	.200	3	10	0	2	2	0	0	0	0	0	0	1	0	2	0	0	0
Stillman, Balt	.111	5	9	0	1	1	0	0	0	0	0	0	2	0	4	0	0	0
Miller, Bos	.333	4	9	3	3	3	0	0	0	1	1	0	1	0	4	0	1	0
Minoso, Chi	.125	3	8	0	1	1	0	0	0	0	0	0	0	0	2	0	0	0
Bradford, Chi	.375	3	8	1	3	6	1	1	0	0	0	0	2	0	1	0	0	0
Freehan, Det	.375	3	8	0	3	3	0	0	0	0	0	0	0	0	1	0	0	0
Porter, Milw	.250	2	8	0	2	2	0	0	0	1	0	1	0	0	0	0	0	0
Rudi, Oak	.125	2	8	0	1	2	1	0	0	1	0	0	0	0	3	0	0	0
Ellis, Tex	.500	3	8	2	4	7	0	0	1	3	0	0	0	0	1	0	0	0
Grich, Balt	.429	2	7	2	3	3	0	0	0	0	0	0	1	0	1	0	0	0
Stanton, Calif	.571	4	7	2	4	9	1	1	1	6	1	0	0	0	2	0	0	0
Hendrick, Clev	.000	3	7	0	0	0	0	0	0	2	0	2	2	0	2	0	1	0
Velez, NY	.429	5	7	2	3	3	0	0	0	4	0	0	5	0	1	0	0	0
Burroughs, Tex	.143	3	7	0	1	1	0	0	0	0	1	0	3	0	1	0	0	0
Bailor, Balt	.333	1	6	0	2	4	0	1	0	1	0	0	0	0	0	0	0	0
Blanks, Clev	.333	3	6	0	2	2	0	0	0	0	0	0	1	0	2	0	1	0
Terrell, Minn	.333	12	6	7	2	2	0	0	0	1	0	0	0	0	0	1	0	0
Gamble, NY	.000	1	6	1	0	0	0	0	0	0	0	0	2	0	2	0	0	0
Bernhardt, NY	.167	2	6	0	1	1	0	0	0	0	0	0	0	0	1	0	0	0
Alvarez, Calif	.200	2	5	2	1	4	0	0	1	3	0	0	0	0	0	0	0	0
Brye, Minn	.400	3	5	1	2	2	0	0	0	0	0	0	0	0	0	0	0	0
Maddox, NY	.600	2	5	1	3	3	0	0	0	0	0	0	0	0	0	0	0	1
Tenace, Oak	.000	2	5	0	0	0	0	0	0	0	0	0	0	0	2	0	0	0
Colbert, Oak	.000	2	5	0	0	0	0	0	0	0	0	0	1	0	3	0	0	0
Holt, Oak	.200	2	5	0	1	2	1	0	0	2	0	0	1	0	2	0	0	0
Pape, Tex	.200	3	5	1	1	1	0	0	0	0	0	0	0	0	0	0	0	0
DeCinces, Balt	.000	1	4	0	0	0	0	0	0	0	0	0	0	0	0	0	0	0
Evans, Bos	.250	1	4	0	1	2	1	0	0	1	0	0	0	0	0	0	0	1
Fisk, Bos	.000	1	4	0	0	0	0	0	0	1	0	0	0	0	1	0	0	0
Spencer, Chi	.000	2	4	0	0	0	0	0	0	0	0	0	0	0	2	0	0	0
Gonzalez, Clev	.500	2	4	0	2	2	0	0	0	1	0	0	0	0	0	0	0	0
Jones, KC	.250	3	4	2	1	1	0	0	0	1	0	0	1	0	0	0	1	0
Chambliss, NY	.250	1	4	0	1	1	0	0	0	0	0	0	0	0	0	0	0	0
Baker, Bos	.000	1	3	0	0	0	0	0	0	0	0	0	0	0	1	0	0	0
Bonds, Calif	.000	1	3	0	0	0	0	0	0	0	0	0	1	0	1	0	0	0
Wohlford, KC	.000	3	3	1	0	0	0	0	0	0	0	0	0	0	1	0	0	0
Ford, Minn	.667	3	3	3	2	6	1	0	1	4	0	0	0	0	1	0	1	0
Gross, Oak	.333	3	3	0	1	1	0	0	0	0	0	0	0	0	0	0	0	0

Player and Club	Pct.	G.	AB.	R.	H.	TB.	2B.	3B.	HR.	RBI.	SH.	SF.	BB.	HP.	SO.	SB.	CS.	GI DP.
Alexander, Oak	.000	19	3	6	0	0	0	0	0	0	0	0	0	0	0	8	3	0
Montgomery, Bos	.500	1	2	2	1	4	0	0	1	3	0	1	1	0	0	0	0	0
Stein, Chi	.000	1	2	0	0	0	0	0	0	0	0	0	0	0	0	0	0	0
Cerone, Clev	.000	1	2	0	0	0	0	0	0	0	0	0	0	0	1	0	0	0
Smith, Clev	.000	2	2	0	0	0	0	0	0	0	0	0	0	0	0	0	0	0
Pruitt, Clev	.500	4	2	1	1	1	0	0	0	0	0	0	0	0	0	0	1	0
Kuiper, Clev	.500	2	2	0	1	1	0	0	0	0	0	0	0	0	0	0	0	0
Howard, Clev	.500	4	2	1	1	1	0	0	0	0	0	0	0	1	0	0	0	0
Lis, Clev	.000	1	2	0	0	0	0	0	0	0	0	0	0	1	0	0	0	0
Rosario, Milw	.000	2	2	0	0	0	0	0	0	0	0	0	0	0	0	1	1	0
Blomberg, NY	.000	1	2	0	0	0	0	0	0	0	0	0	0	0	0	0	0	0
Bando, Oak	.000	2	2	1	0	0	0	0	0	0	0	0	1	0	1	1	0	0
Randle, Tex	.500	1	2	0	1	1	0	0	0	1	0	0	0	0	0	1	0	0
Blair, Balt	.000	1	1	0	0	0	0	0	0	0	1	0	1	0	0	0	0	0
Jones, Calif	.000	2	1	0	0	0	0	0	0	0	1	0	0	0	0	0	0	0
Bochte, Calif	.000	1	1	0	0	0	0	0	0	0	0	0	0	0	1	0	0	0
Bannister, Chi	1.000	4	1	1	1	1	0	0	0	0	0	0	0	0	0	0	0	0
Bell, Chi	.000	1	1	0	0	0	0	0	0	0	0	0	0	0	0	0	0	0
Coggins, NY-Chi	.000	1	1	0	0	0	0	0	0	0	0	0	0	0	0	0	0	0
Fosse, Clev	.000	1	1	0	0	0	0	0	0	0	0	0	0	0	0	0	0	0
Crosby, Clev	.000	1	1	0	0	0	0	0	0	0	0	0	0	0	0	0	0	0
Spikes, Clev	.000	2	1	0	0	0	0	0	0	0	0	0	0	0	1	0	0	0
LeFlore, Det	.000	1	1	1	0	0	0	0	0	0	0	0	0	0	1	0	0	0
Oglivie, Det	1.000	1	1	1	1	4	0	0	1	2	0	0	0	0	0	0	0	0
Cowens, KC	.000	1	1	1	0	0	0	0	0	0	0	0	0	0	1	0	0	0
Poquette, KC	1.000	2	1	1	1	1	0	0	0	2	0	0	0	0	0	0	0	0
Bevacqua, Milw	.000	3	1	2	0	0	0	0	0	0	0	0	0	0	0	0	0	0
Gantner, Milw	.000	2	1	0	0	0	0	0	0	0	0	0	0	0	0	0	0	0
Bowling, Milw	.000	1	1	0	0	0	0	0	0	0	0	0	0	0	0	0	0	0
Moore, Milw	.000	2	1	1	0	0	0	0	0	1	0	0	2	0	0	0	0	0
Roof, Minn-Chi	1.000	1	1	0	1	1	0	0	0	0	0	0	0	0	0	0	0	0
Woods, Oak	.000	1	1	0	0	0	0	0	0	0	0	0	0	0	1	0	0	0
Moates, Tex	.000	7	1	1	0	0	0	0	0	0	0	0	0	0	0	0	0	0
Thompson, Minn-Tex.	.000	1	1	0	0	0	0	0	0	0	0	0	0	0	1	0	0	0
Griffin, Bos	.000	2	0	1	0	0	0	0	0	0	0	0	0	0	0	0	0	0
Lee, Bos	.000	2	0	1	0	0	0	0	0	0	0	0	0	0	0	0	0	0
Remy, Calif	.000	5	0	0	0	0	0	0	0	0	0	0	0	0	0	1	1	0
Torres, Calif	.000	6	0	3	0	0	0	0	0	0	0	0	0	0	0	0	0	0
Briggs, Calif	.000	1	0	0	0	0	0	0	0	0	0	0	0	0	0	0	0	0
Smith, Calif.	.000	1	0	0	0	0	0	0	0	0	0	0	0	0	0	0	0	0
Dade, Calif	.000	1	0	0	0	0	0	0	0	0	0	0	0	0	0	0	0	0
Lopez, Calif	.000	1	0	0	0	0	0	0	0	0	0	0	1	0	0	0	0	0
Nordbrook, Bal-Cal	.000	1	0	0	0	0	0	0	0	0	0	0	0	0	0	0	0	0
Tanana, Calif	.000	1	0	0	0	0	0	0	0	0	0	0	0	0	0	0	0	0
Griffin, Clev	.000	4	0	0	0	0	0	0	0	0	0	0	0	0	0	0	1	0
Waits, Clev	.000	7	0	3	0	0	0	0	0	0	0	0	0	0	0	0	1	0
Manuel, Det	.000	1	0	0	0	0	0	0	0	0	0	0	0	0	0	0	0	0
Stanley, Det	.000	2	0	1	0	0	0	0	0	0	0	0	0	0	0	0	0	0
Meyer, Det	.000	1	0	0	0	0	0	0	0	0	0	0	0	0	0	0	0	0
Kimm, Det	.000	2	0	1	0	0	0	0	0	0	0	0	0	0	0	0	0	0
Patek, KC	.000	1	0	1	0	0	0	0	0	0	0	0	0	0	0	0	0	0
Fitzmorris, KC	.000	1	0	0	0	0	0	0	0	0	0	0	0	0	0	0	0	0
Hall, KC	.000	2	0	0	0	0	0	0	0	0	0	0	0	0	0	0	0	0
J. G. Thomas, Milw..	.000	1	0	0	0	0	0	0	0	0	0	0	1	0	0	0	0	0
Heidemann, Milw	.000	1	0	0	0	0	0	0	0	0	0	0	0	0	0	0	0	0
Joshua, Milw	.000	1	0	1	0	0	0	0	0	0	0	0	0	0	0	0	0	0
Lezcano, Milw	.000	3	0	0	0	0	0	0	0	0	0	0	0	0	0	0	0	0
McKay, Minn	.000	1	0	0	0	0	0	0	0	0	0	0	0	0	0	0	0	0
Gomez, Minn	.000	1	0	0	0	0	0	0	0	0	0	0	0	0	0	0	0	0
Hopkins, Oak	.000	2	0	0	0	0	0	0	0	0	0	0	0	0	0	0	1	0
Lintz, Oak	.000	19	0	5	0	0	0	0	0	0	1	0	1	0	0	9	2	0

OFFICIAL AMERICAN LEAGUE FIELDING AVERAGES

CLUB FIELDING

Club	Pct.	G.	PO.	A.	E.	TC.	DP.	TP.	PB.
Baltimore	.982	162	4406	1870	118	6394	157	0	7
Cleveland	.980	159	4296	1710	121	6127	159	1	10
New York	.980	159	4365	1824	126	6315	141	0	16
Chicago	.979	161	4344	1793	130	6267	155	0	5
Kansas City	.978	162	4417	1858	139	6414	147	0	9
Boston	.978	162	4374	1761	141	6276	148	0	8
Oakland	.977	161	4378	1821	144	6343	130	0	11
California	.977	162	4432	1840	150	6422	139	0	15
Texas	.976	162	4416	1807	156	6379	142	0	11
Milwaukee	.975	161	4306	1718	152	6176	160	0	17
Detroit	.974	161	4294	1961	168	6423	161	0	7
Minnesota	.973	162	4377	1823	172	6372	182	1	11
Totals	.977		52405	21786	1717	75908	1821	2	127

INDIVIDUAL FIELDING

(Position Leader in Capitals)

FIRST BASEMEN

*Throws lefthanded.

Player—Club	Pct.	G.	PO.	A.	E.	DP.
McMullen, Oak.	1.000	26	204	8	0	19
Fairly, Oak.*	1.000	15	121	10	0	10
Lis, Cleve.	1.000	17	107	8	0	10
Carty, Cleve.	1.000	12	79	3	0	8
DeCinces, Balt.	1.000	11	45	5	0	1
SPENCER, Chi.*	.998	143	1206	112	2	116
Yastrzemski, Bos.	.998	94	829	52	2	78
Solaita, 5 K.C.-54 Calif.*	.996	59	485	57	2	33
L. May, Balt.	.996	94	722	62	3	61
Mayberry, K.C.*	.996	160	1484	105	7	132
Tenace, Oak.	.995	70	577	31	3	47
Fregosi, Tex.	.995	26	183	14	1	20
Meyer, Det.	.994	19	168	10	1	15
Chambliss, N.Y.	.994	155	1440	109	9	123
Cooper, Bos.*	.994	66	600	42	4	49

Player—Club	Pct.	G.	PO.	A.	E.	DP.
Thompson, Det.*	.994	117	1157	88	8	104
Briggs, Calif.*	.993	44	274	23	2	32
Stanley, Det.	.992	17	117	9	1	10
Gonzalez, Cleve.*	.992	15	116	8	1	7
Melton, Calif.	.992	30	220	15	2	20
Howard, Cleve.	.991	32	211	20	2	20
Scott, Milw.	.991	155	1393	107	13	133
Muser, Balt.*	.991	109	683	62	7	65
Bochte, Calif.*	.991	59	489	39	5	37
Carew, Minn.	.989	152	1394	108	16	149
Powell, Cleve.	.987	89	698	61	10	76
Baylor, Oak.	.987	69	629	44	9	40
Hargrove, Tex.*	.984	141	1222	110	21	103
L. Johnson, Chi.	.983	34	210	18	4	20
Kusick, Minn.	.977	23	109	17	3	16
Hegan, Milw.*	.969	10	57	6	2	8

(Fewer Than Ten Games)

Player—Club	Pct.	G.	PO.	A.	E.	DP.
Johnson, Bos.	1.000	5	30	1	0	3
Ault, Tex.*	1.000	4	23	0	0	1
Freehan, Det.	1.000	2	16	6	0	2
Crowley, Balt.	1.000	1	13	2	0	1
Rudi, Oak.	1.000	2	12	1	0	2
Fosse, Cleve.	1.000	3	10	1	0	1
D. Nelson, K.C.	1.000	3	9	2	0	3
Robinson, Cleve.	1.000	2	10	0	0	1
C. May, N.Y.	1.000	1	9	0	0	0
Garrett, Calif.	1.000	1	7	0	0	1
Bell, Cleve.	1.000	2	5	1	0	0
Wathan, K.C.	1.000	3	6	0	0	0
Pruitt, Cleve.	1.000	1	5	0	0	0
Sutherland, Milw.	1.000	2	5	0	0	0
Alomar, N.Y.	1.000	1	3	1	0	0
Davis, Calif.	1.000	1	4	0	0	0
Ewing, Chi.	1.000	1	4	0	0	0

Player—Club	Pct.	G.	PO.	A.	E.	DP.
Petrocelli, Bos.	1.000	1	4	0	0	0
Quirk, K.C.	1.000	2	3	0	0	1
Stein, Chi.	1.000	1	3	0	0	0
Ashby, Cleve.	1.000	2	1	1	0	0
Harper, Balt.	1.000	1	2	0	0	0
Rojas, K.C.	1.000	1	1	1	0	0
Stillman, Balt.*	1.000	2	2	0	0	0
Essian, Chi.	1.000	2	1	0	0	0
Oglivie, Det.*	.990	9	98	1	1	13
Baker, Bos.	.981	8	48	3	1	6
Velez, N.Y.	.978	8	43	1	1	4
Gross, Oak.	.966	3	27	1	1	2
Lowenstein, Cleve.	.955	9	81	3	4	8
Kuiper, Cleve.	.920	5	21	2	2	3
Hansen, Milw.*	.000	1	0	0	0	0
Johnson, Milw.	.000	1	0	0	0	0

TRIPLE PLAY: Howard.

SECOND BASEMEN

Player—Club	Pct.	G.	PO.	A.	E.	DP.	Player—Club	Pct.	G.	PO.	A.	E.	DP.
Rojas, K.C.	1.000	40	48	45	0	11	D. Nelson, K.C.	.975	46	70	88	4	14
Heidemann, Milw.	1.000	24	44	44	0	17	Garner, Oak.	.975	159	378	465	22	91
Thompson, Tex.	1.000	14	18	36	0	4	Randolph, N.Y.	.974	124	307	415	19	87
Dauer, Balt.	1.000	10	22	22	0	7	White, K.C.	.973	130	255	387	18	75
Nordbrook,							Guerrero, Calif.	.973	41	80	97	5	19
14 Balt.-1 Calif.	1.000	15	7	4	0	1	Randle, Tex.	.971	113	291	319	18	63
DeCinces, Balt.	.989	17	49	44	1	11	Sutherland,						
Griffin, Bos.	.989	44	77	98	2	15	42 Det.-45 Milw.	.970	87	156	204	11	52
Terrell, Minn.	.988	31	37	46	1	12	Alomar, N.Y.	.970	38	85	108	6	17
KUIPER, Cleve.	.987	128	300	365	9	92	Randall, Minn.	.969	153	327	423	24	124
Grich, Balt.	.985	140	389	400	12	91	Blanks, Cleve.	.966	46	93	104	7	25
Brohamer, Chi.	.984	117	263	334	10	74	Smalley, Tex.	.963	38	82	99	7	19
Johnson, Milw.	.980	100	161	222	8	42	Garcia,						
Doyle, Bos.	.977	113	209	311	12	67	39 Milw.-77 Det.	.962	116	242	314	22	79
Remy, Calif.	.977	133	279	406	16	77	Stein, Chi.	.960	58	118	143	11	34
Scrivener, Det.	.976	43	86	120	5	22	Manuel, Det.	.921	47	36	57	8	8
Dillard, Bos.	.976	17	32	48	2	10							

(Fewer Than Ten Games)

Player—Club	Pct.	G.	PO.	A.	E.	DP.	Player—Club	Pct.	G.	PO.	A.	E.	DP.
Petrocelli, Bos.	1.000	5	9	13	0	4	Lintz, Oak.	1.000	5	2	2	0	0
Sandt, Oak.	1.000	9	7	11	0	1	Wohlford, K.C.	1.000	1	1	2	0	1
Bannister, Chi.	1.000	4	4	12	0	2	McMullen, Oak.	1.000	1	0	1	0	0
Tovar, N.Y.	1.000	3	4	8	0	2	Pape, Tex.	1.000	1	1	0	0	0
Yancy, Chi.	1.000	3	8	4	0	3	Cubbage,						
Pryor, Tex.	1.000	3	4	6	0	1	5 Tex.-2 Minn.	.947	7	9	9	1	3
Gomez, Minn.	1.000	8	4	5	0	1	Stanley, Det.	.833	2	3	2	1	1
Jackson, Calif.	1.000	7	5	3	0	1	Stanley, N.Y.	.800	3	3	1	1	0
Bevacqua, Milw.	1.000	2	0	6	0	0	Beniquez, Tex.	.500	1	1	0	1	0
Carew, Minn.	1.000	7	4	2	0	0	Heise, Bos.	.000	1	0	0	0	0
Dade, Calif.	1.000	2	3	3	0	0							

THIRD BASEMEN

Player—Club	Pct.	G.	PO.	A.	E.	DP.	Player—Club	Pct.	G.	PO.	A.	E.	DP.
Johnson, Milw.	1.000	17	4	15	0	0	Bell, Cleve.	.956	158	104	330	20	23
Gantner, Milw.	.982	24	17	37	1	3	McMullen, Oak.	.952	35	10	30	2	1
RODRIGUEZ, Det.	.978	128	120	280	9	21	Jackson, Calif.	.950	114	85	222	16	19
Thompson, Tex.	.976	39	28	54	2	3	Brett, K.C.	.948	157	140	335	26	22
Stanley, N.Y.	.975	11	7	32	1	3	Stein, Chi.	.943	58	35	98	8	5
Mankowski, Det.	.971	23	20	47	2	8	DeCinces, Balt.	.941	109	96	208	19	9
Bell, Chi.	.970	67	70	124	6	10	Cubbage,						
Chalk, Calif.	.970	49	35	94	4	9	1 Tex.-99 Minn.	.940	100	71	209	18	22
Robinson, Balt.	.969	71	59	126	6	11	Hobson, Bos.	.936	76	60	146	14	11
Heise, Bos.	.968	22	11	19	1	1	Orta, Chi.	.930	49	31	102	10	9
Petrocelli, Bos.	.967	73	57	120	6	11	Howell, Tex.	.926	130	103	245	28	20
Melton, Calif.	.966	21	7	21	1	2	Terrell, Minn.	.923	26	14	34	4	6
Nettles, N.Y.	.965	158	137	383	19	30	Dillard, Bos.	.918	18	16	29	4	4
Bando, Oak.	.962	155	125	304	17	26	McKay, Minn.	.911	41	25	77	10	13
Heidemann, Milw.	.962	40	30	45	3	2	Braun, Minn.	.897	16	7	28	4	3
Money, Milw.	.958	103	96	202	13	21	Quirk, K.C.	.875	11	4	10	2	0

(Fewer Than Ten Games)

Player—Club	Pct.	G.	PO.	A.	E.	DP.	Player—Club	Pct.	G.	PO.	A.	E.	DP.
Brohamer, Chi.	1.000	1	2	4	0	1	Alomar, N.Y.	.800	3	2	2	1	0
Crosby, Cleve.	1.000	1	0	2	0	0	Fregosi, Tex.	.800	5	0	4	1	0
Gomez, Minn.	1.000	4	0	2	0	0	J. G. Thomas, Milw.	.500	1	1	0	1	0
Pryor, Tex.	1.000	1	0	2	0	0	Pape, Tex.	.500	4	0	1	1	0
Bernhardt, N.Y.	1.000	1	0	1	0	0	Grich, Balt.	.000	2	0	0	0	0
Blanks, Cleve.	1.000	2	0	1	0	0	Sandt, Oak.	.000	2	0	0	0	0
Moore, Milw.	1.000	1	0	1	0	0	Dade, Calif.	.000	1	0	0	0	0
Randle, Tex.	1.000	1	0	1	0	0	Torres, Calif.	.000	1	0	0	0	0
Pruitt, Cleve.	.929	6	3	10	1	0	Bannister, Chi.	.000	1	0	0	0	0
Scrivener, Det.	.923	5	3	9	1	1	Essian, Chi.	.000	1	0	0	0	0
Harrah, Tex.	.923	5	4	8	1	1	Ashby, Cleve.	.000	1	0	0	0	0
Rojas, K.C.	.909	6	4	6	1	2	Velez, N.Y.	.000	1	0	0	0	0

SHORTSTOPS

Player—Club	Pct.	G.	PO.	A.	E.	DP.
Garcia, Balt.	1.000	11	15	27	0	7
Quirk, K.C.	1.000	12	2	4	0	1
Gomez, Minn.	.988	24	32	51	1	16
DUFFY, Cleve.	.982638	132	222	344	10	83
Stanley, N.Y.	.982630	110	145	251	7	36
Belanger, Balt.	.982	153	239	545	14	97
Miley, Calif.	.981	14	22	30	1	9
Thompson, 34 Minn.-10 Tex.	.981	44	72	130	4	28
Nordbrook, 12 Balt.-4 Calif.	.978	16	16	29	1	5
Blanks, Cleve.	.977	56	59	109	4	28
Dent, Chi.	.976	158	279	468	18	96
Chalk, Calif.	.971	102	141	293	13	45
Campaneris, Oak.	.969	149	231	490	23	66
Mason, N.Y.	.966	93	128	245	13	47
Sandt, Oak.	.966	29	37	49	3	10
Smalley, 5 Tex.-103 Minn.	.966	108	192	348	19	71
Veryzer, Det.	.966	97	164	313	17	53
Ramirez, Calif.	.966	30	30	82	4	11
White, K.C.	.964	37	41	92	5	14
Yount, Milw.	.963	161	290	510	31	104
Patek, K.C.	.962	143	233	426	26	87
Scrivener, Det.	.961	37	48	101	6	24
Terrell, Minn.	.959	16	28	42	3	9
Burleson, Bos.	.957	152	274	478	34	88
Harrah, Tex.	.955	146	290	473	36	81
Wagner, Det.	.947	39	60	135	11	25
Guerrero, Calif.	.932	41	49	75	9	13
Bannister, Chi.	.886	14	8	23	4	5
Dillard, Bos.	.875	12	10	25	5	7
Smith, Calif.	.625	10	0	5	3	1

(Fewer Than Ten Games)

Player—Club	Pct.	G.	PO.	A.	E.	DP.
Brett, K.C.	1.000	4	6	15	0	1
Manuel, Det.	1.000	4	4	7	0	0
Alomar, N.Y.	1.000	6	5	3	0	1
Bando, Oak.	1.000	5	2	6	0	1
Stein, Chi.	1.000	1	2	2	0	0
Johnson, Milw.	1.000	1	2	1	0	0
McKay, Minn.	1.000	2	2	0	0	0
Stanley, Det.	1.000	3	0	2	0	0
DeCinces, Balt.	1.000	2	1	0	0	0
Hampton, Calif.	1.000	1	0	1	0	0
Nettles, N.Y.	1.000	1	0	1	0	0
Petrocelli, Bos.	1.000	1	0	1	0	0
Pape, Tex.	.968	6	8	22	1	4
Heise, Tex.	.909	9	16	24	4	6
Klutts, N.Y.	.875	2	4	3	1	0
Griffin, Cleve.	.750	6	1	2	1	0
Bailor, Balt.	.000	1	0	0	0	0
Money, Milw.	.000	1	0	0	0	0
Pryor, Tex.	.000	1	0	0	0	0

TRIPLE PLAYS: Duffy, Gomez.

OUTFIELDERS

Player—Club	Pct.	G.	PO.	A.	E.	DP.
Carbo, 1 Bos.-33 Milw.	1.000	34	72	5	0	1
Coggins, 2 N.Y.-26 Chi.°	1.000	28	48	1	0	0
Pruitt, Cleve.	1.000	26	41	3	0	1
Hegan, Milw.°	1.000	20	31	0	0	0
Alexander, Oak.	1.000	23	23	0	0	0
Maddox, N.Y.	1.000	13	21	2	0	1
Jones, K.C.°	1.000	17	21	0	0	0
Nordhagen, Chi.	1.000	10	20	1	0	0
Rosario, Milw.	1.000	12	20	0	0	0
Alvarez, Calif.	1.000	11	12	1	0	0
Muser, Balt.°	1.000	12	10	1	0	0
Shopay, Balt.	1.000	11	6	0	0	0
EVANS, Bos.	.994	145	324	15	2	4
Collins, Calif.°	.994	71	160	3	1	0
Otis, K.C.	.992	152	373	5	3	1
Lemon, Chi.	.992	131	353	12	3	1
Miller, Bos.°	.991	82	220	4	2	1
Moates, Tex.°	.991	66	106	4	1	2
Jones, Calif.°	.990	62	98	6	1	0
Torres, Calif.	.990	105	195	5	2	0
Rudi, Oak.	.989	126	258	6	3	2
Bumbry, Balt.	.989	116	251	9	3	2
Bostock, Minn.	.988	124	320	10	4	2
Bochte, Calif.°	.988	86	162	3	2	1
Bannister, Chi.	.988	43	80	1	1	0
Meyer, Det.	.988	47	76	4	1	1
White, N.Y.	.987	156	380	9	5	1
Burroughs, Tex.	.987	155	289	12	4	3
Hendrick, Cleve.	.987	146	288	13	4	6
Clines, Tex.	.987	103	215	9	3	1
Brye, Minn.	.987	78	147	1	2	0
Manning, Det.	.987	136	359	8	5	1
Oglivie, Det.°	.986	64	136	7	2	0
Beniquez, Tex.	.986	141	410	18	6	3
J. G. Thomas Milw.	.986	94	210	4	3	0
Rivers, N.Y.°	.986	136	407	6	6	0
Cowens, K.C.	.986	148	329	13	5	3
Stanton, Calif.	.985	79	128	1	2	0
Spikes, Cleve.	.985	98	185	7	3	0
Lynn, Bos.°	.984	128	367	13	6	4
Hisle, Minn.	.984	154	361	16	6	1
Grieve, Tex.	.983	52	112	4	2	2
Singleton, Balt.	.983	134	278	9	5	2
Joshua, Milw.°	.982	105	268	10	5	4
Piniella, N.Y.	.982	49	106	4	2	0
Gamble, N.Y.	.981	104	199	10	4	3
Baylor, Oak.	.981	76	152	1	3	0
Yastrzemski, Bos.°	.980	51	93	3	2	0
Blair, Balt.	.979	139	327	6	7	1
Poquette, K.C.	.979	98	188	1	4	0
Smith, Cleve.	.979	50	90	4	2	0
Velez, N.Y.	.979	24	46	1	1	1
Bradford, Chi.	.978	48	91	0	2	0
North, Oak.	.978	144	397	8	9	1
Moore, Milw.	.978	28	42	2	1	0
Garr, Chi.	.978	125	254	7	6	2
Bonds, Calif.	.977	98	199	9	5	3
Wohlford, K.C.	.975	93	189	6	5	0
Bowling, Milw.	.975	13	38	1	1	1
Sharp, Milw.°	.975	56	108	7	3	2
Hairston, Chi.	.973	40	71	1	2	0
LeFlore, Det.	.973	132	381	14	11	1

OUTFIELDERS—Continued

Player—Club	Pct.	G.	PO.	A.	E.	DP.
Lezcano, Milw.	.973	142	345	10	10	3
Darwin, 21 Milw.-17 Bos.	.972	38	68	2	2	0
Lowenstein, Cleve.	.972	61	97	7	3	1
Braun, Minn.	.971	32	64	4	2	0
Randle, Tex.	.971	30	63	4	2	0
Orta, Chi.	.971	77	156	9	5	1
McRae, K.C.	.970	31	63	2	2	0
Staub, Det.	.970	126	218	8	7	3
C. May, 9 Chi.-7 N.Y.	.970	16	32	0	1	0
Stanley, Det.	.969	38	60	2	2	0
Ford, Minn.	.968	139	267	6	9	1
Rice, Bos.	.967	98	199	8	7	0

Player—Club	Pct.	G.	PO.	A.	E.	DP.
Briggs, Calif.°	.967	40	84	3	3	1
Lahoud, 26 Calif.-5 Tex.°	.964	31	54	0	2	0
R. Jackson, Balt.°	.964	121	284	8	11	3
Washington, Oak.°	.963	126	276	10	11	2
Lane, Det.	.960	15	23	1	1	0
Tovar, Oak.	.958	20	23	0	1	0
D. Thomas, Milw.	.955	32	60	3	3	1
Johnson, Det.	.954	90	159	7	8	1
Mora, Balt.	.951	31	55	3	3	0
Kelly, Chi.°	.950	26	37	1	2	0
Munson, N.Y.	.818	11	9	0	2	0

(Fewer Than Ten Games)

Player—Club	Pct.	G.	PO.	A.	E.	DP.
Nyman, Chi.°	1.000	7	13	0	0	0
Murray, N.Y.	1.000	7	9	1	0	0
McMullen, Oak.	1.000	5	8	0	0	0
Dempsey, 4 N.Y.-3 Balt.	1.000	7	6	1	0	0
Gonzalez, Cleve.°	1.000	7	7	0	0	0
Jones, Chi.°	1.000	8	7	0	0	0
Woods, Oak.	1.000	4	7	0	0	0
Mangual, Oak.	1.000	7	4	1	0	0
Locklear, N.Y.	1.000	3	4	0	0	0
Lopez, Calif.	1.000	4	4	0	0	0
Gross, Oak.	1.000	2	3	0	0	0
Stein, Chi.	1.000	1	3	0	0	0
Terrell, Minn.	1.000	6	3	0	0	0
Carty, Cleve.	1.000	1	2	0	0	0
Aaron, Milw.	1.000	1	1	0	0	0

Player—Club	Pct.	G.	PO.	A.	E.	DP.
Jackson, Calif.	1.000	4	1	0	0	0
Robinson, Cleve.	1.000	1	1	0	0	0
Dineen, N.Y.°	.900	4	9	0	1	0
Walling, Oak.°	.889	3	8	0	1	0
Wilson, K.C.	.875	6	6	1	1	0
Bernhardt, N.Y.	.800	4	4	0	1	0
Dade, Calif.	.750	4	2	1	1	0
Harper, Balt.	.000	1	0	0	0	0
L. Johnson, Chi.	.000	1	0	0	1	0
Howard, Cleve.	.000	2	0	0	0	0
Yount, Milw.	.000	1	0	0	0	0
Gomez, Minn.	.000	1	0	0	0	0
Alomar, N.Y.	.000	1	0	0	0	0
Whitfield, N.Y.	.000	1	0	0	0	0
Lintz, Oak.	.000	3	0	0	0	0
Williams, Oak.	.000	1	0	0	0	0

CATCHERS

Player—Club	Pct.	G.	PO.	A.	E.	DP.	PB.
Fahey, Tex.	.993	38	126	19	1	3	3
SUNDBERG, Tex..	.9914	140	719	96	7	11	6
Martinez, KC	.9913	94	420	40	4	4	5
Dempsey, 9 NY-58 Balt ..	.988	67	302	39	4	8	3
Downing, Chi	.988	93	450	38	6	4	1
Varney, Chi	.988	14	76	4	1	0	2
Ashby, Clev	.987	86	475	51	7	7	3
Healy, 6 KC-31 NY	.987	37	134	20	2	0	3
Fosse, Clev	.987	85	483	42	7	9	4
Duncan, Balt	.985	93	371	35	6	9	2
Wathan, KC	.984	23	57	4	1	1	0
Fisk, Bos	.984	133	649	73	12	9	7
Montgomery, Bos..	.983	30	106	12	2	2	1
Tenace, Oak	.983	65	263	25	5	3	4
Freehan, Det	.983	61	312	28	6	2	2
Hendricks, 27 Balt-18 NY	.982	45	147	17	3	2	3

Player—Club	Pct.	G.	PO.	A.	E.	DP.	PB.
Newman, Oak	.981	43	140	18	3	1	0
Munson, NY	.981	121	537	78	12	8	12
Humphrey, Calif	.980	71	397	42	9	4	6
Etchebarren, Calif	.980	102	539	46	12	7	3
Stinson, KC	.979	79	304	30	7	4	3
Wynegar, Minn	.978	137	650	78	16	6	10
Borgmann, Minn ..	.976	24	110	13	3	1	1
Porter, Milw	.975	111	491	52	14	7	12
Haney, Oak	.974	87	290	45	9	2	5
Essian, Chi	.974	77	319	53	10	10	2
Garrett, Calif	.974	15	36	1	1	1	3
Kimm, Det	.970	61	256	33	9	5	3
Moore, Milw	.969	49	207	42	8	1	4
Hosley, Oak	.968	37	79	13	3	0	2
Roof, 12 Minn-4 Chi..	.967	16	76	12	3	3	0
Herrmann, Calif....	.954	27	74	9	4	1	3
Wockenfuss, Det ..	.941	59	221	19	15	5	2
Kusnyer, Milw	.938	14	41	4	3	2	1

(Fewer Than Ten Games)

Player—Club	Pct.	G.	PO.	A.	E.	DP.	PB.
May, Det.	1.000	6	33	5	0	0	0
Pruitt, Clev	1.000	6	24	3	0	1	1
Whitt, Bos	1.000	8	24	0	0	0	0
Ellis, Tex	1.000	7	21	2	0	0	2
Shopay, Balt	1.000	1	8	1	0	0	1

Player—Club	Pct.	G.	PO.	A.	E.	DP.	PB.
Enright, Chi	1.000	2	4	0	0	0	0
Hampton, Calif	1.000	2	2	1	0	1	0
Merchant, Bos	1.000	1	1	0	0	0	0
Cerone, Clev	.963	6	25	1	1	1	2
Nordhagen, Chi	.944	5	15	2	1	0	0

TRIPLE PLAY: Borgmann.

PITCHERS

Player—Club	Pct.	G.	PO.	A.	E.	DP.
FIDRYCH, Det	1.000	31	19	59	0	4
Blyleven,						
12 Minn-24 Tex ..	1.000	36	22	44	0	4
Wise, Bos..............	1.000	34	15	39	0	5
Ruhle, Det	1.000	32	14	28	0	1
Alexander,						
11 Balt-19 NY ...	1.000	30	11	30	0	1
Splittorff, KC°	1.000	26	9	30	0	5
Jenkins, Bos.........	1.000	30	13	23	0	3
Burgmeier, Minn°...	1.000	57	8	26	0	2
Mingori, KC°	1.000	55	9	24	0	1
Bare, Det	1.000	30	6	25	0	2
Briles, Tex	1.000	32	10	18	0	0
F. Martinez,						
11 NY-28 Balt°..	1.000	39	11	15	0	1
Foucault, Tex	1.000	46	4	20	0	3
P. Mitchell, Oak	1.000	26	7	17	0	0
Buskey, Clev	1.000	39	4	18	0	2
Jones, Bos°	1.000	24	8	13	0	2
Boggs, Tex	1.000	13	7	10	0	1
Decker, Minn	1.000	13	4	13	0	0
Flanagan, Balt°	1.000	20	4	13	0	0
Jefferson, Chi.......	1.000	19	3	14	0	2
Gura, KC°	1.000	20	4	12	0	2
Abbott, Oak	1.000	19	3	12	0	0
Carroll, Chi	1.000	29	0	15	0	2
Verhoeven, Calif ...	1.000	21	4	10	0	0
Littell, KC	1.000	60	3	9	0	1
Peterson,						
9 Clev-4 Tex°...	1.000	13	0	12	0	0
Castro, Milw	1.000	39	0	11	0	2
Terpko, Tex	1.000	32	2	8	0	0
Albury, Minn°	1.000	23	1	8	0	0
Champion, Milw	1.000	10	2	6	0	0
Frisella, Milw	1.000	32	1	7	0	0
Johnson, Minn	1.000	18	1	7	0	0
Holdsworth, Balt ...	1.000	16	4	3	0	0
G. Jackson,						
13 Balt-21 NY°..	1.000	34	1	6	0	0
Scott, Calif°	1.000	33	2	4	0	0
Brewer, Calif°	1.000	13	2	2	0	0
Hoerner, Tex°	1.000	41	0	3	0	0
Bruno, KC	1.000	12	0	1	0	0
Ross, Calif	.987	34	23	55	1	1
Palmer, Balt	.987	40	27	49	1	2
Tanana, Calif°	.983	34	12	45	1	1
C. B. Johnson, Chi ..	.981	32	22	30	1	0
Travers, Milw°	.978	34	13	31	1	4
Colborn, Milw........	.977	32	11	32	1	4
Crawford, Det°	.976	32	1	40	1	2
Figueroa, NY	.975	36	16	23	1	0
Thomas, Clev	.974	37	12	26	1	2
Blue, Oak°	.974	37	3	34	1	2
Bahnsen, Oak	.973	35	13	23	1	0
Brown, Clev	.971	32	13	21	1	2
Umbarger, Tex°	.971	30	4	30	1	3
Campbell, Minn	.970	78	12	20	1	1
Hassler,						
14 Calif-19 KC°	.969	33	4	27	1	3
Fingers, Oak.........	.968	70	4	26	1	2
Lindblad, Oak°......	.968	65	9	21	1	1
Eckersley, Clev	.967	36	9	20	1	1
Pattin, KC	.967	44	9	20	1	1
Bosman, Oak	.966	27	9	19	1	2
Hunter, NY	.964	36	24	30	2	2
Grimsley, Balt°	.964	28	8	19	1	0
Augustine, Milw°	.964	39	9	18	1	1
Barrios, Chi	.960	35	10	14	1	3
Grilli, Det	.958	36	5	18	1	1
Fitzmorris, KC	.958	35	19	49	3	4
Garland, Balt	.955	38	27	37	3	2
Slaton, Milw..........	.953	38	18	43	3	2
Holtzman,						
13 Balt-21 NY°..	.953	34	19	42	3	4
Norris, Oak	.952	24	11	29	2	1
Cuellar, Balt°	.952	26	2	18	1	1
Pole, Bos	.950	31	6	13	1	0
Goltz, Minn	.946	36	18	35	3	3
Bird, KC...............	.946	39	14	21	2	1
Perry, Tex	.946	32	11	24	2	1
Forster, Chi°	.939	29	5	26	2	0
Brett,						
2 NY-27 Chi°	.939	29	11	35	3	0
Hartzell, Calif	.938	37	13	32	3	1
Gossage, Chi	.938	31	18	27	3	1
Waits, Clev°	.938	26	10	20	2	2
Hiller, Det°	.938	56	2	13	1	0
Broberg, Milw	.938	20	4	11	1	0
Roberts, Det°	.937	36	6	53	4	6
Willoughby, Bos	.935	54	7	22	2	1
Bibby, Clev	.935	34	10	19	2	2
Todd, Oak	.935	49	7	22	2	1
Dobson, Clev	.933	35	14	28	3	3
House, Bos°	.933	36	3	11	1	0
Ellis, NY	.929	32	19	20	3	0
Hamilton, Chi°	.929	45	4	9	1	1
Singer,						
10 Tex-26 Minn ..	.927	36	7	31	3	0
Lee, Bos°	.923	24	2	22	2	1
Hargan, Tex	.923	35	6	18	2	1
Tiant, Bos	.920	38	12	34	4	4
Murphy,						
15 Mil-37 Bos	.920	52	7	16	2	1
Hood, Clev°	.917	33	10	12	2	0
Lemanczyk, Det	.917	20	8	14	2	0
Tidrow, NY	.917	47	2	9	1	0
Monge, Calif°	.913	32	6	15	2	1
Torrez, Oak	.903	39	19	37	6	4
Bane, Minn°	.900	17	5	4	1	0
Bacsik, Min°	.900	23	3	6	1	0
R. May,						
11 NY-24 Balt°..	.898	35	13	31	5	3
Kirkwood, Calif	.898	28	18	26	5	3
Cleveland, Bos	.897	41	10	25	4	4
Pagan,						
7 NY-20 Balt......	.889	27	6	2	1	0
Hall, KC°	.889	31	1	7	1	0
Vuckovich, Chi	.880	33	3	19	3	0
Redfern, Minn	.880	23	8	14	3	1
Kern, Clev	.875	50	7	14	3	2
Coleman, Det	.875	12	2	19	3	2
Lyle, NY°	.875	64	3	11	2	1
Drago, Calif	.875	43	3	4	1	0
Knapp, Chi...........	.875	11	2	5	1	1
Ryan, Calif...........	.873	39	14	34	7	1
Hughes, Minn	.872	37	13	21	5	2
Busby, KC	.864	13	10	9	3	0
Rodriguez, Milw	.857	45	8	16	4	2
Leonard, Calif	.850	35	11	23	6	2
Miller, Balt	.846	49	1	10	2	1
Barr, Tex°	.833	20	1	14	3	1
Laxton, Det°	.818	26	4	5	2	0

PITCHERS—Continued

Player—Club	Pct.	G.	PO.	A.	E.	DP.	Player—Club	Pct.	G.	PO.	A.	E.	DP.
LaRoche, Clev°	.800	61	3	9	3	0	Sadecki,						
Luebber, Minn	.786	38	5	17	6	1	3 KC-36 Milw°	.600	39	1	2	2	0

(Fewer Than Ten Games)

Player—Club	Pct.	G.	PO.	A.	E.	DP.	Player—Club	Pct.	G.	PO.	A.	E.	DP.
Wood, Chi°	1.000	7	1	12	0	0	Skok, Tex°	1.000	9	0	1	0	0
Kreuger, Bos°	1.000	8	1	8	0	1	York, NY	1.000	3	0	1	0	0
MacCormack. Det	1.000	9	4	3	0	0	Kravec, Chi°	.875	9	0	7	1	0
J. D. Martinez, Bal°	1.000	4	3	4	0	0	Haas, Milw	.875	5	2	5	1	1
Monroe, Chi	1.000	8	5	1	0	0	Beare, Milw	.857	6	2	4	1	1
McGregor, Balt°	1.000	3	2	3	0	0	Overy, Calif	.667	5	0	2	1	0
Guidry, NY°	1.000	7	0	4	0	0	Odom, Chi	.600	8	1	2	2	0
Perzanowski, Tex	1.000	5	2	2	0	0	Dunning, Calif	.500	4	0	1	1	0
Sprague, Milw	1.000	3	0	4	0	1	C. Mitchell, Oak	.500	1	0	1	1	0
Hausman, Milw	1.000	3	1	2	0	0	Wheelock, Calif	.000	2	0	0	0	0
Austin, Milw°	1.000	3	0	2	0	1	Kucek, Chi	.000	2	0	0	0	0
Barker, Tex	1.000	2	0	2	0	0	Otten, Chi	.000	2	0	0	0	0
Cram, KC	1.000	4	2	0	0	0	Raich, Clev	.000	1	0	0	0	0
R. Nelson, KC	1.000	3	1	1	0	0	McClure, KC°	.000	8	0	0	0	0
Parker, Clev	1.000	3	1	1	0	0	Sanders, KC	.000	3	0	0	0	0
Glynn, Det°	1.000	5	0	1	0	0	Pazik, Minn°	.000	5	0	0	0	0
Kobel, Milw°	1.000	3	0	1	0	0	Batton, Oak	.000	2	0	0	0	0

TRIPLE PLAY: Thomas.

OFFICIAL AMERICAN LEAGUE PITCHING AVERAGES

Compiled by Sports Information Center, No. Quincy, Mass.

CLUB PITCHING

Club	ERA	G	CG	Sv	ShO	IP	H	AB	R	ER	HR	SH	SF	Tot. BB	Int. BB	SO	WP	Bk.
New York	3.19	159	62	37	15	1455	1300	5391	575	516	97	53	57	448	16	674	39	3
Kansas City	3.21	162	41	35	12	1472⅔	1356	5499	611	525	83	49	61	493	31	735	29	5
Oakland	3.26	161	39	29	15	1459⅓	1412	5538	598	528	96	83	42	415	42	711	40	2
Baltimore	3.32	162	59	23	16	1468⅔	1396	5479	598	541	80	80	63	489	40	678	37	3
California	3.36	162	64	17	15	1477¼	1323	5479	631	551	95	74	40	553	50	992	27	2
Texas	3.45	162	63	15	15	1472	1464	5582	598	565	106	90	45	461	31	773	46	9
Cleveland	3.47	159	30	46	11	1432	1361	5335	615	552	80	77	47	533	31	928	41	7
Boston	3.52	162	49	27	13	1458	1495	5606	652	570	109	58	46	409	48	673	33	1
Milwaukee	3.64	161	45	27	11	1435⅓	1406	5409	660	581	99	68	51	567	62	677	53	6
Minnesota	3.69	162	29	23	11	1459	1421	5483	655	599	89	53	51	567	39	762	61	12
Detroit	3.87	161	55	20	12	1431⅓	1426	5421	709	615	101	72	55	610	38	738	45	4
Chicago	4.25	161	54	22	10	1448	1460	5487	745	684	87	61	61	600	27	802	40	6
Totals	3.52		590	321	161	17468⅓	16820	65711	7753	6828	1122	818	624	6128	471	9143	491	60

Note—Totals for earned runs for several clubs do not agree with the composite totals for all pitchers of each respective club due to instances in which provisions of Section 10.18 (i) of the Scoring Rules were applied. The following differences are to be noted: Cleveland pitchers add to 554; Detroit, 616; Minnesota, 603; Texas, 567.

PITCHERS' RECORDS

(Top Fifteen Qualifiers for Earned-Run Leadership—162 or More Innings)

Pitcher and Club	ERA	W.	L.	Pct.	G.	GS.	CG.	GF.	Sv.	ShO.	IP.	H.	R.	ER.	HR.	SH.	SF.	Tot. BB.	Int. BB.	HB.	SO.	WP.	Bk.
Fidrych, Mark, Detroit	2.34	19	9	.679	31	29	24	0	0	4	250	217	76	65	12	15	8	53	3	3	97	2	0
Blue, Vida, Oakland*	2.36	18	13	.581	37	37	20	0	6	6	298	268	90	78	9	13	5	63	1	1	166	6	1
Tanana, Frank, California*	2.44	19	10	.655	34	34	23	0	0	2	288	212	88	78	23	14	4	73	5	5	261	5	0
Torrez, Michael, Oakland	2.50	16	12	.571	39	39	16	0	0	0	266	231	93	74	15	16	6	87	2	6	115	5	0
Palmer, James, Baltimore	2.51	22	13	.629	40	40	23	0	0	6	315	255	101	88	20	15	8	84	4	8	159	8	0
Garland, Wayne, Baltimore	2.68	20	7	.741	38	25	14	9	1	0	232	224	71	69	14	10	6	64	6	5	113	5	1
Hartzell, Paul, California	2.77	7	4	.636	37	15	7	14	2	2	166	166	64	51	9	6	4	43	7	10	51	0	0
Travers, William, Milwaukee*	2.81	15	16	.484	36	36	15	0	0	3	240	211	92	75	6	21	4	95	10	5	120	7	1
Byleven, Rikalbert, 12 Minn.-24 Tex.	2.87	13	16	.448	36	36	18	0	0	6	298	283	106	95	8	8	5	81	12	6	219	7	2
Ross, Gary, California	3.00	8	10	.444	31	30	0	4	0	0	225	145	89	75	12	9	11	58	6	12	100	0	0
Campbell, William, Minnesota	3.00	17	5	.773	78	0	0	68	20	0	168	147	63	56	9	7	5	58	11	5	115	0	0
Figueroa, Eduardo, New York	3.01	19	10	.655	36	33	19	1	0	0	257	237	101	86	13	13	9	64	2	11	119	4	0
Tiant, Luis, Boston	3.06	21	12	.636	38	38	19	0	0	3	279	274	136	107	15	11	5	64	4	6	131	1	0
Fitzmorris, Alan, Kansas City	3.06	15	11	.577	35	33	8	0	0	2	220	227	89	75	25	6	10	56	5	6	80	6	3
Cleveland, Reginald, Boston	3.07	10	9	.526	41	14	3	10	2	0	170	159	73	58	13	3	5	61	6	4	76	6	0

*Throws lefthanded.

DEPARTMENTAL LEADERS: W—Palmer, 22; L—Ryan, 18; Pct.—Campbell, 773; G—Campbell, 78; GS—Palmer, 40; CG—Fidrych, 24; GF—Campbell, 68; Sv—Lyle, 23; ShO—Ryan, 7; IP—Ryan, 315; H—Slaton, 315; 1256; R—Hunter, Slaton, 126; ER—Hunter, 117; HR—Hunter, 28; SH—Blyleven, 18; SF—Palmer, 14; Tot.BB—Ryan, 183; Int.BB—Murphy, 14; HB—Blyleven, 12; SO—Ryan, 327; WP—Goltz, 15; Bk—Umbarger, 3.

(All Pitchers—Listed Alphabetically)

Pitcher and Club	ERA	W.	L.	Pct.	G.	GS	CG	GF	Sv.	ShO	IP.	H.	BFP.	R.	ER.	HR.	SH.	SF.	Tot. BB.	Int. BB.	HB.	SO.	WP.	Bk.
Abbott, Glenn, Oakland	5.52	2	4	.333	19	10	0	4	0	0	62	87	283	41	38	6	3	2	16	4	0	27	3	0
Albury, Victor, Minnesota°	3.60	3	1	.750	23	2	0	11	0	0	50	51	221	22	20	5	3	5	24	2	0	23	4	0
Alexander, Doyle, 11 Balt.-19 N.Y.	3.36	13	9	.591	30	25	7	0	0	3	201	172	812	81	75	12	5	9	63	3	4	58	1	0
Augustine, Gerald, Milwaukee°	3.30	9	12	.429	39	24	6	4	1	0	172	167	716	69	63	6	9	2	56	2	4	59	1	0
Austin, Rick, Milwaukee°	5.40	0	2	.000	3	0	0	3	0	0	5	10	26	3	3	1	0	0	4	0	0	3	0	0
Bacsik, Michael, Texas	5.13	3	2	.600	23	0	0	9	0	0	55	66	251	31	26	3	1	2	26	4	0	21	1	0
Bahnsen, Stanley, Oakland	3.34	8	7	.533	35	17	2	10	3	0	143	124	589	52	53	13	6	4	43	2	2	82	2	0
Bane, Edward, Minnesota°	4.63	4	7	.364	17	15	2	0	0	0	79	92	359	55	45	6	4	1	39	3	0	24	0	0
Barker, Leonard, Texas	5.13	7	8	.467	30	21	1	2	0	0	134	157	594	85	69	13	3	6	51	6	0	59	6	1
Barr, Raymond, Detroit.	2.40	1	0	1.000	20	0	0	5	1	0	15	10	56	7	4	2	0	0	4	1	0	7	0	0
Barr, Steven, Texas°	4.56	2	6	.250	20	10	2	3	0	0	68	70	309	51	42	10	3	3	44	0	0	27	1	0
Barrios, Francisco, Chicago	4.31	5	9	.357	35	14	6	13	3	0	142	136	596	72	68	13	7	1	46	3	0	81	2	0
Batton, Christopher, Oakland	9.00	0	0	.000	2	1	0	1	0	0	5	5	19	4	4	0	0	0	4	0	0	4	0	0
Beare, Gary, Milwaukee	3.29	2	3	.400	5	5	2	0	0	0	41	43	173	16	15	4	1	0	15	0	1	32	0	0
Bibby, James, Cleveland	3.20	13	7	.650	34	27	4	2	0	1	163	162	683	66	58	9	9	8	61	1	3	84	3	0
Bird, J. Douglas, Kansas City	3.36	12	10	.545	39	27	5	6	2	0	198	191	808	90	74	17	13	10	63	6	1	107	3	0
Blue, Vida, Oakland°	2.36	18	13	.581	37	37	20	0	0	6	298	283	1205	90	78	14	18	6	63	3	1	166	1	0
Blyleven, Rikalbert, 12 Minn.-24 Tex.	2.87	13	16	.448	36	36	18	0	0	6	298	283	1225	106	95	14	13	5	81	3	12	219	5	1
Boggs, Thomas, Texas	3.50	1	7	.125	13	13	1	0	0	0	90	87	383	52	35	7	6	2	42	1	1	36	7	0
Bosman, Richard, Oakland	4.10	4	2	.667	27	15	3	6	1	0	112	118	459	54	51	13	9	3	34	3	1	34	1	0
Brett, Kenneth, 2 N.Y.-27 Chi.°	3.28	10	12	.455	29	26	9	2	0	2	203	191	835	92	74	13	6	7	62	4	2	92	2	0
Brewer, James, California°	2.70	3	1	.750	13	0	0	7	1	0	20	20	85	8	6	0	1	1	9	1	0	16	0	0
Briles, Nelson, Texas	3.26	11	9	.550	32	31	7	1	0	0	210	224	879	87	76	17	7	6	47	1	0	98	3	0
Broberg, Peter, Milwaukee	4.99	1	7	.125	13	11	1	1	0	0	92	99	437	59	51	5	5	4	72	1	7	28	6	0
Brown, Jackie, Cleveland	4.25	9	11	.450	32	27	5	1	0	0	180	193	777	94	85	14	8	3	55	4	1	104	2	0
Bruno, Thomas, Kansas City	6.88	1	0	1.000	13	0	0	4	0	0	17	20	80	13	13	1	3	1	29	0	0	11	1	0
Burgmeier, Thomas, Minnesota°	2.50	8	1	.889	57	0	0	22	1	0	115	90	456	36	32	3	14	4	32	7	0	45	3	0
Busby, Steven, Kansas City	4.38	3	3	.500	13	13	1	0	0	0	72	58	323	42	35	11	1	3	49	3	3	29	1	0
Buskey, Thomas, Cleveland	3.64	4	4	.500	39	0	0	20	1	0	94	88	391	42	38	7	4	8	34	8	3	32	2	1
Campbell, William, Minnesota	3.00	17	5	.773	78	0	0	68	20	0	168	145	703	63	56	9	9	7	62	11	2	115	4	0
Carroll, Clay, Chicago	2.57	4	4	.500	29	0	0	29	6	0	70	70	311	26	27	4	1	1	29	5	2	38	2	3
Castro, William, Milwaukee°	3.47	0	6	.000	39	0	0	29	8	0	70	70	291	35	27	3	5	0	19	2	1	23	3	0
Champion, B. Billy, Milwaukee	7.13	0	3	.000	20	3	0	3	0	0	24	35	115	19	19	3	5	3	13	1	1	8	0	0
Cleveland, Reginald, Boston.	3.07	10	9	.526	41	14	3	10	1	0	170	159	719	73	58	11	9	3	61	4	3	76	6	0
Colborn, James, Milwaukee	3.70	9	15	.375	32	32	12	0	0	2	226	232	937	97	93	20	7	8	54	5	4	101	6	0
Coleman, Joseph, Detroit	4.84	2	5	.286	12	12	1	0	0	0	67	80	309	44	36	3	1	7	34	0	0	38	6	0
Cram, Gerald, Kansas City	6.75	0	2	.000	5	1	0	2	0	0	4	8	21	3	3	0	1	0	3	0	0	2	0	0
Crawford, James, Detroit°	4.54	1	8	.111	32	5	0	11	2	0	109	115	478	65	55	8	7	10	43	4	0	68	1	0
Cuellar, Miguel, Baltimore°	4.96	4	13	.235	26	19	3	2	0	0	107	129	490	63	59	8	12	5	50	2	1	52	3	0
Decker, George, Minnesota	5.28	2	7	.222	19	12	1	1	0	0	58	60	279	34	34	4	6	0	32	5	0	35	5	0
Dobson, Patrick, Cleveland	3.48	16	12	.571	35	35	12	0	0	0	217	226	919	98	84	13	13	7	65	0	7	117	6	0

Pitcher and Club	ERA.	W.	L.	Pct.	G.	GS.	CG.	GF.	Sv.	ShO.	IP.	H.	BFP.	R.	ER.	HR.	SH.	SF.	Tot. BB.	Int. BB.	HB.	SO.	WP.	Bk.
Drago, Richard, California	4.44	7	8	.467	43	0	0	27	6	0	79	80	346	42	39	7	3	4	31	8	5	43	3	0
Dunning, Steven, California	7.50	0	7	.000	4	4	0	0	0	0	6	9	37	9	5	2	1	1	6	0	0	4	0	0
Eckersley, Dennis, Cleveland	3.44	13	12	.520	36	30	9	3	1	2	199	155	821	82	76	13	10	5	78	2	1	200	6	1
Ellis, Dock, New York	3.18	17	8	.680	32	32	8	0	0	0	212	195	886	83	75	14	12	5	65	5	1	65	1	0
Fidrych, Mark, Detroit	2.34	19	9	.679	31	29	24	2	0	4	250	217	996	76	65	12	13	11	53	3	2	97	4	0
Figueroa, Eduardo, New York	3.01	19	10	.655	34	34	14	0	0	0	257	237	1081	101	86	19	16	11	94	1	2	119	6	1
Fingers, Roland, Oakland	2.47	13	11	.542	70	0	0	62	20	0	135	118	559	40	37	5	5	11	40	10	0	113	9	0
Fitzmorris, Alan, Kansas City	3.07	15	11	.577	35	33	10	8	0	1	220	227	907	89	75	7	6	11	63	4	2	80	1	0
Flanagan, Michael K., Baltimore°	4.13	3	5	.375	20	10	4	1	0	0	85	83	358	41	39	6	0	5	33	1	1	56	1	0
Forster, Terry, Chicago°	4.38	2	12	.143	52	16	0	31	5	0	111	126	486	61	54	7	4	7	41	5	4	70	7	0
Frisella, Daniel, Milwaukee	3.32	8	5	.500	46	0	0	31	9	0	76	68	317	41	28	3	4	7	35	7	1	41	5	0
Garland, Wayne, Baltimore	2.68	20	7	.741	38	25	14	9	0	3	232	224	976	81	69	14	15	3	64	3	7	113	5	0
Glynn, Edward, Detroit°	6.00	0	1	.000	5	0	0	4	0	0	24	22	108	16	16	3	1	0	18	0	1	16	1	0
Goltz, David, Minnesota	3.36	14	14	.500	38	35	13	0	1	1	249	239	1054	113	93	10	7	9	91	3	6	135	6	0
Gossage, Richard, Chicago	3.94	9	17	.346	31	29	15	1	1	1	224	214	956	113	98	14	6	5	90	5	5	135	15	1
Grilli, Stephen, Detroit	4.64	0	1	.000	7	0	0	2	0	0	16	13	72	9	8	1	0	0	12	0	0	6	0	0
Grimsley, Ross, Baltimore°	3.94	8	7	.533	36	28	8	2	0	2	137	143	578	66	60	8	2	2	25	4	3	36	2	0
Guidry, Ronald, New York°	5.63	0	1	1.000	7	0	0	3	0	0	16	20	72	10	10	1	0	1	12	1	0	12	2	0
Gura, Lawrence, Kansas City°	2.29	4	0	1.000	20	7	2	2	0	0	63	47	249	20	16	1	6	0	18	0	1	22	0	0
Haas, Bryan, Milwaukee	3.94	0	1	.500	5	2	0	2	0	0	30	28	134	19	13	2	3	1	12	0	0	25	1	0
Hall, Thomas, Kansas City°	4.50	0	0	.500	31	0	0	13	1	0	90	81	395	55	45	8	6	0	38	4	0	62	3	0
Hamilton, David, Chicago°	3.60	6	6	.636	45	5	2	14	7	0	124	114	537	63	50	8	8	7	36	4	0	63	8	0
Hargan, Steven, Texas	2.77	7	8	.294	35	31	7	0	0	2	166	166	692	63	51	10	9	6	45	3	1	51	3	1
Hartzell, Paul, California	3.61	7	4	.000	33	18	4	7	0	1	147	139	614	68	59	7	5	0	56	5	1	61	6	0
Hassler, Andrew, 14 Cal-19 KC°	6.00	7	12	.600	33	15	0	9	4	0	121	93	15	37	32	2	8	5	67	9	2	61	2	0
Hausman, Thomas, Milwaukee	2.38	5	8	.000	16	0	0	2	0	0	35	41	161	22	20	0	3	1	19	6	0	24	6	0
Hiller, John, Detroit°	5.14	12	8	.800	56	1	0	46	13	0	121	93	510	37	32	7	0	7	67	8	1	117	3	0
Hoerner, Joseph, Texas°	2.03	4	0	.000	41	0	0	19	3	0	40	41	149	9	9	0	1	0	13	2	0	15	1	0
Holdsworth, Fredrick, Baltimore	3.64	14	11	.560	16	0	0	8	0	0	78	89	350	46	42	11	3	1	41	2	0	24	2	1
Holtzman, Kenneth, 13 Bal-21 NY°	4.85	14	11	.560	33	34	16	0	0	0	247	265	1041	108	100	21	12	4	70	1	1	64	2	0
Hood, Donald, Cleveland°	4.30	3	5	.375	33	6	0	9	0	0	44	39	186	24	21	2	0	1	22	1	1	32	2	0
House, Thomas, Boston°	4.98	9	14	.391	37	26	3	2	0	0	177	190	770	113	98	17	5	4	19	3	3	87	5	0
Hughes, James, Minnesota	3.52	15	5	.531	37	34	8	0	0	1	299	268	1226	126	117	28	13	2	73	1	8	173	6	1
Hunter, James, New York	2.54	17	5	.875	36	36	21	0	0	3	299	268	1226	126	117	28	13	2	68	8	3	173	6	1
Jackson, Grant, 13 Bal-21 NY°	8.56	7	5	.286	34	2	0	14	1	0	62	57	310	22	59	5	0	5	25	5	3	39	5	0
Jefferson, Jesse, Chicago	3.27	2	12	.522	32	9	0	7	0	0	62	86	320	52	52	6	2	1	42	0	0	30	4	0
Jenkins, Ferguson, Boston	4.73	12	11	.522	29	29	12	0	0	0	209	201	857	85	76	20	10	5	43	6	5	142	3	0
Johnson, C. Barth, Chicago	2.63	3	1	.750	30	8	2	9	1	0	211	231	901	115	91	20	9	5	62	7	1	91	3	0
Johnson, Thomas, Minnesota	3.38	3	3	.625	28	2	0	10	0	0	118	44	480	44	39	5	12	6	37	5	1	37	7	0
Jones, T. Fredrick, Boston°	2.36	10	6	.588	24	14	4	5	0	0	104	133	464	48	39	7	8	8	26	0	1	45	2	0
Kern, James, Cleveland	4.61	6	12	.333	50	1	0	31	15	0	158	167	675	91	81	12	7	8	50	5	1	111	4	0
Kirkwood, Donald, California	4.80	12	11	.750	21	6	2	6	0	0	52	54	233	31	28	8	8	4	57	7	1	78	0	1
Knapp, R. Christian, Chicago	4.85	3	0	.000	11	8	1	0	0	0	4	6	22	5	5	1	1	0	3	1	1	41	0	1
Kobel, Kevin, Milwaukee°	11.25	0	1	.750	6	6	0	1	0	0	50	49	226	28	27	3	2	0	32	1	1	0	0	0
Kravec, Kenneth, Chicago°	4.86	1	5	.167	9	8	0	0	0	0	50	49	226	28	27	3	2	0	32	1	0	38	3	1

Pitcher and Club	ERA	W	L	Pct.	G	GS	CG	GF	Sv	ShO	IP	H	BFP	R	ER	HR	SH	SF	Tot. BB	Int. BB	HB	SO	WP	Bk.
Kreuger, Richard, Boston*	4.06	2	1	.667	8	4	0	3	0	0	31	31	134	14	14	2	3	1	16	0	0	12	2	0
Kucek, John, Chicago	9.00	0	0	.000	2	0	0	1	0	0	5	9	26	5	5	3	1	1	4	0	0	3	0	0
LaRoche, David, Cleveland*	2.25	1	4	.200	61	0	0	43	21	0	96	57	389	25	24	2	3	5	49	11	1	104	2	0
Laxton, William, Detroit*	4.07	0	1	.000	26	3	0	11	3	0	95	77	410	49	43	13	3	2	51	1	0	74	2	2
Lee, William, Boston*	5.63	5	7	.417	24	14	2	7	0	0	96	124	440	68	60	13	2	2	28	1	1	29	1	0
Lemanczyk, David, Detroit	5.11	4	6	.400	20	10	1	7	1	0	81	86	355	48	46	11	0	0	30	0	5	51	3	0
Leonard, Dennis, Kansas City	3.51	17	10	.630	35	34	21	0	0	3	259	247	1072	113	101	16	12	7	60	5	3	150	0	1
Lindblad, Paul, Oakland*	3.05	6	5	.545	65	0	0	16	5	0	115	111	480	50	39	4	3	11	24	5	0	37	0	1
Littell, Mark, Kansas City	2.08	8	4	.667	60	0	0	37	16	0	104	68	428	26	24	1	7	2	62	3	1	92	7	1
Luebber, Stephen, Minnesota	4.01	4	5	.444	38	12	3	1	0	0	119	109	508	56	53	9	2	7	42	7	2	45	1	1
Lyle, Albert, New York*	2.26	7	8	.467	64	0	0	58	23	0	104	82	420	33	26	5	9	3	42	4	2	61	4	4
MacCormack, Frank, Detroit	5.73	0	1	.000	2	2	0	1	0	0	33	35	156	25	21	1	2	4	34	0	0	14	0	0
Martinez, Felix, 11 NY-28 Bal*	2.31	5	1	.833	39	7	1	21	10	0	70	50	287	20	18	4	9	0	42	3	0	45	0	0
Martinez, J. Dennis, Baltimore	2.57	1	2	.333	4	2	0	1	0	0	28	31	106	19	18	1	0	0	8	0	0	18	0	0
May, Rudolph, 11 NY-24 Bal*	3.72	15	10	.600	35	32	9	1	0	0	220	205	907	105	91	16	9	5	70	0	5	109	3	0
McClure, Robert, Kansas City*	9.00	0	0	.000	8	0	0	1	0	0	4	3	22	4	4	1	0	0	5	0	0	6	0	0
McGregor, Scott, Baltimore*	3.60	0	1	.000	2	0	0	0	0	0	15	17	63	7	6	4	3	0	8	0	0	37	0	0
Miller, Dyar, Baltimore	2.93	2	2	.500	49	0	0	29	9	0	89	73	370	29	29	9	5	5	36	8	3	38	2	0
Mingori, Stephen, Kansas City*	2.33	2	4	.333	55	0	0	27	7	0	85	73	341	23	22	4	6	5	25	8	1	6	1	0
Mitchell, Craig, Oakland	3.00	1	1	.500	13	2	0	7	0	0	35	30	140	13	12	1	2	0	30	0	0	20	0	0
Mitchell, Paul, Oakland	4.25	9	7	.563	26	13	2	2	0	0	118	169	615	74	67	15	4	2	30	0	2	53	0	0
Monge, Isidro, California*	3.36	6	7	.462	32	0	0	7	7	0	108	108	490	50	44	10	5	8	49	0	0	39	1	0
Monroe, Lawrence, Chicago	4.09	2	3	.400	52	7	1	29	0	0	99	100	445	51	45	10	8	0	44	3	1	44	1	0
Murphy, Thomas, 15 Mil-37 Bos	4.18	0	4	.000	24	0	0	2	10	0	28	116	130	13	10	7	3	4	56	14	0	18	4	0
Nelson, Roger, Kansas City	2.00	2	3	.400	8	0	0	5	0	0	9	9	42	2	2	0	1	0	7	0	0	8	1	0
Norris, Michael, Oakland	5.79	2	1	.500	5	5	1	1	0	0	31	31	133	21	18	10	3	4	20	0	0	47	1	0
Odom, Johnny, Chicago	4.50	0	2	.000	5	0	0	3	0	0	70	70	300	37	35	7	3	5	27	1	0	8	1	0
Otten, James, Chicago	6.43	0	2	.000	27	0	0	3	0	0	6	6	32	6	5	2	0	0	3	1	0	5	1	0
Overy, H. Michael, California	4.76	0	2	.000	40	0	0	1	0	0	6	8	29	6	5	5	0	0	27	0	0	8	0	0
Pagan, David, 7 NY-20 Bal	2.51	2	5	.286	44	7	1	5	0	0	70	70	300	51	39	8	14	3	27	1	0	47	0	0
Palmer, James, Baltimore	2.51	22	13	.629	40	40	23	0	0	6	315	255	1256	101	88	20	10	14	84	5	3	159	0	0
Parker, Harry, Cleveland	0.00	0	1	.000	15	0	0	5	0	0	7	7	32	5	0	0	0	0	3	0	0	5	0	0
Pattin, Martin, Kansas City	2.49	8	14	.364	32	23	5	1	0	0	141	114	575	51	39	9	3	4	38	3	0	65	0	1
Pazik, Michael, Minnesota*	7.00	0	3	.000	13	3	0	0	0	0	13	13	43	9	7	4	2	0	4	0	1	6	0	0
Perry, Gaylord, Texas	3.24	15	14	.517	32	32	21	0	0	0	250	232	1005	93	90	14	8	6	52	3	0	143	0	0
Perzanowski, Stanley, Texas	9.75	1	3	.250	5	9	0	0	0	0	62	80	273	38	35	3	3	3	17	1	0	6	0	0
Peterson, Fred, 9 Clev-4 Tex*	5.08	6	5	.545	13	11	1	0	0	0	121	131	528	62	58	8	5	3	48	6	0	23	1	0
Pole, Richard, Boston	4.31	0	1	.000	31	31	6	0	0	0	118	120	500	55	53	6	8	3	63	5	1	49	4	0
Raich, Eric, Cleveland	15.00	0	1	.000	6	6	0	0	0	0	6	15	30	10	10	1	1	0	5	0	0	1	0	0
Redfern, Peter, Minnesota	3.51	8	8	.500	23	23	3	0	0	0	118	105	508	61	46	16	8	11	63	4	1	74	4	0
Roberts, David A., Detroit*	4.00	16	17	.485	36	36	18	0	0	2	252	254	1048	122	112	16	10	7	122	6	1	79	4	0
Rodriguez, Eduardo, Milwaukee	3.64	5	13	.278	45	12	2	26	8	0	136	124	584	68	55	12	7	5	65	5	1	77	5	0
Ross, Gary, California	3.00	8	16	.333	34	0	0	2	0	0	225	224	948	89	75	12	10	3	65	5	4	100	2	0
Ruhle, Vernon, Detroit	3.92	9	12	.429	32	31	9	10	0	1	200	227	865	99	87	19	13	10	59	2	2	88	5	0
Ryan, L. Nolan, California	3.36	17	18	.486	39	39	21	0	1	7	284	193	1196	117	106	13	13	0	183	5	3	327	5	2
Sadecki, Raymond, 3 KC-36 Mil*	3.86	2	0	1.000	39	0	0	10	1	0	42	45	190	20	18	3	0	0	23	3	0	28	5	0

Pitcher and Club	ERA	W.	L.	Pct.	G.	GS.	CG.	GF.	Sv.	ShO.	IP.	H.	BFP.	R.	ER.	HR.	SH.	SF.	Tot. BB.	Int. BB.	HB.	SO.	WP.	Bk.
Sanders, Kenneth, Kansas City	0.00	0	0	.000	3	0	0		0	0	3	3	14	0	0	3		1	4	2	0	1	0	0
Scott, Ralph, California*	3.23	13	10	.565	36	0	0	16	1	0	39	47	172	17	14	9	6	3	12	4	1	10	6	0
Singer, William, 10 Tex-26 Minn	3.68	10	10	.500	36	36	7	0	0	4	237	233	1011	119	97	13	12	12	96	4	11	97	1	1
Skok, Craig, Texas	12.60	0	1	.000	9	0	0	1	0	0	9	13	30			1						5		0
Slaton, James, Milwaukee*	3.44	14	15	.483	38	38	12	0	0	2	293	287	1235	126	112	14	15	12	94	12	6	138	4	1
Splittorff, Paul, Kansas City*	3.96	11	8	.579	38	38	12	0	0	2	159	169	686	79	70	11	8	5	59	5	3	59	1	0
Sprague, Edward, Milwaukee	6.75	0	3	.000	26	1	0	23	6	0	8	14	37		6		1	1	4	0	0	6	0	0
Tanana, Frank, California*	2.44	19	10	.655	34	34	23	0	0	2	288	212	1142	88	78	24	14	4	73	5	1	261	1	0
Terpko, Jeffrey, Texas	2.38	3	3	.500	32	1	0	15	7	0	53	42	222	18	14	3	5	3	29	1	1	24	0	0
Thomas, Stanley, Cleveland	2.29	3	3	.500	37	0	0	24	10	0	106	88	435	33	27	4	1	5	41	2	4	54	1	3
Tiant, Luis, Boston	3.06	21	12	.636	38	38	19	0	0	3	279	274	1136	107	95	24	5	10	64	2	1	131	3	0
Tidrow, Richard, New York	2.64	7	8	.467	49	0	0	22	4	0	92	80	375	29	27	7	10	3	24	1	1	65	1	3
Todd, James, Oakland	3.80	16	12	.571	47	0	0	20	10	0	83	87	362	43	35	25	3	4	34	8	2	23	8	0
Torrez, Michael, Oakland	2.50	16	12	.571	39	39	13	0	0	3	266	231	1094	93	74	5	16	8	87	2	5	115	0	3
Travers, William, Milwaukee*	2.81	15	16	.484	34	34	10	0	0	3	240	211	1006	92	75	6	6	5	95	5	5	120	7	0
Umbarger, James, Texas*	3.15	10	12	.455	21	0	0	13	0	0	37	43	156	15	13	15	8	5	14	4	1	105	1	0
Verhoeven, John, California	3.41	0	0	.000	33	22	7	4	0	1	110	122	500	57	57	21	16	1	54	8	0	23	0	1
Vuckovich, Peter, Chicago	4.66	7	7	.636	26	0	0	15	4	0	124	143	539	60	55	12	7	4	54	4	0	62	2	0
Waits, Richard, Cleveland*	3.99	0	9	.438	54	34	11	0	0	4	2	6	14		6	5	4	8	54	4	1	65	2	0
Wheelock, Gary, California	27.00	0	0	.200	3	0	0	2	0	0	2	6	14	6	6	0	1	0	4	0	1	2	0	0
Willoughby, James, Boston	2.82	3	12	.200	54	0	0	40	10	0	99	94	419	38	31	6	8	1	31	12	2	37	2	0
Wise, Richard, Boston	3.54	14	11	.560	34	34	11	0	0	1	224	218	919	100	88	18	8	8	48	1	1	93	3	0
Wood, Wilbur, Chicago*	2.25	1	0	.571	7	7	5	0	0	0	56	51	225	24	14	1	2	1	11	0	0	31	1	0
York, James, New York	5.40	0	1	1.000	3	0	0	1	0	0	10	14	47	14	6	0	0		4	0	1	6	2	0

NOTE—Following pitchers combined to pitch shutout games: Baltimore (2)—Palmer and Miller, Palmer and Garland; Boston (4)—Pole and Willoughby, Tiant and Willoughby, Jenkins and Murphy, Cleveland, House and Willoughby; California (2)—Ross and Drago, Tanana and Drago; Chicago (5)—Brett and Carroll 2, C. B. Johnson and Hamilton, Brett and Jefferson, Brett and Hamilton; Cleveland (7)—Dobson and LaRoche, Eckersley and Hood, Eckersley and Thomas, Waits and Bibby, Dobson and Kern 2, Bibby and Kern; Kansas City (3)—Busby and Littell, Bird and Littell, Pattin and Mingori; Milwaukee (2)—Colborn and Rodriguez, Travers, Sadecki and Frisella; Minnesota (2)—Luebber and Burgmeier, Redfern and Campbell; New York (2)—Ellis and Lyle, Hunter and Jackson; Oakland (2)—Norris and Fingers 2.

PITCHERS WITH TWO OR MORE CLUBS

(Alphabetically Arranged with Pitcher's First Club on Top)

Pitcher and Club	ERA	W.	L.	Pct.	G.	GS.	CG.	GF.	Sv.	ShO.	IP.	H.	BFP.	R.	ER.	HR.	SH.	SF.	Tot. BB.	Int. BB.	HB.	SO.	WP.	Bk.
Alexander, Baltimore	3.50	3	4	.429	11	6	2	4	0	0	64⅓	58	265	27	25	3	2	4	24	2	0	17	0	1
Alexander, New York	3.29	10	5	.667	19	19	5	0	0	2	136⅔	114	547	54	50	9	5	5	41	0	3	41	0	1
Blyleven, Minnesota	3.12	4	5	.444	12	12	4	0	0	0	95⅓	101	406	39	33	3	7	4	35	5	4	75	0	2
Blyleven, Texas	2.76	9	11	.450	24	24	14	0	0	6	202⅔	182	819	67	62	11	11	0	46	1	8	144	1	0
Brett, New York	0.00	0	0	.000	2	0	0	2	1	0	2⅓	2	9	2	0	0	0	0	0	0	0	2	0	0
Brett, Chicago	3.32	10	12	.455	27	26	16	1	1	0	200⅔	171	826	82	74	9	6	3	76	3	3	91	4	1
Hassler, California	5.13	0	6	.000	14	4	0	7	0	0	47⅓	50	200	31	27	3	4	3	17	2	0	16	1	0
Hassler, Kansas City	2.89	5	6	.455	19	14	4	0	0	0	99⅔	89	414	37	32	2	3	4	39	0	0	45	3	0

Pitcher and Club	ERA	W	L	Pct.	G	GS	CG	GF	Sv.	ShO.	IP.	H.	BFP.	R.	ER.	HR.	SH.	SF.	Tot. BB.	Int. BB.	HB.	SO.	WP.	Bk.
Holtzman, Baltimore	2.86	5	4	.556	13	13	6	0	0	1	97⅔	100	414	34	31	4	6	3	35	2	1	25	3	0
Holtzman, New York	4.17	9	7	.563	21	21	10	0	0	2	149	165	627	74	69	14	5	3	35	0	0	41	7	0
G. Jackson, Baltimore	5.12	1	1	.500	13	13	0	6	3	0	19⅓	19	83	11	11	1	1	1	9	2	2	14	0	0
G. Jackson, New York	1.69	6	0	1.000	21	21	1	8	2	1	58⅓	38	227	11	11	1	2	4	16	0	1	25	2	0
F. Martinez, New York	1.93	2	0	1.000	11	0	0	3	8	0	28	18	108	6	6	1	0	0	14	0	2	14	0	0
F. Martinez, Baltimore	2.59	3	1	.750	28	0	0	18	0	0	41⅔	32	179	13	12	0	4	2	28	3	1	31	2	0
R. May, New York	3.57	4	3	.571	11	11	2	0	1	1	68	49	270	32	27	5	2	1	28	1	0	38	3	0
R. May, Baltimore	3.78	11	7	.611	24	21	5	1	0	1	152⅓	156	637	73	64	11	7	4	42	3	0	71	1	0
Murphy, Milwaukee	7.36	0	1	.000	15	0	0	9	1	0	18⅓	25	94	18	15	2	3	0	9	2	1	7	1	0
Murphy, Boston	3.44	4	5	.444	37	0	0	20	8	0	81	91	351	43	31	5	7	3	25	11	2	32	3	0
Pagan, New York	2.28	1	1	.500	7	2	1	0	1	0	23⅔	18	87	7	6	0	2	0	4	0	0	13	0	0
Pagan, Baltimore	5.98	1	4	.200	20	5	0	5	1	0	46⅔	54	213	31	31	2	6	2	23	1	1	34	4	0
Peterson, Cleveland	5.55	0	3	.000	9	9	0	0	0	0	47	59	204	31	29	3	1	1	10	0	0	19	1	0
Peterson, Texas	3.60	1	0	1.000	4	2	0	1	0	0	15	21	69	7	6	0	0	0	7	0	0	4	0	0
Sadecki, Kansas City	0.00	0	0	.000	3	0	0	9	1	0	4⅔	7	22	0	0	0	1	2	3	0	0	1	0	0
Sadecki, Milwaukee	4.34	2	0	1.000	36	0	0	9	0	0	37⅓	38	168	20	18	2	0	0	20	2	3	27	0	1
Singer, Texas	3.48	4	1	.800	10	10	2	0	0	1	64⅔	56	274	31	25	4	6	2	27	3	5	34	2	1
Singer, Minnesota	3.77	9	9	.500	26	26	5	0	0	3	172	177	737	88	72	9	6	9	69	4	6	63	4	1

1976 A. L. Pitching Against Each Club

Baltimore—88-74

Pitcher	Bos. W–L	Cal. W–L	Chi. W–L	Clev. W–L	Det. W–L	K.C. W–L	Mil. W–L	Minn. W–L	N.Y. W–L	Oak. W–L	Tex. W–L	Totals W–L
Alexander	0–1	0–1	0–0	0–0	2–0	0–1	1–0	0–0	0–0	0–0	0–0	3– 4
Cuellar	0–2	0–2	1–1	0–2	0–1	0–1	2–1	0–1	0–1	0–1	1–0	4–13
Flanagan	0–2	0–0	0–0	0–0	0–0	1–1	1–0	0–0	1–0	0–1	0–0	3– 5
Garland	3–1	1–0	2–0	3–1	4–0	2–0	2–1	0–1	0–1	2–1	1–1	20– 7
Grimsley	0–1	0–0	0–1	2–0	1–1	0–0	0–1	1–0	4–1	0–1	0–1	8– 7
Holdsworth	0–1	0–0	0–0	0–0	1–0	0–0	1–0	0–0	0–0	0–0	2–0	4– 1
Holtzman	1–0	1–0	0–1	0–1	1–0	0–1	0–0	1–0	1–0	0–0	0–1	5– 4
G. Jackson	0–0	1–0	0–0	0–0	0–0	0–0	0–0	0–1	0–0	0–0	0–0	1– 1
F. Martinez	0–0	0–0	0–0	0–0	0–0	0–0	0–1	0–0	2–0	0–0	1–0	3– 1
J. D. Martinez	0–2	0–0	0–0	0–0	1–0	0–0	0–0	0–0	0–0	0–0	0–0	1– 2
R. May	0–0	1–1	0–1	1–2	1–1	1–0	1–1	1–0	3–0	1–1	1–0	11– 7
McGregor	0–0	0–0	0–0	0–0	0–0	0–0	0–0	0–1	0–0	0–0	0–0	0– 1
Miller	0–0	0–0	1–0	0–1	0–2	0–0	1–0	0–0	0–0	0–1	0–0	2– 4
Pagan	0–1	1–0	0–0	0–1	0–0	0–0	0–1	0–1	0–0	0–0	0–0	1– 4
Palmer	3–0	3–0	4–0	1–3	1–1	2–2	2–0	1–3	2–2	1–2	2–0	22–13
Totals	7–11	8–4	8–4	7–11	12–6	6–6	11–7	4–8	13–5	4–8	8–4	88–74

No Decisions—None.

Boston—83-79

Pitcher	Balt. W–L	Cal. W–L	Chi. W–L	Clev. W–L	Det. W–L	K.C. W–L	Mil. W–L	Minn. W–L	N.Y. W–L	Oak. W–L	Tex. W–L	Totals W–L
Cleveland	3–1	0–0	0–0	1–1	1–1	0–1	1–2	0–0	3–0	1–2	0–1	10– 9
House	0–1	0–0	0–0	1–0	0–0	0–0	0–0	0–0	0–2	0–0	0–0	1– 3
Jenkins	1–1	1–1	1–1	1–2	2–1	1–1	2–0	2–0	1–1	0–2	0–1	12–11
Jones	0–0	0–0	0–0	0–1	1–0	1–0	0–0	2–0	0–2	0–0	1–0	5– 3
Kreuger	0–0	0–0	0–0	0–0	0–0	0–0	1–1	0–0	1–0	0–0	0–0	2– 1
Lee	0–0	1–0	0–0	0–2	2–0	0–2	1–0	0–0	1–1	0–0	0–2	5– 7
Murphy	0–0	2–0	0–1	0–1	0–1	0–1	1–0	0–0	0–0	0–1	1–0	4– 5
Pole	0–0	1–0	1–0	0–0	0–0	0–0	3–1	0–1	0–1	1–0	0–1	6– 5
Tiant	2–2	2–0	4–0	3–1	4–0	0–1	2–0	1–2	1–3	1–1	1–2	21–12
Willoughby	2–1	0–2	0–1	0–1	1–0	0–1	0–1	0–0	0–1	0–2	0–2	3–12
Wise	3–1	0–2	0–2	3–0	3–1	1–1	1–1	2–2	0–0	1–0	0–1	14–11
Totals	11–7	7–5	6–6	9–9	14–4	3–9	12–6	7–5	7–11	4–8	3–9	83–79

No Decisions—None.

California—76-86

Pitcher	Balt. W–L	Bos. W–L	Chi. W–L	Clev. W–L	Det. W–L	K.C. W–L	Mil. W–L	Minn. W–L	N.Y. W–L	Oak. W–L	Tex. W–L	Totals W–L
Brewer	0–0	0–0	0–1	2–0	1–0	0–0	0–0	0–0	0–0	0–0	0–0	3– 1
Drago	1–1	0–1	2–0	1–1	0–0	1–2	0–0	0–1	0–0	0–1	2–1	7– 8
Hartzell	0–0	1–0	0–0	0–0	1–2	0–0	1–1	0–1	0–0	1–0	3–0	7– 4
Hassler	0–0	0–1	0–0	0–1	0–1	0–1	0–0	0–1	0–0	0–1	0–0	0– 6
Kirkwood	0–1	0–1	0–2	0–0	1–0	1–1	1–0	1–2	1–1	0–2	1–2	6–12
Monge	0–0	0–0	2–1	0–1	0–0	2–0	0–1	0–2	1–1	1–1	0–0	6– 7
Overy	0–0	0–0	0–0	0–0	0–0	0–1	0–0	0–0	0–0	0–0	0–0	0– 2
Ross	0–3	1–0	0–1	1–0	0–2	1–1	1–3	3–1	0–2	0–1	1–2	8–16
Ryan	1–2	1–3	3–1	2–1	2–0	2–3	1–0	1–2	0–2	2–3	2–1	17–18
Scott	0–0	1–0	0–0	0–0	0–0	0–0	0–0	0–0	2–0	0–0	0–0	3– 0
Tanana	2–1	1–1	4–1	1–1	1–1	1–1	0–2	3–0	1–1	2–1	3–0	19–10
Verhoeven	0–0	0–0	0–0	0–0	0–0	0–0	0–0	0–0	0–0	0–2	0–0	0– 2
Totals	4–8	5–7	11–7	7–5	6–6	8–10	4–8	8–10	5–7	6–12	12–6	76–86

No Decisions—Dunning, Wheelock.

Chicago—64-97

Pitcher	Balt. W–L	Bos. W–L	Cal. W–L	Clev. W–L	Det. W–L	K.C. W–L	Mil. W–L	Minn. W–L	N.Y. W–L	Oak. W–L	Tex. W–L	Totals W–L
Barrios	0–3	0–0	1–2	0–1	0–0	1–0	2–0	0–2	0–0	1–0	0–1	5– 9
Brett	0–1	1–1	1–3	1–1	0–0	1–1	2–0	2–1	1–1	1–2	0–1	10–12
Carroll	0–0	1–0	0–1	0–2	0–0	1–0	0–1	0–0	0–0	2–0	0–0	4– 4
Forster	0–1	0–0	0–1	0–1	1–1	1–2	0–0	0–1	0–2	0–2	0–1	2–12
Gossage	1–2	1–1	3–0	1–0	0–2	0–3	1–2	2–2	0–2	0–2	0–1	9–17
Hamilton	1–0	0–0	0–0	0–1	1–0	1–0	0–0	0–0	0–3	0–0	3–2	6– 6
Jefferson	0–0	0–1	0–1	0–0	0–0	1–1	0–0	0–1	0–0	1–0	0–1	2– 5
C. B. Johnson	0–0	2–1	1–1	0–1	1–3	0–2	1–1	1–2	0–2	1–2	2–1	9–16
Knapp	0–0	0–0	0–0	0–0	1–0	1–0	0–0	0–0	0–0	1–0	0–1	3– 1
Kravec	0–1	0–0	0–1	0–1	0–0	0–0	1–0	0–1	0–0	0–0	0–1	1– 5
Monroe	0–0	0–0	0–1	0–0	0–0	0–0	0–0	0–0	0–0	0–0	0–0	0– 1
Odom	0–0	0–1	0–0	0–0	1–0	0–0	0–0	0–0	0–0	1–1	0–0	2– 2
Vuckovich	1–0	0–0	1–0	1–1	0–0	0–1	0–0	2–0	0–0	0–0	2–1	7– 4
Wood	1–0	1–1	0–0	0–0	1–0	1–0	0–1	0–1	0–0	0–0	0–0	4– 3
Totals	4–8	6–6	7–11	3–9	6–6	8–10	7–5	7–11	1–11	8–9	7–11	64–97

No Decisions—Kucek, Otten.

Cleveland—81-78

Pitcher	Balt. W–L	Bos. W–L	Cal. W–L	Chi. W–L	Det. W–L	K.C. W–L	Mil. W–L	Minn. W–L	N.Y. W–L	Oak. W–L	Tex. W–L	Totals W–L
Bibby	0–2	1–1	0–0	2–0	2–1	1–0	3–1	0–0	1–0	1–0	2–2	13– 7
Brown	0–0	0–1	1–1	0–1	2–1	0–0	3–1	2–1	0–1	0–2	1–1	9–11
Buskey	0–1	1–0	0–1	0–0	1–0	0–0	0–0	0–0	0–1	1–1	1–0	5– 4
Dobson	5–0	2–3	0–2	1–0	0–3	2–0	1–1	2–0	0–1	1–1	0–1	16–12
Eckersley	1–2	2–1	2–0	0–1	1–2	2–1	2–1	2–1	0–1	0–0	0–1	13–12
Hood	0–0	1–0	0–1	0–1	0–0	0–0	1–0	0–0	0–1	0–0	0–1	3– 5
Kern	2–0	1–1	1–0	5–0	0–2	0–1	1–1	0–0	0–1	0–1	1–0	10– 7
LaRoche	0–0	0–1	0–0	0–0	0–0	0–1	0–0	0–0	0–1	0–0	0–0	1– 4
Peterson	0–0	0–0	0–1	0–0	0–0	0–1	0–1	1–0	0–1	0–0	1–0	0– 3
Thomas	2–0	0–1	0–0	0–0	0–0	0–0	0–0	1–0	0–0	1–2	0–0	4– 4
Waits	1–2	1–0	1–1	1–0	0–3	1–0	0–0	0–0	1–2	0–0	0–0	7– 9
Totals	11–7	9–9	5–7	9–3	6–12	6–6	11–6	9–3	4–12	4–8	7–5	81–78

No Decisions—Parker, Raich.

Detroit—74-87

Pitcher	Balt. W–L	Bos. W–L	Cal. W–L	Chi. W–L	Clev. W–L	K.C. W–L	Mil. W–L	Minn. W–L	N.Y. W–L	Oak. W–L	Tex. W–L	Totals W–L
Bare	1–1	1–0	2–0	3–1	0–2	0–1	0–2	0–0	0–1	0–0	0–0	7– 8
Coleman	0–1	0–1	0–0	0–1	0–1	0–0	0–0	0–0	1–1	0–0	0–1	2– 5
Crawford	0–1	0–1	0–1	0–1	0–1	0–0	0–0	0–0	0–0	1–1	2–0	1– 8
Fidrych	1–2	1–2	2–0	1–0	4–0	1–1	2–1	2–1	2–1	0–0	3–0	19– 9
Glynn	0–0	0–1	0–0	0–0	1–0	0–0	0–0	0–0	0–0	0–0	0–0	1– 3
Grilli	0–0	1–0	0–1	0–0	1–0	1–0	0–0	0–0	1–0	0–0	0–0	3– 1
Hiller	1–3	1–0	0–0	1–0	2–0	1–0	5–1	0–1	0–0	0–0	1–1	12– 8
Laxton	0–1	0–0	0–0	0–1	0–0	0–1	0–0	0–2	0–1	0–0	0–1	0– 5
Lemanczyk	1–0	0–2	0–0	0–1	1–0	0–2	0–0	0–0	1–0	0–0	1–1	4– 6
MacCormack	0–0	0–0	0–0	0–1	0–0	0–1	0–1	0–1	0–1	0–0	0–0	0– 5
Roberts	2–1	0–4	1–2	0–0	1–2	1–2	3–2	3–1	3–1	0–1	2–1	16–17
Ruhle	0–2	0–3	1–1	2–1	1–0	1–1	2–0	0–1	1–1	1–1	0–1	9–12
Totals	6–12	4–14	6–6	6–6	12–6	4–8	12–6	4–8	9–8	6–6	5–7	74–87

No Decisions—None.

KANSAS CITY—90-72

Pitcher	Balt. W–L	Bos. W–L	Cal. W–L	Chi. W–L	Clev. W–L	Det. W–L	Mil. W–L	Minn. W–L	N.Y. W–L	Oak. W–L	Tex. W–L	Totals W–L
Bird	1–2	0–2	2–1	1–1	0–0	0–0	2–0	1–0	2–1	3–1	0–2	12–10
Bruno	0–0	1–0	0–0	0–0	0–0	0–0	0–0	0–0	0–0	0–0	0–0	1–0
Busby	1–0	0–0	0–0	0–1	0–1	1–0	0–0	0–0	1–1	0–0	0–0	3–3
Fitzmorris	0–0	3–0	2–2	2–0	1–2	3–1	1–1	2–1	0–0	0–1	1–3	15–11
Gura	0–0	0–0	1–0	1–0	0–0	0–0	0–0	0–0	0–0	1–0	1–0	4–0
Hall	0–0	0–0	0–0	0–1	0–0	0–0	0–0	0–0	0–0	0–0	1–0	1–1
Hassler	0–1	0–0	0–0	2–0	1–0	1–0	1–0	0–2	0–0	0–0	0–3	5–6
Leonard	2–1	1–1	0–0	2–1	1–1	2–1	1–2	2–0	1–0	2–2	3–1	17–10
Littell	1–0	1–0	0–1	1–0	0–1	0–0	0–0	1–2	2–0	0–0	0–0	8–4
Mingori	0–0	0–0	2–0	1–2	1–1	0–1	0–0	0–0	0–1	0–0	1–0	5–5
Pattin	0–2	1–0	2–2	0–1	1–0	0–1	1–1	3–1	0–1	0–4	0–1	8–14
Splittorff	1–0	2–0	1–2	0–1	0–0	1–0	2–0	1–2	2–1	1–1	0–1	11–8
Totals	6–6	9–3	10–8	10–8	6–6	8–4	8–4	10–8	7–5	9–9	7–11	90–72

No Decisions—Cram, McClure, R. Nelson, Sadecki, Sanders.

MILWAUKEE—66-95

Pitcher	Balt. W–L	Bos. W–L	Cal. W–L	Chi. W–L	Clev. W–L	Det. W–L	K.C. W–L	Minn. W–L	N.Y. W–L	Oak. W–L	Tex. W–L	Totals W–L
Augustine	2–2	0–2	3–0	0–2	0–0	1–2	2–0	0–2	0–2	0–0	1–0	9–12
Beare	0–0	0–1	0–0	0–0	1–1	0–1	0–0	0–0	1–0	0–0	0–0	2–3
Broberg	0–0	0–3	0–0	0–0	0–1	0–0	1–1	0–1	0–1	0–0	0–0	1–7
Castro	0–1	0–1	0–0	0–0	2–1	0–0	0–0	0–2	0–0	1–1	1–0	4–6
Champion	0–0	0–0	0–0	0–0	0–0	0–0	0–1	0–0	0–0	0–0	0–0	0–1
Colborn	1–4	2–1	1–1	2–0	0–2	1–1	0–3	0–0	0–1	1–1	1–1	9–15
Frisella	0–0	2–0	0–0	0–0	0–0	0–1	0–1	1–0	1–0	1–0	0–0	5–2
Haas	0–0	0–1	0–0	0–0	0–0	0–0	0–0	0–0	0–0	0–0	0–0	0–1
Kobel	0–0	0–0	0–0	0–0	0–0	0–0	0–0	0–0	0–1	0–0	0–0	0–1
Murphy	0–0	0–0	0–0	0–0	0–0	0–0	0–0	0–0	0–1	0–0	0–0	0–1
Rodriguez	2–3	0–2	0–1	1–1	0–2	0–2	0–0	0–1	0–0	0–1	2–0	5–13
Sadecki	0–0	0–0	1–0	0–0	0–0	1–0	0–0	0–0	0–0	0–0	0–0	2–0
Slaton	1–0	2–0	1–2	0–3	1–1	2–2	0–1	3–0	1–4	2–1	1–1	14–15
Sprague	0–0	0–0	0–0	0–0	0–1	0–1	0–0	0–0	0–0	0–0	0–0	0–2
Travers	1–1	0–1	2–0	2–1	2–2	1–2	1–1	1–2	2–3	0–3	3–0	15–16
Totals	7–11	6–12	8–4	5–7	6–11	6–12	4–8	4–8	5–13	5–7	10–2	66–95

No Decisions—Austin, Hausman.

MINNESOTA—85-77

Pitcher	Balt. W–L	Bos. W–L	Cal. W–L	Chi. W–L	Clev. W–L	Det. W–L	K.C. W–L	Mil. W–L	N.Y. W–L	Oak. W–L	Tex. W–L	Totals W–L
Albury	0–0	0–0	1–0	1–0	0–0	1–0	0–0	0–0	0–1	0–0	0–0	3–1
Bane	0–0	1–0	0–0	1–0	1–1	0–1	0–2	0–1	0–2	0–0	1–0	4–7
Blyleven	0–0	0–0	1–1	0–2	0–1	1–0	1–0	0–0	1–0	0–1	0–0	4–5
Burgmeier	1–0	1–0	0–0	2–0	0–0	1–0	1–0	1–0	0–1	1–0	0–0	8–1
Campbell	2–0	1–0	2–0	1–0	1–0	2–0	2–1	3–1	0–0	2–1	1–2	17–5
Decker	0–1	0–2	0–0	1–1	0–1	0–1	0–0	1–0	0–0	0–0	0–1	2–7
Goltz	1–1	1–3	2–3	0–0	1–2	1–0	1–2	1–0	0–1	4–1	2–1	14–14
Hughes	1–0	0–1	1–3	1–0	0–2	1–1	2–1	0–2	1–1	1–2	2–0	9–14
Johnson	0–1	0–0	0–0	1–0	0–0	0–0	0–0	1–0	0–0	1–0	0–0	3–1
Luebber	0–1	0–0	0–0	0–0	0–0	0–0	0–0	0–0	0–1	1–1	3–1	4–5
Redfern	0–0	1–0	2–1	2–2	0–1	1–0	0–1	0–0	0–1	0–1	2–1	8–8
Singer	3–0	0–1	2–1	2–1	0–1	0–2	1–1	1–0	0–2	1–0	0–1	9–9
Totals	8–4	5–7	10–8	11–7	3–9	8–4	8–10	8–4	2–10	11–7	11–7	85–77

No Decisions—Pazik.

NEW YORK—97-62

Pitcher	Balt. W—L	Bos. W—L	Cal. W—L	Chi. W—L	Clev. W—L	Det. W—L	K.C. W—L	Mil. W—L	Minn. W—L	Oak. W—L	Tex. W—L	Totals W—L
Alexander	0—2	2—0	0—0	1—1	1—0	2—1	1—1	0—0	1—0	1—0	1—0	10—5
Ellis	2—3	1—1	3—0	2—0	2—0	1—2	1—0	2—2	1—0	0—0	2—0	17—8
Figueroa	1—2	3—2	1—1	2—0	1—1	2—1	0—2	4—0	3—0	1—1	1—0	19—10
Holtzman	1—0	0—1	0—0	1—0	2—1	0—3	0—1	2—1	2—0	0—0	1—0	9—7
Hunter	1—5	3—1	2—0	1—0	2—1	0—0	1—2	3—2	1—1	1—2	2—1	17—15
Jackson	0—0	0—0	1—0	1—0	1—0	2—0	0—0	0—0	0—0	1—0	0—0	6—0
Lyle	0—0	1—1	0—1	0—0	2—0	0—1	2—1	1—0	0—1	0—2	1—1	7—8
Martinez	0—0	0—0	0—0	1—0	0—0	0—0	0—0	0—0	0—0	0—0	1—0	2—0
R. May	0—0	0—0	0—1	1—0	1—1	1—1	0—0	0—0	0—0	1—0	0—0	4—3
Pagan	0—0	0—0	0—0	0—0	0—0	0—0	0—0	0—0	1—0	0—0	0—1	1—1
Tidrow	0—1	1—1	0—2	0—0	0—0	0—0	0—0	1—0	1—0	1—1	0—0	4—5
York	0—0	0—0	0—0	1—0	0—0	0—0	0—0	0—0	0—0	0—0	0—0	1—0
Totals	5—13	11—7	7—5	11—1	12—4	8—9	5—7	13—5	10—2	6—6	9—3	97—62

No Decisions—Brett, Guidry.

OAKLAND—87-74

Pitcher	Balt. W—L	Bos. W—L	Cal. W—L	Chi. W—L	Clev. W—L	Det. W—L	K.C. W—L	Mil. W—L	Minn. W—L	N.Y. W—L	Tex. W—L	Totals W—L
Abbott	0—1	0—0	0—1	0—0	0—0	0—1	1—0	1—0	0—1	0—0	0—0	2—4
Bahnsen	1—0	1—0	2—1	1—1	0—0	0—0	0—2	1—0	0—2	2—1	0—0	8—7
Blue	3—0	1—0	1—2	2—1	0—2	1—2	3—1	1—2	2—0	2—1	2—2	18—13
Bosman	0—0	0—1	0—0	1—0	1—0	0—0	0—0	0—0	1—0	0—0	1—1	4—2
Fingers	1—0	1—1	2—0	1—3	3—2	1—1	1—1	1—1	0—1	2—0	0—1	13—11
Lindblad	0—1	1—0	1—0	0—1	0—0	1—0	0—0	1—0	1—2	1—1	0—0	6—5
P. Mitchell	1—1	1—0	1—0	2—0	1—0	1—0	1—0	0—2	0—0	0—2	1—2	9—7
Norris	0—0	1—0	1—1	0—1	0—0	1—0	1—0	0—0	0—0	0—2	0—1	4—5
Todd	0—0	2—0	1—0	1—0	1—0	0—1	0—2	0—1	1—2	1—1	0—1	7—8
Torrez	2—1	0—2	3—1	1—1	3—0	0—1	3—1	1—1	2—1	0—0	1—3	16—12
Totals	8—4	8—4	12—6	9—8	8—4	6—6	9—9	7—5	7—11	6—7	7—11	87—74

No Decisions—Batton, C. Mitchell.

TEXAS—76-86

Pitcher	Balt. W—L	Bos. W—L	Cal. W—L	Chi. W—L	Clev. W—L	Det. W—L	K.C. W—L	Mil. W—L	Minn. W—L	N.Y. W—L	Oak. W—L	Totals W—L
Bacsik	0—0	1—0	0—1	1—1	0—0	0—0	0—0	0—0	0—0	0—0	1—0	3—2
Barker	0—0	0—0	0—0	1—0	0—0	0—0	0—0	0—0	0—0	0—0	0—0	1—0
Barr	0—0	0—0	0—0	0—0	0—0	1—1	0—0	0—2	1—0	0—2	1—0	2—6
Blyleven	0—0	0—0	0—1	1—1	2—1	1—2	0—2	3—0	0—3	0—1	1—0	9—11
Boggs	0—0	0—0	0—1	0—0	0—1	0—0	1—0	0—0	0—1	0—0	0—0	1—7
Briles	0—1	2—1	1—1	2—2	0—0	2—0	1—1	1—1	0—0	2—0	0—0	11—9
Foucault	0—1	1—0	0—1	1—1	1—0	1—0	2—2	0—2	0—1	0—0	2—0	8—8
Hargan	0—1	1—0	0—1	1—1	2—1	1—0	2—0	0—0	0—2	1—1	0—0	8—8
Hoerner	0—1	0—0	0—1	0—0	0—0	0—0	0—0	0—1	0—0	0—1	0—0	0—4
Perry	1—3	1—1	1—1	1—0	2—1	1—1	1—1	0—1	3—1	0—3	4—1	15—14
Peterson	1—0	0—0	0—0	0—0	0—0	0—0	0—0	0—0	0—0	0—0	0—0	1—0
Singer	0—0	1—0	1—1	0—0	0—0	0—0	0—0	1—0	0—0	0—0	0—0	4—1
Skok	0—0	0—0	0—0	0—0	0—1	0—0	0—0	0—0	0—0	0—0	0—0	0—1
Terpko	0—0	0—0	0—0	0—1	0—1	1—1	0—0	0—0	1—1	1—0	0—0	3—3
Umbarger	2—1	2—0	1—3	0—1	1—0	0—0	0—2	0—3	2—2	1—0	1—0	10—12
Totals	4—8	9—3	6—12	11—7	5—7	7—5	11—7	2—10	7—11	3—9	11—7	76—86

No Decisions—Perzanowski.

AMERICAN LEAGUE

PENNANT WINNERS

Year	Club	Manager	W.	L.	Pct.	°G.A.
1901	Chicago	Clark Griffith	83	53	.610	4
1902	Philadelphia	Connie Mack	83	53	.610	5
1903	Boston	James Collins	91	47	.659	14½
1904	Boston	James Collins	95	59	.617	1½
1905	Philadelphia	Connie Mack	92	56	.622	2
1906	Chicago	Fielder Jones	93	58	.616	3
1907	Detroit	Hugh Jennings	92	58	.613	1½
1908	Detroit	Hugh Jennings	90	63	.588	½
1909	Detroit	Hugh Jennings	98	54	.645	3½
1910	Philadelphia	Connie Mack	102	48	.680	14½
1911	Philadelphia	Connie Mack	101	50	.669	13½
1912	Boston	Garland Stahl	105	47	.691	14
1913	Philadelphia	Connie Mack	96	57	.627	6½
1914	Philadelphia	Connie Mack	99	53	.651	8½
1915	Boston	William Carrigan	101	50	.669	2½
1916	Boston	William Carrigan	91	63	.591	2
1917	Chicago	Clarence Rowland	100	54	.649	9
1918	Boston	Edward Barrow	75	51	.595	2½
1919	Chicago	William Gleason	88	52	.629	3½
1920	Cleveland	Tristram Speaker	98	56	.636	2
1921	New York	Miller Huggins	98	55	.641	4½
1922	New York	Miller Huggins	94	60	.610	1
1923	New York	Miller Huggins	98	54	.645	16
1924	Washington	Stanley (Bucky) Harris	92	62	.597	2
1925	Washington	Stanley (Bucky) Harris	96	55	.636	8½
1926	New York	Miller Huggins	91	63	.591	3
1927	New York	Miller Huggins	110	44	.714	19
1928	New York	Miller Huggins	101	53	.656	2½
1929	Philadelphia	Connie Mack	104	46	.693	18
1930	Philadelphia	Connie Mack	102	52	.662	8
1931	Philadelphia	Connie Mack	107	45	.704	13½
1932	New York	Joseph McCarthy	107	47	.695	13
1933	Washington	Joseph Cronin	99	53	.651	7
1934	Detroit	Gordon (Mickey) Cochrane	101	53	.656	7
1935	Detroit	Gordon (Mickey) Cochrane	93	58	.616	3
1936	New York	Joseph McCarthy	102	51	.667	19½
1937	New York	Joseph McCarthy	102	52	.662	13
1938	New York	Joseph McCarthy	99	53	.651	9½
1939	New York	Joseph McCarthy	106	45	.702	17
1940	Detroit	Delmer Baker	90	64	.584	1
1941	New York	Joseph McCarthy	101	53	.656	17
1942	New York	Joseph McCarthy	103	51	.669	9
1943	New York	Joseph McCarthy	98	56	.636	13½
1944	St. Louis	J. Luther Sewell	89	65	.578	1
1945	Detroit	Stephen O'Neill	88	65	.575	1½
1946	Boston	Joseph Cronin	104	50	.675	12
1947	New York	Stanley (Bucky) Harris	97	57	.630	12
1948	Cleveland†	Louis Boudreau	97	58	.626	1
1949	New York	Charles (Casey) Stengel	97	57	.630	1
1950	New York	Charles (Casey) Stengel	98	56	.636	3
1951	New York	Charles (Casey) Stengel	98	56	.636	5
1952	New York	Charles (Casey) Stengel	95	59	.617	2
1953	New York	Charles (Casey) Stengel	99	52	.656	8½
1954	Cleveland	Alfonso Lopez	111	43	.721	8
1955	New York	Charles (Casey) Stengel	96	58	.623	3
1956	New York	Charles (Casey) Stengel	97	57	.630	9
1957	New York	Charles (Casey) Stengel	98	56	.636	8
1958	New York	Charles (Casey) Stengel	92	62	.597	10
1959	Chicago	Alfonso Lopez	94	60	.610	5
1960	New York	Charles (Casey) Stengel	97	57	.630	8

PENNANT WINNERS—Continued

Year Club	Manager	W.	L.	Pct.	°G.A.
1961—New York	Ralph Houk	109	53	.673	8
1962—New York	Ralph Houk	96	66	.593	5
1963—New York	Ralph Houk	104	57	.646	10½
1964—New York	Lawrence (Yogi) Berra	99	63	.611	1
1965—Minnesota	Sabath (Sam) Mele	102	60	.630	7
1966—Baltimore	Henry A. Bauer	97	63	.606	9
1967—Boston	Richard H. Williams	92	70	.568	1
1968—Detroit	E. Mayo Smith	103	59	.636	12
1969—Baltimore (E)°°	Earl S. Weaver	109	53	.673	19
1970—Baltimore (E)°°	Earl S. Weaver	108	54	.667	15
1971—Baltimore (E)°°	Earl S. Weaver	101	57	.639	12
1972—Oakland (W)°°	Richard H. Williams	93	62	.600	5½
1973—Oakland (W)°°	Richard H. Williams	94	68	.580	6
1974—Oakland (W)°°	Alvin Ralph Dark	90	72	.556	5
1975—Boston (E)°°	Darrell D. Johnson	95	65	.594	4½
1976—New York (E)°°	Alfred M. Martin	97	62	.610	10½

°Games ahead of second-place club.   †Defeated Boston in one-game playoff.

°°Won Championship Series.

YEARLY FINISHES

Year	Balt.	Bos.	Calif.	Chi.	Cleve.	Det.	Minn.	N.Y.	Oak.	Wash.
1901	°8	2	....	1	7	3	‡6	5	†4	....
1902	°2	3	....	4	5	7	‡6	8	†1	....
1903	°6	1	....	7	3	5	‡8	4	†2	....
1904	°6	1	....	3	4	7	‡8	2	†5	....
1905	°8	4	....	2	5	3	‡7	6	†1	....
1906	°5	8	....	1	3	6	‡7	2	†4	....
1907	°6	7	....	3	4	1	‡8	5	†2	....
1908	°4	5	....	3	2	1	‡7	8	†6	....
1909	°7	3	....	4	6	1	‡8	5	†2	....
1910	°8	4	....	6	5	3	‡7	2	†1	....
1911	°8	5	....	4	3	2	‡7	6	†1	....
1912	°7	1	....	4	5	6	‡2	8	†3	....
1913	°8	4	....	5	3	6	‡2	7	†1	....
1914	°5	2	....	x6	8	4	‡3	x6	†1	....
1915	°6	1	....	3	7	2	‡4	5	†8	....
1916	°5	1	....	2	6	3	‡7	4	†8	....
1917	°7	2	....	1	3	4	‡5	6	†8	....
1918	°5	1	....	6	2	7	‡3	4	†8	....
1919	°5	6	....	1	2	4	‡7	3	†8	....
1920	°4	5	....	2	1	7	‡6	3	†8	....
1921	°3	5	....	7	2	6	‡4	1	†8	....
1922	°2	8	....	5	4	3	‡6	1	†7	....
1923	°5	8	....	7	3	2	‡4	1	†6	....
1924	°4	7	....	8	6	3	‡1	2	†5	....
1925	°3	8	....	5	6	4	‡1	7	†2	....
1926	°7	8	....	5	2	6	‡4	1	†3	....
1927	°7	8	....	5	6	4	‡3	1	†2	....
1928	°3	8	....	5	7	6	‡4	1	†2	....
1929	°4	8	....	7	3	6	‡5	2	†1	....
1930	°6	8	....	7	4	5	‡2	3	†1	....
1931	°5	6	....	8	4	7	‡3	2	†1	....
1932	°6	8	....	7	4	5	‡3	1	†2	....
1933	°8	7	....	6	4	5	‡1	2	†3	....
1934	°6	4	....	8	3	1	‡7	2	†5	....
1935	°7	4	....	5	3	1	‡6	2	†8	....
1936	°7	6	....	3	5	2	‡4	1	†8	....
1937	°8	5	....	3	4	2	‡6	1	†7	....
1938	°7	2	....	6	3	4	‡5	1	†8	....
1939	°8	2	....	4	3	5	‡6	1	†7	....
1940	°6	x4	....	x4	2	1	‡7	3	†8	....
1941	x°6	2	....	3	x4	x4	x‡6	1	†8	....

YEARLY FINISHES—Continued

Year	Balt.	Bos.	Calif.	Chi.	Cleve.	Det.	Minn.	N.Y.	Oak.	Wash.
1942	*3	2	....	6	4	5	‡7	1	†8	....
1943	*6	7	....	4	3	5	‡2	1	†8	....
1944	*1	4	....	7	x5	2	‡8	3	x†5	....
1945	*3	7	....	6	5	1	‡2	4	†8	....
1946	*7	1	....	5	6	2	‡4	3	†8	....
1947	*8	3	....	6	4	2	‡7	1	†5	....
1948	*6	2	....	8	1	5	‡7	3	†4	....
1949	*7	2	....	6	3	4	‡8	1	†5	....
1950	*7	3	....	6	4	2	‡5	1	†8	....
1951	*8	3	....	4	2	5	‡7	1	†6	....
1952	*7	6	....	3	2	8	‡5	1	†4	....
1953	*8	4	....	3	2	6	‡5	1	†7	....
1954	7	4	....	3	1	5	‡6	2	†8	....
1955	7	4	....	3	2	5	‡8	1	†6	....
1956	6	4	....	3	2	5	‡7	1	†8	....
1957	5	3	....	2	6	4	‡8	1	†7	....
1958	6	3	....	2	4	5	‡8	1	†7	....
1959	6	5	....	1	2	4	‡8	3	†7	....
1960	2	7	....	3	4	6	‡5	1	†8	....
1961	3	6	§8	4	5	2	7	1	x†9	x9
1962	7	8	§3	5	6	4	2	1	†9	10
1963	4	7	§9	2	x5	x5	3	1	†8	10
1964	3	8	§5	2	x6	4	x6	1	†10	9
1965	3	9	§7	2	5	4	1	6	†10	8
1966	1	9	6	4	5	3	2	10	†7	8
1967	x6	1	5	4	8	x2	x2	9	†10	x6
1968	2	4	x8	x8	3	1	7	5	6	10

	EAST DIVISION							WEST DIVISION						
Year	Balt.	Bos.	Cleve.	Det.	N.Y.	Wash.	Mil.	Calif.	Chi.	K.C.	Mil.	Minn.	Oak.	Tex.
1969	1	3	6	2	5	4	....	3	5	4	y6	1	2	....
1970	1	3	5	4	2	6	....	3	6	x4	x4	1	2	....
1971	1	3	6	2	4	5	....	4	3	2	6	5	1	....
1972	3	2	5	1	4	....	6	5	2	4		3	1	6
1973	1	2	6	3	4		5	4	5	2		3	1	6
1974	1	3	4	6	2		5	6	4	5		3	1	2
1975	2	1	4	6	3		5	6	5	2		4	1	3
1976	2	3	4	5	1		6	x4	6	1		3	2	x4

*Record of predecessor St. Louis club. †Predecessor Philadelphia (1901-54), Kansas City (1955-67). ‡Predecessor Washington Club. §Known as Los Angeles Angels from 1961 to September 2, 1965. yPredecessor Seattle club. xTied for position.

Note—In 1901, Milwaukee was eighth. In 1902, St. Louis was second.

LEADING BATSMEN

Year	Player and Club	G.	AB.	R.	H.	TB.	2B.	3B.	HR.	RBI.	B.A.
1901—	Napoleon Lajoie, Philadelphia	131	543	145	229	345	48	13	14	....	.422
1902—	Edward Delahanty, Washington	123	474	103	178	279	41	15	10	....	.376
1903—	Napoleon Lajoie, Cleveland	126	488	90	173	260	40	13	7	....	.355
1904—	Napoleon Lajoie, Cleveland	140	554	92	211	304	50	14	5	....	.381
1905—	Elmer Flick, Cleveland	131	496	71	152	231	29	19	4	....	.306
1906—	George Stone, St. Louis	154	581	91	208	288	24	19	6	....	.358
1907—	Tyrus Cobb, Detroit	150	605	97	212	286	29	15	5	116	.350
1908—	Tyrus Cobb, Detroit	150	581	88	188	276	36	20	4	101	.324
1909—	Tyrus Cobb, Detroit	156	573	116	216	296	33	10	9	115	.377
1910—	Tyrus Cobb, Detroit	140	509	106	196	282	36	13	8	88	.385
1911—	Tyrus Cobb, Detroit	146	591	147	248	367	47	24	8	144	.420
1912—	Tyrus Cobb, Detroit	140	553	119	227	324	30	23	7	90	.410
1913—	Tyrus Cobb, Detroit	122	428	70	167	229	18	16	4	65	.390
1914—	Tyrus Cobb, Detroit	97	345	69	127	177	22	11	2	57	.368
1915—	Tyrus Cobb, Detroit	156	563	144	208	274	31	13	3	95	.369
1916—	Tristram Speaker, Cleveland	151	546	102	211	274	41	8	2	83	.386
1917—	Tyrus Cobb, Detroit	152	588	107	225	336	44	23	7	108	.383
1978—	Tyrus Cobb, Detroit	111	421	83	161	217	19	14	3	64	.382
1919—	Tyrus Cobb, Detroit	124	497	92	191	256	36	13	1	69	.384

LEADING BATSMEN—Continued

Year	Player and Club	G.	AB.	R.	H.	TB.	2B.	3B.	HR.	RBI.	B.A.
1920—	George Sisler, St. Louis	154	631	137	257	399	49	18	19	122	.407
1921—	Harry Heilmann, Detroit	149	602	114	237	365	43	14	19	139	.394
1922—	George Sisler, St. Louis	142	586	134	246	348	42	18	8	105	.420
1923—	Harry Heilmann, Detroit	144	524	121	211	331	44	11	18	115	.403
1924—	George (Babe) Ruth, New York	153	529	143	200	391	39	7	46	121	.378
1925—	Harry Heilmann, Detroit	150	573	97	225	326	40	11	13	133	.393
1926—	Henry Manush, Detroit	136	498	95	188	281	35	8	14	86	.378
1927—	Harry Heilmann, Detroit	141	505	106	201	311	50	9	14	120	.398
1928—	Leon (Goose) Goslin, Washington	135	456	80	173	280	36	10	17	102	.379
1929—	Lew Fonseca, Cleveland	148	566	97	209	301	44	15	6	103	.369
1930—	Aloysius Simmons, Philadelphia	138	554	152	211	392	41	16	36	165	.381
1931—	Aloysius Simmons, Philadelphia	128	513	105	200	329	37	13	22	128	.390
1932—	Dale Alexander, Detroit-Boston	124	392	58	144	201	27	3	8	60	.367
1933—	James Foxx, Philadelphia	149	573	125	204	403	37	9	48	163	.356
1934—	H. Louis Gehrig, New York	154	579	128	210	409	40	6	49	165	.363
1935—	Chas. (Buddy) Myer, Washington	151	616	115	215	288	36	11	5	100	.349
1936—	Lucius Appling, Chicago	138	526	111	204	267	31	7	6	128	.388
1937—	Charles Gehringer, Detroit	144	564	133	209	293	40	1	14	96	.371
1938—	James Foxx, Boston	149	565	139	197	398	33	9	50	175	.349
1939—	Joseph DiMaggio, New York	120	462	108	176	310	32	6	30	126	.381
1940—	Joseph DiMaggio, New York	132	508	93	179	318	28	9	31	133	.352
1941—	Theodore Williams, Boston	143	456	135	185	335	33	3	37	120	.406
1942—	Theodore Williams, Boston	150	522	141	186	338	34	5	36	137	.356
1943—	Lucius Appling, Chicago	155	585	63	192	238	33	2	3	80	.328
1944—	Louis Boudreau, Cleveland	150	584	91	191	255	45	5	3	67	.327
1945—	George Stirnweiss, New York	152	632	107	195	301	32	22	10	64	.309
1946—	Jas. (Mickey) Vernon, Washington	148	587	88	207	298	51	8	8	85	.353
1947—	Theodore Williams, Boston	156	528	125	181	335	40	9	32	114	.343
1948—	Theodore Williams, Boston	137	509	124	188	313	44	3	25	127	.369
1949—	George Kell, Detroit	134	522	97	179	244	38	9	3	59	.343
1950—	William Goodman, Boston	110	424	91	150	193	25	3	4	68	.354
1951—	Ferris Fain, Philadelphia	117	425	63	146	200	30	3	6	57	.344
1952—	Ferris Fain, Philadelphia	145	538	82	176	231	43	3	2	59	.327
1953—	Jas. (Mickey) Vernon, Washington	152	608	101	205	315	43	11	15	115	.337
1954—	Roberto Avila, Cleveland	143	555	112	189	265	27	2	15	67	.341
1955—	Albert Kaline, Detroit	152	588	121	200	321	24	8	27	102	.340
1956—	Mickey Mantle, New York	150	533	132	188	376	22	5	52	130	.353
1957—	Theodore Williams, Boston	132	420	96	163	307	28	1	38	87	.388
1958—	Theodore Williams, Boston	129	411	81	135	240	23	2	26	85	.328
1959—	Harvey Kuenn, Detroit	139	561	99	198	281	42	7	9	71	.353
1960—	James (Pete) Runnels, Boston	143	528	80	169	208	29	2	2	35	.320
1961—	Norman Cash, Detroit	159	535	119	193	354	22	8	41	132	.361
1962—	James (Pete) Runnels, Boston	152	562	80	183	256	33	5	10	60	.326
1963—	Carl Yastrzemski, Boston	151	570	91	183	271	40	3	14	68	.321
1964—	Pedro (Tony) Oliva, Minnesota	161	672	109	217	374	43	9	32	94	.323
1965—	Pedro (Tony) Oliva, Minnesota	149	576	107	185	283	40	5	16	98	.321
1966—	Frank Robinson, Baltimore	155	576	122	182	367	34	2	49	122	.316
1967—	Carl Yastrzemski, Boston	161	579	112	189	360	31	4	44	121	.326
1968—	Carl Yastrzemski, Boston	157	539	90	162	267	32	2	23	74	.301
1969—	Rodney Carew, Minnesota	123	458	79	152	214	30	4	8	56	.332
1970—	Alexander Johnson, California	156	614	85	202	282	26	6	14	86	.329
1971—	Pedro (Tony) Oliva, Minnesota	126	487	73	164	266	30	3	22	81	.337
1972—	Rodney Carew, Minnesota	142	535	61	170	203	21	6	0	51	.318
1973—	Rodney Carew, Minnesota	149	580	98	203	273	30	11	6	62	.350
1974—	Rodney Carew, Minnesota	153	599	86	218	267	30	5	3	55	.364
1975—	Rodney Carew, Minnesota	143	535	89	192	266	24	4	14	80	.359
1976—	George H. Brett, Kansas City	159	645	94	215	298	34	14	7	67	.333

LEADERS IN RUNS SCORED

Year	Player and Club	Runs	Year	Player and Club	Runs
1900—	(Not classed as major)		1905—	Harry Davis, Philadelphia	92
1901—	Napoleon Lajoie, Philadelphia	145	1906—	Elmer Flick, Cleveland	98
1902—	David Fultz, Philadelphia	110	1907—	Samuel Crawford, Detroit	102
1903—	Patrick Dougherty, Boston	108	1908—	Matthew McIntyre, Detroit	105
1904—	Patrick Dougherty, Boston-New York	113	1909—	Tyrus Cobb, Detroit	116

LEADERS IN RUNS SCORED—Continued

Year Player and Club	Runs	Year Pitcher and Club	Runs
1910— Tyrus Cobb, Detroit	106	1944— George Stirnweiss, New York	125
1911— Tyrus Cobb, Detroit	147	1945— George Stirnweiss, New York	107
1912— Edward Collins, Philadelphia	137	1946— Theodore Williams, Boston	142
1913— Edward Collins, Philadelphia	125	1947— Theodore Williams, Boston	125
1914— Edward Collins, Philadelphia	122	1948— Thomas Henrich, New York	138
1915— Tyrus Cobb, Detroit	144	1949— Theodore Williams, Boston	150
1916— Tyrus Cobb, Detroit	113	1950— Dominic DiMaggio, Boston	131
1917— Owen (Donie) Bush, Detroit	112	1951— Dominic DiMaggio, Boston	113
1918— Raymond Chapman, Cleveland	84	1952— Lawrence Doby, Cleveland	104
1919— George (Babe) Ruth, Boston	103	1953— Albert Rosen, Cleveland	115
1920— George (Babe) Ruth, New York	158	1954— Mickey Mantle, New York	129
1921— George (Babe) Ruth, New York	177	1955— Alphonse Smith, Cleveland	123
1922— George Sisler, St. Louis	134	1956— Mickey Mantle, New York	132
1923— George (Babe) Ruth, New York	151	1957— Mickey Mantle, New York	121
1924— George (Babe) Ruth, New York	143	1958— Mickey Mantle, New York	127
1925— John Mostil, Chicago	135	1959— Edward Yost, Detroit	115
1926— George (Babe) Ruth, New York	139	1960— Mickey Mantle, New York	119
1927— George (Babe) Ruth, New York	158	1961— Mantle, New York-Maris, New York	132
1928— George (Babe) Ruth, New York	163	1962— Albert G. Pearson, Los Angeles	115
1929— Charles Gehringer, Detroit	131	1963— W. Robert Allison, Minnesota	99
1930— Aloysius Simmons, Philadelphia	152	1964— Pedro (Tony) Oliva, Minnesota	109
1931— H. Louis Gehrig, New York	163	1965— Zoilo Versalles, Minnesota	126
1932— James Foxx, Philadelphia	151	1966— Frank Robinson, Baltimore	122
1933— H. Louis Gehrig, New York	138	1967— Carl Yastrzemski, Boston	112
1934— Charles Gehringer, Detroit	134	1968— Richard McAuliffe, Detroit	95
1935— H. Louis Gehrig, New York	125	1969— Reginald Jackson, Oakland	123
1936— H. Louis Gehrig, New York	167	1970— Carl Yastrzemski, Boston	125
1937— Joseph DiMaggio, New York	151	1971— Donald Buford, Baltimore	99
1938— Henry Greenberg, Detroit	144	1972— Bobby Murcer, New York	102
1939— Robert (Red) Rolfe, New York	139	1973— Reginald Jackson, Oakland	99
1940— Theodore Williams, Boston	134	1974— Carl Yastrzemski, Boston	93
1941— Theodore Williams, Boston	135	1975— Fred Lynn, Boston	103
1942— Theodore Williams, Boston	141	1976— Roy White, New York	104
1943— George Case, Washington	102		

LEADERS IN HITS

Year Player and Club	Hits	Year Player and Club	Hits
1900— (Not classed as major)		1926— George Burns, Cleveland	216
1901— Napoleon Lajoie, Philadelphia	229	Edgar (Sam) Rice, Washington	216
1902— Charles Hickman, Cleveland	194	1927— Earle Combs, New York	231
1903— Patrick Dougherty, Boston	195	1928— Henry Manush, St. Louis	241
1904— Napoleon Lajoie, Cleveland	211	1929— Dale Alexander, Detroit	215
1905— George Stone, St. Louis	187	Charles Gehringer, Detroit	215
1906— Napoleon Lajoie, Cleveland	214	1930— U. John Hodapp, Cleveland	225
1907— Tyrus Cobb, Detroit	212	1931— H. Louis Gehrig, New York	211
1908— Tyrus Cobb, Detroit	188	1932— Aloysius Simmons, Philadelphia	216
1909— Tyrus Cobb, Detroit	216	1933— Henry Manush, Washington	221
1910— Napoleon Lajoie, Cleveland	227	1934— Charles Gehringer, Detroit	214
1911— Tyrus Cobb, Detroit	248	1935— Joseph Vosmik, Cleveland	216
1912— Tyrus Cobb, Detroit	227	1936— H. Earl Averill, Cleveland	232
1913— Joseph Jackson, Cleveland	197	1937— Roy (Beau) Bell, St. Louis	218
1914— Tristram Speaker, Boston	193	1938— Joseph Vosmik, Boston	201
1915— Tyrus Cobb, Detroit	208	1939— Robert (Red) Rolfe, New York	213
1916— Tristram Speaker, Cleveland	211	1940— Raymond (Rip) Radcliff, St. Louis	200
1917— Tyrus Cobb, Detroit	225	W. Barney McCosky, Detroit	200
1918— George Burns, Philadelphia	178	Roger (Doc) Cramer, Boston	200
1919— Cobb, Detroit-Robert Veach, Detroit	191	1941— Cecil Travis, Washington	218
1920— George Sisler, St. Louis	257	1942— John Pesky, Boston	205
1921— Harry Heilmann, Detroit	237	1943— Richard Wakefield, Detroit	200
1922— George Sisler, St. Louis	246	1944— George Stirnweiss, New York	205
1923— Charles Jamieson, Cleveland	222	1945— George Stirnweiss, New York	195
1924— Edgar (Sam) Rice, Washington	216	1946— John Pesky, Boston	208
1925— Aloysius Simmons, Philadelphia	253	1947— John Pesky, Boston	207

LEADERS IN HITS—Continued

Year Player and Club	Hits	Year Player and Club	Hits
1948— Robert Dillinger, St. Louis	207	1963— Carl Yastrzemski, Boston	183
1949— L. Dale Mitchell, Cleveland	203	1964— Pedro (Tony) Oliva, Minnesota	217
1950— George Kell, Detroit	218	1965— Pedro (Tony) Oliva, Minnesota	185
1951— George Kell, Detroit	191	1966— Pedro (Tony) Oliva, Minnesota	191
1952— J. Nelson Fox, Chicago	192	1967— Carl Yastrzemski, Boston	189
1953— Harvey Kuenn, Detroit	209	1968— Dagoberto Campaneris, Oakland	177
1954— Fox, Chicago-Kuenn, Detroit	201	1969— Pedro (Tony) Oliva, Minnesota	197
1955— Albert Kaline, Detroit	200	1970— Pedro (Tony) Oliva, Minnesota	204
1956— Harvey Kuenn, Detroit	196	1971— Cesar Tovar, Minnesota	204
1957— J. Nelson Fox, Chicago	196	1972— Joseph Rudi, Oakland	181
1958— J. Nelson Fox, Chicago	187	1973— Rodney Carew, Minnesota	203
1959— Harvey Kuenn, Detroit	198	1974— Rodney Carew, Minnesota	218
1960— Orestes (Minnie) Minoso, Chicago	184	1975— George Brett, Kansas City	195
1961— Norman Cash, Detroit	193	1976— George Brett, Kansas City	215
1962— Robert Richardson, New York	209		

ONE-BASE HIT LEADERS

Year Player and Club	1B.	Year Player and Club	1B.
1900— (Not classed as major)		1937— John K. Lewis, Washington	162
1901— Napoleon Lajoie, Philadelphia	154	1938— Melo B. Almada, Wash.-St. Louis	158
1902— Fielder A. Jones, Chicago	148	1939— Roger M. Cramer, Boston	147
1903— Patrick H. Dougherty, Boston	161	1940— Roger M. Cramer, Boston	160
1904— William H. Keeler, New York	164	1941— Cecil H. Travis, Washington	153
1905— William H. Keeler, New York	147	1942— John M. Pesky, Boston	165
1906— William H. Keeler, New York	166	1943— Roger M. Cramer, Detroit	159
1907— Tyrus R. Cobb, Detroit	163	1944— George H. Stirnweiss, New York	146
1908— Matthew W. McIntyre, Detroit	131	1945— Irvin G. Hall, Philadelphia	139
George R. Stone, St. Louis	131	1946— John M. Pesky, Boston	159
1909— Tyrus R. Cobb, Detroit	164	1947— John M. Pesky, Boston	172
1910— Napoleon Lajoie, Cleveland	165	1948— L. Dale Mitchell, Cleveland	162
1911— Tyrus R. Cobb, Detroit	169	1949— L. Dale Mitchell, Cleveland	161
1912— Tyrus R. Cobb, Detroit	167	1950— Philip F. Rizzuto, New York	150
1913— Edward T. Collins, Philadelphia	145	1951— George C. Kell, Detroit	150
1914— John P. McInnis, Philadelphia	160	1952— J. Nelson Fox, Chicago	157
1915— Tyrus R. Cobb, Detroit	161	1953— Harvey E. Kuenn, Detroit	167
1916— Tristram Speaker, Cleveland	160	1954— J. Nelson Fox, Chicago	167
1917— Tyrus R. Cobb, Detroit	151	1955— J. Nelson Fox, Chicago	157
J. Clyde Milan, Washington	151	1956— J. Nelson Fox, Chicago	158
1918— George H. Burns, Philadelphia	141	1957— J. Nelson Fox, Chicago	155
1919— Edgar C. Rice, Washington	144	1958— J. Nelson Fox, Chicago	160
1920— George H. Sisler, St. Louis	171	1959— J. Nelson Fox, Chicago	149
1921— John T. Tobin, St. Louis	179	1960— J. Nelson Fox, Chicago	139
1922— George Sisler, St. Louis	134	1961— Robert C. Richardson, New York	148
1923— Charles D. Jamieson, Cleveland	172	1962— Robert C. Richardson, New York	158
1924— Charles D. Jamieson, Cleveland	168	1963— Albert G. Pearson, Los Angeles	139
1925— Edgar C. Rice, Washington	182	1964— Robert C. Richardson, New York	148
1926— Edgar C. Rice, Washington	167	1965— Donald A. Buford, Chicago	129
1927— Earle B. Combs, New York	166	1966— Luis E. Aparicio, Baltimore	143
1928— Henry E. Manush, St. Louis	161	1967— Horace M. Clarke, New York	140
1929— Earle B. Combs, New York	151	1968— Dagoberto B. Campaneris, Oakland	139
1930— Edgar C. Rice, Washington	158	1969— Horace M. Clarke, New York	146
1931— Oscar D. Melillo, St. Louis	142	1970— Alexander Johnson, California	156
Jonathan T. Stone, Detroit	142	1971— Cesar L. Tovar, Minnesota	171
1932— Henry E. Manush, Washington	145	1972— Rodney C. Carew, Minnesota	143
1933— Henry E. Manush, Washington	167	1973— Rodney C. Carew, Minnesota	156
1934— Roger M. Cramer, Philadelphia	158	1974— Rodney C. Carew, Minnesota	180
1935— Roger M. Cramer, Philadelphia	170	1975— Thurman Munson, New York	151
1936— Raymond A. Radcliff, Chicago	161	1976— George Brett, Kansas City	160

TWO-BASE HIT LEADERS

Year Player and Club	2B.	Year Player and Club	2B.
1900— (Not classed as major)		1902— Harry Davis, Philadelphia	43
1901— Napoleon Lajoie, Philadelphia	48	1903— Ralph Seybold, Philadelphia	43

TWO-BASE HIT LEADERS —Continued

Year	Player and Club	2B.
1904—	Napoleon Lajoie, Cleveland	50
1905—	Harry Davis, Philadelphia	47
1906—	Napoleon Lajoie, Cleveland	49
1907—	Harry Davis, Philadelphia	37
1908—	Tyrus Cobb, Detroit	36
1909—	Samuel Crawford, Detroit	35
1910—	Napoleon Lajoie, Cleveland	51
1911—	Tyrus Cobb, Detroit	47
1912—	Tristram Speaker, Boston	53
1913—	Joseph Jackson, Cleveland	39
1914—	Tristram Speaker, Boston	46
1915—	Robert Veach, Detroit	40
1916—	Graney, Cleveland-Speaker, Cleveland	41
1917—	Tyrus Cobb, Detroit	44
1918—	Tristram Speaker, Cleveland	33
1919—	Robert Veach, Detroit	45
1920—	Tristram Speaker, Cleveland	50
1921—	Tristram Speaker, Cleveland	52
1922—	Tristram Speaker, Cleveland	48
1923—	Tristram Speaker, Cleveland	59
1924—	J. Sewell, Cleveland-Heilmann, Detroit	45
1925—	Martin McManus, St. Louis	44
1926—	George Burns, Cleveland	64
1927—	H. Louis Gehrig, New York	52
1928—	Manush, St. Louis-Gehrig, New York	47
1929—	Manush, St. L.-R. Johnson, Detroit-Gehringer, Detroit	45
1930—	U. John Hodapp, Cleveland	51
1931—	Earl Webb, Boston	67
1932—	Eric McNair, Philadelphia	47
1933—	Joseph Cronin, Washington	45
1934—	Henry Greenberg, Detroit	63
1935—	Joseph Vosmik, Cleveland	47
1936—	Charles Gehringer, Detroit	60
1937—	Roy (Beau) Bell, St. Louis	51
1938—	Joseph Cronin, Boston	51
1939—	Robert (Red) Rolfe, New York	46
1940—	Henry Greenberg, Detroit	50
1941—	Louis Boudreau, Cleveland	45
1942—	Donald Kolloway, Chicago	40
1943—	Richard Wakefield, Detroit	38
1944—	Louis Boudreau, Cleveland	45
1945—	Wallace Moses, Chicago	35
1946—	Jas. (Mickey) Vernon, Washington	51
1947—	Louis Boudreau, Cleveland	45
1948—	Theodore Williams, Boston	44
1949—	Theodore Williams, Boston	39
1950—	George Kell, Detroit	56
1951—	Kell, Det.-Yost, Wash.-Mele, Wash.	36
1952—	Ferris Fain, Philadelphia	43
1953—	Jas. (Mickey) Vernon, Washington	43
1954—	Jas. (Mickey) Vernon, Washington	33
1955—	Harvey Kuenn, Detroit	38
1956—	James Piersall, Boston	40
1957—	Minoso, Chicago-Gardner, Baltimore	36
1958—	Harvey Kuenn, Detroit	39
1959—	Harvey Kuenn, Detroit	42
1960—	John (Tito) Francona, Cleveland	36
1961—	Albert Kaline, Detroit	41
1962—	Floyd Robinson, Chicago	45
1963—	Carl Yastrzemski, Boston	40
1964—	Pedro (Tony) Oliva, Minnesota	43
1965—	Zoilo Versalles, Minnesota	45
	Carl Yastrzemski, Boston	45
1966—	Carl Yastrzemski, Boston	39
1967—	Pedro (Tony) Oliva, Minnesota	34
1968—	C. Reginald Smith, Boston	37
1969—	Pedro (Tony) Oliva, Minnesota	39
1970—	Pedro (Tony) Oliva, Minnesota	36
	Amos Otis, Kansas City	36
	Cesar Tovar, Minnesota	36
1971—	C. Reginald Smith, Boston	33
1972—	Louis Piniella, Kansas City	33
1973—	Salvatore Bando, Oakland	32
	Pedro Garcia, Milwaukee	32
1974—	Joseph Rudi, Oakland	39
1975—	Fred Lynn, Boston	47
1976—	Amos Otis, Kansas City	40

THREE-BASE HIT LEADERS

Year	Player and Club	3B.
1900—	(Not classed as major)	
1901—	James Williams, Baltimore	22
1902—	James Williams, Baltimore	23
1903—	Samuel Crawford, Detroit	25
1904—	Charles (Chick) Stahl, Boston	22
1905—	Elmer Flick, Cleveland	19
1906—	Elmer Flick, Cleveland	22
1907—	Elmer Flick, Cleveland	18
1908—	Tyrus Cobb, Detroit	20
1909—	J. Franklin Baker, Philadelphia	19
1910—	Samuel Crawford, Detroit	19
1911—	Tyrus Cobb, Detroit	24
1912—	Joseph Jackson, Cleveland	26
1913—	Samuel Crawford, Detroit	23
1914—	Samuel Crawford, Detroit	26
1915—	Samuel Crawford, Detroit	19
1916—	Joseph Jackson, Chicago	21
1917—	Tyrus Cobb, Detroit	23
1918—	Tyrus Cobb, Detroit	14
1919—	Robert Veach, Detroit	17
1920—	Joseph Jackson, Chicago	20
1921—	Howard Shanks, Washington	19
1922—	George Sisler, St. Louis	18
1923—	Rice, Washington-Goslin, Washington	18
1924—	Walter Pipp, New York	19
1925—	Leon (Goose) Goslin, Washington	20
1926—	H. Louis Gehrig, New York	20
1927—	Earle Combs, New York	23
1928—	Earle Combs, New York	21
1929—	Charles Gehringer, Detroit	19
1930—	Earle Combs, New York	22
1931—	Roy Johnson, Detroit	19
1932—	Joseph Cronin, Washington	18
1933—	Henry Manush, Washington	17
1934—	W. Benjamin Chapman, New York	13
1935—	Joseph Vosmik, Cleveland	20
1936—	Averill, Cleveland-J. MiMaggio, N.Y.	15
	Rolfe, New York	15

THREE-BASE LEADERS—Continued

Year	Player and Club	3B.
1937—	F. Walker, Chicago-Kreevich, Chicago	16
1938—	J. Geoffrey Heath, Cleveland	18
1939—	John (Buddy) Lewis, Washington	16
1940—	Barney McCosky, Detroit	19
1941—	J. Geoffrey Heath, Cleveland	20
1942—	Stanley Spence, Washington	15
1943—	Lindell, New York-Moses, Chicago	12
1944—	Lindell, N. York-Stirnweiss, N. York	16
1945—	George Stirnweiss, New York	22
1946—	Henry Edwards, Cleveland	16
1947—	Thomas Henrich, New York	13
1948—	Thomas Henrich, New York	14
1949—	L. Dale Mitchell, Cleveland	23
1950—	D. DiMaggio, Doerr, Bos.-Evers, Det.	11
1951—	Orestes (Minnie) Minoso, Clev.-Chi.	14
1952—	Roberto Avila, Cleveland	11
1953—	Manuel (Jim) Rivera, Chicago	16
1954—	Orestes (Minnie) Minoso, Chicago	18
1955—	Mantle, New York-Carey, New York	11
1956—	Minoso, Chicago-Jensen, Boston-Simpson, Kansas City-Lemon, Wash.	11
1957—	McDougald, Bauer, Simpson, New York ..	9
1958—	Victor Power, Kansas City-Cleveland	10

Year	Player and Club	3B.
1959—	W. Robert Allison, Washington	9
1960—	J. Nelson Fox, Chicago	10
1961—	Jacob Wood, Detroit	14
1962—	Gino Cimoli, Kansas City	15
1963—	Zoilo Versalles, Minnesota	13
1964—	Richard Rollins, Minnesota	10
	Zoilo Versalles, Minnesota	10
1965—	Dagoberto Campaneris, Kansas City	12
	Zoilo Versalles, Minnesota	12
1966—	Robert Knoop, California	11
1967—	Paul L. Blair, Baltimore	12
1968—	James Fregosi, California	13
1969—	Delbert Unser, Washington	8
1970—	Cesar Tovar, Minnesota	13
1971—	Freddie Patek, Kansas City	11
1972—	Carlton Fisk, Boston	9
	Joseph Rudi, Oakland	9
1973—	Alonza Bumbry, Baltimore	11
	Rodney Carew, Minnesota	11
1974—	John (Mickey) Rivers, California	11
1975—	George Brett, Kansas City	13
	John Rivers, California	13
1976—	George Brett, Kansas City	14

HOME RUN LEADERS

Year	Player and Club	HR.
1900—	(Not classed as major)	
1901—	Napoleon Lajoie, Philadelphia	14
1902—	Ralph (Socks) Seybold, Philadelphia	16
1903—	John (Buck) Freeman, Boston	13
1904—	Harry Davis, Philadelphia	10
1905—	Harry Davis, Philadelphia	8
1906—	Harry Davis, Philadelphia	12
1907—	Harry Davis, Philadelphia	8
1908—	Samuel Crawford, Detroit	7
1909—	Tyrus Cobb, Detroit	9
1910—	J. Garland (Jake) Stahl, Boston	10
1911—	J. Franklin Baker, Philadelphia	9
1912—	J. Franklin Baker, Philadelphia	10
1913—	J. Franklin Baker, Philadelphia	12
1914—	Baker, Philadelphia-Crawford, Detroit	8
1915—	Robert Roth, Chicago-Cleveland	7
1916—	Walter Pipp, New York	12
1917—	Walter Pipp, New York	9
1918—	Ruth, Boston-Tilly Walker, Phila.	11
1919—	George (Babe) Ruth, Boston	29
1920—	George (Babe) Ruth, New York	54
1921—	George (Babe) Ruth, New York	59
1922—	Kenneth Williams, St. Louis	39
1923—	George (Babe) Ruth, New York	41
1924—	George (Babe) Ruth, New York	46
1925—	Robert Meusel, New York	33
1926—	George (Babe) Ruth, New York	47
1927—	George (Babe) Ruth, New York	60
1928—	George (Babe) Ruth, New York	54
1929—	George (Babe) Ruth, New York	46
1930—	George (Babe) Ruth, New York	49
1931—	Ruth, New York-Gehrig, New York	46
1932—	James Foxx, Philadelphia	58
1933—	James Foxx, Philadelphia	48
1934—	H. Louis Gehrig, New York	49
1935—	Foxx, Philadelphia-Greenberg, Detroit.....	36
1936—	H. Louis Gehrig, New York	49
1937—	Joseph DiMaggio, New York	46
1938—	Henry Greenberg, Detroit	58
1939—	James Foxx, Boston	35

Year	Player and Club	HR.
1940—	Henry Greenberg, Detroit	41
1941—	Theodore Williams, Boston	37
1942—	Theodore Williams, Boston	36
1943—	Rudolph York, Detroit	34
1944—	Nicholas Etten, New York	22
1945—	Vernon Stephens, St. Louis	24
1946—	Henry Greenberg, Detroit	44
1947—	Theodore Williams, Boston	32
1948—	Joseph DiMaggio, New York	39
1949—	Theodore Williams, Boston	43
1950—	Albert Rosen, Cleveland	37
1951—	Gus Zernial, Chicago-Philadelphia	33
1952—	Lawrence Doby, Cleveland	32
1953—	Albert Rosen, Cleveland	43
1954—	Lawrence Doby, Cleveland	32
1955—	Mickey Mantle, New York	37
1956—	Mickey Mantle, New York	52
1957—	Roy Sievers, Washington	42
1958—	Mickey Mantle, New York	42
1959—	Colavito, Cleveland-Killebrew, Wash.	42
1960—	Mickey Mantle, New York	40
1961—	Roger Maris, New York	61
1962—	Harmon Killebrew, Minnesota	48
1963—	Harmon Killebrew, Minnesota	45
1964—	Harmon Killebrew, Minnesota	49
1965—	Anthony Conigiaro, Boston	32
1966—	Frank Robinson, Baltimore	49
1967—	Harmon Killebrew, Minnesota	44
	Carl Yastrzemski, Boston	44
1968—	Frank Howard, Washington	44
1969—	Harmon Killebrew, Minnesota	49
1970—	Frank Howard, Washington	44
1971—	William E. Melton, Chicago	33
1972—	Richard Allen, Chicago	37
1973—	Reginald Jackson, Oakland	32
1974—	Richard Allen, Chicago	32
1975—	Reginald Jackson, Oakland	36
	George Scott, Milwaukee	36
1976—	Graig Nettles, New York	32

LEADERS IN TOTAL BASES

Year	Player and Club	T.B.
1900—	(Not classed as major)	
1901—	Napoleon Lajoie, Philadelphia	345
1902—	John (Buck) Freeman, Boston	287
1903—	John (Buck) Freeman, Boston	281
1904—	Napoleon Lajoie, Cleveland	304
1905—	George Stone, St. Louis	260
1906—	George Stone, St. Louis	288
1907—	Tyrus Cobb, Detroit	286
1908—	Tyrus Cobb, Detroit	276
1909—	Tyrus Cobb, Detroit	296
1910—	Napoleon Lajoie, Cleveland	304
1911—	Tyrus Cobb, Detroit	367
1912—	Joseph Jackson, Cleveland	331
1913—	Samuel Crawford, Detroit	298
1914—	Tristram Speaker, Boston	287
1915—	Tyrus Cobb, Detroit	274
1916—	Joseph Jackson, Chicago	293
1917—	Tyrus Cobb, Detroit	336
1918—	George Burns, Philadelphia	236
1919—	George (Babe) Ruth, Boston	284
1920—	George Sisler, St. Louis	399
1921—	George (Babe) Ruth, New York	457
1922—	Kenneth Williams, St. Louis	367
1923—	George (Babe) Ruth, New York	399
1924—	George (Babe) Ruth, New York	391
1925—	Aloysius Simmons, Philadelphia	392
1926—	George (Babe) Ruth, New York	365
1927—	H. Louis Gehrig, New York	447
1928—	George (Babe) Ruth, New York	380
1929—	Aloysius Simmons, Philadelphia	373
1930—	H. Louis Gehrig, New York	419
1931—	H. Louis Gehrig, New York	410
1932—	James Foxx, Philadelphia	438
1933—	James Foxx, Philadelphia	403
1934—	H. Louis Gehrig, New York	409
1935—	Henry Greenberg, Detroit	389
1936—	Harold Trosky, Cleveland	405
1937—	Joseph DiMaggio, New York	418
1938—	James Foxx, Boston	398
1939—	Theodore Williams, Boston	344
1940—	Henry Greenberg, Detroit	384
1941—	Joseph DiMaggio, New York	348
1942—	Theodore Williams, Boston	338
1943—	Rudolph York, Detroit	301
1944—	John Lindell, New York	297
1945—	George Stirnweiss, New York	301
1946—	Theodore Williams, Boston	343
1947—	Theodore Williams, Boston	335
1948—	Joseph DiMaggio, New York	355
1949—	Theodore Williams, Boston	368
1950—	Walter Dropo, Boston	326
1951—	Theodore Williams, Boston	295
1952—	Albert Rosen, Cleveland	297
1953—	Albert Rosen, Cleveland	367
1954—	Orestes (Minnie) Minoso, Chicago	304
1955—	Albert Kaline, Detroit	321
1956—	Mickey Mantle, New York	376
1957—	Roy Sievers, Washington	331
1958—	Mickey Mantle, New York	307
1959—	Rocco Colavito, Cleveland	301
1960—	Mickey Mantle, New York	294
1961—	Roger Maris, New York	366
1962—	Rocco Colavito, Detroit	309
1963—	Richard Stuart, Boston	319
1964—	Pedro (Tony) Oliva, Minnesota	374
1965—	Zoilo Versalles, Minnesota	308
1966—	Frank Robinson, Baltimore	367
1967—	Carl Yastrzemski, Boston	360
1968—	Frank Howard, Washington	330
1969—	Frank Howard, Washington	340
1970—	Carl Yastrzemski, Boston	335
1971—	C. Reginald Smith, Boston	302
1972—	Bobby Murcer, New York	314
1973—	David L. May, Milwaukee	295
	George Scott, Milwaukee	295
	Salvatore L. Bando, Oakland	295
1974—	Joseph Rudi, Oakland	287
1975—	George Scott, Milwaukee	318
1976—	George Brett, Kansas City	298

RUNS BATTED IN LEADERS

Note—Runs batted in not compiled prior to 1907; officially adopted in 1920.

Year	Player and Club	RBI
1907—	Tyrus Cobb, Detroit	116
1908—	Tyrus Cobb, Detroit	101
1909—	Tyrus Cobb, Detroit	115
1910—	Samuel Crawford, Detroit	115
1911—	Tyrus Cobb, Detroit	144
1912—	J. Franklin Baker, Philadelphia	133
1913—	J. Franklin Baker, Philadelphia	126
1914—	Samuel Crawford, Detroit	112
1915—	Samuel Crawford, Detroit	116
1916—	Walter Pipp, New York	99
1917—	Robert Veach, Detroit	115
1918—	George Burns, Philadelphia	74
	Robert Veach, Detroit	74
1919—	George (Babe) Ruth, Boston	112
1920—	George (Babe) Ruth, New York	137
1921—	George (Babe) Ruth, New York	171
1922—	Kenneth Williams, St. Louis	155
1923—	George (Babe) Ruth, New York	131
1924—	Leon (Goose) Goslin, Washington	129
1925—	Robert Meusel, New York	138
1926—	George (Babe) Ruth, New York	145
1927—	H. Louis Gehrig, New York	175
1928—	George (Babe) Ruth, New York	142
	H. Louis Gehrig, New York	142
1929—	Aloysius Simmons, Philadelphia	157
1930—	H. Louis Gehrig, New York	174
1931—	H. Louis Gehrig, New York	184
1932—	James Foxx, Philadelphia	169
1933—	James Foxx, Philadelphia	163
1934—	H. Louis Gehrig, New York	165
1935—	Henry Greenberg, Detroit	170
1936—	Harold Trosky, Cleveland	162

RUNS BATTED IN LEADERS—Continued

Year	Player and Club	RBI	Year	Player and Club	RBI
1937—	Henry Greenberg, Detroit	183	1956—	Mickey Mantle, New York	130
1938—	James Foxx, Boston	175	1957—	Roy Sievers, Washington	114
1939—	Theodore Williams, Boston	145	1958—	Jack Jensen, Boston	122
1940—	Henry Greenberg, Detroit	150	1959—	Jack Jensen, Boston	112
1941—	Joseph DiMaggio, New York	125	1960—	Roger Maris, New York	112
1942—	Theodore Williams, Boston	137	1961—	Roger Maris, New York	142
1943—	Rudolph York, Detroit	118	1962—	Harmon Killebrew, Minnesota	126
1944—	Vernon Stephens, St. Louis	109	1963—	Richard Stuart, Boston	118
1945—	Nicholas Etten, New York	111	1964—	Brooks Robinson, Baltimore	118
1946—	Henry Greenberg, Detroit	127	1965—	Rocco Colavito, Cleveland	108
1947—	Theodore Williams, Boston	114	1966—	Frank Robinson, Baltimore	122
1948—	Joseph DiMaggio, New York	155	1967—	Carl Yastrzemski, Boston	121
1949—	Theodore Williams, Boston	159	1968—	Kenneth Harrelson, Boston	109
	Vernon Stephens, Boston	159	1969—	Harmon Killebrew, Minnesota	140
1950—	Walter Dropo, Boston	144	1970—	Frank Howard, Washington	126
	Vernon Stephens, Boston	144	1971—	Harmon Killebrew, Minnesota	119
1951—	Gus Zernial, Chicago-Philadelphia	129	1972—	Richard Allen, Chicago	113
1952—	Albert Rosen, Cleveland	105	1973—	Reginald Jackson, Oakland	117
1953—	Albert Rosen, Cleveland	145	1974—	Jeffrey Burroughs, Texas	118
1954—	Lawrence Doby, Cleveland	126	1975—	George Scott, Milwaukee	109
1955—	Raymond Boone, Detroit	116	1976—	Lee May, Baltimore	109
	Jack Jensen, Boston	116			

BATTERS LEADING IN BASES ON BALLS

Note—Bases on balls not included in batting records in American League prior to 1913.

Year	Player and Club	BB.	Year	Player and Club	BB.
1913—	Burton Shotton, St. Louis	102	1945—	Roy Cullenbine, Cleveland-Detroit	112
1914—	Owen (Donie) Bush, Detroit	112	1946—	Theodore Williams, Boston	156
1915—	Edward Collins, Chicago	119	1947—	Theodore Williams, Boston	162
1916—	Burton Shotton, St. Louis	111	1948—	Theodore Williams, Boston	126
1917—	John Graney, Cleveland	94	1949—	Theodore Williams, Boston	162
1918—	Raymond Chapman, Cleveland	84	1950—	Edward Yost, Washington	141
1919—	John Graney, Cleveland	105	1951—	Theodore Williams, Boston	143
1920—	George (Babe) Ruth, New York	148	1952—	Edward Yost, Washington	129
1921—	George (Babe) Ruth, New York	144	1953—	Edward Yost, Washington	123
1922—	L. W. (Whitey) Witt, New York	89	1954—	Theodore Williams, Boston	136
1923—	George (Babe) Ruth, New York	170	1955—	Mickey Mantle, New York	113
1924—	George (Babe) Ruth, New York	142	1956—	Edward Yost, Washington	151
1925—	William Kamm, Chicago	90	1957—	Mickey Mantle, New York	146
	John Mostil, Chicago	90	1958—	Mickey Mantle, New York	129
1926—	George (Babe) Ruth, New York	144	1959—	Edward Yost, Detroit	135
1927—	George (Babe) Ruth, New York	138	1960—	Edward Yost, Detroit	125
1928—	George (Babe) Ruth, New York	135	1961—	Mickey Mantle, New York	126
1929—	Max Bishop, Philadelphia	128	1962—	Mickey Mantle, New York	122
1930—	George (Babe) Ruth, New York	136	1963—	Carl Yastremski, Boston	95
1931—	George (Babe) Ruth, New York	128	1964—	Norman Siebern, Baltimore	106
1932—	George (Babe) Ruth, New York	130	1965—	Rocco Colavito, Cleveland	93
1933—	George (Babe) Ruth, New York	114	1966—	Harmon Killebrew, Minnesota	103
1934—	James Foxx, Philadelphia	111	1967—	Harmon Killebrew, Minnesota	131
1935—	H. Louis Gehrig, New York	132	1968—	Carl Yastrzemski, Boston	119
1936—	H. Louis Gehrig, New York	130	1969—	Harmon Killebrew, Minnesota	145
1937—	H. Louis Gehrig, New York	127	1970—	Frank Howard, Washington	132
1938—	James Foxx, Boston	119	1971—	Harmon Killebrew, Minnesota	114
	Henry Greenberg, Detroit	119	1972—	Richard Allen, Chicago	99
1939—	Harlond Clift, St. Louis	111		Roy White, New York	99
1940—	Charles Keller, New York	106	1973—	John Mayberry, Kansas City	122
1941—	Theodore Williams, Boston	145	1974—	F. Gene Tenace, Oakland	110
1942—	Theodore Williams, Boston	145	1975—	John Mayberry, Kansas City	119
1943—	Charles Keller, New York	106	1976—	D. Michael Hargrove, Texas	97
1944—	Nicholas Etten, New York	97			

BATTERS LEADING IN STRIKEOUTS

Note—Strikeouts not included in batting records in American League prior to 1913.

Year	Player and Club	SO.
1913	Daniel Moeller, Washington	106
1914	August Williams, St. Louis	120
1915	John Lavan, St. Louis	83
1916	Walter Pipp, New York	82
1917	Robert Roth, Cleveland	73
1918	George (Babe) Ruth, Boston	58
1919	Maurice Shannon, Philadelphia-Boston	70
1920	Aaron Ward, New York	84
1921	Robert Meusel, New York	88
1922	James Dykes, Philadelphia	98
1923	George (Babe) Ruth, New York	93
1924	George (Babe) Ruth, New York	81
1925	Martin McManus, St. Louis	69
1926	Anthony Lazzeri, New York	96
1927	George (Babe) Ruth, New York	89
1928	George (Babe) Ruth, New York	87
1929	James Foxx, Philadelphia	70
1930	James Foxx, Philadelphia	66
	Edward Morgan, Cleveland	66
1931	James Foxx, Philadelphia	84
1932	Bruce Campbell, Chicago-St. Louis	104
1933	James Foxx, Philadelphia	93
1934	Harlond Clift, St. Louis	100
1935	James Foxx, Philadelphia	99
1936	James Foxx, Boston	119
1937	Frank Crosetti, New York	105
1938	Frank Crosetti, New York	97
1939	Hank Greenberg, Detroit	95
1940	Samuel Chapman, Philadelphia	96
1941	James Foxx, Boston	103
1942	Joseph Gordon, New York	95
1943	Chester Laabs, St. Louis	105
1944	J. Patrick Seerey, Cleveland	99
1945	J. Patrick Seerey, Cleveland	97
1946	Charles Keller, New York	101
	J. Patrick Seerey, Cleveland	101
1947	Edwin Joost, Philadelphia	110
1948	J. Patrick Seerey, Cleveland-Chicago	102
1949	Richard Kokos, St. Louis	91
1950	Gus Zernial, Chicago	110
1951	Gus Zernial, Chicago-Philadelphia	101
1952	Lawrence Doby, Cleveland	111
	Mickey Mantle, New York	111
1953	Lawrence Doby, Cleveland	121
1954	Mickey Mantle, New York	107
1955	Norbert Zauchin, Boston	105
1956	James Lemon, Washington	138
1957	James Lemon, Washington	94
1958	James Lemon, Washington	120
	Mickey Mantle, New York	120
1959	Mickey Mantle, New York	126
1960	Mickey Mantle, New York	125
1961	Jacob Wood, Detroit	141
1962	Harmon Killebrew, Minnesota	142
1963	David Nicholson, Chicago	175
1964	Nelson Mathews, Kansas City	143
1965	Zoilo Versalles, Minnesota	122
1966	George Scott, Boston	152
1967	Frank Howard, Washington	155
1968	Reginald Jackson, Oakland	171
1969	Reginald Jackson, Oakland	142
1970	Reginald Jackson, Oakland	135
1971	Reginald Jackson, Oakland	161
1972	A. Bobby Darwin, Minnesota	145
1973	A. Bobby Darwin, Minnesota	137
1974	A. Bobby Darwin, Minnesota	127
1975	Jeffrey Burroughs, Texas	155
1976	James Rice, Boston	123

LEADING BASE STEALERS

Year	Player and Club	SB.
1900	(Not classed as major)	
1901	Frank Isbell Chicago	48
1902	Fred (Topsy) Hartsel, Philadelphia	54
1903	Harry Bay, Cleveland	46
1904	Elmer Flick, Clev-Harry Bay, Clev.	42
1905	Daniel Hoffman, Philadelphia	46
1906	Flick, Cleveland-Anderson, Washington	39
1907	Tyrus Cobb, Detroit	49
1908	Patrick Dougherty, Chicago	47
1909	Tyrus Cobb, Detroit	76
1910	Edward Collins, Philadelphia	81
1911	Tyrus Cobb, Detroit	83
1912	J. Clyde Milan, Washington	88
1913	J. Clyde Milan, Washington	74
1914	Frederick Maisel, New York	74
1915	Tyrus Cobb, Detroit	96
1916	Tyrus Cobb, Detroit	68
1917	Tyrus Cobb, Detroit	55
1918	George Sisler, St. Louis	45
1919	Edward Collins, Chicago	33
1920	Edgar (Sam) Rice, Washington	63
1921	George Sisler, St. Louis	35
1922	George Sisler, St. Louis	51
1923	Edward Collins, Chicago	49
1924	Edward Collins, Chicago	42
1925	John Mostil, Chicago	43
1926	John Mostil, Chicago	35
1927	George Sisler, St. Louis	27
1928	Charles (Buddy) Myer, Boston	30
1929	Charles Gehringer, Detroit	27
1930	Martin McManus, Detroit	23
1931	W. Benjamin Chapman, New York	61
1932	W. Benjamin Chapman, New York	38
1933	W. Benjamin Chapman, New York	27
1934	William Werber, Boston	40
1935	William Werber, Boston	29
1936	Lynford Lary, St. Louis	37
1937	Werber, Phila-Chapman, Wash-Bos	35
1938	Frank Crosetti, New York	27
1939	George Case, Washington	51
1940	George Case, Washington	35
1941	George Case, Washington	33
1942	George Case, Washington	44
1943	George Case, Washington	61

LEADING BASE STEALERS—Continued

Year — Player and Club	SB.	Year — Player and Club	SB.
1944— George Stirnweiss, New York	55	1961— Luis Aparicio, Chicago	53
1945— George Stirnweiss, New York	33	1962— Luis Aparicio, Chicago	31
1946— George Case, Cleveland	28	1963— Luis Aparicio, Baltimore	40
1947— Robert Dillinger, St. Louis	34	1964— Luis Aparicio, Baltimore	57
1948— Robert Dillinger, St. Louis	28	1965— Dagoberto Campaneris, Kansas City	51
1949— Robert Dillinger, St. Louis	20	1966— Dagoberto Campaneris, Kansas City	52
1950— Dominic DiMaggio, Boston	15	1967— Dagoberto Campaneris, Kansas City	55
1951— Orestes (Minnie) Minoso, Clev-Chi	31	1968— Dagoberto Campaneris, Kansas City	62
1952— Orestes (Minnie) Minoso, Chicago	22	1969— Tommy Harper, Seattle	73
1953— Orestes (Minnie) Minoso, Chicago	25	1970— Dagoberto Campaneris, Oakland	42
1954— Jack Jensen, Boston	22	1971— Amos Otis, Kansas City	52
1955— Manuel (Jim) Rivera, Chicago	25	1972— Dagoberto Campaneris, Oakland	52
1956— Luis Aparicio, Chicago	21	1973— Tommy Harper, Boston	54
1957— Luis Aparicio, Chicago	28	1974— William North, Oakland	54
1958— Luis Aparicio, Chicago	29	1975— John Rivers, California	70
1959— Luis Aparicio, Chicago	56	1976— William North, Oakland	75
1960— Luis Aparicio, Chicago	51		

SLUGGING LEADERS

Year — Player and Club	Slug. Avg.	Year — Player and Club	Slug. Avg.
1900— (Not classed as major)		1939— James Foxx, Boston	.694
1901— Napoleon Lajoie, Philadelphia	.630	1940— Henry Greenberg, Detroit	.670
1902— Edward Delahanty, Washington	.589	1941— Theodore Williams, Boston	.735
1903— Napoleon Lajoie, Cleveland	.533	1942— Theodore Williams, Boston	.648
1904— Napoleon Lajoie, Cleveland	.549	1943— Rudolph York, Detroit	.527
1905— Elmer Flick, Cleveland	.466	1944— Robert Doerr, Boston	.5278
1906— George Stone, St. Louis	.496	1945— George Stirnweiss, New York	.476
1907— Tyrus Cobb, Detroit	.473	1946— Theodore Williams, Boston	.667
1908— Tyrus Cobb, Detroit	.475	1947— Theodore Williams, Boston	.634
1909— Tyrus Cobb, Detroit	.517	1948— Theodore Williams, Boston	.615
1910— Tyrus Cobb, Detroit	.554	1949— Theodore Williams, Boston	.650
1911— Tyrus Cobb, Detroit	.621	1950— Joseph DiMaggio, New York	.585
1912— Tyrus Cobb, Detroit	.586	1951— Theodore Williams, Boston	.556
1913— Joseph Jackson, Cleveland	.551	1952— Lawrence Doby, Cleveland	.541
1914— Tyrus Cobb, Detroit	.513	1953— Albert Rosen, Cleveland	.613
1915— Jacques F. Fournier, Chicago	.491	1954— Theodore Williams, Boston	.635
1916— Tristram Speaker, Cleveland	.502	1955— Mickey Mantle, New York	.611
1917— Tyrus Cobb, Detroit	.571	1956— Mickey Mantle, New York	.705
1918— George (Babe) Ruth, Boston	.555	1957— Theodore Williams, Boston	.731
1919— George (Babe) Ruth, Boston	.657	1958— Rocco Colavito, Cleveland	.620
1920— George (Babe) Ruth, New York	.847	1959— Albert Kaline, Detroit	.530
1921— George (Babe) Ruth, New York	.846	1960— Roger Maris, New York	.581
1922— George (Babe) Ruth, New York	.672	1961— Mickey Mantle, New York	.687
1923— George (Babe) Ruth, New York	.764	1962— Mickey Mantle, New York	.605
1924— George (Babe) Ruth, New York	.739	1963— Harmon Killebrew, Minnesota	.555
1925— Kenneth Williams, St. Louis	.613	1964— John (Boog) Powell, Baltimore	.606
1926— George (Babe) Ruth, New York	.737	1965— Carl Yastrzemski, Boston	.536
1927— George (Babe) Ruth, New York	.772	1966— Frank Robinson, Baltimore	.637
1928— George (Babe) Ruth, New York	.709	1967— Carl Yastrzemski, Boston	.622
1929— George (Babe) Ruth, New York	.697	1968— Frank Howard, Washington	.552
1930— George (Babe) Ruth, New York	.732	1969— Reginald Jackson, Oakland	.608
1931— George (Babe) Ruth, New York	.700	1970— Carl Yastrzemski, Boston	.592
1932— James Foxx, Philadelphia	.749	1971— Pedro (Tony) Oliva, Minnesota	.546
1933— James Foxx, Philadelphia	.703	1972— Richard Allen, Chicago	.603
1934— H. Louis Gehrig, New York	.706	1973— Reginald Jackson, Oakland	.531
1935— James Foxx, Philadelphia	.636	1974— Richard Allen, Chicago	.563
1936— H. Louis Gehrig, New York	.696	1975— Fred Lynn, Boston	.566
1937— Joseph DiMaggio, New York	.673	1976— Reginald Jackson, Baltimore	.502
1938— James Foxx, Boston	.704		

LEADING PITCHERS IN WINNING PERCENTAGE

(15 OR MORE VICTORIES)

Year	Pitcher	Club	Won	Lost	Pct.
1901	Clark Griffith	Chicago	24	7	.774
1902	William Bernhard	Philadelphia-Cleveland	18	5	.783
1903	Earl Moore	Cleveland	22	7	.759
1904	John Chesbro	New York	41	12	.774
1905	Jess Tannehill	Boston	22	9	.710
1906	Edward Plank	Philadelphia	19	6	.760
1907	William Donovan	Detroit	25	4	.862
1908	Edward Walsh	Chicago	40	15	.727
1909	George Mullin	Detroit	29	8	.784
1910	Albert (Chief) Bender	Philadelphia	23	5	.821
1911	Albert (Chief) Bender	Philadelphia	17	5	.773
1912	Joseph Wood	Boston	34	5	.872
1913	Walter Johnson	Washington	36	7	.837
1914	Albert (Chief) Bender	Philadelphia	17	3	.850
1915	Ernest Shore	Boston	19	8	.704
	George Foster	Boston	19	8	.704
1916	Edward V. Cicotte	Chicago	15	7	.682
1917	Ewell (Reb) Russell	Chicago	15	5	.750
1918	Samuel Jones	Boston	16	5	.762
1919	Edward V. Cicotte	Chicago	29	7	.806
1920	James Bagby	Cleveland	31	12	.721
1921	Carl Mays	New York	27	9	.750
1922	Leslie (Joe) Bush	New York	26	7	.788
1923	Herbert Pennock	New York	19	6	.760
1924	Walter Johnson	Washington	23	7	.767
1925	Stanley Coveleski	Washington	20	5	.800
1926	George Uhle	Cleveland	27	11	.711
1927	Waite Hoyt	New York	22	7	.759
1928	Alvin Crowder	St. Louis	21	5	.808
1929	Robert Grove	Philadelphia	20	6	.769
1930	Robert Grove	Philadelphia	28	5	.848
1931	Robert Grove	Philadelphia	31	4	.886
1932	John Allen	New York	17	4	.810
1933	Robert Grove	Philadelphia	24	8	.750
1934	Vernon Gomez	New York	26	5	.839
1935	Elden Auker	Detroit	18	7	.720
1936	Monte Pearson	New York	19	7	.731
1937	John Allen	Cleveland	15	1	.938
1938	Charles (Red) Ruffing	New York	21	7	.750
1939	Robert Grove	Boston	15	4	.789
1940	Lynwood (Schoolboy) Rowe	Detroit	16	3	.842
1941	Vernon Gomez	New York	15	5	.750
1942	Ernest Bonham	New York	21	5	.808
1943	Spurgeon (Spud) Chandler	New York	20	4	.833
1944	Cecil (Tex) Hughson	Boston	18	5	.783
1945	Harold Newhouser	Detroit	25	9	.735
1946	David (Boo) Ferriss	Boston	25	6	.806
1947	Allie Reynolds	New York	19	8	.704
1948	John Kramer	Boston	18	5	.783
1949	Ellis Kinder	Boston	23	6	.793
1950	Victor Raschi	New York	21	8	.724
1951	Robert Feller	Cleveland	22	8	.733
1952	Robert Shantz	Philadelphia	24	7	.774
1953	Edmund Lopat	New York	16	4	.800
1954	Sandalio Consuegra	Chicago	16	3	.842
1955	Thomas Byrne	New York	16	5	.762
1956	Edward (Whitey) Ford	New York	19	6	.760
1957	Richard Donovan	Chicago	16	6	.727
	Thomas Sturdivant	New York	16	6	.727
1958	Robert Turley	New York	21	7	.750
1959	Robert Shaw	Chicago	18	6	.750
1960	James Perry	Cleveland	18	10	.643

LEADING PITCHERS IN WINNING
PERCENTAGE—Continued

Year	Pitcher	Club	Won	Lost	Pct.
1961—	Edward (Whitey) Ford	New York	25	4	.862
1962—	Raymond Herbert	Chicago	20	9	.690
1963—	Edward (Whitey) Ford	New York	24	7	.774
1964—	Wallace Bunker	Baltimore	19	5	.792
1965—	James (Mudcat) Grant	Minnesota	21	7	.750
1966—	Wilfred (Sonny) Siebert	Cleveland	16	8	.667
1967—	Joel Horlen	Chicago	19	7	.731
1968—	Dennis McLain	Detroit	31	6	.838
1969—	James Palmer	Baltimore	16	4	.800
1970—	Miguel (Mike) Cuellar	Baltimore	24	8	.750
1971—	David McNally	Baltimore	21	5	.808
1972—	James A. Hunter	Oakland	21	7	.750
1973—	James A. Hunter	Oakland	21	5	.808
1974—	Miguel (Mike) Cuellar	Baltimore	22	10	.688
1975—	Michael A. Torrez	Baltimore	20	9	.690
1976—	William Campbell	Minnesota	17	5	.773

LEADING PITCHERS—EARNED-RUN AVERAGE

(Based on Ten Complete Games Through 1950, Then 154 Innings Until A. L. Expanded in 1961, When It Became 162 Innings)

Year	Pitcher and Club	G.	IP.	ERA.	Year	Pitcher and Club	G.	IP.	ERA.
1913—	Johnson, Washington	48	346	1.14	1945—	Newhouser, Detroit	40	313	1.81
1914—	Leonard, Boston	35	222	1.01	1946—	Newhouser, Detroit	37	293	1.94
1915—	Wood, Boston	25	157	1.49	1947—	Chandler, New York	17	128	2.46
1916—	Ruth, Boston	44	324	1.75	1948—	Bearden, Cleveland	37	230	2.43
1917—	Cicotte, Chicago	49	346	1.53	1949—	Parnell, Boston	39	295	2.78
1918—	Johnson, Washington	39	325	1.27	1950—	Wynn, Cleveland	32	214	3.20
1919—	Johnson, Washington	39	290	1.49	1951—	Rogovin, Detroit-Chicago	27	217	2.78
1920—	Shawkey, New York	38	267	2.46	1952—	Reynolds, New York	35	244	2.07
1921—	Faber, Chicago	43	331	2.47	1953—	Lopat, New York	25	178	2.43
1922—	Faber, Chicago	43	353	2.80	1954—	Garcia, Cleveland	45	259	2.64
1923—	S. Coveleski, Cleveland	33	228	2.76	1955—	Pierce, Chicago	33	206	1.97
1924—	Johnson, Washington	38	278	2.72	1956—	Ford, New York	31	226	2.47
1925—	S. Coveleski, Washington	32	241	2.84	1957—	Shantz, New York	30	173	2.45
1926—	Grove, Philadelphia	45	258	2.51	1958—	Ford, New York	30	219	2.01
1927—	Moore, New York	50	213	2.28	1959—	Wilhelm, Baltimore	32	226	2.19
1928—	Braxton, Washington	38	218	2.52	1960—	Baumann, Chicago	47	185	2.68
1929—	Grove, Philadelphia	42	275	2.81	1961—	Donovan, Washington	23	169	2.40
1930—	Grove, Philadelphia	50	291	2.54	1962—	Aguirre, Detroit	42	216	2.21
1931—	Grove, Philadelphia	41	289	2.06	1963—	Peters, Chicago	41	243	2.33
1932—	Grove, Philadelphia	44	292	2.84	1964—	Chance, Los Angeles	46	278	1.65
1933—	Pearson, Cleveland	19	135	2.33	1965—	McDowell, Cleveland	42	273	2.18
1934—	Gomez, New York	38	282	2.33	1966—	Peters, Chicago	30	205	1.98
1935—	Grove, Boston	35	273	2.70	1967—	Horlen, Chicago	35	258	2.06
1936—	Grove, Boston	35	253	2.81	1968—	Tiant, Cleveland	34	258	1.60
1937—	Gomez, New York	34	278	2.33	1969—	Bosman, Washington	31	193	2.19
1938—	Grove, Boston	24	164	3.07	1970—	Segui, Oakland	47	162	2.56
1939—	Grove, Boston	23	191	2.54	1971—	Blue, Oakland	39	312	1.82
1940—	Feller, Cleveland	43	320	2.62	1972—	Tiant, Boston	43	179	1.91
1941—	T. Lee, Chicago	35	300	2.37	1973—	Palmer, Baltimore	38	296	2.40
1942—	Lyons, Chicago	20	180	2.10	1974—	Hunter, Oakland	41	318	2.49
1943—	Chandler, New York	30	253	1.64	1975—	Palmer, Baltimore	39	323	2.09
1944—	Trout, Detroit	49	352	2.12	1976—	Fidrych, Detroit	31	250	2.34

Note—Wilcy Moore pitched only six complete games—he started 12—in 1927, but was recognized as leader because of 213 innings pitched; Ernie Bonham, New York, had 1.91 ERA and ten complete games in 1940, but appeared in only 12 games and 99 innings, and Bob Feller was recognized as leader.

Note—Earned-runs not tabulated in American League prior to 1913.

STRIKEOUT LEADERS—PITCHING

Year	Pitcher and Club	SO.
1900—	(Not classed as major)	
1901—	Denton (Cy) Young, Boston	159
1902—	George (Rube) Waddell, Philadelphia	210
1903—	George (Rube) Waddell, Philadelphia	301
1904—	George (Rube) Waddell, Philadelphia	349
1905—	George (Rube) Waddell, Philadelphia	286
1906—	George (Rube) Waddell, Philadelphia	203
1907—	George (Rube) Waddell, Philadelphia	226
1908—	Edward Walsh, Chicago	269
1909—	Frank Smith, Chicago	177
1910—	Walter Johnson, Washington	313
1911—	Edward Walsh, Chicago	255
1912—	Walter Johnson, Washington	303
1913—	Walter Johnson, Washington	243
1914—	Walter Johnson, Washington	225
1915—	Walter Johnson, Washington	203
1916—	Walter Johnson, Washington	228
1917—	Walter Johnson, Washington	188
1918—	Walter Johnson, Washington	162
1919—	Walter Johnson, Washington	147
1920—	Stanley Coveleski, Cleveland	133
1921—	Walter Johnson, Washington	143
1922—	Urban Shocker, St. Louis	149
1923—	Walter Johnson, Washington	130
1924—	Walter Johnson, Washington	158
1925—	Robert Grove, Philadelphia	116
1926—	Robert Grove, Philadelphia	194
1927—	Robert Grove, Philadelphia	174
1928—	Robert Grove, Philadelphia	183
1929—	Robert Grove, Philadelphia	170
1930—	Robert Grove, Philadelphia	209
1931—	Robert Grove, Philadelphia	175
1932—	Charles (Red) Ruffing, New York	190
1933—	Vernon Gomez, New York	163
1934—	Vernon Gomez, New York	158
1935—	Thomas Bridges, Detroit	163
1936—	Thomas Bridges, Detroit	175
1937—	Vernon Gomez, New York	194
1938—	Robert Feller, Cleveland	240
1939—	Robert Feller, Cleveland	246
1940—	Robert Feller, Cleveland	261
1941—	Robert Feller, Cleveland	260
1942—	Louis (Bobo) Newsom, Washington	113
	Cecil (Tex) Hughson, Boston	113
1943—	Allie Reynolds, Cleveland	151
1944—	Harold Newhouser, Detroit	187
1945—	Harold Newhouser, Detroit	212
1946—	Robert Feller, Cleveland	348
1947—	Robert Feller, Cleveland	196
1948—	Robert Feller, Cleveland	164
1949—	Virgil Trucks, Detroit	153
1950—	Robert Lemon, Cleveland	170
1951—	Victor Raschi, New York	164
1952—	Allie Reynolds, New York	160
1953—	W. William Pierce, Chicago	186
1954—	Robert Turley, Baltimore	185
1955—	Herbert Score, Cleveland	245
1956—	Herbert Score, Cleveland	263
1957—	Early Wynn, Cleveland	184
1958—	Early Wynn, Chicago	179
1959—	James Bunning, Detroit	201
1960—	James Bunning, Detroit	201
1961—	Camilo Pascual, Minnesota	221
1962—	Camilo Pascual, Minnesota	206
1963—	Camilo Pascual, Minnesota	202
1964—	Alphonso Downing, New York	217
1965—	Samuel McDowell, Cleveland	325
1966—	Samuel McDowell, Cleveland	225
1967—	James Lonborg, Boston	246
1968—	Samuel McDowell, Cleveland	283
1969—	Samuel McDowell, Cleveland	279
1970—	Samuel McDowell, Cleveland	304
1971—	Michael Lolich, Detroit	308
1972—	L. Nolan Ryan, California	329
1973—	L. Nolan Ryan, California	383
1974—	L. Nolan Ryan, California	367
1975—	Frank Tanana, California	269
1976—	L. Nolan Ryan, California	327

SHUTOUT LEADERS

Year	Pitcher and Club	ShO.
1900—	(Not classed as major)	
1901—	Clark C. Griffith, Chicago	5
	Denton T. Young, Boston	5
1902—	Adrian Joss, Cleveland	5
1903—	Denton T. Young, Boston	7
1904—	Denton T. Young, Boston	10
1905—	Edward H. Killian, Detroit	8
1906—	Edward A. Walsh, Chicago	10
1907—	Edward S. Plank, Philadelphia	8
1908—	Edward A. Walsh, Chicago	12
1909—	Edward A. Walsh, Chicago	8
1910—	John W. Coombs, Philadelphia	13
1911—	Walter P. Johnson, Washington	6
	Edward S. Plank, Philadelphia	6
1912—	Joseph Wood, Boston	10
1913—	Walter P. Johnson, Washington	12
1914—	Walter P. Johnson, Washington	10
1915—	Walter P. Johnson, Washington	8
1916—	George H. Ruth, Boston	9
1917—	Stanley Coveleski, Cleveland	9
1918—	Walter P. Johnson, Washington	8
	Carl W. Mays, Boston	8
1919—	Walter P. Johnson, Washington	7
1920—	Carl W. Mays, New York	6
1921—	Samuel P. Jones, Boston	5
1922—	George E. Uhle, Cleveland	5
1923—	Stanley Coveleski, Cleveland	5
1924—	Walter P. Johnson, Washington	6
1925—	Theodore A. Lyons, Chicago	5
1926—	Edwin L. Wells, Detroit	4
1927—	Horace M. Lisenbee, Washington	4
1928—	Herbert J. Pennock, New York	5
1929—	George F. Blaeholder, St. Louis	4
	Alvin F. Crowder, St. Louis	4
	Samuel D. Gray, St. Louis	4
	Daniel K. MacFayden, Boston	4
1930—	Clinton H. Brown, Cleveland	3
	George L. Earnshaw, Philadelphia	3
	George W. Pipgras, New York	3
1931—	Robert M. Grove, Philadelphia	4
	Victor G. Sorrell, Detroit	4
1932—	Thomas D. Bridges, Detroit	4
	Robert M. Grove, Philadelphia	4
1933—	Oral C. Hildebrand, Cleveland	6

SHUTOUT LEADERS—Continued

Year	Pitcher and Club	ShO.
1934—	Vernon L. Gomez, New York	6
	Melvin L. Harder, Cleveland	6
1935—	Lynwood T. Rowe, Detroit	6
1936—	Robert M. Grove, Boston	6
1937—	Vernon L. Gomez, New York	6
1938—	Vernon L. Gomez, New York	4
1939—	Charles H. Ruffing, New York	5
1940—	Robert W. Feller, Cleveland	4
	Theodore A. Lyons, Chicago	4
	Albert J. Milnar, Cleveland	4
1941—	Robert W. Feller, Cleveland	6
1942—	Ernest E. Bonham, New York	6
1943—	Spurgeon F. Chandler, New York	5
	Paul H. Trout, Detroit	5
1944—	Paul H. Trout, Detroit	7
1945—	Harold Newhouser, Detroit	8
1946—	Robert W. Feller, Cleveland	10
1947—	Robert W. Feller, Cleveland	5
1948—	Robert G. Lemon, Cleveland	10
1949—	Edward M. Garcia, Cleveland	6
	Ellis R. Kinder, Boston	6
	Virgil O. Trucks, Detroit	6
1950—	Arthur J. Houtteman, Detroit	4
1951—	Allie P. Reynolds, New York	7
1952—	Edward M. Garcia, Cleveland	6
	Allie P. Reynolds, New York	6
1953—	Erwin C. Porterfield, Washington	9
1954—	Edward M. Garcia, Cleveland	5
	Virgil O. Trucks, Chicago	5
1955—	William F. Hoeft, Detroit	7
1956—	Herbert J. Score, Cleveland	5
1957—	James A. Wilson, Chicago	5

Year	Pitcher and Club	ShO.
1958—	Edward C. Ford, New York	7
1959—	Camilo A. Pascual, Washington	6
1960—	Edward C. Ford, New York	4
	James E. Perry, Cleveland	4
	Early Wynn, Chicago	4
1961—	Stephen D. Barber, Baltimore	8
	Camilo A. Pascual, Minnesota	8
1962—	Richard E. Donovan, Cleveland	5
	James L. Kaat, Minnesota	5
	Camilo A. Pascual, Minnesota	5
1963—	Raymond E. Herbert, Chicago	7
1964—	W. Dean Chance, Los Angeles	11
1965—	James T. Grant, Minnesota	6
1966—	Thomas E. John, Chicago	5
	Samuel E. McDowell, Cleveland	5
	Luis C. Tiant, Cleveland	5
1967—	Steven L. Hargan, Cleveland	6
	Joel E. Horlen, Chicago	6
	Thomas E. John, Chicago	6
	Michael S. Lolich, Detroit	6
	James E. McGlothlin, California	6
1968—	Luis C. Tiant, Cleveland	9
1969—	Dennis D. McLain, Detroit	9
1970—	Charles T. Dobson, Oakland	5
	James A. Palmer, Baltimore	5
1971—	Vida Blue, Oakland	8
1972—	L. Nolan Ryan, California	9
1973—	Rikalbert Blyleven, Minnesota	9
1974—	Luis C. Tiant, Boston	7
1975—	James A. Palmer, Baltimore	10
1976—	L. Nolan Ryan, California	7

Major League Baseball Players Association

375 Park Avenue, New York, N. Y. 10022
Telephone—752-0940 (area code 212)

Marvin J. Miller—Executive Director
Richard M. Moss—General Counsel
Secretarial Staff—Sue Carr and Marlene Widrow

EXECUTIVE BOARD

Brooks Robinson—American League Representative
Mike Marshall—National League Representative
Steve Rogers—Pension Committee
Brooks Robinson—Pension Committee
Plus all remaining player representatives

NATIONAL LEAGUE PLAYER REPRESENTATIVES

Mike Marshall—Atlanta Braves
Joe Coleman—Chicago Cubs
Bob Bailey—Cincinnati Reds
Bob Watson—Houston Astros
Tommy John—Los Angeles Dodgers
Steve Rogers—Montreal Expos
Jon Matlack—New York Mets
Bob Boone—Philadelphia Phillies
Jerry Reuss—Pittsburgh Pirates
Lou Brock—St. Louis Cardinals
Brent Strom—San Diego Padres
Jim Barr—San Francisco Giants

AMERICAN LEAGUE PLAYER REPRESENTATIVES

Mark Belanger—Baltimore Orioles
Bill Lee—Boston Red Sox
Paul Hartzell—California Angels
Bucky Dent—Chicago White Sox
Tom Buskey—Cleveland Indians
Dave Roberts—Detroit Tigers
Steve Busby—Kansas City Royals
Mike Hegan—Milwaukee Brewers
Rod Carew—Minnesota Twins
Dock Ellis—New York Yankees
Jim Todd—Oakland Athletics
Nelson Briles—Texas Rangers

EIGHTH CHAMPIONSHIP SERIES

Including

A. L. Playoff Review

A. L. Game Box Scores

A. L. Composite Box Score

N. L. Playoff Review

N. L. Game Box Scores

N. L. Composite Box Score

Chris Chambliss stands on his toes to watch flight of his ninth-inning home run that won the American League pennant for the Yankees.

Yanks Capture A. L. Gonfalon

By JOE MARCIN

With one swing of the bat, New York Yankee first baseman Chris Chambliss propelled his team to its first American League pennant since 1964 and touched off one of the wildest mob scenes in the history of American sports.

With the score tied, 6-6, in the bottom of the ninth inning in the fifth game of the Championship Series, Chambliss sent the first pitch from the Kansas City Royals' fireballing righthander, Mark Littell, over the right field fence. Littell had yielded only one homer during the regular season.

As soon as it was clear that the 1976 American League season was over and the Yankees were winners, Yankee fans, who had been wandering in a desert of pennantless seasons—something to which they were not accustomed—rushed onto the field.

By the time Chambliss reached first base, he was surrounded by spectators. When he reached second, the bag had already been removed by a souvenir collector and Chambliss had to reach out to touch it. He never did reach third and came nowhere near home, although his teammates brought him out later to stamp his feet in the general vicinity of home plate.

The hero of the evening was fortunate to escape without serious injury, as were his teammates. The fans' victory "celebration" turned into an orgy of hoodlumism and looting and resulted in about $100,000 worth of damage being done to the premises.

Chambliss' homer was the climax of an exciting game. After the lead seesawed back and forth in the early going, the Yankees finally managed to carry a 6-3 bulge into the eighth frame. But the Royals' third baseman, George Brett,

GAME OF SATURDAY, OCTOBER 9, AT KANSAS CITY

New York	AB	R	H	RBI	PO	A	Kansas City	AB	R	H	RBI	PO	A
Rivers, cf	5	2	2	0	0	0	Otis, cf	1	0	0	0	0	0
R. White, lf	4	0	1	2	4	0	Wohlford, lf	3	0	0	0	2	0
Munson, c	5	1	1	0	5	2	Brett, 3b	4	0	3	0	1	3
Piniella, dh	4	0	2	0	0	0	McRae, dh	4	0	0	0	0	0
Chambliss, 1b	4	0	2	1	7	0	Mayberry, 1b	3	0	0	0	10	0
Nettles, 3b	4	0	0	0	3	3	Cowens, rf-cf	3	1	1	0	3	0
Maddox, rf	4	0	1	0	4	0	Poquette, lf-rf	3	0	0	1	4	0
Randolph, 2b	4	0	0	0	2	2	F. White, 2b	2	0	0	0	2	3
Stanley, ss	4	1	3	0	2	1	Rojas, ph-2b	1	0	0	0	0	0
Hunter, p	0	0	0	0	0	2	Patek, ss	3	0	1	0	1	3
							Martinez, c	2	0	0	0	4	0
							Quirk, ph	0	0	0	0	0	0
							Wathan, c	0	0	0	0	0	0
							Stinson, ph	1	0	0	0	0	0
							Gura, p	0	0	0	0	0	0
							Littell, p	0	0	0	0	0	0
Totals	38	4	12	3	27	10	Totals	30	1	5	1	27	9

New York	2	0	0	0	0	0	0	0	2	— 4
Kansas City	0	0	0	0	0	0	0	1	0	— 1

New York	IP	H	R	ER	BB	SO
Hunter (Winner)	9	5	1	1	0	5

Kansas City	IP	H	R	ER	BB	SO
Gura (Loser)	8⅔	12	4	3	1	4
Littell	⅓	0	0	0	0	0

Errors—Brett 2. Double play—Kansas City 1. Left on bases—New York 8, Kansas City 2. Two-base hits—Stanley, R. White. Three-base hits—Chambliss, Cowens. Umpires—Brinkman, Haller, Maloney, Barnett, Frantz and McCoy. Time—2:06. Attendance—41,077.

Kansas City's Fred Patek, at 5-feet-4 the smallest player in the majors, was the Royals' big man in the fourth A. L. playoff game with two doubles, a single and three runs batted in.

Chris Chambliss is mobbed by fans as he circles the bases after hitting his pennant-winning homer.

tied the game with a three-run home run. That set the stage for the pulsating finish.

The Yankees had been substantial favorites to win the playoff but the Royals, even after losing ace center fielder Amos Otis because of a leg injury in the first game, battled right down to the wire.

The Series opened in Kansas City and the Royals showed their nervousness by handing the Yanks two runs in the first inning with Brett committing a

GAME OF SUNDAY, OCTOBER 10, AT KANSAS CITY

New York	AB.	R.	H.	RBI.	PO.	A.
Rivers, cf	4	0	0	0	3	0
R. White, lf	4	1	2	0	2	0
Munson, c	5	1	2	1	2	1
Chambliss, 1b	5	0	3	1	9	1
May, dh	5	1	2	0	0	0
Nettles, 3b	3	0	1	0	2	5
Gamble, rf	4	0	1	1	3	0
Randolph, 2b	3	0	0	0	1	3
Stanley, ss	3	0	1	0	0	4
Piniella, ph	1	0	0	0	0	0
Mason, ss	0	0	0	0	1	0
Figueroa, p	0	0	0	0	0	0
Tidrow, p	0	0	0	0	1	0
Totals	37	3	12	3	24	14

Kansas City	AB.	R.	H.	RBI.	PO.	A.
Wohlford, lf	4	1	1	0	2	0
Cowens, cf	5	1	1	0	5	0
Brett, 3b	3	1	1	1	0	1
Mayberry, 1b	4	1	1	1	12	0
McRae, dh	3	0	0	0	0	0
Poquette, rf	3	1	2	2	2	0
F. White, 2b	4	1	1	0	3	5
Patek, ss	4	1	1	1	1	6
Martinez, c	4	0	1	2	2	0
Leonard, p	0	0	0	0	0	0
Splittorff, p	0	0	0	0	0	1
Mingori, p	0	0	0	0	0	0
Totals	34	7	9	7	27	13

New York	0	1	2	0	0	0	0	0	0	– 3
Kansas City	2	0	0	0	0	2	0	3	x	– 7

New York	IP.	H.	R.	ER.	BB.	SO.
Figueroa (Loser)	5⅓	6	4	4	2	2
Tidrow	2⅔	3	3	2	1	0

Kansas City	IP.	H.	R.	ER.	BB.	SO.
Leonard	2⅓	6	3	3	2	0
Splittorff (Winner)	5⅔	4	0	0	2	1
Mingori	1	2	0	0	0	1

Errors—Munson 2, Chambliss, Stanley, Gamble. Double plays—Kansas City 2. Left on bases—New York 11, Kansas City 7. Two-base hits—May, R. White, Munson, Stanley, Nettles, Poquette. Three-base hit—Brett. Stolen bases—Cowens 2, Wohlford. Sacrifice fly—Brett. Umpires—Barnett, Maloney, Haller, Frantz, McCoy and Brinkman. Time—2:45. Attendance—41,091.

GAME OF TUESDAY, OCTOBER 12, AT NEW YORK

Kansas City	AB.	R.	H.	RBI.	PO.	A.
Wohlford, lf	2	1	0	0	0	0
Cowens, cf	4	0	1	0	1	0
Brett, 3b	3	1	2	1	1	0
Mayberry, 1b	4	1	1	0	11	0
McRae, dh	2	0	0	1	0	0
Poquette, rf	3	0	1	1	2	0
Nelson, ph	1	0	0	0	0	0
F. White, 2b	2	0	0	0	1	3
Rojas, ph-2b	1	0	0	0	0	0
Patek, ss	3	0	1	0	3	5
Martinez, c	2	0	0	0	5	1
Quirk, ph	1	0	0	0	0	0
Stinson, c	0	0	0	0	0	0
Hassler, p	0	0	0	0	0	0
Pattin, p	0	0	0	0	0	0
Hall, p	0	0	0	0	0	0
Mingori, p	0	0	0	0	0	0
Littell, p	0	0	0	0	0	1
Totals	28	3	6	3	24	11

New York	AB.	R.	H.	RBI.	PO.	A.
Rivers, cf	5	0	1	0	1	0
R. White, lf	3	1	0	0	0	0
Munson, c	4	1	2	0	5	2
Piniella, dh	2	1	1	0	0	0
May, ph-dh	1	0	0	0	0	0
Chambliss, 1b	4	2	2	3	10	2
Nettles, 3b	3	0	1	1	0	3
Maddox, rf	4	0	1	1	4	0
Randolph, 2b	3	0	1	0	3	3
Stanley, ss	3	0	0	0	3	4
Ellis, p	0	0	0	0	1	0
Lyle, p	0	0	0	0	0	0
Totals	32	5	9	5	27	14

Kansas City	3	0	0	0	0	0	0	0	0	– 3
New York	0	0	0	2	0	3	0	0	x	– 5

Kansas City	IP.	H.	R.	ER.	BB.	SO.
Hassler (Loser)	5*	4	4	4	3	3
Pattin	0†	0	1	1	1	0
Hall	⅓	1	0	0	0	0
Mingori	0‡	1	0	0	0	0
Littell	2⅔	3	0	0	1	2

New York	IP.	H.	R.	ER.	BB.	SO.
Ellis (Winner)	8	6	3	3	2	5
Lyle (Save)	1	0	0	0	1	0

    *Pitched to two batters in sixth.
    †Pitched to one batter in sixth.
    ‡Pitched to one batter in sixth.

Errors—None. Double plays—Kansas City 1, New York 2. Left on bases—Kansas City 3, New York 8. Two-base hits—Poquette, Piniella, Munson, Maddox. Home run—Chambliss. Stolen bases—Wohlford, Chambliss, Randolph. Sacrifice fly—McRae. Hit by pitcher—By Ellis (McRae). Passed ball—Munson. Umpires—Maloney, Haller, Frantz, McCoy, Brinkman and Barnett. Time—3:00. Attendance—56,808.

Yankees' Graig Nettles connects for a two-run homer off Royals' Larry Gura in second inning of fourth game.

pair of misplays. Catfish Hunter subdued the home team easily, giving up only five hits, and the New Yorkers captured the game, 4-1.

In the second contest, the Royals found Yankee 19-game winner Ed Figueroa no puzzle and pounded out a 7-3 triumph.

The Yankees won the third engagement, 5-3, as Chambliss got two hits, including a home run, and drove in three runs.

Hunter was supposed to finish off the underdogs in the fourth game but

Royals' Jamie Quirk slides into third after hitting triple in fourth game. Quirk scored on a sacrifice fly.

GAME OF WEDNESDAY, OCTOBER 13, AT NEW YORK

Kansas City	AB.	R.	H.	RBI.	PO.	A.
Cowens, cf	5	0	0	0	4	0
Poquette, lf-rf	4	0	0	0	3	0
Brett, 3b	4	0	0	0	1	2
Mayberry, 1b	3	1	0	0	9	0
McRae, rf	4	2	2	0	2	0
Wohlford, lf	0	0	0	0	3	0
Quirk, dh	2	1	1	2	0	0
Nelson, ph-dh	1	0	0	0	0	0
Rojas, 2b	3	1	2	1	1	3
F. White, pr-2b	0	1	0	0	0	0
Patek, ss	4	1	3	3	3	3
Martinez, c	3	0	1	1	1	1
Gura, p	0	0	0	0	0	0
Bird, p	0	0	0	0	0	1
Mingori, p	0	0	0	0	0	0
Totals	33	7	9	7	27	10

New York	AB.	R.	H.	RBI.	PO.	A.
Rivers, cf	4	0	1	0	5	0
R. White, lf	4	0	1	0	7	0
Munson, c	4	0	2	0	2	1
Piniella, dh	4	0	0	0	0	0
Chambliss, 1b	4	1	1	0	9	0
Nettles, 3b	4	2	2	3	0	2
Maddox, rf	1	0	0	0	1	0
Gamble, ph-rf	2	1	1	0	1	0
Velez, ph	1	0	0	0	0	0
Randolph, 2b	4	0	1	1	1	1
Stanley, ss	2	0	1	0	1	1
Hendricks, ph	1	0	1	0	0	0
Guidry, pr	0	0	0	0	0	0
Mason, ss	0	0	0	0	0	2
Alomar, ph	1	0	0	0	0	0
Hunter, p	0	0	0	0	0	1
Tidrow, p	0	0	0	0	0	0
Jackson, p	0	0	0	0	0	1
Totals	36	4	11	4	27	9

Kansas City										
Kansas City	0	3	0	2	0	1	0	1	0 – 7
New York	0	2	0	0	0	0	1	0	1 – 4

Kansas City	IP.	H.	R.	ER.	BB.	SO.
Gura	2*	6	2	2	0	0
Bird (Winner)	4⅔	4	1	1	0	1
Mingori (Save)	2⅓	1	1	1	0	0

New York	IP.	H.	R.	ER.	BB.	SO.
Hunter (Loser)	3†	5	5	5	1	0
Tidrow	3⅔	2	1	1	2	0
Jackson	2⅓	2	1	1	1	2

*Pitched to one batter in third.
†Pitched to two batters in fourth.

Error—Bird. Double play—Kansas City 1. Left on bases—Kansas City 5, New York 5. Two-base hits—R. White, Patek 2, McRae, Gamble. Three-base hits—Quirk, McRae. Home runs—Nettles 2. Sacrifice flies—Rojas, Quirk. Umpires—Haller, Frantz, McCoy, Brinkman, Barnett and Maloney. Time—2:50. Attendance—56,355.

things didn't work out that way. The Royals knocked him out of the box in the fourth inning and copped a 7-4 decision to deadlock the Series.

That set up the climactic game of the 1976 American League season wherein Chambliss' big blow was the hit of the year and the near riot that followed was an ugly anti-climax.

GAME OF THURSDAY, OCTOBER 14, AT NEW YORK

Kansas City	AB.	R.	H.	RBI.	PO.	A.
Cowens, cf	4	1	1	0	2	0
Poquette, lf	3	0	0	0	2	0
Wohlford, ph-lf	2	1	1	0	0	0
Brett, 3b	4	2	2	3	0	1
Mayberry, 1b	4	1	2	2	6	1
McRae, rf	4	0	0	3	1	0
Quirk, dh	4	0	0	0	0	0
Rojas, 2b	4	1	1	0	3	2
Patek, ss	4	0	1	0	5	1
Martinez, c	4	0	3	1	3	2
Leonard, p	0	0	0	0	0	0
Splittorff, p	0	0	0	0	0	0
Pattin, p	0	0	0	0	0	0
Hassler, p	0	0	0	0	0	1
Littell, p	0	0	0	0	0	0
Totals	37	6	11	6	24	8

New York	AB.	R.	H.	RBI.	PO.	A.
Rivers, cf	5	3	4	0	2	0
R. White, lf	2	2	1	1	4	0
Munson, c	5	0	3	2	4	0
Chambliss, 1b	4	2	3	3	15	0
May, dh	4	0	0	0	0	0
Alomar, pr-dh	0	0	0	0	0	0
Nettles, 3b	2	0	0	0	0	1
Gamble, rf	2	0	0	0	0	0
Randolph, 2b	3	0	0	0	1	5
Stanley, ss	3	0	0	0	1	5
Figueroa, p	0	0	0	0	0	2
Jackson, p	0	0	0	0	0	0
Tidrow, p	0	0	0	0	0	0
Totals	31	7	11	6	27	13

Kansas City								
Kansas City	2	1	0	0	0	0	3	0 – 6
New York	2	0	2	0	0	2	0	0	1 – 7

None out when winning run scored.

Kansas City	IP.	H.	R.	ER.	BB.	SO.
Leonard	0*	3	2	2	0	0
Splittorff	3⅔	3	2	2	3	1
Pattin	⅓	0	0	0	0	0
Hassler	2⅓	4	2	1	3	1
Littell (Loser)	1⅓‡	1	1	1	0	1

New York	IP.	H.	R.	ER.	BB.	SO.
Figueroa	7†	8	4	4	0	3
Jackson	1	2	2	2	0	1
Tidrow (Winner)	1	1	0	0	1	0

*Pitched to three batters in first.
†Pitched to one batter in eighth.
‡Pitched to one batter in ninth.

Errors—Gamble, Brett. Double play—New York 1. Left on bases—Kansas City 5, New York 9. Two-base hits—Brett, Chambliss. Three-base hit—Rivers. Home runs—Mayberry, Brett, Chambliss. Stolen bases—R. White, Rojas, Chambliss. Sacrifice hits—R. White, Gamble. Sacrifice fly—Chambliss. Umpires—Frantz, McCoy, Brinkman, Barnett, Maloney and Haller. Time—3:13. Attendance—56,821.

NEW YORK YANKEES' BATTING AND FIELDING AVERAGES

Player—Position	G.	AB.	R.	H.	TB.	2B.	3B.	HR.	RBI.	B.A.	PO.	A.	E.	F.A.
Hendricks, ph	1	1	0	1	1	0	0	0	0	1.000	0	0	0	.000
Chambliss, 1b	5	21	5	11	20	1	1	2	8	.524	50	3	1	.981
Munson, c	5	23	3	10	12	2	0	0	3	.435	18	6	2	.923
Rivers, cf	5	23	5	8	10	0	1	0	0	.348	11	0	0	1.000
Stanley, ss	5	15	1	5	7	2	0	0	0	.333	7	15	1	.957
R. White, lf	4	11	1	3	4	1	0	0	0	.273	0	0	0	.000
Piniella, dh-ph	3	8	1	2	3	1	0	0	1	.250	4	0	2	.667
Gamble, rf-ph	5	17	2	4	11	1	0	2	4	.235	5	14	0	1.000
Nettles, 3b	3	9	0	2	3	1	0	0	1	.222	9	0	0	1.000
Maddox, rf	3	10	1	2	3	1	0	0	0	.200	0	0	0	.000
May, dh-ph	5	17	0	2	2	0	0	0	1	.118	8	14	0	1.000
Randolph, 2b	5	0	0	0	0	0	0	0	0	.000	1	0	1	1.000
Ellis, p	1	0	0	0	0	0	0	0	0	.000	0	0	0	.000
Guidry, pr	1	0	0	0	0	0	0	0	0	.000	0	0	0	.000
Lyle, p	2	0	0	0	0	0	0	0	0	.000	0	2	0	1.000
Figueroa, p	2	0	0	0	0	0	0	0	0	.000	0	3	0	1.000
Hunter, p	2	0	0	0	0	0	0	0	0	.000	0	1	0	1.000
Jackson, p	2	0	0	0	0	0	0	0	0	.000	1	2	0	1.000
Mason, ss	3	0	0	0	0	0	0	0	0	.000	1	0	0	1.000
Tidrow, p	2	0	0	0	0	0	0	0	0	.000	0	0	0	.000
Alomar, ph-pr-dh	2	1	0	0	0	0	0	0	0	.000	0	0	0	.000
Velez, ph	1	1	0	0	0	0	0	0	0	.000	0	0	0	.000
Totals	5	174	23	55	84	13	2	4	21	.316	132	60	6	.970

KANSAS CITY ROYALS' BATTING AND FIELDING AVERAGES

Player—Position	G.	AB.	R.	H.	TB.	2B.	3B.	HR.	RBI.	B.A.	PO.	A.	E.	F.A.
Brett, 3b	5	18	4	8	14	1	1	1	5	.444	3	7	3	.769
Patek, ss	5	18	2	7	9	2	0	0	4	.389	13	18	0	1.000
Martinez, c	5	15	0	5	5	0	0	0	4	.333	15	4	0	1.000
Rojas, ph-2b	4	9	2	3	3	0	0	0	1	.333	4	6	0	1.000
Mayberry, 1b	5	18	4	4	7	0	0	1	3	.222	48	1	0	1.000
Cowens, rf-cf	5	21	3	4	6	0	1	0	0	.190	15	0	0	1.000
Poquette, lf-rf	5	16	1	3	5	2	0	0	4	.188	13	0	0	1.000
Wohlford, lf-ph	5	11	3	2	2	0	0	0	0	.182	7	0	0	1.000
Quirk, ph-dh	4	7	1	1	3	0	1	0	2	.143	0	0	0	.000
F. White, 2b-pr	4	8	2	1	1	0	0	0	0	.125	6	11	0	1.000
McRae, dh-rf	5	17	2	2	5	1	1	0	1	.118	5	1	0	1.000
Bird, p	1	0	0	0	0	0	0	0	0	.000	0	1	1	.500
Hall, p	1	0	0	0	0	0	0	0	0	.000	0	0	0	.000
Wathan, c	1	0	0	0	0	0	0	0	0	.000	0	0	0	.000
Gura, p	2	0	0	0	0	0	0	0	0	.000	0	0	0	.000
Hassler, p	2	0	0	0	0	0	0	0	0	.000	0	4	0	1.000
Leonard, p	2	0	0	0	0	0	0	0	0	.000	0	0	0	.000
Pattin, p	2	0	0	0	0	0	0	0	0	.000	0	0	0	.000
Splittorff, p	2	0	0	0	0	0	0	0	0	.000	0	1	0	1.000
Littell, p	3	0	0	0	0	0	0	0	0	.000	0	1	0	1.000
Mingori, p	3	0	0	0	0	0	0	0	0	.000	0	0	0	.000
Otis, cf	1	1	0	0	0	0	0	0	0	.000	1	0	0	1.000
Stinson, ph-c	2	1	0	0	0	0	0	0	0	.000	0	0	0	.000
Nelson, ph-dh	2	2	0	0	0	0	0	0	0	.000	0	0	0	.000
Totals	5	162	24	40	60	6	4	2	24	.247	129	51	4	.978

NEW YORK YANKEES' PITCHING RECORDS

Pitcher	G.	GS.	CG.	IP.	H.	R.	ER.	BB.	SO.	HB.	WP.	W.	L.	Pct.	ERA.
Lyle	1	0	0	1	0	0	0	1	0	0	0	0	0	.000	0.00
Ellis	1	1	0	8	6	3	3	2	5	1	0	1	0	1.000	3.38
Tidrow	3	0	0	7⅓	6	4	3	4	0	0	1	1	0	1.000	3.68
Hunter	2	2	1	12	10	6	6	1	5	0	0	1	1	.500	4.50
Figueroa	2	2	0	12⅓	14	8	8	2	5	0	0	0	1	.000	5.84
Jackson	2	0	0	3⅓	4	3	3	1	3	0	0	0	0	.000	8.10
Totals	5	5	1	44	40	24	23	11	18	1	0	3	2	.600	4.70

No shutouts. Save—Lyle.

KANSAS CITY ROYALS' PITCHING RECORDS

Pitcher	G.	GS.	CG.	IP.	H.	R.	ER.	BB.	SO.	HB.	WP.	W.	L.	Pct.	ERA.
Hall	1	0	0	⅓	1	0	0	0	0	0	0	0	0	.000	0.00
Splittorff	2	0	0	9⅓	7	2	2	5	2	0	0	1	0	1.000	1.93
Bird	1	0	0	4⅔	4	1	1	0	1	0	0	1	0	1.000	1.93
Littell	3	0	0	4⅔	4	1	1	1	3	0	0	1	0	.000	1.93
Mingori	3	0	0	3⅓	4	1	1	0	1	0	0	0	0	.000	2.70
Gura	2	2	0	10⅔	18	6	5	1	4	0	0	0	1	.000	4.22
Hassler	2	1	0	7⅓	8	6	5	6	4	0	0	0	1	.000	6.14
Leonard	2	2	0	2⅓	9	5	5	2	0	0	0	0	0	.000	19.29
Pattin	2	0	0	⅓	1	1	1	1	0	0	0	0	0	.000	27.00
Totals	5	5	0	43	55	23	21	16	15	0	0	2	3	.400	4.40

No shutouts. Save—Mingori.

COMPOSITE SCORE BY INNINGS

New York	4	3	4	2	0	5	1	0	4 — 23		
Kansas City	7	4	0	2	0	3	0	8	0 — 24		

Sacrifice hits—Gamble, R. White.

Sacrifice flies—Brett, Chambliss, McRae, Quirk, Rojas.

Stolen bases—Chambliss 2, Cowens 2, Wohlford 2, Randolph, Rojas, R. White.

Caught stealing—Patek 3, Alomar, Brett, McRae, Munson, Rivers.

Double plays—Randolph and Chambliss; Chambliss, Stanley and Randolph; Stanley and Chambliss; Brett, F. White and Mayberry; Patek, F. White and Mayberry; Patek and Mayberry; Martinez and F. White; Rojas, Patek and Mayberry.

Left on bases—New York 41—8, 11, 8, 5, 9; Kansas City 22—2, 7, 3, 5, 5.

Hit by pitcher—By Ellis (McRae).

Passed ball—Munson.

Balks—None.

Time of games—First game, 2:06; second game, 2:45; third game, 3:00; fourth game, 2:50; fifth game, 3:13.

Attendance—First game, 41,077; second game, 41,091; third game, 56,808; fourth game, 56,355; fifth game, 56,821.

Umpires—Brinkman, Haller, Maloney, Barnett, Frantz and McCoy.

Official scorers—Sid Bordman, Kansas City Star; Phil Pepe, New York Daily News.

Big Red Machine Rolls Over Phils

By JOE MARCIN

For most of the summer, baseball fans had been looking forward to what promised to be a great Championship Series between two fine teams, the Cincinnati Reds and the Philadelphia Phillies, each of whom had been impressive winners in their respective divisions.

But in actual play, the 1976 National League pennant playoffs were a routine affair with the Reds asserting complete mastery over their East Division foe.

The Series began in Philadelphia with each club sending its ace lefthander to the mound, Don Gullett for the Reds and Steve Carlton for the Phils. It was no contest. After a spate of first-inning wildness, Gullett was in command all the way, finishing an eight-inning stint with only one run and two hits against his record.

Carlton, meanwhile, was the victim of some shoddy support. A liner by Pete Rose was misplayed into a triple by right fielder Ollie Brown and that gave Cincinnati one of its runs. The Reds got another of their tallies when Phil third sacker Mike Schmidt passed up an easy throw to first base and attempt-

Reds' Dave Concepcion is hugged by teammates after scoring the winning run in the ninth inning of final National League playoff game. Hugging Concepcion, who tallied on Ken Griffey's infield single, are Joe Morgan (right), Reds' Manager Sparky Anderson (with jacket) and relief pitcher Rawly Eastwick (partially hidden).

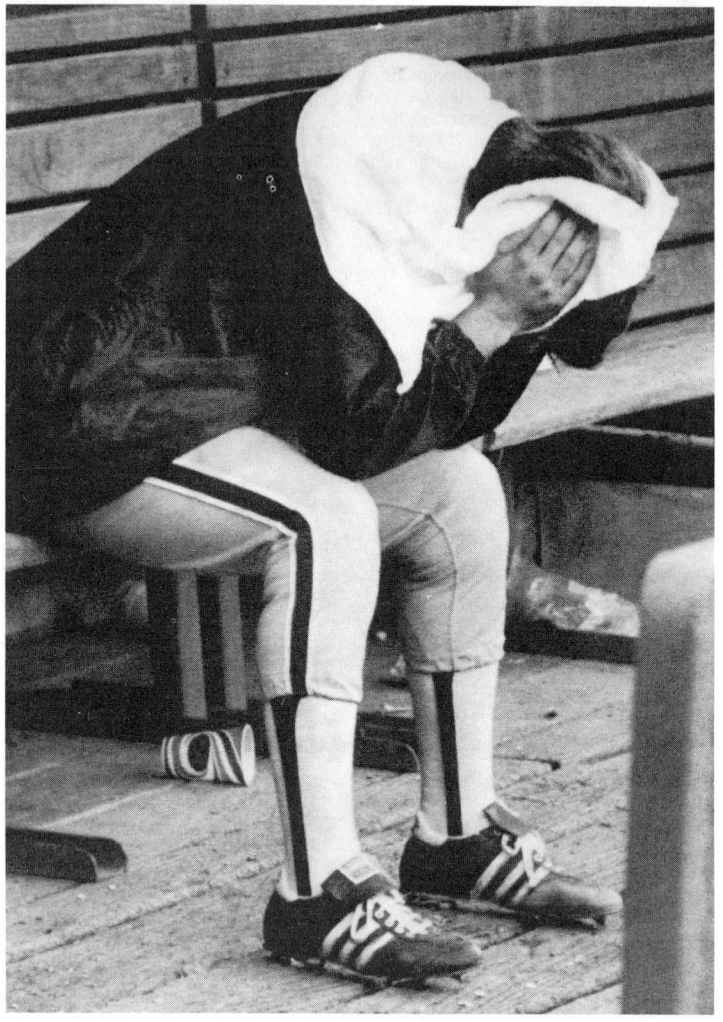

Phils' pitcher Tom Underwood drapes a towel over his head after allowing Ken Griffey's pennant-clinching single.

GAME OF SATURDAY, OCTOBER 9, AT PHILADELPHIA

Cincinnati	AB.	R.	H.	RBI.	PO.	A.	Philadelphia	AB.	R.	H.	RBI.	PO.	A.
Rose, 3b	5	1	3	1	1	2	Cash, 2b	4	1	1	0	2	0
Griffey, rf	4	0	1	0	5	0	Maddox, cf	4	1	2	0	2	0
Morgan, 2b	2	0	0	0	1	1	Schmidt, 3b	3	0	0	1	3	3
Eastwick, p	0	0	0	0	0	1	Luzinski, lf	3	1	1	1	2	0
Perez, 1b	3	0	0	1	8	0	Allen, 1b	3	0	1	0	5	0
Foster, lf	5	1	1	1	4	0	Brown, rf	2	0	0	0	2	0
Bench, c	5	1	2	0	4	2	Johnstone, ph	1	0	1	1	0	0
Concepcion, ss	3	2	1	0	0	2	McCarver, c	3	0	0	0	6	0
Geronimo, cf	4	0	0	0	4	0	McGraw, p	0	0	0	0	0	0
Gullett, p	4	1	2	3	0	0	Tolan, ph	1	0	0	0	0	0
Flynn, 2b	0	0	0	0	0	0	Bowa, ss	3	0	0	0	1	4
Totals	35	6	10	6	27	8	Hutton, ph	1	0	0	0	0	0
							Carlton, p	2	0	0	0	0	0
							Boone, c	1	0	0	0	4	0
							Totals	31	3	6	3	27	7

Cincinnati										
Cincinnati	0	0	1	0	0	2	0	3	0 – 6
Philadelphia	1	0	0	0	0	0	0	0	2 – 3

Cincinnati	IP.	H.	R.	ER.	BB.	SO.
Gullett (Winner)	8	2	1	1	3	4
Eastwick	1	4	2	2	0	0

Philadelphia	IP.	H.	R.	ER.	BB.	SO.
Carlton (Loser)	7*	8	5	4	5	6
McGraw	2	2	1	1	1	4

*Pitched to two batters in eighth.

Error—Schmidt. Double plays—Philadelphia 2. Left on bases—Cincinnati 9, Philadelphia 5. Two-base hits—Rose 2, Concepcion, Bench, Gullett, Cash, Luzinski. Three-base hits—Rose, Griffey. Home run—Foster. Stolen bases—Griffey, Bench, Morgan 2. Sacrifice flies—Schmidt, Perez. Wild pitches—McGraw, Eastwick. Umpires—Sudol, Dale, Stello, Vargo, Harvey and Tata. Time—2:39. Attendance—62,640.

ed, unsuccessfully, to tag a runner off third. Carlton was finally kayoed in the eighth frame and his successor, Tug McGraw, was rapped for a couple of hits resulting in three runs that put the game out of reach for the home team.

After Gullett left the game with an injury to his left leg, the Phils managed to score a pair of runs off reliever Rawly Eastwick. But it was a meaningless gesture and served only to make the final score a respectable 6-3.

The largest crowd ever to see a Championship Series game—62,651— saw Phil righthander Jim Lonborg ride a 2-0 lead and a no-hitter into the sixth inning of the second contest.

But in the sixth he walked leadoff batter Dave Concepcion, who moved to second on a groundout. Rose then got the first hit off Lonborg, a single to right that plated Concepcion. Ken Griffey followed with a single sending Rose to third and took second on the futile throw trying to head off Pete. Lonborg was given the hook and replaced by Gene Garber. Joe Morgan drew an intentional walk to load the bases and Tony Perez then rammed a hot liner down the first base line. Dick Allen was unable to handle it, two runs scored and the sun had begun to set on the Phillies' season.

Allen was charged with an error on the play but many thought that Perez should have been credited with a double.

Cincinnati added another run before the inning was over and again pounded McGraw in the next inning to walk away with a 6-2 victory.

The third game, played at Cincinnati's Riverfront Stadium was the most exciting. The Phils carried a 6-4 lead into the bottom of the ninth but were hit by lightning in the form of successive home runs by the first two batters of the inning, George Foster and Johnny Bench. Both blows came off reliever Ron Reed.

GAME OF SUNDAY, OCTOBER 10, AT PHILADELPHIA

Cincinnati	AB.	R.	H.	RBI.	PO.	A.
Rose, 3b	5	2	2	1	1	2
Griffey, rf	4	1	2	1	4	0
Morgan, 2b	2	1	0	0	5	1
Perez, 1b	3	0	0	1	10	1
Foster, lf	4	0	0	1	0	0
Bench, c	4	0	1	0	4	1
Geronimo, cf	4	0	1	0	1	0
Concepcion, ss	3	1	0	0	1	5
Zachry, p	1	0	0	0	1	3
Driessen, ph	1	0	0	0	0	0
Borbon, p	2	1	0	0	0	0
Totals	33	6	6	4	27	13

Philadelphia	AB.	R.	H.	RBI.	PO.	A.
Cash, 2b	5	0	2	0	0	3
Maddox, cf	4	0	0	0	6	0
Schmidt, 3b	5	0	1	0	0	2
Luzinski, lf	4	1	1	1	4	0
Allen, 1b	3	1	1	0	12	0
Johnstone, rf	4	0	3	0	1	0
Boone, c	3	0	2	1	3	2
Bowa, ss	2	0	0	0	1	4
Lonborg, p	1	0	0	0	0	2
Garber, p	0	0	0	0	0	0
Tolan, ph	1	0	0	0	0	0
McGraw, p	0	0	0	0	0	1
Reed, p	0	0	0	0	0	0
McCarver, ph	1	0	0	0	0	0
Totals	33	2	10	2	27	14

Cincinnati	0	0	0	0	0	4	2	0	0 – 6
Philadelphia	0	1	0	0	1	0	0	0	0 – 2

Cincinnati	IP.	H.	R.	ER.	BB.	SO.
Zachry (Winner)	5	6	2	2	3	3
Borbon (Save)	4	4	0	0	1	0

Philadelphia	IP.	H.	R.	ER.	BB.	SO.
Lonborg (Loser)	5⅓	2	3	1	2	2
Garber	⅔	1	1	0	1	0
McGraw	⅓	2	2	2	0	1
Reed	2⅔	1	0	0	1	1

Error—Allen. Double plays—Cincinnati 2. Left on bases—Cincinnati 5, Philadelphia 10. Home run—Luzinski. Stolen base—Griffey. Sacrifice hits—Boone, Lonborg. Sacrifice fly—Perez. Wild pitch—McGraw. Umpires—Dale, Stello, Vargo, Harvey, Tata and Sudol. Time—2:24. Attendance—62,651.

GAME OF TUESDAY, OCTOBER 12, AT CINCINNATI

Philadelphia	AB.	R.	H.	RBI.	PO.	A.
Cash, 2b	4	0	1	1	6	5
Maddox, cf	5	1	1	1	1	0
Schmidt, 3b	5	1	3	1	1	4
Luzinski, lf	4	0	1	1	0	0
Reed, p	1	0	0	0	0	0
Garber, p	0	0	0	0	0	0
Underwood, p	0	0	0	0	0	0
Allen, 1b	3	0	0	0	11	0
Martin, lf	1	1	0	1	0	0
Johnstone, rf	4	1	3	1	2	0
Boone, c	3	0	0	0	1	0
Harmon, pr	0	1	0	0	0	0
Oates, c	1	0	0	0	1	0
Bowa, ss	3	1	1	1	0	3
Kaat, p	2	0	1	0	0	1
Tolan, lf-1b	0	0	0	0	1	0
Totals	36	6	11	6	25	13

Cincinnati	AB.	R.	H.	RBI.	PO.	A.
Rose, 3b	4	0	1	0	0	1
Griffey, rf	5	1	2	1	2	0
Morgan, 2b	3	1	0	0	3	3
Perez, 1b	4	1	2	1	9	1
Foster, lf	3	1	1	2	3	0
Bench, c	3	2	1	1	3	1
Concepcion, ss	4	1	1	0	1	5
Geronimo, cf	3	0	1	2	5	0
Nolan, p	0	0	0	0	1	0
Sarmiento, p	1	0	0	0	0	0
Borbon, p	0	0	0	0	0	0
Lum, ph	1	0	0	0	0	0
Eastwick, p	0	0	0	0	0	0
Armbrister, ph	0	0	0	0	0	0
Totals	31	7	9	7	27	11

Philadelphia	0	0	0	1	0	0	2	2	1 – 6
Cincinnati	0	0	0	0	0	0	4	0	3 – 7

One out when winning run scored.

Philadelphia	IP.	H.	R.	ER.	BB.	SO.
Kaat	6*	2	2	2	2	1
Reed	2†	5	4	4	1	1
Garber (Loser)	0‡	1	1	1	0	0
Underwood	⅓	1	0	0	2	0

Cincinnati	IP.	H.	R.	ER.	BB.	SO.
Nolan	5⅔	6	1	1	2	1
Sarmiento	1	2	2	2	1	0
Borbon	⅓	0	0	0	0	0
Eastwick (Winner)	2	3	3	2	2	1

*Pitched to two batters in seventh.
†Pitched to two batters in ninth.
‡Pitched to one batter in ninth.

Errors—Rose, Perez. Double plays—Philadelphia 1, Cincinnati 1. Left on bases—Philadelphia 10, Cincinnati 6. Two-base hits—Maddox, Schmidt 2, Luzinski, Johnstone, Bowa. Three-base hits—Johnstone, Geronimo. Home runs —Foster, Bench. Sacrifice hits—Kaat, Armbrister. Sacrifice flies—Cash, Foster. Wild pitch—Eastwick. Umpires— Stello, Vargo, Harvey, Tata, Sudol and Dale. Time—2:43. Attendance—55,047.

Reds' Tony Perez (24) welcomes home Johnny Bench in seventh inning of final playoff game after Cesar Geronimo's triple scored two runs.

After Bench's homer Garber relieved and stayed only long enough to give up a single to Concepcion. Lefty Tom Underwood came on and loaded the bases on a walk, a sacrifice and another walk. Griffey then ended the 1976 National League season by chopping a high bounding hit off the glove of first baseman Bobby Tolan. Concepcion raced home with the run that gave the Reds a 7-6 triumph and their second straight flag.

Reds' George Foster catches Bob Boone's long fly ball against the left field wall in the third game of the National League playoffs at Riverfront Stadium.

PHILADELPHIA PHILLIES' BATTING AND FIELDING AVERAGES

Player–Position	G.	AB.	R.	H.	TB.	2B.	3B.	HR.	RBI.	B.A.	PO.	A.	E.	F.A.
Johnstone, ph-rf	3	9	1	7	10	1	1	0	2	.778	3	0	0	1.000
Kaat, p	1	2	0	1	1	0	0	0	0	.500	0	1	0	1.000
Cash, 2b	3	13	1	4	5	1	0	0	1	.308	8	8	0	1.000
Schmidt, 3b	3	13	1	4	6	2	0	0	2	.308	4	9	1	.929
Boone, c	3	7	0	2	2	0	0	0	1	.286	8	2	0	1.000
Luzinski, lf	3	11	2	3	8	2	0	1	3	.273	6	0	0	1.000
Maddox, cf	3	13	2	3	4	1	0	0	1	.231	9	0	0	1.000
Allen, 1b	3	9	1	2	2	0	0	0	0	.222	28	0	1	.966
Bowa, ss	3	8	1	1	2	1	0	0	1	.125	2	11	0	1.000
Garber, p	2	0	0	0	0	0	0	0	0	.000	0	0	0	.000
Harmon, pr	1	0	1	0	0	0	0	0	0	.000	0	0	0	.000
McGraw, p	2	0	0	0	0	0	0	0	0	.000	0	1	0	1.000
Underwood, p	1	0	0	0	0	0	0	0	0	.000	0	0	0	.000
Hutton, ph	1	1	0	0	0	0	0	0	0	.000	0	0	0	.000
Lonborg, p	1	1	0	0	0	0	0	0	0	.000	0	2	0	1.000
Martin, lf	1	1	1	0	0	0	0	0	0	.000	1	0	0	1.000
Oates, c	1	1	0	0	0	0	0	0	0	.000	1	0	0	1.000
Reed, p	2	1	0	0	0	0	0	0	0	.000	0	0	0	.000
Brown, rf	1	2	0	0	0	0	0	0	0	.000	2	0	0	1.000
Carlton, p	1	2	0	0	0	0	0	0	0	.000	0	0	0	.000
Tolan, ph-lf-1b	3	2	0	0	0	0	0	0	0	.000	1	0	0	1.000
McCarver, c-ph	2	4	0	0	0	0	0	0	0	.000	6	0	0	1.000
Totals	3	100	11	27	40	8	1	1	11	.270	79	34	2	.983

CINCINNATI REDS' BATTING AND FIELDING AVERAGES

Player–Position	G.	AB.	R.	H.	TB.	2B.	3B.	HR.	RBI.	B.A.	PO.	A.	E.	F.A.
Gullett, p	1	4	1	2	3	1	0	0	3	.500	0	0	0	.000
Rose, 3b	3	14	3	6	10	2	1	0	2	.429	2	5	1	.875
Griffey, rf	3	13	2	5	7	0	1	0	2	.385	11	0	0	1.000
Bench, c	3	12	3	4	8	1	0	1	1	.333	11	4	0	1.000
Concepcion, ss	3	10	4	2	3	1	0	0	0	.200	2	12	0	1.000
Perez, 1b	3	10	1	2	2	0	0	0	3	.200	27	2	1	.967
Geronimo, cf	3	11	0	2	4	0	1	0	2	.182	10	0	0	1.000
Foster, lf	3	12	2	2	8	0	0	2	4	.167	7	0	0	1.000
Armbrister, ph	1	0	0	0	0	0	0	0	0	.000	0	0	0	.000
Eastwick, p	2	0	0	0	0	0	0	0	0	.000	0	1	0	1.000
Flynn, 2b	1	0	0	0	0	0	0	0	0	.000	0	0	0	.000
Nolan, p	1	0	0	0	0	0	0	0	0	.000	1	0	0	1.000
Driessen, ph	1	1	0	0	0	0	0	0	0	.000	0	0	0	.000
Lum, ph	1	1	0	0	0	0	0	0	0	.000	0	0	0	.000
Sarmiento, p	1	1	0	0	0	0	0	0	0	.000	0	0	0	.000
Zachry, p	1	1	0	0	0	0	0	0	0	.000	1	3	0	1.000
Borbon, p	2	2	1	0	0	0	0	0	0	.000	0	0	0	.000
Morgan, 2b	3	7	2	0	0	0	0	0	0	.000	9	5	0	1.000
Totals	3	99	19	25	45	5	3	3	17	.253	81	32	2	.983

CINCINNATI REDS' PITCHING RECORDS

Pitcher	G.	GS.	CG.	IP.	H.	R.	ER.	BB.	SO.	HB.	WP.	W.	L.	Pct.	ERA.
Borbon	2	0	0	4⅓	4	0	0	1	0	0	0	0	0	.000	0.00
Gullett	1	1	0	8	2	1	1	3	4	0	0	1	0	1.000	1.13
Nolan	1	1	0	5⅔	6	1	1	2	1	0	0	0	0	.000	1.59
Zachry	1	1	0	5	6	2	2	3	3	0	0	1	0	1.000	3.60
Eastwick	2	0	0	3	7	5	4	2	1	0	2	1	0	1.000	12.00
Sarmiento	1	0	0	1	2	2	2	1	0	0	0	0	0	.000	18.00
Totals	3	3	0	27	27	11	10	12	9	0	2	3	0	1.000	3.33

No shutouts. Save—Borbon.

PHILADELPHIA PHILLIES' PITCHING RECORDS

Pitcher	G.	GS.	CG.	IP.	H.	R.	ER.	BB.	SO.	HB.	WP.	W.	L.	Pct.	ERA.
Underwood	1	0	0	⅓	1	0	0	2	0	0	0	0	0	.000	0.00
Lonborg	1	1	0	5⅓	3	1	1	2	2	0	0	0	1	.000	1.69
Kaat	1	1	0	6	2	2	2	2	1	0	0	0	0	.000	3.00
Carlton	1	1	0	7	8	5	4	5	6	0	0	0	1	.000	5.14
Reed	2	0	0	4⅔	6	4	4	2	2	0	0	0	0	.000	7.71
McGraw	2	0	0	2⅓	3	3	3	1	5	0	2	0	0	.000	11.57
Garber	2	0	0	⅔	2	2	1	1	0	0	0	0	1	.000	13.50
Totals	3	3	0	26⅓	25	19	15	15	16	0	2	0	3	.000	5.13

No shutouts or saves.

COMPOSITE SCORE BY INNINGS

Cincinnati	0	0	1	0	0	6	6	3	3 — 19
Philadelphia	1	1	0	1	1	0	2	2	3 — 11

Sacrifice hits—Armbrister, Boone, Kaat, Lonborg.

Sacrifice flies—Perez 2, Foster, Cash, Schmidt.

Stolen bases—Griffey 2, Morgan 2, Bench.

Caught stealing—Geronimo, Maddox.

Double plays—Morgan unassisted; Rose, Bench and Perez; Concepcion, Morgan and Perez; Schmidt unassisted; Schmidt and Cash; Bowa, Cash and Allen.

Left on bases—Cincinnati 20—9, 5, 6; Philadelphia 25—5, 10, 10.

Hit by pitcher—None.

Passed balls—None.

Balks—None.

Time of games—First game, 2:39; second game, 2:24; third game, 2:43.

Attendance—First game, 62,640; second game, 62,651; third game, 55,047.

Umpires—Sudol, Dale, Stello, Vargo, Harvey and Tata.

Official scorers—Bob Hertzel, Cincinnati Enquirer; Bob Kenney, Camden Courier-Post.

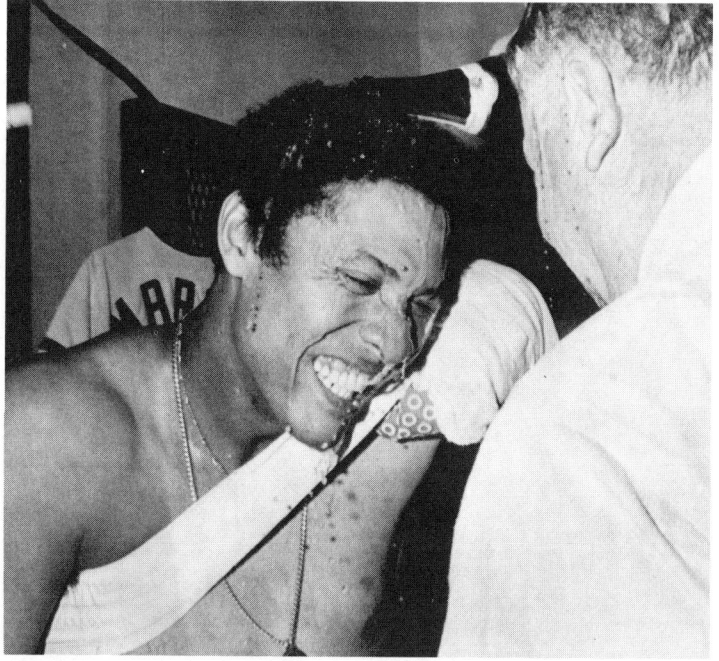

Reds' Tony Perez is doused with champagne in locker room after Cincinnati's 7-6 title-winning triumph over the Phillies.

1976 WORLD SERIES

Including

Review of '76 Series

Official Play-By-Play, Each Game

Official Composite Box Score

World Series Tables—Attendance, Money, Results

Manager Sparky Anderson waves to fans lining the parade route as the Reds are welcomed back to Cincinnati following their World Series victory over the New York Yankees.

World Series

WORLD SERIES CHAMPIONS, 1903-1976

New York, A. L.	20	1923-27-28-32-36-37-38-39-41-43-47-49-50-51-52-53-56-58-61-62
St. Louis, N. L.	8	1926-31-34-42-44-46-64-67
New York, N. L.	6	1905-21-22-33-54 (Giants). 1969 (Mets)
Philadelphia, A.L.	5	1910-11-13-29-30
Boston, A.L.	5	1903-12-15-16-18
Cincinnati, N.L.	4	1919-40-75-76
Pittsburgh, N.L.	4	1909-25-60-71
Los Angeles, N.L.	3	1959-63-65
Detroit, A.L.	3	1935-45-68
Oakland, A.L.	3	1972-73-74
Chicago, A.L.	2	1906-17
Chicago, N. L.	2	1907-08
Cleveland, A. L.	2	1920-48
Baltimore, A.L.	2	1966-70
Boston, N. L.	1	1914
Washington, A.L.	1	1924
Brooklyn, N. L.	1	1955
Milwaukee, N.L.	1	1957

American League has won 43, National League 30.

RESULTS OF WORLD SERIES GAMES OF 1976

Game	Where Played	Date	Winner		Winner	Loser	Att.
First	Cincinnati	Oct. 16	Cincinnati	5-1	Gullett	Alexander	54,826
Second	Cincinnati	Oct. 17	Cincinnati	4-3	Billingham	Hunter	54,816
Third	New York	Oct. 19	Cincinnati	6-2	Zachry	Ellis	56,667
Fourth	New York	Oct. 21	Cincinnati	7-2	Nolan	Figueroa	56,700

ROSTERS OF ELIGIBLES FOR WORLD SERIES

Cincinnati Reds—Santo Alcala, Edison R. Armbrister, Robert S. Bailey, Johnny L. Bench, John E. Billingham, Pedro Borbon, David I. Concepcion, Daniel Driessen, Rawlins J. Eastwick, Robert D. Flynn, George A. Foster, Cesar F. Geronimo, G. Kenneth Griffey, Donald E. Gullett, Michael K. Lum, William H. McEnaney, Joe L. Morgan, Gary L. Nolan, Fredie H. Norman, Atanasio R. Perez, William F. Plummer, Peter E. Rose, Manuel E. Sarmiento, Joel R. Youngblood, Patrick P. Zachry, George L. (Sparky) Anderson, manager; Theodore B. Kluszewski, George R. Scherger, Lawrence W. Shepard and Russell E. Nixon, coaches; Larry M. Starr, trainer.

New York Yankees—Doyle L. Alexander, Santos Alomar, C. Christopher Chambliss, Dock P. Ellis, Eduardo Figueroa, Oscar C. Gamble, Ronald A. Guidry, Francis X. Healy, Elrod J. Hendricks, Kenneth D. Holtzman, James A. Hunter, Grant D. Jackson, Albert W. Lyle, Elliott Maddox, James P. Mason, Carlos May, Thurman L. Munson, Graig Nettles, Louis V. Piniella, William L. Randolph, John M. Rivers, Frederick B. Stanley, Richard W. Tidrow, Otoniel Velez, Roy H. White, Alfred M. (Billy) Martin, manager; Lawrence P. Berra, Elston G. Howard, Richard D. Howser, Robert G. Lemon and Eugene R. Michael, coaches; Gene Monahan, trainer.

By JOE MARCIN

The Cincinnati Reds became the first National League team to win two consecutive World Series since the New York Giants of 1921 and 1922 when they swept past the New York Yankees in four straight games.

The New Yorkers were making their first appearance in the Classic since 1964 and their subsequent sorry showing bore no resemblance at all to the great Yankee teams of the past that took World Series victories as a matter of course.

The 1976 World Series was the first in which the designated hitter was used. As a concession to the American League, Commissioner Bowie Kuhn ordered that the DH be used in the Series in alternating years. As a concession to television, Kuhn ordered that the first Sunday game be played at night. Both decisions provoked considerable criticism from fans and the press.

Kuhn also made and then rescinded another decision regarding the use by the Yankees of walkie-talkies to help them position their outfielders. The Yankees had been doing it during the season and Kuhn said they could do it in the World Series. But after the first inning of the opening game he withdrew his approval, claiming the original okay had been to use one man in the stands but that the Yankees had violated the agreement by using three men roaming the upper deck. Later, when the Yankees went back to the one-man-in-the-stands operation, permission was again granted. Overall, it was an inconsequential thing with no bearing on the play. But one got the impression watching the Yankee outfielders that they could use all the help they could get.

Cincinnati had its star southpaw, Don Gullett, primed for the Saturday opener—the only game played by daylight—and he was opposed by a surprise starter, righthander Doyle Alexander. The Yankees had used much of their pitching strength in the playoffs and could not open with their big ace, Catfish Hunter, as they would have liked to do.

The Reds' second baseman, Joe Morgan, set the tone of the Series when he rapped an Alexander fast ball over the fence for a home run in the first inning. The Yankees tied the score in the second on a double by designated hitter Lou Piniella, who moved to third on an infield out and scored on a sacrifice fly by Graig Nettles. But it was the only scoring the Yankees could manage during the afternoon.

The Reds went ahead for good in the third frame on a triple by shortstop Dave Concepcion and a sacrifice fly by Pete Rose. The score climbed to 3-1 in the sixth on a walk to Rose, a forceout by Ken Griffey, his steal of second and a single by Tony Perez.

Alexander went to the showers in the seventh without retiring a batter. George Foster singled and scored on Johnny Bench's triple. Sparky Lyle replaced Alexander and uncorked a wild pitch, permitting Bench to score.

Gullett kept the Yankees under control while in the game but he was forced to leave the contest in the eighth inning when he suffered the dislocation of a tendon in an ankle. Later it was revealed that the ankle would have to be placed in a cast and the lefty was through for the Series. As events turned out, he wasn't needed anymore. Righthander Pedro Borbon relieved Gullett and retired all five batters he faced.

Hunter was on the mound in the second game and he was opposed by lefty Fred Norman. It was a cold Sunday night and that seemed to bother Hunter. In the second inning the Reds jumped off to a 3-0 lead. Danny Driessen, the first designated hitter ever to be used by the National League, doubled to center and scored on Foster's single. After Foster was thrown out on an attempted steal, Bench doubled to left center. Cesar Geronimo drew a walk and Concepcion delivered a run-producing single. Rose then walked to load the bases and Geronimo scored on Griffey's sacrifice fly.

But the Yankees came back. They got a run in the fourth on singles by Thurman Munson, Chris Chambliss and Nettles and knocked out Norman in the seventh on a single by Willie Randolph, an RBI double by Fred Stanley and a single by Roy White. Jack Billingham replaced Norman and the tying run came home while a forceout was made at second base.

Hunter had settled down after his early troubles and assumed full command of the game. It looked like extra innings were in order when he retired the first two Reds in the bottom of the ninth. But a throwing error by shortstop Stanley enabled Griffey to reach second base. Morgan was given an intentional base on balls so that Hunter could have the presumed advantage of pitching to the righthanded-hitting Perez. But the Cincinnati first sacker ruined the strategy by lining the first pitch to left field for a single. Griffey scored and the Reds took a 2-0 advantage in the Series.

After a day off for travel, the scene for the third game shifted to refurbished Yankee Stadium and in this contest the American Leaguers were hoist by their own petard—the designated hitter. Driessen, the DH for the Reds, had a single, double, homer and walk and scored two runs. Carlos May, the Yankee DH, was 0 for 4.

Dock Ellis, a former National Leaguer, started on the hill for the Yankees and lasted less than four innings. In the second frame, Driessen singled, stole second and rode home on Foster's double. A single by Bench, a forceout, another steal and a single by Concepcion added two more. Driessen hit his homer in the fourth.

The Yankees picked up a run in their half of the fourth on singles by Chambliss and Oscar Gamble wrapped around a walk. They got another in the seventh when Jim Mason, who had replaced Stanley at shortstop in the fifth inning, hit a home run. After Mason's circuit clout, a walk to Rivers and a two-out single by Munson drove Cincinnati starter Pat Zachry off the mound. But reliever Will McEnaney then slammed the door.

The Cincinnati team got two more runs in the eighth on singles by Rose, Griffey and Foster, with a double by Morgan thrown in for good measure.

A day of rain held off the Reds' clinching the championship but they finished off the job when play resumed on Thursday night. After the Yankees opened the scoring in their first turn at bat on a single by Munson and a double by Chambliss, The Reds took command in the fourth inning. Morgan walked, stole second and scored on Foster's single. Bench then blasted a homer high off the screen on the left field foul pole and the Reds took a 3-1 lead.

The Yanks crept within a run in the fifth when Rivers was safe on a bloop single, stole second and scored on Munson's single. Reds' starter Gary Nolan nursed the slender margin into the seventh. When Munson singled with two out, Cincinnati skipper Sparky Anderson brought in McEnaney to face the Bombers' cleanup hitter, Chambliss. Once again the lefthander was equal to the task, getting Chambliss on a ground ball to Morgan and pitching hitless ball the rest of the way to earn his second save.

The Reds put the icing on the cake in their final turn at bat. Perez walked and moved to second on a wild pitch. With Driessen at the plate, action was suspended for several minutes while National League umpire Bruce Froemming ejected Yankee Manager Billy Martin for throwing a baseball onto the field. Martin and A.L. ump Bill Deegan, working behind the plate, had been verbally jousting throughout the game. When play resumed and Driessen drew a walk, starter Ed Figueroa was replaced by Dick Tidrow. Perez advanced to third on Foster's fly to deep center. Bench then came to the plate and hit a line shot into the left field seats for a three-run homer. Geronimo and Concepcion then belted successive doubles to complete the scoring and Sparky Lyle came in to finally put out the fire.

The Yankees went down 1-2-3 in the ninth and the Series was over.

If the 1975 World Series was one of the most exciting ever played, the 1976 World Series was one of the dullest. The superiority of the Reds was so pronounced that there was little element of suspense.

Bench, who batted .533 and had two homers, a triple and a double and six runs batted in, was voted the No. 1 star of the Series. His counterpart, Munson, batted .529 and finished up with six straight hits, tyimg a Series record. He was a heroic figure in a losing cause.

The Reds made great use of their overall speed, stealing seven bases, while the Yankees could manage but one.

Among the spectators for the games played at Yankee Stadium was Joe DiMaggio. He must have wondered to himself at the incompetence of the Yankee outfielders and some errant base running that was a far cry from the Yankee efficiency of their fabled past.

Reds' Dave Concepcion, who tripled in the third inning of the opening game of the World Series, slides back into third on a pickoff attempt. Yankee third baseman Graig Nettles makes the play. Concepcion then scored decisive run of opener on a sacrifice fly.

AT CINCINNATI **Game 1** OCTOBER 16

New York	AB.	R.	H.	PO.	A.	E.
Rivers, cf	4	0	0	3	0	0
White, lf	4	0	1	4	0	0
Munson, c	4	0	1	5	1	0
Piniella, dh	3	1	1	0	0	0
bMay, dh	1	0	0	0	0	0
Chambliss, 1b	3	0	1	4	0	1
Nettles, 3b	3	0	0	3	0	0
Maddox, rf	2	0	1	0	0	0
cGamble	1	0	0	0	0	0
Randolph, 2b	2	0	0	3	2	0
Stanley, ss	1	0	0	2	3	0
aVelez	1	0	0	0	0	0
Mason, ss	0	0	0	0	1	0
Alexander, p	0	0	0	0	1	0
Lyle, p	0	0	0	0	0	0
Totals	29	1	5	24	8	1

Cincinnati	AB.	R.	H.	PO.	A.	E.
Rose, 3b	2	0	0	2	2	0
Griffey, rf	4	1	0	2	0	0
Morgan, 2b	4	1	1	3	4	0
Perez, 1b	4	0	3	11	0	0
Driessen, dh	4	0	0	0	0	0
Foster, lf	3	1	2	0	0	0
Bench, c	3	1	2	5	1	0
Geronimo, cf	3	0	1	2	0	1
Concepcion, ss	3	1	1	2	3	0
Gullett, p	0	0	0	0	1	0
Borbon, p	0	0	0	0	1	0
Totals	30	5	10	27	12	1

```
New York ......................................  0   1   0     0   0   0     0   0   0 – 1
Cincinnati .....................................  1   0   1     0   0   1     2   0   x – 5
```

New York	IP.	H.	R.	ER.	BB.	SO.
Alexander (Loser)	6*	9	5	5	2	1
Lyle	2	1	0	0	0	3

Cincinnati	IP.	H.	R.	ER.	BB.	SO.
Gullett (Winner)	7⅓	5	1	1	3	4
Borbon	1⅔	0	0	0	0	0

*Pitched to two batters in seventh.

Bases on balls—Off Gullett 3 (Stanley, Maddox, Randolph), off Alexander 2 (Foster, Rose).

Strikeouts—By Gullett 4 (Rivers, Munson, Stanley, Velez), by Alexander 1 (Morgan), by Lyle 3 (Concepcion, Griffey, Perez).

aStruck out for Stanley in seventh. bFiled out for Piniella in eighth. cFouled out for Maddox in ninth. Runs batted in—Nettles, Morgan, Rose, Perez, Bench. Two-base hits—Piniella, Perez, Geronimo. Three-base hits—Concepcion, Maddox, Bench. Home run—Morgan. Stolen base—Griffey. Caught stealing—Perez, Rivers. Sacrifice flies—Nettles, Rose. Double plays—Alexander, Randolph and Chambliss; Randolph, Stanley and Chambliss; Morgan, Concepcion and Perez; Morgan and Perez. Wild pitch—Lyle. Hit by pitcher—By Gullett (Chambliss). Left on bases—New York 6, Cincinnati 4. Umpires—Weyer (N.L.) plate, DiMuro (A.L.) first base, B. Williams (N.L.) second base, Deegan (A.L.) third base, Froemming (N.L.) left field, Phillips (A.L.) right field. Time—2:10. Attendance—54,826.

FIRST INNING

New York—Rivers struck out. White's ground ball was deflected by Rose to Concepcion who threw the batter out by a step. Munson fanned. No runs, no hits, no errors, none left.

Cincinnati—Rose flied to Rivers. Griffey lined to White. Morgan homered into the lower right field stands. Perez grounded a single to left-center. Perez was out attempting to steal, Munson to Stanley. One run, two hits, no errors, none left.

SECOND INNING

New York—Piniella lined a double to right. Chambliss grounded sharply to Morgan, Piniella moving to third. Nettles flied deep to Geronimo, Piniella scoring after the catch. Maddox bounced to Rose. One run, one hit, no errors, none left.

Cincinnati—Driessen flied to Rivers in deep right-center. Foster walked. Bench grounded into a double play, Alexander to Randolph to Chambliss. No runs, no hits, no errors, none left.

THIRD INNING

New York—Randolph grounded to Concepcion. Stanley was called out on strikes. Rivers grounded to Morgan. No runs, no hits, no errors, none left.

Cincinnati—Geronimo popped to Nettles. Concepcion lined a triple to the wall in left-center. Rose flied deep to Rivers, Concepcion scoring after the catch. Griffey popped to Nettles. One run, one hit, no errors, none left.

FOURTH INNING

New York—White lined to Rose who leaped to make the catch. Munson flied to Griffey in shallow right. Piniella grounded out, Perez unassisted. No runs, no hits, no errors, none left.

Cincinnati—Morgan flied to White in left-center. Perez grounded a double inside the third-base bag. Driessen flied to White in left-center, Perez holding second. Perez was automatically out when he was struck by Foster's ground ball as Nettles was attempting to make the play. Foster was credited with a hit and Nettles with the putout. No runs, two hits, no errors, one left.

FIFTH INNING

New York—Chambliss lined a single to left. Nettles grounded into a double play, Morgan to Concepcion to Perez. Maddox grounded a triple down the left field line. Randolph flied deep to Geronimo. No runs, two hits, no errors, one left.

Cincinnati—Bench lined a single to center. Geronimo bounced into a double play, Randolph to Stanley to Chambliss. Concepcion grounded to Stanley who made a good play on the slowly-hit ball near second base. No runs, one hit, no errors, none left.

SIXTH INNING

New York—Stanley walked. Attempting to sacrifice, Rivers forced Stanley, Gullett to Concepcion. Rivers was out stealing, Bench to Morgan. White reached second when Geronimo dropped his liner to left-center. Munson lined a single to right, White stopping at third. Piniella hit a looping liner to Morgan in short center. No runs, one hit, one error, two left.

Cincinnati—Rose walked. Griffey forced Rose, Stanley to Randolph. Morgan fanned as Griffey stole second. Perez grounded a single to left scoring Griffey. Driessen fouled to Munson. One run, one hit, no errors, one left.

SEVENTH INNING

New York—Chambliss was hit by a pitched ball. Nettles grounded to Morgan who tagged Chambliss and threw to Perez for the double play. Maddox walked. Randolph walked. Velez batted for Stanley and struck out. No runs, no hits, no errors, two left.

Cincinnati—Mason went to shortstop for New York. Foster lined a single to left. Bench lined a hit off the wall in right and when the carom eluded Maddox, Foster scored and Bench went all the way to third. It was ruled a triple. Lyle replaced Alexander on the mound for New York. Bench scored on a wild pitch. Geronimo looped a double to left-center. Concepcion struck out. Rose grounded to Mason, Geronimo advancing to third on the play. Griffey fanned. Two runs, three hits, no errors, one left.

EIGHTH INNING

New York—Rivers fouled to Bench. White lined a single to left. Borbon came in to pitch for Cincinnati, replacing Gullett who had suffered an ankle injury while pitching to Rivers. Munson tapped to Borbon who made a good play on the roller down the third base line, getting the batter by a step, White moving to second. May batted for Piniella and lined to Griffey. No runs, one hit, no errors, one left.

Cincinnati—Morgan lined to Randolph. Perez struck out but had to be tagged by Munson who did not hold the third strike. Driessen was safe when Chambliss fumbled his ground ball and Lyle made no move to cover first. Foster flied to White in short left. No runs, no hits, one error, one left.

NINTH INNING

New York—Chambliss grounded to Perez who made the play unassisted. Nettles lined to Perez who made a backhanded grab. Gamble batted for Maddox and fouled to Rose near the third base box seats. No runs, no hits, no errors, none left.

A few Yankees huddle around a heater in the dugout to ward off the chill during second game of the World Series.

AT CINCINNATI   *Game* 2   OCTOBER 17

New York	AB.	R.	H.	PO.	A.	E.
Rivers, cf	5	0	0	6	0	0
White, lf	3	0	1	6	0	0
Munson, c	4	1	1	7	1	0
Piniella, rf	4	0	2	1	0	0
Chambliss, 1b	4	0	2	2	0	0
Nettles, 3b	4	0	1	2	1	0
Maddox, dh	3	0	0	0	0	0
aMay, dh	1	0	0	0	0	0
Randolph, 2b	4	1	1	2	0	0
Stanley, ss	3	1	1	0	0	1
Hunter, p	0	0	0	0	1	0
Totals	35	3	9	26	3	1

Cincinnati	AB.	R.	H.	PO.	A.	E.
Rose, 3b	4	0	0	0	0	0
Griffey, rf	4	1	0	1	0	0
Morgan, 2b	4	0	2	6	3	0
Perez, 1b	5	0	2	8	1	0
Driessen, dh	4	1	2	0	0	0
Foster, lf	4	0	1	2	0	0
Bench, c	4	1	2	3	0	0
Geronimo, cf	2	1	0	4	0	0
Concepcion, ss	4	0	1	2	3	0
Norman, p	0	0	0	0	1	0
Billingham, p	0	0	0	1	0	0
Totals	35	4	10	27	8	0

New York	0	0	0		1	0	0		2	0 — 3
Cincinnati	3	0	0		0	0	0		0	0 1 — 4

Two out when winning run scored.

New York	IP.	H.	R.	ER.	BB.	SO.
Hunter (Loser)	8⅔	10	4	3	4	5

Cincinnati	IP.	H.	R.	ER.	BB.	SO.
Norman	6⅓	9	3	3	2	2
Billingham (Winner)	2⅔	0	0	0	0	1

Bases on balls—Off Norman 2 (Stanley, White), off Hunter 4 (Geronimo 2, Rose, Morgan).

Strikeouts—By Norman 2 (Maddox 2), by Billingham 1 (Randolph), by Hunter 5 (Foster 2, Concepcion, Bench, Rose).

aGrounded out for Maddox in eighth. Runs batted in—Nettles, Stanley, Munson, Foster, Concepcion, Griffey, Perez. Two-base hits—Driessen, Bench, Stanley. Three-base hit—Morgan. Stolen bases—Morgan, Concepcion. Caught stealing—Foster. Sacrifice fly—Griffey. Double play—Concepcion, Morgan and Perez. Left on bases—New York 7, Cincinnati 10. Umpires—DiMuro (A.L.) plate, B. Williams (N.L.) first base, Deegan (A.L.) second base, Froemming (N.L.) third base, Phillips (A.L.) left field, Weyer (N.L.) right field. Time—2:33. Attendance—54,816.

FIRST INNING

New York—Rivers flied to Geronimo. White popped to Morgan in short center. Munson flied to Griffey in short right-center. No runs, no hits, no errors, none left.

Cincinnati—Rose lined deep to White. Griffey flied to White in deep left-center. Morgan lined a single to center. Morgan stole second. Perez popped to Nettles near the pitching mound. No runs, one hit, no errors, one left.

SECOND INNING

New York—Piniella beat out a hit to deep short where Concepcion fielded the ball but could not make the throw. Chambliss flied to Geronimo in deep center, Piniella holding first. Nettles flied to Foster in left-center. Maddox struck out. No runs, one hit, no errors, one left.

Cincinnati—Driessen doubled to the wall in center. Foster lined a single to center scoring Driessen. Foster was out trying to steal, Munson to Randolph. Bench doubled to left-center. Geronimo walked. Concepcion looped a single to right-center, Bench scoring and Geronimo going to third. Concepcion stole second. On the play, Munson threw to third attempting to get Geronimo and Nettles made a diving stop of the wild throw. Rose walked, filling the bases. Griffey flied to Rivers in short center and Geronimo scored after the catch, Concepcion and Rose holding their bases. Morgan fouled to Munson who made a fine catch near the New York dugout on the third base side. Three runs, four hits, no errors, two left.

THIRD INNING

New York—Randolph flied to Geronimo. Stanley walked. Rivers grounded out to Perez unassisted, Stanley going to second. White popped to Morgan. No runs, no hits, no errors, one left.

Cincinnati—Perez lined a single to right. Driessen hit a high bouncer to Chambliss and beat the throw to Hunter covering first for a single, Perez stopping at second. Foster fanned. Bench flied to White, both runners holding their bases. Geronimo walked to load the bases. Concepcion struck out. No runs, two hits, no errors, three left.

FOURTH INNING

New York—Munson beat out a ground ball to Rose who made the play to his left but could not throw out the runner. Piniella flied to Foster, Munson holding first. Chambliss lined a single to left, Munson stopping at second. Nettles singled to center, Munson scoring and Chambliss going to third, and on the throw to third Nettles went to second. Maddox fanned on a pitch in the dirt, Bench making the tag for the out. Randolph bounced sharply to Concepcion who made a good play to his left. One run, three hits, no errors, two left.

Cincinnati—Rose lined deep to White. Griffey flied deep to Rivers. Morgan lined a triple to left-center. Perez flied to Rivers who made a running catch in short right-center. No runs, one hit, no errors, one left.

FIFTH INNING

New York—Stanley popped to Concepcion. Rivers grounded to Concepcion. White walked. Munson tapped to Norman. No runs, no hits, no errors, one left.

Cincinnati—Driessen flied to White. Foster grounded sharply to Nettles. Bench struck out. No runs, no hits, no errors, none left.

SIXTH INNING

New York—Piniella grounded a single to left. Chambliss lined a single to center, Piniella stopping at second. Nettles fouled to Morgan near the stands behind first base, both runners holding their bases. Maddox grounded into a double play, Concepcion to Morgan to Perez. No runs, two hits, no errors, one left.

Cincinnati—Geronimo popped to Nettles. Concepcion lined to Piniella. Rose fanned. No runs, no hits, no errors, none left.

SEVENTH INNING

New York—Randolph lined a single to center. Stanley doubled into the left field corner scoring Randolph. Rivers flied to Geronimo, Stanley holding second. White singled to left, Stanley stopping at third. Billingham replaced Norman on the mound for Cincinnati. Munson bounced to Morgan who threw to Concepcion, forcing White, Stanley scoring. Piniella's ground ball behind second was fumbled by Morgan but he recovered in time to step on the bag, forcing Munson. Two runs, three hits, no errors, one left.

Cincinnati—Griffey flied to Rivers in short center. Morgan fouled to Munson who reached over the railing near the New York dugout to make a spectacular catch. Perez popped to Randolph. No runs, no hits, no errors, none left.

EIGHTH INNING

New York—Chambliss was out on a hard hit ground ball to Morgan. Nettles lined to Perez who made a leaping catch. May batted for Maddox and grounded to Perez who threw to Billingham covering first for the out. No runs, no hits, no errors, none left.

Cincinnati—Driessen flied to Rivers in right-center. Foster struck out. Bench lined a single to left. Geronimo tapped to Hunter. No runs, one hit, no errors, one left.

NINTH INNING

New York—Randolph was called out on strikes. Stanley popped to Morgan. Rivers bounced out to Perez unassisted. No runs, no hits, no errors, none left.

Cincinnati—Concepcion flied to Rivers in shallow center. Rose flied to White. Griffey grounded slowly to Stanley whose wild throw to first went into the Cincinnati dugout, Griffey reaching second on the error. Morgan was intentionally passed. Perez lined a single to left, Griffey scoring the winning run. One run, one hit, one error, two left.

Reds' Tony Perez (4 showing on uniform) is mobbed by teammates after driving in winning run in ninth inning of the second game.

AT NEW YORK   Game 3   OCTOBER 19

Cincinnati	AB.	R.	H.	PO.	A.	E.
Rose, 3b	5	1	2	1	1	0
Griffey, rf	4	0	1	0	0	0
Morgan, 2b	4	1	1	2	0	1
Perez, 1b	4	0	0	7	2	0
Driessen, dh	3	2	3	0	0	0
Foster, lf	4	1	2	4	0	0
Bench, c	4	0	2	8	0	0
Geronimo, cf	4	1	1	3	0	0
Concepcion, ss	4	0	1	1	2	0
Zachry, p	0	0	0	0	2	1
McEnaney, p	0	0	0	1	0	0
Totals	36	6	13	27	7	2

New York	AB.	R.	H.	PO.	A.	E.
Rivers, cf	4	0	2	1	0	0
White, lf	3	0	0	1	0	0
Munson, c	5	0	3	6	2	0
Chambliss, 1b	5	1	1	11	1	0
May, dh	4	0	0	0	0	0
Nettles, 3b	2	0	0	1	4	0
Gamble, rf	3	0	1	2	0	0
bPiniella, rf	1	0	0	0	0	0
Randolph, 2b	4	0	0	4	4	0
Stanley, ss	1	0	0	1	2	0
aHendricks	1	0	0	0	0	0
Mason, ss	1	1	1	0	1	0
cVelez	1	0	0	0	0	0
Ellis, p	0	0	0	0	0	0
Jackson, p	0	0	0	0	3	0
Tidrow, p	0	0	0	0	0	0
Totals	35	2	8	27	17	0

```
Cincinnati ...... 0  3  0   1  0  0   0  2  0 — 6
New York ........ 0  0  0   1  0  0   1  0  0 — 2
```

Cincinnati	IP.	H.	R.	ER.	BB.	SO.
Zachry (Winner)	6⅔	6	2	2	5	6
McEnaney (Save)	2⅓	2	0	0	0	1

New York	IP.	H.	R.	ER.	BB.	SO.
Ellis (Loser)	3⅓	7	4	4	0	1
Jackson	3⅔*	4	2	2	0	3
Tidrow	2	2	0	0	1	1

*Pitched to three batters in eighth.

Bases on balls—Off Tidrow 1 (Driessen), off Zachry 5 (Nettles 2, White 2, Rivers).

Strikeouts—By Ellis 1 (Perez), by Jackson 3 (Concepcion, Morgan, Geronimo), by Tidrow 1 (Rose), by Zachry 6 (Chambliss 2, Rivers, May, Nettles, Randolph), by McEnaney 1 (Velez).

aFlied out for Stanley in fourth. bGrounded out for Gamble in eighth. cStruck out for Mason in ninth. Runs batted in—Foster 2, Geronimo, Concepcion, Driessen, Morgan, Gamble, Mason. Two-base hits—Foster, Driessen, Morgan. Home runs—Driessen, Mason. Stolen bases—Driessen, Geronimo. Caught stealing—Bench. Double plays—Stanley, Randolph and Chambliss; Nettles and Chambliss; Nettles, Randolph and Chambliss; Perez and Concepcion. Left on bases—Cincinnati 4, New York 11. Umpires—B. Williams (N.L.) plate, Deegan (A.L.) first base, Froemming (N.L.) second base, Phillips (A.L.) third base, Weyer (N.L.) left field, DiMuro (A.L.) right field. Time—2:40. Attendance—56,667.

FIRST INNING

Cincinnati—Rose looped a single to right. Griffey bounced out to Chambliss unassisted, Rose moving to second. Morgan rolled out to Chambliss unassisted, Rose going to third. Perez popped to Randolph in short right. No runs, one hit, no errors, one left.

New York—Rivers bunted to the left of the mound and was safe at first on Zachry's bad throw. Rivers was picked off first on a snap throw from Zachry to Perez. White popped to Rose in front of the plate. Munson grounded a single to center. Chambliss struck out. No runs, one hit, one error, one left.

SECOND INNING

Cincinnati—Driessen's high bouncer was deflected by Ellis to Randolph who fielded the ball behind second base but his throw pulled Chambliss off the bag. It was ruled a hit. Driessen stole second as Munson dropped the pitch. Foster's drive to right-center bounced over the wall for a ground-rule double, Driessen scoring. Bench hit a soft liner that Chambliss leaped for and deflected to Randolph who threw to Ellis covering first but Bench beat the throw for a hit, Foster stopping at third. Geronimo forced Bench, Stanley to Randolph, Foster scoring. Geronimo broke for second and was safe when Munson's perfect throw got away from Stanley. It was ruled a stolen base. Concepcion looped a single to left scoring Geronimo. Rose bounced into a double play, Stanley to Randolph to Chambliss. Three runs, four hits, no errors, none left.

New York—May bounced out to Perez unassisted. Nettles walked. Gamble lined to Geronimo. Randolph flied to Foster. No runs, no hits, no errors, one left.

Reds' Johnny Bench connects for a two-run homer in the fourth inning of the fourth game of the World Series. The Yanks' Ed Figueroa is the pitcher and catching is Thurman Munson. The blow gave the Reds a 3-1 lead.

THIRD INNING

Cincinnati—Griffey tapped to Nettles who made a good play to his left. Morgan bounced to Randolph. Perez fanned. No runs, no hits, no errors, none left.

New York—Stanley tried to check his swing but tapped to Zachry. Rivers struck out and was tagged by Bench who did not hold the third strike. White walked. Munson lined to Geronimo. No runs, no hits, no errors, one left.

FOURTH INNING

Cincinnati—Driessen lined a homer into the stands in right-center. Foster grounded to Randolph who made a great play behind second to get the runner by a step. Bench lined a single to right. Jackson replaced Ellis on the mound for New York. Bench was picked off first and tagged out, Jackson to Chambliss to Stanley. Geronimo lined to Gamble. One run, two hits, no errors, none left.

New York—Chambliss grounded a single to center. May struck out. Nettles walked. Gamble lined a single to center, Chambliss scoring and Nettles stopping at second. Randolph fouled to Bench. Hendricks batted for Stanley and flied to Foster in left-center. One run, two hits, no errors, two left.

FIFTH INNING

Cincinnati—Mason went to shortstop for New York. Concepcion struck out. Rose's tap in front of the plate was fielded by Munson who threw to Chambliss for the out. Griffey flied to White in left-center. No runs, no hits, no errors, none left.

New York—Rivers looped a single to left just out of Concepcion's reach. White walked. Munson lined to Perez who threw to Concepcion, doubling Rivers. Chambliss struck out. No runs, one hit, no errors, one left.

SIXTH INNING

Cincinnati—Morgan struck out. Perez grounded to Jackson who knocked the ball down and threw to Chambliss for the out. Driessen's fly to center fell in front of the diving Rivers for a double. Foster flied to Gamble in short right. No runs, one hit, no errors, one left.

New York—May flied to Geronimo. Nettles struck out. Gamble popped to Morgan in short right. No runs, no hits, no errors, none left.

SEVENTH INNING

Cincinnati—Bench smashed a ground ball to Jackson who stabbed the ball behind his back and threw to Chambliss for the out. Geronimo fanned. Concepcion flied to Rivers. No runs, no hits, no errors, none left.

New York—Randolph struck out. Mason lined a home run into the lower right field stands. Rivers walked. White forced Rivers. Rose to Morgan. Munson lined a single to right, White stopping at second. McEnaney replaced Zachry on the mound for Cincinnati. Chambliss bounced to Perez who threw to McEnaney covering first for the out. One run, two hits, no errors, two left.

EIGHTH INNING

Cincinnati—Rose lined a single to center. Griffey grounded a single to right, Rose racing to third. Morgan doubled inside the first base bag, Rose scoring and Griffey stopping at third. Tidrow replaced Jackson on the mound for New York. Perez bounced to Mason and Griffey was caught in a rundown and tagged out, Mason to Munson to Nettles to Munson, Morgan taking third and Perez second on the play. Driessen was purposely passed, loading the bases. Foster lined a single to left, White missing a shoestring catch, Morgan scoring and the bases remaining filled. Bench bounced to Nettles who stepped on third, forcing Driessen, and then threw to Chambliss for the double play. Two runs, four hits, no errors, two left.

New York—May grounded to Concepcion. Nettles grounded to Morgan who booted the ball into foul territory, Nettles reaching second on the error. Piniella batted for Gamble and grounded to Concepcion, Nettles advancing to third. Randolph flied to Foster who made a running catch in left-center. No runs, no hits, one error, one left.

NINTH INNING

Cincinnati—Geronimo lined a single to left. Concepcion bounced into a double play, Nettles to Randolph to Chambliss. Rose struck out. No runs, one hit, no errors, none left.

New York—Velez batted for Mason and struck out. Rivers lined a single to right. White fouled to Perez. Munson grounded a single to right, Rivers stopping at second. Chambliss flied to Foster. No runs, two hits, no errors, two left.

AT NEW YORK Game 4 OCTOBER 21

Cincinnati	AB.	R.	H.	PO.	A.	E.	New York	AB.	R.	H.	PO.	A.	E.
Rose, 3b	5	0	1	3	0	0	Rivers, cf	5	1	1	4	0	0
Griffey, rf	5	0	0	2	0	0	White, lf	5	0	0	2	0	0
Morgan, 2b	3	1	1	2	3	1	Munson, c	4	1	4	3	3	0
Perez, 1b	3	1	0	6	1	0	Chambliss, 1b	4	0	1	9	2	0
Driessen, dh	3	1	1	0	0	0	May, dh	3	0	0	0	0	0
Foster, lf	3	1	1	8	0	0	bPiniella, dh	1	0	0	0	0	0
Bench, c	4	2	2	2	1	0	Nettles, 3b	3	0	2	2	3	0
Geronimo, cf	4	1	2	3	0	1	Gamble, rf	4	0	0	1	0	0
Concepcion, ss	3	0	2	1	3	1	Randolph, 2b	4	0	0	4	2	0
Nolan, p	0	0	0	0	1	0	Stanley, ss	1	0	0	1	2	0
McEnaney, p	0	0	0	0	0	0	aHendricks	1	0	0	0	0	0
Totals	33	7	9	27	9	2	Mason, ss	0	0	0	1	0	0
							cVelez	1	0	0	0	0	0
							Figueroa, p	0	0	0	0	1	0
							Tidrow, p	0	0	0	0	0	0
							Lyle, p	0	0	0	0	0	0
							Totals	36	2	8	27	13	0

Cincinnati	0	0	0	3	0	0	0	0	4 — 7
New York	1	0	0	0	1	0	0	0	0 — 2

Cincinnati	IP.	H.	R.	ER.	BB.	SO.
Nolan (Winner)	6⅔	8	2	2	1	1
McEnaney (Save)	2⅓	0	0	0	1	1

New York	IP.	H.	R.	ER.	BB.	SO.
Figueroa (Loser)	8*	6	5	5	5	2
Tidrow	⅓	3	2	2	0	0
Lyle	⅔	0	0	0	0	0

*Pitched to two batters in ninth.

Bases on balls—Off Figueroa 5 (Foster, Concepcion, Morgan, Perez, Driessen), off Nolan 1 (Stanley), off McEnaney 1 (Nettles).

Strikeouts—By Figueroa 2 (Foster, Geronimo), by Nolan 1 (Randolph), by McEnaney 1 (Velez).

aFouled out for Stanley in sixth. bFlied out for May in eighth. cStruck out for Mason in ninth. Runs batted in—Foster, Bench 5, Concepcion, Chambliss, Munson. Two-base hits—Rose, Chambliss, Geronimo, Concepcion. Home runs—Bench 2. Stolen bases—Geronimo, Morgan, Rivers. Caught stealing—Foster, Nettles, Concepcion. Double play—Stanley, Nettles, Chambliss and Randolph. Wild pitch—Figueroa. Left on bases—Cincinnati 4, New York 9. Umpires—Deegan (A.L.) plate, Froemming (N.L.) first base, Phillips (A.L.) second base, Weyer (N.L.) third base, Di-Muro (A.L.) left field, B. Williams (N.L.) right field. Time—2:36. Attendance—56,700.

FIRST INNING

Cincinnati—Rose lined a hit down the left field line that bounced into the stands for a ground-rule double. Griffey bounced to Stanley and Rose was caught in a rundown and tagged out, Stanley to Nettles who then threw to Chambliss and Griffey was trapped off first and tagged out, Chambliss to Randolph, for a double play. Morgan bounced out, Chambliss unassisted. No runs, one hit, no errors, none left.

New York—Rivers popped to Concepcion. White grounded to Morgan who fumbled the ball but recovered in time to throw out the batter. Munson looped a single to right-center. Chambliss lined a double to left-center scoring Munson. May grounded to Concepcion who made a lunging one-handed grab behind second base and threw to Perez for the out. One run, two hits, no errors, one left.

SECOND INNING

Cincinnati—Perez grounded to Chambliss unassisted. Driessen flied to White in short left. Foster walked. Foster was out attempting to steal, Munson to Randolph. No runs, no hits, no errors, none left.

New York—Nettles tried to check his swing but tapped to Nolan. Gamble popped to Rose near the pitching mound. Randolph flied to Geronimo who raced in for a shoestring catch. No runs, no hits, no errors, none left.

THIRD INNING

Cincinnati—Bench popped to Randolph. Geronimo looped a single to left-center. Geronimo stole second. Concepcion walked. Rose forced Concepcion, Chambliss to Stanley. Geronimo going to third. Griffey's ground ball was deflected by Figueroa to Randolph who threw the batter out on a close play. No runs, one hit, no errors, two left.

New York—Stanley walked on four pitches. Rivers flied to Foster in short left. White flied to Griffey in deep right-center. Munson lined a single to right, Stanley stopping at second. Chambliss grounded to Morgan who fumbled the ball for an error, loading the bases. May lined to Foster. No runs, one hit, one error, three left.

FOURTH INNING

Cincinnati—Morgan walked. Perez lined to Rivers in left-center, Morgan holding first. Morgan stole second. Driessen fouled to Munson behind the plate. Foster lined a single to left, Morgan scoring. Bench lined a homer just inside the left field foul pole, Foster scoring ahead of him. Geronimo grounded to Stanley who made the stop in deep short and followed with a strong throw to get the batter by a step. Three runs, two hits, no errors, none left.

New York—Nettles grounded a single to right-center. Gamble grounded to Perez and both runners were safe when Concepcion dropped Perez' throw to second. Trying to sacrifice, Randolph missed the pitch and Nettles was trapped off second and tagged out, Bench to Concepcion to Rose, Gamble holding first. Randolph was called out on strikes. Stanley lined to Griffey. No runs, one hit, one error, one left.

FIFTH INNING

Cincinnati—Concepcion bounced to Nettles. Rose flied to White. Griffey fouled to Nettles. No runs, no hits, no errors, none left.

New York—Rivers looped a single to right. White flied to Foster in short left. Rivers stole second. Munson singled on the ground into center field scoring Rivers. Chambliss lined to Foster in left-center. May bounced to Morgan. One run, two hits, no errors, one left.

SIXTH INNING

Cincinnati—Morgan lined a single to left-center. Perez rolled softly to Nettles, Morgan moving to second. Driessen popped to Randolph. Foster struck out. No runs, one hit, no errors, one left.

New York—Nettles' hard ground ball took a high bounce over Morgan's head for a single. Gamble popped to Morgan. Randolph flied to Geronimo. Hendricks batted for Stanley and fouled to Perez. No runs, one hit, no errors, one left.

SEVENTH INNING

Cincinnati—Mason went in to play shortstop for New York. Bench flied to Gamble in short right. Geronimo took a called third strike. Concepcion lined a single to center. Concepcion was thrown out stealing, Munson to Mason. No runs, one hit, no errors, none left.

New York—Rivers flied to Foster in short left-center. White flied to Geronimo who made a running catch in short center. Munson grounded a single to center for his fourth hit of the game. McEnaney replaced Nolan as the Cincinnati pitcher. Attempting to check his swing, Chambliss rolled to Morgan. No runs, one hit, no errors, one left.

EIGHTH INNING

Cincinnati—Rose flied to Rivers in left-center. Griffey's tap in front of the plate was fielded quickly by Munson who threw to Chambliss for the out. Morgan flied to Rivers in deep right-center. No runs, no hits, no errors, none left.

New York—Piniella batted for May and lined to Foster. Nettles walked. Gamble flied to Foster in left-center. Randolph forced Nettles, Concepcion to Morgan. No runs, no hits, no errors, one left.

NINTH INNING

Cincinnati—Perez walked. Perez advanced to second on a wild pitch. Driessen walked. Tidrow replaced Figueroa on the mound for New York. Foster flied to Rivers, Perez advancing to third after the catch and Driessen holding first. Bench lined a home run into the left field stands, Perez and Driessen scoring ahead of him. Geronimo grounded a hit down the first base line and was awarded a ground-rule double when the ball was touched by spectators in foul territory reaching over the low fence. Concepcion also was awarded two bases when his ground ball past third base went into foul territory and was interfered with by the crowd, Geronimo scoring. Lyle replaced Tidrow on the mound for New York. Rose bounced sharply to Randolph, Concepcion moving to third. Griffey grounded out to Chambliss unassisted. Four runs, three hits, no errors, one left.

New York—Velez batted for Mason and fanned. Rivers lined to Rose. White flied to Foster in left-center. No runs, no hits, no errors, none left.

CINCINNATI REDS' BATTING AND FIELDING AVERAGES

Player—Position	G.	AB.	R.	H.	TB.	2B.	3B.	HR.	RBI.	BB.	IBB.	SO.	B.A.	PO.	A.	E.	F.A.
Bench, c	4	15	4	8	17	1	1	2	6	0	0	1	.533	18	2	0	1.000
Foster, lf	4	14	3	6	7	1	0	0	4	2	0	3	.429	14	0	0	1.000
Concepcion, ss	4	14	1	5	8	1	1	0	3	1	0	3	.357	6	11	1	.944
Driessen, dh	4	14	4	5	10	2	0	1	1	2	1	0	.357	0	0	0	.000
Morgan, 2b	4	15	3	5	11	1	1	1	2	2	1	2	.333	13	10	2	.920
Perez, 1b	4	16	1	5	6	1	0	0	2	1	0	2	.313	32	4	0	1.000
Geronimo, cf	4	13	3	4	6	2	0	0	1	2	0	2	.308	12	0	1	.923
Rose, 3b	4	16	1	3	4	1	0	0	1	2	0	2	.188	6	3	0	1.000
Griffey, rf	4	17	2	1	1	0	0	0	1	0	0	1	.059	5	0	0	1.000
McEnaney, p	2	0	0	0	0	0	0	0	0	0	0	0	.000	1	0	0	1.000
Borbon, p	1	0	0	0	0	0	0	0	0	0	0	0	.000	0	1	0	1.000
Billingham, p	1	0	0	0	0	0	0	0	0	0	0	0	.000	1	0	0	1.000
Gullett, p	1	0	0	0	0	0	0	0	0	0	0	0	.000	0	1	0	1.000
Nolan, p	1	0	0	0	0	0	0	0	0	0	0	0	.000	0	1	0	1.000
Norman, p	1	0	0	0	0	0	0	0	0	0	0	0	.000	0	1	0	1.000
Zachry, p	1	0	0	0	0	0	0	0	0	0	0	0	.000	0	2	1	.667
Totals	4	134	22	42	70	10	3	4	21	12	2	16	.313	108	36	5	.966

NEW YORK YANKEES' BATTING AND FIELDING AVERAGES

Player—Position	G.	AB.	R.	H.	TB.	2B.	3B.	HR.	RBI.	BB.	IBB.	SO.	B.A.	PO.	A.	E.	F.A.
Mason, ss	3	1	1	1	4	0	0	0	0	0	0	0	1.000	1	2	0	1.000
Munson, c	4	17	2	9	9	0	0	0	2	0	0	1	.529	21	7	0	1.000
Piniella, dh-rf-ph	4	9	1	3	4	1	0	0	0	0	0	0	.333	1	0	0	1.000
Chambliss, 1b	4	16	1	5	6	1	0	0	1	0	0	2	.313	26	3	1	.967
Nettles, 3b	4	12	0	3	3	0	0	0	2	3	0	1	.250	8	8	0	1.000
Maddox, rf-dh	2	5	0	1	3	0	1	0	0	1	0	2	.200	0	0	0	.000
Rivers, cf	4	18	1	3	3	0	0	0	0	1	0	2	.167	14	0	0	1.000
Stanley, ss	4	6	1	1	2	1	0	0	1	3	0	1	.167	4	7	1	.917
White, lf	4	15	0	2	2	0	0	0	0	3	0	0	.133	13	0	0	1.000
Gamble, ph-rf	3	8	0	1	1	0	0	0	1	0	0	0	.125	3	0	0	1.000
Randolph, 2b	4	14	1	1	1	0	0	0	0	1	0	3	.071	13	8	0	1.000
Hendricks, ph	2	2	0	0	0	0	0	0	0	0	0	0	.000	0	0	0	.000
Velez, ph	3	3	0	0	0	0	0	0	0	0	0	3	.000	0	0	0	.000
May, ph-dh	4	9	0	0	0	0	0	0	0	0	0	1	.000	0	0	0	.000
Tidrow, p	2	0	0	0	0	0	0	0	0	0	0	0	.000	0	0	0	.000
Lyle, p	2	0	0	0	0	0	0	0	0	0	0	0	.000	0	0	0	.000
Alexander, p	1	0	0	0	0	0	0	0	0	0	0	0	.000	0	1	0	1.000
Ellis, p	1	0	0	0	0	0	0	0	0	0	0	0	.000	0	0	0	.000
Figueroa, p	1	0	0	0	0	0	0	0	0	0	0	0	.000	0	1	0	1.000
Hunter, p	1	0	0	0	0	0	0	0	0	0	0	0	.000	0	1	0	1.000
Jackson, p	1	0	0	0	0	0	0	0	0	0	0	0	.000	0	3	0	1.000
Totals	4	135	8	30	38	3	1	1	8	12	0	16	.222	104	41	2	.986

May flied out for Piniella in eighth inning of first game; grounded out for Maddox in eighth inning of second game.

Gamble popped out for Maddox in ninth inning of first game.

Velez struck out for Stanley in seventh inning of first game; struck out for Mason in ninth inning of third game; struck out for Mason in ninth inning of fourth game.

Hendricks flied out for Stanley in fourth inning of third game; fouled out for Stanley in sixth inning of fourth game.

Piniella grounded out for Gamble in eighth inning of third game; flied out for May in eighth inning of fourth game.

CINCINNATI REDS' PITCHING RECORDS

Pitcher	G	GS	CG	IP	H	R	ER	HR	BB	IBB	SO	HB	WP	W	L	Pct.	ERA.
McEnaney	2	0	0	4⅓	2	0	0	0	1	0	2	0	0	0	0	.000	0.00
Billingham	1	0	0	2⅔	0	0	0	0	0	1	0	0	0	1	0	1.000	0.00
Borbon	1	0	0	1⅔	0	0	0	0	0	0	0	0	0	0	0	.000	0.00
Gullett	1	1	0	7⅓	5	1	1	0	3	0	4	1	0	1	0	1.000	1.23
Nolan	1	1	0	6⅔	8	2	2	0	1	0	1	0	0	1	0	1.000	2.70
Zachry	1	1	0	6⅔	6	2	2	1	5	0	6	0	0	1	0	1.000	2.70
Norman	1	1	0	6⅓	9	3	3	0	2	0	2	0	0	0	0	.000	4.26
Totals	4	4	0	36	30	8	8	1	12	0	16	1	0	4	0	1.000	2.00

Saves—McEnaney 2.

NEW YORK YANKEES' PITCHING RECORDS

Pitcher	G	GS	CG	IP	H	R	ER	HR	BB	IBB	SO	HB	WP	W	L	Pct.	ERA.
Lyle	2	0	0	2⅔	1	0	0	0	0	0	3	0	1	0	0	.000	0.00
Hunter	1	1	1	8⅔	10	4	3	0	4	1	5	0	0	0	1	.000	3.12
Jackson	1	0	0	3⅔	4	2	2	0	0	0	3	0	0	0	1	.000	4.91
Figueroa	1	1	0	8	6	5	5	1	5	0	2	0	1	0	1	.000	5.63
Alexander	1	1	0	6	9	5	5	1	2	0	1	0	0	0	1	.000	7.50
Tidrow	2	0	0	2⅓	5	2	2	1	1	1	1	0	0	0	0	.000	7.71
Ellis	1	1	0	3⅓	7	4	4	1	0	0	1	0	0	0	1	.000	10.80
Totals	4	4	1	34⅔	42	22	21	4	12	2	16	0	2	0	4	.000	5.45

COMPOSITE SCORE BY INNINGS

Cincinnati	1	6	1	4	0	1	2	2	5	–	22
New York	1	1	0	2	1	0	3	0	0	–	8

Sacrifice hits—None.

Sacrifice flies—Nettles, Rose, Griffey.

Stolen bases—Geronimo 2, Morgan 2, Concepcion, Driessen, Griffey, Rivers.

Caught stealing—Foster 2, Bench, Concepcion, Perez, Rivers.

Double plays—Alexander, Randolph, and Chambliss; Randolph, Stanley and Chambliss; Stanley, Randolph and Chambliss; Nettles, Randolph and Chambliss; Nettles and Chambliss; Stanley, Nettles, Chambliss and Randolph; Morgan, Concepcion and Perez; Morgan and Perez; Concepcion, Morgan and Perez; Perez and Concepcion.

Passed balls—None.

Hit by pitcher—By Gullett (Chambliss).

Balks—None.

Bases on balls—Off Figueroa 5 (Concepcion, Driessen, Foster, Morgan, Perez), off Hunter 4 (Geronimo 2, Morgan, Rose), off Alexander 2 (Foster, Rose), off Tidrow 1 (Driessen), off Zachry 5 (Nettles 2, White 2, Rivers), off Gullett 3 (Maddox, Randolph, Stanley), off Norman 2 (Stanley, White), off Nolan 1 (Stanley), off McEnaney 1 (Nettles).

Strikeouts—By Hunter 5 (Foster 2, Concepcion, Bench, Rose), by Jackson 3 (Concepcion, Morgan, Geronimo), by Lyle 3 (Concepcion, Griffey, Perez), by Figueroa 2 (Foster, Geronimo), by Alexander 1 (Morgan), by Ellis 1 (Perez), by Tidrow 1 (Rose), by Zachry 6 (Chambliss 2, May, Nettles, Randolph, Rivers), by Gullett 4 (Munson, Rivers, Stanley, Velez), by Norman 2 (Maddox 2), by McEnaney 2 (Velez 2), by Billingham 1 (Randolph), by Nolan 1 (Randolph).

Left on bases—Cincinnati 22—4, 10, 4, 4; New York 33—6, 7, 11, 9.

Time of games—First game, 2:10; second game, 2:33; third game, 2:40; fourth game, 2:36.

Attendance—First game, 54,826; second game, 54,816; third game, 56,667; fourth game, 56,700. Total, 223,009.

Umpires—Weyer (N.L.), DiMuro (A.L.), B. Williams (N.L.), Deegan (A.L.), Froemming (N.L.), Phillips (A.L.).

Official scorers—Richard Dozer, Chicago Tribune; Earl Lawson, Cincinnati Post; Dick Young, New York Daily News; Jack Lang, Long Island Press.

WORLD SERIES RESULTS

Year—Winner   Loser
1903—Boston A. L., 5 games; Pittsburgh N. L., 3 games.
1904—No Series.
1905—New York N. L., 4 games; Philadelphia A. L., 1 game.
1906—Chicago A. L., 4 games; Chicago N. L., 2 games.
1907—Chicago N. L., 4 games; Detroit A. L., 0 games; 1 tie.
1908—Chicago N. L., 4 games; Detroit A. L., 1 game.
1909—Pittsburgh N. L., 4 games; Detroit A. L., 3 games.
1910—Philadelphia A. L., 4 games; Chicago N. L., 1 game.
1911—Philadelphia A. L., 4 games; New York N. L., 2 games.
1912—Boston A. L., 4 games; New York N. L., 3 games; 1 tie.
1913—Philadelphia A. L., 4 games; New York N. L., 1 game.
1914—Boston N. L., 4 games; Philadelphia A. L., 0 games.
1915—Boston A. L., 4 games; Philadelphia N. L., 1 game.
1916—Boston A. L., 4 games; Brooklyn N. L., 1 game.
1917—Chicago A. L., 4 games; New York N. L., 2 games.
1918—Boston A. L., 4 games; Chicago N. L., 2 games.
1919—Cincinnati N. L., 5 games; Chicago A. L., 3 games.
1920—Cleveland A. L., 5 games; Brooklyn N. L., 2 games.
1921—New York N. L., 5 games; New York A. L., 3 games.
1922—New York N. L., 4 games; New York A. L., 0 games; 1 tie.
1923—New York A. L., 4 games; New York N. L., 2 games.
1924—Washington A. L., 4 games; New York N. L., 3 games.
1925—Pittsburgh N. L., 4 games; Washington A. L., 3 games.
1926—St. Louis N. L., 4 games; New York A. L., 3 games.
1927—New York A. L., 4 games; Pittsburgh N. L., 0 games.
1928—New York A. L., 4 games; St. Louis N. L., 0 games.
1929—Philadelphia A. L., 4 games; Chicago N. L., 1 game.
1930—Philadelphia A. L., 4 games; St. Louis N. L., 2 games.
1931—St. Louis N. L., 4 games; Philadelphia A. L., 3 games.
1932—New York A. L., 4 games; Chicago N. L., 0 games.
1933—New York N. L., 4 games; Washington A. L., 1 game.
1934—St. Louis N. L., 4 games; Detroit A. L., 3 games.
1935—Detroit A. L., 4 games; Chicago N. L., 2 games.
1936—New York A. L., 4 games; New York N. L., 2 games.
1937—New York A. L., 4 games; New York N. L., 1 game.
1938—New York A. L., 4 games; Chicago N. L., 0 games.
1939—New York A. L., 4 games; Cincinnati N. L., 0 games.
1940—Cincinnati N. L., 4 games; Detroit A. L., 3 games.
1941—New York A. L., 4 games; Brooklyn N. L., 1 game.
1942—St. Louis N. L., 4 games; New York A. L., 1 game.
1943—New York A. L., 4 games; St. Louis N. L., 1 game.
1944—St. Louis N. L., 4 games; St. Louis A. L., 2 games.
1945—Detroit A. L., 4 games; Chicago N. L., 3 games.
1946—St. Louis N. L., 4 games; Boston A. L., 3 games.
1947—New York A. L., 4 games; Brooklyn N. L., 3 games.
1948—Cleveland A. L., 4 games; Boston N. L., 2 games.
1949—New York A. L., 4 games; Brooklyn N. L., 1 game.
1950—New York A. L., 4 games; Philadelphia N. L., 0 games.
1951—New York A. L., 4 games; New York N. L., 2 games.
1952—New York A. L., 4 games; Brooklyn N. L., 3 games.
1953—New York A. L., 4 games; Brooklyn N. L., 2 games.
1954—New York N. L., 4 games; Cleveland A. L., 0 games.
1955—Brooklyn N. L., 4 games; New York A. L., 3 games.
1956—New York A. L., 4 games; Brooklyn N. L., 3 games.
1957—Milwaukee N. L., 4 games; New York A. L., 3 games.
1958—New York A. L., 4 games; Milwaukee N. L., 3 games.
1959—Los Angeles N. L., 4 games; Chicago A. L., 2 games.
1960—Pittsburgh N. L., 4 games; New York A. L., 3 games.
1961—New York A. L., 4 games; Cincinnati N. L., 1 game.
1962—New York A. L., 4 games; San Francisco N. L., 3 games.
1963—Los Angeles N. L., 4 games; New York A. L., 0 games.
1964—St. Louis N. L., 4 games; New York A. L., 3 games.
1965—Los Angeles N. L., 4 games; Minnesota A. L., 3 games.
1966—Baltimore A. L., 4 games; Los Angeles N. L., 0 games.
1967—St. Louis N. L., 4 games; Boston A. L., 3 games.
1968—Detroit A. L., 4 games; St. Louis N. L., 3 games.
1969—New York N. L., 4 games; Baltimore A. L., 1 game.
1970—Baltimore A. L., 4 games; Cincinnati N. L., 1 game.
1971—Pittsburgh N. L., 4 games; Baltimore A. L., 3 games.
1972—Oakland A. L., 4 games; Cincinnati N. L., 3 games.
1973—Oakland A. L., 4 games; New York N. L., 3 games.
1974—Oakland A. L., 4 games; Los Angeles N. L., 1 game.
1975—Cincinnati N. L., 4 games; Boston A. L., 3 games.
1976—Cincinnati N. L., 4 games; New York A. L., 0 games.

WORLD SERIES ATTENDANCE, MONEY

Year	Games	Attendance	Gate Receipts	Players' Tot.	W. Share	L. Share
1903	8	100,429	$ 50,000.00	$ 32,612.00	$ 1,182.00	$ 1,316.25
1905	5	91,723	68,436.81	27,394.20	1,142.00	832.22
1906	6	99,845	106,550.00	33,401.70	1,874.63	439.50
1907	5	78,068	101,728.50	54,933.39	2,142.85	1,945.96
1908	5	62,232	94,975.50	46,114.92	1,317.58	870.00
1909	7	145,295	188,302.50	66,924.90	1,825.22	1,274.76
1910	5	124,222	173,980.00	79,071.93	2,062.79	1,375.16
1911	6	179,851	342,364.50	127,910.61	3,654.58	2,436.39
1912	8	252,037	490,833.00	147,572.28	4,024.68	2,566.47
1913	5	151,000	325,980.00	135,164.16	3,246.36	2,164.22
1914	4	111,009	225,739.00	121,898.94	2,812.28	2,031.65
1915	5	143,351	320,361.50	144,899.55	3,780.25	2,520.17
1916	5	162,859	385,590.50	162,927.45	3,910.26	2,834.82
1917	6	186,654	425,878.00	152,888.58	3,669.32	2,442.21
1918	6	128,483	179,619.00	69,527.70	1,102.51	671.09
1919	8	236,928	722,414.00	260,349.66	5,207.07	3,254.36
1920	7	178,737	564,800.00	214,882.74	4,168.00	2,419.60
1921	8	269,976	900,233.00	292,522.23	5,265.00	3,510.00
1922	5	185,947	605,475.00	247,309.71	4,545.71	2,842.86
1923	6	301,430	1,063,815.00	368,783.04	6,143.49	4,112.88
1924	7	283,665	1,093,104.00	331,092.51	5,959.64	3,820.29
1925	7	282,848	1,182,854.00	339,664.19	5,332.72	3,734.60
1926	7	328,051	1,207,864.00	372,300.51	5,584.51	3,417.75
1927	4	201,705	783,217.00	399,440.67	5,782.24	3,985.47
1928	4	199,072	777,290.00	419,736.60	5,813.20	4,181.30
1929	5	190,490	859,494.00	388,086.66	5,620.57	3,782.01
1930	6	212,619	953,772.00	·323,865.00	5,038.07	3,536.68
1931	7	231,567	1,030,723.00	320,303.46	4,467.59	3,023.00
1932	4	191,998	713,377.00	363,822.27	5,231.77	4,244.60
1933	5	163,076	679,365.00	284,665.68	4,256.72	3,019.86
1934	7	281,510	1,031,341.00	327,950.46	5,389.57	3,354.68
1935	6	286,672	1,073,794.00	397,360.24	6,544.76	4,198.53
1936	6	302,924	1,204,399.00	460,002.66	6,430.55	4,655.58
1937	5	238,142	985,994.00	459,629.35	6,471.11	4,489.96
1938	4	200,833	851,166.00	434,094.66	5,728.76	4,674.87
1939	4	183,849	745,329.09	431,117.84	5,541.89	4,193.39
1940	7	281,927	1,222,328.21	404,414.04	5,803.62	3,531.81
1941	5	235,773	1,007,762.00	474,184.54	5,943.31	4,829.40
1942	5	277,101	1,105,249.00	427,579.41	6,192.53	3,351.77
1943	5	277,312	1,105,784.00	488,005.74	6,139.46	4,321.96
1944	6	206,708	906,122.00	309,590.91	4,626.01	2,743.79
1945	7	333,457	1,492,454.00	475,579.04	6,443.34	3,930.22
1946	7	250,071	1,052,900.00	304,141.05	3,742.34	2,140.89
1947	7	389,763	1,781,348.92	493,674.82	5,830.03	4,081.19
1948	6	358,362	1,633,685.56	548,214.99	6,772.07	4,570.73
1949	5	236,716	1,129,627.88	490,855.84	5,626.74	4,272.74
1950	4	196,009	953,669.03	486,371.21	5,737.95	4,081.34
1951	6	341,977	1,633,457.47	560,562.37	6,446.09	4,951.03
1952	7	340,706	1,622,753.01	500,003.28	5,982.65	4,200.64
1953	6	307,350	1,779,269.44	691,341.61	8,280.68	6,178.42
1954	4	251,507	1,566,203.38	881,763.72	11,147.90	6,712.50
1955	7	362,310	2,337,515.34	737,853.59	9,768.21	5,598.58
1956	7	345,903	2,183,254.59	758,561.63	8,714.76	6,934.34
1957	7	394,712	2,475,978.94	709,027.55	8,924.36	5,606.06
1958	7	393,909	2,397,223.03	726,044.55	8,759.10	5,896.08
1959	6	420,784	2,628,809.44	893,301.40	11,231.18	7,257.17
1960	7	349,813	2,230,627.88	682,144.82	8,417.94	5,214.64
1961	5	223,247	1,480,059.95	645,928.28	7,389.13	5,356.37
1962	7	376,864	2,878,891.11	893,281.71	9,882.74	7,291.49
1963	4	247,279	1,995,189.09	1,017,546.43	12,794.00	7,874.32
1964	7	321,807	2,243,187.96	696,520.15	8,622.19	5,309.29
1965	7	364,326	2,975,041.60	885,612.21	10,297.43	6,634.36
1966	4	220,791	2,047,142.46	1,044,042.65	11,683.04	8,189.36
1967	7	304,085	2,350,607.10	705,878.44	8,314.81	5,115.23
1968	7	379,670	3,018,113.40	879,761.08	10,936.66	7,078.71
1969	5	272,378	2,857,782.78	*1,734,696.37	*18,338.18	*14,904.21
1970	5	253,183	2,599,170.26	*1,714,305.14	*18,215.78	*13,687.59
1971	7	351,091	3,049,803.46	*1,742,325.31	*18,164.58	*13,906.46
1972	7	363,149	3,954,542.99	*1,882,178.15	*20,705.01	*15,080.25
1973	7	358,289	3,923,968.37	*1,992,461.17	*24,617.57	*14,950.18
1974	5	260,004	3,007,194.00	*2,045,442.79	*22,219.09	*15,703.97
1975	7	308,272	3,380,579.91	*1,826,264.97	*19,060.46	*13,325.87
1976	4	223,009	2,498,416.53	*2,467,835.98	*26,366.68	*19,935.48

*Total combined figures for World Series and League Championship Series.

NOTE—Losers' shares in 1903-05-07 and winners' in 1906-08-07 include club owners' slices which were added to their teams' player pools.

1976 ALL-STAR GAME

Including

Review of '76 Game

Official Box Score

Official Play-By-Play

Results of Previous Games

All-Star Game Another A.L. Humiliation

By JOE MARCIN

If the All-Star Game had been a prize fight, it would have been stopped early. The National Leaguers took time out from their own intra-mural activities on the evening of July 13 to administer their annual whipping to the American League by a score of 7-1 in a game that quickly lost much of its competitiveness.

The victory gave the senior circuit a five-game winning skein and its 13th triumph out of the last 14 games in the series that began in 1933.

To help commemorate our nation's Bicentennial, the game was played in Philadelphia and 63,974 spectators, including President Gerald R. Ford (himself to join the American Leaguers as a loser several months hence), sat in on the carnage at Veterans Stadium.

American League Manager Darrell Johnson, who, as it turned out, was to enter the ranks of the unemployed four days later when he was dismissed by the Boston Red Sox, chose for his starting pitcher the Detroit Tigers' colorful rookie, Mark Fidrych. The young righthander had been the sensation of the baseball world with his exploits and antics on the mound, including "talking" to the ball between pitches. But his sorcery was ineffectual against the National League.

After the San Diego Padres' Randy Jones pitched a scoreless first half of the opening inning, the Cincinnati Reds' redoubtable Pete Rose led off the home nine's first turn at bat with a single and immediately tallied on a triple by the Los Angeles Dodgers' Steve Garvey. Garvey crossed the plate when the Reds' George Foster grounded out.

Fidrych was tagged for a couple of hits in the second frame but managed to struggle through without being scored upon. He was succeeded in the third canto by the New York Yankees' Catfish Hunter. The rich righthander should have been throwing dollar bills to the plate instead of a baseball. The Reds' Joe Morgan singled with one out and then Foster drilled a long blast far over the left field fence to make the score 4-0.

It was evident at this point that school was out for the junior loop, but the rules demand that, except in inclement weather, the contest go on for nine innings.

Jones tossed three shutout stanzas and was followed to the hill by the New York Mets' Tom Seaver and the San Francisco Giants' John (The Count) Montefusco for two innings apiece and the Los Angeles Dodgers' Rick Rhoden and the Houston Astros' Ken Forsch for an inning each. Except for Seaver, they were all puzzles to the A.L. batters. The Mets' veteran hurler yielded a home run to the Boston Red Sox' Fred Lynn in the fourth frame. Lynn's hit was one of only five that his club could muster.

Boston's Luis Tiant blanked the Nationals in the two innings he worked but the California Angels' hard-throwing lefty, Frank Tanana, was bombarded for three runs in the eighth round. Tanana gave up a walk, two singles and a homer. The latter blow was by the Astros' Cesar Cedeno.

But it scarcely mattered. The Americans were already thoroughly defeated by that time. Except for Lynn's homer, they expired meekly inning after inning.

Cincinnati's Foster, making his first All-Star Game appearance, won Most Valuable Player honors.

As a matter of fact, the National League victory was heavily tinged with red, the Cincinnati Red variety. There were five Reds voted to the starting line-up and Anderson added two more. Among them, they accounted for four runs scored, four runs batted in and seven of their club's ten hits.

The Reds' Sparky Anderson, pilot of the National Leaguers, could just sit back and enjoy the game. No matter which button he pushed, it was the right one.

The crowd was the third largest in All-Star Game history, surpassed only by the throngs at games played in Cleveland's Municipal Stadium in 1935 and 1954.

The gate receipts of $772,346 were a new record for the affair.

An estimated 60 million people watched the proceedings on ABC-TV. The competition on NBC and CBS was the Democratic National Convention and the Nielsen ratings proved what everybody knew all along—even a bad baseball game is preferred viewing to a conclave of politicians spouting windy oratory.

For the record, the series now stands at 28 victories for the Nationals, 18 for the Americans and one tie.

The American League dominated the early years of the All-Star Game but obviously its talent of recent seasons is a far cry from the halcyon days of Babe Ruth, Lou Gehrig, Jimmie Foxx, Bob Feller and Ted Williams. Meanwhile, the National League, even while losing such super All-Star Game performers as Stan Musial, Willie Mays and Juan Marichal, still appears to have come up with enough good players to maintain superiority.

FIRST INNING

Americans—LeFlore grounded a single to left. Carew bounced into a double play, Morgan to Concepcion to Garvey. Brett walked on four pitches. Munson forced Brett, Concepcion to Morgan. No runs, one hit, no errors, one left.

Nationals—Rose lined a single to center. Garvey's fly ball to right fell in front of Staub and then bounced past him for a triple, Rose scoring. Morgan flied to Staub in shallow right, Garvey holding third. Foster grounded slowly to Grich, Garvey scoring. Luzinski fouled to Carew. Two runs, two hits, no errors, none left.

SECOND INNING

Americans—Lynn fouled to Garvey near the first base dugout. Harrah bounced to Rose. Staub lined a single to right. Grich attempted to check his swing but tapped to Concepcion. No runs, one hit, no errors, one left.

Nationals—Bench lined a single to left. Kingman fouled to Carew. Bench broke for second on the hit-and-run and Concepcion grounded a single to center, Bench racing to third. Concepcion advanced to second when a pitch got away from Munson, Bench holding third. It was ruled a passed ball. Jones struck out. Rose rolled to Carew who threw to Fidrych covering first for the out. No runs, two hits, no errors, two left.

THIRD INNING

Americans—McRae batted for Fidrych and, trying to check his swing, tapped to Jones. LeFlore struck out. Carew grounded to Morgan, who threw to Jones covering first for the out. No runs, no hits, no errors, none left.

Nationals—Hunter was the new pitcher for the Americans. Garvey fouled to Carew. Morgan grounded a single to center. Foster homered over the wall in left-center, Morgan scoring ahead of him. Luzinski flied to LeFlore. Bench fanned. Two runs, two hits, no errors, none left.

FOURTH INNING

Americans—Seaver took the mound for the Nationals. Brett flied to Kingman in right-center. Munson popped to Concepcion in short center. Lynn homered into the stands in right, near the foul line. Harrah popped to Morgan. One run, one hit, no errors, none left.

Nationals—Kingman struck out. Concepcion flied to LeFlore in short left. Seaver fanned. No runs, no hits, no errors, none left.

FIFTH INNING

Americans—Foster moved from center to right, Cedeno went to center, Bowa went to shortstop and Boone was the new catcher for the Nationals. Staub lined a single to right. Grich grounded into a double play, Morgan to Bowa to Garvey. Rivers batted for Hunter and struck out. No runs, one hit, no errors, none left.

Nationals—Rivers remained in the game in right field, Yastrzemski went to left, Belanger to short, Fisk came in to catch and Tiant was the new pitcher for the Americans. Rose tripled to the wall in right-center. Garvey grounded to Brett who made a backhanded stop and threw to Carew for the out, Rose holding third. Morgan popped to Grich. Foster grounded to Belanger. No runs, one hit, no errors, one left.

SIXTH INNING

Americans—Oliver went to right field, Cash to second base, Perez to first base, Schmidt to third base and Montefusco was the new pitcher for the Nationals. Yastrzemski popped to Bowa in short left near the foul line. Carew walked. Brett flied to Cedeno in deep right-center. Carew stole second. Fisk fouled to Boone. No runs, no hits, no errors, one left.

Nationals—Money went to third base and Garner to second base for the Americans. Luzinski fouled to Carew. Cedeno struck out. Boone popped to Belanger in short center. No runs, no hits, no errors, none left.

SEVENTH INNING

Americans—Oliver moved from right to left field and Griffey went to right field for the Nationals. Lynn fanned but had to be tagged by Boone when the third strike was in the dirt. Belanger flied to Griffey in short right. Wynegar batted for Tiant and walked. Garner struck out. No runs, no hits, no errors, one left.

Nationals—Patek went to shortstop and Tanana was the new pitcher for the Americans. Bowa flied to Rivers in right-center. Schmidt grounded to Patek. Oliver grounded to Carew who threw to Tanana covering first for the out. No runs, no hits, no errors, none left.

EIGHTH INNING

Americans—Russell went to short and Rhoden took the mound for the Nationals. Rivers beat out a high chop to Rhoden to the left of the mound. Yastrzemski grounded into a double play, Cash to Russell to Perez. Carew lined to Oliver in left-center. No runs, one hit, no errors, none left.

Nationals—Cash grounded a single to left. Perez walked. Russell grounded into a double play, Money to Garner to Carew, Cash going to third. Griffey grounded a single to center, Cash scoring. Cedeno homered over the left field fence, Griffey scoring ahead of him. Boone flied to Rivers. Three runs, three hits, no errors, none left.

NINTH INNING

Americans—Cey went to third base and Forsch was the new pitcher for the Nationals. Money popped to Cash. Chambliss batted for Fisk and grounded to Russell. Otis batted for Lynn and struck out. No runs, no hits, no errors, none left.

AMERICANS	AB	R	H	RBI	PO	A
LeFlore (Tigers), lf	2	0	1	0	2	0
Yastrzemski (Red Sox), lf	2	0	0	0	0	0
Carew (Twins), 1b	3	0	0	0	9	2
Brett (Royals), 3b	2	0	0	0	0	1
Money (Brewers), 3b	1	0	0	0	0	1
Munson (Yankees), c	2	0	0	0	4	0
Fisk (Red Sox), c	1	0	0	0	1	0
dChambliss (Yankees)	1	0	0	0	0	0
Lynn (Red Sox), cf	3	1	1	1	0	0
eOtis (Royals)	1	0	0	0	0	0
Harrah (Rangers), ss	2	0	0	0	0	0
Belanger (Orioles), ss	1	0	0	0	1	1
Patek (Royals), ss	0	0	0	0	0	1
Staub (Tigers), rf	2	0	2	0	1	0
Tiant (Red Sox), p	0	0	0	0	0	0
cWynegar (Twins)	0	0	0	0	0	0
Tanana (Angels), p	0	0	0	0	1	0
Grich (Orioles), 2b	2	0	0	0	1	1
Garner (Athletics), 2b	1	0	0	0	1	1
Fidrych (Tigers), p	0	0	0	0	1	0
aMcRae (Royals)	1	0	0	0	0	0
Hunter (Yankees), p	0	0	0	0	0	0
bRivers (Yankees), rf	2	0	1	0	2	0
Totals	29	1	5	1	24	8

NATIONALS	AB	R	H	RBI	PO	A
Rose (Reds), 3b	3	1	2	0	0	1
Oliver (Pirates), rf-lf	1	0	0	0	1	0
Garvey (Dodgers), 1b	3	1	1	1	6	0
Cash (Phillies), 2b	1	1	1	0	1	1
Morgan (Reds), 2b	3	1	1	0	2	3
Perez (Reds), 1b	0	0	0	0	2	0
Foster (Reds), cf-rf	3	1	1	3	0	0
Montefusco (Giants), p	0	0	0	0	0	0
Russell (Dodgers), ss	1	0	0	0	1	2
Luzinski (Phillies), lf	3	0	0	0	0	0
Griffey (Reds), rf	1	1	1	1	0	0
Bench (Reds), c	2	0	1	0	1	0
Cedeno (Astros), cf	2	1	1	2	1	0
Kingman (Mets), rf	2	0	0	0	1	0
Boone (Phillies), c	2	0	0	0	5	0
Concepcion (Reds), ss	2	0	1	0	2	3
Bowa (Phillies), ss	1	0	0	0	2	1
Rhoden (Dodgers), p	0	0	0	0	0	0
Cey (Dodgers), 3b	0	0	0	0	0	0
Jones (Padres), p	1	0	0	0	1	1
Seaver (Mets), p	1	0	0	0	0	0
Schmidt (Phillies), 3b	1	0	0	0	0	0
Forsch (Astros), p	0	0	0	0	0	0
Totals	33	7	10	7	27	12

```
Americans ..............................  0   0   0     1   0   0     0   0   0 — 1
Nationals  ..............................  2   0   2     0   0   0     0   3   x — 7
```

Americans	IP	H	R	ER	BB	SO
Fidrych (Tigers)	2	4	2	2	0	1
Hunter (Yankees)	2	2	2	2	0	3
Tiant (Red Sox)	2	1	0	0	0	1
Tanana (Angels)	2	3	3	3	1	0

Nationals	IP	H	R	ER	BB	SO
Jones (Padres)	3	2	0	0	1	1
Seaver (Mets)	2	2	1	1	0	1
Montefusco (Giants)	2	0	0	0	2	2
Rhoden (Dodgers)	1	1	0	0	0	0
Forsch (Astros)	1	0	0	0	0	1

Winning pitcher—Jones. Losing pitcher—Fidrych.

aGrounded out for Fidrych in third. bStruck out for Hunter in fifth. cWalked for Tiant in seventh. dGrounded out for Fisk in ninth. eStruck out for Lynn in ninth. Errors—None. Double plays—Morgan, Concepcion and Garvey; Morgan, Bowa and Garvey; Cash, Russell and Perez; Money, Garner and Carew. Left on bases—Americans 4, Nationals 3. Three-base hits—Garvey, Rose. Home runs—Foster, Lynn, Cedeno. Stolen base—Carew. Passed ball—Munson. Bases on balls—Off Jones 1 (Brett), off Montefusco 2 (Carew, Wynegar), off Tanana 1 (Perez). Strikeouts—By Jones 1 (LeFlore), by Seaver 1 (Rivers), by Montefusco 2 (Lynn, Garner), by Forsch 1 (Otis), by Fidrych 1 (Jones), by Hunter 3 (Bench, Kingman, Seaver), by Tiant 1 (Cedeno). Umpires—Wendelstedt (NL) plate, Neudecker (AL) first base, Olsen (NL) second base, Denkinger (AL) third base, Davidson (NL) left field, Evans (AL) right field. Time—2:12. Attendance—63,974. Official scorers—Richard Dozer, Chicago Tribune; Ray Kelly, Philadelphia Bulletin, and Bill Liston, Boston Herald-American.

RESULTS OF PREVIOUS GAMES

1933—At Comiskey Park, Chicago, July 6. Americans 4, Nationals 2. Managers —Connie Mack, John McGraw. Winning pitcher—Lefty Gomez. Losing pitcher— Bill Hallahan. Attendance—47,595.

1934—At Polo Grounds, New York, July 10. Americans 9, Nationals 7. Managers—Joe Cronin, Bill Terry. Winning pitcher—Mel Harder. Losing pitcher—Van Mungo. Attendance—48,363.

1935—At Municipal Stadium, Cleveland, July 8. Americans 4, Nationals 1. Managers—Mickey Cochrane, Frankie Frisch. Winning pitcher—Lefty Gomez. Losing pitcher—Bill Walker. Attendance—69,831.

1936—At Braves Field, Boston, July 7. Nationals 4, Americans 3. Managers— Charlie Grimm, Joe McCarthy. Winning pitcher—Dizzy Dean. Losing pitcher— Lefty Grove. Attendance—25,556.

1937—At Griffith Stadium, Washington, July 7. Americans 8, Nationals 3. Managers—Joe McCarthy, Bill Terry. Winning pitcher—Lefty Gomez. Losing pitcher— Dizzy Dean. Attendance—31,391.

1938—At Crosley Field, Cincinnati, July 6. Nationals 4, Americans 1. Managers —Bill Terry, Joe McCarthy. Winning pitcher—Johnny Vander Meer. Losing pitcher—Lefty Gomez. Attendance—27,067.

1939—At Yankee Stadium, New York, July 11. Americans 3, Nationals 1. Managers—Joe McCarthy, Gabby Hartnett. Winning pitcher—Tommy Bridges. Losing pitcher—Bill Lee. Attendance—62,892.

1940—At Sportsman's Park, St. Louis, July 9. Nationals 4, Americans 0. Managers—Bill McKechnie, Joe Cronin. Winning pitcher—Paul Derringer. Losing pitcher—Red Ruffing. Attendance—32,373.

1941—At Briggs Stadium, Detroit, July 8. Americans 7, Nationals 5. Managers— Del Baker, Bill McKechnie. Winning pitcher—Ed Smith. Losing pitcher—Claude Passeau. Attendance—54,674.

1942—At Polo Grounds, New York, July 6. Americans 3, Nationals 1. Managers —Joe Cronin, Leo Durocher. Winning pitcher—Spud Chandler. Losing pitcher— Mort Cooper. Attendance—34,178.

1943—At Shibe Park, Philadelphia, July 13 (night game). Americans 5, Nationals 3. Managers—Joe McCarthy, Billy Southworth. Winning pitcher—Dutch Leonard. Losing pitcher—Mort Cooper. Attendance—31,938.

1944—At Forbes Field, Pittsburgh, July 11 (night game). Nationals 7, Americans 1. Managers—Billy Southworth, Joe McCarthy. Winning pitcher—Ken Raffensberger. Losing pitcher—Tex Hughson. Attendance—29,589.

1945—No game played.

1946—At Fenway Park, Boston, July 9. Americans 12, Nationals 0. Managers— Steve O'Neill, Charlie Grimm. Winning pitcher—Bob Feller. Losing pitcher— Claude Passeau. Attendance—34,906.

1947—At Wrigley Field, Chicago, July 8. Americans 2, Nationals 1. Managers— Joe Cronin, Eddie Dyer. Winning pitcher—Frank Shea. Losing pitcher—Johnny Sain. Attendance—41,123.

1948—At Sportsman's Park, St. Louis, July 13. Americans 5, Nationals 2. Managers—Bucky Harris, Leo Durocher. Winning pitcher—Vic Raschi. Losing pitcher—Johnny Schmitz. Attendance—34,009.

1949—At Ebbets Field, Brooklyn, July 12. Americans 11, Nationals 7. Managers—Lou Boudreau, Billy Southworth. Winning pitcher—Virgil Trucks. Losing pitcher—Don Newcombe. Attendance—32,577.

1950—At Comiskey Park, Chicago, July 11. Nationals 4, Americans 3 (14 innings). Managers—Burt Shotton, Casey Stengel. Winning pitcher—Ewell Blackwell. Losing pitcher—Ted Gray. Attendance—46,127.

1951—At Briggs Stadium, Detroit, July 10. Nationals 8, Americans 3. Managers—Eddie Sawyer, Casey Stengel. Winning pitcher—Sal Maglie. Losing pitcher—Ed Lopat. Attendance—52,075.

1952—At Shibe Park, Philadelphia, July 8. Nationals 3, Americans 2 (five innings—rain). Managers—Leo Durocher, Casey Stengel. Winning pitcher—Bob Rush. Losing pitcher—Bob Lemon. Attendance—32,785.

1953—At Crosley Field, Cincinnati, July 14. Nationals 5, Americans 1. Managers—Chuck Dressen, Casey Stengel. Winning pitcher—Warren Spahn. Losing pitcher— Allie Reynolds. Attendance—30,846.

1954—At Municipal Stadium, Cleveland, July 13. Americans 11, Nationals 9. Managers—Casey Stengel, Walter Alston. Winning pitcher—Dean Stone. Losing pitcher—Gene Conley. Attendance—68,751.

1955—At Milwaukee County Stadium, Milwaukee, July 12. Nationals 6, Americans 5 (12 innings). Managers—Leo Durocher, Al Lopez. Winning pitcher—Gene Conley. Losing pitcher—Frank Sullivan. Attendance—45,643.

1956—At Griffith Stadium, Washington, July 10. Nationals 7, Americans 3. Managers—Walter Alston, Casey Stengel. Winning pitcher—Bob Friend. Losing pitcher—Billy Pierce. Attendance—28,843.

1957—At Busch Stadium, St. Louis, July 9. Americans 6, Nationals 5. Managers—Casey Stengel, Walter Alston. Winning pitcher—Jim Bunning. Losing pitcher—Curt Simmons. Attendance—30,693.

1958—At Memorial Stadium, Baltimore, July 8. Americans 4, Nationals 3. Managers—Casey Stengel, Fred Haney. Winning pitcher—Early Wynn. Losing pitcher—Bob Friend. Attendance—48,829.

1959 (first game)—At Forbes Field, Pittsburgh, July 7. Nationals 5, Americans 4. Managers—Fred Haney, Casey Stengel. Winning pitcher—Johnny Antonelli. Losing pitcher—Whitey Ford. Attendance—35,277.

1959 (second game)—At Memorial Coliseum, Los Angeles, August 3. Americans 5, Nationals 3. Managers—Casey Stengel, Fred Haney. Winning pitcher—Jerry Walker. Losing pitcher—Don Drysdale. Attendance—55,105.

1960 (first game)—At Municipal Stadium, Kansas City, July 11. Nationals 5, Americans 3. Managers—Walter Alston, Al Lopez. Winning pitcher—Bob Friend. Losing pitcher—Bill Monbouquette. Attendance—30,619.

1960 (second game)—At Yankee Stadium, New York, July 13. Nationals 6, Americans 0. Managers—Walter Alston, Al Lopez. Winning pitcher—Vern Law. Losing pitcher—Whitey Ford. Attendance—38,362.

1961 (first game)—At Candlestick Park, San Francisco, July 11. Nationals 5, Americans 4 (10 innings). Managers—Danny Murtaugh, Paul Richards. Winning pitcher—Stu Miller. Losing pitcher—Hoyt Wilhelm. Attendance—44,115.

1961 (second game)—At Fenway Park, Boston, July 31. Americans 1, Nationals 1 (nine-inning tie, stopped by rain). Managers—Paul Richards, Danny Murtaugh. Attendance—31,851.

1962 (first game)—At District of Columbia Stadium, Washington, July 10. Nationals 3, Americans 1. Managers—Fred Hutchinson, Ralph Houk. Winning pitcher—Juan Marichal. Losing pitcher—Camilo Pascual. Attendance—45,480.

1962 (second game)—At Wrigley Field, Chicago, July 30. Americans 9, Nationals 4. Managers—Ralph Houk, Fred Hutchinson. Winning pitcher—Ray Herbert. Losing pitcher—Art Mahaffey. Attendance—38,359.

1963—At Municipal Stadium, Cleveland, July 9. Nationals 5, Americans 3. Managers—Alvin Dark, Ralph Houk. Winning pitcher—Larry Jackson. Losing pitcher—Jim Bunning. Attendance—44,160.

1964—At Shea Stadium, New York, July 7. Nationals 7, Americans 4. Managers—Walter Alston, Al Lopez. Winning pitcher—Juan Marichal. Losing pitcher—Dick Radatz. Attendance—50,850.

1965—At Metropolitan Stadium, Bloomington (Minnesota), July 13. Nationals 6, Americans 5. Managers—Gene Mauch, Al Lopez. Winning pitcher—Sandy Koufax. Losing pitcher—Sam McDowell. Attendance—46,706.

1966—At Busch Memorial Stadium, St. Louis, July 12. Nationals 2, Americans 1 (10 innings). Managers—Walter Alston, Sam Mele. Winning pitcher—Gaylord Perry. Losing pitcher—Pete Richert. Attendance—49,936.

1967—At Anaheim Stadium, Anaheim (California), July 11. Nationals 2, Americans 1 (15 innings). Managers—Walter Alston, Hank Bauer. Winning pitcher—Don Drysdale. Losing pitcher—Jim Hunter. Attendance—46,309.

1968—At Astrodome, Houston, July 9 (night). Nationals 1, Americans 0. Managers—Red Schoendienst, Dick Williams. Winning pitcher—Don Drysdale. Losing pitcher—Luis Tiant. Attendance—48,321.

1969—At Robert F. Kennedy Memorial Stadium, Washington, July 23. Nationals 9, Americans 3. Managers—Red Schoendienst, Mayo Smith. Winning pitcher—Steve Carlton. Losing pitcher—Mel Stottlemyre. Attendance—45,259.

1970—At Riverfront Stadium, Cincinnati, July 14 (night). Nationals 5, Americans 4 (12 innings). Managers—Gil Hodges, Earl Weaver. Winning pitcher—Claude Osteen. Losing pitcher—Clyde Wright. Attendance—51,838.

1971—At Tiger Stadium, Detroit, July 13 (night). Americans 6, Nationals 4. Managers—Earl Weaver, George (Sparky) Anderson. Winning pitcher—Vida Blue. Losing pitcher—Dock Ellis. Attendance—53,559.

1972—At Atlanta Stadium, Atlanta, July 25 (night). Nationals 4, Americans 3 (10 innings). Managers—Danny Murtaugh, Earl Weaver. Winning pitcher—Tug McGraw. Losing pitcher—Dave McNally. Attendance—53,107.

1973—At Royals Stadium, Kansas City, July 24 (night). Nationals 7, Americans 1. Managers—George (Sparky) Anderson, Dick Williams. Winning pitcher—Rick Wise. Losing pitcher—Bert Blyleven. Attendance—40,849.

1974—At Three Rivers Stadium, Pittsburgh, July 23 (night). Nationals 7, Americans 2. Managers—Yogi Berra, Dick Williams. Winning pitcher—Ken Brett. Losing pitcher—Luis Tiant. Attendance—50,706.

1975—At Milwaukee County Stadium, Milwaukee, July 15 (night). Nationals 6, Americans 3. Managers—Walter Alston, Alvin Dark. Winning pitcher—Jon Matlack. Losing pitcher—Jim Hunter. Attendance—51,480.

JOE MORGAN
• CINCINNATI REDS •
MAJOR LEAGUE
PLAYER OF THE YEAR

JOE BURKE
• KANSAS CITY ROYALS •
MAJOR LEAGUE EXECUTIVE

DANNY OZARK
• PHILADELPHIA PHILLIES •
MAJOR LEAGUE MANAGER

VERN RAPP
• DENVER •
MINOR LEAGUE MANAGER

ART TEECE
• SALT LAKE CITY •
MINOR LEAGUE EXECUTIVE
IN CLASS AAA

PAT PUTNAM
• ASHEVILLE •
MINOR LEAGUE PLAYER

WOODROW REID
• CHATTANOOGA •
MINOR LEAGUE EXECUTIVE
IN CLASS AA

The Sporting News

NO. **1**

MEN

of

1976

DON BUCHHEISTER
• CEDAR RAPIDS •
MINOR LEAGUE EXECUTIVE
IN CLASS A

REVIEW OF 1976

Including

Summation of Year's Activities

MVP Tables, All-Star Teams

Homers by Parks

By JEROME HOLTZMAN

It was a year of uncommon activity and enormous change. The reserve clause, which had withstood repeated assault since its introduction, by secret agreement, in 1879, finally succumbed, much to the dismay of the club owners, and underwent severe modifications, an action that lengthened the already impressive sequence of victories by the Major League Baseball Players Association.

Twenty-four players took full advantage of this new and sudden opportunity to break with their clubs. By refusing to sign their 1976 contracts they opted for, and at the season's end, were rewarded with their free agency. They then went on the open market. Frantic bidding followed. Half of these free agents reaped the anticipated bounty: record-setting multi-year million-dollar contracts which sent player salaries soaring as never before.

The free agents were absorbed back into the system with a so-called re-entry draft, a complex auction arrangement which allowed the clubs to declare simultaneous negotiation rights to the players of their choice. This draft was held on November 4 at the Plaza Hotel in New York City and was attended by Marvin Miller, executive director of the Players Association, who had expressed apprehension about the possibility of owner collusion.

Bill Campbell First Free Agent to Sign

Two days later Bill Campbell, a star relief pitcher previously with the Minnesota Twins, had the distinction of becoming the first free agent to make a new connection. Campbell signed a four-year, $1,000,000 contract with the Boston Red Sox, a remarkable bonanza considering that Campbell's 1976 pay was $23,000.

Within the next three weeks, 11 more players, all front-liners and many of them of all-star caliber, agreed to similar multi-million dollar proposals, putting the torch to Miller's suspicions that the owners would conspire to keep the prices down. Super star Reggie Jackson was the last of the big-name free agents to sign and got the biggest haul: $3,000,000 from the New York Yankees for a five-year contract.

The free agency issue, which was triggered by the historic Messersmith decision, was the dominant story of the year and had considerable side effects. Among them: a 17-day spring training lockout by the owners, which was finally ended by order of Commissioner Kuhn; and a multi-million dollar damage suit brought against Commissioner Bowie Kuhn by Oakland's Charlie Finley, the second time in history an owner challenged the authority of the commissioner in open court.

Finley Sells Three Stars

At almost the last hour before the tolling of the June 15th trading deadline, Finley sold three of his star players, Joe Rudi, Rollie Fingers and Vida Blue. Rudi and Fingers went to the Boston Red Sox for $1,000,000 each and Blue to the New York Yankees for $1,500,000. All had been playing out their options and would have become free agents at season's end and able to sign with a new club with Finley receiving no compensation in exchange. (Blue, as it turned out had been signed by Finley just prior to the "sale.") Commissioner Kuhn voided these sales as "not in the best interests of baseball."

Otherwise, comparatively routine events continued apace. The American

League, confronted with a lingering $32,500,000 suit by the City of Seattle and the State of Washington, avoided the hazards of litigation by expanding from 12 to 14 teams. It was a unilateral action expected to prompt companion expansion from the National League. But the National League, after considerable debate, remained at 12 teams.

Seattle and Toronto Enter American League

Seattle and Toronto were awarded the new franchises. There was no problem annexing Seattle which the A. L. had abandoned in 1970 after one year of inept operation that resulted in a bankruptcy. But the Americans had considerably more difficulty acquiring Toronto, a territory also regarded with favor by a majority of the National League owners who were aware of the tremendous gate potential of a Toronto vs. Montreal rivalry.

Initially, Toronto was wooed by the N. L. In early February, the financially troubled San Francisco Giants were "sold" to a Toronto group after "an agreement in principle" had been reached. But the sale was conditional and blocked on March 4 when the Giants were purchased for $8,000,000 by Bob Lurie, wealthy San Francisco realtor, and Arthur (Bud) Herseth, a Phoenix, Ariz. cattle baron, each of whom put up $4,000,000 and vowed to keep the Giants anchored in San Francisco.

Once the Lurie-Herseth purchase was consummated, the American League moved swiftly and approved Toronto as its 14th club; the expansion to Seattle had previously been announced. The A. L., at this point, most likely would have relinquished Toronto to the N. L. with the stipulation that both leagues would remain fixed at 13 teams and that this imbalance would trigger immediate interleague play. The N. L. considered this at a subsequent meeting but refused.

Braves and Astros Change Ownerships

In addition to the San Francisco Giants, two other clubs changed ownerships in 1976. R. E. (Ted) Turner, an internationally known yachtsman, bought the Atlanta Braves for a reported $12-million, to be paid on a 12-year installment plan. The purchase was made in the name of Turner Communications and gave the Braves local ownership for the first time. Bill Bartholomay, who was among the sellers, remained as chairman of the board.

Judge Roy Hofheinz, the man who built the Astrodome, which he called the "eighth wonder of the world," sold the Houston Astros to the General Electric Credit Corporation and the Ford Motor Credit Corporation. The deal was announced on June 24 and finalized on October 7. The credit companies had been major lenders to the Astros since 1972 and had been operating the club since June, 1975, when debts of more than $38,000,000 forced Hofheinz to relinquish control of his once vast Astrodomain empire.

All three of the franchises which changed ownerships in 1976 enjoyed home attendance increases. There were modest gains at Houston and at San Francisco but the increase at Atlanta was quite dramatic. Though they finished last in the National League West, the Braves drew 818,179 paid admissions, a boost of 283,507 from the previous year.

Rise in Attendance

Despite what seemed to be constant labor-management turmoil and the absence of genuine pennant races in any of the four divisions, the 24 major league clubs, combined, had a record gate of 31,318,331. Four clubs, also a record, topped the two million mark in attendance. The New York Yankees, who returned to Yankee Stadium, which had been renovated at a cost estimated at $100,000,000, led the American League with a home gate of 2,012,434.

The other three clubs in the 2,000,000 bracket were in the National League and were the Cincinnati Reds, the Philadelphia Phillies and the Los Angeles Dodgers. In a remarkable coincidence, they went over the 2,000,000 mark on successive days and/or nights. The Dodgers drew their 2,000,000th fan on Friday, August 20, the Phillies on August 21, the Reds on August 22. The world champion Reds led all clubs at the gate with 2,629,708 for the regular season, fourth highest in major league history.

It was another vigorous confirmation of baseball's spectator appeal and demonstrated anew the game's ability not only to survive but to thrive in the face of ever increasing litigation and mounting off-the-field problems. When the year began the owners still hadn't recovered from the crucial Messersmith decision given on December 23, 1975, by Arbitrator Peter Seitz, a ruling that was to have enormous effect on player salaries.

Review of Messersmith Case

A brief history is necessary:

Andy Messersmith, a star pitcher, had signed a one-year $90,000 contract in 1974 with the Dodgers. As a result of a dispute over the terms of his 1975 contract, he played the entire 1975 season without a contract. The Dodgers simply renewed his contract in accordance with paragraph 10 (a) of the Uniform Players Contract which contained a renewal clause that was the centerpiece of the reserve system; 10 (a) in effect, allowed a club to continue renewing a player's contract into perpetuity.

At the end of the 1975 season, Messersmith and pitcher Dave McNally of the Montreal Expos, who had also played without a contract before retiring in mid-season, appealed to the Players Association which took the immediate position that Messersmith and McNally were free agents. When the owners disagreed, the Players Association filed a grievance contending Messersmith was free to sign with any club.

The owners countered by insisting that the alleged claims did not come in the ambit of baseball's grievance procedure of the collective bargaining agreement and was not arbitrable.

The owners then applied to a federal district court in Kansas City to enjoin the proceedings. At the behest of the judge, the parties agreed to go ahead with the arbitration hearing with the understanding the court would hear and determine the jurisdictional question afterward.

Arbitrator Seitz, after a lengthy analysis, held that the renewal clause was not perpetual, but was for only one year; after this one year there was no contractural bond between player and club. Players who played out their renewal year were free to negotiate with any major league team. Therefore, Messersmith was declared a free agent. And Seitz was fired by the owners who under the Basic Agreement were entitled to dismiss an arbitrator at the conclusion of any particular grievance.

C. C. Johnson Spink, in his January 17 "We Believe" column in THE SPORTING NEWS quoted Seitz as saying:

"I am not a new Abraham Lincoln freeing the slaves. I was striking a blow at the reserve clause. I was just interpreting the renewal clause as a lawyer and as an elderly arbitrator."

Then Spink, in a prophetic paragraph, predicted: "The Seitz ruling gave the reserve clause a resounding whack and is likely to result in higher player salaries whether or not a large number of players switch to other clubs. Players are expected to demand, and obtain, long-term contracts at a higher pay level than now prevails."

Owners Lose in Court

Stunned, the owners appealed the Seitz decision to the U. S. District Court of the Western District of Missouri. Judge John W. Oliver delivered a 45-page opinion on February 4 upholding Seitz. The owners then appealed to a three-judge panel of the Eighth District Court of Appeals which on March 9 affirmed Judge Oliver's opinion. The only remaining appeal would have been to the U. S. Supreme Court but the owners acknowledged defeat and made no further appeal.

Marvin Miller objected to these appeals, insisting they were in violation of the Basic Agreement which states that an arbitrator's decision is to be binding and that there shall be no recourse to the courts by either side. This litigation, as Miller feared, delayed and to some extent halted labor-management negotiations on the Basic Agreement which had expired on December 31, 1975, eight days after Seitz had announced his ruling.

But the delays, as it turned out, were to be considerably more beneficial to the players than the owners. In the beginning, many of the players didn't grasp the full consequence of the Messersmith decision. For that matter, neither did Miller, nor Richard Moss, the attorney for the Players Association.

It wasn't until three or four weeks later, when Miller and Moss were on the road and in the midst of a series of regional player meetings, that all of the subtleties emerged. Among them was to be a crucial speculation: the possibility of litigation against the Players Association, collectively, and Miller and Moss, individually, if the Messersmith decision was bartered, in part or in full, during the on-going negotiations in exchange for improvement in either the Basic Agreement, or the players' Benefit Plan, or both.

Player Threats

There was never any specific identification of which players voiced these threats. But it was generally believed among them were Joe Torre and Tom Seaver of the New York Mets, Darold Knowles of the Chicago Cubs and Ken Holtzman of the Oakland A's, all veterans. The possibility of such litigation took both sides by surprise. Miller insisted it was not part of a premeditated plan by the Association. Some club executives, who had suffered because of Miller's brilliance, refused to believe him.

This threat of a law suit, or suits, in this situation was a problem unique to professional sports. It would not arise at United States Steel or at General Motors in which the union is the exclusive bargaining representative for all employees covered by the contract. In sports, there are both individual and league union contracts.

Hence, Miller had reason to fear that if the Association, in its negotiations, yielded a player's individual rights, the Association would be liable for damages. Whether such a suit would have been successful was difficult to determine. There was no specific pattern of precedent; the labor laws were far from certain.

In the first few weeks following the Messersmith decision there were indications the Association, in its desire for a new and improved package, was ready to agree to a new reserve system that would have softened the effects of the Messersmith ruling despite a pronouncement by Miller that "the owners aren't going to flim-flam the players out of this one."

If the owners had not twice appealed to the courts, if they had moved to an uncommonly swift conclusion of negotiations, it is possible, and perhaps likely, that they would have escaped with a comparatively minimal revision of the reserve clause.

Delay Favors Players

But the longer they delayed, the more the players had time to study and discuss among themselves the potential effects of their victory. They discovered that by refusing to sign their 1976 contracts they could play out their renewal, or option year, as Messersmith had done, and become free agents at the end of the season.

There was also the possibility that even if they signed for the 1976 season they could play out their options in 1977—providing they didn't relinquish this assumed privilege during their negotiations. As for those players who had previously signed multi-year contracts which would still be in effect beyond 1977, the Association also assumed the position that these players could also play out their options at the expiration of their existing contracts.

This program would allow almost every major leaguer, in either 1976 or 1977, to avail himself of the Messersmith benefits. But the owners were unwilling to concede the Seitz ruling had effects beyond Messersmith and McNally and insisted a new reserve system, when agreed upon, should be retroactive; i.e., players who signed their 1976 contracts would be bound to their clubs as before. To compromise, they proposed a new reserve system in which a player could become a free agent after nine years of major league service.

Nine years was much too long, Miller insisted, but he did recommend a possible solution. The owners could indemnify the Association and its officers from the threatened litigation from disgruntled players who claimed their rights had been abrogated by a collective agreement; or they could ask individual players to sign waivers stating they would not initiate litigation. "I think they probably could get a majority of the players to do this," Miller said.

The owners refused and with each turn of the screw the players became increasingly aware of their free agency opportunities. Reading the mood of the players, Miller also hardened in his resistance. There was no further discussion of owner indemnification.

In retrospect, this refusal by the owners may have been a mistake. In view of the subsquent bidding for free agents it may have been more economical, and orderly, for the moguls to invest in such a legal war chest, particularly since there was no guarantee that suits brought by individual players would have been successful.

Owners Submit Proposal

The pressure mounted. On February 11, the owners submitted their nine-year free agency proposal. Ten days later the players rejected this offer. Commissioner Bowie Kuhn, trying to steer a middle course, expressed disappointment on the lack of progress. Said Kuhn: "I can foresee trouble in achieving agreement at the bargaining table because the players now have too strong a position. I think the Seitz decision upset the balance of power, so to speak."

Miller countered: "I think the majority of players are willing to make a compromise on a retroactive reserve system. But the arbitrator's ruling gave all the players certain legal contractual rights. Not every player would be willing to bargain these away. Many are represented by lawyers and agents.

"I'm tired of the owners big mouthing that there is no legal liability and that the Players Association can do as it pleases. This dispute involves tremendous legal liabilities that the Players Association is not about to undertake. I have invited the owners' representatives to write a letter stating that the clubs assume full liability in this matter but the owners are not interested in assuming this liability."

Training Camps Not Opened

Two days later, on February 23, the owners revealed the spring training camps would not open until a new labor contract was agreed upon. National League President Charles Feeney made the announcement after a meeting of the owners' Player Relations Committee. Said Feeney: "We have reluctantly but unanimously voted to delay the opening of spring training."

One owner, Bill Veeck, who had recently returned to baseball as president of the Chicago White Sox, indicated he would not honor the lockout. Said Veeck, in defiance: "It's common knowledge that the White Sox are against postponing spring training. In the old days it was 15-1 against me. Now it's 23-1. I think my fellow owners have stuck their heads in the sand. Sometimes it seems to me that Marvin Miller is the only one who makes sense. He can't negotiate away the court's decision. If you were a player, would you let him?"

Miller responded in kind. "Bill Veeck is an interesting and intelligent man," Miller said. "He's different. I'll say that."

Miller also took this occasion to blast the owners. "The whole thing is comical," Miller declared. "For the first time in history an industry that is not threatened by any strike action from its employees is shutting down on its own volition."

American League president Lee MacPhail hurried to Chicago for a closed-door conference with Veeck, still a maverick at the age of 62. MacPhail warned Veeck that the White Sox would be slapped with a severe fine, which one newspaper estimated at $500,000. "The idea of playing baseball and negotiating at the same time is not desirable," MacPhail said.

Veeck Opens Camp

Veeck, however, was advised he could open his Sarasota, Fla. spring camp, if he wished, providing only minor leaguers were in uniform. There would be a violation only if any of the players on the Sox' 40-man winter roster participated. The Chicago newspapers, in big headlines, announced: "VEECK TO OPEN SOX CAMP."

The ChiSox did launch drills on March 1, the traditional opening day for spring training. Twenty-five players worked out but 24 were farmhands not on the parent roster; the 25th was veteran outfielder Cleon Jones, a free agent trying for a comeback.

"I quit like a dog," Veeck told Tom Fitzgerald of The Chicago Sun-Times. "As much as it grieves me, I am turning tail and running. But this is not an unconditional surrender. I'm complying with the letter of the rules, not the spirit."

Young Ted Turner, a rookie owner who appears to have maverick potential, followed Veeck's lead in dissent. Turner also opened the Atlanta Braves' spring camp in West Palm Beach, Fla., with nine minor leaguers reporting. Later, the Braves and White Sox engaged in two exhibition games but no major leaguers participated.

Players Work Out On Their Own

About 50 major leaguers also began working out but did so on their own. Some two dozen players, from a variety of clubs, joined together and participated in impromptu drills at Bradenton, Fla. Pete Rose simultaneously led about a dozen of his Cincinnati teammates in workouts at a Little League complex in West Tampa, Fla. A scattering of players was also limbering up and running wind sprints in Arizona and California.

Rose, longtime Cincinnati super star, was critical of Miller and the Players Association.

"We must remember that it's give and take," Rose said. "It can't be all take for the players."

Milwaukee first baseman George Scott, another veteran, also spoke against the Association. "I'm for protecting the owners," Scott said. "I don't see how they can operate without the reserve clause. I think the players should stop crying about slavery and worry about baseball. If they played as hard as they complain, they'd all be super stars."

Negotiations continued. By this time the Association's Executive Board, which included the 24 player representatives, and the owners' Player Relations Committee, had gathered in St. Petersburg, Fla. On March 12, after another unsuccessful meeting, the Association announced a "get-tough" policy. All players were advised to halt their unofficial workouts.

Said Tom Seaver of the New York Mets, who had organized the group in Bradenton: "If we continue working out at this time we are only helping the owners while undercutting our own negotiators." Miller agreed that this decision to stop training strengthened the Association's bargaining position.

Editorial Comment In The Sporting News

THE SPORTING NEWS, in a March 13 editorial titled, "Time Is Growing Short," admonished the owners:

"Closing the camps won't help solve the problem. Such a move has to be viewed by the players as a challenge to their resolve. The Messersmith decision has put baseball in a state of turmoil. It isn't world shaking but it surely will jolt a 100-year old professional sport if that sport's own people don't find a solution and quickly."

On March 14, Commissioner Kuhn expressed optimism and told the Associated Press:

"I can't offer you a hard date but the spring camps will be opened and we will have baseball on time. The season will not be delayed. This has been a frustrating time for all of us. My job is to keep these guys meeting and working for a solution."

At this point there had been 29 negotiation sessions without significant progress. But there was considerable movement on March 15th when the owners' Player Relations Committee submitted its "best and final offer" in a 10-page proposal which included a surrender on the crucial reserve clause issue.

The owners agreed that players who don't sign their contracts in either 1976 or 1977 could become free agents, a concession that gave all 600 major leaguers full Messersmith benefits. The owners also agreed the new reserve system would permit players to become free agents after eight major league seasons, instead of nine, as previously proposed.

In addition, a player with seven years of major league service could ask to be traded between the end of the World Series and November 1. The player could designate up to four clubs to which he did not want to be traded. If not traded by March 21 of the following year, he would become a free agent.

Said John Gaherin, the owners' negotiator: "This is our final, our last proposal. A lot of clubs are not in favor of what we're doing. Some clubs fear that it could result in bankruptcies. But these proposals were offered to get spring training started and baseball back on the track though we know the problems that are being created along with it."

The Association's Executive Board met in Tampa, Fla. on March 17. Miller insisted there was no formal vote taken but it was later revealed that the player representatives, in turn, expressed their sentiments. The result of this informal poll revealed that 17 clubs were in favor of rejecting the owners' so-called "final offer." Five clubs favored acceptance. Two clubs were not represented.

Split In Players' Ranks

It must be understood that in all of the players' previous actions through the years, Miller had emphasized the necessity for unanimity. The Association, he repeatedly advised, was not likely to succeed in its goal if splintered. This 17-5 "vote" revealed a serious split. Taking the lead from the players, Miller immediately adopted a conciliatory approach.

In the press conference following this meeting Miller conceded the tone of the meeting was "somewhat conciliatory" and said the players "are now prepared to agree" to a structured free agency "along the general lines suggested by the owners."

What wasn't palatable to the players, Miller said, was the portion of the proposal limiting the negotiation rights of the free agents to eight clubs. There was no such restriction on Messersmith. Miller did concede this aspect of the owners' package, which also included pension and minimum salary increases, could be settled in future bargaining sessions.

Kuhn Opens Training Camps

Less than a half-hour later, Commissioner Kuhn, from his New York City office, made the following announcement:

"Because I think it is now vital that spring training get underway without further delay, I have directed that all camps be opened by the earliest possible time."

The lockout had ended; by March 19 all of the 24 big league spring camps were in full swing.

Joseph Durso, baseball writer for The New York Times, told of the reaction in St. Petersburg:

"When the great shutdown of the baseball business ended after 17 days, a bartender named Hoot Gibson stopped the music and announced the news to the crowd. The noise of the St. Patrick's Day revelers subsided, they listened, then the lounge erupted in the loudest cheers and whistles of the night.

"When the St. Petersburg Times appeared the next morning—at a time when the British pound was slipping, the Prime Minister was resigning and the American political primaries were raging—the lead headline trumpeted the news across all eight columns of page one: 'Play Ball, Kuhn Orders.' "

Spring training was completed without further incident. Negotiations continued and, at times, were spiced with angry declarations from both sides. Tentative agreement was reached on July 12, the day before the All-Star Game in Philadelphia, on new four-year packages covering the Basic Agreement and the Players' Benefit Plan. The players, by an overwhelming majority, approved both contracts and announcement of this approval was made jointly on August 9, concluding 13 months of sustained effort.

Players' Gains

A partial list of the Association's gains follow:

Players playing with unsigned (i.e., renewed) contracts in 1976 to become free agents after the 1976 season; players with unsigned contracts in 1977 to become free agents after the 1977 season; players with multi-year contracts to become free agents at the end of the next regular season, if they don't sign a new contract prior to that time.

A free agent shall be eligible to negotiate with a maximum of 12 clubs (13 beginning in 1977) that have acquired, through a re-entry selection procedure, the rights to negotiate with him. In addition, the player's previous club, if it so desires, can also negotiate with him.

Any player with at least six years of major league service may, following the conclusion of the championship season, become a free agent by notifying his club in writing.

Any player with at least five years of major league service may, following the conclusion of a championship season, demand a trade by notifying his club in writing during the period between October 15 (or the end of the World Series, whichever is later) and 15 days thereafter. The club must consummate a trade by the following March 15, or the player becomes a free agent, unless the player has retracted his notice.

Minimum salaries increased to $19,000 for 1976 and 1977, and to $21,000 in 1978 and 1979.

Salary arbitration, providing the request is made by both the player and the club.

If a player's contract is terminated in spring training, he shall receive 30 days' termination pay; if terminated during the season, he shall receive the remainder of that year's salary.

Effective in 1977, clubs shall not schedule or re-schedule, if practicable, more than 19 consecutive days without an off-day. No club shall be scheduled for more than two days off in any seven-day period.

If a player is optioned for at least 20 days in one major league season, the option counts against the number permitted. (The previous provision was 30 days).

The clubs, in each of the years from 1976 through 1979, are to make annual contributions to the players' pension fund of $8,300,000—an annual increase of $1,850,000.

It was another feather in the cap of Marvin Miller who, during the course of negotiations, observed his 10th year as the head of the Players Association. Some few owners did express relief that peace had come, for at least four years. But a surprising large cluster of owners, certainly more than in previous years, voiced displeasure with the performance of John Gaherin, their labor counsel, and with the Player Relations Committee which had been expanded from six to eight members in another futile attempt to overwhelm Miller and Moss.

Bob Howsam, president of the Cincinnati Reds and supposedly a hardliner, was added to the committee on the assumption he would be a tough bargainer. Apparently he wasn't. Ted Bonda, the chief executive officer of the Cleveland Indians, was also named to the committee which included Ed Fitzgerald, Milwaukee, chairman; Dan Galbreath, Pittsburgh; Clark Griffith, Minnesota; John McHale, Montreal, and league presidents Feeney and MacPhail.

Gussie Busch Speaks Out

Gussie Busch, the 77-year-old autocrat who owns the St. Louis Cardinals, was outspoken in his criticism of Gaherin and the Player Relations Committee. So were Charlie Finley of Oakland, Calvin Griffith, Minnesota, and Jerold Hoffberger, Baltimore. McHale of Montreal, a committee member, threatened to resign in disappointment with the committee's performance.

"We have been kicked in the teeth," said Busch, who insisted half of the N. L. owners never did approve the final settlement with the Association. Finley was equally upset and declared: "We've been hornswoggled. And it's our own fault. And we're going to pay for it."

The Atlanta Braves were the first to pay. Messersmith, appropriately, was the first to benefit from the new order. The bidding on the 30-year old righthander, a two-time 20-game winner, didn't begin until mid-March, after the owners had lost their second appeal on the Seitz decision.

Unlike the re-entry draft at the end of the 1976 season, which was accompanied by frantic million dollar offers for big-name free agents, there was comparatively little movement to acquire Messersmith. This was especially so in the first two weeks and was interpreted as an indication that the clubs were reluctant to acknowledge his free agency.

Owners Accused Of Collusion

Herb Osmond of Newport Beach, Calif., Messersmith's agent, accused the owners of collusion. Marvin Miller also hinted of an owner conspiracy, a charge that gained credence with the revelation that Walter O'Malley of the Los Angeles Dodgers told his fellow owners he wouldn't sign any free agents; i.e., the O'Malley message was "I won't touch your free agents, if you don't touch mine."

Ten months later, when testifying at the Bowie Kuhn vs. Charlie Finley trial, O'Malley admitted he came to a meeting of owners in New York City armed with a "White Paper" on the Dodgers' position on free agents. They wouldn't sign any and instead would replace their departing stars with players from their farm system. O'Malley delivered this statement on March 20, scarcely a week after Messersmith's free agency had been certified by the Eighth District Court of Appeals.

Publicly, the Dodgers assumed an opposite posture. When Messersmith expressed hope that the Dodgers would sign him, Walter O'Malley responded by saying "We've told Andy if at any time he wants to come back and talk to us, fine. We're not abandoning him."

Dodgers' Offer to Messersmith

The Dodgers' final offer to Messersmith, which he had refused, was a three-year, no-trade package for $540,000. The breakdown was for $150,000 for 1975, which would have been retroactive and was $35,000 more than his salary for that season; $170,000 for 1976, and $220,000 for 1977. Apparently this offer was renewed but not increased after Messersmith was on the open market.

The Chicago White Sox and California Angels were among the first to enter bids. The White Sox reportedly offered $750,000 for four years, the Angels $600,000 for three years. The Atlanta Braves, San Diego Padres, St. Louis Cardinals, Pittsburgh Pirates and New York Mets also made offers; those entered by the Pirates, Cardinals and Mets were remarkably low, leading to the belief that these clubs were primarily protecting themselves against possible charges of collusion.

Yankees Announce Agreement

The New York Yankees, on March 31, announced that they had entered into a four-year $1,000,000 agreement with Herb Osmond, Messersmith's agent. Part of Messersmith's salary, reportedly, was to be in the form of deferred payments over a 20-year period with the understanding the deferred money was to draw six percent interest.

Gabe Paul, Yankee president, insisted he had bargained in good faith and that there was a deal. But Osmond claimed there was no binding agreement, that the Yankees had reversed their position on the interest accrual of the deferred payments. The matter was brought to Commissioner Kuhn who, after a hearing, decided the agreement was not binding.

Another hassle followed, this one with the California Angels who announced they would sign Messersmith, if he passed a physical examination. This was in response to reports that Messersmith's arm might not be sound, a report which was dismissed by Dodger general manager Al Campanis "as a lot of baloney." Said Campanis: "There's nothing wrong with his arm."

Messersmith's Physical Condition

Dr. Frank Jobe, an orthopedist, who treats both Dodger and Angel players, did the examining and reported Messersmith had some arthritic change in the elbow but that it was not uncommon and something most pitchers eventually experienced. Dr. Jobe had also looked at Messersmith the previous season, said the elbow looked the same as it did the year before and added: "He never missed a turn (with the Dodgers) last year and he didn't even ask for an aspirin."

Messersmith Signs With Atlanta

Two days later, on April 10, Messersmith signed a "lifetime" contract with the Atlanta Braves. Actually, it was a three-year package for $1,000,000, and included a $400,000 bonus for signing and a no-trade clause. Said Atlanta owner Ted Turner, "Andy Messersmith will be with the Braves as long as I am. His contract is forever—until death or old age do us part."

But elsewhere the bonds were loosening. On March 10, the traditional date when the clubs automatically renew contracts of holdouts, a survey revealed that 193 players had refused to sign 1976 contracts and, in effect, had begun playing out their options. This number, most likely, would have been lower if the players, as in the past, had access to salary arbitration but because of the severity of the dispute, salary arbitration was suspended in 1976.

The owners did have one weapon and many of them used it: the prerogative to slash any player's salary by 20 percent. Veteran pitcher Ken Holtzman, who was active in and privy to Association affairs, made a study of the list of the 193 unsigned players. Said Holtzman in a March 20 interview with Dave Anderson of The New York Times:

"About 85 of these players were cut the maximum 20 percent. There were 24 Atlanta players who hadn't signed and all of them were cut 20 percent. Twenty-one Minnesota players took the 20 percent cut. Oakland was next with nine (Holtzman was included in this group.) The Orioles renewed Jim Palmer and cut him 20 percent but the Mets didn't cut Tom Seaver. The Phillies cut Dick Allen 20 percent, from $250,000 to $200,000, but all the Boston Red Sox players who hadn't signed got a raise."

Unsigned Players

As the season progressed, the number of unsigned players continued to dwindle. By May 15, a month before the trading deadline, the list had thinned to 62, according to a Sporting News survey taken by assistant managing editor Ralph Ray. At this point, Minnesota and Baltimore led, each with ten unsigned players. Oakland was third with seven. Of these 62 holdouts, 42 were American Leaguers.

The biggest fear, by the owners, was that their unsigned players would go the route, as Messersmith and McNally had done the year before. The clubs would not be entitled to compensation for such losses. Desperate for some return, several owners began trading their unsigned players for other unsigned players, with the hope that the dissidents would be more likely to capitulate, if in a new setting.

Oakland and Baltimore Swap Unsigned Players

On April 2, Oakland and Baltimore entered into such a swap. Oakland owner Charlie Finley traded two of his stars, pitcher Holtzman and outfielder Reggie Jackson, both unsigned, to the Orioles for outfielder Don Baylor and pitchers Mike Torrez and Paul Mitchell. Of the three Baltimore players, only Baylor was unsigned.

As could be expected, this deal created considerable comment. Ferguson Jenkins, Boston Red Sox pitcher, was quoted as saying: "Finley must be crazy. He has destroyed his Oakland club." Many of the Oakland players were also dismayed at the loss of teammates Jackson and Holtzman. But most managers considered it an even deal. Said Darrell Johnson of the Red Sox: "It looks like a standoff to me. I don't think it will have much effect on either club.''

Baltimore general manager Hank Peters expressed confidence he could sign Holtzman and Jackson. Peters was wrong. He signed neither. Delighted to be free from Finley, Holtzman immediately joined the Orioles. Jackson went into semi-seclusion and sat out for a month.

Orioles Irked by Jackson's Absence

"When is the Messiah coming?" asked pitcher Jim Palmer who along with many of the other Baltimore players was angry because of Jackson's pro-longed absence. The Orioles lacked power and Jackson's delay further weak-ened the club. Finally, Jackson did surface and there were more hard feelings when his teammates heard of the financial deal the Orioles gave him.

First, G. M. Peters restored Jackson's 20 percent pay cut, which had been invoked by Finley and had reduced his 1976 salary by $28,000—from $140,000 to $112,000. In addition, Jackson was given a $60,000 raise, hiking his total salary to $200,000. Peters later indicated he agreed to this sweetheart deal with the mistaken belief that Jackson, at a time later in the season, would sign with the Orioles.

The Orioles still had 10 other unsigned players when Jackson reported. There were complaints of a "double standard" by the other unsigned players, especially Holtzman whose 20 percent cut was not restored. The other Balti-more players also playing with a cut were angry because Peters had told them he was merely following "club policy."

Twins Trade Bert Blyleven

Owner Calvin Griffith of Minnesota, who like Finley operates as his own general manager, also had problems signing his players. Griffith followed Fin-ley's lead and on June 1 unloaded Bert Blyleven, the Twins' pitching ace, in a six-player deal with the Texas Rangers. For two unsigned players, Blyleven and infielder Danny Thompson, who was to die of leukemia, the Twins re-ceived pitchers Bill Singer and Jim Gideon and infielders Roy Smalley and Mike Cubbage—plus an undisclosed sum of cash estimated at $250,000.

It was a remarkably shrewd deal by Griffith who has a well-deserved rep-utation for running an economical operation. There was no question that Bly-leven, one of the American League's best pitchers, was underpaid. Blyleven had asked for a $60,000 pay increase. This would have lifted his 1976 salary to $125,000. Griffith countered with an offer of $85,000. Blyleven refused and said he would play out his option.

Had the Twins kept Blyleven and Thompson for the full season they wouldn't have received compensation in exchange. By trading them, the Twins got four players, all of whom had signed: three frontliners and an out-standing minor league pitching prospect in Gideon, plus an enormous amount of cash. Griffith's fellow-owners applauded him for his sagacity, including Finley who was to make the next move. And it was a blockbuster!

Finley's Blockbuster

At almost the last hour before the midnight tolling of the June 15 trading deadline, Finley announced he had sold three of his star Oakland players for a total of $3,500,000. It was the biggest money deal in baseball history. Pitcher

Vida Blue was peddled to the New York Yankees for $1,500,000, and outfielder Joe Rudi and relief pitcher Rollie Fingers went to the Boston Red Sox for $1,000,000 each.

Finley made the announcement in Chicago. By coincidence, Commissioner Kuhn and American League president Lee MacPhail were also in Chicago. Hearing of the sales, Kuhn telephoned Finley. Kuhn expressed surprise and also his displeasure. He questioned the wisdom of such a multi-million dollar player auction and indicated he already was giving thought to voiding the deals.

"Commissioner, it's none of your damn business," Finley said. When Kuhn continued to voice his opinion that the sales were somewhat irregular, Finley suggested they meet in the coffee shop at the Pick-Congress Hotel which is in the next block from Finley's Michigan Boulevard insurance office. Also present were Finley's son, Paul, and Alexander (Sandy) Hadden, baseball's secretary-treasurer. Hadden was traveling with Kuhn.

The sale of Rudi, Fingers and Blue made headlines everywhere. "I had no alternative," Finley told newsmen. "I'm disappointed with the necessity of having to make these sales. But I just refused to let these players drive me into bankruptcy with their astronomical salary demands."

Finley Blasts Kapstein

Finley also blasted Jerry Kapstein, an agent who represented Fingers and Rudi and also Gene Tenace, Campy Campaneris and Don Baylor, other A's who had refused to sign. "Kapstein kept me in the dark continuously," charged Finley. "He never made one trip to come in and talk to me."

That Rudi and Fingers had not signed was apparently of no great concern to Dick O'Connell, the executive vice-president and trade-maker for the Red Sox. Just as Hank Peters of Baltimore was confident he could sign Holtzman and Jackson, so was O'Connell of his ability to negotiate with Rudi and Fingers and satisfy their demands.

The Yankees, however, told Finley they would not take this chance with Blue; their purchase of Blue would be made only if he was signed. Hastily, Finley advised Blue of the impending sale. Terms were agreed upon. Blue was to receive a three-year package of $485,000. His 1976 salary would be raised from $80,000 to $140,000. Blue would also be paid $140,000 in 1977 and $205,000 in 1978.

After his midnight meeting with Finley in Chicago, Kuhn returned to his New York City office and began consulting with baseball's powerful six-man Executive Council, asking for their views. These informal talks, it was later revealed, in the federal court of Judge Frank McGarr, resulted in a 3-3 deadlock.

Kuhn Given Advice

League presidents MacPhail and Feeney advised Kuhn to allow the deals to stand. So did John Fetzer of Detroit whose Tigers, less than 40 hours earlier, had made an unsuccessful $1,000,000 bid for Blue's contract. Walter O'Malley of Los Angeles, John McHale of Montreal and Ed Fitzgerald of Milwaukee urged Kuhn to void the transfers.

Kuhn called for a hearing on June 17. Officials from the Yankees and Red Sox, along with Finley and Marvin Miller were asked to attend. In the meantime, the three players involved, Kuhn said, were to remain on the active list of the Oakland club but would not be allowed to participate in any games until he made a final determination.

A spokesman for the commissioner refused to disclose the specific questions which Kuhn wanted answered but said: "There is no indication of any wrongdoing, and the commissioner is not suggesting any wrongdoing. But there are some questions to be answered. That's the purpose of the hearing."

Kuhn Cancels Deals

The next day, much to the surprise of almost everyone, Kuhn announced he was canceling the deals. Speaking at a jammed press conference, Kuhn said: "I am disallowing the assignments in the best interests of baseball." Then he added: "The commissioner is left with the lonely job of deciding integrity and confidence. I have to weigh public opinion."

Kuhn's Decision

The full text of Kuhn's decision follows:

"Pursuant to the major league agreement and rules, I conducted a hearing yesterday into the question of whether the recent assignments of the contracts of Oakland players Joe Rudi, Rollie Fingers and Vida Blue to the New York and Boston clubs should be approved by this office or whether such transactions should be disapproved as inconsistent with the best interests of baseball, the integrity of the game and the maintenance of public confidence in it.

"While the clubs and the Players Association argued that the assignments were in accordance with the terms of applicable rules, none of the participants made a persuasive argument as to the overriding considerations of whether these transactions are consistent with the public's confidence in baseball. I can not accept the narrow view that these considerations should be ignored.

"Shorn of much of its finest talent in exchange for cash, the Oakland club, which has been a divisional champion for the last five years, has little chance to compete effectively in its division. Whether other players will be available to restore the club by using the cash involved is altogether speculative although Mr. Finley vigorously argues his ability to do so.

"Public confidence in the integrity of club operations and in baseball would be greatly undermined should such assignments not be restrained. While I am of course aware that there have been sales of player contracts in the past, there has been no instance in my judgment which had the potential for harm to our game as do these assignments, particularly in the present unsettled circumstances of baseball's reserve system and in the highly competitive circumstances we find in today's sports and entertainment world.

"Nor can I persuade myself that the spectacle of the Yankees and Red Sox buying contracts of star players in the prime of their careers for cash sums totalling $3,500,000 is anything but devastating to baseball's reputation for integrity and to public confidence in the game, even though I can well understand that their motive is a good faith effort to strengthen their clubs. If such transactions now and in the future were permitted, the door would be opened wide to the buying success of the more affluent clubs, public suspicion would be aroused, traditional and sound methods of player development and acquisition would be undermined and our efforts to preserve the competitive balance would be greatly impaired.

"I can not help but conclude that I would be remiss in exercising my powers as commissioner pursuant to the major league agreement and Major League Rule 12 if I did not act now to disapprove these assignments. If, as contended by the participants, the commissioner lacks the power to prevent a development so harmful to baseball as this, then our system of self regulation for the good of the game and the public is a virtual mirage. I think the commissioner's power is clear and binding and its exercise vital to the best interests of the game and accordingly the assignments here involved are disapproved."

Reaction

The reaction was enormous. Though no precise surveys were taken, the initial response was critical of Kuhn, by an approximate three to one majority. Finley, of course, shouted the loudest and immediately announced he would bring suit. "Bowie Kuhn is acting like the village idiot," said Finley. "Even if he thinks he's God, we're going to show him he can't upset the courts of the land."

Marvin Miller of the Players Association sided with Finley. Said Miller: "The big criminal act was that the Red Sox and Yankees, by making these deals, had set a fair market value on the players purchased. The owners themselves had set a standard which they never wanted. It established that Blue is a player of such caliber to be worth $1,500,000—before he even sits down to talk salary—and that similarly Rudi and Fingers are worth $1,000,000 each."

As others were to do later, Miller also said he didn't understand Kuhn's statement that the sales had upset competitive balance. "I'm puzzled," Miller declared. "I don't know what the commissioner means when he says he is concerned about competitive balance. The Yankees haven't won a pennant in 12 years and the Red Sox have never won a World Series.

"What is the great balance that they are worrying about disturbing? The Oakland club has won its divisional championship for the last five years. Baltimore has won its division in five of the last seven years. Pittsburgh has won five titles in the last six years, and Cincinnati four in the last six. It's a myth to contend there is such a thing as competitive balance."

Miller also charged that Kuhn once again "had done his master's bidding." Milton Richman, sports editor of the United Press International, took a similar view and wrote: "If this great landmark decision of his finishes Bowie Kuhn, as it so easily could, then the whole thing can be laid at the door of Walter O'Malley. He was the one who called the shot."

The Sporting News Editorial

Said THE SPORTING NEWS, in an editorial titled 'Commissioner's Strange Behavior:' "There is no question that Kuhn has authority to act in what he deems to be 'the best interests of baseball.' But he doesn't have unlimited authority. He is no absolute czar . . . and has grossly overstepped his authority and has plunged baseball into a morass of litigation that will only harm the game and which, in the end, could result in Kuhn himself losing his job."

More Press Comment

Veteran scribe Bob Broeg, in his column in THE SPORTING NEWS simply said: "Egad, for once I find myself siding with Charlie Finley. What a revoltin' development."

Leonard Koppett, also writing in THE SPORTING NEWS, commented: "If a commissioner—any commissioner—can make such a finding and have such an effect in this case, why can't a commissioner in some other year decide it would be 'good for baseball' to have a winner in a big market like New York rather than in Baltimore, or that a nice close pennant race would be 'good for baseball,' rather than a runaway winner like the 1936 Yankees or the 1975 Cincinnati Reds?"

It was easily the most spectacular dismantlement of a championship club since Connie Mack broke up his 1929-31 Philadelphia A's and Rick Talley of the Chicago Tribune refused to blame Finley. Said Talley: "In truth it wasn't Finley who broke up the Oakland A's. It was the players. They fought him at the negotiation table and let it be known they wanted out and would have become free agents available to the highest bidder."

Busch and Wrigley Side With Finley

Cardinal owner Gussie Busch applauded Finley. "If I was in Finley's position," said Busch, "I would have done the same thing." Philip K. Wrigley, longtime owner of the Chicago Cubs, also sided with Finley. "I don't see why the sales weren't approved," Wrigley declared. "They were according to the rules and regulations. I couldn't understand why the commissioner got mixed up in this in the first place."

Asked Dick O'Connell of the Red Sox: "Who do we check with now if we want to buy a player? Who determines if his batting average is low enough, or if the price is low enough?"

Kuhn's Defenders

But Kuhn also had his defenders.

Said Walter O'Malley of Los Angeles: "It was a tough decision to make and I must say I would go along with him. This highlights the absolute necessity for a reserve clause. The rich teams would have all the players and the poor teams none."

Minnesota owner Calvin Griffith, who also came to Kuhn's defense, called it "a dark day for baseball," and then added: "It is a terrible thing when two clubs, the Yankees and the Red Sox, start bidding to see who can buy a championship club. This shows that what the owners have been saying about the wealthy clubs getting the top players has been true."

Ernie Banks, the one-time Chicago Cub slugger, commended Kuhn for his courage. Said Banks: "The fans have a right to see top players on a lot of teams, not overloading one team and giving the fans nothing much on those other teams."

Joe Falls of Detroit was one of the few sportswriters to champion Kuhn's decision. Wrote Falls in THE SPORTING NEWS: "In this whole affair, as I see it, Bowie Kuhn stands the tallest because somebody had to defend the morals of baseball and he did it. If you are a realist you can mount your arguments against Kuhn and win them all. But if you've ever edged forward on your seat as Vida Blue prepared to make his 3-and-2 pitch to Carl Yastrzemski, with two outs and the runners going, you can understand why Kuhn acted as he did. If that is too difficult to comprehend, then you might do better reading the Wall Street Journal rather than the sports pages."

Finley Files Suit

As he said he would, Finley initiated litigation against Kuhn. Neil Papiano of Los Angeles, who was to serve as Finley's attorney, filed a $10 million damage suit in Chicago on June 25 charging that Kuhn had conspired to deprive Finley of his rightful money from the sale of his three players, and also charging violation of several of Finley's civil rights. Named as co-defendants were the American and National leagues, the major league's Executive Council and the Boston Red Sox and New York Yankees.

Though it was to be many months before the entire affair was resolved, the dispute did have one immediate and somewhat unexpected effect. It revealed to the players, as never before, their worth on the open market. Aware now, in some instances, that their contracts were worth $1,000,000—or more—unsigned players everywhere increased their salary demands and simultaneously stiffened in their resolve to become free agents.

The number of potential free agents, however, had been steadily decreasing. The traditional date when clubs must renew contracts of unsigned players was on March 11, almost a full month before the opening of the championship season. On this date there were 193 unsigned players; i.e., players whose contracts were renewed by their clubs.

As of May 1, six weeks before the June 15 trading deadline, the list of dissatisfied players had dropped to 62—42 in the American League and 20 in the National. At this point the Baltimore Orioles and Minnesota Twins led with 10 unsigned players. Oakland was third with seven.

Unsigned Players

By August 1, it was estimated that 39 players still hadn't signed. Baltimore was now in the undisputed lead with seven and Minnesota and Oakland tied for second with six each. Though not among the leaders, the Boston Red Sox had been unable to satisfy the money demands of catcher Carlton Fisk, outfielder Fred Lynn and shortstop Rick Burleson, all high-quality performers and all represented by Jerry Kapstein of Providence, R. I., an agent who had approximately 60 players in his stable.

Their inability to sign Fisk, Lynn and Burleson also hurt the Red Sox on the field. There was no question that the club's overall performance suffered. But by agreeing to paying a total of $2,000,000 for Rudi and Fingers—in the aborted deals with Finley—the Red Sox had to up the ante for their three unsigned stars. Eventually, they straggled into the fold. Fisk and Burleson signed on August 3. Lynn agreed to terms on August 8, the same date when a new four-year agreement with the Players Association went into effect.

The New Agreement

The new collective contract included a severely modified reserve clause system and also provided for a complex re-entry arrangement for the players who went the full season without a contract, and hence had become free agents. A total of 22 players went the distance. Two others, veteran sluggers Willie McCovey and Nate Colbert, both of whom had been given their releases, were also eligible for the re-entry draft.

Finley was the biggest single loser. Six Oakland players, not including McCovey, were on the re-entry list of free agents. The Baltimore Orioles lost four players, the California Angels three and the Minnesota Twins two. No other club lost more than one.

A complete list of the 22 players who played out their contracts follows:

OAKLAND (6)—Sal Bando, Don Baylor, Campy Campaneris, Rollie Fingers, Joe Rudi and Gene Tenace.

BALTIMORE (4)—Wayne Garland, Bobby Grich, Reggie Jackson and Royle Stillman.

CALIFORNIA (3)—Paul Dade, Tim Nordbrook and Billy Smith.

MINNESOTA (2)—Bill Campbell and Eric Soderholm.

YANKEES (1)—Doyle Alexander.

PHILADELPHIA (1)—Dave Cash.

SAN DIEGO (1)—Tito Fuentes.

CINCINNATI (1)—Don Gullett.

PITTSBURGH (1)—Richie Hebner.

SAN FRANCISCO (1)—Gary Matthews.

CHICAGO CUBS (1)—Steve Stone.

The re-entry draft was held on November 4 at the Plaza Hotel in New York City and was limited to the 24 existing clubs; i.e., the new Seattle and Toronto expansion franchises were not allowed to participate. The drafting clubs, in inverse order of the 1976 standings, were permitted to select negotiation rights to as many players as were eligible, except that when a player had been selected by 12 clubs other than his own his name was removed from the list.

There were a total of 17 selection rounds and 13 players were selected by the maximum 12 clubs. These 13 players were: Tenace, Baylor, Rudi, Matthews, Gullett, Campbell, Garland, Fingers, Grich, Bando, Cash, Alexander and Jackson. Tenace was the first to be chosen by 12 clubs, and Jackson the last. The clubs could negotiate only with the players they selected and basically were limited to signing only two free agents.

The first deadline for signing free agents was February 15 but by this time virtually all of the signings were completed.

It is virtually impossible to present a completely accurate listing of the terms obtained by each of the free agents but the following table of the 13 most sought after free agents and their total money package has been compiled from newspaper reports:

Players	Length of Contract	Total Package	New Team
Reggie Jackson	5 Yrs.	$3,000,000	New York Yankees
Joe Rudi	5 Yrs.	2,090,000	California Angels
Don Gullett	6 Yrs.	2,000,000	New York Yankees
Gene Tenace	5 Yrs.	1,815,000	San Diego Padres
Bobby Grich	5 Yrs.	1,750,000	California Angels
Rollie Fingers	6 Yrs.	1,600,000	San Diego Padres
Dave Cash	5 Yrs.	1,500,000	Montreal Expos
Sal Bando	5 Yrs.	1,400,000	Milwaukee Brewers
Gary Matthews	5 Yrs.	1,200,000	Atlanta Braves
Don Baylor	6 Yrs.	1,020,000	California Angels
Bill Campbell	5 Yrs.	1,000,000	Boston Red Sox
Wayne Garland	10 Yrs.	1,000,000	Cleveland Indians
Campy Campaneris	5 Yrs.	950,000	Texas Rangers

New Millionaires

Each of these signings was trumpeted with big headlines as the nation's fans, as well as other players, gaped in awe at the growing list of new millionaires. Agent Kapstein, from his Rhode Island office, orchestrated the signings, and for maximum publicity, released them one at a time. Of Kapstein's 60 some clients, 11 played out their options; nine of the 11 hit the million-dollar jackpot.

Marvin Miller, who had feared owner collusion and the possibility they would try to prevent a free market, expressed delight and, in the main, had kind words for management and complimented the moguls on their spirit to observe the letter of the law. But it wasn't necessarily fellowship that triggered the boom. It was the desire, essentially, of several of the more wealthy owners to buy themselves a pennant with the belief that a flag or a World Series triumph is accompanied by instant immortality. Ray Kroc of San Diego, Gene Autry of the California Angels and George Steinbrenner of the New York Yankees dominated the market and, together, made millionaires out of seven players.

High batting averages or impressive statistics were not a necessity. Sal Bando, previously of Oakland and who was 60th in the American League in batting with a .240 average, got $1,400,000 from the Milwaukee Brewers in a package that included a 20-year schedule of deferred payments. Two other Oakland players, Gene Tenace and Don Baylor, didn't hit .250 either but also participated in the bonanza. Reggie Jackson, who batted .277 for the season, got the biggest haul, $3,000,000 from the Yankees and apparently had an even larger offer, which he refused, from the Montreal Expos.

Braves Sign Gary Matthews

That the free agents were pursued with vigor was best illustrated by the Atlanta Braves who lassooed Gary Matthews, a young outfielder who had played out his contract with the San Francisco Giants. Atlanta owner Ted Turner threw a ball-park party in Matthews' honor immediately after the end of the National League season and also heralded his arrival by buying billboard space near the Atlanta airport proclaiming "Welcome Gary Matthews."

Atlanta scribe Wayne Minshew, who was among the more than 300 local celebrities to attend the party, reported that "Matthews seemed bewildered by all the attention but was so pleased that the next day he was in the Atlanta suburbs house-hunting." The Braves subsequently acquired negotiation rights to Matthews and signed him to a long-term contract though he had at least one higher salary offer from another club.

So intense was the competition for free agents that several clubs were accused of tampering. According to the ground rules there was to be no contact with potential free agents until after the regular league season. But John Alevizos, who was later relieved of his duties as the Atlanta general manager, twice met with Matthews during the late stages of the National League campaign.

Giants Charge Braves With Tampering

The Giants, who didn't want to lose Matthews, charged the Braves with tampering. Commissioner Kuhn held a hearing in late September and fined the Atlanta club $10,000. For a time it also appeared likely Kuhn would further punish the Braves by preventing them from acquiring negotiation rights to

Matthews. Kuhn took no such action. But he later re-opened and closed the Matthews affair by suspending owner Turner for one year.

The Turner suspension came as a surprise and was announced on January 2, 1977, while Kuhn was in the midst of his three-week court battle with Finley. Some scribes and baseball executives, as well, interpreted this action as an attempt, by Kuhn, to demonstrate to the federal judge hearing the case of the constant vigilance and discipline required against errant owners.

Some Owners Are Unhappy

Though the re-entry draft went off without significant complaints by the Players Association, it was quite clear that not all of the clubs were pleased with the results. Said Ewing Kauffman, the Kansas City owner: "Few of us are happy with what's happened. These million-dollar salaries could easily price us out of the market. Reasonable entitlement to a good wage is one thing: greed is another."

Donald Grant, the front office chief of the New York Mets, expressed similar fear. Grant said the Mets had made substantial offers to Reggie Jackson and Bobby Grich "but to increase the offers would have been senseless. I can't tell the other clubs what to do but it appears they are overextending themselves."

Observed Calvin Griffith, the chief executive officer of the Minnesota Twins: "Sports today are sick. If I'm going to stay in business, I'm going to need a rich partner."

Though there was no way of knowing with total accuracy, it can be said that probably as many as half of the clubs did not make any big money offers for the free agents. One club, the Cincinnati Reds, revealed it would not bid for any free agents, an announcement that was made prior to the draft for negotiation rights.

Bob Howsam, president of the Reds, issued the following statement: "In fairness to the players who have won the world championship for us two years in a row and considering the way our organization is structured, we do not think it would be right for the Cincinnati club to get into bidding contests that must come out of this draft."

Historians may wish to note that Finley did participate in the re-entry draft and acquired negotiation rights to almost all of the eligible free agents but made only token bids for their services. Said Finley, as he watched his former Oakland players being signed by other clubs, "What the owners are doing is stupid. They're going to bankrupt themselves."

Finley's Suit Proceeds

Finley's multi-million dollar damage suit against Kuhn, after several delays, opened on December 16 in the Chicago courtroom of federal judge Frank McGarr who heard the case without a jury. The litigation consumed 15 trial days and included a parade of 20 witnesses, seven of whom testified in behalf of Finley, 13 for Kuhn.

The basic question was whether or not Kuhn had the authority to void Finley's June sale of players Rudi, Fingers and Blue, particularly since they were made without any violation of the existing rules. It was the second time in baseball history than an owner sued the commissioner. The late Phil Ball of St. Louis also sued Judge Kenesaw Mountain Landis, baseball's first commissioner, in 1931 when Landis freed Fred Bennett, an obscure outfielder whom the Browns had been "covering up" in the minors. Ball lost the case at the district court level and did not appeal.

The Toronto Situation

In addition to his massive problems with Finley, Commissioner Kuhn was also faced with the implied threat of legal action by the entire American League. This occurred in early April when Kuhn ordered the A. L. to halt its plans to annex the Toronto territory as its 14th franchise. The A. L. had passed a resolution on March 21 to put a club in Toronto and five days later approved the purchase of the franchise, for $7,000,000, by Labatt's brewing Co.

Don McDougall, president of Labatt's, previously had made an unsuccessful $12,000,000 bid for the San Francisco Giants and expressed delight that Toronto finally had a major league club. The A. L. owners were also pleased. Said John Fetzer, owner of the Detroit Tigers: "The Labatt company has a solid and strong economic base. You can't run a baseball club on a shoestring."

The National League had also shown considerable interest in acquiring the Toronto territory, primarily because it would provide a natural rival for its Montreal club. Many of the N. L. owners, and particularly Charlie Bronfman of the Expos, expressed severe disappointment when the planned sale and simultaneous transfer of the San Francisco franchise to Toronto failed to go through, as anticipated.

Commissioner Kuhn was also upset because of his previous pledges to the Congress that the city of Washington, D. C. would be awarded a franchise in the next wave of expansion.

Kuhn then stepped into the fray and urged the A. L. to find a solution to the Washington problem, and gave them a week to do so. Failing this, Kuhn said, he would then consider a request by the National League to move into both Washington and Toronto.

American League Bucks Kuhn

American League president Lee MacPhail refused to yield and said his league "intends to go forward with its plans for Toronto" and then added: "This is obviously an interleague fight. We agree to meet with the commissioner and the National League to consider any suggestion for Washington but they must not involve or adversely affect the Toronto and Seattle territories or other American League franchises."

American League owners then watched with considerable interest as the N. L. moguls, on Kuhn's suggestion, convened in Chicago on April 26. The N. L. was expected to claim Toronto at this meeting but in a surprise move voted against expansion.

N. L. Votes Not To Go To Toronto

Whereas a unanimous vote was required, five N. L. clubs voted against further expansion, an action which, in effect, rebuffed Kuhn but did settle the Toronto question without further dispute.

Los Angeles owner Walter O'Malley, who led the fight for Toronto, told his fellow owners: "Gentlemen, we are making a mistake."

Majors Enjoy Record Attendance

This constant turmoil was limited to the executive suite. There was no such frenzy on the playing field, much to the dismay of the owners. But despite the absence of close pennant races in all four divisions, there was a record total attendance of 31,318,331 at the major league level. The American League continued to inch closer to the perennially more successful National League with a record gate of 14,657,802. The N. L. total attendance was 16,660,529.

Players from the Cincinnati Reds and New York Yankees, the two pennant winning clubs, won the year's principal awards. Outfielder George Foster of Cincinnati and catcher Thurman Munson of the Yankees were selected for the Player of the Year Bulova Accuquartz watches given annually by THE SPORTING NEWS. In addition to his major league-leading 121 RBIs, Foster batted .306 for the season and hit 29 homers. Munson hit .302, with 17 homers and 105 runs batted in.

The Sporting News Awards

Other SPORTING NEWS awards went to Randy Jones of San Diego, National League Pitcher of the Year; Jim Palmer, Baltimore, American League Pitcher of the Year; Larry Herndon, San Francisco outfielder, National League Rookie Player of the Year; Clarence (Butch) Metzger, San Diego, N. L. Rookie Pitcher of the Year; catcher Butch Wynegar, Minnesota, A. L. Rookie Player of the Year, and Mark Fidrych, Detroit, A. L. Rookie Pitcher of the Year. Joe Burke, executive vice-president and general manager of the Kansas City Royals, won honors as the Major League Executive of the Year, and Danny Ozark of the Phillies was named Major League Manager of the Year.

The Sporting News All-Star Teams

Major league players, allowed to vote only for opponents, selected the following All-Star teams for THE SPORTING NEWS:

AMERICAN LEAGUE

Chris Chambliss, New York, 1b; Bobby Grich, Baltimore, 2b; George Brett, Kansas City, 3b; Mark Belanger, Baltimore, ss; Thurman Munson, New York, c; Joe Rudi, Oakland, lf; Mickey Rivers, New York, cf, and Reggie Jackson, Baltimore, rf; Hal McRae, Kansas City, dh; righthanded pitcher Jim Palmer, Baltimore, and lefthanded pitcher Frank Tanana, California.

NATIONAL LEAGUE

Willie Montanez, Atlanta, 1b; Joe Morgan, Cincinnati, 2b; Mike Schmidt, Philadelphia, 3b; Dave Concepcion, Cincinnati, ss; Bob Boone, Philadelphia, c; George Foster, Cincinnati, lf; Cesar Cedeno, Houston, cf; Ken Griffey, Cincinnati, rf; Don Sutton, Los Angeles, righthanded pitcher; Randy Jones, San Diego, lefthanded pitcher.

THE SPORTING NEWS All-Star fielding teams, chosen by team managers and a selected group of baseball writers and sports announcers, follow:

AMERICAN LEAGUE

George Scott, Milwaukee, 1b; Bobby Grich, Baltimore, 2b; Aurelio Rodriguez, Detroit, 3b; Mark Belanger, Baltimore, ss; Jim Sundberg, Texas, c; outfielders Joe Rudi, Oakland, Dwight Evans, Boston, and Rick Manning, Cleveland, and pitcher Jim Palmer, Baltimore.

NATIONAL LEAGUE

Steve Garvey, Los Angeles, 1b; Joe Morgan, Cincinnati, 2b; Mike Schmidt, Philadelphia, 3b; Dave Concepcion, Cincinnati, ss; Johnny Bench, Cincinnati, c; outfielders Cesar Cedeno, Houston, Cesar Geronimo, Cincinnati, and Garry Maddox, Philadelphia, and pitcher Jim Kaat, Philadelphia.

Most Valuable Player Awards

Cincinnati's Joe Morgan repeated as the National League's Most Valuable Player in the annual balloting conducted by the Baseball Writers' Association of America. Morgan finished with 311 points and was named on all 24 ballots, getting 19 first-place votes and five seconds, and was the first player since Ernie Banks of the Cubs to win back-to-back MVP trophies. George Foster was second to Morgan in the voting with 221 points and Mike Schmidt third with 179.

Name	1	2	3	4	5	6	7	8	9	10	Tot.
Joe Morgan	19	5	..	..	..	..	..	..	..	..	311
George Foster	5	9	6	1	1	1	1	..	..	..	221
Mike Schmidt	..	5	10	3	3	3	..	..	..	..	179
Pete Rose	..	5	2	4	1	2	6	..	..	2	131
Garry Maddox	..	..	4	4	3	3	..	..	2	1	98
Bill Madlock	..	..	..	3	..	3	..	1	5	2	51
Steve Garvey	..	..	..	2	2	2	2	1	1	2	51
Greg Luzinski	..	..	1	..	3	2	2	1	1	..	49
Ken Griffey	..	..	..	..	5	2	1	1	..	2	49
Randy Jones	..	..	..	3	..	4	..	2	..	1	48
Bob Watson	..	..	..	..	..	1	4	4	1	3	38
Al Oliver	..	..	..	1	1	1	..	1	4	1	30
Rawly Eastwick	..	..	1	..	1	..	2	1	..	1	26
Jerry Koosman	..	..	..	1	..	..	2	..	1	3	20
Steve Carlton	..	..	..	..	1	..	2	..	1	..	16
Dave Cash	..	..	..	..	1	..	1	1	1	..	15
J. R. Richard	..	..	..	1	..	..	..	1	1	..	12
Rick Monday	..	..	..	..	1	..	..	1	1	..	11
Dave Kingman	..	..	..	..	..	..	..	3	..	2	11
Dave Parker	..	..	..	..	1	..	..	..	2	..	10
Bill Robinson	..	..	..	1	..	..	..	..	1	..	9
Don Sutton	..	..	..	..	..	..	..	1	1	2	7
Ron Cey	..	..	..	..	..	..	1	..	1	..	6
Willie Montanez	..	..	..	..	..	..	..	1	..	1	4
Lou Brock	..	..	..	..	..	..	..	1	..	..	3
Cesar Cedeno	..	..	..	..	..	..	..	1	..	..	3
Cesar Geronimo	..	..	..	..	..	..	..	1	..	..	3
Richie Zisk	..	..	..	..	..	..	..	1	..	..	3
Larry Bowa	..	..	..	..	..	..	..	..	1	..	1

Thurman Munson of the Yankees won the American League's Most Valuable Player award, the first Yankee and the first catcher to win this honor since Elston Howard in 1963. Munson had 18 first-place votes, four seconds and two thirds for 304 points. Kansas City's George Brett, the league's batting champion, was also named on all 24 ballots and was second to Munson with 217 points. Mickey Rivers of the Yankees was third with 179½.

Name	1	2	3	4	5	6	7	8	9	10	Tot.
Thurman Munson..	18	4	2	..	..	..	..	..	..	..	304
George Brett	2	14	7	1	..	..	..	..	..	..	217
Mickey Rivers	1	6	6	5	3	2	..	..	..	½	179½
Hal McRae	..	..	1	6	1	3	3	4	2	..	99
Chris Chambliss	..	..	..	3	2	3	4	1	1	2½	71½
Rod Carew	1	..	1	..	3	..	4	3	2	2	71
Amos Oits	1	..	..	1	3	2	1	1	1	..	58
Bill Campbell	..	..	3	2	1	..	..	2	2	2	56
Lee May	..	..	1	..	2	3	2	1	1	3	51
Jim Palmer	..	..	..	2	3	2	..	1	1	..	47
Mark Fidrych	1	..	..	1	..	1	1	2	2	1	41
Joe Rudi	..	..	..	1	2	2	..	..	2	2	35
Sal Bando	..	..	1	1	2	..	..	1	..	1	31
Carl Yastrzemski...	..	..	1	..	..	..	2	2	1	2	26
Frank Tanana	..	..	..	..	..	1	3	..	..	2	19
Reggie Jackson	..	..	1	..	..	1	1	..	..	..	17
Graig Nettles	..	..	..	..	1	..	1	1	2	..	17
Gene Tenace	..	..	..	1	..	..	..	2	..	..	13
Rollie Fingers	..	..	..	..	1	..	1	..	..	2	12
Vida Blue	..	..	..	..	..	1	..	..	2	1	10
Ed Figueroa	..	..	..	..	..	1	..	..	2	..	9
Sparky Lyle	..	..	..	..	..	1	..	1	..	..	8
Ron LeFlore	..	..	..	..	..	..	1	..	1	..	6
Mark Littell	..	..	..	..	..	1	..	..	..	..	5
Rico Carty	..	..	..	..	..	..	..	1	1	..	5
Roy White	..	..	..	..	..	..	..	1	..	..	3
Luis Tiant	..	..	..	..	..	..	..	..	1	1	3
John Mayberry......	..	..	..	..	..	..	..	..	..	1	1
Butch Wynegar	..	..	..	..	..	..	..	..	..	1	1

The Cy Young awards, also given annually by the BBWAA, were won by San Diego's Randy Jones in the National League, and by Baltimore's Jim Palmer in the American. Jones, who was 16-3 at the All-Star break and finished with a 22-14 record, got 96 points; Palmer, who was 22-13, totaled 108 points. Runners-up were Jerry Koosman of the New York Mets in the N. L. with 69½ points, and Detroit's Mark Fidrych in the A. L. with 51.

Fidrych, who had a 19-9 record and was the major leagues' biggest single gate attraction, won the BBWAA's American League Rookie of the Year trophy, and got 22 out of a possible 24 votes. Catcher Butch Wynegar of Minnesota drew the other two votes. Pitchers Butch Metzger of San Diego and Pat Zachry of Cincinnati finished in a tie for the National League Rookie of the Year award, each receiving 11 votes. It was the first tie in the history of the BBWAA's rookie awards.

Other winners of awards given by THE SPORTING NEWS were Pat Putnam, first baseman for the Asheville Tourists in the Western Carolinas League,

Minor League Player of the Year; Vern Rapp of Denver, Minor League Manager of the Year; Art Teece, Salt Lake City, Triple A Executive of the Year; Woodrow Reid of Chattanooga, Double A Executive of the Year, and Don (Bucky) Buchheister, Cedar Rapids, Ia., Class A Executive of the Year.

Major League Attendance for 1976

AMERICAN LEAGUE

	Home	Away
Baltimore	1,058,609	1,307,920
Boston	1,895,846	1,297,969
California	1,006,774	1,090,168
Chicago	914,945	1,151,428
Cleveland	948,776	1,176,491
Detroit	1,467,020	1,308,570
Kansas City	1,680,265	1,227,619
Milwaukee	1,012,164	977,054
Minnesota	715,394	1,089,625
New York	2,012,434	1,579,626
Oakland	780,593	1,392,109
Texas	1,164,982	1,059,223

A.L. 1976 Total—14,657,802

NATIONAL LEAGUE

	Home	Away
Atlanta	818,179	1,200,561
Chicago	1,026,217	1,338,085
Cincinnati	2,629,708	1,841,310
Houston	886,146	1,211,254
Los Angeles	2,386,301	1,524,649
Montreal	646,704	1,174,360
New York	1,468,754	1,392,593
Philadelphia	2,480,150	1,518,160
Pittsburgh	1,025,945	1,412,042
St. Louis	1,207,079	1,421,775
San Diego	1,458,478	1,265,230
San Francisco	626,868	1,360,510

N.L. 1976 Total—16,660,529

MAJOR LEAGUE UMPIRES ASSOCIATION

President—Bob Engel, National League
Vice-President—Dave Phillips, American League
Secretary-Treasurer—Billy Williams, National League

John L. Cifelli, Attorney-Negotiator
Citizens Federal Building
Chicago Heights, Ill. 60411
754-5311 (312)

BOARD OF DIRECTORS
Bob Engel, National League
Dave Phillips, American League
Marty Springstead, American League
Bruce Froemming, National League
Paul Runge, National League
Lee Weyer, National League
Jim Evans, American League

Jackson First Choice In Re-Entry Draft

By LARRY WIGGE

Baseball's first free-agent re-entry draft was held November 4, 1976. Twenty-four players, who had not signed contracts in 1976 and played out their options, were available on the open market to all other major league clubs.

Reggie Jackson, slugging outfielder of the Baltimore Orioles, was the first player selected. Montreal was the first of 13 teams to draft the 30-year-old outfielder. Jackson later signed with the New York Yankees. Each player could be chosen by 12 clubs, in addition to his 1976 team.

The draft was formulated in an agreement between management and the Players Association as an outgrowth of the landmark decision by arbitrator Peter Seitz and upheld in two court appeals granting free agency to pitchers Andy Messersmith and Dave McNally in December, 1975.

In addition to Jackson, 12 players were selected by 13 clubs: Yankee pitcher Doyle Alexander; Oakland third baseman Sal Bando; Oakland outfielder Don Baylor; Minnesota relief pitcher Bill Campbell; Philadelphia second baseman Dave Cash; Oakland relief pitcher Rollie Fingers; Baltimore pitcher Wayne Garland; Baltimore second baseman Bobby Grich; Cincinnati pitcher Don Gullett; San Francisco outfielder Gary Matthews; Oakland outfielder Joe Rudi, and Oakland catcher Gene Tenace.

The Boston Red Sox were the first team to sign a re-entry prize when they inked Campbell, THE SPORTING NEWS' American League Fireman of the Year, to a long-term pact.

As spring training began, all but three of the 24 players had signed with new clubs. Besides Jackson, the Yankees signed Gullett; the California Angels signed Baylor, Grich and Rudi; the San Diego Padres inked Fingers and Tenace.

Alexander and the former Oakland shortstop, Bert Campaneris, signed with Texas; Bando chose the Milwaukee Brewers; Cash went to Montreal; Garland and Paul Dade signed with Cleveland; Matthews went to Atlanta and former Pittsburgh third baseman Richie Hebner signed with Philadelphia. The White Sox signed Tim Nordbrook, Eric Soderholm, Royle Stillman and Steve Stone, and Billy Smith agreed to terms with Baltimore.

Phillies' slugger Richie Allen was added to the list of free agents shortly after the re-entry proceedings. A special draft for Allen was held November 12. Only the Oakland A's opted for the controversial first baseman who remained unsigned.

The following is a list of the free-agent players and the teams which selected them in the re-entry draft. The numbers in parentheses after each team indicate the round in which the player was selected; capital letters indicate the player's former club selected him:

DOYLE ALEXANDER (13): Rangers (5), Tigers (6), Indians (6), Twins (6), Red Sox (7), Pirates (7), Dodgers (7), Expos (8), Athletics (8), Angels (9), Giants (9), White Sox (10), YANKEES.

SAL BANDO (13): Brewers (1), Twins (1), Rangers (3), Pirates (3), Cardinals (6), Giants (6), Orioles (6), Tigers (7), Indians (7), Mets (7), Royals (7), White Sox (8), ATHLETICS.

DON BAYLOR (13): Rangers (1), White Sox (2), Angels (2), Indians (2), Yankees (2), Brewers (3), Cubs (3), Orioles (3), Phillies (3), Royals (3), Mets (4), Twins (4), ATHLETICS.

BERT CAMPANERIS (12): Rangers (2), Expos (7), Twins (7), Yankees (7), Angels (8), Indians (8), Red Sox (8), Mets (8), Phillies (8), Orioles (9), White Sox (11), ATHLETICS.

BILL CAMPBELL (13): Cardinals (1), Red Sox (1), Cubs (2), Royals (2), Astros (3), Athletics (3), Dodgers (3), Expos (4), Tigers (4), Phillies (4), Angels (5), White Sox (6), TWINS.

DAVE CASH (13): Tigers (2), Expos (3), Twins (3), Red Sox (6), Athletics (6), White Sox (7), Orioles (7), Brewers (8), Giants (8), Dodgers (8), Royals (8), Yankees (8), PHILLIES.

NATE COLBERT (0): Not selected.

PAUL DADE (3): Athletics (16), Indians (19), ANGELS.

ROLLIE FINGERS (13): Giants (1), Cardinals (2), Red Sox (3), Tigers (5), Orioles (5), Expos (6), Padres (6), Rangers (6), Pirates (6), Dodgers (6), Phillies (6), Royals (6), ATHLETICS.

TITO FUENTES (7); Tigers (8); Pirates (9), Phillies (10), Giants (11), Athletics (13), White Sox (15), PADRES.

WAYNE GARLAND (13): Indians (1), Twins (2), Tigers (3), White Sox (4), Giants (4), Rangers (4), Cubs (4), Athletics (4), Royals (4), Dodgers (5), Yankees (5), Brewers (6), ORIOLES.

BOBBY GRICH (13): Tigers (1), Athletics (1), Yankees (1), Padres (2), Red Sox (2), Mets (3), Cardinals (4), Expos (5), Giants (5), Royals (5), Brewers (7), Angels (7), ORIOLES.

DON GULLETT (13): Dodgers (1), Braves (2), Yankees (3), Indians (4), Orioles (4), White Sox (5), Cardinals (5), Red Sox (5), Mets (5), Pirates (5), Athletics (5), Phillies (5), REDS.

RICHIE HEBNER (8): Braves (4), Rangers (7), Athletics (7), Phillies (7), Orioles (8), White Sox (9), Giants (10), PIRATES.

REGGIE JACKSON (13): Expos (1), Dodgers (2), Braves (3), Padres (5), Angels (6), Mets (6), Yankees (6), Giants (7), Pirates (8), Athletics (9), Phillies (9), White Sox (14), ORIOLES.

GARY MATTHEWS (13): Braves (1), Astros (1), Mets (1), Expos (2), Athletics (2), Padres (4), Angels (4), Pirates (4), Yankees (4), Brewers (5), Indians (5), Twins (5), GIANTS.

WILLIE McCOVEY (0): Not selected.

TIM NORDBROOK (5): Athletics (15), White Sox (17), Royals (19), Rangers (20), ANGELS.

JOE RUDI (13): White Sox (1), Padres (1), Angels (1), Pirates (1), Orioles (1), Phillies (1), Giants (2), Mets (2), Cardinals (3), Brewers (4), Red Sox (4), Dodgers (4), ATHLETICS.

BILLY SMITH (9): Royals (9), Yankees (9), Orioles (10), Athletics (11), White Sox (12), Giants (12), Red Sox (19), Rangers (21), ANGELS.

ERIC SODERHOLM (4): Athletics (14), Rangers (19), White Sox (20), TWINS.

ROYLE STILLMAN (3): Athletics (10), Pirates (19), White Sox (21).

STEVE STONE (6): Rangers (8), Tigers (9), Indians (9), Athletics (12), White Sox (13), CUBS.

GENE TENACE (13): Cubs (1), Royals (1), Brewers (2), Astros (2), Pirates (2), Orioles (2), Phillies (2), White Sox (3), Padres (3), Angels (3), Giants (3), Indians (3), ATHLETICS.

Homers by Parks for 1976

NATIONAL LEAGUE

	At Atl.	At Chi.	At Cin.	At Hou.	At L.A.	At Mon.	At N.Y.	At Phil.	At Pitt.	At St.L.	At S.D.	At S.F.	Totals 1976	Totals 1975
Atlanta	43	6	5	2	6	7	1	2	3	1	4	2	82	107
Chicago	3	71	1	2	5	7	2	5	4	1	1	3	105	95
Cincinnati	9	15	73	4	4	6	4	5	8	4	6	3	141	124
Houston	8	3	5	30	2	2	3	3	2	2	3	6	66	84
Los Angeles	1	10	6	3	42	0	2	5	3	9	5	5	91	118
Montreal	2	8	4	4	2	45	6	5	7	2	4	5	94	98
New York	10	16	4	0	7	2	43	4	8	6	1	1	102	101
Philadelphia	3	11	5	1	5	4	6	63	4	4	2	2	110	125
Pittsburgh	6	5	3	4	3	4	7	8	54	6	7	3	110	138
St. Louis	3	6	3	0	0	4	6	7	3	27	2	2	63	81
San Diego	6	2	4	3	6	3	2	1	1	3	30	3	64	78
San Francisco	5	2	6	4	8	2	4	4	0	2	4	44	85	84
1976 Totals	99	155	119	57	90	86	86	112	98	67	68	76	1113	....
1975 Totals	121	125	122	83	116	110	100	119	108	85	71	73	....	1233

AT ATLANTA (99): Atlanta (43)—Wynn 12, Henderson 6, Montanez 5, Williams 4, Gaston 3, Correll 2, Lacy 2, Paciorek 2, Royster 2, Asselstine, Evans, May, Niekro, Perez. **Chicago (3)**—LaCock, Madlock, Monday. **Cincinnati (9)**—Foster 3, Concepcion, Driessen, Griffey, Lum, Perez, Rose. **Houston (8)**—Cedeno 2, Roberts 2, Cabell, Cruz, Niekro, Watson. **Los Angeles (1)**—Buckner. **Montreal (2)**—Foli, Mangual. **New York (10)**—Kingman 5, Hodges 3, Garrett, Harrelson. **Philadelphia (3)**—Johnstone, Schmidt, Tolan. **Pittsburgh (3)**—Robinson 2, Moose, Rooker, Sanguillen, Zisk. **St. Louis (3)**—Ferguson, McBride, Simmons. **San Diego (6)**—Grubb 2, Turner 2, Hernandez, Winfield. **San Francisco (5)**—Matthews 2, Herndon, Murcer, Thomasson.

AT CHICAGO (155): Atlanta (6)—Henderson 2, Chaney, Correll, Royster, Williams. **Chicago (71)**—Monday 20, Morales 12, Madlock 11, Cardenal 7, LaCock 4, Mitterwald 4, Swisher 4, Wallis 4, Trillo 2, Rosello, Thornton, Tyrone. **Cincinnati (15)**—Foster 3, Perez 3, Bench 2, Driessen 2, Griffey 2, Morgan 2, Rose. **Houston (5)**—Cedeno, Cruz, Richard. **Los Angeles (10)**—Cey 3, Cruz 3, Buckner, Goodson, Russell, Yeager. **Montreal (8)**—Jorgensen 2, Foli, Mackanin, Parrish, Valentine, White, Williams. **New York (16)**—Kingman 6, Phillips 4, Milner 2, Foster, Kranepool, Mazzilli, Stearns. **Philadelphia (11)**—Schmidt 7, Maddox 2, Boone, McCarver, Maddox. **Pittsburgh (5)**—Stargell 2, Zisk 2, Hebner. **St. Louis (4)**—Crawford 2, Ferguson, Hernandez, Simmons, Smith. **San Diego (2)**—W. Davis, Rader. **San Francisco (2)**—Matthews, Mercer.

AT CINCINNATI (119): Atlanta (5)—Correll, Montanez, Office, Paciorek, Royster. **Chicago (1)**—Trillo. **Cincinnati (73)**—Foster 15, Morgan 13, Bench 12, Perez 9, Rose 7, Bailey 4, Concepcion 4, Driessen 3, Plummer 3, Armbrister 2, Griffey 2, Geronimo. **Houston (5)**—Cedeno 3, Roberts, Watson. **Los Angeles (4)**—Garvey 3, Goodson, Russell, Smith. **Montreal (4)**—Carter, Mackanin, Thornton, Valentine. **New York (4)**—Ayala, Kranepool, Milner, Torre. **Philadelphia (5)**—Allen, Johnstone, Luzinski, Maddox, Schmidt. **Pittsburgh (3)**—Zisk 2, Robinson. **St. Louis (3)**—Brock, Crawford, Kessinger. **San Diego (4)**—W. Davis, Ivie, Kendall, Rader. **San Francisco (6)**—Speier 2, Evans, Murcer, Perez, Thomasson.

AT HOUSTON (57): Atlanta (2)—Gilbreath, Henderson. **Chicago (2)**—Monday, Summers. **Cincinnati (4)**—Bench, Foster, Morgan, Perez. **Houston (30)**—Watson 9, Cedeno 8, Johnson 5, Herrmann 2, Roberts 2, Cabell, Cruz, Dierker, Richard. **Los Angeles (3)**—Cey, Ferguson, Smith. **Montreal (4)**—Mangual, Parrish, Rivera, Thornton. **New York (0). Philadelphia (1)**—Schmidt. **Pittsburgh (2)**—Oliver 2, Moreno, Sanguillen. **St. Louis (0). San Diego (2)**—Almon, Grubb, Torres. **San Francisco (4)**—Alexander, Matthews, Speier, Thomasson.

AT LOS ANGELES (90): Atlanta (6)—Montanez 2, Wynn 2, May, Williams. **Chicago (5)**—Monday 2, LaCock, Morales, Thornton. **Cincinnati (4)**—Perez 2, Foster, Morgan. **Houston (2)**—Watson 2. **Los Angeles (42)**—Cey 12, Garvey 6, Yeager 5, Buckner 4, Lopes 4, Smith 4, Baker 3, Cruz, Ferguson, Rhoden, Russell. **Montreal (2)**—Lyttle, Valentine. **New York (7)**—Kingman 4, Milner 2, Kranepool. **Philadelphia (5)**—Allen 3, Luzinski, Schmidt. **Pittsburgh (5)**—Hebner, Parker, Stargell 3. **St. Louis (0). San Diego (6)**—Winfield 3, W. Davis, Ivie, Torres. **San Francisco (8)**—Murcer 4, Matthews 2, Rader, Thomasson.

AT MONTREAL (86): Atlanta (7)—Office 2, Henderson, Paciorek, Royster, Williams, Wynn. **Chicago (7)**—Monday 3, LaCock, Mitterwald, Morales, Swisher. **Cincinnati (6)**—Morgan 2, Bench, Concepcion, Flynn, Lum. **Houston (2)**—Herrmann, Roberts. **Los Angeles (0). Montreal (45)**—Unser 7, Carter 5, Foote 4, Mackanin 4, Parrish 4, Thornton 4, Valentine 3, Williams 3, Foli 2, Jorgensen 2, Morales 2, Colbert, Garrett, Mangual, Rivera, White. **New York (2)**—Garrett, Unser. **Philadelphia (4)**—Luzinski 2, Schmidt 2. **Pittsburgh (4)**—Hebner 2, Oliver, Parker. **St. Louis (4)**—Cruz, Hernandez, Mumphrey, Simmons. **San Diego (5)**—McCovey, Rader, Winfield. **San Francisco (2)**—Matthews, Reitz.

AT NEW YORK (86): Atlanta (1)—Correll. **Chicago (2)**—Monday, Morales. **Cincinnati (4)**—Concepcion 2, Foster, Morgan. **Houston (3)**—Cedeno, Johnson, Watson. **Los Angeles (2)**—Garvey, Smith. **Montreal (4)**—Colbert, Garrett, Morales, Parrish, Thornton, Valentine. **New York (43)**—Kingman 16, Milner 7, Kranepool 6, Torre 3, Boisclair 2, Garrett 2, Ro. Baldwin, Grote, Hodges, Mazzilli, Staiger, Stearns, Unser. **Philadelphia (6)**—Schmidt 3, Christenson 2, Luzinski. **Pittsburgh (7)**—Stargell 2, Dyer, Hebner, Moreno, Robertson, Zisk. **St. Louis (6)**—Anderson, Crawford, Ferguson, Hernandez, McBride, Smith. **San Diego (2)**—Winfield 2. **San Francisco (4)**—Evans, Matthews, Murcer, Perez.

AT PHILADELPHIA (112): Atlanta (2)—May, Montanez. **Chicago (5)**—Monday 2, Madlock, Summers, Trillo. **Cincinnati (5)**—Foster 3, Bailey, Morgan. **Houston (3)**—Johnson 2, Cruz. **Los Angeles (5)**—Cey 2, Garvey, Goodson, Russell. **Montreal (5)**—Williams 2, Jorgensen, Morales, Scanlon. **New York (4)**—Kingman 2, Grote, Mangual. **Philadelphia (63)**—Schmidt 17, Luzinski 15, Allen 9, Brown 4, Tolan 4, Boone 3, Maddox 3, Johnstone 2, McCarver 2, Cash, Kaat, Martin, Vukovich. **Pittsburgh (8)**—Parker 2, Robinson 2, Stargell 2, Zisk 2, Hebner. **St. Louis (7)**—Smith 3, Cruz 2, Brock, Harris. **San Diego (1)**—Turner. **San Francisco (4)**—Evans 3, Matthews.

AT PITTSBURGH (98): Atlanta (3)—Gaston, Henderson, Lacy. **Chicago (4)**—Madlock 2, LaCock, Monday. Cincinnati (8)—Morgan 5, Griffey, Perez, Rose. **Houston (3)**—Cedeno, DaVanon, Roberts. **Los Angeles (3)**—Cey, Russell, Yeager. **Montreal (7)**—Mackanin 2, Foli, Foote, Parrish, Thornton, Williams. **New York (8)**—Kingman 3, Milner 2, Kranepool, Staiger, Torre. **Philadelphia (4)**—Schmidt 2, Allen, Luzinski. **Pittsburgh (54)**—Robinson 14, Stargell 11, Oliver 9, Zisk 8, Parker 5, Dyer 2, Hebner 2, Helms, Robertson, Stennett. **St. Louis (3)**—Cruz, Forsch, Smith. **San Diego (1)**—Winfield. **San Francisco (0).**

AT ST. LOUIS (67): Atlanta (1)—Williams. **Chicago (1)**—Morales. **Cincinnati (4)** Foster 2, Perez, Plummer. **Houston (2)**—Cedeno, Johnson. **Los Angeles (9)**—Cey 3, Ferguson 3, Smith 3. **Montreal (2)**—Foli, Jorgensen. **New York (6)**—Unser 3, Grote, Millan, Milner. **Philadelphia (4)**—Schmidt 2, Brown, Martin. **Pittsburgh (6)**—Robinson 2, Parker, Reynolds, Stargell, Zisk. **St. Louis (27)**—Cruz 9, Crawford 4, Hernandez 4, Brock 2, Smith 2, Tyson 2, Ferguson, McBride, Simmons, Templeton. **San Diego (3)**—Ivie, McCovey, Winfield. **San Francisco (2)**—Evans 2.

AT SAN DIEGO (68): Atlanta (4)—Henderson 2, Office, Williams. **Chicago (1)**—Monday. **Cincinnati (6)**—Bailey, Concepcion, Foster, Geronimo, Lum, Morgan. **Houston (2)**—Watson 2. **Los Angeles (5)**—Garvey 2, Yeager 2, Ferguson. **Montreal (4)**—Roenicke 2, Foote, Williams. **New York (1)**—Kingman. **Philadelphia (2)**—Hutton, Johnstone. **Pittsburgh (7)**—Parker 3, Zisk 3, Stennett. **St. Louis (2)**—Crawford, Simmons. **San Diego (30)**—Rader 5, Ivie 4, McCovey 4, Winfield 4, W. Davis 2, Fuentes 2, Grubb 2, Torres 2, Turner 2, Champion, Kendall, Rettenmund. **San Francisco (4)**—Murcer 3, Thomasson.

AT SAN FRANCISCO (76): Atlanta (2)—Wynn 2. **Chicago (3)**—Cardenal, Summers, Wallis. **Cincinnati (3)**—Driessen, Foster, Perez. **Houston (3)**—Cedeno, Howard, Johnson. **Los Angeles (5)**—Yeager 2, Baker, Buckner, Cey. **Montreal (5)**—Parrish 3, Foote, Thornton. **New York (1)**—Grote. **Philadelphia (2)**—Allen, Schmidt. **Pittsburgh (3)**—Hebner, Stargell, Zisk. **St. Louis (2)**—Clarey, Tyson. **San Diego (3)**—McCovey, Rader, Rettenmund. **San Francisco (44)**—Murcer 12, Matthews 11, Reitz 4, Evans 3, Hill 3, Thomasson 3, Clark 2, Montanez 2, Thomas 2, Alexander, Herndon.

AMERICAN LEAGUE

	At Balt.	At Bos.	At Calif.	At Chi.	At Clev.	At Det.	At K.C.	At Milw.	At Minn.	At N.Y.	At Oak.	At Tex.	Totals 1976	1975
Baltimore	58	5	4	6	8	6	4	6	4	6	2	10	119	124
Boston	5	71	1	4	4	17	0	6	4	9	8	5	134	134
California	1	4	24	2	4	5	3	2	5	4	7	2	63	55
Chicago	0	5	3	31	4	2	5	4	2	4	5	8	73	94
Cleveland	5	10	2	1	40	1	2	3	5	6	5	5	85	153
Detroit	3	4	3	4	9	51	1	4	9	5	6	2	101	125
Kansas City	1	9	1	2	0	3	37	0	2	2	6	6	65	118
Milwaukee	6	4	5	3	2	4	1	45	2	5	7	5	88	146
Minnesota	3	2	5	8	3	7	1	3	34	5	7	3	81	121
New York	4	7	4	0	5	11	3	6	8	67	2	3	120	110
Oakland	7	7	4	3	5	3	10	3	5	2	56	8	113	151
Texas	3	4	3	1	3	3	1	6	3	3	7	40	80	134
1976 Totals	96	132	59	65	83	113	72	88	86	118	113	97	1122	......
1975 Totals	91	157	76	96	164	146	91	135	163	106	118	122	......	1465

AT BALTIMORE (96): Baltimore (58)—R. Jackson 12, L. May 12, Grich 8, Singleton 7, Bumbry 6, DeCinces 5, Duncan 2, Mora 2, Robinson 2, Belanger, Blair. **Boston (5)**—Rice 2, Darwin, Evans, Lynn. **California (1)**—Solaita. **Chicago (0). Cleveland (5)**—Hendrick 2, Bell, Robinson, Spikes. **Detroit (3)**—Johnson, Rodriguez, Veryzer. **Kansas City (1)**—Mayberry. **Milwaukee (6)**—Aaron, Heidemann, Lezcano, Money, D. Thomas, R. G. Thomas. **Minnesota (3)**—Hisle 2, Ford. **New York (6)**—Nettles 2, Randolph, White. **Oakland (7)**—Bando 2, Baylor, McMullen, Rudi, Tenace, Williams. **Texas (3)**—Harrah 2, Howell.

AT BOSTON (132): Baltimore (5)—Grich 2, Bumbry, Duncan, R. Jackson. **Boston (71)**—Rice 12, Fisk 10, Yastrzemski 10, Cooper 9, Evans 9, Hobson 5, Lynn 4, Burleson 3, Petrocelli 3, Montgomery 2, Baker, Carbo, Darwin, Whitt. **California (4)**—Jackson 2, Davis, Solaita. **Chicago (5)**—Downing 2, Bell, Bradford, Brohamer. **Cleveland (10)**—Carty 3, Hendrick 3, Bell 2, Blanks, Manning. **Detroit (4)**—Thompson 2, Oglivie, Rodriguez. **Kansas City (9)**—Otis 3, Cowens, Jones, Martinez, McRae, Stinson, White. **Milwaukee (4)**—Garcia, Heidemann, Money, Scott. **Minnesota (2)**—Hisle, Kusick. **New York (7)**—Munson 3, Nettles 2, C. May, Rivers. **Oakland (7)**—Tenace 3, Baylor 2, Bando, Garner. **Texas (4)**—Ellis, Grieve, Harrah, Howell.

AT CALIFORNIA (59): Baltimore (4)—R. Jackson, L. May, Mora, Singleton. **Boston (1)**—Rice. **California (24)**—Bonds 6, Melton 3, Solaita 3, Davis 2, Jones 2, Torres 2, Alvarez, Briggs, Collins, Humphrey, Jackson, Stanton. **Chicago (3)**—Kelly, Lemon, Spencer. **Cleveland (2)**—Hendrick, Robinson. **Detroit (3)**—Freehan, LeFlore, Rodriguez. **Kansas City (1)**—Martinez. **Milwaukee (5)**—Aaron, Hegan, Porter, Scott, R. G. Thomas. **Minnesota (5)**—Ford 2, Carew, Hisle, Wynegar. **New York (4)**—Chambliss, Gamble, Hendricks, White. **Oakland (4)**—Bando 2, Baylor, Rudi. **Texas (3)** Burroughs, Hargrove, Harrah.

AT CHICAGO (65): Baltimore (6) DeCinces 2, L. May 2, Bumbry, R. Jackson. **Boston (4)**—Fisk 2, Montgomery, Yastrzemski. **California (2)**—Bochte, Collins. **Chicago (31)**—Orta 8, Spencer 5, L. Johnson 4, Brohamer 3, Stein 3, Lemon 2, Varney 2, Bell, Bradford, Dent, Kelly. **Cleveland (1)**—Fosse. **Detroit (4)**—Horton 2, Thompson 2. **Kansas City (2)**—Mayberry, D. Nelson. **Milwaukee (3)**—Darwin, Hegan, Scott. **Minnesota (8)**—Wynegar 2, Bostock, Braun, Carew, Ford, Hisle, Smalley. **New York (0). Oakland (3)**—Fairly, Tenace, Washington. **Texas (1)**—Harrah.

AT CLEVELAND (83): Baltimore (4)—DeCinces, Duncan, L. May, Singleton. **Boston (4)**—Burleson, Cooper, Evans, Fisk. **California (4)**—Bonds, Melton, Solaita, Torres. **Chicago (4)**—Bradford, Downing, Kelly, Spencer. **Cleveland (40)**—Hendrick 11, Carty 6, Powell 5, Blanks 4, Bell 3, Lowenstein 2, Manning 2, Smith 2, Ashby, Duffy, Fosse, Robinson, Spikes. **Detroit (9)**—Horton 3, Garcia, Mankowski, Oglivie, Staub, Thompson, Wockenfuss. **Kansas City (0). Milwaukee (2)**—Lezcano 2. **Minnesota (3)**—Braun, Kusick, Wynegar. **New York (3)**—Chambliss, Piniella, Rivers, Velez, White. **Oakland (5)**—Rudi 2. **Milwaukee (3)**—Baylor. **Texas (3)**—Burroughs 2, Harrah.

AT DETROIT (113): Baltimore (6)—L. May 2, Blair, DeCinces, Grich, Singleton. **Boston (17)**—Rice 5, Yastrzemski 4, Cooper 2, Burleson, Dillard, Evans, Fisk, Hobson, Lynn. **California (3)**—Jackson 2, Alvarez, Guerrero, Jones. **Chicago (2)**—Lemon, Spencer. **Cleveland (1)**—Hendrick. **Detroit (51)**—Staub 9, Oglivie 8, Thompson 7, Horton 5, Rodriguez 5, Johnson 4, Freehan 2, Meyer 2, Scrivener 2, Stanley 2, Wockenfuss 2, Garcia, Kimm, LeFlore. **Kansas**

City (3)—McRae, Otis, Poquette. **Milwaukee (4)**—Money 3, Hegan. **Minnesota (7)**—Ford 2, Brye, Cubbage, Hisle, Kusick, Wynegar. **New York (11)**—Chambliss 3, Munson 3, White 2, Hendricks, Nettles, Rivers. **Oakland (3)**—Tenace 2, Rudi. **Texas (3)**—Grieve 2, Hargrove.

    AT KANSAS CITY (72): Baltimore (8)—R. Jackson 3, L. May 2, Bumbry, Grich, Singleton. **Boston (0). California (3)**—Herrmann 2, Jones. **Chicago (5)**—Bell, Brohamer, Garr, Orta, Spencer. **Cleveland (2)**—Ashby, Hendrick. **Detroit (1)**—Thompson. **Kansas City (37)**—Mayberry 10, Otis 10, Brett 6, McRae 4, Cowens 2, Martinez 2, Poquette, Quirk, Wohlford. **Milwaukee (1)**—Joshua. **Minnesota (1)**—Kusick. **New York (3)**—Munson 3. **Oakland (10)**—Bando 4, Baylor 3, Garner, Rudi, Tenace. **Texas (1)**—Grieve.

    AT MILWAUKEE (88): Baltimore (6)—R. Jackson 3, L. May 2, Muser. **Boston (6)**—Cooper 2, Hobson 2, Darwin, Yastrzemski. **California (2)**—Bonds, Melton. **Chicago (4)**—Spencer 3, Bradford. **Cleveland (3)**—Lis 2, Manning. **Detroit (4)**—LeFlore, Oglivie, Staub, Thompson. **Kansas City (0). Milwaukee (45)**—Scott 12, Aaron 6, Money 5, Lezcano 4, J. G. Thomas 4, Joshua 3, Porter 3, D. Thomas 2, Carbo, Hegan, Moore, Rosario, Sutherland, Yount. **Minnesota (3)**—Borgmann, Cubbage, Kusick. **New York (6)**—Nettles 3, Munson 2, Chambliss. **Oakland (3)**—Tenace 2, Rudi. **Texas (6)**—Grieve 2, Harrah 2, Fahey, Lahoud.

    AT MINNESOTA (86): Baltimore (4)—Singleton 2, DeCinces, L. May. **Boston (4)**—Evans, Lynn, Rice, Yastrzemski. **California (5)**—Jackson 3, Bochte, Collins. **Chicago (2)**—Brohamer, Orta. **Cleveland (5)**—Carty 2, Hendrick 2, Manning. **Detroit (9)**—Freehan 2, Thompson 2, Garcia, Horton, LeFlore, Stanley, Staub. **Kansas City (2)**—Mayberry, Otis. **Milwaukee (2)**—Porter, Scott. **Minnesota (34)**—Ford 8, Hisle 6, Kusick 6, Carew 4, Wynegar 4, Bostock, Braun, Brye, Cubbage, Randall, Smalley. **New York (8)**—Nettles 4, Chambliss, Gamble, Munson, White. **Oakland (5)**—Washington 2, Williams 2, Tenace. **Texas (6)**—Harrah 3, Burroughs 2, Grieve.

    AT NEW YORK (118): Baltimore (6)—R. Jackson 2 DeCinces, Garcia, Grich, Hendricks. **Boston (9)**—Rice 3, Yastrzemski 3, Burleson 2, Fisk. **California (5)**—Collins, Jones, Solaita, Torres. **Chicago (4)**—Brohamer, Garr, Kelly, Varney. **Cleveland (6)**—Ashby 2, Carty, Manning, Powell, Spikes. **Detroit (5)**—Oglivie 2, Staub 2, Horton. **Kansas City (2)**—Martinez, McRae. **Milwaukee (5)**—Carbo, Hegan, Joshua, Moore, D. Thomas. **Minnesota (5)**—Bostock, Carew, Ford, Oliva, Wynegar. **New York (67)**—Nettles 18, Gamble 15, Chambliss 10, White 8, Munson 5, Rivers 5, Piniella 2, Hendricks, C. May, Stanley, Velez. **Oakland (2)**—Rudi, Washington. **Texas (3)**—Hargrove, Howell, Sundberg.

    AT OAKLAND (113): Baltimore (8)—Harper, Mora. **Boston (8)**—Evans 2, Fisk 2, Lynn 2, Rice, Yastrzemski. **California (7)**—Bonds 2, Jones, Melton, Solaita, Stanton, Torres. **Chicago (5)**—Orta 2, Spencer 2, Stein. **Cleveland (5)**—Hendrick 3, Carty, Duffy. **Detroit (6)**—Horton 2, Johnson, Oglivie, Stanley, Staub. **Kansas City (2)**—Otis 2. **Milwaukee (6)**—Aaron 2, Carbo, Scott, R. G. Thomas, Yount. **Minnesota (7)**—Ford 4, Bostock, Carew, Hisle. **New York (2)**—Mason, Nettles. **Oakland (56)**—Bando 16, Tenace 9, Garner 6, Williams 6, Baylor 5, McMullen 4, Rudi 4, Fairly 2, North 2, Hosley, Washington. **Texas (7)**—Grieve 2, Howell 2, Burroughs, Fregosi, Pape.

    AT TEXAS (97): Baltimore (10)—R. Jackson 4, L. May 2, Mora 2, Blair, Robinson. **Boston (5)**—Evans 2, Cooper, Lynn. **California (2)**—Solaita, Torres. **Chicago (8)**—Bell 2, Garr 2, Orta 2, Dent, Kelly. **Cleveland (5)**—Powell 3, Bell, Hendrick. **Detroit (2)**—Oglivie, Thompson. **Kansas City (6)**—Brett, McRae, Otis, Patek, Stinson, White. **Milwaukee (5)**—Money 2, Moore, Scott, R. G. Thomas. **Minnesota (3)**—Carew, Ford, Hisle. **New York (3)**—Alomar, C. May, Nettles. **Oakland (8)**—Bando 2, Baylor 2, Tenace 2, Campaneris, Rudi. **Texas (40)**—Burroughs 12, Grieve 11, Hargrove 4, Harrah 4, Howell 3, Sundberg 2, Fregosi, Randle, Smalley, Thompson.

NO-HITTERS

Including

Review of Four '76 No-Hitters
Official Box Score of Each

BATTING, PITCHING FEATURES
THE SPORTING NEWS AWARDS

Including

BBWAA Awards

MAJOR LEAGUE FARM SYSTEMS
HALL OF FAME ELECTION

Including

Feature of Electees

All Hall-of-Famers Listed According to Years Selected

Dierker Heads No-Hit Quartet in 1976

By LARRY WIGGE

Trudging along for five innings at his usual deliberate pace, Houston's Larry Dierker suddenly became excited. The no-hit dream which had eluded him four times was to become a reality July 9, 1976.

The 29-year-old Astro righthander hurled the first no-hitter of the 1976 season in the majors. Three other no-hitters were authored by Pittsburgh's John Candelaria, San Francisco's John Montefusco and a combined effort by Johnny Odom and Francisco Barrios of the Chicago White Sox.

Dierker's gem was a 6-0 shutout of the Montreal Expos at Houston's Astrodome.

"I couldn't help notice how excited Larry was late in the game," said shortstop Roger Metzger, who noted that Dierker normally never showed any excitement and just plodded along.

"He worked at his usual pace for five innings," said Metzger. "Then he was really speeding it up. He was pounding his fist into his glove. He was really keyed up."

The senior man on Houston manager Bill Virdon's pitching staff, Dierker pitched perfect ball for eight innings in a game against the New York Mets in 1966. He lost the perfect game, the no-hitter, the shutout and the game, 1-0, in the ninth inning.

Houston Astros' pitcher Larry Dierker shows his style while pitching a no-hitter against the Montreal Expos. It was the first for Dierker, who struck out eight batters and walked only four, winning the game, 6-0.

Larry was one out away from a no-hitter against the Braves in 1969. He maintained a 0-0 deadlock before departing for a pinch-hitter in the 12th inning at Atlanta. The Astros lost, 3-2 in 13 innings.

He also pitched one-hitters against San Diego in 1971 and the Mets in 1972.

Dierker said he felt he was going to make it this time. He had promised that if he ever got close to a no-hitter again, he wouldn't give anybody a pitch to hit. However, Virdon lauded Larry for challenging the hitters and throwing it by them.

Dierker struck out eight batters and walked four en route to the no-hitter. He struck out Pepe Mangual and Jim Lyttle and got Mike Jorgensen on a harmless grounder to first base in the ninth.

A good play by second baseman Rob Andrews, another by third baseman Enos Cabell and two long running catches by center fielder Jose Cruz helped save the dream for Dierker.

AT HOUSTON—JULY 9

Montreal	AB.	R.	H.	RBI.	E.
Mangual, cf	4	0	0	0	0
Lyttle, rf	4	0	0	0	0
Jorgensen, lf	4	0	0	0	0
Thornton, 1b	1	0	0	0	1
Parrish, 3b	2	0	0	0	1
Mackanin, 2b	2	0	0	0	0
L. Johnson, c	2	0	0	0	0
Foote, ph	1	0	0	0	0
Kerrigan, p	0	0	0	0	0
Frias, ss	2	0	0	0	0
Foli, ph-ss	1	0	0	0	0
Stanhouse, p	1	0	0	0	0
Carrithers, p	0	0	0	0	0
Dwyer, ph	1	0	0	0	0
Warthen, p	0	0	0	0	0
Morales, ph-c	1	0	0	0	0
Totals	26	0	0	0	2

Houston	AB.	R.	H.	RBI.	E.
Gross, rf	4	0	0	0	0
Andrews, 2b	4	0	2	1	0
Cabell, 3b	4	0	1	0	0
Watson, 1b	3	2	2	0	0
Cruz, cf	4	1	2	1	0
C. Johnson, lf	4	1	0	0	0
Howard, lf	0	0	0	0	0
Herrmann, c	3	1	2	2	0
Metzger, ss	3	1	2	1	0
DIERKER, p	3	0	0	1	0
Totals	32	6	11	6	0

Montreal	0	0	0	0	0	0	0	0	0—0
Houston	0	2	0	2	2	0	0	0	x—6

Montreal	IP.	H.	R.	ER.	BB.	SO.
Stanhouse (L. 6-4)	3⅔	6	4	4	4	0
Carrithers	1⅓	3	2	1	0	1
Warthen	2	2	0	0	0	1
Kerrigan	1	0	0	0	0	1

Houston	IP.	H.	R.	ER.	BB.	SO.
DIERKER (W. 8-8)	9	0	0	0	4	8

Double plays—Montreal 3, Houston 1. Left on bases—Montreal 3, Houston 7. Two-base hit—Cruz. Home run—Herrmann (1). Stolen bases—Thornton, Watson. Sacrifice fly—DIERKER. Wild pitch—Stanhouse. Umpires—McSherry, A. Williams, Gorman and Pryor. Time—2:26. Attendance—12,511.

At Oakland on July 28, there were so many runners on base when Johnny Odom and Francisco Barrios of the White Sox combined for a 2-1 no-hit victory against the A's that Barrios admitted he was unaware of the hitless game until the ninth inning.

After walking nine batters in five innings, Odom departed to the clubhouse. Barrios issued two bases on balls in his four-inning stint.

"I didn't look at the scoreboard until the ninth inning," said Barrios, a 23-year-old righthander from Mexico. "Then I saw no hit."

"I just couldn't take it. I couldn't watch," said Odom, who listened to the game and paced in the clubhouse. "Who would have thought I'd get a no-hitter at age 31?" And it came after I had been in the minors for three months."

Odom was making only his second start for Chicago after pitching in the International League and the American Association.

The former Oakland righthander, who helped the A's to three consecutive

World Series triumphs in 1972-73-74, had to pitch out of several jams against his old mates.

In the third inning, Odom walked the bases loaded. But a double play ended the threat. He walked two more batters in the fourth, when a throwing error by catcher Jim Essian let Oakland score its only run.

The only tough fielding chances, however, came while Barrios was on the mound.

A deep fly was caught by Jorge Orta in left-center field and a bad-hop grounder was speared by shortstop Bucky Dent.

The greatest threat to the no-hitter came in the ninth when Sal Bando opened the inning with a slow roller to second baseman Jack Brohamer. Bando argued vehemently when umpire George Maloney called him out on a close play.

"He was out by two steps," said a sharp-eyed Bucky Dent.

AT OAKLAND–JULY 28

Chicago	AB.	R.	H.	RBI.	E.	Oakland	AB.	R.	H.	RBI.	E.
Hairston, rf	3	0	2	0	0	North, cf	3	0	0	0	0
Nordhagen, ph-rf	2	0	0	0	0	Campaneris, ss	2	0	0	0	0
Garr, cf-lf	4	0	2	0	0	Rudi, lf	3	0	0	0	0
Orta, lf	3	0	0	0	0	Williams, dh	1	1	0	0	0
Bannister, cf	0	0	0	0	0	Lintz, pr-dh	0	0	0	0	0
Kelly, dh	2	0	0	0	0	Baylor, ph-dh	1	0	0	0	0
L. Johnson, ph-dh	1	0	0	0	0	Bando, 3b	2	0	0	0	1
Stein, 3b	4	0	2	0	0	Tenace, c	3	0	0	0	0
Spencer, 1b	3	2	2	1	0	Washington, rf	3	0	0	0	0
Brohamer, 2b	4	0	1	0	0	McMullen, 1b	3	0	0	0	0
Dent, ss	4	0	1	1	0	Garner, 2b	3	0	0	0	0
Essian, c	4	0	0	0	1	Torrez, p	0	0	0	0	0
ODOM, p	0	0	0	0	0	Lindblad, p	0	0	0	0	0
BARRIOS, p	0	0	0	0	0	Fingers, p	0	0	0	0	0
Totals	34	2	10	2	1	Totals	24	1	0	0	1

Chicago 0   1   0   0   0   1   0   0   0 – 2
Oakland 0   0   0   1   0   0   0   0   0 – 1

Chicago	IP.	H.	R.	ER.	BB.	SO.	Oakland	IP.	H.	R.	ER.	BB.	SO.
ODOM (W. 2-0)	5*	0	1	0	9	3	Torrez	5	7	1	1	1	2
BARRIOS (Save 2)	4	0	0	0	2	2	Lindblad (L. 4-3)	2⅓	2	1	1	0	0
							Fingers	1⅔	1	0	0	1	2

*Pitched to one batter in sixth.

Double plays–Chicago 3, Oakland 2. Left on bases–Chicago 8, Oakland 7. Two-base hits–Spencer, Brohamer. Home run–Spencer (7). Stolen bases–Kelly, North, Washington, Lintz. Sacrifice hit–Orta. Umpires–Goetz, Maloney, McKean and Bremigan. Time–2:31. Attendance–3,367.

On August 9, lefthander John Candelaria became the second Pirate–Nick Maddox in 1907 was the other–to pitch a no-hitter in Pittsburgh when he blanked Los Angeles, 2-0.

"This is something I've dreamed about since I was a little boy," said Candelaria. "It's something every kid dreams about."

Candelaria, a popular 22-year-old hurler known as the Candy Man, was honored prior to the game when each fan was given a candy bar as he passed through the turnstiles.

Candelaria turned in a powerful performance. He struck out seven and walked one. The Dodgers had only three base runners, all in the fourth inning.

Steve Yeager drew a one-out walk. After losing pitcher Doug Rau forced Yeager for the second out, shortstop Frank Taveras misplayed a grounder by Dave Lopes for an error and third baseman Bill Robinson booted a one-hop grounder by Ted Sizemore. The bases were loaded.

Pirate Pitcher John Candelaria gets hug from catcher Duffy Dyer after the 22-year-old lefty hurled no-hitter against the Los Angeles Dodgers. Candelaria permitted the Dodgers only three base runners, all in the fourth inning.

Candelaria forced Bill Russell to bounce to second baseman Rennie Sten-nett to end the inning. He then proceeded to retire the next 18 batters in order.

In the ninth, Candelaria needed only three pitches to retire Lopes on a grounder to short and Sizemore on a foul fly to right. Russell again stepped to the plate. The Candy Man got the final out on a fly to short center field, nabbed by Al Oliver, who brushed against Taveras while making the play.

"My legs were shaking on that one," Candelaria admitted.

AT PITTSBURGH—AUGUST 9

Los Angeles	AB.	R.	H.	RBI.	E.	Pittsburgh	AB.	R.	H.	RBI.	E.
Lopes, cf	4	0	0	0	0	Taveras, ss	4	0	1	0	1
Sizemore, 2b	4	0	0	0	0	Stennett, 2b	4	0	0	0	0
Russell, ss	4	0	0	0	1	Oliver, cf	2	0	1	0	0
Garvey, 1b	3	0	0	0	0	Stargell, 1b	3	0	0	0	0
Cey, 3b	3	0	0	0	0	Zisk, lf	3	1	1	0	0
Baker, rf	3	0	0	0	0	Parker, rf	3	1	1	0	0
Buckner, lf	1	0	0	0	0	Robinson, 3b	3	0	1	2	1
Lacy, ph-lf	2	0	0	0	0	Dyer, c	3	0	0	0	0
Yeager, c	2	0	0	0	0	CANDELARIA, p	3	0	0	0	0
Rau, p	2	0	0	0	0	Totals	28	2	5	2	2
Auerbach, ph	1	0	0	0	0						
Hough, p	0	0	0	0	1						
Totals	29	0	0	0	1						

Los Angeles				0	0	0		0	0	0		0	0	0 – 0
Pittsburgh				0	0	0		0	2	0		0	0	x – 2

Los Angeles	IP.	H.	R.	ER.	BB.	SO.	Pittsburgh	IP.	H.	R.	ER.	BB.	SO.
Rau (L. 10-9)	7	5	2	2	1	6	CANDELARIA (W. 11-4)	9	0	0	0	1	7
Hough	1	0	0	0	0	0							

Double play—Los Angeles 1. Left on bases—Los Angeles 3, Pittsburgh 3. Two-base hit—Robinson. Stolen base—Stennett. Umpires—Colosi, Montague, Weyer and Runge. Time—1:45. Attendance—9,860.

AT ATLANTA—SEPTEMBER 29

San Francisco	AB.	R.	H.	RBI.	E.	Atlanta	AB.	R.	H.	RBI.	E.
Herndon, cf	5	0	2	1	0	Royster, 3b	3	0	0	0	1
Perez, 2b	5	0	0	0	0	Gilbreath, 2b	3	0	0	0	0
Matthews, lf	5	2	2	0	0	Montanez, 1b	3	0	0	0	0
Murcer, rf	4	2	1	2	0	May, lf	3	0	0	0	0
Alexander, c	4	2	1	0	0	Asselstine, cf	3	0	0	0	0
Thomasson, 1b	4	0	2	2	0	Paciorek, rf	3	0	0	0	0
Thomas, 3b	4	1	1	1	0	Murphy, c	3	0	0	0	1
LeMaster, ss	3	2	3	3	0	Chaney, ss	2	0	0	0	0
MONTEFUSCO, p	4	0	0	1	0	Capra, p	0	0	0	0	0
Totals	38	9	12	9	0	Wynn, ph	1	0	0	0	0
						Easterly, p	0	0	0	0	0
						Hanna, p	1	0	0	0	0
						Camp, p	0	0	0	0	0
						Rockett, ph-ss	1	0	0	0	0
						Gaston, ph	1	0	0	0	0
						Totals	27	0	0	0	2

San Francisco				0	4	0		1	3	0		0	0	1 – 9
Atlanta				0	0	0		0	0	0		0	0	0 – 0

San Francisco	IP.	H.	R.	ER.	BB.	SO.	Atlanta	IP.	H.	R.	ER.	BB.	SO.
M'TEFUSCO (W. 16-14)	9	0	0	0	1	4	Easterly (L. 1-1)	1⅔	6	4	4	0	1
							Hanna	2⅓*	4	4	3	2	0
							Camp	2	0	0	0	0	1
							Capra	3	2	1	1	0	2

*Pitched to four batters in fifth.

Double play—Atlanta 1. Left on bases—San Francisco 5, Atlanta 1. Two-base hits—LeMaster, Matthews, Murcer. Three-base hit—LeMaster. Sacrifice fly—LeMaster. Umpires—Davidson, Colosi, Olsen and Weyer. Time—1:59. Attendance—1,369.

John (The Count) Montefusco cradles a bottle of champagne given him by Atlanta Owner Ted Turner after the San Francisco Giants' ace righthander pitched a no-hitter against the Braves.

The only hard-hit ball against the Giants' John Montefusco in his no-hitter at Atlanta, September 29, was a liner by rookie Dale Murphy right at second baseman Marty Perez to end the eighth inning. Montefusco breezed to a 9-0 victory.

"Tonight, I only wanted to stop Willie Montanez from getting a hit," the brash Montefusco said, referring to a feud with his ex-teammate. "And I stopped the whole team."

Montefusco struck out four and permitted only one baserunner in his near-perfect effort, a walk to Jerry Royster in the fourth. Royster again became important to The Count when he flied to right fielder Bobby Murcer for the final out of the 26-year-old righthander's masterpiece.

On a night when Montefusco was a doubtful starter, he captivated a sparse Atlanta gathering on Fan Appreciation Night. They cheered the visitor's every movement.

"I was kind of sick the last three days. But, I wanted to pitch," Montefusco had explained at the time. "I really didn't feel too good before the game. But now I feel great. What a difference two hours can make."

Rick Wise Leader in Low-Hit Games

By CHRIS ROEWE

The 1976 major league season featured 68 pitching performances in which the opposition was able to produce no more than two safeties.

Four no-hit games were pitched—three in the National and one in the American. A. L. hurlers also spun eight one-hit games and 30 two-hitters for a total of 39 low-hit efforts. Senior circuit pitchers authored two one-hit gems and 24 two-hitters.

Rick Wise was the leader in low-hit efforts, pitching two one-hitters and a pair of two-hitters. The veteran Boston righthander shut out the Tigers on two hits at Boston, May 24, permitted only one single in blanking the Twins in their own ball park, June 14, pitched his second one-hitter in two weeks in whitewashing the Orioles at Fenway Park, June 29, and hurled his fourth and last shutout of the year before the hometown fans, September 9, the Tigers again getting only two hits.

Joaquin Andujar, rookie righthander of the Houston Astros, topped N. L. hurlers in this department with three two-hit games. On June 1 he stopped the hard-hitting Reds in the Astrodome, 2-1, blanked the Cubs, 2-0, in his next start in the first game of a doubleheader at Houston, June 6, and limited the Dodgers to two singles in beating them, 5-2, also at Houston, September 4.

Two other A. L. pitchers authored three two-hitters. Mike Torrez of Oakland mystified the Orioles on April 30, the Angels on September 3 and Kansas City on September 28. The Angels' Nolan Ryan numbered the Brewers, White Sox and Athletics among his victims. The fireballer's last two starts of the campaign produced two-hit shutouts—3-0 over the White Sox, September 29, and 1-0 over Oakland, October 3.

The White Sox' Ken Brett missed a no-hit game by the narrowest of margins. With two out in the ninth at Anaheim Stadium, May 26, Jerry Remy was credited with a hit on a slow roller that the third baseman could not handle. The White Sox won on 10 innings, the Angels getting their second hit of the game in their last time at bat.

A complete list of one-hit and two-hit games follows:

AMERICAN LEAGUE
One-Hit Games

May 7	Bare, Detroit vs. Chicago, 5-0—Garr, single in fourth.
May 24	Eckersley (eight innings) and Thomas (one inning), Cleveland vs. Baltimore, 4-0—Bumbry, single in first.
June 14	Wise, Boston vs. Minnesota, 5-0—Terrell, single in third.
June 21	Blyleven, Texas vs. Oakland, 1-0—McMullen, single in fifth.
June 26	Pattin (seven and two-thirds innings) and Mingori (one and one-third innings), Kansas City vs. California, 3-0—Collins, single in sixth.
June 29	Wise, Boston vs. Baltimore, 2-0—Blair, single in sixth.
Aug. 10	Palmer, Baltimore vs. Minnesota, 2-0—Cubbage, single in second.
Aug. 28	Blue, Oakland vs. Detroit, 5-2—Stanley, homer in ninth.

Two-Hit Games

April 13	Slaton, Milwaukee vs. Detroit, 1-0—Oglivie, single in first; Rodriguez, double in second.
April 17	Roberts, Detroit vs. California, 2-0—Bochte, single in seventh; Chalk, single in eighth.
April 21	Palmer (eight and two-thirds innings) and Miller (one-third inning), Baltimore vs. California, 5-1—Bochte, single in fifth; Remy, single in ninth.
April 23	Eckersley, Cleveland vs. Oakland, 3-0—Williams, single in second; Washington, single in ninth.
April 26	Tanana, California vs. Milwaukee, lost, 7-1—Money, homer in first; Yount, single in fourth.
April 28	Roberts, Detroit vs. Oakland, 8-1—Campaneris, single in third; McMullen, double in ninth.
April 30	Torrez, Oakland vs. Baltimore, 11-1—Bumbry, single in sixth; Robinson, single in eighth.
May 5	Palmer, Baltimore vs. Chicago, 2-0—Kelly, single in first; Garr, single in ninth.
May 15	Fidrych, Detroit vs. Cleveland, 2-1—Bell and Manning, singles in seventh.

May 24 Wise, Boston vs. Detroit, 3-0—Johnson, single in first; LeFlore, single in third.
May 26 Brett (10 innings) and Carroll (one inning), Chicago vs. California, 1-0—Remy, single in ninth; Melton,
        single in tenth.
June 15 Ryan, California vs. Milwaukee, 1-0—Money, single in first; Sutherland, single in eighth.
June 17 Ross, California vs. Milwaukee, 2-0—Porter, single in sixth; Joshua, single in ninth.
June 21 Garland, Baltimore vs. Boston, 2-0—Petrocelli, single in eighth; Miller, single in ninth.
July 4 Redfern (six and two-thirds innings), Albury (no inning) and Campbell (two and one-third innings), Min-
        nesota vs. California, 9-5 (second game)—Guerrero, single and Jackson, homer, in seventh.
July 16 Holtzman, New York vs. Texas, 3-0—Burroughs, single in fourth; Howell, single in seventh.
July 26 Blyleven, Texas vs. Minnesota, 3-0—Braun, single in fourth; Kusick, single in seventh.
Aug. 2 Alexander, New York vs. Detroit, 1-0—Staub, single in seventh; Johnson, single in ninth.
Aug. 7 Luebber (eight and two-thirds innings) and Campbell (one-third inning), Minnesota vs. Texas, 3-1—How-
        ell and Hargrove, singles in ninth.
Aug. 11 Tanana, California vs. Boston, 6-0—Evans, single in second; Burleson, single in sixth.
Aug. 20 Hassler, Kansas City vs. Milwaukee, 3-0—Sutherland, single in second; Lezcano, single in sixth.
Aug. 31 Goltz, Minnesota vs. Milwaukee, 4-0 (first game)—Sharp, single in seventh; Johnson, single in eighth.
Sept. 3 Torrez, Oakland vs. California, 3-0—Torres, singles in third and fifth.
Sept. 9 Wise, Boston vs. Detroit, 5-0—Mankowski and Oglivie, singles in seventh.
Sept. 15 Garland, Baltimore vs. Detroit, 1-0 (six innings)—Staub, single in first; Johnson, single in second.
Sept. 25 Goltz, Minnesota vs. California, 6-0—Collins, single in first; Guerrero, single in ninth.
Sept. 25 Tiant, Boston vs. Baltimore, 1-0—R. Jackson, single in fourth; Duncan, single in sixth.
Sept. 28 Torrez, Oakland vs. Kansas City, 1-0—McRae, single in second; Rojas, single in fifth.
Sept. 29 Ryan, California vs. Chicago, 3-0—Garr, single in first; Spencer, double in ninth.
Oct. 3 Ryan, California vs. Oakland, 1-0—Gross, single in fourth; Garner, single in sixth.

NATIONAL LEAGUE
One-Hit Games

June 4 Messersmith, Atlanta vs. Montreal, 2-0—Mangual, single in ninth.
Oct. 2 Niekro, Atlanta vs. Cincinnati, 3-0—Geronimo, double in ninth.

Two-Hit Games

April 25 Candelaria, Pittsburgh vs. San Francisco, 3-0—Murcer, single in first; Montanez, double in fifth.
May 8 Alcala (seven innings) and Borbon (two innings), Cincinnati vs. Chicago, 14-4—Cardenal, single in first;
        Madlock, homer in fifth.
May 9 Strom, San Diego vs. New York, 4-0—Torre, single in seventh; Harrelson, single in ninth.
May 9 Rogers, Montreal vs. San Francisco, 8-0 (second game)—Murcer, single in first; Rader, single in third.
May 15 Warthen, Montreal vs. Atlanta, 6-1 (second game)—Lacy, single in first; Perez, single in seventh.
June 1 Andujar, Houston vs. Cincinnati, 2-1—Flynn, single in fifth; Perez, single in ninth.
June 1 Halicki, San Francisco vs. Los Angeles, 6-0—Lopes, single in fourth; Garvey, single in seventh.
June 4 R. Reuschel, Chicago vs. Houston, lost 1-0—Cedeno, single in first; Cruz, single in second.
June 6 Andujar, Houston vs. Chicago, 2-0 (first game)—Madlock, single in fourth; Cardenal, single in ninth.
June 12 D'Acquisto (six innings), Moffitt (two innings) and Heaverlo (one inning), San Francisco vs. New York,
        lost, 3-1—Milner, double in third; Kingman, single in seventh.
June 18 Seaver, New York vs. San Francisco, 3-2—Evans, homer in fifth; Thomas, triple in sixth.
June 23 Richard (eight innings) and Forsch (one inning), Houston vs. Los Angeles, lost, 1-0—Rhoden, single and
        Buckner, double in sixth.
July 5 Hooton, Los Angeles vs. Philadelphia, 6-0—Maddox, single in third and double in eighth.
July 11 Halicki, San Francisco vs. Chicago, 2-0—Cardenal, single in seventh; Swisher, single in eighth.
July 18 Lolich, New York vs. Atlanta, 2-0—Chaney, single in seventh; Wynn, single in fourth.
July 21 Demery (eight and two-thirds innings) and Giusti (one-third inning), Pittsburgh vs. Houston (second
        game), 6-1—Cruz, single in seventh; Watson, single in ninth.
July 26 Dierker, Houston vs. San Diego, 7-0—Hernandez, single in third; Grubb, double in fourth.
Aug. 3 Hooton, Los Angeles vs. Houston, 2-0—Gross and Cedeno, singles in first.
Aug. 21 Sutton, Los Angeles vs. Pittsburgh, 5-1—Parker, homer in eighth; Sanguillen, double in ninth.
Sept. 4 Zachry, Cincinnati vs. Atlanta, 5-1—Paciorek and Correll, singles in second.
Sept. 4 Andujar, Houston vs. Los Angeles, 5-2—Lopes, single in first; Smith, single in sixth.
Sept. 11 Koosman, New York vs. St. Louis, 4-1—Mumphrey, single in sixth; Simmons, single in seventh.
Sept. 18 Halicki (four innings) and Lavelle (five innings), San Francisco vs. Cincinnati, 5-0—Rose, double in first;
        Geronimo, single in fifth.
Sept. 21 Warthen, Montreal vs. New York, 4-0—Mazzilli, singles in fifth and eighth.

Another 300-Strikeout Season for Ryan

By LARRY WIGGE

For a record fourth time in his major league career, California righthander Nolan Ryan struck out more than 300 batters in 1976 as he captured his fourth strikeout title in the last five seasons.

Ryan fanned 327 American League batters and surpassed the major league mark of three 300-strikeout seasons he had shared with Sandy Koufax and two pre-1900 pitchers—Tim Keefe and Amos Rusie.

Angel teammate Frank Tanana, who had 261 strikeouts during the season, struck out 15 Oakland batters September 6. However, California lost 2-1 after Tanana had departed.

The only other big league hurler to reach the 15-strikeout mark in 1976 was Ryan, who had three such games.

On June 19, Ryan posted 15 strikeouts against the Red Sox in a 5-3 victory. He fanned 17 Tigers at Detroit on August 18 in an 11-inning 5-4 triumph. In a 3-2 victory at Chicago September 10, Ryan whiffed 18 White Sox. It was the fourth time in Ryan's career that he had as many as 18 strikeouts in a game.

Tom Seaver of the Mets, who led the National League in strikeouts with 235, extended his major league record for most consecutive seasons with 200 or more strikeouts to nine.

Seaver's teammate, Mickey Lolich, who announced his retirement after the season, fanned 120 to bring his lifetime total to 2,799. He ranks fifth on the all-time list.

A complete recap of all 15-strikeout performances in 1976 follows:

Date	Pitcher—Club—Opp.	Place	IP.	H.	R.	ER.	BB.	SO.	Result
June 19	—Ryan, Angels vs. Red Sox	H	9	6	3	2	4	15	W 5-3
Aug. 18*	—Ryan, Angels vs. Tigers	A	10	9	4	3	5	17	W 5-4
Sept. 6†	—Tanana, Angels vs. A's	H	10	8	1	1	4	15	L 1-2
Sept. 10	—Ryan, Angels vs. White Sox	A	9	3	2	2	9	18	W 3-2

*Did not complete 11-inning game.   †Not involved in 11-inning decision.

Ryan had 10 or more strikeouts 13 times in '76, boosting his career total of 10-strikeout games to 84. Tanana, with 11 similar efforts, combined with Ryan for 24 of the 52 A. L. big strikeout contests. There were only 26 such strikeout totals in the N. L.

Following is a list of all pitchers with 10-strikeout games and number of times achieved:

AMERICAN LEAGUE: Baltimore (3)—Palmer 2, Garland. Boston (1)—Tiant. California (25)—Ryan 13, Tanana 11, Ross. Chicago (4)—Brett, Gossage, Knapp, Kravec. Cleveland (8)—Eckersley 8. Detroit—None. Kansas City—None. Milwaukee (1)—Slaton. Minnesota (2)—Blyleven, Goltz. New York—None. Oakland (2)—Blue, P. Mitchell. Texas (6)—Blyleven 2, Perry 2, Hargan, Umbarger.

NATIONAL LEAGUE: Atlanta (2)—Niekro, Ruthven. Chicago—None. Cincinnati (2)—Norman 2. Houston (4)—Richard 3, Cosgrove. Los Angeles—None. Montreal (1)—Dunning. New York (10)—Koosman 4, Seaver 4, Matlack, Swan. Philadelphia (2)—Carlton 2. Pittsburgh (2)—Candelaria 2. St. Louis (1)—McGlothen. San Diego—none. San Francisco (2)—Halicki, Montefusco.

Campbell and Eastwick Best in Relief

By CHRIS ROEWE

Bill Campbell of the Twins and Rawly Eastwick of the Reds were the winners of the Fireman of the Year awards presented annually by THE SPORTING NEWS to the top relief pitchers in each major league.

With one point given for each save and one for each victory in relief, both Campbell and Eastwick totaled 37 points. The Twin righthander led all relievers in wins with 17 and had 20 saves while Eastwick led in saves with 26 and won 11 for the world champion Reds.

Campbell had quite a year for the Twins. His 78 games pitched led all A. L. moundsmen and his 168 innings set a league record for a relief pitcher. The old mark was 165 innings by Eddie Fisher of the White Sox in 1965. Campbell's 17 wins tied the A. L. record for victories by a reliever, set by John Hiller of the Tigers in 1974.

The A. L. Fireman Derby was a close contest from start to finish with veteran rescue artists Rollie Fingers of the A's and Sparky Lyle of the Yankees in contention all of the way. Fingers finished second with 20 saves and 13 victories and Lyle was third with seven wins and a league-leading 23 saves.

Eastwick had no real competition and won the N. L. race going away. The young Cincinnati righthander, who finished second in 1975, his rookie year, had a seven-point advantage over the second-place finisher, Charlie Hough of the Dodgers. Hough, who took over as Los Angeles' premier fireman after the trade of Mike Marshall to the Braves, totaled 30 points, one more than Skip Lockwood, who won recognition as top man in the Mets' bullpen.

Last year's Fireman Award winners did not challenge the winners. The Cardinals' Al Hrabosky, defending N. L. titlist, finished in seventh place with 21 points and Rich Gossage of the White Sox, the 1975 A. L. winner, was converted to a starting pitcher by Paul Richards, who returned to the helm of the Chicago club.

A complete list of saves and victories in relief by major league pitchers in 1976 follows:

AMERICAN LEAGUE

Pitcher—Club	Saves	Relief Wins	Tot. Pts.	Pitcher—Club	Saves	Relief Wins	Tot. Pts.
Campbell, Minnesota	20	17	37	Carroll, Chicago	6	4	10
Fingers, Oakland	20	13	33	Rodriguez, Milwaukee	8	2	10
Lyle, New York	23	7	30	Burgmeier, Minnesota	1	8	9
Hiller, Detroit	13	11	24	Jackson, Balt-New York	4	5	9
Kern, Cleveland	15	9	24	Miller, Baltimore	7	2	9
Littell, Kansas City	16	8	24	Hoerner, Texas	8	0	8
LaRoche, Cleveland	21	1	22	Cleveland, Boston	2	5	7
Hamilton, Chicago	10	6	16	Thomas, Cleveland	6	1	7
F. Martinez, NY-Balt.	10	5	15	Buskey, Cleveland	1	5	6
Mingori, Kansas City	10	5	15	Grilli, Detroit	3	3	6
Frisella, Milwaukee	9	5	14	Holdsworth, Baltimore	2	4	6
Drago, California	6	7	13	Pattin, Kansas City	5	1	6
Foucault, Texas	5	8	13	Scott, California	3	3	6
Murphy, Milwaukee-Boston	9	4	13	Bahnsen, Oakland	0	5	5
Tidrow, New York	10	3	13	Bird, Kansas City	2	3	5
Willoughby, Boston	10	3	13	Brewer, California	2	3	5
Castro, Milwaukee	8	4	12	Garland, Baltimore	1	4	5
Lindblad, Oakland	5	6	11	Hargan, Texas	1	4	5
Todd, Oakland	4	7	11	House, Boston	4	1	5

Pitcher—Club	Saves	Relief Wins	Tot. Pts.
Bibby, Cleveland	1	3	4
Gura, Kansas City	1	3	4
Lee, Boston	3	1	4
Verhoeven, California	4	0	4
Albury, Minnesota	0	3	3
Bacsik, Texas	0	3	3
Barrios, Chicago	3	0	3
Hood, Cleveland	1	2	3
Johnson, Minnesota	0	3	3
Sadecki, Milwaukee	1	2	3
Terpko, Texas	0	3	3
Alexander, Balt-New York	0	2	2
Brett, New York-Chicago	2	0	2
Brown, Cleveland	0	2	2
Crawford, Detroit	2	0	2
Eckersley, Cleveland	1	1	2
Hall, Kansas City	1	1	2
Hartzell, California	2	0	2
Hughes, Minnesota	0	2	2
Laxton, Detroit	2	0	2
Lemanczyk, Detroit	0	2	2
Luebber, Minnesota	2	0	2
Monge, California	0	2	2
Vuckovich, Chicago	0	2	2

One Save—Briles, Texas; Cuellar, Baltimore; Forster, Chicago; Gossage, Chicago; Pagan, New York-Baltimore.

One Relief Win—Abbott, Oakland; Augustine, Milwaukee; Bruno, Kansas City; Jenkins, Boston; Jones, Boston; Knapp, Chicago; J. D. Martinez, Baltimore; Pole, Boston; York, New York.

NATIONAL LEAGUE

Pitcher—Club	Saves	Relief Wins	Tot. Pts.
Eastwick, Cincinnati	26	11	37
Hough, Los Angeles	18	12	30
Lockwood, New York	19	10	29
Metzger, San Diego	16	11	27
Forsch, Houston	19	4	23
Lavelle, San Francisco	12	10	22
Hrabosky, St. Louis	13	8	21
Garber, Philadelphia	11	9	20
Marshall, LA-Atlanta	14	6	20
Moffitt, San Francisco	14	6	20
Reed, Philadelphia	14	6	20
McGraw, Philadelphia	11	7	18
Murray, Montreal	13	4	17
Sutter, Chicago	10	6	16
Devine, Atlanta	9	5	14
Knowles, Chicago	9	5	14
Tekulve, Pittsburgh	9	5	14
Moose, Pittsburgh	10	3	13
Borbon, Cincinnati	8	4	12
Giusti, Pittsburgh	6	5	11
Sosa, Atlanta-Los Angeles	4	6	10
McEnaney, Cincinnati	7	2	9
Apodaca, New York	5	3	8
Pentz, Houston	5	3	8
Zamora, Chicago	3	5	8
Greif, San Diego-St. Louis	6	1	7
P. Reuschel, Chicago	3	4	7
Coleman, Chicago	4	2	6
Demery, Pittsburgh	2	4	6
Griffin, Houston	0	5	5
Heaverlo, San Francisco	1	4	5
Hernandez, Pitts-Chicago	3	2	5
Leon, Atlanta	3	2	5
Sarmiento, Cincinnati	0	5	5
Wallace, St. Louis	2	3	5
Dal Canton, Atlanta	1	3	4
Schueler, Philadelphia	3	1	4
Walker, St. Louis	3	1	4
Caldwell, San Francisco	2	1	3
Freisleben, San Diego	1	2	3
Garman, Chicago	1	2	3
Granger, Montreal	2	1	3
Hardy, Houston	3	0	3
Kerrigan, Montreal	1	2	3
Rasmussen, St. Louis	0	3	3
Scherman, Montreal	1	2	3
Schultz, Chicago	2	1	3
Stanhouse, Montreal	1	2	3
Twitchell, Philadelphia	1	2	3
Underwood, Philadelphia	2	1	3
Wall, Los Angeles	1	2	3
Barlow, Houston	0	2	2
Billingham, Cincinnati	1	1	2
Darcy, Cincinnati	2	0	2
Espinosa, New York	0	2	2
Folkers, San Diego	0	2	2
Fryman, Montreal	2	0	2
Gullett, Cincinnati	1	1	2
Henderson, Cincinnati	0	2	2
Reuss, Pittsburgh	2	0	2
Sambito, Houston	1	1	2
Sanders, New York	1	1	2
Taylor, Montreal	0	2	2
Torrealba, Atlanta	2	0	2
Williams, San Francisco	1	1	2
Zachry, Cincinnati	0	2	2

One Save—Beard, Atlanta; Candelaria, Pittsburgh; Curtis, St. Louis; Frisella, St. Louis; Kison, Pittsburgh; Lerch, Philadelphia; Lonborg, Philadelphia; McLaughlin, Houston; Messersmith, Atlanta; Moret, Atlanta; R. Reuschel, Chicago; Reynolds, San Diego; Rogers, Montreal; Rooker, Pittsburgh; Toms, San Francisco.

One Relief Win—Alcala, Cincinnati; Capilla, St. Louis; Carrithers, Montreal; Downing, Los Angeles; Dressler, San Francisco; Frailing, Chicago; Halicki, San Francisco; Hall, New York; Hinton, Cincinnati; Johnson, San Diego; Lang, Montreal; Myrick, New York; Norman, Cincinnati; Proly, St. Louis; Spillner, San Diego; Sutton, Los Angeles.

Blyleven Best in 1-0 Battles

By CHRIS ROEWE

The number of 1-0 games zoomed to 71 in 1976, an increase of 28 over the previous season.

Bert Blyleven was the leader in 1-0 victories with four. Traded by the Twins to the Rangers, June 1, the righthander with the explosive curve blanked the A's on one hit in 10 innings, June 21, stopped the White Sox, again in 10 innings, June 26, whitewashed the Angels, August 5, and shut out the Royals, September 25. Blyleven also was the loser in two minimum-score games, dropping tough decisions to the White Sox and Angels.

Home runs provided the only scores in 15 of these struggles. Jerry Morales of the Cubs assumed the hero role twice, providing the only run needed by Steve Stone on August 6 and Ray Burris on September 19.

The complete list of 1-0 games, including the winning and losing pitchers and the innings in which the runs were scored, follows:

AMERICAN LEAGUE (34)

Date		Winner	Loser	Inning
APRIL—				
9	–	*Palmer, Baltimore	Jenkins, Boston	
13	–	Slaton, Milwaukee	*Hiller, Detroit	9
26	–	*Colborn, Milw.	Tanana, California	1
27	–	Ellis, New York	Perry, Texas	9
MAY—				
12	–	Singer, Texas	*Kirkwood, California	8
22	–	Hunter, New York	*House, Boston	11
25	–	Travers, Milw.	Ellis, New York	11
26	–	*Brett, Chicago	Kirkwood, California	11
JUNE—				
2	–	*Hamilton, Chicago	Umbarger, Texas	11
15	–	Ryan, California	Colborn, Milwaukee	6
21	–	Blyleven, Texas	P. Mitchell, Oakland	10
25	–	Ellis, New York	Travers, Milwaukee	10
26	–	Blyleven, Texas	Brett, Chicago	10
29	–	Fitzmorris, K. C.	Goltz, Minnesota	10
JULY—				
2	–	B. Johnson, Chi.	Blyleven, Texas	1
9	–	Leonard, K. C.	Fidrych, Detroit	4
16	–	Fidrych, Detroit	*Fingers, Oakland	11
27	–	Blue, Oakland	Gossage, Chicago	7
28	–	Roberts, Detroit	Augustine, Milwaukee	9
29	–	R. May, Baltimore	Fidrych, Detroit	4
AUGUST—				
2	–	Alexander, N. Y.	Roberts, Detroit	3
3	–	Eckersley, Cleve.	*Murphy, Boston	10
5	–	Blyleven, Texas	Ross, California	2
24	–	Augustine, Milw.	*Foucault, Texas	10
SEPTEMBER—				
7	–	*Redfern, Minn.	Perry, Texas	3
10a	–	Bare, Detroit	Cleveland, Boston	1
11	–	Torrez, Oakland	Briles, Texas	8
15b	–	Garland, Balt.	Roberts, Detroit	8
20	–	Ryan, California	Blyleven, Texas	6
25	–	Blyleven, Texas	Hassler, Kansas City	4
25	–	Tiant, Boston	Grimsley, Baltimore	5
28	–	Torrez, Oakland	Pattin, Kansas City	7
OCTOBER—				
2	–	*Cleveland, Boston	J. D. Martinez, Balt.	1
3	–	Ryan, California	Torrez, Oakland	7

NATIONAL LEAGUE (37)

Date		Winner	Loser	Inning
APRIL—				
10	–	Matlack, N. Y.	*Fryman, Montreal	4
21	–	*Barlow, Houston	*Wall, Los Angeles	16
MAY—				
12	–	*Garman, Chicago	*Moffitt, San Fran.	11
23‡	–	Mon'fusco, S. F.	*Leon, Atlanta	10
JUNE—				
4	–	Cosgrove, Houston	R. Reuschel, Chicago	2
17	–	Lockwood, N. Y.	*Hough, Los Angeles	14
23	–	Rhoden, Los Ang.	*Richard, Houston	6
25	–	Halicki, S. F.	Hooton, Los Angeles	9
JULY—				
5	–	*Renko, Chicago	Strom, San Diego	6
6	–	Richard, Houston	*Lockwood, New York	10
11	–	Andujar, Houston	Rogers, Montreal	5
16	–	Halicki, S. F.	Kaat, Philadelphia	9
17	–	Andujar, Houston	*Seaver, New York	1
25	–	Rau, Los Angeles	*Freisleben, S. Diego	7
25	–	McLaughlin, Hou.	Halicki, San Fran.	10
28	–	*Giusti, Pitts.	*Sanders, New York	13
AUGUST—				
4	–	Ruthven, Atlanta	Jones, San Diego	9
4	–	Richard, Houston	*Rau, Los Angeles	6
6†	–	Stone, Chicago	*Kerrigan, Montreal	9
15	–	Koosman, N. Y.	*Nolan, Cincinnati	5
19	–	Can'laria, Pitts.	Barr, San Francisco	4
22	–	Matlack, N. Y.	*Jones, San Diego	7
SEPTEMBER—				
1	–	*Hrabosky, St. L.	*Eastwick, Cincinnati	11
1	–	Koosman, N. Y.	Montefusco, San Fran.	8
1	–	McLaughlin, Hou.	*Kaat, Philadelphia	7
3	–	Seaver, New York	*Carlton, Philadelphia	4
5	–	*Hrabosky, St. L.	*Coleman, Chicago	11
5	–	Fryman, Montreal	*Reuss, Pittsburgh	8
8	–	*Halicki, S. F.	*Hough, Los Angeles	11
17†	–	Devine, Atlanta	*Hough, Los Angeles	12
19‡	–	Fryman, Montreal	LaGrow, St. Louis	8
19	–	Burris, Chicago	*Lonborg, Philadelphia	2
28	–	Richard, Houston	Hooton, Los Angeles	1
29	–	Renko, Chicago	Demery, Pittsburgh	6
29	–	*Wall, Los Ang.	*Sambito, Houston	7
OCTOBER—				
3†	–	Rooker, Pit'burgh	Denny, St. Louis	6
3‡	–	Reuss, Pittsburgh	Falcone, St. Louis	9

*Did not pitch complete game. †First game of doubleheader. ‡Second game of doubleheader. aFive innings. bSix innings.

Phillies Lead in Grand Slams

By CHRIS ROEWE

There were 51 grand-slam homers hit in the majors in 1976, one fewer than the previous year. National League hitters produced 28 and 23 were slugged by American League batsmen.

Club leader in grand slams was Philadelphia with seven. Greg Luzinski hit two and one each were slugged by Richie Allen, Bob Boone, Ollie Brown, Garry Maddox and Bobby Tolan. Baltimore was the A.L. leader with six.

Best individual total was three, shared by John Milner of the Mets, Rod Carew of the Twins and the Orioles' Reggie Jackson. The lefthanded-hitting Jackson connected off three lefthanded pitchers—Jerry Augustine of the Brewers and Ken Brett and Terry Forster of the White Sox.

Jackson and teammate Lee May both hit homers with the bases loaded in a doubleheader with the White Sox at Baltimore, August 14. May rapped his fourmaster in the first game and Jackson homered in the nightcap, both blows providing the winning margin as the Orioles won two free-scoring games, 8-6 and 6-5.

Willie Stargell's grand slam on August 5 was the 10th of his career. The Pirate slugger became the eighth National Leaguer to hit 10 or more.

The complete list of grand-slam homers with the inning in which each was hit in parentheses, follows:

AMERICAN LEAGUE (23)

APRIL
27   Staub, Detroit vs. Fingers, Oakland .... (8)

MAY
12   R. Jackson, Balt. vs. Augustine, Mil. .... (6)
15†   Bonds, California vs. Redfern, Minn. .... (6)
21   DeCinces, Baltimore vs. Bare, Det. .... (1)
22   Singleton, Baltimore vs. Crawford, Det. .... (9)
29   Manning, Cleveland vs. Murphy, Mil. .... (10)

JUNE
22   Bell, Chicago vs. Busby, Kansas City .... (3)
22   Darwin, Boston vs. R. May, Baltimore........ (1)
25*   Harrah, Texas vs. Hamilton, Chicago .... (9)
26   Carew, Minnesota vs. P. Mitchell, Oak. .... (2)

JULY
4†   Carew, Minnesota vs. Monge, California .... (8)
4†   Jackson, California vs. Campbell, Minn. .... (7)
7   Cubbage, Minnesota vs. Castro, Mil. .... (8)
22   Spikes, Cleveland vs. Tanana, Calif............ (1)
25   Stanton, California vs. Foucault, Texas ...... (11)
30   Wynegar, Minnesota vs. Bosman, Oakland   (5)

AUGUST
7   Chambliss, New York vs. R. May, Balt...... (9)
14*   L. May, Baltimore vs. Forster, Chi. .... (2)
14†   R. Jackson, Baltimore vs. Brett, Chi......... (5)
22*   R. Jackson, Baltimore vs. Forster, Chi. ...... (9)

SEPTEMBER
9   Carew, Minnesota vs. Hargan, Texas .... (7)
10   Gamble, New York vs. Slaton, Milwaukee .. (8)
29   Nettles, New York vs. Tiant, Boston............ (2)

NATIONAL LEAGUE (28)

APRIL
13   Winfield, San Diego vs. Wall, L. A. .... (7)
24   Luzinski, Phila. vs. Messersmith, Atl. .... (3)

MAY
5   Tolan, Philadelphia vs. Niekro, Houston .... (6)
9   Griffey, Cincinnati vs. Zamora, Chicago .... (3)
21   Winfield, San Diego vs. Nolan, Cin. .... (1)
23   Foster, Cincinnati vs. Folkers, S. D............ (6)
25   Murcer, San Fran. vs. Richard, Hous. .... (5)
28   Crawford, St. Louis vs. Swan, New York .... (5)

JUNE
7   Cey, Los Angeles vs. Reed, Phila. .... (1)
18   Madlock, Chicago vs. Leon, Atlanta .... (7)
22   Paciorek, Atlanta vs. Cosgrove, Hous. .... (3)
23†   Evans, San Francisco vs. Folkers, S. D....... (3)
26   Rivera, Montreal vs. Reuss, Pitts.............. (3)
26   Milner, New York, vs. Bonham, Chicago..... (3)
27   Boone, Phila. vs. McGlothen, St. L. .... (4)

JULY
1   Milner, New York vs. Wallace, St. L. .... (6)
2   Allen, Philadelphia vs. Reuss, Pitt............. (5)
5   Morgan, Cincinnati vs. Dunning, Mont........ (5)
25   Brown, Philadelphia vs. Giusti, Pitts.......... (8)

AUGUST
1*   Luzinski, Philadelphia vs. Apodaca, N. Y... (5)
3†   Maddox, Philadelphia vs. Stone, Chi. .... (4)
5   Stargell, Pittsburgh vs. Matlack, N. Y. .... (6)
14   Watson, Hous. vs. Candelaria, Pitts. .... (6)

SEPTEMBER
6   Morgan, Cincinnati vs. Richard, Houston ... (3)
15*   Ferguson, St. Louis vs. Lolich, New York .. (3)
27   Milner, New York vs. Lang, Montreal .... (6)
29   Garrett, Montreal vs. Seaver, New York .... (4)
29   Rader, San Diego vs. Norman, Cincinnati .. (1)

*First game of doubleheader. †Second game of doubleheader.

— 329 —

Schmidt Tenth to Club Four Homers in Game

By LARRY WIGGE

Wind-swept Wrigley Field was the site of nine home runs April 17, including a record four homers by Philadelphia's strongboy third baseman Mike Schmidt, as the Phillies outslugged the Chicago Cubs, 18-16, in one of the most bizarre games of 1976.

Schmidt became only the 10th player in major league history to club four home runs in a game. The last was San Francisco's Willie Mays on April 30, 1961.

Demoted from his usual third spot to sixth in the batting order because he was hitting a dismal .167, Schmidt responded with five hits. In his previous four big league seasons, Mike had connected for only five homers at the cozy Chicago ball park.

In a game in which the Cubs jumped to a 12-1 lead after three innings, only to be beaten in 10 innings, Schmidt started his memorable day with a fly ball to center field in the second inning.

After a leadoff single in the fourth, Schmidt followed with four consecutive round-trippers.

Against Cub starter Rick Reuschel, Mike cleared the left field screen with a man on base in the fifth and skied a solo shot for the circuit in the seventh.

Reliever Paul Reuschel was the victim of Schmidt's third homer, a three-run clout to center in the eighth. Darold Knowles served up a fastball to Schmidt's liking in the 10th for a two-run homer over the left-center field wall.

The box score of Schmidt's record-tying performance follows:

AT CHICAGO–APRIL 17

Philadelphia	AB.	R.	H.	RBI.	E.
Cash, 2b	6	1	2	2	0
Bowa, ss	6	3	3	1	0
Johnstone, rf	5	2	4	2	0
Luzinski, lf	5	0	1	1	0
Brown, lf	0	0	0	0	0
Allen, 1b	5	2	1	2	0
SCHMIDT, 3b	6	4	5	8	0
Maddox, cf	5	2	2	1	0
McGraw, p	0	0	0	0	0
McCarver, ph	1	1	1	0	0
Underwood, p	0	0	0	0	0
Lonborg, p	0	0	0	0	0
Boone, c	6	1	3	1	0
Carlton, p	1	0	0	0	0
Schueler, p	0	0	0	0	0
Garber, p	0	0	0	0	0
Hutton, ph	0	0	0	0	0
Reed, p	0	0	0	0	0
Martin, ph	1	0	0	0	0
Twitchell, p	0	0	0	0	0
Tolan, ph-cf	3	2	2	0	0
Totals	50	18	24	18	0

Chicago	AB.	R.	H.	RBI.	E.
Monday, cf	6	3	4	4	0
Cardenal, lf	5	1	1	0	0
Summers, lf	0	0	0	0	0
Mitterwald, ph	1	0	0	0	0
Wallis, lf	1	0	0	0	0
Madlock, 3b	7	2	3	3	0
Morales, rf	5	2	1	0	0
Thornton, 1b	4	3	1	1	0
Trillo, 2b	5	0	2	3	0
Swisher, c	6	1	3	4	0
Rosello, ss	4	1	2	1	0
Kelleher, ss	2	0	1	0	0
R. Reuschel, p	1	2	0	0	0
Garman, p	0	0	0	0	0
Knowles, p	0	0	0	0	0
P. Reuschel, p	0	0	0	0	0
Schultz, p	0	0	0	0	0
Adams, ph	1	1	1	0	0
Totals	48	16	19	16	0

Philadelphia	0	1	0	1	2	0	3	5	3	3 –	18
Chicago	0	7	5	1	0	0	0	0	2	1 –	16

Philadelphia	IP.	H.	R.	ER.	BB.	SO.
Carlton	1⅔	7	7	7	2	1
Schueler	⅔	3	3	3	0	0
Garber	⅔	2	2	2	1	1
Reed	2	1	1	1	1	1
Twitchell	2	0	0	0	1	1
McGraw (W. 1-1)	2	4	2	2	1	2
Underwood	⅔	2	1	1	0	1
Lonborg (Save 1)	⅓	0	0	0	0	0

Chicago	IP.	H.	R.	ER.	BB.	SO.
R. Reuschel	7	14	7	7	1	4
Garman	⅔	4	5	5	1	1
Knowles (L. 1-1)	1⅓*	3	4	4	1	0
P. Reuschel	0†	3	2	2	0	0
Schultz	1	0	0	0	0	0

*Pitched to one batter in tenth.
†Pitched to three batters in tenth.

Double plays—Philadelphia 1, Chicago 1. Left on bases—Philadelphia 8, Chicago 12. Two-base hits—Cardenal, Madlock, Thornton, Boone, Adams. Three-base hits—Johnstone, Bowa. Home runs—Maddox, Swisher, Monday 2, SCHMIDT 4, Boone. Sacrifice hits—R. Reuschel, Johnstone. Sacrifice flies—Luzinski, Cash. Hit by pitcher—By Schueler (R. Reuschel), by Garber (Thornton), by Twitchell (Monday). Balk—Schultz. Umpires—Vargo, Olsen, Davidson and Rennert. Time—3:42. Attendance—28,287.

In addition to Schmidt's big-homer game, five other major leaguers hit three home runs in a game in 1976.

Boston's Carl Yastrzemski, with the only American League three-homer bonanza, started the power show at Detroit May 19. Three days later, St. Louis' Reggie Smith capped his three-homer game in the ninth for a victory at Philadelphia.

Dave Kingman of the New York Mets exhibited his muscle for three homers at Los Angeles June 4. Pittsburgh's Bill Robinson hit three against the Padres at Three Rivers Stadium in a 15-inning loss the following day, and Gary Matthews of San Francisco homered three times against Houston September 25.

Following is a complete listing of all three-homer games in 1976:

Date	Player—Opposition	Place	AB.	R.	H.	2B.	3B.	HR.	RBI.	Result
April 17*	Schmidt, Phillies vs. Cubs	A	6	4	5	0	0	4	8	W 18-16
May 19	Yastrzemski, Red Sox vs. Tigers	A	4	4	4	0	0	3	4	W 9-2
May 22	Smith, Cardinals vs. Phillies	A	5	3	3	0	0	3	5	W 7-6
June 4	Kingman, Mets vs. Dodgers	A	5	3	3	0	0	3	8	W 11-0
June 5†	Robinson, Pirates vs. Padres	H	8	3	4	0	0	3	4	L 11-9
Sept. 25	Matthews, Giants vs. Astros	H	4	3	3	0	0	3	5	W 10-0

*10-inning game. †15-inning game.

Kingman paced the majors with seven multiple-homer games in 1976. A listing of players with two or more homers in a game and the number of times achieved follows:

AMERICAN LEAGUE: Baltimore (2)—L. May 2. Boston (5)—Rice 3, Yastrzemski 2. California (2)—Herrmann, Jones. Chicago (1)—L. Johnson. Cleveland (5)—Carty 2, Hendrick 2, Powell. Detroit (3)—Oglivie, Stanley, Thompson. Kansas City (3)—Mayberry 2, Otis. Milwaukee—None. Minnesota (2)—Ford, Wynegar. New York (6)—Nettles 4, Gamble, White. Oakland (6)—Tenace 3, Bando 2, Baylor. Texas (4)—Harrah 2, Burroughs, Grieve.

NATIONAL LEAGUE: Atlanta (4)—Wynn 2, Gaston, Montanez. Chicago (4)—Monday 3, Morales. Cincinnati (11)—Foster 3, Morgan 3, Armbrister, Bailey, Bench, Concepcion, Perez. Houston (2)—Watson 2. Los Angeles (3)—Cey, Cruz, Smith. Montreal (1)—Parrish. New York (9)—Kingman 7, Milner, Torre. Philadelphia (6)—Schmidt 4, Allen, Christenson. Pittsburgh (3)—Robinson 2, Parker. St. Louis (1)—Smith. San Diego (1)—Grubb. San Francisco (7)—Matthews 3, Murcer 3, Evans.

Jose Cardenal Joins Select Company

By CHRIS ROEWE

Jose Cardenal became a member of the select group of major leaguers who have made more than five hits in one game when he had six safeties as the Cubs edged the Giants, 6-5, in the first of two games at Candlestick Park, May 2.

The much-traveled Chicago outfielder singled in the first, doubled in a run in the fourth, hit a two-run homer in the fifth, beat out a hit in the eighth, popped out in the 10th, singled in the 12th and singled home the winning run in the 14th.

Cardenal was the third Cub among the last seven members admitted to this exclusive group. Don Kessinger had 6-for-6 in 1971 and Bill Madlock duplicated in 1975.

Fourteen other players made five hits in one game in 1976. No hitter accomplished the feat more than once.

Slugging Mike Schmidt of the Phillies enjoyed a big day at Wrigley Field, April 17, when he smashed four homers and single in a slugfest won by the Phillies, 18-16. Details of his feat are included in another feature in this book.

Records of all players with five or more hits in one game follow:

Date	Player–Opposition	Place	AB	R	H	2B	3B	HR	RBI	Result
April 17	Schmidt, Phillies vs. Cubs (10 innings)	A	6	4	5	0	0	4	8	W 18-16
April 19	McBride, Cardinals vs. Mets (17 innings)	H	8	1	5	2	0	0	0	L 4-3
April 28	Crawford, Cardinals vs. Giants (16 innings)	A	7	1	5	0	0	0	0	W 4-2
May 2*	Cardenal, Cubs vs. Giants (14 innings)	A	7	2	6	1	0	1	4	W 6-5
May 18	Kuiper, Indians vs. Yankees (16 innings)	H	8	1	5	0	0	0	0	L 11-6
May 30*	Cey, Dodgers vs. Reds	A	5	2	5	3	0	0	2	W 6-5
June 4	Concepcion, Reds vs. Cardinals	A	6	1	5	0	0	0	2	W 11-2
June 15	Poquette, Royals vs. Tigers	H	6	5	5	2	0	1	2	W 21-7
June 22	Stennett, Pirates vs. Cubs	A	6	2	5	0	0	0	2	W 10-7
June 29	Geronimo, Reds vs. Padres (14 innings)	A	6	3	5	0	1	1	3	W 12-5
July 2*	Rose, Reds vs. Astros (14 innings)	H	7	2	5	1	0	0	0	L 10-8
July 18*	Herrmann, Astros vs. Expos (10 innings)	A	5	2	5	0	0	1	4	W 7-6
Aug. 16	Brock, Cardinals vs. Padres	H	6	0	5	0	0	0	2	L 11-7
Aug. 22	Campaneris, Athletics vs. Red Sox (11 inn.)	A	6	0	5	1	0	0	2	W 7-6
Sept. 9	Brett, Royals vs. Angels (10 innings)	H	5	2	5	0	0	0	1	W 6-5

*First game of doubleheader.

The majors' longest batting streak of 1976 was fashioned by Ron LeFlore, fleet center fielder of the Tigers, who hit safely in 30 consecutive games from April 17 through May 27. The string ended when Ed Figueroa and Tippy Martinez of the Yankees combined to collar him in four trips to the plate, May 28. LeFlore banged out 51 hits in 130 at-bats in this stretch for a .392 average. He scored 21 runs and drove in 14, numbering 12 doubles, three triples and one homer among his safeties.

Another center fielder, Rowland Office of the Braves, hit safely in 29 straight games for the longest National League skein. Starting on May 23, Office made 51 hits in 125 times at bat for a red-hot .408 mark before going hitless in three tries against Don Stanhouse of the Expos on June 24.

Streaks of 15 or more games were also enjoyed by these players: 20 games—Mickey Rivers, Yankees; 19 games—Chris Chambliss, Yankees; Joe Morgan, Reds; Cesar Cedeno, Astros; 18 games—Carlton Fisk and Jim Rice, Red Sox; Ray Fosse, Indians; George Foster, Reds; 17 games—Fred Lynn,

Red Sox; Jorge Orta, White Sox; Chris Chambliss, Yankees; Toby Harrah, Rangers; Bill Madlock, Cubs; 16 games—Duane Kuiper, Indians; Robin Yount, Brewers; John Milner, Mets; 15 games—Rick Manning, Indians; Jay Johnstone and Garry Maddox, Phillies; Lou Brock, Cardinals; Willie Montanez, Giants.

Three players made four or more hits in one game on six occasions. Batting champion George Brett of the Royals and the Reds' Dave Concepcion each had one five-hit game and five four-hit games while Dave Parker of the Pirates had six four-hit efforts.

The complete list of players with four or more hits in one game follows:

AMERICAN LEAGUE: Baltimore (4)—Belanger 3, Bumbry. Boston (15)—Yastrzemski 3, Dillard 2, Doyle 2, Lynn 2, Rice 2, Burleson, Cooper, Evans, Fisk. California (2)—Bochte, Jackson. Chicago (11)—Garr 3, Spencer 2, Bradford, Dent, L. Johnson, Kelly, Orta, Stein. Cleveland (12)—Kuiper 4, Blanks 2, Carty 2, Manning 2, Fosse, Hendrick. Detroit (13)—LeFlore 4, Horton, Johnson, Meyer, Oglivie, Staub, Sutherland, Thompson, Veryzer, Wagner. Kansas City (13)—Brett 6, McRae 2, Otis 2, Poquette 2, Mayberry. Milwaukee (9)—Yount 3, Money 2, Hegan, Johnson, Joshua, Sharp. Minnesota (11)—Bostock 3, Carew 2, Hisle 2, Brye, Oliva, Thompson, Wynegar. New York (16)—Munson 4, Nettles 3, White 3, Piniella 2, Rivers 2, Chambliss, Randolph. Oakland (5)—Campaneris 3, North, Washington. Texas (10)—Beniquez 2, Clines 2, Hargrove 2, Burroughs, Grieve, Howell, Thompson.

NATIONAL LEAGUE: Atlanta (9)—Gilbreath 2, Office 2, Henderson, Lacy, Montanez, Paciorek, Royster. Chicago (14)—Cardenal 3, Morales 3, Madlock 2, Monday 2, Biittner, LaCock, Mitterwald, Swisher. Cincinnati (20)—Concepcion 6, Foster 4, Rose 4, Geronimo 2, Armbrister, Driessen, Griffey, Youngblood. Houston (16)—Cabell 3, Cedeno 3, Gross 3, Andrews 2, Johnson 2, Watson 2, Herrmann. Los Angeles (13)—Garvey 4, Buckner 3, Cey 2, Russell 2, Sizemore, Smith, Yeager. Montreal (5)—Foli 2, Jorgensen, Valentine, White. New York (5)—Grote, Harrelson, Kingman, Phillips, Stearns. Philadelphia (14)—Johnstone 5, Cash 4, Luzinski 2, Bowa, Schmidt, Tolan. Pittsburgh (16)—Parker 6, Oliver 3, Robinson 2, Sanguillen 2, Stennett 2, Taveras. St. Louis (13)—Brock 3, Simmons 3, Harris 2, Crawford, Fairly, McBride, Mumphrey, Tyson. San Diego (8)—Fuentes 3, W. Davis, Grubb, Ivie, Kendall, Turner. San Francisco (8)—Montanez 2, Thomasson 2, Evans, Matthews, Murcer, Speier.

Jose Morales Sets Pinch-Hitter Marks

Bruce Boisclair of the Mets and Steve Braun of the Twins were the majors' leading pinch-hitters in 1976.

Boisclair, a rookie outfielder, batted .571, with 12 hits in 21 at-bats to lead all National League pinch-hitters. Braun hit safely five times in nine tries to lead American League emergency swingers with a .556 average.

Jose Morales of the Expos had a record-setting year as a pinch-hitter. Morales established major league seasonal marks for appearances (82), official at-bats (78) and hits (25). His .321 average included three homers and 24 RBIs.

NATIONAL LEAGUE PINCH-HITTING
(Compiled by Elias Sports Bureau)

CLUB PINCH-HITTING

Club	AB.	H.	HR.	RBI.	Pct.	Club	AB.	H.	HR.	RBI.	Pct.
New York	187	54	4	24	.289	Philadelphia	217	50	1	21	.230
Los Angeles	200	54	1	28	.270	San Francisco	226	49	2	21	.217
Pittsburgh	178	45	3	30	.253	Montreal	264	56	5	34	.212
Atlanta	201	50	5	28	.249	San Diego	213	42	3	34	.197
Cincinnati	214	52	5	32	.243	Chicago	235	44	4	24	.187
St. Louis	223	53	3	22	.238	Totals	2560	597	38	320	.233
Houston	202	48	2	22	.238						

Individual Pinch-Hitting
(10 or More At-Bats)

Player-Club	AB.	H.	HR.	RBI.	Pct.	Player-Club	AB.	H.	HR.	RBI.	Pct.
Boisclair, N.Y.	21	12	1	1	.571	Hernandez, St.L.	17	4	0	0	.235
Milner, N.Y.	12	6	0	4	.500	McCovey, S.D.	17	4	1	8	.235
Robinson, Pitt.	11	5	1	3	.455	Vail, N.Y.	17	4	0	0	.235
Dyer, Pitt.	12	5	0	2	.417	Phillips, N.Y.	13	3	0	0	.231
Grote, N.Y.	10	4	0	1	.400	Torre, N.Y.	35	8	0	3	.229
Sizemore, L.A.	13	5	0	1	.385	Adams, S.F.	59	13	0	3	.220
Bailey, Cin.	27	10	0	5	.370	Fairly, St.L.	46	10	0	6	.217
Rivera, Mtl.	14	5	0	0	.357	McCarver, Phil.	42	9	0	1	.214
Ott, Pitt.	17	6	0	3	.353	Lee, L.A.	14	3	0	1	.214
Paciorek, Atl.	20	7	0	1	.350	Turner, S.D.	25	5	0	3	.200
Helms, Pitt.	23	8	1	6	.348	Henderson, Atl.	10	2	1	3	.200
Brown, Phil.	27	9	1	8	.333	Thomas, S.F.	10	2	0	0	.200
Anderson, St.L.	21	7	0	2	.333	Thornton, Chi.-Mtl.	21	4	1	3	.190
Boone, Phil.	12	4	0	1	.333	LaCock, Chi.	37	7	1	1	.189
Moore, Atl.	12	4	0	2	.333	Biittner, Mtl.-Chi.	32	6	0	2	.188
Morales, Mtl.	78	25	3	24	.321	May, Atl.	44	8	0	2	.182
Mota, L.A.	38	12	0	12	.316	Ontiveros, S.F.	44	8	0	1	.182
Crawford, St.L.	16	5	0	0	.313	Driessen, Cin.	34	6	2	7	.176
Boswell, Hou.	65	20	0	12	.308	Milbourne, Hou.	17	3	0	0	.176
Rudolph, St.L.	13	4	0	1	.308	Harris, St.L.	23	4	0	2	.174
Gaston, Atl.	40	12	1	10	.300	W. Davis, S.D.	12	2	0	2	.167
Rettenmund, S.D.	40	12	2	9	.300	Johnstone, Phil.	12	2	0	2	.167
Cruz, Hou.	10	3	0	0	.300	Rader, S.F.	12	2	0	3	.167
Griffey, Cin.	10	3	0	0	.300	Dwyer, Mtl.-N.Y.	37	6	0	0	.162
Mumphrey, St.L.	10	3	0	0	.300	Wallis, Chi.	26	4	0	2	.154
Lacy, Atl.-L.A.	17	5	0	1	.294	Youngblood, Cin.	33	5	0	0	.152
Tyrone, Chi.	14	4	0	4	.286	Kirkpatrick, Pitt.	40	6	0	3	.150
Locklear, S.D.	29	8	0	6	.276	Cruz, L.A.	20	3	0	0	.150
Goodson, L.A.	55	15	1	7	.273	Ferguson, L.A.-St.L.	14	2	1	1	.143
Martin, Phil.	22	6	0	3	.273	Ayala, N.Y.	15	2	1	2	.133
Oliver, Pitt.	11	3	0	2	.273	DaVanon, Hou.	15	2	0	1	.133
Roberts, Hou.	26	7	1	4	.269	Tolan, Phil.	33	4	0	2	.121
Arnold, S.F.	45	12	0	5	.267	Melendez, St.L.-S.D.	25	3	0	1	.120
Hutton, Phil.	19	5	0	0	.263	Garrett, N.Y.-Mtl.	17	2	0	3	.118
Williams, Atl.-Mtl.	19	5	0	3	.263	White, Mtl.	17	2	0	1	.118
Armbrister, Cin.	27	7	0	0	.259	Robertson, Pitt.	26	3	0	5	.115
Lum, Cin.	39	10	1	9	.256	Cromartie, Mtl.	14	1	0	0	.071
Summers, Chi.	47	12	1	5	.255	Gross, Hou.	14	1	0	0	.071
Howard, Hou.	24	6	0	2	.250	Walton, L.A.	15	1	0	1	.067
Lyttle, Mtl.-L.A.	20	5	1	3	.250	Adams, Chi.	16	1	0	0	.063
Thomasson, S.F.	16	4	2	5	.250	Mitterwald, Chi.	16	1	0	0	.063
Brock, St.L.	12	3	0	2	.250	Kubiak, S.D.	39	2	0	0	.051
Taylor, Phil.	21	5	0	2	.238	Jorgensen, Mtl.	14	0	0	0	.000

Bruce Boisclair

Jose Morales

Steve Braun

AMERICAN LEAGUE PINCH-HITTING
(Compiled by Sports Information Center)

Club Pinch-Hitting

Club	AB.	H.	HR.	RBI.	Pct.
New York	101	30	0	20	.297
Oakland	96	25	1	13	.260
Minnesota	133	34	3	30	.256
Texas	80	20	0	13	.250
Cleveland	106	25	1	22	.236
Detroit	134	30	5	21	.224
California	149	33	1	22	.221
Baltimore	109	23	2	19	.211
Chicago	107	22	1	13	.206
Kansas City	140	28	0	14	.200
Boston	76	13	2	11	.171
Milwaukee	116	16	0	10	.138
Totals	1347	299	16	208	.222

Individual Pinch-Hitting
(7 or More At-Bats)

Player-Club	AB.	H.	HR.	RBI.	Pct.
Braun, Minnesota	9	5	0	4	.556
May, Chicago-N. Y.	15	7	0	6	.467
Bostock, Minnesota	9	4	0	2	.444
Pruitt, Cleveland	7	3	0	1	.429
Healy, K. C.-New York	7	3	0	0	.429
Bochte, California	7	3	0	1	.429
Ewing, Chicago	7	3	0	1	.429
Harper, Baltimore	10	4	0	0	.400
Davis, Calif.-K. C.	21	8	0	7	.381
Gamble, New York	16	6	0	5	.375
Cubbage, Tex.-Minn.	8	3	0	3	.375
Kelly, Chicago	20	7	0	4	.350
McMullen, Oakland	27	9	1	8	.333
Stanley, Detroit	19	6	0	4	.316
Robinson, Cleveland	16	5	1	7	.313
Johnson, Detroit	16	5	0	2	.313
Solaita, K. C.-Calif.	13	4	0	2	.308
Mora, Baltimore	10	3	1	4	.300
Powell, Cleveland	10	3	0	3	.300
Sharp, Milwaukee	17	5	0	1	.294
Miller, Boston	17	5	0	2	.294
Blanks, Cleveland	14	4	0	4	.286
Melton, California	26	7	0	5	.269
Rojas, Kansas City	28	7	0	2	.250
Crowley, Baltimore	16	4	0	2	.250
Muser, Baltimore	16	4	0	3	.250
Doyle, Boston	8	2	0	0	.250
Stein, Chicago	8	2	0	1	.250
Thompson, Minn.-Texas	8	2	0	3	.250
L. Johnson, Chicago	17	4	1	4	.235
Oglivie, Detroit	39	9	3	9	.231
Williams, Oakland	13	3	0	1	.231
Meyer, Detroit	36	8	1	3	.222
Oliva, Minnesota	32	7	1	5	.219
Quirk, Kansas City	32	7	0	6	.219
Piniella, New York	14	3	0	4	.214
Velez, New York	14	3	0	1	.214
Fregosi, Texas	15	3	0	2	.200
Stanton, California	15	3	0	3	.200
Aaron, Milwaukee	10	2	0	2	.200
Blair, Baltimore	11	2	0	2	.182
Hosley, Oakland	11	2	0	0	.182
Tovar, Oak.-New York	11	2	0	0	.182
Carbo, Bos.-Milwaukee	12	2	0	0	.167
Brye, Minnesota	12	2	0	1	.167
Garrett, California	12	2	0	0	.167
Hendricks, Balt.-N. Y.	12	2	0	0	.167
Darwin, Milw.-Boston	19	3	1	3	.158
Lahoud, Calif.-Tex.	21	3	0	1	.143
Bumbry, Baltimore	7	1	0	0	.143
Hansen, Milwaukee	7	1	0	1	.143
Poquette, Kansas City	7	1	0	1	.143
Porter, Milwaukee	7	1	0	1	.143
Lowenstein, Cleveland	16	2	0	0	.125
Wohlford, Kansas City	16	2	0	1	.125
Money, Milwaukee	8	1	0	1	.125
Howell, Texas	8	1	0	0	.125
Jones, California	18	2	0	1	.111
Jones, Kansas City	9	1	0	0	.111
Sutherland, Det.-Milw.	9	1	0	0	.111
Hegan, Milwaukee	10	1	0	1	.100
Kusick, Minnesota	35	3	0	2	.086
J. G. Thomas, Mil'kee	12	1	0	2	.083
Stillman, Baltimore	15	1	0	1	.067
Spikes, Cleveland	8	0	0	0	.000
Cooper, Boston	9	0	0	1	.000
D. Nelson, Kansas City	16	0	0	0	.000

The Sporting News AWARDS

THE SPORTING NEWS MVP AWARDS

AMERICAN LEAGUE				NATIONAL LEAGUE		
Year	Player	Club	Points	Player	Club	Points
1929	Al Simmons, Philadelphia, of		40	No selection		
1930	Joseph Cronin, Washington, ss		52	William Terry, New York, 1b		47
1931	H. Louis Gehrig, New York, 1b		40	Charles Klein, Philadelphia, of		40
1932	James Foxx, Philadelphia, 1b		56	Charles Klein, Philadelphia, of		46
1933	James Foxx, Philadelphia, 1b		49	Carl Hubbell, New York, p		64
1934	H. Louis Gehrig, New York, 1b		51	Jerome Dean, St. Louis, p		57
1935	Henry Greenberg, Detroit, 1b		64	J. Floyd Vaughan, Pitts., ss		42
1936	H. Louis Gehrig, New York, 1b		55	Carl Hubbell, New York, p		61
1937	Charles Gehringer, Detroit, 2b		78	Joseph Medwick, St. Louis, of		70
1938	James Foxx, Boston, 1b		305	Ernest Lombardi, Cincinnati, c		229
1939	Joseph DiMaggio, N. York, of		280	William Walters, Cincinnati, p		303
1940	Henry Greenberg, Detroit, of		292	Frank McCormick, Cinn., 1b		274
1941	Joseph DiMaggio, N. York, of		291	Adolph Camilli, Brooklyn, 1b		300
1942	Joseph Gordon, New York, 2b		270	Morton Cooper, St. Louis, p		263
1943	Spurgeon Chandler, N. Y., p		246	Stanley Musial, St. Louis, of		267
1944	Robert Doerr, Boston, 2b			Martin Marion, St. Louis, ss		
1945	Edward J. Mayo, Detroit, 2b			Thomas Holmes, Boston, of		

THE SPORTING NEWS PLAYER, PITCHER OF YEAR

1948—Louis Boudreau, Cleveland, ss
    Robert Lemon, Cleveland, p
1949—Theodore Williams, Boston, of
    Ellis Kinder, Boston, p
1950—Philip Rizzuto, New York, ss
    Robert Lemon, Cleveland, p
1951—Ferris Fain, Philadelphia, 1b
    Robert Feller, Cleveland, p
1952—Luscious Easter, Cleveland, 1b
    Robert Shantz, Philadelphia, p
1953—Albert Rosen, Cleveland, 3b
    Erv (Bob) Porterfield, Wash., p
1954—Roberto Avila, Cleveland, 2b
    Robert Lemon, Cleveland, p
1955—Albert Kaline, Detroit, of
    Edward Ford, New York, p
1956—Mickey Mantle, New York, of
    W. William Pierce, Chicago, p
1957—Theodore Williams, Boston, of
    W. William Pierce, Chicago, p
1958—Jack Jensen, Boston, of
    Robert Turley, New York, p
1959—J. Nelson Fox, Chicago, 2b
    Early Wynn, Chicago, p
1960—Roger Maris, New York, of
    Charles Estrada, Baltimore, p
1961—Roger Maris, New York, of
    Edward Ford, New York, p
1962—Mickey Mantle, New York, of
    Richard Donovan, Cleveland, p
1963—Albert Kaline, Detroit, of
    Edward Ford, New York, p

1948—Stanley Musial, St. Louis, of-1b
    John Sain, Boston, p
1949—Enos Slaughter, St. Louis, of
    Howard Pollet, St. Louis, p
1950—Ralph Kiner, Pittsburgh, of
    C. James Konstanty, Phila., p
1951—Stanley Musial, St. Louis, of
    Elwin Roe, Brooklyn, p
1952—Henry Sauer, Chicago, of
    Robin Roberts, Philadelphia, p
1953—Roy Campanella, Brooklyn, c
    Warren Spahn, Milwaukee, p
1954—Willie Mays, New York, of
    John Antonelli, New York, p
1955—Edwin Snider, Brooklyn, of
    Robin Roberts, Philadelphia, p
1956—Henry Aaron, Milwaukee, of
    Donald Newcombe, Brooklyn, p
1957—Stanley Musial, St. Louis, 1b
    Warren Spahn, Milwaukee, p
1958—Ernest Banks, Chicago, ss
    Warren Spahn, Milwaukee, p
1959—Ernest Banks, Chicago, ss
    Samuel Jones, San Francisco, p
1960—Richard Groat, Pittsburgh, ss
    Vernon Law, Pittsburgh, p
1961—Frank Robinson, Cincinnati, of
    Warren Spahn, Milwaukee, p
1962—Maurice Wills, Los Angeles, ss
    Donald Drysdale, Los Angeles, p
1963—Henry Aaron, Milwaukee, of
    Sanford Koufax, Los Angeles, p

PLAYER, PITCHER OF YEAR—Continued

AMERICAN LEAGUE	NATIONAL LEAUGE

Year	Player Club	Player Club
1964	Brooks Robinson, Baltimore, 3b Dean Chance, Los Angeles, p	Kenton Boyer, St. Louis, 3b Sanford Koufax, Los Angeles, p
1965	Pedro (Tony) Oliva, Minn., of James Grant, Minnesota, p	Willie Mays, San Francisco, of Sanford Koufax, Los Angeles, p
1966	Frank Robinson, Baltimore, of James Kaat, Minnesota, p	Roberto Clemente, Pittsburgh, of Sanford Koufax, Los Angeles, p
1967	Carl Yastrzemski, Boston, of Jim Lonborg, Boston, p	Orlando Cepeda, St. Louis, 1b Mike McCormick, San Fran., p
1968	Ken Harrelson, Boston, of Denny McLain, Detroit, p	Pete Rose, Cincinnati, of Bob Gibson, St. Louis, p
1969	Harmon Killebrew, Minn., 1b-3b Denny McLain, Detroit, p	Willie McCovey, San Fran., 1b Tom Seaver, New York, p
1970	Harmon Killebrew, Minn., 3b Sam McDowell, Cleveland, p	Johnny Bench, Cin., c Bob Gibson, St. Louis, p
1971	Pedro (Tony) Oliva, Minn., of Vida Blue, Oakland, p	Joe Torre, St. Louis, 3b Ferguson Jenkins, Chicago, p
1972	Richie Allen, Chicago, 1b Wilbur Wood, Chicago, p	Billy Williams, Chicago, of Steve Carlton, Philadelphia, p
1973	Reggie Jackson, Oakland, of Jim Palmer, Baltimore, p	Bobby Bonds, San Francisco, of Ron Bryant, San Francisco, p
1974	Jeff Burroughs, Texas, of Jim Hunter, Oakland, p	Lou Brock, St. Louis, of Mike Marshall, Los Angeles, p
1975	Fred Lynn, Boston, of Jim Palmer, Baltimore, p	Joe Morgan, Cincinnati, 2b Tom Seaver, New York, p
1976	Thurman Munson, New York, c Jim Palmer, Baltimore, p	George Foster, Cincinnati, of Randy Jones, San Diego, p

FIREMAN (Relief Pitcher) OF THE YEAR

Year	American League	National League
1960	Mike Fornieles, Boston	Lindy McDaniel, St. Louis
1961	Luis Arroyo, New York	Stu Miller, San Francisco
1962	Dick Radatz, Boston	Roy Face, Pittsburgh
1963	Stu Miller, Baltimore	Lindy McDaniel, Chicago
1964	Dick Radatz, Boston	Al McBean, Pittsburgh
1965	Eddie Fisher, Chicago	Ted Abernathy, Chicago
1966	Jack Aker, Kansas City	Phil Regan, Los Angeles
1967	Minnie Rojas, California	Ted Abernathy, Cincinnati
1968	Wilbur Wood, Chicago	Phil Regan, L.A.-Chicago
1969	Ron Perranoski, Minnesota	Wayne Granger, Cincinnati
1970	Ron Perranoski, Minnesota	Wayne Granger, Cincinnati
1971	Ken Sanders, Milwaukee	Dave Giusti, Pittsburgh
1972	Sparky Lyle, New York	Clay Carroll, Cincinnati
1973	John Hiller, Detroit	Mike Marshall, Montreal
1974	Terry Forster, Chicago	Mike Marshall, Los Angeles
1975	Rich Gossage, Chicago	Al Hrabosky, St. Louis
1976	Bill Campbell, Minnesota	Rawly Eastwick, Cincinnati

THE SPORTING NEWS ROOKIE AWARDS

1946—Combined selection—Delmer Ennis, Philadelphia, N. L., of
1947—Combined selection—Jack Robinson, Brooklyn, 1b
1948—Combined selection—Richie Ashburn, Philadelphia, N. L., of

THE SPORTING NEWS ROOKIE AWARDS—Continued

AMERICAN LEAGUE		NATIONAL LEAGUE	
Year	Player Club	Player Club	
1949—Roy Sievers, St. Louis, of		Donald Newcombe, Brooklyn, p	
1950—Combined selection—Edward Ford, New York, A. L., p			
1951—Orestes Minoso, Chicago, of		Willie Mays, New York, of	
1952—Clinton Courtney, St. Louis, c		Joseph Black, Brooklyn, p	
1953—Harvey Kuenn, Detroit, ss		James Gilliam, Brooklyn, 2b	
1954—Robert Grim, New York, p		Wallace Moon, St. Louis, of	
1955—Herbert Score, Cleveland, p		William Virdon, St. Louis, of	
1956—Luis Aparicio, Chicago, ss		Frank Robinson, Cincinnati, of	
1957—Anthony Kubek, New York, inf-of		Edward Bouchee, Philadelphia, 1b	
(No pitcher named)		Jack Sanford, Philadelphia, p	
1958—Albert Pearson, Washington, of		Orlando Cepeda, San Francisco, 1b	
Ryne Duren, New York, p		Carlton Willey, Milwaukee, p	
1959—W. Robert Allison, Washington, of		Willie McCovey, San Francisco, 1b	
1960—Ronald Hansen, Baltimore, ss		Frank Howard, Los Angeles, of	
1961—Richard Howser, Kansas City, ss		Billy Williams, Chicago, of	
Donald Schwall, Boston, p		Kenneth Hunt, Cincinnati, p	
1962—Thomas Tresh, New York, of-ss		Kenneth Hubbs, Chicago, 2b	
1963—Peter Ward, Chicago, 3b		Peter Rose, Cincinnati, 2b	
Gary Peters, Chicago, p		Raymond Culp, Philadelphia, p	
1964—Pedro (Tony) Oliva, Minn., of		Richard Allen, Philadelphia, 3b	
Wallace Bunker, Baltimore, p		William McCool, Cincinnati, p	
1965—Curtis Blefary, Baltimore, of		Joseph Morgan, Houston, 2b	
Marcelino Lopez, California, p		Frank Linzy, San Francisco, p	
1966—Tommie Agee, Chicago, of		Tommy Helms, Cincinnati, 3b	
James Nash, Kansas City, p		Donald Sutton, Los Angeles, p	
1967—Rod Carew, Minnesota, 2b		Lee May, Cincinnati, 1b	
Tom Phoebus, Baltimore, p		Dick Hughes, St. Louis, p	
1968—Del Unser, Washington, of		Johnny Bench, Cincinnati, c	
Stan Bahnsen, New York, p		Jerry Koosman, New York, p	
1969—Carlos May, Chicago, of		Coco Laboy, Montreal, 3b	
Mike Nagy, Boston, p		Tom Griffin, Houston, p	
1970—Roy Foster, Cleveland, of		Bernie Carbo, Cincinnati, of	
Bert Blyleven, Minnesota, p		Carl Morton, Montreal, p	
1971—Chris Chambliss, Cleveland, 1b		Earl Williams, Atlanta, c	
Bill Parsons, Milwaukee, p		Reggie Cleveland, St. Louis, p	
1972—Carlton Fisk, Boston, c		Dave Rader, San Francisco, c	
Dick Tidrow, Cleveland, p		Jon Matlack, New York, p	
1973—Al Bumbry, Baltimore, of		Gary Matthews, San Fran., of	
Steve Busby, Kansas City, p		Steve Rogers, Montreal, p	
1974—Mike Hargrove, Texas, 1b		Greg Gross, Houston, of	
Frank Tanana, California, p		John D'Acquisto, San Francisco, p	
1975—Fred Lynn, Boston, of		Gary Carter, Montreal, of-c	
Dennis Eckersley, Cleveland, p		John Montefusco, San Francisco, p	
1976—Butch Wynegar, Minnesota, c		Larry Herndon, San Francisco, of	
Mark Fidrych, Detroit, p		Butch Metzger, San Diego, p	

MAJOR LEAGUE EXECUTIVE

Year Executive Club	Year Executive Club
1936—Branch Rickey, St. Louis NL	1944—Wm. O. DeWitt, St. Louis AL
1937—Edward Barrow, New York AL	1945—Philip K. Wrigley, Chicago NL
1938—Warren Giles, Cincinnati NL	1946—Thomas A. Yawkey, Boston AL
1939—Larry MacPhail, Brooklyn NL	1947—Branch Rickey, Brooklyn NL
1940—W. O. Briggs, Sr., Detroit AL	1948—Bill Veeck, Cleveland AL
1941—Edward Barrow, New York AL	1949—Robt. Carpenter, Phila'phia NL
1942—Branch Rickey, St. Louis NL	1950—George Weiss, New York AL
1943—Clark Griffith, Washington AL	1951—George Weiss, New York AL

MAJOR LEAGUE EXECUTIVE—Continued

Year	Executive	Club
1952	George Weiss, New York AL	
1953	Louis Perini, Milwaukee NL	
1954	Horace Stoneham, N. York NL	
1955	Walter O'Malley, Brooklyn NL	
1956	Gabe Paul, Cincinnati NL	
1957	Frank Lane, St. Louis NL	
1958	Joe L. Brown, Pittsburgh NL	
1959	E. J. (Buzzie) Bavasi, L.A. NL	
1960	George Weiss, New York AL	
1961	Dan Topping, New York AL	
1962	Fred Haney, Los Angeles AL	
1963	Vaughan (Bing) Devine, St.L.NL	
1964	Vaughan (Bing) Devine, St.L.NL	
1965	Calvin Griffith, Minnesota AL	
1966	Lee MacPhail, Commissioner's Office	
1967	Dick O'Connell, Boston AL	
1968	James Campbell, Detroit AL	
1969	John Murphy, New York NL	
1970	Harry Dalton, Baltimore AL	
1971	Cedric Tallis, Kansas City AL	
1972	Roland Hemond, Chicago AL	
1973	Bob Howsam, Cincinnati NL	
1974	Gabe Paul, New York AL	
1975	Dick O'Connell, Boston AL	
1976	Joe Burke, Kansas City AL	

MAJOR LEAGUE MANAGER

Year	Manager	Club
1936	Joe McCarthy, New York AL	
1937	Bill McKechnie, Boston NL	
1938	Joe McCarthy, New York AL	
1939	Leo Durocher, Brooklyn NL	
1940	Bill McKechnie, Cincinnati NL	
1941	Billy Southworth, St. Louis NL	
1942	Billy Southworth, St. Louis NL	
1943	Joe McCarthy, New York AL	
1944	Luke Sewell, St. Louis AL	
1945	Ossie Bluege, Washington AL	
1946	Eddie Dyer, St. Louis NL	
1947	Bucky Harris, New York AL	
1948	Bill Meyer, Pittsburgh NL	
1949	Casey Stengel, New York AL	
1950	Red Rolfe, Detroit AL	
1951	Leo Durocher, New York NL	
1952	Eddie Stanky, St. Louis NL	
1953	Casey Stengel, New York AL	
1954	Leo Durocher, New York NL	
1955	Walter Alston, Brooklyn NL	
1956	Birdie Tebbetts, Cincinnati NL	
1957	Fred Hutchinson, St. Louis NL	
1958	Casey Stengel, New York AL	
1959	Walter Alston, Los Angeles NL	
1960	Danny Murtaugh, Pitts. NL	
1961	Ralph Houk, New York AL	
1962	Bill Rigney, Los Angeles AL	
1963	Walter Alston, Los Angeles NL	
1964	Johnny Keane, St. Louis NL	
1965	Sam Mele, Minnesota AL	
1966	Hank Bauer, Baltimore AL	
1967	Dick Williams, Boston AL	
1968	Mayo Smith, Detroit AL	
1969	Gil Hodges, New York NL	
1970	Danny Murtaugh, Pittsburgh NL	
1971	Charlie Fox, San Francisco NL	
1972	Chuck Tanner, Chicago AL	
1973	Gene Mauch, Montreal NL	
1974	Bill Virdon, New York AL	
1975	Darrell Johnson, Boston AL	
1976	Danny Ozark, Philadelphia NL	

MAJOR LEAGUE PLAYER

Year	Player	Club
1936	Carl Hubbell, New York NL	
1937	Johnny Allen, Cleveland AL	
1938	Johnny Vander Meer, Cinn. NL	
1939	Joe DiMaggio, New York AL	
1940	Bob Feller, Cleveland AL	
1941	Ted Williams, Boston AL	
1942	Ted Williams, Boston AL	
1943	Spud Chandler, New York AL	
1944	Marty Marion, St. Louis NL	
1945	Hal Newhouser, Detroit AL	
1946	Stan Musial, St. Louis NL	
1947	Ted Williams, Boston AL	
1948	Lou Boudreau, Cleveland AL	
1949	Ted Williams, Boston AL	
1950	Phil Rizzuto, New York AL	
1951	Stan Musial, St. Louis NL	
1952	Robin Roberts, Philadelphia NL	
1953	Al Rosen, Cleveland AL	
1954	Willie Mays, New York NL	
1955	Duke Snider, Brooklyn NL	
1956	Mickey Mantle, New York AL	
1957	Ted Williams, Boston AL	
1958	Bob Turley, New York AL	
1959	Early Wynn, Chicago AL	
1960	Bill Mazeroski, Pittsburgh NL	
1961	Roger Maris, New York AL	
1962	Maury Wills, Los Angeles NL	
	Don Drysdale, Los Angeles NL	

MAJOR LEAGUE PLAYER—Continued

Year	Player	Club
1963	Sandy Koufax, Los Angeles NL	
1964	Ken Boyer, St. Louis NL	
1965	Sandy Koufax, Los Angeles NL	
1966	Frank Robinson, Baltimore AL	
1967	Carl Yastrzemski, Boston AL	
1968	Denny McLain, Detroit AL	
1969	Willie McCovey, San Fran. NL	

Year	Player	Club
1970	Johnny Bench, Cin. NL	
1971	Joe Torre, St. Louis NL	
1972	Billy Williams, Chicago NL	
1973	Reggie Jackson, Oakland AL	
1974	Lou Brock, St. Louis NL	
1975	Joe Morgan, Cincinnati NL	
1976	Joe Morgan, Cincinnati NL	

MINOR LEAGUE EXECUTIVE (HIGHER CLASSIFICATIONS)
(Restricted to Class AAA Starting in 1963)

Year	Executive	Club
1936	Earl Mann, Atlanta, Southern	
1937	Robt. LaMotte, Savannah, Sally	
1938	Louis McKenna, St. Paul, A.A.	
1939	Bruce Dudley, Louisville, A.A.	
1940	Roy Hamey, Kansas City, A.A.	
1941	Emil Sick, Seattle, PCL	
1942	Bill Veeck, Milwaukee, A.A.	
1943	Clar. Rowland, Los Angeles, PCL	
1944	William Mulligan, Seattle, PCL	
1945	Bruce Dudley, Louisville, A.A.	
1946	Earl Mann, Atlanta, Southern	
1947	Wm. Purnhage, Waterloo, I.I.I.	
1948	Ed. Glennon, Bir'ham, Southern	
1949	Ted Sullivan, Indianapolis, A.A.	
1950	Cl. (Brick) Laws, Oakland, PCL	
1951	Robert Howsam, Denver, West.	
1952	Jack Cooke, Toronto, Int.	
1953	Richard Burnett, Dallas, Texas	
1954	Edward Stumpf, Indpls., A.A.	
1955	Dewey Soriano, Seattle, PCL	
1956	Robert Howsam, Denver, A.A.	

Year	Executive	Club
1957	John Stiglmeier, Buffalo, Int.	
1958	Ed. Glennon, Bir'ham, Southern	
1959	Ed. Leishman, Salt Lake, PCL	
1960	Ray Winder, Little Rock, Sou.	
1961	Elten Schiller, Omaha, A.A.	
1962	Geo. Sisler, Jr., Rochester, Int.	
1963	Lewis Matlin, Hawaii, PCL	
1964	Ed. Leishman, San Diego, PCL	
1965	Harold Cooper, Columbus, Int.	
1966	John Quinn, Jr., Hawaii, PCL	
1967	Hillman Lyons, Richmond, Int.	
1968	Gabe Paul, Jr., Tulsa, PCL	
1969	Bill Gardner, Louisville, Int.	
1970	Dick King, Wichita, A.A.	
1971	Carl Steinfeldt, Jr., Roch'ter, Int.	
1972	Don Labbruzzo, Evansville, A.A.	
1973	Merle Miller, Tucson, PCL	
1974	John Carbray, Sacramento, PCL	
1975	Stan Naccarato, Tacoma, PCL	
1976	Art Teece, Salt Lake City, PCL	

MINOR LEAGUE EXECUTIVE (LOWER CLASSIFICATIONS)
(Separate Awards for Class AA and Class A Started in 1963)

Year	Executive	Club
1950	H. Cooper, Hutch'son, West. A.	
1951	O. W. (Bill) Hayes, T'ple, B.S.	
1952	Hillman Lyons, Danville, MOV	
1953	Carl Roth, Peoria, III	
1954	James Meaghan, Cedar R., III	
1955	John Petrakis, Dubuque, MOV	
1956	Marvin Milkes, Fresno, Calif.	
1957	Richard Wagner, L'coln, West.	
1958	Gerald Waring, Macon, Sally	
1959	Clay Dennis, Des Moines, III	
1960	Hubert Kittle, Yakima, Northw.	
1961	David Steele, Fresno, California	
1962	John Quinn, Jr., S. Jose, Calif.	
1963	Hugh Finnerty, Tulsa, Texas	
	Ben Jewell, M. Valley, Pioneer	
1964	Glynn West, B'ham, Southern	
	Jas. Bayens, Rock Hill, W. Car.	

Year	Executive	Club
1965	Dick Butler, Dallas-Ft.W., Tex.	
	Ken. Blackman, Quad C., Midw.	
1966	Tom Fleming, Evansville, South.	
	Cappy Harada, Lodi, California	
1967	Robt. Quinn, Reading, East.	
	Pat Williams, Spar'burg, W. C.	
1968	Phil Howser, Charlotte, South.	
	Merle Miller, Burlington, Midw.	
1969	Charlie Blaney, Albuq., Tex.	
	Bill Gorman, Visalia, Calif.	
1970	Carl Sawatski, Arkansas, Tex.	
	Bob Williams, Bakersfield, Calif.	
1971	Miles Wolff, Savannah, Dixie A.	
	Ed Holtz, Appleton, Midwest	
1972	John Begzos, S. Antonio, Texas	
	Bob Piccinini, Modesto, Calif.	

MINOR LEAGUE EXECUTIVE (LOWER CLASSIFICATIONS)
(Continued)
(Separate Awards for Class AA and Class A Started in 1963)

Year	Executive	Club
1973	Dick Kravitz, Jacksonville, Sou.	
	Fritz Colschen, Clinton, Midw.	
1974	Jim Paul, El Paso, Texas	
	Bing Russell, Portland, N'west	
1975	Jim Paul, El Paso, Texas	
	Cordy Jensen, Eugene, N'west	
1976	Woodrow Reid, Chat'ooga, Sou.	
	—Don Buchheister, Ced. Rap., Mid.	

MINOR LEAGUE MANAGER

Year	Manager	Club
1936	Al Sothoron, Milwaukee, A.A.	
1937	Jake Flowers, Salis'y, East. Sh.	
1938	Paul Richards, Atlanta, South.	
1939	Bill Meyer, Kansas City, A.A.	
1940	Larry Gilbert, Nashville, South.	
1941	Burt Shotton, Columbus, A.A.	
1942	Eddie Dyer, Columbus, A.A.	
1943	Nick Cullop, Columbus, A.A.	
1944	Al Thomas, Baltimore, Int.	
1945	Lefty O'Doul, San Fran., PCL	
1946	Clay Hopper, Montreal, Int.	
1947	Nick Cullop, Milwaukee, A.A.	
1948	Casey Stengel, Oakland, PCL	
1949	Fred Haney, Hollywood, PCL	
1950	Rollie Hemsley, Columbus, A.A.	
1951	Charlie Grimm, Milw., A.A.	
1952	Luke Appling, Memphis, South.	
1953	Bobby Bragan, Hollywood, PCL	
1954	Kerby Farrell, Indpls., A.A.	
1955	Bill Rigney, Minneapolis, A.A.	
1956	Kerby Farrell, Indpls., A.A.	
1957	Ben Geraghty, Wichita, A.A.	
1958	Cal Ermer, Birmingham, South.	
1959	Pete Reiser, Victoria, Texas	
1960	Mel McGaha, Toronto, Int.	
1961	Kerby Farrell, Buffalo, Int.	
1962	Ben Geraghty, Jackson'le, Int.	
1963	Rollie Hemsley, Indpls., Int.	
1964	Harry Walker, Jacks'vle., Int.	
1965	Grady Hatton, Okla. City, PCL	
1966	Bob Lemon, Seattle, PCL	
1967	Bob Skinner, San Diego, PCL	
1968	Jack Tighe, Toledo, Int.	
1969	Clyde McCullough, Tide., Int.	
1970	Tom Lasorda, Spokane, PCL	
1971	Del Rice, Salt Lake City, PCL	
1972	Hank Bauer, Tidewater, Int.	
1973	Joe Morgan, Charleston, Int.	
1974	Joe Altobelli, Rochester, Int.	
1975	Joe Frazier, Tidewater, Int.	
1976	Vern Rapp, Denver, A.A.	

MINOR LEAGUE PLAYER

Year	Player	Club
1936	Jn. Vander Meer, Durham, Pied.	
1937	Charlie Keller, Newark, Int.	
1938	Fred Hutchinson, Seattle, PCL	
1939	Lou Novikoff, Tulsa-Los A'les.	
1940	Phil Rizzuto, Kansas City, A.A.	
1941	John Lindell, Newark, Int.	
1942	Dick Barrett, Seattle, PCL	
1943	Chet Covington, Scranton, East.	
1944	Rip Collins, Albany, Eastern	
1945	Gil Coan, Chattanooga, South.	
1946	Sibby Sisti, Indianapolis, A.A.	
1947	Hank Sauer, Syracuse, Int.	
1948	Gene Woodling, S. F., PCL	
1949	Orie Arntzen, Albany, Eastern	
1950	Frank Saucier, San Ant'o, Tex.	
1951	Gene Conley, Hartford, Eastern	
1952	Bill Skowron, Kans. City, A.A.	
1953	Gene Conley, Toledo, A.A.	
1954	Herb Score, Indianapolis, A.A.	
1955	John Murff, Dallas, Texas	
1956	Steve Bilko, Los Angeles, PCL	
1957	Norm Siebern, Denver, A.A	
1958	Jim O'Toole, Nashville, South.	
1959	Frank Howard, Victoria-Spok.	
1960	Willie Davis, Spokane, PCL	
1961	Howie Koplitz, Bir'ham, South.	
1962	Bob Bailey, Columbus, Int.	
1963	Don Buford, Indianapolis, Int.	
1964	Mel Stottlemyre, Richm'd., Int.	
1965	Joe Foy, Toronto, International	
1966	Mike Epstein, Rochester, Int.	
1967	Johnny Bench, Buffalo, Int.	
1968	Merv Rettenmund, Roch'ter, Int.	
1969	Danny Walton, Okla. City, A.A.	
1970	Don Baylor, Rochester, Int.	
1971	Bobby Grich, Rochester, Int.	
1972	Tom Paciorek, Albuq'que, PCL	
1973	Steve Ontiveros, Phoenix, PCL	
1974	Jim Rice, Pawtucket, Int.	
1975	Hector Cruz, Tulsa, A.A.	
1976	Pat Putnam, Asheville, W. Car.	

Baseball Writers' Association Awards
Most Valuable Player Citations
CHALMERS AWARD

	AMERICAN LEAGUE			NATIONAL LEAGUE		
Year	Player	Club	Points	Player	Club	Points
1911	Tyrus Cobb, Detroit, of		64	Frank Schulte, Chicago, of		29
1912	Tristram Speaker, Boston, of		59	Lawrence Doyle, N. Y., 2b		48
1913	Walter Johnson, Washington, p		54	Jacob Daubert, Brooklyn, 1b		50
1914	Edward Collins, Phila., 2b		63	John Evers, Boston, 2b		50

LEAGUE AWARDS

	AMERICAN LEAGUE			NATIONAL LEAGUE		
Year	Player	Club	Points	Player	Club	Points
1922	George Sisler, St. Louis, 1b		59	No selection		
1923	George Ruth, New York, of		64	No selection		
1924	Walter Johnson, Washington, p		55	Arthur Vance, Brooklyn, p		74
1925	Roger Peckinpaugh, Wash., ss		45	Rogers Hornsby, St. Louis, 2b		73
1926	George Burns, Cleveland, 1b		63	Robert O'Farrell, St. Louis, c		79
1927	H. Louis Gehrig, New York, 1b		56	Paul Waner, Pittsburgh, of		72
1928	Gordon Cochrane, Phila., c		53	James Bottomley, St. Louis, 1b		76
1929	No selection			Rogers Hornsby, Chicago, 2b		60

BASEBALL WRITERS' ASSOCIATION MVP AWARDS

	AMERICAN LEAGUE			NATIONAL LEAGUE		
Year	Player	Club	Points	Player	Club	Points
1931	Robert Grove, Philadelphia, p		78	Frank Frisch, St. Louis, 2b		65
1932	James Foxx, Philadelphia, 1b		75	Charles Klein, Phila., of		78
1933	James Foxx, Philadelphia, 1b		74	Carl Hubbell, New York, p		77
1934	Gordon Cochrane, Detroit, c		67	Jerome Dean, St. Louis, p		78
1935	Henry Greenberg, Detroit, 1b		*80	Charles Hartnett, Chicago, c		75
1936	H. Louis Gehrig, New York, 1b		73	Carl Hubbell, New York, p		60
1937	Charles Gehringer, Detroit, 2b		78	Joseph Medwick, St. Louis, of		70
1938	James Foxx, Boston, 1b		305	Ernest Lombardi, Cincinnati, c		229
1939	Joseph DiMaggio, N. York, of		280	William Walters, Cincinnati, p		303
1940	Henry Greenberg, Detroit, of		292	Frank McCormick, Cinn., 1b		274
1941	Joseph DiMaggio, N. York, of		291	Adolph Camilli, Brooklyn, 1b		300
1942	Joseph Gordon, New York, 2b		270	Morton Cooper, St. Louis, p		263
1943	Spurgeon Chandler, N. Y., p		246	Stanley Musial, St. Louis, of		267
1944	Harold Newhouser, Detroit, p		236	Martin Marion, St. Louis, ss		190
1945	Harold Newhouser, Detroit, p		236	Philip Cavarretta, Chicago, 1b		279
1946	Theodore Williams, Boston, of		224	Stanley Musial, St. Louis, 1b		319
1947	Joseph DiMaggio, N. York, of		202	Robert Elliott, Boston, 3b		205
1948	Louis Boudreau, Cleveland, ss		324	Stanley Musial, St. Louis, of		303
1949	Theodore Williams, Boston, of		272	Jack Robinson, Brooklyn, 2b		264
1950	Philip Rizzuto, New York, ss		284	C. James Konstanty, Phila., p		286
1951	Lawrence Berra, New York, c		184	Roy Campanella, Brooklyn, c		243
1952	Robert Shantz, Phila., p		280	Henry Sauer, Chicago, of		226
1953	Albert Rosen, Cleveland, 3b		*336	Roy Campanella, Brooklyn, c		297
1954	Lawrence Berra, New York, c		230	Willie Mays, New York, of		283
1955	Lawrence Berra, New York, c		218	Roy Campanella, Brooklyn, c		226
1956	Mickey Mantle, N. Y., of		*336	Donald Newcombe, Brkn., p		223
1957	Mickey Mantle, New York, of		233	Henry Aaron, Milwaukee, of		239
1958	Jack Jensen, Boston, of		233	Ernest Banks, Chicago, ss		283
1959	J. Nelson Fox, Chicago, 2b		295	Ernest Banks, Chicago, ss		232½
1960	Roger Maris, New York, of		225	Richard Groat, Pittsburgh, ss		276

BASEBALL WRITERS' ASSOCIATION MVP AWARDS—Cont.

	AMERICAN LEAGUE				NATIONAL LEAGUE		
Year	Player	Club	Points		Player	Club	Points
1961	Roger Maris, New York, of		202		Frank Robinson, Cincinnati, of		219
1962	Mickey Mantle, New York, of		234		Maurice Wills, Los Angeles, ss		209
1963	Elston Howard, New York, c		248		Sanford Koufax, Los Angeles, p		237
1964	Brooks Robinson, Balti., 3b		269		Kenton Boyer, St. Louis, 3b		243
1965	Zoilo Versalles, Minn., ss		275		Willie Mays, San Francisco, of		224
1966	Frank Robinson, Balti., of		*280		Roberto Clemente, Pitts., of		218
1967	Carl Yastrzemski, Boston, of		275		Orlando Cepeda, St. Louis, 1b		*280
1968	Dennis McLain, Detroit, p		*280		Robert Gibson, St. Louis, p		242
1969	Harmon Killebrew, Minn., 1-3b		294		Willie McCovey, San Fran., 1b		265
1970	John (Boog) Powell, Balti., 1b		234		Johnny Bench, Cincinnati, c		326
1971	Vida Blue, Oakland, p		268		Joseph Torre, St. Louis, 3b		318
1972	Richie Allen, Chicago, 1b		321		Johnny Bench, Cincinnati, c		263
1973	Reggie Jackson, Oak., of		*336		Pete Rose, Cincinnati, of		274
1974	Jeff Burroughs, Texas, of		248		Steve Garvey, Los Angeles, 1b		270
1975	Fred Lynn, Boston, of		326		Joe Morgan, Cincinnati, 2b		321½
1976	Thurman Munson, N. Y., c		304		Joe Morgan, Cincinnati, 2b		311

*Unanimous selection.

BASEBALL WRITERS' ASSOCIATION ROOKIE AWARDS

1947 — Combined selection — Jack Robinson, Brooklyn, 1b.
1948 — Combined selection — Alvin Dark, Boston, N. L., ss.

Year	Player	Club	Votes		Player	Club	Votes
1949	Roy Sievers, St. Louis, of		10		Donald Newcombe, Brkn, p		21
1950	Walter Dropo, Boston, 1b		15		Samuel Jethroe, Boston, of		11
1951	Gilbert McDougald, N. Y., 3b		13		Willie Mays, New York, of		18
1952	Harry Byrd, Philadelphia, p		9		Joseph Black, Brooklyn, p		19
1953	Harvey Kuenn, Detroit, ss		23		James Gilliam, Brooklyn, 2b		11
1954	Robert Grim, New York, p		15		Wallace Moon, St. Louis, of		17
1955	Herbert Score, Cleveland, p		18		William Virdon, St. Louis, of		15
1956	Luis Aparicio, Chicago, ss		22		Frank Robinson, Cincinnati, of		*24
1957	Anthony Kubek, N. Y., inf-of		23		John Sanford, Philadelphia, p		16
1958	Albert Pearson, Washington, of		14		Orlando Cepeda, S. Fran., 1b		*†21
1959	W. Robert Allison, Wash., of		18		Willie McCovey, San Fran., 1b		*24
1960	Ronald Hansen, Baltimore, ss		22		Frank Howard, Los Angeles, of		12
1961	Donald Schwall, Boston, p		7		Billy Williams, Chicago, of		10
1962	Thomas Tresh, New York, of-ss		13		Kenneth Hubbs, Chicago, 2b		19
1963	Gary Peters, Chicago, p		10		Peter Rose, Cincinnati, 2b		17
1964	Pedro (Tony) Oliva, Minn., of		19		Richard Allen, Philadelphia, 3b		18
1965	Curtis Blefary, Baltimore, of		12		James Lefebvre, Los Ang., 2b		13
1966	Tommie Agee, Chicago, of		16		Tommy Helms, Cincinnati, 3b		12
1967	Rod Carew, Minnesota, 2b		19		Tom Seaver, New York, p		11
1968	Stan Bahnsen, New York, p		17		Johnny Bench, Cincinnati, c		10½
1969	Lou Piniella, Kansas City, of		9		Ted Sizemore, Los Angeles, 2b		14
1970	Thurman Munson, N. Y., c		23		Carl Morton, Montreal, p		11
1971	Chris Chambliss, Cleveland, 1b		11		Earl Williams, Atlanta, c		18
1972	Carlton Fisk, Boston, c		*24		Jon Matlack, New York, p		19
1973	Al Bumbry, Baltimore, of		13½		Gary Matthews, San Fran., of		11
1974	Mike Hargrove, Texas, 1b		16½		Bake McBride, St. Louis, of		16
1975	Fred Lynn, Boston, of		23		John Montefusco, San Fran., p		12
1976	Mark Fidrych, Detroit, p		22		Butch Metzger, San Diego, p		11
					Pat Zachry, Cincinnati, p		11

*Unanimous selection. †Three writers did not vote.

CY YOUNG MEMORIAL AWARD

Year	Pitcher	Club	Votes
1956—Donald Newcombe, Brkn			10
1957—Warren Spahn, Milwaukee			15
1958—Robert Turley, N. Y., A. L.			5
1959—Early Wynn, Chicago, A.L.			13
1960—Vernon Law, Pittsburgh			8
1961—Edward Ford, N. Y., A. L.			9
1962—Don Drysdale, L.A., N.L.			14
1963—Sanford Koufax, L.A., N.L.			*20
1964—Dean Chance, L. A., A. L.			17
1965—Sanford Koufax, L.A., N.L.			*20
1966—Sanford Koufax, L.A., N.L.			*20
1967—A. L.—Jim Lonborg, Boston			18
N. L.—M. McCormick, S. F.			18
1968—A. L.—Dennis McLain, Det.			*20
N. L.—Bob Gibson, St. L.			*20
1969—A. L.—Dennis McLain, Det.			10
Mike Cuellar, Balt.			10
N. L.—Tom Seaver, N. Y.			23

Year	Pitcher	Club	Votes
1970—A. L.—Jim Perry, Minn.			†55
N. L.—Bob Gibson, St. L.			†118
1971—A. L.—Vida Blue, Oakland			†98
N. L.—Fergy Jenkins, Chi.			†97
1972—A. L.—Gaylord Perry, Cleve.			†64
N. L.—Steve Carlton, Phil.			*†120
1973—A. L.—Jim Palmer, Balt.			†88
N. L.—Tom Seaver, N. Y.			†71
1974—A. L.—Jim Hunter, Oakland			†90
N. L.—Mike Marshall, L. A.			†96
1975—A. L.—Jim Palmer, Balt.			†98
N. L.—Tom Seaver, N. Y.			†98
1976—A. L.—Jim Palmer, Balt.			†108
N. L.—Randy Jones, S. D.			†96

*Unanimous selection. †Point system used.

Major League Farm Systems for 1977

*Indicates working agreement. All other clubs owned outright.

AMERICAN LEAGUE

BALTIMORE (4): AAA–*Rochester. AA–*Charlotte. A–*Miami. Rookie–Bluefield.

BOSTON (5): AAA–*Pawtucket. AA–*Bristol, Conn. A–*Elmira, *Winston-Salem, Winter Haven.

CALIFORNIA (5): AAA–*Salt Lake City. AA–*El Paso. A–*Quad Cities, *Salinas. Rookie–*Idaho Falls.

CHICAGO (4): AAA–*Iowa. AA–*Knoxville. A–*Appleton. Rookie–Sarasota.

CLEVELAND (4): AAA–*Toledo. AA–*Jersey City. A–*Waterloo, *Batavia.

DETROIT (4): AAA–*Evansville. AA–*Montgomery. A–*Lakeland. Rookie–*Bristol, Va.

KANSAS CITY (4): AAA–Omaha. AA–*Jacksonville. A–*Daytona Beach. Rookie–Sarasota.

MILWAUKEE (4): AAA–*Spokane. AA–*Holyoke. A–*Burlington, Ia., *Newark.

MINNESOTA (5): AAA–*Tacoma. AA–Orlando. A–*Visalia, *Wisconsin Rapids. Rookie–*Elizabethton.

NEW YORK (4): AAA–*Syracuse. AA–*West Haven. A–*Oneonta, Fort Lauderdale. ,

OAKLAND (4): AAA–*San Jose. AA–*Chattanooga. A–*Modesto. Rookie–*Medicine Hat.

SEATTLE (1): A–*Bellingham.

TEXAS (4): AAA–*Tucson. AA–*Tulsa. A–*Asheville. Rookie–Sarasota.

TORONTO (1): A–*Utica.

NATIONAL LEAGUE

ATLANTA (4): AAA–Richmond. AA–Savannah. A–Greenwood. Rookie–Kingsport.

CHICAGO (5): AAA–*Wichita. AA–Midland. A–*Pompano Beach, *Geneva. Rookie–Bradenton.

CINCINNATI (6): AAA–*Indianapolis. AA–*Three Rivers. A–*Shelby, *Tampa, *Eugene. Rookie–Billings.

HOUSTON (4): AAA–*Charleston, W. Va. AA–*Columbus, Ga. A–Cocoa. Rookie–Sarasota.

LOS ANGELES (5): AAA–Albuquerque. AA–*San Antonio. A–*Lodi, *Clinton. Rookie–*Lethbridge.

MONTREAL (5): AAA–*Denver. AA–*Quebec City. A–*West Palm Beach, Jamestown. Rookie–Sarasota.

NEW YORK (5): AAA–*Tidewater. AA–*Jackson. A–*Lynchburg, *Wausau, *Little Falls.

PHILADELPHIA (5): AAA–*Oklahoma City. AA–*Reading. A–Peninsula, Spartanburg, *Auburn.

PITTSBURGH (6): AAA–*Columbus, O. AA–*Shreveport. A–*Charleston, S. C., *Salem, *Niagara Falls. Rookie–Bradenton.

ST. LOUIS (6): AAA–*New Orleans. AA–*Arkansas. A–*Gastonia, *St. Petersburg. Rookie–*Calgary, *Johnson City.

SAN DIEGO (4): AAA–*Hawaii. AA–*Amarillo. A–*Walla Walla, *Reno.

SAN FRANCISCO (5): AAA–*Phoenix. AA–*Waterbury. A–*Fresno, *Cedar Rapids. Rookie–Great Falls.

ERNIE BANKS

JOE SEWELL

AL LOPEZ

HALL OF FAME

FOR 1977

AMOS RUSIE

MARTIN DIHIGO

JOHN HENRY LLOYD

Cooperstown Admits Six New Members

By CHRIS ROEWE

Six more names were added to the list of Cooperstown immortals in the 1977 elections to bring the total of honorees to 163. The Baseball Writers' Association selected Ernie Banks, longtime Chicago Cubs' slugging star; the Committee on Veterans honored shortstop Joe Sewell, catcher and manager Al Lopez and pitcher Amos Rusie; the Special Committee on Negro Leagues named shortstop John Henry Lloyd and Martin Dihigo, who played all positions.

Banks was the eighth player to be honored in his first year of eligibility. Others with that distinction were Bob Feller, Sandy Koufax, Mickey Mantle, Stan Musial, Jackie Robinson, Warren Spahn and Ted Williams.

With 383 ballots submitted by 10-year members of the BBWAA, the 75 percent needed for election meant that a candidate had to get at least 288 votes. Banks qualified easily with 321. Eddie Mathews finished second with 239 votes. Others named by more than 200 writers were the late Gil Hodges with 224, Enos Slaughter 222 and Duke Snider 212.

Purchased by the Cubs from the Kansas City Monarchs of the Negro American League, Ernie Banks, then 22, played his first major league game on September 17, 1953, and went on to sparkle in a Cub uniform for 19 seasons, finally retiring from active play in 1971. His 2,583 hits included more than 1,000 extra-base blows—512 homers, 90 triples and 407 doubles—in compiling a lifetime batting mark of .274. Banks hit more than 40 homers in five different seasons and led the N. L. in homers in 1958 and 1960. He was the league leader in RBIs in 1958-59. Ernie was installed at shortstop when he joined the Cubs and he remained the regular at that position through 1960. His fielding percentage of .985 in 1959 is still the major league record. In 1961 Banks was shifted to first base where he performed for the balance of his career. Ernie was named Most Valuable Player in 1958-59. He served as a coach for the Cubs in 1972-73 and since 1974 has been an instructor in their farm system.

Joseph Wheeler Sewell was a pint-sized infielder who had a major league lifetime batting average of .312 for 14 seasons. Purchased by Cleveland from New Orleans of the Southern Association in September, 1920, to replace shortstop Ray Chapman who had died as the result of being hit in the head with a pitch, Joe immediately became an Indian fixture and rarely missed a game as he played shortstop, second base and third base through the 1930 season. He finished his career as the third baseman for the New York Yankees in 1931-32-33. Joe coached for the Yankees in 1934-35, scouted for Cleveland from 1952 through 1962 and for the Yankees in 1963. Sewell is best remembered as the toughest hitter to strike out. He fanned only 114 times in his 14 years in the majors and only four times in both 1925 and 1929. Two brothers also played in the majors—Tommy, an infielder who had a brief trial with the Cubs in 1927, and Luke, an American League catcher who later managed in both major leagues. Joe, now 78, lives in retirement in Tuscaloosa, Ala.

A fine defensive catcher, Alfonso Raymond Lopez played for 19 seasons in the majors in the period from 1928 through 1947. Al saw service with Brooklyn, the Boston Braves and Pittsburgh before winding up his playing career with Cleveland in the American League in 1947. Lopez was named manager of the Indians in 1951 and in six years had five second-place finishes and one pennant-winner. His 1954 club won 111 games, still an American League record. In 1957 Al took over as manager of the White Sox, a post he held through 1965. His 1959 club won the A. L. pennant, first for a White Sox team since 1919. Lopez returned briefly as Chicago skipper in 1968, finishing the season after Eddie Stanky was dismissed and starting the 1969 season before being replaced by Don Gutteridge. Lopez still holds the record for most games caught in the majors (1,918) and is tied with Gabby Hartnett for most years catching 100 or more games in the National League (12). Al is now 68 and makes his home in Tampa, Fla.

Amos Wilson Rusie was a righthanded fastballer who won 241 games in 10 National League seasons. Pitching for Indianapolis, New York and Cincinnati in the period from 1889 through 1901, Rusie had three 30-victory years. His finest year was 1894 when he was 36-13 for New York. Rusie fanned 1,953, whiffing more than 300 in 1890-91-92. He pitched a no-hit game against Brooklyn, July 31, 1891. Rusie died at Seattle, Wash., December 6, 1942.

John Henry Lloyd was primarily a shortstop but played all infield positions in his career in the Negro major leagues which extended from 1905 through 1931. A lefthanded batter, Lloyd was a consistent .300 hitter and his range at shortstop earned him the title of the Black Honus Wagner. Lloyd died on March 19, 1964 when he was 79 years old.

Martin Dihigo played in the Negro majors in the period from 1923 through 1945. A versatile player who played every position well, Dihigo was a Cuban who played several seasons in Latin America and in Mexico. Rated by some of his contemporaries as the greatest player of all time, Dihigo was Cuba's Minister of Sports when he died in 1971 at age 65.

Immediately following the selection of Lloyd and Dihigo, the Special Committee on Negro Leagues announced it was disbanding and would not meet again. In the seven years of its existence the committee voted nine stars of the Negro major leagues into the Hall of Fame. In addition to Lloyd and Dihigo those honored were Satchel Paige, Josh Gibson, Buck Leonard, Monte Irvin, Cool Papa Bell, Judy Johnson and Oscar Charleston.

The complete tabulation of the voting by the BBWAA follows: Ernie Banks, 321; Eddie Mathews, 239; Gil Hodges, 224; Enos Slaughter, 222; Duke Snider, 212; Don Drysdale, 197; Pee Wee Reese, 163; Nellie Fox, 152; Jim Bunning, 146; George Kell, 141; Richie Ashburn, 139; Red Schoendienst, 105; Lew Burdette, 85; Roger Maris, 72; Al Dark, 66; Harvey Kuenn, 57; Ted Kluszewski, 55; Mickey Vernon, 52; Walker Cooper, 45; Elston Howard, 43; Don Newcombe, 43; Don Larsen, 39; ElRoy Face, 33; Curt Flood, 16; Ken Boyer, 14; Bobby Thomson, 10; Del Crandall, 8; Harvey Haddix, 7; Vern Law, 5; Vic Wertz, 4; Bill White, 4; Dick Groat, 4; Camilo Pascual, 3; Johnny Podres, 3.

Following is a complete list of those enshrined in the Hall of Fame prior to 1977 with the vote by which each enrollee was elected:

1936—Tyrus Cobb (222), John (Honus) Wagner (215), George (Babe) Ruth (215), Christy Mathewson (205), Walter Johnson (189), named by Baseball Writers Association of America. Total ballots cast, 226.

1937—Napoleon Lajoie (168), Tristram Speaker (165), Denton (Cy) Young (153), named by the BBWAA. Total ballots cast, 201. George Wright, Morgan G. Bulkeley, Byron Bancroft Johnson, John J. McGraw, Cornelius McGillicuddy (Connie Mack), named by Centennial Commission.

1938—Grover C. Alexander (212), named by BBWAA. Total ballots, 262. Henry Chadwick, Alexander J. Cartwright, named by Centennial Commission.

1939—George Sisler (235), Edward Collins (213), William Keeler (207), Louis Gehrig, named by BBWAA. (Gehrig by special election after retirement from game was announced). Total ballots cast, 274. Albert G. Spalding, Adrian C. Anson, Charles A. Comiskey, William (Buck) Ewing, Charles Radbourn, William A. (Candy) Cummings, named by committee of old-time players and writers.

1942—Rogers Hornsby (182), named by BBWAA. Total ballots cast, 233.

1944—Judge Kenesaw M. Landis, named by committee on old timers.

1945—Hugh Duffy, Jimmy Collins, Hugh Jennings, Ed Delahanty, Fred Clarke, Mike Kelly, Wilbert Robinson, Jim O'Rourke, Dennis (Dan) Brouthers and Roger Bresnahan, named by committee on old-timers.

1946—Jesse Burkett, Frank Chance, Jack Chesbro, Johnny Evers, Clark Griffith, Tom McCarthy, Joe McGinnity, Eddie Plank, Joe Tinker, Rube Waddell and Ed Walsh, named by committee on old timers.

1947—Carl Hubbell (140), Frank Frisch (136), Gordon (Mickey) Cochrane (128) and Robert (Lefty) Grove (123), named by BBWAA. Total ballots, 161.

1948—Herbert J. Pennock (94) and Harold (Pie) Traynor (93), named by BBWAA. Total ballots cast, 121.

1949—Charles Gehringer (159), named by BBWAA in runoff election. Total ballots cast, 187. Charles (Kid) Nichols and Mordecai (Three-Finger) Brown, named by committee on old-timers.

1951—Mel Ott (197) and Jimmie Foxx (179), named by BBWAA. Total ballots cast, 226.

1952—Harry Heilmann (203) and Paul Waner (195), named by BBWAA. Total ballots cast, 234.

1953—Jerome (Dizzy) Dean (209) and Al Simmons (199), named by BBWAA. Total ballots cast, 264. Charles Albert (Chief) Bender, Roderick (Bobby) Wallace, William Klem, Tom Connolly, Edward G. Barrow and William Henry (Harry) Wright, named by the new Committee on Veterans.

1954—Walter (Rabbit) Maranville (209), William Dickey (202) and William Terry (195), named by BBWAA. Total ballots cast, 252.

1955—Joe DiMaggio (223), Ted Lyons (217), Arthur (Dazzy) Vance (205) and Charles (Gabby) Hartnett (195), named by BBWAA. Total ballots cast, 251. J. Franklin (Home Run) Baker and Ray Schalk, named by Committee on Veterans.

1956—Hank Greenberg (164) and Joe Cronin (152), named by BBWAA. Total ballots cast, 193.

1957—Joseph V. McCarthy and Sam Crawford, named by Committee on Veterans.

1959—Zachariah (Zack) Wheat, named by Committee on Veterans.

1961—Max Carey and William Hamilton, named by Committee on Veterans.

1962—Bob Feller (150) and Jackie Robinson (124), named by BBWAA. Total ballots cast, 160. Bill McKechnie and Edd Roush, named by Committee on Veterans.

1963—Eppa Rixey, Edgar (Sam) Rice, Elmer Flick and John Clarkson, named by Committee on Veterans.

1964—Luke Appling (189), named by BBWAA in runoff election. Total ballots cast, 225. Urban (Red) Faber, Burleigh Grimes, Tim Keefe, Heinie Manush, Miller Huggins and John Montgomery Ward, named by Committee on Veterans.

1965—James (Pud) Galvin, named by Committee on Veterans.

1966—Ted Williams (282), named by BBWAA. Total ballots cast, 302. Casey Stengel, named by Committee on Veterans.

1967—Charles (Red) Ruffing (266), named by BBWAA in runoff election. Total ballots cast, 306. Branch Rickey and Lloyd Waner, named by Committee on Veterans.

1968—Joseph (Ducky) Medwick (240), named by BBWAA. Total ballots cast, 283. Leon (Goose) Goslin and Hazen (Kiki) Cuyler, named by Committee on Veterans.

1969—Stan (The Man) Musial (317) and Roy Campanella (270), named by BBWAA. Total ballots cast, 340. Stan Coveleski and Waite Hoyt, named by Committee on Veterans.

1970—Lou Boudreau (232), named by BBWAA. Total ballots cast, 300. Earle Combs, Jesse Haines and Ford Frick, named by Committee on Veterans.

1971—Chick Hafey, Rube Marquard, Joe Kelley, Dave Bancroft, Harry Hooper, Jake Beckley and George Weiss, named by Committee on Veterans. Satchel Paige, named by Special Committee on Negro Leagues.

1972—Sandy Koufax (344), Yogi Berra (339) and Early Wynn (301), named by BBWAA. Total ballots cast, 396. Lefty Gomez, Will Harridge and Ross Youngs, named by Committee on Veterans. Josh Gibson and Walter (Buck) Leonard, named by Special Committee on Negro Leagues.

1973—Warren Spahn (316), named by BBWAA. Total ballots cast, 380. Roberto Clemente (393), in special election by BBWAA in which 424 ballots were cast. Billy Evans, George Kelly and Mickey Welch, named by Committee on Veterans. Monte Irvin, named by Special Committee on Negro Leagues.

1974—Mickey Mantle (322) and Whitey Ford (284), named by BBWAA. Total ballots cast, 365. Jim Bottomley, Sam Thompson and Jocko Conlan, named by Committee on Veterans. James (Cool Papa) Bell, named by Special Committee on Negro Leagues.

1975—Ralph Kiner (273), named by BBWAA. Total ballots cast, 362. Earl Averill, Bucky Harris and Billy Herman, named by Committee on Veterans. William (Judy) Johnson, named by Special Committee on Negro Leagues.

1976—Robin Roberts (337) and Bob Lemon (305), named by BBWAA. Total ballots cast, 388. Roger Connor, Cal Hubbard and Fred Lindstrom, named by Committee on Veterans. Oscar Charleston, named by Special Committee on Negro Leagues.

✶☉✶

Hotels of Major League Teams

AMERICAN LEAGUE

AT BALTIMORE: Baltimore Hilton–Detroit, Minnesota, Texas. **Cross Keys Inn**–Boston, California, Kansas City, Milwaukee, Oakland, Seattle, Toronto. **Hilton Inn**–Chicago, Cleveland, New York.

AT BOSTON: Holiday Inn (Somerville)–Seattle. **Sheraton-Boston**–All clubs except Seattle.

AT CALIFORNIA: Grand–Detroit, Minnesota. **Hyatt House Anaheim**–Boston, Chicago, Cleveland, Kansas City, New York, Oakland, Texas, Toronto. **Hyatt House Long Beach**–Baltimore (except August 5, 6 & 7 at Hyatt House Anaheim). **Inn at the Park**–Milwaukee. **South Coast Plaza (Costa Mesa)**–Seattle.

AT CHICAGO: Continental Plaza–New York. **Executive House**–Detroit, Milwaukee. **Sheraton Plaza**–Baltimore, Boston, Kansas City, Minnesota, Seattle, Texas, Toronto. **Water Tower Hyatt**–California, Cleveland, Oakland.

AT CLEVELAND: Holiday Inn (North Randall)–Seattle. **Hollenden House**–All clubs except Seattle.

AT DETROIT: Ponchartrain–All clubs except Oakland and Seattle. **Detroit Plaza**–Seattle. **Sheraton Southfield**–Oakland.

AT KANSAS CITY: Sheraton Royal–All clubs.

AT MILWAUKEE: Marc Plaza–Chicago, Cleveland, Oakland, Seattle. **Pfister**–All other clubs. Oakland will stay at Pfister September 16, 17 & 18.

AT MINNESOTA: Leamington–All clubs except California and Seattle. **Radisson**–California and Seattle.

AT NEW YORK: New York Sheraton–All clubs except Detroit and Seattle. **St. Moritz**–Seattle. **Roosevelt**–Detroit.

AT OAKLAND: Hilton–Minnesota, Seattle, Texas. **Oakland Hyatt House**–All other clubs.

AT SEATTLE: Hilton–Boston (at Washington Plaza August 2 & 3), Chicago, Kansas City, Minnesota (at Sea Tac Motor Inn July 26, 27 & 28), Toronto. **Olympic**–Texas. **Sea Tac Motor Inn**–Baltimore. **Seattle Hyatt House**–Oakland. **University Tower**–New York. **Washington Plaza**–California (at Sheraton Renton July 24 & 25), Cleveland (at Sea Tac Motor Inn August 22), Detroit, Milwaukee.

AT TEXAS: Inn of Six Flags (Arlington)–New York, Oakland, Toronto. **Rodeway Inn (Arlington)**–Cleveland, Detroit. **Sheraton-Dallas**–Baltimore, Boston, California, Chicago, Detroit, Milwaukee, Minnesota. **Sheraton Safari**–Seattle.

AT TORONTO: Sheraton Centre–California, Texas. **Royal York**–Kansas City. **Toronto**–All clubs except California, Texas and Kansas City.

NATIONAL LEAGUE

AT ATLANTA: Marriott–All clubs.

AT CHICAGO: Executive House–Atlanta. **Hyatt House**–San Francisco. **Hyatt Regency**–Los Angeles, Montreal. **Sheraton Plaza**–Cincinnati, Houston, New York, Philadelphia, Pittsburgh, St. Louis, San Diego.

AT CINCINNATI: Stouffer's Inn–Atlanta, New York, Philadelphia, Pittsburgh, St. Louis. **Terrace Hilton**–Chicago, Houston, Los Angeles, Montreal, San Diego, San Francisco.

AT HOUSTON: Marriott–Atlanta, Chicago, Cincinnati, Los Angeles, Montreal, San Diego. **Shamrock Hilton**–New York, Philadelphia, Pittsburgh, St. Louis, San Francisco.

AT LOS ANGELES: Hyatt Regency–Atlanta, Chicago, Houston, New York, Pittsburgh, St. Louis. **Los Angeles Hilton**–Cincinnati. **Sheraton West**–Montreal, San Diego. **Wilshire Hyatt House**–Philadelphia, San Francisco.

AT MONTREAL: Loew's La Cite–All clubs except Chicago, Philadelphia, Pittsburgh. **Queen Elizabeth**–Chicago, Philadelphia, Pittsburgh.

AT NEW YORK: New York Sheraton—Cincinnati, Houston, Philadelphia, Pittsburgh, St. Louis, San Diego, San Francisco. **Roosevelt**—Atlanta. **Waldorf Astoria**—Chicago, Los Angeles, Montreal.

AT PHILADELPHIA: Hilton Inn—Los Angeles. **Holiday Inn**—Chicago, New York, St. Louis, San Diego, San Francisco. **Marriott**—Montreal. **Philadelphia Hilton**—Atlanta, Cincinnati, Pittsburgh. **Philadelphia Sheraton**—Houston.

AT PITTSBURGH: Carlton House—Cincinnati, San Francisco. **Hyatt House**—Philadelphia. **Pittsburgh Hilton**—Chicago, Los Angeles, Montreal, New York, St. Louis, San Diego. **William Penn**—Atlanta, Houston.

AT ST. LOUIS: Breckenridge Pavilion—Chicago. **Chase-Park Plaza**—Atlanta, Houston, New York. **Stouffer's Inn**—Cincinnati, Los Angeles, Montreal, Philadelphia, Pittsburgh, San Diego, San Francisco.

AT SAN DIEGO: Sheraton Harbor Island—Atlanta, Chicago, Montreal, New York, Pittsburgh, St. Louis. **Town & Country**—Cincinnati, Houston, Los Angeles, Philadelphia, San Francisco.

AT SAN FRANCISCO: Jack Tar—Chicago, San Diego. **San Francisco Hilton**—Atlanta, Los Angeles, Montreal, New York, Philadelphia, Pittsburgh. **Sheraton Palace**—Cincinnati, Houston, St. Louis.

Baltimore Deals Made Headlines in '76

By CHRIS ROEWE

Baltimore was involved in the two biggest trades of 1976, dealing with Oakland shortly before the season opened and with the Yankees at the trading deadline.

On April 2 the Orioles sent outfielder Don Baylor and pitchers Mike Torrez and Paul Mitchell to the A's in exchange for outfielder Reggie Jackson and pitchers Ken Holtzman and Bill Van Bommel, the latter a righthander with no major league experience.

Both Jackson and Holtzman brought contract disputes with them and when the Orioles were unable to satisfy Holtzman's demands he was included in a 10-player trade with the Yankees, June 15. Along with the lefthander the Orioles dealt pitchers Doyle Alexander, Grant Jackson and Jimmy Freeman and catcher Ellie Hendricks to the Bombers for pitchers Rudy May, Tippy Martinez, Dave Pagan and Scott McGregor and catcher Rick Dempsey.

Pitcher Andy Messersmith signed with the Braves, April 10, after having won his free agency in a legal battle over the interpretation of the reserve clause. It was a landmark case that resulted in 25 major league players becoming free agents at the end of the season for the purpose of a "re-entry draft," which is discussed elsewhere in this book.

The Twins could not meet the financial requests of their young pitching star, Bert Blyleven, and on June 1 they reluctantly traded him with ill-fated shortstop Danny Thompson to the Rangers for pitchers Bill Singer and Jim Gideon, infielders Roy Smalley and Mike Cubbage and cash estimated at $250,000.

One manager was included in the transactions of 1976. The Pirates traded popular catcher Manny Sanguillen and an estimated $100,000 in cash to the Athletics for the services of manager Chuck Tanner, November 5.

The winter meetings, usually the scene of many player shifts, produced only 14 transactions. The most surprising move was the Rangers' trade on December 9 of their young home-run hitting outfielder, Jeff Burroughs, to the Braves for outfielders Ken Henderson and Dave May, pitchers Carl Morton, Roger Moret and Adrian Devine and cash estimated at $250,000.

A chronological listing of major league deals follows:

January 7—Tigers signed outfielder Alex Johnson, a free agent.

January 8—Yankees purchased pitcher Jim York from Astros and assigned him to Syracuse.

January 9—Cardinals purchased infielder Terry Hughes from Rhode Island, Red Sox' affiliate, and assigned him to Tulsa.

January 12—Angels traded pitcher Bill Rothan, on El Paso roster, to Cardinals for outfielder Dick Sharon, on Tulsa roster; Rothan was assigned to Arkansas and Sharon to Salt Lake City.

January 13—Brewers signed outfielder Vada Pinson, a free agent.

January 27—Yankees released outfielder Walt Williams.

February 3—Cardinals purchased pitcher Tom Walker, on Evansville roster, from Tigers and assigned him to Tulsa.

February 11—Twins released outfielder John Briggs.

February 13—Dodgers signed pitcher Ron Bryant, a free agent, and assigned him to Albuquerque.

February 14—Expos signed pitcher Wayne Granger, a free agent, and assigned him to Denver.

February 15—Red Sox signed shortstop Gene Michael, a free agent.

February 20—Angels purchased catcher Ed Herrmann from Yankees.

February 24—Yankees signed outfielder-first baseman Tommy Davis, released by Orioles.

February 24—Mets traded pitcher George Stone to Rangers for pitcher Bill Hands; Stone was assigned to Sacramento and Hands to Tidewater.

March 2—Cardinals traded second baseman Ted Sizemore to Dodgers for outfielder Willie Crawford.

March 3—Red Sox traded pitcher Dick Drago to Angels for outfielders John Balaz and Dick Sharon and infielder Dave Machemer; Sharon and Machemer were assigned from Salt Lake City to Rhode Island.

March 5—Angels acquired pitcher Chuck Ross from Red Sox, completing deal of June 14, 1975, in which Red Sox obtained second baseman Denny Doyle from Angels.

March 21—Dodgers traded outfielder Jesus Alvarez and cash to Angels for catcher Ellie Rodriguez; Alvarez was assigned to Salt Lake City.

March 24—Rangers released shortstop Leo Cardenas.

March 26—Mets released outfielder Joe Lovitto.

March 29—Yankees released shortstop Eddie Brinkman.

March 30—White Sox released pitcher Cecil Upshaw.

March 30—Mets released outfielder Jesus Alou.

April 1—Phillies signed outfielder-first baseman Bobby Tolan, released by Padres.

April 2—Rangers released pitcher Clyde Wright.

April 2—Cardinals purchased pitcher Lerrin LaGrow from Tigers and assigned him to Tulsa.

April 2—Athletics traded outfielder Reggie Jackson and pitchers Ken Holtzman and Bill Van Bommel to Orioles for outfielder Don Baylor and pitchers Mike Torrez and Paul Mitchell.

April 3—White Sox signed outfielder Cleon Jones, a free agent.

April 5—Cardinals assigned shortstop Bob Hrapmann from Arkansas to Midland, Cubs' affiliate, to complete deal in which Cardinals acquired shortstop Don Kessinger, October 28, 1975.

April 5—White Sox released pitcher Claude Osteen.

April 5—Brewers released outfielder Vada Pinson.

April 5—Reds traded outfielder Merv Rettenmund to Padres for shortstop Rudy Meoli and cash; Meoli was assigned to Indianapolis.

April 6—Athletics signed infielder Ken McMullen, released by Dodgers.

April 7—Yankees released outfielder-first baseman Tommy Davis.

April 7—Red Sox released pitcher Diego Segui.

April 7—Reds traded outfielder Terry Crowley to Braves for pitcher Mike Thompson, assigned to Indianapolis.

April 7—Cardinals traded pitcher Harry Parker to Indians for pitcher Roric Harrison; Parker was assigned to Toledo and Harrison to Tulsa.

April 8—Padres traded pitcher Danny Frisella to Cardinals for pitcher Ken Reynolds, assigned to Hawaii, and pitcher Bob Stewart, assigned from Arkansas to Amarillo.

April 8—Giants released pitcher Tom Bradley.

April 8—Angels purchased pitcher Wayne Simpson from Phillies and assigned him to Salt Lake City.

April 9—Orioles signed outfielder Tommy Harper, a free agent.

April 10—Braves signed pitcher Andy Messersmith who had won his free agency in a contract dispute with the Dodgers.

April 13—Cubs purchased catcher Randy Hundley from Padres.

April 14—Pirates signed pitcher Tom Hilgendorf, released by Phillies, and assigned him to Charleston, W. Va.

April 19—Phillies purchased catcher Tim Blackwell, on Rhode Island roster, from Red Sox.

April 19—Athletics purchased catcher Tim Hosley from Cubs and assigned him to Tucson.

April 22—Cubs released pitcher Tom Dettore.

April 29—White Sox signed infielder Roland (Sonny) Jackson, a free agent, and assigned him to Iowa.

May 3—White Sox released outfielder Cleon Jones.

May 3—Twins released pitcher Ray Corbin.

May 4 Red Sox released shortstop Gene Michael.

May 7—Mets traded pitcher Tom Hall to Royals for infielder Bryan Jones, assigned from Waterloo to Lynchburg, and cash.

May 7—Athletics released infielder Teddy Martinez.

May 13—Brewers signed pitcher Ray Sadecki, released by Royals.

May 16—Yankees traded pitcher Larry Gura to Royals for catcher Fran Healy.

May 17—Cubs traded first baseman Andy Thornton to Expos for pitcher Steve Renko and outfielder-first baseman Larry Biittner.

May 18—White Sox traded outfielder Carlos May to Yankees for pitcher Ken Brett and outfielder Rich Coggins.

May 19—Cardinals traded outfielder Luis Melendez to Padres for pitcher Bill Greif.

May 26—Orioles signed outfielder Terry Crowley, released by Braves, and assigned him to Rochester.

May 28—Indians traded pitcher Fritz Peterson to Rangers for pitcher Stan Perzanowski and cash; Perzanowski was assigned to Toledo.

May 28—Indians purchased pitcher Cardell Camper from Cardinals and assigned him to Toledo.

May 29—Cardinals traded infielder Mario Guerrero, on Tulsa roster, to Angels for catcher Ed Jordan, assigned from El Paso to Arkansas, and a player to be named; Angels assigned first baseman-outfielder Ed Kurpiel from Salt Lake City to Tulsa to complete deal, July 30.

June 1—Twins traded pitcher Bert Blyleven and shortstop Danny Thompson to Rangers for pitcher Bill Singer, infielders Roy Smalley and Mike Cubbage and pitcher Jim Gideon, latter assigned to Tacoma, and cash estimated at $250,000.

June 2—Giants traded outfielder Von Joshua to Brewers for a player to be named later; deal was completed with a cash payment.

June 2—Angels signed outfielder-first baseman Tommy Davis, a free agent.

June 3—Red Sox traded outfielder Bernie Carbo and cash to Brewers for pitcher Tom Murphy and outfielder Bobby Darwin.

June 4—Red Sox released first baseman Deron Johnson.

June 6—Angels traded catcher Ed Herrmann to Astros for catcher Terry Humphrey and pitcher Mike Barlow, both assigned to Salt Lake City.

June 7—Cardinals traded pitcher Danny Frisella to Brewers for a player to be named later; outfielder Sam Mejias was assigned to Tulsa, June 23 to complete deal.

June 8—Tigers traded pitcher Joe Coleman to Cubs for cash and a player to be named later.

June 9—Athletics signed first baseman Nate Colbert, released by Expos, and assigned him to Tucson.

June 10—Brewers traded second baseman Pedro Garcia to Tigers for second baseman Gary Sutherland.

June 13—Braves traded third baseman-first baseman Darrell Evans and shortstop Marty Perez to Giants for first baseman Willie Montanez, shortstop Craig Robinson, outfielder Jerald (Jake) Brown, latter assigned to Savannah, and infielder Mike Eden, assigned from Phoenix to Richmond.

June 15—Brewers released pitcher Ed Sprague.

June 15—Rangers purchased outfielder Joe Lahoud from Angels.

June 15—White Sox traded catcher Richard (Pete) Varney to Braves for pitcher Johnny Odom, assigned from Richmond to Iowa.

June 15—Cardinals traded outfielder Reggie Smith to Dodgers for catcher-outfielder Joe Ferguson, outfielder Bobby Detherage and infielder Freddie Tisdale, latter assigned from Lodi to St. Petersburg.

June 15—Orioles traded pitchers Ken Holtzman, Doyle Alexander and Grant Jackson, catcher Ellie Hendricks and pitcher Jimmy Freeman, latter assigned from Rochester to Syracuse, to Yankees for pitchers Rudy May, Felix (Tippy) Martinez, Dave Pagan and Scott McGregor and catcher Rick Dempsey.

June 20—Brewers released pitcher Billy Champion.

June 22—Mets traded infielder Jack Heidemann to Brewers for pitcher Tom Deidel, assigned from Berkshire to Jackson, and cash.

June 23—Dodgers traded pitcher Mike Marshall to Braves for pitcher Elias Sosa and infielder Lee Lacy.

July 5—Royals purchased pitcher Andy Hassler from Angels.

July 8—Expos released pitcher Fred Scherman.

July 10—Padres traded outfielder Gene Locklear to Yankees for a player to be named later; Locklear was assigned to Syracuse; Yankees assigned pitcher Rick Sawyer from Syracuse to Padres to complete deal, July 31.

July 14—Angels purchased first baseman Tolia (Tony) Solaita from Royals.

July 14—White Sox traded outfielder Rich Coggins to Phillies for outfielder Wayne Nordhagen, on Oklahoma City roster; Coggins was assigned to Oklahoma City.

July 21—Mets traded outfielder Del Unser and infielder Wayne Garrett to Expos for outfielders Jim Dwyer and Jose (Pepe) Mangual.

July 24—Braves traded catcher-first baseman Earl Williams to Expos for a player to be named later; deal was completed with a cash payment.

July 24—White Sox released outfielder Charles (Buddy) Bradford.

August 3—Padres purchased pitcher Tom Griffin from Astros.

August 9—White Sox signed catcher Phil Roof, released by Twins.

August 11—Dodgers signed outfielder Jim Lyttle, a free agent.

August 30—Athletics purchased first baseman Willie McCovey from Padres.

September 1—Yankees signed infielder-outfielder Cesar Tovar, released by Athletics.

September 3—Cardinals traded outfielder Mike Easler, on Tulsa roster, to Angels for infielder Ron Farkas, assigned from El Paso to Tulsa, September 7.

September 8—Cubs purchased pitcher Ramon Hernandez from Pirates.

September 9—Angels purchased infielder Tim Nordbrook from Orioles.

September 10—White Sox signed coach Orestes Minoso to a player contract; released him, October 6.

September 14—Athletics purchased first baseman-outfielder Ron Fairly from Cardinals.

September 17—Royals purchased pitcher Ken Sanders from Mets.

September 20—Royals purchased outfielder-first baseman Tommy Davis from Angels.

September 29—Mariners purchased pitcher Dave Johnson from Rochester, Orioles' affiliate.

October 15—Mariners purchased pitcher Jim Minshall from Pirates.

October 20—Cardinals traded outfielder Willie Crawford, infielder-outfielder Vic Harris and pitcher John Curtis to Giants for pitchers John D'Acquisto and Mike Caldwell and catcher Dave Rader.

October 21—Blue Jays purchased catcher Phil Roof from Iowa, White Sox' affiliate; Blue Jays assigned pitcher Larry Anderson to White Sox to complete deal, January 5, 1977.

October 22—Blue Jays purchased infielder Dave Hilton, outfielder John Scott and infielder-catcher Dave Roberts from Hawaii, Padres' affiliate.

October 22—Cardinals traded pitcher Mike Wallace to Rangers for pitcher Johnny Ike Sutton, assigned from Sacramento to New Orleans.

October 22—Mariners purchased infielder Kurt Bevacqua from Spokane, Brewers' affiliate.

October 22—Mariners purchased catcher Larry Cox from Tacoma, Twins' affiliate.

October 22—Mariners purchased pitcher Diego Segui from Hawaii, Padres' affiliate.

October 22—Mariners purchased infielder Jose Baez from Albuquerque, Dodgers' affiliate.

October 24—Mariners purchased pitcher Tommy Moore from Sacramento, Rangers' affiliate.

November 1—Dodgers released outfielder Jim Lyttle.

November 2—Dodgers released outfielder Leron Lee.

November 2—Expos released pitcher Chuck Taylor.

November 2—Phillies released infielder Tony Taylor.

November 5—Pirates traded catcher Manny Sanguillen and cash estimated at

$100,000 to Athletics for manager Chuck Tanner.

November 5—Athletics purchased second baseman Tommy Helms from Pirates.

November 5—Blue Jays traded pitcher Al Fitzmorris to Indians for catcher Alan Ashby and first baseman-outfielder Doug Howard, latter on Toledo roster.

November 5—Blue Jays purchased pitcher Chuck Hartenstein from Hawaii, Padres' affiliate.

November 6—Cardinals traded pitchers Bill Greif and Angel Torres and outfielder Sam Mejias to Expos for pitcher Steve Dunning, infielder Pat Scanlon and outfielder Tony Scott, latter on Denver roster.

November 6—Cardinals released pitcher Lloyd Allen and infielder Lee Richard.

November 6—Mariners purchased pitcher John Montague from Oklahoma City, Phillies' affiliate.

November 6—Tigers purchased infielder Luis Alvarado from Cardinals.

November 6—Reds traded outfielder Tommy Spencer to White Sox for infielder Hugh Yancy, on Iowa roster; Spencer was assigned to Iowa and Yancy to Indianapolis.

November 6—Reds traded pitcher Tom Carroll to Pirates for pitcher Jim Sadowski, on Charleston, W. Va., roster; Carroll was assigned to Charleston and Sadowski to Indianapolis.

November 8—Rangers traded pitcher Art DeFilippis, on Sacramento roster, to Reds for pitcher Mike Thompson, on Indianapolis roster; DeFilippis was assigned to Indianapolis and Thompson to Sacramento.

November 9—Athletics released outfielder Billy Williams.

November 18—Orioles traded catcher Dave Duncan to White Sox for outfielder Pat Kelly.

November 23—Astros traded pitcher Larry Dierker and infielder Jerry DaVanon to Cardinals for catcher-outfielder Joe Ferguson and outfielder Bobby Detherage, latter assigned to Memphis.

November 29—Astros signed outfielder Jim Fuller, a free agent.

November 29—Yankees purchased outfielder Jim Wynn from Braves.

December 2—Expos released pitcher Clay Kirby.

December 3—Angels traded third baseman Bill Melton to Indians for cash and a player to be named later.

December 6—Indians traded outfielder John Lowenstein and catcher Rick Cerone to Blue Jays for first baseman Rico Carty.

December 6—Brewers traded pitcher Jim Colborn and catcher Darrell Porter to Royals for outfielder Jim Wohlford, infielder Jamie Quirk and a player to be named later.

December 6—Red Sox traded first baseman Cecil Cooper to Brewers for first baseman George Scott and outfielder Bernie Carbo.

December 6—Brewers purchased catcher Larry Haney from Athletics.

December 6—Twins purchased outfielder Glenn Adams from Giants.

December 6 Royals purchased infielder Bob Heise from Red Sox.

December 7—Mariners traded pitcher Grant Jackson to Pirates for infielders Craig Reynolds and Jim Sexton.

December 8—Indians traded outfielder George Hendrick to Padres for outfielder Johnny Grubb, catcher Fred Kendall and shortstop Hector Torres.

December 8—Astros traded outfielder Greg Gross to Cubs for infielder Julio Gonzalez.

December 8—In three-club deal, Cubs traded outfielder-first baseman Pete LaCock to the Royals, the Mets sent outfielder Jim Dwyer from Tidewater to Wichita, Cubs' affiliate, and the Mets were to receive a player from the Royals later; Royals assigned outfielder Sheldon Mallory to Tidewater, Mets' affiliate, to complete deal, December 13.

December 9—Rangers traded outfielder Jeff Burroughs to the Braves for outfielders Ken Henderson and Dave May, pitchers Carl Morton, Roger Moret and Adrian Devine and cash estimated at $250,000.

December 9—Cardinals traded first baseman-outfielder Ed Kurpiel, on New Orleans roster, to Mets for outfielder Leon Brown and first baseman Brock Pemberton, both on Tidewater roster; Kurpiel was assigned to Tidewater and Brown and Pemberton to New Orleans.

December 10—Cardinals traded pitcher Lynn McGlothen to Giants for third baseman Ken Reitz.

December 10—Indians traded pitcher Jackie Brown to Expos for first baseman Andy Thornton.

December 10—White Sox traded pitchers Terry Forster and Rich Gossage to Pirates for outfielder Richie Zisk and pitcher Silvio Martinez.

December 13—Braves purchased pitcher Steve Kline from Toledo, Indians' affiliate.

December 13—Royals released pitcher Ken Sanders.

December 14—Brewers released pitcher Ray Sadecki.

December 15—Tigers released catcher Bill Freehan.

December 16—Tigers released outfielder Alex Johnson and second baseman Pedro Garcia.

December 16—Reds traded first baseman Tony Perez and pitcher Will McEnaney to Expos for pitchers Woodie Fryman and Dale Murray.

December 17—Orioles released outfielder Tommy Harper.

December 17—Yankees released infielder-outfielder Cesar Tovar.

December 20—Dodgers traded infielder Ted Sizemore to Phillies for catcher Johnny Oates and a player to be named later; pitcher R. Quency Hill was assigned by the Phillies to Albuquerque, Dodgers' affiliate, to complete the deal, January 4, 1977.

December 21—Orioles released pitcher Mike Cuellar.

Seven Selected in Major League Draft

The major league draft opened the proceedings at the 75th annual winter meetings held at the Hilton Hotel in Los Angeles and seven players were chosen for the $25,000 draft price.

Tom Carroll, a righthander who had a couple of flings with the Cincinnati Reds, was the first player chosen in the draft. The Montreal Expos tabbed the 24-year-old from the Pittsburgh organization. Carroll was 4-3 with Cincinnati in 1974 and 4-1 in '75. He became Pirate property in a minor league trade only a month before the draft.

The expansion Seattle Mariners opted for first baseman-outfielder Charles Beamon, a 23-year-old performer from the Kansas City Royals' farm system.

Roger Freed, two-time National Association Player of the Year (1970 and 1976), was chosen by the St. Louis Cardinals from Montreal's Denver club.

The Chicago Cubs picked lefthander Guillermo Hernandez from the Philadelphia system and former major leaguers Teddy Martinez, an infielder, and outfielder Rich Chiles were picked by the Dodgers and Twins, respectively.

Martinez spent five years with the New York Mets and had also seen service with St. Louis and Oakland. He was taken from the Cincinnati chain. Chiles was grabbed from Houston's Memphis club. He had spent parts of three seasons with the Astros and one year with the Mets.

Outfielder Mike Dimmel was chosen by the Baltimore Orioles to complete the draft. He had been a Dodger farmhand.

Three Hall of Famers Die in 1976

By CHRIS ROEWE

Baseball mourned the passing of many of its illustrious players and executives in 1976.

Three stars enshrined in the Hall of Fame were among the decedents—outfielders Max Carey and Earle Combs and pitcher Red Faber.

Carey, whose real name was Maximilian Carnarius, was a National League outfielder from 1910 through 1929. He had his greatest years with Pittsburgh where he won fame as a base stealer. His 738 stolen bases is the second highest total in modern National League history. Max coached for Pittsburgh in 1930 and managed Brooklyn in 1932-33. He was 86 when he died at Miami Beach, Fla., May 30. Carey was elected to the Hall of Fame in 1961.

Earle Combs is best remembered as the center fielder and leadoff man for the 1927 New York Yankees, perhaps the greatest club of all time. Combs had his finest season that year, batting .356 and leading the league in hits and triples. Earle batted .325 in a 12-year career with the Yankees that began in 1924. He later served as a coach with the Yankees, St. Louis Browns, Boston Red Sox and Philadelphia Phillies. Combs, 77, died at Richmond, Ky., July 21, just seven years after being named to the Cooperstown shrine.

Urban Charles (Red) Faber, 88, died at Chicago, September 25. Faber spent his entire 20-year major league career that began in 1914 with the Chicago White Sox, winning 254 games. Red led the league in earned-run average in 1921-22 and worked 300 or more innings in four seasons. He was the star of the 1917 World Series, winning three games as the Sox defeated the New York Giants, four games to two. Faber won election to the Hall of Fame in 1964.

Four players, a manager and a chief executive, all of whom were active on the major league scene in 1976, died during the year and in the early days of January, 1977.

Tom Yawkey, popular owner of the Boston Red Sox since 1933 who brought three pennants to Boston, died there, July 9, at 73. Bob Moose, 29-year-old Pittsburgh pitcher, was killed in an auto accident near Martins Ferry, O., October 9. Danny Murtaugh, 59, Pittsburgh manager, who had announced his retirement at the end of the 1976 season, died of a heart attack at Chester, Pa., December 2; an infielder with the Phillies, Braves and Pirates in the period from 1941 through 1951, Murtaugh was a longtime Pittsburgh employee who served four hitches as Pirate skipper. Danny Thompson, shortstop who broke into the majors with Minnesota in 1970 and was traded to the Texas Rangers during the 1976 season, lost a courageous battle with leukemia at Rochester, Minn., December 10. Like Moose he was only 29. Danny Frisella, a major league pitcher since 1967 who was with St. Louis and Milwaukee in 1976, was killed in a dune buggy accident near Phoenix, Ariz., January 1, 1977. He was 30. Mike Miley, 23-year-old shortstop with the California Angels for parts of the 1975 and 1976 seasons, was killed in an auto crash at Baton Rouge, La., January 6, 1977.

The names of quite a few other prominent baseball people were found in the obituary columns in 1976. Among the more familiar were Larry Gardner, American League third baseman for 17 seasons who played for four World Series winners; Jim Konstanty, one of the game's greatest relief pitchers who won Most Valuable Player honors while leading the Phillies to a pennant in 1950; Jimmy Dykes, regular third baseman for the Philadelphia Athletics when they won consecutive pennants in 1929-30-31 and the manager of six major league clubs; Lon Warneke, great righthander who won 192 games for the Chicago Cubs and St. Louis Cardinals; Fred Marberry, one of the first hurlers to win acclaim as a relief artist; John Quinn, National League executive for many years with the Boston and Milwaukee Braves and the Phillies; George Earnshaw, teammate of Jimmy Dykes at Philadelphia in the pennant years of 1929-30-31 who won 67 games in that period; Wes Ferrell, righthander who won 20 or more games each year from 1929 through 1932, his first four full seasons in the majors.

An alphabetical listing of baseball deaths in 1976 follows:

George Wilson (Bill) Aiton, 85, outfielder with the St. Louis Browns briefly in 1912, at Van Nuys, Calif., August 16.

William Askew (Chick) Autry, 91, first baseman-outfielder with Cincinnati in 1907 and 1909 and the Boston Braves in 1909, at Santa Rosa, Calif., January 16.

William Mallory Bagwell, 80, outfielder with the Boston Braves in 1923 and Philadelphia Athletics in 1925, at Choudrant, La., October 5.

Daniel Robert Bankhead, 55, the first Negro to pitch in the major leagues when he appeared in four games for Brooklyn in 1947, at Houston, Tex., May 2; also pitched for Brooklyn in 1950-51; hit home run in first time at bat in major leagues, August 26, 1947.

Joseph Howard Berry, Jr., 79, infielder with the New York Giants briefly in 1921-22, at Philadelphia, Pa., April 29.

Frank Leo Brazill, 77, infielder with the Philadelphia Athletics in 1921-22 and a scout for the New York Giants in 1940-41, at Oakland, Calif., November 3.

Roland D. Burke, 63, managing editor of The Sporting Goods DEALER, sister publication of THE SPORTING NEWS, from 1969 until his death at St. Louis, Mo., August 1.

Robert Butler, 58, scout for Minnesota from 1965 through 1974 and a member of the Major League Scouting Bureau when he died at Lincoln, R.I., September 17.

Max George Carey (Maximilian Carnarius), 86, outfielder and premier base stealer and a member of the Hall of Fame, at Miami Beach, Fla., May 30; played with Pittsburgh from 1910 through 1926 and with Brooklyn from 1926 through 1929; coached for Pittsburgh in 1930 and managed Brooklyn in 1932-33; made 2,665 hits in compiling a lifetime major league batting average of .285; holds major league mark for most years leading league in stolen bases (10); stole 738 bases, second highest total in modern National League history; was credited with 51 steals in 53 attempts in 1922; elected to Hall of Fame in 1961.

Ollie A. Carnegie, 77, outfielder with Buffalo in the International League from 1931 through 1941 and again in 1945, at Buffalo, N. Y., October 4; holds International League home run record with 258; named most valuable player in 1938 when he batted .330 with 45 homers and 134 RBIs.

Paul Chervinko, 65, catcher with Brooklyn in 1937-38, at Danville, Ill., June 3.

Mark Joseph Christman, 62, major league infielder and scout, at St. Louis, Mo., October 9; played with Detroit in 1938-39, the St. Louis Browns in 1939 and from 1943 through 1946 and Washington in 1947-48-49; scouted for Washington in 1957, New York Yankees from 1959 through 1973, Oakland in 1974 and Los Angeles in 1975-76; was regular third baseman for the Browns in 1944 when they won their only pennant.

Earle Bryan Combs, 77, outfielder with the New York Yankees from 1924 through 1935 and a member of the Hall of Fame, at Richmond, Ky., July 21; made 1,866 hits in compiling a major league lifetime batting mark of .325; as the center fielder and leadoff man for the 1927 Yankees, generally considered the greatest team of all time, he batted .356 and led league in hits (231), triples (23) and putouts by an outfielder (411); also led league in triples with 21 in 1928 and 22 in 1930; batted .350 in World Series play with 21 hits in 60 times at bat in the Series of 1926-27-28-32; career was shortened when he crashed into the wall at Sportsman's Park, St. Louis, July 24, 1934, suffering a fractured skull; coached for the Yankees from 1935 through 1944, St. Louis Browns in 1947, Boston Red

Sox from 1948 through 1952 and Philadelphia Phillies in 1954; named to Hall of Fame in 1970.

Robert Daniel Cooney, 68, pitcher with the St. Louis Browns in 1931-32, at Glens Falls, N. Y., May 5.

Chester Rogers Covington, 65, pitcher with the Philadelphia Phillies briefly in 1944, at Pembroke Park, Fla., June 11; named minor league Player of the Year by THE SPORTING NEWS in 1943 when he won 21 games, pitched a perfect game and had an ERA of 1.51 for Scranton of the Eastern League.

Bernard Aloysius Culloton, 80, pitcher with Pittsburgh briefly in 1925-26, at Kingston, N. Y., November 30.

George Willard (Skeets) Dickey, 60, catcher with the Boston Red Sox in 1935-36 and Chicago White Sox in 1941-42 and 1946-47 and a brother of Bill Dickey, former catcher for the New York Yankees who is a member of the Hall of Fame, at DeWitt, Ark., June 16.

Sylvester Urban (Blix) Donnelly, 62, pitcher with the St. Louis Cardinals in 1944-45-46, Philadelphia Phillies from 1946 through 1950 and Boston Braves in 1951, at Olivia, Minn., June 20; made two relief appearances in the all-St. Louis World Series of 1944 and did not allow a run in six innings as the Cardinals defeated the Browns.

Thomas B. Dowd, 74, traveling secretary of the Boston Red Sox from 1946 through 1968 and a former National Football League official, at Boston, Mass., February 19.

Thomas Patrick Dunn, 75, umpire in the National League from 1939 through 1946, at Prince Georges Co., Md., January 20.

Edward Fant (Bull) Durham, 68, pitcher with the Boston Red Sox from 1929 through 1932 and Chicago White Sox in 1933, at Chester, S. C., April 27.

James Joseph Dykes, 79, major league infielder and manager, at Philadelphia, Pa., June 15; played with the Philadelphia Athletics from 1918 through 1932 and Chicago White Sox from 1933 through 1939; made 2,256 hits in compiling a major league lifetime batting mark of .280; was regular third baseman for the Athletics when they won consecutive pennants in 1929-30-31; served as player-manager and manager of the White Sox from 1934 to May 25, 1946; coached for the Athletics in 1949-50 and served as manager from May 26, 1950 through the 1953 season; managed Baltimore in 1954; coached for Cincinnati from 1955 until August 14, 1958 when he was named manager for the balance of the season; began the 1959 season as a Pittsburgh coach and was named Detroit manager, May 3, a post he held until August 3, 1960, when he and Joe Gordon, Cleveland manager, swapped jobs; managed Cleveland in 1961, coached for Milwaukee in 1962 and Kansas City in 1963-64.

George Livingston Earnshaw, 76, pitcher who was one of the mainstays of the staff of the Philadelphia Athletics when they won consecutive pennants in 1929-30-31, at Little Rock, Ark., December 1; pitched for the Athletics from 1928 through 1933, the Chicago White Sox in 1934-35, Brooklyn in 1935-36 and St. Louis Cardinals in 1936; had marks of 24-8, 22-13 and 21-7 in 1929-30-31 and won four games and lost three in the World Series of those years.

Eugene Birminghouse Elliott, 88, outfielder with the New York Yankees briefly in 1911, at Huntingdon, Pa., January 5.

Joseph Michael Erautt, 55, catcher with the Chicago White Sox briefly in 1950-51, at Portland, Ore., October 6.

Urban Charles (Red) Faber, 88, a member of the Hall of Fame, whose entire major league career was spent with the Chicago White Sox for whom he pitched from 1914 through 1933, at Chicago, Ill., September 25; had four 20-win seasons, finishing with 254 victories and 212 losses in the majors; led league in earned-run average in two consecutive years, 1921-22; pitched 300 or more innings in 1915 and 1920-21-22; pitched in four games of the 1917 World Series, including three starting assignments, winning three and losing one as the White Sox defeated the New York Giants in six games; worked as a coach for the White Sox in 1946-47-48; named to Hall of Fame in 1964.

James Alexander Ferguson, 79, pitcher with New York, Boston and Washington of the American League and Philadelphia and Brooklyn of the National League in the period from 1918 through 1929, at Camarillo, Calif., April 28.

Richard Robert Ferrell, 21, catcher with Great Falls of the Pioneer Rookie League in 1976, of injuries suffered in an auto accident, at Billings, Mont., September 11.

Wesley Cheek Ferrell, 68, pitcher who had six 20-win seasons in the major leagues and a brother of Rick Ferrell, major league catcher from 1929 through 1947, at Sarasota, Fla., December 9; pitched for Cleveland from 1927 through 1933, Boston Red Sox from 1934 through 1937, Washington in 1937-38, New York Yankees in 1938-39, Brooklyn in 1940 and Boston Braves in 1941; won 20 or more games in his first four full seasons in the majors, 1929 through 1932; pitched a no-hit game against St. Louis, April 29, 1931; holds major league record for most homers hit by a pitcher in one season (9), in 1931; major league totals were 193 wins and 128 losses.

George (Rube) Foster, 88, pitcher with the Boston Red Sox from 1913 through 1917, at Bokoshe, Okla., March 1; had record of 19-8 in 1915 and won two complete-game victories for the Red Sox as they defeated Philadelphia in the World Series of that year.

James Gerald (Jumbo) Foster, 51, scout for Pittsburgh from 1954 through 1958 and Baltimore from 1966 through 1974 and a member of the Major League Scouting Bureau in 1975, at Aloha, Ore., January 12.

Marion John Fricano, 52, pitcher with the Philadelphia Athletics in 1952-53-54 and Kansas City in 1955, at Tijuana, Mex., May 18.

Daniel Vincent Frisella, 30, pitcher with the New York Mets from 1967 through 1972, Atlanta in 1973-74, San Diego in 1975, St. Louis in 1976 and Milwaukee in 1976, in dune buggy accident near Phoenix, Ariz., January 1, 1977.

Milton Galatzer, 68, outfielder with Cleveland from 1933 through 1936 and Cincinnati in 1939, at San Francisco, Calif., January 29.

William Lawrence (Larry) Gardner, 89, third baseman with the Boston Red Sox from 1908 through 1917, Philadelphia Athletics in 1918 and Cleveland from 1919 through 1924, at St. George, Vt., March 11; starred for four World Series winners—the Red Sox of 1912-15-16 and Indians of 1920; served for many years as baseball coach and later athletic director at the University of Vermont.

Eusebio Miguel Gonzales, 83, shortstop with the Boston Red Sox briefly in 1918, at Havana, Cuba, February 14.

Robert Lyndon Hasbrook, 82, first baseman-second baseman with the Chicago White Sox briefly in 1916-17, at Garland, Tex., February 9.

Robert Clay Hopper, 75, minor league outfielder from 1926 through 1941 and a manager in the top minor leagues from 1946 through 1956, at Greenwood, Miss., April 17; managed Montreal in the International League in 1946 where Jackie Robinson played his first season in Organized Ball.

Frank William Kellert, 52, first baseman with the St. Louis Browns in 1953, Baltimore in 1954, Brooklyn in 1955 and Chicago Cubs in 1956, at Oklahoma City, Okla., November 19.

Stanley Keyes, 73, outfielder in the minor leagues from 1924 through 1940 who led the Southern Association in homers and RBIs while with Nashville in 1932, at Pontiac, Mich., April 10.

George A. Kingsley, 79, president and chief officer of the Portland Beavers of the Pacific Coast League from 1957 through 1966, at Portland, Ore., July 30.

Louis Frank Klein, 57, infielder with the St. Louis Cardinals in 1943, 1945-46 and 1949, Cleveland in 1951 and Philadelphia Athletics in 1951, at Metairie, La., June 20; jumped to the outlaw Mexican League in June, 1946 and was declared ineligible to play in Organized Ball; was reinstated in June, 1949, and returned to Cardinals; shared managerial reins with the Chicago Cubs in 1961-62 and 1965 under the club's policy of having coaches split the manager's duties; coached for Cubs from 1966 through 1974 and was a Cub scout from October, 1974 until his death.

Casimir James (Jim) Konstanty, 59, great relief pitcher for the Philadelphia Phillies and the National League's Most Valuable Player in 1950, at Oneonta, N. Y., June 11; pitched for Cincinnati in 1944, the Boston Braves in 1946, the Phillies from 1948 through 1954, New York Yankees in 1954-55-56 and St. Louis Cardinals in 1956; had mark of 16-7 for the pennant-winning Phillies of 1950 and started the first game of the World Series, losing to the Yankees, 1-0.

John William (Tex) Kraus, 57, pitcher with the Philadelphia Phillies in 1943 and 1945 and New York Giants in 1946, at San Antonio, Tex., January 2.

Ernest George Krueger, 85, catcher with Cleveland, the New York Yankees, Brooklyn, New York Giants and Cincinnati in the period from 1913 through 1925, at Waukegan, Ill., April 22; caught the first six innings and scored the run for Brooklyn in the famous

26-inning 1-1 tie game with Boston, May 1, 1920; caught in 160 games and batted .339 for Indianapolis of the American Association in 1924.

Richard Edward Lajeskie, 50, infielder with the New York Giants briefly in 1946, at Ramsey, N. J., August 15.

Albert Wesley Lakeman, 57, catcher with Cincinnati from 1942 through 1947, the Philadelphia Phillies in 1947-48, Boston Braves in 1949 and Detroit in 1954, at Spartanburg, S. C., May 25; served as a coach for the Boston Red Sox in 1963-64 and in 1967-68-69; scouted for Milwaukee in 1971-72-73.

Otis Samuel Lambeth, 86, pitcher with Cleveland in 1916-17-18, at Moran, Kan., June 5.

Walter Edward Lynch, 79, catcher with the Boston Red Sox briefly in 1922, at Daytona Beach, Fla., December 21.

Duane Frederick (Duke) Maas, 47, pitcher with Detroit in 1955-56-57, Kansas City in 1958 and the New York Yankees from 1958 through 1961, at Mt. Clemens, Mich., December 7; one of 13 players involved in a trade between Kansas City and Detroit, November 20, 1957.

Harry William (Swede) Malmberg, 50, second baseman with Detroit in 1955, at San Francisco, Calif., October 29; coached for Boston in 1963-64 and managed in the minors from 1965 through 1975.

Paul Augustus Maloy, 83, pitcher with the Boston Red Sox briefly in 1913, at Sandusky, O., March 18.

Fred (Firpo) Marberry, 77, one of the great relief pitchers in major league history, at Mexia, Tex., June 30; pitched for Washington from 1923 through 1932, Detroit in 1933-34-35, the New York Giants and Washington in 1936; major league totals were 147 victories and 89 defeats; umpired in the American League for part of the 1935 season.

Myron Winthrop (Mike) McCormick, 58, outfielder with Cincinnati from 1940 through 1943 and in 1946, the Boston Braves in 1946-47-48, Brooklyn in 1949, New York Giants in 1950, Chicago White Sox in 1950 and Washington in 1951, at Los Angeles, Calif., April 14; played in all games of the World Series of 1940 and 1948 with a composite batting average of .288.

Wallace McKenna, 57, president of the Carolina League from 1970 through 1976, at Lynchburg, Va., December 3.

Emile Michael Meola, 70, pitcher with the Boston Red Sox briefly in 1933 and 1936 and St. Louis Browns in 1936, at Fair Lawn, N. J., September 1.

Michael Wilfred Miley, 23, shortstop with the California Angels in 1975-76, in auto crash near Baton Rouge, La., January 6, 1977.

John Kenneth Miljus, 80, pitcher with Brooklyn in 1917 and in 1920-21, Pittsburgh in 1927-28 and Cleveland in 1928-29, at Polson, Mont., February 11.

Graham Edward (Eddie) Moore, 77, versatile infielder who played with five major league clubs in the period from 1923 through 1934, at Fort Myers, Fla., February 10; played second base for Pittsburgh in all seven games of the 1925 World Series, won by the Pirates over Washington.

Robert Ralph Moose, 29, pitcher with Pittsburgh from 1967 through 1976, in auto accident near Martins Ferry, O., October 9; had 76-71 record with Pirates including a 14-3 mark in 1969; pitched no-hit game against New York, September 20, 1969.

Daniel Edward Murtaugh, 59, major league second baseman and manager who served four hitches as Pittsburgh skipper, at Chester, Pa., December 2; played for the Philadelphia Phillies in 1941-42-43 and 1946, Boston Braves in 1947 and Pittsburgh from 1948 through 1951; coached for Pittsburgh in 1956-57; replaced Bobby Bragan as Pirate manager, August 3, 1957, and held the post through 1964; scouted for the Pirates in 1965-66-67; replaced Harry Walker as Pirate manager, July 18, 1967 and finished the season; served as director of player development for Pittsburgh in 1968-69; returned as Pirate manager in 1970-71; worked as a Pirate scout in 1972-73 until he replaced Bill Virdon as manager, September 7, 1973, a post he held through 1976; led Pirates to world championships in 1960 and 1971 and East Division titles in 1970-74-75.

Elmer Glenn Myers, 82, pitcher with the Philadelphia Athletics from 1915 through 1918, Cleveland in 1919-20 and Boston Red Sox in 1920-21-22, at Collingwood, N. J., July 29.

Ernest Alonzo Nevers, 72, pitcher with the St. Louis Browns in 1926-27-28 and one of the country's greatest all-round athletes who was elected to the college and professional football Halls of Fame, at San Rafael, Calif., May 3.

Henry Kauhane (Prince) Oana, 68, who saw brief service with the Philadelphia Phillies as an outfielder in 1934 and as a pitcher with Detroit in 1943 and 1945, at Austin, Tex., June 19.

James Leo O'Neill, 83, infielder with Washington in 1920 and 1923, at Chambersburg, Pa., September 5; one of four brothers who played in major leagues including Stephen, longtime American League catcher who also managed in both majors.

Harry George Otis, 89, pitcher with Cleveland in 1909, at Trenton, N. J., January 29.

Frank Parenti, 77, active in Organized Ball from 1923 through 1969 as a minor league infielder and manager, and a scout for the Chicago White Sox from 1949 through 1969, at St. Petersburg, Fla., January 1.

John Paul Pasek, 70, catcher with Detroit in 1933 and the Chicago White Sox in 1934, at Niagara Falls, N. Y., March 13.

Alfred Frederick Platte, 86, outfielder with Detroit briefly in 1913, at Grand Rapids, Mich., August 29.

George W. Pratt, 62, Pittsburgh scout from 1952 through 1966, at Merry Hill, N. C., February 12.

John Joseph Quinn, 68, major league executive for many years and member of a prominent baseball family, at Stanton, Calif., September 20; worked in the front office of the Boston Red Sox from 1929 through 1935, served as secretary of the Boston Braves from 1936 until 1945 when he was named general manager, a post he held for the Boston and later Milwaukee Braves through the 1958 season when he resigned to become general manager of the Philadelphia Phillies, a job he maintained until his dismissal in June, 1972; his father, J. A. Robert Quinn, at one time was the principal owner of the Boston Red Sox and later a top executive of the Boston Braves, St. Louis Browns and Brooklyn Dodgers; two sons have been active in O. B.—Robert E. is the director of minor league operations for the Cleveland Indians and John J., Jr. for several years was the general manager of the Hawaii club of the Pacific Coast League.

Glen David (Rip) Russell, 61, first baseman and third baseman with the Chicago Cubs from 1939 through 1942 and Boston Red Sox in 1946-47, at Los Alamitos, Calif., September 26.

Claire Hodgson Ruth, 76, widow of the immortal Babe Ruth, at New York City, October 25.

Henry William Scheer, 75, infielder with the Philadelphia Athletics in 1922-23, at New Haven, Conn., March 21.

Carey Isom Selph, 74, infielder with the St. Louis Cardinals in 1929 and Chicago White Sox in 1932, at Houston, Tex., February 24.

John Joseph Shovlin, 85, infielder with Pittsburgh briefly in 1911 and the St. Louis Browns in 1919-20, at Bethesda, Md., February 16.

William Franklin Skiff, 81, catcher who saw brief service with Pittsburgh in 1921 and the New York Yankees in 1926, at New York City, December 25; in Organized Ball for 55 years, starting in 1916; worked for Yankees from 1947 through 1966, serving as minor league manager and scout.

Danny Leon Thompson, 29, shortstop with the Minnesota Twins from 1970 through 1976 and Texas Rangers in 1976, of leukemia at Rochester, Minn., December 10.

Albert Tooley, 89, shortstop with Brooklyn in 1911-12, at Marshall, Mich., August 17.

Leo Alphonse Townsend, 85, pitcher with the Boston Braves briefly in 1920-21, at Mobile, Ala., December 3.

Lonnie Warneke, 67, National League pitcher and umpire, at Hot Springs, Ark., June 23; pitched for the Chicago Cubs from 1930 through 1936, St. Louis Cardinals from 1937 through 1942 and the Cubs in 1942-43 and 1945; won 192 games in the majors, enjoying three 20-win seasons; led league in victories (22) winning percentage (.786) and ERA. (2.37) in 1932; pitched no-hit game against Cincinnati, August 30, 1941; won two games and lost one in the World Series of 1932 and 1935; umpired in the National League from 1949 through 1955.

Thomas Austin Yawkey, 73, owner of the Boston Red Sox from 1933 until his death at Boston, Mass., July 9; one of baseball's most generous and well-liked chief executives, his teams won pennants in 1946, 1967 and 1975 but were never able to bring the world championship to Boston.

Presidents of Minor Leagues for '77

CLASS AAA

American Association—Joe Ryan, P. O. Box 382, Wichita, Kan. 67201

International League—Roy Jackson, P. O. Box 530, Paoli, Pa. 19301

Mexican League—Lic. Antonio Ramirez (Muro), Campos Eliseos 169-202, Mexico 5, D. F., Mexico

Pacific Coast League—Roy Jackson, P. O. Box 530, Paoli, Pa. 19301

CLASS AA

Eastern League—P. Patrick McKernan, 26 Spadina Parkway, Pittsfield, Mass. 01201

Southern League—Billy Hitchcock, Box 528, Opelika, Ala. 36801

Texas League—Carl Sawatski, P. O. Box 5240, Little Rock, Ark. 72205

CLASS A

California League—E. W. (Bill) Wickert, 677 Santa Barbara Road, Berkeley, Calif. 94707

Carolina League—Jim Mills, 516-C Clay St., Cary, N. C. 27511

Florida State League—George MacDonald, Jr., P. O. Box 414, Lakeland, Fla. 33802

Gulf States League—Howard L. Green, 1244 Karla Drive, Hurst, Tex. 76053

Mexican Center League—Lic. Antonio Ramirez (Muro), Campos Eliseos 169-202, Mexico 5, D. F., Mexico

Midwest League—William K. Walters, P. O. Box 444, Burlington, Ia. 52601

New York-Pennsylvania League—Vincent M. McNamara, Box 98, South Park Station, Buffalo, N.Y. 14220

Northwest League—Bob Richmond, P. O. Box 848, Eugene, Ore. 97401

Western Carolinas League—John H. Moss, P. O. Box 49, Kings Mountain, N. C. 28086

ROOKIE CLASSIFICATION

Appalachian League—Chauncey DeVault, P. O. Box 927, Bristol, Va. 24201

Gulf Coast League—George MacDonald, Jr., P. O. Box 414, Lakeland, Fla. 33802

Pioneer League—Ralph C. Nelles, P. O. Box 570, Billings, Mont. 59103

Bobby Bragan—National Association President

Official Minor League Averages

Official Averages Of All Triple A, Double A and A Leagues, Plus Rookie Leagues

American Association

CLASS AAA

Leading Batter
MIKE EASLER
Tulsa

League President
JOE RYAN

Leading Pitcher
JOE HENDERSON
Indianapolis

CHAMPIONSHIP WINNERS IN PREVIOUS YEARS

1902 – Indianapolis	.683
1903 – St. Paul	.657
1904 – St. Paul	.646
1905 – Columbus	.658
1906 – Columbus	.615
1907 – Columbus	.584
1908 – Indianapolis	.601
1909 – Louisville	.554
1910 – Minneapolis	.637
1911 – Minneapolis	.600
1912 – Minneapolis	.636
1913 – Milwaukee	.599
1914 – Milwaukee	.590
1915 – Minneapolis	.597
1916 – Louisville	.605
1917 – Indianapolis	.588
1918 – Kansas City	.589
1919 – St. Paul	.610
1920 – St. Paul	.701
1921 – Louisville	.583
1922 – St. Paul	.641
1923 – Kansas City	.675
1924 – St. Paul	.578
1925 – Louisville	.635
1926 – Louisville	.629
1927 – Toledo	.601
1928 – Indianapolis	.593
1929 – Kansas City	.665
1930 – Louisville	.608
1931 – St. Paul	.623
1932 – Minneapolis	.595
1933 – Columbus*	.604
Minneapolis	.562

1934 – Minneapolis	.570
Columbus*	.556
1935 – Minneapolis	.591
1936 – Milwaukee†	.584
1937 – Columbus†	.584
1938 – St. Paul	.596
Kansas City (2nd)‡	.556
1939 – Kansas City	.695
Louisville (4th)†	.490
1940 – Kansas City	.625
Louisville (4th)†	.500
1941 – Columbus†	.621
1942 – Kansas City	.549
Columbus (3rd)‡	.532
1943 – Milwaukee	.596
Columbus (3rd)‡	.532
1944 – Milwaukee	.667
Louisville (3rd)†	.574
1945 – Milwaukee	.604
Louisville (3rd)†	.545
1946 – Louisville†	.601
1947 – Kansas City	.608
Milwaukee (3rd)‡	.513
1948 – Indianapolis	.649
St. Paul (3rd)‡	.558
1949 – St. Paul	.608
Indianapolis (2nd)‡	.604
1950 – Minneapolis	.584
Columbus (3rd)‡	.549
1951 – Milwaukee†	.623
1952 – Milwaukee	.656
Kansas City (2nd)‡	.578
1953 – Toledo	.584

Kansas City (2nd)‡	.571
1954 – Indianapolis	.625
Louisville (2nd)‡	.556
1955 – Minneapolis†	.597
1956 – Indianapolis†	.597
1957 – Wichita	.604
Denver (2nd)‡	.584
1958 – Charleston	.589
Minneapolis (3rd)‡	.536
1959 – Louisville§	.599
Omaha§	.516
Minneapolis (2nd)‡	.586
1960 – Denver	.571
Louisville (2nd)‡	.556
1961 – Indianapolis	.573
Louisville (2nd)‡	.533
1962 – Indianapolis	.605
Louisville (4th)‡	.486
1963-1968 – Did not operate.
1969 – Omaha	.607
1970 – Omaha*	.529
Denver	.504
1971 – Indianapolis	.604
Denver*	.521
1972 – Wichita	.621
Evansville*	.593
1973 – Iowa	.610
Tulsa*	.504
1974 – Indianapolis	.578
Tulsa*	.567
1975 – Evansville*	.566
Denver	.596

*Won playoff (East vs. West). †Won championship and four-team playoff. ‡Won four-team playoff. §Respective Eastern and Western division winners.

STANDING OF CLUBS AT CLOSE OF SEASON, SEPTEMBER 2

EASTERN DIVISION

Club	Omaha	Iowa	Ind.	Evan.	Den.	O.C.	Tul.	Wich.	W.	L.	T.	Pct.	G.B.
Omaha (Royals)	....	13	17	14	9	10	8	7	78	58	0	.574	......
Iowa (White Sox)	11	....	12	10	11	7	6	11	68	68	1	.500	10
Indianapolis (Reds)	7	12	....	16	3	6	8	10	62	73	0	.459	15½
Evansville (Tigers)	10	14	8	....	2	2	9	10	55	81	0	.404	23

WESTERN DIVISION

Club	Omaha	Iowa	Ind.	Evan.	Den.	O.C.	Tul.	Wich.	W.	L.	T.	Pct.	G.B.
Denver (Expos)	7	5	13	14	....	15	15	17	86	50	1	.632	......
Oklahoma City (Phillies)	6	9	10	14	9	....	13	11	72	63	0	.533	13½
Tulsa (Cardinals)	8	10	7	7	9	11	....	13	65	70	0	.481	20½
Wichita (Cubs)	9	5	6	6	7	12	11	....	56	79	0	.415	29½

Iowa club represented Des Moines, Iowa.

Major league affiliations in parentheses.

Playoff—Denver defeated Omaha, four games to two.

Regular-Season Attendance—Denver, 202,444; Evansville, 100,696; Indianapolis, 139,615; Iowa, 124,575; Oklahoma City, 122,287; Omaha, 120,799; Tulsa, 135,474; Wichita, 124,107. Total, 1,069,997. All-Star Game, 6,737. Playoffs, 10,391.

Managers: Denver—Vern Rapp; Evansville—Fred Hatfield; Indianapolis—Jim Snyder; Iowa—Loren Babe; Oklahoma City—Jim Bunning; Omaha—Billy Gardner; Tulsa—Ken Boyer; Wichita—Howard (Doc) Edwards.

All-Star Team: 1B—Freed, Denver; 2B—Staggs, Omaha; 3B—Scanlon, Denver; SS—Templeton, Tulsa; Utility—Rodney Scott, Denver; OF—Easler, Tulsa; Ewing, Iowa; Cromartie, Denver; Bosetti, Oklahoma City; C—Patchin, Omaha; Nahorodny, Oklahoma City; P—Lerch, Oklahoma City; Montague, Oklahoma City; Manager—Rapp, Denver.

(Compiled by Ed Williams, League Statistician, Shawnee, Okla.)

CLUB BATTING

Club	G.	AB.	R.	OR.	H.	TB.	2B.	3B.	HR.	RBI.	SH.	SF.	BB.	Int. BB.	HP.	SO.	SB.	CS.	LOB.	Pct.
Denver	137	4376	748	602	1253	2064	216	65	149	680	62	33	496	63	34	795	147	60	933	.286
Okla. City	135	4512	701	586	1285	1933	232	58	100	640	68	47	428	49	41	718	126	56	968	.285
Tulsa	135	4469	609	622	1211	1853	236	35	112	561	31	36	445	35	21	736	64	55	950	.271
Iowa	137	4380	592	620	1132	1607	225	26	66	534	68	31	549	62	12	690	99	56	998	.258
Evansville	136	4230	533	650	1093	1572	188	42	69	483	45	42	535	47	26	657	94	41	995	.258
Wichita	135	4308	545	663	1107	1669	156	23	120	493	48	26	472	33	33	704	78	30	960	.257
Omaha	136	4311	631	557	1100	1729	179	54	114	574	40	28	586	54	28	831	86	37	996	.255
Indianapolis	135	4224	514	573	1023	1507	184	27	82	473	59	30	482	54	17	718	101	46	905	.242

INDIVIDUAL BATTING

(Leading Qualifiers for Batting Championship—367 or More Plate Appearances)

*Bats lefthanded.   †Switch-hitter.

Player and Club	G.	AB.	R.	H.	TB.	2B.	3B.	HR.	RBI.	SH.	SF.	BB.	HP.	SO.	SB.	CS.	Pct.
Easler, Michael, Tulsa*	118	378	75	133	246	31	2	26	77	0	4	43	2	68	9	8	.352
Ewing, Samuel, Iowa*	101	350	51	123	196	26	1	15	81	1	4	30	0	43	4	3	.351
Cromartie, Warren, Denver*	120	396	65	129	209	25	11	11	68	3	4	56	2	48	1	5	.326
Iorg, Dane, Okla City*	106	443	65	142	214	24	15	6	38	0	1	21	0	84	25	13	.321
Templeton, Garry, Tulsa†	122	398	88	123	274	21	2	42	102	2	6	73	4	75	7	5	.309
Freed, Roger, Denver	134	483	93	149	215	24	9	8	54	5	4	60	7	73	26	7	.308
Smith, Lonnie, Okla City	103	312	65	96	175	21	2	18	78	1	2	55	2	57	0	1	.308
Scanlon, J. Patrick, Den*	115	388	62	119	174	15	2	12	54	0	6	68	2	48	4	2	.307
Ward, Chris, Wichita*	115	388	62	119	174	15	2	12	54	0	6	68	2	48	4	2	.307
Scott, Rodney, Denver	114	375	75	115	150	20	6	1	26	3	2	53	3	66	35	15	.307

Departmental Leaders: G—Staggs, 136; AB—Bamberger, 504; R—Smith, 93; H—Bosetti, 154; TB—Freed, 274; 2B—Alvarado, 38; 3B—Templeton, 15; HR—Freed, 42; RBI—Freed, 102; SH—Spencer, 10; SF—Nordhagen, 10; BB—Staggs, 89; HP—Gonzalez, 11; SO—Martz, 106; SB—Bosetti, 42; CS—R. Scott, 15.

(All Players—Listed Alphabetically)

Player and Club	G.	AB.	R.	H.	TB.	2B.	3B.	HR.	RBI.	SH.	SF.	BB.	HP.	SO.	SB.	CS.	Pct.
Adams, Robert M., Evans	105	338	32	89	128	16	4	5	44	1	4	25	1	40	4	0	.263
Adams, R. Michael, Wichita	36	92	17	28	43	2	2	3	9	0	0	23	1	15	1	2	.304
Albin, Donald, Denver	40	22	4	2	3	1	0	0	3	0	0	0	0	9	0	0	.091
Alfonso, Carlos, Ind	17	3	0	0	0	0	0	0	0	1	0	1	0	1	0	0	.000
Allen, Lloyd, Denver	34	48	2	7	8	1	0	0	4	2	1	0	0	19	0	0	.146
Alvarado, Luis, Tulsa	130	490	65	137	212	38	2	11	72	1	7	37	1	62	3	5	.280
Andrews, Fred, Okla City	97	360	46	107	141	20	4	2	48	2	3	27	1	48	8	9	.297
Arroyo, Fernando, Evans	44	28	1	2	2	0	0	0	1	3	1	1	0	6	0	0	.071
Atkinson, William, Denver*	51	15	0	3	3	0	0	0	2	0	0	0	0	5	0	0	.200
Baird, Harry, Omaha	50	8	0	0	0	0	0	0	0	0	0	0	0	5	0	0	.000

Player and Club	G.	AB.	R.	H.	TB.	2B.	3B.	HR.	RBI.	SH.	SF.	BB.	HP.	SO.	SB.	CS.	Pct.
Ballinger, Mark, Omaha	17	31	4	6	7	1	0	0	1	2	0	0	1	10	0	0	.194
Bannister, Alan, Iowa	32	118	24	29	44	6	0	3	12	2	0	23	0	19	12	3	.246
Bass, A. Earl, Tulsa	24	39	5	6	8	2	0	0	4	2	0	4	0	9	0	0	.154
Bastable, John, Okla City	66	172	31	47	76	8	3	5	31	0	1	20	1	29	2	3	.273
Bell, Kevin, Iowa	51	165	24	47	71	12	0	4	24	1	0	21	0	44	3	1	.285
Best, Kurt, Iowa	24	7	0	1	1	0	0	0	1	1	0	1	1	4	0	0	.143
Blackwell, Gary, Tulsa	26	53	6	6	10	1	0	1	2	0	0	3	1	8	1	1	.113
Blair, Dennis, Denver	25	37	1	1	1	0	0	0	1	3	0	3	0	18	0	0	.027
Blateric, Stephen, Iowa	22	6	0	0	0	0	0	0	0	0	0	1	0	2	0	0	.000
Boitano, Danny, Okla City	50	9	1	1	1	0	0	0	1	0	0	0	0	6	0	0	.111
Bolek, Kenneth, Evans*	3	2	2	1	1	0	0	0	0	1	0	1	0	1	0	0	.500
Bosetti, Richard, Okla C	123	504	82	154	206	25	6	5	52	7	3	43	6	59	42	14	.306
Bright, William, Wichita*	94	225	25	57	90	9	0	8	36	0	2	21	1	36	1	0	.253
Brookens, Edward, Evans	1	1	0	1	1	0	0	0	0	0	0	0	0	0	0	0	1.000
Bruno, Thomas, Omaha	20	43	3	4	5	1	0	0	4	3	1	2	0	26	0	0	.093
Buskey, Michael, Okla City	122	387	54	104	143	25	4	2	45	6	4	49	7	52	6	5	.269
Butkus, Stanley, Tulsa	57	12	1	1	2	1	0	0	1	0	0	2	0	6	0	1	.083
Capilla, Douglas, Tulsa*	50	13	1	2	2	0	0	0	0	0	0	1	0	5	0	0	.154
Cappuzzello, George, Evans	11	13	1	0	0	0	0	0	0	1	0	0	0	7	0	0	.000
Carroll, Thomas, Ind*	29	49	5	9	13	4	0	0	7	3	0	1	0	19	0	0	.184
Cash, Ronald, Evansville	81	229	23	58	79	10	1	3	28	1	3	21	0	47	3	4	.253
Chant, Charles, Tulsa	59	185	20	52	76	12	0	4	31	1	1	17	1	30	2	5	.281
Christenson, Gary, Evans*	16	11	3	1	1	0	0	0	1	1	0	3	0	2	0	0	.091
Clancy, Stephen, Wichita	94	268	21	61	77	7	0	3	18	1	2	35	4	38	0	1	.228
Clarey, Douglas, Tulsa	63	167	29	38	71	8	2	7	31	1	1	31	2	35	1	0	.228
Coggins, Richard, Okla C*	36	123	19	31	42	5	0	2	14	1	0	14	0	14	6	2	.252
Collins, Gregory, 27 Wich-5 Ia	32	70	8	17	22	2	0	1	8	1	1	7	1	11	0	0	.243
Coluccio, Robert, Iowa*	125	356	55	87	149	20	9	8	48	3	2	61	1	62	23	6	.244
Contreras, Arnaldo, Okla C†	25	3	0	0	0	0	0	0	1	0	0	0	0	2	0	0	.000
Cox, James, Denver	78	226	29	62	107	11	5	8	37	1	4	26	0	47	3	3	.274
Cram, Gerald, Omaha	51	31	5	8	12	1	0	1	3	1	0	3	0	10	0	0	.258
Cripe, David, Omaha	74	195	27	53	84	8	1	7	23	0	0	28	2	23	0	0	.272
Cromartie, Warren, Denver*	107	415	69	140	186	12	5	8	60	5	3	22	3	27	27	8	.337
Crosby, Edward, Tulsa*	95	259	21	60	68	4	2	0	26	3	7	40	3	23	0	2	.232
Crosby, Kenneth, Wichita	36	15	2	1	2	1	0	0	1	2	0	5	0	8	0	0	.067
Dancy, William, Okla City†	18	39	3	9	13	2	1	0	4	0	1	2	0	11	1	0	.231
Darcy, Patrick, Ind	16	35	2	4	4	0	0	0	2	0	1	0	1	17	0	0	.114
Darichuk, Greg, Evans*	2	2	0	1	1	0	0	0	0	0	0	0	0	1	0	0	.500
Davis, William N., Ind*	17	11	0	1	1	0	0	0	0	0	0	2	0	1	0	0	.091
Dawson, Andre, Denver	74	240	51	84	171	19	4	20	46	1	0	23	3	50	10	1	.350
Day, Charles, Evansville*	114	308	42	82	128	15	5	7	34	3	2	38	0	43	1	0	.266
Decker, George, Evansville	12	21	0	0	0	0	0	0	0	1	0	0	0	9	0	0	.000
DeFreites, Arturo, Ind	42	153	14	42	56	14	0	0	13	0	0	2	0	26	0	3	.275
de los Santos, Ramon, Tul*	10	0	0	0	0	0	0	0	0	0	0	0	0	0	0	0	.000
DeMola, Donald, Denver	1	0	0	0	0	0	0	0	0	0	0	0	0	0	0	0	.000
Denevi, Michael, Omaha	15	34	3	4	4	0	0	0	1	0	0	3	1	11	0	0	.118
Detherage, Robert, Tulsa	21	71	13	15	22	4	0	1	1	0	0	6	0	20	1	1	.211
Dlugach, Michael, Iowa	34	51	3	15	16	1	0	0	2	1	0	6	0	6	0	0	.294
Droege, William, Wichita	74	227	28	56	73	9	1	2	26	2	1	26	2	36	7	1	.247
Drumright, David, Denver	21	9	0	2	2	0	0	0	1	0	0	1	0	4	0	0	.222
Dunn, Ronald, Wichita	105	381	48	94	181	18	3	21	48	2	2	28	1	71	3	1	.247
Dunning, Steven, Denver	4	7	0	0	0	0	0	0	0	2	0	1	0	3	0	0	.000
Easler, Michael, Tulsa*	118	378	75	133	246	31	2	26	77	0	4	43	2	68	9	8	.352
Enright, George, Iowa	108	271	29	68	88	9	1	3	29	5	3	36	1	47	0	0	.251
Enyart, Terry, Denver	45	27	1	3	3	0	0	0	3	2	0	3	0	13	0	0	.111
Erickson, G. Charles, Iowa	18	25	3	5	6	1	0	0	1	0	0	3	0	4	0	0	.200
Eschen, James, Evansville†	132	454	61	115	149	16	3	4	35	3	6	81	3	29	21	9	.253
Estrada, Manuel, Iowa	117	368	50	91	128	18	2	5	30	4	4	42	3	45	4	1	.247
Ewing, Samuel, Iowa*	101	350	51	123	196	26	1	15	81	1	4	30	0	43	4	3	.351
Ferrer, Sergio, Okla City†...	89	226	33	60	72	9	0	1	10	6	2	35	2	20	4	3	.265
Frailing, Kenneth, Wich*	11	19	0	4	5	1	0	0	3	0	2	0	4	0	0	0	.211
Franklin, Anthony, 1 In-20 Wich†	21	69	16	23	29	-2	2	0	7	1	1	14	0	8	1	3	.333
Freed, Roger, Denver	122	398	88	123	274	21	2	42	102	0	2	73	4	75	7	5	.309
Freeman, Jimmy, Tulsa*	12	8	0	0	0	0	0	0	0	1	0	3	0	4	0	0	.000
Gamble, John, Evansville	90	224	26	47	57	7	0	1	20	3	3	28	1	41	6	2	.210
Garcia, Nelson, Tulsa†	25	100	13	24	37	2	1	3	7	2	0	4	0	13	5	1	.240
Garcia, Ruben, Omaha	4	1	0	0	0	0	0	0	0	0	0	0	0	0	0	0	.000
Geisel, J. David, Wichita*	10	17	1	1	1	0	0	0	0	1	0	4	0	8	0	0	.059
Glynn, Edward, Evansville	28	53	3	11	11	0	0	0	1	1	0	3	0	24	0	0	.208
Godby, Danny, Indianapolis	55	104	5	17	19	2	0	0	4	3	0	12	0	20	0	1	.163
Gonzales, Daniel, Evans*	37	108	15	33	48	6	0	3	14	0	0	6	1	7	2	1	.306
Gonzalez, Julio, Wichita	128	484	59	136	167	12	5	3	41	3	1	24	11	53	27	6	.281
Goodman, Bobbie, Denver	1	0	0	0	0	0	0	0	0	0	0	2	0	0	0	0	.000
Granger, Wayne, Denver	26	10	0	0	0	0	0	0	0	0	0	0	0	5	0	0	.000
Gronlund, David, Denver	22	38	3	5	5	0	0	0	4	5	0	1	0	10	0	0	.132

Player and Club	G.	AB.	R.	H.	TB.	2B.	3B.	HR.	RBI.	SH.	SF.	BB.	HP.	SO.	SB.	CS.	Pct.
Grow, Lorin, Indianapolis*	11	7	0	1	1	0	0	0	1	0	1	0	2	0	0	0	.143
Guerrero, Mario, Tulsa	29	81	7	19	27	2	0	2	4	2	0	8	0	8	0	0	.235
Hairston, Jerry, Iowa*	94	325	53	94	139	24	3	5	65	4	1	68	0	41	8	8	.289
Harmon, Thomas, Tulsa*	84	262	28	71	84	13	0	0	22	2	2	21	1	15	1	0	.271
Harrison, Roric, Tulsa	16	17	3	5	9	1	0	1	3	0	0	2	0	8	0	0	.294
Hasbach, David, Omaha	13	32	5	6	6	0	0	0	6	2	1	1	0	13	0	0	.188
Henderson, Joseph, Ind*	54	23	2	4	7	0	0	1	2	0	0	3	0	11	0	0	.174
Hernaiz, Jesus, Okla City	24	13	0	2	2	0	0	0	1	0	0	0	0	5	0	0	.154
Hernandez, Guillermo, OC*	25	24	1	2	2	0	0	0	4	6	2	0	1	10	0	0	.048
Hill, R. Quency, Okla C*	47	11	1	2	2	0	0	0	3	1	0	1	0	1	0	0	.182
Hinton, Richard, Indiana*	39	21	2	3	6	0	0	1	2	0	1	4	0	7	0	0	.143
Hiser, Gene, 35 Wich-76 Ia*	111	303	35	75	99	16	1	2	29	7	2	39	1	39	5	4	.248
Hughes, Terry, Tulsa	27	102	11	21	34	4	0	3	15	0	0	5	1	11	0	0	.206
Hume, Thomas, Indianapolis	27	58	6	10	14	1	0	1	3	6	0	4	0	18	0	0	.172
Iorg, Dane, Okla City*	120	396	65	129	209	25	11	11	68	3	4	56	2	48	1	5	.326
Jackson, Roland, Iowa*	84	220	32	60	77	11	0	2	22	3	0	20	0	12	6	3	.273
Johnson, L. Doby, Denver	84	235	37	68	126	14	1	14	43	2	2	30	1	45	12	2	.289
Johnson, Robert D., Omaha†	23	19	2	3	4	1	0	0	0	0	0	2	0	14	0	0	.158
Jones, Ruppert, Omaha*	102	359	65	94	184	15	9	19	73	1	5	59	3	90	16	5	.262
Jones, Terrence, Okla City	44	80	11	18	21	3	0	0	5	1	2	4	2	16	5	1	.225
Keener, Joseph, Denver	27	67	7	10	12	2	0	0	7	0	0	3	0	34	0	0	.149
Kemp, Steven, Evansville*	52	171	37	66	119	14	3	11	38	1	1	40	3	35	3	1	.386
Kennedy, Junior, Ind.	122	348	53	87	116	15	4	2	44	6	3	60	1	54	11	4	.250
Kerrigan, Joseph, Denver	22	4	1	1	1	0	0	0	0	0	0	0	0	3	0	0	.250
Kimm, Bruce, Evansville	2	6	1	2	6	1	0	1	1	0	0	2	0	0	1	0	.333
Kinard, Rudolph, Denver	54	161	26	42	55	5	4	0	13	3	1	20	0	20	1	2	.261
Kirkpatrick, William, Den	4	1	0	0	0	0	0	0	0	1	0	2	0	0	0	0	.000
Kiser, Larry, Okla City	21	32	3	6	7	1	0	0	3	0	0	5	0	2	0	0	.188
Knapp, R. Christian, Iowa	11	25	3	6	6	0	0	0	3	6	1	2	0	12	0	0	.240
Kniffin, Charles, Okla C	16	23	1	2	2	0	0	0	3	4	1	1	0	3	0	0	.087
Knight, C. Ray, Ind.	110	396	47	106	166	24	3	10	41	2	1	36	1	50	2	3	.268
Knox, John C., 3 Ev-92 Ind*	95	211	18	45	53	4	2	0	18	2	0	23	0	31	2	1	.213
Komadina, Tony, Iowa*	3	4	0	0	0	0	0	0	0	0	0	0	0	4	0	0	.000
Kravec, Kenneth, Iowa*	30	46	2	5	5	0	0	0	0	7	0	0	0	22	0	0	.109
Kremmel, James, Wichita*	26	1	1	0	0	0	0	0	0	3	0	0	0	0	0	0	.000
Krukow, Michael, Wichita	26	47	1	10	10	0	0	0	4	0	1	2	0	22	0	0	.213
Kucek, John, Iowa	22	43	1	4	4	0	0	0	2	2	1	0	0	13	0	0	.093
Kurpiel, Edward, Tulsa*	29	82	14	23	35	3	0	3	16	0	0	18	0	19	2	0	.280
LaGrow, Lerrin, Tulsa	26	54	3	8	9	1	0	0	1	2	0	4	0	22	0	0	.148
Lambe, Bryan, Evansville	86	206	38	54	71	11	3	0	13	3	1	32	1	26	17	2	.262
Lamont, Gene, Evansville*	96	269	23	63	91	13	0	5	25	1	5	36	2	47	2	1	.234
Lamp, Dennis, Wichita	30	47	6	9	9	0	0	0	2	0	3	0	0	17	0	0	.191
Lance, Gary, Omaha†	26	51	3	7	7	0	0	0	3	5	0	5	0	21	0	0	.137
Landreth, Larry, Denver	26	52	6	3	4	1	0	0	3	4	0	1	2	25	0	0	.058
Landrum, Terry, Tulsa	9	24	1	6	7	1	0	0	1	0	0	1	3	6	1	3	.250
Lane, Marvin, Evansville	85	276	46	80	146	13	7	13	61	2	3	48	2	67	3	3	.290
Lang, Robert, Denver	8	9	2	2	4	0	1	0	0	4	0	0	0	2	0	0	.222
LaRussa, Anthony, Iowa	107	332	53	86	109	11	0	4	34	1	4	40	3	43	10	6	.259
Lee, Leon, Tulsa	116	371	64	104	170	18	3	14	48	1	1	51	3	57	0	1	.280
Leibowitz, David, Tulsa	1	1	0	0	0	0	0	0	0	0	0	0	0	0	0	0	.000
Lemanczyk, David, Evans.	7	19	2	3	4	1	0	0	1	0	0	0	0	6	0	0	.158
Lerch, Randy, Okla City*	32	80	7	21	32	4	2	1	14	4	0	3	0	14	0	0	.263
Lyttle, James, Denver*	25	92	15	26	51	5	4	4	11	2	0	16	3	19	1	1	.283
MacCormack, Frank, Evans	15	21	2	2	2	0	0	0	1	0	4	1	4	14	0	0	.095
Makowski, Thomas, Evans	17	6	0	0	0	0	0	0	0	0	0	0	2	0	0	0	.000
Mallory, Sheldon, Omaha*	110	346	66	91	142	22	7	5	29	3	1	64	0	44	21	12	.263
Mankowski, Philip, Evans.*	122	413	50	119	159	21	2	5	49	4	3	38	3	40	3	1	.288
Manuel, Jerry, Evansville†	11	44	6	8	12	1	0	1	3	2	0	2	3	9	0	1	.182
Marshall, Keith, Ind	108	256	36	67	79	7	1	1	21	2	1	37	4	30	6	4	.262
Martin, Bill, Tulsa	1	1	0	0	0	0	0	0	0	0	0	0	0	0	0	0	.000
Martinez, Teodoro, Ind†	85	310	45	79	101	15	2	1	19	1	2	18	1	45	25	10	.255
Martz, Gary, Omaha	131	436	72	106	198	18	4	22	62	0	2	56	4	106	0	3	.243
McClain, Harold, Iowa*.	38	33	2	2	3	1	0	0	2	1	0	2	0	24	0	0	.061
McClure, Robert, Omaha†	21	43	3	11	11	0	0	0	5	3	0	5	1	15	0	0	.256
McKinney, Lynn, Omaha†	9	16	0	2	2	0	0	0	2	1	0	0	0	7	0	0	.125
McMillan, Thomas, Iowa	23	82	13	17	19	0	1	0	2	0	7	0	17	1	1		.207
Mejias, Samuel, Tulsa	70	263	49	85	122	13	3	6	30	1	1	21	0	46	6	9	.323
Meoli, Rudolph, Ind*.	120	403	63	105	155	23	6	5	51	4	4	82	1	48	22	7	.261
Meyerrose, Michael, Evans	42	7	1	1	1	0	0	0	0	0	0	2	0	1	0	0	.143
Molinaro, Robert, Evans*	135	491	72	142	205	27	9	6	67	0	4	50	3	38	20	10	.289
Montague, John, Okla City	28	68	5	12	16	1	0	1	7	4	1	3	0	20	0	0	.176
Moore, Donnie, Wichita*	33	54	4	7	8	1	0	0	5	3	1	0	0	14	0	0	.130
Moran, C. William, Iowa	7	1	0	1	1	0	0	0	0	0	0	0	0	0	0	0	1.000
Morrison, James, Okla City	126	422	79	122	205	17	6	18	71	3	5	40	6	83	17	5	.289
Mumphrey, Jerry, Tulsa†	19	68	14	23	37	9	1	1	8	0	0	13	0	6	6	2	.338

Player and Club	G.	AB.	R.	H.	TB.	2B.	3B.	HR.	RBI.	SH.	SF.	BB.	HP.	SO.	SB.	CS.	Pct.
Murphy, Brian, Omaha	105	332	27	74	91	10	2	1	35	5	1	42	1	50	0	2	.223
Nahorodny, William, Okla C	114	391	74	114	211	22	3	23	78	2	3	34	5	83	7	1	.292
Navarrete, Juan, Denver*	77	245	29	71	88	5	6	0	30	4	5	18	1	20	9	3	.290
Nelson, Roger E., Omaha	52	11	0	1	1	0	0	0	1	1	0	0	0	3	0	0	.091
Nettles, Morris, Iowa*	48	100	16	19	30	5	0	2	8	0	0	17	0	15	4	2	.190
Nordhagen, Wayne, 82 OC-17 Ia	99	350	56	106	181	30	6	11	78	0	10	31	1	46	0	0	.303
Nyman, Nyls, Iowa*	104	380	60	107	157	27	4	5	36	2	2	34	1	42	7	10	.282
Odom, Johnny, Iowa	3	10	1	2	2	0	0	0	0	0	0	0	0	4	0	0	.200
Oliver, Robert, Okla City	96	295	40	96	149	17	3	10	55	1	2	9	0	40	1	1	.325
Olsen, Lewis, Omaha	25	51	5	5	5	0	0	0	1	3	0	5	0	22	0	0	.098
Ortenzio, Frank, Omaha	129	447	61	113	192	29	4	14	81	1	3	64	4	88	1	2	.253
Otten, James, Iowa	39	38	2	6	6	0	0	0	1	3	0	2	0	12	0	0	.158
Papi, Stanley, Denver	108	318	46	86	133	23	6	4	53	2	2	23	4	65	4	7	.270
Patchin, Steven, Omaha	109	353	47	106	162	15	4	11	50	0	3	38	1	34	0	1	.300
Patterson, Paul, Iowa*	8	1	0	0	0	0	0	0	0	0	0	0	0	1	0	0	.000
Payne, Larry, Indianapolis	27	48	0	11	12	1	0	0	6	5	0	1	0	16	0	0	.229
Perkins, Craig, Omaha	50	113	12	32	53	3	0	6	27	1	2	5	1	18	0	0	.283
Pirtle, Gerald, Wichita	50	14	2	3	3	0	0	0	0	3	0	1	0	4	0	0	.214
Potter, Michael, Tulsa	111	352	44	95	156	20	1	13	51	3	7	35	2	70	1	2	.270
Prall, Wilfred, Wichita*	35	29	2	2	6	1	0	1	1	2	0	2	0	10	0	0	.069
Proly, Michael, Iowa	51	15	0	4	4	0	0	0	1	0	0	0	0	4	0	0	.267
Putman, Eddy, Wichita	12	44	2	12	18	3	0	1	6	0	0	3	0	10	0	0	.273
Rapp, Vernon, Denver	1	1	0	1	1	0	0	0	0	0	0	0	0	0	0	1	1.000
Reece, Robert, Denver	93	248	39	67	99	15	4	3	33	4	0	28	0	27	2	0	.270
Reed, Kenneth, Iowa	14	19	1	1	1	0	0	0	0	0	0	0	0	2	0	0	.053
Revering, David, Ind*	123	407	63	118	223	20	2	27	77	0	7	68	0	76	1	0	.290
Robles, Sergio, Tulsa	6	20	0	3	3	0	0	0	1	0	0	1	0	2	0	0	.150
Roenicke, Gary, Denver	77	252	56	73	130	11	5	12	44	2	2	41	5	39	4	1	.290
Roof, Phillip, Iowa	10	25	2	6	13	1	0	2	5	0	0	1	0	4	0	0	.240
Rothan, William, Tulsa	8	3	0	0	0	0	0	0	0	0	0	0	0	0	0	0	.000
Ruberto, John, Indianapolis	40	83	3	21	23	2	0	0	6	1	1	7	0	13	0	0	.253
Sarmiento, Manuel, Ind	43	10	0	1	1	0	0	0	0	2	0	0	0	1	0	0	.100
Scanlon, J. Patrick, Den*	103	312	65	96	175	21	2	18	78	1	2	55	2	57	0	1	.308
Scarce, G. McCurdy, Ind*	45	14	0	1	2	1	0	0	0	1	0	1	0	9	0	0	.071
Schneck, David, Ind*	126	391	56	98	180	21	2	19	59	3	2	21	2	61	15	4	.251
Schultz, C. Budd, Wichita	13	8	0	2	2	0	0	0	1	1	0	1	0	0	0	0	.250
Scott, Anthony, Denver†	106	328	63	102	165	21	9	8	45	0	1	25	1	67	18	6	.311
Scott, Rodney, Denver	114	375	75	115	150	20	6	1	26	3	2	53	3	66	35	15	.307
Sember, Michael, Wichita	69	216	26	52	60	5	0	1	16	2	0	26	1	58	6	4	.241
Seoane, Manuel, Okla City	21	37	2	2	5	0	0	1	1	5	0	1	0	23	0	0	.054
Shaffer, Duane, Iowa	58	12	1	2	2	0	0	0	0	0	1	0	0	6	0	0	.167
Sielicki, John, Tulsa*	12	20	3	5	6	1	0	0	1	1	0	2	0	8	0	0	.250
Slayback, William, Evans	30	30	1	4	4	0	0	0	1	5	0	1	0	7	0	0	.133
Smith, Lonnie, Okla City	134	483	93	149	215	24	9	8	54	5	4	60	7	73	26	7	.308
Solomon, Eddie, Tulsa	9	21	2	4	4	0	0	0	4	2	1	0	0	5	0	0	.190
Sovern, Jeffrey, Ind	103	328	30	68	94	8	0	6	33	1	1	38	6	47	1	1	.207
Spencer, H. Thomas, Ind	126	419	47	100	146	17	4	7	43	10	5	43	0	67	12	8	.239
Sperring, Robert, Wichita	94	298	34	71	129	3	13	38	3	1	31	3	66	4	0		.238
Squires, Michael, Iowa*	124	336	37	85	111	18	1	2	40	3	4	50	1	32	10	7	.253
Staggs, Stephen, Omaha	136	492	92	139	202	20	14	5	50	3	2	89	4	55	27	7	.283
Stoddard, Timothy, Iowa	12	8	0	0	0	0	0	0	0	0	0	0	0	6	0	0	.000
Stodgel, Douglas, Wichita	86	210	19	57	74	9	1	2	21	4	1	18	1	14	3	1	.271
Strampe, Robert, Denver†	4	6	0	0	0	0	0	0	0	1	0	0	0	5	0	0	.000
Sudakis, William, Omaha†	85	275	46	78	141	19	1	14	49	1	3	44	0	46	1	1	.284
Sutter, H. Bruce, Wichita	7	2	0	0	0	0	0	0	0	0	0	0	0	1	0	0	.000
Sykes, Robert, Evansville*	24	37	2	4	5	1	0	0	2	4	0	4	0	16	0	0	.108
Tabb, Jerry, Wichita*	124	395	60	114	194	21	1	19	67	2	4	50	2	52	3	1	.289
Tamargo, John, Tulsa†	113	346	44	96	147	21	3	8	48	0	1	46	1	32	0	1	.277
Taylor, Bruce, Evansville	48	12	0	1	1	0	0	0	0	0	0	3	0	6	0	0	.083
Taylor, Charles G., Denver	37	10	1	0	0	0	0	0	0	2	0	2	0	7	0	0	.000
Temple, V. James, Okla C	8	2	0	0	0	0	0	0	0	0	0	0	0	0	0	0	.000
Templeton, Garry, Tulsa†	106	443	65	142	214	24	15	6	38	0	1	21	0	84	25	13	.321
Terlecky, Gregory, Iowa	35	40	4	3	5	0	1	0	4	2	0	4	0	14	0	0	.075
Thomas, Roy, Iowa	27	55	5	14	19	2	0	1	6	4	0	6	0	23	0	0	.255
Thompson, Jason, Evans*	4	16	3	5	14	0	0	3	6	0	0	1	0	9	0	0	.313
Thompson, Michael, Ind	21	29	2	2	3	1	0	0	0	0	0	4	0	19	0	0	.069
Throop, George, Omaha	3	1	1	1	1	0	0	0	0	0	0	0	0	0	0	0	1.000
Tyrone, James, Wichita	124	459	72	123	199	14	1	20	57	2	2	48	3	57	17	7	.268
Tyrone, O. Wayne, Wichita	28	84	18	24	59	7	2	8	21	1	0	14	0	25	0	0	.286
Valentine, Ellis, Denver	57	204	31	63	95	9	1	7	32	1	3	22	1	25	14	5	.309
Valle, John, Louisville	22	68	4	12	15	3	0	0	8	1	2	14	0	12	0	1	.176
Velazquez, Carlos, Okla C	3	3	0	0	0	0	0	0	0	0	0	0	0	0	0	0	.000
Wagner, Mark, Evansville	107	304	32	79	101	9	5	1	22	1	3	50	2	60	8	5	.260
Walker, R. Thomas, Tulsa	21	47	2	5	5	0	0	0	2	3	0	1	0	15	0	0	.106
Wallace, David, Okla City	53	13	0	1	1	0	0	0	0	2	0	0	0	7	0	0	.077

Player and Club	G.	AB.	R.	H.	TB.	2B.	3B.	HR.	RBI.	SH.	SF.	BB.	HP.	SO.	SB.	CS.	Pct.
Ward, Chris, Wichita*	115	388	62	119	174	15	2	12	54	0	6	68	2	48	4	2	.307
Warthen, Daniel, Denver†	8	12	3	2	2	0	0	0	2	0	0	2	1	3	0	0	.167
Washington, U. L., Omaha†	30	120	20	30	49	3	2	4	16	0	0	16	0	31	14	4	.250
Waterbury, Steven, Tulsa	28	46	4	11	18	1	0	2	10	1	0	2	0	8	0	0	.239
Wathan, John, Omaha	24	84	4	13	18	5	0	0	6	0	0	5	0	16	0	0	.155
Werner, Donald, Ind	38	112	14	23	32	4	1	1	12	1	2	12	1	27	4	0	.205
Wilcox, Milton, 9 Wich-18 Ev	27	42	4	8	11	3	0	0	5	2	1	1	0	9	0	0	.190
Wiles, Randall, Tulsa*	12	7	0	0	0	0	0	0	0	0	0	1	0	6	0	0	.000
Wright, Gary, Omaha*	19	16	1	2	2	0	0	0	2	3	0	2	0	4	0	0	.125
Yancy, Hugh, Iowa	73	258	31	73	100	11	2	4	44	4	2	32	0	26	1	2	.283
York, James, Iowa	5	4	1	2	3	1	0	0	1	0	0	0	0	0	0	0	.500
Zahn, Geoffrey, Wichita*	21	47	5	6	7	1	0	0	2	3	0	6	0	7	0	0	.128
Zamora, Oscar, Wichita	14	3	0	1	2	1	0	0	1	0	0	0	0	1	0	0	.333
Zdeb, Joseph, Omaha	117	372	57	111	146	8	6	5	44	1	4	47	2	69	6	0	.298

GRAND-SLAM HOME RUNS—Clarey, Cromartie, Dawson, Day, L. Johnson, Kurpiel, Lane, LaRussa, Mankowski, Molinaro, Papi, Patchin, Perkins, Revering, Tamargo, 1 each.

AWARDED FIRST BASE ON INTERFERENCE—Navarrete 3 (Werner 2, Stodgel); Hiser 2 (Ruberto, Wathan); Bosetti (Werner), Droege (Adams), Dunn (Adams), Hernaiz (Reece), Krukow (Johnson), Otten (Patchin).

CLUB FIELDING

Club	G.	PO.	A.	E.	DP.	PB.	Pct.	Club	G.	PO.	A.	E.	DP.	PB.	Pct.
Indianapolis	135	3373	1437	136	129	14	.973	Omaha	136	3395	1431	177	116	9	.965
Denver	137	3382	1474	152	124	6	.970	Wichita	135	3354	1457	182	134	23	.964
Iowa	137	3455	1439	154	112	16	.969	Tulsa	135	3438	1442	192	131	10	.962
Oklahoma City	135	3438	1382	166	144	18	.967	Evansville	136	3307	1427	192	130	18	.961

Triple Plays—Oklahoma City 2; Wichita 1.

INDIVIDUAL FIELDING

*Throws lefthanded.

FIRST BASEMEN

Player and Club	G.	PO.	A.	E.	DP.	Pct.	Player and Club	G.	PO.	A.	E.	DP.	Pct.
SQUIRES, Iowa*	112	823	47	4	69	.995	Lee, Tulsa	79	404	17	6	49	.986
Revering, Ind	120	1051	75	7	103	.994	Hughes, Tulsa	18	136	9	2	20	.986
Cash, Evansville	66	482	42	3	45	.994	Ward, Wichita*	10	67	1	1	3	.986
Oliver, Okla City	60	451	31	4	42	.992	Adams, Evansville	34	254	21	5	25	.982
Ortenzio, Omaha	123	1044	81	10	88	.991	Tamargo, Tulsa	38	298	15	6	21	.981
Cox, Denver	34	201	20	2	20	.991	Cromartie, Denver*	14	95	6	2	5	.981
Tabb, Wichita	115	1016	46	11	95	.990	Ewing, Iowa	39	279	26	8	21	.974
Day, Evansville*	43	309	22	4	29	.988	Sovern, Indianapolis	11	72	4	2	7	.974
Iorg, Okla City	87	695	64	10	78	.987	Kurpiel, Tulsa*	10	66	5	2	7	.973
Freed, Denver	107	905	65	14	79	.986	O. Tyrone, Wichita	13	80	6	3	8	.966

Triple Plays—Iorg, 2; Tabb, 1.

(Fewer Than Ten Games)

Player and Club	G.	PO.	A.	E.	DP.	Pct.	Player and Club	G.	PO.	A.	E.	DP.	Pct.
Martz, Omaha	9	60	6	0	3	1.000	Gamble, Evansville	1	8	0	0	2	1.000
Patchin, Omaha	7	52	3	0	7	1.000	Werner, Indianapolis	1	7	0	0	3	1.000
Sperring, Wichita	9	51	2	0	0	1.000	Clancy, Wichita	1	4	0	0	0	1.000
Knight, Indianapolis	5	34	2	0	4	1.000	Dlugach, Iowa	4	2	0	0	0	1.000
Thompson, Evansville*	4	29	7	0	2	1.000	Harmon, Tulsa	1	2	0	0	0	1.000
LaRussa, Iowa	6	24	3	0	2	1.000	Johnson, Denver	1	2	0	0	1	1.000
Putman, Wichita	2	17	1	0	2	1.000	Potter, Tulsa	1	1	0	0	0	1.000
DeFreites, Ind	3	15	1	0	0	1.000	Blackwell, Tulsa	1	1	0	0	0	1.000
Schneck, Ind*	2	12	0	0	1	1.000	Eschen, Evansville	6	61	6	1	6	.985
Bastable, Okla City	5	11	0	0	1	1.000	Hairston, Iowa	7	53	4	2	6	.966
Nahorodny, Okla City	1	8	1	0	2	1.000	Hiser, Wich-Iowa*	2	12	1	2	1	.867
Lane, Evansville	3	7	1	0	0	1.000							

SECOND BASEMEN

Player and Club	G.	PO.	A.	E.	DP.	Pct.	Player and Club	G.	PO.	A.	E.	DP.	Pct.
Manuel, Evansville	11	25	29	1	6	.982	Guerrero, Tulsa	17	37	45	3	10	.965
Knox, Evans-Ind	47	77	104	4	17	.978	Estrada, Iowa	70	122	160	11	27	.962
Sperring, Wichita	10	18	27	1	3	.978	Ferrer, Okla City	44	81	113	8	36	.960
Kinard, Denver	49	108	144	6	32	.977	Cox, Denver	34	62	58	5	12	.960
KENNEDY, Ind	96	204	277	12	62	.976	Staggs, Omaha	136	273	389	30	82	.957
LaRussa, Iowa	18	38	45	2	13	.976	Adams, Wichita	13	20	25	2	3	.957
Eschen, Evansville	118	240	306	16	69	.972	Stodgel, Wichita	17	24	30	3	7	.947
Alvarado, Tulsa	112	243	317	17	76	.971	Gonzalez, Wichita	100	235	293	30	79	.946
Navarrete, Denver	62	118	152	8	35	.971	Dancy, Okla City	12	21	23	3	6	.936
Yancy, Iowa	58	115	165	9	39	.969	Clarey, Tulsa	10	12	17	2	5	.935
Andrews, Okla City	93	210	231	15	63	.967							

Triple Plays—Gonzalez, Dancy, 1 each.

SECOND BASEMEN—Continued

(Fewer Than Ten Games)

Player and Club	G.	PO.	A.	E.	DP.	Pct.	Player and Club	G.	PO.	A.	E.	DP.	Pct.
Denevi, Omaha	3	8	10	0	5	1.000	Dlugach, Iowa	1	0	2	0	0	1.000
Franklin, Wichita	3	6	7	0	1	1.000	Hairston, Iowa	1	1	0	0	0	1.000
Crosby, Tulsa	3	2	9	0	4	1.000	R. Scott, Denver	8	18	19	2	3	.949
Martinez, Ind	2	3	8	0	2	1.000	Gamble, Evansville	7	20	14	4	4	.895
Dunn, Wichita	2	7	3	0	1	1.000	Lambe, Evansville	1	3	2	1	2	.833
Papi, Denver	2	2	6	0	0	1.000	Harmon, Tulsa	1	0	0	1	0	.000
Reed, Iowa	2	3	4	0	1	1.000							

THIRD BASEMEN

Player and Club	G.	PO.	A.	E.	DP.	Pct.	Player and Club	G.	PO.	A.	E.	DP.	Pct.
Martinez, Ind	11	8	14	0	1	1.000	Scanlon, Denver	97	59	179	17	13	.933
Jackson, Iowa	26	23	36	1	2	.983	Cripe, Omaha	58	41	108	11	9	.931
Papi, Denver	46	28	76	2	10	.981	Clarey, Tulsa	44	30	72	8	7	.927
Franklin, Wichita	16	16	28	1	5	.978	Sudakis, Omaha	77	66	119	15	7	.925
Stodgel, Wichita	16	12	22	1	4	.971	Crosby, Tulsa	59	29	104	11	9	.924
Oliver, Okla City	17	17	44	2	1	.968	Mankowski, Evans.	113	75	217	25	16	.921
DUNN, Wichita	102	77	220	11	20	.964	LaRussa, Iowa	56	45	97	14	9	.910
Knight, Indianapolis	106	102	179	13	13	.956	Bell, Iowa	50	39	100	16	7	.897
Alvarado, Tulsa	16	6	15	1	1	.955	Gamble, Evansville	23	11	48	9	4	.868
Knox, Indianapolis	13	5	26	2	0	.939	Lee, Tulsa	26	25	42	13	5	.838
Morrison, Okla City	119	100	239	24	22	.934							

Triple Plays—Morrison, 2.

(Fewer Than Ten Games)

Player and Club	G.	PO.	A.	E.	DP.	Pct.	Player and Club	G.	PO.	A.	E.	DP.	Pct.
Murphy, Omaha	2	4	7	0	0	1.000	Bastable, Okla City	4	1	6	1	1	.875
Hairston, Iowa	3	2	3	0	0	1.000	Adams, Evansville	3	1	6	1	0	.875
Templeton, Tulsa	3	1	3	0	0	1.000	Meoli, Indianapolis	8	4	9	2	2	.867
J. Tyrone, Wichita	1	1	1	0	1	1.000	Ewing, Iowa	4	4	5	2	0	.818
Eschen, Evansville	1	1	1	0	0	1.000	Cox, Denver	8	0	8	2	1	.800
Estrada, Iowa	1	1	0	0	0	1.000	Sovern, Indianapolis	3	2	6	2	0	.800
Coluccio, Iowa	1	1	0	0	0	1.000	Denevi, Omaha	5	0	3	1	0	.750
Dlugach, Iowa	1	0	1	0	0	1.000	O. Tyrone, Wichita	3	1	3	2	0	.667
Hughes, Tulsa	8	6	12	1	0	.947	R. Scott, Denver	1	1	1	2	0	.500
Yancy, Iowa	6	3	10	1	0	.929	Sperring, Wichita	1	0	1	1	0	.500
Reed, Iowa	5	3	6	1	0	.900	Lambe, Evansville	1	0	0	1	0	.000
Navarrete, Denver	9	5	17	3	2	.880							

SHORTSTOPS

Player and Club	G.	PO.	A.	E.	DP.	Pct.	Player and Club	G.	PO.	A.	E.	DP.	Pct.
Crosby, Tulsa	28	56	95	3	16	.981	Papi, Denver	61	81	121	12	21	.944
Martinez, Ind	17	26	49	2	12	.974	Gonzalez, Wichita	30	40	91	8	11	.942
McMillan, Iowa	23	33	72	3	9	.972	Kennedy, Ind	14	22	43	4	5	.942
MEOLI, Indianapolis	106	157	326	17	71	.966	Estrada, Iowa	36	70	115	12	28	.939
Buskey, Okla City	120	194	379	29	91	.952	Templeton, Tulsa	101	177	316	34	66	.935
Jackson, Iowa	35	55	100	8	20	.951	Gamble, Evansville	38	62	83	11	20	.929
Bannister, Iowa	32	64	106	9	22	.950	Wagner, Evansville	103	148	297	36	58	.925
Yancy, Iowa	11	12	25	2	4	.949	Ferrer, Okla City	28	43	69	10	26	.918
Murphy, Omaha	100	153	305	25	43	.948	Sember, Wichita	51	69	143	21	28	.910
Sperring, Wichita	64	90	186	15	39	.948	Washington, Omaha	30	48	102	15	22	.909
R. Scott, Denver	95	142	266	24	51	.944							

(Fewer Than Ten Games)

Player and Club	G.	PO.	A.	E.	DP.	Pct.	Player and Club	G.	PO.	A.	E.	DP.	Pct.
Sudakis, Omaha	1	1	7	0	0	1.000	Navarrete, Denver	3	5	2	1	0	.875
Reed, Iowa	3	2	4	0	0	1.000	Clarey, Tulsa	4	4	9	2	2	.867
Hairston, Iowa	1	0	1	0	0	1.000	LaRussa, Iowa	7	8	14	5	3	.815
Dunn, Wichita	1	0	1	0	0	1.000	Eschen, Evansville	3	4	4	2	1	.800
Guerrero, Tulsa	6	8	15	1	4	.958	Mejias, Tulsa	1	0	1	1	0	.500
Denevi, Omaha	6	7	11	2	0	.900							

OUTFIELDERS

Player and Club	G.	PO.	A.	E.	DP.	Pct.	Player and Club	G.	PO.	A.	E.	DP.	Pct.
NYMAN, Iowa*	98	194	3	0	0	1.000	Bastable, Okla City	13	16	0	0	0	1.000
A. Scott, Denver	93	162	7	0	2	1.000	Coluccio, Iowa	113	228	13	3	0	.988
Hiser, Wichita-Iowa*	92	125	7	0	1	1.000	Valentine, Denver	57	122	8	2	2	.985
Lambe, Evansville	64	76	4	0	1	1.000	Mallory, Omaha*	98	155	8	3	4	.982
Mumphrey, Iowa	19	42	4	0	1	1.000	Droege, Wichita	67	104	4	2	1	.982
Iorg, Oklahoma City	26	36	2	0	1	1.000	Hairston, Iowa	82	143	5	3	0	.980
Blackwell, Tulsa	17	18	0	0	0	1.000	Dawson, Denver	70	97	2	2	0	.980

OFFICIAL BASEBALL GUIDE

OUTFIELDERS—Continued

Player and Club	G.	PO.	A.	E.	DP.	Pct.		Player and Club	G.	PO.	A.	E.	DP.	Pct.
Lyttle, Denver	25	49	1	1	1	.980		Ward, Wichita*	106	164	8	8	0	.955
Spencer, Ind	122	268	11	6	2	.979		Potter, Tulsa	103	158	5	8	0	.953
Cromartie, Denver*	94	179	7	4	3	.979		Martinez, Ind	54	78	1	4	0	.952
Lane, Evansville	80	170	5	4	2	.978		O. Tyrone, Wichita	11	19	1	1	0	.952
Jones, Okla City	24	40	1	1	0	.976		Garcia, Tulsa	25	55	3	3	1	.951
Ewing, Iowa	36	33	6	1	1	.975		Molinaro, Evansville	131	211	12	12	4	.949
J. Tyrone, Wichita	121	191	11	6	2	.971		Kemp, Evansville*	52	91	2	5	1	.949
Nordhagen, OC-Iowa*	92	154	9	5	1	.970		Freed, Denver	15	15	3	1	0	.947
Day, Evansville*	51	94	3	3	1	.970		LaRussa, Iowa	13	17	0	1	0	.944
Zdeb, Omaha	109	209	7	7	1	.969		Coggins, Okla City*	32	46	1	3	1	.940
Bosetti, Okla City	123	273	12	9	1	.969		Smith, Okla City	129	200	4	14	1	.936
Jones, Omaha*	99	243	2	8	0	.968		Schneck, Ind*	125	161	12	12	3	.935
Mejias, Tulsa	68	141	9	5	1	.968		Detherage, Tulsa	19	27	2	2	0	.935
Valle, Evansville	22	29	0	1	0	.967		Sember, Wichita	11	13	0	1	0	.929
Kurpiel, Tulsa*	19	29	0	1	0	.967		Bright, Wichita	65	89	7	8	2	.923
Chant, Tulsa	52	106	6	4	1	.966		Gonzales, Evansville	34	40	1	4	0	.911
Godby, Indianapolis	34	23	2	1	0	.962		Nettles, Iowa	36	28	2	3	0	.909
Marshall, Ind	101	135	8	6	3	.960		DeFreites, Ind	39	48	1	6	0	.891
Roenicke, Denver	76	110	9	5	2	.960		Adams, Wichita	12	14	0	3	0	.824
Easler, Tulsa	109	172	16	8	4	.959		R. Scott, Denver	10	4	0	1	0	.800
Martz, Omaha	120	196	11	9	1	.958								

(Fewer Than Ten Games)

Player and Club	G.	PO.	A.	E.	DP.	Pct.		Player and Club	G.	PO.	A.	E.	DP.	Pct.
Landrum, Tulsa	8	17	0	0	0	1.000		Sovern, Indianapolis	4	4	0	0	0	1.000
Sperring, Wichita	9	14	1	0	0	1.000		Cox, Denver	7	9	3	1	0	.923
Adams, Evansville	7	8	2	0	0	1.000		Wathan, Omaha	1	1	0	1	0	.500
Jackson, Iowa	9	4	0	0	0	1.000		Harmon, Tulsa	1	0	0	1	0	.000

CATCHERS

Player and Club	G.	PO.	A.	E.	DP.	PB.	Pct.		Player and Club	G.	PO.	A.	E.	DP.	PB.	Pct.
Putman, Wichita	11	62	8	0	4	2	1.000		Wathan, Omaha	21	127	14	3	3	3	.979
Erickson, Iowa	14	54	3	0	0	0	1.000		Enright, Iowa	104	529	56	13	5	10	.978
Perkins, Omaha	28	129	4	1	2	2	.993		Johnson, Denver	73	352	51	9	5	4	.978
REECE, Denver	86	389	49	4	8	2	.991		Collins, Wich-Iowa	29	122	14	3	0	3	.978
Nahorodny, Okla C	106	598	49	7	8	12	.989		Werner, Ind	36	201	28	6	3	2	.974
Dlugach, Iowa	17	75	10	1	2	0	.988		Adams, Evansville	56	287	36	9	5	5	.973
Clancy, Wichita	93	504	45	7	5	14	.987		Patchin, Omaha	87	467	31	15	3	4	.971
Lamont, Evansville	85	467	47	7	8	13	.987		Ruberto, Ind	32	139	17	5	1	4	.969
Harmon, Tulsa	79	451	44	7	6	4	.986		Tamargo, Tulsa	64	365	30	13	2	4	.968
Sovern, Ind	84	446	45	8	6	8	.984		Ewing, Iowa	28	64	6	3	0	3	.959
Bastable, Okla C	34	184	18	4	0	6	.981		Stodgel, Wichita	28	113	12	8	5	5	.940

(Fewer Than Ten Games)

Player and Club	G.	PO.	A.	E.	DP.	PB.	Pct.		Player and Club	G.	PO.	A.	E.	DP.	PB.	Pct.
Roof, Iowa	8	42	4	0	0	1	1.000		Sudakis, Omaha	2	16	1	0	1	0	1.000
Robles, Tulsa	6	28	4	0	0	1	1.000		Goodman, Denver	1	1	0	0	0	1	1.000
Lee, Tulsa	5	20	2	0	0	1	1.000		Nordhagen, Iowa	4	28	3	2	0	1	.939
Kimm, Evansville	2	21	0	0	0	0	1.000		Iorg, Okla City	1	10	2	1	1	0	.923

PITCHERS

Player and Club	G.	PO.	A.	E.	DP.	Pct.		Player and Club	G.	PO.	A.	E.	DP.	Pct.
MONTAGUE, Okla City	28	15	26	0	2	1.000		Fraling, Wichita*	10	1	8	0	0	1.000
Bass, Tulsa	19	8	25	0	1	1.000		Kniffin, Okla City*	16	2	6	0	1	1.000
LaGrow, Tulsa	25	3	28	0	0	1.000		Best, Iowa	24	1	6	0	0	1.000
Otten, Iowa	38	9	19	0	3	1.000		Schultz, Wichita*	13	2	5	0	2	1.000
Crosby, Wichita	36	7	20	0	0	1.000		Scarce, Ind*	45	1	3	0	0	1.000
Kucek, Iowa	22	6	20	0	0	1.000		Wiles, Tulsa*	12	0	4	0	0	1.000
Darcy, Indianapolis	16	6	18	0	2	1.000		Zamora, Wichita	14	0	2	0	0	1.000
Kravec, Iowa*	24	2	22	0	3	1.000		Lerch, Okla City*	29	16	39	1	7	.982
Wright, Omaha*	19	2	18	0	0	1.000		Payne, Indianapolis	27	14	31	1	2	.978
Atkinson, Denver	51	3	16	0	0	1.000		Olsen, Omaha	25	14	22	1	3	.973
Sielicki, Tulsa*	11	3	15	0	1	1.000		Henderson, Ind	54	10	19	1	3	.967
Granger, Denver	26	7	10	0	0	1.000		Krukow, Wichita	26	6	21	1	4	.964
Shaffer, Iowa	58	6	8	0	1	1.000		Lance, Omaha	25	20	29	2	1	.961
Baird, Omaha*	50	6	6	0	1	1.000		McClain, Iowa*	38	4	19	1	1	.958
Taylor, Evansville	47	1	10	0	1	1.000		Bruno, Omaha	20	5	18	1	3	.958
Drumright, Denver	19	3	8	0	0	1.000		Waterbury, Tulsa	28	9	9	1	1	.947
Contreras, Okla City	25	2	8	0	0	1.000		Carroll, Indianapolis	27	11	23	2	3	.944
Christenson, Evans*	16	2	7	0	0	1.000		Zahn, Wichita*	21	8	25	2	0	.943
Harrison, Tulsa	15	3	6	0	0	1.000		Kiser, Okla City*	21	14	18	2	2	.941

PITCHERS—Continued

Player and Club	G.	PO.	A.	E.	DP.	Pct.
Nelson, Omaha	52	3	13	1	1	.941
Capilla, Tulsa*	49	3	13	1	0	.941
Hasbach, Omaha	13	3	13	1	0	.941
Knapp, Iowa	11	5	11	1	0	.941
Slayback, Evansville	30	7	24	2	2	.939
Hume, Indianapolis	27	12	33	3	2	.938
Pirtle, Wichita	50	5	10	1	2	.938
Boitano, Okla City	50	6	9	1	1	.938
Hinton, Indianapolis*	37	4	11	1	1	.938
Thompson, Ind	21	6	9	1	3	.938
Gronlund, Denver	19	2	13	1	0	.938
Albin, Denver	35	6	23	2	1	.935
Blair, Denver	25	9	20	2	1	.935
Thomas, Iowa	27	15	27	3	1	.933
Seoane, Okla City	21	5	23	2	1	.933
Hill, Okla City*	47	2	12	1	0	.933
Landreth, Denver	26	5	22	2	3	.931
Cram, Omaha	51	8	26	3	0	.919
Wilcox, Wichita-Evans	27	9	25	3	4	.919
Glynn, Evansville	24	9	24	3	2	.917
Taylor, Denver	37	4	7	1	1	.917
Arroyo, Evansville	44	10	17	3	4	.900
Kerrigan, Denver	22	1	8	1	0	.900
Lamp, Wichita	30	3	41	5	2	.898
Wallace, Okla City	53	6	11	2	1	.895
MacCormack, Evans	15	7	17	3	1	.889
Walker, Tulsa	21	5	11	2	0	.889
Makowski, Evansville*	17	2	6	1	0	.889
Alfonso, Indianapolis	16	1	7	1	0	.889
Terlecky, Iowa	35	9	21	4	0	.882
Proly, Tulsa	50	1	14	2	1	.882
Hernaiz, Okla City	24	6	9	2	2	.882
Ballinger, Omaha	17	7	8	2	1	.882
Butkus, Tulsa	57	6	16	3	0	.880
Meyerrose, Evansville	42	6	15	3	2	.875
Sarmiento, Ind	43	3	4	1	2	.875
Keener, Denver	27	13	27	6	0	.870
Johnson, Omaha	22	2	11	2	0	.867
McClure, Omaha*	21	5	26	5	2	.861
Blateric, Denver	22	1	5	1	0	.857
Moore, Wichita	24	12	29	7	3	.854
Hernandez, Okla C*	25	2	21	4	1	.852
Prall, Wichita	33	3	19	4	1	.846
Decker, Evansville	12	8	8	3	1	.842
Allen, Tulsa	33	9	33	8	2	.840
Kremmel, Wichita*	26	1	4	1	2	.833
Day, Evansville	13	2	3	1	0	.833
Enyart, Denver*	45	4	10	3	0	.824
Cappuzzello, Evans*	11	2	6	2	0	.800
Davis, Indianapolis	17	3	8	3	2	.786
Sykes, Evansville*	24	4	25	8	2	.784
Freeman, Tulsa*	12	1	2	1	0	.750
Stoddard, Iowa	12	0	3	1	0	.750
de los Santos, Tulsa*	10	0	0	1	0	.000

(Fewer Than Ten Games)

Player and Club	G.	PO.	A.	E.	DP.	Pct.
Geisel, Wichita	9	1	6	0	0	1.000
Warthen, Denver*	8	1	5	0	0	1.000
Sutter, Wichita	7	0	5	0	0	1.000
Komadina, Iowa*	3	1	4	0	0	1.000
Strampe, Denver	4	2	2	0	0	1.000
Dunning, Denver	4	1	3	0	0	1.000
Patterson, Iowa	8	1	1	0	0	1.000
York, Iowa	5	0	2	0	0	1.000
Temple, Okla City	8	0	1	0	0	1.000
Garcia, Omaha*	4	0	1	0	0	1.000
Velazquez, Okla City	1	0	0	1		1.000
LaRussa, Iowa	3	0	1	0	0	1.000
Moran, Iowa	7	0	1	0	0	1.000
Lemanczyk, Evansville	7	5	11	1	2	.941
McKinney, Omaha	9	5	9	1	0	.933
Solomon, Tulsa	8	0	11	1	0	.917
Grow, Indianapolis*	9	1	9	1	0	.909
Lang, Denver	8	2	12	2	0	.875
Odom, Iowa	3	3	1	1	1	.800
Kirkpatrick, Denver	4	2	1	1	0	.750
Rothan, Tulsa	8	1	3	2	0	.667

The following players do not have any recorded accepted chances at the positions indicated; therefore, are not listed in the fielding averages for those particular positions: Alvarado, of; Blackwell, 2b; Brookens, p; Cash, 3b-ss; Cox, ss-c-p; Cripe, ss; E. Crosby, of; DeMola, p; Gonzalez, 3b; Harmon, 3b-ss-p; Hinton*, of; Jackson, 2b; Lee, of; Martin, ss-of; Martinez, 1b; Morrison, ss; Patchin, of; Rapp, c; Ruberto, 3b; Squires*, p; Stodgel, ss; Templeton, of; Throop, p. Bolek, Darichuk, and Leibowitz appeared as pinch-hitters only.

CLUB PITCHING

Club	G.	CG.	ShO.	Sv.	IP.	H.	R.	ER.	HR.	BB.	Int. BB.	HB.	SO.	WP.	Bk.	ERA.
Omaha	136	32	8	33	1132	1105	557	449	83	404	56	18	693	55	7	3.57
Oklahoma City	135	31	11	22	1146	1170	586	497	95	418	40	18	732	51	3	3.90
Tulsa	135	24	9	21	1146	1261	622	511	102	481	53	25	771	50	6	4.01
Indianapolis	135	19	11	27	1124	1040	573	507	89	610	61	29	729	44	5	4.06
Iowa	137	28	10	27	1152	1165	620	522	106	497	48	30	773	65	4	4.08
Denver	137	24	6	36	1127	1137	602	516	125	525	29	33	689	48	3	4.12
Evansville	136	24	6	22	1102	1124	650	527	88	601	59	33	712	60	6	4.30
Wichita	135	34	9	20	1118	1202	663	537	124	457	51	26	750	42	5	4.32

PITCHERS' RECORDS
(Leading Qualifiers for Earned-Run Average Leadership—109 or More Innings)
*Throws lefthanded.

Pitcher—Club	G.	GS.	CG.	ShO.	W.	L.	Sv.	Pct.	IP.	H.	R.	ER.	HR.	BB.	Int. BB.	HB.	SO.	WP.	ERA.
Henderson, Ind	54	1	0	0	7	3	10	.700	109	73	29	28	8	66	8	2	80	2	2.31
Montague, Okla C	28	28	11	6	14	6	0	.700	144	115	57	51	11	51	0	2	120	7	2.64
Allen, Tulsa	33	18	4	2	11	6	2	.647	154	163	64	48	8	56	6	3	90	5	2.81
Otten, Iowa	38	14	3	1	6	6	7	.500	133	140	51	43	11	45	3	4	79	6	2.91
McClure, Omaha*	21	21	9	2	9	8	0	.529	133	133	61	44	9	41	2	2	91	6	2.98
Krukow, Wichita	26	20	6	2	7	9	0	.438	144	142	61	53	9	47	2	6	108	6	3.31
Lerch, Okla City*	29	29	11	2	13	11	0	.542	207	203	91	77	10	47	3	2	152	7	3.35
Olsen, Omaha	25	25	7	2	9	7	0	.563	155	159	68	58	7	36	4	4	59	3	3.37

| | | | | | | | | | | | | | | | Int. | | | | |
Pitcher–Club	G.	GS.	CG.	ShO.	W.	L.	Sv.	Pct.	IP.	H.	R.	ER.	HR.	BB.	BB.	HB.	SO.	WP.	ERA.
Keener, Denver	27	27	7	1	14	4	0	.778	176	173	74	66	15	59	0	5	82	5	3.38
McClain, Iowa*	38	12	3	1	7	8	1	.467	117	120	59	46	11	38	12	2	52	4	3.54

Departmental Leaders: G–Shaffer, 58; GS–Lerch, 29; CG–Lerch, Montague, 11; ShO–Montague, 6; W–Keener, Montague, 14; L–Lamp, 14; Sv–Nelson, Shaffer, 16; Pct.–Cram, .786; IP–Lerch, 207; H–Lerch, 203; R–Carroll, Lance, 103; ER–Carroll, 89; HR–Moore, 25; BB–Payne, 101; IBB–McClain, 12; HB–Payne, 10; SO–Lerch, 152; WP–Thomas, 17.

(All Pitchers–Listed Alphabetically)

| | | | | | | | | | | | | | | | Int. | | | | |
Pitcher–Club	G.	GS.	CG.	ShO.	W.	L.	Sv.	Pct.	IP.	H.	R.	ER.	HR.	BB.	BB.	HB.	SO.	WP.	ERA.
Albin, Denver	35	5	0	0	5	6	2	.455	80	101	53	44	13	25	3	1	43	6	4.95
Alfonso, Ind	16	1	0	0	2	1	0	.667	31	28	19	16	2	23	2	1	15	3	4.65
Allen, Tulsa	33	18	4	2	11	6	2	.647	154	163	64	48	8	56	6	3	90	5	2.81
Arroyo, Evans	44	9	2	0	5	8	10	.385	102	120	74	54	13	41	10	5	56	2	4.76
Atkinson, Denver	51	0	0	0	4	1	15	.667	79	79	36	35	9	47	6	1	61	3	3.99
Baird, Omaha*	50	0	0	0	4	1	5	.800	57	46	18	14	3	31	8	0	34	3	2.21
Ballinger, Omaha	17	14	3	1	6	2	0	.750	88	62	38	31	5	36	1	1	61	5	3.17
Bass, Tulsa	19	19	2	2	8	6	0	.571	118	103	54	51	15	39	1	2	76	3	3.89
Best, Iowa	24	1	0	0	3	4	1	.429	37	44	32	30	4	15	3	1	30	0	7.30
Blair, Denver	25	25	0	0	9	4	0	.692	122	131	73	61	14	84	3	8	91	15	4.50
Blateric, Iowa	22	0	0	0	2	3	2	.400	39	47	25	19	3	9	6	2	24	4	4.38
Boitano, Okla C	50	0	0	0	3	5	7	.375	70	65	39	33	8	54	7	0	50	7	4.24
Brookens, Evans	1	1	0	0	0	0	0	.000	3	4	0	0	0	1	0	0	1	0	0.00
Bruno, Omaha	20	18	3	0	9	4	0	.692	114	115	59	48	16	38	4	1	79	2	3.79
Butkus, Tulsa	57	0	0	0	5	6	3	.455	80	93	43	32	5	39	10	0	53	3	3.60
Capilla, Tulsa*	49	0	0	0	4	4	1	.500	57	59	38	31	6	45	8	2	58	4	4.89
Cappuzzello, Ev*	11	6	4	0	1	4	0	.200	49	50	22	15	3	20	2	0	37	5	2.76
Carroll, Ind	27	27	4	2	9	12	0	.429	149	159	103	89	19	88	7	3	83	6	5.38
Christenson, Ev*	16	7	0	0	3	4	0	.429	50	60	40	38	8	33	3	1	29	5	6.84
Contreras, Okla C	25	0	0	0	1	2	4	.333	27	26	9	8	1	18	3	2	17	1	2.67
Cox, Denver	1	1	0	0	0	0	0	.000	1	0	0	0	0	1	0	0	0	0	0.00
Cram, Omaha	51	1	0	0	11	3	9	.786	102	100	45	39	10	28	8	4	58	7	3.44
Crosby, Wichita	36	7	2	0	3	4	5	.429	97	91	45	37	10	45	6	2	95	1	3.43
Darcy, Ind	16	16	2	0	5	7	0	.417	103	95	53	49	6	59	8	1	58	2	4.28
Davis, Ind	17	5	0	0	1	4	0	.200	50	56	28	22	5	27	2	2	31	5	3.96
Day, Evansville*	13	0	0	0	1	0	0	1.000	32	23	17	14	3	21	0	0	17	0	3.94
Decker, Evans	12	12	0	0	1	10	0	.091	57	62	57	44	7	43	2	2	35	11	6.95
de los Santos, Tul*	10	0	0	0	2	0	0	.000	10	13	10	7	1	8	2	0	8	1	6.30
DeMola, Denver	1	0	0	0	0	1	0	.000	2	3	4	4	1	1	0	0	0	0	18.00
Drumright, Denver	19	3	1	0	5	4	1	.556	53	38	26	25	8	17	1	1	25	1	4.63
Dunning, Denver	4	3	1	0	3	0	0	1.000	23	20	7	7	2	5	0	0	11	0	2.74
Enyart, Denver*	45	12	0	0	7	6	4	.538	105	115	61	54	11	50	3	5	59	2	4.63
Frailing, Wich*	10	8	0	0	2	3	1	.400	52	57	30	26	6	12	1	0	23	2	4.50
Freeman, Tulsa*	12	6	0	0	1	2	1	.333	40	49	30	21	6	25	0	1	29	3	4.73
Garcia, Omaha*	4	0	0	0	1	0	0	1.000	5	3	2	0	0	7	1	0	4	3	0.00
Geisel, Wichita*	9	8	3	1	2	4	0	.333	50	50	33	28	7	25	1	2	27	0	5.04
Glynn, Evansville*	24	24	5	2	9	7	0	.563	148	146	79	59	8	82	7	1	92	5	3.59
Granger, Denver	26	1	0	0	3	1	6	.750	44	42	16	12	5	15	2	2	18	0	2.45
Gronlund, Denver	19	17	5	1	10	3	1	.769	106	107	60	51	13	52	0	5	54	3	4.33
Grow, Ind*	9	6	0	0	0	4	0	.000	32	32	23	18	6	24	4	1	13	2	5.06
Harmon, Tulsa	1	0	0	0	0	0	0	.000	0	3	6	5	1	2	0	0	0	0	......
Harrison, Tulsa	15	9	0	0	2	4	1	.333	55	67	30	29	4	31	4	2	35	4	4.75
Hasbach, Omaha	13	13	4	1	7	4	0	.636	83	65	36	32	6	31	2	1	62	1	3.47
Henderson, Ind	54	1	0	0	7	3	10	.700	109	73	29	28	8	66	8	2	80	2	2.31
Hernaiz, Okla C	24	4	0	0	4	1	1	.800	50	53	34	26	3	25	1	1	27	4	4.68
Hernandez, OC*	25	23	3	1	8	9	0	.471	135	154	82	68	18	30	5	2	88	1	4.53
Hill, Okla City*	47	2	0	0	5	6	6	.455	67	63	34	29	3	36	6	3	42	3	3.90
Hinton, Ind*	37	6	1	0	2	5	7	.286	81	81	29	27	9	25	4	3	53	1	3.00
Hume, Ind	27	27	8	3	9	12	0	.429	182	178	91	83	10	62	8	1	111	4	4.10
Johnson, Omaha	22	5	1	0	1	5	1	.167	66	77	42	38	6	22	2	1	49	8	5.18
Keener, Denver	27	27	7	1	14	4	0	.778	176	173	74	66	15	59	0	5	82	5	3.38
Kerrigan, Denver	22	0	0	0	2	0	1	1.000	32	26	13	12	2	12	3	0	13	2	3.38
Kirkpatrick, Den	4	2	0	0	1	1	0	.500	12	20	11	8	1	3	1	0	4	0	6.00
Kiser, Okla C*	21	15	1	0	4	5	0	.444	107	107	64	53	6	61	6	2	64	7	4.46
Knapp, Iowa	11	11	6	2	7	2	0	.778	81	63	24	23	5	28	1	1	74	0	2.56
Kniffin, Okla C*	16	13	2	0	4	6	0	.400	76	79	40	36	13	27	0	1	40	1	4.26
Komadina, Iowa*	3	3	0	0	0	1	0	.000	13	12	8	7	1	10	0	3	7	1	4.85
Kravec, Iowa*	24	22	5	2	8	5	0	.615	131	103	68	63	13	89	4	2	142	4	4.33
Kremmel, Wichita*	26	1	0	0	1	2	0	.333	44	57	37	32	6	27	2	3	37	3	6.55
Krukow, Wichita	26	20	6	2	7	9	0	.438	144	142	61	53	9	47	2	6	108	6	3.31
Kucek, Iowa	22	20	2	0	5	9	0	.357	124	130	68	58	9	55	2	1	78	9	4.21
LaGrow, Tulsa	25	25	6	1	6	10	0	.375	161	171	81	74	17	45	5	3	108	4	4.14
Lamp, Wichita	30	25	6	0	8	14	1	.364	153	182	94	69	15	52	10	6	98	7	4.06
Lance, Omaha	25	25	5	1	10	10	0	.500	157	166	103	76	16	57	9	1	65	3	4.36

Pitcher–Club	G.	GS.	CG.	ShO.	W.	L.	Sv.	Pct.	IP.	H.	R.	ER.	HR.	BB.	Int. BB.	HB.	SO.	WP.	ERA.
Landreth, Denver	26	26	7	1	13	9	0	.591	155	128	77	64	15	83	2	2	118	6	3.72
Lang, Denver	8	7	1	0	0	3	0	.000	42	53	37	35	7	23	1	0	27	3	7.50
LaRussa, Iowa	3	0	0	0	0	0	0	.000	3	3	1	1	0	0	0	0	2	0	3.00
Lemanczyk, Evans	7	7	3	1	5	2	0	.714	48	36	16	14	4	18	3	0	27	2	2.63
Lerch, Okla City*	29	29	11	2	13	11	0	.542	207	203	91	77	10	47	3	2	152	7	3.35
MacCormack, Evans*	15	13	2	1	4	4	0	.500	74	63	33	28	3	51	1	4	60	9	3.41
Makowski, Evans*	17	3	0	0	0	3	0	.000	44	52	32	31	4	25	2	2	19	5	6.34
McClain, Iowa*	38	12	3	1	7	8	1	.467	117	120	59	46	11	38	12	2	52	8	3.54
McClure, Omaha*	21	21	9	2	9	8	0	.529	133	133	61	44	9	41	2	2	91	6	2.98
McKinney, Omaha	9	8	0	0	2	3	0	.400	47	59	27	24	2	19	4	0	31	0	4.60
Meyerrose, Evans	42	1	0	0	3	3	2	.500	83	88	46	35	6	40	6	1	53	7	3.80
Montague, Okla C	28	28	11	6	14	6	0	.700	194	183	72	57	11	51	0	2	120	7	2.64
Moore, Wichita	24	24	9	2	7	11	0	.389	152	170	96	80	25	61	4	1	92	6	4.74
Moran, Iowa	7	0	0	0	2	1	0	.667	10	12	9	8	0	5	0	1	11	1	7.20
Nelson, Omaha	52	0	0	0	6	6	16	.500	60	49	27	20	2	31	8	3	56	7	3.00
Odom, Iowa	3	3	1	0	3	0	0	1.000	21	21	6	6	3	11	0	0	18	3	2.57
Olsen, Omaha	25	25	7	2	9	7	0	.563	155	159	68	58	7	36	4	4	59	3	3.37
Otten, Iowa	38	14	3	1	6	6	7	.500	133	140	51	43	11	45	3	4	79	6	2.91
Patterson, Iowa	8	0	0	0	0	1	0	.000	10	11	10	9	3	10	0	0	5	0	8.10
Payne, Ind	27	27	2	1	9	9	0	.500	161	147	96	81	17	101	6	10	128	11	4.86
Pirtle, Wichita	50	0	0	0	8	7	9	.533	80	77	41	33	8	25	4	1	64	3	3.71
Prall, Wichita*	33	15	2	1	5	10	0	.333	115	135	83	71	14	59	3	0	63	2	5.56
Proly, Tulsa	50	0	0	0	6	4	11	.600	67	71	28	20	5	13	4	1	28	5	2.69
Rothan, Tulsa	8	3	0	0	2	0	0	.000	17	22	9	6	1	9	1	2	11	5	3.18
Sarmiento, Ind	43	0	0	0	11	5	6	.688	65	49	21	20	5	24	5	1	51	1	2.77
Scarce, Ind*	45	1	0	0	2	4	4	.333	68	66	35	27	3	43	5	3	33	4	3.57
Schultz, Wichita*	13	2	1	1	1	1	0	.500	32	28	15	12	2	15	1	1	22	2	3.38
Seoane, Okla City	21	21	3	0	8	7	0	.533	117	144	69	62	10	24	1	1	69	8	4.77
Shaffer, Iowa	58	0	0	0	9	8	16	.529	88	91	44	36	11	36	6	5	62	2	3.68
Sielicki, Tulsa*	11	11	1	0	2	6	0	.250	63	77	38	33	2	35	1	0	35	2	4.71
Slayback, Evans	30	18	2	0	3	13	2	.188	113	119	81	70	11	58	7	6	81	4	5.58
Solomon, Tulsa	8	8	4	1	5	2	0	.714	56	42	19	15	2	16	1	3	49	2	2.41
Squires, Iowa*	1	0	0	0	0	0	0	.000	2	5	4	4	0	1	0	0	1	0	18.00
Stoddard, Iowa	12	2	0	0	0	0	0	.000	29	37	20	18	1	15	1	0	20	2	5.59
Strampe, Denver	4	4	0	0	0	4	0	.000	17	20	17	12	3	12	1	2	6	0	6.35
Sutter, Wichita	7	0	0	0	2	1	1	.667	12	9	3	2	1	4	1	0	16	1	1.50
Sykes, Evansville*	24	21	3	1	8	11	0	.421	118	137	71	56	6	71	3	3	70	3	4.27
Taylor, Evansville	47	0	0	0	6	7	8	.462	68	60	35	31	4	52	6	5	58	1	4.10
Taylor, Denver	37	0	0	0	4	1	6	.800	63	58	20	19	6	16	2	0	43	2	2.71
Temple, Okla City	8	0	0	0	1	2	0	.333	10	12	5	5	1	8	1	0	3	1	4.50
Terlecky, Iowa	35	21	2	1	10	6	0	.625	132	144	92	74	16	51	4	5	63	4	5.05
Thomas, Iowa	27	26	6	1	6	11	0	.353	168	167	89	70	15	72	6	2	103	17	3.75
Thompson, Ind	21	18	2	1	5	7	0	.417	93	76	46	41	5	68	2	1	73	6	3.97
Throop, Omaha	3	0	0	0	1	0	0	1.000	5	4	2	2	0	3	0	0	7	3	3.60
Velazquez, Okla C	3	0	0	0	0	0	0	.000	6	10	5	5	1	1	0	0	2	0	7.50
Walker, Tulsa	21	16	5	2	9	5	2	.643	115	132	62	48	11	24	4	2	80	0	3.76
Wallace, Okla C	53	0	0	0	7	3	4	.700	80	69	42	38	10	36	7	2	58	4	4.28
Warthen, Denver*	8	4	2	1	4	0	0	1.000	34	22	17	12	0	20	1	1	34	0	3.18
Waterbury, Tulsa	28	18	2	0	6	10	0	.375	123	162	97	80	16	79	4	4	91	8	5.85
Wilcox, 9 Wi-18 Ev	27	18	3	0	6	7	0	.462	130	141	72	55	11	63	11	4	94	3	3.81
Wiles, Tulsa*	12	2	0	0	0	1	0	.000	30	34	15	13	2	15	2	0	20	1	3.90
Wright, Omaha*	19	6	0	0	2	5	2	.286	59	67	29	25	1	24	3	0	37	4	3.81
York, Iowa	5	2	0	0	0	1	0	.000	14	15	10	9	0	7	0	1	4	2	5.79
Zahn, Wichita*	21	21	5	1	8	8	0	.500	137	142	81	65	16	61	9	2	66	8	4.27
Zamora, Wichita	14	0	0	0	2	3	2	.400	22	29	22	18	2	6	3	1	20	1	7.36

BALKS—Payne, 3; Bruno, Meyerrose, Solomon, Sykes, 2 each; Baird, Best, Boitano, Butkus, Capilla, Cappuzzello, Cram, Drumright, Hasbach, Hinton, Keener, Kiser, Kravec, Krukow, MacCormack, McClure, Moore, Olsen, Otten, Pirtle, Prall, Sielicki, Thomas, Thompson, Walker, Wallace, Warthen, Wilcox, 1 each.

COMBINATION SHUTOUTS—Landreth-Albin, Enyart-Granger, Denver; Brookens-Wilcox, Evansville; Thompson-Henderson-Hinton, Payne-Hinton-Sarmiento, Payne-Hinton-Henderson, Davis-Scarce-Sarmiento, Indianapolis; Odom-Shaffer, Kravec-Kucek, Iowa; Hill-Wallace, Seoane-Hill, Oklahoma City; Ballinger-Baird, Omaha; Bass-Proly, Tulsa; Prall-Sutter, Wichita.

NO-HIT GAMES—Montague, Oklahoma City, defeated Omaha, 1-0, May 25 (seven innings); Hasbach, Omaha, defeated Tulsa, 4-0, June 2 (seven innings); Knapp, Iowa, defeated Evansville, 3-0, June 13 (seven innings); Glynn, Evansville, defeated Iowa, 3-0, July 15 (seven innings).

International League

CLASS AAA

Leading Batter
RICHARD DAUER
Rochester

League President
GEORGE SISLER, JR.

Leading Pitcher
DENNIS MARTINEZ
Rochester

CHAMPIONSHIP WINNERS IN PREVIOUS YEARS

1884—Trenton .520	1924—Baltimore .709	1953—Rochester .630
1885—Syracuse .584	1925—Baltimore .633	Montreal (2nd)† .586
1886—Utica .646	1926—Toronto .657	1954—Toronto .630
1887—Toronto .644	1927—Buffalo .667	Syracuse (4th)§ .510
1888—Syracuse .723	1928—Rochester .549	1955—Montreal .617
1889—Detroit .649	1929—Rochester .613	Rochester (4th)† .497
1890—Detroit .617	1930—Rochester .629	1956—Toronto .566
1891—Buffalo (reg. season) .727	1931—Rochester .601	Rochester (2nd)† .553
Buffalo (supplem'l) .680	1932—Newark .649	1957—Toronto .575
1892—Providence .615	1933—Newark .622	Buffalo (2nd)† .571
Binghamton* .667	Buffalo (4th)† .494	1958—Montreal‡ .588
1893—Erie .606	1934—Newark .608	1959—Buffalo .582
1894—Providence .696	Toronto (3rd)† .559	Havana (3rd)† .523
1895—Springfield .687	1935—Montreal .597	1960—Toronto‡ .649
1896—Providence .602	Syracuse (2nd)† .565	1961—Columbus .597
1897—Syracuse .632	1936—Buffalo‡ .610	Buffalo (3rd)† .559
1898—Montreal .586	1937—Newark‡ .717	1962—Jacksonville .610
1899—Rochester .624	1938—Newark‡ .684	Atlanta (3rd)† .539
1900—Providence .616	1939—Jersey City .582	1963—Syracuse x .533
1901—Rochester .642	Rochester (2nd)† .556	Indianapolis† .562
1902—Toronto .669	1940—Rochester .611	1964—Jacksonville .589
1903—Jersey City .642	Newark (2nd)† .594	Rochester (4th)† .532
1904—Buffalo .657	1941—Newark .649	1965—Columbus .582
1905—Providence .638	Montreal (2nd)† .584	Toronto (3rd)† .556
1906—Buffalo .607	1942—Newark .601	1966—Rochester .565
1907—Toronto .619	Syracuse (3rd)† .513	Toronto (2nd-tied)† .558
1908—Baltimore .593	1943—Toronto .625	1967—Richmond .574
1909—Rochester .596	Syracuse (3rd)† .536	Toledo (3rd)† .525
1910—Rochester .601	1944—Baltimore‡ .553	1968—Toledo .565
1911—Rochester .645	1945—Montreal .621	Jacksonville (4th)† .514
1912—Toronto .595	Newark (2nd)† .582	1969—Tidewater .563
1913—Newark .625	1946—Montreal‡ .649	Syracuse (3rd)† .536
1914—Providence .617	1947—Jersey City .610	1970—Syracuse‡ .600
1915—Buffalo .632	Syracuse (3rd)† .575	1971—Rochester‡ .614
1916—Buffalo .586	1948—Montreal‡ .614	1972—Louisville .563
1917—Toronto .604	1949—Buffalo .584	Tidewater (3rd)† .545
1918—Toronto .693	Montreal (3rd)† .545	1973—Charleston .586
1919—Baltimore .671	1950—Rochester .609	Pawtucket y† .534
1920—Baltimore .719	Baltimore (3rd)† .556	1974—Memphis .613
1921—Baltimore .717	1951—Montreal‡ .617	Rochester x‡ .611
1922—Baltimore .689	1952—Montreal .629	1975—Tidewater‡ .610
1923—Baltimore .677	Rochester (3rd)† .619	

*Won split-season playoff. †Won four-team playoff. ‡Won championship and four-team playoff. §Defeated Havana in game to decide fourth place, then won four-team playoff. xLeague was divided into Northern, Southern divisions. yLeague divided into American, National divisions. (NOTE—Known as Eastern League in 1884, New York State League in 1885, International League in 1886-87, International Association in 1888, International League in 1889-90, Eastern Association in 1891, and Eastern League from 1892 until 1912.)

STANDING OF CLUBS AT CLOSE OF SEASON, SEPTEMBER 3

Club	Roch.	Syr.	Mem.	Rich.	R.I.	Char.	Tide.	Tol.	W.	L.	T.	Pct.	G.B.
Rochester (Orioles)	..	11	10	15	11	15	13	13	88	50	0	.638	....
Syracuse (Yankees)	9	..	12	9	11	13	11	17	82	57	0	.590	6½
Memphis (Astros)	10	8	..	12	11	10	6	12	69	69	0	.500	19
Richmond (Braves)	5	11	8	..	9	13	11	12	69	71	0	.493	20
Rhode Island (Red Sox)	9	9	9	11	..	9	12	9	68	70	0	.493	20
Charleston (Pirates)	4	7	8	7	9	..	12	15	62	73	0	.459	24½
Tidewater (Mets)	6	8	14	9	8	8	..	7	60	78	0	.435	28
Toledo (Indians)	7	3	8	8	11	5	13	..	55	85	0	.393	34

Rhode Island club represented Pawtucket, R. I.
Tidewater club represented Norfolk and Portsmouth, Va.

Major league affiliations in parentheses.

Playoffs—Syracuse defeated Memphis, three games to none; Richmond defeated Rochester, three games to one; Syracuse defeated Richmond, three games to one (for Governor's Cup).

Regular-Season Attendance—Charleston, 72,543; Memphis, 92,973; Rhode Island, 106,052; Richmond, 109,636; Rochester, 258,101; Syracuse, 187,397; Tidewater, 106,458; Toledo, 106,106. Total, 1,039,266. All-Star Game, 3,827. Playoffs, 29,441.

Managers: Charleston—Tim Murtaugh; Memphis—Jim Beauchamp; Rhode Island—Joe Morgan; Richmond—Jack McKeon; Rochester—Joe Altobelli; Syracuse—Bobby Cox; Tidewater—Tom Burgess; Toledo—Joe Sparks.

All-Star Team: 1B—Lis, Toledo; 2B—Dauer, Rochester; 3B—Hobson, Rhode Island; SS—Klutts, Syracuse; OF—Dilone, Charleston; Moreno, Charleston; Whitfield, Syracuse; C—Stearns, Tidewater; P—Martinez, Rochester; McGregor, Syracuse-Rochester; Manager—Altobelli, Rochester.

(Compiled by Ed Williams, League Statistician, Shawnee, Okla.)

CLUB BATTING

Club	G.	AB.	R.	OR.	H.	TB.	2B.	3B.	HR.	RBI.	SH.	SF.	Int. BB.	BB.	HP.	SO.	SB.	CS.	LOB.	Pct.
Charleston	135	4505	623	656	1265	1843	192	28	110	558	24	33	419	59	24	755	224	75	938	.281
Memphis	138	4622	674	705	1287	1778	201	31	76	602	47	42	506	48	39	610	148	59	1005	.278
Toledo	140	4620	702	790	1275	1847	202	41	96	644	39	38	585	55	19	615	121	53	1032	.276
Richmond	140	4568	678	645	1258	1784	193	42	83	610	83	39	593	54	29	699	59	42	1080	.275
Rochester	138	4384	690	524	1204	1834	205	31	121	638	41	55	600	63	31	633	49	37	1049	.275
Syracuse	139	4554	681	645	1243	1830	219	37	98	627	60	44	593	67	39	677	71	49	1063	.273
Rhode Island	138	4546	632	647	1213	1845	181	23	135	588	33	43	564	37	31	741	60	33	1063	.267
Tidewater	138	4428	566	634	1148	1642	173	36	83	513	62	38	516	56	23	669	124	70	999	.259

INDIVIDUAL BATTING
(Leading Qualifiers for Batting Championship—378 or More Plate Appearances)
*Bats lefthanded. †Switch-hitter.

Player and Club	G.	AB.	R.	H.	TB.	2B.	3B.	HR.	RBI.	SH.	SF.	BB.	HP.	SO.	SB.	CS.	Pct.
Dauer, Richard, Rochester	132	524	84	176	241	26	3	11	78	6	3	46	3	38	2	5	.3358
Dilone, Miguel, Char†	100	408	63	137	159	7	6	1	17	1	0	37	3	33	61	21	.3357
Moore, Alvin, Richmond	103	398	58	131	169	23	3	3	72	2	5	49	1	35	3	3	.329
Cacek, Craig, Memphis	132	475	86	154	204	24	1	8	63	1	6	82	4	42	3	3	.324
Gonzalez, J. Fernando, Char	119	443	53	142	220	31	4	13	70	1	5	20	2	64	4	8	.321
Norris, James, Toledo*	133	435	92	139	197	23	7	7	68	4	1	118	0	45	40	11	.320
Klutts, Gene, Syracuse	119	430	75	137	237	22	3	24	80	2	6	35	4	87	3	3	.319
Moreno, Omar, Charleston*	94	330	70	104	138	11	7	3	36	1	4	55	1	77	55	9	.315
Gonzalez, Orlando, Toledo*	98	357	49	111	139	17	4	1	45	4	3	35	3	39	19	5	.311
Stearns, John, Tidewater	102	332	64	103	154	17	2	10	45	3	0	71	4	29	11	8	.310

Departmental Leaders: G—Coleman, Pemberton, Whitfield, 138; AB—Whitfield, 525; R—Lis, 93; H—Dauer, 176; TB—Lis, 245; 2B—J. Gonzalez, 31; 3B—A. Garcia, 10; HR—Baker, 36; RBI—Lis, 103; SH—Ruiz, 20; SF—Duncan, 11; BB—Beall, 135; HP—Baker, 10; SO—Baker, 139; SB—Dilone, 61; CS—Dilone, 21.

(All Players—Listed Alphabetically)

Player and Club	G.	AB.	R.	H.	TB.	2B.	3B.	HR.	RBI.	SH.	SF.	BB.	HP.	SO.	SB.	CS.	Pct.
Allietta, Robert, Memphis	72	236	32	58	76	6	0	4	29	8	0	20	2	22	0	0	.246
Alston, Wendell, Syracuse*	130	516	87	145	225	26	9	12	66	7	0	56	0	49	18	10	.281
Andrew, Kim, Rhode Island	109	348	55	100	124	9	3	3	30	3	2	64	2	27	10	5	.287
Andrews, Robert, Memphis	22	80	16	26	41	3	3	2	14	0	0	17	0	8	5	0	.325
Angelini, Norman, Rich*	42	3	0	0	0	0	0	0	1	0	0	0	0	3	0	0	.000
Armas, Antonio, Charleston	114	409	62	96	185	24	1	21	67	2	4	34	1	120	7	3	.235
Asselstine, Brian, Rich*	122	458	73	134	182	23	5	5	58	4	2	52	2	40	11	6	.293

Player and Club	G.	AB.	R.	H.	TB.	2B.	3B.	HR.	RBI.	SH.	SF.	BB.	HP.	SO.	SB.	CS.	Pct.
Augustine, David, Char	100	297	40	77	107	9	3	5	24	2	2	11	4	43	10	1	.259
Autry, Albert, Richmond	32	19	0	1	1	0	0	0	2	3	0	1	0	9	0	0	.053
Aviles, Ramon, Rhode Is	134	421	50	108	137	17	3	2	42	6	3	47	1	21	4	2	.257
Ayala, Benigno, Tidewater	87	293	41	66	115	9	2	12	48	1	4	24	1	56	5	0	.225
Bailor, Robert, Rochester	36	103	21	32	47	10	1	1	12	2	2	9	2	9	8	1	.311
Bair, C. Douglas, Char	45	5	0	0	0	0	0	0	0	0	0	1	2	0	0	.000
Baker, Jack, Rhode Island	133	469	72	119	243	16	0	36	80	1	6	57	10	139	2	1	.254
Balaz, John, Rhode Island	133	480	69	114	207	21	0	24	69	0	4	38	2	120	1	3	.238
Baldwin, Rick, Tidewater*	46	6	1	2	3	1	0	0	1	0	1	0	0	1	0	0	.333
Baldwin, Robert, Tidewater*	133	495	66	134	215	20	5	17	72	6	5	43	1	61	18	13	.271
Beall, Robert, Richmond†	109	350	85	107	163	19	5	9	55	7	1	135	2	71	4	5	.306
Beard, Michael, Richmond*	14	5	1	2	2	0	0	0	1	1	0	0	0	0	0	0	.400
Beene, Fred, Toledo	36	1	0	0	0	0	0	0	0	0	0	0	0	0	0	0	.000
Belloir, Robert, Richmond	35	93	16	24	34	4	0	2	9	2	1	15	0	10	3	1	.258
Benson, Wayne, Syracuse	11	25	2	4	4	0	0	0	1	0	5	0	8	0	1	.160
Bergman, David, Syracuse*	134	455	68	134	182	23	2	7	65	4	8	77	2	73	17	6	.295
Bernard, Dwight, Tidewater	17	9	3	3	6	0	0	1	1	0	0	0	4	0	0	.333
Bernhardt, Juan, Syracuse	101	380	41	115	163	24	0	8	57	3	7	22	5	37	1	3	.303
Blackwell, Timothy, R I†	2	3	0	0	0	0	0	0	0	0	0	0	0	1	0	0	.000
Bladt, Richard, Syracuse	130	453	81	129	185	21	4	9	60	4	6	70	8	59	10	8	.285
Bonnell, R. Barry, Rich	66	227	36	64	96	13	2	5	31	7	2	18	3	29	3	3	.282
Breazeale, James, Richmond*	25	69	11	18	36	3	0	5	19	0	1	13	0	8	0	0	.261
Brown, Leon, Tidewater	21	78	14	25	33	5	0	1	13	2	0	7	1	6	4	1	.321
Bruhert, Michael, Tidewater	7	2	0	0	0	0	0	0	0	0	0	0	0	2	0	0	.000
Cacek, Craig, Memphis	132	475	85	154	204	24	1	8	63	1	6	82	4	42	3	3	.324
Camp, Rick, Richmond	51	9	0	0	0	0	0	0	0	2	0	1	0	7	0	0	.000
Capra, Lee, Richmond	4	1	0	0	0	0	0	0	0	0	0	1	0	1	0	0	.000
Cerone, Richard, Toledo	96	339	38	86	138	19	0	11	49	6	2	45	3	38	2	2	.254
Champion, B. Billy, Rich	12	4	0	0	0	0	0	0	0	0	0	0	0	3	0	0	.000
Cheadle, David, 9 Rich-5 Char*	14	2	0	0	0	0	0	0	0	1	0	1	0	0	0	0	.000
Chiles, Richard, Memphis*	79	288	40	87	130	14	1	9	47	2	3	35	2	20	1	1	.302
Coleman, David, Rhode Is	138	515	73	143	220	29	6	12	66	1	5	48	3	88	1	4	.278
Coletta, Christopher, R I*	82	209	30	57	83	8	0	6	21	0	1	18	0	29	4	1	.273
Collins, Donald, Richmond	24	5	1	0	0	0	0	0	0	1	0	1	0	3	0	0	.000
Collins, Jimmie, Richmond*	80	266	35	78	105	11	5	2	29	0	1	22	2	45	7	6	.293
Crowley, Terrence, Roch*	20	69	4	18	31	7	0	2	7	1	0	9	0	10	1	1	.261
Dancy, William, Tidewater†	42	138	10	35	44	5	2	0	20	2	2	9	0	20	1	4	.254
Darrow, Darrell, Syracuse	42	112	16	23	32	3	0	2	12	5	0	21	0	19	2	2	.205
Dauer, Richard, Rochester	132	524	84	176	241	26	3	11	78	6	3	46	3	38	2	5	.336
DeFreites, Arturo, Toledo	81	304	43	86	150	14	4	14	62	0	3	9	3	54	4	0	.283
DeJohn, Mark, Tidewater†	111	332	27	66	85	10	3	1	22	11	1	37	2	48	0	2	.199
de la Rosa, Jesus, Memphis	80	265	28	71	89	12	0	2	29	2	2	24	4	60	10	4	.268
Delgado, Luis, Rhode Is*	2	2	1	1	2	1	0	0	1	0	0	0	0	0	0	0	.500
Diaz, Baudilio, Rhode Is	62	117	10	29	42	1	0	4	18	3	2	15	0	16	0	0	.248
Didier, Robert, Richmond†	47	152	21	36	42	3	0	1	16	6	5	11	2	18	0	0	.237
Diggle, Ronnie, Tidewater*	111	358	48	94	138	13	2	9	39	3	3	67	0	67	6	6	.263
Dillard, Stephen, Rhode Is	34	135	17	31	39	5	0	1	9	3	3	10	0	16	11	4	.230
Dilone, Miguel, Char†	100	408	63	137	159	7	6	1	17	1	0	37	3	33	61	21	.336
Dineen, Kerry, Syracuse*	59	166	21	42	60	12	3	0	22	3	5	31	1	19	7	3	.253
Duncan, Taylor, Rochester	127	447	50	121	182	24	2	11	69	3	11	39	1	42	4	3	.271
Dusan, Gene, Toledo†	18	46	3	10	10	0	0	0	6	0	0	5	0	11	0	1	.217
Dwyer, James, Tidewater*	8	26	0	5	6	1	0	0	1	0	0	4	0	4	0	0	.192
Easterly, James, Richmond†	40	26	3	3	4	1	0	0	0	4	0	1	0	9	0	0	.115
Eden, E. Michael, Rich†	54	191	37	58	82	7	4	3	17	3	2	34	0	30	4	0	.304
Edwards, Michael, Charleston	62	223	24	46	62	3	2	3	21	1	3	6	1	27	6	5	.206
Englishbey, Stephen, Mem*	15	37	3	6	10	1	0	1	3	0	0	4	1	11	1	0	.162
Espinosa, Arnulfo, Tide	14	15	1	0	0	0	0	0	0	0	0	0	0	10	0	0	.000
Fiore, Michael, Rochester*	109	358	54	96	152	16	2	12	64	0	6	78	1	48	0	0	.268
Foster, Leonard, Tidewater	71	230	26	66	94	11	1	5	39	1	2	17	2	28	6	3	.287
Fuller, James, Rochester	78	269	46	61	131	9	2	19	55	0	4	42	4	92	1	2	.227
Galasso, Robert, Rochester*	26	1	0	0	0	0	0	0	0	0	0	0	0	1	0	0	.000
Garcia, Alfonso, Rochester	130	450	75	124	164	11	10	3	44	6	3	36	4	65	12	6	.276
Garcia, Nelson, Toledo†	18	38	8	8	12	1	0	1	4	1	0	0	0	1	0	2	.211
Gardner, Arthur, Memphis*	118	496	73	141	196	23	4	8	54	4	1	26	1	68	34	17	.284
Gardner, Vassie, Toledo	62	235	29	55	73	13	1	1	23	0	1	21	2	34	10	5	.234
Geach, Jeffrey, Richmond	133	486	60	147	211	19	6	11	70	5	5	36	0	44	6	5	.302
Gonzalez, J. Fernando, Char	119	443	53	142	220	31	4	13	70	1	5	20	2	64	4	8	.321
Gonzalez, Orlando, Toledo*	98	357	49	111	139	17	4	1	45	4	3	35	3	39	19	5	.311
Griffin, Alfredo, Toledo†	22	88	5	19	28	7	1	0	6	3	0	4	0	13	0	1	.216
Grose, Jeffrey, Tidewater*	26	4	1	0	0	0	0	0	0	0	0	2	0	1	0	0	.000
Guidry, Ronald, Syracuse*	23	0	1	0	0	0	0	0	0	0	0	0	0	0	0	0	.000
Hammon, Randal, Tidewater	11	8	0	2	2	0	0	0	3	1	0	0	0	5	0	0	.250
Hanna, Preston, Richmond	29	5	1	2	2	0	0	0	0	2	0	0	0	1	0	0	.400
Harlow, Larry, Rochester*	130	442	81	109	152	22	0	7	47	4	1	73	4	65	5	10	.247
Heidemann, Jack, Tidewater	37	149	26	53	76	9	1	4	27	4	1	13	2	19	4	2	.356

HOCKEY REGISTER

More than 575 pages . . . the complete career playing record of players in the NHL, WHA, AHL, CHL, WHL and amateur leagues . . . Lists all outstanding records and achievements of each player, also personal data . . . The only book of its kind published . . . A MUST for all hockey fans. Annually in Dec.

Price $5.00.

Plus 50c postage and handling.

PRO AND AMATEUR HOCKEY GUIDE

More than 320 pages . . . Official Statistics of Professional and Amateur Leagues, Club Directories, All-Star Teams, All-Time Records for all Pro Leagues, Draft Lists, Stanley Cup Records . . . includes teams and colleges in both the United States and Canada and international teams . . . Photos. Annually in December.

Price $3.00.

Plus 50c postage and handling.

THE SPORTING NEWS' NATIONAL FOOTBALL GUIDE

Club directories of all NFL and WFL teams, complete NFL statistics. Diagrams of NFL stadia. All-time records and many other features, plus photos. Annually in August.

Price $3.00.

Plus 50c postage and handling.

OFFICIAL AMERICAN FOOTBALL LEAGUE HISTORY

Complete statistics and review of 1969 season, team records, 1960-69; all-time AFL records, records of championship, All-Star and Super-Bowl Games.   Price $4.00.

Plus 50c postage and handling.

FOOTBALL REGISTER

Complete season-by-season records of active National Football League players and coaches. Annually in September.

Price $5.00.

Plus 50c postage and handling.

OFFICIAL NFL, AND COLLEGE FOOTBALL SCHEDULES AND RECORDS

Pocket-size. Pro and College Schedules—All-Star Teams—Final Standings. Previous year results. Published annually in July.

Price 50 cents.

Plus 25c postage and handling.

Player and Club	G.	AB.	R.	H.	TB.	2B.	3B.	HR.	RBI.	SH.	SF.	BB.	HP.	SO.	SB.	CS.	Pct.
Heil, Charles, 8 Roch-28 Tide*	36	107	6	20	21	1	0	0	7	0	1	6	0	12	0	1	.187
Heise, Benjamin, Toledo	65	200	23	48	63	3	3	2	26	0	2	20	0	21	2	1	.240
Hobson, Clell, Rhode Island	90	360	56	103	201	21	1	25	72	1	6	33	0	81	1	1	.286
Howard, Douglas, Toledo	70	273	33	84	122	14	0	8	45	0	2	5	0	25	2	0	.308
Howard, Larry, Memphis	5	18	0	3	4	1	0	0	0	0	0	0	0	3	0	0	.167
Humphrey, Terryal, Memphis	74	259	50	92	155	21	3	12	59	2	4	34	5	31	1	0	.355
Howe, Arthur, Memphis	40	135	13	29	44	3	0	4	21	2	0	10	3	14	0	0	.215
Hunter, Harold, Rhode Is	127	424	46	123	148	16	0	3	51	3	7	49	7	50	0	0	.290
Hutto, James, Rochester	86	247	31	60	98	15	1	7	32	3	3	35	4	48	0	2	.243
Irwin, Dennis, Syracuse	29	96	12	26	43	3	1	4	10	2	1	13	1	18	1	0	.271
Javier, I. Alfredo, Mem	107	417	54	120	186	24	3	12	63	4	3	13	9	71	9	5	.288
Johnson, James, Memphis	23	62	13	13	16	3	0	0	4	2	0	7	0	12	0	0	.210
Jones, Odell, Charleston	16	9	0	2	2	0	0	0	2	0	0	2	0	3	0	0	.222
Jones, Timothy, Charleston	24	16	0	3	3	0	0	0	1	1	0	2	0	3	0	0	.188
Kammeyer, Robert, Syracuse*	7	2	0	0	0	0	0	0	0	0	0	1	0	2	0	0	.000
Kelley, Thomas, Tidewater	7	2	0	0	0	0	0	0	0	0	0	0	0	0	0	0	.000
Kelly, J. Thomas, Roch*	127	405	71	117	196	19	3	18	70	7	5	85	4	71	2	2	.289
Kidder, James, Tidewater	43	113	10	28	39	5	0	2	12	4	1	6	0	17	3	2	.248
Klenda, David, Tidewater*	25	9	1	1	2	1	0	0	0	0	0	0	0	5	0	0	.111
Kleven, Jay, Tidewater	55	155	11	27	33	3	0	1	13	2	3	16	0	24	0	1	.174
Klutts, Gene, Syracuse	119	430	75	137	237	22	3	24	80	2	6	35	4	87	3	3	.319
Lacey, John, Richmond*	32	80	14	25	29	4	0	0	10	3	0	13	2	10	1	0	.313
LaCorte, Frank, Richmond	14	3	0	0	0	0	0	0	0	1	0	0	0	3	0	0	.000
Langford, J. Rick, Charleston	17	20	2	4	8	1	0	1	5	1	0	0	0	9	0	0	.200
Lantigua, Manuel, Tidewater	15	37	1	10	11	1	0	0	3	0	1	3	0	7	1	0	.270
Lis, Joseph, Toledo	126	425	93	130	245	23	1	30	103	0	9	97	3	85	1	4	.306
Locklear, Gene, Syracuse*	16	60	7	18	29	3	1	2	8	0	0	9	2	10	2	0	.300
Lora, Luis, Tidewater*	72	266	34	75	99	8	5	2	26	4	5	15	0	32	19	8	.282
Louis, Alberto, Charleston	31	110	13	33	40	4	0	1	9	0	1	5	0	15	9	3	.300
Macha, Kenneth, Charleston	126	458	68	138	211	29	1	14	77	0	2	55	4	73	14	3	.301
Machemer, David, Rhode Is	108	308	57	87	108	4	7	1	27	3	1	66	1	31	2	8	.282
Maddox, Jerry, Richmond	27	71	14	14	24	4	0	2	8	2	0	7	0	10	1	0	.197
Mahler, Michael, Richmond†	17	5	0	1	1	0	0	0	0	1	0	0	0	3	0	0	.200
Makowski, Thomas, Tidewater	14	1	0	0	0	0	0	0	0	2	0	0	0	1	0	0	.000
Marshall, David, Charleston	5	10	3	3	3	0	0	0	0	0	0	11	0	1	1	0	.300
Martinez, J. Dennis, Roch	26	1	0	0	0	0	0	0	0	0	0	0	0	0	0	0	.000
Martinez, Silvio, Charleston	8	7	0	2	2	0	0	0	0	0	0	0	0	3	0	0	.286
Matchick, J. Thomas, 40 Ro-53 S*	93	321	41	85	119	16	3	4	44	5	3	28	0	63	0	0	.265
McCutchin, James, Toledo	31	3	0	0	0	0	0	0	0	0	0	0	0	1	0	0	.000
McElwain, Eugene, Syracuse	10	1	0	0	0	0	0	0	0	0	0	0	0	1	0	0	.000
McGregor, Scott, 18 Syr-15 Roch†	33	8	0	3	4	1	0	0	2	0	0	2	0	1	1	0	.375
McGrew, Alvin, 13 Roch-41 Syr.	54	126	20	23	34	4	2	1	8	4	1	23	1	28	1	2	.183
McLaren, John, Memphis	36	82	7	18	25	1	0	2	12	1	2	16	0	13	0	0	.220
McMillan, Thomas, Toledo	107	374	57	91	121	11	5	3	40	9	4	45	0	42	13	4	.243
Mendoza, John, Charleston	7	29	3	6	12	0	0	2	4	0	0	2	1	5	0	0	.207
Merchant, J. Anderson, RI*	68	203	34	60	81	12	0	3	22	3	1	51	3	18	0	0	.296
Milbourne, Lawrence, Mem†	71	292	45	95	126	12	2	5	31	4	4	14	3	27	12	4	.325
Miller, Richard E., Tide*	75	253	33	70	91	11	2	2	15	4	1	29	2	52	12	6	.277
Minshell, James, Charleston	37	1	0	0	0	0	0	0	0	1	0	0	0	1	0	0	.000
Monzon, Daniel F., Memphis	53	149	23	36	45	9	0	0	24	2	2	34	0	17	2	1	.242
Moore, Alvin, Richmond	103	398	53	131	169	23	3	3	72	2	5	49	1	35	3	3	.329
Mora, Andres, Rochester	18	67	17	22	46	6	0	6	15	1	1	4	0	20	0	1	.328
Moreno, Omar, Charleston*	94	330	70	104	138	11	7	3	36	1	4	55	1	7	55	9	.315
Morlan, John, Charleston	24	7	1	1	1	0	0	0	0	0	0	1	0	0	0	0	.143
Murphy, Dale, Richmond	18	50	10	13	28	1	1	4	8	0	1	1	0	12	0	0	.260
Murray, Eddie, Rochester†	54	168	35	46	89	6	2	11	40	1	4	34	1	27	3	1	.274
Nettles, Morris, Toledo*	65	197	27	50	56	4	1	0	10	0	0	30	0	35	7	5	.254
Newhauser, Donald, Char	32	2	0	0	0	0	0	0	0	0	0	0	0	2	0	0	.000
Nicosia, Steven, Char	117	378	59	99	143	20	0	8	49	1	2	47	2	66	5	3	.262
Nolan, Joseph, Richmond*	32	87	9	25	33	6	1	0	9	0	0	19	0	3	0	0	.287
Norrid, Timothy, Toledo	39	106	14	26	33	2	1	1	15	0	1	21	1	22	0	0	.245
Norris, James, Toledo*	133	435	92	139	197	23	7	7	68	4	1	118	0	45	40	11	.320
Odom, Johnny, Richmond	17	10	4	0	0	0	0	0	0	0	0	0	0	5	0	0	.000
Oliver, David J., Toledo*	128	486	78	136	162	12	4	2	42	8	3	62	1	40	7	4	.280
Oliver, Richard, Toledo	46	147	14	34	45	5	0	2	11	2	1	19	1	37	0	0	.231
Osborn, Danny, Richmond	56	10	1	2	2	0	0	0	1	0	0	0	3	0	0	0	.000
Page, Mitchell, Charleston*	126	456	76	134	223	21	1	22	83	2	4	55	3	84	23	7	.294
Parker, William, Syracuse	29	88	12	19	24	5	0	0	8	1	0	12	0	26	1	0	.216
Pemberton, Brock, Tide†	138	520	64	151	200	26	7	3	58	4	5	58	4	30	4	5	.290
Perez, Ramon, Memphis	16	66	7	15	17	0	1	0	4	1	0	2	0	12	3	2	.227
Perry, Kenneth, Tidewater	28	99	15	26	31	5	2	2	10	0	0	10	1	20	3	0	.263
Pichardo, Nelson, Syracuse	35	109	13	26	29	3	0	0	8	4	1	2	2	11	1	2	.239
Polinsky, Robert, Syracuse*	46	2	0	0	0	0	0	0	0	0	0	0	0	0	0	0	.000
Price, Raymond, Charleston	26	18	1	2	2	0	0	0	2	1	0	0	0	5	1	0	.111
Puhl, Terry, Memphis*	105	372	50	99	125	17	3	1	39	2	1	60	1	57	18	8	.266

Player and Club	G.	AB.	R.	H.	TB.	2B.	3B.	HR.	RBI.	SH.	SF.	BB.	HP.	SO.	SB.	CS.	Pct.
Ramos, Domingo, Syracuse	11	39	7	10	14	2	1	0	8	0	0	4	0	11	0	0	.256
Reynolds, G. Craig, Char*	126	497	57	144	170	18	1	2	47	8	3	35	2	34	12	7	.290
Rhea, Marc, Memphis	130	446	64	121	165	18	4	6	64	5	9	52	2	79	18	2	.271
Ricks, Edward, Syracuse	26	0	3	0	0	0	0	0	0	0	0	0	0	0	0	0	.000
Robinson, Craig, Richmond	26	67	4	11	12	1	0	0	4	0	1	10	0	19	1	1	.164
Rockett, Patrick, Richmond	66	200	34	49	75	8	0	6	25	3	0	20	5	36	1	1	.245
Rodriguez, Adriano, Toledo	56	146	16	27	37	4	0	2	14	0	0	6	1	32	0	2	.185
Ruiz, Manuel, Richmond	135	447	58	121	151	17	5	1	55	20	3	50	4	72	10	7	.254
Sadowski, James, Charleston	28	18	1	3	3	0	0	0	1	0	0	0	0	6	0	0	.167
Sanders, Reginald, Richmond	118	446	55	121	198	21	4	16	69	1	5	27	3	85	1	0	.271
Sealy, Randall, Charleston	5	3	0	1	1	0	0	0	0	0	0	0	0	1	0	0	.333
Sexton, Jimmy, Charleston	49	154	21	42	61	8	1	3	12	0	0	12	0	25	13	1	.273
Sharon, Richard, Rhode Is	77	246	28	57	88	5	1	8	38	2	1	28	0	72	5	1	.232
Sherrill, Dennis, Syracuse	5	10	0	0	0	0	0	0	0	0	0	1	2	6	0	0	.000
Shopay, Thomas, Rochester*	55	173	29	60	83	9	1	4	19	2	2	24	1	7	9	3	.347
Skaggs, David, Rochester	85	252	40	61	79	8	2	2	27	5	4	32	1	28	1	0	.242
Smith, Tommy A., Toledo*	69	284	58	95	158	18	9	9	54	1	5	23	0	24	11	5	.335
Solari, Dennis, Tidewater	42	4	0	0	0	0	0	0	0	0	0	0	0	2	0	0	.000
Sosa, Jose Memphis	42	0	1	0	0	0	0	0	0	0	0	0	0	0	0	0	.000
Stearns, John, Tidewater	102	332	64	103	154	17	2	10	45	3	0	71	4	29	11	8	.310
Stearns, William, Syracuse	74	196	23	43	60	8	0	3	27	5	1	29	0	28	0	0	.219
Stelmaszek, Richard, Syr*	74	214	30	47	63	10	0	2	23	7	0	49	0	26	0	1	.220
Stillman, Royle, Rochester*	56	185	26	54	79	8	1	5	44	0	2	32	1	21	1	0	.292
Tate, Randall, Tidewater	27	6	0	0	0	0	0	0	0	0	0	2	0	0	5	0	.000
Taveras, Alejandro, Mem	128	447	70	103	124	9	6	0	42	5	5	56	2	43	31	8	.230
Tevlin, Creighton, Roch*	5	18	5	5	8	1	1	0	2	0	0	4	0	2	0	0	.278
Thomas, T. William, Char	61	195	36	46	87	6	1	11	32	0	3	29	0	49	3	4	.236
Todd, Jackson, Tidewater	27	21	1	1	1	0	0	0	0	1	0	1	2	11	0	0	.048
Trapp, Randolph, Tidewater	130	385	64	90	138	11	2	11	38	4	2	79	1	94	27	8	.234
Varney, Richard, Richmond	34	105	16	25	41	4	0	4	16	0	1	13	2	19	1	0	.238
Velazquez, Federico, Rich	11	36	2	6	12	0	0	2	5	0	1	4	0	10	0	0	.167
Webb, Henry, Tidewater	19	4	0	0	0	0	0	0	0	0	0	0	0	4	0	0	.000
Werner, Donald, Richmond	49	151	19	40	49	1	1	2	21	0	2	36	1	46	2	4	.265
Whisenton, Larry, Richmond*	1	1	0	0	0	0	0	0	0	0	0	0	0	0	0	0	.000
Whitfield, Terry, Syr*	138	525	81	152	237	25	6	16	89	0	4	56	5	71	2	4	.290
Whitt, Ernest, Rhode Is*	90	304	33	81	122	16	2	7	42	4	1	39	2	32	1	3	.266
Williams, Steven, Char*	37	2	0	0	0	0	0	0	0	0	0	0	1	0	0	0	.000
Wright, James C., Rhode Is	39	0	1	0	0	0	0	0	0	0	0	0	0	0	0	0	.000
Yancy, Hugh, Toledo	34	136	22	40	58	12	0	2	21	1	1	20	1	16	3	1	.294
Zeber, George, Syracuse†	118	397	59	99	137	16	2	6	43	6	5	63	6	60	4	4	.249

The following pitchers had no plate appearances primarily through use of designated-hitters, listed alphabetically by club, games in parentheses.

CHARLESTON—Hilgendorf, Thomas (2).

MEMPHIS—Bannister, Floyd (1); Barlow, Michael (9); Culpepper, David (2); Elenes, Larry (7); Hardy, H. Lawrence (29); Konieczny, Douglas (20); Larson, Daniel (17); Lemongello, Mark (30); McLaughlin, Michael (20); Roberge, Bertrand (2); Rothermel, Russell (44); Sambito, Joseph (5); Selak, Ronald (31); Siebert, Paul (18); Sprinkle, Charles (5); Stanton, Michael (21).

RHODE ISLAND—Aase, Donald (10); Barr, Mark (45); Bomback, Mark (18); Brayton, Roswell (22); Burton, Jim (30); Farias, Thomas (43); Jones, T. Fredrick (5); Kreuger, Richard (35); LaRose, H. John (14); Paxton, Michael (19); Percival, Curran (8); Ripley, Allen (5); Spencer, Gerald (7); Watkins, Kenneth (21).

RICHMOND—McLaughlin, Joey (1).

ROCHESTER—Babcock, Robert (34); Flanagan, Michael K. (7); Freeman, Jimmy (14); Holdsworth, Fredrick (14); Johnson, David C. (36); Kirkpatrick, William (12); Robson, Gary (6); Stein, W. Randolph (27); Stephenson, C. Earl (34); Van Bommel, William (9); Willis, Michael (21).

SYRACUSE—Anderson, Richard L. (6); Beattie, James (17); Clay, Kenneth (30); Delgatti, Scott (2); Heinold, Douglas (17); Mersch, Neal (20); Patterson, Gilbert (10); Reynolds, Kenneth (7); Sawyer, Richard (19); Sielicki, John (15); York, James (22).

TIDEWATER—Myrick, Robert (13).

TOLEDO—Andersen, Larry (6); Arsenault, Edward (1); Camper, Cardell (18); Kinney, Dennis (3); Kline, Steven (26); Linnert, Thomas (10); Parker, Harry (25); Perzanowski, Stanley (16); Raich, Eric (30); Reynolds, Robert (16); Strickland, James (46); Werd, Norman (8).

GRAND-SLAM HOME RUNS—Bergman, Heise, Klutts, 2 each; Allietta, Beall, Fuller, Humphrey, Javier, Murphy, Puhl, Smith, Stelmaszek, Whitt, Zeber, 1 each.

AWARDED FIRST BASE ON INTERFERENCE—Aviles 2 (J. Stearns, W. Stearns), Maddox 2 (Diaz, Kleven); Coleman (Kleven), Diggle (Cerone), Monzon (Rodriguez), Nicosia (Stelmaszek), Pemberton (Hutto).

CLUB FIELDING

Club	G.	PO.	A.	E.	DP.	PB.	Pct.
Rochester	138	3426	1505	140	174	8	.972
Richmond	140	3558	1586	154	155	15	.971
Rhode Island	138	3527	1520	152	121	7	.971
Tidewater	138	3477	1484	150	129	14	.971
Charleston	135	3430	1300	158	101	15	.968
Toledo	140	3534	1696	177	131	12	.967
Syracuse	139	3580	1673	180	153	27	.967
Memphis	138	3564	1542	202	122	13	.962

Triple Plays—Richmond, Tidewater, 1 each.

INDIVIDUAL FIELDING

FIRST BASEMEN

*Throws lefthanded.

Player and Club	G.	PO.	A.	E.	DP.	Pct.
Bernhardt, Syracuse	18	164	13	0	21	1.000
Coleman, Rhode Is...	24	84	7	0	8	1.000
Murray, Rochester	31	275	12	2	37	.993
BERGMAN, Syr*	122	1199	80	10	107	.9922
Baker, Rhode Is	132	1049	84	9	73	.9921
Lis, Toledo	81	790	45	1	67	.992
Fiore, Rochester*	85	713	50	6	59	.992
Gonzalez, Toledo*	42	391	46	4	33	.991
Pemberton, Tide*	138	1179	83	13	114	.990
Whitt, Rhode Is	28	92	4	1	10	.990
Sanders, Richmond	90	736	44	9	82	.989
Lacey, Richmond*	24	173	11	2	21	.989
Cacek, Memphis	130	1167	105	18	108	.986
Beall, Richmond*	30	270	22	4	21	.986
Kelly, Rochester*	17	131	13	2	13	.986
Breazeale, Richmond	10	62	3	1	3	.985
Page, Charleston	124	1044	66	20	63	.982

Triple Play—Pemberton.

(Fewer Than Ten Games)

Player and Club	G.	PO.	A.	E.	DP.	Pct.
Howard, Toledo	9	92	6	0	7	1.000
Norris, Toledo*	8	79	2	0	11	1.000
Macha, Charleston	9	65	3	0	6	1.000
Howe, Memphis	8	57	4	0	1	1.000
Matchick, Syracuse	4	24	3	0	1	1.000
Crowley, Rochester*	2	14	1	0	2	1.000
Thomas, Charleston	1	10	0	0	2	1.000
Stillman, Rochester*	1	8	2	0	0	1.000
R. Oliver, Toledo	1	8	0	0	2	1.000
Dauer, Rochester	1	3	0	0	0	1.000
Norrid, Toledo	1	3	0	0	0	1.000
Ayala, Tidewater	1	2	0	0	0	1.000
Hutto, Rochester	7	60	3	1	8	.984
DeFreites, Toledo	2	14	0	1	2	.933
Armas, Charleston	2	3	0	1	3	.929
Didier, Richmond	2	9	0	1	1	.900

SECOND BASEMEN

Player and Club	G.	PO.	A.	E.	DP.	Pct.
Machemer, Rhode Is	13	24	32	0	3	1.000
Gonzalez, Char	26	56	82	3	18	.979
Heise, Toledo	21	46	49	2	11	.979
Dancy, Tidewater	42	100	118	5	18	.978
DAUER, Rochester	129	272	398	17	103	.975
Edwards, Charleston	58	133	145	7	18	.975
Andrews, Memphis	22	38	75	3	19	.974
Ruiz, Richmond	133	336	458	23	109	.972
D. Oliver, Toledo	124	255	443	21	101	.971
Zeber, Syracuse	114	237	377	19	82	.970
Milbourne, Memphis	61	114	206	10	38	.970
Sexton, Charleston	47	83	105	6	16	.969
DeJohn, Tidewater	36	74	116	6	19	.969
Monzon, Memphis	17	28	35	2	5	.969
Hunter, Rhode Is	96	198	271	16	55	.967
Perry, Tidewater	28	62	73	5	28	.964
Rhea, Memphis	36	66	96	8	16	.953
Reynolds, Char	11	13	27	2	2	.952
Darrow, Syracuse	24	41	61	6	15	.944
Kidder, Tidewater	31	72	67	9	19	.939
Dillard, Rhode Is	34	87	107	13	16	.937
Perez, Memphis	12	20	39	8	5	.881

(Fewer Than Ten Games)

Player and Club	G.	PO.	A.	E.	DP.	Pct.
Mora, Rochester	7	8	15	0	1	1.000
Foster, Tidewater	2	6	6	0	2	1.000
Geach, Richmond	3	1	2	0	1	1.000
Shopay, Rochester	1	0	2	0	1	1.000
Trapp, Tidewater	1	1	0	0	0	1.000
Johnson, Memphis	1	0	1	0	1	1.000
Pichardo, Syracuse	7	11	19	1	5	.968
Matchick, Roch-Syr	6	7	16	1	3	.958
Heidemann, Tidewater ..	4	9	13	1	4	.957
Moore, Richmond	9	18	20	2	4	.950
Andrew, Rhode Island	8	11	24	2	6	.946
Parker, Syracuse	1	0	1	1	0	.500

THIRD BASEMEN

Player and Club	G.	PO.	A.	E.	DP.	Pct.
Monzon, Memphis	28	23	36	0	2	1.000
Bailor, Rochester	10	7	18	0	1	1.000
Lis, Toledo	19	15	41	1	2	.982
Hunter, Rhode Is	32	31	48	3	8	.963
Heise, Toledo	24	12	33	2	3	.957
TRAPP, Tidewater	97	79	177	12	16	.955
Hobson, Rhode Is	88	89	200	14	18	.954
Duncan, Rochester	104	65	182	12	14	.954
Foster, Tidewater	22	21	41	3	7	.954
Geach, Richmond	104	75	188	13	26	.953
Gonzalez, Char	57	52	95	8	7	.948
Yancy, Toledo	34	30	78	7	7	.939
Belloir, Richmond	10	11	20	2	4	.939
Matchick, Roch-Syr	64	44	103	10	17	.936
Machemer, Rhode Is	18	10	30	3	2	.930
Parker, Syracuse	11	7	19	2	2	.929
Bernhardt, Syracuse	82	66	174	19	24	.927
R. Oliver, Toledo	42	33	109	11	13	.927
Howe, Memphis	65	36	115	14	13	.915
Maddox, Rochester	25	21	33	5	2	.915
Stearns, Tidewater	21	18	39	6	2	.905
Norrid, Toledo	34	24	67	11	8	.892
Rhea, Memphis	40	26	79	14	10	.882
Macha, Charleston	70	56	99	24	7	.866

(Fewer Than Ten Games)

Player and Club	G.	PO.	A.	E.	DP.	Pct.
Perez, Memphis	4	2	10	0	1	1.000
Mora, Rochester	1	3	0	0	0	1.000
Howard, Toledo	1	2	1	0	0	1.000
Kidder, Tidewater	2	1	1	0	0	1.000
McLaren, Memphis	1	1	1	0	1	1.000
Bladt, Syracuse	2	0	1	0	0	1.000
Moore, Richmond	7	9	17	1	3	.963
Johnson, Memphis	8	3	9	1	0	.923
Pichardo, Syracuse	9	9	14	2	2	.920
Dilone, Charleston	7	11	17	4	3	.875
Augustine, Char	4	1	5	1	0	.857
Mendoza, Charleston	2	2	4	1	0	.857
Eden, Richmond	3	1	4	1	1	.833
Darrow, Syracuse	4	6	13	4	2	.826
Heidemann, Tidewater ..	5	3	8	3	1	.786
Murray, Rochester	3	3	0	1	0	.750
Shopay, Rochester	3	1	2	1	0	.750
Klutts, Syracuse	3	0	3	2	0	.600
Hutto, Rochester	1	1	0	1	0	.500
Andrew, Rhode Is	1	0	0	1	0	.000

SHORTSTOPS

Player and Club	G.	PO.	A.	E.	DP.	Pct.
Heise, Toledo	14	28	43	2	8	.973
DeJohn, Tidewater	76	113	221	10	39	.971
Robinson, Richmond	26	40	89	5	24	.963
Belloir, Richmond	17	30	47	3	13	.963
Heidemann, Tidewater ..	27	40	74	5	8	.958
AVILES, Rhode Is	134	238	452	35	75	.952
Taveras, Memphis	127	211	367	30	65	.951
Milbourne, Memphis	14	18	39	3	5	.950
Garcia, Rochester	129	241	473	38	112	.949
Klutts, Syracuse	114	191	290	28	83	.945
McMillan, Toledo	106	174	362	32	55	.944
Griffin, Toledo	22	44	71	7	14	.943
Ramos, Syracuse	10	13	20	2	2	.943
Eden, Richmond	43	69	118	12	23	.940
Pichardo, Syracuse	11	23	39	4	8	.939
Reynolds, Charleston	120	185	235	29	55	.935
Rockett, Richmond	60	94	186	21	28	.930
Foster, Tidewater	41	68	113	14	32	.928
Augustine, Char	17	20	31	4	3	.927
Machemer, Rhode Is	20	9	21	3	2	.909

Triple Plays–DeJohn, Eden, 1 each.

(Fewer Than Ten Games)

Player and Club	G.	PO.	A.	E.	DP.	Pct.
Sherrill, Syracuse	5	8	11	0	2	1.000
Bailor, Rochester	1	3	6	0	2	1.000
Sexton, Charleston	2	2	4	0	1	1.000
Ruiz, Richmond	3	2	2	0	2	1.000
Edwards, Charleston	2	0	1	0	0	1.000
D. Oliver, Toledo	1	1	0	0	0	1.000
Duncan, Rochester	8	17	26	1	8	.977
Mendoza, Charleston	5	11	7	1	3	.947
Johnson, Memphis	4	8	12	3	3	.870
Darrow, Syracuse	6	12	14	4	4	.867
Hobson, Rhode Is	2	2	4	1	0	.857
Dauer, Rochester	3	1	4	1	2	.833

OUTFIELDERS

Player and Club	G.	PO.	A.	E.	DP.	Pct.
Beall, Richmond*	67	102	3	0	1	1.000
McGrew, Roch-Syr	44	78	3	0	1	1.000
Geach, Richmond	17	22	1	0	0	1.000
Coletta, Rhode Is*	38	18	0	0	0	1.000
Gonzalez, Charleston	10	12	1	0	0	1.000
Bergman, Syracuse*	12	2	2	0	0	1.000
MORENO, Charleston* ..	93	200	17	1	2	.995
Kelly, Rochester*	103	192	15	2	2	.990
Howard, Toledo	60	87	6	1	1	.989
Diggle, Tidewater	82	146	5	2	1	.987
Robt. Baldwin, Tide*	133	259	11	4	3	.985
Puhl, Memphis	104	191	5	3	1	.985
Nettles, Toledo*	61	131	2	2	0	.985
Dineen, Syracuse*	54	104	3	2	1	.982
Bladt, Syracuse	99	190	14	4	2	.981
Asselstine, Richmond	115	237	9	5	1	.980
Stillman, Rochester*	42	48	2	1	1	.980
Coleman, Rhode Is...	136	275	10	6	0	.979
Bonnell, Richmond	64	134	4	3	1	.979
Lora, Tidewater*	57	136	5	3	0	.979
Thomas, Charleston	40	83	7	2	0	.978
Smith, Toledo	67	162	4	4	0	.976
Shopay, Rochester	43	80	1	2	0	.976
Dilone, Charleston	88	191	9	5	0	.976
Harlow, Rochester*	126	308	12	9	1	.973
Balaz, Rhode Island...	133	210	8	6	0	.973
Moore, Richmond	88	134	7	4	1	.972
Miller, Tidewater	65	131	8	4	3	.972
Armas, Charleston	79	197	8	6	1	.972
Javier, Memphis	92	164	6	5	1	.971
Norris, Toledo*	91	154	5	5	0	.970
Louis, Charleston	30	63	2	2	0	.970
Whitt, Rhode Island	18	31	1	1	0	.969
Brown, Tidewater	12	28	0	1	0	.966
J. Collins, Rich	73	98	11	4	1	.965
Gardner, Toledo	60	107	2	4	0	.965
Sharon, Rhode Is	77	162	9	8	1	.955
Chiles, Memphis*	52	96	9	5	2	.955
Augustine, Char	75	121	4	6	1	.954
Gonzalez, Toledo*	54	103	1	5	0	.954
Rhea, Memphis	14	19	1	1	0	.952
Alston, Syracuse	102	183	6	11	2	.945
Machemer, Rhode Is	70	72	8	5	1	.941
Ayala, Tidewater	32	45	2	3	0	.940
Whitfield, Syracuse	124	208	13	15	3	.936
Gardner, Memphis*	99	265	12	21	1	.930
Mora, Rochester	10	13	0	1	0	.929
Fuller, Rochester	68	93	5	8	2	.925
Trapp, Tidewater	30	37	5	4	2	.913
Macha, Charleston	14	10	0	1	0	.909
de la Rosa, Memphis	57	89	8	10	0	.907
DeFreites, Toledo	26	38	0	4	0	.905
Heil, Roch-Tide*	16	24	1	3	0	.893
Murray, Rochester	21	13	1	2	0	.875

Triple Play–J. Collins.

(Fewer Than Ten Games)

Player and Club	G.	PO.	A.	E.	DP.	Pct.
Werner, Richmond	9	21	0	0	0	1.000
Englishbey, Memphis* ..	4	7	0	0	0	1.000
Tevlin, Rochester*	5	6	0	0	0	1.000
Sanders, Richmond	4	3	1	0	0	1.000
Cacek, Memphis	2	3	1	0	0	1.000
Matchick, Rochester	1	2	1	0	0	1.000
Stearns, Syracuse	5	2	0	0	0	1.000
Page, Charleston	3	2	0	0	0	1.000
Delgado, Rhode Is*	2	2	0	0	0	1.000
Eden, Richmond	2	1	0	0	0	1.000
Bernhardt, Syracuse	1	1	0	0	0	1.000
Monzon, Memphis	1	1	0	0	0	1.000
Murphy, Richmond	1	0	1	0	0	1.000
Dwyer, Tidewater*	7	14	0	1	0	.933
Garcia, Toledo	7	16	1	2	0	.895
Locklear, Syracuse	8	14	0	2	0	.875
Johnson, Memphis	5	3	1	1	0	.800
Rodriguez, Toledo	1	2	2	1	0	.800
Benson, Syracuse	4	2	0	1	0	.667

CATCHERS

Player and Club	G.	PO.	A.	E.	DP.	PB.	Pct.
Merchant, Rhode Is...	44	214	24	0	0	4	1.000
Nolan, Richmond...	27	134	14	0	1	3	1.000
Marshall, Char...	5	31	4	0	0	1	1.000
Shopay, Rochester	3	4	0	0	0	0	1.000
Blackwell, Rhode Is	2	3	1	0	0	0	1.000
Macha, Charleston...	24	101	14	1	0	2	.991
ALLIETTA, Memphis	72	378	33	4	3	3	.990
Skaggs, Rochester	85	408	50	5	11	3	.989
Didier, Richmond	43	247	35	3	2	1	.989
Nicosia, Char	111	616	57	8	2	12	.988
Diaz, Rhode Island	58	222	28	3	3	0	.988
Varney, Richmond	33	154	13	2	1	4	.988

CATCHERS—Continued

Player and Club	G.	PO.	A.	E.	DP.	PB.	Pct.
Kleven, Tidewater	52	277	33	4	4	8	.987
Rodriguez, Toledo	53	200	33	3	2	5	.987
Stearns, Syracuse	62	242	40	4	5	13	.986
Whitt, Rhode Is	70	333	53	6	8	3	.985
Stearns, Tidewater	84	398	61	8	8	4	.983
Stelmaszek, Syr	67	306	35	6	10	10	.983
McLaren, Memphis	33	142	15	3	0	3	.981
Hutto, Rochester	59	288	21	7	2	5	.978
Werner, Richmond	36	194	22	5	6	3	.977
Humphrey, Memphis	40	251	17	7	2	6	.975
Irwin, Syracuse	29	145	11	5	0	4	.969
Dusan, Toledo	14	48	2	2	0	2	.962
Cerone, Toledo	87	351	50	18	4	5	.957
Lantigua, Tide	15	58	5	3	0	2	.955
Murphy, Richmond	14	60	8	4	0	4	.944
Howard, Memphis	4	32	2	2	1	1	.944

Triple Plays—Nolan, Stearns (Tidewater), 1 each.

PITCHERS

Player and Club	G.	PO.	A.	E.	DP.	Pct.
BEENE, Toledo	33	10	24	0	2	1.000
Easterly, Richmond*	33	6	26	0	1	1.000
Kreuger, Rhode Is*	35	7	23	0	1	1.000
Paxton, Rhode Is	19	6	18	0	1	1.000
Polinsky, Syracuse	46	6	17	0	0	1.000
Espinosa, Tidewater	14	2	20	0	0	1.000
McCutchin, Toledo	31	6	15	0	0	1.000
Osborn, Richmond	54	3	16	0	3	1.000
Rick Baldwin, Tide	46	2	17	0	0	1.000
Stein, Rochester	24	8	10	0	0	1.000
Angelini, Richmond*	42	3	14	0	0	1.000
Solari, Tidewater	42	2	15	0	1	1.000
Watkins, Rhode Is	21	1	16	0	1	1.000
Hardy, Memphis	29	9	7	0	1	1.000
Morlan, Charleston	24	2	12	0	0	1.000
Hammon, Tidewater	11	5	9	0	0	1.000
Mersch, Syracuse	20	6	7	0	0	1.000
Camper, Toledo	18	2	10	0	0	1.000
Linnert, Toledo*	10	6	6	0	0	1.000
Aase, Rhode Island	10	4	8	0	2	1.000
Kammeyer, Syracuse	10	3	9	0	0	1.000
Freeman, Rochester*	12	3	8	0	2	1.000
Makowski, Tide*	14	3	6	0	2	1.000
Minshall, Charleston	37	2	5	0	0	1.000
Beard, Richmond*	14	3	3	0	0	1.000
Brayton, Rhode Is*	22	3	1	0	0	1.000
LaRose, Rhode Is*	14	2	2	0	0	1.000
Myrick, Tidewater*	13	1	3	0	0	1.000
McElwain, Syracuse*	10	1	2	0	1	1.000
Kirkpatrick, Roch	12	0	2	0	0	1.000
McGregor, Syr-Roch*	24	15	36	1	0	.981
Raich, Toledo	29	20	24	1	0	.978
Selak, Memphis	31	14	29	1	1	.977
Sadowski, Charleston	28	13	26	1	1	.975
Sawyer, Syracuse	19	11	25	1	2	.973
Martinez, Rochester	25	10	25	1	3	.972
Burton, Rhode Is*	28	7	26	1	0	.971
Hanna, Richmond	27	8	25	1	2	.971
Strickland, Toledo*	46	9	19	1	0	.966
Willis, Rochester*	27	4	21	1	1	.962
Kline, Toledo	26	13	35	2	5	.960
Patterson, Syr	10	7	16	1	0	.958
Galasso, Rochester	25	3	19	1	0	.957
Mahler, Richmond*	17	2	20	1	2	.957
Ricks, Syracuse	22	4	17	1	4	.955
Grose, Tidewater*	26	4	16	1	1	.952
Klenda, Tidewater	25	2	18	1	2	.952
Bomback, Rhode Is	18	9	29	2	1	.950
Bernard, Tidewater	15	4	15	1	0	.950
McLaughlin, Memphis	20	14	23	2	1	.949
Sosa, Memphis	41	5	13	1	2	.947
Parker, Toledo	25	9	23	2	1	.941
Beattie, Syracuse	17	9	23	2	2	.941
Rothermel, Memphis*	44	5	11	1	3	.941
Bair, Charleston	45	5	10	1	0	.938
Webb, Tidewater	19	5	10	1	0	.938
Todd, Memphis	26	8	34	3	2	.933
Johnson, Rochester	36	5	9	1	0	.933
Siebert, Memphis*	18	5	9	1	0	.933
Sielicki, Syracuse*	15	5	9	1	0	.933
Langford, Charleston	16	8	19	2	0	.931
T. Jones, Charleston	24	17	36	4	3	.930
Clay, Syracuse	30	13	37	4	2	.926
Newhauser, Char	32	2	10	1	1	.923
Reynolds, Toledo	45	4	19	2	0	.920
Heinold, Syracuse	17	10	22	3	2	.914
Farias, Rhode Is	43	7	14	2	1	.913
Wright, Rhode Is	37	10	20	3	1	.909
Camp, Richmond	49	14	24	4	3	.905
Price, Charleston	24	9	9	2	0	.900
York, Syracuse	22	1	8	1	0	.900
Barr, Rhode Island	45	6	27	4	0	.892
Larson, Memphis	17	10	20	4	1	.882
Babcock, Rochester	34	4	18	3	2	.880
Konieczny, Memphis	20	6	16	3	0	.880
Autry, Richmond	32	2	19	3	0	.875
Cheadle, Rich-Char*	14	1	6	1	0	.875
Champion, Richmond	12	3	4	1	0	.875
Odom, Richmond	12	8	12	3	2	.870
O. Jones, Charleston	16	3	9	2	1	.857
Guidry, Syracuse*	22	3	3	1	1	.857
Stanton, Memphis	21	9	25	6	1	.850
Holdsworth, Rochester	14	7	10	3	4	.850
Stephenson, Roch*	34	3	13	3	1	.842
Lemongello, Memphis	30	6	28	7	2	.829
D. Collins, Rich*	23	1	8	2	0	.818
Tate, Tidewater	27	7	18	6	2	.806
Perzanowski, Toledo	16	4	10	4	0	.778
Williams, Char*	37	3	6	3	0	.750
LaCorte, Richmond	14	4	3	1	2	.727

Triple Play—Grose.

(Fewer Than Ten Games)

Player and Club	G.	PO.	A.	E.	DP.	Pct.
Werd, Toledo*	8	3	4	0	1	1.000
Sambito, Memphis*	5	3	2	0	1	1.000
Elenes, Memphis	7	2	2	0	0	1.000
Barlow, Memphis	9	0	3	0	1	1.000
Kelley, Tidewater	7	1	2	0	0	1.000
Capra, Richmond	4	0	3	0	0	1.000
Roberge, Memphis	2	1	2	0	0	1.000
Van Bommel, Roch	9	1	1	0	1	1.000
Sealy, Charleston	5	2	0	0	0	1.000
Jones, Rhode Island*	5	0	2	0	0	1.000
Bannister, Memphis*	1	0	2	0	1	1.000
Reynolds, Syracuse*	7	1	1	0	0	1.000
Anderson, Syracuse	6	0	1	0	0	1.000
Robson, Rochester	6	1	0	0	0	1.000
Kinney, Toledo*	3	0	1	0	0	1.000
Delgatti, Syracuse	2	1	0	0	0	1.000
Hilgendorf, Char.*	2	0	1	0	0	1.000
Baker, Rhode Island	2	0	1	0	0	1.000
Spencer, Rhode Is	7	4	12	1	0	.941
Flanagan, Rochester*	7	0	11	1	2	.917
Martinez, Charleston	8	3	7	1	0	.909
Andersen, Toledo	6	0	6	1	0	.857
Ripley, Rhode Island	5	2	3	1	0	.833
Percival, Rhode Is	8	1	5	2	0	.750
Bruhert, Tidewater	7	0	4	3	0	.571

The following players do not have any recorded accepted chances at the positions indicated; therefore, are not listed in the fielding averages for those particular positions: Andrew, of; Arsenault, p; Asselstine, 2b; Bailor, of; Bernhardt, 2b; Coletta*, ss; Culpepper, p; Dancy, ss; Diaz, of; Geach, ss; Hunter, ss; Matchick, p; J. McLaughlin, p; Nicosia, 1b; R. Oliver, of; W. Parker, p; Sprinkle, p; Whitt, 3b.

CLUB PITCHING

Club	G.	CG.	ShO.	Sv.	IP.	H.	R.	ER.	HR.	BB.	Int. BB.	HB.	SO.	WP.	Bk.	ERA.
Rochester	138	57	15	17	1142	1110	524	445	77	442	31	29	649	53	8	3.51
Syracuse	139	42	2	27	1193	1272	645	532	85	560	45	33	651	51	12	4.01
Richmond	140	34	6	18	1186	1201	645	540	87	641	61	19	736	74	6	4.10
Tidewater	138	35	5	24	1159	1205	634	534	82	558	47	36	680	59	13	4.15
Rhode Island	138	32	8	18	1176	1201	647	580	100	576	87	22	694	45	10	4.44
Charleston	135	36	7	17	1143	1167	656	568	113	603	53	29	692	66	9	4.47
Memphis	138	35	7	24	1188	1305	705	610	120	559	71	31	751	55	9	4.62
Toledo	140	34	2	12	1178	1432	790	680	138	437	44	36	546	46	6	5.20

PITCHERS' RECORDS

(Leading Qualifiers for Earned-Run Average Leadership—112 or More Innings)

*Throws lefthanded.

Pitcher–Club	G.	GS.	CG.	ShO.	W.	L.	Sv.	Pct.	IP.	H.	R.	ER.	HR.	BB.	Int. BB.	HB.	SO.	WP.	ERA.
Martinez, Roch	25	23	16	1	14	8	0	.636	180	148	64	50	15	50	2	6	140	2	2.50
Sawyer, Syracuse	19	18	8	0	9	4	0	.692	134	125	55	41	10	38	4	5	65	4	2.75
Autry, Richmond	32	18	8	2	9	6	0	.600	161	142	58	51	9	77	8	1	109	12	2.85
Todd, Tidewater	26	26	13	2	13	9	0	.591	201	204	75	65	6	53	5	3	125	3	2.91
Easterly, Rich.*	33	16	4	2	7	6	0	.538	137	133	56	45	5	88	9	4	91	10	2.96
McGregor, 11 Sy-13 Ro*	24	23	14	6	12	6	0	.667	162	159	59	55	8	40	2	2	83	4	3.06
Bair, Charleston	45	0	0	0	7	10	8	.412	122	102	48	43	6	57	3	1	108	7	3.17
Langford, Char.	16	16	9	2	9	5	0	.643	121	106	51	43	8	48	7	1	95	4	3.20
Galasso, Roch	25	23	9	2	13	5	0	.722	141	132	70	54	11	66	1	2	75	10	3.45
T. Jones, Char	24	24	10	2	7	10	0	.412	161	173	86	65	14	73	8	4	73	6	3.63

Departmental Leaders: G—Osborn, 54; GS—Burton, 28; CG—Martinez (Roch.), 16; ShO—McGregor, 6; W—Martinez (Roch.), 14; L—Tate, 14; Sv—Baldwin, 14; Pct.—Galasso, .722; IP—Todd, 201; H—Lemongello, 208; R—Burton, 110; ER—Burton, 105; HR—Kline, 25; BB—Burton, 112; IBB—Barr, 13; HB—Tate, 10; SO—Martinez (Roch.), 140; WP—Burton, 18.

(All Pitchers—Listed Alphabetically)

Pitcher–Club	G.	GS.	CG.	ShO.	W.	L.	Sv.	Pct.	IP.	H.	R.	ER.	HR.	BB.	Int. BB.	HB.	SO.	WP.	ERA.
Aase, Rhode Island	10	9	2	1	5	2	0	.714	54	42	23	20	3	34	2	0	40	1	3.33
Andersen, Toledo	6	5	0	0	0	2	0	.000	23	47	33	33	5	6	1	2	8	2	12.91
Anderson, Syracuse	6	0	0	0	0	0	1	.000	9	5	3	3	0	8	1	1	4	1	3.00
Angelini, Rich*	42	1	0	0	6	5	3	.545	74	71	43	30	1	40	8	4	67	8	3.65
Arsenault, Toledo	1	0	0	0	0	0	0	.000	5	10	7	7	3	3	0	0	2	0	12.00
Autry, Richmond	32	18	8	2	9	6	0	.600	161	142	58	51	9	77	8	1	109	12	2.85
Babcock, Roch	34	4	0	0	7	6	3	.538	91	107	63	51	5	47	3	3	53	3	5.04
Bair, Charleston	45	0	0	0	7	10	8	.412	122	102	48	43	6	57	3	1	108	7	3.17
Baker, Rhode Is	2	0	0	0	0	0	0	.000	4	1	0	0	0	0	0	0	2	0	0.00
Rick Baldwin, Tide	46	0	0	0	8	4	14	.667	74	53	20	19	1	36	11	5	35	2	2.31
Bannister, Mem.*	1	1	0	0	1	0	0	1.000	6	7	1	1	0	3	0	0	6	0	1.50
Barlow, Memphis	9	0	0	0	2	0	2	1.000	11	10	6	6	3	6	1	0	8	0	4.91
Barr, Rhode Is	45	14	5	1	10	10	4	.500	146	165	79	66	10	56	13	4	65	1	4.07
Beard, Rich.*	14	1	1	0	1	0	0	1.000	21	24	8	7	1	6	1	0	8	1	3.00
Beattie, Syracuse	17	17	2	0	5	5	0	.500	100	106	76	67	8	80	3	5	74	7	6.03
Beene, Toledo	33	17	7	0	7	9	0	.438	181	206	86	76	21	48	8	0	88	7	3.78
Bernard, Tide	15	13	1	0	1	9	0	.100	90	109	74	64	9	61	4	1	47	3	6.40
Bomback, Rhode Is	18	18	3	1	5	7	0	.417	120	130	60	54	10	60	5	1	63	1	4.05
Brayton, RI*	22	0	0	0	2	1	1	.667	29	21	9	8	2	12	3	0	8	1	2.48
Bruhert, Tide	7	2	0	0	0	2	0	.000	22	25	23	13	1	19	0	3	18	6	5.32
Burton, Rhode Is*	28	28	5	1	11	7	0	.611	169	167	110	105	19	112	8	4	106	18	5.59
Camp, Richmond	49	14	4	1	10	11	7	.476	164	177	90	78	9	68	10	2	85	10	4.28
Camper, Toledo	18	17	3	1	4	8	0	.333	95	101	65	57	14	40	2	3	58	5	5.40
Capra, Richmond	4	4	0	0	2	1	0	.667	14	13	8	8	2	8	0	0	6	0	5.14
Champion, Rich	12	7	1	0	3	4	0	.429	45	48	29	24	4	25	2	0	19	5	4.80
Cheadle, 9 Rch-5 Chr*	14	7	0	0	2	3	0	.400	36	33	25	20	3	24	1	1	20	1	5.00
Clay, Syracuse	30	24	8	1	11	8	1	.579	168	202	94	77	6	67	5	2	87	8	4.13
D. Collins, Rich.*	23	14	4	0	4	6	0	.400	88	109	58	49	9	50	1	1	40	8	5.01
Culpepper, Mem	2	0	0	0	0	0	0	.000	1	1	0	0	0	1	0	0	1	0	0.00
Delgatti, Syr	2	0	0	0	0	0	1	.000	3	3	2	2	0	1	0	0	1	1	6.00
Easterly, Rich.*	33	16	4	2	7	6	0	.538	137	133	56	45	5	88	9	4	91	10	2.96
Elenes, Memphis	7	0	0	0	0	1	0	.000	13	11	6	5	0	14	2	1	14	1	3.46
Espinosa, Tide	14	14	6	1	7	3	0	.700	108	106	40	35	6	34	4	2	66	0	2.92
Farias, Rhode Is	43	7	0	0	4	6	0	.400	105	105	49	45	10	58	10	3	70	5	3.86
Flanagan, Roch.*	7	7	6	1	6	1	0	.857	51	40	16	12	4	14	2	1	24	1	2.12

Pitcher–Club	G.	GS.	CG.	ShO.	W.	L.	Sv.	Pct.	IP.	H.	R.	ER.	HR.	BB.	Int. BB.	HB.	SO.	WP.	ERA.
Freeman, Roch.*	12	7	0	0	2	3	0	.400	47	43	25	20	2	37	2	2	35	4	3.83
Galasso, Roch	25	23	9	2	13	5	0	.722	141	132	70	54	11	66	1	2	75	10	3.45
Grose, Tidewater*	26	18	3	0	3	12	0	.200	120	115	78	61	15	88	1	2	85	7	4.58
Guidry, Syracuse*	22	0	0	0	5	1	9	.833	40	16	5	3	0	13	3	0	50	0	0.68
Hammon, Tidewater	11	10	1	0	3	5	0	.375	66	74	40	37	7	23	4	1	30	1	5.05
Hanna, Richmond	27	18	3	0	4	9	0	.308	126	126	81	74	8	84	1	1	47	4	5.29
Hardy, Memphis	29	0	0	0	2	1	5	.667	52	55	38	24	6	18	4	0	30	5	4.15
Heinold, Syracuse	17	16	4	0	4	9	0	.308	97	128	59	51	7	33	2	2	30	4	4.73
Hilgendorf, Char.*	2	0	0	0	0	0	0	.000	5	7	8	3	3	1	0	0	2	0	5.40
Holdsworth, Roch.	14	13	5	0	5	4	0	.556	98	102	43	38	8	41	3	2	54	4	3.49
Johnson, Rochester	36	0	0	0	11	5	7	.688	74	65	28	23	3	28	6	0	44	5	2.80
O. Jones, Char	16	16	2	1	2	7	0	.222	84	81	49	46	7	43	1	4	47	3	4.93
Jones, Rhode Is.*	5	4	0	0	0	0	0	.000	20	30	22	22	4	9	2	1	12	2	9.90
T. Jones, Char	24	24	10	2	7	10	0	.412	161	173	86	65	14	73	8	4	73	6	3.63
Kammeyer, Syr	10	6	2	0	3	1	1	.750	42	49	21	19	5	16	1	1	13	1	4.07
Kelley, Tidewater	7	1	1	0	0	1	0	.000	23	34	18	16	1	11	0	0	17	4	6.26
Kinney, Toledo*	3	0	0	0	0	0	0	.000	3	2	1	1	0	1	0	0	4	0	3.00
Kirkpatrick, Roch	12	4	0	0	1	0	0	1.000	35	45	16	15	2	8	0	0	13	2	3.86
Klenda, Tidewater	25	7	3	1	5	4	2	.556	91	88	38	34	5	36	4	1	52	4	3.36
Kline, Toledo	26	23	8	0	9	10	0	.474	157	195	102	88	25	41	5	5	60	1	5.04
Konieczny, Mem	20	16	6	0	6	10	0	.375	105	135	81	71	12	53	6	1	48	3	6.09
Kreuger, Rhode Is.*	35	2	0	0	9	4	4	.692	80	65	28	27	4	35	7	1	51	2	3.04
LaCorte, Rich	14	13	0	0	3	3	0	.500	78	91	55	46	9	47	0	2	77	4	5.31
Langford, Char	16	16	9	2	9	5	0	.643	121	106	51	43	8	48	7	1	95	4	3.20
LaRose, Rhode Is.*	14	1	0	0	0	3	2	.000	27	33	17	15	2	18	3	0	15	2	5.00
Larson, Memphis	17	17	6	1	7	4	0	.636	118	132	68	57	9	60	7	4	79	5	4.35
Lemongello, Mem	30	23	3	0	10	6	0	.625	165	208	102	83	22	51	10	4	62	0	4.53
Linnert, Toledo*	10	2	2	0	2	4	0	.333	33	41	23	21	2	11	1	3	18	2	5.73
Mahler, Rich*	17	14	5	0	5	9	1	.357	84	95	63	54	14	40	7	2	52	6	5.79
Makowski, Tide.*	14	7	2	0	3	2	0	.600	50	51	24	21	5	25	1	1	30	2	3.78
Martinez, Roch	25	23	16	1	14	8	0	.636	180	148	64	50	15	50	2	6	140	2	2.50
Martinez, Char	8	8	1	0	2	4	0	.333	44	59	30	29	6	18	2	1	31	4	5.93
Matchick, Syr	1	0	0	0	0	0	0	.000	1	1	0	0	0	2	0	0	0	1	0.00
McCutchin, Toledo	31	18	1	0	6	10	2	.375	122	162	89	73	10	63	6	2	37	4	5.39
McElwain, Syr.*	10	0	0	0	1	0	0	1.000	22	23	12	10	5	16	1	1	8	1	4.09
McGregor, 11 Sy-13 Ro*	24	23	14	6	12	6	0	.667	162	159	59	55	8	40	2	2	83	4	3.06
McLaughlin, Rich	1	0	0	0	0	0	0	.000	1	1	1	1	0	1	0	0	1	0	9.00
McLaughlin, Mem	20	19	7	2	8	9	0	.471	147	137	71	60	13	53	3	3	117	6	3.67
Mersch, Syracuse	20	4	1	0	4	3	0	.571	56	68	35	33	10	27	6	1	27	2	5.30
Minshall, Char	37	2	0	0	6	3	0	.667	77	106	56	46	10	48	6	3	59	3	5.38
Morlan, Char	24	16	3	0	6	7	0	.462	120	118	80	77	20	75	6	5	66	6	5.78
Myrick, Syr	13	0	0	0	2	0	0	1.000	24	22	10	7	1	10	0	0	22	2	2.63
Newhauser, Char	32	0	0	0	5	2	6	.714	51	45	22	17	2	36	4	0	26	5	3.00
Odom, Richmond	12	12	4	0	4	3	0	.571	74	72	42	29	6	42	4	0	57	3	3.53
Osborn, Richmond	54	1	0	0	8	5	6	.615	89	71	31	26	8	44	9	1	60	2	2.63
Parker, Toledo	25	23	9	0	9	11	0	.450	159	188	103	90	22	39	3	3	70	5	5.09
Parker, Syracuse	1	0	0	0	0	0	0	.000	2	4	6	5	1	3	0	0	2	2	22.50
Patterson, Syr	10	10	6	0	7	2	0	.778	77	71	30	25	1	34	1	1	40	2	2.92
Paxton, Rhode Is	19	19	5	2	7	6	0	.538	126	108	64	58	10	61	10	2	92	1	4.14
Percival, Rhode Is	8	6	1	1	1	3	0	.250	26	43	26	24	4	10	4	1	18	1	8.31
Perzanowski, Tol	16	10	1	0	4	3	0	.571	66	82	48	42	3	34	1	9	36	6	5.73
Polinsky, Syr	46	1	0	0	4	8	13	.333	93	83	44	34	5	49	9	3	67	2	3.29
Price, Charleston	24	21	3	1	6	11	0	.353	115	135	86	73	13	44	5	3	62	6	5.71
Raich, Toledo	29	18	3	0	3	9	2	.250	141	163	87	75	13	46	5	3	42	2	4.79
Reynolds, Syr.*	7	2	0	0	1	2	0	.333	11	18	14	12	0	14	1	0	8	3	9.82
Reynolds, Toledo	45	0	0	0	6	10	3	.375	85	98	43	35	3	42	10	2	56	2	3.71
Ricks, Syracuse	22	18	4	0	10	6	0	.625	123	129	73	58	13	81	2	6	68	7	4.24
Ripley, Rhode Is.	5	5	3	0	3	2	0	.600	39	40	19	17	3	16	1	0	33	3	3.92
Roberge, Memphis	2	1	0	0	0	0	0	.000	10	11	5	3	2	3	0	0	8	2	2.70
Robson, Roch	6	0	0	0	1	0	0	1.000	9	13	4	4	0	4	0	1	4	0	4.00
Rothermel, Mem.*	44	1	0	0	7	1	4	.875	62	66	26	22	6	24	5	2	44	2	3.19
Sadowski, Char	28	24	8	1	9	8	0	.529	163	160	86	75	14	95	8	3	74	12	4.14
Sambito, Mem.*	5	3	0	0	3	0	0	1.000	27	37	19	19	6	13	1	0	17	2	6.33
Sawyer, Syracuse	19	18	8	0	9	4	0	.692	134	125	55	41	10	38	4	5	65	4	2.75
Sealy, Charleston	5	5	0	0	1	2	0	.333	25	32	21	15	4	11	0	2	13	4	5.40
Selak, Memphis	31	21	4	1	4	12	1	.250	163	162	100	94	15	105	11	1	112	10	5.19
Siebert, Mem.*	18	10	3	0	8	3	0	.727	94	104	43	39	12	34	7	2	47	3	3.73
Sielicki, Syr.*	15	12	1	0	8	2	1	.800	82	87	38	27	4	32	1	1	39	1	2.96
Solari, Tide	42	1	0	0	6	4	7	.600	86	84	33	26	3	22	7	2	45	2	2.72
Sosa, Memphis	41	5	1	0	4	10	12	.286	80	86	56	50	5	35	7	5	56	13	5.63
Spencer, Rhode Is	7	7	2	0	1	2	0	.333	35	34	21	20	4	20	5	1	17	3	5.14
Sprinkle, Mem	5	0	0	0	1	1	0	.500	6	8	7	7	2	3	1	1	2	1	10.50
Stanton, Memphis	21	21	5	1	6	11	0	.353	128	135	88	69	5	67	6	9	101	5	4.85
Stein, Rochester	24	22	2	1	5	6	0	.455	110	120	71	67	9	58	1	6	51	9	5.48

Pitcher–Club	G.	GS.	CG.	ShO.	W.	L.	Sv.	Pct.	IP.	H.	R.	ER.	HR.	BB.	Int. BB.	HB.	SO.	WP.	ERA.
Stephenson, Roch.*	34	0	0	0	4	3		.571	46	36	8	6	0	22	7	3	30	6	1.17
Strickland, Tol.*	46	1	0	0	4	7	5	.364	87	98	74	63	11	58	2	3	60	9	6.52
Tate, Tidewater	27	25	4	0	7	14	0	.333	122	136	96	84	13	93	4	10	58	14	6.20
Todd, Tidewater	26	26	13	2	13	9	0	.591	201	204	75	65	6	53	5	3	125	3	2.91
Van Bommel, Roch	9	0	0	0	0	2	1	.000	17	20	12	9	1	12	0	0	7	3	4.76
Watkins, Rhode Is	21	0	0	0	4	2	1	.667	60	55	30	23	2	31	9	2	28	1	3.45
Webb, Tidewater	19	14	1	1	2	9	1	.182	81	104	65	55	9	47	2	5	50	9	6.11
Werd, Toledo*	8	6	0	0	1	2	0	.333	21	39	29	19	6	5	0	1	7	1	8.14
Williams, Char.*	37	3	0	0	2	4	3	.333	49	38	30	25	5	51	3	2	33	6	4.59
Willis, Roch.*	27	22	11	4	12	6	2	.667	156	161	81	73	13	39	4	2	80	2	4.21
Wright, Rhode Is	37	18	6	0	6	12	3	.333	136	162	90	76	13	44	5	2	74	3	5.03
York, Syracuse	22	1	0	0	6	1	0	.857	59	74	42	35	6	22	3	3	24	4	5.34

BALKS—Camp, 5; Grose, Hammon, 4 each; Stanton, 3; Babcock, Barr, Camper, Clay, Farias, Kreuger, Langford, Price, Raich, Selak, Sielicki, 2 each; Baldwin, Beattie, Beene, Bruhert, Burton, Elenes, Flanagan, Galasso, O. Jones, Jones (RI), T. Jones, Kammeyer, Kirkpatrick, Klenda, Konieczny, LaCorte, Larson, Martinez (Roch.), McElwain, McGregor, Mersch, Morlan, Paxton, Polinsky, Reynolds (Syr.), Ricks, Rothermel, Sadowski, Sealy, Stein, Tate, Todd, Werd, Willis, Wright, 1 each.

COMBINATION SHUTOUTS—Lemongello-Selak, Konieczny-Sosa, Memphis; Aase-Kreuger, Rhode Island; Cheadle-Osborn, Richmond; Stein-Stephenson-Johnson, Rochester; Kline-Beene, Toledo.

NO-HIT GAME—Langford, Charleston, defeated Memphis, 11-0, May 30.

INTERNATIONAL LEAGUE HALL OF FAME

★ ★ ★ ★

John Berly	Rube Parnham	Herb Pennock
Jack Bentley	Charley Keller	Dick Porter
Bruno Betzel	Billy Kelly	Pat Powers
Joe Boley	Ernest J. Lanigan	Jimmy Ripple
Ike Boone	Fritz Maisel	Jackie Robinson
Joe Brown	Al Mamaux	Dick Rudolph
Ollie Carnegie	William J. Manley	Ben Sankey
Rip Collins	Joe McCarthy	George Selkirk
Estel Crabtree	Frank McGowan	Frank Shaughnessy
Jack Dunn	Fred Merkle	Harry Smythe
George Earnshaw	Bill Meyer	Billy Southworth
Jewel Ens	Howard Moss	George Stallings
Luke Hamlin	William J. Murray	Tommy Thomas
Ed Holly	Glenn Nelson	George Toporcer
Dan Howley	Jack Ogden	Dixie Walker
Fred Hutchinson	Steve O'Neill	Jimmy Walsh
Merwin Jacobson	Ed Onslow	George Wiltse

Mexican League

CLASS AAA

Leading Batter
LARRY FRITZ
Durango

League President
ANTONIO RAMIREZ M.

Leading Pitcher
GARY RYERSON
Tampico

CHAMPIONSHIP WINNERS IN PREVIOUS YEARS

1955—Mexico City Tigers* ...... .539	1963—Puebla .... .606	1971—Jalisco§ .... .558
1956—Mexico City Reds .... .692	1964—Mexico City Reds .... .586	Saltillo .... .593
1957—Yucatan .... .567	1965—Mexico City Tigers........ .590	1972—Saltillo .... .636
Mex. C. Reds (2nd)† .... .550	1966—Mexico City Tigers‡ ...... .614	Cordoba§ .... .541
1958—Nuevo Laredo .... .625	Mexico City Reds .... .571	1973—Saltillo .... .656
1959—Poza Rica .... .575	1967—Jalisco .... .607	Mexico City Reds x ...... .590
Mex. C. Reds (3rd)† ..... .507	1968—Mexico City Reds .... .586	1974—Jalisco .... .627
1960—Mexico City Tigers....... .538	1969—Reynosa .... .591	Mexico City Reds x ...... .551
1961—Veracruz .... .575	1970—Aguila§ .... .580	1975—Tampico x .... .541
1962—Monterrey .... .592	Mexico City Reds .... .607	Cordoba .... .649

*Defeated Nuevo Laredo, two games to none, in playoff for pennant. †Won four-team playoff. ‡Won split-season playoff. §League divided into Northern, Southern divisions: won two-team playoff. xLeague divided into Northern. Southern zones; sub-divided into Eastern, Western divisions; won eight-team playoff.

STANDING OF CLUBS AT CLOSE OF SEASON, AUGUST 8

SOUTHERN ZONE
WESTERN DIVISION

Club	Pu.	Ag.	MT.	Du.	Cor.	MR.	PR.	Tam.	Ju.	UL.	Sal.	Chi.	Rey.	Coa.	Mon.	NL.	W.	L.	T.	Pct.	G.B.
Puebla............	..	8	7	8	6	7	5	4	2	5	4	4	4	6	3	7	80	55	2	.593	......
Ag'calientes	6	..	8	7	6	3	3	4	4	4	3	6	3	3	3	68	66	2	.507	11½
Mex. Tigers ..	7	6	..	7	3	0	6	1	1	1	2	4	3	4	6	3	54	78	0	.409	24½
Durango	6	7	7	..	4	5	2	2	3	2	4	1	2	1	3	5	54	79	1	.406	25

EASTERN DIVISION

Club																	W.	L.	T.	Pct.	G.B.
Cordoba	2	2	4	4	..	9	10	10	4	3	2	7	6	5	5	5	78	53	1	.595	......
Mexico Reds....	1	5	8	3	5	..	5	10	3	4	5	5	5	4	6	6	75	63	0	.543	6½
Poza Rica	3	5	2	6	3	9	..	7	3	5	4	2	5	4	5	5	68	67	0	.504	12
Tampico	4	3	7	6	4	4	7	..	2	4	4	4	3	4	5	5	66	68	0	.493	13½

NORTHERN ZONE
WESTERN DIVISION

Club																	W.	L.	T.	Pct.	G.B.
Juarez	5	4	7	5	3	5	5	6	..	7	5	6	5	3	4	4	74	61	1	.548	......
Union Lag	3	4	7	6	5	4	3	3	7	..	7	7	4	5	6	4	75	62	0	.547	......
Saltillo	4	3	5	4	4	3	4	4	5	7	..	8	3	6	3	6	72	61	1	.541	1
Chihuahua	4	5	4	5	1	3	6	3	8	7	6	..	3	2	5	5	67	68	0	.496	7

EASTERN DIVISION

Club	Pu.	Ag.	MT.	Du.	Cor.	MR.	PR.	Tam.	Ju.	UL.	Sal.	Chi.	Rey.	Coa.	Mon.	NL.	W.	L.	T.	Pct.	G.B.
Reynosa	4	2	5	5	2	3	2	5	3	4	5	5	..	8	7	7	67	68	1	.496	......
Coahuila	1	2	2	7	1	4	4	2	5	3	4	5	5	..	8	7	61	66	1	.480	2
Monterrey	4	5	2	3	3	2	2	3	4	2	5	6	5	9	..	8	59	75	0	.440	7½
Nuevo Laredo	1	5	3	3	3	2	3	3	4	4	2	3	7	6	5	..	54	82	0	.397	13½

Tampico club represented Tampico and Ciudad Madero.
Union Laguna club represented Gomez Palacio and Torreon.
Coahuila club represented Monclova and Sabinas.

Forfeited Game—Coahuila forfeited to Saltillo (game not played).

Playoffs—Juarez defeated Coahuila, four games to one; Union Laguna defeated Reynosa, four games to one; Cordoba defeated Aguascalientes, four games to one; Mexico City Reds defeated Puebla, four games to two. Union Laguna defeated Juarez, four games to two; Mexico City Reds defeated Cordoba, four games to two. Mexico City Reds defeated Union Laguna, four games to two for league championship.

Regular-Season Attendance—Aguascalientes, 305,397; Chihuahua, 229,155; Coahuila, 256,459; Cordoba, 225,649; Durango, 143,980; Juarez, 262,535; Mexico City Reds, 351,416; Mexico City Tigers, 178,896; Monterrey, 214,636; Nuevo Laredo, 169,504; Poza Rica, 229,029; Puebla, 213,996; Reynosa, 101,828; Saltillo, 101,439; Tampico, 227,287; Union Laguna, 192,134. Total, 3,548,340. Playoffs, 393,916. No all-star game.

Managers: Aguascalientes—Pompeyo Davalillo; Chihuahua—Miguel Gaspar; Coahuila—Wilfredo Calvino; Cordoba—Napoleon Reyes; Durango—Alan Gallagher, Jorge Fitch; Juarez—Jose Guerrero; Mexico City Reds—Benjamin Reyes Chavez; Mexico City Tigers—Jose Luis Garcia; Monterrey—Miguel Sotelo, Jesus Valtier; Nuevo Laredo—Vinicio Garcia; Poza Rica—David Garcia; Puebla—Clemente Carrera; Reynosa—Jorge Fitch, Marte de Alejandro; Saltillo—Enrique Izquierdo, Gregorio Luque; Tampico—Benjamin Valenzuela, Ronaldo Camacho; Union Laguna—Moises Camacho.

All-Star Team: 1B—Pierce, Puebla; 2B—Briones, Juarez; 3B—DelMoral, Juarez; SS—Villaescusa, Mexico City Reds; OF—Davalillo, Puebla; Ford, Reynosa; Suarez, Mexico City Reds; C—Estrada, Puebla; DH—Walseth, Puebla; P—Romo, Mexico City Reds; Pollorena, Union Laguna; Manager—Guerrero, Juarez.

(Compiled by Antonio Silva Vidaurry, League Statistician, Mexico, D. F.)

CLUB BATTING

Club	G.	AB.	R.	OR.	H.	TB.	2B.	3B.	HR.	RBI.	SH.	SF.	BB.	Int. BB.	HP.	SO.	SB.	CS.	LOB.	Pct.
Puebla	137	4596	683	545	1328	1913	184	22	119	646	36	46	467	53	39	597	27	33	1010	.289
Aguascalientes	136	4477	586	633	1287	1663	148	60	36	536	46	47	422	42	37	638	102	104	939	.287
Juarez	136	4307	555	505	1225	1611	160	32	54	513	79	52	423	77	27	484	149	88	944	.284
Mexico Reds	138	4496	555	532	1276	1620	155	51	29	503	81	36	394	57	47	470	62	49	1000	.284
Durango	134	4428	594	650	1255	1679	158	31	68	550	59	31	443	38	36	636	73	58	913	.283
Saltillo	133	4280	545	457	1197	1617	163	22	71	491	84	32	388	55	42	486	43	45	959	.280
Laguna	137	4387	589	538	1208	1661	160	43	69	534	71	42	420	42	36	560	121	78	912	.275
Cordoba	132	4149	547	422	1133	1557	194	40	50	512	82	44	414	53	61	609	65	50	916	.273
Chihuahua	135	4303	533	584	1165	1573	134	35	68	477	60	38	419	45	42	534	44	39	962	.271
Tampico	134	4363	500	479	1159	1547	137	14	71	458	71	42	446	35	40	600	49	47	1016	.268
Mexico Tig	132	4240	503	599	1135	1438	150	45	21	456	59	30	400	40	36	620	68	57	907	.268
Reynosa	136	4395	510	519	1163	1578	178	48	47	466	80	34	410	49	29	637	59	80	959	.265
Coahuila	127	4050	482	472	1067	1492	162	25	71	436	30	23	372	48	29	613	46	42	834	.263
Poza Rica	135	4192	461	491	1087	1397	136	30	39	424	92	29	399	48	35	563	44	61	932	.259
Nuevo Laredo	136	4465	443	599	1123	1449	140	24	46	389	74	26	348	55	25	708	47	43	958	.252
Monterrey	134	4243	389	450	996	1357	131	22	62	357	70	30	380	40	41	744	124	84	889	.235

INDIVIDUAL BATTING

(Leading Qualifiers for Batting Championship—373 or More Plate Appearances)

*Bats lefthanded. †Switch-hitter.

Player and Club	G.	AB.	R.	H.	TB.	2B.	3B.	HR.	RBI.	SH.	SF.	BB.	HP.	SO.	SB.	CS.	Pct.
Fritz, Lawrence, Ags*	104	310	57	110	159	16	3	9	65	2	4	83	3	51	7	6	.355
Noriega, Fco. Javier, Ags	107	328	50	116	154	17	3	5	39	4	4	37	7	48	8	9	.354
Suarez, Miguel, Mex. R*	132	492	62	171	202	18	5	1	53	12	0	24	3	25	2	1	.348
Del Moral, Jose, Jua.	116	450	68	156	220	21	2	13	66	9	8	23	1	47	9	9	.347
Batista, Rafael, Cor*	126	415	70	139	218	36	2	13	91	1	5	67	10	81	2	2	.335
Vazquez, M. Efrain, Lar†	106	392	55	131	176	28	4	3	55	1	4	35	2	40	2	2	.334
Walseth, Michael, Pue*	137	512	93	171	273	34	3	24	107	1	5	71	3	67	0	1	.334
Davalillo, Victor, Pue*	123	501	84	167	216	23	1	8	63	2	3	38	1	30	5	4	.333
Ford, Lambert, Rey*	133	501	76	166	214	11	17	1	39	10	1	69	1	43	10	11	.331
Pierce, L. Jack, Pue*	132	486	90	161	291	20	1	36	118	0	4	60	5	73	1	2	.331
Bravo, Angel, Ags*	127	463	72	153	198	13	13	2	44	2	6	54	1	47	12	17	.330

Departmental Leaders: G—Sommers, Walseth, 137; AB—Sommers, 538; R—Moore, 108; H—Suarez, Walseth, 171; TB—Pierce, 291; 2B—Batista, 36; 3B—L. Ford, 17; HR—Pierce, 36; RBI—Pierce, 118; SH—A. Briones, 21; SF—H. Garcia, Roque, 10; BB—Moore, 129; HP—Mendez, 11; SO—Jacinto Hernandez, 117; SB—A. Briones, 68; CS—A. Briones, 28.

(All Players—Listed Alphabetically)

Player and Club	G.	AB.	R.	H.	TB.	2B.	3B.	HR.	RBI.	SH.	SF.	BB.	HP.	SO.	SB.	CS.	Pct.
Abarca, David, Ags	2	1	1	0	0	0	0	0	0	0	0	0	0	0	0	0	.000
Acosta, Teolindo, Lar*	101	384	48	106	111	5	0	0	19	4	3	37	3	16	7	5	.276
Aguilar, Enrique, Ags	107	170	31	43	50	3	2	0	10	3	1	10	0	25	2	5	.253
Aguilar, Jose L., M. Tig†	115	324	39	95	106	7	2	0	27	3	3	63	1	43	5	5	.293
Aguirre, Trinidad, Mex. R	81	254	24	59	75	8	1	2	22	10	1	12	1	35	2	2	.232
Alcaide, Jose, Ags*	29	85	11	28	43	5	2	2	14	0	1	9	0	14	1	0	.329
Alcaraz, A. Luis, Cor	116	385	50	117	168	25	1	8	54	5	2	58	3	49	1	0	.304
Allen, Kim, Dur	66	254	45	77	86	6	0	1	19	3	1	29	4	16	34	10	.303
Alou, Jesus, Cor	39	141	16	37	47	7	0	1	20	3	1	10	1	8	1	2	.262
Alvarado, Alejandro, Tam*	95	325	35	98	106	8	0	0	20	8	0	28	2	9	3	8	.302
Alvarado, Natanael, Cor	106	397	68	113	139	16	5	0	28	7	4	27	6	76	16	10	.285
Alvarez, Arturo, Lar*	103	333	27	89	119	18	3	2	28	4	2	24	2	54	4	4	.267
Alvarez, Manuel, Cor*	112	411	64	119	184	25	5	10	52	5	4	38	4	77	1	4	.290
Anaya, Jesus, Ags	7	10	2	1	1	0	0	0	0	0	0	1	1	1	0	0	.100
Arano, Antonio, Lar	6	19	1	2	2	0	0	0	0	0	0	0	0	2	0	0	.105
Arauz, Lorenzo, M. Tig*	4	7	0	0	0	0	0	0	0	0	0	1	0	5	0	0	.000
Armas, Abel, Ags*	1	2	0	0	0	0	0	0	0	0	0	0	0	2	0	0	.000
Arvizu, Juan, PR	41	94	8	12	17	2	0	1	10	4	1	28	0	28	0	1	.128
Ashford, Samuel, Lar*	71	267	31	66	96	8	2	6	30	1	3	16	1	53	1	0	.247
Barron, Rafael, Mex. R	94	271	14	52	58	4	1	0	18	7	4	9	2	37	3	4	.192
Batista, Rafael, Cor*	126	415	70	139	218	36	2	13	91	1	5	67	10	81	2	2	.335
Bazan, Elias, Rey*	1	0	1	0	0	0	0	0	0	0	0	0	0	0	0	0	.000
Benitez, Jose Luis, Ags	46	124	9	22	31	2	2	1	12	2	1	3	1	30	0	1	.177
Bernal, Arturo, Mon*	107	316	23	80	121	14	3	7	33	1	0	26	2	54	4	3	.253
Blanco, C. Oswaldo, Jua	134	448	78	130	181	16	4	9	62	1	8	77	3	92	13	14	.290
Blessitt, Isaiah, Coa	88	309	40	73	127	15	6	9	31	0	1	27	1	76	5	7	.236
Bojorquez, Jose, 38 Cor-87 Tam	125	410	48	120	148	18	2	2	39	10	9	40	2	57	2	5	.293
Bourque, Patrick, Mex. R*	112	386	65	125	173	14	8	6	52	1	4	70	6	47	7	2	.324
Bravo, Angel, Ags*	127	463	72	153	198	13	13	2	44	2	6	54	1	47	12	17	.330
Breazeale, James, Dur*	124	435	55	140	224	24	0	20	104	0	1	68	2	49	0	1	.322
Briones, Antonio, Jua	136	528	93	168	209	22	5	3	51	21	6	44	2	38	68	28	.318
Briones, Eleazar, Mon	102	259	13	44	52	3	1	1	10	8	1	13	5	49	2	2	.170
Brookins, Landon, Chi	127	434	62	137	225	21	8	17	76	1	0	56	10	49	9	9	.316
Brown, Curtis, Lag	130	462	79	140	196	17	9	7	65	6	7	54	5	54	6	6	.303
Buckner, James, Mon*	79	269	32	83	108	9	2	4	23	1	3	33	1	35	17	10	.309
Calvo, Bernardo, Ags	99	327	27	101	116	7	4	0	39	3	4	21	1	41	4	5	.309
Camarero, Rolando, Ags	96	255	17	57	79	11	1	3	30	0	5	19	0	48	2	5	.224
Camargo, Fernando, Mon	67	105	7	20	27	2	1	1	7	2	0	12	1	24	1	2	.190
Canada, Romel, Lag*	133	468	87	141	241	24	5	22	80	2	5	67	3	50	32	12	.301
Cantres, Angel L., Rey	88	294	32	81	113	15	4	3	30	1	1	33	7	55	6	6	.276
Cardona, Candelario, Sal	84	249	31	67	81	8	3	0	13	3	1	16	5	40	3	5	.269
Castillo, Roberto, Rey	1	2	0	0	0	0	0	0	0	0	0	0	0	0	0	0	.000
Castro, Alberto, Lag	1	2	0	1	1	0	0	0	1	0	1	0	0	0	0	0	.500
Castro, Arnoldo, Coa	115	400	37	104	133	15	1	4	45	6	2	15	1	35	3	1	.260
Cerda, Benjamin, Dur	119	440	67	140	199	21	1	12	67	4	6	42	3	49	1	1	.318
Cervantes, Eduardo, Chi	21	37	2	5	6	1	0	0	4	0	0	4	0	9	0	0	.135
Cervantes, Eraclio, Chi	6	7	1	3	6	1	1	0	2	0	0	2	0	0	0	0	.429
Cervantes, Refugio, M. Tig†	131	468	58	132	179	23	9	2	51	7	5	27	8	71	1	1	.282
Chavarin, Ubaldo, Rey	12	34	3	7	8	1	0	0	2	0	1	4	0	5	0	0	.206
Chavez, Carlos, Tam	2	1	1	0	0	0	0	0	0	0	0	0	0	0	0	0	.000
Chavez, Francisco, 17 La-105 Ta	122	427	50	98	115	12	1	1	41	9	4	48	3	79	8	2	.230
Chavez, J. Guadalupe, Sal*	127	461	63	135	180	27	3	4	41	16	4	50	5	40	6	8	.293
Chavez, Juan de Dios, Pue	131	429	43	101	125	15	3	1	47	9	3	28	5	89	3	2	.235
Chavez, Rene, Chi	7	0	4	0	0	0	0	0	0	0	0	0	0	0	0	0	.000
Christiansen, David, Lag	84	266	39	84	131	17	3	8	37	4	3	44	5	37	3	2	.316
Clark, James, Mex. R	130	466	61	136	178	15	3	7	65	2	7	46	2	49	2	5	.292
Clayton, Leonardo, Mon*	21	21	2	2	2	0	0	0	1	0	2	0	8	3	1		.095
Colon, Raul, PR*	128	436	53	135	177	22	4	4	63	2	4	51	3	65	14	8	.310
Contreras, Edgardo, Pue	2	3	0	0	0	0	0	0	0	0	1	0	0	0	0	0	.000
Contreras, Raul, Lar	1	2	0	0	0	0	0	0	0	0	0	0	0	2	0	0	.000
Cordova, Ernesto, Dur	1	2	0	0	0	0	0	0	0	0	0	1	0	1	0	0	.000
Corella, Jaime, M. Tig	4	9	1	3	7	1	0	1	3	0	0	0	0	1	0	0	.333
Crawford, Alfred, Ags	98	366	70	118	159	14	6	5	44	4	1	19	7	38	22	11	.322
Cruz, Domingo, Sal	120	434	53	135	157	12	2	2	55	9	1	29	3	44	5	3	.311
Cruz, Julio, Tam	1	0	0	0	0	0	0	0	0	0	0	1	0	0	0	0	.000
Cummings, Michael, Lar	6	22	1	5	5	0	0	0	1	1	0	2	0	4	1	0	.227
Davalillo, Victor, Pue*	123	501	84	167	216	23	1	8	63	2	3	38	1	30	5	4	.333
Davila, Angel, Cor*	7	9	2	2	2	0	0	0	2	0	1	1	0	3	0	0	.222
Davila, L. Alberto, Jua	108	268	31	66	81	5	5	0	19	5	2	35	3	38	5	2	.246
De Hoyos, Arnoldo, Coa*	127	466	85	141	176	18	4	3	37	2	1	57	5	36	11	9	.303
Del Moral, Jose, Jua	116	450	68	156	220	21	2	13	66	9	8	23	1	47	9	9	.347
Diaz, Albino, PR	97	323	44	95	120	12	5	1	27	11	3	24	1	31	4	7	.294
Diaz Rdz., Arsenio, PR	126	448	56	121	171	15	4	9	67	4	3	29	2	54	5	8	.270
Diaz, Cesar, Ags	4	0	1	0	0	0	0	0	0	0	0	0	0	1	1	0	.000

Player and Club	G	AB	R	H	TB	2B	3B	HR	RBI	SH	SF	BB	HP	SO	SB	CS	Pct
Diaz, Hector, Rey	41	131	14	33	52	10	3	1	12	4	1	10	0	34	0	4	.252
Dugan, James H., Coa	118	430	63	135	216	27	3	16	69	3	1	40	3	110	7	6	.314
Duran, Roberto, Cor*	62	161	23	45	59	5	3	1	20	5	2	27	9	31	1	3	.280
Elguezabal, Jose A., Pue	21	52	11	14	17	1	1	0	4	2	1	4	1	9	0	0	.269
Elizondo, Fernando, Sal	34	81	7	16	19	1	1	0	4	2	0	5	0	11	1	0	.198
Enriquez, Graciano, Chi	133	503	48	139	173	12	5	4	47	5	5	21	3	54	2	5	.276
Escalante, Sergio, M.Tig*	1	0	1	0	0	0	0	0	0	0	0	0	0	0	0	0	.000
Escalante, Victor, 29 M.Tig-30 Tam	59	109	17	26	27	1	0	0	3	3	0	24	1	16	1	1	.239
Espino, Hector, Tam	96	337	49	100	167	7	0	20	65	0	4	49	2	13	1	3	.297
Espinosa, Ernesto, 53 Mon-30 Rey	83	295	24	72	85	7	3	0	22	10	2	21	5	29	7	0	.244
Espinosa, Nestor, M.Tig	1	1	0	1	2	1	0	0	3	1	0	0	0	0	0	0	1.000
Esquivel, Ramiro, Tam	28	78	8	16	22	3	0	1	7	1	1	2	1	12	0	1	.205
Estrada, Francisco, Pue	110	350	30	90	105	8	2	1	35	4	5	44	4	20	0	2	.257
Fabela, Victor, Coa	44	87	5	23	34	2	0	3	10	1	0	15	4	9	0	2	.264
Faudoa, Victor, Chi*	109	342	26	93	119	11	6	1	19	2	1	28	3	46	1	3	.272
Felix, Fernando, Lag	134	472	57	133	174	13	5	6	66	6	8	22	3	58	19	11	.282
Felix, Victor, Lag	116	419	64	115	143	10	9	4	42	8	4	49	4	65	13	8	.274
Figueroa, Baldemar, Lar	121	429	44	113	133	10	2	2	24	8	0	26	2	54	7	8	.263
Figueroa, Leobardo, Tam	70	217	27	49	59	3	2	1	13	5	0	17	7	24	11	5	.226
Flores, Ignacio, Mon	6	4	1	1	1	0	0	0	0	0	0	0	0	0	0	0	.250
Ford, Lambert, Rey*	133	501	76	166	214	11	17	1	39	10	1	69	1	43	10	11	.331
Ford, Theodore, 44 Dur-87 M.Reds	131	459	85	151	208	16	7	9	71	2	2	85	3	62	3	5	.329
Fritz, Lawrence J., Ags*	104	310	57	110	159	16	3	9	65	2	4	83	3	51	7	6	.355
Fuentes, Antonio, PR	90	242	26	68	79	8	0	1	26	6	1	19	0	23	1	2	.281
Galliher, Marvin, Rey	32	122	13	37	50	8	1	1	10	1	0	14	1	8	5	2	.303
Gamundi, Timoteo, M.Tig	108	364	43	101	123	10	3	2	33	10	1	20	5	57	12	7	.277
Garcia, Bulmaro, 43 Tam-40 Cor	83	274	24	61	68	7	0	0	15	12	0	12	8	23	0	3	.223
Garcia, Eden, Jua	6	15	0	3	6	1	1	0	1	1	0	0	0	0	0	0	.200
Garcia, Humberto, Rey	127	459	59	114	191	26	3	15	83	4	10	36	3	93	8	9	.248
Garcia, Nicolas, Tam	2	5	0	1	1	0	0	0	0	0	0	0	0	2	0	0	.200
Garza, Carlos, M.Tig†	115	332	49	81	111	12	3	4	41	2	2	79	1	74	0	4	.244
Garza, Gustavo, 24 Lar-12 Rey*	36	94	3	20	22	2	0	0	6	2	0	8	0	16	0	1	.213
Garzon, Felix, M.Tig	61	175	20	59	66	7	0	0	21	4	2	14	2	25	3	2	.337
Gaspar, Miguel, Chi	2	2	0	2	3	1	0	0	0	0	0	0	0	0	0	0	1.000
Gaytan, Ricardo, Sal	10	8	2	2	3	1	0	0	3	0	0	0	0	4	0	0	.250
Gil, T. Gustavo, PR	11	30	3	1	1	0	0	0	2	0	0	4	0	4	0	0	.033
Gongora, Gerardo, Tam	59	120	8	22	25	3	0	0	6	3	1	7	0	26	0	0	.183
Gonzalez, Arturo, Mon	84	202	12	37	48	7	2	0	10	7	1	9	2	37	6	6	.183
Gonzalez, Efrain, Lag	1	1	0	0	0	0	0	0	0	0	0	0	0	1	0	0	.000
Gonzalez, Wenceslao, PR	83	218	23	54	88	5	1	9	29	0	1	27	6	58	1	2	.248
Grant, Tim, Dur	15	61	8	17	25	1	2	1	8	1	0	10	1	14	4	4	.279
Grijalva, Raul, Rey*	25	98	10	22	22	0	0	0	1	0	0	10	1	14	4	1	.224
Guerrero, Leobardo, Ags	122	444	70	135	165	12	9	0	48	15	4	37	2	52	22	18	.304
Guillen, Norberto, 2 Coa-48 Lar	50	97	5	18	21	3	0	0	5	4	1	4	1	21	0	0	.186
Gutierrez, Eduardo, Rey	1	1	0	0	0	0	0	0	0	0	0	0	0	0	0	0	.000
Gutierrez, Guillermo, Dur*	1	1	0	0	0	0	0	0	0	0	0	0	0	0	0	0	.000
Gutierrez, Leon, Cor	31	75	6	15	17	2	0	0	2	3	0	6	0	5	2	0	.200
Guzman, Luis Fernando, Dur	1	2	0	0	0	0	0	0	0	0	0	0	0	6	0	0	.000
Guzman, Ramiro, Tam†	6	12	0	2	2	0	0	0	0	0	0	1	0	0	0	0	.167
Guzman, Ubaldo, M.Tig	4	6	0	0	0	0	0	0	0	1	0	1	0	5	0	0	.000
Hart, James, Ags	28	89	6	28	34	3	0	1	13	0	2	17	0	18	1	1	.315
Heras, Roberto, M.Tig	13	26	1	5	7	2	0	0	3	1	0	0	0	6	0	0	.192
Hernandez, Jacinto, Lar	136	448	41	95	141	11	4	9	45	7	1	58	1	17	4	7	.212
Hernandez L., Jose, Rey	61	177	14	39	47	6	1	0	24	3	0	16	0	42	1	4	.220
Hernandez, Jose Maria, Dur	76	215	25	52	72	6	4	2	27	3	0	13	0	44	1	1	.242
Hernandez, Pedro, Pue	11	21	1	6	6	0	0	0	2	0	0	0	0	7	0	0	.286
Hernandez, Rafael, Lar	14	40	4	12	14	2	0	0	4	1	0	1	0	7	0	0	.300
Hernandez Z., Ramon, M.Reds	133	524	56	137	160	13	5	0	41	20	3	26	1	28	10	6	.261
Hdz, Rodolfo, 71 Dur-44 Cor	115	417	56	118	163	23	2	6	62	4	8	31	4	44	1	4	.283
Hdz, Salvador, M.Tig	58	155	21	32	42	5	1	1	19	5	0	20	1	18	3	6	.206
Howard, Charles, Tam†	91	299	46	69	100	8	1	7	26	0	2	41	7	45	5	1	.231
Ibarra, Humberto, Lag*	47	73	3	11	12	1	0	0	3	0	1	7	0	15	0	1	.151
Jackson, Alfonso, Lar	92	238	14	46	55	6	0	1	17	10	1	11	7	48	0	1	.193
Jimenez, Alfonso, Pue	131	427	51	98	132	12	2	6	42	3	5	50	2	54	3	7	.230
Juarez, Clemente, PR	1	2	0	0	0	0	0	0	0	0	0	0	0	1	0	0	.000
Juarez, Marcelo, 81 Sal-41 Lar	122	463	67	138	166	20	1	2	49	11	6	41	6	42	7	4	.298
Kilpatrick, Cleo, 44 Dur-19 Cor†	63	229	32	70	97	7	4	4	28	0	1	17	1	27	2	3	.306
King, Harold, Coa*	112	374	52	105	163	20	1	12	63	0	5	64	3	67	1	1	.281
Koegel, Peter, PR	51	153	15	33	46	4	0	3	19	1	3	16	0	27	0	0	.216
Lara, Armando, M.Tig	130	472	50	131	165	18	5	2	59	6	6	42	7	53	4	4	.278
Lara, Cesar, Coa	22	34	3	10	10	0	0	0	1	0	0	0	0	6	0	0	.294
Lara, Francisco, Pue	131	521	85	142	163	12	3	1	34	8	4	38	8	34	5	7	.273
Lara, Santos, PR	19	34	2	3	4	1	0	0	0	0	1	0	1	8	0	0	.088
Lazaro, Alfredo, Lag	75	183	23	38	54	7	0	3	13	5	1	23	2	43	3	6	.208
Lazaro, Manuel, Lag	83	225	29	55	60	3	1	0	12	7	0	9	1	37	4	6	.244

Player and Club	G	AB	R	H	TB	2B	3B	HR	RBI	SH	SF	BB	HP	SO	SB	CS	Pct.
Leal, Felipe, Lar	28	52	5	11	17	0	0	2	8	0	0	5	0	15	1	0	.212
Lee, Leron, Mon*	116	400	51	110	174	13	3	15	57	2	6	50	4	72	14	7	.275
Leon, Eduardo, Tam	122	409	33	113	142	8	0	7	40	12	6	45	1	82	4	2	.276
Leon, Ricardo, Tam*	53	189	21	54	70	7	0	3	14	1	2	11	0	19	0	0	.286
Lizarraga, Miguel, Lag	40	66	4	13	14	1	0	0	5	2	0	11	0	20	0	0	.197
Lizarraga, Raul, Tam	15	42	5	10	13	1	1	0	5	1	0	3	0	10	0	1	.238
Lolich, Ronald J., Chi	28	91	17	30	41	5	0	2	25	0	2	10	2	8	0	0	.330
Lopez, Baudel, M.Reds*	120	404	59	108	132	12	6	0	42	6	3	50	9	41	7	6	.267
Lopez, Jaime, Chi	126	482	53	147	162	11	2	0	31	7	5	28	0	26	1	3	.305
Lopez, Juan Manuel, Rey	13	32	1	5	9	2	1	0	1	1	0	0	0	15	0	1	.156
Lopez, Lorenzo, Tam	116	410	46	127	167	20	1	6	62	9	3	21	5	49	3	9	.310
Lopez, Ricardo, Tam	1	3	1	1	1	0	0	0	0	0	0	1	0	0	0	0	.333
Lopez, Victor Manuel, Lag	136	480	61	153	216	28	1	11	82	4	5	55	3	49	20	11	.319
Lugo, Gabriel, Sal	132	487	82	149	244	17	3	24	95	3	4	40	8	42	2	2	.306
Lugo, Manuel, Dur	5	2	2	0	0	0	0	0	0	0	0	0	0	1	0	0	.000
Lugo, Pedro, PR	26	48	5	9	9	0	0	0	3	2	0	3	1	9	0	0	.188
Luque, Gregorio, Sal	68	228	18	57	72	5	2	2	20	5	2	4	4	7	0	0	.250
Mariscal, Alfredo, PR*	2	4	0	2	2	0	0	0	0	0	0	0	0	1	0	0	.500
Marquez, Francisco, Ags	104	320	30	73	93	12	1	2	30	1	3	21	10	71	2	7	.228
Martinez, Antonio, Lar†	26	83	2	21	24	0	0	1	9	0	3	6	1	7	0	2	.253
Martinez, Humberto, Rey	61	139	13	23	30	3	2	0	13	4	2	8	2	23	2	6	.165
Martinez, Javier, 1 Lar-1 Coa	2	2	0	0	0	0	0	0	0	0	0	0	1	0	0	0	.000
Martinez C., Juan, Mon	100	301	32	65	121	15	1	13	46	1	3	31	3	104	4	7	.216
Martinez, Raul, Dur	1	1	0	0	0	0	0	0	0	0	0	0	0	0	0	0	.000
Matias, John Roy, Jua*	136	502	68	154	206	18	2	10	72	3	7	47	3	26	3	2	.307
McRae, Norman, Chi	4	2	2	0	0	0	0	0	0	0	0	0	0	1	0	0	.000
Mena, Rigoberto, Sal	100	333	20	72	87	15	0	0	32	9	1	31	2	8	1	0	.216
Mendez, Roberto, Dur	128	465	86	135	167	16	2	4	40	18	4	67	11	50	4	6	.290
Mendoza, Luis Alonso, Rey	34	28	7	4	6	2	0	0	4	1	1	1	0	5	0	0	.143
Mendoza, Porfirio, Jua	11	27	3	4	4	0	0	0	4	1	1	1	0	5	0	0	.148
Mendoza, Saul, Coa	122	407	36	97	142	17	2	8	39	5	1	44	4	47	5	3	.238
Mere, Luis, M.Reds	1	2	0	0	0	0	0	0	0	0	0	1	0	1	0	0	.000
Minoso, Orestes (Jr.), Dur	13	55	17	20	28	3	1	1	4	1	0	4	1	11	4	0	.364
Molina, Jose Maria, Ags	15	18	0	1	1	0	0	0	0	0	0	2	1	6	0	0	.056
Montes Correa, Jose, Rey	21	54	4	10	11	1	0	0	2	3	0	5	0	9	2	0	.185
Montoya, Ramon, M.Reds	1	3	1	2	2	0	0	0	0	0	0	0	0	1	0	0	.667
Montoya, Raul, Jua	112	375	38	93	112	13	0	2	26	5	1	28	4	23	32	8	.248
Moore, Curtis, Chi*	131	404	108	114	220	18	2	28	72	0	2	129	3	80	14	5	.282
Mora, Jesus, Ags	2	6	0	2	2	0	0	0	0	0	0	0	0	0	0	0	.333
Morales, Alfredo, Chi	63	146	14	25	29	2	1	0	9	8	0	14	3	21	1	0	.171
Morales, Carlos, Pue	14	24	0	9	10	1	0	0	5	0	0	1	1	9	0	0	.375
Morales, Guillermo, Tam	2	2	0	0	0	0	0	0	0	0	0	0	0	1	0	0	.000
Moreno, Angel, Ags*	3	7	0	1	1	0	0	0	0	0	0	0	0	3	0	0	.143
Moreno, Jose Luis, Coa	3	7	0	1	1	0	0	0	0	0	0	0	0	1	0	0	.143
Munoz, Edward, Mon*	47	188	36	50	76	8	3	4	10	1	0	18	1	23	14	5	.266
Munoz, Jose Luis, Jua	32	21	6	6	9	1	1	0	0	0	1	0	1	5	0	1	.286
Munoz, Romulo, M.Tig	76	222	18	54	75	15	0	2	23	2	0	11	0	47	0	0	.243
Murrell, Ivan, 3 Dur-64 Lar-38 Sal‡	105	383	52	108	163	17	1	12	60	1	1	33	0	82	7	0	.282
Navarrete, Carlos, M.Reds	85	232	21	64	76	7	1	1	17	6	1	8	3	25	0	0	.276
Nettles, James W., Jua*	62	168	25	33	46	10	0	1	13	1	1	45	2	26	3	4	.196
Nieblas, Armando, Mon	1	0	1	0	0	0	0	0	0	0	0	0	0	0	0	0	.000
Noriega, Fco. Javier, Ags	107	328	50	116	154	17	3	5	39	4	4	37	7	48	8	9	.354
Ochoa, David, Cor	5	7	0	1	1	0	0	0	0	0	0	1	0	0	2	0	.143
Oliveras, Max, PR	41	138	8	32	39	5	1	0	15	3	1	9	2	24	1	1	.232
Oquendo, Ismael, 26 Sal-86 PR*	112	382	43	111	169	16	3	12	42	5	1	45	5	48	6	9	.291
Ornelas, Rafael, Sal	112	363	44	106	135	8	3	5	47	11	4	44	1	55	2	7	.292
Ornelas, Roberto, 35 Lag-56 Dur	91	261	26	62	82	6	4	2	20	6	0	25	0	57	4	2	.238
Orozco, Arturo, Chi	108	326	38	77	130	11	0	14	55	3	3	39	4	84	0	2	.236
Orozco, Victor, Jua	41	111	8	26	30	1	0	1	12	3	1	6	0	14	1	1	.234
Ortiz U., Alfredo, Mex. R*	18	27	4	11	13	2	0	0	7	0	0	3	0	7	0	0	.407
Ortiz, Jose Manuel, Mon	127	409	27	101	122	15	0	2	36	5	3	32	5	57	7	10	.247
Ortiz, Osvaldo, Rey	127	471	60	146	217	21	7	12	76	4	7	43	2	48	5	8	.310
Osuna, Carlos, Lar	20	58	2	6	6	0	0	0	1	0	0	3	0	13	1	0	.103
Osuna, Elpidio, Jua	127	423	41	124	164	23	1	5	67	3	6	44	4	66	9	6	.293
Pactwa, Joseph, Tam*	56	135	28	39	79	4	0	12	33	0	1	39	1	34	0	1	.289
Padilla, Manuel, Rey	8	24	3	7	12	2	0	1	1	0	0	2	0	9	0	0	.292
Paredes, Jesus, Cor	88	290	39	85	110	7	3	4	35	4	1	23	3	43	7	8	.293
Parker, William D., Mon	42	140	17	37	71	9	2	7	20	3	1	17	0	30	4	1	.264
Parra, Manuel, 18 Cor-90 Lar	108	364	41	98	156	15	5	11	51	6	4	14	1	92	1	1	.269
Paul, Michael, Tam*	6	16	3	2	2	0	0	0	0	0	0	2	0	8	0	0	.125
Payan, Daniel, Chi	9	21	4	7	8	1	0	0	5	1	2	0	0	3	1	0	.333
Peralta, Luis, Jua	118	340	44	84	114	9	3	5	34	6	4	40	2	37	2	5	.247
Peralta, Vicente, PR	100	290	22	65	74	4	1	1	27	8	4	26	1	36	1	3	.224
Perez, Alfredo, Lag	8	7	0	0	0	0	0	0	0	0	0	0	0	0	0	0	.000
Perez, Jose Luis, Ags*	22	72	7	23	29	4	1	0	9	0	0	6	0	9	0	1	.319

Player and Club	G.	AB.	R.	H.	TB.	2B.	3B.	HR.	RBI.	SH.	SF.	BB.	HP.	SO.	SB.	CS.	Pct.
Perez, Luis A., Lar	7	9	1	0	0	0	0	0	0	1	0	1	0	1	0	0	.000
Pettaway, Nat, 18 PR-105 Sal*	123	416	63	123	195	22	1	16	56	2	3	62	4	110	7	12	.296
Phillips, Adolfo, Coa	16	66	13	13	20	2	1	1	3	0	0	9	1	20	7	2	.197
Pierce, L. Jack, Pue*	132	486	90	161	291	20	1	36	118	0	4	60	5	73	1	2	.331
Pineda, Juan Jose, Ags	2	1	1	0	0	0	0	0	0	0	0	1	0	1	0	0	.000
Plascencia, Obed, M. Tig	54	181	20	54	64	4	0	2	34	0	1	20	2	11	0	2	.298
Plascencia, Rigoberto, M. Tig	39	150	13	35	47	4	4	0	19	0	1	11	0	23	2	0	.233
Prieto, Juvencio, Cor	68	125	14	32	39	7	0	0	10	3	1	8	1	14	3	3	.256
Ramirez, Gustavo, Chi	121	453	54	118	129	9	1	0	32	9	5	18	5	22	5	3	.260
Ramirez, Manuel, 30 Dur-32 Lag	62	125	14	43	41	7	0	0	7	2	0	9	1	28	2	2	.272
Raygoza, German, M. Tig	1	1	0	1	3	0	1	0	0	0	0	0	0	0	0	0	1.000
Rey, Arturo, Tam	94	279	17	51	65	8	0	2	26	4	1	23	5	44	1	0	.183
Reyes, Jose, Cor	3	9	0	2	3	1	0	0	1	0	0	0	0	1	0	0	.222
Rivera, Carlos, M. Tig	129	475	70	136	174	13	11	1	47	2	5	19	2	52	10	7	.286
Rivera, Eduardo, 16 Sal-92 Cor	108	320	32	70	94	12	3	2	39	7	3	33	5	46	0	2	.219
Rivero, Gener, Cor	117	349	38	91	107	6	5	0	26	15	0	21	4	28	7	4	.261
Robinson, Lee, Mon	20	60	7	12	15	0	0	1	3	2	1	11	0	13	0	0	.200
Robles, Alejandro, 2 Ags-126 PR*	128	427	53	131	156	17	4	0	47	16	5	33	2	31	3	11	.307
Robles, Rigoberto, Ags	17	17	4	0	0	0	0	0	0	0	0	4	0	3	0	0	.000
Rodriguez, Francisco, Ags	130	468	66	126	170	19	5	5	84	3	9	42	3	57	7	4	.269
Rdz., Gerardo, 21 Pue-85 Dur	106	350	45	89	150	16	3	13	54	2	5	45	6	90	1	2	.254
Rodriguez, Jose, Jua	80	251	16	73	100	8	2	5	45	12	1	12	0	28	1	0	.290
Rodriguez, Juan, Mex. R	16	50	1	9	11	2	0	0	6	0	0	4	0	4	0	1	.180
Rodriguez M., Leonardo, Mon	115	349	34	84	92	6	1	0	17	14	0	28	5	43	8	3	.241
Rodriguez, Roberto, Lar*	36	113	16	39	43	2	1	0	7	3	1	11	0	10	2	2	.345
Roque, Jorge, Cor	124	410	55	112	173	24	8	7	65	3	10	63	3	64	20	8	.273
Rosario, Santiago, Mex. R*	67	211	30	60	85	5	4	4	39	1	2	24	1	27	4	2	.284
Rosas, Clemente, 38 Dur-58 Lag	96	305	25	65	85	6	1	4	35	4	3	9	1	46	0	1	.213
Rubio, Arturo, Lar	96	329	33	76	90	6	4	0	10	0	0	20	1	23	5	8	.231
Ruiz, Porfirio, Coa	99	315	25	70	85	9	3	0	19	2	3	9	2	38	1	1	.222
Saiz, Francisco, PR*	103	329	38	87	109	13	3	1	27	9	2	37	4	44	1	2	.264
Salado, Jose, Cor	43	142	7	30	34	2	1	0	12	4	1	9	3	15	0	1	.211
Salazar, Rolando, Lar	62	145	11	30	35	5	0	0	10	3	0	14	2	30	2	1	.207
Saldana, Ruben, Mon	99	292	18	64	75	6	1	1	19	7	2	22	2	39	3	8	.219
Salinas, Hilario, Cor	4	9	0	2	2	0	0	0	0	0	0	0	0	0	0	0	.222
Salinas, Mercedes, Chi	70	187	12	36	39	3	0	0	16	11	4	8	2	20	1	0	.193
Sanchez, Celerino, Coa	99	359	44	102	154	15	2	11	56	0	3	31	1	40	1	5	.284
Sanchez, Leonides, PR	66	191	18	47	49	2	0	0	10	4	0	12	0	17	1	2	.246
Sanchez, Raul, Lag*	96	313	40	80	105	9	8	0	39	4	2	40	2	34	8	6	.256
Sanders, Clement R., Mon	88	310	26	71	90	5	1	4	25	1	6	38	0	54	9	5	.229
Sandoval, Rodolfo, Rey	57	175	16	42	50	8	0	0	18	0	2	11	0	20	0	1	.240
Santana, Blas, Lag	133	513	66	157	195	17	6	3	48	12	2	18	6	38	10	7	.306
Santiago, Jose, Lag	19	38	2	8	12	1	0	1	4	0	1	0	0	9	1	0	.211
Sauceda, Ramiro, Mon	5	1	1	1	1	0	0	0	0	0	0	0	0	0	0	0	1.000
Sauceda, Victor, Mon	103	359	28	80	101	13	1	2	29	7	1	13	6	71	20	12	.223
Serna, Manuel, Rey	119	406	50	99	129	12	0	6	37	16	3	50	2	63	4	8	.244
Serratos, Ramon, Rey	89	219	39	51	63	6	3	0	12	0	0	22	0	24	11	4	.233
Silverio, Tomas, Tam*	134	487	73	152	219	23	7	10	54	8	8	61	1	75	11	8	.312
Solis, Jesus, Lar	1	1	0	0	0	0	0	0	0	0	0	0	0	0	0	0	.000
Sommers, Jesus, Pue	137	538	81	157	234	26	3	15	79	2	5	38	4	61	2	3	.292
Sosa, Emilio, PR	24	64	3	11	11	0	0	0	2	7	0	6	0	7	0	0	.172
Sosa Pena, Fausto, PR	6	10	1	3	3	0	0	0	1	0	0	0	0	1	0	0	.300
Soto M., Carlos, Lar	26	71	4	12	16	1	0	2	5	0	1	5	1	20	0	0	.169
Soto, Gregorio, Ags	14	15	0	0	0	0	0	0	0	0	0	1	0	6	0	0	.000
Soto, Jose, Jua*	1	1	0	0	0	0	0	0	0	0	0	0	0	0	0	0	.000
Sposito, Gustavo V., 59 Chi-32 Ags-28 Sal	119	425	48	120	150	12	6	2	43	8	4	36	0	43	12	9	.282
Stennett, Renaldo, Rey*	45	184	16	53	63	1	0	3	16	0	2	4	3	15	2	3	.288
Suarez, Miguel, Mex. R*	132	492	62	171	202	18	5	1	53	12	0	24	3	25	2	1	.348
Talley, Joseph, Pue*	132	456	82	147	252	33	3	22	87	0	7	82	0	104	8	5	.322
Terrazas, Martin, 6 Tig-4 Cor	10	14	0	2	2	0	0	0	2	0	0	2	0	2	1	0	.143
Texidor, Esteban, Tam	4	5	0	2	2	0	0	0	0	0	0	0	0	1	0	0	.400
Thompson, Albert, Lar	24	84	7	13	27	2	0	4	12	0	1	14	1	19	1	0	.155
Tiburcio, Edgardo, M. Tig*	102	306	26	84	98	9	1	1	36	7	3	35	1	40	0	6	.275
Torres, Jose Nemesio, Mon	15	20	0	1	1	0	0	0	2	0	0	3	0	6	1	1	.050
Torres, Reyes, Chi	132	460	47	117	136	12	2	1	41	9	3	23	5	63	5	3	.254
Torres, Victor, Tam	24	96	6	30	35	5	0	0	12	0	2	2	1	4	2	1	.313
Tovar, Jose de Jesus, Coa	92	183	18	32	35	3	0	0	7	6	2	11	0	42	3	0	.175
Trevino, Carlos, 51 Coa-3 Lar-34 Sal	88	290	30	71	92	12	0	3	40	3	3	25	2	44	1	0	.245
Trevino, Juan, 3 Cor-70 Sal	73	222	22	52	61	7	1	0	20	7	1	7	1	27	1	0	.234
Valdez, Jose Humberto, M.Tig	3	0	1	0	0	0	0	0	0	0	0	0	0	0	0	0	.000
Valenzuela, Carlos, Rey	127	389	35	106	128	19	0	1	36	7	0	50	5	67	0	6	.272
Valenzuela, Jose Maria, Dur	115	374	35	94	123	16	5	1	36	11	4	24	2	82	1	4	.251
Valle, Guadalupe, M.Tig	74	136	13	17	30	4	3	1	13	3	0	4	2	48	2	0	.125
Valle, Hector, Jua	6	22	1	6	7	1	0	0	3	0	0	0	0	2	0	0	.273

Player and Club	G.	AB.	R.	H.	TB.	2B.	3B.	HR.	RBI.	SH.	SF.	BB.	HP.	SO.	SB.	CS.	Pct.
Vallejano, Rodolfo, Tam	1	1	0	0	0	0	0	0	0	0	0	0	0	0	0	0	.000
Vazquez M., Efrain, Lar†	106	392	55	131	176	28	4	3	55	1	4	35	2	40	2	4	.334
Vazquez, Nicolas, Coa	123	445	48	126	154	15	2	3	37	3	2	38	4	56	2	5	.283
Vega, Abelardo, Mex.R	118	392	44	106	143	18	5	3	52	4	4	47	7	53	3	5	.270
Vega, Valenciano, Jua	67	194	16	51	62	4	2	1	17	7	1	4	0	15	0	3	.263
Velo, Waldo, Dur	1	1	0	1	1	0	0	0	0	0	0	0	0	0	0	0	1.000
Villaescusa, Antonio, Mex.R	132	479	63	134	170	24	6	0	49	10	6	11	9	45	19	10	.280
Villagomez, David, Mex.R	7	13	1	1	1	0	0	0	0	0	0	0	8	0	0		.077
Villalobos, Gonzalo, Ags	128	476	42	123	140	9	4	0	46	6	2	24	0	52	5	8	.258
Villalobos, Lauro, Dur	134	441	46	120	133	9	2	0	31	12	1	25	3	33	11	10	.272
Villarreal, Glen, Lar	24	58	7	16	18	2	0	0	6	1	1	6	0	3	1	1	.276
Villela, Rig Pascual, Dur	122	434	34	106	129	10	2	3	48	1	4	25	2	56	4	2	.244
Walseth, Michael, Pue*	137	512	93	171	273	24	3	24	107	1	5	71	3	67	0	1	.334
Webster, Ramon Alb, Sal*	70	260	31	67	88	11	2	2	21	5	4	19	1	18	4	3	.258
Wilkins, Vernon L., Tam*	13	27	3	5	6	1	0	0	4	0	2	4	0	4	1	0	.185
Williams, James, 13 Mon-46 Jua-59 Chi	118	416	43	111	143	17	6	1	47	2	7	41	6	57	4	7	.267
Wissell, Richard J., Rey*	93	326	33	84	119	20	3	3	39	3	3	23	0	38	1	1	.258
Yepez, Francisco, PR	123	362	46	80	97	9	4	0	22	10	0	39	8	49	7	5	.221
Zamudio, Hector, M.Tig	95	364	49	100	124	14	2	2	21	3	1	20	3	35	25	13	.275
Zabala, Faustino, Cor	8	25	4	6	6	0	0	0	3	1	1	1	1	3	0	0	.240
Zavala, Alfredo, Pue	34	99	9	29	33	4	0	0	4	2	1	5	0	14	0	0	.293
Zuniga, Faustino, Pue	36	112	13	21	28	4	0	1	4	1	0	6	2	20	0	0	.188

The following pitchers had no plate appearances primarily through use of designated-hitters, listed alphabetically by club, games in parentheses:

AGUASCALIENTES—Abraham, Brian (11); Byron Quiroz, Ricardo (19); Cervantes, Antonio (6); Cervantes, Lauro (6); Figueroa, Agustin (17); Garcia, Ruben (33); Hernandez S., Rafael (5); Marcano, Gilberto (21); Pina, Horacio (27); Sanchez, Salvador (2); Valle, Urbano (18).

CHIHUAHUA—Adame, Arnulfo (29); Allen, James (13); Guzman, Ramon (42); Jacobo, Elias (4); Martinez, Gabriel (2); Montoya, Saul (26); Pena, Paulino (4); Rios, Wilfredo (9); Sandoval, Rodrigo (11); Soto, J. Francisco (35); Tafoya, Daniel (4).

COAHUILA—Baney, Richard (6); Barbosa, Antonio (9); Buentello, Israel (33); Cisneros, Alfonso (46); Cutler, Bradley (12); Dominguez, Herminio (23); Esquivel, Saul (12); Lee, Won Kuk (29); Rauch, Robert (17); Solis M., Francisco (28); Tatar, Jay (5); Vega, Fernando Luis (7).

CORDOBA—Arano, Ramon (29); Barojas, Salome (15); Castillo, Enrique (9); Gutierrez, Pablo (32); Lagunas, Crescencio (29); Pena, Jose (34); Pizarro, Juan Ramon (20); Romo, Vicente (25); Uzcanga, Gilberto (3).

DURANGO—Acosta L., Eduardo (16); Cazares, Sergio (9); Felix, Jose (10); Figueroa, Domingo (8); Holly, Jeffrey (5); Moran, C. William (13); Norton, Thomas (22); Saucedo, Oscar (15); Uresti, Crisanto (3).

JUAREZ—Aguilar, Rafael (29); Fajardo, Ignacio (36); Garcia, Rafael (25); Hambright, Roger (36); Lersch, Barry (36); Lozano, Francisco (36); Orea, Diacono (38); Snook, Frank (3).

MEXICO CITY REDS—Gamez, Rodrigo (12); Hutson, G. Herbert (22); Jimenez, Juan (10); Lopez, Aurelio (59); Pereda, Pablo (2); Reynoso, Jesus (2); Rodriguez, Manuel (31); Romo, Enrique (29); Shanahan, P. Gregory (22).

MEXICO CITY TIGERS—Agundez, Victor (37); Delgado, Julio (3); Icedo, Enrique (12); Johnson, Tomas (9); Limon, Jose (5); Lopez, Fernando (40); Munguia, Ramon (5); Nuno, Ramiro (32); Pina, Javier R. (2); Raygoza, Guillermo (7); Saldivar, Arturo (1); San Miguel, Jesus (27); Suby, Juan (11); Villanueva, Luis (44).

MONTERREY—Bernal, Othon (1); Carrasco, Carlos (28); Cruz, Concepcion (30); Garcia, Jose Luis (11); Henninger, Richard (33); Martinez H., Francisco (42); Penalver, Luis (38); Rodriguez, Pilar (9); Troedson, Richard (12); Volkening, Larry (23).

NUEVO LAREDO—Acosta M., Eduardo (4); Ayon, Andres (3); Campbell, Richard (6); Delfin, Justino (15); Fox, Timothy (3); Kekich, Michael (10); Mellado, Oscar (4); Palacios, Raul (1); Valdivia, Miguel (2); Valenzuela, Hector (41).

POZA RICA—Brunet, George (30); Cavanaugh, Carl (29); Franco, David (22); Hernandez, Angel (39); Madrigal, Hector (38); Moroyoqui, Regino (5); Saldana, Eulogio (10); Sandate, Ricardo (31).

PUEBLA—Acosta, Cecilio (28); Beltran, Manuel (27); Bracamontes, Ignacio (27); Ezcarrega, Ernesto (28); Monteagudo, Aurelio (31); Mota, Francisco (30); Nevarez, Ismael (3); Officer, James (4); Pereira, Manuel (33); Salomon, Porfirio (27).

REYNOSA—Aponte, Bonifacio (28); Campoy, Alejandro (29); Lanfranco, Guadalupe (30); Nagy, Michael (30); Ochoa, Jose Roberto (22); Salgado, Octavio (33); Salinas, Guadalupe (30).

SALTILLO—Ahumada, Alejo (28); Armas, Tomas (27); Gage-Cole, Murray (17); Goodwin, Donnell (20); McCoy, Patrick (26); Menendez, Rolando (1); Solis, Miguel (25); Soto, Alvaro (33); Verdugo, Roberto (18).

TAMPICO—Almada, Guillermo (9); Maya, Antonio (1); Nieto, Rodolfo (4); Olivo, Milciades (10); Ryerson, Gary (30).

UNION LAGUNA—Beltran, Eleazar (22); Beltran, Margarito (4); Bonfils, Peter (35); Castillo, Andres (22); Gonzalez, Guillermo (44); Oliva, Ernesto (2); Pena, Manuel (11); Pollorena, Antonio (32); Torres F., Jesus (1); Tovar, Pedro (31).

TWO CLUBS—DeLaTorre, Adolfo (12 Union Laguna, 9 Durango); Fabela, Wilfredo (15 Mexico City Reds, 8 Chihuahua); Gamez, Raul (1 Nuevo Laredo, 28 Puebla); Garcia, Victor (9 Tampico, 27 (Nuevo Laredo); Hernandez, David (3 Saltillo, 18 Nuevo Laredo, 6 Coahuila); Kokor, Steven (12 Aguascalientes, 18 Chihuahua); Lara, Gilberto (20 Nuevo

Laredo, 6 Saltillo); Martinez A., Francisco (10 Nuevo Laredo, 10 Coahuila); Maytorena, Francisco (9 Tampico, 30 Union Laguna); Meza, Alfredo (29 Mexico City Tigers, 6 Saltillo); Munoz, Adan (18 Cordoba, 10 Puebla); Orea, Ignacio (1 Reynosa, 4 Juarez); Perez, Gregorio (10 Aguascalientes, 14 Chihuahua); Sifuentes, Francisco (3 Cordoba, 16 Nuevo Laredo); Valenzuela, Humberto (7 Mexico City Reds, 11 Nuevo Laredo); Valles, Reynaldo (2 Tampico, 10 Cordoba).

GRAND-SLAM HOME RUNS—Diaz Rdz., Espino, A. Orozco, Pactwa, Pierce, 2 each; Batista, A. Briones, Brookins, Canada, Clark, Dugan, T. Ford, Rodolfo Hernandez, Howard, M. Juarez, Kilpatrick, King, F. Lara, Lee, G. Lugo, Martinez C., Matias, Rafael Ornelas, Paredes, F. Rodriguez, Thompson, A. Vega, 1 each.

AWARDED FIRST BASE ON INTERFERENCE—H. Garcia 4 (Navarrete, L. Peralta, G. Rodriguez, M. Salinas); Alcaraz 3 (Koegel, Navarrete, L. Peralta); J. Aguilar (G. Rodriguez), F. Chavez (E. Rivera), D. Cruz (E. Briones), Espino (G. Rodriguez), Gongora (G. Rodriguez), Marquez (L. Peralta), H. Martinez (L. Peralta), V. Peralta (A. Orozco), C. Rivera (M. Salinas), F. Rodriguez (L. Peralta), Ruiz (E. Briones), Saiz (L. Peralta), Webster (Barron).

CLUB FIELDING

Club	G.	PO.	A.	E.	DP.	PB.	Pct.	Club	G.	PO.	A.	E.	DP.	PB.	Pct.
Saltillo	133	3333	1529	110	138	15	.978	Durango	134	3390	1550	146	153	25	.971
Cordoba	132	3324	1449	111	116	19	.977	Reynosa	136	3486	1521	149	120	26	.971
Union Laguna	137	3474	1393	115	133	12	.977	Tampico	134	3456	1555	153	122	12	.970
Monterrey	134	3480	1550	124	144	11	.976	Chihuahua	135	3360	1377	149	112	19	.970
Coahuila	127	3228	1326	126	111	21	.973	Mexico Tigers	132	3327	1441	151	121	20	.969
Mexico Reds	138	3504	1479	138	97	25	.973	Aguascalientes	136	3495	1570	167	167	21	.968
Juarez	136	3429	1476	141	103	14	.972	Poza Rica	135	3366	1415	159	93	23	.967
Puebla	137	3522	1572	150	136	15	.971	Nuevo Laredo	136	3495	1510	180	112	29	.965

Triple Play—Reynosa.

INDIVIDUAL FIELDING

*Throws lefthanded.

FIRST BASEMEN

Player and Club	G.	PO.	A.	E.	DP.	Pct.	Player and Club	G.	PO.	A.	E.	DP.	Pct.
Walseth, Pue.	17	145	4	0	11	1.000	Fritz, Ags*	51	379	34	5	47	.988
Osuna, Jua	10	84	6	0	6	1.000	King, Coa	29	228	17	3	20	.988
Alcaide, Ags*	10	63	3	0	11	1.000	Sanders, Mon	87	856	39	11	72	.988
Hto. Garcia, Rey	54	441	33	1	40	.998	Rod. Hdz., Dur-Cor	19	144	13	2	21	.987
Wissell, Rey*	47	400	33	1	37	.998	Parra, Cor-Lar	72	580	35	8	41	.987
C. Garza, M. Tig.	25	203	13	1	15	.995	Dugan, Coa	54	428	22	6	44	.987
Ibarra, Lag*	42	194	7	1	18	.995	Koegel, PR	26	203	9	3	13	.986
Webster, Sal*	44	384	16	2	30	.995	L. Lopez, Tam	30	261	17	4	18	.986
Espino, Tam	76	700	50	4	66	.995	Saldana, Mon	27	240	14	4	26	.984
CERVANTES, M. Tig	105	914	63	6	79	.9938	Camarero, Ags	59	406	35	7	51	.984
F. Felix, Lag	111	903	46	6	98	.9937	Alvarez, Lar*	71	601	40	11	59	.983
Bourque, M. Reds*	104	871	65	6	60	.9936	Hart, Ags	12	96	9	2	10	.981
Blanco, Jua	125	1061	57	8	91	.993	Valencian, Dur	22	151	3	3	10	.981
Rosario, M. Reds*	30	240	18	2	18	.992	Pettaway, PR-Sal*	49	472	26	10	46	.980
Batista, Cor*	121	1069	76	9	93	.992	Pierce, Pue	119	1076	65	23	103	.980
Breazeale, Dur	102	895	39	8	107	.992	Galliher, Rey	32	282	23	7	27	.978
C. Trevino, Coa-Lar-Sal	78	652	43	6	63	.991	Howard, Tam	16	122	6	3	12	.977
Oquendo, Sal-Pr*	72	375	17	4	39	.990	Calvo, Ags	26	199	20	6	28	.973
Robles, PR*	56	423	32	5	31	.989	Martinez, Mon	19	129	4	4	18	.971
Lopez, Chi	126	1030	56	12	88	.989	Diaz Rdz., PR	12	90	4	3	7	.969
Faudoa, Chi*	12	86	3	1	6	.989	Clayton, Mon	10	46	4	2	2	.962
							Colon, PR*	13	116	7	5	8	.961

Triple Play—Garcia.

(Fewer Than Ten Games)

Player and Club	G.	PO.	A.	E.	DP.	Pct.	Player and Club	G.	PO.	A.	E.	DP.	Pct.
Lopez, Lag	8	72	2	0	6	1.000	Davalillo, Pue*	2	2	1	0	0	1.000
R. Leon, Tam*	7	68	6	0	5	1.000	McRae, Chi	2	2	0	0	0	1.000
J.M. Lopez, Rey	7	69	4	0	4	1.000	Peralta, Jua	1	2	0	0	1	1.000
Christiansen, Lag	4	29	1	0	1	1.000	Orozco, Jua	1	1	0	0	0	1.000
O. Plascencia, M. Tig.	4	28	0	0	2	1.000	Payan, Chi	1	1	0	0	1	1.000
Robinson, Mon	3	26	1	0	4	1.000	Morales, Chi	1	1	0	0	0	1.000
Bouorquez, Cor	2	22	1	0	2	1.000	Leal, Lar	1	1	0	0	0	1.000
Salado, Cor	2	12	1	0	0	1.000	Congora, Tam	7	46	1	1	1	.979
A. Martinez, Lar	2	12	0	0	0	1.000	Fabela, Coa	9	40	3	1	7	.977
Bravo, Ags*	5	11	0	0	1	1.000	Thompson, Lar*	5	38	2	1	1	.975
Soto, Lar	1	8	0	0	1	1.000	Clark, Mex Reds	5	37	0	1	2	.974
Duran, Cor*	1	7	0	0	1	1.000	Arvizu, Pue	4	28	2	1	6	.968
Ortiz U., M. Reds*	1	7	0	0	0	1.000	C. Morales, Pue	3	26	1	1	3	.964
Perez, Lag	4	6	0	0	1	1.000	Matias, Jua*	7	22	4	1	2	.963
JM. Hdz., Dur	2	6	0	0	0	1.000	Paul, Tam*	4	35	4	2	1	.951
Guzman, Dur	1	5	0	0	1	1.000	Pactwa, Tam*	2	7	1	1	1	.889
JM. Ortiz, Mon	2	4	0	0	1	1.000	Mariscal, PR*	1	6	1	1	0	.875
Castro, Coa	1	4	0	0	0	1.000	Camargo, Mon	1	6	0	1	0	.857
Osv. Ortiz, Rey	1	4	0	0	0	1.000							

SECOND BASEMEN

Player and Club	G.	PO.	A.	E.	DP.	Pct.	Player and Club	G.	PO.	A.	E.	DP.	Pct.
Zavala, Pue	13	29	29	0	5	1.000	Robles, Ags	13	17	14	1	4	.969
MENDEZ, Dur	128	347	389	7	94	.991	M. Lazaro, Lag	71	145	155	10	31	.968
Castro, Coa	97	205	233	5	59	.989	Hernandez, M. Tig	53	104	112	8	22	.964
J. M. Ortiz, Mon	125	320	369	9	57	.987	Garcia, Tam-Cor	43	93	115	8	28	.963
Alcaraz, Cor	110	248	277	8	58	.985	A. Lazaro, Lag	68	136	121	10	44	.963
Briones, Jua	136	342	394	14	80	.981	Sanchez, PR	62	120	160	11	38	.962
Lugo, Dur	132	292	374	13	89	.981	Tovar, Coa	58	95	83	7	18	.962
Hernandez, Mex. Reds	128	311	342	13	56	.980	Figueroa, Lar	96	230	221	18	54	.962
Lara, PR	14	22	28	1	5	.980	Calvo, Ags	13	23	27	2	5	.962
Zamudio, M. Tigers	71	159	183	7	42	.980	Serratos, Rey	52	107	116	9	28	.961
Chavez, Lag-Tam	118	312	326	16	82	.976	Reyes Torres, Chi	132	340	324	27	78	.961
Serna, Rey	94	223	244	13	43	.973	Salazar, Lar	42	96	95	8	16	.960
Fuentes, PR	27	30	39	2	9	.972	V. Escalante, M. Tig	16	32	34	4	5	.943
Chavez, Pue	130	320	335	19	91	.972	Aguilar, Ags	13	24	25	3	11	.942
Guerrero, Ags	116	330	330	20	99	.971	Ed. Cervantes, Chi	16	17	13	2	6	.938
Oliveras, PR	39	89	104	6	21	.970	Cesar Lara, Coa	19	22	31	4	6	.930

Triple Play—Serratos.

(Fewer Than Ten Games)

Player and Club	G.	PO.	A.	E.	DP.	Pct.	Player and Club	G.	PO.	A.	E.	DP.	Pct.
Hernandez, Dur	7	17	22	0	6	1.000	Prieto, Cor	2	2	1	0	0	1.000
Espinosa, Mon	7	16	20	0	4	1.000	Ramirez, Lag	2	1	1	0	1	1.000
Alvarez, Cor	5	11	15	0	3	1.000	Clayton, Mon	1	0	2	0	0	1.000
Torres, Mon	8	14	10	0	7	1.000	Flores, Mon	1	1	1	0	0	1.000
Ortiz, Rey	6	11	12	0	4	1.000	Rodriguez, Mon	1	1	1	0	1	1.000
Gustavo Gil, PR	7	9	12	0	4	1.000	Morales, Chi	2	0	1	0	0	1.000
Howard, Tam	4	8	12	0	4	1.000	Arvizu, PR	1	0	1	0	0	1.000
Vega, Mex. Reds	3	5	14	0	1	1.000	Martinez, Dur	1	0	1	0	0	1.000
E. Leon, Tam	4	8	6	0	4	1.000	Camarero, Ags	1	0	1	0	0	1.000
Rivera, M. Tigers	8	8	4	0	1	1.000	Saldana, Mon	5	8	5	1	3	.929
Sposito, Sal	1	7	2	0	0	1.000	Ashford, Lar	3	6	5	1	1	.917
Fausto Sosa, PR	3	6	2	0	0	1.000	Aguirre, Mex. Reds	9	17	15	3	2	.914
Hernandez, Cor	2	3	3	0	0	1.000	Diaz, Rey	1	5	2	1	1	.875
Barron, Mex. Reds	1	2	3	0	0	1.000	Lopez, Lag	2	0	5	1	0	.833
Munoz, M. Tigers	1	2	2	0	0	1.000	Arano, Lar	1	3	1	1	0	.800
Contreras, Pue	2	3	0	0	0	1.000	Figueroa, Tam	1	1	0	1	1	.500

SHORTSTOPS

Player and Club	G.	PO.	A.	E.	DP.	Pct.	Player and Club	G.	PO.	A.	E.	DP.	Pct.
Ramirez, Dur	11	9	12	0	4	1.000	Arvizu, PR	10	15	23	2	4	.950
RODRIGUEZ, Mon	113	194	383	13	64	.978	Morales, Chi	62	75	141	12	21	.947
Gener Rivero, Cor	116	192	397	16	61	.974	Ramirez, Chi	93	145	242	23	49	.944
Raul Montoya, Jua	94	189	286	15	44	.969	J. Hernandez, Lar	136	265	514	49	74	.941
Rodriguez, Ags	128	235	438	23	88	.967	Vega, Jua	35	54	121	12	17	.936
Lopez, Lag	128	238	416	23	71	.966	M. Lazaro, Lag	10	9	20	2	5	.935
Jimenez, Pue	131	250	476	28	77	.963	Valle, M. Tigers	49	47	120	12	18	.933
Espinosa, Mon-Rey	57	100	159	10	28	.963	Escalante, M. Tig-Tam	35	44	57	8	9	.927
Mendoza, Coa	122	219	399	24	74	.963	Diaz, Rey	37	62	101	13	18	.926
Chavez, Sal	126	247	447	27	90	.963	Montes, Rey	21	34	51	7	8	.924
Grijalva, Rey	25	35	77	5	10	.957	Aguilar, Ags	14	18	39	5	7	.919
Villaescusa, Mex. Reds	132	259	400	30	50	.956	Bulm. Garcia, Cor	10	5	17	2	3	.917
Rivera, M. Tigers	101	184	337	25	47	.954	Rod. Hdz.,Dur-Cor	19	27	48	7	8	.915
Yepez, PR	121	179	361	26	61	.954	Elizondo, Sal	16	22	35	6	3	.905
Villalobos, Dur	130	264	435	34	95	.954	Zavala, Pue	10	13	22	5	3	.875
Serna, Rey	32	52	71	6	16	.953	Lizarraga, Tam	10	6	16	4	3	.846
E. Leon, Tam	114	184	359	27	69	.953							

Triple Play—Serna.

(Fewer Than Ten Games)

Player and Club	G.	PO.	A.	E.	DP.	Pct.	Player and Club	G.	PO.	A.	E.	DP.	Pct.
Gil, PR	4	3	9	0	2	1.000	Lara, PR	2	1	0	0	0	1.000
Chavarin, Rey	4	7	2	0	1	1.000	Sosa, PR	2	0	1	0	0	1.000
Lara, Coa	1	3	4	0	1	1.000	O. Plascencia, M. Tig	1	1	0	0	0	1.000
Garza, M. Tigers	2	2	4	0	0	1.000	Mendoza, Jua	7	8	16	1	2	.960
Torres, Chi	6	2	3	0	0	1.000	Sanchez, PR	4	7	9	1	4	.941
Manuel Alvarez, Cor	5	3	2	0	0	1.000	Hernandez Z., M. Reds	7	10	12	2	0	.917
Sposito, Chi	2	2	2	0	0	1.000	Chavez, Lag	3	1	10	1	1	.917
Ortiz, Rey	1	1	3	0	0	1.000	Munoz, Jua	4	0	12	2	1	.857
Aguirre, Mex. Reds	1	2	0	0	0	1.000	Tovar, Coa	8	6	7	3	0	.813
Diaz, PR	2	1	1	0	0	1.000	Parker, Mon	5	3	9	4	4	.750
Lugo, Dur	1	1	1	0	0	1.000	Pineda, Ags	2	0	2	1	0	.667
Vega, Mex. Reds	1	1	1	0	0	1.000	Hernandez, Dur	1	0	1	1	0	.500

THIRD BASEMEN

Player and Club	G.	PO.	A.	E.	DP.	Pct.
Tovar, Coa	30	24	35	1	4	.983
SANTANA, Lag	133	166	298	15	27	.969
Rivera, M. Tigers	34	28	63	3	6	.968
Fuentes, PR	43	27	57	3	3	.966
Sanchez, Coa.	98	100	185	12	18	.960
Calvo, Ags	43	27	81	5	9	.956
Parker, Mon	42	28	78	5	8	.955
Elizondo, Sal	11	7	14	1	1	.955
Figueroa, Lar	24	24	36	3	2	.952
Garcia, Tam-Cor	23	14	45	3	2	.952
Mena, Sal	100	73	193	14	12	.950
Cerda, Dur	116	119	250	20	30	.949
Bojorquez, Cor-Tam	99	81	211	16	19	.948
Espinosa, Mon	25	24	66	5	5	.947
Saldana, Mon	56	48	111	9	14	.946
Brookins, Chi	58	45	95	8	7	.946
Ortiz, Rey	121	123	270	23	27	.945
Torres, Tam	24	20	47	4	4	.944
Vazquez, Lar	91	78	188	16	10	.943
Sommers, Pue	136	131	270	25	24	.941
Diaz Rdz., PR	85	75	193	17	18	.940
Vega, Mex. Reds	111	105	195	20	14	.938
Ramirez, Chi.	35	34	48	6	6	.932
R. Hdz., Dur-Cor	31	29	52	6	3	.931
Garza, M. Tigers	34	33	59	7	9	.929
Sposito, Chi-Ags-Sal	102	70	219	23	15	.926
Arvizu, PR	23	16	45	5	1	.924
Alvarez, Cor	96	71	201	23	14	.922
Aguirre, Mex. Reds	26	15	53	6	4	.919
Del Moral, Jua	116	126	246	34	19	.916
Noriega, Ags	75	68	105	16	14	.915
Martinez C., Mon.	28	13	39	5	8	.912
Garzon, M. Tigers	58	36	89	15	8	.893
O. Plascencia, M. Tig.	20	17	33	6	4	.893
Montoya, Jua	17	12	27	5	3	.886
Osuna, Lar	19	10	35	7	1	.865
Ramirez, Dur-Lag	12	7	12	4	2	.826

(Fewer Than Ten Games)

Player and Club	G.	PO.	A.	E.	DP.	Pct.
E. Leon, Tam	8	3	6	0	0	1.000
Anaya, Ags	5	4	5	0	0	1.000
Castro, Coa	3	5	4	0	1	1.000
Guerrero, Ags	4	0	6	0	1	1.000
Ortiz, Mon	3	1	2	0	1	1.000
Camarero, Ags	3	0	3	0	0	1.000
Orozco, Chi	1	3	0	0	0	1.000
Serna, Rey	3	1	1	0	0	1.000
F. Chavez, Tam	1	0	2	0	0	1.000
Rodriguez, Pue	2	0	1	0	0	1.000
Valle, M. Tigers	2	0	1	0	0	1.000
Cervantes, Chi	2	0	1	0	0	1.000
Williams, Chi	1	0	1	0	0	1.000
Ochoa, Cor	1	0	1	0	0	1.000
A. Lazaro, Lag	8	11	13	1	2	.960
Zavala, Pue	6	2	12	1	0	.933
Martinez, Rey	9	10	16	2	1	.929
Vega, Jua	2	5	6	1	2	.917
Alvarado, Cor	5	4	6	1	2	.909
L. Gutierrez, Cor	2	6	3	1	1	.900
Arano, Lar	5	3	12	2	0	.882
Villarreal, Lar	6	4	3	1	0	.875
Mendoza, Jua	4	1	6	1	0	.875
Barron, Mex. Reds	7	6	13	3	1	.864
Hernandez, Dur	5	3	11	3	1	.824
Chavarin, Rey	8	4	12	5	2	.762
Aguilar, Ags	7	1	6	3	1	.700
Howard, Tam	2	2	0	1	0	.667
Castillo, Rey	1	0	2	2	0	.500

OUTFIELDERS

Player and Club	G.	PO.	A.	E.	DP.	Pct.
Prieto, Cor	53	60	2	0	0	1.000
Zamudio, M. Tigers	27	32	5	0	0	1.000
Sosa, PR	22	27	3	0	1	1.000
Sposito, Chi-Ags	12	27	3	0	0	1.000
Fabela, Coa	18	30	0	0	0	1.000
Vega, Jua	25	24	5	0	0	1.000
Peralta, Jua	15	27	0	0	0	1.000
Rodriguez, Mex. R	10	16	1	0	1	1.000
Camarero, Ags	12	12	0	0	0	1.000
Gonzalez, PR	11	11	0	0	0	1.000
LEE, Mon	111	199	11	1	2	.9952
Ornelas, Sal	102	176	9	1	2	.9946
Enriquez, Chi	133	309	14	2	3	.994
Paredes, Cor	82	145	5	1	0	.993
Lara, Pue	128	230	16	2	3	.992
Suarez, Mex. Reds*	78	101	2	1	0	.990
Ford, D-Mex. R	100	176	16	2	1	.990
Faudoa, Chi*	89	179	13	2	2	.990
Munoz, M. Tigers	53	86	10	1	4	.990
Osuna, Jua	61	90	2	1	0	.989
Ford, Rey*	133	305	17	4	2	.988
Murrell, Dur-Lar-Sal	101	215	7	3	2	.987
Rodriguez, Lar*	34	71	3	1	0	.987
Lopez, Mex Reds	118	262	14	4	0	.986
V.M. Felix, Lag	108	200	6	3	1	.986
Cruz, Sal	113	190	11	3	0	.985
Davalillo, Pue*	122	310	15	5	2	.985
De Hoyos, Coah*	126	312	7	5	2	.985
Davila, Jua	105	227	12	4	1	.984
Aguirre, Mex Reds	33	57	1	1	0	.983
Juarez, Sal-Lar	120	271	16	5	2	.983
Clark, Mex Reds	114	216	12	4	4	.983
Brown, Lag	129	322	9	6	0	.982
Allen, Dur	66	156	8	3	0	.982
Crawford, Ags	90	155	7	3	3	.982
F. Felix, Lag	32	50	4	1	1	.982
Ashford, Lar	66	156	4	3	2	.982
Matias, Jua*	71	147	10	3	0	.981
Cantres, Rey	88	138	11	3	1	.980
L. Lopez, Tam	72	142	4	3	1	.980
Ornelas, Lag-Dur	65	135	11	3	0	.980
Nettles, Jua*	62	135	6	3	0	.979
V. Sauceda, Mon	95	220	10	5	0	.979
Gonzalez, Mon	66	129	6	3	0	.978
Villalobos, Ags	127	289	19	7	6	.978
R. Plascencia, M Tig	35	80	6	2	1	.977
Phillips, Coa	16	42	1	1	0	.977
Grant, Dur*	15	41	2	1	1	.977
Buckner, Mon*	76	118	10	3	2	.977
Saiz, PR*	84	119	8	3	0	.977
J. Perez, Ags*	19	38	4	1	1	.977
Garcia, Rey	70	120	1	3	0	.976
Silverio, Tam*	133	297	23	8	4	.976
Williams, Mon-Jua-Chi*	100	219	6	6	0	.974
Hernandez, Dur	44	70	5	2	1	.974
Bravo, Ags*	111	178	7	5	2	.974
Brookins, Chi	76	127	9	4	1	.971
Gamundi, M Tig	103	252	13	8	1	.971
Roque, Cor	121	344	17	10	2	.971
Munoz, Mon*	46	94	5	3	0	.971
Acosta, Lar*	87	156	6	5	1	.970
Canada, Lag	132	250	8	8	1	.970
Howard, Tam	50	62	1	2	1	.969
Cardona, Sal	76	138	14	5	3	.968
Duran, Cor*	39	58	2	2	0	.968
Vazquez, Coa	123	228	4	8	1	.967
Aguilar, M Tig	73	134	10	5	3	.966
Rubio, Lar	92	161	11	6	1	.966

OUTFIELDERS—Continued

Player and Club	G.	PO.	A.	E.	DP.	Pct.
Villela, Dur	108	186	14	7	3	.966
Figueroa, Tam	60	81	3	3	0	.966
Talley, Pue*	130	259	12	10	5	.964
Diaz Rdz., PR	19	27	0	1	0	.964
Dugan, Coa	15	27	0	1	0	.964
Alvarado, Cor	93	152	7	6	0	.964
Rodriguez, Jua	73	143	11	6	3	.963
Moore, Chi	52	96	4	4	0	.962
Garza, Lar-Rey*	25	46	4	2	0	.962
Alvarado, Tam*	81	141	6	6	1	.960
Colon, PR*	111	226	15	10	2	.960
Lolich, Chi	21	46	2	2	0	.960
Lara, M Tigers	129	244	21	12	4	.957
Diaz, PR	59	114	10	6	1	.954
Zuniga, Pue	29	56	6	3	0	.954
Robles, PR*	69	110	6	6	0	.951
Martinez, Rey	39	38	0	2	0	.950
Rosario, Mex Reds*	10	17	2	1	1	.950
Stennett, Rey	45	70	4	4	1	.949
Gutierrez, Cor	26	36	1	2	0	.949
Oquendo, Sal-PR*	64	91	7	6	0	.942
Valenzuela, Dur	19	30	2	2	1	.941
Blessitt, Coa	87	124	9	9	0	.937
Hernandez Lara, Rey	44	61	5	5	1	.930
Minoso, Dur	13	24	2	2	0	.929
Aguilar, Ags	59	56	7	5	2	.926
Kilpatrick, Dur-Cor*	58	89	5	8	0	.922
R. Leon, Tam*	15	26	3	3	0	.906
Martinez C., Mon	13	20	1	4	0	.840

(Fewer Than Ten Games)

Player and Club	G.	PO.	A.	E.	DP.	Pct.
Alou, Cor	6	16	0	0	0	1.000
Sanchez, Lag*	9	13	0	0	0	1.000
Calvo, Ags	8	10	1	0	0	1.000
Wilkins, Tam*	9	9	0	0	0	1.000
Villagomez, Mex R	6	9	0	0	0	1.000
Guzman, Tam	3	8	1	0	0	1.000
Morales, Pue	4	6	0	0	0	1.000
Lizarraga, Tam	3	6	0	0	0	1.000
Guerrero, Ags	6	3	2	0	0	1.000
Villalobos, Dur	3	4	1	0	1	1.000
Elguezabal, Pue	2	5	0	0	0	1.000
Mora, Ags	2	5	0	0	0	1.000
Noriega, Ags	2	5	0	0	0	1.000
Ochoa, Lar	1	4	1	0	0	1.000
Erac. Cervantes, Chi	5	4	0	0	0	1.000
Rodriguez, Dur	3	3	0	0	0	1.000
Walseth, Pue	3	3	0	0	0	1.000
Reyes, Cor	2	3	0	0	0	1.000
Montoya, Mex R	1	3	0	0	0	1.000
Guzman, M Tig	3	6	0	0	0	1.000
Davila, Cor*	2	2	0	0	0	1.000
Oliveras, PR	2	2	0	0	0	1.000
Perez, Lag	2	2	0	0	0	1.000
Gutierrez, Dur	1	1	1	0	0	1.000
Trevino, Lar	1	2	0	0	0	1.000
Bojorquez, Cor	5	1	0	0	0	1.000
Ramirez, Dur	3	1	0	0	0	1.000
Arauz, M. Tig*	2	1	0	0	0	1.000
Perez, Lar	2	1	0	0	0	1.000
Mendoza, Rey	1	1	0	0	0	1.000
Navarrete, Mex R	1	1	0	0	0	1.000
Pettaway, Sal*	1	1	0	0	0	1.000
Martinez, Lar	9	16	1	1	0	.944
Salazar, Lar	7	17	2	2	1	.905
Soto, Ags	9	8	0	1	0	.889
Alcaide, Ags*	5	11	2	2	0	.867
Cummings, Lar	6	9	1	2	0	.833
Barron, Mex R	4	4	0	1	0	.800
Gongora, Tam	4	3	0	1	0	.750
Alvarez, Lar*	5	5	0	2	0	.714
Moreno, Coa	3	1	0	1	0	.500

CATCHERS

Player and Club	G.	PO.	A.	E.	DP.	PB.	Pct.
Lugo, PR	24	112	11	0	0	2	1.000
Diaz Rdz., PR	12	80	0	0	0	4	1.000
Lizarraga, Jua	34	73	7	0	1	1	1.000
Heras, M. Tig	11	43	4	0	5	1	1.000
Orozco, Jua	38	124	13	1	1	5	.993
RIVERA, Sal-Cor	101	472	56	5	8	14	.991
Benitez, Ags	45	184	22	2	1	8	.990
Ruiz, Coa	99	532	77	6	6	13	.990
Luque, Sal	55	255	36	3	4	4	.990
Soto, Lar	16	77	20	1	0	5	.990
Salado, Cor	41	162	25	2	1	6	.989
Rosas, Dur-Lag	83	366	54	5	1	8	.988
Salinas, Chi	62	277	43	4	8	7	.988
Gongora, Tam	41	133	18	2	2	5	.987
Valenzuela, Dur	38	182	35	3	7	12	.986
Rey, Tam	93	464	42	7	5	5	.986
Guillen, Coa-Lar	48	183	19	3	1	11	.985
Valenzuela, Rey	126	623	89	11	7	23	.985
Peralta, PR	98	583	65	11	3	13	.983
Briones, Mon	102	412	53	8	0	7	.983
King, Coa	34	154	20	3	3	7	.983
Trevino, Cor-Sal	73	300	46	6	1	5	.983
Tiburcio, M. Tig	95	441	56	9	6	15	.982
Estrada, Pue	117	469	67	10	3	9	.982
Jackson, Lar	89	373	48	8	3	11	.981
Robinson, Mon	18	88	14	2	3	3	.981
Esquivel, Tam	25	129	15	3	2	2	.980
Marquez, Ags	99	493	65	13	15	13	.977
Navarrete, Mex R	82	373	54	10	1	10	.977
Christiansen, Lag	73	266	32	7	3	6	.977
Orozco, Chi	80	333	40	9	5	11	.976
Peralta, Jua	102	399	41	12	3	8	.973
Barron, Mex R	83	393	45	12	6	15	.973
Camargo, Mon	61	122	14	4	2	1	.971
Sandoval, Rey	11	57	11	2	2	0	.971
Molina, Ags	12	26	8	1	1	0	.971
Elguezabal, Pue	16	52	8	2	0	4	.968
R. Hernandez, Lar	14	45	7	2	1	3	.963
Rodriguez, Pue-Dur	85	369	56	17	5	12	.962
Mendoza, Rey	26	46	4	2	0	3	.962
Aguilar, M. Tig	36	132	10	6	2	4	.959
Koegel, PR	15	82	9	4	1	4	.958
Hernandez, Pue		19	3	4	0	0	.846

(Fewer Than Ten Games)

Player and Club	G.	PO.	A.	E.	DP.	PB.	Pct.
Garcia, Jua	6	20	2	0	0	1	1.000
Terrazas, M. Tig-Cor.	7	17	1	0	1	1	1.000
Corella, M. Tig	3	15	2	0	0	0	1.000
Alvarado, Cor	6	9	1	0	0	1	1.000
Hernandez, Dur	3	0	3	0	0	0	1.000
Morales, Tam	2	3	0	0	0	0	1.000
Salinas, Cor	1	3	0	0	0	0	1.000
Gonzalez, Lag	2	2	0	0	0	0	1.000
Castro, Lag	1	1	0	0	0	0	1.000
Prieto, Cor	1	1	0	0	0	0	1.000
Clark, Mex R	1	0	1	0	0	0	1.000
Valle, Jua	6	19	5	1	0	0	.960
Payan, Chi	5	13	3	1	0	1	.941
Gaytan, Sal	9	10	0	1	0	3	.909
Noriega, Ags	2	2	0	1	0	0	.667

PITCHERS

Player and Club	G.	PO.	A.	E.	DP.	Pct.
NAGY, Rey	30	15	58	0	2	1.000
Orea, Jua	38	17	40	0	1	1.000
Vallejano, Tam	31	15	41	0	4	1.000
Salomon, Pue	27	8	41	0	5	1.000
Ortiz, Mex R*	23	9	28	0	0	1.000
Madrigal, PR	38	4	32	0	0	1.000
Acosta L., Dur	16	9	25	0	3	1.000
Espinoza, M. Tig	43	10	23	0	0	1.000
Carrasco, Mon	28	6	27	0	4	1.000
Campoy, Rey	29	13	18	0	1	1.000
Cruz, Tam	21	8	23	0	2	1.000
Garcia, Tam-Lar	36	4	26	0	3	1.000
Valenzuela, Lar	41	5	24	0	0	1.000
Munoz, Cor-Pue	28	4	23	0	0	1.000
Lopez, Mex R	59	5	21	0	2	1.000
Chavez, Chi	33	10	15	0	1	1.000
Perez, Ags-Chih*	24	5	20	0	2	1.000
Maytorena, Tam-Lag	39	5	19	0	0	1.000
Agundez, M. Tig	37	7	17	0	1	1.000
Castillo, Rey	13	6	18	0	2	1.000
Castillo, Lag	22	3	19	0	3	1.000
Solis, Lar	36	3	17	0	2	1.000
Gutierrez, Cor	32	3	17	0	1	1.000
Valdez, M. Tig	39	3	16	0	1	1.000
Mota, Pue	30	2	16	0	1	1.000
Verdugo, Lar	18	4	14	0	1	1.000
Troedson, Mon*	12	3	15	0	2	1.000
Velo, Dur-Ags	36	5	12	0	1	1.000
Meza, M. Tig-Sal*	35	3	14	0	0	1.000
Hernandez, PR	39	3	13	0	2	1.000
Dominguez, Coa*	23	2	14	0	0	1.000
Valle, Ags*	18	3	13	0	1	1.000
Salgado, Rey	33	3	12	0	0	1.000
Mariscal, Sal-PR*	23	4	10	0	0	1.000
Kekich, Lar*	10	1	13	0	1	1.000
Fabela, Mex R-Chi	23	2	10	0	0	1.000
Sifuentes, Cor-Lar*	19	2	10	0	1	1.000
Pereira, Pue	33	2	9	0	0	1.000
Soto, Sal	33	1	8	0	2	1.000
Cruz, Mon	30	1	8	0	0	1.000
Martinez, Dur	19	3	4	0	0	1.000
Delfin, Lar	15	1	6	0	1	1.000
Saucedo, Dur	15	0	7	0	0	1.000
Gonzalez, Lag*	14	2	4	0	0	1.000
Olivo, Tam	10	2	4	0	0	1.000
Byron Quiroz, Ags	19	2	3	0	0	1.000
Esquivel, Coa	12	2	3	0	0	1.000
Suby, M. Tig	11	1	4	0	0	1.000
Vatias, Jua*	13	1	3	0	2	1.000
Garcia, Mon*	11	1	3	0	0	1.000
Contreras, Lar*	12	0	3	0	0	1.000
Sandoval, Chi	11	0	3	0	1	1.000
Escalante, M. Tig*	26	1	1	0	0	1.000
Pena, Lag*	11	0	2	0	0	1.000
Saldana, PR	10	0	2	0	0	1.000
Penalver, Mon	38	17	46	1	3	.984
Ahumada, Sal	28	11	39	1	5	.980
McCoy, Sal	26	15	33	1	1	.980
Diaz, Ags	24	11	36	1	5	.979
Arano, Cor	29	10	32	1	2	.977
Garcia, Lar-Tam	45	4	37	1	2	.976
Ezcarrega, Pue	28	9	31	1	3	.976
Soto, Chi	35	6	33	1	0	.975
Pizarro, Cor*	20	8	30	1	3	.974
Cordoba, Dur	31	10	27	1	3	.974
Brunet, PR*	30	8	28	1	0	.973
Garcia, Jua	25	11	24	1	0	.972
Acosta, Pue	28	3	31	1	0	.971
Bracamontes, Pue*	27	7	26	1	3	.971
G. Raygoza, M. Tig	47	8	23	1	2	.969
Buentello, Coa	33	8	23	1	1	.969
Armas, Sal*	27	2	28	1	0	.968
Texidor, Tam-Dur	17	7	19	1	1	.963

Player and Club	G.	PO.	A.	E.	DP.	Pct.
Villanueva, M. Tig*	44	6	19	1	3	.962
Leal, Lar	27	18	31	2	4	.961
Romo, Cor	25	16	33	2	2	.961
Pollorena, Lag	32	14	34	2	2	.960
Romo, Mex R	29	17	31	2	2	.960
Kokor, Ags-Chi	30	11	36	2	2	.959
Salinas, Rey	30	20	25	2	0	.957
Solis, Sal	25	8	37	2	2	.957
Beltran, Pue	27	5	17	1	0	.957
Guzman, Chi	42	1	20	1	0	.955
Pina, Ags	27	15	47	3	4	.954
Lersch, Jua	36	14	27	2	0	.953
Hernandez, Sal-Lar-Coa	27	12	28	2	4	.952
Norton, Dur	22	7	13	1	0	.952
Gutierrez, Dur*	21	1	18	1	2	.950
Lagunas, Cor	29	7	29	2	5	.947
Pena, Cor	34	17	36	3	6	.946
Mere, Mex R	31	7	28	2	1	.946
Hutson, Mex R	22	9	25	2	0	.944
Armas, Ags*	31	5	12	1	0	.944
Aguilar, Jua	29	3	14	1	0	.944
Gage Cole, Sal	17	6	11	1	0	.944
Moran, Dur	13	4	13	1	2	.944
Cutler, Coa*	12	4	13	1	1	.944
Aponte, Rey	28	5	28	2	1	.943
Gutierrez, Rey	23	7	26	2	2	.943
Bonfils, Lag*	35	9	40	3	1	.942
Solis, Coa*	28	3	13	1	1	.941
Montova, Chi*	26	7	8	1	0	.938
Paul, Tam*	24	6	37	3	2	.935
Cavanaugh, PR	29	12	28	3	1	.930
Moreno, Ags*	24	6	20	2	0	.929
Martinez, Lar-Coa	37	3	10	1	0	.929
Monteagudo, Pue	31	11	27	3	1	.927
Henninger, Mon	33	5	32	3	1	.925
Kuk Lee, Coa	29	8	36	4	3	.917
Volkening, Mon	23	7	26	3	5	.917
Lanfranco, Rey*	30	6	11	1	2	.917
Ochoa, Rey	22	5	6	1	0	.917
Barojas, Cor	15	2	9	1	1	.917
Adame, Chi	29	3	29	3	0	.914
Garcia, Ags	33	5	16	2	1	.913
Hambright, Jua	36	10	42	5	4	.912
Pactwa, Tam*	19	7	23	3	0	.909
McRae, Chi	27	5	25	3	1	.909
San Miguel, M. Tig	27	2	18	2	1	.909
Rauch, Coa	17	7	13	2	0	.909
Nieblas, Mon	20	2	8	1	0	.909
Jimenez, Mex R	10	2	8	1	0	.909
Tovar, Lag	31	9	20	3	0	.906
Shanahan, Mex R	22	4	25	3	2	.906
Ryerson, Tam*	30	6	41	5	1	.904
R. Lopez, Tam	28	6	22	3	0	.903
Martinez H., Mon*	42	3	34	4	2	.902
Fajardo, Jua	36	2	15	2	0	.895
Lopez, M. Tig	40	4	20	3	1	.889
Beltran, Lag	22	0	16	2	0	.889
De La Torre, Lag-Dur	21	4	12	2	1	.889
Lugo, Dur	21	0	8	1	0	.889
M. Rodriguez, Mex R	31	4	19	3	0	.885
Franco, PR	22	6	16	3	0	.880
Allen, Chi*	13	4	18	3	0	.880
Guzman, Dur	31	2	19	3	1	.875
Soto, Jua*	28	5	9	2	1	.875
Abraham, Ags*	11	3	10	2	1	.867
Goodwin, Sal	26	8	23	5	1	.861
Lozano, Jua*	36	4	8	2	0	.857
Abarca, Ags	20	5	7	2	0	.857
Marcano, Ags	21	14	15	5	0	.853
Sandate, PR*	31	10	33	8	0	.843
Nuno, M. Tig	32	3	12	3	1	.833
Gamez, Mex R*	12	1	4	1	0	.833

PITCHERS- Continued

Player and Club	G.	PO.	A.	E.	DP.	Pct.
Cisneros, Coa	46	0	9	2	0	.818
Gamez, Lar-Pue*	29	1	8	2	0	.818
Lara, Lar-Sal*	26	4	9	3	1	.813
Diaz, Rey	23	3	5	2	0	.800
Santiago, Lag	43	5	8	4	3	.765
Martinez A., Lar-Coa*	20	3	3	2	0	.750
Felix, Dur	10	2	4	2	1	.750
Figueroa, Ags	17	1	2	1	0	.750
Ibarra, Lag*	14	1	2	1	0	.750
Valenzuela, Mex R-Lar	18	3	5	3	1	.727
Bazan, Rey*	20	1	3	2	0	.667
Valles, Tam-Cor*	12	0	2	1	0	.667
Icedo, M Tig*	12	0	0	1	0	.000

(Fewer Than Ten Games)

Player and Club	G.	PO.	A.	E.	DP.	Pct.
Campbell, Lar*	6	3	8	0	1	1.000
Lee Baney, Coa	6	1	6	0	0	1.000
Rios, Chi*	8	0	6	0	0	1.000
Almada, Tam*	9	1	4	0	1	1.000
Gmo. Raygoza, M Tig	7	0	5	0	0	1.000
Officer, Pue*	4	1	4	0	0	1.000
Johnson, M Tig	9	2	2	0	0	1.000
A. Cervantes, Ags	6	0	4	0	0	1.000
Fox, Lar	3	1	3	0	1	1.000
Castillo, Cor	9	0	3	0	0	1.000
Arauz, M Tig*	5	1	2	0	0	1.000
Mellado, Lar	4	0	3	0	0	1.000
Reynoso, Mex R	2	1	2	0	0	1.000
Rodriguez, Mon	9	0	2	0	0	1.000
L. Cervantes, Ags	6	1	1	0	0	1.000
Davila, Cor*	5	1	1	0	0	1.000
Munguia, M Tig	5	0	2	0	0	1.000
Holly, Dur*	5	0	2	0	0	1.000
Hernandez S., Ags	5	1	1	0	0	1.000
Snook, Jua	3	1	1	0	1	1.000
Oliva, Lag	2	1	1	0	1	1.000
Saucedo, Mon	1	1	1	0	0	1.000
Cazares, Dur*	9	0	1	0	0	1.000
Limon, M Tig	5	0	1	0	0	1.000
Orea, Jua-Rey	5	0	1	0	0	1.000
Beltran, Lag	4	0	1	0	0	1.000
Nieto, Tam*	4	0	1	0	0	1.000
Uresti, Dur	3	0	1	0	0	1.000
Nevarez, Pue	3	0	1	0	0	1.000
Delgado, M Tig*	3	0	1	0	0	1.000
Valdivia, Lar	2	0	1	0	0	1.000
E. Leon, Tam	1	0	1	0	0	1.000
Avon, Lar	3	0	7	1	0	.875
Vega, Coa	7	1	6	1	0	.875
Barbosa, Coa*	9	2	9	2	1	.846
Figueroa, Dur*	8	0	2	1	0	.667
Acosta M., Lar	4	1	1	1	0	.667
Chavez, Tam	4	1	1	1	0	.667
Tatar, Coa	5	0	2	2	0	.500
Sanchez, Ags*	2	0	0	1	0	.000

NOTE: No compilation made of fielders who had no chances.

CLUB PITCHING

Club	G.	CG.	ShO.	Sv.	IP.	H.	R.	ER.	HR.	BB.	Int. BB.	HB.	SO.	WP.	Bk.	ERA.
Cordoba	132	63	18	20	1108	1054	422	324	48	330	50	43	552	17	0	2.63
Monterrey	134	70	12	7	1160	1168	450	344	53	337	70	24	562	24	1	2.67
Poza Rica	135	76	15	12	1122	1094	491	345	50	312	34	20	782	43	1	2.77
Tampico	134	61	21	9	1152	1145	479	360	61	341	32	42	642	36	2	2.81
Saltillo	133	76	14	10	1111	1098	457	369	61	357	37	26	539	40	5	2.99
Puebla	137	59	14	16	1174	1259	545	407	64	379	51	37	538	22	0	3.12
Reynosa	136	63	16	6	1162	1113	519	406	53	466	74	48	632	31	5	3.14
Coahuila	127	34	15	20	1076	1107	472	376	45	426	45	24	617	34	1	3.14
Mexico Reds	138	57	18	19	1168	1201	532	416	47	385	31	57	702	62	2	3.21
Juarez	136	62	11	12	1143	1167	505	413	52	403	48	41	523	41	4	3.25
Nuevo Laredo	136	45	15	10	1165	1214	599	440	66	404	32	20	606	58	3	3.40
Aguascalientes	136	56	8	16	1165	1227	633	453	67	541	65	60	633	56	2	3.50
Union Laguna	137	54	13	10	1158	1175	538	452	72	439	71	39	501	65	4	3.51
Durango	134	57	8	15	1130	1334	650	452	78	438	36	37	552	74	2	3.60
Chihuahua	135	57	10	9	1120	1212	584	452	61	471	49	47	554	37	2	3.63
Mexico Tigers	132	12	6	24	1109	1246	599	459	40	516	52	37	564	40	4	3.72

PITCHERS' RECORDS

(Leading Qualifiers for Earned-Run Average Leadership—110 or More Innings)

*Throws lefthanded.

Pitcher–Club	G.	GS.	CG.	ShO.	W.	L.	Sv.	Pct.	IP.	H.	R.	ER.	HR.	BB.	Int. BB.	HB.	SO.	WP.	ERA.
Ryerson, Tampico*	30	23	17	10	16	7	2	.696	184	150	43	31	0	35	3	2	122	3	1.52
Nagy, Reynosa	30	28	24	4	16	11	1	.593	232	195	71	47	4	56	9	7	113	4	1.82
Romo, Mexico Reds	29	27	19	5	20	4	0	.833	233	169	60	49	5	56	2	10	239	4	1.89
Moran, Durango	13	13	12	2	9	4	0	.692	112	88	36	24	5	25	0	3	88	4	1.93
Paul, Tampico*	24	23	12	6	11	7	0	.611	172	162	49	37	6	30	2	3	124	2	1.94
Martinez, H., Mon*	42	20	11	2	15	11	1	.577	193	183	51	43	6	60	13	8	120	2	2.01
Penalver, Mon	38	29	17	0	10	13	2	.435	251	240	83	57	12	44	7	2	133	1	2.04
Cisneros, Coahuila	46	3	0	0	5	4	15	.556	110	91	36	27	4	34	4	1	87	2	2.17
Sandate, Poza R*	31	29	22	4	14	13	1	.519	215	183	82	53	6	58	4	1	220	7	2.22
Hutson, Mex Reds	22	22	9	3	13	7	0	.650	154	147	52	38	3	53	2	5	62	5	2.22

Departmental Leaders: G—A. Lopez, 59; GS—Lersch, 33; CG—Pollorena, 26; ShO—Ryerson, 10; W—Pollorena, 20; L—Madrigal, 16; Sv—A. Lopez, 16; Pct.—Romo (MR), .833; IP—Pollorena, 252; H—Hambright, 248; R—Chavez (Chi), 103; HR—Armas (Sal), 18; BB—Bonfils, 95; IBB—Henninger, 17; HB—Pena (Cor), 18; SO—Romo (MR), 239; WP—Bonfils, 19.

OFFICIAL BASEBALL GUIDE

(All Pitchers—Listed Alphabetically)

Pitcher–Club	G.	GS.	CG.	ShO.	W.	L.	Sv.	Pct.	IP.	H.	R.	ER.	HR.	BB.	Int. BB.	HB.	SO.	WP.	ERA.
Abarca, Ags	20	7	1	0	4	4	0	.500	55	81	46	29	3	22	4	2	38	7	4.75
Abraham, Ags*	11	11	5	0	3	6	0	.333	64	79	48	33	4	20	4	0	35	3	4.64
Acosta, Pue	28	18	7	0	7	8	1	.467	124	157	73	52	8	46	6	8	53	2	3.77
Acosta L., Dur	16	16	7	1	6	8	0	.429	121	136	53	38	4	51	4	2	52	11	2.83
Acosta M., Lar	4	4	0	0	0	2	0	.000	18	38	20	15	3	1	0	0	8	0	7.50
Adame, Chi	29	12	6	2	6	6	2	.500	110	128	52	40	9	27	5	3	43	2	3.27
Aguilar, Jua	29	1	0	0	5	5	0	.500	77	95	33	27	3	27	2	5	21	5	3.16
Agundez, M.Tig	37	11	1	0	6	7	4	.462	106	133	52	45	5	30	11	0	30	6	3.82
Ahumada, Sal	28	27	15	3	14	9	0	.609	191	199	74	60	7	78	7	6	98	4	2.83
Allen, Chi*	13	10	2	0	2	6	1	.250	70	88	41	30	6	26	2	3	31	1	3.86
Almada, Tam*	9	1	1	0	0	2	0	.000	20	31	16	12	4	1	0	1	6	0	5.40
Aponte, Rey	26	14	2		10	11	0	.476	178	153	69	53	8	86	6	10	119	1	2.68
Arano, Cor	29	28	10	4	14	9	0	.609	184	197	72	59	10	39	9	5	75	2	2.89
Arauz, M.Tig*	5	0	0	0	0	0	0	.000	5	5	6	5	0	6	0	0	3	1	7.50
Armas, Ags*	31	0	0	0	0	5	3	.000	42	44	29	21	4	28	6	4	16	4	4.50
Armas, Sal*	27	23	17	2	10	12	1	.455	164	183	83	68	18	20	6	2	74	0	3.73
Ayon, Lar	3	3	1	0	1	2	0	.333	22	20	12	7	1	12	3	0	7	0	2.86
Baney, Coa	6	6	1	0	1	4	0	.200	33	35	12	11	4	10	1	0	9	0	3.00
Barbosa, Coa*	9	8	0	0	1	2	0	.333	36	43	18	13	1	9	0	0	24	1	3.25
Barojas, Cor	15	3	0	0	3	1	0	.750	43	32	12	9	2	14	2	3	17	2	1.88
Bazan, Rey*	20	0	0	0	0	2	0	.000	26	22	16	12	1	22	3	0	15	3	4.15
Beltran, E., Lag	22	13	2	0	4	7	0	.364	94	100	50	44	6	46	7	5	53	14	4.21
Beltran, M., Lag	4	0	0	0	0	1	0	.000	9	10	7	5	0	4	1	0	2	0	5.00
Beltran, Pue	27	5	2	0	5	5	3	.500	78	95	39	30	4	20	0	0	44	2	3.46
Bernal, Mon	1	0	0	0	0	0	0	.000	0	0	0	0	0	0	0	0	0	0	0.00
Bonfils, Lag*	35	32	12	0	15	8	1	.652	226	208	88	74	13	95	8	7	125	19	2.95
Bracamontes, Pue*	27	25	12	3	15	5	0	.750	186	191	66	46	10	44	1	4	88	0	2.23
Brunet, PR*	30	25	13	1	10	12	0	.455	172	193	89	63	7	74	4	1	132	13	3.30
Buentello, Coa	33	21	4	1	9	6	0	.600	140	148	60	50	6	52	5	4	67	6	3.21
Byron Quiroz, Ags	19	0	0	0	4	1	3	.800	32	35	31	19	2	29	5	6	24	6	5.34
Campbell, Lar*	6	6	1	0	1	3	0	.250	31	30	18	14	1	18	0	0	24	2	4.06
Campoy, Rey	29	13	3	1	5	10	0	.333	105	116	62	53	10	48	10	4	39	3	4.54
Carrasco, Mon	28	20	12	1	11	9	1	.550	169	178	64	50	11	47	7	3	61	4	2.66
Castillo, Lag	22	19	4	2	6	8	0	.429	109	114	62	55	8	54	6	1	49	12	4.54
Castillo, Cor	9	0	0	0	0	0	1	.000	11	15	2	2	1	8	3	0	5	0	1.64
Castillo, Rey	13	8	6	1	5	5	0	.500	72	52	16	14	1	36	4	4	56	1	1.75
Cavanaugh, PR	29	27	14	4	16	9	1	.640	182	209	80	59	10	33	4	11	99	9	2.92
Cazares, Dur*	9	1	0	0	0	2	0	.000	19	24	15	12	1	11	2	0	8	3	5.68
Cervantes, A., Ags	6	2	0	0	0	1	0	.000	18	17	12	9	1	10	0	1	6	0	4.50
Cervantes, L., Ags	6	0	0	0	0	0	0	.000	12	11	4	4	0	6	1	0	3	1	3.00
Chavez, Tam	4	0	0	0	0	0	0	.000	7	9	2	2	0	2	0	1	3	1	2.57
Chavez, Chi	33	31	17	0	15	13	0	.536	218	216	103	72	4	88	7	7	115	5	2.97
Cisneros, Coa	46	3	0	0	5	4	15	.556	112	91	36	27	4	34	4	1	87	2	2.17
Contreras, Lar*	12	2	0	0	0	2	0	.000	15	16	11	6	0	16	1	2	13	2	3.60
Cordova, Dur	31	27	11	2	10	15	0	.400	172	234	87	63	8	47	2	5	75	5	3.30
Cruz, Mon	30	0	0	0	1	6	2	.143	55	54	19	14	3	28	7	0	24	2	2.29
Cruz, Tam	21	15	4	0	3	11	1	.214	102	124	65	45	8	30	2	6	59	4	3.97
Cutler, Coa*	12	12	4	1	6	5	0	.545	70	90	39	30	6	16	2	2	20	0	3.86
Davila, Cor*	5	1	0	0	1	2	0	.333	8	13	3	1	0	7	5	0	4	0	1.13
DeLaTorre, 12 Lag-9 Du	21	8	3	1	2	7	0	.222	74	101	48	40	6	26	5	2	18	3	4.86
Delfin, Lar	15	0	0	0	2	4	4	.333	33	31	14	9	0	10	2	1	23	1	2.45
Delgado, M.Tig*	3	0	0	0	0	2	0	.000	4	4	6	6	0	7	0	0	2	0	13.50
Diaz, Ags	24	23	12	0	12	8	0	.600	173	165	79	54	12	82	7	8	79	11	2.81
Diaz, Rey	23	2	0	0	5	0	2	1.000	54	58	28	22	1	30	9	7	31	1	3.67
Dominguez, Coa	23	12	2	1	4	7	0	.364	95	121	46	40	3	47	2	1	55	1	3.79
Escalante, M.Tig*	26	3	0	0	3	2	1	.600	46	54	34	28	4	37	1	2	22	6	5.48
Espinosa, M.Tig	43	20	4	2	11	13	3	.458	146	159	74	59	6	71	5	5	93	0	3.64
Esquivel, Coa	12	2	0	0	1	1	0	.500	38	40	22	18	3	25	1	2	14	7	4.26
Ezcarrega, Pue	28	26	12	4	15	8	1	.652	178	201	91	69	9	52	8	2	62	3	3.49
Fabela, 15 M.Reds-8 Chi	23	5	0	0	2	1	0	.667	55	63	30	23	4	27	0	2	21	1	3.76
Fajardo, Jua	36	5	2	0	6	3	1	.667	70	74	40	31	1	31	5	4	18	2	3.99
Faudoa, Chi*	1	0	0	0	0	0	0	.000	1	0	0	0	0	0	0	0	0	0	0.00
Felix, Dur	10	7	1	0	1	2	0	.333	46	61	32	23	3	13	1	2	11	2	4.50
Figueroa, Ags	17	0	0	0	2	0	1	1.000	22	34	16	13	2	6	2	1	4	0	5.32
Figueroa, Dur*	8	4	0	0	1	4	0	.200	22	31	21	14	3	16	2	2	13	1	5.73
Fox, Lar	3	3	1	0	0	2	0	.000	17	16	7	6	0	8	1	0	8	0	3.18
Franco, PR	20	7	0		7	7	0	.500	125	123	55	37	5	44	3	1	55	6	2.66
Gage-Cole, Sal	17	5	0	0	2	3	1	.400	52	57	29	20	5	21	4	3	19	2	3.46
Gamez, 1 Lar-28 Pue*	29	6	0	0	3	3	0	.500	22	22	7	4	1	10	3	0	10	0	1.64
Gamez, Mex.R*	12	1	0	0	0	0	0	.000	8	23	16	14	0	17	2	0	6	3	15.75
Garcia, Mon*	11	0	0	0	1	0	0	.000	3	3	3	3	0	3	0	0	2	6	4.74
Garcia, 12 Lar-33 Tam	45	9	3	0	9	9	3	.500	147	155	63	44	3	32	5	5	67	7	2.69
Garcia, Jua	25	21	15	2	11	8	2	.579	155	143	60	52	5	73	2	3	122	12	3.02

Pitcher–Club	G	GS	CG	ShO	W	L	Sv	Pct.	IP	H	R	ER	HR	BB	Int. BB	HB	SO	WP	ERA
Garcia, Ags	33	14	5	0	7	8	4	.467	123	141	64	49	6	65	8	2	45	4	3.59
Garcia, 9 Tam-27 Lar	36	18	8	3	16	9	1	.640	167	154	70	52	12	55	3	2	92	10	2.80
Gonzalez, Mon	2	0	0	0	0	0	0	.000	4	4	0	0	0	1	0	0	1	0	0.00
Gonzalez, Lag*	14	2	0	0	0	2	0	.000	35	58	37	28	7	16	3	2	16	4	7.20
Goodwin, Sal	20	15	2	11	8	0	.579	148	130	59	44	6	55	4	1	71	6	2.68
Gutierrez, Rey	23	10	5	2	5	5	1	.500	91	85	31	24	4	41	4	1	63	4	2.37
Gutierrez, Dur*	21	15	5	1	4	9	1	.308	89	101	59	38	9	42	3	6	46	9	3.84
Gutierrez, Cor	32	2	1	0	4	6	8	.400	81	71	31	23	5	18	8	7	38	0	2.56
Guzman, Dur	31	3	1	0	3	5	1	.375	82	101	65	39	8	28	3	2	54	2	4.28
Ramon Guzman, Chi	42	7	3	1	11	6	4	.647	104	97	50	35	7	42	7	6	81	4	3.03
Hambright, Jua	36	32	17	4	17	11	0	.607	250	248	90	75	7	91	9	6	133	7	2.70
Henninger, Mon	33	30	14	4	10	15	0	.400	195	197	83	70	10	63	17	3	89	6	3.23
Hernandez, PR	39	1	0	0	3	2	4	.600	112	86	47	34	4	27	6	1	74	0	2.73
Hdz., 3 Sal-18 Lar-6 Coa	27	22	4	2	7	9	2	.438	140	159	76	60	7	45	4	3	63	10	3.86
Hernandez Lara, Rey	1	0	0	0	0	0	0	.000	2	5	3	3	1	2	0	0	0	0	13.50
Hernandez S., Ags	5	0	0	0	0	0	0	.000	5	4	0	0	0	2	0	0	1	0	0.00
Holly, Dur*	5	4	1	0	1	4	0	.200	17	30	22	15	2	11	0	0	5	3	7.94
Hutson, Mex.R	22	22	9	3	13	7	0	.650	154	147	52	38	3	53	2	5	62	5	2.22
Ibarra, Lag*	14	1	0	0	0	1	0	.000	32	45	32	23	2	19	2	1	12	2	6.47
Icedo, M.Tig*	12	4	0	0	1	2	0	.333	12	21	20	11	0	11	3	0	3	0	8.25
Jacobo, Chi*	4	0	0	0	0	0	0	.000	6	4	2	2	0	3	0	0	0	0	3.00
Jimenez, Mex.R	10	4	1	0	2	4	1	.333	32	44	21	16	5	6	3	0	9	2	4.50
Johnson, M.Tig	9	3	0	0	1	2	0	.333	23	22	11	8	0	5	0	0	5	3	3.13
Kekich, Lar*	10	9	3	1	3	2	0	.600	72	45	20	16	1	32	0	0	67	4	2.00
Kokor, 12 Ags-18 Chi	30	28	12	2	10	14	0	.417	181	189	89	69	12	55	3	6	96	2	3.43
Lagunas, Cor	29	22	10	1	12	7	1	.632	161	173	70	57	8	39	5	0	48	0	3.19
Lanfranco, Rey*	30	10	2	1	6	6	2	.500	99	103	53	42	5	21	3	3	46	2	3.82
Lara, 20 Lar-6 Sal*	26	10	2	0	2	8	0	.200	65	78	43	33	3	34	1	3	40	3	4.57
Leal, Lar	27	27	15	7	9	14	0	.391	205	195	73	54	11	59	4	3	118	6	2.37
Lee, Coa	29	29	15	6	16	9	0	.640	212	204	79	54	5	74	9	5	137	2	2.29
Lersch, Jua	36	33	10	0	11	12	0	.478	199	219	101	78	12	43	8	4	63	7	3.53
Leon, Tam	1	0	0	0	0	0	0	.000	7	12	5	4	0	1	0	0	0	0	5.14
Limon, M.Tig	5	0	0	0	0	0	0	.000	10	13	3	2	0	5	1	1	7	0	1.80
Lopez, Mex.R	59	2	0	0	4	11	16	.267	98	111	61	49	5	49	4	7	65	16	4.50
Lopez, M.Tig	40	23	1	0	4	12	0	.250	119	144	86	62	6	75	4	3	64	6	4.69
Lopez, Tam	28	11	6	2	4	5	1	.444	107	83	33	26	7	30	5	3	66	1	2.19
Lozano, Jua*	36	3	0	0	3	4	1	.429	60	72	43	34	5	18	3	3	29	3	5.10
Lugo, Dur	21	1	1	0	2	0	8	1.000	52	63	14	12	3	19	1	1	19	4	2.08
Madrigal, PR	38	23	16	3	15	16	5	.484	209	202	77	52	10	50	11	3	148	6	2.24
Marcano, Ags	21	19	9	2	9	9	0	.500	149	132	67	51	9	45	7	5	106	8	3.08
Mariscal, 4 Sal-19 PR*	23	9	3	1	3	8	1	.273	83	69	43	36	6	20	2	2	39	1	3.90
M'tinez A.10 Lar-10 Coa*	20	1	0	0	2	2	0	.000	23	29	19	17	1	11	2	0	13	4	6.65
Martinez H., Mon*	42	20	11	2	15	11	1	.577	193	183	51	43	6	60	13	8	120	2	2.01
Martinez, Chi	2	0	0	0	0	0	0	.000	2	8	6	5	0	2	0	0	1	0	22.50
Martinez, 22 Lar-15 Coa	37	3	1	0	5	7	1	.417	91	111	66	53	2	41	9	1	31	4	5.24
Martinez, Dur	19	0	0	0	2	0	0	.000	45	53	30	22	5	24	4	3	19	5	4.40
Matias, Jua*	13	0	0	0	5	1	3	.833	23	17	3	3	0	8	2	0	8	0	1.17
Maya, Tam	1	0	0	0	0	0	0	.000	1	1	0	0	0	0	0	0	1	0	0.00
Maytorena, 9 Ta-30 Lag	39	6	1	0	6	6	5	.500	97	106	37	29	6	27	5	6	64	0	2.69
McCoy, Sal	26	23	12	2	11	10	1	.524	194	166	75	57	2	75	3	4	136	12	2.64
McRae, Chi	27	22	7	3	9	8	0	.529	136	135	71	53	2	84	6	4	62	7	3.51
Mellado, Lar	4	0	0	0	0	0	0	.000	6	7	2	2	0	0	0	0	6	0	3.00
Menendez, Sal*	1	0	0	0	0	0	0	.000	1	2	0	0	0	0	0	0	0	0	0.00
Mere, Mex.R	31	17	2	0	8	9	2	.471	131	133	62	50	6	43	5	10	66	9	3.44
Meza, 29 M.Tig-6 Sal*	35	4	0	0	4	4	2	.500	74	87	39	28	4	36	5	1	35	3	3.41
Monteagudo, Pue	31	24	16	3	15	8	3	.652	193	186	70	55	11	37	7	10	133	4	2.56
Montoya, Chi*	26	4	0	0	2	2	1	.500	67	93	52	45	3	37	3	5	30	2	6.04
Moran, Dur	13	12	2	9	4	0	.692	112	88	36	24	5	25	0	3	88	4	1.93
Moreno, Ags*	24	16	4	0	5	5	1	.500	103	128	64	48	7	53	6	7	51	7	4.19
Moroyoqui, PR	3	0	0	0	0	0	0	.000	9	13	7	6	1	4	0	0	5	6	6.00
Mota, Pue	30	4	1	0	4	2	2	.667	102	107	52	36	8	34	9	2	52	5	3.18
Munguia, M.Tig	2	0	0	0	1	0	0	1.000	13	20	8	5	0	3	0	1	7	3	3.46
Munoz, 18 Cor-10 Pue	28	10	3	1	6	7	4	.462	106	113	43	36	4	36	5	1	43	1	3.06
Nagy, Rey	30	28	24	4	16	11	1	.593	232	195	71	47	4	56	9	7	113	4	1.82
Nevarez, Pue	3	0	0	0	0	1	0	.000	7	8	7	6	0	9	0	0	2	0	7.71
Nieblas, Mon	20	4	1	1	1	2	0	.333	59	72	33	19	2	24	4	1	23	3	2.90
Nieto, Tam*	4	0	0	0	0	0	0	.000	3	0	0	0	0	2	0	0	0	0	0.00
Norton, Dur	22	22	12	0	11	8	0	.579	146	153	89	61	9	82	3	6	53	9	3.76
Nuno, M.Tig	32	0	0	0	3	3	0	.500	62	71	40	34	1	44	5	4	24	0	4.94
Ochoa, Rey	22	4	0	0	1	2	0	.333	45	54	43	33	3	30	5	3	27	2	6.60
Officer, Pue*	4	2	0	0	0	2	0	.000	12	11	11	9	1	9	0	0	5	1	6.75
Oliva, Lag	2	0	0	0	0	0	0	.000	3	3	5	0	4	4	0	0	0	0	0.00
Olivo, Tam	10	5	1	0	2	2	0	.500	33	43	20	16	4	14	4	4	15	0	4.36
D. Orea, Jua	38	31	18	3	15	13	1	.536	223	210	81	69	10	69	12	12	104	5	2.78
I. Orea, 1 Rey-4 Jua	5	2	0	0	0	1	0	.000	8	10	7	2	9	1	0	1	0	15.75

Pitcher–Club	G	GS	CG	ShO	W	L	Sv	Pct.	IP	H	R	ER	HR	BB	Int. BB	HB	SO	WP	ERA
Ortiz U., Mex.R*	23	22	7	3	6	11	0	.353	141	168	73	55	7	33	5	4	60	4	3.51
Pactwa, Tam*	19	19	7	0	6	10	0	.375	110	101	66	45	5	78	1	7	67	8	3.68
Palacios, Lar	1	0	0	0	0	0	0	.000	0	0	0	0	0	1	0	0	0	0	0.00
Paul, Tam*	24	23	12	6	11	7	0	.611	172	162	49	37	6	30	2	3	124	2	1.94
Pena, Cor	34	28	18	4	18	7	6	.720	222	186	73	56	9	77	8	18	135	3	2.27
Pena, Lag*	11	0	0	0	0	1	0	.000	32	31	10	10	4	19	1	1	16	1	2.81
Pena, Chi	4	0	0	0	0	0	0	.000	1	2	1	1	0	2	0	0	1	2	9.00
Penalver, Mon	38	29	17	0	10	13	2	.435	251	240	83	57	12	44	7	2	133	1	2.04
Pereda, Mex.R	2	0	0	0	0	0	0	.000	1	2	2	2	0	0	0	0	1	2	18.00
Pereira, Pue	33	0	0	0	4	2	5	.667	62	58	26	19	4	14	6	2	21	2	2.76
Perez 10 Ags-14 Chi*	24	14	6	1	10	4	0	.714	109	130	56	46	3	48	4	2	65	6	3.80
Pina, Ags	27	22	14	3	9	9	1	.500	187	157	75	53	9	77	8	15	153	1	2.55
Pina, M.Tig	2	1	0	0	0	1	0	.000	2	6	6	5	0	4	0	1	0	0	22.50
Pizarro, Cor*	20	20	10	2	11	8	0	.579	143	130	58	42	2	43	2	0	76	7	2.64
Pollorena, Lag	32	32	26	8	20	9	0	.690	252	214	77	69	11	52	15	8	117	4	2.46
Rauch, Coa	17	17	4	1	6	9	0	.400	114	105	56	44	6	71	4	3	93	9	3.47
German Raygoza, M.Tig	47	10	0	0	8	7	8	.533	143	144	55	43	4	40	8	8	60	3	2.71
Gui'rmo Raygoza, M.Tig	7	4	0	0	0	2	0	.000	12	18	11	10	0	5	0	1	5	1	7.50
Reynoso, Mex.R	2	0	0	0	0	1	0	.000	4	3	1	1	0	4	1	0	3	0	2.25
Rios, Chi*	8	3	0	1	3	0	0	.250	24	30	19	16	0	20	5	0	11	2	6.00
Rivera, M.Tig	1	0	0	0	0	0	0	.000	0	2	1	1	0	1	0	0	0	0	......
M. Rodriguez, Mex.R	31	16	5	3	8	6	0	.571	118	155	83	71	6	51	5	6	34	5	5.42
P. Rodriguez, Mon	9	2	0	0	0	2	0	.000	13	25	16	12	1	2	0	1	5	2	8.31
Romo, Mex.R	29	27	19	5	20	4	0	.833	233	169	60	49	5	56	2	10	239	4	1.89
Romo, Cor	25	25	13	5	11	9	0	.550	176	150	67	49	6	38	4	7	113	2	2.51
Ryerson, Tam*	30	23	17	10	16	7	2	.696	184	150	43	31	0	35	3	2	122	3	1.52
Saldana, PR	10	1	1	0	1	1	0	.000	24	32	19	13	2	6	0	1	15	2	4.88
Saldivar, M.Tig	1	0	0	0	0	1	0	.000	2	1	2	2	0	0	0	0	0	0	9.00
Salgado, Rey	33	11	5	1	6	7	0	.462	114	110	43	34	8	31	9	3	56	2	2.68
Salinas, Rey	30	24	4	1	8	9	0	.471	145	159	94	69	7	62	12	6	69	6	4.28
Salomon, Pue	27	25	7	0	11	9	0	.550	157	177	86	65	7	90	9	9	51	3	3.73
SanMiguel, M.Tig	27	11	0	0	4	4	1	.000	66	72	31	23	4	22	4	3	27	2	3.14
Sanchez, Ags*	2	2	0	0	0	0	0	.000	7	11	9	6	3	3	0	0	1	1	7.71
Sandate, PR*	31	29	22	4	14	13	1	.519	215	183	82	53	6	58	4	1	220	7	2.22
Sandoval, Chi	11	2	0	0	0	3	0	.000	17	28	20	15	2	7	0	6	6	1	7.94
Santiago, Lag	43	2	0	0	13	6	5	.684	86	85	39	32	5	47	9	1	30	2	3.35
Sauceda, Mon	1	0	0	0	0	0	0	.000	2	1	0	0	0	1	0	0	1	0	0.00
Saucedo, Dur	15	1	1	0	2	1	0	.667	43	49	16	14	2	8	1	2	24	2	2.93
Shanahan, Mex.R	22	22	14	2	12	8	0	.600	173	175	67	45	5	47	2	10	133	11	2.34
Sifuentes, 3 Cor-16 Lar*	19	9	1	0	1	5	0	.167	52	52	36	28	2	42	1	2	28	6	4.85
Silverio, Tam*	1	0	0	0	0	0	0	.000	6	14	7	5	2	3	0	0	1	0	7.50
Snook, Jua	3	3	0	0	0	0	0	.000	11	14	9	8	2	4	0	3	2	0	6.55
Solis M., Coa	28	0	0	0	4	4	5	.500	60	44	16	15	1	31	7	5	28	1	2.25
Solis, Lar	36	2	0	0	2	5	1	.286	83	85	40	31	6	28	2	4	28	4	3.36
Solis C., Sal	25	24	14	3	14	7	0	.667	175	172	67	55	14	43	7	5	74	6	2.83
Soto, Sal	33	0	0	0	3	3	5	.500	67	58	15	14	3	22	2	1	27	7	1.88
Soto, Jua*	28	5	0	0	1	3	4	.250	72	68	35	29	5	31	5	0	22	0	3.63
Soto, Chi	35	14	7	1	6	9	1	.400	145	148	65	52	9	55	8	7	47	2	3.23
Suby, M.Tig	11	1	0	0	0	2	0	.000	23	36	17	10	2	9	0	1	16	2	3.91
Tafoya, Chi	4	0	0	0	0	0	0	.000	3	9	5	4	2	3	0	0	2	1	12.00
Tatar, Coa	5	2	0	0	1	3	0	.250	24	30	17	14	1	5	1	0	15	0	5.25
Texidor, 14 Tam-3 Dur	17	9	2	0	2	10	0	.167	73	88	51	35	9	26	2	0	42	4	4.32
Torres F., Lag	1	0	0	0	0	0	0	.000	0	1	1	0	0	2	0	0	0	0	......
Tovar, Lag	31	24	8	3	11	10	0	.524	162	164	69	55	7	41	10	4	33	3	3.06
Troedson, Mon*	12	12	5	0	4	8	0	.333	75	67	33	26	2	21	2	3	34	1	3.12
Uresti, Dur	3	0	0	0	0	0	0	.000	7	12	7	5	2	3	0	1	4	1	6.43
Uzcanga, Cor	3	0	0	0	0	0	0	.000	7	4	0	0	0	5	0	2	2	0	0.00
Valdez, M.Tig	39	20	4	0	6	6	3	.500	130	117	53	42	3	54	4	4	87	5	2.91
Valdivia, Lar	2	0	0	0	0	1	0	.000	8	3	4	1	0	4	0	0	4	1	1.13
Hector Valenzuela, Lar	41	24	8	2	8	14	2	.364	180	209	90	66	13	29	6	1	59	2	3.30
Hto. Valenzuela, 7 Mex.R-11 Lar	18	2	0	0	1	3	0	.250	51	63	33	28	8	12	2	3	16	0	4.94
Valle, Ags*	18	8	3	1	6	2	1	.750	65	60	29	22	0	29	3	6	19	3	3.05
Vallejano, Tam	31	26	9	1	13	10	0	.565	203	221	87	69	14	60	10	7	74	10	3.06
Valles, 2 Tam-10 Cor*	12	0	0	0	0	0	0	.000	20	17	8	5	2	19	1	1	15	0	2.25
Vega, Coa	7	6	3	0	4	1	0	.800	44	50	20	15	3	11	0	0	25	0	3.07
Verdugo, Sal	18	7	3	1	3	4	0	.429	69	70	25	23	2	22	1	2	22	2	3.00
Velo, 26 Dur-10 Ags	36	13	3	0	5	10	6	.333	119	135	75	52	8	48	13	3	71	11	3.93
Villalobos, Dur	1	0	0	0	0	0	0	.000	4	5	1	1	0	1	0	0	3	1	2.25
Villanueva, M.Tig*	20	2	0	0	2	7	8	.438	120	122	49	33	4	53	3	2	82	2	2.48
Volkening, Mon	23	17	10	2	7	8	0	.467	125	127	57	43	3	35	11	1	65	2	3.10

BALKS–D. Orea, Salinas, Solis C., 3 each; Bonfils, Espinosa, F. Lopez, 2 each; Abarca, Aponte, E. Beltran, R. Castillo, L. Cervantes, R. Chavez, D. Figueroa, N. Garcia (Lar), G. Gonzalez, Goodwin, R. Guzman, Hambright,

Henninger, D. Hernandez (Lar), R. Lopez, M. Rodriguez, Sandate, Shanahan, J. Solis, A. Soto, Tatar, Uresti, Vallejano, 1 each.

COMBINATION SHUTOUTS—Valle-Garcia, Aguascalientes; McRae-Cuzman, Chihuahua; Cutler-Solis M., Barbosa-Buentello-Cisneros, Dominguez-Cisneros, Cutler-Cisneros, Rauch-Cisneros, Coahuila; Barojas-Lagunas, Pizarro-P. Gutierrez, Cordoba; Cordova-Guzman, Durango; Lersch-Fajardo-Soto, Lersch-Hambright-Matias, Juarez; M. Rodriguez-Jimenez, Mere-A. Lopez, Mexico Reds; Valdez-Villanueva-Espinosa, Johnson-Villanueva-Valdez, Espinosa-German Raygoza, Gmo. Raygoza-Villanueva, Mexico Tigers; Troedson-P. Rodriguez, Martinez H.,-Cruz, Monterrey; Brunet-Madrigal, Franco-Madrigal, Poza Rica; Acosta-Pereira, Bracamontes-Pereira, Beltran-Pereira, Puebla; Aponte-Lanfranco, Salinas-Bazan-Campoy, Salinas-Bazan, Reynosa; Ahumada-Meza, Saltillo; Pactwa-N. Garcia, Vallejano-N. Garcia, Tampico.

NO-HIT GAMES—None.

Pacific Coast League

CLASS AAA

Leading Batter
PAUL DADE
Salt Lake City

League President
ROY JACKSON

Leading Pitcher
DIEGO SEGUI
Hawaii

CHAMPIONSHIP WINNERS IN PREVIOUS YEARS

1903—Los Angeles ... .630	Hollywood* ... .650	1955—Seattle ... .552
1904—Tacoma ... .589	1931—Hollywood ... .626	1956—Los Angeles ... .637
Tacoma§ ... .571	San Francisco* ... .608	1957—San Francisco ... .601
Los Angeles§ ... .571	1932—Portland ... .587	1958—Phoenix ... .578
1905—Tacoma ... .583	1933—Los Angeles ... .610	1959—Salt Lake City ... .552
Los Angeles* ... .604	1934—Los Angeles z ... .786	1960—Spokane ... .601
1906—Portland ... .657	Los Angeles z ... .689	1961—Tacoma ... .630
1907—Los Angeles ... .608	1935—Los Angeles ... .648	1962—San Diego ... .604
1908—Los Angeles ... .585	San Francisco* ... .608	1963—Spokane ... .620
1909—San Francisco ... .623	1936—Portland‡ ... .549	Oklahoma City a ... .632
1910—Portland ... .567	1937—Sacramento ... .573	1964—Arkansas ... .609
1911—Portland ... .589	San Diego (3rd)† ... .545	San Diego a ... .576
1912—Oakland ... .591	1938—Los Angeles ... .590	1965—Oklahoma City a ... .628
1913—Portland ... .559	Sacramento (3rd)† ... .537	Portland ... .547
1914—Portland ... .574	1939—Seattle ... .580	1966—Seattle a ... .561
1915—San Francisco ... .570	Sacramento (4th)† ... .500	Tulsa ... .578
1916—Los Angeles ... .601	1940—Seattle‡ ... .629	1967—San Diego a ... .574
1917—San Francisco ... .561	1941—Seattle‡ ... .598	Spokane ... .541
1918—Vernon ... .569	1942—Sacramento ... .590	1968—Tulsa a ... .642
Los Angeles (2nd) x ... .548	Seattle (3rd)† ... .539	Spokane ... .586
1919—Vernon ... .613	1943—Los Angeles ... .710	1969—Tacoma a ... .589
1920—Vernon ... .556	S. Francisco (2nd)† ... .574	Eugene ... .603
1921—Los Angeles ... .574	1944—Los Angeles ... .586	1970—Spokane a ... .644
1922—San Francisco ... .638	S. Francisco (3rd)† ... .509	Hawaii ... .671
1923—San Francisco ... .617	1945—Portland ... .622	1971—Salt Lake City a ... .534
1924—Seattle ... .545	S. Francisco (4th)† ... .525	Tacoma ... .545
1925—San Francisco ... .643	1946—San Francisco‡ ... .628	1972—Albuquerque a ... .622
1926—Los Angeles ... .599	1947—Los Angeles†† ... .567	Eugene ... .534
1927—Oakland ... .615	1948—Oakland‡ ... .606	1973—Tucson ... .583
1928—San Francisco* ... .630	1949—Hollywood‡ ... .583	Spokane a ... .563
Sacramento§§ ... .626	1950—Oakland ... .590	1974—Spokane a ... .549
San Francisco§§ ... .626	1951—Seattle‡ ... .593	Albuquerque ... .535
1929—Mission ... .643	1952—Hollywood ... .606	1975—Salt Lake City ... .556
Hollywood* ... .592	1953—Hollywood ... .589	Hawaii a ... .611
1930—Los Angeles ... .576	1954—San Diego y ... .604	

*Won split-season playoff. †Won four-team playoff. ‡Won pennant and four-team playoff. §Tied for second-half title with Tacoma winning playoff. §§Tied for second-half title, with Sacramento winning playoff. ††Ended regular season in tie with San Francisco and won one-game playoff for pennant, then won four-club playoff. xWon playoff from first-place Vernon and awarded championship. yDefeated Hollywood in one-game playoff for pennant. zWon both halves, no playoff. aLeague was divided into Northern, Southern divisions in 1963, 1969-70-71, and Eastern, Western divisions in 1964 through 1968 and 1972 to present; won two-team playoff. NOTE—Championship awarded to playoff winner, 1936-37.

STANDING OF CLUBS AT CLOSE OF SEASON, SEPTEMBER 7

EASTERN DIVISION

Club	S.L.C.	Phx.	Alb.	Tuc.	Haw.	Tac.	Sac.	Spo.	W.	L.	T.	Pct.	G.B.
Salt Lake City (Angels)	....	21	23	22	6	4	8	6	90	54	0	.625	....
Phoenix (Giants)	11	....	19	17	6	6	7	9	75	67	0	.528	14
Albuquerque (Dodgers)	9	13	....	18	7	6	7	6	66	78	0	.458	24
Tucson (Athletics)	10	13	14	....	6	4	5	2	54	88	0	.380	35

WESTERN DIVISION

Club	S.L.C.	Phx.	Alb.	Tuc.	Haw.	Tac.	Sac.	Spo.	W.	L.	T.	Pct.	G.B.
Hawaii (Padres)	6	6	5	6	....	17	15	22	77	68	0	.531	....
Tacoma (Twins)	8	6	6	8	16	....	11	21	76	69	0	.524	1
Sacramento (Rangers)	4	5	5	7	17	21	....	12	71	72	0	.497	5
Spokane (Brewers)	6	3	6	10	10	11	19	....	65	78	0	.455	11

Hawaii and Tacoma finished regular season tied for first place; Hawaii defeated Tacoma in one game to break tie. Game of May 7 forfeited by Hawaii to Tacoma (no game played, no statistics).
Hawaii club represented Honolulu, Hawaii.

Major league affiliations in parentheses.

Playoff—Hawaii defeated Salt Lake City, three games to two.

Regular-Season Attendance—Albuquerque, 169,278; Hawaii, 306,236; Phoenix, 151,207; Sacramento, 82,324; Salt Lake City, 239,321; Spokane, 116,646; Tacoma, 192,758; Tucson, 102,514. Total, 1,360,284. Playoffs, 3,936. No all-star game.

Managers: Albuquerque—Stan Wasiak; Hawaii—Roy Hartsfield; Phoenix—Everett (Rocky) Bridges; Sacramento—Rich Donnelly; Salt Lake City—James F. Williams; Spokane—Frank Howard; Tacoma—Cal Ermer; Tucson—Harry Bright, A. Lee Stange.

All-Star Team: 1B—Ault, Sacramento; 2B—Wills, Sacramento; 3B—Gross, Tucson; SS—LeMaster, Phoenix; OF—Clark, Phoenix; Gaspar, Hawaii; Lopez, Salt Lake City; C—Alexander, Phoenix; DH—Gorinski, Tacoma; P—Wiley, Tacoma; Knepper, Phoenix. Manager—Williams, Salt Lake City.

(Compiled by William J. Weiss, League Statistician, San Mateo, Calif.)

CLUB BATTING

Club	G.	AB.	R.	OR.	H.	TB.	2B.	3B.	HR.	RBI.	SH.	SF.	BB.	Int. BB.	HP.	SO.	SB.	CS.	LOB.	Pct.
Sacramento	143	4846	828	948	1470	2296	201	38	183	754	37	41	491	29	31	630	60	43	1040	.303
Salt Lake City	144	4846	852	703	1400	2024	231	72	83	738	40	63	613	32	36	683	261	95	1034	.293
Hawaii	144	4821	746	666	1395	2023	216	44	108	680	54	44	595	35	31	567	106	44	1137	.289
Albuquerque	144	4706	721	756	1361	1988	240	72	81	670	26	46	495	45	21	709	231	79	963	.289
Tucson	142	4751	742	848	1363	2074	235	43	130	674	16	48	579	34	26	780	153	54	1058	.287
Spokane	143	4710	711	782	1300	1936	236	29	114	650	28	42	503	18	21	645	41	25	976	.276
Phoenix	142	4643	732	708	1268	1918	212	75	96	667	7	38	540	26	22	759	73	43	955	.273
Tacoma	144	4635	733	654	1251	1896	163	40	134	669	56	33	605	34	45	769	74	33	1068	.270

INDIVIDUAL BATTING

(Leading Qualifiers for Batting Championship—389 or More Plate Appearances)

*Bats lefthanded. †Switch-hitter.

Player and Club	G.	AB.	R.	H.	TB.	2B.	3B.	HR.	RBI.	SH.	SF.	BB.	HP.	SO.	SB.	CS.	Pct.
Dade, L. Paul, SLC	91	320	66	116	154	18	4	4	65	4	9	45	1	28	26	2	.363
Beasley, Lewis, Sac*	129	473	87	166	262	25	4	21	86	2	3	31	3	50	16	5	.351
Lopez, Carlos, SLC	123	448	95	157	227	19	12	9	88	1	6	36	2	49	30	16	.350
Bevacqua, Kurt, Spo	95	356	70	120	180	24	0	12	49	3	5	57	0	47	2	4	.337
Richards, Eugene, Haw*	137	522	102	173	239	24	9	8	59	8	1	91	6	75	19	7	.331
Smith, Keith, Sac	111	403	71	131	220	20	0	23	73	3	0	14	3	40	4	5	.325
Wills, Elliott T., Sac†	117	432	91	140	250	20	6	26	95	0	8	58	8	54	12	4	.324
Gross, Wayne D., Tuc*	115	395	77	128	229	30	7	19	75	0	4	71	2	57	5	4	.324
Cruz, Cirilo, Sac*	127	476	69	154	225	20	6	13	83	3	3	37	4	68	1	2	.324
Clark, Jack, Phx	131	470	111	152	264	29	16	17	86	0	2	72	0	73	16	10	.323

(Dade becomes league batting champion under provisions of Official Baseball Rule 10.23 (a), although falling ten short of the required 389 plate appearances. If ten AB were added to his total of 320, his batting average would still lead the league.)

Departmental Leaders: G—Gaspar, 144; AB—Picciolo, 570; R—Ault, 112; H—Richards, 173; TB—Ault, 278; 2B—McKinney, 34; 3B—Clark, 16; HR—Gorinski, 28; RBI—Gorinski, 110; SH—Champion, 10; SF—Dade, B. Smith, 9; BB—Maloof, 116; HP—Speed, 9; SO—Gorinski, 130; SB—Burke, 63; CS—Flores, 18.

(All Players—Listed Alphabetically)

Player and Club	G.	AB.	R.	H.	TB.	2B.	3B.	HR.	RBI.	SH.	SF.	BB.	HP.	SO.	SB.	CS.	Pct.
Alberts, Francis, SLC	31	106	15	32	46	5	0	3	23	0	3	11	1	16	1	1	.302
Alexander, Gary, Phx	109	360	59	115	208	18	12	17	76	0	2	45	1	100	4	3	.319
Allietta, Robert, SLC	36	115	16	29	41	1	3	9	0	0	11	1	5	0	2	.252
Almon, William, Haw	129	454	67	132	161	16	2	3	44	5	2	35	5	67	21	8	.291
Alvarez, J. M. Orlando, SLC	93	357	64	113	169	18	4	10	63	2	3	40	0	63	16	7	.317
Astroth, Jonathan, Sac*	77	257	52	82	147	11	0	18	60	0	1	53	0	40	0	0	.319
Ault, Douglas, Sac	143	536	112	168	278	25	5	25	83	0	5	51	5	66	3	3	.313
Baez, Jose, Alb	107	392	54	121	171	30	4	4	49	2	2	39	0	39	14	6	.309
Barker, Leonard, Sac	27	1	0	0	0	0	0	0	0	1	0	0	1	0	0	.000
Barlow, Michael, SLC*	25	1	0	1	2	1	0	0	0	0	0	0	0	0	0	1	1.000
Bass, Randy, Tac*	141	451	73	126	210	15	3	21	76	1	5	107	3	91	3	0	.279
Batton, Christopher, Tuc	24	2	0	0	0	0	0	0	0	0	0	0	0	1	0	0	.000
Beasley, Lewis, Sac*	129	473	87	166	262	25	4	21	86	2	3	31	3	50	16	5	.351
Bevacqua, Kurt, Spo	95	356	70	120	180	24	0	12	49	3	3	57	0	47	2	4	.337
Bianco, Thomas, Spot	118	447	71	120	176	26	0	10	61	0	4	40	4	66	2	4	.268
Boggs, Thomas, Sac	19	2	0	0	0	0	0	0	0	0	0	0	0	1	0	0	.000
Bordes, Charles, Sac	44	116	10	25	30	2	0	1	10	4	1	15	0	19	0	1	.216
Bowling, Stephen, Spo	137	470	59	125	212	25	7	16	92	7	5	42	2	94	7	1	.266
Briggs, Dan, SLC†	56	219	41	66	107	14	3	7	42	0	3	19	7	33	2	1	.301
Burke, Glenn, Alb	116	467	72	140	198	17	10	7	53	0	7	18	0	71	63	13	.300
Ceci, Samuel, Spo	89	282	34	66	81	8	2	1	27	5	1	19	1	24	0	0	.234
Champion, R. Michael, Haw	141	501	64	134	192	21	5	9	65	10	4	28	2	63	3	4	.267
Christensen, Bruce, Phx*	89	287	25	69	77	6	1	0	30	0	3	30	0	21	1	1	.240
Clark, Jack, Phx	131	470	111	152	264	29	16	17	86	0	2	72	0	73	16	10	.323
Colbert, Nathan, Tuc	64	210	35	52	102	12	1	12	44	0	1	26	1	52	5	2	.248
Collins, David, SLC†	35	138	28	49	70	13	4	0	12	3	2	18	1	14	19	7	.360
Collins, Terry, Alb*	67	174	23	42	62	4	5	2	24	4	3	19	3	21	6	3	.241
Colzie, Richard, Tuc	9	9	3	5	6	1	0	0	0	0	0	3	1	0	0	0	.556
Cornutt, Terry, Phx	41	2	0	0	0	0	0	0	0	0	0	0	0	0	0	0	.000
Corrigan, Lawrence, Alb*	22	2	0	1	1	0	0	0	0	0	0	0	0	0	0	0	.500
Cox, Larry, Tac	135	457	61	121	189	22	5	12	66	2	2	45	4	58	3	0	.265
Criscione, David, Sac	117	392	56	115	179	13	3	15	62	5	8	38	1	53	1	3	.293
Cristelli, Patrick, SLC*	29	1	0	1	1	0	0	0	0	0	0	0	0	0	0	0	1.000
Cruz, Cirilo, Sac*	127	476	69	154	225	20	6	13	83	3	3	37	4	68	1	2	.324
Cruz, Henry, Alb*	24	82	15	25	34	4	1	1	12	0	0	15	0	5	6	4	.305
Cruz, Julio L., Alb*	20	69	11	17	23	2	2	0	6	0	1	6	1	9	12	2	.246
Dade, L. Paul, SLC	91	320	66	116	154	18	4	4	65	4	9	45	1	28	26	2	.363
Danforth, Perry, Spo*	75	236	28	62	82	7	2	3	20	1	2	5	3	38	5	1	.263
Darrow, Darrell, SLC	78	268	35	55	70	8	2	1	25	7	3	18	1	36	12	2	.205
De Filippis, Arthur, Sac*	26	6	1	4	5	1	0	0	2	0	0	1	0	0	0	0	.667
DeJesus, Ivan, Alb	108	405	69	123	185	27	7	7	64	3	6	46	3	70	31	7	.304
Dettore, Thomas, Hawaii*	29	2	0	0	0	0	0	0	0	0	0	0	0	0	0	0	.000
Dillard, Jay, Phx	9	3	0	0	0	0	0	0	0	0	0	0	0	2	0	0	.000
Dimmel, Michael, Alb	64	236	34	60	88	6	5	4	27	2	1	21	1	44	8	5	.254
Dobson, Charles, SLC	27	1	1	1	1	0	0	0	0	0	0	0	0	0	0	0	1.000
Doherty, John, 17 SLC-33 Haw‡	50	154	21	45	60	12	0	1	26	2	0	29	0	19	4	3	.292
Doyle, Brian, Sac*	96	393	65	114	146	15	4	3	32	5	1	20	0	32	9	6	.290
Dupree, Michael, Haw	26	6	2	2	2	0	0	0	1	0	0	0	1	0	0	.333
Eden, E. Michael, Phx†	56	212	34	69	88	13	3	0	20	0	2	30	1	13	7	4	.325
Ellis, Robert, Spo	96	294	47	88	123	15	1	6	48	0	4	57	1	56	3	0	.299
Epperly, Thomas, Tac	64	155	20	37	60	6	1	5	19	1	1	20	0	41	0	1	.239
Fairey, James, Haw*	92	294	40	88	139	13	7	8	57	3	8	28	2	26	2	0	.299
Farkas, Ronald, SLC	7	24	0	4	5	1	0	0	3	0	0	2	3	1	0	.167
Farr, Theodore, Alb	5	12	1	2	5	0	0	1	1	0	0	4	1	4	0	0	.167
Flores, Gilberto, SLC	112	468	88	151	188	16	9	1	48	0	2	43	4	39	40	18	.323
Forry, Dewey, Alb	37	9	1	2	2	0	0	0	0	0	0	1	0	0	0	1	.222
Frazier, Frederic, SLC*	37	123	15	31	46	6	3	1	22	1	3	14	0	14	5	2	.252
Gallagher, Robert, Phx*	125	442	65	114	158	16	5	6	61	0	3	43	3	70	4	2	.258
Gallino, David, Tuc	6	21	1	3	3	0	0	0	1	0	0	1	0	2	0	0	.143
Garrett, H. Adrian, Phx*	31	126	20	39	69	3	0	9	31	0	2	10	1	20	0	0	.310
Gaspar, Rodney, Haw†	144	564	98	166	209	22	3	5	49	6	3	103	1	36	4	8	.294
George, Frankie, SLC	113	421	79	124	188	22	3	12	74	3	5	54	2	56	17	9	.295
Gomez, Juan, Tuc	27	78	6	11	13	2	0	0	2	0	0	5	2	11	0	0	.141
Gomez, Luis, Tac	12	32	3	6	7	1	0	0	0	0	0	1	0	2	0	0	.188
Gorinski, Robert, Tac	138	544	93	155	264	21	2	28	110	2	6	31	5	130	3	5	.285
Gross, Wayne, Tuc*	115	395	77	128	229	30	7	19	75	0	4	71	2	57	5	4	.324
Hahn, Donald, Phx	70	267	49	81	126	14	2	9	34	0	1	28	1	43	1	3	.303
Hale, John, Alb*	103	352	66	113	194	31	7	12	62	0	5	54	1	56	15	4	.321
Hampton, Isaac, SLC†	118	364	77	97	167	23	1	15	60	5	1	71	3	105	20	2	.266
Hansen, Robert, Spo*	99	360	57	109	178	15	3	16	80	0	5	42	1	28	1	1	.303
Heintzelman, Thomas, Phx	136	502	92	139	230	26	10	15	103	1	8	46	2	86	9	2	.277
Herndon, Larry, Phx	14	57	8	14	21	2	1	1	5	0	0	5	0	14	2	1	.246
Hilton, J. David, Haw	126	475	61	137	228	27	8	16	77	6	3	55	1	59	5	3	.288
Hockenbery, Charles, SLC†	31	1	0	0	0	0	0	0	0	0	0	0	0	1	0	0	.000

Player and Club	G.	AB.	R.	H.	TB.	2B.	3B.	HR.	RBI.	SH.	SF.	BB.	HP.	SO.	SB.	CS.	Pct.
Holt, James, Tuc*	94	312	31	105	148	22	3	5	34	0	1	22	0	33	1	1	.337
Hopkins, Donald, Tuc*	98	330	50	87	102	9	3	0	18	0	1	23	1	55	42	9	.264
Hosley, Timothy, Tuc	62	210	46	67	123	9	1	15	54	0	5	37	1	34	5	4	.319
Hudson, Charles, 5 SL-29 Tuc*	34	1	0	0	0	0	0	0	0	0	0	1	0	0	0	0	.000
Hudson, Rex, Alb†	18	0	1	0	0	0	0	0	0	0	0	0	0	0	0	0	.000
Huntz, Stephen, Haw*	85	264	33	57	88	11	1	6	30	3	3	51	0	31	1	0	.216
Hypes, Kyle, Phx†	18	1	0	0	0	0	0	0	0	0	0	0	0	0	0	0	.000
Jackson, Ronnie, SLC	10	33	9	12	20	2	0	2	10	0	1	8	0	5	1	0	.364
James, Philip, Phx*	130	456	78	136	206	30	11	6	71	0	6	70	1	50	5	6	.298
Jones, Robert, Sac*	26	93	16	33	72	5	2	10	29	0	1	9	2	24	2	1	.355
Knepper, Robert, Phx*	35	20	0	3	3	0	0	0	0	0	0	1	0	11	0	0	.150
Kobel, Kevin, Spo	32	1	0	0	0	0	0	0	0	0	0	0	0	0	0	0	.000
Kurpiel, Edward, SLC*	83	263	42	69	112	16	6	5	37	0	2	49	2	53	3	1	.262
Kusnyer, Arthur, Spo	55	203	40	66	112	9	2	11	45	1	4	23	1	38	1	0	.325
Landestoy, Rafael, Alb	140	463	68	128	162	14	7	2	54	7	6	42	2	52	28	15	.276
LeMaster, Johnnie, Phx	105	380	60	94	130	14	5	4	35	1	2	37	1	67	11	7	.247
Leonard, Jeffrey, Alb	7	27	2	8	15	2	1	1	6	0	0	0	0	10	0	0	.296
Lieppman, Keith, Tuc	32	64	8	13	19	1	1	1	8	2	1	2	0	15	1	0	.203
Lind, Jackson, Alb†	89	255	35	69	103	13	3	5	37	1	4	50	0	43	1	2	.271
Lintz, Larry, Tuc†	7	24	3	6	6	0	0	0	2	0	0	3	0	4	0	0	.250
Lopez, Carlos, SLC	123	448	95	157	227	19	12	9	88	1	6	36	2	49	30	16	.350
Lopez, Juan, Spo	98	327	28	63	81	7	1	3	31	3	3	13	1	44	1	1	.193
Magner, Richard, Alb	49	145	20	45	53	6	1	0	17	2	1	16	0	24	4	0	.310
Mahlberg, Gregory, Sac	85	247	46	62	100	8	3	8	23	3	1	52	1	40	1	1	.251
Maloof, Jack, Tac*	130	445	94	125	158	18	3	3	39	9	2	116	5	51	15	8	.281
Mangual, Angel, Tuc	42	164	24	45	68	9	4	2	25	0	2	12	0	24	3	3	.274
Martin, Joseph, Phx*	71	230	17	58	66	5	0	1	25	2	0	21	0	14	0	0	.252
Martinson, Michael, SLC	53	152	18	32	36	4	0	0	16	2	2	10	1	22	4	3	.211
McDermott, Terrence, Alb	14	48	2	12	17	0	1	1	8	0	0	4	0	13	0	1	.250
McKay, David, Tac	63	211	31	52	69	6	1	3	22	6	2	20	5	42	4	1	.246
McKinney, C. Richard, Tuc	129	458	84	145	257	34	6	22	95	0	6	63	2	56	1	1	.317
Mejias, Samuel, Spo	51	123	13	29	37	8	0	0	13	0	2	9	0	18	3	0	.236
Miley, Michael, SLC†	119	394	75	108	166	22	9	6	60	4	8	86	3	65	28	9	.274
Miller, C. Bruce, Phx	87	351	44	92	119	17	2	2	37	0	2	22	1	28	1	0	.262
Minton, Gregory, Phx†	15	3	1	0	0	0	0	0	0	0	0	0	0	2	0	0	.000
Moharter, David, Sac*	50	1	0	1	1	0	0	0	1	0	0	0	0	0	0	0	1.000
Mull, Jack, Phx	8	23	1	3	4	1	0	0	2	0	0	2	1	6	0	0	.130
Murphy, Dwayne, Tuc*	52	179	32	42	62	7	2	3	11	0	0	37	1	31	15	1	.235
Newman, Jeffrey, Tuc	68	231	23	62	90	11	1	5	38	1	4	14	2	52	1	1	.268
Norwood, Willie, Tac	128	439	84	133	203	21	2	15	68	9	1	42	7	72	14	0	.303
Nottle, Edward, Sac	6	1	0	0	0	0	0	0	0	0	0	0	1	0	0	0	.000
Overy, H. Michael, SLC	39	1	0	0	0	0	0	0	0	0	0	0	0	1	0	0	.000
Pape, Kenneth, Sac	38	149	23	42	56	6	1	2	16	0	1	22	0	22	0	0	.282
Pasley, Kevin, Alb	122	461	68	148	196	24	9	2	60	2	5	14	3	26	8	2	.321
Pepitone, Joseph, Haw*	13	54	5	12	15	0	0	1	3	0	0	2	1	9	1	0	.222
Picciolo, Robert, Tuc	139	570	78	170	212	19	4	5	54	5	4	22	2	78	20	6	.298
Pitts, Gaylen, Tuc	106	310	56	81	131	14	0	12	53	5	3	66	1	65	15	5	.261
Plank, Edward, Phx	29	3	0	0	0	0	0	0	0	0	0	0	0	0	0	0	.000
Poepping, Michael, Tuc	122	342	47	77	145	11	6	15	57	3	1	45	4	79	1	2	.225
Pryor, Gregory, Sac	122	495	71	136	190	21	3	9	51	4	4	30	3	38	4	5	.275
Pyka, Terry, Sac	64	188	33	51	65	5	0	3	21	5	3	28	0	37	3	4	.271
Ramirez, Orlando, SLC	8	27	4	5	9	1	0	1	4	0	0	3	0	7	0	1	.185
Renick, W. Richard, Tac	77	255	50	80	138	5	1	17	50	1	2	44	5	47	1	3	.314
Reynolds, Tommie, Spo	116	415	57	111	183	33	3	11	60	0	5	50	4	46	0	0	.267
Riccelli, Frank, Phx*	31	8	2	1	3	0	0	0	0	0	0	0	1	4	0	0	.125
Richards, Eugene, Haw*	137	522	102	173	239	24	9	8	59	8	1	91	6	75	19	7	.331
Roberts, David W., Haw	106	366	54	91	140	17	1	10	53	4	6	30	7	55	2	4	.249
Robles, Sergio, Alb	17	48	5	10	13	0	0	1	5	0	0	2	0	10	0	1	.208
Roderick, Barry, Tac*	37	110	10	28	37	2	2	1	15	2	1	9	0	7	1	1	.255
Rosario, Angel, Spo†	111	421	87	126	196	24	2	14	42	3	1	64	0	57	7	5	.299
Sain, Thomas, Tac	45	155	18	30	53	5	3	4	18	0	0	18	3	1	1	1	.194
Sakata, Lenn, Spo	141	510	64	143	206	23	5	10	70	1	3	29	1	65	6	4	.280
Sands, Charles, Tuc*	85	249	62	73	144	15	1	18	58	1	5	100	5	71	0	0	.293
Sanner, Dale, Tuc*	18	27	6	8	10	0	1	0	3	0	0	0	0	7	0	0	.296
Scott, John, Haw	133	517	83	163	241	25	4	15	82	3	4	36	2	47	38	7	.315
Sheldon, Bob, Spo*	75	260	56	72	89	12	1	1	19	2	1	51	2	21	3	4	.277
Simpson, Joe, Alb*	108	419	77	131	176	19	7	4	60	2	2	52	0	44	40	11	.313
Simpson, Wayne, SLC	28	1	0	0	0	0	0	0	0	0	0	0	0	0	0	0	.000
Smith, Billy E., SLC*	115	396	64	114	157	16	9	3	60	7	9	53	6	45	22	9	.288
Smith, Cleopherus, Alb	141	489	66	116	207	27	2	20	84	1	3	65	6	129	0	1	.237
Smith, J. Theodore, Tuc	3	11	1	1	1	0	0	0	0	0	0	0	0	2	0	0	.091
Smith, Keith, Sac	111	403	71	131	220	20	0	23	73	3	0	14	3	40	4	5	.325
Soderholm, Dale, Tuc	59	159	20	34	43	4	1	1	21	3	0	21	2	42	3	2	.214
Speed, Horace, Phx	134	448	75	109	192	19	5	18	73	1	4	73	9	128	12	4	.243
Stabelfeldt, David, Phx	2	5	0	0	0	0	0	0	0	0	0	0	0	0	0	0	.000

Player and Club	G.	AB.	R.	H.	TB.	2B.	3B.	HR.	RBI.	SH.	SF.	BB.	HP.	SO.	SB.	CS.	Pct.
Stone, Gerard, Haw†	61	179	27	46	66	4	2	4	22	2	1	59	1	26	0	1	.257
Sutton, Johnny, Sac	60	8	1	2	2	0	0	0	0	0	0	0	0	2	0	0	.250
Thomas, Donald, Sac	31	107	7	22	31	1	1	2	13	2	0	13	0	32	0	1	.206
Thompson, Bobby, Sac†	20	66	17	21	36	3	0	4	11	0	1	18	1	10	4	1	.318
Toms, Thomas, Phx	51	1	1	1	1	0	0	0	0	0	0	0	0	0	0	0	1.000
Valentine, Robert, Haw	120	395	67	120	186	23	2	13	89	3	7	47	2	32	9	0	.304
Van Wyck, James, Tac	83	244	28	62	71	3	3	0	17	7	0	25	1	23	2	0	.254
Verhoeven, John, SLC	28	2	0	1	1	0	0	0	0	0	0	0	0	0	0	0	.500
Walton, Daniel, Alb†	60	219	40	64	105	13	2	8	45	0	1	34	1	45	5	1	.292
Weathers, S. Michael, Tuc	112	370	38	97	128	18	2	3	34	0	3	34	2	55	2	5	.262
Wheelock, Gary, SLC	35	10	2	3	3	0	0	0	3	0	0	4	0	3	0	0	.300
Wilfong, Robert, Tac*	69	220	41	67	90	8	3	3	16	6	3	36	3	22	8	1	.305
Wills, Elliott, Sac†	117	433	91	140	250	20	6	26	95	0	8	58	8	54	12	4	.324
Wolfe, W. Scott, Phx	33	112	10	18	22	2	1	0	7	1	3	12	1	22	0	0	.161
Woods, Alvis, Tac*	121	416	60	118	159	15	4	6	74	4	6	35	1	40	13	9	.284
Woods, Gary L., Tac	137	526	79	162	220	22	6	8	67	6	5	32	3	73	28	13	.308

The following pitchers had no plate appearances primarily through use of designated hitters, listed alphabetically by club, games in parentheses:

ALBUQUERQUE—Barrett, Charles N. (1); Lesslie, Robert W. (27); Lewallyn, Dennis D. (25); Mestek, Robert K. (5); Nitz, Rick C. (23); Rautzhan, Clarence G. (40); Seberger, Michael C. (Tac 14-Alb 15); Sells, David W. (35); Selma, Richard J. (41); Wilson, Billy D. (3).

HAWAII—Freisleben, David J. (7); Hartenstein, Charles O. (39); Johnson, Jerry M. (17); McAllen, John S. (25); McSpadden, Galen W. (4); Reynolds, Kenneth L. (8); Segui, Diego P. (21); Shellenback, James P. (27); Shirley, Robert C. (13); Watt, Eddie D. (35); Wehrmeister, David T. (23).

PHOENIX—Bryant, Ronald R. (Alb 13-Phx 8); Dressler, Robert A. (6); Quezada, Silvano (45); Wegener, Michael D. (32).

SACRAMENTO—Bacsik, Michael J. (12); Bostic, Jerry G. (28); Clyde, David E. (5); Harper, David B. (15); Moore, Tommy J. (33); Skok, Craig R. (25); Soroko, Mark E. (8); Steen, Michael L. (7).

SALT LAKE CITY—Lange, Richard O. (31); Pitlock, Lee P. (Tuc 8-SLC 35); Quintana, L. Joaquin (15); Ryerson, Gary L. (6); Stumpp, Richard C. (1); Wright, G. Lamar (14).

SPOKANE—Anderson, Lawrence D. (34); Austerman, Carl R. (4); Austin, Rick G. (42); Barker, Jeffrey E. (2); Beare, Gary R. (6); Currence, D. Lafayette (13); Edge, Claude L. (1); Haas, Bryan E. (30); Hausman, Thomas M. (22); Ruling, Stephen M. (37); Strampe, Robert E. (Haw 4-Spo 20); Velazquez, Carlos (33); Widmar, A. J. Thomas (36); Wrona, Ron R. (12).

TACOMA—Ausman, Paul D. (10); Bane, Edward N. (15); Bemis, Gregg S. (18); Bethke, Rick A. (17); Butler, William F. (38); Garvin, T. Jared (7); Gideon, James L. (Sac 9-Tac 18); Johnson, Thomas R. (45); Maneely, Robert J. (11); May, Davis E. (16); Pazik, Michael J. (22); Redfern, Peter I. (4); Veintidos, Juan R. (26); Wiley, Mark E. (34).

TUCSON—Bradley, Thomas W. (22); Foor, James E. (26); Griffin, Alan A. (26); Hooten, M. Leon (35); Kirby, Wayne M. (7); Lacey, Robert J. (29); Lysander, Richard E. (17); McCatty, Steven E. (5); Mevring, Bradley C. (1); Mitchell, Craig S. (26); Mitchell, Paul M. (4); Norris, Michael K. (6); Quiros, Gustavo A. (2); Scarbery, Randy J. (18); Taylor, Randall T. (10); Tronerud, Ricky J. (4).

GRAND-SLAM HOME RUNS—Beasley, Bowling, Ellis, Gorinski, Hansen, 2 each; Alexander, Astroth, Bianco, Gallagher, Garrett, Heintzelman, Hosley, Kusnyer, C. Lopez, J. Lopez, Mahlberg, Pitts, Richards, Roberts, J. Simpson, C. Smith, Speed, G. Woods, 1 each.

AWARDED FIRST BASE ON CATCHER'S INTERFERENCE—C. Lopez 3 (Roberts 2, Cox); Astroth (Cox); Danforth (Criscione); Hampton (Cox); McKinney (Stone).

CLUB FIELDING

Club	G.	PO.	A.	E.	DP.	PB.	Pct.	Club	G.	PO.	A.	E.	DP.	PB.	Pct.
Phoenix	142	3575	1660	146	147	20	.973	Salt Lake City	144	3701	1579	187	155	22	.966
Hawaii	144	3671	1608	171	150	16	.969	Tacoma	144	3587	1562	185	154	12	.965
Spokane	143	3601	1554	167	156	18	.969	Sacramento	143	3584	1658	191	170	25	.965
Tucson	142	3577	1482	172	120	18	.967	Albuquerque	144	3599	1717	208	150	12	.962

Triple Plays—None.

INDIVIDUAL FIELDING

*Throws lefthanded

FIRST BASEMAN

Player and Club	G.	PO.	A.	E.	DP.	Pct.	Player and Club	G.	PO.	A.	E.	DP.	Pct.
Gallagher, Phx*	11	79	8	0	9	1.000	B. Smith, SLC	38	333	16	4	36	.989
Bass, Tac	67	569	51	3	61	.995	Lieppman, Tuc	27	170	5	2	14	.989
Valentine, Haw	66	545	25	3	61	.995	Colbert, Tuc	59	493	21	6	47	.988
Gross, Tuc	26	187	15	1	21	.995	Briggs, SLC*	44	371	34	6	31	.985
Sheldon, Spo	73	628	52	4	70	.994	C. Smith, Alb	133	1162	78	20	128	.984
JAMES, Phx*	120	1144	62	9	117	.993	Holt, Tuc	54	414	22	7	32	.984
Doherty, SLC-Haw*	46	393	15	3	42	.993	Roberts, Haw	12	119	8	2	19	.984
Garrett, Haw	28	283	19	2	24	.993	Kurpiel, SLC*	43	345	33	7	44	.982
Heintzelman, Phx	15	121	15	1	9	.993	Hansen, Spo*	43	347	30	7	42	.982
Ault, Sac*	143	1259	99	13	163	.991	Pepitone, Haw*	10	93	9	2	6	.981
Bianco, Spo	27	209	19	2	19	.991	Alberts, SLC	10	73	3	6	8	.927
Maloof, Tac*	89	650	53	8	78	.989							

FIRST BASEMEN -Continued
(Fewer Than Ten Games)

Player and Club	G.	PO.	A.	E.	DP.	Pct.	Player and Club	G.	PO.	A.	E.	DP.	Pct.
Reynolds, Spo	9	66	3	0	10	1.000	Magner, Alb	1	3	2	0	0	1.000
Huntz, Haw	7	50	5	0	3	1.000	Poepping, Tac	2	2	1	0	0	1.000
Alexander, Phx	2	11	1	0	2	1.000	Lind, Alb	5	24	4	1	2	.966
J. Simpson, Alb*	2	10	0	0	1	1.000	McDermott, Alb	8	65	8	4	5	.948
C. Lopez, SLC	1	8	1	0	1	1.000	Hampton, SLC	3	21	0	2	4	.913
C. Cruz, Sac*	1	5	0	0	0	1.000							

SECOND BASEMEN

Player and Club	G.	PO.	A.	E.	DP.	Pct.	Player and Club	G.	PO.	A.	E.	DP.	Pct.
Bordes, Sac	15	34	40	0	8	1.000	Miller, Phx	35	77	121	6	26	.971
J. Cruz, SLC	15	26	46	1	12	.986	Pitts, Tuc	34	70	100	5	20	.971
Wilfong, Tac	69	163	191	6	51	.983	Doyle, Sac	12	32	36	2	9	.971
Heintzelman, Phx	95	223	303	11	83	.980	Lind, Alb	13	24	37	2	6	.968
Darrow, SLC	78	164	248	11	48	.974	Baez, Alb	96	214	314	18	75	.967
B. Smith, SLC	19	35	40	2	17	.974	Frazier, SLC	33	60	129	7	30	.964
Van Wyck, Tac	30	51	58	3	13	.974	Christensen, Phx	14	31	43	3	9	.961
CHAMPION, Haw	141	317	453	22	113	.9722	Renick, Tac	52	95	122	10	39	.956
Weathers, Tuc	107	219	296	15	58	.9717	Landestoy, Alb	36	82	128	10	25	.955
Sakata, Spo	141	327	428	22	107	.9717	Pyka, Sac	10	36	25	7	8	.897
Wills, Sac	113	297	350	19	96	.971							

(Fewer Than Ten Games)

Player and Club	G.	PO.	A.	E.	DP.	Pct.	Player and Club	G.	PO.	A.	E.	DP.	Pct.
Dade, SLC	7	14	11	0	3	1.000	Danforth, Spo	6	11	17	1	6	.966
T. Collins, Alb	4	5	2	0	1	1.000	Hilton, Haw	5	10	9	1	0	.950
Wolfe, Phx	2	4	3	0	1	1.000	Lintz, Tuc	7	21	20	4	7	.911
Hampton, SLC	2	2	4	0	1	1.000	Sheldon, Spo	1	1	3	1	1	.800
Sain, Tac	2	2	3	0	1	1.000	Roberts, Haw	1	1	2	1	0	.750
Bevacqua, Spo	2	2	1	0	0	1.000	McKay, Tac	1	2	0	1	0	.667
Roderick, Tac	1	2	1	0	1	1.000							

THIRD BASEMAN

Player and Club	G.	PO.	A.	E.	DP.	Pct.	Player and Club	G.	PO.	A.	E.	DP.	Pct.
Bordes, Sac	15	34	40	0	8	1.000	Lind, Alb	26	16	48	5	4	.928
Danforth, Spo	16	12	17	1	1	.967	Bianco, Spo	88	75	177	20	22	.926
T. Collins, Alb	33	17	54	3	4	.959	Doyle, Sac	72	45	149	16	14	.924
Miller, Phx	44	27	102	6	7	.956	Pitts, Tuc	58	47	106	13	8	.922
B. Smith, SLC	30	14	51	3	5	.956	Epperly, Tac	26	19	48	6	5	.918
Christensen, Phx	59	37	107	7	17	.954	DeJesus, Alb	25	13	63	7	4	.916
HILTON, Haw	116	75	248	19	27	.944	Sain, Tac	41	39	79	11	8	.915
McKay, Tuc	62	38	123	10	13	.942	Landestoy, Alb	36	23	56	8	3	.908
Jackson, SLC	10	14	18	2	1	.941	Huntz, Haw	28	24	39	7	7	.900
Renick, Tac	24	22	55	5	2	.939	Baez, Alb	10	9	16	3	3	.893
Bevacqua, Spo	53	49	86	9	9	.938	Thomas, Sac	31	30	72	14	13	.879
Dade, SLC	78	41	122	11	18	.937	Eden, Phx	14	7	22	5	2	.853
Gross, Tuc	83	68	148	15	22	.935	Walton, Alb	23	14	35	9	3	.845
Heintzelman, Phx	26	23	49	5	7	.935	Hampton, SLC	26	14	31	11	2	.804
Pape, Sac	23	15	52	5	4	.931							

(Fewer Than Ten Games)

Player and Club	G.	PO.	A.	E.	DP.	Pct.	Player and Club	G.	PO.	A.	E.	DP.	Pct.
Gallino, Tuc	6	8	9	0	1	1.000	Magner, Alb	1	0	1	0	0	1.000
Valentine, Haw	5	2	13	0	1	1.000	Farkas, SLC	6	4	16	1	1	.952
Criscione, Sac	7	4	3	0	0	1.000	Clark, Phx	8	1	14	1	2	.938
G. Woods, Tuc	2	1	3	0	0	1.000	Weathers, Tuc	5	1	10	3	4	.786
Holt, Tuc	1	2	0	0	0	1.000	Ellis, Spo	1	0	3	1	0	.750
J. Cruz, SLC	2	1	1	0	0	1.000	Roderick, Tac	1	0	1	1	0	.500

SHORTSTOPS

Player and Club	G.	PO.	A.	E.	DP.	Pct.	Player and Club	G.	PO.	A.	E.	DP.	Pct.
B. Smith, SLC	22	33	63	2	9	.980	Landestoy, Alb	62	112	214	18	41	.948
Van Wyck, Tac	56	80	173	8	38	.969	Almon, Haw	129	248	395	36	85	.947
PICCIOLO, Tuc	138	220	429	22	73	.967	Pryor, Sac	122	158	409	32	90	.947
L. Gomez, Tac	11	25	34	2	8	.967	Miller, Phx	10	14	21	2	2	.946
Danforth, Spo	11	11	18	1	7	.967	Roderick, Tac	32	48	103	9	31	.944
Miley, SLC	118	211	359	29	90	.952	DeJesus, Alb	83	148	278	28	60	.938
Wolfe, Phx	31	40	118	8	26	.952	Bevacqua, Spo	48	64	110	13	30	.930
LeMaster, Phx	104	151	349	26	66	.951	Doyle, Sac	17	21	56	6	13	.928
Huntz, Haw	12	17	41	3	10	.951	Soderholm, Tac	57	108	154	22	28	.923
J. Lopez, Spo	97	146	281	23	61	.949							

SHORTSTOPS—Continued
(Fewer Than Ten Games)

Player and Club	G.	PO.	A.	E.	DP.	Pct.	Player and Club	G.	PO.	A.	E.	DP.	Pct.
Pitts, Tuc	5	8	11	0	2	1.000	Ramirez, SLC	8	8	20	4	6	.875
T. Collins, Alb	3	8	8	0	1	1.000	Pape, Sac	9	7	19	6	6	.813
Valentine, Haw	4	7	8	0	2	1.000	Champion, Haw	1	1	1	1	0	.500
Heintzelman, Phx	1	2	3	0	0	1.000	McKay, Tac	1	0	0	1	0	.000
Christensen, Phx	2	0	1	0	0	1.000							

OUTFIELDERS

Player and Club	G.	PO.	A.	E.	DP.	Pct.	Player and Club	G.	PO.	A.	E.	DP.	Pct.
Herndon, Phx	14	38	3	0	1	1.000	C. Cruz, Sac*	125	214	16	8	3	.966
James, Phx*	13	30	1	0	0	1.000	Dimmel, Alb	64	106	6	4	0	.966
Briggs, SLC*	13	27	0	0	0	1.000	Danforth, Spo	40	53	2	2	0	.965
T. Collins, Alb	21	21	2	0	0	1.000	C. Lopez, SLC	98	123	9	5	0	.964
Gross, Tuc	14	18	1	0	0	1.000	Alvarez, SLC	80	127	5	5	2	.964
Holt, Tuc	10	18	0	0	0	1.000	D. Collins, SLC*	30	50	3	2	0	.964
Criscione, Sac	14	12	1	0	0	1.000	Pyka, Sac	43	76	2	3	0	.963
Sanner, Tuc	12	9	0	0	0	1.000	A. Woods, Tac*	113	219	11	9	3	.962
Gallagher, Phx*	77	138	2	1	1	.993	Valentine, Haw	20	24	1	1	0	.962
POEPPING, Tac	104	203	6	2	2	.991	J. Simpson, Alb*	101	183	15	8	2	.961
Gaspar, Haw*	144	317	17	4	1	.988	Clark, Phx	111	187	9	8	2	.961
Bowling, Spo	133	290	16	4	4	.987	Speed, Phx	134	268	12	12	0	.959
Hale, Alb	100	167	8	3	2	.983	Beasley, Sac	125	226	10	10	0	.959
McKinney, Tuc	107	149	13	3	0	.982	Reynolds, Spo	51	83	6	4	1	.957
Jones, Sac*	26	51	4	1	1	.982	K. Smith, Sac	87	119	10	6	1	.956
Rosario, Spo	110	240	7	6	3	.976	Richards, Haw*	137	231	13	12	2	.953
George, SLC	106	192	8	5	2	.976	Fairey, Haw*	11	20	0	1	0	.952
Eden, Phx	21	39	2	1	0	.976	Ellis, Spo	67	111	5	6	1	.951
Burke, Alb	106	258	9	7	2	.974	Thompson, Sac	20	53	4	3	1	.950
Flores, SLC	100	219	8	6	0	.974	Mejias, Spo	50	80	3	5	0	.943
Norwood, Tac	126	274	6	8	1	.972	Mangual, Tuc	42	80	2	5	1	.943
Murphy, Tuc	52	125	6	4	2	.970	Scott, Haw	131	209	13	14	3	.941
Hopkins, Tuc	86	179	7	6	1	.969	Gorinski, Tac	114	199	8	13	1	.941
Hahn, Phx	70	140	6	5	1	.967	H. Cruz, Alb*	20	38	4	4	0	.913
G. Woods, Tuc	130	354	11	13	6	.966	Hampton, SLC	11	15	3	2	0	.900

(Fewer Than Ten Games)

Player and Club	G.	PO.	A.	E.	DP.	Pct.	Player and Club	G.	PO.	A.	E.	DP.	Pct.
C. Smith, Alb	7	16	1	0	0	1.000	Bevacqua, Spo	1	1	0	0	0	1.000
Leonard, Alb	7	14	0	0	0	1.000	Maloof, Tac*	9	13	1	1	0	.933
Bianco, Spo	7	10	1	0	0	1.000	J. T. Smith, Tuc	3	9	0	1	0	.900
Walton, Alb	3	6	0	0	0	1.000	Pasley, Alb	6	8	1	1	0	.900
DeFilippis, Sac*	1	4	0	0	0	1.000	Landestoy, Alb	7	9	1	2	0	.833
J. Cruz, SLC	1	3	0	0	0	1.000	Colzie, Tuc	4	4	1	1	0	.833
Lind, Alb	1	3	0	0	0	1.000	Dade, SLC	4	4	0	1	0	.800
B. Smith, SLC	1	1	1	0	0	1.000	Astroth, Sac	9	6	0	2	0	.750
Magner, Alb	4	1	0	0	0	1.000	McDermott, Alb	1	2	0	1	0	.667
Forry, Alb	3	1	0	0	0	1.000	Mahlberg, Sac	1	0	0	1	0	.000

CATCHERS

Player and Club	G.	PO.	A.	E.	DP.	PB.	Pct.	Player and Club	G.	PO.	A.	E.	DP.	PB.	Pct.
Astroth, Sac	12	45	6	0	0	2	1.000	Alexander, Phx	88	387	62	13	3	11	.972
Mull, Phoenix	8	45	5	0	0	1	1.000	Robles, Alb	14	56	10	2	0	0	.971
Martinson, SLC	49	274	19	2	3	3	.993	Cox, Tac	134	641	104	23	15	9	.970
MAHLBERG, Sac	76	401	34	4	4	9	.991	Kusnyer, Spo	39	182	14	6	2	6	.970
Ceci, Spo	83	369	48	6	7	2	.986	J. Gomez, Tac	26	108	20	4	4	3	.970
Pasley, Alb	107	558	82	10	6	10	.985	Hampton, SLC	76	475	49	17	9	16	.969
Stone, Haw	59	290	22	5	2	7	.984	Magner, Alb	31	132	16	5	2	2	.967
Epperly, Tac	17	54	7	1	1	3	.984	Newman, Tuc	67	311	26	13	1	6	.963
Martin, Phx	52	244	24	5	1	8	.982	Hosley, Tuc	48	208	36	11	0	5	.957
Criscione, Sac	66	316	33	8	3	14	.978	Ellis, Spo	25	145	9	7	1	10	.957
Allietta, SLC	33	204	14	5	0	3	.978	Sands, Tuc	11	28	4	2	1	4	.941
Roberts, Haw	89	459	52	13	5	9	.975								

PITCHERS

Player and Club	G.	PO.	A.	E.	DP.	Pct.	Player and Club	G.	PO.	A.	E.	DP.	Pct.
KOBEL, Spo*	32	11	32	0	2	1.000	T. Johnson, Tac	45	5	13	0	1	1.000
Riccelli, Phx*	30	13	22	0	1	1.000	Toms, Phx	51	3	14	0	1	1.000
Rautzhan, Alb*	40	11	19	0	2	1.000	Wrona, Spo	12	7	9	0	1	1.000
Lacey, Tuc*	29	7	23	0	2	1.000	McAllen, Haw*	25	2	14	0	2	1.000
Skok, Sac*	25	7	22	0	0	1.000	Butler, Tac*	38	3	11	0	1	1.000
Wegener, Phx	32	7	14	0	2	1.000	Bryant, Alb-Phx*	21	0	13	0	1	1.000
Harper, Sac	15	7	11	0	1	1.000	Verhoeven, SLC	28	4	8	0	0	1.000

PITCHERS—Continued

Player and Club	G.	PO.	A.	E.	DP.	Pct.	Player and Club	G.	PO.	A.	E.	DP.	Pct.
May, Tac	16	3	7	0	0	1.000	Wiley, Tac	34	14	20	3	0	.919
Shirley, Haw*	13	2	8	0	0	1.000	L. Barker, Sac	27	11	22	3	1	.917
Pitlock, Tuc-SLC*	43	0	8	0	2	1.000	Nitz, Alb	23	7	26	3	3	.917
Currence, Spo*	13	1	6	0	0	1.000	Cornutt, Phx	41	7	15	2	0	.917
Wright, SLC*	14	0	7	0	0	1.000	Foor, Tuc*	26	3	8	1	0	.917
Lysander, Tuc	17	1	3	0	0	1.000	Dobson, SLC	23	2	9	1	1	.917
Ausman, Tac*	10	0	2	0	0	1.000	Lange, SLC	30	11	32	4	3	.915
Anderson, Spo	34	12	24	1	3	.973	Forry, Alb	32	3	7	1	0	.909
Gideon, Sac-Tac	27	13	21	1	2	.971	Overy, SLC	39	2	8	1	0	.909
C. Hudson, SLC-Tuc*	33	7	24	1	0	.969	Wheelock, SLC	27	18	29	5	2	.904
C. Mitchell, Tuc	26	6	24	1	2	.968	Moore, Sac	33	13	32	5	3	.900
Knepper, Phx*	29	6	45	2	4	.962	DeFilippis, Sac*	24	2	7	1	1	.900
Batton, Tuc	24	10	14	1	1	.960	R. Hudson, Alb	16	4	13	2	2	.895
Sutton, Sac	59	10	14	1	1	.960	Hockenbery, SLC	31	10	23	4	0	.892
Velazquez, Spo	33	7	17	1	2	.960	Segui, Haw	21	9	24	4	1	.892
Haas, Spo	30	2	22	1	2	.960	Boggs, Sac*	18	12	20	4	5	.889
Moharter, Sac*	50	5	18	1	3	.958	Cristelli, SLC	27	5	25	4	0	.882
Bostic, Sac*	28	9	13	1	2	.957	Ruling, Spo	37	11	18	4	3	.879
Dupree, Haw	20	8	14	1	1	.957	Hartenstein, Haw	39	7	14	3	1	.875
Minton, Phx	13	5	16	1	0	.955	Maneely, Tac	11	5	2	1	0	.875
Lewallyn, Alb	25	14	41	3	4	.948	Seberger, Tac-Alb	29	4	22	4	2	.867
Lesslie, Alb	27	14	40	3	0	.947	Sells, Alb	35	13	23	6	3	.857
Quezada, Phx	45	6	12	1	0	.947	Hypes, Phx*	18	4	13	3	1	.850
Widmar, Spo	36	13	21	2	1	.944	Barlow, SLC	25	1	10	2	1	.846
Veintidos, Tac	26	13	20	2	3	.943	Hooten, Tuc	35	5	16	4	0	.840
Hausman, Spo	22	9	22	2	2	.939	Austin, Spo*	42	6	9	3	1	.833
Dettore, Haw	28	7	53	4	3	.938	Quintana, SLC*	15	0	5	1	0	.833
Bradley, Tuc	22	6	9	1	0	.938	Strampe, Haw-Spo	24	5	14	4	1	.826
Bacsik, Sac	12	10	5	1	0	.938	Wehrmeister, Haw	23	3	11	3	2	.824
Plank, Phx	29	10	19	2	1	.935	Corrigan, Alb	21	2	12	3	1	.824
Griffin, Tuc	26	8	20	2	0	.933	Shellenback, Haw*	27	4	14	4	1	.818
Pazik, Tac*	22	4	24	2	2	.933	Bane, Tac*	14	5	13	5	1	.783
Bethke, Tac*	17	1	13	1	0	.933	Selma, Alb	41	1	9	3	0	.769
W. Simpson, SLC	28	11	30	3	0	.932	Bemis, Tac*	18	1	4	2	0	.714
Watt, Haw	35	5	8	1	0	.929	Scarbery, Tuc	18	0	9	4	0	.692
J. Johnson, Haw	17	7	16	2	0	.920							

(Fewer Than Ten Games)

Player and Club	G.	PO.	A.	E.	DP.	Pct.	Player and Club	G.	PO.	A.	E.	DP.	Pct.
Dressler, Phx	6	3	14	0	0	1.000	J. Barker, Spo	2	1	0	0	0	1.000
Reynolds, Haw*	8	2	15	0	1	1.000	Barrett, Alb	1	1	0	0	0	1.000
Soroko, Sac	8	3	13	0	0	1.000	McCatty, Tuc	5	0	1	0	0	1.000
Beare, Spo	6	3	8	0	0	1.000	Holt, Tuc	2	0	1	0	0	1.000
Freisleben, Haw	7	2	6	0	0	1.000	Lind, Alb	2	0	1	0	0	1.000
Dillard, Phx	9	2	5	0	0	1.000	Poepping, Tac	1	0	1	0	0	1.000
Redfern, Tac	4	2	2	0	0	1.000	Stumpp, SLC	1	0	1	0	0	1.000
McSpadden, Haw*	4	0	4	0	0	1.000	Garvin, Tac*	7	4	14	2	3	.900
Clyde, Sac*	5	1	2	0	0	1.000	Ryerson, SLC*	6	2	3	1	0	.833
Mestek, Alb	5	1	1	0	0	1.000	Norris, Tuc	5	0	8	2	3	.800
Kirby, Tuc	7	0	2	0	0	1.000	Nottle, Sac	6	2	1	2	0	.600
Austerman, Spo	4	0	2	0	0	1.000	Steen, Sac	7	1	2	0	0	.600
Wilson, Alb	3	0	2	0	0	1.000							

The following players do not have any recorded accepted chances at the positions indicated; therefore, are not listed in the fielding averages for those particular positions: Cristelli, of; Dupree, of; Edge, of; Epperly, of; George, 2b; L. Gomez, 2b; Kurpiel*, of; Magner, 2b; Meyring, p; P. Mitchell, p; Quiros, p; Renick, p; Sheldon, of; Sutton, of; Taylor, p; Tronerud, p. Farr and Stabelfeldt appeared as designated hitters only.

CLUB PITCHING

Club	G.	CG.	ShO.	Sv.	IP.	H.	R.	ER.	HR.	BB.	Int. BB.	HB.	SO.	WP.	Bk.	ERA.
Tacoma	144	54	12	21	1196	1243	654	544	106	594	34	32	643	63	4	4.09
Hawaii	144	57	10	18	1224	1262	666	586	115	437	19	32	698	40	4	4.31
Salt Lake City	144	29	2	29	1234	1326	703	596	119	529	38	36	903	42	14	4.35
Albuquerque	144	44	5	25	1200	1373	756	602	93	561	47	26	686	50	12	4.52
Phoenix	142	26	9	32	1192	1312	708	613	72	501	40	19	629	60	7	4.63
Spokane	143	28	4	22	1200	1403	782	670	103	607	39	35	615	75	9	5.03
Tucson	142	40	3	19	1192	1424	848	741	108	541	26	15	617	51	7	5.59
Sacramento	143	37	3	24	1195	1465	948	806	206	651	13	34	714	71	5	6.07

PITCHERS' RECORDS

(Leading Qualifiers for Earned-Run Average Leadership—115 or More Innings)

*Throws lefthanded.

Pitcher—Club	G.	GS.	CG.	ShO.	W.	L.	Sv.	Pct.	IP.	H.	R.	ER.	HR.	BB.	Int. BB.	HB.	SO.	WP.	ERA.
Segui, Hawaii	21	17	10	1	11	5	1	.688	147	117	64	52	19	51	1	1	105	5	3.18
Seberger, 14 Tac-15 Al	29	9	4	0	7	7	1	.500	119	135	55	46	9	37	4	3	60	4	3.48
Lewallyn, Alb	25	25	13	2	15	10	0	.600	180	207	98	71	12	61	2	1	62	4	3.55
R. Hudson, Alb	16	16	5	0	8	5	0	.615	121	112	60	49	11	40	2	3	94	4	3.64
Wiley, Tacoma	34	31	16	2	15	15	0	.500	219	267	116	90	19	39	6	4	96	5	3.70
Wheelock, SLC	27	27	11	1	15	8	0	.652	201	206	100	85	15	54	1	4	138	4	3.81
Veintidos, Tac	26	22	9	2	11	8	0	.579	163	155	82	69	17	107	2	1	99	4	3.81
Lange, SLC	30	28	6	0	12	7	0	.632	193	216	102	86	17	65	5	1	107	4	4.01
Pazik, Tac*	22	21	12	3	14	6	0	.737	152	134	73	70	14	76	6	1	75	3	4.14
W. Simpson, SLC	28	28	9	0	13	6	0	.684	174	189	98	82	19	72	5	13	131	4	4.24

Departmental Leaders: G—Sutton, 59; GS—Wiley, 31; CG—Dettore, Wiley, 16; ShO—Knepper, Pazik, 3; W—Lewallyn, Plank, Wheelock, Wiley, 15; L—Dettore, Wiley, 15; Sv—Toms, 21; Pct.—Pazik, .737; IP—Wiley, 219; H—Wiley, 267; R—Sells, 123; ER—Haas, 106; HR—DeFilippis, 36; BB—Gideon, 120; 1BB—Quezada, 10; HB—Dettore, Simpson, 13; SO—Wheelock, 138; WP—Anderson, 25.

(All Pitchers—Listed Alphabetically)

Pitcher—Club	G.	GS.	CG.	ShO.	W.	L.	Sv.	Pct.	IP.	H.	R.	ER.	HR.	BB.	Int. BB.	HB.	SO.	WP.	ERA.
Anderson, Spo	34	23	4	0	9	11	0	.450	145	158	110	99	12	100	4	3	89	25	6.14
Ausman, Tac*	10	0	0	0	0	0	1	.000	17	11	3	1	0	7	1	1	8	0	0.53
Austerman, Spo	4	3	0	0	0	2	0	.000	12	25	16	15	1	5	0	0	2	1	11.25
Austin, Spo*	42	0	0	0	3	4	11	.429	74	74	36	32	4	49	5	3	57	1	3.89
Bacsik, Sac	12	12	3	0	4	3	0	.571	77	101	51	39	11	31	0	2	43	5	4.56
Bane, Tacoma*	14	14	3	1	4	5	0	.444	78	79	49	32	4	41	1	2	40	2	3.69
J. Barker, Spo	2	0	0	0	0	0	0	.000	3	6	4	4	1	0	0	1	0	1	12.00
L. Barker, Sac	27	27	4	0	11	10	0	.524	141	140	103	87	19	96	0	9	92	16	5.55
Barlow, SLC	25	0	0	0	5	1	4	.833	50	52	23	20	4	19	3	6	40	2	3.60
Barrett, Alb	1	1	0	0	0	1	0	.000	2	4	5	5	0	3	1	0	1	0	22.50
Batton, Tuc	24	24	6	0	10	12	0	.455	157	182	106	94	18	82	3	0	77	3	5.39
Beare, Spokane	6	5	3	0	1	4	0	.200	40	33	15	13	1	15	1	0	36	2	2.93
Bemis, Tac*	18	0	0	0	3	3	1	.500	28	36	24	22	8	16	0	0	19	2	7.07
Bethke, Tac*	17	5	1	1	1	4	0	.200	49	55	38	34	4	51	0	0	30	18	6.24
Boggs, Sac	18	18	6	0	6	11	0	.353	115	153	101	88	23	60	0	2	77	6	6.89
Bostic, Sac*	28	9	3	0	3	4	1	.429	94	143	89	80	17	47	1	3	49	8	7.66
Bradley, Tuc	22	22	7	0	5	9	0	.357	123	173	110	89	13	37	1	2	65	5	6.51
Bryant, 13 Al-8 Ph*	21	12	1	0	2	7	0	.222	71	86	71	63	7	70	2	7	48	9	7.99
Butler, Tac*	38	10	2	1	4	6	5	.400	103	104	52	44	7	64	4	1	65	2	3.84
Clyde, Sac*	5	5	0	0	0	4	0	.000	27	38	29	26	5	18	0	0	21	2	8.67
Cornutt, Phx	41	0	0	0	7	0	5	1.000	57	90	45	37	4	48	6	2	56	2	3.43
Corrigan, Alb	21	14	1	0	3	7	0	.300	101	118	70	48	10	56	5	4	49	1	4.28
Cristelli, SLC	27	25	1	0	11	10	0	.524	137	161	101	87	20	72	1	3	80	5	5.72
Currence, Spo*	13	7	0	0	3	3	0	.500	43	53	32	28	5	29	1	2	20	3	5.86
DeFilippis, Sac*	24	16	1	0	8	6	0	.571	109	134	89	89	36	72	0	2	94	3	7.35
Dettore, Haw	28	28	16	1	11	15	0	.423	210	222	117	101	15	76	3	13	105	8	4.33
Dillard, Phx	9	8	0	0	1	6	0	.143	36	53	41	39	1	23	2	2	20	4	9.75
Dobson, SLC	23	9	1	0	3	3	2	.500	61	74	41	37	8	24	1	1	48	0	5.46
Dressler, Phx	6	6	2	0	5	1	0	.833	48	46	7	6	0	11	1	0	18	0	1.13
Dupree, Haw	20	11	4	2	4	4	1	.500	95	90	37	36	6	43	3	2	60	2	3.41
Edge, Spo	1	1	0	0	0	0	0	.000	⅓	4	2	2	1	1	0	0	0	0	54.00
Foor, Tuc*	26	0	0	0	1	2	3	.333	51	59	27	23	5	20	2	1	25	0	4.06
Forry, Alb	32	2	0	0	4	4	3	.500	69	63	33	32	4	35	1	1	42	5	4.17
Freisleben, Haw	7	7	2	1	2	3	0	.400	41	46	25	21	7	18	0	2	23	0	4.61
Garvin, Tac*	7	7	5	0	4	3	0	.571	55	52	27	25	9	22	2	3	36	0	4.09
Gideon, 9 Sac-18 Tac	27	24	6	1	5	9	0	.357	146	161	115	89	12	120	1	6	69	20	5.49
Griffin, Tuc	26	21	7	2	7	10	0	.412	147	168	109	99	16	76	2	2	65	5	6.06
Haas, Spo	30	28	9	0	13	9	0	.591	172	208	116	106	22	86	0	1	130	3	5.55
Harper, Sac	15	14	6	0	5	7	0	.417	91	111	68	55	17	38	1	0	54	3	5.44
Hartenstein, Haw	39	3	3	0	11	5	7	.688	96	89	38	34	4	20	4	3	59	1	3.19
Hausman, Spo	22	18	3	1	4	10	1	.286	111	135	81	70	8	38	4	6	40	1	5.68
Hockenbery, SLC	31	13	1	0	5	6	1	.455	109	134	76	61	9	54	9	4	61	7	5.04
Holt, Tuc	2	0	0	0	0	0	0	.000	4	8	6	6	1	3	0	0	2	1	13.50
Hooten, Tuc	35	9	1	0	2	8	7	.200	90	93	65	56	8	44	4	0	42	4	5.60
C. Hudson, 5 SLC-28 Tc*	33	10	5	1	6	5	0	.545	137	154	88	75	9	61	0	1	55	5	4.93
R. Hudson, Alb	16	16	5	0	8	5	0	.615	121	112	60	49	11	40	2	3	94	4	3.64
Hypes, Phx*	18	18	0	0	8	7	0	.727	86	92	46	41	1	37	0	1	41	4	4.29
J. Johnson, Haw	17	17	7	1	7	8	0	.467	115	127	69	59	14	36	2	1	73	3	4.62
T. Johnson, Tac	45	0	0	0	7	6	13	.538	89	75	21	18	4	20	7	7	65	1	1.82
Kirby, Tuc	7	0	0	0	0	2	1	.000	20	22	18	18	1	14	1	1	15	3	8.10
Knepper, Phx*	29	29	13	3	14	10	0	.583	205	209	96	98	14	72	1	2	130	14	4.30
Kobel, Spo*	32	20	3	2	7	12	0	.368	131	153	86	80	14	43	6	6	56	4	5.50
Lacey, Tuc*	29	12	3	0	3	9	1	.250	105	139	73	69	5	26	1	2	35	4	5.91

Pitcher–Club	G.	GS.	CG.	ShO.	W.	L.	Sv.	Pct.	IP.	H.	R.	ER.	HR.	BR.	Int. BB.	HB.	SO.	WP.	ERA.
Lange, SLC	30	28	6	0	12	7	0	.632	193	216	102	86	17	65	5	1	107	4	4.01
Lesslie, Alb	27	27	8	1	7	14	0	.333	172	213	120	98	17	85	6	6	112	3	5.13
Lewallyn, Alb	25	25	13	2	15	10	0	.600	180	207	98	71	12	61	2	1	62	4	3.55
Lind, Alb	2	0	0	0	0	0	0	.000	5	6	2	2	0	1	0	0	3	0	3.60
Lysander, Tuc	17	0	0	0	2	2	0	.500	28	41	21	20	2	15	2	0	21	1	6.43
Maneely, Tac	11	6	0	0	0	1	0	.000	36	39	29	26	2	23	1	4	14	3	6.50
May, Tac	16	5	1	1	7	3	0	.700	46	50	24	21	2	24	1	2	22	4	4.11
McAllen, Haw*	25	2	0	0	4	2	0	1.000	68	70	34	31	4	31	0	3	23	3	4.10
McCatty, Tuc	5	0	0	0	1	1	0	.500	10	13	8	7	1	7	0	0	5	0	6.30
McSpadden, Haw*	4	2	0	0	0	1	0	.000	19	24	12	11	2	6	0	0	7	0	5.21
Mestek, Alb	5	0	0	0	0	1	0	.000	12	15	8	8	0	5	0	0	5	1	6.00
Meyring, Tuc	1	0	0	0	0	0	0	.000	1	4	4	4	0	1	0	0	0	0	36.00
Minton, Phx	13	12	0	0	4	5	0	.444	74	91	57	46	2	32	3	6	31	2	5.59
C. Mitchell, Tuc	26	26	8	0	8	13	0	.381	170	178	104	93	14	70	3	2	105	12	4.92
P. Mitchell, Tuc	4	4	0	0	3	1	0	.750	23	22	7	6	1	8	0	0	17	1	2.35
Moharter, Sac*	50	1	0	0	2	3	6	.400	70	100	66	59	16	27	2	1	40	7	7.59
Moore, Sac	33	13	6	1	10	7	4	.588	124	123	82	64	15	81	0	3	80	4	4.65
Nitz, Alb	23	18	7	0	8	6	0	.571	118	139	77	67	12	53	4	3	57	3	5.11
Norris, Tuc	5	5	2	0	2	1	0	.667	33	28	15	14	1	23	0	2	19	1	3.82
Nottle, Sac	6	0	0	0	0	0	0	.000	21	22	9	7	0	4	0	0	6	0	3.00
Overy, SLC	39	0	0	0	9	5	10	.643	79	54	20	18	5	46	5	0	99	0	2.05
Pazik, Tac*	22	21	12	3	14	5	0	.737	152	134	73	70	14	76	6	1	75	3	4.14
Pitlock, 8 Tc-35 SLC*	43	1	0	0	5	3	5	.625	76	84	64	57	9	67	3	4	91	4	6.75
Plank, Phx	29	27	6	0	15	10	0	.600	174	213	112	99	14	43	4	1	62	7	5.12
Poepping, Tac	1	0	0	0	0	0	0	.000	1	6	6	6	3	0	0	0	1	0	54.00
Quezada, Phx	45	7	2	0	5	10	6	.333	117	132	69	59	9	37	10	1	59	4	4.54
Quintana, SLC*	15	5	0	0	3	1	0	.750	39	36	20	19	5	21	0	1	28	1	4.38
Quiros, Tuc	2	0	0	0	0	0	0	.000	2	2	3	0	0	1	0	0	2	0	0.00
Rautzhan, Alb*	40	4	0	0	3	5	3	.375	81	97	50	38	4	41	9	0	48	5	4.22
Redfern, Tac	4	4	2	0	2	1	0	.667	27	23	8	8	2	9	0	1	18	0	2.67
Renick, Tac	1	0	0	0	0	0	0	.000	1	0	0	0	0	1	0	0	0	0	0.00
Reynolds, Haw*	8	8	2	1	5	1	0	.833	60	58	28	25	3	21	0	0	44	2	3.75
Riccelli, Phx*	30	30	3	0	9	11	0	.450	166	181	110	91	9	114	1	1	95	10	4.93
Ruling, Spo	37	16	1	0	6	8	4	.429	136	152	80	66	6	101	5	10	68	11	4.37
Ryerson, SLC*	6	5	0	0	1	1	0	.500	23	37	22	18	3	7	0	0	13	0	7.04
Scarbery, Tac	18	7	1	0	4	8	2	.333	69	97	58	43	9	33	6	1	48	4	5.61
Seberger, 14 Tac-15 Alb	29	9	4	0	7	7	1	.500	119	135	55	46	9	37	4	3	60	4	3.48
Segui, Haw	21	17	10	1	11	5	1	.688	147	117	64	52	19	51	1	1	105	5	3.18
Sells, Alb	35	21	5	1	8	11	2	.421	157	198	123	90	10	76	8	2	89	11	5.16
Selma, Alb	41	0	0	0	2	6	17	.250	51	48	26	21	3	31	5	0	45	2	3.71
Shellenback, Haw*	27	11	5	1	7	5	2	.583	109	119	52	47	10	29	2	0	49	5	3.88
Shirley, Haw*	13	13	4	0	5	5	0	.500	81	91	62	47	12	24	1	2	47	2	5.22
W. Simpson, SLC	28	28	9	0	13	6	0	.684	174	189	98	82	19	72	5	13	131	8	4.24
Skok, Sac*	25	13	4	0	8	3	1	.727	115	157	87	79	19	41	1	3	60	5	6.18
Soroko, Sac	8	6	1	0	1	6	0	.143	37	50	32	30	5	17	1	2	13	0	7.30
Steen, Spo	7	0	0	0	0	0	0	.000	15	21	11	10	2	18	1	0	8	2	6.00
Strampe, 4 Haw-20 Spo	24	14	3	0	7	7	0	.500	106	117	71	58	8	71	3	3	62	13	4.92
Stumpp, SLC	1	1	0	0	0	0	0	.000	2	5	3	3	1	2	1	0	1	0	13.50
Sutton, Sac	59	0	0	0	10	5	12	.667	99	116	79	59	15	53	6	4	47	8	5.36
Taylor, Tuc	10	0	0	0	1	3	0	.250	19	32	15	14	0	8	1	1	3	1	6.63
Toms, Phx	51	0	0	0	4	6	21	.400	72	68	24	17	1	21	6	0	56	4	2.13
Tronerud, Tuc	4	0	0	0	0	0	2	.000	6	3	1	1	3	0	0	3	0	1.50
Veintidos, Tac	26	22	9	2	11	8	0	.579	163	155	82	69	17	107	2	1	99	4	3.81
Velazquez, Spo	33	0	0	0	4	1	5	.800	71	93	41	34	12	17	2	1	27	2	4.31
Verhoeven, SLC	28	0	0	0	7	2	8	.778	60	53	19	15	2	18	1	1	56	3	2.25
Watt, Haw	35	0	0	0	4	2	5	.667	60	53	29	27	2	20	3	1	39	2	4.05
Wegener, Phx	32	2	0	0	3	2	0	.600	98	110	65	55	9	55	5	1	45	7	5.05
Wehrmeister, Haw	23	22	4	1	6	11	0	.353	112	137	85	72	15	54	0	3	61	6	5.79
Wheelock, SLC	27	27	11	1	15	8	0	.652	201	206	100	85	15	54	1	4	138	4	3.81
Widmar, Spo	36	11	2	0	5	6	1	.455	131	175	91	74	9	39	3	1	46	6	5.08
Wiley, Tac	34	31	16	2	15	15	0	.500	219	267	116	90	19	39	6	4	96	5	3.70
Wilson, Alb	3	1	0	0	0	0	0	.000	5	10	11	10	0	5	1	0	3	1	18.00
Wright, SLC*	14	2	0	0	0	2	0	.000	27	31	24	18	5	17	3	1	21	4	6.00
Wrona, Spo	12	0	0	0	0	1	0	.000	34	36	15	13	2	16	4	0	21	3	3.25

BALKS—Lesslie, Simpson, 4 each; Corrigan, Cristelli, Dillard, Forry, Haas, Hooten, C. Hudson (Tucson), Lacey, Nitz, Overy, Selma, 2 each; Anderson, Ausman, Austerman, Bane, Boggs, Cornutt, Currence, Dettore, Dobson, Edge, Foor, Gideon (Sac.), Hausman, Hockenbery, Hypes, Lange, May, Moore, Plank, Quezada, Quintana, Riccelli, Shellenback, Skok, Steen, Strampe (Spo.), Velazquez, Verhoeven, Watt, Wehrmeister, Wheelock, Wiley, 1 each.

COMBINATION SHUTOUTS—Forry-Selma, Albuquerque; Segui-Hartenstein, Hawaii; Dressler-Quezada 2, Hypes-Quezada, Hypes-Cornutt, Knepper-Toms, Plank-Toms, Phoenix; Barker-Moore, Sacramento; Lange-Quintana, Salt Lake City; Widmar-Austin, Spokane; Gideon-Johnson, Tacoma.

NO-HIT GAMES—None.

Eastern League

CLASS AA

Leading Batter
DANNY THOMAS
Berkshire

League President
PAT McKERNAN

Leading Pitcher
PAUL MOSKAU
Three Rivers

CHAMPIONSHIP WINNERS IN PREVIOUS YEARS

1923—Williamsport .... .661	1943—Scranton .... .630	1959—Springfield† .... .607
1924—Williamsport .... .654	Elmira (2nd)‡ .... .568	1960—Williamsport y .... .551
1925—York§ .... .583	1944—Hartford .... .723	Springfield (3rd)y....... .496
Williamsport§ .... .583	Binghamton (4th)‡ ...... .474	1961—Springfield .... .612
1926—Scranton .... .627	1945—Utica .... .615	1962—Williamsport .... .593
1927—Harrisburg .... .630	Albany (3rd)‡ .... .564	Elmira (2nd)‡ .... .514
1928—Harrisburg .... .603	1946—Scranton† .... .691	1963—Charleston .... .593
1929—Binghamton .... .597	1947—Utica† .... .652	1964—Elmira .... .586
1930—Wilkes-Barre .... .572	1948—Scranton† .... .636	1965—Pittsfield .... .607
1931—Harrisburg .... .597	1949—Albany .... .664	1966—Elmira .... .633
1932—Wilkes-Barre .... .561	Binghamton (4th)‡ ...... .500	1967—Binghamton z .... .586
1933—Binghamton .... .690	1950—Wilkes-Barre‡ .... .652	Elmira .... .532
1934—Binghamton .... .694	1951—Wilkes-Barre .... .612	1968—Pittsfield .... .604
Williamsport* .... .603	Scranton (2nd)† .... .562	Reading (2nd)‡............. .579
1935—Scranton .... .657	1952—Albany .... .603	1969—York .... .640
Binghamton* .... .580	Binghamton (2nd)‡ ...... .562	1970—Waterbury a .... .560
1936—Scranton* .... .609	1953—Reading .... .682	Reading a .... .553
Elmira .... .629	Binghamton (2nd)‡ ...... .636	1971—Three Rivers .... .569
1937—Elmira† .... .622	1954—Wilkes-Barre .... .576	Elmira b .... .561
1938—Binghamton .... .622	Albany (3rd)‡ .... .540	1972—West Haven b................. .600
Elmira (3rd)‡ .... .522	1955—Reading .... .613	Three Rivers .... .559
1939—Scranton† .... .571	Allentown (2nd)‡ .... .565	1973—Reading b .... .551
1940—Scranton .... .568	1956—Schenectady† .... .609	Pittsfield .... .551
Binghamton (2nd)‡ ...... .554	1957—Binghamton .... .607	1974—Thetford Mines (2nd)c .. .536
1941—Wilkes-Barre .... .630	Reading (3rd)‡ .... .529	Pittsfield (2nd) .... .496
Elmira (3rd)‡ .... .514	1958—Lancaster x .... .568	1975—Reading .... .613
1942—Albany .... .600	Binghamton (6th)‡ ...... .493	Bristol* .... .587
Scranton (2nd)‡ .... .593		

*Won split-season playoff. †Won championship and four-team playoff. ‡Won four-team playoff. §Tied for pennant, York winning playoff. xLeague was divided into Northern, Southern divisions and played a split season; Lancaster over-all season leader. yPlayoff finals canceled after one game because of rain with Williamsport and Springfield declared playoff co-champions. zLeague was divided into Eastern, Western divisions; Binghamton won playoff. aTied for pennant, Waterbury winning playoff. bLeague was divided into American, National divisions; won playoff. cLeague was divided into American and National divisions; won four-team playoff. (NOTE—Known as New York-Pennsylvania League prior to 1938.)

STANDING OF CLUBS AT CLOSE OF SEASON, SEPTEMBER 4
SOUTH DIVISION

Club	W.H.	Bris.	Read.	Wmpt.	T.R.	Q.C.	Berk.	Wat.	W.	L.	T.	Pct.	G.B.
West Haven (Yankees)	....	12	13	14	8	12	11	10	80	59	0	.576	......
Bristol (Red Sox)	12	....	9	15	10	8	8	12	74	60	1	.552	3½
Reading (Phillies)	6	11	....	10	5	7	3	12	54	82	0	.397	24½
Williamsport (Indians)	6	4	14	....	4	2	11	7	48	91	0	.345	32

NORTH DIVISION

Club	W.H.	Bris.	Read.	Wmpt.	T.R.	Q.C.	Berk.	Wat.	W.	L.	T.	Pct.	G.B.
Three Rivers (Reds)	10	8	13	14	....	14	15	9	83	55	2	.601	......
Quebec City (Expos)	6	10	10	16	17	....	10	9	78	59	1	.569	4½
Berkshire (Brewers)	9	9	17	9	2	8	....	14	68	68	0	.500	14
Waterbury (Dodgers)	10	6	6	13	9	8	10	....	62	73	0	.459	19½

Berkshire represented Pittsfield, Mass.
Major league affiliations in parentheses.
Playoff—West Haven defeated Three Rivers three games to none for league championship.
Regular-Season Attendance—Berkshire, 23,561; Bristol, 38,637; Quebec City, 54,061; Reading, 71,152; Three Rivers, 62,655; Waterbury, 64,912; West Haven 28,331; Williamsport, 53,757. Total, 397,066. Playoffs, 2,528. No all-star game.
Managers: Berkshire—John Felske; Bristol—John Kennedy; Quebec City—Lance Nichols; Reading—Bob Wellman, Granville Hamner; Three Rivers—Roy Matjyka; Waterbury—Don LeJohn; West Haven—Pete Ward; Williamsport—John (Red) Davis.
All-Star Team: 1B—Guerrero, Waterbury; 2B—Meyers, Bristol; 3B—Gantner, Berkshire; SS—Oester, Three Rivers; OF—Henderson, Three Rivers; Berg, Bristol; Murray, West Haven; Thomas, Berkshire; C—Blackwell, Reading; P—Hannahs, Quebec City; Moskau, Three Rivers; Manager—Roy Matjyka, Three Rivers.

(Compiled by Howe News Bureau, Chicago, Ill.)

CLUB BATTING

Club	G.	AB.	R.	OR.	H.	TB.	2B.	3B.	HR.	RBI.	SH.	SF.	Int. BB.	BB.	HP.	SO.	SB.	CS.	LOB.	Pct.
Bristol	135	4238	520	481	1106	1406	131	32	35	446	84	31	534	28	25	491	94	52	1006	.261
Waterbury	135	4407	505	600	1150	1548	157	47	49	454	76	31	362	43	40	543	107	49	942	.261
Three Rivers	140	4283	508	415	1095	1492	159	35	56	444	82	31	455	39	28	659	125	68	932	.256
Berkshire	136	4287	559	589	1094	1562	166	19	88	505	49	37	432	33	53	727	114	46	942	.255
West Haven	139	4258	556	482	1069	1505	196	27	62	476	79	30	505	44	22	556	144	55	914	.251
Quebec City	138	4176	555	467	1048	1539	173	27	88	499	47	39	496	38	42	712	160	70	897	.251
Williamsport	139	4411	491	617	1086	1407	161	29	34	416	49	34	473	34	31	709	96	59	995	.246
Reading	136	4218	475	518	1001	1463	150	24	88	417	22	32	446	27	31	712	79	44	910	.237

INDIVIDUAL BATTING
(Leading Qualifiers for Batting Championship—378 or More Plate Appearances)

*Bats lefthanded.   †Switch-hitter.

Player and Club	G.	AB.	R.	H.	TB.	2B.	3B.	HR.	RBI.	SH.	SF.	BB.	HP.	SO.	SB.	CS.	Pct.
Thomas, Danny, Berkshire	115	381	78	124	234	17	3	29	83	1	6	50	12	78	15	2	.325
Berg, Richard, Bristol*	129	492	73	158	192	15	5	3	46	13	1	61	1	70	24	11	.321
Henderson, Stephen, TR	134	506	90	158	255	24	11	17	61	3	2	55	5	82	44	17	.312
Aaron, Wilmer, Wmpt†	119	461	60	142	169	19	4	0	31	4	0	32	7	56	34	10	.308
Guerrero, Pedro, Wat.	132	495	73	151	216	30	10	5	66	0	1	52	0	72	23	7	.305
Jones, Darryl, West Haven	126	456	57	135	195	24	6	8	61	10	4	26	1	33	5	7	.296
Washington, Ronald, Wat.	115	436	61	128	169	9	10	4	32	9	1	29	8	45	14	6	.294
Gantner, James, Berk*	126	403	56	118	159	21	1	6	53	4	4	74	4	50	25	12	.293
Davis, Richard, Berkshire	126	470	70	136	210	24	1	16	69	5	5	19	2	51	10	3	.289
Cage, Wayne, Wmpt*	117	416	46	119	166	11	3	10	42	2	1	46	0	72	9	3	.286
Murray, Larry, WH†	126	472	92	135	205	26	4	12	55	2	5	56	4	56	59	12	.286

Departmental Leaders: G—Thompson, 139; AB—Webb, 533; R—Murray, 92; H—Berg, Henderson, 158; TB—Henderson, 255; 2B—Guerrero, 30; 3B—Henderson, 11; HR—Thomas, 29; RBI—Thomas, 83; SH—Berg, Bowen, Harer, 13; SF—Crowley, Hart, L. Jones, 8; BB—Castle, 87; HP—Thomas, 12; SO—Fitzgerald, 134; SB—Murray, 59; CS—Henderson, 17.

(All Players—Listed Alphabetically)

Player and Club	G.	AB.	R.	H.	TB.	2B.	3B.	HR.	RBI.	SH.	SF.	BB.	HP.	SO.	SB.	CS.	Pct.
Aaron, Wilmer, Wmpt†	119	461	60	142	169	19	4	0	31	4	0	32	7	56	34	10	.308
Allenson, Gary, Bristol	50	160	18	38	48	7	0	1	20	2	4	22	1	21	0	2	.238
Andersen, Larry, Wmpt	1	2	0	1	1	0	0	0	0	0	0	1	0	1	0	0	.500
Armstrong, Michael, TR	24	21	0	2	2	0	0	0	2	0	2	0	8	0	0	.095
Arnold, Robert L., WH	1	1	0	0	0	0	0	0	0	0	0	0	0	1	0	0	.000
Arsenault, Edward, Wmpt	2	2	0	1	1	0	0	0	0	0	0	0	0	0	0	.500
Baker, David, Reading	35	107	10	17	22	2	0	1	5	1	1	10	2	7	0	0	.159
Begnaud, Gary, Reading	134	458	68	118	213	20	3	23	78	1	4	64	2	79	2	0	.258
Bellini, Riccardo, Wmpt	43	136	11	29	34	5	0	0	9	5	0	11	1	18	1	5	.213
Benedetti, Ludwig, Bris.	88	263	35	64	69	3	1	0	21	6	1	20	0	20	7	3	.243

Player and Club	G	AB	R	H	TB	2B	3B	HR	RBI	SH	SF	BB	HP	SO	SB	CS	Pct.
Bennett, Michael, Bris*	16	41	4	6	10	1	0	1	3	0	0	8	0	6	0	0	.146
Benson, Wayne, West Haven	38	108	13	19	22	3	0	0	5	1	0	17	0	9	1	1	.176
Berg, Richard, Bristol*	129	492	73	158	192	15	5	3	46	13	1	61	1	70	24	11	.321
Bernazard, Antonio, QC†	106	334	35	72	89	8	3	1	26	9	0	28	5	42	6	11	.216
Biagini, Gregory, QC†	128	420	57	104	166	23	3	11	53	4	4	57	0	94	1	3	.248
Blackwell, Timothy, Read†	91	299	29	74	94	10	2	2	25	3	1	42	2	44	5	2	.247
Bowen, Samuel, Bristol	127	433	60	92	136	20	3	6	44	13	3	82	1	86	16	5	.212
Brayton, Roswell, Bristol	1	1	0	0	0	0	0	0	0	0	0	0	0	1	0	0	.000
Brenizer, Todd, Reading	2	2	0	0	0	0	0	0	0	0	0	0	0	0	0	0	.000
Brennan, Thomas, Wmpt	1	2	0	0	0	0	0	0	0	0	0	0	0	0	0	0	.000
Bridges, Keith, Wmpt	12	37	5	8	10	0	1	0	2	0	0	8	1	4	1	3	.216
Brown, John E., Wmpt*	26	72	8	14	18	0	2	0	4	2	0	6	0	23	1	2	.194
Brusstar, Warren, Reading	1	1	0	0	0	0	0	0	0	0	0	0	0	0	0	0	.000
Buffamoyer, John, Berk	88	240	18	48	60	6	0	2	19	3	0	20	3	63	0	2	.200
Cage, Wayne, Wmpt*	117	416	46	119	166	11	3	10	42	2	1	46	0	72	9	3	.286
Carrion, Leonel, QC	120	421	66	114	155	24	4	3	43	2	2	55	7	57	41	9	.271
Castle, Donald, WH*	124	378	58	93	159	15	3	15	75	1	7	87	1	62	1	0	.246
Chandler, Jeff, TR†	22	16	4	7	10	3	0	0	2	6	0	1	0	1	0	0	.438
Cleverly, Gary, Wmpt*	5	18	1	1	1	0	0	0	0	0	0	1	0	5	0	0	.056
Contreras, Arnaldo, Read†	1	2	0	0	0	0	0	0	0	0	0	0	0	2	0	0	.000
Coulson, Steven, WH*	122	438	61	119	160	21	7	2	45	10	1	50	2	33	12	8	.272
Cox, W. Ted, Bristol	110	399	39	111	139	13	3	3	53	4	5	43	0	55	2	4	.278
Creech, T. Edwin, QC	132	477	57	119	150	16	0	5	53	10	3	28	0	44	28	8	.249
Crowley, Raymond, QC*	121	356	48	95	154	16	5	11	56	4	8	71	4	67	2	1	.267
Cruz, Todd, Reading	123	424	34	98	126	11	1	5	32	2	1	12	3	76	3	2	.231
Cunningham, Mark, QC	27	69	10	10	15	2	0	1	3	0	0	18	1	16	4	1	.145
Cuoco, Richard, Wat†	1	3	1	1	1	0	0	0	0	0	0	0	0	0	0	0	.333
Dancy, William, Reading†	59	238	45	65	94	10	5	3	25	1	2	15	1	19	1	5	.273
Danson, J. Roger, Berk	56	150	19	30	37	1	0	2	10	1	0	14	4	37	5	3	.200
Davis, Kenzie, Berkshire	66	226	31	55	79	7	1	5	28	3	2	23	2	55	10	2	.243
Davis, Richard, Berkshire	126	470	70	136	210	24	1	16	69	5	5	19	2	51	10	3	.289
Davis, William N., TR†	22	6	2	4	4	0	0	0	1	0	0	0	0	1	0	0	.667
Dawson, Andre, Quebec City	40	143	27	51	81	6	0	8	27	0	2	12	3	21	9	3	.357
Denton, David, Bristol	5	13	1	3	3	0	0	0	0	0	0	2	0	0	0	0	.231
Detherage, Robert, Wat	14	45	9	13	26	1	0	4	11	2	1	4	0	10	0	1	.289
Dimmel, Michael, Wat	55	207	20	55	69	5	3	1	23	2	3	17	3	31	10	7	.266
Dolf, Michael, Wmpt	111	354	34	80	107	14	2	3	36	2	5	44	1	69	3	4	.226
Drumright, David, QC	2	0	1	0	0	0	0	0	0	0	0	0	0	0	0	0	.000
Dumoulin, Daniel, TR	4	3	0	2	2	0	0	0	0	1	0	0	1	0	0	0	.667
Dyes, Andrew, Quebec City	106	337	49	77	144	15	5	14	57	0	4	39	7	96	18	11	.228
Erardi, J. Gregory, Berk	1	1	0	0	0	0	0	0	0	1	0	0	0	0	0	0	.000
Ervin, Terrence, Berk	40	114	12	25	38	4	3	1	17	0	0	10	1	31	1	1	.219
Espy, Duane, Berkshire	134	504	76	126	168	19	4	5	40	10	6	42	3	63	20	6	.250
Farr, Theodore, Waterbury	17	66	5	12	15	3	0	0	4	0	1	2	1	21	1	1	.182
Ferreyra, Raul, Three Rivers	1	0	0	0	0	0	0	0	0	0	0	1	0	0	0	0	.000
Fischetti, Arthur, Wat†	5	19	5	7	8	1	0	0	2	0	0	4	1	1	2	1	.368
Fischlin, Michael, WH	91	248	16	38	53	7	1	2	20	12	1	25	3	50	5	6	.153
Fitzgerald, Daniel, Read	133	438	64	99	186	20	2	21	59	0	4	60	7	134	25	10	.226
Ford, Edward, Bristol†	111	356	47	88	113	8	4	3	38	9	1	23	0	33	10	6	.247
Fry, Jerry, Quebec City	100	296	28	73	98	13	0	4	27	5	3	28	2	38	4	1	.247
Gantner, James, Berk*	126	403	56	118	159	21	1	6	53	4	4	74	4	50	25	12	.293
Garcia, Nelson, Waterbury†	52	201	26	55	74	8	4	1	17	5	1	4	1	14	7	1	.274
Gardner, Gerald, Read	48	154	18	37	46	4	1	1	14	1	2	21	3	24	3	2	.240
Gardner, Vassie, Wmpt	74	270	36	72	99	14	2	3	42	1	4	27	0	44	8	5	.267
Geigel, German, Read*	26	83	11	22	24	2	0	0	3	2	0	7	0	10	1	1	.265
Gibson, John, Reading*	9	22	2	5	6	1	0	0	2	0	1	3	0	5	0	0	.227
Gill, Sheldon, West Haven*	39	111	11	27	29	2	0	0	14	1	0	11	0	20	0	0	.243
Glass, Robert, Wat*	60	192	12	44	63	7	0	4	24	4	0	16	2	22	0	0	.229
Gonzalez, Ernest, Read	45	171	25	41	52	9	1	0	5	2	1	22	0	29	9	4	.240
Grace, Michael, Three Rivers	132	430	38	102	131	14	3	3	45	10	5	33	2	87	2	6	.237
Graumann, A. Dean, TR	88	230	20	51	61	7	0	1	17	9	1	18	0	28	10	5	.222
Greenhalgh, Daniel, Read	1	1	0	0	0	0	0	0	0	0	0	0	0	1	0	0	.000
Griffin, Alfredo, Wmpt†	58	200	22	55	58	3	0	0	17	8	0	14	4	29	13	4	.275
Grossman, Robert, Wmpt	1	2	0	0	0	0	0	0	0	1	0	0	0	1	0	0	.000
Grow, Lorin, TR*	15	12	1	2	2	0	0	0	0	0	0	0	0	2	0	0	.167
Guarnaccia, John, Read*	68	219	28	45	80	4	2	9	26	0	1	32	3	59	6	1	.205
Guerra, Richard, Wmpt	75	253	31	72	108	17	2	5	40	3	4	28	2	38	2	0	.285
Guerrero, Pedro, Wat	132	495	73	151	216	30	10	5	66	0	1	52	0	72	23	7	.305
Hall, Raymond, Berk	89	248	29	53	65	5	0	1	21	4	1	36	10	42	10	6	.214
Hance, Mark, Waterbury	86	296	35	80	101	11	2	2	33	7	5	38	1	28	3	3	.270
Hannah, J. Michael, Wmpt	55	172	22	36	53	5	3	2	19	0	1	39	1	22	5	1	.209
Harer, Wayne, Bristol†	135	468	58	122	147	11	4	2	49	13	2	65	0	51	16	8	.261
Harris, LaMart, QC	2	3	0	1	1	0	0	0	0	0	0	0	0	1	0	0	.333
Harris, Wiley, Three Rivers	16	49	0	14	16	2	0	0	8	1	0	3	0	5	0	1	.286
Hart, J. Michael, QC†	129	420	65	108	174	13	1	17	70	1	8	70	5	68	29	13	.257

Player and Club	G.	AB.	R.	H.	TB.	2B.	3B.	HR.	RBI.	SH.	SF.	BB.	HP.	SO.	SB.	CS.	Pct.
Hassey, Ronald, Wmpt*	21	68	6	19	22	3	0	0	8	0	0	4	1	9	0	0	.279
Haug, Steven, WH	35	90	3	20	22	2	0	0	5	1	1	3	0	8	0	0	.222
Heinold, Douglas, WH	1	1	0	0	0	0	0	0	0	1	0	0	0	0	0	0	.000
Heise, Benjamin, Wmpt	23	81	10	17	20	1	1	0	6	0	0	4	0	10	1	1	.210
Helget, Dale, Bristol*	3	4	0	1	1	0	0	0	3	0	1	1	0	0	0	0	.250
Henderson, Stephen, TR	134	506	90	158	255	24	11	17	61	3	2	55	5	82	44	17	.312
Hickey, Robert, Wmpt†	7	22	2	6	7	1	0	0	2	1	0	4	0	3	1	0	.273
Hiss, William, Wmpt	5	15	2	1	1	0	0	0	0	0	0	3	0	3	0	0	.067
Holle, Gary, Berkshire	4	14	1	2	2	0	0	0	0	0	0	1	2	3	2	0	.143
Hoyt, D. LaMarr, WH	1	0	1	0	0	0	0	0	0	0	0	0	0	0	0	0	.000
Hughes, John D., Read	49	144	7	29	37	3	1	1	11	0	3	11	0	21	1	1	.201
Iorg, Garth, WH†	78	273	31	75	97	17	1	1	24	5	1	16	1	35	15	3	.275
Irwin, Dennis, WH	98	308	28	63	83	18	1	0	25	6	2	33	4	63	9	4	.205
Isaac, Luis, Williamsport	64	195	7	31	41	8	1	0	18	0	4	9	1	33	0	0	.159
Ithier, Pedro, Wmpt	33	127	13	22	25	3	0	0	10	2	1	10	0	11	3	3	.173
Jacobs, Ronald, Berk	27	79	9	21	24	3	0	0	10	0	2	5	0	22	0	0	.266
Jones, Darryl, WH	126	456	57	135	195	24	6	8	61	10	4	26	1	33	5	7	.296
Jones, Lynn, Three Rivers	131	418	41	105	128	17	0	2	36	8	8	36	3	30	13	5	.251
Jones, Terrence, Read	18	59	4	6	8	0	1	0	3	0	0	4	0	7	3	2	.102
Kammeyer, Robert, WH	1	1	0	0	0	0	0	0	0	1	0	0	0	0	0	0	.000
Kessler, C. Bradford, TR	43	132	16	29	47	3	0	5	15	1	1	14	1	45	3	0	.220
Kinard, Rudolph, QC	62	227	31	62	76	12	1	0	15	5	2	14	1	26	8	2	.273
Kinney, Dennis, Wmpt*	1	1	0	0	0	0	0	0	0	0	0	0	1	0	0	0	.000
Klein, Mark, Reading	1	2	0	0	0	0	0	0	0	0	0	0	0	2	0	0	.000
Klobas, Russell, Read	66	228	31	58	93	12	1	7	30	0	1	31	2	39	11	3	.254
Krause, Guy, Quad City*	75	228	34	48	84	9	3	7	33	3	1	38	3	73	1	0	.211
Krsnich, Joseph, Bris*	125	423	51	116	146	16	1	4	36	5	3	67	5	53	3	5	.274
LaCoss, Michael, TR	25	39	2	7	10	3	0	0	1	5	0	6	0	12	0	0	.179
Lindsey, David, Berk*	130	446	49	105	169	22	0	14	72	0	3	55	4	81	4	2	.235
Linnert, Thomas, Wmpt	1	1	0	0	0	0	0	0	0	0	0	0	0	1	0	0	.000
Lucich, Mark, TR*	127	368	38	90	118	13	3	3	32	0	3	29	4	38	2	2	.245
Magner, Richard, Wat	11	43	5	11	13	0	1	0	4	3	0	1	1	9	1	0	.256
Manderbach, Gary, Read	1	2	0	0	0	0	0	0	0	0	0	0	0	2	0	0	.000
Manning, Anthony, Wmpt	22	79	9	19	21	2	0	0	7	1	1	3	0	6	0	3	.241
Mantlo, Gerald, Berk	60	130	12	20	27	7	0	0	12	0	3	8	2	30	0	0	.154
McCall, Larry, WH*	5	0	3	0	0	0	0	0	0	0	0	0	0	0	0	0	.000
McDermott, Terrence, Wat	28	96	12	22	42	8	0	4	18	0	1	3	1	19	0	0	.229
McElwain, Eugene, WH*	1	1	0	0	0	0	0	0	0	0	0	0	0	1	0	0	.000
McGrew, Alvin, WH	24	62	7	18	21	1	1	0	9	2	0	10	0	10	2	0	.290
Meyer, William, Wat	16	49	6	12	15	1	1	0	2	3	1	7	2	12	1	0	.245
Meyers, Charles, Bris*	103	341	44	88	119	12	2	5	30	9	2	25	3	29	2	1	.258
Moore, David M., TR	27	15	1	3	3	0	0	0	3	3	0	2	0	7	0	0	.200
Moran, E. Michael, Wmpt	5	13	1	2	4	0	1	0	0	0	0	4	0	2	1	0	.154
Moreland, B. Keith, Read	61	199	7	52	57	5	0	0	7	4	2	20	1	14	0	2	.261
Moskau, Paul, TR	40	69	4	20	24	1	0	1	9	3	0	4	1	7	0	0	.290
Moss, Barry, TR†	111	306	42	85	111	14	3	2	29	4	2	45	6	37	4	3	.278
Murray, Larry, WH†	126	472	92	135	205	26	4	12	55	2	5	56	4	56	59	12	.286
Mutz, Thomas, TR*	99	288	39	70	91	9	0	4	38	0	4	61	1	28	1	2	.243
Navarrete, Juan, QC*	52	179	24	49	63	4	2	2	11	2	0	15	1	8	9	5	.274
Norman, Daniel, TR	134	491	64	134	223	20	9	17	63	3	2	48	0	85	33	11	.273
Norrid, Timothy, Wmpt*	101	352	49	94	119	15	2	2	23	4	2	58	2	78	5	3	.267
Oester, Ronald, TR†	138	447	57	110	132	14	4	0	44	11	2	47	2	68	6	8	.246
Oliver, Richard, Wmpt	35	127	14	35	43	8	0	0	12	0	2	8	1	15	1	1	.276
Oliveros, Eudaldo, Read	96	298	28	72	88	9	2	1	22	1	2	34	4	47	5	2	.242
Ollar, C. Richard, Wat*	75	261	30	75	89	14	0	0	18	9	2	29	2	21	2	2	.287
Palat, Edward, WH	38	107	13	24	34	4	0	2	9	1	0	15	0	24	0	0	.224
Patterson, Gilbert, WH	1	1	0	0	0	0	0	0	0	0	0	0	0	0	0	0	.000
Phillips, Lanny, Bristol	115	379	45	105	141	15	3	5	43	5	3	61	6	32	6	4	.277
Pichardo, Nelson, WH	70	228	25	58	65	7	0	0	17	7	0	10	2	14	7	3	.254
Plut, Stephen, Waterbury*	63	219	24	53	64	5	3	0	23	5	3	24	1	24	5	0	.242
Poff, John, Reading*	124	443	47	115	164	18	2	9	51	3	6	42	0	56	1	4	.260
Pyka, Garry, Berk	34	132	9	29	39	6	2	0	10	2	2	5	1	18	1	1	.220
Rasmussen, Neil, Berk	97	286	24	72	89	10	2	1	22	6	1	12	0	48	1	1	.252
Redmon, Glenn, Wmpt	61	220	30	59	76	11	0	2	21	3	2	20	1	14	0	1	.268
Reilly, Charles, Bris.	51	136	14	34	40	4	1	0	18	3	3	25	4	11	8	3	.250
Riggleman, James, Wat	84	287	38	75	111	14	2	6	39	1	4	31	1	47	4	5	.261
Robson, Gary, Wmpt	1	2	0	1	1	0	0	0	0	0	0	0	0	1	0	0	.500
Roderick, Barry, Wat*	55	182	11	43	51	4	2	0	22	3	0	20	2	13	2	1	.236
Rogers, Randell, Wat.	125	399	36	93	112	9	2	2	27	12	2	26	1	50	4	4	.233
Rothschild, Lawrence, TR	31	10	2	3	3	0	0	0	0	0	0	0	0	3	0	0	.300
Salter, Robert, Read	17	52	2	7	8	1	0	0	3	1	0	5	0	7	0	0	.135
Santo Domingo, Rafael, TR†	84	222	25	46	50	4	0	0	16	9	0	15	1	40	4	3	.207
Schafer, Randall, QC	79	245	22	59	83	12	0	4	24	2	2	21	2	57	0	2	.241
Servoss, Robert, Wmpt*	84	289	28	68	90	11	4	1	28	1	2	29	1	34	5	5	.235
Severns, Billy, Berk*	129	463	66	130	166	14	2	6	38	10	1	58	3	55	10	5	.281

Player and Club	G.	AB.	R.	H.	TB.	2B.	3B.	HR.	RBI.	SH.	SF.	BB.	HP.	SO.	SB.	CS.	Pct.
Sherrill, Dennis, WH	37	109	12	20	22	2	0	0	4	5	0	8	2	18	2	2	.183
Shirley, Steven, Wat*	2	5	1	2	2	0	0	0	0	0	0	1	0	1	0	0	.400
Smith, Gary, West Haven	3	7	1	3	3	0	0	0	1	0	0	1	0	1	0	0	.429
Soriano, Hilario, Wat	13	48	1	6	7	1	0	0	0	1	0	3	0	13	0	0	.125
Standley, Donald, Wat	1	1	0	1	1	0	0	0	0	0	0	0	0	0	0	0	1.000
Sutcliffe, Richard, Wat*	2	5	1	0	0	0	0	0	2	1	0	0	0	3	0	0	.000
Tarbell, Steven, Bristol	72	242	19	61	72	4	2	1	32	2	1	19	4	18	0	0	.252
Thomas, Danny, Berkshire	115	381	78	124	234	17	3	29	83	1	6	50	12	78	15	2	.325
Thompson, Marvin, WH	139	472	68	131	171	27	2	3	50	11	3	71	1	46	22	6	.278
Tufts, Greg, Wmpt	9	26	1	3	3	0	0	0	1	0	0	3	1	8	0	0	.115
Unsoeld, Mark, TR	75	206	22	51	69	11	2	1	25	2	1	35	2	44	3	5	.248
Villaran, Miguel, Wat	59	189	16	41	62	4	1	5	18	1	0	15	2	26	3	1	.217
Vukovich, John, Read	47	171	15	41	65	9	0	5	16	0	0	11	1	27	3	3	.240
Washington, Ronald, Wat	115	436	61	128	169	9	10	4	32	9	1	29	8	45	14	6	.294
Washko, Patrick, Wmpt†	48	146	18	36	59	5	0	6	20	3	2	28	5	32	1	2	.247
Webb, Marvin, Wat	135	533	64	147	206	19	5	10	63	8	5	27	6	35	20	9	.276
Weese, Gary, Wmpt	1	3	0	0	0	0	0	0	0	0	0	0	0	2	0	0	.000
Werd, Norman, Wmpt*	2	6	0	1	1	0	0	0	0	0	0	0	0	1	0	0	.167
Werth, Dennis, WH	125	386	56	91	164	20	1	17	57	2	5	66	1	69	4	3	.236
Westlake, Claiborne, QC*	8	24	1	6	6	0	0	0	0	0	0	1	0	4	0	0	.250
Westmoreland, Claude, Wat	37	128	13	23	31	3	1	1	6	0	0	9	1	25	5	0	.180
White, Thomas, Read*	1	1	0	0	0	0	0	0	0	0	0	0	0	0	0	0	.000
Whitt, Ernest, Bris*	26	87	12	19	30	2	3	1	10	0	1	10	0	5	0	0	.218
Yoder, Kris, Wmpt	81	241	23	42	49	5	1	0	17	7	3	29	1	63	1	3	.174

The following pitchers had no plate appearances primarily through use of designated-hitters, listed alphabetically by club, games in parentheses).

BERKSHIRE—Alexander, Robert R. (14); Austerman, Carl (23); Beare, Gary (22); Cort, Barry (25); Currence, D. Lafayette (17); Deidel, Thomas (10); Hinds, Samuel (30); Jensen, R. Lawrence (20); McLaurine, W. Lee (60); Morris, John E. (25); Sorensen, Larry (7); Wrona, Ron (7).

BRISTOL—LaRose, H. John (19); Newcomer, F. Breen (6); Paxton, Michael (8); Percival, Curran (14); Proctor, John (23); Rainey, Charles (22); Remmerswaal, Wilhelmus (11); Ripley, Allen (23); Ross, Charles (19); Stanley, Robert (27); Suter, W. Burke (16); Vosk, James (40).

QUEBEC CITY—Ewell, Mark (24); Fierbaugh, N. Randolph (25); Gingrich, Jeffrey (33); Gronlund, David (6); Hanna, Donald (7); Hannahs, Gerald (26); Horstmann, Gary (18); Kerrigan, Joseph (8); Leonhard, David (8); Rawley, Shane (25); Riley, Edward (33); Rushing, Kenneth (37); Schatzeder, Daniel (5).

READING—Bell, Oliver (5); Gregson, Glenn (43); Hernaiz, Jesus (8); Kniffin, Charles (11); Wright, James L. (20).

THREE RIVERS—Niewczyk, James (10).

WATERBURY—Badcock, W. Thomas (35); Bobinger, Mitchell (24); McNulty, Steven (6); Mestek, Robert (20); O'Brien, Steven (36); Slocum, W. Douglas (25); Van Der Beek, James (5).

WEST HAVEN—Anderson, Richard L. (19); Beattie, James (8); Diorio, Ronald (40); Fleshman, Richard (12); Mersch, Neal (10); Rajsich, David (30).

WILLIAMSPORT—Arnold, John (6); Bockewitz, Stanley (24); Flanagan, Donald (12); Mahan, George (13); McGough, Thomas (24); Skiba, Daniel (2).

GRAND-SLAM HOME RUNS—Castle, Lindsey, 2 each; Crowley, Cruz, Dawson, Dyes, Ervin, Fitzgerald, Guarnaccia, Palat, Thomas, Vukovich, 1 each.

AWARDED FIRST BASE ON INTERFERENCE—Biagini (Hance), Harer (Fry), Irwin (Blackwell), Navarrete (Hance), Phillips (Blackwell), Reilly (Fry), Villaran (Mutz).

OBSTRUCTION—Badcock on Creech, Norrid on Ford.

CLUB FIELDING

Club	G.	PO.	A.	E.	DP.	PB.	Pct.
Bristol	135	3413	1580	149	128	12	.971
Three Rivers	140	3473	1553	150	134	19	.971
Berkshire	138	3358	1440	148	96	15	.970
Quebec City	138	3369	1467	185	128	16	.963

Club	G.	PO.	A.	E.	DP.	PB.	Pct.
West Haven	139	3449	1558	199	119	16	.962
Reading	136	3328	1502	192	106	14	.962
Williamsport	139	3461	1508	203	118	22	.961
Waterbury	135	3450	1417	212	110	28	.958

Triple Plays—None.

INDIVIDUAL FIELDING

*Throws lefthanded.

FIRST BASEMEN

Player and Club	G.	PO.	A.	E.	DP.	Pct.
Hannah, Wmpt	19	110	10	0	8	1.000
Rasmussen, Berk	14	74	5	0	4	1.000
Werth, W H	74	635	58	3	55	.996
Kessler, T R	33	308	25	2	25	.994
HARER, Bris*	135	1340	88	10	121	.993
Begnuad, Read	131	1144	89	10	88	.992
Crowley, Q C*	83	699	39	6	62	.992
Lucich, T R*	115	916	53	9	91	.991

Player and Club	G.	PO.	A.	E.	DP.	Pct.
Lindsey, Berk*	114	1021	62	11	74	.990
Cage, Wmpt*	116	1043	79	13	94	.989
Thomas, Berk	12	76	4	1	7	.988
Biagini, Q C	57	447	50	7	47	.986
Guerrero, Wat	132	1129	96	19	100	.985
Castle, W H*	70	618	43	14	48	.979
Moss T R	10	78	4	4	4	.953

FIRST BASEMEN—Continued

(Fewer Than Ten Games)

Player and Club	G.	PO.	A.	E.	DP.	Pct.	Player and Club	G.	PO.	A.	E.	DP.	Pct.
Holle, Berk*	4	37	3	0	2	1.000	Mantlo, Berk	1	5	0	0	1	1.000
Poff, Read*	2	18	6	0	2	1.000	Tarbell, Read	1	1	0	0	0	1.000
McDermott, Wat	2	22	1	0	1	1.000	Unsoeld, R	6	31	0	1	1	.969
Tufts, Wmpt	1	11	0	0	1	1.000	Brown, Wmpt*	6	51	3	2	4	.964
Washko, Wmpt	1	9	0	0	0	1.000	Hughes, Read	4	21	0	1	2	.955
Benedetti, Bris	2	8	0	0	1	1.000	Villaran, Wat	1	5	0	2	1	.714

SECOND BASEMEN

Player and Club	G.	PO.	A.	E.	DP.	Pct.	Player and Club	G.	PO.	A.	E.	DP.	Pct.
Rasmussen, Berk	16	29	26	0	4	1.000	Pichardo, W H	52	86	148	9	23	.963
Redmon, Wmpt	54	147	170	6	38	.981	Santo Domingo, T R	72	89	186	11	41	.962
Roderick, Wat	51	109	105	5	23	.977	Iorg, W H	78	172	236	18	45	.958
Meyers, Bris	89	187	262	11	48	.976	Coulson, W H	12	20	35	3	9	.948
Kinard, Q C	31	67	75	4	19	.973	Washington, Wat	47	117	124	14	31	.945
Vukovich, Read	36	60	115	5	14	.972	Dancy, Read	58	132	171	18	36	.944
Graumann, T R	81	133	205	10	44	.971	Reilly, Bris	51	97	133	14	31	.943
Bellini, Wmpt	42	96	112	7	24	.967	Aaron, Wmpt	21	47	52	6	9	.943
Oliveros, Read	40	76	98	6	6	.967	Creech, Q C	10	17	21	3	3	.927
Villaran, Wat	18	44	43	3	7	.967	Ithier, Wmpt	14	34	26	5	4	.923
ESPY, Berk	126	285	337	22	62	.966	Webb, Wat	21	45	54	9	11	.917
Bernazard, Q C	103	227	257	18	70	.964							

(Fewer Than Ten Games)

Player and Club	G.	PO.	A.	E.	DP.	Pct.	Player and Club	G.	PO.	A.	E.	DP.	Pct.
Oliver, Wmpt	9	15	16	0	6	1.000	Cleverly, Wmpt	1	0	2	0	1	1.000
Denton, Bris	4	12	10	0	2	1.000	Moreland, Read	3	8	6	1	2	.933
Fischlin, W H	1	4	4	0	1	1.000	Hickey, Wmpt	2	5	9	2	2	.875
Meyer, Wat	1	1	3	0	0	1.000							

THIRD BASEMEN

Player and Club	G.	PO.	A.	E.	DP.	Pct.	Player and Club	G.	PO.	A.	E.	DP.	Pct.
Moss, TR	12	10	27	1	2	.974	Oliveros, Read	19	11	30	3	3	.932
Klobas, Read	57	48	124	8	18	.956	Moreland, Read	58	54	93	12	2	.925
GANTNER, Berk	124	118	292	20	18	.953	Benedetti, Bris	41	37	81	10	5	.922
Cox, Bristol	109	73	208	14	23	.952	Norrid, Wmpt	101	90	174	23	16	.920
Cunningham, QC	27	17	43	3	4	.952	Rasmussen, Berk	13	4	29	3	1	.917
Grace, TR	130	123	294	23	33	.948	Coulson, WH	96	44	178	24	11	.902
Creech, QC	67	45	124	11	9	.939	Oliver, Wmpt	25	31	52	10	7	.892
Webb, Wat	42	29	79	7	12	.939	Biagini, QC	47	27	68	14	4	.872
Washington, Wat	65	53	125	12	7	.937	Dolf, Wmpt	10	4	15	3	0	.864
Thompson, WH	34	22	64	6	3	.935	Riggleman, Wat	14	22	26	14	4	.774

(Fewer Than Ten Games)

Player and Club	G.	PO.	A.	E.	DP.	Pct.	Player and Club	G.	PO.	A.	E.	DP.	Pct.
McDermott, Wat	5	7	6	0	0	1.000	Hance, Wat	6	6	12	2	2	.900
Hannah, Wmpt	6	4	9	0	0	1.000	Fischlin, WH	8	5	18	4	0	.852
Vukovich, Read	2	2	7	0	1	1.000	Pichardo, WH	5	1	9	2	1	.833
Redmon, Wmpt	1	2	3	0	0	1.000	Fry, QC	7	10	4	3	0	.824
Jacobs, Berk	1	3	1	0	1	1.000	Begnaud, Read	3	2	4	2	0	.750
Kinard, QC	1	1	3	0	0	1.000	Villaran, Wat	7	1	10	7	1	.611
Reilly, Bris	1	0	1	0	0	1.000	Thomas, Berk	2	0	1	1	0	.500
Jones, WH	2	1	0	0	0	1.000							

SHORTSTOPS

Player and Club	G.	PO.	A.	E.	DP.	Pct.	Player and Club	G.	PO.	A.	E.	DP.	Pct.
Navarrete, QC	52	86	144	3	31	.987	Oester, TR	138	233	408	38	84	.944
Benedetti, Bris	28	42	99	4	18	.972	Fischlin, WH	83	141	231	23	52	.942
Heise, Wmpt	23	40	90	5	14	.963	Griffin, Wmpt	58	86	172	17	25	.938
Hall, Berk	82	124	231	15	47	.959	Rogers, Wat	122	192	372	41	52	.932
Villaran, Wat	13	21	43	3	8	.955	Sherrill, WH	37	64	115	13	20	.932
FORD, Bris	110	193	356	27	68	.953	Ithier, Wmpt	19	31	50	6	13	.931
Creech, QC	61	108	189	15	46	.952	Cruz, Reading	123	203	388	53	62	.918
Rasmussen, Berk	25	29	48	4	9	.951	Pyka, Berk	34	52	90	13	11	.916
Kinard, QC	32	61	95	9	19	.945	Thompson, WH	20	23	43	8	8	.892
Pichardo, WH	13	20	32	3	5	.945	Dolf, Wmpt	22	37	67	16	9	.867

SHORTSTOPS–Continued

(Fewer Than Ten Games)

Player and Club	G.	PO.	A.	E.	DP.	Pct.	Player and Club	G.	PO.	A.	E.	DP.	Pct.
Redmon, Wmpt	5	7	20	0	2	1.000	Santo Domingo, TR	4	4	10	1	1	.933
Dancy, Read	2	4	7	0	1	1.000	Oliveros, Read	5	2	10	1	2	.923
Oliver, Wmpt	1	3	5	0	2	1.000	Vukovich, Read	9	6	18	3	0	.889
Bellini, Wmpt	2	3	4	0	2	1.000	Hiss, Wmpt	5	9	11	3	0	.870
Gantner, Berk	2	2	2	0	1	1.000	Graumann, TR	1	1	3	1	0	.800
Cleverly, Wmpt	3	7	10	1	3	.944	Moran, Wmpt	4	3	9	5	3	.706

OUTFIELDERS

Player and Club	G.	PO.	A.	E.	DP.	Pct.	Player and Club	G.	PO.	A.	E.	DP.	Pct.
Washko, Wmpt	45	83	2	0	0	1.000	Jones, TR	128	196	5	8	0	.962
Palat, WH	31	43	2	0	0	1.000	Thompson, WH	95	161	14	7	5	.962
Castle, WH*	16	26	0	0	0	1.000	Guarnaccia, Read*	68	140	11	6	4	.962
Geigel, Read*	15	23	2	0	0	1.000	Jones, Reading	10	25	0	1	0	.962
Oliveros, Read	12	22	2	0	0	1.000	Carrion, QC	118	236	9	10	3	.961
Espy, Berk	10	16	1	0	0	1.000	Danson, Berk	47	88	5	4	0	.959
Garcia, Wmpt	52	158	5	1	3	.994	Gardner, Wmpt	74	152	3	7	1	.957
Ollar, Wat*	66	119	5	1	0	.992	Westmoreland, Wat	36	82	6	4	0	.957
JONES, WH	111	190	9	2	3	.990	Fitzgerald, Read	131	249	8	12	0	.955
Severns, Berk*	127	259	11	3	3	.989	Riggleman, Wat	46	77	3	4	1	.952
Servoss, Wmpt	83	227	9	3	1	.987	Hannah, Wmpt	12	18	2	1	0	.952
Thomas, Berk	65	116	9	2	2	.984	Krsnich, Bris	86	165	8	9	1	.951
Phillips, Bris	95	163	6	3	1	.983	Dimmel, Wat	55	135	2	7	0	.951
Norman, TR	132	230	13	5	4	.980	Dolf, Wmpt	74	106	10	6	2	.951
R. Davis, Berk	83	157	4	4	0	.976	Ervin, Berk	33	72	6	4	1	.951
Detherage, Wat	14	38	2	1	1	.976	Poff, Read*	108	162	10	9	2	.950
Murray, WH	126	268	12	8	1	.972	Coulson, WH	13	18	1	1	0	.950
Krause, QC	45	67	3	2	0	.972	Gardner, Read	43	87	6	5	0	.949
Manning, Wmpt	15	33	2	1	0	.972	Aaron, Wmpt	61	98	7	6	0	.946
Henderson, TR	125	260	12	8	1	.971	Hart, QC	118	166	4	10	0	.944
Plut, Wat	59	117	15	4	4	.971	Berg, Bris*	93	145	2	9	0	.942
Webb, Wat	66	124	6	4	1	.970	Dawson, QC	37	89	3	6	2	.939
Bowen, Bris	127	274	15	10	3	.967	McGrew, WH	16	14	0	1	0	.933
Moss, TR	33	57	1	2	0	.967	Harris, QC	15	12	0	1	0	.923
K. Davis, Berk	54	127	6	5	0	.964	Guerra, Wmpt	31	44	3	4	0	.922
Bridges, Wmpt	12	25	2	1	1	.964	Dyes, QC	99	159	17	17	4	.912
Gonzalez, Read	19	25	1	1	1	.963	Brown, Wmpt*	17	19	0	2	0	.905
							Benson, WH	27	49	8	7	3	.891

(Fewer Than Ten Games)

Player and Club	G.	PO.	A.	E.	DP.	Pct.	Player and Club	G.	PO.	A.	E.	DP.	Pct.
Fischetti, Wat	5	11	0	0	0	1.000	Smith, WH*	2	4	0	0	0	1.000
Klobas, Read	6	5	2	0	1	1.000	Blackwell, Read	1	2	0	0	0	1.000
Hickey, Wmpt	4	4	2	0	0	1.000	Fry, QC	2	1	0	0	0	1.000
Lucich, TR*	6	6	0	0	0	1.000	Yoder, Wmpt	5	14	1	1	0	.938
Glass, Wat	5	4	1	0	0	1.000	Meyer, Wat	8	12	1	1	0	.929
Roderick, Wat	5	5	0	0	0	1.000	Biagini, QC	7	6	1	1	1	.875
Harris, QC	2	4	0	0	0	1.000	Bennett, Bris	7	9	3	3	0	.800

CATCHERS

Player and Club	G.	PO.	A.	E.	DP.	PB.	Pct.	Player and Club	G.	PO.	A.	E.	DP.	PB.	Pct.
Whitt, Bris	26	127	25	1	2	6	.993	Schafer, QC	62	340	37	10	0	10	.974
MUTZ, TR	91	465	61	4	7	11	.992	Allenson, Bris	46	190	36	6	1	1	.974
Isaac, Wmpt	50	239	40	3	1	8	.989	Gill, WH	23	102	8	3	2	1	.973
Tarbell, Bris	66	272	25	4	2	3	.987	Salter, Read	17	89	7	3	1	0	.970
Unsoeld, TR	57	247	40	4	4	8	.986	Buffamoyer, Berk	88	360	52	13	3	9	.969
Irwin, WH	93	491	52	9	9	12	.984	Baker, Read	26	137	21	5	0	3	.969
Jacobs, Berk	24	114	8	2	0	3	.984	Mantlo, Berk	48	146	12	5	4	3	.969
Blackwell, Read	87	425	64	10	6	7	.980	Soriano, Wat	13	74	9	3	1	3	.965
Hance, Wat	72	381	53	10	3	15	.977	Yoder, Wmpt	75	331	43	15	6	7	.961
Haug, WH	27	112	18	3	2	2	.977	Glass, Wat	38	166	16	8	1	9	.958
Magner, Wat	11	69	12	2	1	1	.976	Hassey, Wmpt	15	63	10	4	0	6	.948
Fry, QC	80	408	41	12	3	6	.974	Hughes, Read	12	56	5	4	1	4	.938

(Fewer Than Ten Games)

Player and Club	G.	PO.	A.	E.	DP.	PB.	Pct.	Player and Club	G.	PO.	A.	E.	DP.	PB.	Pct.
Guerra, Wmpt	5	17	1	0	1	1	1.000	McDermott, Wat	3	8	1	0	0	0	1.000
Helget, Bris	3	8	3	0	1	2	1.000	Werth, WH	4	21	3	4	0	1	.857
Oliveros, Read	1	7	2	0	0	0	1.000								

PITCHERS

Player and Club	G.	PO.	A.	E.	DP.	Pct.	Player and Club	G.	PO.	A.	E.	DP.	Pct.
MOSKAU, TR	26	12	45	0	4	1.000	Percival, Bris	14	4	12	1	1	.941
Rawley, QC*	25	9	37	0	4	1.000	Moore, TR	26	9	35	3	3	.936
Ross, Bristol*	19	11	23	0	3	1.000	Heinold, WH	11	3	25	2	2	.933
Ripley, Bris	21	7	26	0	0	1.000	White, Reading*	20	2	12	1	0	.933
Riley, QC	33	5	27	0	1	1.000	Chandler, TR*	22	4	23	2	0	.931
LaRose, Bris*	19	3	28	0	1	1.000	Davis, TR	22	5	7	1	0	.923
Austerman, Berk	23	4	25	0	1	1.000	Proctor, Bris	23	2	10	1	0	.923
Rothschild, TR	30	9	20	0	3	1.000	Beare, Berk	22	8	26	3	0	.919
Gibson, Read*	22	5	23	0	1	1.000	Greenhalgh, Read	24	13	20	3	4	.917
Robson, Wmpt	19	6	19	0	0	1.000	Dumoulin, TR	38	9	13	2	2	.917
Anderson, WH	19	10	14	0	0	1.000	McLaurine, Berk*	60	2	20	2	3	.917
Klein, Reading	22	8	15	0	0	1.000	Mahan, Wmpt	13	3	8	1	0	.917
Mersch, WH	10	8	13	0	0	1.000	Brayton, Bris*	15	0	11	1	1	.917
Linnert, Wmpt*	21	4	17	0	1	1.000	Ferreyra, TR	25	4	7	1	1	.917
Vosk, Bristol	40	4	14	0	1	1.000	Fleshman, WH	12	5	16	2	0	.913
Flanagan, Wmpt	12	4	12	0	0	1.000	Erardi, Berk	61	1	20	2	1	.913
Arsenault, Wmpt	45	5	10	0	1	1.000	Andersen, Wmpt	21	10	41	5	6	.911
Slocum, Wat	25	6	8	0	1	1.000	McCall, WH	31	17	24	4	2	.911
Kinney, Wmpt*	33	5	9	0	0	1.000	Gingrich, QC	33	5	35	4	5	.909
Deidel, Berk*	10	1	10	0	0	1.000	Rainey, Bris	22	10	10	2	1	.909
Jensen, Berk*	20	1	8	0	0	1.000	Van Der Beek, Wat	30	6	13	2	0	.905
Alexander, Berk	14	0	7	0	0	1.000	Stanley, Bris	27	12	44	6	6	.903
Arnold, WH	13	1	4	0	0	1.000	Fierbaugh, QC	25	9	27	4	1	.900
McElwain, WH*	21	0	5	0	0	1.000	Suter, Bristol	16	8	19	3	1	.900
Contreras, Read	12	0	4	0	0	1.000	Shirley, Wat*	24	6	21	3	1	.900
Hoyt, WH	25	18	36	1	3	.982	Grow, TR*	13	3	15	2	2	.900
Hinds, Berk	30	16	30	1	5	.979	Currence, Berk*	17	1	8	1	0	.900
LaCoss, TR	25	9	36	1	3	.978	Mestek, Wat	20	8	18	3	1	.897
Kammeyer, WH	18	11	25	1	2	.973	Badcock, Wat*	35	1	25	3	1	.897
Brusstar, Read	27	24	37	2	3	.968	Cort, Berkshire	25	8	26	4	4	.895
Rushing, QC*	37	4	21	1	2	.962	Hannahs, QC*	26	9	33	5	2	.894
Werd, Wmpt*	19	3	21	1	3	.960	McGough, Wmpt	24	3	10	2	0	.867
O'Brien, Wat	36	2	22	1	0	.960	Morris, Berk	25	4	8	2	0	.857
Brennan, Wmpt	11	5	18	1	3	.958	Gregson, Read	43	6	9	3	0	.833
Sutcliffe, Wat	30	15	30	2	2	.957	Armstrong, TR	24	10	12	5	0	.815
Bockewitz, Wmpt*	24	4	16	1	1	.952	Rajsich, WH*	30	3	9	3	0	.800
Ewell, QC	24	5	14	1	0	.950	Horstmann, QC	18	1	7	2	1	.800
Drumright, QC	18	4	14	1	1	.947	Bobinger, Wat*	24	10	17	7	0	.794
Brenizer, Read*	39	5	13	1	1	.947	Diorio, WH	40	4	7	3	1	.786
Standley, Wat	47	8	26	2	5	.944	Grossman, Wmpt	21	7	5	5	0	.706
Kniffin, Read*	11	1	16	1	3	.944	Patterson, WH	13	3	14	8	1	.680
Wright, Read	20	14	19	2	1	.943	Weese, Wmpt	11	1	4	3	0	.625

(Fewer Than Ten Games)

Player and Club	G.	PO.	A.	E.	DP.	Pct.	Player and Club	G.	PO.	A.	E.	DP.	Pct.
Manderbach, Read*	8	9	15	0	2	1.000	Hernaiz, Read	8	3	2	0	0	1.000
Paxton, Bristol	8	7	16	0	1	1.000	Sorensen, Berk	7	1	2	0	0	1.000
Beattie, WH	8	8	13	0	4	1.000	Rasmussen, Berk	2	1	0	0	0	1.000
Gronlund, QC	6	2	12	0	1	1.000	Skiba, Wmpt	2	0	1	0	0	1.000
Schatzeder, QC*	5	1	10	0	1	1.000	Wrona, Berk	7	1	7	1	0	.889
Arnold, Wmpt*	6	2	9	0	1	1.000	McNulty, Wat	6	1	3	1	1	.800
Bell, Reading*	7	3	7	0	1	1.000	Hanna, QC*	7	2	2	2	0	.667
Newcomer, Bris*	6	1	7	0	1	1.000	Leonhard, QC	8	0	0	1	0	.000
Kerrigan, QC	8	1	6	0	0	1.000							

The following pitchers do not have any recorded accepted chances; therefore, are not listed in the fielding averages for that position: Harer*, Lindsey*, Mantlo, Niewczyk*, Ollar*, Remmerswaal.

Cuoco, Farr, Westlake appeared as designated hitters and/or pinch-hitters only.

CLUB PITCHING

Club	G.	CG.	ShO.	Sv.	IP.	H.	R.	ER.	HR.	BB.	Int. BB.	HB.	SO.	WP.	Bk.	ERA.
Three Rivers	140	60	27	21	1158	995	415	326	70	427	24	40	667	34	6	2.53
West Haven	139	64	17	18	1150	1066	482	360	61	355	46	33	679	34	6	2.82
Quebec City	138	48	14	21	1123	1010	467	377	54	486	13	29	700	65	9	3.02
Bristol	135	64	16	20	1138	1060	481	384	56	413	45	32	559	36	2	3.04
Reading	136	54	9	13	1109	1061	518	420	45	483	56	39	662	55	4	3.41
Waterbury	135	40	6	23	1150	1111	600	457	65	536	43	24	652	68	6	3.58
Berkshire	136	34	3	28	1119	1173	589	507	70	494	23	31	582	60	16	4.08
Williamsport	139	52	10	12	1154	1173	617	524	79	509	36	44	608	49	8	4.09

PITCHERS' RECORDS

(Leading Qualifiers for Earned-Run Average Leadership—112 or More Innings)

*Throws lefthanded.

Pitcher—Club	G.	GS.	CG.	ShO.	W.	L.	Sv.	Pct.	IP.	H.	R.	ER.	HR.	BB.	Int. BB.	HB.	SO.	WP.	ERA.
Moskau, Three R	26	23	11	6	13	6	0	.684	180	134	42	31	5	58	0	4	124	3	1.55
Gingrich, Que C	33	18	10	2	10	4	0	.714	152	125	39	32	5	27	2	9	89	6	1.89
Rothschild, TR	30	12	10	5	11	3	5	.786	123	96	33	28	7	29	2	4	75	6	2.05
Wright, Reading	20	20	10	4	13	5	0	.722	147	124	51	39	2	56	4	7	107	4	2.39
Hannahs, Que C*	26	26	14	5	20	6	0	.769	173	144	56	46	11	88	1	1	126	13	2.39
Ross, Bristol*	19	14	9	1	11	5	0	.688	119	101	38	33	3	34	4	4	52	1	2.50
Hoyt, West Haven	25	25	14	4	15	8	0	.652	180	169	66	50	6	46	6	8	103	5	2.50
Kammeyer, West H	18	18	10	1	4	13	0	.235	125	123	60	36	3	48	12	6	61	3	2.59
Stanley, Bristol	27	27	13	4	15	9	0	.625	186	176	76	55	8	83	6	11	78	2	2.66
Rawley, Que C*	25	25	11	2	11	7	0	.611	164	143	55	49	11	79	1	3	113	8	2.69

Departmental Leaders: G—Erardi, 61; GS—Brusstar, Stanley, 27; CG—Brusstar, 19; ShO—Moskau, 6; W—Hannahs, 20; L—Brusstar, 17; Sv—Vosk, 16; Pct.—Rothschild, .786; IP—Brusstar, 199; H—Sutcliffe, 187; R—Fierbaugh, 93; ER—McGough, 83; HR—McGough, 17; BB—Shirley, 97; IBB—Brusstar, Kammeyer, 12; HB—Stanley, 11; SO—Hannahs, 126; WP—Brusstar, Hannahs, Hinds, Shirley, Van Der Beek, 13.

(All Pitchers—Listed Alphabetically)

Pitcher—Club	G.	GS.	CG.	ShO.	W.	L.	Sv.	Pct.	IP.	H.	R.	ER.	HR.	BB.	Int. BB.	HB.	SO.	WP.	ERA.
Alexander, Berk	14	4	1	0	0	5	0	.000	29	43	37	34	2	26	4	0	10	0	10.55
Andersen, Wmpt*	21	15	12	1	9	6	0	.600	133	117	47	40	4	34	5	0	74	1	2.71
Anderson, West H	19	19	7	1	10	4	0	.714	124	117	61	48	10	48	3	3	88	3	3.48
Armstrong, TR	24	24	5	0	10	10	0	.500	146	143	77	57	16	52	2	4	91	5	3.51
Arnold, Wmpt*	6	6	0	0	1	3	0	.250	27	34	20	18	1	26	0	0	12	0	6.00
Arnold, West H	13	0	0	0	1	0	1	1.000	23	28	20	18	4	9	2	1	8	0	7.04
Arsenault, Wmpt	45	0	0	0	3	5	0	.273	60	63	40	31	5	37	6	5	40	4	4.65
Austerman, Berk	23	19	4	0	7	9	0	.438	105	138	79	60	10	46	3	5	44	8	5.14
Badcock, Wat*	35	3	2	0	5	2	6	.714	99	87	43	28	3	67	5	1	67	2	2.55
Beare, Berkshire	22	21	10	2	10	10	0	.500	139	138	55	46	3	47	1	2	71	5	2.98
Beattie, West H	8	8	3	0	5	2	0	.714	60	47	19	15	2	33	0	1	48	5	2.25
Bell, Reading*	7	7	0	0	4	2	0	.667	30	32	13	13	2	17	1	1	10	3	3.90
Bobinger, Wat*	24	24	8	2	10	9	0	.526	154	137	84	71	14	81	4	4	85	9	4.15
Bockewitz, Wmpt*	24	6	4	1	5	3	1	.625	83	70	33	24	6	48	2	3	51	3	2.60
Brayton, Bristol*	15	3	0	0	1	2	0	.333	45	50	15	13	3	8	1	0	22	1	2.60
Brenizer, Reading*	39	3	0	0	4	4	4	.500	63	58	29	21	1	45	7	2	46	10	3.00
Brennan, Wmpt	11	11	2	1	3	4	0	.429	61	63	37	30	4	40	0	9	22	3	4.43
Brusstar, Reading	27	27	19	2	10	17	0	.370	199	167	83	60	4	90	12	4	119	13	2.71
Chandler, TR*	22	20	6	3	10	5	0	.667	131	118	57	48	7	56	0	6	64	3	3.30
Contreras, Read	12	0	0	0	2	1	2	.667	29	19	14	12	1	20	1	5	22	2	3.72
Cort, Berkshire	25	24	5	0	14	5	0	.737	148	144	55	46	6	45	0	1	68	7	2.80
Currence, Berk*	17	11	5	0	4	5	1	.444	77	88	47	40	6	33	0	0	57	5	4.68
Davis, Three R	22	0	0	0	5	1	4	.833	45	43	15	11	3	23	4	2	22	1	2.20
Deidel, Berk*	10	5	0	0	5	1	0	.833	39	43	21	20	5	20	0	2	22	1	4.62
Diorio, West H	40	0	0	0	3	3	7	.500	58	52	17	10	3	17	1	1	26	3	1.55
Drumright, Que C	18	2	1	1	4	1	5	.800	58	34	9	8	0	18	0	1	16	0	1.24
Dumoulin, Three R	38	0	0	0	5	1	9	.667	58	50	27	13	2	26	3	0	35	5	2.02
Erardi, Berkshire	61	1	0	0	8	4	10	.667	102	91	46	37	5	51	4	3	62	8	3.26
Ewell, Quebec C	24	4	0	0	1	5	4	.167	54	61	37	30	4	21	2	3	27	1	5.00
Ferreyra, Three R	25	1	1	1	5	2	2	.714	44	44	17	14	2	13	3	3	16	2	2.86
Fierbaugh, Que C.	25	24	5	0	8	13	0	.381	148	148	93	73	7	70	1	3	91	9	4.44
Flanagan, Wmpt	12	11	4	0	4	6	0	.400	83	73	39	34	4	32	2	2	30	3	3.69
Fleshman, West H	12	11	3	1	5	5	0	.500	80	68	30	22	4	27	5	3	44	2	2.48
Gibson, Reading*	22	19	4	1	4	11	0	.267	107	130	83	76	8	64	6	3	73	5	6.39
Gingrich, Que C	33	18	10	2	10	4	0	.714	152	125	39	32	5	27	2	9	89	6	1.89
Greenhalgh, Read	24	24	9	2	5	14	0	.263	160	170	70	57	12	38	2	4	89	3	3.21
Gregson, Reading	43	1	1	0	0	6	5	.000	67	62	27	20	1	35	9	2	30	7	2.69
Gronlund, Que C	6	5	1	0	3	1	0	.750	36	24	15	11	0	21	0	0	27	1	2.75
Grossman, Wmpt	21	12	1	0	3	6	0	.333	75	81	53	44	10	62	2	3	43	7	5.28
Grow, Three R*	13	13	8	4	7	5	0	.583	98	70	21	20	5	36	1	1	59	3	1.84
Hanna, Quebec C	7	7	0	0	1	2	0	.333	30	37	19	11	1	22	0	1	23	7	3.30
Hannahs, Que C*	26	26	14	5	20	6	0	.769	173	144	56	46	11	88	1	1	126	13	2.39
Harer, Bristol*	1	0	0	0	0	0	0	.000	2	0	0	0	0	3	0	0	0	0	0.00
Heinold, West H	11	11	5	2	7	3	0	.700	74	67	14	11	2	10	2	1	35	2	1.34
Hernaiz, Reading	8	0	0	0	1	1	0	.500	23	16	5	5	0	9	0	1	11	0	1.96
Hinds, Berkshire	30	26	6	0	12	10	0	.545	180	177	87	79	15	68	4	4	85	13	3.95
Horstmann, QC	18	4	1	0	1	2	1	.333	46	57	33	29	3	24	2	1	18	5	5.67
Hoyt, West Haven	25	25	14	4	15	8	0	.652	180	169	66	50	6	46	6	8	103	5	2.50
Jensen, Berk*	20	2	1	0	2	1	1	.667	57	79	47	46	7	29	0	2	26	1	7.26
Kammeyer, West H	18	18	10	1	4	13	0	.235	125	123	60	36	3	48	12	6	61	3	2.59
Kerrigan, Que C.	8	0	0	0	1	1	4	.500	15	9	5	4	0	5	1	0	6	1	2.40
Kinney, Wmpt*	33	1	0	0	1	2	4	.333	67	76	31	27	3	24	4	4	59	5	3.63

Pitcher–Club	G.	GS.	CG.	ShO.	W.	L.	Sv.	Pct.	IP.	H.	R.	ER.	HR.	BB.	Int. BB.	HB.	SO.	WP.	ERA.
Klein, Reading	22	13	5	1	4	7	1	.364	107	108	53	44	6	35	6	3	63	4	3.70
Kniffin, Reading*	11	11	5	2	4	6	0	.400	81	77	27	22	3	22	4	1	46	1	2.44
LaCoss, Three R	25	25	9	2	12	10	0	.545	162	148	66	53	9	53	1	10	80	1	2.94
LaRose, Bristol*	19	14	5	1	8	6	0	.571	108	105	45	32	3	30	4	3	65	1	2.67
Leonhard, Que C	8	1	0	0	0	0	0	.000	17	16	11	6	1	13	0	1	10	1	3.18
Lindsey, Berk*	1	0	0	0	0	0	0	.000	2	1	0	0	0	2	0	0	1	0	0.00
Linnert, Wmpt*	21	4	0	0	1	4	2	.200	74	62	28	21	2	29	2	5	45	3	2.55
Mahan, Wmpt	13	13	3	2	2	8	0	.200	70	83	46	42	4	33	1	1	37	3	5.40
Manderbach, Read*	8	6	1	0	2	3	1	.400	35	33	16	14	0	17	2	1	16	0	3.60
Mantlo, Berkshire	1	0	0	0	0	0	0	.000	4	6	3	3	1	1	0	0	3	1	6.75
McCall, West H	31	20	10	2	11	10	2	.524	159	160	68	52	12	28	7	0	93	1	2.94
McElwain, W H*	21	1	0	0	0	3	4	.000	35	46	29	26	1	19	1	0	23	3	6.69
McGough, Wmpt	24	24	10	2	7	12	0	.368	145	172	92	83	17	52	3	2	57	9	5.15
McLaurine, Berk*	60	0	0	0	3	8	14	.273	81	76	25	22	6	33	7	1	61	5	2.44
McNulty, Wat	6	5	0	0	3	0	0	.000	24	37	26	18	2	9	0	0	11	2	6.75
Mersch, West H	10	10	6	1	6	2	0	.750	70	65	27	21	7	18	0	1	41	0	2.70
Mestek, Waterbury	20	20	8	2	6	10	0	.375	136	140	67	56	7	48	4	3	85	9	3.71
Moore, Three R	26	22	10	4	7	12	1	.368	159	138	55	51	13	68	7	6	95	5	2.89
Morris, Berkshire	25	12	0	0	2	4	2	.333	74	67	51	43	1	59	0	10	28	6	5.23
Moskau, Three R	26	23	11	6	13	6	0	.684	180	134	42	31	5	58	0	4	124	3	1.55
Newcomer, Bris*	6	4	0	0	3	0	0	.000	25	20	12	12	1	12	1	0	11	1	4.32
Niewczyk, T R*	10	0	0	0	1	0	1	1.000	12	11	5	2	1	13	1	0	6	0	1.50
O'Brien, Wat	36	1	1	0	5	2	2	.714	110	102	51	33	3	41	9	3	53	6	2.70
Ollar, Wat*	1	0	0	0	0	0	0	.000	2	3	2	2	1	2	0	0	1	0	9.00
Patterson, W H	13	13	6	2	9	2	0	.818	100	67	30	23	2	27	3	3	64	3	2.07
Paxton, Bristol	8	7	5	1	4	3	0	.571	51	38	15	14	3	16	0	1	36	1	2.47
Percival, Bristol	14	14	8	2	8	4	0	.667	97	82	42	34	5	34	3	3	47	2	3.15
Proctor, Bristol	23	4	2	0	3	4	2	.429	71	68	27	23	5	16	3	1	29	2	2.92
Rainey, Bristol	22	13	3	1	7	4	0	.636	101	109	67	49	9	63	5	1	31	11	4.37
Rajsich, West H*	30	3	0	0	4	4	4	.500	61	57	36	28	5	25	4	5	45	4	4.13
Rasmussen, Berk	2	0	0	0	0	0	0	.000	5	4	4	0	0	3	0	0	3	0	0.00
Rawley, Que C*	25	25	11	2	11	7	0	.611	164	143	55	49	11	79	1	3	113	8	2.69
Remmerswaal, Bris	1	0	0	0	0	0	0	.000	1/3	3	2	2	0	1	0	0	0	1	54.00
Riley, Quebec	33	17	5	2	9	10	1	.474	118	101	51	47	7	68	2	3	77	5	3.58
Ripley, Bristol	21	14	3	1	10	10	0	.500	161	161	67	58	7	39	8	3	88	6	3.24
Robson, Wmpt	19	19	10	2	6	13	0	.316	137	120	61	54	6	37	2	7	77	2	3.55
Ross, Bristol*	19	14	9	1	11	5	0	.688	119	101	38	33	3	34	4	4	52	1	2.50
Rothschild, TR	30	12	10	5	11	3	5	.786	123	96	33	28	7	29	2	4	75	6	2.05
Rushing, Que C*	37	0	0	0	7	4	6	.636	85	73	28	17	2	20	1	2	58	6	1.80
Schatzeder, Q C*	5	5	0	0	2	3	0	.400	28	38	16	14	2	10	0	1	19	2	4.50
Shirley, Wat*	24	24	4	0	5	14	0	.263	125	115	79	57	6	97	0	0	69	13	4.10
Skiba, Wmpt	2	2	0	0	0	2	0	.000	6	15	12	12	1	3	1	0	1	0	18.00
Slocum, Wat	25	14	1	0	4	7	0	.364	88	95	66	60	9	56	0	1	60	4	6.14
Sorensen, Berk	7	6	1	0	0	3	0	.000	41	44	19	15	1	16	0	1	25	0	3.29
Standley, Wat	47	1	0	0	8	6	15	.571	83	61	17	13	2	34	11	1	24	6	1.41
Stanley, Bristol	27	27	13	4	15	9	0	.625	186	176	76	55	8	83	6	11	78	2	2.66
Sutcliffe, Wat	30	26	8	0	10	11	0	.476	187	187	90	66	14	45	6	9	121	3	3.18
Suter, Bristol	16	13	5	1	5	5	0	.500	90	91	52	43	5	39	5	2	50	4	4.30
Van Der Beek, Wat	30	17	8	2	9	9	0	.500	142	147	75	53	4	56	4	2	77	13	3.36
Vosk, Bristol	40	1	0	0	2	5	16	.286	82	56	22	16	4	35	5	3	50	3	1.76
Weese, Wmpt	11	0	0	0	1	3	0	.250	32	27	24	21	3	11	1	2	23	2	5.91
Werd, Wmpt*	19	15	6	0	2	11	0	.154	99	117	54	43	9	31	5	1	37	3	3.91
White, Reading*	20	5	0	0	1	5	0	.167	62	78	45	37	5	35	2	5	30	3	5.37
Wright, Reading	20	20	10	0	13	5	0	.722	147	124	51	39	2	56	4	7	107	4	2.39
Wrona, Berkshire	7	5	0	0	1	3	0	.250	36	34	16	16	2	15	0	0	16	0	4.00

BALKS—Currence, 5; Cort, Linnert, 3 each; Bobinger, Chandler, Dumoulin, Erardi, Fierbaugh, Gingrich, Grossman, McCall, Patterson, Rawley, Wrona, 2 each; Alexander, Arsensault, Bell, Davis, Deidel, Ewell, Flanagan, Gronlund, Hannahs, Hoyt, Jensen, Klein, Manderbach, McElwain, McGough, McLaurine, Mestek, Moskau, Newcomer, O'Brien, Ross, Sutcliffe, Van Der Beek, Wright, 1 each.

COMBINATION SHUTOUTS—Austerman-Jensen-Erardi, Berkshire; Brayton-Vosk, Rainey-Newcomer-Proctor-Vosk, Bristol; Rawley-Drumright, Rawley-Riley, Quebec City; Bell-Brenizer, Reading; LaCoss-Dumoulin, Moskau-Dumoulin, Three Rivers; Shirley-Stanley 2, Waterbury; Fleshman-Diorio, Heinold-McElwain, Rajsich-Diorio-McElwain, West Haven; Flanagan-Linnert-Arsenault, Williamsport.

NO-HIT-GAME—Patterson, West Haven, defeated Williamsport, 1-0, June 28.

Southern League

Leading Batter
LARRY FOSTER
Knoxville

League President
BILLY HITCHCOCK

CHAMPIONSHIP WINNERS IN PREVIOUS YEARS

1904—Macon .598	Knoxville* .634	Augusta (3rd)† .543
1905—Macon .625	1930—Greenville* .620	1956—Jacksonville‡ .621
1906—Savannah .637	Macon .643	1957—Augusta .636
1907—Charleston .620	1931-35—Did not operate.	Charlotte (2nd)† .562
1908—Jacksonville .694	1936—Jacksonville .652	1958—Augusta .550
1909—Chattanooga* .738	Columbus* .650	Macon (3rd)† .500
Augusta .702	1937—Columbus .572	1959—Knoxville .557
1910—Columbus .588	Savannah (3rd)† .565	Gastonia (4th)† .504
Columbia .710	1938—Savannah .574	1960—Columbia .597
1911—Columbus* .681	Macon (2nd)† .570	Savannah (3rd)† .561
Columbia .632	1939—Columbus .601	1961—Asheville .635
1912—Jacksonville* .679	Augusta (2nd)† .597	1962—Savannah .662
Columbus .632	1940—Savannah .627	Macon (3rd)† .576
1913—Savannah .754	Columbus (2nd)† .583	1963—Augusta* .661
Savannah .593	1941—Macon .643	Lynchburg .662
1914—Savannah* .667	Columbus (2nd)† .636	1964—Lynchburg .579
Albany .650	1942—Charleston .620	1965—Columbus .572
1915—Macon .588	Macon (2nd)† .585	1966—Mobile .629
Columbus* 686	1943-45—Did not operate.	1967—Birmingham .604
1916—Augusta* .617	1946—Columbus .568	1968—Asheville .614
Columbia .631	Augusta (4th)† .547	1969—Charlotte .579
1917—Charleston .741	1947—Columbus .575	1970—Columbus .569
Columbia* .667	Savannah (2nd)† .563	1971—Did not operate as league—
1918—Did not operate.	1948—Charleston .572	clubs were members of Dixie Asso-
1919—Columbia .585	Greenville (3rd)† .549	ciation.
1920—Columbia .633	1949—Macon‡ .623	1972—Asheville .583
1921—Columbia .642	1950—Macon‡ .588	Montgomery§ .561
1922—Charleston .625	1951—Montgomery .607	1973—Montgomery§ .580
1923—Charlotte* .653	1952—Columbia .649	Jacksonville .559
Macon .580	Montgomery (3rd)† .558	1974—Jacksonville .565
1924—Augusta .612	1953—Jacksonville .679	Knoxville§ .533
1925—Spartanburg .620	Savannah (2nd)† .571	1975—Orlando .587
1926—Greenville .662	1954—Jacksonville .593	Montgomery§ .545
1927—Greenville .622	Savannah (2nd)† .571	
1928—Asheville .664	1955—Columbia .636	
1929—Asheville .605		

*Won split-season playoff. †Won four-club playoff. ‡Won championship and four-club playoff. §League was divided into Eastern and Western divisions; won playoffs.

STANDING OF CLUBS AT CLOSE OF FIRST HALF, JUNE 22

EAST DIVISION						WEST DIVISION					
Club	W.	L.	T.	Pct.	G.B.	Club	W.	L.	T.	Pct.	G.B.
Charlotte (Orioles)	37	28	1	.569	......	Chattanooga (Athletics)	34	30	1	.531	......
Savannah (Braves)	33	27	0	.550	1½	Knoxville (White Sox)	35	31	0	.530	......
Orlando (Twins)	35	32	0	.522	3	Montgomery (Tigers)	25	34	0	.424	6½
Jacksonville (Royals)	31	37	0	.456	7½	Columbus (Astros)	26	37	2	.413	7½

STANDING OF CLUBS AT CLOSE OF SECOND HALF, SEPTEMBER 2

EAST DIVISION						WEST DIVISION					
Club	W.	L.	T.	Pct.	G.B.	Club	W.	L.	T.	Pct.	G.B.
Orlando (Twins)	40	32	0	.556	......	Montgomery (Tigers)	56	22	0	.718	......
Jacksonville (Royals)	35	35	0	.500	4	Chattanooga (Athletics)	36	38	0	.486	18
Charlotte (Orioles)	37	38	0	.493	4½	Columbus (Astros)	32	43	0	.427	22½
Savannah (Braves)	36	44	0	.450	8	Knoxville (White Sox)	26	46	0	.361	27

COMPOSITE STANDING OF CLUBS AT CLOSE OF SEASON, SEPTEMBER 2

EAST DIVISION

Club	Orl.	Char.	Sav.	Jax.	Mon.	Chat.	Knx.	Col.	W.	L.	T.	Pct.	G.B.
Orlando (Twins)	....	11	9	8	11	11	14	11	75	64	0	.540	......
Charlotte (Orioles)	9	....	12	10	7	10	13	13	74	66	1	.529	1½
Savannah (Braves)	11	8	....	13	10	8	11	8	69	71	0	.493	6½
Jacksonville (Royals)	11	10	7	....	7	12	8	11	66	72	0	.478	8½

WEST DIVISION

Club	Orl.	Char.	Sav.	Jax.	Mon.	Chat.	Knx.	Col.	W.	L.	T.	Pct.	G.B.
Montgomery (Tigers)	9	13	10	12	....	12	11	14	81	56	0	.591	......
Chattanooga (Athletics)	9	10	12	8	8	....	14	9	70	68	1	.507	11½
Knoxville (White Sox)	6	7	9	12	7	6	....	14	61	77	0	.442	20½
Columbus (Astros)	9	7	12	9	6	9	6	....	58	80	2	.420	23½

Major league affiliations in parentheses.

Playoffs—Orlando defeated Charlotte, 1 game to none for East Division championship. Montgomery defeated Chattanooga, 1 game to none for West Division championship. Montgomery defeated Orlando, three games to one for League Championship.

Regular-Season Attendance—Charlotte, 113,559; Chattanooga, 135,144; Columbus, 50,171; Jacksonville, 69,343; Knoxville, 38,046; Montgomery, 59,754; Orlando, 41,951; Savannah, 58,361. Total, 566,329. All-Star Game, 4,207. Playoffs, 7,694.

Managers: Charlotte—Jim Schaffer; Chattanooga—Rene Lachemann; Columbus—Leo Posada; Jacksonville—E. William (Billy) Scripture; Knoxville—Gordon Lund; Montgomery—Les Moss; Orlando—Dick Phillips; Savannah—Tommie Aaron.

All-Star Team: 1B—Murray, Charlotte; 2B—Doyle, Charlotte; 3B—Parrill, Charlotte; SS—Gulliver, Montgomery; Utility—Brookens, Montgomery; OF—Bryant, Chattanooga; Budaska, Chattanooga; Foster, Knoxville; Cannon, Columbus; C—Murphy, Savannah; DH—Obradovich, Orlando; P—Ford, Charlotte; DeBarr, Montgomery; Manager—Lachemann, Chattanooga.

(Compiled by Howe News Bureau, Chicago, Ill.)

CLUB BATTING

Club	G.	AB.	R.	OR.	H.	TB.	2B.	3B.	HR.	RBI.	SH.	Int. SF.	BB.	HP.	SO.	SB.	CS.	LOB.	Pct.
Montgomery	137	4201	584	478	1101	1571	180	31	76	523	50	43	524	24	35	611	131	44	861	.262
Charlotte	141	4443	534	486	1151	1605	183	41	63	478	26	39	439	26	29	523	59	43	946	.259
Chattanooga	139	4241	534	558	1068	1425	144	39	45	466	57	40	576	33	34	678	167	101	1059	.252
Orlando	139	4404	550	532	1097	1535	164	35	68	500	68	43	582	47	42	593	65	49	1038	.249
Savannah	140	4289	540	508	1063	1448	145	30	60	474	77	46	469	34	41	643	138	51	937	.248
Jacksonville	138	4317	459	442	1056	1391	152	24	45	417	54	34	371	16	40	585	95	40	887	.245
Columbus	140	4282	447	530	1031	1293	116	28	30	386	54	43	432	18	53	703	124	67	935	.241
Knoxville	138	4257	444	558	1012	1385	170	31	47	398	47	42	507	13	33	695	56	44	980	.238

INDIVIDUAL BATTING

(Leading Qualifiers for Batting Championship—378 or More Plate Appearances)

*Bats lefthanded. †Switch-hitter.

Player and Club	G.	AB.	R.	H.	TB.	2B.	3B.	HR.	RBI.	SH.	SF.	BB.	HP.	SO.	SB.	CS.	Pct.
Foster, Larry, Knoxville	106	338	53	105	160	14	1	13	57	0	3	82	6	72	10	4	.311
Corcoran, Timothy, Mon*	129	437	66	135	185	25	5	5	60	7	5	57	2	33	13	1	.309
Bryant, Derek, Chattanooga	134	467	70	141	181	14	10	2	50	6	4	64	1	31	42	16	.302
Doyle, Blake, Charlotte*	134	529	72	158	187	16	5	1	53	4	7	30	2	20	11	9	.299
Cannon, Joseph, Columbus*	127	478	64	142	169	13	4	2	40	6	6	21	8	102	39	15	.297
Beamon, Charles, Jack*	138	500	58	143	158	12	0	1	47	6	7	49	5	40	16	6	.286
Tevlin, Creighton, Char*	113	393	47	112	133	14	2	1	23	4	2	38	4	29	5	5	.285

Player and Club	G.	AB.	R.	H.	TB.	2B.	3B.	HR.	RBI.	SH.	SF.	BB.	HP.	SO.	SB.	CS.	Pct.
Small, G. Henry, Savannah	134	468	56	132	186	26	2	8	62	3	3	33	10	48	2	2	.282
Gates, Joseph, Jack*	124	386	63	108	135	14	5	1	21	2	2	64	5	71	25	9	.280
Parrill, Martin, Char*	115	413	50	113	182	17	2	16	66	1	6	31	0	45	1	2	.274

Departmental Leaders: G—Beamon, Obradovich, 138; AB—Doyle, 529; R—Obradovich, 84; H—Doyle, 158; TB—Obradovich, 205; 2B—Seidholz, 28; 3B—Bryant, Liranzo, 10; HR—Obradovich, 21; RBI—Obradovich, 68; SH—Albert, 17; SF—Wolfe, 13; BB—Obradovich, 113; HB—Obradovich, Small, 10; SO—Obradovich, 104; SB—Bryant, Cador, 42; CS—Bryant, 16.

(All Players—Listed Alphabetically)

Player and Club	G.	AB.	R.	H.	TB.	2B.	3B.	HR.	RBI.	SH.	SF.	BB.	HP.	SO.	SB.	CS.	Pct.
Adams, Robert Melvin, Mon	7	30	6	7	12	2	0	1	6	0	0	2	0	2	1	0	.233
Albert, Richard, Savannah	116	353	44	81	106	19	0	2	27	17	3	62	4	71	4	2	.229
Alexander, Roger G., Sav	1	0	1	0	0	0	0	0	0	0	0	0	0	0	0	0	.000
Alfaro, Jose, Columbus	1	1	0	0	0	0	0	0	0	0	0	0	0	0	0	0	.000
Alonso, Julio, Montgomery	1	2	0	0	0	0	0	0	0	0	0	0	0	1	0	0	.000
Alvarez, Jose R., Columbus...........	57	136	10	22	25	1	1	0	9	6	2	33	1	30	3	1	.162
Aranzamendi, Jorge, Sav...............	44	109	6	16	19	3	0	0	9	7	2	14	3	23	1	0	.147
Arcia, Jose R., Columbus	93	289	21	64	77	10	0	1	19	3	2	21	6	48	4	0	.221
Argenti, Robert, Chat†	62	170	19	36	42	4	1	0	8	5	0	13	2	19	6	3	.212
Arline, James, Savannah*	123	396	51	92	122	14	5	2	29	6	3	38	1	103	16	10	.232
Arthur, Albert, Orlando	1	2	0	0	0	0	0	0	0	0	0	0	0	2	0	0	.000
Bates, Charles, Mon....................	111	346	33	91	126	18	4	3	33	7	3	41	4	63	1	3	.263
Beach, Randolph, Orlando	27	78	10	16	21	5	0	0	6	3	0	15	2	11	1	0	.205
Beamon, Charles, Jack*	138	500	58	143	158	12	0	1	47	6	7	49	5	40	16	6	.286
Beaurivage, Ronald, Chat*	55	145	21	28	41	6	2	1	19	2	3	40	2	31	1	4	.193
Benedict, Bruce, Savannah	24	73	10	21	22	1	0	0	7	1	1	13	1	8	0	1	.288
Bethke, Rick, Orlando*	1	0	1	0	0	0	0	0	0	0	0	0	0	0	0	0	.000
Blaylock, Gary, Jack*	103	340	35	77	114	14	1	7	43	1	4	22	2	49	1	1	.226
Bochy, Bruce, Columbus...............	69	230	9	53	59	6	0	0	16	1	1	14	0	30	0	3	.230
Bonnell, R. Barry, Sav	51	188	31	42	70	6	2	6	23	4	2	17	1	16	7	0	.223
Brandenburg, Gary, Char.............	51	153	15	30	40	5	1	1	16	2	0	21	1	18	1	1	.196
Brazell, Ted, Montgomery	66	185	13	40	51	4	2	1	16	0	0	27	3	19	3	0	.216
Brookens, Thomas, Mon	137	492	76	127	192	22	5	11	56	6	5	66	6	65	21	7	.258
Brown, Jerald, Savannah	37	106	10	26	32	3	0	1	11	5	2	11	0	17	0	1	.245
Bryan, James, Charlotte*	103	326	34	79	97	13	1	1	22	1	2	39	0	37	2	5	.242
Bryant, Derek, Chattanooga	134	467	70	141	181	14	10	2	50	6	4	64	1	31	42	16	.302
Budaska, Mark, Chat†.................	131	420	63	111	154	18	2	7	55	1	4	91	3	93	17	11	.264
Butera, Salvatore, Orlando	90	267	45	73	90	8	0	3	28	4	0	52	5	20	1	1	.273
Cacciatore, Frank, Mon*.............	9	25	3	5	6	1	0	0	2	0	0	4	0	5	0	0	.200
Cador, Roger, Savannah*	132	429	68	105	128	13	2	2	46	2	3	63	3	57	42	8	.245
Cannon, Joseph, Columbus*...........	127	478	64	142	169	13	4	2	40	6	6	21	8	102	39	15	.297
Carter, Gregory, Mon	1	3	0	0	0	0	0	0	0	0	0	0	0	2	0	0	.000
Caughey, Wayne, Orlando*	96	323	40	80	103	8	6	1	29	6	5	35	2	29	8	8	.248
Collins, Gregory, Knx	31	89	8	23	32	6	0	1	7	0	0	10	0	15	0	0	.258
Collins, Jimmie, Sav*	5	17	1	2	5	0	0	1	3	0	0	2	0	1	0	1	.118
Concepcion, Onix, Jack	5	13	1	4	4	0	0	0	4	0	0	1	0	4	0	0	.308
Connoly, Kevin, Sav*..................	11	35	1	5	5	0	0	0	4	0	2	3	0	5	0	0	.143
Corcoran, Timothy, Mon*.............	129	437	66	135	185	25	5	5	60	7	5	57	2	33	13	1	.309
Cosey, D. Ray, Chat*.................	8	38	6	11	16	3	1	0	2	0	0	0	0	9	1	1	.289
Cox, Jeffrey, Chat	36	131	20	38	48	3	2	1	14	1	1	13	4	15	9	6	.290
Crane, Mark, Montgomery	9	14	2	1	1	0	0	0	0	1	0	2	0	3	1	0	.071
Crosta, James, Knoxville	46	137	6	28	31	3	0	0	4	4	0	16	0	17	2	2	.204
Denevi, Michael, Jack	100	307	34	70	88	16	1	0	27	5	1	20	4	41	1	4	.228
Dinzey, Amado, Savannah†	29	66	3	10	13	0	0	1	3	1	1	3	0	22	0	0	.152
Dlugach, Michael, Knx	36	107	11	22	24	2	0	0	8	1	0	16	1	21	1	0	.206
Doyle, Blake, Charlotte*	134	529	72	158	187	16	5	1	53	4	7	30	2	20	11	9	.299
Drake, Kevin, Columbus	128	437	50	117	137	6	4	2	33	6	3	25	5	88	22	3	.268
Duncan, Richard, Orlando*	115	364	34	80	106	10	2	4	33	3	4	34	2	35	10	3	.220
Edwards, David, Orlando	55	209	32	61	90	10	5	3	26	2	1	26	6	30	1	2	.292
Englishbey, Stephen, Col*.............	41	135	9	19	30	2	0	3	10	1	2	16	1	26	1	2	.141
Fleming, John, Jack	91	294	26	59	86	6	3	5	25	2	2	11	1	28	1	3	.201
Flowers, Burnel, Mon*	80	320	47	101	113	7	1	1	20	1	0	21	0	24	41	13	.316
Foley, Marvis, Knoxville*	126	414	44	104	126	12	2	2	36	5	7	41	2	45	3	4	.251
Foster, Larry, Knoxville	106	338	53	105	160	14	1	13	57	0	3	82	6	72	10	4	.311
Gates, Joseph, Jack*	124	386	63	108	135	14	5	1	21	2	2	64	5	71	25	9	.280
Gatlin, Michael, Orlando	33	90	8	19	26	5	1	0	9	3	1	8	0	19	2	0	.211
Gaudet, James, Jack	15	50	5	15	19	4	0	0	4	1	0	5	0	13	1	1	.300
Gomez, Juan A., Chat	6	12	0	1	1	0	0	0	1	0	2	0	2	0	0	0	.083
Gonzales, Daniel, Mon*	77	271	26	79	107	10	3	4	31	1	2	19	1	31	5	2	.292
Gulliver, Glenn, Mon*	51	130	26	36	54	10	1	2	22	2	1	30	2	14	2	3	.277
Haines, Dennis, Chat*	100	311	38	88	124	11	5	5	44	4	6	48	0	60	1	3	.283
Heil, Charles, Jack†	17	52	2	5	7	2	0	0	7	0	1	2	0	5	0	0	.096
Hrovat, Dale, Jacksonville	1	1	0	0	0	0	0	0	0	0	0	0	0	1	0	0	.000
Ingalls, Richard, Jack*	87	230	15	48	54	4	1	0	13	10	0	25	0	14	1	3	.209

Player and Club	G.	AB.	R.	H.	TB.	2B.	3B.	HR.	RBI.	SH.	SF.	BB.	HP.	SO.	SB.	CS.	Pct.
Jata, Paul, Orlando	22	62	6	15	19	1	0	1	6	0	1	11	0	9	0	0	.242
Kemp, Steven, Montgomery*	73	256	41	74	119	17	2	8	43	0	2	33	2	35	3	1	.289
Kennedy, Kevin, Charlotte	40	123	21	27	31	4	0	0	5	2	1	18	5	19	2	1	.220
Keough, Matthew, Chat	124	420	43	88	125	13	3	6	52	8	2	32	3	91	10	2	.210
Kilpatrick, Cleo, Knx*	49	176	26	45	56	4	2	1	11	0	2	12	2	31	8	1	.256
Koegel, Peter, Jack	87	310	29	89	131	15	0	9	54	0	2	33	3	33	1	2	.287
Lacey, John, Savannah*	84	274	38	73	93	7	2	3	35	1	1	35	1	39	6	5	.266
Laseter, Thomas, Jack	92	309	38	74	118	11	3	9	36	3	0	20	6	51	0	1	.239
Lieppman, Keith, Chat	63	213	28	46	65	8	1	3	29	2	4	19	0	30	6	1	.216
Liranzo, Rafael, Charlotte	135	486	55	127	199	25	10	9	61	1	5	21	2	78	6	5	.261
Lonchar, John, Orlando	75	224	23	57	72	10	1	1	28	6	1	26	0	24	0	0	.254
Long, David, Savannah*	6	22	1	11	15	1	0	1	4	0	0	1	0	3	0	0	.500
Lynch, Terrance, Mon	94	276	47	83	122	16	4	5	44	2	4	41	3	47	4	1	.301
Maddox, Jerry, Savannah	98	316	53	83	121	13	2	7	41	4	3	57	7	37	1	4	.263
Marple, M. Daniel, 6 Char-39 Mon*	45	125	15	27	32	3	1	0	6	6	2	27	0	18	3	2	.216
May, Davis, Orlando	2	0	1	0	0	0	0	0	0	0	0	0	0	0	1	0	.000
Melendez, William, Col	14	35	4	9	11	2	0	0	7	2	1	7	0	6	0	0	.257
Melvin, Kenneth, Jack	120	353	35	77	99	13	0	3	27	2	3	45	4	78	6	3	.218
Mollenhauer, Robert, Chat	120	395	42	99	121	14	1	2	33	6	3	39	2	39	7	7	.251
Murphy, Dale, Savannah	104	352	37	94	153	13	5	12	55	1	6	25	1	61	6	1	.267
Murphy, Dwayne, Chat*	68	200	32	52	61	6	0	1	23	4	3	50	1	42	18	12	.260
Murphy, Scott, Charlotte	48	158	14	40	51	6	1	1	11	1	0	18	0	16	1	1	.253
Murray, Eddie, Charlottet	88	299	46	89	144	15	2	12	46	0	2	43	1	41	11	3	.298
Nasif, Ralph, Montgomery	65	229	26	52	71	10	0	3	29	2	2	8	1	34	8	1	.227
Nickeson, Robert, Char	63	145	14	23	29	1	1	1	7	4	1	24	0	28	1	4	.159
Noah, Russell, Orlando*	119	382	49	87	138	12	6	9	45	4	1	62	0	89	3	4	.228
Norton, Fred, Knoxville	120	451	48	102	141	16	7	3	31	8	1	35	5	76	5	4	.226
Obradovich, James, Orlando*	138	441	84	117	205	17	4	21	68	5	3	113	10	104	1	1	.265
Ondina, Michael, Knoxville*	121	415	56	108	163	24	5	7	49	2	7	69	3	94	6	5	.260
O'Rear, John, Charlotte	125	413	53	99	131	15	7	1	41	2	4	36	4	53	7	4	.240
Palmer, Robert, Knoxville	106	338	24	75	107	17	3	3	35	3	3	34	6	67	0	2	.222
Parker, Darrell, Jack‡	49	168	17	39	57	5	2	3	18	2	2	8	1	23	1	2	.232
Parrill, Martin, Char*	115	413	50	113	182	17	2	16	66	1	6	31	0	45	1	2	.274
Parrish, Lance, Mont	107	340	46	75	130	9	2	14	55	3	3	38	1	95	0	1	.221
Perez, Ramon, Columbus	103	357	50	94	110	8	4	0	18	5	1	43	5	36	20	8	.263
Perkins, Craig, Jack	39	126	12	34	57	8	0	5	15	0	1	20	1	19	2	0	.270
Perlozzo, Samuel, Orlando	126	456	48	123	143	18	1	0	51	13	2	40	7	25	10	10	.270
Pisker, Donald, Columbus*	37	109	9	32	37	3	1	0	18	3	1	17	0	32	0	1	.294
Portley, Calvin, Columbust	116	330	44	83	93	6	2	0	19	6	4	61	4	56	12	13	.252
Puhl, Terry, Columbus*	28	98	13	28	36	5	0	1	14	3	0	16	0	12	11	2	.286
Puig, Richard, Knoxville*	118	414	39	81	120	13	4	6	25	8	3	39	1	62	11	5	.196
Pujols, Luis, Columbus	53	142	12	28	36	2	0	2	16	1	3	10	8	21	1	2	.197
Ramirez, Milton, Jack	129	401	28	101	121	13	2	1	35	12	4	15	1	25	1	2	.252
Reed, Kenneth, Knoxville	48	134	11	26	35	7	1	0	7	2	2	26	0	15	1	2	.194
Rickman, Richard, Char*	12	39	4	4	7	0	0	1	4	1	0	3	0	3	1	0	.103
Rima, Thomas, Columbus*	108	330	25	83	102	8	4	1	30	2	3	38	2	28	8	6	.252
Robinson, Bruce, Chat*	76	230	23	46	68	3	2	5	29	3	1	26	3	49	7	2	.200
Rockett, Patrick, Savannah	42	144	13	32	38	1	1	1	13	7	2	12	1	12	2	1	.222
Ryan, Albert, Savannah	29	85	14	19	21	2	0	0	5	3	0	13	1	12	9	2	.224
Ryan, Craig, Charlotte*	121	408	54	104	174	16	6	14	54	0	1	57	4	92	4	1	.255
Ryan, Terry, Orlando*	1	0	1	0	0	0	0	0	0	0	0	0	0	0	0	0	.000
Sain, Thomas, Orlando	76	289	27	70	93	13	2	2	22	4	0	19	2	33	3	3	.242
Sanner, Dale, Chat*	27	86	13	24	26	2	0	0	8	1	0	11	0	18	1	2	.279
Seidholz, Donn, Knoxville	131	460	40	119	178	28	2	9	65	4	10	26	2	70	3	4	.259
Serrano, Martin, Jack	18	51	5	11	12	1	0	0	4	1	2	4	0	4	1	0	.216
Shipley, Ted, Orlando	90	265	23	54	69	6	0	3	23	5	5	26	2	41	10	5	.204
Sigman, S. Lee, Chat	24	55	5	5	7	2	0	0	5	3	0	2	2	14	0	1	.091
Sinatro, Gregory, Chat‡	84	264	31	76	95	10	3	1	29	5	3	33	9	40	13	7	.288
Small, G. Henry, Savannah	134	468	56	132	186	26	2	8	62	3	3	33	10	48	2	2	.282
Smith, Calvin, Savannah*	113	394	46	98	114	3	5	1	30	8	0	27	5	43	28	11	.249
Stegman, David, Mont	61	188	31	50	58	8	0	0	20	4	6	33	5	24	15	7	.266
Stoddard, Timothy, Knox	1	1	0	0	0	0	0	0	1	0	0	1	0	0	0	0	.000
Tatis, Fernando, Columbus	129	447	49	119	176	26	5	7	66	3	7	31	6	80	0	4	.266
Taylor, Robert, Mont	21	36	6	6	7	1	0	0	1	0	2	2	0	4	0	2	.167
Tevlin, Creighton, Char*	113	393	47	112	133	14	2	1	23	4	2	38	4	29	5	5	.285
Thayer, Gregory, Orlando	2	1	1	0	0	0	0	0	0	0	0	0	0	0	0	0	.000
Thomasson, Harold, Jack	16	38	2	4	5	1	0	0	2	0	0	1	0	14	0	0	.105
Trammell, Alan, Mont	21	56	4	10	10	0	0	0	2	1	0	7	0	12	3	0	.179
Trella, Stephen, Mont	1	0	1	0	0	0	0	0	0	0	0	0	0	0	0	0	.000
Twellman, Thomas, Col	71	207	21	30	33	3	0	0	7	3	2	17	3	13	2	5	.145
Tyler, Michael, Columbus*	32	79	11	17	23	4	1	0	6	2	2	11	1	7	0	0	.215
Valle, John, Montgomery	74	232	45	58	116	11	1	15	53	0	5	35	4	34	6	0	.250
Vanderhook, H. Randolph, Char	90	272	30	63	81	10	1	2	25	0	4	41	2	22	1	1	.232
Velazquez, Federico, Sav	109	356	32	81	133	15	2	11	51	4	8	23	1	53	7	2	.228
Viefhaus, Stephen, Mont	79	227	24	47	62	6	0	3	26	5	4	33	1	49	2	0	.207

Player and Club	G.	AB.	R.	H.	TB.	2B.	3B.	HR.	RBI.	SH.	SF.	BB.	HP.	SO.	SB.	CS.	Pct.
Walling, Dennis, Chat*	115	369	48	95	147	15	5	9	42	1	5	58	1	51	20	14	.257
Ward, Gary, Orlando	132	475	50	119	167	17	2	9	65	7	6	44	1	62	8	4	.251
Wheeler, Edward, Knox	123	413	51	99	129	16	4	2	40	1	3	68	3	66	5	10	.240
Whisenton, Larry, Sav*	32	107	24	40	52	5	2	1	16	3	4	17	1	13	6	1	.374
Whiting, Don, Charlotte*	121	412	39	103	145	27	3	3	46	1	4	40	4	47	5	5	.250
Willeford, Jerry, Col*	1	2	0	0	0	0	0	0	0	0	0	0	0	0	0	0	.000
Williams, Mark, Chat*	46	170	17	60	74	11	0	1	17	0	0	11	1	13	7	5	.353
Willis, James, Columbus	128	440	46	91	139	11	2	11	58	1	3	51	3	88	1	2	.207
Wilson, Willie, Jack	107	388	54	98	126	13	6	1	35	7	3	26	7	72	37	3	.253
Wolf, Michael, Knoxville	122	370	27	75	83	8	0	0	22	9	1	32	2	44	1	1	.203
Wolfe, Lawrence, Orlando	136	476	67	126	193	24	5	11	61	3	13	71	3	59	6	8	.265

The following pitchers had no plate appearances primarily through use of designated hitters, listed alphabetically by club, games in parentheses:

CHARLOTTE—Chevez, Antonio (11); Darr, Michael (27); Flinn, John (24); Ford, David (27); Johnson, Duane (7); Miller, Randall (39); Pagnozzi, Michael (27); Parrott, Michael (5); Smith, Myrl (24); Van Bommel, William (16); Walker, Robert H. (14); Ward, Gregory (25).

CHATTANOOGA—Abraham, Brian (7); Bell, Ronald (21); Boyd, T. Randy (22); Hagman, David (5); Harrell, Clarence (7); Hile, Michael (7); Kingman, Brian (26); Kirby, Wayne (32); Lysander, Richard (18); McCatty, Steven (36); Peach, Russell (27); Salas, Bobby Ray (6); Scarbery, Randy (9); Stegman, Dennis (11); Taylor, Randall (40); Tronerud, Ricky (22); Wibberley, Christopher (8).

COLUMBUS—Aloi, David (29); Bannister, Floyd (3); Cuen, Eleno (8); Culpepper, David (36); DeMerritt, Martin (3); Dixon, Thomas (27); Elenes, Larry (20); Lopez, Marcelino (4); Miller, Richard L. (3); Ray, James F. (8); Roznovsky, Ronald (36); Sambito, Joseph (12); Sprinkle, Charles (20); Williams, Richard A. (27).

JACKSONVILLE—Ballinger, Mark (21); Bernard, Edward (12); Branch, Roy (26); Cowan, Edward (7); Garcia, Ruben (26); McGilberry, Randall (44); McKinney, Lynn (17); Meyring, Bradley (3); Osburn, L. Patrick (34); Overstreet, David (23); Paschall, William (21); Quisenberry, Daniel (9); Viebrock, Alan (7); Williams, Gary G. (23); Williams, Michael W. (6); Wright, Gary Evan (9).

KNOXVILLE—Best, Kurt (25); Bock, Paul (29); Combs, Robert (34); Frost, C. David (20); Knapp, R. Christian (11); Komadina, Tony (26); Monroe, Lawrence (29); Moran, C. William (6); Norton, Thomas (3); Smith, Barry (29); Stinson, Homer (8); Williams, Leo (23); Wortham, Richard (11).

MONTGOMERY—Bruchanski, Kenneth (33); Burnside, Sheldon (12); Cappuzzello, George (17); Christenson, Gary (12); Corr, Larry (1); DeBarr, Dennis (43); Harris, Frank (21); Ibarguen, Michael (7); Kenyon, Frank (2); Mercier, Ronald (5); Meyerrose, Michael (22); Morris, John S. (12); Rozema, David (19); Tobik, David (18); Treuel, Ralph (6).

ORLANDO—Ausman, Paul (12); Bemis, Gregg (13); Corbin, A. Ray (2); Garvin, T. Jared (23); Gressick, Jeffrey (5); Harris, William H. (14); Holly, Jeffrey (25); Lerner, Lewis (13); Smith, Charles D. (31).

SAVANNAH—Box, Robert (22); Bradford, Larry (23); Campbell, David A. (42); Davey, Michael (10); Figueroa, Domingo (22); Lusic, George (30); Mahler, Michael (8); McLaughlin, Joey (24); McWilliams, Larry (16); Rios, Wilfredo (9); Sevillano, Jose (28); Stephenson, C. Earl (7).

GRAND-SLAM HOME RUNS: Walling, 2; Budaska, Foley, Kemp, Kilpatrick, Lynch, Murray, Nasif, Palmer, Parrish, Puhl, Ramierz, Robinson, 1 each.

AWARDED FIRST BASE ON INTERFERENCE: Blaylock 3 (Lonchar, Robinson, Vanderhook); Bryant (Dale Murphy), Cador (Parrish), Maddox (Palmer), Dale Murphy (Haines), Ondina (Parrish), Perez (Parrish).

CLUB FIELDING

Club	G.	PO.	A.	E.	DP.	PB.	Pct.	Club	G.	PO.	A.	E.	DP.	PB.	Pct.
Columbus	140	3452	1462	134	110	11	.973	Montgomery	137	3342	1487	156	135	26	.969
Orlando	139	3555	1621	143	130	10	.973	Jacksonville	138	3465	1404	167	112	9	.967
Savannah	140	3449	1403	143	108	11	.971	Chattanooga	139	3456	1440	173	104	18	.966
Charlotte	141	3514	1487	154	135	8	.970	Knoxville	138	3443	1547	180	165	10	.965

Triple Plays—Savannah 2, Chattanooga 1.

INDIVIDUAL FIELDING

*Throws lefthanded.

FIRST BASEMEN

Player and Club	G.	PO.	A.	E.	DP.	Pct.	Player and Club	G.	PO.	A.	E.	DP.	Pct.
Haines, Chattanooga	23	157	9	0	5	1.000	Beamon, Jack.*	44	312	41	4	28	.989
Bates, Montgomery	84	709	62	2	76	.997	Ryan, Charlotte	62	547	33	7	60	.988
Corcoran, Mon.*	56	478	46	2	38	.996	Obradovich, Orl.*	124	1187	75	17	107	.987
Small, Savannah	65	518	38	3	50	.995	Blaylock, Jack.*	82	708	47	10	62	.987
Noah, Orlando*	19	147	13	1	7	.994	Foley, Knoxville	67	634	41	9	85	.987
WILLIS, Columbus	109	927	78	7	87	.993	Lieppman, Chat	62	505	34	7	36	.987
Wheeler, Knoxville	66	575	21	4	52	.993	Sinatro, Chat	13	123	5	2	8	.985
Lacey, Savannah	78	640	32	6	48	.991	Tatis, Columbus	33	268	17	5	14	.983
Murray, Charlotte	77	746	45	9	60	.989	Koegel, Jacksonville	20	160	18	4	11	.978
Beaurivage, Chat.*	48	436	18	5	37	.989							

FIRST BASEMEN—Continued

(Fewer Than Ten Games)

Player and Club	G.	PO.	A.	E.	DP.	Pct.	Player and Club	G.	PO.	A.	E.	DP.	Pct.
Murphy, Charlotte	2	13	1	0	3	1.000	Rima, Columbus	1	2	0	0	0	1.000
Heil, Jacksonville*	2	11	1	0	3	1.000	Velazquez, Savannah	1	2	0	0	0	1.000
Cacciatore, Mon*	2	11	1	0	1	1.000	Nasif, Montgomery	2	1	0	0	0	1.000
Collins, Savannah	1	9	1	0	0	1.000	Foster, Knoxville	8	69	4	2	12	.973
Arcia, Columbus	1	7	0	0	1	1.000	Budaska, Chat.*	5	22	0	1	1	.957
Kemp, Montgomery*	1	5	0	0	1	1.000	Brandenburg, Char	1	2	0	1	1	.667
Maddox, Savannah	1	3	1	0	1	1.000	Keough, Chattanooga	1	2	0	1	0	.667
Dlugach, Knoxville	1	3	1	0	0	1.000	Melendez, Columbus	1	0	0	1	0	.000
Perkins, Jack	1	4	0	0	1	1.000							

Triple Plays—Small 2, Budaska.

SECOND BASEMEN

Player and Club	G.	PO.	A.	E.	DP.	Pct.	Player and Club	G.	PO.	A.	E.	DP.	Pct.
PERLOZZO, Orlando	124	321	380	6	84	.992	Doyle, Charlotte	132	297	375	24	97	.966
Ryan, Savannah	22	48	51	1	7	.990	Brookens, Mon	137	310	389	25	93	.965
Cox, Chattanooga	12	28	42	1	6	.986	Smith, Savannah	111	247	281	20	60	.964
Murphy, Charlotte	10	15	32	1	4	.979	Puig, Knoxville	109	209	310	23	79	.958
Gates, Jacksonville	105	195	267	11	55	.977	Alvarez, Columbus	12	9	13	1	1	.957
Albert, Savannah	15	29	50	2	9	.975	Serrano, Jack	15	28	31	3	8	.952
Portley, Columbus	115	226	342	15	61	.974	Caughey, Orlando	19	42	36	4	4	.951
Mollenhauer, Chat	75	146	184	11	40	.968	Argenti, Jack	62	116	142	15	26	.945
Crosta, Knoxville	29	60	89	5	21	.968	Ingalls, Jack	23	43	43	6	6	.935
Twellman, Columbus	17	23	37	2	6	.968							

(Fewer Than Ten Games)

Player and Club	G.	PO.	A.	E.	DP.	Pct.	Player and Club	G.	PO.	A.	E.	DP.	Pct.
Nickeson, Chat	5	2	9	0	0	1.000	Perez, Columbus	7	17	14	2	6	.939
Bryant, Chattanooga	2	1	2	0	0	1.000	Concepcion, Jack	3	8	15	2	1	.920
Tatis, Columbus	1	2	0	0	0	1.000	Reed, Knoxville	8	22	20	4	3	.913

Triple Plays—Ryan, Mollenhauer.

THIRD BASEMEN

Player and Club	G.	PO.	A.	E.	DP.	Pct.	Player and Club	G.	PO.	A.	E.	DP.	Pct.
Murphy, Charlotte	14	13	28	0	1	1.000	Maddox, Savannah	98	104	185	18	24	.941
Twellman, Columbus	53	48	111	5	13	.970	Keough, Chattanooga	118	110	252	23	18	.940
Sain, Orlando	23	22	53	3	5	.962	Albert, Savannah	39	38	54	6	4	.939
Denevi, Jack	86	83	180	13	21	.953	Seidholz, Knoxville	103	92	231	24	27	.931
Nasif, Montgomery	11	8	12	1	2	.952	Sinatro, Chat	25	13	54	5	3	.931
PARRILL, Charlotte	114	72	197	14	23	.951	Alvarez, Columbus	26	20	43	5	2	.926
Perez, Columbus	54	58	69	7	7	.948	Viefhaus, Mon	64	57	123	16	18	.918
Wolfe, Orlando	110	87	231	19	15	.944	Valle, Montgomery	43	36	97	12	8	.917
Ingalls, Jack	47	32	69	6	6	.944	Rickman, Charlotte	11	6	25	3	1	.912
Foley, Knoxville	14	7	26	2	3	.943	Bates, Montgomery	24	15	53	7	5	.907
Crosta, Knoxville	14	10	23	2	2	.943	Thomasson, Jack	14	15	22	5	3	.881

(Fewer Than Ten Games)

Player and Club	G.	PO.	A.	E.	DP.	Pct.	Player and Club	G.	PO.	A.	E.	DP.	Pct.
Nickeson, Chat	4	2	4	0	0	1.000	Rima, Columbus	9	6	11	2	1	.895
Ryan, Savannah	7	3	3	0	1	1.000	Caughey, Orlando	7	8	16	3	1	.889
Vanderhook, Char	3	0	4	0	2	1.000	Melvin, Jacksonville	8	7	9	2	1	.889
Mollenhauer, Chat	4	2	1	0	0	1.000	Crane, Montgomery	3	2	5	2	1	.778
Pujols, Columbus	2	1	0	0	0	1.000	Ramirez, Jack	2	2	1	2	0	.600
Reed, Knoxville	8	7	16	1	0	.958	Willis, Columbus	2	0	1	1	0	.500
Arcia, Columbus	5	10	11	1	0	.955							

SHORTSTOPS

Player and Club	G.	PO.	A.	E.	DP.	Pct.	Player and Club	G.	PO.	A.	E.	DP.	Pct.
Trammell, Mon	21	40	64	2	11	.981	Ramirez, Jack	128	197	322	30	51	.945
Mollenhauer, Chat	47	57	121	5	16	.973	Caughey, Orlando	62	108	181	17	24	.944
Keough, Chattanooga	10	11	21	1	4	.970	Alvarez, Columbus	18	23	45	4	7	.944
WOLF, Knoxville	122	216	368	19	90	.968	Denevi, Jack	14	15	36	3	6	.944
Perez, Columbus	43	57	119	6	25	.967	Rockett, Savannah	42	62	119	11	16	.943
Taylor, Montgomery	16	16	41	2	10	.966	Aranzamendi, Sav	41	53	102	10	19	.939
Arcia, Columbus	85	146	223	17	43	.956	Nickeson, Chat	58	74	135	16	23	.929
Murphy, Charlotte	19	23	63	4	13	.956	Nasif, Montgomery	53	79	135	17	31	.926
O'Rear, Charlotte	125	197	394	28	75	.955	Gulliver, Mon	51	75	124	16	24	.926
Shipley, Orlando	85	122	286	20	52	.953	Reed, Knoxville	15	25	35	10	11	.857
Cox, Chattanooga	25	48	72	6	10	.952	Sigman, Chattanooga	24	27	58	15	11	.850
Albert, Savannah	65	96	188	15	29	.950							

SHORTSTOPS—Continued
(Fewer Than Ten Games)

Player and Club	G.	PO.	A.	E.	DP.	Pct.
Ingalls, Jack	1	3	3	0	1	1.000
Concepcion, Jack	1	2	3	0	1	1.000
Perlozzo, Orlando	1	4	0	0	0	1.000
Rickman, Charlotte	1	1	3	0	1	1.000
Twellman, Columbus	2	2	1	0	1	1.000
Viefhaus, Mon	9	16	30	2	5	.958
Seidholz, Knoxville	6	10	20	3	5	.909
Serrano, Jack	2	1	5	1	2	.857
Crane, Montgomery	3	2	9	2	0	.846

Triple Play—Aranzamendi.

OUTFIELDERS

Player and Club	G.	PO.	A.	E.	DP.	Pct.
Whisenton, Savannah*	32	60	4	0	0	1.000
Noah, Orlando*	31	45	5	0	0	1.000
Heil, Jacksonville*	14	16	3	0	0	1.000
Murphy, Chattanooga	60	138	6	1	2	.993
WALLING, Chat	104	241	8	2	2	.992
Drake, Columbus	125	310	12	5	2	.985
Beach, Orlando	25	62	5	1	0	.985
Pisker, Columbus*	35	52	6	1	1	.983
Gonzales, Mon	77	98	8	2	3	.981
Small, Savannah	38	47	4	1	0	.981
Edwards, Orlando	51	134	2	3	0	.978
Corcoran, Mon*	71	129	3	3	0	.978
Kemp, Montgomery	58	86	4	2	2	.978
Sain, Orlando	52	114	4	3	0	.975
Laseter, Jack	70	112	5	3	1	.975
Puhl, Columbus	28	76	1	2	0	.975
Parker, Jack	23	36	3	1	1	.975
Arline, Savannah*	120	245	14	7	2	.974
Ondina, Knoxville	121	182	8	5	2	.974
Liranzo, Charlotte	134	318	8	9	1	.973
Stegman, Mon	61	105	2	3	1	.973
Wilson, Jack	107	273	5	8	2	.972
Melvin, Jack	106	196	9	6	4	.972
Beamon, Jack*	105	167	8	5	1	.972
Reed, Knoxville	14	32	2	1	0	.971
Gatlin, Orlando	26	33	0	1	0	.971
Budaska, Chat*	90	148	11	5	2	.970
Foster, Knoxville	81	121	9	4	1	.970
Cannon, Columbus	124	238	12	8	2	.969
Duncan, Orlando	113	204	16	7	4	.969
F. Norton, Knx	118	287	11	10	3	.968
Cador, Savannah*	129	259	12	9	0	.968
Flowers, Mon*	80	117	3	4	1	.968
Tevlin, Charlotte*	101	171	6	6	2	.967
Rima, Columbus	85	140	8	5	2	.967
Whiting, Charlotte*	86	139	4	5	1	.966
Englishbey, Col*	29	54	0	2	0	.964
Ward, Orlando	132	235	16	10	3	.962
Bonnell, Savannah	51	117	6	5	2	.961
Kilpatrick, Knx*	49	87	8	4	2	.960
Brown, Savannah	33	68	3	3	0	.959
Bryant, Chattanooga	113	214	9	10	3	.957
Bryan, Charlotte*	97	166	7	8	2	.956
Williams, Chat*	39	101	6	5	2	.955
Dinzey, Savannah	25	31	2	2	1	.943
Marple, Char-Mon	25	32	0	2	0	.941
Lynch, Montgomery	41	51	7	4	1	.935
Ingalls, Jack	18	26	1	2	0	.931
Wheeler, Knoxville	25	33	1	5	1	.872

(Fewer Than Ten Games)

Player and Club	G.	PO.	A.	E.	DP.	Pct.
Sanner, Chattanooga	5	11	2	0	1	1.000
Seidholz, Knoxville	9	8	0	0	0	1.000
Valle, Montgomery	3	6	0	0	0	1.000
Collins, Savannah	3	5	0	0	0	1.000
Adams, Montgomery	5	5	0	0	0	1.000
Cacciatore, Mon*	4	4	0	0	0	1.000
Crane, Montgomery	2	2	1	0	1	1.000
Keough, Chattanooga	2	2	0	0	0	1.000
Perkins, Jack	2	2	0	0	0	1.000
Ryan, Charlotte	3	2	0	0	0	1.000
Crosta, Knoxville	1	1	0	0	0	1.000
Pujols, Columbus	1	1	0	0	0	1.000
Cosey, Chattanooga*	7	16	1	1	0	.944
Sinatro, Chat	8	12	1	1	0	.933
Alvarez, Columbus	5	10	0	1	0	.909
Long, Savannah*	6	8	1	2	1	.818

Triple Play—Sanner.

CATCHERS

Player and Club	G.	PO.	A.	E.	DP.	PB.	Pct.
Melendez, Col	13	53	6	0	0	1	1.000
Pujols, Columbus	43	184	21	1	1	5	.995
Brazell, Mon	38	165	23	1	3	4	.995
Kennedy, Char	39	210	24	2	3	5	.992
Collins, Knx	21	103	21	1	2	3	.992
Koegel, Jack	42	239	21	3	2	5	.989
Brandenburg, Char	32	143	11	2	2	1	.987
Velazquez, Sav	32	134	16	2	2	1	.987
Gaudet, Jack	15	63	9	1	0	0	.986
Foley, Knoxville	25	114	19	2	2	3	.985
PARRISH, Mon	104	600	79	11	10	22	.9840
Butera, Orlando	74	326	41	6	8	4	.9839
Lonchar, Orlando	68	263	39	5	6	5	.984
Benedict, Sav	23	107	12	2	1	1	.983
Haines, Chat	67	288	27	6	6	4	.981
Bochy, Columbus	63	266	45	6	0	2	.981
Murphy, Savannah	85	444	40	10	5	9	.980
Vanderhook, Char	72	355	47	8	3	2	.980
Tyler, Columbus	30	125	20	3	2	3	.980
Fleming, Jack	75	374	47	10	4	3	.977
Robinson, Chat	72	320	46	10	11	12	.973
Palmer, Knoxville	90	349	62	14	12	4	.967
Dlugach, Knx	10	33	5	2	0	0	.950

(Fewer Than Ten Games)

Player and Club	G.	PO.	A.	E.	DP.	PB.	Pct.
Jata, Orlando	9	37	2	0	0	1	1.000
Adams, Montgomery	1	3	2	0	0	1	1.000
Carter, Mon	1	1	0	0	0	0	1.000
Perkins, Jack	7	43	9	2	0	1	.963
Gomez, Chat	6	22	3	2	1	2	.926
Connolly, Sav	3	11	1	1	0	0	.923
Willeford, Col	1	4	0	1	0	1	.800

Triple Plays—Benedict, Murphy.

PITCHERS

Player and Club	G.	PO.	A.	E.	DP.	Pct.	Player and Club	G.	PO.	A.	E.	DP.	Pct.
McLAUGHLIN, Sav	24	13	27	0	3	1.000	Monroe, Knoxville	29	18	39	4	3	.934
Arthur, Orlando	41	3	28	0	2	1.000	G. Williams, Jack*	23	10	18	2	3	.933
Box, Savannah*	22	2	22	0	1	1.000	DeBarr, Mon*	43	8	20	2	2	.933
Sevillano, Savannah	28	3	20	0	1	1.000	Bruchanski, Mon	33	11	15	2	2	.929
Burnside, Mon*	12	2	19	0	1	1.000	Taylor, Chat	40	4	9	1	0	.929
Osburn, Jacksonville*	14	4	17	0	3	1.000	Thayer, Orlando	24	8	29	3	1	.925
McWilliams, Sav*	16	6	12	0	1	1.000	Trella, Montgomery	23	18	18	3	1	.923
Bradford, Savannah*	23	5	13	0	1	1.000	Lysander, Chat	18	10	14	2	0	.923
Alonso, Montgomery*	23	2	10	0	1	1.000	Frost, Knoxville	20	3	21	2	1	.923
Culpepper, Columbus	36	3	9	0	1	1.000	Branch, Jack	25	7	28	3	0	.921
Wortham, Knoxville*	11	2	7	0	2	1.000	Stegman, Chat	11	4	7	1	1	.917
Bernard, Jacksonville	12	4	4	0	0	1.000	Williams, Knx	23	2	9	1	1	.917
Combs, Knoxville	34	0	8	0	1	1.000	Elenes, Columbus	18	5	15	2	2	.909
Ryan, Orlando*	11	2	5	0	0	1.000	Williams, Columbus	24	14	24	4	1	.905
Morris, Montgomery	12	1	6	0	1	1.000	Komadina, Knx*	26	4	14	2	0	.900
Walker, Charlotte	14	2	5	0	1	1.000	Best, Knoxville	25	4	5	1	0	.900
Sprinkle, Columbus	20	3	3	0	1	1.000	Pagnozzi, Char*	27	13	28	5	3	.891
Smith, Charlotte*	24	2	4	0	0	1.000	Bemis, Orlando*	13	2	6	1	0	.889
Garvin, Orlando*	23	8	49	1	1	.983	Figueroa, Sav*	22	1	7	1	0	.889
Alexander, Sav	24	12	34	1	1	.979	Smith, Orlando	31	10	13	3	1	.885
Roznovsky, Col	36	15	28	1	1	.977	Darr, Charlotte	27	12	26	5	2	.884
Paschall, Jack	21	17	22	1	1	.975	Holly, Orlando*	25	4	11	2	1	.882
Ward, Charlotte	25	11	23	1	1	.971	Alfaro, Columbus	24	3	19	3	0	.880
Peach, Chat*	27	3	27	1	0	.968	Van Bommel, Char	'16	4	3	1	1	.875
Overstreet, Jack	23	13	16	1	2	.967	Tobik, Montgomery	18	1	6	1	0	.875
Aloi, Columbus	29	17	38	2	0	.965	Stoddard, Knx	20	7	34	6	3	.872
Bethke, Orlando*	10	1	23	1	0	.960	Ausman, Orlando*	12	2	4	1	1	.857
Sambito, Columbus*	12	11	13	1	1	.960	Chevez, Charlotte	11	4	18	4	0	.846
Cappuzzello, Mon*	17	8	16	1	1	.960	Smith, Knoxville	27	4	18	4	1	.846
Ford, Charlotte	27	10	32	2	2	.955	Tronerud, Chat	22	2	9	2	0	.846
Rozema, Montgomery	19	8	13	1	1	.955	Garcia, Jack*	26	2	9	2	1	.846
Kirby, Chattanooga	32	5	16	1	1	.955	Miller, Charlotte	39	1	10	2	0	.846
Dixon, Columbus	27	9	32	2	0	.953	Campbell, Savannah	42	1	10	2	0	.846
Christenson, Mon*	12	3	17	1	1	.952	Ballinger, Jack	21	1	4	1	1	.833
Harris, Orlando*	14	4	15	1	2	.950	McKinney, Jack	17	13	26	8	2	.830
Bell, Chattanooga	21	6	13	1	1	.950	Davey, Savannah*	10	4	5	2	1	.818
Lusic, Savannah	30	7	12	1	1	.950	Bock, Knoxville*	29	1	11	3	1	.800
Kingman, Chat	26	18	19	2	2	.949	Meyerrose, Mon	22	3	5	2	2	.800
Harris, Montgomery	21	15	19	2	1	.944	Hrovat, Jack	20	1	6	2	1	.778
Knapp, Knoxville	11	3	14	1	3	.944	McGilberry, Jack	44	4	5	4	0	.692
May, Orlando	18	7	25	2	2	.941	Boyd, Chattanooga*	22	0	2	1	0	.667
Flinn, Charlotte	24	9	23	2	1	.941	Lerner, Orlando	13	0	1	2	0	.333
McCatty, Chat	36	1	15	1	3	.941							

(Fewer Than Ten Games)

Player and Club	G.	PO.	A.	E.	DP.	Pct.	Player and Club	G.	PO.	A.	E.	DP.	Pct.
Mahler, Savannah*	8	5	11	0	0	1.000	Stephenson, Sav*	7	0	3	0	0	1.000
Bannister, Col*	3	3	9	0	0	1.000	Ray, Columbus	8	0	3	0	0	1.000
Gressick, Orlando*	5	2	10	0	1	1.000	Corbin, Orlando	2	1	1	0	0	1.000
Scarbery, Chat	9	1	8	0	0	1.000	Viefhaus, Mon	3	0	2	0	0	1.000
Stinson, Knoxville*	8	1	7	0	1	1.000	Meyring, Jack	3	0	2	0	0	1.000
Viebrock, Jack*	7	3	4	0	0	1.000	Mercier, Mon	5	0	2	0	0	1.000
M. Williams, Jack*	6	2	4	0	0	1.000	Corr, Montgomery	1	0	1	0	0	1.000
Abraham, Chat*	7	1	5	0	0	1.000	Kenyon, Mon*	2	1	0	0	0	1.000
Rios, Savannah*	9	3	3	0	0	1.000	DeMerritt, Col	3	0	1	0	0	1.000
Wright, Jack*	9	2	4	0	0	1.000	Lopez, Columbus*	4	1	0	0	0	1.000
T. Norton, Knx	3	1	4	0	1	1.000	Wibberley, Chat	8	1	0	0	0	1.000
Moran, Knoxville	6	0	5	0	0	1.000	Parrott, Charlotte	5	1	6	1	0	.875
Salas, Chattanooga	6	2	3	0	0	1.000	Treuel, Montgomery	6	1	3	1	0	.800
Ibarguen, Mon	7	2	3	0	0	1.000	Harrell, Chat	7	1	3	1	1	.800
Quisenberry, Jack	9	0	5	0	1	1.000	Hile, Chattanooga*	7	1	3	2	0	.667
Hagman, Chattanooga	5	1	3	0	0	1.000	Cuen, Columbus	8	3	1	2	0	.667
Cowan, Jacksonville	7	1	3	0	0	1.000	Miller, Columbus*	3	0	1	1	0	.500
Johnson, Charlotte	7	2	2	0	0	1.000							

The following players do not have any recorded accepted chances at the positions indicated; therefore, are not listed in the fielding averages for those particular positions: Beamon*, p; Keough, p; Melvin, p; Noah*, p; Sanner, c.

CLUB PITCHING

Club	G.	CG.	ShO.	Sv.	IP.	H.	R.	ER.	HR.	BB.	Int. BB.	HB.	SO.	WP.	Bk.	ERA.
Jacksonville	138	56	15	10	1155	949	442	347	48	519	42	45	650	44	7	2.70
Charlotte	141	66	12	21	1155	1046	486	410	54	457	10	26	650	34	10	3.15
Montgomery	137	38	17	26	1114	977	478	390	49	445	27	46	720	58	6	3.15
Savannah	140	59	11	14	1150	1112	508	418	57	436	20	48	630	41	7	3.27
Orlando	139	55	13	16	1185	1129	532	453	66	541	18	23	572	49	8	3.44
Columbus	140	61	12	7	1151	1113	530	445	60	513	34	35	591	44	13	3.48
Chattanooga	139	37	12	22	1152	1124	558	456	53	454	29	31	569	33	11	3.56
Knoxville	138	49	13	18	1148	1129	558	476	47	535	31	53	649	56	6	3.73

PITCHERS' RECORDS

(Leading Qualifiers for Earned-Run Average Leadership—112 or More Innings)

*Throws lefthanded.

Pitcher—Club	G.	GS.	CG.	ShO.	W.	L.	Sv.	Pct.	IP.	H.	R.	ER.	HR.	BB.	Int. BB.	HB.	SO.	WP.	ERA.
Rozema, Montgomery	19	18	10	4	12	4	0	.750	126	98	29	22	6	15	1	3	96	3	1.57
McKinney, Jack	17	17	8	3	10	5	0	.667	128	97	37	23	5	51	2	6	65	5	1.62
Frost, Knoxville	20	20	10	1	8	7	0	.533	136	121	43	36	6	32	2	2	88	6	2.38
Dixon, Columbus	27	23	11	2	11	10	0	.524	167	145	58	45	6	49	0	2	98	6	2.43
Ford, Charlotte	27	27	19	4	17	7	0	.708	212	188	76	59	12	31	0	3	121	3	2.50
Thayer, Orlando	24	22	9	4	10	7	0	.588	168	129	60	49	8	99	1	6	102	12	2.63
Kingman, Chat	26	26	10	2	14	11	0	.560	184	167	69	54	9	47	0	5	101	3	2.64
R. Williams, Col	24	19	10	3	7	7	0	.500	146	134	49	43	7	46	6	0	53	3	2.65
Arthur, Orlando	41	7	4	0	10	10	9	.500	139	142	47	41	8	25	4	1	57	1	2.65
Paschall, Jack	21	18	8	0	9	8	0	.529	145	126	53	43	7	31	5	2	88	0	2.67

Departmental Leaders: G—McGilberry, 44; GS—Aloi, Monroe, 28; CG—Ford, 19; ShO—Ford, May, Rozema, Thayer, 4; W—Ford, 17; L—Aloi, 16; Sv—Ra. Miller, 19; Pct.—DeBarr, .846; IP—Ford, 212; H—Aloi, Ford, 188; R—Pagnozzi, 95; ER—Pagnozzi, 87; HR—Garvin, 16; BB—Darr, 120; IBB—McGilberry, 10; HB—Alexander, F. Harris, 13; SO—Ford, 121; WP—Monroe, 13.

(All Pitchers—Listed Alphabetically)

Pitcher—Club	G.	GS.	CG.	ShO.	W.	L.	Sv.	Pct.	IP.	H.	R.	ER.	HR.	BB.	Int. BB.	HB.	SO.	WP.	ERA.
Abraham, Chat*	7	0	0	0	2	0	0	1.000	14	19	5	4	0	6	0	0	5	0	2.57
Alexander, Sav	24	24	13	1	10	11	0	.476	169	157	78	61	6	65	3	13	109	6	3.25
Alfaro, Columbus	24	22	7	1	7	7	0	.500	127	115	63	56	7	87	2	6	72	11	3.97
Aloi, Columbus	29	28	12	3	7	16	0	.304	185	188	91	77	12	92	4	9	89	5	3.75
Alonso, Mon*	23	0	0	0	3	3	4	.500	41	39	23	17	0	18	4	0	24	3	3.73
Arthur, Orlando	41	7	4	0	10	10	9	.500	139	142	47	41	8	25	4	1	57	1	2.65
Ausman, Orlando*	12	3	0	0	2	1	2	.667	33	39	19	15	2	16	0	2	19	1	4.09
Ballinger, Jack	21	2	1	1	6	2	1	.750	37	28	7	6	1	22	5	2	22	3	1.46
Bannister, Col*	3	3	1	1	0	0	0	1.000	24	16	4	4	1	14	0	1	20	2	1.50
Beamon, Chat*	1	0	0	0	0	0	0	.000	⅔	0	0	0	0	0	0	0	0	0	0.00
Bell, Chattanooga	21	21	6	1	8	7	0	.533	142	129	63	53	10	24	0	3	76	1	3.36
Bemis, Orlando*	13	13	2	0	1	6	0	.143	58	55	47	45	9	51	1	3	43	7	6.98
Bernard, Jack	12	8	2	0	2	6	0	.250	52	48	19	15	3	16	2	1	30	2	2.60
Best, Knoxville	25	0	0	0	2	5	10	.286	45	42	20	18	3	20	6	2	27	0	3.60
Bethke, Orlando*	10	10	3	1	5	2	0	.714	64	54	23	17	0	40	1	0	29	3	2.39
Bock, Knoxville*	29	4	1	1	6	3	3	.667	54	50	30	26	2	42	5	3	31	3	4.33
Box, Savannah*	22	16	8	3	8	6	0	.571	112	96	42	40	6	56	4	7	44	6	3.21
Boyd, Char*	22	2	0	0	1	1	2	.500	34	33	17	9	2	13	0	2	25	1	2.38
Bradford, Sav*	23	23	5	1	7	7	0	.500	136	144	65	47	2	55	0	1	90	5	3.11
Branch, Jack	25	23	8	0	6	11	0	.353	157	116	67	54	6	73	3	12	93	5	3.10
Bruchanski, Mon	33	7	0	0	7	4	4	.636	103	90	35	29	2	36	3	4	49	8	2.53
Burnside, Mon*	12	12	7	2	6	5	0	.545	79	62	31	24	5	20	2	5	43	4	2.73
Campbell, Savannah	42	0	0	0	7	5	6	.583	83	70	26	22	2	31	2	4	63	2	2.39
Cappuzzello, Mon*	17	17	4	1	7	7	0	.500	117	102	57	46	4	65	2	1	105	5	3.54
Chevez, Charlotte	11	10	5	1	7	3	0	.700	77	58	20	16	2	19	1	1	42	1	1.87
Christenson, Mon*	12	10	4	1	4	2	1	.667	66	70	29	24	4	25	1	2	24	2	3.27
Combs, Knoxville	34	1	0	0	4	4	2	.500	74	84	46	41	8	34	0	1	36	1	4.99
Corbin, Orlando	2	2	0	0	1	0	0	1.000	10	10	7	7	0	4	0	0	6	1	6.30
Corr, Montgomery	1	0	0	0	0	0	0	.000	5	4	3	3	0	3	0	0	4	1	5.40
Cowan, Jack	7	0	0	0	1	0	0	1.000	5	3	2	2	0	5	0	0	2	2	3.60
Cuen, Columbus	8	1	0	0	0	0	0	.000	29	40	23	21	4	20	0	2	6	0	6.52
Culpepper, Col	36	1	1	0	3	5	4	.375	68	64	29	24	5	28	7	0	25	2	3.18
Darr, Charlotte	27	27	14	2	12	12	0	.500	177	153	86	76	8	120	0	3	98	10	3.86
Davey, Savannah*	10	10	3	0	2	4	0	.333	65	58	30	23	3	25	1	2	32	1	3.05
DeBarr, Mon*	43	0	0	0	11	2	10	.846	99	92	36	26	3	35	5	1	78	4	2.36
DeMerritt, Col	3	0	0	0	1	1	0	.500	7	4	3	3	1	6	0	0	5	2	3.86
Dixon, Columbus	27	23	11	2	11	10	0	.524	167	145	58	45	6	49	0	2	98	6	2.43
Elenes, Columbus	18	16	8	0	4	11	1	.267	112	104	51	45	4	56	1	7	80	7	3.62
Figueroa, Sav*	22	3	2	0	2	3	1	.400	61	66	24	18	3	33	0	4	21	5	2.66
Flinn, Charlotte	24	21	10	0	9	8	0	.529	148	151	62	47	4	28	0	7	76	2	2.86

Pitcher–Club	G	GS	CG	ShO	W	L	Sv	Pct.	IP	H	R	ER	HR	BB	Int. BB	HB	SO	WP	ERA
Ford, Charlotte	27	27	19	4	17	7	0	.708	212	188	76	59	12	31	0	3	121	3	2.50
Frost, Knoxville	20	20	10	1	8	7	0	.533	136	121	43	36	6	32	2	2	88	6	2.38
Garcia, Jack*	26	6	4	2	6	2	3	.750	67	48	18	14	3	28	3	0	38	4	1.88
Garvin, Orlando*	23	23	15	1	11	9	0	.550	178	163	73	67	16	50	3	2	91	4	3.39
Gressick, Orlando*	5	5	1	0	3	0	0	.000	26	32	21	16	2	15	1	0	14	4	5.54
Hagman, Chat	5	5	1	1	1	3	0	.250	27	34	17	14	4	8	0	0	9	0	4.67
Harrell, Chat	7	1	0	0	0	2	0	.000	18	18	13	9	0	15	0	1	15	3	4.50
F. Harris, Mon	21	20	6	1	12	4	0	.750	152	126	54	46	12	37	0	13	75	3	2.72
W. Harris, Orl*	14	14	8	1	9	4	0	.692	100	90	37	29	3	51	0	2	45	4	2.61
Hile, Chat*	7	3	0	0	0	1	0	.000	18	21	16	13	0	19	0	0	4	1	6.50
Holly, Orlando*	25	5	2	0	5	5	3	.500	96	98	35	29	0	26	3	1	46	2	2.72
Hrovat, Jacksonville	20	0	0	0	1	3	1	.250	35	29	16	12	2	20	2	1	13	1	3.09
Ibarguen, Mon	7	4	0	0	1	3	0	.250	29	30	10	10	1	15	0	1	24	0	3.10
Johnson, Knoxville	7	3	1	0	0	2	0	.000	25	33	16	14	0	17	1	0	12	3	5.04
Kenyon, Mon*	2	0	0	0	0	0	0	.000	2	4	2	2	0	0	0	0	4	0	9.00
Keough, Chat	2	0	0	0	0	0	0	.000	2	1	0	0	0	0	0	0	0	0	0.00
Kingman, Chat	26	26	10	2	14	11	0	.560	184	167	69	54	9	47	0	5	101	3	2.64
Kirby, Chat	32	11	2	1	4	9	2	.308	100	106	56	44	5	57	6	3	64	5	3.96
Knapp, Knoxville	11	10	3	0	7	3	0	.700	83	58	26	22	2	42	1	7	68	1	2.39
Komadina, Knx*	26	13	4	2	4	11	1	.267	98	98	58	50	4	55	1	4	53	8	4.59
Lerner, Orlando	13	0	0	0	1	1	0	.500	26	30	11	10	0	17	0	2	18	1	3.46
Lopez, Columbus*	4	0	0	0	0	0	1	.000	3	4	6	6	1	7	0	0	1	0	18.00
Lusic, Savannah	30	11	6	0	6	8	3	.429	106	112	53	44	8	32	3	3	54	3	3.74
Lysander, Chat	18	18	7	2	7	6	0	.538	118	108	47	42	6	34	3	1	31	2	3.20
Mahler, Savannah*	8	7	4	1	3	5	0	.375	53	44	21	19	4	20	3	4	38	0	3.23
May, Orlando	18	18	7	4	10	5	0	.667	129	121	52	43	5	53	0	3	61	5	3.00
McCatty, Chat	36	2	0	0	5	4	3	.556	77	73	44	27	5	31	4	0	40	2	3.16
McGilberry, Jack	44	0	0	0	3	6	5	.333	61	51	28	22	1	43	10	0	62	3	3.25
McKinney, Jack	17	17	8	3	10	5	0	.667	128	97	37	23	5	51	2	6	65	5	1.62
McLaughlin, Sav	24	24	11	2	12	8	0	.600	169	165	69	52	8	44	1	2	70	3	2.77
McWilliams, Sav*	16	14	3	0	3	8	1	.273	74	82	41	38	4	33	3	5	37	5	4.62
Melvin, Jack	2	0	0	0	0	0	0	.000	5	5	6	5	0	0	0	2	4	1	9.00
Mercier, Mon	5	2	0	0	0	2	0	.000	12	22	14	13	1	5	0	2	7	2	9.75
Meyerrose, Mon	22	0	0	0	2	4	3	.333	37	29	9	7	0	13	5	1	24	2	1.70
Meyring, Jack	3	3	0	0	0	0	0	.000	12	23	14	10	2	5	0	3	2	0	7.50
Ra. Miller, Char	39	0	0	0	3	1	19	.750	62	47	11	10	2	15	2	1	43	2	1.45
Miller, Columbus*	3	3	0	0	0	2	0	.000	11	22	10	8	1	3	0	0	10	0	6.55
Monroe, Knoxville	29	28	11	3	11	14	0	.440	195	183	73	63	2	75	8	11	113	13	2.91
Moran, Knoxville	6	6	3	1	2	3	0	.400	35	34	19	10	1	19	1	1	21	3	2.57
Morris, Mon	12	9	0	0	2	3	0	.400	36	37	31	25	0	36	1	1	18	4	6.25
Noah, Orlando*	3	0	0	0	0	0	0	.000	4	4	4	4	1	6	0	0	4	0	9.00
T. Norton, Knx	3	3	0	0	0	3	0	.000	12	12	14	13	1	14	1	3	7	3	9.75
Osburn, Jack*	14	14	7	2	7	4	0	.636	93	75	30	24	2	44	0	4	52	7	2.32
Overstreet, Jack	23	20	7	1	7	11	0	.389	138	120	56	44	3	71	2	8	62	4	2.87
Pagnozzi, Char*	27	26	7	1	12	11	0	.522	169	155	95	87	7	119	1	3	106	6	4.63
Parrott, Charlotte	5	4	0	0	0	2	0	.000	17	19	13	10	1	10	1	0	3	2	5.29
Paschall, Jack	21	18	8	0	9	8	0	.529	145	126	53	43	7	31	5	2	88	0	2.67
Peach, Chat*	27	26	4	1	10	9	0	.526	166	155	78	70	5	96	2	9	100	6	3.80
Quisenberry, Jack	9	0	0	0	0	0	0	.000	12	8	6	3	0	4	2	0	6	0	2.25
Ray, Columbus	8	3	0	0	1	1	0	.500	13	20	19	17	1	14	0	0	5	3	11.77
Rios, Savannah*	9	0	0	0	2	1	0	.667	18	11	3	3	1	4	0	0	8	0	1.50
Rozema, Montgomery	19	18	10	4	12	4	0	.750	126	98	39	22	6	15	1	3	96	3	1.57
Roznovsky, Col	36	9	3	0	7	12	1	.368	112	136	73	57	5	42	8	2	42	2	4.58
Ryan, Orlando*	11	3	0	0	2	2	1	.500	25	31	19	18	3	10	1	0	5	0	6.48
Salas, Chat	6	3	1	0	0	1	0	.000	23	17	4	4	0	11	1	0	9	1	1.57
Sambito, Col*	12	12	8	1	8	2	0	.800	100	77	27	20	2	23	2	2	61	0	1.80
Scarbery, Col	9	9	5	3	6	2	0	.750	65	55	18	17	1	12	0	0	29	0	2.35
Sevillano, Savannah	28	8	4	2	6	5	3	.545	93	97	52	48	9	30	0	1	57	4	4.65
B. Smith, Knx	27	16	3	0	1	12	1	.077	119	128	81	71	6	61	2	3	48	3	5.37
C. Smith, Orlando	31	14	4	1	8	9	1	.471	129	131	77	63	9	78	3	1	32	4	4.40
Smith, Charlotte*	24	0	0	0	5	3	1	.625	47	38	15	14	1	18	1	1	34	1	2.68
Sprinkle, Col	20	0	0	0	1	6	0	.143	45	44	23	19	3	26	4	4	24	1	3.80
Stegman, Chat	11	8	1	0	1	7	0	.125	40	68	52	45	2	28	1	4	8	3	10.13
Stephenson, Sav*	7	0	0	0	1	0	0	1.000	11	10	4	4	1	8	0	2	7	1	3.27
Stinson, Knoxville*	8	3	1	0	2	0	0	1.000	37	40	19	14	0	18	1	4	24	1	3.41
Stoddard, Knoxville	20	19	9	0	9	8	0	.529	140	147	55	45	5	60	2	3	62	5	2.89
Taylor, Chat	40	0	0	0	6	3	13	.667	58	46	24	17	1	22	8	1	21	2	2.64
Thayer, Orlando	24	22	9	4	10	7	0	.588	168	129	60	49	8	99	1	6	102	12	2.63
Tobik, Montgomery	18	8	0	0	4	5	4	.444	63	56	33	26	5	32	2	1	44	1	3.71
Trella, Montgomery	23	23	7	3	9	7	0	.563	124	101	64	57	6	72	1	6	94	11	4.14
Treuel, Montgomery	6	6	0	0	1	1	0	.500	16	10	17	12	0	17	0	5	9	4	6.75
Tronerud, Chat	22	2	0	0	1	1	2	.800	46	49	17	17	1	16	4	1	25	0	3.33
Van Bommel, Char	16	4	0	0	3	3	0	.500	65	43	18	13	2	22	0	2	40	2	1.80
Viebrock, Jack*	7	0	0	0	0	0	0	.000	13	8	4	4	1	7	2	0	3	1	2.77

Pitcher—Club	G.	GS.	CG.	ShO.	W.	L.	Sv.	Pct.	IP.	H.	R.	ER.	HR.	BB.	Int. BB.	HB.	SO.	WP.	ERA.
Viefhaus, Mon..............	2	0	0	0	0	0	0	.000	6	5	1	1	0	1	0	0	2	1	1.50
Walker, Charlotte.............	14	1	0	0	0	0	1	.000	33	26	10	7	1	15	1	0	18	0	1.91
Ward, Charlotte	25	18	10	1	6	14	0	.300	141	135	64	57	14	43	2	5	57	2	3.64
Wibberley, Chat	8	2	0	0	1	1	0	.500	19	25	18	17	2	15	0	1	5	4	8.05
G. Williams, Jack*	23	22	9	3	7	9	0	.438	145	118	52	45	7	65	0	2	86	3	2.79
L. Williams, Knx	23	5	0	0	1	3	1	.250	51	74	41	35	2	25	1	5	15	2	6.18
M. Williams, Jack*..........	6	4	1	0	0	3	0	.000	27	29	21	15	5	24	2	0	9	1	5.00
R. Williams, Col	24	19	10	3	7	7	0	.500	146	134	49	43	7	46	6	0	53	3	2.65
Wortham, Knoxville*.........	11	10	4	1	4	2	0	.667	68	58	33	32	5	38	0	4	56	7	4.24
Wright, Jack*	9	1	1	0	1	1	0	.500	22	17	6	6	0	10	2	2	13	2	2.45

BALKS—Pagnozzi, Thayer, 5 each; R. Williams, 4; Alfaro, Bannister, Bell, Combs, Darr, Hagman, Kirby, Paschall, Peach, Roznovsky, Stinson, Trella, G. Williams, 2 each; Alonso, Bemis, Box, Bradford, Branch, Burnside, Davey, DeBarr, Dixon, Elenes, Figueroa, Ford, Harrell, Mahler, May, Melvin, Ra. Miller, Overstreet, Rios, Sambito, Sevillano, B. Smith, C. Smith, Taylor, Tobik, Tronerud, Ward, L. Williams, 1 each.

COMBINATION SHUTOUTS—Van Bommel-Parrott-Miller, Parrott-Van Bommel-Miller, Pagnozzi-Miller, Charlotte; Salas-Abraham, Chattanooga; Aloi-Culpepper, Columbus; Overstreet-Garcia (2), Branch-McGilberry, Jacksonville; Stinson-Smith, Monroe-Bock, Frost-Komadina, Monroe-Best, Knoxville; Harris-Alonso, Trella-Alonso, Ibarguen-DeBarr, Harris-DeBarr, Rozema-Christenson, Montgomery; Bethke-Smith, Orlando; Alexander-Campbell, Savannah.

NO-HIT GAMES—Trella, Montgomery, defeated Jacksonville, 1-0, April 24 (seven innings); Ballinger, Jacksonville, defeated Columbus, 3-0, June 4 (seven innings); Burnside, Montgomery, defeated Charlotte, 8-0, June 24 (seven innings).

Texas League

CLASS AA

Leading Batter
FRED FRAZIER
El Paso

League President
CARL SAWATSKI

CHAMPIONSHIP WINNERS IN PREVIOUS YEARS

1888 – Dallas .... .671	1918 – Dallas .... .584	1941 – Houston .... .673
1889 – Houston .... .551	1919 – Shreveport* .... .677	Dallas (4th)§ .... .519
1890 – Galveston .... .705	Fort Worth .... .651	1942 – Beaumont .... .605
1892 – Houston .... .741	1920 – Fort Worth .... .703	Shreveport (2nd)§ .... .576
Houston .... .613	Fort Worth .... .750	1943-44-45 – Did not operate.
1895 – Dallas .... .754	1921 – Fort Worth .... .691	1946 – Fort Worth .... .656
Fort Worth* .... .750	Fort Worth .... .662	Dallas (2nd)§ .... .591
1896 – Fort Worth .... .757	1922 – Fort Worth .... .694	1947 – Houston‡ .... .623
Houston* .... .679	Fort Worth .... .711	1948 – Fort Worth‡ .... .601
Galveston .... .548	1923 – Fort Worth .... .632	1949 – Fort Worth .... .649
1897 – San Antonio† .... .657	1924 – Fort Worth .... .689	Tulsa (2nd)§ .... .584
Galveston† .... .717	Fort Worth .... .763	1950 – Beaumont .... .595
1898 – League disbanded.	1925 – Fort Worth .... .711	San Antonio (4th)§........ .513
1899 – Galveston .... .632	Fort Worth y .... .653	1951 – Houston‡ .... .619
Galveston .... .762	1926 – Dallas .... .574	1952 – Dallas .... .571
1900-01 – Did not operate.	1927 – Wichita Falls .... .654	Shreveport (3rd)§ .... .522
1902 – Corsicana .... .866	1928 – Houston* .... .679	1953 – Dallas‡ .... .571
Corsicana .... .682	Wichita Falls .... .731	1954 – Shreveport .... .559
1903 – Paris-Waco .... .615	1929 – Dallas* .... .588	Houston (2nd)§............ .553
Dallas* .... .648	Wichita Falls .... .620	1955 – Dallas .... .581
1904 – Corsicana* .... .615	1930 – Wichita Falls .... .697	Shreveport (3rd)§ .... .540
Fort Worth .... .800	Fort Worth* .... .632	1956 – Houston‡ .... .623
1905 – Fort Worth .... .545	1931 – Houston** .... .625	1957 – Dallas .... .662
1906 – Fort Worth .... .677	Houston .... .734	Houston (2nd)§............ .630
Cleburne x .... .609	1932 – Beaumont* .... .640	1958 – Fort Worth .... .582
1907 – Austin .... .629	Dallas .... .727	Cor. Christi (3rd)§ ...... .507
1908 – San Antonio .... .664	1933 – Houston .... .623	1959 – Victoria .... .589
1909 – Houston .... .601	San Antonio (4th)§........ .523	Austin (2nd)§ .... .548
1910 – Dallas† .... .586	1934 – Galveston‡ .... .579	1960 – Rio Grande Valley ...... .590
Houston† .... .586	1935 – Oklahoma City‡ .... .590	Tulsa (3rd)§ .... .528
1911 – Austin .... .575	1936 – Dallas .... .604	1961 – Amarillo .... .643
1912 – Houston .... .626	Tulsa (3rd)§ .... .519	San Antonio (3rd)§ ...... .532
1913 – Houston .... .620	1937 – Oklahoma City .... .635	1962 – El Paso .... .571
1914 – Houston† .... .671	Fort Worth (3rd)§ .... .535	Tulsa (2nd)§ .... .550
Waco† .... .671	1938 – Beaumont .... .635	1963 – San Antonio .... .564
1915 – Waco .... .592	1939 – Houston .... .606	Tulsa (3rd)§ .... .529
1916 – Waco .... .587	Fort Worth (4th)§ .... .540	1964 – San Antonio‡ .... .607
1917 – Dallas .... .600	1940 – Houston‡ .... .652	1965 – Tulsa .... .574

Albuquerque xx .... .550	1970–Albuquerque** .... .615	1973–San Antonio .... .590
1966–Arkansas .... .579	Memphis .... .507	Memphis xx .... .558
1967–Albuquerque .... .557	1971–Did not operate as league–	El Paso .... .555
1968–Arkansas .... .586	clubs were members of Dixie	1974–Victoria xx .... .581
El Paso xx.................... .562	Association.	1975–Lafayette xxx .... .558
1969–Amarillo .... .593	1972–Alexandria .... .600	Midland xxx .... .604
Memphis xx .... .504	El Paso xx...................... .557	

*Won split-season playoff. †No playoff for title. ‡Finished first and won four-club playoff. §Won four-club play-off. xTitle to Cleburne by default. yTied with Dallas in second half and won playoff for championship. zFort Worth disbanded. **Tied with Beaumont at end of first half and won title in best-of-five series played as part of second half schedule. xxLeague divided into Eastern, Western divisions; won two-team playoff. xxxLeague divided into Eastern, Western divisions; declared co-champions when playoffs were not completed. NOTE–Championship awarded to winner of four-team playoff, 1933-51; first-place team and playoff winner co-champions, 1952-64.

STANDING OF CLUBS AT CLOSE OF SEASON, SEPTEMBER 6

EASTERN DIVISION

Club	Shrev.	Jack.	Ark.	Laf.	Amar.	ElP.	S.A.	Mid.	W.	L.	T.	Pct.	G.B.
Shreveport (Pirates)	..	14	19	19	4	3	6	5	70	66	0	.515	......
Jackson (Mets)	18	..	17	18	2	5	3	6	69	66	0	.511	½
Arkansas (Cardinals)	13	15	..	16	2	2	4	7	59	76	0	.437	10½
Lafayette (Giants)	13	14	16	..	2	5	4	3	58	76	0	.433	11

WESTERN DIVISION

Club	Shrev.	Jack.	Ark.	Laf.	Amar.	ElP.	S.A.	Mid.	W.	L.	T.	Pct.	G.B.
Amarillo (Padres)	6	8	8	5	..	17	21	16	81	54	0	.600	......
El Paso (Angels)	7	5	8	4	14	..	18	21	77	56	0	.579	3
San Antonio (Rangers)	4	6	5	7	11	14	..	16	63	71	0	.470	17½
Midland (Cubs)	5	4	3	7	16	11	16	..	62	74	0	.456	19½

Arkansas club represented Little Rock, Ark.

Major league affiliations in parentheses.

Playoff–Amarillo defeated Shreveport, three games to two.

Regular-Season Attendance–Amarillo, 76,799; Arkansas, 90,255; El Paso, 181,746; Jackson, 86,069; Lafayette, 35,808; Midland, 66,457; San Antonio, 60,122; Shreveport, 47,930. Total, 645,186. Playoffs, 10,089. All-Star Game, 6,134.

Managers: Amarillo–Bob Miller; Arkansas–Jack Krol; El Paso–Bobby Knoop; Jackson–John Antonelli; Lafayette–John Van Ornum; Midland–Dennis Sommers; San Antonio–Orlando Martinez; Shreveport–John Lipon.

All-Star Team: 1B–Aikens, El Paso; 2B–Frazier, El Paso; 3B–Farkas, El Paso; SS–Mulliniks, El Paso; OF–Reynolds, Amarillo; Louis, Shreveport; Mazzilli, Jackson; DH–Delyon, Amarillo; C–Bradley, Lafayette; P–Dillard, Lafayette; Poloni, San Antonio; Manager–Miller, Amarillo.

(Compiled by Ed Williams, League Statistician, Shawnee, Okla.)

CLUB BATTING

Club	G.	AB.	R.	OR.	H.	TB.	2B.	3B.	HR.	RBI.	SH.	SF.	BB.	HP.	SO.	SB.	CS.	LOB.	Pct.
El Paso	133	4468	843	679	1335	2032	253	39	122	742	27	42	572	22	27	796	94	30	984	.299
Amarillo	135	4545	776	615	1330	1885	229	49	76	685	55	48	617	27	16	736	109	39	1105	.293
Midland	136	4493	636	717	1233	1707	162	42	76	551	53	36	620	27	16	734	60	36	1019	.274
San Antonio	134	4166	611	718	1120	1565	166	27	75	555	46	33	603	21	30	705	120	51	1005	.269
Lafayette	134	4368	542	577	1132	1602	177	28	79	485	59	22	461	32	19	643	58	29	1007	.259
Shreveport	136	4426	569	525	1144	1675	200	41	83	499	60	37	441	36	23	792	129	49	951	.258
Arkansas	135	4318	525	594	1116	1462	156	26	46	446	52	28	466	38	21	631	55	30	1004	.258
Jackson	135	4316	515	592	1054	1462	161	38	57	449	45	38	446	37	28	699	76	40	953	.244

INDIVIDUAL BATTING

(Leading Qualifiers for Batting Championship–367 or More Plate Appearances)

*Bats lefthanded.   †Switch-hitter.

Player and Club	G.	AB.	R.	H.	TB.	2B.	3B.	HR.	RBI.	SH.	SF.	BB.	SO.	SB.	CS.	Pct.
Frazier, Frederic, El Paso	83	309	73	114	162	22	4	6	72	1	7	41	16	2	1	.369
Reynolds, Donald, Amarillo	125	453	94	151	241	19	7	19	85	3	7	86	72	8	6	.333
Delyon, Eugene, Amarillo	128	475	83	157	222	25	8	8	90	1	6	83	85	15	5	.331
Young, John, Arkansas*	119	420	71	135	208	33	2	12	73	0	1	63	54	5	1	.321
Friedman, Martin, El P*	118	435	97	139	184	27	3	4	55	4	5	92	63	25	9	.320
Aikens, Willie, El Paso*	133	514	99	163	285	24	4	30	117	0	4	64	114	10	3	.317
Farkas, Ronald, El Paso	115	371	77	117	159	18	6	4	49	2	1	70	70	1	4	.315
Mulliniks, S. Rance, El P*	90	333	81	105	156	22	4	7	51	5	4	68	61	20	4	.315
Huisman, William, Midland	116	428	70	134	195	19	6	10	58	6	3	56	35	15	4	.313
Menees, H. Eugene, Amar	113	375	59	117	155	14	6	4	47	13	2	53	43	8	5	.312

Frazier did not have the required number of plate appearances but when charged with five official at bats to reach the qualification plateau he thus became the leader with .363 average. Under the provisions of scoring rule 10.23a, Frazier, El Paso, qualified for the batting championship.

Departmental Leaders: G—Djakonow, Kim, 134; AB—Kim, 537; R—Aikens, 99; H—Kim, 164; TB—Aikens, 285; 2B—Young, 33; 3B—Louis, 12; HR—Aikens, 30; RBI—Aikens, 117; SH—Hrapmann, 14; SF—Robert Mitchell, 9; BB—Mazzilli, 111; HP—Iorg, Mazzilli, 7; SO—Rush, 123; SB—Chauncey, 31; CS—Mazzilli, 15.

(All Players—Listed Alphabetically)

Player and Club	G.	AB.	R.	H.	TB.	2B.	3B.	HR.	RBI.	SH.	SF.	BB.	HP.	SO.	SB.	CS.	Pct.
Aikens, Willie, El Paso*	133	514	99	163	285	24	4	30	117	0	4	64	6	114	10	3	.317
Alberts, Francis, El Paso	53	195	43	61	115	8	2	14	40	0	2	28	1	21	3	0	.313
Alfano, Donnie, Amarillo*	50	62	6	15	20	3	1	0	11	4	3	5	0	12	0	0	.242
Anderson, Richard E., Shrev	28	42	3	6	6	0	0	0	1	0	1	0	1	15	0	0	.143
Andrews, John M., Laf	127	444	49	104	154	19	2	9	47	5	4	36	4	66	7	6	.234
Andrews, John R., Jack*	42	4	1	1	3	0	1	0	1	0	0	0	0	2	0	0	.250
Ashford, Thomas, Amarillo	132	519	91	141	206	29	0	12	67	6	6	55	3	77	10	3	.272
Astroth, Jonathan, San A*	29	85	16	27	32	5	0	0	13	1	0	27	0	15	1	0	.318
Baker, Charles, Amarillo	109	385	44	104	137	19	1	4	64	2	4	27	3	67	7	6	.270
Barnes, Craig, Lafayette*	118	360	60	95	176	15	3	20	57	4	2	58	2	76	1	1	.264
Barrow, Melvin, San An	65	199	24	57	75	9	0	3	33	3	2	32	5	20	5	1	.286
Bauers, Wayne, Jackson	96	251	33	59	73	5	0	3	18	1	2	22	2	36	2	3	.235
Bengston, Richard, Jack	32	121	14	25	33	6	1	0	7	2	1	12	0	26	0	0	.207
Bernard, Dwight, Jackson	9	15	0	2	2	0	0	0	1	0	0	0	0	11	0	0	.133
Bialas, David, Arkansas	123	391	57	99	131	14	6	2	29	1	0	46	0	45	3	1	.253
Blackwell, Gary, Arkansas	52	145	13	32	37	5	0	0	8	1	0	14	3	18	0	1	.221
Blomberg, Steven, Shrev	92	312	40	65	96	7	0	8	23	4	1	18	1	80	18	2	.208
Bolick, Frank, San An	4	3	1	1	1	0	0	0	1	0	0	1	0	1	0	0	.333
Bradley, J. Richard, Laf	101	363	55	98	149	14	2	11	47	0	2	36	0	52	3	0	.270
Brandt, Randy, Shrev*	6	1	0	0	0	0	0	0	0	0	0	0	0	0	0	0	.000
Brookens, Timothy, San An	43	117	16	25	35	4	0	2	10	2	1	24	1	49	4	1	.214
Brown, Jerald, Lafayette	44	92	8	24	28	4	0	0	12	0	1	12	0	15	1	0	.261
Bruhert, Michael, Jackson	17	25	3	7	9	0	1	0	4	6	0	0	0	7	0	0	.280
Bucci, Michael, San An	54	150	19	38	50	4	1	2	16	1	0	23	0	38	3	5	.253
Butcher, Clifton, Amarillo*	23	1	0	1	1	0	0	0	0	0	0	0	0	0	0	0	1.000
Camper, Cardell, Arkansas	7	9	0	0	0	0	0	0	0	3	0	1	5	0	0	0	.000
Cariel, Rafael, Shreveport	87	271	28	70	95	9	5	2	33	4	2	20	3	21	5	2	.258
Castillo, E. Manuel, Ark†	116	355	36	99	114	11	2	0	35	1	5	19	2	32	4	2	.279
Caudill, William, Arkansas	27	48	1	8	8	0	0	0	1	3	0	1	0	15	0	0	.167
Chauncey, Keathel, San An*	118	357	63	95	119	13	1	3	47	1	4	61	2	49	31	6	.266
Chew, Earle, Midland	99	339	47	88	126	10	8	4	45	1	0	38	0	79	9	4	.260
Coe, Roger, Amarillo*	20	3	0	0	0	0	0	0	0	0	0	0	0	2	0	0	.000
Cornejo, N. Mardie, Jackson	48	6	0	1	1	0	0	0	0	3	0	0	0	1	0	0	.167
Covert, Mark, Arkansas	26	34	2	1	1	0	0	0	3	0	3	1	1	16	0	0	.029
Craig, Rockne, Amarillo	83	294	55	75	107	16	2	4	35	0	2	41	1	42	9	4	.255
Cruz, Julio L., El Paso	13	49	9	16	22	4	1	0	9	2	1	5	0	6	3	1	.327
Cuellar, Robert, San An	49	1	0	0	0	0	0	0	0	0	0	0	0	0	0	0	.000
Daves, William, Arkansas	38	101	8	31	37	2	2	0	7	1	1	9	1	18	0	0	.307
Davis, Rodney, Shreveport	55	9	1	2	2	0	0	0	0	0	0	4	0	0	0	2	.222
Deidel, Thomas, Jackson*	12	11	0	0	0	0	0	0	1	0	2	0	6	0	0	0	.000
del Orbe, F. Lazaro, Laf	40	107	13	23	29	2	2	0	9	6	0	2	0	19	1	0	.215
de los Santos, German, Laf	23	68	6	20	28	6	1	0	10	0	1	2	0	14	0	0	.294
de los Santos, Ramon, Ark*	26	3	0	0	0	0	0	0	0	0	0	0	0	2	0	0	.000
Delyon, Eugene, Amarillo	128	475	83	157	222	25	8	8	90	1	6	83	1	85	15	5	.331
Detherage, Robert, Ark	41	148	18	44	58	3	1	3	18	1	3	18	0	23	3	1	.297
Dillard, Jay, Lafayette	20	30	1	1	1	0	0	0	4	4	1	3	1	13	0	0	.033
Divison, Julio, Lafayette	33	32	2	2	2	0	0	0	2	0	1	0	8	0	0	0	.063
Djakonow, Paul, Shreveport	134	441	68	107	191	25	4	17	58	4	5	72	5	95	2	1	.243
Donohue, Thomas, El Paso	37	135	22	44	66	9	2	3	23	1	0	4	1	34	6	0	.326
Doyle, Brian, San Antonio*	25	86	15	30	37	2	1	1	7	1	0	7	1	3	7	1	.349
Droege, William, Midland	40	155	33	48	79	12	2	5	28	2	3	19	2	27	3	1	.310
Drumright, Keith, Midland*	42	163	22	52	57	3	1	0	14	1	1	18	0	9	5	4	.319
Duncan, Douglas, San An	65	177	18	50	72	11	1	3	20	1	1	25	1	34	1	1	.282
Duran, Daniel, San An*	112	377	45	96	141	13	1	10	50	2	2	49	4	64	2	4	.255
Dyer, James, Jackson*	32	101	6	17	23	4	1	0	6	0	0	10	0	33	2	1	.168
Edelen, Benny, Arkansas	39	109	13	25	35	4	0	2	12	1	0	13	0	23	0	1	.229
Edwards, Michael, Shrev.	53	209	28	67	95	12	2	4	23	4	0	18	1	24	18	9	.321
Ervin, Terrence, Jackson	44	147	14	37	50	5	1	2	19	0	1	10	0	41	5	1	.252
Farkas, Ronald, El Paso	115	371	77	117	159	18	6	4	49	2	1	70	1	70	1	4	.315
Franklin, Anthony, Midland	67	232	32	55	75	8	3	2	20	5	1	35	0	29	15	4	.237
Frazier, Frederic, El Paso	83	309	73	114	162	22	4	6	72	1	7	41	4	16	2	1	.369
Friedman, Martin, El P*	118	435	97	139	184	27	3	4	55	4	5	92	2	63	25	9	.320
Fuqua, Lafayette	18	24	2	4	5	1	0	0	6	0	1	1	0	13	0	0	.167
Geisel, J. David, Midland*	20	2	1	1	1	0	0	0	1	1	0	0	0	1	0	0	.500
Gerhardt, A. Russell, Am*	25	3	0	1	1	0	0	0	0	0	0	0	0	1	0	0	.333

Player and Club	G.	AB.	R.	H.	TB.	2B.	3B.	HR.	RBI.	SH.	SF.	BB.	HP.	SO.	SB.	CS.	Pct.
Gifford, William, Jackson*	2	8	0	2	2	0	0	0	1	0	0	1	0	3	0	0	.250
Goddard, Joseph, Amarillo	1	0	0	0	0	0	0	0	0	0	0	1	0	0	0	0	.000
Gonzalez, L. Antonio, Laf*	24	15	0	4	5	1	0	0	1	3	0	2	0	4	0	0	.267
Gonzalez, Michael, Shrev	27	31	4	6	11	2	0	1	5	2	0	2	0	7	0	0	.194
Goodwin, Danny, El Paso*	63	220	43	67	102	17	0	6	39	0	1	35	2	52	2	0	.305
Gordon, Karl, Midland	3	2	1	0	0	0	0	0	0	0	0	1	0	0	0	0	.000
Gordon, Michael, Midland†	120	430	47	106	165	23	3	10	61	4	3	46	3	104	0	0	.247
Gray, Gary, San Antonio	124	443	74	135	235	27	8	19	109	1	8	40	4	71	7	1	.305
Grundler, Frank, Shrev	126	432	61	120	167	13	2	10	49	3	3	54	0	75	19	2	.278
Gunter, Chester, Shrev	40	20	4	7	10	0	0	1	3	2	0	1	0	8	0	0	.350
Gustavson, Duane, Midland	17	54	4	10	12	2	0	0	4	1	0	7	1	16	0	0	.185
Hamilton, William, Amar†	122	433	76	116	188	29	5	11	70	5	1	72	3	66	6	4	.268
Hammon, Randal, Jackson	15	20	1	5	5	0	0	0	2	2	0	0	0	8	0	0	.250
Hargis, Gary, Shreveport	130	493	51	134	166	21	1	3	39	10	2	14	2	47	19	6	.272
Heinen, Joseph, Lafayette	52	6	0	1	1	0	0	0	0	0	0	0	0	0	0	0	.167
Hernandez, Joseph, Mid	40	157	19	44	63	6	5	1	15	0	1	16	0	21	3	0	.280
Hodges, Ronald A., Laf	9	15	0	4	4	0	0	0	1	1	0	1	0	1	0	0	.267
Hopkins, Randolph, Shrev*	56	7	2	0	0	0	0	0	0	2	0	2	0	6	0	0	.000
Hrapmann, Robert, Midland†	126	438	49	106	133	12	3	3	36	14	1	32	1	75	5	3	.242
Huisman, William, Midland	116	428	70	134	195	19	6	10	58	6	3	56	0	35	15	4	.313
Husband, Paul, Arkansas	56	148	20	34	58	10	1	4	24	2	0	13	1	23	1	0	.230
Iorg, Lee, Jackson	130	490	59	131	174	21	2	6	59	1	5	36	7	31	6	4	.267
Jackson, Roy, Jackson	20	26	3	3	3	0	0	0	0	1	0	0	1	6	0	0	.115
Jaramillo, Rudolph, San An	90	304	35	78	108	7	4	5	48	3	4	22	1	37	10	4	.257
Jordan, Edward, 16 El P-65 Ark	81	250	24	52	77	11	1	4	23	1	2	33	0	41	0	0	.208
Kidder, James, Jackson	56	204	32	49	68	6	5	1	19	4	1	28	0	25	0	1	.240
Kim, Wendell, Lafayette	134	537	71	164	213	21	5	6	45	5	0	63	4	45	4	7	.305
Klenda, David, Jackson*	15	3	0	1	1	0	0	0	0	0	0	0	0	0	0	0	.333
Kremmel, James, Midland*	15	1	0	0	0	0	0	0	0	0	0	0	0	0	0	0	.000
Kubski, Gilbert, El Paso*	99	310	36	85	117	15	4	3	38	4	4	13	1	36	5	0	.274
Kurosaki, Ryan, Arkansas	45	16	1	1	1	0	0	0	1	2	0	0	0	5	0	0	.063
Landreaux, Kenneth, El P*	21	59	15	13	24	3	1	2	11	1	1	8	1	9	0	0	.220
Landrum, Terry, Arkansas	99	359	49	99	139	13	3	7	45	2	3	32	1	74	13	7	.276
Lanthorn, Eugene, Laf	38	12	1	0	0	0	0	0	0	0	0	0	0	7	0	0	.000
Lantigua, Manuel, Arkansas	66	224	18	48	62	7	2	1	22	1	3	13	0	26	0	0	.214
Lebron, Juan, Shreveport	1	1	0	0	0	0	0	0	0	0	0	0	0	1	0	0	.000
Lentine, James, Arkansas	27	73	7	14	25	2	0	3	6	0	2	14	0	9	1	1	.192
Leyva, Nicholas, Arkansas	48	153	16	38	53	4	1	3	26	0	3	12	2	33	0	1	.248
Litle, R. Gene, Jackson	19	14	0	0	0	0	0	0	0	0	0	2	0	10	0	0	.000
Little, D. Jeffrey, Laf	30	25	2	5	6	1	0	0	2	2	0	2	0	6	0	0	.200
Lora, Luis, Jackson*	37	120	17	28	39	5	0	2	15	0	0	14	2	12	4	1	.233
Louis, Alberto, Shreveport	65	263	47	85	130	9	12	4	32	1	4	14	1	50	24	7	.323
Marin, Arturo, Lafayette	71	200	15	43	54	8	0	1	16	3	1	10	2	24	2	0	.215
Martin, Joseph, Laf*	16	43	5	11	15	1	0	1	7	0	0	11	0	1	0	0	.256
Martinez, Orlando, San An†	2	6	3	1	1	0	0	0	0	0	0	2	0	2	0	0	.167
Martinez, Silvio, Shrev	19	19	2	2	2	0	0	0	0	2	0	1	0	13	0	0	.105
Mazzilli, Lee, Jackson†	131	439	91	128	200	21	6	13	43	1	4	111	7	69	28	15	.292
Menees, H. Eugene, Amar	113	375	59	117	155	14	6	4	47	13	2	53	2	43	8	5	.312
Milke, George, Jackson	18	26	3	3	4	1	0	0	2	0	0	2	0	15	0	0	.115
Miller, Richard E., Jack*	27	75	11	25	36	4	2	1	8	1	0	19	0	10	1	0	.333
Minaya, Felix, Jackson	80	239	27	58	70	10	1	0	26	2	3	19	3	22	5	2	.243
Mitchell, Robert D., Amar*	131	519	95	148	176	14	7	0	57	11	9	69	2	37	11	12	.285
Mitchell, Ronald, Shrev	131	486	62	122	195	28	6	11	60	3	4	41	2	84	4	6	.251
Muhlstock, Andrew, Laf	35	10	2	2	2	0	0	0	1	1	0	5	0	4	0	0	.200
Mulliniks, S. Rance, El P*	90	333	81	105	156	22	4	7	51	5	4	68	6	61	20	4	.315
Murphy, Michael, Arkansas	64	11	0	1	2	1	0	0	0	0	0	3	0	1	0	0	.091
Nakamoto, Brian, San An	112	321	62	91	144	13	2	12	56	2	5	79	2	77	4	3	.283
Nelson, David G., Shrev	23	18	1	3	3	0	0	0	1	0	0	1	0	10	0	0	.167
Nelson, J. Douglas, Shrev*	31	47	6	11	13	2	0	0	7	2	0	4	1	11	0	0	.234
Oberkfell, Kenneth, Ark*	128	456	64	131	163	19	2	3	47	4	3	61	3	45	2	3	.287
Ortiz, Jose L., Midland	109	361	67	103	132	10	2	5	30	7	4	93	3	42	25	8	.285
Pagel, Karl, Midland*	15	43	3	8	11	0	0	1	2	1	0	6	0	21	0	0	.186
Pavlick, Gregory, Jackson	19	13	1	1	2	1	0	0	0	2	0	1	0	6	0	0	.077
Peltier, Dwayne, Shrev	42	93	9	14	20	3	0	1	7	1	0	17	1	28	1	1	.151
Pepper, C. Anthony, Laf*	121	396	56	102	164	15	4	13	64	1	3	44	0	51	8	1	.258
Perez, D. Francisco, Jack	23	82	11	22	25	3	0	0	4	3	1	5	1	10	0	0	.268
Perry, Kenneth, Jackson	66	245	32	75	137	13	5	13	43	2	2	26	1	32	11	6	.306
Person, Carl, El Paso	34	121	20	29	37	5	1	0	15	0	2	10	1	18	3	0	.240
Pinkerton, C. Wayne, SA†	65	204	19	47	60	7	0	2	18	5	0	14	0	50	2	1	.230
Prather, Billy, Lafayette	13	29	1	7	8	1	0	0	2	0	0	3	0	6	0	1	.241
Prewitt, Larry, Jackson†	32	27	2	7	7	0	0	0	2	1	0	1	0	10	0	0	.259
Putman, Eddy, Midland	97	331	48	97	136	18	0	7	54	1	6	50	4	42	1	1	.293
Pyka, Terry, San Antonio	33	130	25	42	60	12	0	2	17	1	0	17	3	17	6	3	.323
Rainbolt, Rayburn, San An	42	0	1	0	0	0	0	0	0	0	0	0	0	0	0	0	.000
Ramirez, Orlando, El Paso	31	133	20	30	41	4	2	1	14	2	2	10	1	27	5	2	.226
Ramsey, Michael, Arkansas†	84	288	26	79	87	6	1	0	24	2	1	23	1	32	8	4	.274

Player and Club	G.	AB.	R.	H.	TB.	2B.	3B.	HR.	RBI.	SH.	SF.	BB.	HP.	SO.	SB.	CS.	Pct.
Reedy, Jerome, San Antonio	82	278	43	76	87	8	0	1	26	1	2	49	0	20	4	3	.273
Replogle, Andrew, Arkansas	18	30	1	4	4	0	0	0	2	3	0	1	0	7	0	0	.133
Reynolds, Donald, Amarillo	125	453	94	151	241	19	7	19	85	3	7	86	2	72	8	6	.333
Riggleman, James, Arkansas	47	154	29	46	72	9	1	5	25	1	2	19	2	13	1	1	.299
Robles, Sergio, Arkansas	44	133	12	37	42	5	0	0	15	0	1	11	0	12	0	0	.278
Rodriguez, Felix, Shrev*	32	62	1	7	8	1	0	0	5	0	0	3	0	5	0	1	.113
Rolle, Shadrach, Jackson†	95	318	36	72	104	9	7	3	35	3	5	25	1	54	12	5	.226
Rosado, Luis, Jackson	110	386	39	106	161	22	3	9	49	4	6	22	0	66	0	1	.275
Rosseau, Ernest, Arkansas*	116	346	51	94	109	9	3	0	23	1	1	46	1	35	13	6	.272
Rothan, William, Arkansas	30	18	2	2	2	0	0	0	2	0	0	0	0	7	0	0	.111
Rowland, Michael, Laf	26	34	2	4	8	1	0	1	3	4	0	5	0	11	0	0	.118
Rush, Lawrence, El Paso	101	370	55	98	163	19	2	14	64	1	3	32	2	123	0	0	.265
Saferight, Harry, Shrev*	103	351	36	93	144	18	3	9	52	2	5	40	2	53	0	0	.265
Sander, Richard, Jackson	6	9	1	1	1	0	0	0	1	0	0	0	0	4	0	0	.111
Sanderlin, Thomas, San An	124	400	54	109	123	11	0	1	33	5	3	31	0	58	10	6	.273
Sanner, Dale, Shreveport*	37	140	16	37	50	8	1	1	12	1	0	12	0	24	4	1	.264
Schmidt, E. Eugene, Laf	24	18	2	1	1	0	0	0	0	2	0	3	1	7	0	0	.056
Scott, Michael, Jackson	7	14	2	1	1	0	0	0	1	1	0	0	0	5	0	0	.071
Scurry, Rodney, Shrev*	25	26	1	6	8	2	0	0	2	1	0	2	0	12	0	0	.231
Sealy, Randall, Shrev	15	17	2	1	2	1	0	0	2	2	0	1	0	7	0	0	.059
Sember, Michael, Midland	54	187	25	47	62	2	2	3	23	1	3	31	0	42	9	3	.251
Senn, Terrence, Jackson	108	362	32	84	97	13	0	0	38	2	2	35	2	43	0	0	.232
Sexton, Jimmy, Shreveport	59	207	43	67	97	14	2	4	30	2	3	30	2	35	11	4	.324
Shirley, Robert, Amarillo*	16	1	0	0	0	0	0	0	0	0	0	0	0	1	0	0	.000
Silicato, Thomas, San An	12	50	7	12	13	1	0	0	3	1	1	2	0	1	2	0	.240
Slater, Robert, El Paso	3	11	4	4	6	2	0	0	0	0	0	0	0	3	0	0	.364
Stabelfeldt, David, Laf	29	92	5	26	36	5	1	1	9	1	0	4	0	17	0	0	.283
Standart, Richard, Shrev*	41	8	1	1	1	0	0	0	0	0	0	2	0	0	0	0	.125
Staniland, Stephen, Ark	27	48	3	6	7	1	0	0	1	0	0	5	0	15	1	0	.125
Steen, Michael, San An	33	1	0	0	0	0	0	0	0	0	0	0	0	1	0	0	.000
Stimac, Craig, Amarillo	31	86	13	25	40	6	0	3	14	1	2	7	0	21	1	1	.291
Stone, Michael, Arkansas	15	40	7	10	13	0	0	1	7	1	2	4	0	17	0	0	.250
Stouffer, Blair, San An*	22	62	8	14	22	5	0	1	5	3	0	10	1	11	0	0	.226
Stroughter, Stephen, El P*	116	460	82	136	216	27	4	15	85	1	3	43	0	77	5	4	.296
Stupy, Terry, El Paso	72	242	39	70	95	13	0	4	30	3	1	30	4	18	3	2	.289
Sweet, Rick, Amarillo†	117	412	63	116	160	22	5	4	67	6	2	58	4	41	3	5	.282
Thomas, Donald G., San An	105	339	39	83	109	14	0	4	36	5	3	56	3	58	3	4	.245
Thomas, James L., San An	61	156	15	31	39	6	1	0	16	2	1	28	0	36	2	1	.199
Thompson, Bobby, San An†	87	320	63	91	125	5	7	5	24	7	1	34	2	52	26	12	.284
Thompson, V. Scott, Mid*	116	425	47	121	157	11	2	7	54	4	5	35	1	58	9	5	.285
Tisdale, Freddie, Ark*	9	10	1	1	1	0	0	0	0	0	0	1	0	4	0	0	.100
Torres, Angel, Arkansas*	53	22	2	5	5	0	0	0	2	1	0	0	0	6	0	0	.227
Turner, Darrell, Midland	25	1	0	0	0	0	0	0	0	0	0	0	0	1	0	0	.000
Tyrone, O. Wayne, Midland	50	180	35	50	88	6	1	10	36	0	1	37	0	31	2	0	.278
Umfleet, R. Michael, Mid*	97	348	55	106	136	14	2	4	48	5	2	73	1	60	5	1	.305
Urrea, John, Arkansas	24	38	2	4	4	0	0	0	3	12	0	6	0	6	0	0	.105
Verban, Steve, Midland*	78	217	31	57	76	6	2	3	22	0	2	27	0	44	3	1	.263
Walton, Reginald, Laf	132	471	52	119	168	21	5	6	50	1	4	42	3	62	17	2	.253
Waterbury, Steven, Ark	1	1	0	0	0	0	0	0	0	0	0	0	0	1	0	0	.000
Wiles, Randall, Arkansas*	22	13	0	0	0	0	0	0	0	0	0	1	0	4	0	0	.000
Wilhelm, James, Amarillo	132	495	92	154	221	32	7	7	76	2	4	52	5	53	13	4	.311
Wittmayer, Kurt, Amar	10	29	5	9	10	1	0	0	2	1	0	8	1	4	0	0	.310
Wojcik, Stephen, Jackson*	31	25	1	2	2	0	0	0	0	1	0	0	0	13	0	0	.080
Wolfe, W. Scott, Lafayette	35	116	12	29	39	5	1	1	12	7	1	16	2	18	1	1	.250
Wrenn, Luther, Shreveport	126	420	52	111	163	25	3	7	56	7	8	71	2	74	4	7	.264
Yeglinski, John, Laf*	123	435	66	131	186	25	3	8	48	2	1	69	1	46	3	5	.301
Yost, Edgar, Jackson	83	266	25	53	67	5	0	3	25	2	2	29	2	56	0	0	.199
Young, John, Arkansas*	119	420	71	135	208	33	2	12	73	0	1	63	2	54	5	1	.321
Zagarino, Joe, El Paso	43	149	17	28	51	8	0	5	20	0	1	13	0	40	1	0	.188

The following pitchers had no plate appearances primarily through use of designated-hitters, listed alphabetically by club, games in parentheses:

AMARILLO—Allen, Michael (15); Bernal, Victor (44); Bovee, Rodney (5); Eichelberger, Juan (12); Franklin, John (17); Joseph, William (1); Lentz, Michael (11); McSpadden, Galen (19); Mura, Stephen (7); Owchinko, Robert (13); Rehn, Bradley (4); Stewart, Robert (13).

EL PASO—Barrientos, Virgilio (42); Boyle, Gary (2); Caneira, John (25); Dorsey, James (26); Gibbon, Charles (14); Kuhaulua, Fred (13); McQueen, R. Leroy (15); Meche, Carl (11); Moore, Balor (25); Nolan, Robert (27); Panick, Francis (14); Roslund, John (20); Ross, Gary (7); Stumpp, Richard (4); Whiteley, Thomas (38); Wright, G. Lamar (11).

MIDLAND—Beckman, Bernhard (26); Doland, Wayne (25); Groover, Lawrence (31); Hamrick, Stephen (29); Junge, Gary (41); Riley, George (8); Rogers, Charles (28); Temple, V. James (36).

SAN ANTONIO—Bright, G. Donald (33); Byrd, Jeffrey (26); Clancy, James (23); Harper, David (4); Holman, C. Edward (26); Norman, Ronald (20); Poloni, John (24); Shubert, Richard (25).

SHREVEPORT—Thomas, Gerard (2).

GRAND-SLAM HOME RUNS—Droege, 2; Aikens, Alberts, Bradley, Husband, Miller, Pepper, Perry, Sweet, V. Thompson, Umfleet, Wilhelm, 1 each.

AWARDED FIRST BASE ON CATCHER'S INTERFERENCE—Barnes 2 (Stone 2).

CLUB FIELDING

Club	G.	PO.	A.	E.	DP.	PB.	Pct.	Club	G.	PO.	A.	E.	DP.	PB.	Pct.
Lafayette	134	3340	1505	161	98	18	.968	Shreveport	136	3475	1514	204	128	12	.961
Arkansas	135	3345	1302	160	107	22	.967	Midland	136	3467	1519	217	124	11	.958
Amarillo	135	3455	1544	190	134	18	.963	Jackson	135	3403	1543	216	117	22	.958
El Paso	133	3348	1353	185	105	21	.962	San Antonio	134	3245	1476	213	119	26	.957

Triple Plays—El Paso, San Antonio, 1 each.

INDIVIDUAL FIELDING

*Throws lefthanded.

FIRST BASEMEN

Player and Club	G.	PO.	A.	E.	DP.	Pct.	Player and Club	G.	PO.	A.	E.	DP.	Pct.
Bialas, Arkansas	19	163	6	0	12	1.000	Rush, El Paso	21	172	16	3	13	.984
ROSADO, Jackson	100	908	55	8	77	.992	Young, Arkansas*	115	914	43	18	80	.982
Gustavson, Midland	14	113	10	1	12	.992	Aikens, El Paso	113	971	52	20	77	.981
Duran, San An*	103	907	68	10	77	.990	Sweet, Amarillo	23	203	9	4	16	.981
Mitchell, Shrev	129	1158	92	17	115	.987	Bengston, Jackson	32	302	28	7	23	.979
Pepper, Lafayette*	81	699	43	10	48	.987	Putman, Midland	32	258	9	6	18	.978
Delyon, Amarillo	48	428	30	6	41	.987	Tyrone, Midland	12	79	3	2	9	.976
Thompson, Midland*	83	734	47	11	68	.986	Gray, San Antonio	32	221	12	6	21	.975
Hamilton, Amarillo	61	617	33	10	56	.985	Barnes, Lafayette*	55	563	30	17	24	.972

Triple Plays—Aikens, Duran, 1 each.

(Fewer Than Ten Games)

Player and Club	G.	PO.	A.	E.	DP.	Pct.	Player and Club	G.	PO.	A.	E.	DP.	Pct.
M. Gordon, Midland	2	20	1	0	1	1.000	Verban, Midland	1	2	0	0	0	1.000
Jaramillo, San An	3	14	0	0	1	1.000	Castillo, Arkansas	1	2	0	0	0	1.000
Craig, Amarillo	1	13	1	0	2	1.000	Stimac, Amarillo	1	1	0	0	0	1.000
Rodriguez, Shrev*	2	9	0	0	1	1.000	Grundler, Shrev	6	54	5	1	3	.983
Riggleman, Ark	1	8	0	0	0	1.000	Brown, Lafayette	6	35	1	1	3	.973
Gonzalez, Shreveport	1	6	0	0	1	1.000	Senn, Jackson	4	34	1	1	1	.972
Alberts, El Paso	1	4	0	0	0	1.000	Alfano, Amarillo*	3	20	1	1	0	.955
Nakamoto, San An	1	2	1	0	1	1.000	Saferight, Shrev	4	17	0	3	0	.850

SECOND BASEMEN

Player and Club	G.	PO.	A.	E.	DP.	Pct.	Player and Club	G.	PO.	A.	E.	DP.	Pct.
Cruz, El Paso	13	23	21	0	3	1.000	Dumright, Midland	36	92	106	9	20	.957
KIM, Lafayette	133	294	360	11	61	.983	Mulliniks, El Paso	18	34	44	4	5	.951
Farkas, El Paso	12	25	31	1	9	.982	Djakonow, Shrev	34	91	72	9	22	.948
Castillo, Arkansas	39	86	91	4	15	.978	Brookens, San An	15	28	45	4	4	.948
Hargis, Shreveport	73	165	218	10	51	.975	Franklin, Midland	56	145	174	18	41	.947
Oberkfell, Ark	70	170	169	9	38	.974	Kidder, Jackson	56	142	156	17	37	.946
Menees, Amarillo	112	216	368	16	84	.973	Edwards, Shrev	27	66	75	8	19	.946
Frazier, El Paso	82	172	214	12	44	.970	Pyka, San Antonio	33	89	88	15	17	.922
Leyva, Arkansas	29	52	67	4	16	.967	Baker, Amarillo	10	13	32	4	3	.918
Reedy, San Antonio	70	147	211	13	41	.965	Wittmayer, Amar	10	11	34	5	5	.900
Huisman, Midland	51	115	174	11	28	.963	D. Thomas, San An	10	22	29	6	3	.895
Perry, Jackson	66	129	200	13	39	.962							

Triple Play—Reedy.

(Fewer Than Ten Games)

Player and Club	G.	PO.	A.	E.	DP.	Pct.	Player and Club	G.	PO.	A.	E.	DP.	Pct.
Slater, El Paso	3	11	12	0	2	1.000	del Orbe, Lafayette	1	1	1	0	0	1.000
Mitchell, Amarillo	3	4	10	0	2	1.000	Silicato, San An	7	16	18	1	8	.971
Ramirez, El Paso	2	5	9	0	1	1.000	Senn, Jackson	9	26	37	3	10	.955
Delyon, Amarillo	1	3	1	0	0	1.000	Minaya, Jackson	4	10	8	1	1	.947
Edelen, Arkansas	1	0	4	0	0	1.000	Marin, Lafayette	3	5	4	1	1	.900
Mitchell, Shrev	1	0	4	0	0	1.000	Grundler, Shrev	4	3	4	1	0	.875
K. Gordon, Midland	1	1	2	0	0	1.000	Kubski, El Paso	5	8	9	3	1	.850
Person, El Paso	2	0	2	0	0	1.000							

THIRD BASEMEN

Player and Club	G.	PO.	A.	E.	DP.	Pct.	Player and Club	G.	PO.	A.	E.	DP	Pct.
Senn, Jackson	29	14	59	2	4	.973	Bucci, San Antonio	18	10	32	4	2	.913
D. THOMAS, San An	92	84	200	14	20	.953	Djakonow, Shrev	97	74	180	25	19	.910
Zagarino, El Paso	43	34	78	7	9	.941	Rolle, Jackson	84	73	189	28	15	.903
Huisman, Midland	36	32	57	6	9	.937	Farkas, El Paso	79	56	145	22	14	.901
Andrews, Lafayette	123	87	301	28	16	.933	Grundler, Shrev	23	22	42	7	1	.901
Leyva, Arkansas	11	8	20	2	1	.933	Perez, Jackson	21	18	46	7	3	.901
Castillo, Arkansas	52	42	103	11	9	.929	Edelen, Arkansas	27	16	55	8	5	.899
Umfleet, Midland	96	84	185	22	15	.924	Peltier, Shrev	16	13	31	6	1	.880
Riggleman, Ark	44	28	73	9	10	.918	Doyle, San Antonio	23	25	50	11	10	.872
Ashford, Amarillo	122	100	274	34	33	.917							

Triple Plays—Farkas, D. Thomas, 1 each.

THIRD BASEMEN—Continued

(Fewer Than Ten Games)

Player and Club	G.	PO.	A.	E.	DP.	Pct.	Player and Club	G.	PO.	A.	E.	DP.	Pct.
Mitchell, Amarillo	9	0	19	0	1	1.000	Rosado, Jackson	1	1	0	0	0	1.000
Sweet, Amarillo	3	4	5	0	1	1.000	Gray, San Antonio	1	0	1	0	0	1.000
Hrapmann, Midland	2	5	2	0	1	1.000	Tyrone, Midland	5	4	11	1	1	.938
Lantigua, Jackson	2	1	6	0	0	1.000	Rush, El Paso	6	5	18	2	0	.920
Barrow, San Antonio	3	2	4	0	0	1.000	de los Santos, Laf	8	5	17	2	2	.917
Franklin, Midland	2	2	4	0	0	1.000	Brookens, San An	5	6	7	2	1	.867
del Orbe, Lafayette	2	1	4	0	0	1.000	Delyon, Amarillo	3	2	4	1	0	.857
Baker, Amarillo	1	1	2	0	0	1.000	Stupy, El Paso	8	3	12	3	1	.833
Minaya, Jackson	1	0	2	0	1	1.000	Gifford, Jackson	2	0	4	1	1	.800
Marin, Lafayette	2	1	0	0	0	1.000	Bialas, Arkansas	1	2	2	1	0	.800

SHORTSTOPS

Player and Club	G.	PO.	A.	E.	DP.	Pct.	Player and Club	G.	PO.	A.	E.	DP.	Pct.
Franklin, Midland	11	18	31	1	9	.980	Farkas, El Paso	29	53	79	11	18	.923
Hargis, Shreveport	58	87	171	7	22	.974	Edwards, Shrev	26	37	82	10	22	.922
del Orbe, Lafayette	29	40	105	5	12	.967	HRAPMANN, Midland	101	167	302	42	58	.918
Oberkfell, Ark	58	89	152	9	28	.964	Sexton, Shreveport	54	76	159	21	29	.918
Mulliniks, El Paso	73	106	203	16	39	.951	Ramsey, Arkansas	79	109	231	32	42	.914
Pinkerton, San An	65	92	198	15	33	.951	Mitchell, Amarillo	45	68	116	19	23	.906
Marin, Lafayette	59	90	163	13	32	.951	Stouffer, San An	21	36	60	12	9	.889
Ramirez, El Paso	29	43	73	6	7	.951	Sember, Midland	27	36	85	16	14	.883
Minaya, Jackson	58	98	181	16	31	.946	Dyer, Jackson	30	45	76	19	12	.864
Wolfe, Lafayette	35	52	121	11	12	.940	Reedy, San Antonio	13	19	33	9	10	.852
Baker, Amarillo	86	130	315	32	58	.933	Brookens, San An	22	20	48	12	12	.850
Senn, Jackson	53	83	178	19	26	.932	de los Santos, Laf	15	12	39	9	4	.850

(Fewer Than Ten Games)

Player and Club	G.	PO.	A.	E.	DP.	Pct.	Player and Club	G.	PO.	A.	E.	DP.	Pct.
Kim, Lafayette	1	3	3	0	1	1.000	Bucci, San Antonio	2	2	5	1	1	.875
Djakonow, Shrev	1	2	1	0	0	1.000	Ashford, Amarillo	8	12	14	4	1	.867
Martinez, San An	1	1	2	0	0	1.000	Barrow, San Antonio	9	13	17	5	2	.857
Person, El Paso	8	19	14	2	6	.943	Silicato, San An	4	7	6	4	1	.765
D. Thomas, San An	5	3	18	2	7	.913	Doyle, San Antonio	2	3	3	2	0	.750

OUTFIELDERS

Player and Club	G.	PO.	A.	E.	DP.	Pct.	Player and Club	G.	PO.	A.	E.	DP.	Pct.
Bucci, San Antonio	29	36	4	0	1	1.000	Yeglinski, Laf*	115	193	11	7	3	.967
Landreaux, El Paso	19	32	4	0	1	1.000	Reynolds, Amarillo	119	201	11	8	2	.964
Person, El Paso	26	35	0	0	0	1.000	Pagel, Midland*	15	22	5	1	0	.964
Tyrone, Midland	19	27	5	0	0	1.000	Louis, Shreveport	65	133	7	6	1	.959
Baker, Amarillo	10	19	3	0	0	1.000	Chew, Midland	95	187	9	9	3	.956
Putman, Midland	11	17	2	0	0	1.000	Kubski, El Paso	92	126	12	7	3	.952
Delyon, Amarillo	10	16	0	0	0	1.000	Blackwell, Ark	38	78	1	4	0	.952
Craig, Amarillo	70	135	3	1	0	.993	Detherage, Ark	40	74	3	4	1	.951
Hernandez, Mid*	40	103	6	1	0	.991	Sember, Midland	24	35	1	2	0	.947
Rush, El Paso	44	77	5	1	0	.988	Bauers, Jackson	54	83	5	5	0	.946
ROSSEAU, Ark	92	117	3	2	0	.984	Stroughter, El P	116	191	16	12	3	.945
Grundler, Shrev	76	141	5	3	0	.980	Iorg, Jackson*	129	232	20	15	1	.944
Sanderlin, Laf	117	224	9	5	4	.979	Husband, Arkansas	37	64	4	4	0	.944
Wrenn, Shrev	120	177	4	4	0	.978	Ervin, Jackson	36	61	6	4	2	.944
Wilhelm, Amarillo	128	317	7	8	2	.976	Bialas, Arkansas	89	126	5	8	1	.942
Nakamoto, San An	82	115	9	3	2	.976	Jaramillo, San An	82	102	5	7	1	.939
Mitchell, Amarillo	68	115	7	3	1	.976	Droege, Midland	40	70	3	5	0	.936
Verban, Midland	76	113	3	3	1	.975	Ortiz, Midland	90	102	8	8	1	.932
Blomberg, Shrev	88	205	17	6	4	.974	Walton, Lafayette	125	153	8	12	0	.931
Sanner, Shrev	37	69	4	2	1	.973	Lentine, Arkansas	27	59	2	5	1	.924
Barrow, San An	41	62	7	2	1	.972	Thompson, San An	86	172	10	16	0	.919
Thompson, Mid*	20	32	3	1	0	.972	Lora, San Antonio*	34	62	2	7	0	.901
Mazzilli, Jackson	129	262	8	8	2	.971	Saferight, Shrev	22	33	2	4	0	.897
Barnes, Lafayette*	39	66	2	2	0	.971	Miller, Jackson	23	28	3	4	1	.886
Friedman, El Paso*	117	284	27	10	3	.969	Pepper, Lafayette*	24	35	1	5	0	.878
Chauncey, San An*	111	170	13	6	3	.968	Senn, Jackson	10	8	0	2	0	.800
Landrum, Arkansas	99	201	12	7	3	.968							

(Fewer Than Ten Games)

Player and Club	G.	PO.	A.	E.	DP.	Pct.	Player and Club	G.	PO.	A.	E.	DP.	Pct.
Alfano, Amarillo*	6	8	1	0	0	1.000	J. Thomas, San An	2	1	0	0	0	1.000
Cuellar, San An	1	2	1	0	0	1.000	Tisdale, Arkansas	1	1	0	0	0	1.000
Astroth, San An	2	2	0	0	0	1.000	Brown, Lafayette	7	9	0	1	0	.900
Stimac, Amarillo	1	2	0	0	0	1.000	Hrapmann, Midland	7	8	1	1	0	.900
Gerhardt, Amar*	1	2	0	0	0	1.000	Rodriguez, Shrev*	6	4	0	1	0	.800
Gray, San Antonio	4	1	0	0	0	1.000	Riggleman, Arkansas	1	2	0	1	0	.667

CATCHERS

Player and Club	G.	PO.	A.	E.	DP.	PB.	Pct.
Rosado, Jackson	2	5	1	0	0	0	1.000
Hamilton, Amar.	41	220	17	1	2	9	.996
JORDAN, El P-Ark.	76	476	31	3	7	13	.994
Stupy, El Paso	65	394	36	5	3	6	.989
Nakamoto, San An	23	71	6	1	0	2	.987
Astroth, San An	24	125	9	2	0	2	.985
Stabelfeldt, Laf.	23	118	16	2	2	6	.985
Martin, Lafayette	12	62	5	1	0	4	.985
Yost, Jackson	74	390	42	7	7	16	.984
Duncan, San An	54	285	29	5	5	13	.984
Cariel, Shrev	76	408	56	8	9	5	.983
M. Gordon, Mid	109	588	69	13	8	9	.981
Goodwin, El Paso	36	195	12	4	3	9	.981
Saferight, Shrev	67	361	28	8	2	7	.980
Robles, Arkansas	34	232	21	6	1	1	.977
Daves, Arkansas	33	189	23	5	0	7	.977
Bradley, Laf	93	495	53	13	7	6	.977
Donohue, El Paso	25	146	22	4	2	4	.977
Putman, Midland	30	104	13	3	3	2	.975
Lantigua, Jackson	63	220	38	7	4	6	.974
Sweet, Amarillo	84	420	35	15	13	7	.968
Stimac, Amarillo	13	53	7	2	0	2	.968
J. Thomas, San An	51	233	19	9	4	9	.966
Stone, Arkansas	11	78	3	3	1	3	.964
Gustavson, Midland	4	23	2	1	0	0	.962
Prather, Lafayette	8	38	1	5	1	2	.886

PITCHERS

Player and Club	G.	PO.	A.	E.	DP.	Pct.
ROWLAND, Lafayette	26	8	28	0	0	1.000
Clancy, San Antonio	23	8	27	0	0	1.000
Gonzalez, Shrev	24	7	24	0	1	.1.000
Dillard, Lafayette	18	5	25	0	1	1.000
Prewitt, Jackson	29	11	18	0	1	1.000
Schmidt, Lafayette.	24	8	19	0	0	1.000
Milke, Jackson	18	11	16	0	0	1.000
Sealy, Shreveport	15	8	18	0	0	1.000
Fuqua, Lafayette	18	4	21	0	1	1.000
Heinen, Lafayette.	52	9	15	0	0	1.000
D. Nelson, Shrev	23	7	17	0	0	1.000
Holman, San An*	26	3	20	0	0	1.000
Replogle, Arkansas	16	1	22	0	1	1.000
Davis, Shreveport	55	4	18	0	2	1.000
Franklin, Amarillo.	17	8	14	0	3	1.000
Muhlstock, Laf	35	10	11	0	2	1.000
Gibbon, El Paso*	14	1	20	0	1	1.000
Owchinko, Amarillo*	13	6	15	0	4	1.000
Cuellar, San An	48	3	17	0	0	1.000
Rainbolt, San An	41	4	16	0	0	1.000
Little, Lafayette*	29	3	17	0	2	1.000
Temple, Midland	36	5	14	0	0	1.000
Staniland, Arkansas	27	2	17	0	0	1.000
Jackson, Jackson	20	7	11	0	2	1.000
Pavlick, Jackson	19	0	16	0	1	1.000
Wright, El Paso*	11	3	13	0	1	1.000
Beckman, Midland*	26	1	13	0	0	1.000
Whiteley, El Paso	38	4	8	0	0	1.000
Deidel, Jackson*	12	1	11	0	0	1.000
Bright, San An	32	2	9	0	1	1.000
Litle, Jackson	19	2	8	0	0	1.000
Panick, El Paso	14	3	7	0	0	1.000
de los Santos, Ark*	26	0	9	0	0	1.000
Wiles, Arkansas	21	1	8	0	0	1.000
Roslund, El Paso*	20	3	5	0	1	1.000
Meche, El Paso	11	0	6	0	0	1.000
Alfano, Amarillo*	28	3	2	0	0	1.000
Kuhaulua, El Paso*	13	0	4	0	0	1.000
Byrd, San Antonio	26	9	32	1	2	.976
Gunter, Shreveport	39	9	23	1	2	.970
Coe, Amarillo*	20	11	21	1	1	.970
McSpadden, Amar*	19	6	26	1	3	.970
Gerhardt, Amarillo*	24	7	24	1	1	.969
Kurosaki, Arkansas	45	4	17	1	4	.955
Torres, Arkansas*	48	8	12	1	2	.952
Cornejo, Jackson	48	3	17	1	0	.952
Nolan, El Paso*	27	5	34	2	0	.951
Murphy, Arkansas	64	2	17	1	2	.950
Covert, Arkansas	26	5	14	1	1	.950
Norman, San An*	25	7	12	1	0	.950
Shirley, Amarillo*	16	5	13	1	0	.947
Hammon, Jackson	15	8	9	1	0	.944
J. Nelson, Shrev*	26	4	29	2	1	.943
Hamrick, Midland*	29	15	34	3	2	.942
Rothan, Arkansas	30	4	12	1	0	.941
Doland, Midland	29	17	31	3	1	.941
Shubert, San An*	25	3	28	2	1	.939
Bruhert, Jackson	17	3	27	2	2	.938
Rogers, Midland	28	14	29	3	1	.935
Divison, Lafayette	33	7	33	3	1	.930
Standart, Shrev	41	3	10	1	0	.929
Scurry, Shreveport*	24	2	24	2	2	.929
Gonzalez, Laf*	22	7	15	2	1	.917
Allen, Amarillo	15	3	8	1	1	.917
Geisel, Midland*	20	2	9	1	0	.917
Anderson, Shreveport	28	5	38	4	4	.915
Wojcik, Jackson*	31	7	23	3	2	.909
Poloni, San An*	24	2	26	3	0	.903
Junge, Midland	41	5	4	1	0	.900
Caudill, Arkansas	27	5	20	3	2	.893
Turner, Midland	25	4	19	3	1	.885
Bernal, Amarillo	44	3	12	2	2	.882
Lanthorn, Lafayette	38	3	12	2	1	.882
Hopkins, Shreveport*	56	4	18	3	1	.880
Andrews, Jackson*	42	5	9	2	1	.875
Stewart, Amarillo	13	3	4	1	0	.875
Urrea, Arkansas	24	7	24	5	2	.861
Lentz, Amarillo*	11	1	5	1	0	.857
Kremmel, Midland*	15	4	7	2	0	.846
Martinez, Shreveport	16	9	22	6	0	.838
Caneira, El Paso	25	6	9	3	1	.833
Butcher, Amarillo	23	1	4	1	0	.833
Steen, San Antonio*	32	2	12	3	3	.824
McQueen, El Paso	15	2	7	2	0	.818
Moore, El Paso*	25	3	37	9	0	.816
Eichelberger, Amar	11	5	12	4	1	.810
Dorsey, El Paso	26	8	25	8	2	.805
Groover, Midland*	29	2	5	3	0	.700
Barrientos, El Paso	42	2	7	4	0	.692
Klenda, Jackson	15	2	4	3	0	.667

(Fewer Than Ten Games)

Player and Club	G.	PO.	A.	E.	DP.	Pct.
Hodges, Lafayette	9	7	15	0	1	1.000
Bernard, Jackson	9	4	11	0	1	1.000
Mura, Amarillo	7	2	12	0	0	1.000
Harper, San Antonio	1	1	7	0	1	1.000
Camper, Arkansas	7	0	6	0	0	1.000
Boyle, El Paso	2	0	3	0	0	1.000
Ross, El Paso	7	1	1	0	0	1.000
Brandt, Shreveport*	6	0	2	0	0	1.000
Rehn, Amarillo	4	0	2	0	0	1.000
Bovee, Amarillo*	5	0	1	0	0	1.000
Stumpp, El Paso	4	0	1	0	0	1.000
Bolick, San Antonio	3	0	1	0	0	1.000
Chauncey, San An*	2	0	1	0	0	1.000
Waterbury, Arkansas	1	0	1	0	0	1.000
Sander, Jackson	6	3	8	1	1	.917
Scott, Jackson	7	5	5	1	1	.909
Riley, Midland*	8	6	12	3	0	.857
Thomas, Shreveport*	2	0	0	1	0	.000

The following players do not have any recorded accepted chances at the positions indicated; therefore, are not listed in the fielding averages for those particular positions: Astroth, 1b; Baker, p; Donohue, of; Jaramillo, 3b; Joseph*, p; Kim, of; Leyva, ss; Ronald Mitchell, of-p; Nakamoto, 3b; Stupy, of; Sweet, of; Goddard and Lebron appeared as pinch-hitters only.

CLUB PITCHING

Club	G.	CG.	ShO.	Sv.	IP.	H.	R.	ER.	HR.	BB.	Int. BB.	HB.	SO.	WP.	Bk.	ERA.
Shreveport	136	23	12	30	1158	1090	525	420	68	499	27	18	705	57	6	3.26
Jackson	135	35	12	21	1134	1176	592	467	69	495	36	20	658	66	3	3.71
Lafayette	134	35	11	11	1113	1110	577	488	86	443	31	39	660	41	5	3.95
Arkansas	135	23	8	24	1115	1100	594	493	70	551	48	16	849	46	5	3.98
Amarillo	136	39	7	24	1156	1269	717	562	82	581	38	23	644	44	2	4.38
Midland	135	31	5	26	1116	1296	679	568	95	526	12	19	751	39	13	4.58
El Paso	133															
San Antonio	134	32	6	23	1082	1188	718	601	66	667	32	36	685	89	3	5.00

PITCHERS' RECORDS
(Leading Qualifiers for Earned-Run Average Leadership—109 or More Innings)

*Throws lefthanded.

Pitcher–Club	G.	GS.	CG.	ShO.	W.	L.	Sv.	Pct.	IP.	H.	R.	ER.	HR.	BB.	Int. BB.	HB.	SO.	WP.	ERA.
Dillard, Lafayette	18	18	8	3	8	5	0	.615	133	100	41	34	6	63	2	4	68	3	2.30
Jackson, Jackson	20	20	8	4	8	6	0	.571	132	136	51	44	8	39	2	0	82	2	3.00
Anderson, Shrev	28	26	4	0	7	14	0	.333	164	164	75	58	11	60	5	4	105	7	3.18
McSpadden, Amar*	19	19	10	2	10	7	0	.588	133	132	55	48	12	44	1	1	67	7	3.25
Shirley, Amar*	16	16	6	0	9	5	0	.643	111	113	55	41	3	39	2	2	90	4	3.32
Bruhert, Jackson	17	17	7	1	6	6	0	.500	114	116	56	43	3	36	2	3	50	6	3.39
Poloni, San An*	24	23	8	2	11	7	0	.611	143	191	76	54	6	43	2	4	91	7	3.40
J. Nelson, Shrev*	26	26	5	1	10	7	0	.588	153	144	71	60	10	82	2	0	93	3	3.53
Nolan, El Paso	27	20	9	3	15	3	1	.833	140	165	67	57	8	42	2	2	89	1	3.66
Rowland, Lafayette	26	26	5	2	5	14	0	.263	161	157	76	66	16	59	1	3	87	6	3.69

Departmental Leaders: G–Murphy, 64; GS–Hamrick, 29; CG–Rogers, 15; ShO–Martinez, 7; W–Caneira, Nolan, 15; L–Rogers, 16; Sv–Bernal, 19; Pct.–Nolan, .833; IP–Rogers, 196; H–Rogers, 238; R–Moore, 110; ER–Clancy, 89; HR–Doland, Moore, Rowland, 16; BB–Moore, 113; IBB–Murphy, 11; HB–Rainbolt, Schmidt, 6; SO–Caudill, 140; WP–Byrd, 20.

(All Pitchers—Listed Alphabetically)

Pitcher–Club	G.	GS.	CG.	ShO.	W.	L.	Sv.	Pct.	IP.	H.	R.	ER.	HR.	BB.	Int. BB.	HB.	SO.	WP.	ERA.
Alfano, Amarillo*	28	1	0	0	3	1	1	.750	48	54	28	22	3	35	0	1	36	6	4.13
Allen, Amarillo	15	11	3	1	7	4	1	.636	82	85	29	23	2	15	0	2	33	5	2.52
Anderson, Shrev	28	26	4	0	7	14	0	.333	164	164	75	58	11	60	5	4	105	7	3.18
Andrews, Jackson*	1	0	0	0	0	0	0	.000	1	0	0	0	0	0	0	0	1	0	0.00
Baker, Amarillo	1	0	0	0	0	0	0	.000	0	0	0	0	0	0	0	0	0	0	0.00
Barrientos, El P	42	0	0	0	6	2	12	.750	83	83	35	30	8	30	2	2	70	3	3.25
Beckman, Mid*	26	12	1	1	7	4	0	.636	95	119	77	57	9	63	2	5	61	10	5.40
Bernal, Amarillo	44	0	0	0	5	7	19	.417	68	65	33	31	6	24	3	2	55	8	4.10
Bernard, Jackson	9	9	3	0	2	5	0	.286	54	48	28	25	3	32	0	1	33	0	4.17
Bolick, San An	3	0	0	0	0	0	0	.000	7	15	10	7	1	3	0	0	3	0	9.00
Bovee, Amarillo*	5	0	0	0	0	1	1	.000	2	5	3	1	0	2	0	1	1	0	4.50
Boyle, El Paso	2	0	0	0	0	0	0	.000	8	10	7	6	1	5	0	0	2	0	6.75
Brandt, Shrev*	6	0	0	0	1	0	1	1.000	6	4	1	0	0	0	0	0	5	0	0.00
Bright, San An	32	3	0	2	6	4	2	.250	74	64	38	37	6	36	3	1	50	7	4.50
Bruhert, Jackson	17	17	7	1	6	6	0	.500	114	116	56	43	3	36	2	3	50	6	3.39
Butcher, Amar	23	1	1	0	5	1	3	.833	50	56	31	23	2	26	0	1	14	4	4.14
Byrd, San Antonio	26	26	7	1	7	11	0	.389	143	152	106	83	2	107	3	4	86	20	5.22
Camper, Arkansas	7	7	1	1	1	3	0	.250	35	33	22	20	6	25	0	0	25	0	5.14
Caneira, El Paso	25	22	5	0	15	4	0	.789	149	182	85	75	13	55	0	1	95	6	4.53
Caudill, Arkansas	27	27	6	1	6	15	0	.286	140	128	79	69	8	84	8	4	140	4	4.44
Chauncey, San An*	2	0	0	0	0	0	0	.000	4	7	2	0	0	2	0	0	0	0	0.00
Clancy, San An	23	23	5	0	6	8	0	.429	125	133	94	89	5	98	3	5	77	10	6.41
Coe, Amarillo*	20	15	6	0	7	3	0	.700	123	135	62	51	5	46	3	1	31	3	3.73
Cornejo, Jackson	48	0	0	0	6	6	11	.500	78	82	36	20	2	24	9	1	41	3	2.31
Covert, Arkansas	26	26	4	2	7	8	0	.467	117	118	67	62	12	90	4	1	65	5	4.77
Cuellar, San An	48	1	0	0	9	5	15	.643	85	67	30	25	3	31	6	3	63	1	2.65
Davis, Shreveport	55	0	0	0	2	5	14	.286	76	76	29	19	3	28	5	0	26	6	2.25
Deidel, Jackson*	12	11	2	2	3	5	0	.375	65	64	47	34	4	31	1	1	39	4	4.71
de los Santos, Ark*	26	0	0	0	2	2	1	.500	42	38	21	12	3	17	2	1	46	4	2.57
Dillard, Lafayette	18	18	8	3	8	5	0	.615	133	100	41	34	6	63	2	4	68	3	2.30
Divison, Lafayette	33	18	7	0	6	13	2	.316	145	164	89	76	15	33	4	3	88	1	4.72
Doland, Midland	29	26	4	1	13	6	0	.684	163	173	96	81	16	61	2	4	70	7	4.53
Dorsey, El Paso	26	26	3	0	9	9	0	.500	164	188	104	82	14	77	2	3	101	9	4.50
Eichelberger, Amar	11	11	3	0	2	6	0	.250	66	77	50	41	8	45	2	0	41	10	5.59

Pitcher–Club	G.	GS.	CG.	ShO.	W.	L.	Sv.	Pct.	IP.	H.	R.	ER.	HR.	BB.	Int. BB.	HB.	SO.	WP.	ERA.
Franklin, Amar	17	9	4	0	7	5	0	.583	89	94	49	41	6	35	0	3	47	5	4.15
Fuqua, Lafayette	18	16	3	0	5	6	0	.455	90	101	48	41	1	22	1	0	50	3	4.10
Geisel, Midland	20	16	4	0	5	8	0	.385	107	114	59	44	1	45	3	1	59	3	3.70
Gerhardt, Amar*	24	14	4	1	9	2	0	.818	115	140	67	59	8	38	1	0	58	4	4.62
Gibbon, El Paso*	14	14	3	0	5	3	0	.625	73	80	42	36	5	32	0	2	47	4	4.44
Gonzalez, Laf*	22	15	2	1	4	7	0	.364	89	115	67	60	9	39	1	5	44	3	6.07
Gonzalez, Shrev	24	19	2	0	7	6	1	.538	112	102	60	56	10	61	2	4	68	7	4.50
Groover, Mid*	29	3	1	0	2	0	1	1.000	84	99	70	46	9	53	3	2	38	4	4.93
Gunter, Shrev	39	1	0	0	6	3	4	.667	91	94	49	42	6	29	2	2	65	9	4.15
Hammon, Jackson	15	15	6	2	7	7	0	.500	91	85	39	31	5	35	2	1	50	7	3.07
Hamrick, Midland*	29	29	7	2	11	11	0	.500	185	172	104	87	13	112	3	1	132	3	4.23
Harper, San An	4	4	2	0	3	1	0	.750	29	31	11	10	1	7	0	1	17	1	3.10
Heinen, Lafayette	52	0	0	0	5	2	3	.714	76	59	33	27	7	44	5	4	61	4	3.20
Hodges, Lafayette	9	8	5	1	4	4	0	.500	52	44	22	20	5	20	2	3	29	1	3.46
Holman, San An*	26	19	3	1	6	11	0	.353	111	142	79	70	9	66	2	4	75	6	5.68
Hopkins, Shrev*	56	0	0	0	8	9	5	.471	97	93	42	33	7	48	6	2	58	3	3.06
Jackson, Jackson	20	20	8	4	8	6	0	.571	132	136	51	44	8	39	2	0	82	2	3.00
Joseph, Amar*	1	1	1	0	0	1	0	.000	8	6	4	4	2	1	0	1	4	0	4.50
Junge, Midland	41	0	0	0	3	2	8	.600	64	70	35	26	5	28	6	0	32	0	3.66
Klenda, Jackson	15	0	0	0	3	0	4	1.000	28	22	4	2	1	11	2	0	20	0	0.64
Kremmel, Mid*	15	0	0	0	1	7	1	.125	33	26	25	16	2	29	3	1	22	3	4.36
Kuhaulua, El P*	13	0	0	0	1	2	3	.333	26	30	15	13	0	24	1	0	27	3	4.50
Kurosaki, Arkansas	45	0	0	0	6	2	6	.714	83	75	31	30	2	26	7	1	49	2	3.25
Lanthorn, Laf	38	0	0	0	3	4	4	.429	71	69	39	33	4	25	3	5	27	3	4.18
Lentz, Amarillo*	11	10	0	0	5	3	0	.625	51	53	37	31	6	25	0	2	43	4	5.47
Litle, Jackson	19	4	0	0	1	2	0	.333	67	77	45	40	12	35	1	1	41	2	5.37
Little, Lafayette*	29	17	2	0	4	9	1	.308	110	107	67	60	9	59	1	3	66	3	4.91
Martinez, Shrev	16	16	8	7	8	4	0	.667	104	74	29	28	8	33	0	2	71	1	2.42
McQueen, Jackson	15	0	0	0	2	2	0	.000	39	54	25	20	3	12	1	0	23	0	4.62
McSpadden, Amar*	19	19	10	2	10	7	0	.588	133	132	55	48	12	44	1	1	67	7	3.25
Meche, El Paso	3	1	0	2	3	1	0	.400	29	35	15	10	1	10	0	0	11	0	3.10
Milke, Jackson	18	18	3	0	4	7	0	.364	87	99	51	40	6	28	1	3	67	4	4.14
Mitchell, Shrev	2	0	0	0	1	0	0	.000	4	4	4	2	2	0	3	2	0	0	4.50
Moore, El Paso*	25	25	4	1	6	12	0	.333	141	153	110	87	16	113	1	5	86	8	5.55
Muhlstock, Laf	35	4	1	0	8	4	1	.667	90	98	41	33	9	38	8	3	87	8	3.30
Mura, Amarillo	7	7	3	0	4	2	0	.667	59	48	22	17	1	27	2	0	50	2	2.59
Murphy, Arkansas	64	1	0	0	7	10	13	.412	95	86	42	30	4	48	11	1	83	4	2.84
D. Nelson, Shrev	23	11	0	0	6	4	1	.600	86	84	38	26	4	18	0	2	53	4	2.72
J. Nelson, Shrev*	26	26	5	1	10	7	0	.588	153	144	71	60	10	82	2	0	93	3	3.53
Nolan, El Paso*	27	20	9	3	15	3	1	.833	140	165	67	57	8	42	2	2	85	1	3.66
Norman, San An*	25	18	1	0	6	8	0	.429	99	121	96	82	11	82	4	2	65	10	7.45
Owchinko, Amar*	13	13	4	2	6	2	0	.750	91	86	36	33	7	38	0	0	69	2	3.26
Panick, El Paso	14	9	1	0	3	5	0	.375	57	74	48	42	8	26	2	1	39	1	6.63
Pavlick, Jackson	19	0	0	0	4	1	0	.800	56	68	35	28	3	19	4	3	21	5	4.50
Poloni, San An*	24	23	8	2	11	7	0	.611	143	191	76	54	6	43	2	4	91	7	3.40
Prewitt, Jackson	29	17	2	1	9	6	0	.600	113	101	64	54	4	90	3	4	83	14	4.30
Rainbolt, San An	41	4	0	0	5	7	2	.417	102	116	78	66	9	65	4	6	57	9	5.82
Rehn, Amarillo	4	0	0	0	0	0	0	.000	6	14	11	8	3	1	0	0	5	3	12.00
Replogle, Ark	16	15	2	1	4	6	0	.400	80	93	55	45	4	35	2	0	41	4	5.06
Riley, Midland*	8	8	1	0	1	5	0	.167	47	61	37	34	1	36	0	3	29	0	6.51
Rogers, Midland	28	28	15	1	11	16	0	.407	196	238	107	82	14	54	5	4	97	4	3.77
Roslund, El Paso*	20	1	0	0	5	3	0	.625	69	72	33	29	2	29	1	1	49	1	3.78
Ross, El Paso	7	0	0	0	1	0	1	1.000	14	17	6	4	2	3	0	0	8	0	2.57
Rothan, Arkansas	30	5	0	0	4	1	0	.800	74	78	40	36	5	29	2	2	52	4	4.38
Rowland, Lafayette	26	26	5	2	5	14	0	.263	161	157	76	66	16	59	1	3	87	6	3.69
Sander, Jackson	6	6	0	0	1	3	0	.250	27	44	31	24	8	18	1	2	14	4	8.00
Schmidt, Lafayette	24	12	2	1	6	8	0	.429	96	96	54	47	5	41	3	6	53	6	4.41
Scott, Jackson	7	7	2	1	3	3	0	.500	44	34	20	14	3	14	1	0	19	1	2.86
Scurry, Shrev*	24	24	1	0	8	8	0	.500	123	120	71	53	4	83	1	2	83	8	3.88
Sealy, Shreveport	15	13	3	1	5	5	0	.500	80	83	35	31	5	28	0	0	40	8	3.49
Shirley, Amar*	16	16	6	9	5	0	0	.643	111	113	55	41	3	39	2	2	90	4	3.32
Shubert, San An*	25	13	3	1	3	4	1	.429	89	79	64	55	10	87	3	5	48	13	5.56
Standart, Shrev	41	0	0	0	2	0	4	1.000	59	48	23	12	0	25	3	0	37	0	1.83
Staniland, Ark	27	27	4	0	6	11	0	.353	147	151	88	69	11	62	4	3	121	7	4.22
Steen, San An*	32	0	0	0	5	3	1	.625	71	70	34	23	3	40	2	1	53	5	2.92
Stewart, Amar	13	7	1	0	2	4	0	.333	49	72	43	36	4	23	2	3	29	1	6.61
Stumpp, El Paso	4	0	0	0	0	0	0	.000	4	11	7	7	1	3	0	0	3	0	15.75
Temple, Midland	36	0	0	0	4	3	14	.571	59	52	26	17	0	34	6	1	47	2	2.59
Thomas, Shrev*	2	0	0	0	0	0	0	.000	2	0	0	0	0	1	0	0	1	0	0.00
Torres, Arkansas	48	0	0	0	2	5	3	.286	95	82	50	36	3	60	3	0	77	8	3.41
Turner, Midland	25	14	6	4	12	0	0	.250	123	144	83	71	12	66	5	1	57	8	5.20
Urrea, Arkansas	24	24	5	2	11	8	0	.579	151	167	71	63	8	45	3	3	113	3	3.75
Waterbury, Ark	1	1	0	0	0	1	0	.000	3	4	5	5	1	5	1	0	1	1	15.00
Whiteley, El Paso	38	1	0	0	5	4	3	.556	57	75	43	35	5	33	0	1	61	1	5.53
Wiles, Arkansas*	21	2	1	0	4	4	1	.500	53	47	23	16	2	25	1	0	36	0	2.72

Pitcher—Club	G.	GS.	CG.	ShO.	W.	L.	Sv.	Pct.	IP.	H.	R.	ER.	HR.	BB.	Int. BB.	HB.	SO.	WP.	ERA.
Wojcik, Jackson*	31	11	2	1	6	5	0	.545	115	141	64	50	6	53	4	0	62	7	3.91
Wright, El Paso*	11	11	3	0	4	4	0	.500	61	67	37	35	8	32	0	1	44	2	5.16

BALKS—Nolan, 5; Dillard, Moore, J. Nelson, 3 each; Barrientos, Byrd, Caudill, Eichelberger, 2 each; Anderson, Bernal, Caneira, Deidel, Gonzalez (Laf), Hamrick, Heinen, Kurosaki, Martinez, McQueen, Milke, Panick, Poloni, Sealy, Staniland, Turner, Urrea, Wojcik, 1 each.

COMBINATION SHUTOUTS—Urrea-Kurosaki, Replogle-Kurosaki, Arkansas; Caneira-Meche, El Paso; Dillard-Lanthorn, Litle-Muhlstock, Litle-Divison, Lafayette; Doland-Temple, Geisel-Temple, Midland; Byrd-Cuellar, San Antonio; Scurry-Davis-Standart, Sealy-Davis-Standart, Gonzalez-Gunter, Shreveport.

NO-HIT GAMES—Beckman, Midland, defeated San Antonio, 5-0, June 8 (seven innings); Rowland, Lafayette, defeated Jackson, 1-0, August 5 (seven innings).

California League

CLASS A

CHAMPIONSHIP WINNERS IN PREVIOUS YEARS

1914—Fresno .571	1956—Fresno‡ .650	1967—San Jose§ .676
1915—Modesto .857	1957—Visalia x .622	Modesto .586
1916-40—Did not operate.	Salinas (4th)* .504	1968—San Jose .629
1941—Fresno .643	1958—Fresno* .639	Fresno§ .623
S. Barbara (2nd)* .597	Bakersfield .672	1969—Stockton§ .600
1942—Santa Barbara† .642	1959—Bakersfield .592	Visalia .614
1943-44-45—Did not operate.	Modesto§ .643	1970—Bakersfield .667
1946—Stockton‡ .600	1960—Reno .614	Bakersfield .671
1947—Stockton‡ .679	Reno .657	1971—Visalia§ .583
1948—Fresno .607	1961—Reno .743	Fresno .500
S. Barbara (3rd)* .529	Reno .643	1972—Modesto§ .547
1949—Bakersfield .612	1962—San Jose§ .686	Bakersfield .629
San Jose (4th)* .543	Reno .587	1973—Lodi§ .657
1950—Ventura .607	1963—Modesto .589	Bakersfield .571
Modesto (2nd)* .586	Stockton§ .687	1974—Fresno§ .607
1951—Santa Barbara‡ .599	1964—Fresno .638	San Jose .579
1952—Fresno‡ .629	Fresno .600	1975—Reno .614
1953—San Jose‡ .664	1965—San Jose .586	Reno .614
1954—Modesto‡ .623	Stockton§ .614	
1955—Stockton .733	1966—Modesto .577	
Fresno§ .718	Modesto .671	

*Won four-club playoff. †League disbanded June 28. ‡Won championship and four-club playoff. §Won split-season playoff. xWon both halves of split-season.

STANDING OF CLUBS AT CLOSE OF FIRST HALF, JUNE 20

Club	W.	L.	T.	Pct.	G.B.	Club	W.	L.	T.	Pct.	G.B.
Salinas (Angels)	48	23	0	.676	......	Modesto (Athletics)	32	38	0	.457	15½
Fresno (Giants)	41	29	0	.586	6½	Lodi (Dodgers)	30	39	0	.435	17
Reno (Twins/Padres)	33	37	0	.471	14½	San Jose (Indians)	26	44	0	.371	21½

STANDING OF CLUBS AT CLOSE OF SECOND HALF, AUGUST 27

Club	W.	L.	T.	Pct.	G.B.	Club	W.	L.	T.	Pct.	G.B.
Reno (Twins/Padres)	42	25	0	.627	......	Modesto (Athletics)	33	34	0	.493	9
Salinas (Angels)	43	26	0	.623	......	Lodi (Dodgers)	34	37	0	.479	10
Fresno (Giants)	36	34	0	.514	7½	San Jose (Indians)	19	51	0	.271	24½

COMPOSITE STANDING OF CLUBS AT CLOSE OF SEASON, AUGUST 27

Club	Sal.	Fr.	Reno	Mod.	Lodi	S.J.	W.	L.	T.	Pct.	G.B.
Salinas (Angels)	..	15	15	19	19	23	91	49	0	.650	......
Fresno (Giants)	13	..	14	16	17	17	77	63	0	.550	14
Reno (Twins/Padres)	13	14	..	13	19	16	75	62	0	.547	14½
Modesto (Athletics)	9	12	12	..	13	19	65	72	0	.474	24½
Lodi (Dodgers)	9	11	9	15	..	20	64	76	0	.457	27
San Jose (Indians)	5	11	12	9	8	..	45	95	0	.321	46

Major League affiliations in parentheses.

Playoffs—Reno defeated Salinas, three games to one.

Regular-Season Attendance—Fresno, 62,377; Lodi, 28,886; Modesto, 48,295; Reno, 38,226; Salinas, 69,887; San Jose, 98,437. Total, 346,108. Playoffs, 6,162. No All-star game.

Managers: Fresno—Andy Gilbert; Lodi—James B. Williams; Modesto—George Farson; Reno—John Goryl; Salinas—Del Crandall; San Jose—Harold (Gomer) Hodge.

All-Star Team: 1B—Argee, Modesto; 2B—Cruz, Salinas; 3B—Rayford, Salinas; SS—Anderson, Salinas; Utility—Cash, Fresno; OF—Bosley, Salinas; Bhagwat, Fresno, Powell, Reno; C—Graham, Reno; P—Califano, Salinas; Greenfield, Fresno; Hagman, Modesto; Heydeman, Lodi; Manager—Crandall, Salinas.

(Compiled by William J. Weiss, League Statistician, San Mateo, Calif.)

CLUB BATTING

Club																			Pct.
Reno	137	4733	915	806	1417	2072	191	67	110	784	66	44	679	42	39	842	120	42	1135	.299
Salinas	140	4627	829	652	1336	1869	205	47	46	725	42	55	696	29	33	806	288	77	1100	.289
Fresno	140	4786	848	784	1340	1967	205	34	118	740	47	47	688	29	35	733	78	33	1153	.280
Lodi	140	4655	731	753	1302	1791	209	38	68	643	43	47	600	24	34	728	110	64	1074	.280
Modesto	140	4416	698	755	1214	1683	166	36	77	595	59	40	629	27	35	832	171	42	1032	.275
San Jose	140	4542	639	910	1200	1595	163	35	54	559	49	45	592	20	38	804	103	65	1073	.264

INDIVIDUAL BATTING

(Leading Qualifiers for Batting Championship–378 or More Plate Appearances)

*Bats lefthanded.   †Switch-hitter.

Player and Club	G.	AB.	R.	H.	TB.	2B.	3B.	HR.	RBI.	SH.	SF.	BB.	HP.	SO.	SB.	CS.	Pct.
Argee, Daniel, Mod*	132	455	80	162	231	35	5	8	85	3	11	86	4	56	12	1	.356
Estes, Frank, Reno*	130	528	101	184	262	29	14	7	111	8	6	45	1	44	23	7	.348
Powell, Hosken, Reno*	126	484	118	167	228	22	9	7	73	2	3	90	6	45	26	8	.345
Bhagwat, Thomas, Fr	99	334	67	111	152	11	6	6	63	0	10	44	3	54	18	8	.332
Smith, Thomas, Sal*	123	460	72	152	235	34	8	11	86	2	4	28	3	50	5	4	.330
Rushde, Michael, Lodi*	133	509	93	168	239	29	9	8	85	2	7	60	3	87	18	3	.330
Leonard, Jeffrey, Lodi	134	527	105	171	211	26	4	2	72	4	3	86	1	78	90	17	.324
Bosley, Thaddis, Sal*	134	527	105	171	211	26	4	2	72	4	3	86	1	78	90	17	.324
Graham, Daniel, Reno*	132	482	96	154	281	26	7	29	115	1	7	102	3	121	3	1	.320
Massari, Daniel, SJ*	135	525	80	165	238	32	7	9	81	5	5	45	1	47	7	8	.314

Departmental Leaders : G—Strong, 140; AB—Johnston, 598; R—Powell, 118; H—Estes, 184; TB—Graham, 281; 2B—Argee, 35; 3B—Estes, 14; HR—Graham, 29; RBI—Graham, 115; SH—Mantick, 16; SF—Argee, 11; BB—Littlejohn, 103; SO—LoGrande, 153; SB—Bosley, 90; CS—Bosley, 17.

(All Players–Listed Alphabetically)

Player and Club	G.	AB.	R.	H.	TB.	2B.	3B.	HR.	RBI.	SH.	SF.	BB.	HP.	SO.	SB.	CS.	Pct.
Aaron, Wilmer, SJ†	12	42	6	16	17	1	0	0	4	0	0	4	0	7	0	1	.381
Ahu, Aran, Reno	111	394	75	110	187	17	6	16	80	2	3	59	5	117	10	2	.279
Allen, Kim, Sal	39	120	30	37	46	9	0	0	22	1	1	25	3	17	19	0	.308
Amerson, Archie, Reno	135	508	96	164	234	23	5	18	95	7	4	60	3	97	4	3	.323
Anderson, James, Sal.	136	469	67	124	158	14	4	4	51	9	5	59	0	58	7	3	.264
Argee, Daniel, Mod*	132	455	80	162	231	35	5	8	85	3	11	86	4	56	12	1	.356
Barrett, Charles, Lodi	26	2	0	0	0	0	0	0	0	0	0	0	0	2	0	0	.000
Beitey, Daniel, Fr.	25	2	0	2	2	0	0	0	0	1	0	0	0	0	0	0	1.000
Bellini, Riccardo, SJ	91	296	51	81	99	8	5	0	24	5	4	56	1	46	7	8	.274
Bhagwat, Thomas, Fr	133	482	107	161	260	27	3	22	106	4	10	94	2	57	4	3	.334
Bosley, Thaddis, Sal*	134	527	105	171	211	26	4	2	72	4	3	86	1	78	90	17	.324
Bothwell, Monte, Mod*	66	181	33	50	74	10	1	4	20	0	1	30	4	51	2	2	.276
Boutin, Thomas, Fr*	9	28	2	6	6	0	0	0	3	0	0	8	0	5	0	0	.214
Brenly, Robert, Fr.	17	60	16	22	30	3	1	1	9	1	0	12	0	17	1	0	.367
Brisbin, Steve, Sal	28	1	0	0	0	0	0	0	0	0	0	0	0	1	0	0	.000
Brown, John E., SJ*	53	156	25	35	47	3	3	1	19	5	1	30	1	37	9	1	.224
Califano, Kenneth, Sal*	30	1	0	1	1	0	0	0	0	0	0	0	0	0	0	0	1.000
Cardoza, Donald, Lodi*	138	532	86	147	210	31	1	10	98	3	10	55	2	43	0	2	.276
Carrion, Reyes, Reno	8	12	3	3	3	0	0	0	0	0	0	1	0	2	0	0	.250
Cash, Michael, Fr.	139	541	91	153	249	24	3	22	102	0	3	42	6	59	4	2	.283
Castillo, Anthony, Reno	81	282	44	69	101	11	0	7	41	3	4	25	2	62	1	1	.245
Coil, C. Martin, Fr.	7	17	0	4	5	1	0	0	2	0	0	0	0	3	0	0	.235
Colzie, Richard, Mod	108	336	56	95	132	14	4	5	45	7	1	53	2	40	17	4	.283
Cosey, D. Ray, Mod*	91	373	73	114	214	19	3	25	69	3	1	31	3	96	21	7	.306
Cox, Jeffrey, Mod	70	241	55	75	99	11	2	3	29	3	2	37	3	27	24	5	.311
Cruz, Julio, Sal†	96	348	92	107	128	12	3	1	45	9	6	81	1	33	68	13	.307
Culligan, Timothy, SJ*	63	196	19	42	58	5	1	3	24	1	2	19	0	46	2	1	.214
Cuoco, Richard, Lodi†	87	288	34	74	87	9	2	0	24	2	1	31	1	41	4	3	.257
de la Cruz, Gerardo, Lodi	28	99	12	26	33	2	1	1	13	1	2	7	0	22	2	3	.263
Derryberry, Timothy, Reno*	45	122	14	25	32	5	1	0	10	4	1	11	5	28	2	0	.205
D'Innocenzio, Richard, Fr.	37	73	16	16	18	2	0	0	5	1	0	27	0	21	2	0	.219
Drake, Harold, Reno	120	455	70	127	175	13	4	9	66	11	4	35	2	61	11	5	.279
Drevnak, David, Sal*	17	51	5	8	15	2	1	1	9	0	0	3	0	23	2	1	.157
Dusan, Gene, SJ†	57	158	22	44	47	3	0	0	20	3	0	33	0	24	2	1	.278
Elrod, James, Fr.	124	464	71	125	199	22	2	16	80	4	8	39	4	69	4	1	.269
Estes, Frank, Reno*	130	528	101	184	262	29	14	7	111	8	6	45	1	44	23	7	.348
Farr, Theodore, Lodi	53	167	28	46	45	10	1	9	36	0	3	36	4	28	2	0	.275
Flores, Martin, Fr*	26	3	0	1	1	0	0	0	0	0	0	0	0	0	0	0	.333
French, Martin, Reno	23	4	1	1	1	0	0	0	1	0	0	1	0	2	0	0	.250
Gallino, David, Mod	105	293	45	70	76	4	1	0	33	5	2	42	1	41	11	2	.239
Garcia, Pedro J., SJ†	51	139	15	26	32	2	2	0	7	3	0	4	0	38	2	4	.187
Garrison, Marvin, Lodi	117	447	71	111	146	18	1	5	40	4	2	63	3	104	18	11	.248
Gatlin, Michael, Reno	66	247	55	80	126	12	8	6	48	4	4	46	0	51	6	2	.324
George, Larry, Mod	3	7	0	0	0	0	0	0	0	0	0	0	0	0	0	0	.000
Goodwin, Danny, Sal*	38	139	24	43	60	7	2	2	30	0	1	28	0	28	4	2	.309
Graham, Daniel, Reno*	132	482	96	154	281	26	7	29	115	1	7	102	3	121	3	1	.320
Greenfield, Monroe, Fr	47	1	1	1	1	0	0	0	0	0	0	0	0	0	0	0	1.000
Griffin, Alfredo, SJ†	64	224	40	58	63	3	1	0	17	2	2	26	3	46	9	6	.259

Player and Club	G.	AB.	R.	H.	TB.	2B.	3B.	HR.	RBI.	SH.	SF.	BB.	HP.	SO.	SB.	CS.	Pct.
Hancock, R. Garry, SJ*	135	526	56	162	209	22	5	5	77	3	10	22	0	37	4	7	.308
Harmon, Larry, SJ	3	4	2	1	1	0	0	0	0	3	0	0	4	0	2	0	.250
Harrison, Mack, Mod†	64	142	21	28	35	2	1	1	9	7	1	12	1	31	7	1	.197
Hassey, Ronald, SJ*	22	62	7	19	26	4	0	1	7	0	0	10	2	3	0	2	.306
Heredia, Ubaldo, Lodi	14	1	1	0	0	0	0	0	0	0	0	0	0	0	0	0	.000
Heydeman, Gregory, Lodi	27	4	1	0	0	0	0	0	0	1	0	0	1	0	1	0	.000
Hickey, Robert, SJ†	26	93	14	18	20	0	1	0	7	3	1	19	0	18	4	4	.194
Hicks, Joseph, Reno	8	11	1	1	3	0	1	0	2	0	0	5	0	0	1	0	.091
Hodge, Harold, SJ†	7	18	1	5	7	2	0	0	4	1	0	1	0	5	0	0	.278
Howerton, Ricky, SJ	78	210	22	52	63	5	0	2	28	1	3	45	2	33	4	1	.248
Ithier, Pedro, SJ	69	262	37	74	92	11	2	1	30	4	2	25	7	21	15	6	.282
Johnston, Gregory B., Fr*	139	598	86	153	194	15	4	6	67	2	8	52	2	103	19	6	.256
Jones, Henry, Lodi	110	393	50	112	122	6	2	0	33	10	1	53	0	49	14	10	.285
Jones, Michael, Mod†	45	140	18	32	42	6	2	0	17	2	1	23	1	37	5	3	.229
Judge, S. Franklin, Sal	26	51	10	12	15	3	0	0	8	4	0	6	3	7	2	0	.235
Kelley, Steven, Sal	29	1	0	0	0	0	0	0	0	0	0	0	0	0	0	0	.000
Kelly, D. Patrick, Sal	111	396	63	124	164	24	2	4	50	2	2	28	5	83	15	8	.313
Killingsworth, Samuel, Sal	6	10	3	2	2	0	0	0	3	0	0	7	0	4	1	0	.200
Kolarek, Frank, Mod	60	151	21	29	42	4	0	3	19	3	0	27	4	56	0	0	.192
Kownacki, Robert, Lodi	34	106	11	22	30	5	0	1	9	1	0	15	2	31	2	0	.208
Larson, Duane, Reno†	23	77	16	25	31	2	2	0	3	1	0	24	0	5	0	2	.325
Leisle, Rodney, Reno	48	148	29	32	62	7	1	7	26	0	0	23	3	49	0	0	.216
Leonard, Jeffrey, Lodi	133	509	93	168	239	29	9	8	85	2	7	60	3	87	18	3	.330
Littlejohn, Dennis, Fr	124	416	93	102	169	15	2	16	56	2	2	103	0	120	7	1	.245
LoGrande, Angelo, SJ	132	494	70	125	213	25	3	19	77	1	5	47	6	153	3	1	.253
Malinoff, Jeffrey, Sal*	1	3	0	0	0	0	0	0	0	0	0	0	0	1	0	0	.000
Manning, Anthony, SJ	9	26	3	8	11	0	0	1	2	0	0	4	3	1	0	0	.308
Mantick, Dennis, Reno	136	550	100	158	180	12	5	0	56	16	4	75	4	68	17	7	.287
Marin, Arturo, Fr	37	133	24	36	53	7	2	2	26	1	0	16	4	15	0	2	.271
Massari, Daniel, SJ*	135	525	80	165	238	32	7	9	81	5	5	45	1	47	7	8	.314
Maxwell, J. Rodney, Sal*	33	1	0	0	0	0	0	0	0	0	0	0	0	1	0	0	.000
McNeely, Ronald, Mod*	26	101	18	37	48	8	0	1	11	3	0	18	0	6	4	1	.366
McNulty, Steven, Lodi	15	2	0	0	0	0	0	0	0	0	0	0	0	2	0	0	.000
McQueen, R. Leroy, Sal	26	2	0	0	0	0	0	0	0	0	0	0	0	1	0	0	.000
Medeiros, Gary, Mod	96	305	27	84	93	9	0	0	41	6	4	19	3	27	3	1	.275
Menees, H. Eugene, Reno	25	88	24	31	37	4	1	0	12	2	2	23	2	13	8	2	.352
Miller, K. Randall, Reno	5	9	2	1	1	0	0	0	1	0	1	0	5	0	6	1	.111
Mitchell, Howard, Fr	136	528	108	151	226	28	4	13	69	12	2	101	5	72	20	8	.286
Moran, E. Michael, SJ†	109	389	84	102	115	6	2	1	37	8	1	86	5	69	20	6	.262
Necoechea, Steven, Mod*	21	48	1	11	14	1	1	0	5	0	1	3	0	11	0	0	.229
Nickeson, Robert, Mod	25	77	9	18	20	0	1	0	14	0	4	11	0	17	3	0	.234
Paris, Bret, Fr†	2	2	0	1	1	0	0	0	0	0	0	0	0	0	0	0	.500
Parsons, Casey, Fr*	42	167	30	54	64	6	2	0	10	2	1	20	0	14	6	2	.323
Patterson, Michael, Mod*	80	236	42	62	93	7	3	6	33	1	1	22	1	50	11	2	.263
Pebley, Edward, Mod†	92	323	43	97	126	15	4	2	45	2	4	44	2	44	10	1	.300
Peguero, Pablo, Lodi	56	185	18	42	51	3	0	2	21	2	2	11	0	22	1	4	.227
Perconte, John, Lodi*	68	252	58	72	84	7	1	1	19	7	2	54	3	23	19	10	.286
Person, Carl, Sal	13	27	5	5	6	1	0	0	1	0	0	3	0	3	1	0	.185
Peters, James, Sal*	125	425	63	132	182	19	8	5	74	2	6	55	3	96	13	11	.311
Plut, Stephen, Lodi*	34	118	17	27	36	1	1	2	17	0	2	19	1	19	2	1	.229
Powell, Hosken, Reno*	126	484	118	167	228	22	9	7	73	2	3	90	6	45	26	8	.345
Preseren, Kenneth, SJ*	13	35	1	4	4	0	0	0	0	0	0	4	0	9	0	0	.114
Rametta, Steven, SJ	59	209	26	49	78	15	1	4	25	1	2	13	1	18	4	2	.234
Ramirez, Nolan, Mod	49	133	12	33	44	5	3	0	17	2	1	30	0	29	0	2	.248
Rayford, Floyd, Sal	125	462	73	126	172	19	6	5	67	4	5	41	5	85	17	3	.273
Richards, David, Lodi	26	70	10	16	20	1	0	1	5	1	0	6	2	9	0	2	.229
Rodriguez, Michael, Mod	29	82	14	12	19	4	0	1	8	0	1	10	0	32	5	1	.146
Roman, Rosendo, SJ	78	202	25	39	47	3	1	1	17	3	1	32	0	48	9	4	.193
Rushde, Michael, Lodi*	123	460	72	152	235	34	8	11	86	2	4	28	3	50	5	4	.330
Sauer, Henry, Sal	114	368	63	92	137	15	3	8	58	0	6	72	4	82	16	4	.250
Scala, Dominic, Mod	38	103	15	20	40	3	1	5	13	1	0	15	0	28	2	0	.194
Schaefer, Douglas, Fr	28	3	0	0	0	0	0	0	0	1	0	0	0	2	0	0	.000
Sigman, S. Lee, Mod	40	94	17	23	30	1	0	2	9	1	0	10	3	25	1	0	.245
Smith, J. Theodore, Mod	55	157	34	42	76	3	2	9	35	0	0	57	2	58	3	1	.268
Smith, Thomas, Sal†	99	334	67	111	152	11	6	6	63	0	10	44	3	54	18	8	.332
Snider, Kelly, Lodi*	12	50	6	11	15	4	0	0	2	0	0	7	0	5	1	0	.220
Soriano, Hilario, Lodi	38	126	14	35	46	6	1	1	16	3	0	6	0	27	1	1	.278
Stabelfeldt, David, Fr	28	92	12	27	36	3	0	2	19	0	0	7	0	17	1	0	.293
Stimac, Craig, Reno	22	65	8	20	34	2	3	2	16	0	0	5	0	14	1	1	.308
Strong, Garret, Fr*	140	535	86	159	227	25	5	11	97	7	7	61	8	58	4	2	.297
Stupy, Terry, Sal	35	101	26	26	36	6	2	0	13	1	0	27	1	4	4	1	.257
Sularz, Guy, Fr	134	497	87	135	167	22	5	0	60	8	6	87	4	58	6	6	.272
Tallman, William, Fr	27	3	0	0	0	0	0	0	0	0	0	0	0	0	0	0	.000
Texidor, Esteban, Sal	21	1	0	0	0	0	0	0	0	0	0	0	0	1	0	0	.000
Tisdale, Freddie, Lodi*	51	196	38	59	88	18	1	3	31	0	4	20	1	30	5	3	.301

Player and Club	G.	AB.	R.	H.	TB.	2B.	3B.	HR.	RBI.	SH.	SF.	BB.	HP.	SO.	SB.	CS.	Pct.
Tomski, Jeffrey, SJ	42	117	15	28	38	5	1	1	17	0	3	29	1	38	0	0	.239
Tufts, Glenn, SJ	53	147	15	40	58	6	0	4	26	0	2	31	4	54	1	1	.272
Volk, Daniel, Lodi	30	88	17	24	35	2	3	1	12	1	0	18	2	19	2	0	.273
Walls, Gary, Reno	17	17	6	4	5	1	0	0	2	0	0	3	1	2	0	0	.235
Washington, Malvin, Salt	10	19	4	5	7	2	0	0	6	1	1	4	0	6	0	1	.263
Washko, Patrick, SJ†	7	22	3	7	13	3	0	1	7	0	0	3	1	6	0	1	.318
Weirum, Ronald, Lodi*	87	268	39	69	89	11	3	1	38	4	5	73	4	46	1	3	.257
Westmoreland, Claude, Lod	76	288	55	88	139	12	3	11	58	0	2	36	3	66	13	4	.306
Whitehead, Steven, Sal*	46	151	23	43	82	10	4	7	28	2	3	22	2	28	4	0	.285
Williams, Mark, Mod*	36	111	15	29	38	3	0	2	12	1	1	14	1	7	2	1	.261
Wilson, Billy, Lodi	24	2	0	1	1	0	0	0	0	0	0	0	0	0	0	0	.500
Wilson, Randolph, Sal*	117	411	68	112	203	16	0	25	97	2	5	70	1	83	5	3	.273
Wirth, Alan, Fr	28	4	0	0	0	0	0	0	0	0	0	0	0	1	0	0	.000
Wittmayer, Kurt, Reno	72	250	56	76	89	7	3	0	26	5	2	46	1	49	7	2	.304
Wolfe, W. Scott, Fr	40	137	18	31	59	5	1	7	28	2	1	15	0	23	0	0	.226
Woodard, Darrell, Mod	104	333	49	91	97	2	2	0	26	9	3	34	0	61	28	6	.273
Wulfemeyer, Mark, Sal	20	1	0	0	0	0	0	0	0	0	0	0	0	0	0	0	.000
Zagarino, Joe, Sal	61	207	38	55	92	11	1	8	28	0	1	29	1	44	3	3	.266

The following pitchers had no plate appearances primarily through use of designated hitters, listed alphabetically by club, games in parentheses:

FRESNO—Cline, Steven T. (30); Dyer, Paul J.* (4); Myers, David L. (6); Scarcella, Jerome M. (19); Steen, Rick J. (7); Thompson, Robert E. (30).

LODI—Evans, James (3); Keefe, Kevin P. (37); Kunkler, G. Martin* (13); Lake, Michael A. (22); Phillips, Charles D.* (11); Power, Ted H. (13); Smith, Daniel R. (29); Tennant, Michael G. (8); Todd, Guy D. (21); Wouters, Leonard W. (13).

MODESTO—Baxter, Thomas R. (18); Bowman, Kenneth M. (25); Boyd, T. Randy (10); Braun, Barton L. (19); Camacho, Ernest C. (10); Cochran, Gregory M. (21); Green, C. Randall (9); Hagman, David J. (30); Hile, Michael A.* (2); Joyce, Kevin M.* (3); Meyl, Brian A.* (5); O'Brien, Patrick A. (9); Owens, Maddison† (1); Peregud, Richard A. (25); Quiros, Gustavo (61); Salas, Bobby R. (24); Spitzack, Gary R.† (4); Stegman, Dennis E. (5); Wibberley, Christopher F. (4); Zoss, Richard S. (23).

RENO—Bovee, Rodney J.* (18); Eichelberger, Juan T. (13); Garcia, David (30); Gill, Ronald A. (48); Gressick, Jeffrey J.* (16); Joseph, William C.† (10); Lee, Randall A.* (9); MacPherson, Bruce I. (7); Messman, Michael A. (22); Quintero, Frank (20); Rehn, Bradley S. (23); Stewart, Robert L. (13); Thormodsgard, Paul G. (16); Veselic, Robert M. (7); Wells, James D. (4); Wilkes, Gregory E. (28).

SALINAS—Botting, Ralph W.* (10); Kuhaulua, Fred M.* (30); O'Donnell, Thomas J.* (7); Panick, Francis S. (9); Perez, Carlos J. (30); Roslund, John C. (22); Stumpp, Richard C.* (47).

SAN JOSE—Alvarez, Miguel A. (13); Amenita, Thomas J. (4); Arnold, John T. * (17); Arp, Ronnie J. (13); Brennan, Thomas M. (16); Bullard, Larkin E. (10); Flanagan, Donald (12); Forgie, Raymond W. (3); Harvey, M. Craig (6); Jones, Michael E. (30); Kinney, Dennis P.* (11); Klein, Stephen J.† (15); Mahan, George K. (12); Melson, Gary L. (3); Narleski, Steven C. (16); Rodriguez, Julian L. (5); Schuler, David P. (54); Skiba, Daniel J. (23); Smith, Reggie T. (8); Weese, Gary L. (4); Widner, Steven E. (32); Wihtol, Alexander A. (51).

GRAND-SLAM HOME RUNS—Argee, Cardoza, Cash, Drevnak, Graham, Kelly, Leisle, Littlejohn, Marin, Rayford, Scala, Sauer, J. T. Smith, Strong, R. Wilson, 1 each.

AWARDED FIRST BASE ON CATCHER'S INTERFERENCE—Rushde 3 (Castillo 2, Rodriguez); Cuoco 2 (Howerton 2); Brenly (Medeiros), Maham (Graham), Kelly (Howerton), Sauer (Tomski).

CLUB FIELDING

Club	G.	PO.	A.	E.	DP.	PB.	Pct.	Club	G.	PO.	A.	E.	DP.	PB.	Pct.
Salinas	140	3582	1548	194	139	45	.964	San Jose	140	3489	1397	232	127	43	.955
Lodi	140	3563	1552	234	130	26	.956	Reno	137	3533	1622	246	127	34	.954
Fresno	140	3623	1601	240	127	30	.956	Modesto	137	3444	1472	253	114	33	.951

Triple Play—Salinas.

INDIVIDUAL FIELDING

*Throws lefthanded.

FIRST BASEMEN

Player and Club	G.	PO.	A.	E.	DP.	Pct.	Player and Club	G.	PO.	A.	E.	DP.	Pct.
Massari, SJ*	23	183	7	1	20	.995	Argee, Mod*	132	1150	91	22	101	.983
Snider, Lodi*	12	130	9	1	9	.993	Bothwell, Mod*	11	51	4	1	4	.982
ESTES, Reno*	113	1097	51	13	93	.989	Strong, Fr*	140	1285	76	28	111	.980
Cardoza, Lodi*	126	1116	104	16	109	.987	LoGrande, SJ	112	878	41	19	86	.980
Dusan, SJ	10	71	4	1	7	.987	Stupy, Sal	28	227	17	7	14	.972
Wilson, Sal*	80	660	50	11	70	.985	Graham, Reno	21	131	10	5	18	.966
Zagarino, Sal	34	287	18	5	36	.984							

Triple Play—Stupy.

(Fewer Than Ten Games)

Player and Club	G.	PO.	A.	E.	DP.	Pct.	Player and Club	G.	PO.	A.	E.	DP.	Pct.
Gatlin, Reno	4	33	3	0	5	1.000	Coil, Fr	1	1	0	0	0	1.000
Killingsworth, Sal	3	32	3	0	3	1.000	Tufts, SJ	2	11	1	1	1	.923
Smith, Sal	3	24	2	0	1	1.000	Farr, Lodi	2	6	1	1	2	.875
Hancock, SJ*	1	6	0	0	0	1.000	Ahu, Reno	1	3	0	1	0	.750
Person, Sal	2	2	0	0	0	1.000							

SECOND BASEMEN

Player and Club	G.	PO.	A.	E.	DP.	Pct.	Player and Club	G.	PO.	A.	E.	DP.	Pct.
Bellini, SJ	55	152	134	4	28	.986	Cox, Mod	56	100	161	11	29	.960
CRUZ, Sal	96	234	314	10	77	.982	Tisdale, Lodi	14	45	65	5	14	.957
Woodard, Mod	50	93	135	6	27	.974	Mitchell, Fr	135	307	413	34	88	.955
Perconte, Lodi	67	141	223	12	41	.968	Whitehead, Sal	27	74	84	8	20	.952
Cuoco, Lodi	53	123	151	9	33	.968	Moran, SJ	⸗72	180	224	21	51	.951
Mantick, Reno	136	344	501	30	100	.966	Judge, Sal	15	24	30	4	5	.931
Harrison, Mod	38	67	110	7	18	.962	Pebley, Mod	10	17	19	5	3	.878
Ithier, SJ	13	35	39	3	8	.961							

Triple Play—Cruz

(Fewer Than Ten Games)

Player and Club	G.	PO.	A.	E.	DP.	Pct.	Player and Club	G.	PO.	A.	E.	DP.	Pct.
Rayford, Sal	8	19	18	0	5	1.000	Person, Sal	1	5	4	1	2	.900
Cash, Fr	4	11	12	0	2	1.000	Nickeson, Mod	3	4	5	1	3	.900
Aaron, SJ	4	4	10	0	1	1.000	Jones, Lodi	2	2	6	1	0	.889
Drake, Reno	1	1	3	0	1	1.000	Garcia, SJ	1	0	1	1	0	.500
Sularz, Fr	5	6	10	1	1	.941							

THIRD BASEMEN

Player and Club	G.	PO.	A.	E.	DP.	Pct.	Player and Club	G.	PO.	A.	E.	DP.	Pct.
Stimac, Reno	12	5	19	1	0	.960	Harrison, Mod	12	8	22	3	5	.909
Mences, Reno	21	14	61	4	1	.949	Drake, Reno	76	63	155	23	11	.905
RAYFORD, Sal	108	67	202	16	21	.944	Nickeson, Mod	18	8	27	4	3	.897
Gallino, Mod	50	43	104	9	6	.942	Bellini, SJ	23	19	24	5	4	.896
Garcia, SJ	24	25	31	4	2	.933	de la Cruz, Lodi	22	14	35	6	5	.891
Pebley, Mod	15	7	21	2	1	.933	Ramirez, Mod	34	35	60	14	6	.872
Weirum, Lodi	84	56	143	15	16	.930	Leisle, Reno	28	14	57	12	5	.855
Zagarino, Sal	14	15	23	3	3	.927	Whitehead, Sal	14	6	23	5	5	.853
Sularz, Fr	43	31	84	10	2	.920	Moran, SJ	22	14	26	7	1	.851
Rametta, SJ	54	48	130	16	17	.918	Westmoreland, Lodi	31	21	65	19	3	.819
Cash, Fr	92	82	158	23	15	.913	Scala, Mod	28	22	38	18	2	.769

(Fewer Than Ten Games)

Player and Club	G.	PO.	A.	E.	DP.	Pct.	Player and Club	G.	PO.	A.	E.	DP.	Pct.
Preseren, SJ	8	6	9	0	2	1.000	Cuoco, Lodi	8	3	18	1	2	.955
Roman, SJ	5	3	7	0	1	1.000	Culligan, SJ	6	8	11	1	2	.950
Graham, Reno	4	1	9	0	0	1.000	Cox, Mod	7	2	7	1	0	.900
Stupy, Sal	4	1	8	0	0	1.000	Brenly, Fr	4	2	6	1	1	.889
Judge, Sal	4	1	4	0	1	1.000	Person, Sal	6	3	15	3	4	.857
Elrod, Fr	5	1	3	0	0	1.000	Harmon, SJ	3	0	2	1	0	.667
Medeiros, Mod	1	0	2	0	0	1.000	Hassey, SJ	1	1	1	1	0	.667
Woodard, Mod	1	0	1	0	0	1.000	Tufts, SJ	2	0	3	3	1	.500

SHORTSTOPS

Player and Club	G.	PO.	A.	E.	DP.	Pct.	Player and Club	G.	PO.	A.	E.	DP.	Pct.
Garcia, SJ	11	17	24	2	4	.953	Sularz, Fr	61	101	175	27	35	.911
Marin, Fr	37	75	129	11	20	.949	Griffin, SJ	60	91	145	24	28	.908
JONES, Lodi	108	195	326	31	70	.944	Woodard, Mod	46	71	103	18	16	.906
Anderson, Sal	136	188	406	40	69	.937	Wittmayer, Reno	72	95	223	35	42	.901
Cox, Mod	11	17	26	3	3	.935	Larson, Reno	23	36	73	12	16	.901
Ithier, SJ	56	84	145	19	23	.923	Sigman, Mod	40	52	84	16	13	.895
Gallino, Mod	62	90	170	23	36	.919	Kownacki, Lodi	30	48	81	19	11	.872
Wolfe, Fr	40	66	136	18	27	.918	Drake, Reno	44	82	123	33	27	.861

Triple Play—Anderson

(Fewer Than Ten Games)

Player and Club	G.	PO.	A.	E.	DP.	Pct.	Player and Club	G.	PO.	A.	E.	DP.	Pct.
Preseren, SJ	8	6	12	0	3	1.000	Whitehead, Sal	2	1	6	1	3	.875
Mitchell, Fr	1	1	3	0	1	1.000	Carrion, Reno	5	2	13	3	2	.833
Moran, SJ	7	12	21	1	7	.971	Bellini, SJ	3	6	13	4	4	.826
Cash, Fr	3	7	9	1	1	.941	Judge, Sal	5	8	8	5	2	.762
Cuoco, Lodi	7	7	13	2	3	.909	Paris, Fr	2	1	2	1	0	.750
Leisle, Reno	1	1	7	1	3	.889	Colzie, Mod	1	0	5	2	1	.714
Nickeson, Mod	5	8	7	2	1	.882							

OUTFIELDERS

Player and Club	G.	PO.	A.	E.	DP.	Pct.	Player and Club	G.	PO.	A.	E.	DP.	Pct.
Estes, Reno*	14	15	0	0	0	1.000	BOSLEY, Sal*	133	285	13	7	3	.977
Stimac, Reno	10	15	0	0	0	1.000	Garrison, Lodi	112	258	5	7	2	.974
Walls, Reno	16	9	0	0	0	1.000	Williams, Mod*	22	33	0	1	0	.971
McNeely, Mod	26	64	3	1	0	.985	Amerson, Reno	134	235	7	8	2	.968
Allen, Sal	33	58	2	1	0	.984	Parsons, Fr	41	56	4	2	1	.968
Smith, Sal	77	130	4	3	1	.978	Sauer, Sal	112	165	7	6	0	.966

OUTFIELDERS—(Continued)

Player and Club	G.	PO.	A.	E.	DP.	Pct.
Johnston, Fr*	139	311	13	12	2	.964
Massari, SJ*	112	181	9	7	0	.964
Bhagwat, Fr	132	147	14	6	3	.964
Hancock, SJ*	131	209	20	9	4	.962
Powell, Reno*	117	171	8	7	2	.962
Culligan, SJ	49	69	5	3	0	.961
Bothwell, Mod*	42	64	7	3	2	.959
Gatlin, Reno	62	82	3	4	0	.955
Derryberry, Reno	44	79	6	4	1	.955
Roman, SJ	73	137	5	7	1	.953
Colzie, Mod	100	167	11	9	2	.952
Brown, SJ*	49	85	1	5	0	.945
Cosey, Mod*	91	195	6	12	0	.944
Rushde, Lodi*	114	157	18	11	3	.941
Volk, Lodi*	24	46	2	3	0	.941
Leonard, Lodi*	133	214	13	15	3	.938
Drevnak, Sal*	10	14	1	1	0	.938
Elrod, Fr	84	135	13	10	1	.937
Jones, Mod	43	86	2	6	1	.936
Peters, Sal*	77	113	13	9	1	.933
D'Innocenzio, Fr	32	28	0	2	0	.933
Westmoreland, Lodi	30	62	6	5	0	.932
Hickey, SJ	21	51	2	4	0	.930
Patterson, Mod	66	95	5	8	1	.926
Plut, Lodi	11	18	2	2	0	.909
Smith, Mod	37	50	0	6	0	.893
Ahu, Reno	42	51	4	7	0	.887

Triple Play - Bosley

(Fewer Than Ten Games)

Player and Club	G.	PO.	A.	E.	DP.	Pct.
Hicks, Reno	8	10	0	0	0	1.000
Manning, SJ	2	5	0	0	0	1.000
Boutin, Fr*	4	4	0	0	0	1.000
Tisdale, Lodi	2	4	0	0	0	1.000
Necochea, Mod*	2	3	1	0	0	1.000
Rodriguez, Mod	3	3	0	0	0	1.000
Cardoza, Lodi*	2	2	1	0	0	1.000
George, Mod	3	2	0	0	0	1.000
Dusan, SJ	1	1	0	0	0	1.000
Gallino, Mod	1	1	0	0	0	1.000
Pebley, Mod	1	1	0	0	0	1.000
Washko, SJ	7	12	1	1	1	.929
Woodard, Mod	3	9	0	1	0	.900
Garcia, SJ	9	18	0	2	0	.900

CATCHERS

Player and Club	G.	PO.	A.	E.	DP.	PB.	Pct.
Rayford, Sal	13	76	6	0	0	2	1.000
Richards, Lodi	17	84	13	1	0	3	.990
Dusan, SJ	38	230	27	4	3	9	.985
Farr, Lodi	43	215	19	4	0	12	.983
CASTILLO, Reno	77	448	63	11	1	21	.979
Howerton, SJ	68	327	36	8	2	13	.978
Medeiros, Mod	80	396	44	11	1	13	.976
Kelly, Sal	104	612	60	19	8	31	.973
Graham, Reno	66	374	52	12	3	12	.973
Soriano, Lodi	37	229	21	7	1	5	.973
Littlejohn, Fr	123	807	127	27	10	21	.972
Peguero, Lodi	54	288	44	10	5	6	.971
Stabelfeldt, Fr	15	83	9	3	1	9	.968
Kolarek, Mod	58	200	35	9	4	13	.963
Tomski, SJ	41	215	27	10	0	14	.960
Rodriguez, Mod	15	66	8	4	2	7	.949
Goodwin, Sal	28	168	13	10	0	12	.948

(Fewer Than Ten Games)

Player and Club	G.	PO.	A.	E.	DP.	PB.	Pct.
Coil, Fr	3	19	3	0	0	3	1.000
Culligan, SJ	1	5	1	0	0	3	1.000
Stupy, Sal	1	5	0	0	0	0	1.000
Miller, Reno	3	4	0	0	0	1	1.000
Scala, Mod	2	3	0	0	0	0	1.000
Hassey, SJ	8	54	1	1	0	4	.982

PITCHERS

Player and Club	G.	PO.	A.	E.	DP.	Pct.
KELLEY, Sal	28	11	17	0	2	1.000
Braun, Mod	19	11	16	0	1	1.000
Stewart, Reno	13	7	16	0	0	1.000
Peregud, Mod	25	6	17	0	0	1.000
Arnold, SJ*	17	2	20	0	1	1.000
Lake, Lodi*	22	6	12	0	0	1.000
Quiros, Mod	61	8	8	0	0	1.000
Klein, SJ	15	4	10	0	1	1.000
Garcia, Reno	30	3	11	0	1	1.000
Alvarez, SJ	12	2	11	0	1	1.000
Thompson, Fr*	30	2	10	0	2	1.000
Kinney, SJ*	11	1	9	0	0	1.000
Smith, Lodi	29	1	8	0	0	1.000
Joseph, Reno*	10	2	6	0	0	1.000
Texidor, Sal	20	2	5	0	0	1.000
Todd, Lodi	21	1	4	0	1	1.000
Rehn, Reno	23	0	4	0	0	1.000
Boyd, Mod*	10	0	3	0	1	1.000
Califano, SJ	28	17	45	2	4	.969
Thormodsgard, Reno	16	7	17	1	1	.960
Zoss, Mod*	23	6	16	1	1	.957
Heydeman, Lodi	27	17	25	2	2	.955
Wilkes, Reno	28	8	32	2	0	.952
Kuhaulua, Sal*	30	4	15	1	0	.950
French, Reno	23	3	16	1	2	.950
Cline, Fr	30	6	30	2	0	.947
Brisbin, Sal	27	9	21	2	1	.938
Gressick, Reno*	16	3	12	1	1	.938
Schaefer, Fr	28	13	16	2	1	.935
Maxwell, Sal*	33	6	23	2	3	.935
Cochran, Mod	21	15	24	3	1	.929
Scarcella, Fr	19	3	10	1	1	.929
Beitey, Fr	25	2	11	1	0	.929
Gill, Reno	48	2	10	1	0	.923
Wilson, Lodi	24	13	22	3	3	.921
Perez, Sal	30	15	29	4	3	.917
Flanagan, SJ	12	0	11	1	0	.917
Tallman, Fr	27	7	34	4	2	.911
Greenfield, Fr	47	4	33	4	1	.902
Bowman, Mod	25	13	24	4	1	.902
Flores, Fr*	26	6	21	3	0	.900
Salas, Mod	23	6	3	1	0	.900
Jones, SJ	30	3	23	3	1	.897
Barrett, Lodi	26	14	37	6	0	.895
Stumpp, Sal	47	4	13	2	3	.895
Mahan, SJ	12	3	14	2	1	.895
Power, Lodi	13	1	7	1	0	.889
Botting, Sal*	10	0	8	1	0	.889
Roslund, Sal*	22	3	5	1	1	.889
Wirth, Fr	28	9	30	5	2	.886
Hagman, Mod	30	7	16	3	2	.885
Schuler, SJ*	54	2	11	2	0	.867
Heredia, Lodi	14	6	13	3	1	.864
Baxter, Mod	18	5	7	2	0	.857

PITCHERS—Continued

Player and Club	G.	PO.	A.	E.	DP.	Pct.
McQueen, Sal	26	2	4	1	0	.857
Wulfemeyer, Sal	19	4	7	2	0	.846
Skiba, SJ	23	3	13	3	0	.842
Wouters, Lodi	13	4	1	1	0	.833
Kunkler, Lodi*	13	6	12	4	0	.818
Camacho, Mod	10	2	7	2	1	.818
Bovee, Reno*	18	0	9	2	1	.818
Widner, SJ*	31	2	15	4	3	.810
Wihtol, SJ	51	1	15	4	1	.800
Keefe, Lodi	37	3	5	2	0	.800

Player and Club	G.	PO.	A.	E.	DP.	Pct.
Eichelberger, Reno	13	3	7	3	0	.769
Narleski, SJ	16	1	9	3	0	.769
Brennan, SJ	16	4	15	6	1	.760
Phillips, Lodi*	11	2	4	2	0	.750
Quintero, Reno	20	3	7	4	0	.714
Arp, SJ	13	0	5	2	0	.714
McNulty, Lodi	15	1	8	4	0	.692
Messman, Reno	22	2	8	5	0	.667
Bullard, SJ	10	0	1	1	0	.500

(Fewer Than Ten Games)

Player and Club	G.	PO.	A.	E.	DP.	Pct.
Lee, Reno*	9	3	7	0	0	1.000
Green, Mod	9	3	3	0	0	1.000
O'Brien, Mod*	9	1	5	0	0	1.000
MacPherson, Reno	7	0	6	0	0	1.000
Rodriguez, SJ	5	0	4	0	0	1.000
Veselic, Reno	7	2	1	0	0	1.000
Panick, Sal	9	0	3	0	0	1.000
Harvey, SJ	6	0	3	0	0	1.000
Forgie, SJ	3	0	3	0	0	1.000
Smith, SJ	8	1	1	0	0	1.000
Weese, SJ	4	1	1	0	1	1.000
Steen, Fr	7	0	2	0	1	1.000

Player and Club	G.	PO.	A.	E.	DP.	Pct.
Stegman, Mod	5	1	0	0	0	1.000
Dyer, Fr*	4	1	0	0	0	1.000
Spitzack, Mod*	4	0	1	0	0	1.000
Joyce, Mod	3	0	1	0	0	1.000
Myers, Fr	6	3	7	1	1	.909
Tennant, Lodi	8	4	9	2	0	.867
Wells, Reno*	4	1	3	1	1	.800
Wibberley, Mod	4	0	3	1	0	.750
O'Donnell, Sal*	7	1	1	1	0	.667
Evans, Lodi*	3	1	1	1	0	.667
Melson, SJ	2	0	0	1	0	.000

The following players do not have any recorded accepted chances at the positions indicated; therefore, are not listed in the fielding averages for those particular positions: Amenita, p; Colzie, p; Hile*, p; Meyl, p; Owens, p; T. Smith, 3b; Sularz, of; Washington, of.

Hodge and Malinoff were used as designated-hitters only.

CLUB PITCHING

Club	G.	CG.	ShO.	Sv.	IP.	H.	R.	ER.	HR.	BB.	Int. BB.	HB.	SO.	WP.	Bk.	ERA.
Salinas	140	20	5	30	1194	1163	652	518	62	677	28	38	827	86	6	3.90
Lodi	140	47	4	19	1188	1287	753	566	98	632	23	40	787	90	16	4.29
Modesto	137	22	2	23	1148	1326	755	584	114	523	23	24	675	74	16	4.58
Fresno	140	48	4	17	1208	1373	784	648	71	690	28	36	867	101	6	4.83
Reno	137	41	7	20	1178	1270	806	640	82	673	22	31	802	113	5	4.89
San Jose	140	24	4	15	1163	1389	910	707	71	689	46	45	788	83	8	5.47

PITCHERS' RECORDS
(Leading Qualifiers for Earned-Run Average Leadership—112 or More Innings)
*Throws lefthanded.

Pitcher–Club	G.	GS.	CG.	ShO.	W.	L.	Sv.	Pct.	IP.	H.	R.	ER.	HR.	BB.	Int. BB.	HB.	SO.	WP.	ERA.
Greenfield, Fr	47	1	1	0	12	9	15	.571	114	111	48	31	3	47	5	7	92	6	2.45
Heydeman, Lodi	27	27	12	2	11	10	0	.524	195	198	98	75	11	99	2	5	159	18	3.46
Cochran, Mod	21	21	4	0	9	8	0	.529	133	170	76	55	9	55	1	2	86	10	3.72
Perez, Sal	30	29	3	0	13	8	0	.619	167	184	90	71	12	70	2	4	71	8	3.83
Brisbin, Sal	27	23	7	2	14	8	0	.636	159	152	91	70	9	100	2	5	103	16	3.96
Bowman, Mod	25	21	3	0	7	8	0	.467	146	178	89	66	18	49	2	2	73	5	4.07
Wilson, Lodi	24	23	11	1	12	11	0	.522	174	193	99	81	15	65	2	6	74	6	4.19
Cline, Fr	30	4	2	0	7	4	0	.636	112	113	66	53	9	59	4	4	76	13	4.26
Schaefer, Fr	28	28	12	1	11	8	0	.579	178	172	100	85	12	111	4	2	154	13	4.30
Wilkes, Reno	28	26	10	1	13	7	0	.650	177	189	122	89	10	76	2	8	111	15	4.53

Departmental Leaders: G–Quiros, 61; GS–Perez, 29; CG–Heydeman, Schaefer, Wirth, 12; ShO–MacPherson, 3; W–Califano, 15; L–Skiba, 13; Sv–Quiros, 18; Pct.–Califano, .833; IP–Heydeman, 195; H–Wirth, 227; R–Wirth, 125; ER–Tallman, 103; HR–Bowman, 18; BB–Schaefer, 111; IBB–Gill, 9; HB–Maxwell, 9; SO–Heydeman, 159; WP–Heydeman, 18.

(All Pitchers—Listed Alphabetically)

Pitcher–Club	G.	GS.	CG.	ShO.	W.	L.	Sv.	Pct.	IP.	H.	R.	ER.	HR.	BB.	Int. BB.	HB.	SO.	WP.	ERA.
Alvarez, SJ	12	10	2	0	3	3	0	.500	65	87	46	39	3	36	3	0	27	4	5.40
Amenita, F	4	0	0	0	0	0	0	.000	1	5	11	11	1	7	0	1	0	0	99.00
Arnold, SJ*	17	16	3	0	6	8	1	.429	93	84	76	59	5	74	0	7	74	7	5.71
Arp, SJ	13	2	0	0	2	0	0	.000	21	38	29	19	1	16	1	0	9	4	8.14
Barrett, Lodi	26	26	11	1	12	10	0	.545	183	199	109	98	16	72	0	6	86	14	4.82
Baxter, Mod	18	11	2	1	4	3	1	.571	74	67	37	30	6	38	3	5	49	3	3.65
Beitey, Fr	25	17	5	0	8	7	1	.533	111	161	85	71	10	52	3	4	56	8	5.76
Botting, Sal*	10	9	0	0	4	2	0	.667	44	55	35	28	4	36	0	3	39	4	5.73

Pitcher–Club	G.	GS.	CG.	ShO.	W.	L.	Sv.	Pct.	IP.	H.	R.	ER.	HR.	BB.	Int. BB.	HB.	SO.	WP.	ERA.
Bovee, Reno*	18	1	0	0	1	2	1	.333	28	33	24	18	1	24	2	3	18	3	5.79
Bowman, Mod	25	21	3	0	7	8	0	.467	146	178	89	66	18	49	2	2	73	5	4.07
Boyd, Mod*	10	3	0	0	0	2	2	.000	23	30	19	14	3	12	1	0	13	4	5.48
Braun, Mod	19	13	2	0	5	8	0	.385	93	125	75	64	17	33	3	1	52	1	6.19
Brennan, SJ	16	11	3	0	3	9	0	.250	72	95	64	46	6	37	3	5	28	2	5.75
Brisbin, Sal	27	23	7	2	14	8	0	.636	159	152	91	70	9	100	2	5	103	16	3.96
Bullard, SJ	10	0	0	0	0	3	0	.000	19	27	21	17	0	15	0	2	8	3	8.05
Califano, Sal*	28	28	3	1	15	3	0	.833	163	171	99	90	13	90	2	3	118	11	4.97
Camacho, Mod	10	10	0	0	3	4	0	.429	56	69	47	35	3	39	1	2	29	7	5.63
Cline, Fr	30	4	2	0	7	4	0	.636	112	113	66	53	9	59	4	4	76	13	4.26
Cochran, Mod	21	21	4	0	9	8	0	.529	133	170	76	55	9	55	1	2	86	10	3.72
Colzie, Mod	2	0	0	0	0	0	0	.000	3	0	0	0	0	1	0	0	1	0	0.00
Dyer, Fr*	4	0	0	0	0	0	0	.000	5	2	3	3	0	11	0	1	1	0	5.40
Eichelberger, Reno	13	13	4	0	6	1	0	.857	89	71	48	35	3	63	0	0	77	8	3.54
Evans, Lodi*	3	2	0	0	1	0	0	1.000	8	12	8	8	1	5	0	0	5	1	9.00
Flanagan, SJ	12	11	3	0	6	5	0	.545	80	81	38	24	0	23	2	1	45	3	2.70
Flores, Fr*	26	26	4	0	10	9	0	.526	151	164	103	84	17	94	2	2	130	15	5.01
Forgie, SJ	3	2	0	0	0	1	0	.000	7	15	13	9	1	7	0	0	3	0	11.57
French, Reno	23	18	5	0	6	7	2	.462	118	136	89	76	15	41	2	2	65	14	5.80
Garcia, Reno	30	12	3	0	8	5	1	.615	109	103	75	57	4	80	2	2	84	11	4.71
Gill, Reno	48	0	0	0	6	7	14	.462	92	98	47	33	4	45	9	3	67	8	3.23
Green, Mod	9	5	0	0	1	2	0	.333	31	42	26	22	2	11	0	1	8	0	6.39
Greenfield, Fr	47	1	1	0	12	9	15	.571	114	111	48	31	3	47	5	7	92	6	2.45
Gressick, Reno*	16	11	4	1	4	4	0	.500	65	67	37	33	4	64	2	0	52	6	4.57
Hagman, Mod	30	7	3	0	9	3	0	.750	105	102	45	35	6	29	1	4	54	4	3.00
Harvey, SJ	6	0	0	0	0	0	0	.000	7	10	10	7	1	10	1	0	1	2	9.00
Heredia, Lodi	14	14	5	0	4	9	0	.308	89	98	66	51	10	42	0	2	60	7	5.16
Heydeman, Lodi	27	27	12	2	11	10	0	.524	195	198	98	75	11	99	2	5	159	18	3.46
Hile, Mod*	2	0	0	0	0	1	0	.000	3	6	8	2	1	2	0	0	1	0	6.00
Jones, SJ	30	16	3	1	4	12	0	.250	119	142	86	72	11	68	6	6	94	11	5.45
Joseph, Reno*	10	4	0	0	1	3	0	.250	33	50	37	25	0	24	0	2	16	5	6.82
Joyce, Mod*	3	0	0	0	0	0	0	.000	5	5	4	4	0	5	0	0	3	3	7.20
Keefe, Lodi	37	0	0	0	5	7	11	.417	60	58	25	22	5	36	4	1	60	2	3.30
Kelley, Sal	28	17	2	0	7	4	2	.636	107	99	57	43	1	52	5	5	78	9	3.62
Kinney, SJ*	11	0	0	0	4	1	3	.800	22	21	12	8	3	10	0	1	16	2	3.27
Klein, SJ	15	14	1	1	3	6	0	.333	76	88	58	49	5	59	1	3	68	5	5.80
Kuhaulua, Sal*	30	0	0	0	3	1	4	.750	86	70	30	23	1	53	1	1	103	6	2.41
Kunkler, Lodi*	13	13	3	0	6	6	0	.333	83	85	56	39	9	50	3	4	54	7	4.23
Lake, Lodi*	22	7	2	0	2	6	0	.250	67	82	60	39	10	51	1	3	37	5	5.24
Lee, Reno*	9	0	0	0	1	1	0	.500	26	24	11	9	2	15	1	1	12	1	3.12
MacPherson, Reno	7	6	3	3	5	0	0	1.000	47	43	20	16	7	13	0	0	23	4	3.06
Mahan, SJ	12	12	3	0	3	7	0	.300	81	92	54	51	7	31	0	3	59	3	5.67
Maxwell, Sal*	33	18	4	0	10	11	1	.476	137	121	89	71	4	94	2	9	81	12	4.66
McNulty, Sal	15	13	1	0	5	5	0	.500	84	95	62	41	6	56	2	2	46	7	4.39
McQueen, Mod	26	0	0	0	3	2	5	.600	39	44	13	11	1	11	2	2	29	1	2.54
Melson, SJ	2	0	0	0	1	0	0	1.000	2	2	3	2	0	3	0	0	1	0	9.00
Messman, Reno	22	6	1	0	1	6	1	.143	64	77	63	52	5	44	1	2	46	11	7.31
Meyl, Mod*	5	2	0	0	0	3	0	.000	11	13	16	11	3	9	0	1	10	1	9.00
Myers, Fr	6	2	0	0	2	0	0	1.000	36	39	21	18	2	30	1	1	25	5	4.50
Narleski, SJ	16	2	0	0	0	2	0	.000	37	35	35	24	3	28	6	2	16	0	5.84
O'Brien, Mod*	9	0	0	0	1	0	1	1.000	15	13	13	12	1	0	17	2	0	11	2	6.60
O'Donnell, Sal*	7	0	0	0	0	3	0	.000	15	13	9	6	1	15	1	0	5	1	3.60
Owens, Mod	1	1	0	0	0	1	0	.000	2	5	8	7	0	6	0	0	3	4	31.50
Panick, Sal	9	0	0	0	1	0	1	1.000	15	19	7	6	2	4	0	0	16	0	3.60
Peregud, Mod	25	19	3	0	5	11	0	.313	123	147	92	72	11	60	5	2	50	11	5.27
Perez, Sal	30	29	3	0	13	8	0	.619	167	184	90	71	12	70	2	4	71	8	3.83
Phillips, Lodi*	11	0	0	0	1	1	3	.500	24	26	21	14	1	14	1	5	24	2	5.25
Power, Lodi	13	5	2	0	1	3	1	.250	51	46	34	26	3	44	1	3	58	11	4.59
Quintero, Reno	20	10	1	0	5	6	0	.455	65	68	51	42	5	49	0	3	50	11	5.82
Quiros, Mod	61	0	0	0	6	5	18	.545	101	102	45	35	11	36	4	1	91	3	3.12
Rehn, Reno	23	1	0	0	5	2	1	.714	53	62	37	30	6	42	0	1	54	7	5.09
Rodriguez, SJ	5	2	0	0	0	1	0	.000	11	10	8	6	0	13	1	1	6	5	4.91
Roslund, Sal*	22	0	0	0	4	0	5	1.000	37	28	18	11	1	20	2	0	35	2	2.68
Salas, Mod	23	9	2	1	5	7	1	.417	92	90	59	44	10	41	0	1	63	7	4.30
Scarcella, Fr	19	3	0	0	2	1	1	.667	57	62	42	42	3	58	2	5	31	8	6.63
Schaefer, Fr	28	28	12	1	11	8	0	.579	178	172	100	85	12	111	4	2	154	13	4.30
Schuler, SJ*	54	0	0	0	4	7	6	.364	89	126	82	47	3	38	7	2	62	3	4.75
Skiba, SJ	23	23	5	1	6	13	0	.316	135	162	113	93	13	69	5	4	83	6	6.20
Smith, Lodi	29	1	0	0	3	2	4	.600	59	54	30	13	4	26	2	1	50	3	1.98
Smith, SJ	8	0	0	0	1	0	0	.000	12	10	4	4	0	2	0	0	8	1	3.00
Spitzack, Mod*	4	0	0	0	1	0	0	1.000	6	11	6	6	2	2	0	0	4	0	9.00
Steen, Fr	7	0	0	0	1	0	0	.000	11	27	19	16	1	11	1	0	5	2	13.09
Stegman, Mod	5	0	0	0	0	0	0	.000	5	14	12	12	0	12	0	0	2	0	21.60
Stewart, Reno	13	12	4	1	6	1	0	.857	82	92	47	41	7	24	0	1	39	2	4.50

Pitcher—Club	G.	GS.	CG.	ShO.	W.	L.	Sv.	Pct.	IP.	H.	R.	ER.	HR.	BB.	Int. BB.	HB.	SO.	WP.	ERA.
Stumpp, Sal	47	0	0	0	6	3	11	.667	76	61	35	24	3	36	3	2	54	2	2.84
Tallman, Fr	27	27	10	1	11	10	0	.524	184	213	122	103	3	101	1	1	135	11	5.04
Tennant, Lodi	8	8	0	0	0	4	0	.000	36	58	37	30	3	29	0	1	23	2	7.50
Texidor, Sal	20	0	0	0	4	1	1	.800	67	76	39	32	6	36	6	1	44	8	4.30
Thompson, Fr*	30	0	0	0	3	2	0	.600	67	82	50	43	4	40	0	3	48	8	5.78
Thormodsgard, Reno	16	15	6	0	6	8	0	.429	104	119	58	49	5	42	1	3	67	5	4.24
Todd, Lodi	21	0	0	0	2	1	0	.667	38	49	29	17	2	18	3	0	21	2	4.03
Veselic, Reno	7	2	0	0	1	1	0	.500	19	22	22	22	2	21	0	0	16	0	10.42
Weese, SJ	4	0	0	0	2	0	0	.000	6	5	3	2	0	5	1	0	5	2	3.00
Wells, Reno*	4	0	0	0	1	0	0	.000	9	19	18	12	2	6	0	0	5	2	12.00
Wibberley, Mod	4	2	0	0	2	1	0	.667	17	22	12	8	1	7	0	1	15	0	4.24
Widner, SJ*	31	13	1	1	1	5	0	.167	107	134	86	66	3	78	1	4	76	9	5.55
Wihtol, SJ	51	2	0	0	1	6	5	.143	101	120	58	52	5	60	8	3	99	11	4.63
Wilkes, Reno	28	26	10	1	13	7	0	.650	177	189	122	89	10	76	2	×	111	15	4.53
Wilson, Lodi	24	23	11	1	12	11	0	.522	174	193	99	81	15	65	2	6	74	6	4.19
Wirth, Fr	28	28	12	0	11	12	0	.478	181	227	125	94	7	76	5	6	114	12	4.67
Wouters, Lodi	13	1	0	0	2	1	0	.667	37	35	17	12	2	25	2	1	30	3	2.92
Wulfemeyer, Sal	19	16	1	1	7	3	0	.700	81	70	40	32	4	60	0	3	51	6	3.56
Zoss, Mod*	23	13	3	0	7	5	0	.583	105	113	63	48	11	59	0	1	58	8	4.11

BALKS—Barrett 5; Camacho, Cochran, Flores, Heydeman, 3 each; Braun, Brisbin, Evans, French, Kelley, Lake, Quiros, Thompson, Zoss, 2 each; Alvarez, Baxter, Califano, Gill, Hagman, Harvey, Heredia, Jones, Joseph, Klein, Kunkler, Mahan, McNulty, Myers, Narleski, Owens, Peregud, Perez, Power, Scarcella, Schuler, Wells, Widner, Wirth, 1 each.

COMBINATION SHUTOUTS—Schaefer-Greenfield, Wirth-Greenfield, Wirth-Greenfield, Fresno; Thormodsgard-Gill, Reno; Wulfemeyer-Maxwell, Salinas.

NO-HIT GAMES—Baxter, Modesto, defeated Salinas, 1-0, May 2 (seven innings); Brisbin, Salinas, defeated Fresno, 2-0, August 18 (seven innings).

Carolina League

CLASS A

CHAMPIONSHIP WINNERS IN PREVIOUS YEARS

1945—Danville .... .681	HP-Thomasville .... .622	1967—Durham x (West.) .... .536
1946—Greensboro .... .599	1958—Danville .... .576	Raleigh (East.) .... .542
Raleigh (2nd)† .... .563	Burlington (4th)† .... .511	1968—Salem (West.) .... .607
1947—Burlington .... .613	1959—Raleigh .... .600	Ral-Dur (East.) .... .597
Raleigh (3rd)† .... .574	Wilson (2nd)† .... .550	H P-Thom. y (W.) .... .493
1948—Raleigh .... .592	1960—Greensboro‡ .... .636	1969—Rocky M (East.) .... .569
Martinsville (2nd)† .... .570	Burlington .... .586	Salem (West.) .... .542
1949—Danville .... .601	1961—Wilson .... .594	Ral-Dur z (East.) .... .560
Burlington (4th)† .... .500	1962—Durham .... .636	1970—Winston-Salem‡ .... .586
1950—Winston-Salem* .... .693	Wilson .... .600	Burlington .... .597
1951—Danville .... .600	Kinston(2nd)† .... .593	1971—Peninsula‡ .... .647
Wins-Salem (2nd)† ..... .583	1963—Kinston§ .... .538	Kinston .... .623
1952—Raleigh .... .581	Greensboro§ .... .590	1972—Salem‡ .... .657
Reidsville (4th)† .... .536	Wilson (2nd)† .... .535	Burlington .... .632
1953—Raleigh .... .593	1964—Kinston§ .... .572	1973—Lynchburg .... .588
Danville (2nd)† .... .572	Winston-Salem§† .... .590	Winston-Salem .... .557
1954—Fayetteville* .... .628	1965—Peninsula§ .... .597	1974—Salem .... .671
Danville (2nd)† .... .533	Durham§ .... .580	Salem .... .582
1955—HP-Thomasville .... .580	Tidewater† .... .528	1975—Rocky Mount .... .667
Fayetteville (4th)† ...... .523	1966—Kinston§ .... .547	Rocky Mount .... .614
1956—HP-Thomasville .... .591	Winston-Salem§ .... .586	
1957—Durham .... .632	Rocky Mount† .... .533	

*Won championship and four-club playoff. †Won four-club playoff. ‡Won split-season playoff. §League was divided into Eastern, Western divisions. xWon eight-club, two-division playoff.
yWon eight-club, two-division playoff against Raleigh-Durham.
zWon eight-club, two-division playoff against Burlington.

STANDING OF CLUBS AT CLOSE OF FIRST HALF, JUNE 24

Club	W.	L.	T.	Pct.	G.B.	Club	W.	L.	T.	Pct.	G.B.
Winston-Salem (Red Sox)	42	26	0	.618	......	Salem (Pirates)	35	32	0	.522	6½
Peninsula (Phillies)	36	31	0	.537	5½	Lynchburg (Mets)	27	42	0	.391	15½

STANDING OF CLUBS AT CLOSE OF SECOND HALF, SEPTEMBER 2

Club	W.	L.	T.	Pct.	G.B.	Club	W.	L.	T.	Pct.	G.B.
Winston-Salem (Red Sox)	38	31	0	.551	......	Peninsula (Phillies)	35	34	1	.507	3
Lynchburg (Mets)	37	33	0	.529	1½	Salem (Pirates)	33	37	1	.471	5½

FINAL STANDING OF CAROLINA LEAGUE VS. WESTERN CAROLINAS LEAGUE

Club	W.	L.	T.	Pct.	G.B.	Club	W.	L.	T.	Pct.	G.B.
Winston-Salem (Red Sox)	12	4	0	.750	......	Spartanburg (Phillies) W/C....	8	8	0	.500	4
Salem (Pirates)	10	6	0	.625	2	Charleston (Pirates) W/C	6	10	0	.375	6
Peninsula (Phillies)	9	6	0	.600	2½	Asheville (Rangers) W/C	5	10	0	.333	6½
Lynchburg (Mets)	9	7	0	.563	3	Greenwood (Braves) W/C	4	12	0	.250	8

COMPOSITE STANDINGS OF CLUBS AT CLOSE OF SEASON, SEPTEMBER 2

Club	W.-S.	Pen.	Sal.	Lyn.	Ash.	Gwd.	Cha.	Spa.	W.	L.	T.	Pct.	G.B.
Winston-Salem (Red Sox)	....	25	23	20	3	4	3	2	80	57	0	.584	......
Peninsula (Phillies)	18	....	22	22	3	1	3	2	71	65	1	.522	8½
Salem (Pirates)	15	22	....	26	2	3	2	3	68	69	1	.496	12
Lynchburg (Mets)	20	17	18	....	2	4	2	1	64	75	0	.460	17
Asheville (Rangers)	1	0	2	2	....	21	22	28	76	62	0	.551	......
Greenwood (Braves)	0	3	1	0	18	....	30	23	75	64	0	.540	1½
Charleston (Pirates)	1	1	2	2	18	14	....	21	59	80	0	.424	17½
Spartanburg (Phillies)	2	2	1	3	16	17	18	....	59	80	0	.424	17½

Major league affiliations in parentheses.

Peninsula represented Hampton, Va.

Playoff—None.

Regular-Season Attendance—Lynchburg, 46,302; Peninsula, 41,367; Salem, 30,387; Winston-Salem, 49,314. Total, 167,370. All-Star Game, 712. No playoff.

Managers: Lynchburg—Jack Aker; Peninsula—Cal Emery; Salem—Steve Demeter; Winston-Salem—Anthony Torchia.

All-Star Team: 1B—Brant, Lynchburg; 2B—Lozano, Lynchburg; 3B—Evans, Winston-Salem; SS—DeLiza, Salem; Ryczek, Peninsula; OF—Delgado, Winston-Salem; Huizenga, Winston-Salem; Brown, Peninsula; DH—McClure, Winston-Salem; C—O'Berry, Winston-Salem; P—Newcomer, Salem; Whitson, Salem; Manager—Torchia, Winston-Salem.

(Compiled by Howe News Bureau, Chicago, Ill.)

CLUB BATTING

Club	G.	AB.	R.	OR.	H.	TB.	2B.	3B.	HR.	RBI.	SH.	SF.	BB.	Int. BB.	HP.	SO.	SB.	CS.	LOB.	Pct.
Winston-Salem	137	4467	641	529	1152	1687	201	44	82	569	47	50	572	35	28	757	130	54	1017	.258
Peninsula	137	4465	567	523	1126	1557	162	46	59	503	40	40	435	21	36	736	146	48	947	.252
Lynchburg	139	4433	581	646	1092	1548	187	55	53	483	54	49	487	24	42	805	162	64	904	.246
Salem	138	4499	570	581	1104	1567	178	51	61	493	34	28	506	16	42	727	74	32	1036	.245

INDIVIDUAL BATTING

(Leading Qualifiers for Batting Championship—378 or More Plate Appearances)

*Bats lefthanded. †Switch-hitter.

Player and Club	G.	AB.	R.	H.	TB.	2B.	3B.	HR.	RBI.	SH.	SF.	BB.	HP.	SO.	SB.	CS.	Pct.
Brown, Rogers Lee, Pen†	102	393	68	137	199	18	10	8	41	1	1	33	0	67	42	12	.349
Delgado, Luis, Win-Salem†	122	486	79	143	197	21	6	7	48	10	7	34	5	53	52	11	.294
Cruz, Pablo N., Salem	110	390	56	110	144	21	2	3	34	7	1	54	4	23	12	2	.282
Foster, Otis, Win-Salem	122	408	62	115	186	27	4	12	83	0	7	95	4	65	5	2	.282
Covert, W. David, Lynch*	120	451	62	127	163	21	6	1	48	1	4	32	4	71	6	4	.282
Dean, John W., Salem*	106	393	54	109	161	18	2	10	53	0	1	43	1	57	3	3	.277
McClure, Paul, Win-Salem*	108	347	47	96	147	26	5	5	61	3	7	56	0	68	3	3	.277
Lozano, David, Lynchburg	125	436	89	119	148	10	8	1	37	5	2	87	4	65	35	11	.273
Evans, Ronald, Win-Salem	123	425	73	115	187	22	1	16	66	1	3	81	1	76	20	5	.271
Brant, Marshall, Lynch	135	476	75	123	238	32	7	23	93	0	11	54	3	89	13	7	.258

Departmental Leaders: G—DeLiza, 138; AB—DeLiza, 518; R—Lozano, 89; H—Delgado, 143; TB—Brant, 238; 2B—Brant, 32; 3B—Brown, 10; HR—Brant, 23; RBI—Brant, 93; SH—Delgado, 10; SF—Brant, 11; BB—Foster, 95; HP—Marshall, 8; SO—Yearby, 91; SB—Delgado, 52; CS—Brown, 12.

(All Players—Listed Alphabetically)

Player and Club	G.	AB.	R.	H.	TB.	2B.	3B.	HR.	RBI.	SH.	SF.	BB.	HP.	SO.	SB.	CS.	Pct.
Baker, David, Peninsula	40	125	10	24	33	6	0	1	10	1	1	7	2	14	2	0	.192
Beck, Thomas, Peninsula	62	187	20	43	57	7	2	1	23	9	2	22	1	27	8	1	.230
Bernazard, Oscar, Salem*	87	292	41	62	100	16	5	4	27	2	3	58	2	48	3	2	.212
Black, Randy Lee, Pen*	54	166	19	36	58	4	6	2	17	1	0	15	0	41	6	3	.217
Boyland, Dorian, Salem*	71	245	27	66	95	12	4	3	31	0	3	21	7	63	1	2	.269
Brady, James, Salem	18	65	10	15	20	3	1	0	11	1	2	13	1	11	0	0	.231
Brant, Marshall, Lynch	135	476	75	123	238	32	7	23	93	0	11	54	3	89	13	7	.258
Breining, Fred, Salem	1	1	0	0	0	0	0	0	0	0	0	0	0	0	0	0	.000
Brown, Rogers Lee, Pen†	102	393	68	137	199	18	10	8	41	1	1	33	0	67	42	12	.349
Bryant, Robert, Lynch*	51	160	23	51	62	5	3	0	15	2	2	13	1	34	12	6	.319
Buba, Mark, Win-Salem	75	239	40	71	81	6	2	0	18	4	1	30	2	27	4	4	.297
Burkholder, Terry, Salem	60	219	29	48	64	9	2	1	12	2	1	29	2	62	7	2	.219
Coletta, Matthew, Win-Salem	85	281	46	70	104	10	3	6	34	5	4	46	2	64	5	3	.249
Contreras, Rafael O., Lyn	116	392	48	98	139	17	6	4	38	8	3	43	3	55	15	9	.250
Covert, W. David, Lynch*	120	451	62	127	163	21	6	1	48	1	4	32	4	71	6	4	.282
Cruz, Pablo N., Salem	110	390	56	110	144	21	2	3	34	7	1	54	4	23	12	2	.282
Cruz, Ruben, Lynchburg*	1	1	0	0	0	0	0	0	0	0	0	0	0	0	0	0	.000
Dean, John W., Salem*	106	393	54	109	161	18	2	10	53	0	1	43	1	57	3	3	.277
de Armas, Rolando, Pen	100	298	15	68	78	10	0	0	35	4	2	21	2	26	1	1	.228
DelCarmen, Manuel, Pen	66	189	21	43	50	2	1	1	12	5	1	23	0	40	10	7	.228
Delgado, Luis, Win-Salem†	122	486	79	143	197	21	6	7	48	10	7	34	5	53	52	11	.294
DeLiza, Juan, Salem	138	518	48	122	164	22	4	4	38	4	3	27	1	62	14	4	.236
DeMeo, Robert, Peninsula	24	55	3	10	11	1	0	0	1	0	0	3	1	11	0	0	.182
Dyer, James, Lynchburg	58	144	13	20	23	3	0	0	3	5	0	9	0	50	4	0	.139
Evans, Ronald, Win-Salem	123	425	73	115	187	22	1	16	66	1	3	81	1	76	20	5	.271
Felt, William, Peninsula	22	68	5	11	21	4	0	2	8	0	0	8	0	6	0	0	.162
Fisher, Glenn, Win-Salem	16	41	5	13	17	2	1	0	3	1	1	5	1	8	0	1	.317
Foster, Otis, Win-Salem	122	408	62	115	186	27	4	12	83	0	7	95	4	65	5	2	.282
Galante, Joseph, Salem	1	1	0	0	0	0	0	0	0	0	0	0	0	0	0	0	.000
Garcia, Luis R., Lynch	67	230	29	53	88	15	4	4	19	2	2	31	1	50	4	4	.230
Geigel, German, Pen*	96	314	43	76	95	5	4	2	20	2	2	23	4	51	8	2	.242
Gerlecz, Steven, Salem	86	283	40	66	83	8	3	1	20	6	2	31	4	53	3	7	.233

Player and Club	G.	AB.	R.	H.	TB.	2B.	3B.	HR.	RBI.	SH.	SF.	BB.	HP.	SO.	SB.	CS.	Pct.
Gifford, William, Lynch*	54	167	8	46	56	10	0	0	19	2	2	15	0	27	1	0	.275
Grady, Charles, Lynch*	50	96	11	17	33	3	2	3	12	0	0	18	0	25	0	0	.177
Greenstein, Stuart, Lynch	14	48	7	15	21	4	1	0	8	2	0	6	0	5	1	1	.313
Guarnaccia, John, Pen*	61	159	27	37	66	5	0	8	25	2	4	33	4	44	5	0	.233
Hall, John H., Salem	1	1	0	0	0	0	0	0	0	0	0	1	0	0	0	0	.000
Harper, Glenn, Lynchburg	2	2	0	1	1	0	0	0	0	0	0	0	0	0	0	0	.500
Holland, Alfred, Salem	1	1	1	1	1	0	0	0	0	0	0	0	0	0	0	0	1.000
Hough, Stanley, Lynchburg	99	288	39	70	94	8	2	4	26	4	3	25	5	50	6	5	.243
Hubal, Joseph, Win-Salem	1	1	0	0	0	0	0	0	0	0	0	0	0	1	0	0	.000
Hughes, John D., Peninsula	57	205	27	55	90	14	0	7	33	1	0	24	4	36	0	2	.268
Huizenga, Kenneth, W-Salem	119	430	69	102	194	28	5	18	73	2	6	40	5	83	5	5	.237
Johnston, James, Salem*	2	1	0	0	0	0	0	0	0	1	0	0	0	0	0	0	.000
Jones, Bryan, Lynchburg	48	137	26	28	45	6	1	3	16	2	1	27	1	24	7	2	.204
Jurak, Edward, Win-Salem	113	401	49	88	110	6	2	4	35	6	4	33	2	56	9	6	.219
Kesses, Steven, Lynchburg	87	306	39	86	105	9	2	2	29	4	1	30	5	63	15	2	.281
LaTorre, Gary, Win-Salem	15	41	5	8	8	0	0	0	1	1	0	3	0	6	0	2	.195
Lebron, Juan, Salem	94	330	33	90	122	19	5	1	37	1	2	14	2	29	1	2	.273
Littleton, Larry, Salem	82	284	50	76	133	10	4	13	59	2	0	51	3	75	1	1	.268
Lozano, David, Lynchburg	125	436	89	119	148	10	8	1	37	5	2	87	4	65	35	11	.273
Manos, Peter, Peninsula	1	0	0	0	0	0	0	0	0	0	0	1	0	0	0	0	.000
Marshall, David F., Salem	88	288	35	63	77	5	3	1	26	0	4	36	8	34	2	2	.219
Matuszek, Leonard, Pen*	47	166	23	46	66	9	1	3	21	1	2	22	2	23	1	1	.277
McClure, Paul, Win-Salem*	108	347	47	96	147	26	5	5	61	3	7	56	0	68	3	3	.277
McCormack, Donald, Pen	94	291	29	68	105	9	5	6	36	3	1	21	4	52	2	3	.234
Minaya, Felix, Lynchburg	18	61	6	15	20	1	2	0	5	1	1	2	0	11	4	1	.246
Moreland, B. Keith, Pen	78	294	38	83	111	12	2	4	47	0	7	17	4	15	2	2	.282
Morello, Lawrence, Win-Sal	69	212	28	62	86	13	1	3	26	0	1	37	1	30	2	0	.292
Muriel, Arnaldo, Peninsula	1	1	0	0	0	0	0	0	0	0	0	0	0	1	0	0	.000
Nelson, Paul, Salem*	119	404	49	88	132	9	4	9	51	3	3	43	0	90	11	3	.218
O'Berry, P. Michael, W-S	111	330	51	66	98	12	4	4	32	3	4	58	1	85	1	2	.200
Olivares, Oswaldo, Lynch*	20	44	3	5	5	0	0	0	3	0	2	5	0	6	2	0	.114
Oliveras, Max, Salem	45	145	18	41	49	3	1	1	15	3	2	19	1	15	3	1	.283
Ortiz, Leonardo, Salem	69	225	28	44	80	8	5	6	32	1	1	7	2	46	3	0	.196
Patterson, W. O. Ricky, Lyn	19	41	5	2	6	1	0	1	3	1	0	1	7	12	2	1	.049
Peltier, Dwayne, Salem	1	4	0	1	1	0	0	0	0	0	0	0	0	2	0	0	.250
Perez, Francisco, Lynch	93	319	34	73	98	14	4	1	29	5	6	24	1	48	4	4	.229
Pinkney, Charles, Win-Salem	70	192	17	49	62	5	1	2	21	0	2	15	0	34	11	6	.255
Plante, Gerald, Peninsula	3	0	1	0	0	0	0	0	0	0	0	0	0	0	0	0	.000
Powers, Stephen, Salem*	29	66	13	17	25	5	0	1	10	1	0	18	0	4	1	0	.258
Raco, Gary, Salem	55	180	23	45	66	4	4	3	23	0	0	26	2	34	4	0	.250
Reedy, Jerome, Peninsula	47	178	30	51	60	9	0	0	20	3	5	21	1	10	8	5	.287
Rodriguez, Felix A., Sal*	49	163	15	39	49	6	2	0	14	0	0	15	2	17	5	1	.239
Ryczek, Martin, Peninsula	121	361	32	76	84	8	0	0	20	3	3	22	2	67	7	4	.211
Schneider, Jeffery, Pen†	2	0	1	0	0	0	0	0	0	0	0	0	0	0	0	0	.000
Shankle, James, Win-Salem	92	296	35	72	105	13	7	2	36	3	2	26	4	57	3	0	.243
Skalisky, Rocky, Pen*	83	165	25	53	73	6	1	4	31	1	2	13	0	7	1	1	.321
Smoak, James, Peninsula	131	434	74	110	148	14	9	2	39	3	4	47	0	80	31	3	.253
Tarbell, Steven, Win-Salem	4	16	3	6	6	0	0	0	0	0	1	0	2	0	0	.375
Trevino, Alejandro, Lynch	94	284	17	57	72	11	2	0	31	3	6	24	1	49	5	1	.201
Tyler, David, Win-Salem	93	321	32	76	99	10	2	3	32	7	1	13	0	41	10	4	.237
Waller, Richard, Win-Salem	1	0	0	0	0	0	0	0	0	0	0	0	0	0	0	0	.000
Yearby, Melvin, Peninsula	113	378	50	93	146	19	5	8	62	0	2	54	3	91	10	1	.246
Yost, Steven, Lynchburg	112	352	47	86	131	17	5	6	49	7	3	41	6	70	26	6	.244
Ysursa, Nicolas, Peninsula	16	38	6	6	6	0	0	0	2	0	1	5	0	7	2	0	.158

The following pitchers had no plate appearances primarily through the use of designated hitters, listed alphabetically by club, games in parentheses:

LYNCHBURG—Berenguer, Juan (28); Clark, Russell (8); Cummings, Charles (17); Driskill, Donald (44); Feola, Lawrence (21); Gorgie, Alex (16); Jackson, Roy (7); Leonard, Robert P. (13); Pacella, John (26); Sander, Richard (21); Speck, R. Clifford (10).

PENINSULA—Bell, Oliver (6); Bradford, Gregory (12); Ciammachilli, Frank (27); Fowler, Don (24); Hernandez, Angel (24); Kirkpatrick, Michael (3); Manderbach, Gary (16); Saucier, Kevin (14); Stone, Gregory (24); Taylor, Jack W. (6); Wertz, Larry (23).

SALEM—Anthony, Paul (12); Brandt, Randy (21); Clites, Robert (4); Davis, Dennis (24); Kavanagh, Michael (6); Kreke, Donald (2); Tapia, Mark (2); Thomas, Gerard (22); Whitson, Edward (26).

WINSTON-SALEM—Bigos, Walter (28); Cross, Wilfred (13); Faust, Alvin (32); Herlihy, Ronald (31); Medina, Freddy (12); Moore, Michael S. (24); Newcomer, F. Breen (25); Poole, Bruce (28); Tagliarino, John (2); Tudor, John (27); Welch, Phillip (28).

GRAND-SLAM HOME RUNS—Littleton, 2; Foster, Huizenga, Lebron, O'Berry, Yearby, 1 each.

AWARDED FIRST BASE ON INTERFERENCE—Shankle 2 (Marshall, Trevino); McClure (Olson).

CLUB FIELDING

Club	G.	PO.	A.	E.	DP.	PB.	Pct.
Peninsula	137	3511	1613	198	115	21	.963
Winston-Salem	137	3554	1488	200	114	18	.962
Lynchburg	139	3562	1511	211	120	28	.960
Salem	138	3493	1399	206	102	21	.960

Triple Plays—None.

INDIVIDUAL FIELDING

*Throws lefthanded.

FIRST BASEMEN

Player and Club	G.	PO.	A.	E.	DP.	Pct.
Matuszek, Peninsula	46	426	34	1	27	.998
Rodriguez, Salem*	14	114	4	1	11	.992
de Armas, Peninsula	62	560	19	6	45	.990
Oliveras, Salem	33	265	19	3	23	.990
McClure, Win.-Salem*	22	165	10	2	15	.989
BRANT, Lynchburg	135	1208	69	15	101	.988
Foster, Win.-Salem	115	988	75	14	83	.987
Cruz, Salem	55	443	23	6	34	.987
Felt, Peninsula	17	156	6	3	14	.982
Brown, Peninsula	25	206	11	6	15	.973
Boyland, Salem*	36	305	8	12	25	.963

(Fewer Than Ten Games)

Player and Club	G.	PO.	A.	E.	DP.	Pct.
Contreras, Lynch.	1	5	0	0	0	1.000
Gerlecz, Salem	1	1	0	0	0	1.000
McCormack, Pen.	1	1	0	0	0	1.000
Ysursa, Peninsula	1	1	0	0	0	1.000
LaTorre, Win.-Salem	5	30	3	1	2	.971
Lebron, Salem	6	30	3	1	0	.971
Covert, Lynchburg*	5	31	0	1	1	.969

SECOND BASEMEN

Player and Club	G.	PO.	A.	E.	DP.	Pct.
de Armas, Peninsula	14	5	6	0	1	1.000
Cruz, Salem	30	67	77	3	19	.980
LOZANO, Lynchburg	125	283	356	20	76	.970
Buba, Win.-Salem	71	153	167	10	43	.970
Beck, Peninsula	62	125	146	10	32	.964
Gerlecz, Salem	45	89	100	8	20	.959
Brady, Salem	18	43	44	4	8	.956
DelCarmen, Pen.	32	59	72	7	14	.949
Tyler, Win.-Salem	78	194	187	21	34	.948
Burkholder, Salem	51	89	115	14	26	.936
Reedy, Peninsula	47	114	123	22	25	.915

(Fewer Than Ten Games)

Player and Club	G.	PO.	A.	E.	DP.	Pct.
Trevino, Lynchburg	7	12	20	0	0	1.000
Ysursa, Peninsula	2	0	2	0	1	1.000
Dyer, Lynchburg	1	1	0	0	0	1.000
Garcia, Lynchburg	6	5	10	1	0	.938
Jones, Lynchburg	7	11	14	3	3	.893
Minaya, Lynchburg	3	9	10	3	0	.864
Oliveras, Salem	1	1	1	1	1	.667
Ryczek, Peninsula	1	0	2	1	0	.667

THIRD BASEMEN

Player and Club	G.	PO.	A.	E.	DP.	Pct.
Oliveras, Salem	13	15	29	2	1	.957
Trevino, Lynchburg	14	17	23	2	2	.952
EVANS, Win.-Salem	120	97	264	20	19	.948
de Armas, Peninsula	12	8	25	2	1	.943
Gifford, Lynchburg	46	28	64	6	2	.939
Marshall, Salem	24	15	43	4	3	.935
Perez, Lynchburg	38	25	103	11	11	.921
Moreland, Peninsula	78	50	216	26	19	.911
Dean, Salem	96	79	175	26	15	.907
Garcia, Lynchburg	44	34	103	14	6	.907
Ryczek, Peninsula	14	10	29	4	2	.907
Brown, Peninsula	39	30	76	14	7	.883
Coletta, Win.-Salem	18	15	34	8	5	.860

(Fewer Than Ten Games)

Player and Club	G.	PO.	A.	E.	DP.	Pct.
Minaya, Lynchburg	5	10	16	0	3	1.000
Shankle, Win.-Salem	3	1	6	0	0	1.000
DeMeo, Peninsula	3	0	4	0	0	1.000
Ysursa, Peninsula	2	1	2	0	0	1.000
McCormack, Peninsula	3	0	2	0	0	1.000
Fisher, Win.-Salem	1	1	0	0	0	1.000
Gerlecz, Salem	9	5	10	2	0	.882
Raco, Salem	3	2	5	1	0	.875
Jones, Lynchburg	1	1	2	1	0	.750
Tyler, Win.-Salem	1	1	2	1	0	.750

SHORTSTOPS

Player and Club	G.	PO.	A.	E.	DP.	Pct.
Fisher, Win.-Salem	13	16	36	2	4	.963
Perez, Lynchburg	55	75	140	13	26	.943
RYCZEK, Peninsula	107	138	360	35	41	.934
DelCarmen, Pen.	35	40	95	10	19	.931
Ysursa, Peninsula	10	9	31	3	1	.930
DeLiza, Salem	138	199	388	54	62	.916
Jones, Lynchburg	26	33	59	9	14	.911
Jurak, Win.-Salem	113	168	346	55	58	.903
Dyer, Lynchburg	56	82	148	25	30	.902

(Fewer Than Ten Games)

Player and Club	G.	PO.	A.	E.	DP.	Pct.
Minaya, Lynchburg	4	7	20	0	1	1.000
Evans, Win.-Salem	3	3	9	0	1	1.000
Moreland, Peninsula	1	0	5	0	0	1.000
Marshall, Salem	1	1	2	0	1	1.000
Tyler, Win.-Salem	9	10	27	3	4	.925
Garcia, Lynchburg	9	8	11	3	1	.864
Trevino, Lynchburg	6	5	20	4	1	.862
Coletta, Win.-Salem	1	1	5	1	2	.857
Gifford, Lynchburg	3	0	8	2	0	.800

OUTFIELDERS

Player and Club	G.	PO.	A.	E.	DP.	Pct.	Player and Club	G.	PO.	A.	E.	DP.	Pct.
Bryant, Lynchburg	49	104	4	0	2	1.000	Nelson, Salem*	115	215	16	8	5	.967
Marshall, Salem	22	49	5	0	0	1.000	Coletta, Win.-Salem	65	100	13	4	2	.966
Skalisky, Peninsula	14	30	2	0	1	1.000	Morello, Win.-Salem	31	50	3	2	1	.964
Greenstein, Lynch	13	16	2	0	0	1.000	Geigel, Peninsula*	93	118	6	5	0	.961
Lebron, Salem	10	13	1	0	0	1.000	Smoak, Peninsula	126	267	6	12	2	.958
Black, Peninsula*	52	92	5	1	0	.990	Gerlecz, Salem	22	23	0	1	0	.958
Littleton, Salem	80	164	8	2	1	.989	Covert, Lynchburg*	73	128	5	6	1	.957
DELGADO, Win.-S.*	121	241	11	3	5	.988	Guarnaccia, Pen.*	56	84	6	4	2	.957
Brown, Peninsula	41	63	2	1	1	.985	Yearby, Peninsula	80	98	4	5	0	.953
Rodriguez, Salem	34	57	1	1	0	.983	Bernazard, Salem*	85	100	10	6	1	.948
McClure, Win.-Salem*	39	52	1	1	0	.981	Yost, Lynchburg	107	192	5	12	1	.943
Huizenga, Win.-Salem	118	279	14	6	4	.980	Raco, Salem	50	74	5	5	0	.940
Contreras, Lynch.	113	230	10	7	1	.972	Pinkney, Win.-Salem	56	90	6	7	2	.932
Kesses, Lynchburg	70	118	6	4	1	.969	Olivares, Lynch.*	17	20	3	2	1	.920

(Fewer Than Ten Games)

Player and Club	G.	PO.	A.	E.	DP.	Pct.	Player and Club	G.	PO.	A.	E.	DP.	Pct.
Hough, Lynchburg	4	10	2	0	1	1.000	Cruz, Salem	1	1	0	0	0	1.000
Shankle, Win.-Salem	4	7	0	0	0	1.000	Grady, Lynchburg	1	1	0	0	0	1.000
LaTorre, Win.-Salem	6	5	0	0	0	1.000	Boyland, Salem*	7	6	0	1	0	.857
Oliveras, Salem	2	2	0	0	0	1.000	Garcia, Lynchburg	3	0	0	1	0	.000
Powers, Salem	3	2	0	0	0	1.000							

CATCHERS

Player and Club	G.	PO.	A.	E.	DP.	PB.	Pct.	Player and Club	G.	PO.	A.	E.	DP.	PB.	Pct.
Baker, Peninsula	35	199	17	0	4	2	1.000	DeMeo, Peninsula	22	82	11	1	4		.989
Hughes, Peninsula	20	105	12	0	2	5	1.000	Ortiz, Salem	67	460	46	6	4	9	.988
Patterson, Lynch.	7	26	2	0	1	3	1.000	McCormack, Pen.	75	389	46	7	7	10	.984
Oliveras, Salem	1	7	0	0	0		1.000	O'Berry, Win.-Salem.	110	608	59	13	10	11	.981
Hall, Salem	1	0	2	0	0		1.000	Lebron, Salem	38	274	22	6	0	9	.980
HOUGH, Lynchburg..	78	405	35	5	4	7	.989	Shankle, Win.-Salem.	39	209	20	5	1	7	.979
Marshall, Salem	44	236	23	3	5	3	.989	Trevino, Lynch.	68	366	67	12	8	18	.973

PITCHERS

Player and Club	G.	PO.	A.	E.	DP.	Pct.	Player and Club	G.	PO.	A.	E.	DP.	Pct.
MANDERBACH, Pen.*..	16	3	29	0	0	1.000	Johnston, Salem	33	4	8	1	3	.923
Wertz, Peninsula*	23	7	23	0	1	1.000	Waller, Win.-Salem	27	7	16	2	1	.920
Skalisky, Peninsula	22	7	20	0	1	1.000	Fowler, Peninsula	24	10	22	3	1	.914
Tudor, Win.-Salem*	25	6	15	0	0	1.000	Newcomer, Win.-Sal*	25	9	22	3	1	.912
Hernandez, Peninsula	24	3	16	0	1	1.000	Whitson, Salem	26	12	38	5	1	.909
Galante, Salem	22	2	16	0	0	1.000	Cummings, Lynchburg*	17	1	18	2	0	.905
Schneider, Pen.*	29	0	17	0	1	1.000	Thomas, Salem*	22	1	18	2	0	.905
Hall, Salem	15	5	9	0	1	1.000	Sander, Lynchburg	21	8	18	3	2	.897
Cross, Win.-Salem	13	3	8	0	0	1.000	Manos, Peninsula	51	3	23	3	0	.897
Bradford, Peninsula*	12	0	9	0	0	1.000	Herlihy, Win.-Salem	30	7	9	2	1	.889
Medina, Win.-Salem	12	3	6	0	0	1.000	Speck, Lynchburg	10	2	6	1	0	.889
Cruz, Lynchburg*	40	2	6	0	0	1.000	Breining, Salem	31	3	18	3	0	.875
Ciammachilli, Pen.	27	6	23	1	1	.967	Feola, Lynchburg*.	21	2	12	2	0	.875
Faust, Winston-Salem	32	11	32	2	2	.956	Holland, Salem*	39	2	12	2	0	.875
Powers, Salem	10	5	16	1	1	.955	Anthony, Salem*	12	5	15	3	0	.870
Harper, Lynchburg	37	7	11	1	1	.947	Davis, Salem	23	7	25	5	1	.865
Welch, Win.-Salem*	28	2	15	1	0	.944	Poole, Win.-Salem*	28	3	23	5	0	.839
Berenguer, Lynch.	28	4	29	2	4	.943	Gorgie, Lynchburg	16	7	12	4	0	.826
Saucier, Peninsula*	14	2	14	1	1	.941	Leonard, Lynchburg	13	2	7	2	0	.818
Driskill, Lynchburg	44	6	10	1	1	.941	Stone, Peninsula	24	2	10	3	0	.800
Bigos, Winston-Salem	28	17	26	3	3	.935	Pacella, Lynchburg	26	11	23	10	1	.773
Brandt, Salem*	21	0	24	2	1	.923	Moore, Winston-Salem ..	24	4	6	3	0	.769

(Fewer Than Ten Games)

Player and Club	G.	PO.	A.	E.	DP.	Pct.	Player and Club	G.	PO.	A.	E.	DP.	Pct.
Clark, Lynchburg	8	2	6	0	0	1.000	Tagliarino, Win.-Salem ..	2	0	1	0	0	1.000
Clites, Salem	4	0	3	0	0	1.000	Tapia, Salem	2	0	1	0	0	1.000
Taylor, Peninsula	6	0	3	0	0	1.000	Jackson, Lynchburg	7	3	11	1	0	.933
Hubal, Winston-Salem ..	2	1	1	0	1	1.000	Kavanagh, Salem	6	0	4	1	0	.800
Nelson, Salem*	2	0	1	0	0	1.000	Bell, Peninsula*	6	2	1	1	0	.750
Kreke, Salem	2	0	1	0	0	1.000							

The following players do not have any recorded accepted chances at the positions indicated; therefore, are not listed in the fielding averages for those particular positions: Kirkpatrick, p; Plante, of. Muriel, Peltier and Tarbell appeared as designated hitters/pinch hitters only.

OFFICIAL BASEBALL GUIDE

CLUB PITCHING

Club	G.	CG.	ShO.	Sv.	IP.	H.	R.	ER.	HR.	BB.	Int. BB.	HB.	SO.	WP.	Bk.	ERA.
Winston-Salem	137	44	16	24	1185	1101	529	411	56	421	13	26	767	70	7	3.12
Peninsula	137	35	10	23	1170	1056	523	407	61	487	33	39	723	85	13	3.13
Salem	138	44	8	20	1164	1122	581	455	72	499	16	31	932	42	12	3.52
Lynchburg	139	50	6	19	1187	1133	646	502	53	597	29	50	732	90	16	3.81

PITCHERS' RECORDS
(Leading Qualifiers for Earned-Run Average Leadership—112 or More Innings)
*Throws lefthanded.

Pitcher–Club	G.	GS.	CG.	ShO.	W.	L.	Sv.	Pct.	IP.	H.	R.	ER.	HR.	BB.	Int. BB.	HB.	SO.	WP.	ERA.
Manos, Peninsula	51	0	0	0	9	4	17	.692	116	67	24	15	5	31	11	1	86	7	1.16
Ciammachilli, Pen	27	13	5	0	13	6	2	.684	137	123	46	36	8	46	2	3	103	6	2.36
Newcomer, W-S*	25	24	13	4	14	6	0	.700	175	155	60	46	7	34	0	0	108	4	2.37
Faust, Win-Salem	32	13	6	1	11	5	1	.688	155	145	60	43	9	33	1	0	87	6	2.50
Whitson, Salem	26	26	16	2	15	9	0	.625	203	168	75	57	7	65	4	5	186	7	2.53
Fowler, Peninsula	24	24	11	4	15	7	0	.682	169	152	61	50	6	67	2	6	84	17	2.66
Poole, Win-Salem*	28	27	9	3	11	9	0	.550	187	161	71	58	6	75	1	6	136	12	2.79
Sander, Lynchburg	21	21	15	1	11	8	0	.579	168	145	66	56	8	65	5	0	108	3	3.00
Waller, Win-Salem	27	24	8	2	13	9	0	.591	160	155	83	54	9	53	0	5	127	6	3.04
Bigos, Win-Salem	28	19	3	2	10	6	1	.625	137	131	56	48	6	41	1	4	56	10	3.15

Departmental Leaders: G—Manos, 51; GS—Berenguer, 28; CG—Whitson, 16; ShO—Fowler, Newcomer, 4; W—Fowler, Whitson, 15; L—Davis, 14; Sv—Manos, 17; Pct.—Newcomer, .700; IP—Whitson, 203; H—Berenguer, 175; R—Pacella, 97; ER—Berenguer, 75; HR—Breining, 14; BB—Berenguer, 118; IBB—Manos, 11; HB—Berenguer, 13; SO—Whitson, 186; WP—Feola, Fowler, 17.

(All Pitchers—Listed Alphabetically)

Pitcher–Club	G.	GS.	CG.	ShO.	W.	L.	Sv.	Pct.	IP.	H.	R.	ER.	HR.	BB.	Int. BB.	HB.	SO.	WP.	ERA.
Anthony, Salem*	12	11	1	0	3	5	0	.375	63	54	33	28	6	30	0	0	39	2	4.00
Bell, Peninsula*	6	6	0	0	0	1	0	.000	25	32	16	12	6	14	0	0	10	5	5.76
Berenguer, Lynch	28	28	10	2	10	13	0	.435	187	175	89	75	4	118	2	13	114	12	3.61
Bigos, Win-Salem	28	19	3	2	10	6	1	.625	137	131	56	48	6	41	1	4	56	10	3.15
Bradford, Pen*	12	10	2	1	2	3	0	.400	56	62	33	25	3	21	1	4	24	3	4.02
Brandt, Salem*	21	20	3	0	10	7	0	.588	121	151	79	53	5	30	1	8	84	2	3.94
Breining, Salem	31	13	5	0	9	4	0	.692	127	127	70	49	14	58	0	4	106	6	3.47
Ciammachilli, Pen	27	13	5	0	13	6	2	.684	137	123	46	36	8	46	2	3	103	6	2.36
Clark, Lynchburg	8	8	1	0	1	3	0	.250	39	43	26	22	0	20	2	1	26	0	5.08
Clites, Salem	4	3	2	2	0	0	1	1.000	21	12	2	2	0	9	0	2	17	0	0.86
Cross, Win-Salem	13	2	0	0	0	2	0	.000	36	31	14	11	4	17	0	1	23	3	2.75
Cruz, Lynchburg*	40	0	0	0	2	4	4	.333	52	56	31	20	0	28	2	1	56	6	3.46
Cummings, Lynch*	17	17	3	0	4	6	0	.400	85	87	48	34	9	34	2	1	58	5	3.60
Davis, Win-Salem	23	20	7	0	5	14	0	.263	138	130	88	74	12	84	1	4	107	9	4.83
Driskill, Lynch	44	0	0	0	4	12	6	.250	70	70	29	19	3	31	3	5	46	8	2.44
Faust, Win-Salem	32	13	6	1	11	5	1	.688	155	145	60	43	9	33	1	0	87	6	2.50
Feola, Lynchburg*	21	3	1	0	1	3	0	.250	53	54	45	38	2	51	0	8	23	17	6.45
Fowler, Peninsula	24	24	11	4	15	7	0	.682	169	152	61	50	6	67	2	6	84	17	2.66
Galante, Salem	22	9	3	1	4	6	0	.400	96	97	46	43	7	41	1	3	92	3	4.03
Gorgie, Lynchburg	16	12	4	0	5	6	0	.455	91	113	65	48	6	25	1	1	65	5	4.75
Hall, Salem	15	10	2	0	1	7	0	.125	77	82	47	40	9	34	2	1	60	2	4.68
Harper, Lynchburg	37	2	0	0	6	8	3	.429	93	95	64	54	6	61	5	4	48	11	5.23
Herlihy, Win-Salem	30	0	0	0	2	2	11	.500	53	35	13	11	0	20	0	2	37	1	1.87
Hernandez, Pen	24	7	3	1	5	2	1	.714	93	85	30	23	3	26	2	1	59	5	2.23
Holland, Salem*	39	4	1	0	4	2	13	.667	76	59	32	25	1	45	2	2	72	1	2.96
Hubal, Win-Salem	2	0	0	0	0	1	0	.000	5	5	8	7	1	7	0	0	2	1	12.60
Jackson, Lynchburg	7	7	4	0	2	3	0	.400	55	51	26	21	2	15	3	1	19	1	3.44
Johnston, Salem	33	2	0	0	8	4	7	.667	72	54	20	16	2	23	0	1	63	3	2.00
Kavanagh, Salem	6	6	0	0	2	3	0	.400	28	33	18	14	3	16	1	0	18	2	4.50
Kirkpatrick, Pen	3	0	0	0	0	0	0	.000	5	4	3	3	3	0	0	1	5	0	5.40
Kreke, Salem	2	0	0	0	0	0	0	.000	3	3	1	1	1	1	0	0	3	2	1.50
Leonard, Lynchburg	13	5	2	0	4	2	0	.667	54	56	28	22	3	19	1	1	19	1	3.67
Manderbach, Pen*	16	14	6	2	5	9	0	.357	95	77	43	30	6	38	3	2	69	12	2.84
Manos, Peninsula	51	0	0	0	9	4	17	.692	116	67	24	15	5	31	11	1	86	7	1.16
Medina, Win-Salem	12	4	0	0	1	1	0	.500	39	38	39	32	2	31	3	0	26	8	7.38
Moore, Win-Salem	24	18	1	1	10	7	0	.588	96	101	63	46	6	60	1	6	51	11	4.31
Nelson, Salem*	2	0	0	0	0	0	0	.000	4	5	2	2	0	2	0	0	2	1	4.50
Newcomer, W-S*	25	24	13	4	14	6	0	.700	175	155	60	46	7	34	0	0	108	4	2.37
Pacella, Lynchburg	26	26	9	3	12	11	0	.522	185	151	97	67	5	83	2	9	119	14	3.26
Poole, Win-Salem*	28	27	9	3	11	9	0	.550	187	161	71	58	6	75	1	6	136	12	2.79
Powers, Salem	10	9	4	0	4	3	0	.571	65	63	23	17	2	24	2	1	42	1	2.35
Sander, Lynchburg	21	21	15	1	11	8	0	.579	168	145	66	56	8	65	5	0	108	3	3.00
Saucier, Pen*	14	14	3	0	5	3	0	.625	82	73	32	24	2	25	1	3	35	2	2.63
Schneider, Pen*	29	13	3	0	4	7	2	.364	103	103	48	45	6	46	6	3	77	6	3.93

Pitcher–Club	G.	GS.	CG.	ShO.	W.	L.	Sv.	Pct.	IP.	H.	R.	ER.	HR.	BB.	Int. BB.	HB.	SO.	WP.	ERA.
Skalisky, Pen	22	14	1	0	4	9	0	.308	91	92	57	44	6	46	1	4	51	4	4.35
Speck, Lynchburg	10	10	1	0	4	2	0	.667	55	37	32	26	5	47	1	5	31	7	4.25
Stone, Peninsula	24	6	0	0	3	5	1	.375	88	76	66	48	7	74	1	9	78	13	4.91
Tagliarino, W-S	2	0	0	0	0	0	0	.000	3	6	3	3	0	1	0	0	1	0	9.00
Tapia, Salem	2	0	0	0	0	1	0	.000	3	2	2	2	0	2	0	0	1	0	6.00
Taylor, Peninsula	6	1	0	0	0	0	0	.000	18	11	7	5	1	4	1	0	9	0	2.50
Thomas, Salem*	22	5	0	1	4	0	.200	65	82	43	32	3	35	2	0	40	1	4.43
Tudor, Win-Salem*	25	5	3	0	5	2	5	.714	82	77	26	25	2	28	1	0	76	2	2.74
Waller, Win-Salem	27	24	8	2	13	9	0	.591	160	155	83	54	9	53	0	5	127	6	3.04
Welch, Win-Salem*	28	1	1	0	3	7	6	.300	57	61	33	27	4	21	5	2	37	6	4.26
Wertz, Peninsula*	23	15	1	0	6	9	0	.400	92	99	54	43	3	46	2	3	37	5	4.21
Whitson, Salem	26	26	16	2	15	9	0	.625	203	168	75	57	7	65	4	5	186	7	2.53

BALKS—Schneider, 6; Holland, Pacella, Sander, 3 each; Berenguer, Driskill, Gorgie, Manos, Medina, Newcomer, Thomas, Waller, Wertz, 2 each; Anthony, Bigos, Brandt, Breining, Cruz, Galante, Hall, Harper, Hernandez, Jackson, Johnston, Leonard, Manderbach, Stone, Whitson, 1 each.

COMBINATION SHUTOUTS—Wertz-Hernandez, Saucier-Stone, Peninsula; Anthony-Johnston, Brandt-Holland, Galante-Johnston, Salem; Moore-Faust, Poole-Welch, Bigos-Tudor, Winston-Salem.

NO-HIT GAMES—Waller, Winston-Salem, defeated Charleston (Western Carolinas League), 4-1, May 25 (seven innings); Fowler, Peninsula, defeated Lynchburg, 3-0, July 18.

Florida State League

CLASS A

CHAMPIONSHIP WINNERS IN PREVIOUS YEARS

1919 – Sanford* .... .605	1946 – Orlando§ .... .681	1962 – Sarasota .... .689
Orlando* .... .703	1947 – St. Augustine .... .625	Fort Lauderdale† .... .623
1920 – Tampa .... .654	Gainesville (2nd)‡ ...... .584	1963 – Sarasota .... .645
Tampa .... .722	1948 – Orlando .... .643	Sarasota .... .667
1921 – Orlando .... .635	Daytona B'ch (2nd)‡ .... .616	1964 – Fort Lauderdale† ...... .629
1922 – St. Petersburg............. .503	1949 – Gainesville .... .635	St. Petersburg............. .594
St. Petersburg............. .618	St. Augustine (3rd)‡ .... .556	1965 – Fort Lauderdale .... .627
1923 – Orlando .... .667	1950 – Orlando .... .629	Fort Lauderdale .... .634
Orlando .... .678	DeLand (3rd)‡ .... .590	1966 – Leesburg† .... .781
1924 – Lakeland .... .695	1951 – DeLand§ .... .643	St. Petersburg............. .700
Lakeland .... .683	1952 – DeLand x .... .704	1967 – St. Petersburg y........ .691
1925 – St. Petersburg............. .667	Palatka (3rd)‡ .... .569	Orlando .... .638
Tampa† .... .696	1953 – Daytona Beach† .... .657	1968 – Miami .... .613
1926 – Sanford .... .647	DeLand .... .703	Orlando z .... .579
Sanford .... .623	1954 – Jacksonville Beach .... .629	1969 – Miami a .... .606
1927 – Orlando† .... .600	Lakeland† .... .594	Orlando .... .606
Miami .... .661	1955 – Orlando .... .671	1970 – Miami b .... .662
1928-35 – Did not operate.	Orlando .... .643	St. Petersburg............. .600
1936 – Gainesville .... .542	1956 – Cocoa .... .614	1971 – Miami b .... .667
St. Augustine (4th)† .... .492	Cocoa .... .671	Daytona Beach .... .586
1937 – Gainesville§............... .616	1957 – Palatka .... .629	1972 – Miami c .... .562
1938 – Leesburg .... .626	Tampa† .... .681	Daytona Beach .... .606
Gainesville (2nd)‡ ...... .615	1958 – St. Petersburg........... .732	1973 – St. Petersburg d .... .575
1939 – Sanford§ .... .787	St. Petersburg........... .681	West Palm Beach......... .580
1940 – Daytona Beach .... .619	1959 – Tampa .... .591	1974 – West Palm Beach d ..... .598
Orlando (4th)‡ .... .507	St. Petersburg†........... .612	Ft. Lauderdale .... .626
1941 – St. Augustine .... .659	1960 – Lakeland .... .731	1975 – St. Petersburg d .... .652
Leesburg (4th)‡ .... .488	Palatka† .... .614	Miami .... .581
1942-45 – Did not operate.	1961 – Tampa† .... .710	
	Sarasota .... .696	

*Split-season playoff abandoned after each team won three games. †Won split-season playoff. ‡Won four-club playoff. §Won championship and four-club playoff. xWon both halves of split season.

yLeague divided into Eastern and Western divisions with split season. St. Petersburg and Orlando won both halves of split season; St. Petersburg won playoff.

zLeague divided into Eastern and Western divisions. Miami won regular-season pennant on basis of highest won-lost percentage. Orlando won four-club playoff involving first two teams in each division.

aLeague divided into Southern and Central divisions. Miami won playoff between division leaders. (NOTE – Pennant awarded to playoff winner in 1936.)

bLeague divided into Eastern and Western divisions. Miami won regular-season pennant on basis of highest won-loss percentage, and also won four-club playoff involving first two teams in each division.

cLeague divided into Eastern and Western divisions. Won four-club playoff involving first two teams in each division.

dLeague divided into Northern and Southern divisions. Won four-club playoff involving first two teams in each division.

STANDING OF CLUBS AT CLOSE OF SEASON, AUGUST 28

NORTHERN DIVISION

Club	Tam.	Lak.	StP.	W.H.	Mia.	FtL.	WPB.	PB.	W.	L.	T.	Pct.	G.B.
Tampa (Reds)	....	18	20	17	4	5	4	8	76	60	0	.559	......
Lakeland (Tigers)	13	....	15	21	6	8	5	6	74	64	0	.536	3
St. Petersburg (Cardinals)	14	19	....	17	5	6	3	6	70	71	0	.496	8½
Winter Haven (Red Sox)	17	13	16	....	6	3	6	4	65	76	0	.461	13½

SOUTHERN DIVISION

Club	Tam.	Lak.	StP.	W.H.	Mia.	FtL.	WPB.	PB.	W.	L.	T.	Pct.	G.B.
Miami (Orioles)..................................	6	4	5	4	....	13	26	21	79	63	0	.556	......
Ft. Lauderdale (Yankees)	2	2	4	7	21	....	20	21	77	62	0	.554	½
West Palm Beach (Expos).............	6	5	7	4	8	14	....	19	63	79	0	.444	16
Pompano Beach (Cubs)	2	3	4	6	13	13	15	....	56	85	0	.397	22½

Major league affiliations in parentheses.

Playoffs—Lakeland defeated Miami, two games to none; Tampa defeated Ft. Lauderdale, two games to none. Lakeland defeated Tampa, two games to none.

Managers: Ft. Lauderdale—Michael Ferraro; Lakeland—Jim Leyland; Miami—Len Johnston; Pompano Beach—Jack Hiatt; St. Petersburg—Hal Lanier; Tampa—Ronald Brand; West Palm Beach—Gordon MacKenzie; Winter Haven—Rac Slider.

Regular-Season Attendance—Ft. Lauderdale, 52,290; Lakeland, 53,397; Miami, 42,672; Pompano Beach, 21,590; St. Petersburg, 70,128; Tampa, 104,021; West Palm Beach, 127,361; Winter Haven, 12,480. Total, 483,939. Playoffs, 5,848. No all-star game.

All-Star Team: 1B—Chism, Miami; 2B—Ireland, Pompano Beach; 3B—Whitaker, Lakeland; SS—Ramos, Ft. Lauderdale; Utility—Boras, St. Petersburg; OF—Michael, Lakeland; Edwards, Miami; Stenholm, Ft. Lauderdale; Koza, Winter Haven; C—Shippy, Lakeland; Ramos, West Palm Beach; P—Murphy, Lakeland; Mayo, Miami; Niemann, Ft. Lauderdale; Pekarcik, Tampa; Manager—Brand, Tampa.

(Compiled by Howe News Bureau, Chicago, Ill.)

CLUB BATTING

Club	G.	AB.	R.	OR.	H.	TB.	2B.	3B.	HR.	RBI.	SH.	SF.	BB.	Int. BB.	HP.	SO.	SB.	CS.	LOB.	Pct.
St. Petersburg ..	141	4413	550	570	1137	1447	170	28	28	471	59	48	487	33	33	589	57	26	1017	.258
Lakeland	138	4195	557	495	1060	1362	131	42	29	469	52	46	542	24	38	623	190	53	966	.253
Miami	142	4384	528	494	1101	1327	133	27	13	442	82	37	541	33	28	618	181	90	1002	.251
Ft. Lauderdale .	139	4365	527	504	1096	1466	167	34	45	453	49	36	444	25	51	605	102	59	972	.251
Winter Haven ..	141	4413	575	551	1084	1475	169	30	54	504	40	39	572	27	38	749	69	34	1044	.246
Pomp. Beach ..	141	4231	516	619	1001	1265	124	28	28	429	54	27	468	10	45	825	110	44	915	.237
W. Palm Beach	142	4275	484	522	990	1318	139	24	47	422	64	33	510	22	60	695	120	40	993	.232
Tampa	136	4107	429	411	951	1180	107	22	26	360	70	39	405	32	35	682	193	69	894	.232

INDIVIDUAL BATTING
(Leading Qualifiers for Batting Championship -383 or More Plate Appearances)
*Bats lefthanded.   †Switch-hitter.

Player and Club	G.	AB.	R.	H.	TB.	2B.	3B.	HR.	RBI.	SH.	SF.	BB.	HP.	SO.	SB.	CS.	Pct.
Smith, Bobby, Miami*	108	346	63	112	128	10	3	0	30	2	2	35	1	32	18	17	.324
Whitaker, Louis, Lakeland*	124	434	70	129	154	12	5	1	62	2	5	55	3	51	48	13	.297
Edwards, Marshall, Miami*	123	449	69	133	142	7	1	0	34	8	1	44	5	42	57	15	.296
Michael, William, Lakeland*	103	368	58	109	140	9	8	2	37	2	2	39	1	42	21	7	.296
Boras, Scott, St. Pete*	129	437	63	129	169	22	6	2	44	7	6	56	6	38	2	0	.295
Stapleton, David, Win Haven	118	400	67	115	144	13	2	4	38	5	4	53	6	33	12	6	.288
Chism, Thomas, Miami*	123	401	51	115	151	20	2	4	62	2	6	69	2	34	2	3	.287
Shippy, Gregory, Lakeland	108	356	47	102	147	21	0	8	60	1	3	37	5	39	3	1	.287
Koza, David, Winter Haven	137	502	67	141	219	22	1	18	83	0	6	35	5	67	0	2	.281
Chapman, Nathan, Ft. Laud*	120	430	58	120	151	19	3	2	35	6	0	37	1	40	18	15	.279
Weicker, George, Tampa	123	373	45	104	134	19	1	3	48	3	6	60	7	59	9	5	.279

Departmental Leaders: G—Randall, 140; AB—Koza, 502; R—Whitaker, 70; H—Koza, 141; TB—Koza, 219; 2B—Boras, Garcia, Koza, Mays, McAlister, Stenholm, 22; 3B—Michael, 8; HR—Koza, 18; RBI—Koza, 83; SH—Draimin, Jarquin, 13; SF—Stenholm, 10; BB—McAlister, 94; HP—Gingrich, 12; SO—Grandy, 127; SB—M. Edwards, 57; CS—B. Smith, 17.

(All Players—Listed Alphabetically)

Player and Club	G.	AB.	R.	H.	TB.	2B.	3B.	HR.	RBI.	SH.	SF.	BB.	HP.	SO.	SB.	CS.	Pct.
Anderson, J. William, Tampa	14	22	1	0	0	0	0	0	0	0	0	1	1	7	0	0	.000
Anderson, Michael D., PB	72	178	23	47	49	2	0	0	15	7	0	20	3	30	5	1	.264
Aponte, Luis, Winter Haven	1	0	1	0	0	0	0	0	0	0	0	0	0	0	0	0	.000
Bartell, Michael, Lakeland†	102	314	34	79	97	10	1	2	27	4	4	38	2	55	10	2	.252
Bashaw, Lawrence, St. Pete	57	13	1	1	1	0	0	0	1	0	0	0	5	0	0	.077
Bautista, Antonio, Ft. Laud	37	112	16	32	40	3	1	1	12	1	1	11	2	16	4	2	.286
Bengston, Richard, WPB	102	334	44	78	111	12	0	7	32	3	3	42	3	51	1	1	.234
Bertolotti, Fulvio, St.P.	19	39	2	8	8	0	0	0	1	0	0	3	1	7	0	0	.205
Bird, William R., Tampa†	108	313	34	64	78	9	1	1	26	5	5	27	5	34	4	7	.204
Bombard, Marc, Tampa	11	12	0	1	1	0	0	0	0	0	0	1	0	4	0	0	.083
Boras, Scott, St. Pete*	129	437	63	129	169	22	6	2	44	7	6	56	6	38	2	0	.295
Boyer, David, St. Pete	86	236	18	55	65	5	1	1	29	1	2	28	2	37	0	0	.233
Brummer, Glenn, St. Pete	113	367	41	96	112	14	1	0	41	2	2	26	6	40	5	2	.262
Bugden, Gerald, St. Pete*	10	11	0	0	0	0	0	0	0	1	0	0	0	2	0	0	.000
Caffrey, Martin, Ft. Laud	1	2	0	0	0	0	0	0	0	0	0	0	0	1	0	0	.000
Carter, Dwight, Lakeland	109	317	50	81	126	10	4	9	46	0	6	67	8	86	9	4	.256
Carter, Gregory, Lakeland	1	3	0	1	1	0	0	0	2	0	0	1	0	2	0	0	.333
Chapman, Nathan, Ft. Laud*	120	430	58	120	151	19	3	2	35	6	0	37	1	40	18	15	.279
Chism, Thomas, Miami*	123	401	51	115	151	20	2	4	62	2	6	69	2	34	2	3	.287
Cias, Darryll, Miami	52	156	16	25	30	3	1	0	14	1	2	16	0	34	2	2	.160
Cipolla, Mitchell, WPB	4	12	3	4	4	0	0	0	0	0	0	4	0	4	0	0	.333
Clarey, Douglas, St. Pete	3	8	0	3	3	0	0	0	1	0	0	1	0	1	0	0	.375
Clarke, William, Miami	136	490	48	131	153	14	4	0	63	7	7	51	0	34	11	11	.267
Combe, Geoffrey, Tampa	48	20	2	1	1	0	0	0	1	0	0	5	0	9	0	0	.050
Cook, Stephen, Miami	24	58	6	16	27	3	1	2	8	0	0	8	2	16	0	0	.276

Player and Club	G.	AB.	R.	H.	TB.	2B.	3B.	HR.	RBI.	SH.	SF.	BB.	HP.	SO.	SB.	CS.	Pct.
Corbett, Douglas, Tampa	45	7	0	0	0	0	0	0	0	1	0	0	1	0	0		.000
Crockett, Claude, St. Pete	111	286	47	83	114	16	3	3	32	1	0	35	4	47	5	3	.290
Cunningham, Mark, W Palm B	58	166	24	28	37	4	1	1	13	6	1	14	5	29	5	0	.169
Dahl, Gregory, Tampa	82	262	25	65	90	11	1	4	29	0	0	11	1	48	7	2	.248
Darichuk, Greg, Lakeland*	7	25	6	6	6	0	0	0	1	0	0	3	2	7	0	0	.240
Daves, William, St. Pete	9	22	2	8	8	0	0	0	3	0	0	2	0	2	0	0	.364
Davidson, Randall, Tampa	68	179	20	44	50	3	0	1	13	3	2	8	1	13	17	2	.246
Davis, Ronald, Pom Beach	1	2	0	0	0	0	0	0	0	0	0	0	0	2	0	0	.000
DeLeon, Luis, Winter Haven	91	266	30	47	59	6	3	0	15	4	2	26	5	59	5	1	.177
Diaz, Vicente, Lakeland	16	45	2	7	8	1	0	0	3	1	0	6	0	6	0	0	.156
Diering, Charles, St. Pete	42	153	24	32	37	3	1	0	6	1	0	15	1	24	4	0	.209
Donaghu, Raymond, St. Pete	31	10	2	1	1	0	0	0	0	1	0	0	0	7	0	0	.100
Draimin, Sheldon, Miami†	125	384	44	81	96	9	3	0	34	13	3	59	3	57	10	12	.211
Draper, James, Lakeland	73	209	20	39	50	4	2	1	21	6	0	30	0	24	1	1	.187
Drury, Kevin, Pompano Beach	116	414	43	100	113	11	1	0	34	6	2	24	2	36	14	5	.242
Dull, Timothy, Tampa	15	14	3	2	3	1	0	0	0	1	0	2	0	5	0	0	.143
Duval, Michael, Tampa*	120	402	46	91	102	5	3	0	26	6	1	27	2	60	39	10	.226
Edelen, Benny, St. Pete	17	29	4	10	13	1	1	0	1	1	0	0	0	2	0	0	.345
Edge, Evan, Tampa*	11	21	0	3	3	0	0	0	2	0	0	2	0	5	0	0	.143
Eduardo, Hector, St. Pete	15	7	0	0	0	0	0	0	0	0	0	0	0	1	0	0	.000
Edwards, John, Winter Haven	31	88	7	19	22	3	0	0	10	0	2	9	0	9	0	0	.216
Edwards, Marshall, Miami*	123	449	69	133	142	7	1	0	34	8	1	44	5	42	57	15	.296
Espino, Juan, Ft. Lauderdale	39	118	18	30	53	5	3	4	20	1	2	11	4	28	1	2	.254
Estevez, Bernardo, Ft. Laud	2	4	0	0	0	0	0	0	0	1	0	0	0	0	0	0	.000
Evans, Godfrey, WPB	109	338	29	78	82	4	0	0	30	7	3	30	4	45	9	2	.231
Figueroa, Jesus, Ft. Laud*	108	385	50	95	106	7	2	0	30	7	1	43	9	31	21	9	.247
Filkins, Leslie, Lakeland*	132	472	54	111	143	17	3	3	46	2	2	59	2	43	19	8	.235
Finch, Joel, Winter Haven	1	1	0	0	0	0	0	0	0	0	0	1	0	0	0	0	.000
Fitzgerald, Daniel Richard, Mia	75	217	17	39	47	5	0	1	20	4	3	21	1	57	2	1	.180
Flesh, Henry, Miami*	117	350	48	81	105	10	4	2	26	6	1	65	3	69	20	4	.231
Garboza, T. Antonio, WH*	75	236	35	52	92	7	3	9	33	2	1	34	6	78	1	0	.220
Garcia, Damaso, Ft. Laud	124	412	55	109	142	22	4	1	41	4	3	30	7	60	18	6	.265
Garrison, Venoy, Lakeland	130	409	53	106	139	15	6	2	51	4	5	49	6	55	17	6	.259
Gates, Eddie, W. Palm Beach	118	368	48	91	133	20	5	4	44	2	3	58	9	67	8	3	.247
Gavillan, Pedro, WPB	33	90	6	20	21	1	0	0	8	2	0	4	1	14	0	0	.222
Gingrich, Gary, WPB†	116	421	55	103	121	14	2	0	36	7	4	45	12	30	29	5	.245
Goodman, Bobbie, WPB	54	167	16	39	62	6	1	5	24	4	3	20	0	49	1	0	.234
Grandy, Eric, Pomp. Beach	138	418	62	101	141	11	7	5	45	4	4	67	9	127	15	4	.242
Gustavson, Duane, Pomp. Bch	74	234	34	61	80	8	4	1	29	1	3	26	2	39	2	0	.261
Hakala, Keith, Lakeland	2	3	0	0	0	0	0	0	0	0	0	2	0	1	0	0	.000
Hampton, Robert, Win Haven	118	411	39	106	146	17	4	5	51	2	3	20	0	78	0	3	.258
Harris, LaMart, WPB	62	188	10	40	48	6	1	0	4	3	0	9	4	37	11	2	.213
Harrison, Robert, St. Pete*	9	9	0	1	1	0	0	0	0	0	0	2	0	1	0	0	.111
Heath, Michael, Ft. Laud	80	267	28	71	99	16	3	2	30	4	0	13	1	43	0	2	.266
Helget, Dale, Winter Haven*	22	67	4	18	26	2	3	0	3	0	0	8	0	13	0	0	.269
Herman, Gregory, St. Pete*	1	1	0	0	0	0	0	0	0	0	0	0	0	0	0	0	.000
Hernandez, Joseph, Pom Bch	103	370	40	97	121	14	2	2	40	4	1	22	3	29	11	7	.262
Herr, Thomas, St. Pete†	82	275	47	74	82	6	1	0	21	5	6	42	3	18	12	3	.269
Hill, Ronald, Pomp. Beach	74	205	23	43	59	9	2	1	22	1	2	23	1	57	4	0	.210
Hogestyn, Donald, Ft. Laud	20	59	7	19	21	2	0	0	6	0	2	18	1	7	0	2	.322
Hoskin, Larry, Pomp. Beach*	11	36	1	5	6	1	0	0	4	0	0	6	0	8	1	0	.139
Houser, Brett, St. Pete	41	7	0	1	1	0	0	0	0	2	0	3	0	2	0	0	.143
Hughes, Stephen, Tampa	125	446	53	109	120	9	1	0	28	6	3	37	2	55	29	12	.244
Huntington, John, Tampa*	33	8	1	0	0	0	0	0	0	1	0	0	0	2	0	0	.000
Husband, Paul, St. Pete	35	76	10	20	27	4	0	1	13	0	0	3	0	8	0	0	.263
Ireland, Timothy, Pomp. Bch	126	402	56	98	123	10	3	3	39	7	4	63	8	60	17	10	.244
Jackson, Erskine, Miami	92	265	35	69	104	16	5	3	39	3	3	29	0	55	10	1	.260
Jackson, Melvin, Lakeland	134	437	63	106	118	8	2	0	37	12	9	52	0	53	48	3	.243
Jarquin, Gersan, Miami	92	284	33	69	77	8	0	0	24	13	0	24	7	24	10	6	.243
Jensen, Kelly, Tampa	2	5	0	0	0	0	0	0	0	0	0	0	0	3	0	0	.000
Johnson, Bryan, Pomp. Bch*	13	22	1	6	8	2	0	0	3	1	1	1	0	5	0	0	.273
Johnson, David M., St. Pete	22	35	2	5	5	0	0	0	4	0	0	3	0	11	1	1	.143
Johnson, Jerry D., St. Pete	3	3	0	0	0	0	0	0	0	0	0	0	0	0	0	0	.000
Keatley, Gregory, Pomp. Bch	61	200	28	43	65	4	0	6	30	0	1	26	3	56	3	1	.215
Kibbee, Thomas, Miami	1	0	1	0	0	0	0	0	0	0	0	0	0	0	0	0	.000
Koritko, Michael, Win Haven	53	195	39	61	84	10	2	3	28	1	0	17	0	23	6	1	.313
Koza, David, Winter Haven	137	502	67	141	219	22	1	18	83	0	6	35	5	67	0	2	.281
Krause, Guy, W. Palm Bch†	53	163	26	35	54	5	1	4	21	2	2	39	2	39	0	1	.215
Krenchicki, Wayne, Miami	133	459	38	109	125	14	1	0	35	6	6	36	0	46	25	11	.237
Krul, Herbert, Lakeland*	47	99	23	26	32	4	1	0	12	2	2	31	0	12	1	0	.263
Kuchar, Edward, Ft. Laud*	8	18	0	2	2	0	0	0	0	0	0	5	0	3	0	0	.111
Kuhnhoff, Donald, Miami	100	283	41	71	78	5	1	0	31	9	2	62	2	39	11	7	.251
Lake, Steven, Miami	1	1	0	1	1	0	0	0	0	0	0	0	0	0	0	0	1.000
Lamprecht, Randy, Win Hav*	35	95	13	27	30	3	0	0	18	3	3	28	1	17	0	1	.284
Lentine, James, St. Pete	113	389	58	107	131	14	2	2	58	2	3	48	5	63	6	1	.275

Player and Club	G.	AB.	R.	H.	TB.	2B.	3B.	HR.	RBI.	SH.	SF.	BB.	HP.	SO.	SB.	CS.	Pct.
Leyva, Nicholas, St. Pete	70	237	32	66	83	11	0	2	28	0	2	17	1	31	3	3	.278
Luis, Beban, Ft. Lauderdale	72	234	26	56	78	7	3	3	29	1	1	6	5	55	3	3	.239
Lyle, Donald, Tampa	100	312	33	90	131	14	3	7	42	9	2	21	3	49	11	5	.288
Lynch, Terrance, Lakeland	4	14	2	3	5	0	1	0	4	0	0	3	0	7	0	1	.214
MacQuarrie, David, WPB	3	1	1	0	0	0	0	0	0	0	0	0	0	0	0	0	.000
Martindale, Denzel, St. Pete	29	68	6	16	18	2	0	0	4	1	1	7	1	8	0	2	.235
Martinez, Ronald, Lakeland	80	204	17	33	41	4	2	0	16	7	5	18	6	48	3	3	.162
Mayer, Robert, Tampa†	1	1	0	0	0	0	0	0	0	0	0	0	0	0	0	0	.000
Mays, Henry, St. Petersburg	123	391	49	103	141	22	2	4	54	2	8	49	0	35	6	2	.263
McAlister, Richard, WH*	128	407	49	97	130	22	4	1	51	1	3	94	1	72	2	2	.238
McDonald, James, Ft. Laud*	129	448	51	104	149	19	4	6	40	4	1	56	1	58	7	3	.232
McMullen, Dale, W Palm B	120	410	41	89	140	18	3	9	46	5	4	41	4	78	6	4	.217
McPherson, George, Tampa*	16	25	4	3	3	0	0	0	1	0	0	5	0	10	4	0	.120
Meek, Stanley, St. Pete*	21	41	2	12	13	1	0	0	5	2	1	2	0	5	0	0	.293
Meyer, A. Theis, St. Pete	25	24	4	6	7	1	0	0	2	5	0	5	0	4	1	0	.250
Michael, William, Lakeland*	103	368	58	109	140	9	8	2	37	2	2	39	1	42	21	7	.296
Miles, Arthur, W Palm B*	122	407	49	101	130	12	4	3	35	7	3	52	1	56	21	13	.248
Moretto, Tony, Tampa*	76	218	16	53	60	7	0	0	11	3	1	27	0	45	9	4	.243
Narron, Jerry, Ft. Laud*	119	412	35	101	136	17	0	6	56	1	6	42	4	37	0	2	.245
O'Brien, Daniel, St. Pete	26	55	9	13	18	5	0	0	6	2	1	4	1	7	1	0	.236
Ormsby, B. Bancroft, WH	34	106	16	23	29	2	2	0	14	0	2	19	1	17	1	0	.217
Pagel, Karl, P Beach*	41	134	21	34	50	6	2	2	12	0	0	16	2	41	1	0	.254
Pastore, Frank, Tampa	21	23	1	1	1	0	0	0	0	4	0	1	0	10	0	0	.043
Pekarcik, Lawrence, Tampa	26	46	1	7	7	0	0	0	3	4	0	3	0	8	0	0	.152
Peoples, Charles, P Beach	48	138	12	31	35	4	0	0	10	2	0	6	1	27	0	0	.225
Perez, Benjamin, Ft. Laud	97	281	31	60	63	1	1	0	18	10	5	18	3	31	9	7	.214
Perez, Julio, W Palm B†	43	121	13	22	25	1	1	0	7	2	0	17	0	6	4	2	.182
Pettinger, Ronald, P Beach	22	61	4	8	9	1	0	0	3	0	0	7	0	13	0	0	.131
Phillips, Randolph, PB*	18	52	5	7	9	2	0	0	1	0	0	4	0	14	0	1	.135
Pisarkiewicz, Michael, St.P*	129	415	51	106	160	17	5	9	59	2	8	74	0	59	7	3	.255
Polonio, Ivan, Win Hav	1	0	1	0	0	0	0	0	0	0	0	0	0	0	0	0	.000
Purcell, Gary, Win Hav*	126	415	53	101	150	19	3	8	51	1	4	59	2	69	9	2	.243
Ramos, Domingo, Ft. Laud	103	328	34	79	96	11	3	0	29	5	1	36	2	41	1	1	.241
Ramos, Roberto, W Palm B	101	297	29	81	103	9	2	3	39	2	2	46	4	63	3	3	.273
Randall, Aaron, P Beach†	140	491	57	133	184	21	3	8	64	1	2	37	1	73	18	4	.271
Redd, Dexter, Lakeland*	130	440	56	115	147	15	7	1	40	9	3	41	3	79	10	4	.261
Reed, Steven, Tampa	13	19	0	1	1	0	0	0	1	3	1	0	0	9	0	0	.053
Replogle, Andrew, St. Pete	11	26	0	4	4	0	0	0	3	4	1	1	0	8	0	0	.154
Richter, Gary, Tampa	36	97	14	18	21	1	1	0	6	3	1	18	1	15	5	0	.186
Ritschel, Rickey, St. Pete	33	8	0	0	0	0	0	0	0	4	0	1	0	4	0	0	.000
Rivera, Ivan, Win Hav*	125	396	61	100	117	15	1	0	34	6	0	65	1	82	15	4	.253
Robinson, Randall, Miami*	18	41	3	10	11	1	0	0	4	1	0	8	0	18	0	0	.244
Rose, Edwin, Winter Haven	118	413	52	102	126	16	1	2	36	8	4	40	2	51	11	9	.247
Rosinski, Brian, P Beach	32	123	12	32	40	4	2	0	21	1	0	13	1	36	3	0	.260
Schmidt, David, Win Hav	69	217	29	48	68	8	0	4	28	3	4	30	6	31	6	1	.221
Seibert, Kurt, P Beach†	58	178	29	47	51	2	1	0	12	3	2	31	1	25	4	3	.264
Shankle, James, Win Hav	3	13	0	2	3	1	0	0	1	0	0	0	0	2	0	0	.154
Shartzer, Steven, St. Pete	102	334	36	85	100	13	1	0	28	4	4	11	0	33	1	1	.254
Shippy, Gregory, Lakeland	108	356	47	102	147	21	0	8	60	1	3	37	5	39	3	1	.287
Smith, Bobby G., Miami*	108	346	63	112	128	10	3	0	30	2	2	35	1	32	18	17	.324
Smith, Garry, Ft. Laud	16	52	11	21	33	7	1	1	6	0	1	4	2	8	0	0	.404
Smith, Randy, St. Pete	1	1	0	0	0	0	0	0	0	0	0	0	0	0	0	0	.000
Sorey, Ronald, W Palm B	22	80	8	21	32	5	0	2	9	0	0	11	4	19	5	1	.263
Soto, Mario, Tampa	26	45	1	4	5	1	0	0	0	5	0	3	0	17	0	0	.089
Spilman, W. Harry, Tampa*	118	361	50	90	130	12	5	6	35	3	3	65	4	48	6	8	.249
Staggs, Ronald, W Palm B*	25	77	9	13	21	2	0	2	6	0	0	11	2	17	0	0	.169
Stapleton, David, Win Hav	118	400	67	115	144	13	2	4	38	5	4	53	3	32	12	6	.288
Stenholm, Richard, Ft. Laud*	108	365	51	100	173	22	3	15	71	0	10	59	3	64	1	1	.274
Stephenson, Kevin, Win Hav	1	1	0	0	0	0	0	0	0	0	0	0	0	0	0	0	.000
Stewart, Willis, P Beach	89	200	20	41	43	2	0	0	11	6	2	23	2	61	5	3	.205
Stitzinger, Gregory, PB	78	238	30	50	60	8	1	0	27	4	3	30	4	56	6	3	.210
Stone, Michael, St. Pete	26	60	5	17	26	3	0	2	7	0	0	9	1	14	0	0	.283
Strelitz, Leonard, St. Pete	24	40	4	5	7	2	0	0	3	2	0	7	0	8	0	0	.125
Styles, Marlon, Tampa*	71	182	15	40	54	3	1	3	21	2	2	34	2	48	7	4	.220
Thomas, Randall, St. Pete	17	46	2	6	6	0	0	0	2	0	0	3	0	14	0	0	.130
Thompson, Lloyd, W Palm B	26	80	9	16	16	0	0	0	2	3	0	12	2	11	2	1	.200
Tisdale, Freddie, St. Pete*	55	166	17	46	64	4	2	2	16	0	2	6	0	17	1	2	.277
Travis, James, P Beach	61	136	15	17	19	2	0	0	7	5	0	23	1	31	1	2	.125
Upshaw, Willie, Ft. Laud*	84	263	20	60	75	6	0	3	22	3	1	28	5	31	6	2	.228
Valdez, Julio, Win Hav	76	185	12	25	30	3	1	0	10	4	1	34	2	48	1	2	.135
Villa, Joseph, Miami	78	201	15	39	52	8	1	1	17	7	1	13	2	61	3	0	.194
Walker, Duane, Tampa*	29	91	9	19	20	1	0	0	3	1	0	7	0	19	17	4	.209
Waller, Reginald, Tampa	112	328	30	80	88	6	1	0	40	4	5	25	5	55	23	3	.244
Waters, Darnell, Ft. Laud	65	171	34	37	49	3	3	1	8	1	1	27	1	47	13	2	.216
Watkins, Thomas, Tampa	90	277	25	61	77	5	4	1	24	3	5	18	1	45	6	3	.220

Player and Club	G.	AB.	R.	H.	TB.	2B.	3B.	HR.	RBI.	SH.	SF.	BB.	HP.	SO.	SB.	CS.	Pct.
Weicker, George, Tampa	123	373	45	104	144	19	1	3	48	3	8	60	7	59	9	5	.279
Welsh, William, W Palm B	110	294	32	66	86	11	3	1	26	8	2	44	3	39	13	2	.224
Westlake, Claiborne, WPB*	42	150	9	42	63	6	0	5	32	0	3	5	0	23	0	0	.280
Whitaker, Louis, Lakeland*	124	434	70	129	154	12	5	1	62	2	5	55	3	51	48	13	.297
Wiencek, Gary, Lakeland	21	46	1	7	8	1	0	0	4	0	0	11	0	13	0	0	.152
Witt, Harold, St. Pete	32	87	12	18	22	4	0	0	4	2	0	25	1	26	2	3	.207
Wood, W. Christopher, WPB	32	111	15	23	29	3	0	1	8	1	0	6	0	18	2	0	.207
Wright, Dave, Fort Laud	1	4	0	0	0	0	0	0	0	0	0	0	0	3	0	0	.000

The following pitchers had no plate appearances primarily through use of designated hitters, listed alphabetically, games in parentheses.

FORT LAUDERDALE—Alcantara, Jose (22); Curnal, James (13); Delgatti, Scott (2); Diehl, Gregory (29); Fleshman, Richard (12); Kruppa, Kenneth* (23); Lewis, Timothy* (14); Lysgaard, James (15); Melvin, Douglas (22); Niemann, Randy (25); Robles, Julio (6); Slagle, Roger (14); Trotter, Joseph* (5).

LAKELAND—Alonso, Julio* (16); Baker, Steven (19); Brewer, Donald (1); Burns, Michael (1); Burnside, Sheldon (10); Dinkelmeyer, John (22); Elders, Michael (15); Grafton, Garry (22); Graves, Lary (12); Halstead, David (13); Harris, Frank (7); McManus, Dana (35); Mercier, Ronald (21); Murphy, John* (24); Murray, James* (5); Reinke, Jeffrey* (16); Taylor, James M.* (16); Tobik, David (6); Treuel, Ralph (8); Underwood, Patrick* (12); Young, Kip (10).

MIAMI—Bird, William D. (24); Broomis, Gregory (35); Brown, Michael T. (11); Chevez, Antonio (13); Curry, William (4); Mayo, Ricky (25); Parrott, Michael (5); Reimann, Richard (18); Rineer, Jeffrey* (33); Smith, Bryn (23); Snyder, Vernon (2); Stewart, Samuel (23); Walker, Robert H. (9).

POMPANO BEACH—Barreto, Miguel (17); Baumgardner, Frank (44); Dimick, Raymond (24); Faley, J. David (40); Ledbetter, Charles (25); Lucchesi, Jeffrey* (26); Martone, Fredrick (9); Moore, Michael D. (7); Reilly, William (5); Riley, George* (20); Smith, Lee (26); Taylor, Michael (24); Von Ahnen, William* (33).

TAMPA—Ferrara, Salvatore (5); Lear, Rickey (6); Ortiz, J. Antonio* (4); Sanchez, Luis M. (2); Winkelbauer, Thomas (4).

WEST PALM BEACH—Bastian, Jose (9); Dues, Hal (24); Ewell, Mark (5); Finlayson, Michael (22); Gerdes, Robert (19); Hanna, Donald (3); Hill, William (14); Horn, Larry (25); Horstmann, Gary (8); Lindell, Richard (8); Ratzer, Stephen (57); Schatzeder, Daniel* (12); Tenenini, Robert (43).

WINTER HAVEN—Agosto, Juan* (28); Burke, Steven (27); Caldera, V. Jose† (24); Hardeman, W. Gary (27); Nuss, Edward (19); Remmerswaal, Wilhelmus (39); Smithson, B. Mike (11); Suter, W. Burke (8).

GRAND SLAM HOME RUNS—Gates, Hampton, Keatley, Krause, Miles, Wood, 1 each.

AWARDED FIRST BASE ON INTERFERENCE—Hoskin (Shippy), Randall (Narron), Stenholm (Villa), Stewart (Espino), Upshaw (Villa).

CLUB FIELDING

Club	G.	PO.	A.	E.	DP.	PB.	Pct.	Club	G.	PO.	A.	E.	DP.	PB.	Pct.
Tampa	136	3449	1453	162	101	27	.967	Lakeland	138	3366	1412	189	109	15	.962
Miami	142	3560	1653	195	116	31	.964	West Palm Beach	142	3447	1373	192	104	27	.962
St. Petersburg	141	3474	1409	183	96	15	.964	Winter Haven	141	3459	1624	216	118	29	.959
Ft. Lauderdale	139	3466	1478	191	136	23	.963	Pompano Beach	141	3379	1364	209	122	38	.958

Triple Plays—Pompano Beach 2, Tampa 1, Lakeland 1.

INDIVIDUAL FIELDING

*Throws lefthanded

FIRST BASEMEN

Player and Club	G.	PO.	A.	E.	DP.	Pct.	Player and Club	G.	PO.	A.	E.	DP.	Pct.
Robinson, Miami*	15	118	11	0	9	1.000	Chism, Miami*	110	1063	94	16	79	.986
Boyer, St. Pete	14	106	8	0	12	1.000	Krause, WPB	25	209	10	3	15	.986
Goodman, WPB	10	79	7	0	6	1.000	Spilman, Tampa	112	986	70	16	73	.985
Hoskin, PB*	8	59	7	0	6	1.000	McDonald, Ft. L*	128	1127	63	19	114	.984
Westlake, WPB	6	42	8	0	6	1.000	Randall, PB*	124	1003	73	18	95	.984
Darichuk, Lake*	5	42	1	0	3	1.000	Hill, P Beach	11	59	2	1	4	.984
Stapleton, WH	5	30	2	0	2	1.000	McAlister, WH	90	792	74	15	69	.983
Koritko, WH	2	20	0	0	2	1.000	Pisarkiewicz, St.P*	125	1024	67	20	77	.982
Krul, Lakeland	1	8	1	0	0	1.000	Flesh, Miami*	17	142	15	4	15	.975
Bird, Tampa	3	8	1	0	0	1.000	Staggs, WPB*	15	137	11	4	11	.974
Watkins, Tampa	1	4	0	0	0	1.000	Thompson, WPB	4	30	2	1	1	.970
Dahl, Tampa	2	4	0	0	0	1.000	Shartzer, St. Pete	6	53	6	2	2	.967
Welsh, WPB	1	3	0	0	0	1.000	Gustavson, PB	4	24	3	1	1	.964
Bengston, WPB	89	749	50	7	54	.991	Pettinger, PB	4	24	1	1	3	.962
Weicker, Tampa	29	204	13	2	14	.991	Bartell, Lake	3	22	1	1	3	.958
Narron, Ft. Laud	13	103	5	1	10	.991	Cias, Miami	2	12	0	1	3	.923
GARRISON, Lake	130	1137	55	15	87	.988	B. G. Smith, Mia*	3	14	0	2	1	.875
Garboza, WH	51	483	41	7	32	.987							

Triple Plays—Randall 2; Garrison, Spilman, 1 each.

SECOND BASEMEN

Player and Club	G.	PO.	A.	E.	DP.	Pct.	Player and Club	G.	PO.	A.	E.	DP.	Pct.
Ormsby, Win Hav	1	1	4	0	1	1.000	Hogestyn, Ft.L	10	18	20	1	4	.974
Stapleton, WH	33		64	100	3	14	.982	Richter, Tampa	24	52	58	3	12	.973
Evans, WPB	12	20	31	1	5	.981	Herr, St. Pete	31	65	76	4	17	.972

SECOND BASEMEN—Continued

Player and Club	G.	PO.	A.	E.	DP.	Pct.
Cunningham, WPB	23	43	56	3	8	.971
GARCIA, Ft. Laud	124	273	353	21	83	.968
Drury, P Beach	35	66	87	5	18	.968
Davidson, Tampa	31	60	59	4	10	.967
Ireland, P Beach	115	252	309	20	64	.966
Watkins, Tampa	68	149	188	12	30	.966
Jarquin, Miami	46	97	126	8	23	.965
Rose, Win Hav	116	218	374	23	58	.963
Gingrich, WPB	49	105	140	10	30	.961
Tisdale, St. Pete	19	32	37	3	8	.958
Boras, St. Pete	66	134	162	14	26	.955
Draper, Lakeland	69	135	178	15	38	.954
Bartell, Lakeland	75	168	173	17	27	.953
Hughes, Tampa	29	51	68	6	16	.952
Martindale, St.P	5	7	12	1	2	.950
Kuhnhoff, Miami	90	187	236	28	44	.938
Witt, St. Pete	26	49	70	8	10	.937
Miles, WPB	64	127	149	19	29	.936
Perez, Ft. Laud	10	31	35	6	7	.917
Draimin, Miami	13	21	33	5	5	.915
Perez, WPB	2	1	4	1	0	.833

Triple Plays–Richter, Drury, Ireland.

THIRD BASEMEN

Player and Club	G.	PO.	A.	E.	DP.	Pct.
Kuhnhoff, Miami	4	0	8	0	1	1.000
Jarquin, Miami	3	3	2	0	0	1.000
Hampton, Win Hav	1	1	3	0	0	1.000
Martindale, St. P	3	2	2	0	0	1.000
Hughes, Tampa	2	2	1	0	0	1.000
Watkins, Tampa	4	2	0	0	0	1.000
Waters, Ft. Laud	1	1	0	0	0	1.000
Phillips, P Beach	2	1	0	0	0	1.000
Krenchicki, Miami	26	21	61	1	1	.988
Cunningham, WPB	34	20	59	2	3	.975
Bartell, Lake	10	11	17	1	2	.966
Koritko, Win Hav	27	23	55	3	4	.963
Hogestyn, Ft. Laud	11	11	13	1	2	.960
Bird, Tampa	49	46	86	7	7	.950
Leyva, St. Pete	36	26	65	5	1	.948
Kuchar, Ft. Laud	8	3	15	1	0	.947
Thompson, WPB	21	15	36	3	3	.944
Perez, WPB	29	23	42	4	4	.942
Stapleton, Win Hav	79	67	145	14	16	.938
Evans, WPB	44	40	50	6	5	.938
D. Carter, Lake	10	10	20	2	2	.938
Weicker, Tampa	84	69	153	15	10	.937
Bautista, Ft. Laud	33	26	40	5	5	.930
Boyer, St. Pete	52	27	98	10	6	.926
WHITAKER, Lake	123	99	267	30	30	.924
Draimin, Miami	112	82	216	25	15	.923
Richter, Tampa	10	6	18	2	0	.923
Perez, Ft. Laud	79	59	138	18	13	.916
Drury, P Beach	7	7	3	1	0	.909
Boras, St. Pete	50	27	83	12	7	.902
Heath, Ft. Laud	22	22	35	7	2	.891
Travis, P Beach	40	35	54	11	8	.890
Stitzinger, PB	72	51	103	21	5	.880
Bengston, WPB	14	13	16	4	0	.879
Dahl, Tampa	2	1	6	1	0	.875
Stewart, PB	31	29	42	12	1	.855
Krause, WPB	8	8	15	4	2	.852
Ormsby, Win Hav	17	8	31	8	2	.830
Jackson, Miami	1	2	2	1	0	.800
Valdez, Win Hav	21	4	25	9	3	.763
Garboza, Win Hav	11	3	13	5	2	.762
Cias, Miami	3	0	2	1	0	.667
Clarey, St. Pete	2	1	2	2	0	.600

Triple Plays–Weicker, Whitaker.

SHORTSTOPS

Player and Club	G.	PO.	A.	E.	DP.	Pct.
Hakala, Lakeland	1	0	2	0	0	1.000
Stapleton, Win Hav	1	0	1	0	0	1.000
Witt, St. Pete	1	1	0	0	0	1.000
Leyva, St. Pete	28	43	63	2	11	.981
Thomas, St. Pete	17	18	46	2	7	.970
KRENCHICKI, Miami	111	169	378	18	60	.968
Koritko, Win Hav	5	12	17	1	6	.967
Hughes, Tampa	99	131	298	18	44	.960
Drury, P Beach	81	123	212	15	48	.957
Perez, Ft. Laud	10	14	28	2	8	.955
Heath, Ft. Laud	26	47	72	6	18	.952
Martindale, St.P	20	22	37	3	8	.952
Evans, WPB	56	101	151	14	24	.947
Valdez, Win Hav	50	74	117	11	16	.946
Jarquin, Miami	37	61	123	12	21	.939
Seibert, PB	55	80	118	13	24	.938
Herr, St.P	51	68	135	14	18	.935
Ramos, Ft.L	103	150	343	35	57	.934
Ormsby, WH	11	15	27	3	2	.933
Gingrich, WPB	58	91	113	15	19	.932
Bird, Tam	47	67	113	14	22	.928
Diering, St.P	38	61	101	13	17	.926
Bartell, Lak	5	5	16	2	0	.913
Jackson, Lak	134	200	375	56	53	.911
DeLeon, WH	86	130	252	39	46	.907
Anderson, Tam	4	3	6	1	1	.900
Travis, PB	23	24	37	9	9	.871
Miles, WPB	33	49	95	23	17	.862
Thompson, WPB	2	2	4	1	0	.857
Estevez, Ft.L	2	3	4	2	1	.778

Triple Play–Seibert.

OUTFIELDERS

Player and Club	G.	PO.	A.	E.	DP.	Pct.
Cias, Mia	42	57	5	0	1	1.000
Stewart, PB	47	45	6	0	0	1.000
Sorey, WPB	16	27	4	0	2	1.000
Upshaw, Ft.L*	12	22	0	0	0	1.000
Ireland, PB	7	9	2	0	0	1.000
McPherson, Tam*	5	8	1	0	1	1.000
Gingrich, WPB	5	8	0	0	0	1.000
Stapleton, WH	1	3	0	0	0	1.000
Wright, Ft.L	1	3	0	0	0	1.000
Seibert, PB	1	2	0	0	0	1.000
Stitzinger, PB	2	2	0	0	0	1.000
Peoples, PB	1	1	0	0	0	1.000
Styles, Tam	1	1	0	0	0	1.000
HERNANDEZ, PB*	101	247	17	2	3	.992
Duval, Tam	114	216	12	2	4	.991
Filkins, Lak*	132	220	14	4	6	.983
Lyle, Tam	97	163	12	3	0	.983
Edwards, Mia*	117	240	14	5	1	.981
Welsh, WPB	106	195	10	4	2	.981
Harris, WPB	54	95	5	2	0	.980
Mays, St.P	115	246	7	6	0	.977
Figueroa, Ft.L*	108	226	11	6	3	.975
Krause, WPB	20	32	5	1	0	.974
Redd, Lak*	122	206	10	6	2	.973
Flesh, Mia*	94	131	13	4	5	.973
Anderson, PB	69	136	7	4	0	.973

OUTFIELDERS—Continued

Player and Club	G.	PO.	A.	E.	DP.	Pct.	Player and Club	G.	PO.	A.	E.	DP.	Pct.
Pagel, PB*	40	68	4	2	3	.973	Waters, Ft.L	43	65	1	3	0	.957
Purcell, WH	123	192	7	6	3	.971	McMullen, WPB	111	167	15	9	2	.953
Wood, WPB	19	30	2	1	0	.970	Walker, Tam*	25	36	5	2	0	.953
Cook, Mia	21	28	3	1	0	.969	Hampton, WH	112	152	17	10	3	.944
Shartzer, St.P	85	115	7	4	2	.968	Stenholm, Ft.L*	73	109	8	7	2	.944
Smith, Ft.L*	16	27	3	1	0	.968	Luis, Ft.L	62	98	4	6	2	.944
Chapman, Ft.L*	118	252	14	9	2	.967	Koritko, WH	20	31	2	2	2	.943
Watkins, Tam	19	28	1	1	0	.967	Miles, WPB	21	28	1	2	1	.935
Michael, Lak*	96	194	6	7	2	.966	Crockett, St.P	84	146	7	11	0	.933
Clarke, Mia	135	172	9	7	0	.963	Wiencek, Lak	16	14	0	1	0	.933
Moretto, Tam	67	122	9	5	2	.963	Jackson, Mia	26	48	3	4	2	.927
Martinez, Lak	73	146	6	6	2	.962	Rosinski, PB	30	48	3	4	0	.927
Koza, WH*	69	94	8	4	0	.962	Tisdale, St.P	27	34	3	3	1	.925
Husband, St.P	17	23	0	1	0	.958	Boyer, St.P	5	8	0	1	0	.889
Grandy, PB	134	210	14	10	3	.957	Randall, PB*	16	25	2	4	0	.871
Lentine, St.P	109	193	7	9	1	.957	B.G. Smith, Mia*	8	13	1	3	0	.824
Waller, Tam	106	169	7	8	3	.957	Hill, PB	1	1	0	1	0	.500
Rivera, WH*	112	174	2	8	0	.957	Jarquin, Mia	3	1	0	1	0	.500
Gates, WPB	92	145	9	7	0	.957	Anderson, Tam	5	0	0	1	0	.000

CATCHERS

Player and Club	G.	PO.	A.	E.	DP.	PB.	Pct.	Player and Club	G.	PO.	A.	E.	DP.	PB.	Pct.
Helget, WH	21	98	20	0	0	5	1.000	Espino, Ft.L	36	170	20	3	2	6	.984
Edge, Tam	7	35	3	0	0	2	1.000	Keatley, PB	41	189	22	4	3	6	.981
Cipolla, WPB	4	33	1	0	0	2	1.000	Krul, Lak	39	133	19	3	1	4	.981
Daves, St.P	8	29	2	0	0	0	1.000	McAlister, WH	12	49	4	1	1	2	.981
Johnson, PB	8	23	4	0	0	3	1.000	Styles, Tam	64	312	35	7	5	13	.980
Bengston, WPB	2	13	0	0	0	0	1.000	Hill, PB	26	121	16	3	2	4	.979
G. Carter, Lak	1	7	1	0	0	0	1.000	Peoples, PB	41	198	27	5	5	19	.978
Harrison, St.P	1	5	0	0	0	0	1.000	Schmidt, WH	64	329	33	10	3	7	.973
J. Johnson, St.P	2	3	1	0	0	0	1.000	Jackson, Mia	14	69	2	2	1	2	.973
Wiencek, Lak	2	4	0	0	0	0	1.000	Fitzgerald, Mia	75	365	36	12	4	16	.971
Garrison, Lak	1	1	0	0	0	0	1.000	Ramos, WPB	86	417	60	15	6	15	.970
Lamprecht, WH	31	162	21	1	3	9	.995	Dahl, Tam	74	326	45	12	3	11	.969
Stone, St.P	22	110	17	1	3	1	.992	Gustavson, PB	12	49	4	1	1	2	.969
Diaz, Lak	16	106	10	1	0	4	.991	Heath, Ft.L	18	74	14	3	3	7	.967
Gavillan, WPB	31	154	17	2	4	5	.988	Villa, Mia	76	334	48	14	5	13	.965
NARRON, FTL	92	460	51	7	7	10	.9864	Goodman, WPB	27	117	17	5	2	5	.964
Brummer, St.P	106	644	77	10	5	10	.9863	Bertolotti, St.P	18	82	9	4	0	4	.958
Edwards, WH	28	112	17	2	4	6	.985	Bird, Tam	1	0	0	0	0	1	.000
Shippy, Lak	91	449	47	8	5	7	.984								

Triple Play—Peoples.

PITCHERS

Player and Club	G.	PO.	A.	E.	DP.	Pct.	Player and Club	G.	PO.	A.	E.	DP.	Pct.
Kibbee, Mia	19	17	19	0	4	1.000	Parrott, Mia	5	0	3	0	0	1.000
D. Johnson, St.P*	22	5	23	0	2	1.000	Trotter, Ft.L*	5	0	3	0	0	1.000
Diehl, Ft.L	29	8	19	0	3	1.000	Lear, Tam	6	2	1	0	0	1.000
Chevez, Mia	13	8	16	0	0	1.000	Ferrara, Tam	5	0	2	0	0	1.000
Slagle, Ft.L	14	7	17	0	1	1.000	Moore, PB	7	0	2	0	0	1.000
Finlayson, WPB	22	13	11	0	0	1.000	Martone, PB*	9	0	2	0	1	1.000
Meek, St.P*	21	4	19	0	0	1.000	Flesh, Mia*	1	0	1	0	0	1.000
McManus, Lak	35	7	16	0	5	1.000	Snyder, Mia	2	0	1	0	0	1.000
Reed, Tam	13	2	16	0	1	1.000	Mayer, Tam*	4	0	1	0	0	1.000
Bombard, Tam*	11	6	11	0	1	1.000	Smith, St.P*	4	0	1	0	0	1.000
Smithson, WH	11	9	8	0	1	1.000	Treuel, Lak	8	1	0	0	0	1.000
Alonso, Lak*	16	2	13	0	1	1.000	Elders, Lak	15	0	1	0	0	1.000
Baker, Lak	19	3	12	0	1	1.000	Stewart, Mia	23	19	35	1	1	.982
Houser, St.P	41	7	8	0	0	1.000	O'Brien, St.P	24	9	29	1	0	.974
Young, Lak	10	6	7	0	1	1.000	Mercier, Lak	21	7	26	1	2	.971
Walker, Mia	9	3	8	0	0	1.000	Hardeman, WH	27	11	22	1	3	.971
Schatzeder, WPB*	10	1	10	0	0	1.000	Replogle, St.P	11	10	22	1	2	.970
Hill, WPB	14	3	7	0	1	1.000	Murphy, Lak*	24	3	29	1	0	.970
Halstead, Lak	13	0	9	0	1	1.000	Combe, Tam	47	11	17	1	2	.966
Caffrey, Ft.L	17	6	3	0	1	1.000	Tenenini, WPB	43	8	19	1	1	.964
Lewis, Ft.L*	14	2	6	0	1	1.000	Bashaw, St.P	57	6	21	1	2	.964
Ewell, WPB	5	2	4	0	0	1.000	Remmerswaal, WH	39	11	13	1	0	.960
Robles, Ft.L	6	2	4	0	0	1.000	Burnside, Lak*	10	5	18	1	1	.958
Horstmann, WPB	8	1	5	0	0	1.000	Ratzer, WPB	57	4	18	1	2	.957
Barreto, PB	17	2	4	0	1	1.000	Von Ahnen, PB*	33	6	15	1	2	.955
Ortiz, Tam*	4	2	2	0	0	1.000	Bird, Mia	24	17	21	2	0	.950
Delgatti, Ft.L	2	2	1	0	0	1.000	Mayo, Mia	25	22	34	3	0	.949
Curry, Mia	4	1	2	0	0	1.000	Niemann, Ft.L*	25	13	42	3	4	.948

PITCHERS—Continued

Player and Club	G.	PO.	A.	E.	DP.	Pct.	Player and Club	G.	PO.	A.	E.	DP.	Pct.
Gerdes, WPB	19	10	8	1	0	.947	Underwood, Lak*	12	0	15	2	1	.882
Faley, PB	40	6	12	1	0	.947	Dull, Tam	15	4	11	2	1	.882
Pekarcik, Tam	26	14	35	3	2	.942	Lucchesi, PB*	26	8	7	2	0	.882
Corbett, Tam	45	8	23	2	1	.939	Tobik, Lak	6	0	7	1	0	.875
Finch, WH	21	20	24	3	1	.936	Soto, Tam	26	12	22	5	1	.872
Alcantara, Ft.L	22	3	26	2	1	.935	Meyer, St.P	25	6	13	3	0	.864
Jensen, Tam	23	12	17	2	1	.935	Lindell, WPB	8	3	9	2	0	.857
Fleshman, Ft.L	12	5	9	1	0	.933	Curnal, Ft.L	13	5	7	2	0	.857
Polonio, WH	20	6	8	1	1	.933	Lysgaard, Ft.L	15	3	9	2	1	.857
Donaghu, St.P	30	4	10	1	1	.933	Bugden, St.P*	10	2	4	1	0	.857
MacQuarrie, WPB	21	7	20	2	0	.931	Grafton, Lak	22	2	4	1	1	.857
Stephenson, WH	26	14	25	3	2	.929	Melvin, Ft.L	22	13	28	7	1	.854
Huntington, Tam*	32	1	12	1	0	.929	Bastian, WPB	9	5	11	3	1	.842
B.N. Smith, Mia	23	12	26	3	2	.927	Caldera, WH*	24	7	12	4	1	.826
Harris, Lak	7	4	8	1	1	.923	Dimick, PB	24	8	10	4	1	.818
Horn, WPB	25	9	26	3	3	.921	Riley, PB*	20	11	29	10	2	.800
Rineer, Mia*	33	6	17	2	0	.920	Nuss, WH	19	7	9	4	0	.800
Agosto, WH*	28	6	28	3	1	.919	Dinkelmeyer, Lak	22	1	7	2	0	.800
Burke, WH	27	18	38	5	1	.918	Smith, PB	26	1	10	3	0	.786
Strelitz, St.P	24	11	22	3	0	.917	Baumgardner, PB	44	4	10	4	0	.778
Graves, Lak	12	2	9	1	1	.917	Suter, WH	8	4	6	3	1	.769
Taylor, Lak*	16	3	8	1	0	.917	Broomis, Mia	35	3	9	4	1	.750
Taylor, PB	24	12	20	3	1	.914	Hanna, WPB	3	2	1	1	1	.750
Wright, Ft.L	36	3	7	1	0	.909	Winkelbauer, Tam	4	1	2	1	0	.750
Davis, PB	18	14	25	4	1	.907	Reilly, PB	5	2	1	1	0	.750
Reimann, Mia	18	5	14	2	0	.905	Herman, St.P*	10	1	2	1	0	.750
Dues, WPB	24	18	29	5	3	.904	Reinke, Lak*	16	0	3	1	0	.750
Edelen, St.P	15	3	14	2	2	.895	Kruppa, Ft.L*	23	1	7	3	1	.727
Ritschel, St.P	33	3	14	2	0	.895	Brown, Mia	11	1	6	3	0	.700
Pastore, Tam	21	12	13	3	0	.893	Burns, Lak	1	0	1	1	0	.500
Aponte, WH	48	4	19	3	2	.885	Eduardo, St.P	15	0	0	2	0	.000
Ledbetter, PB	25	9	21	4	2	.882							

Triple Plays—Murphy, Davis.

The following players do not have any recorded accepted chances at the positions indicated; therefore, are not listed in the fielding averages for those particular positions: W. R. Bird, 2b-of-p; Brewer, p; Heath, p; Murray*, p; Sanchez, p; Waller, p. Lake, Lynch and Shankle appeared as designated hitters and/or pinch-hitters only.

CLUB PITCHING

Club	G.	CG.	ShO.	Sv.	IP.	H.	R.	ER.	HR.	BB.	Int. BB.	HB.	SO.	WP.	Bk.	ERA.
Tampa	136	43	17	21	1116	986	411	321	36	407	48	30	622	67	12	2.59
Miami	142	63	14	12	1187	1063	494	368	23	475	19	48	704	60	9	2.79
Ft. Lauderdale	139	52	14	17	1155	1063	504	381	37	448	29	46	639	49	11	2.97
West Palm Beach	142	49	14	12	1149	1052	522	391	40	450	12	30	676	55	12	3.06
Lakeland	138	42	19	19	1122	988	495	383	35	568	35	42	631	66	17	3.07
Winter Haven	141	36	8	20	1153	1066	551	428	18	498	21	44	723	87	10	3.34
St. Petersburg	141	28	10	21	1158	1105	570	446	49	510	29	42	802	73	10	3.47
Pompano Beach	141	48	8	12	1126	1097	619	493	32	613	13	46	589	88	12	3.94

PITCHERS' RECORDS

(Leading Qualifiers for Earned-Run Average Leadership—114 or More Innings)

*Throws lefthanded.

Pitcher—Club	G.	GS.	CG.	ShO.	W.	L.	Sv.	Pct.	IP.	H.	R.	ER.	HR.	BB.	Int. BB.	HB.	SO.	WP.	ERA.
Remmerswaal, WH	39	7	3	1	7	6	10	.538	119	94	40	23	1	40	3	3	118	6	1.74
Soto, Tam	26	25	13	3	13	7	0	.650	197	142	54	41	6	80	11	1	124	13	1.87
Pekarcik, Tam	26	26	12	8	14	7	0	.667	172	138	50	37	7	48	1	1	71	8	1.94
Dues, WPB	24	24	10	3	12	10	0	.545	162	120	57	37	5	69	1	2	114	9	2.06
Melvin, Ft.L	22	21	6	0	6	7	0	.462	142	137	61	38	2	55	4	7	48	8	2.41
Finlayson, WPB	22	20	14	2	10	8	0	.556	145	118	44	39	5	32	2	1	68	4	2.42
Stewart, Mia	23	22	12	2	12	8	0	.600	182	147	65	49	2	86	5	4	79	8	2.42
Murphy, Lak*	24	24	5	2	11	5	0	.688	157	149	50	43	1	80	0	3	58	1	2.46
Mayo, Mia	25	25	14	3	15	7	0	.682	180	164	64	50	3	69	1	11	99	6	2.50
Jensen, Tam	23	21	9	3	7	10	0	.412	131	114	47	37	6	53	6	3	96	4	2.54

Departmental Leaders: G—Bashaw, Ratzer, 57; GS—Pekarcik, 26; CG—Ledbetter, 16; ShO—Pekarcik, 8; W—Mayo, 15; L—Hardeman, Ledbetter, 13; Sv—Combe, 13; Pct.—Diehl, .733; IP—Soto, 197; H—Ledbetter, 184; R—Ledbetter, 78; ER—Ledbetter, 70; HR—O'Brien, 8; BB—Stewart, 86; IBB—Combe, McManus, 13; HB—Burke, Niemann, 14; SO—Soto, 124; WP—Von Ahnen, 19.

(All Pitchers—Listed Alphabetically)

Pitcher–Club	G.	GS.	CG.	ShO.	W.	L.	Sv.	Pct.	IP.	H.	R.	ER.	HR.	BB.	Int. BB.	HB.	SO.	WP.	ERA.
Agosto, WH*	28	13	3	0	5	11	0	.313	107	97	70	55	1	69	0	1	80	8	4.63
Alcantara, FtL	22	22	14	2	11	8	0	.579	162	144	54	46	2	48	3	8	86	4	2.56
Alonso, Lak*	16	4	2	0	4	5	4	.444	45	39	18	13	2	14	4	0	22	3	2.60
Aponte, WH	48	0	0	0	3	4	6	.429	78	83	42	30	0	23	6	3	45	11	3.46
Baker, Lak	19	17	5	2	5	4	0	.556	97	83	38	27	1	61	2	2	60	7	2.51
Barreto, PB	17	1	0	0	0	2	0	.000	29	32	14	10	2	18	0	1	13	2	3.10
Bashaw, StP	57	0	0	0	8	5	12	.615	79	60	22	11	1	27	5	2	54	1	1.25
Bastian, WPB	9	9	2	0	2	4	0	.333	60	55	33	22	3	19	0	2	27	2	3.30
Baumgardner, PB	44	2	1	0	5	8	5	.385	91	89	46	37	2	56	5	2	51	5	3.66
Bird, Mia	24	13	7	2	7	5	3	.583	117	122	48	35	1	27	0	4	74	2	2.69
Bird, Tam	1	0	0	0	0	0	0	.000	1	0	0	0	0	1	0	0	0	0	0.00
Bombard, Tam*	11	7	2	1	3	2	0	.600	51	48	17	13	2	15	3	1	31	2	2.29
Brewer, Lak	1	0	0	0	0	0	0	.000	3	2	2	2	1	0	0	0	2	0	6.00
Broomis, Mia	35	2	0	0	5	5	6	.500	68	58	23	14	1	17	1	0	46	3	1.85
Brown, Mia	11	7	0	0	2	4	0	.333	40	30	28	19	4	41	0	1	25	6	4.28
Bugden, StP*	10	6	1	0	1	4	0	.200	35	47	26	24	2	20	1	1	28	3	6.17
Burke, WH	27	25	9	2	10	10	0	.500	170	147	77	58	3	71	2	14	103	10	3.07
Burns, Lak	1	1	0	0	1	0	0	1.000	6	5	2	2	0	3	0	0	4	0	3.00
Burnside, Lak*	10	10	5	0	6	3	0	.667	76	61	30	22	2	25	1	4	54	1	2.61
Caffrey, FtL	17	1	0	0	2	1	0	.667	48	64	33	23	2	25	3	1	22	3	4.31
Caldera, WH*	24	3	0	0	3	3	0	.500	60	62	30	23	1	27	2	2	43	8	3.45
Chevez, Mia	13	13	6	1	9	2	0	.818	94	73	27	22	2	18	2	4	88	4	2.11
Combe, FtL	47	1	0	0	9	2	13	.818	102	78	31	24	1	39	13	2	63	5	2.12
Corbett, Tam	45	2	0	0	10	5	5	.667	85	86	25	21	1	22	6	4	37	5	2.22
Curnal, FtL	13	9	5	3	7	3	1	.700	72	52	29	22	1	43	2	1	56	2	2.75
Curry, Mia	4	0	0	0	0	0	0	.000	4	3	0	0	0	4	0	0	1	0	0.00
Davis, PB	18	17	12	1	8	8	0	.500	115	110	62	48	1	51	2	10	78	14	3.76
Delgatti, FtL	2	2	0	0	0	0	0	.000	7	5	3	3	0	4	0	0	3	1	3.86
Diehl, FtL	29	12	4	1	11	4	4	.733	112	110	47	36	4	15	0	2	51	2	2.89
Dimick, PB	24	8	1	0	1	3	1	.250	66	56	43	34	0	52	1	1	32	4	4.64
Dinkelmeyer, Lak	22	0	0	0	4	5	3	.444	38	32	23	17	3	18	3	0	41	1	4.03
Donaghu, StP	30	5	0	0	1	4	0	.200	64	64	39	35	3	34	0	4	40	8	4.92
Dues, WPB	24	24	10	3	12	10	0	.545	162	120	57	37	5	69	1	2	114	8	2.06
Dull, Tam	15	11	2	0	5	8	1	.385	65	75	42	33	4	17	3	3	29	4	4.57
Edelen, StP	15	12	5	0	5	6	0	.455	79	80	34	26	4	20	1	2	43	1	2.96
Eduardo, StP	15	3	0	0	1	2	0	.333	35	21	23	18	2	29	0	1	29	6	4.63
Elders, Lak	15	0	0	0	0	5	3	.000	26	33	18	9	1	5	1	0	17	0	3.12
Ewell, WPB	5	0	0	0	1	0	0	1.000	11	7	2	1	0	1	0	0	3	0	0.82
Faley, PB	40	13	5	1	7	8	2	.467	113	79	48	42	6	78	0	7	70	9	3.35
Ferrara, Tam	5	1	0	0	0	0	0	.000	13	14	9	7	0	9	1	1	9	2	4.85
Finch, WH	21	21	5	1	9	9	0	.500	125	125	59	45	3	41	3	1	66	10	3.24
Finlayson, WPB	22	20	14	2	10	8	0	.556	145	118	44	39	5	32	2	1	68	4	2.42
Flesh, Mia*	1	0	0	0	0	0	0	.000	1	1	0	0	0	1	0	0	1	0	0.00
Fleshman, FtL	12	6	4	1	6	3	0	.667	60	47	18	13	3	8	2	0	30	1	1.95
Gerdes, WPB	19	13	3	1	4	10	1	.286	104	106	50	37	5	40	2	3	82	7	3.20
Grafton, Lak	22	1	0	0	2	3	3	.400	39	25	16	14	0	31	1	5	26	4	3.23
Graves, Lak	12	5	0	0	0	4	0	.000	38	42	37	30	2	33	1	3	21	7	7.11
Halstead, Lak	13	4	1	0	2	4	1	.333	35	40	22	20	2	17	1	4	17	4	5.14
Hanna, WPB	3	3	0	0	0	1	0	.000	5	11	12	9	0	11	0	1	2	3	16.20
Hardeman, WH	27	16	1	1	2	13	0	.133	99	88	54	47	0	56	2	4	60	10	4.27
Harris, Lak	7	7	4	1	3	2	0	.600	43	32	19	12	2	11	0	1	30	0	2.51
Heath, FtL	1	0	0	0	0	0	0	.000	1	1	0	0	0	0	0	0	1	0	0.00
Herman, StP*	10	0	0	0	0	1	0	.000	14	17	11	6	1	7	2	2	8	2	3.86
Hill, WPB	14	9	1	0	1	7	0	.125	60	70	38	24	4	24	2	3	25	0	3.60
Horn, WPB	25	23	6	1	7	9	0	.438	148	132	71	56	6	73	0	5	85	9	3.41
Horstmann, WPB	8	0	0	0	0	1	0	.000	19	19	7	6	0	10	0	0	8	0	2.84
Houser, StP	41	1	0	0	5	2	5	.714	74	52	25	19	0	40	1	6	92	4	2.31
Huntington, Tam*	32	8	0	0	2	3	1	.400	72	65	32	25	2	43	1	1	44	7	3.13
Jensen, Tam	23	21	9	3	7	10	0	.412	131	114	47	37	6	53	6	3	96	4	2.54
D. Johnson, StP*	22	22	2	1	4	9	0	.308	117	115	59	50	5	78	2	3	78	8	3.85
Kibbee, Mia	19	14	6	1	5	7	1	.417	100	91	43	33	1	32	1	3	50	3	2.97
Kruppa, FtL*	23	0	0	0	3	5	2	.375	44	42	27	21	4	13	0	1	36	2	4.30
Lear, Tam	6	0	0	0	1	0	0	1.000	16	13	2	0	0	5	0	0	6	1	0.00
Ledbetter, PB	25	23	16	1	11	13	0	.458	169	184	78	70	2	48	1	2	87	6	3.73
Lewis, FtL*	14	10	1	0	3	4	0	.429	60	53	24	23	5	33	2	1	44	1	3.45
Lindell, WPB	8	1	0	0	3	4	0	.429	33	40	20	17	0	19	0	0	17	3	4.64
Lucchesi, PB*	26	8	1	0	3	6	2	.333	74	69	35	32	3	30	0	1	23	3	3.89
Lysgaard, FtL	15	15	2	1	4	7	0	.364	75	71	46	36	4	35	1	3	50	5	4.32
MacQuarrie, WPB	21	21	7	3	7	10	0	.412	133	109	63	51	4	79	0	5	94	11	3.45
Martone, PB*	9	0	0	0	1	0	0	.667	9	8	2	2	0	5	2	0	4	0	2.00
Mayer, Tam*	4	0	0	0	2	0	0	1.000	6	3	0	0	0	3	0	0	5	1	0.00
Mayo, Mia	25	25	14	3	15	7	0	.682	180	164	64	50	3	69	1	11	99	6	2.50
McManus, Lak	35	8	1	1	9	5	5	.643	99	100	38	30	4	45	13	5	59	8	2.73

Pitcher–Club	G	GS	CG	ShO	W	L	Sv	Pct.	IP	H	R	ER	HR	BB	Int. BB	HB	SO	WP	ERA
Meek, StP*	21	17	4	1	9	8	0	.529	121	99	48	37	5	48	1	4	81	6	2.75
Melvin, FtL	22	21	6	0	6	7	0	.462	142	137	61	38	2	55	4	7	48	8	2.41
Mercier, Lak	21	20	8	1	10	6	0	.625	128	105	50	42	3	51	5	8	70	7	2.95
Meyer, StP	25	14	2	1	8	6	2	.571	104	95	45	33	6	39	1	3	89	8	2.86
Moore, PB	7	0	0	0	1	0	0	1.000	10	6	0	0	0	4	1	2	2	0	0.00
Murphy, Lak*	24	24	5	2	11	5	0	.688	157	149	50	43	1	80	0	3	58	1	2.46
Murray, Lak*	5	0	0	0	0	0	0	.000	12	14	7	6	0	8	0	0	4	2	4.50
Niemann, FtL*	25	25	10	2	9	10	0	.474	190	173	74	60	3	73	6	14	79	11	2.84
Nuss, WH	19	18	3	0	6	7	0	.462	94	104	53	47	3	42	1	1	56	5	4.50
O'Brien, StP	24	23	6	1	11	7	0	.611	153	147	74	55	8	43	5	3	99	10	3.24
Ortiz, Tam*	4	0	0	0	1	0	0	1.000	11	16	11	10	1	4	0	0	3	1	8.18
Parrott, Mia	5	4	0	0	3	0	0	1.000	25	20	10	7	1	15	0	5	23	4	2.52
Pastore, Tam	21	19	2	0	5	7	0	.417	107	101	50	37	0	34	2	3	54	5	3.11
Pekarcik, Tam	26	26	12	8	14	7	0	.667	172	138	50	37	7	48	1	7	71	8	1.94
Polonio, WH	20	3	0	0	3	2	0	.600	52	49	31	28	3	41	0	2	24	7	4.85
Ratzer, WPB	57	1	0	0	8	8	5	.500	100	112	50	38	3	19	3	1	48	1	3.42
Reed, Tam	13	13	3	0	4	7	0	.364	69	71	30	26	5	21	1	3	40	3	3.39
Reilly, PB	5	2	1	0	1	0	0	1.000	24	21	12	10	0	12	0	2	12	1	3.75
Reimann, Mia	18	11	1	0	0	9	0	.000	76	92	50	42	1	34	1	4	34	4	4.97
Reinke, Lak*	16	1	0	0	2	4	0	.333	28	31	17	11	0	22	0	1	19	5	3.54
Remmerswaal, WH	39	7	3	1	7	6	10	.538	119	94	40	23	1	40	3	3	118	6	1.74
Replogle, StP	11	11	4	0	5	5	0	.500	77	68	40	30	1	37	2	0	55	3	3.51
Riley, PB*	20	19	6	3	7	10	1	.412	114	122	73	49	2	47	0	3	76	6	3.87
Rineer, Mia*	33	0	0	0	8	3	2	.727	72	62	32	21	2	35	3	2	33	6	2.63
Ritschel, StP	33	6	0	0	1	5	1	.167	66	89	50	44	4	38	7	2	30	5	6.00
Robles, FtL	6	3	0	0	1	3	0	.250	19	21	17	13	3	1?	0	2	4	1	6.16
Sanchez, Tam	2	1	0	0	0	2	0	.000	8	11	4	4	1	5	1	1	5	1	4.50
Schatzeder, WPB*	10	4	2		5	3	0	.625	64	49	29	19	2	20	0	2	49	3	2.67
Slagle, FtL	14	13	6	2	6	3	0	.667	96	86	36	24	1	35	2	3	70	4	2.25
B. N. Smith, Mia	23	22	14	2	10	10	0	.500	164	140	72	51	3	62	3	9	119	7	2.80
Smith, PB	26	18	2	1	4	8	0	.333	101	120	76	60	7	74	0	3	52	6	5.35
Smith, StP*	4	1	0	0	0	1	1	.000	9	7	7	7	1	3	0	2	8	3	7.00
Smithson, WH	11	10	2	0	4	3	1	.571	64	63	27	22	1	20	2	5	29	1	3.09
Snyder, Mia	2	1	0	0	0	1	0	.000	6	11	7	6	1	2	0	0	5	1	9.00
Soto, Tam	26	25	13	3	13	7	0	.650	197	142	54	41	6	80	11	1	124	13	1.87
Stephenson, WH	26	17	5	0	7	6	1	.538	124	107	51	39	2	54	0	5	47	6	2.83
Stewart, Mia	23	22	12	2	12	8	0	.600	182	147	65	49	2	86	5	4	79	8	2.42
Strelitz, StP	24	20	4	0	11	6	0	.647	134	136	67	51	6	47	1	7	68	5	3.43
Suter, WH	8	8	5	2	6	2	0	.750	61	47	17	11	0	14	0	3	52	5	1.62
Taylor, Lak*	16	8	0	0	2	3	0	.400	60	47	33	26	3	50	0	1	27	2	3.90
Taylor, PB	24	22	2	0	2	11	0	.154	127	114	76	57	6	69	0	5	53	13	4.04
Tenenini, WPB	43	2	1	0	3	4	6	.429	104	104	53	35	3	34	2	5	54	4	3.03
Tobik, Lak	6	5	4	2	3	1	0	.750	42	28	11	5	1	15	1	0	29	6	1.07
Treuel, Lak	8	3	0	0	1	0	0	.000	17	13	17	16	2	28	0	4	16	6	8.47
Trotter, FtL*	5	0	0	0	0	0	0	.000	10	14	15	9	2	9	1	1	9	1	8.10
Underwood, Lak*	12	12	5	3	6	2	0	.750	77	63	26	19	0	32	0	0	45	2	2.22
Von Ahnen, PB*	33	8	1	0	4	7	1	.364	83	87	54	42	1	69	1	7	36	19	4.55
Walker, Mia	9	8	3	0	3	2	0	.600	59	49	25	19	1	32	2	1	28	5	2.90
Waller, Tam	1	0	0	0	0	0	0	.000	1	2	1	1	0	0	0	0	0	0	9.00
Winkelbauer, Tam	4	1	0	0	0	1	0	.000	8	9	6	5	0	8	0	0	5	5	5.63
Wright, FtL	36	0	0	0	8	4	8	.667	59	43	21	14	1	39	3	2	50	3	2.14
Young, Lak	10	8	2	0	4	2	0	.667	55	44	21	17	4	18	2	1	30	0	2.78

BALKS: Soto, 6; Murphy, B. N. Smith, 4 each; Baker, Dues, Ledbetter, Martone, McManus, Nuss, Slagle, 3 each; Burnside, Curnal, Davis, Diehl, Faley, Gerdes, Graves, D. Johnson, Lindell, Meyer, O'Brien, Pastore, Stephenson, Stewart, Strelitz, 2 each; Agosto, Alcantara, Aponte, Bashaw, Bastian, Caffrey, Combe, Corbett, Dimick, Elders, Finlayson, Hanna, Hill, Horn, Huntington, Mayo, Meek, Melvin, Mercier, Niemann, Pekarcik, Reimann, Remmerswaal, Riley, Smithson, Suter, Taylor (Lak), Walker, 1 each.

COMBINATION SHUTOUTS—Lysgaard-Curnal, Lewis-Melvin, Ft. Lauderdale; Murphy-Grafton, Mercier-Grafton, Murphy-McManus, Underwood-Dinkelmeyer, Mercier-Taylor-McManus, Baker-Elders, Young-Alonso, Lakeland; Smith-Snyder, Chevez-Broomis, Mayo-Rineer, Miami; Smith-Faley, Pompano Beach; Replogle-Bashaw, Edelen-Bashaw, Meyer-Houser, O'Brien-Edelen, Meyer-Bashaw, Meek-Houser, St. Petersburg; Soto-Corbett, Pekarcik-Combe, Tampa; Dues-Ratzer 2, West Palm Beach; Finch-Aponte, Winter Haven.

NO-HIT GAMES—Harris, Lakeland, defeated St. Petersburg, 7-0, April 25; Riley, Pompano Beach, defeated Ft. Lauderdale, 10-0, July 11 (seven innings); Stewart, Miami, defeated Winter Haven, 1-0, July 20 (seven innings); Dues, West Palm Beach, defeated Pompano Beach, 2-0, August 1 (six innings); Kibbee, Miami, defeated Pompano Beach, 1-0, August 12 (seven innings—PERFECT).

Gulf States League

CLASS A

STANDING OF CLUBS AT CLOSE OF FIRST HALF, JULY 15

EASTERN DIVISION						WESTERN DIVISION					
Club	W.	L.	T.	Pct.	G.B.	Club	W.	L.	T.	Pct.	G.B.
Baton Rouge	25	17	0	.595	......	Corpus Christi	27	10	0	.730	......
Seguin	20	19	0	.513	3½	Victoria	25	16	0	.610	4
Beeville	11	33	0	.250	15	Rio Grande Valley	12	25	0	.324	15

STANDING OF CLUBS AT CLOSE OF SECOND HALF, AUGUST 28

EASTERN DIVISION						WESTERN DIVISION					
Club	W.	L.	T.	Pct.	G.B.	Club	W.	L.	T.	Pct.	G.B.
*Baton Rouge	18	10	0	.643	......	Corpus Christi	23	17	0	.575	......
Beeville	22	20	0	.524	3	Rio Grande Valley	20	15	0	.571	½
Seguin	9	29	0	.237	14	Victoria	18	19	0	.486	3½

*Baton Rouge withdrew from league, August 13.
Rio Grande Valley club represented Harlingen, Texas.
Forfeit—Seguin forfeited to Corpus Christi, August 24.
No club affilated with major league farm system.

Playoffs—Seguin defeated Beeville, two games to none, for Eastern Division title. Corpus Christi defeated Seguin, three games to none for League Championship.

Regular-Season Attendance—Baton Rouge, 42,133; Beeville, 12,580; Corpus Christi, 74,280; Rio Grande Valley, 15,996; Seguin, 10,106; Victoria, 16,886. Total, 171,981. No attendance figures available for playoffs.

Managers: Baton Rouge—Matt Batts; Beeville—Bob Leach; Corpus Christi—Leo Mazzone; Rio Grande Valley—Ted Uhlaender; Seguin—Jimmy Smith; Victoria—Kenny Richardson.

(Compiled by Buck Francis, League Statistician, Corpus Christi, Texas)

CLUB BATTING

Club	G.	AB.	R.	H.	TB.	2B.	3B.	HR.	RBI.	SH.	SF.	BB.	HP.	SO.	SB.	CS.	Pct.
Corpus Christi	77	2594	556	802	1200	142	32	64	471	29	34	370	8	329	92	36	.309
Victoria	78	2462	451	699	941	96	25	32	349	24	45	307	10	284	141	37	.284
Baton Rouge	70	2119	327	568	783	86	24	27	273	20	13	283	18	256	79	25	.268
Rio Grande Valley	72	2360	390	623	839	84	21	30	328	34	31	348	18	383	84	13	.264
Beeville	86	2728	433	712	949	111	18	30	347	15	33	394	15	455	96	28	.261
Seguin	77	2319	278	581	733	63	16	19	220	22	23	284	9	365	123	37	.251

INDIVIDUAL BATTING
(Leading Qualifiers for Batting Championship—216 or More Plate Appearances)
*Bats lefthanded.   †Switch-hitter.

Player and Club	G.	AB.	R.	H.	TB.	2B.	3B.	HR.	RBI.	SH.	SF.	BB.	HP.	SO.	SB.	Pct.
Krizmanich, Mike, CC*	64	264	65	102	147	23	8	2	47	5	3	37	2	12	15	.386
Rainey, Jim, CC.	54	248	57	89	123	9	2	7	57	2	7	40	3	22	9	.359
Wells, Greg, Beeville	81	320	63	114	153	17	5	4	78	3	4	33	3	35	9	.356
Moore, Calvin, Victoria	67	259	49	90	113	7	2	4	50	5	7	17	1	17	33	.347
Lollis, Ronald, CC	64	228	60	78	120	17	5	5	49	6	2	36	1	21	4	.342
Capehart, James, CC*	74	283	63	95	173	20	5	16	87	0	5	41	0	30	8	.336
Pagnotta, Michael, CC	62	251	57	83	129	16	3	8	59	3	6	20	1	10	3	.331
Lemmons, Jim, Beeville*	65	272	48	87	117	17	2	3	38	5	5	9	2	26	11	.320
Sinovich, Mark, CC	74	262	48	83	136	20	0	11	64	6	5	45	2	34	2	.317
Greene, Steven, Victoria†	76	282	77	89	109	11	3	1	23	4	0	50	0	40	62	.316

Departmental Leaders: G—Osofsky, 83; AB—Wells, 320; R—Greene, 77; H—Wells, 114; TB—Capehart, 173; 2B—Krizmanich, 23; 3B—Krizmanich, 8; HR—Capehart, 16; RBI—Capehart, 87; SH—Osofsky, 10; SF—Torres, 8; BB—Brockway, 56; HP—Buckner, 4; SO—Register, 64; SB—Greene, 62.

(All Players—Listed by Percentage)

Player and Club	G.	AB.	R.	H.	TB.	2B.	3B.	HR.	RBI.	SH.	SF.	BB.	HP.	SO.	SB.	Pct.
Gesquiere, Mark, RGV	18	2	1	1	1	0	0	0	0	0	0	0	0	1	0	.500
Leja, Robert, Bee*	14	7	0	3	3	0	0	0	0	0	0	3	0	0	0	.429
Krizmanich, Mike, CC*	64	264	65	102	147	23	8	2	47	5	3	37	2	12	15	.386

Player and Club	G.	AB.	R.	H.	TB.	2B.	3B.	HR.	RBI.	SH.	SF.	BB.	HP.	SO.	SB.	Pct.
Riddell, Steve, Seg	4	13	2	5	5	0	0	0	2	0	1	3	0	0	2	.385
Benson, Randy, BR	11	24	5	9	14	3	1	0	2	0	0	2	0	4	0	.375
Allen, Sterling, BR	42	155	27	57	84	8	2	5	24	1	0	5	1	15	9	.368
Rainey, Jim, CC	54	248	57	89	123	9	2	7	57	2	7	40	3	22	9	.359
Seid, Richard, Seg	24	87	10	31	39	5	0	1	16	2	1	6	0	4	2	.356
Wells, Gregory, Bee	81	320	63	114	153	17	5	4	78	3	4	33	3	35	9	.356
Taylor, Robert, BR	32	125	21	44	54	6	2	0	10	1	0	8	0	5	3	.352
Fogg, Kevin, BR	19	80	15	28	35	5	1	0	9	0	0	9	0	3	7	.350
Hill, Rickey, RGV	34	123	19	43	58	9	0	2	24	2	6	15	1	10	1	.350
Moore, Calvin, Vic	67	259	49	90	113	7	2	4	50	5	7	17	1	17	33	.347
Lollis, Ronald, CC	64	228	60	78	120	17	5	5	49	6	2	36	1	21	4	.342
Capehart, James, CC*	74	283	63	95	173	20	5	16	87	0	5	41	0	30	8	.336
Dunlap, Fred, BR	3	12	1	4	5	1	0	0	2	0	1	1	0	3	0	.333
Delgado, Juan, Bee†	3	9	0	3	4	1	0	0	2	0	0	2	0	3	0	.333
Daniels, Robert, Seg*	2	6	0	2	3	1	0	0	0	0	0	0	1	0	0	.333
Pagnotta, Michael, CC	62	251	57	83	129	16	3	8	59	3	6	20	1	10	3	.331
Lemmons, Jim, Bee*	65	272	48	87	117	17	2	3	38	5	5	9	2	26	11	.320
Sinovich, Mark, CC	74	262	48	83	136	20	0	11	64	6	5	45	2	34	2	.317
Greene, Steven, Vic†	76	282	77	89	109	11	3	1	23	4	0	50	0	40	62	.316
Osofsky, Alvin, Bee†	83	297	42	90	118	15	2	3	47	10	6	46	2	31	12	.303
Buckner, Richard, Bee	80	303	70	91	111	6	4	2	34	6	1	47	4	23	27	.300
Torres, Anthony, Vic	52	185	42	55	77	9	5	1	31	2	8	24	1	11	0	.297
Bonitto, Arturo, RGV	67	264	37	78	111	14	5	3	31	1	1	13	0	21	5	.295
Register, Jerome, Seg	71	261	30	77	104	5	2	6	43	0	2	29	1	64	22	.295
Fornash, Eugene, Seg	70	252	42	74	102	6	2	6	23	2	0	47	0	29	14	.294
Keenum, Larry, BR	48	184	20	54	72	7	1	3	25	4	2	13	2	5	2	.293
Holoubek, Rick, Vic	70	232	39	68	87	7	0	4	28	2	0	33	0	20	9	.293
McLish, John, RGV*	71	263	46	76	88	6	3	0	34	6	1	41	3	27	19	.289
Wallace, Curtis, BR	62	229	34	66	98	12	4	4	37	2	6	28	0	18	5	.288
Jacobs, David R., Seg	57	206	32	59	76	6	1	3	30	1	1	21	2	13	9	.286
Davis, John, Bee	13	49	5	14	21	1	0	2	14	1	0	6	0	7	0	.286
Hughes, Timothy, Seg	10	21	3	6	6	0	0	0	1	0	1	0	0	10	0	.286
Farrow, Willie, Seg†	11	7	1	2	2	0	0	0	2	0	0	2	0	3	0	.286
Ornest, Michael, Vic†	42	135	19	38	60	11	1	3	24	1	3	14	0	13	3	.281
Cole, Winston, BR	54	179	31	50	66	5	1	3	22	0	0	27	0	11	4	.279
Lair, Ronald, CC	55	179	33	50	69	4	0	5	18	2	1	29	0	28	6	.279
Hiller, Mark, CC†	72	276	65	77	96	10	3	1	40	3	3	45	0	34	6	.279
Lawrence, Stan, Seg*	67	251	38	70	83	7	3	0	14	0	1	39	0	22	30	.279
Pompa, Eliseo, RGV*	32	126	19	35	41	4	1	0	12	0	0	11	1	9	5	.278
James, Charles, Vic	76	274	56	76	111	9	4	6	39	3	3	26	3	13	10	.277
Hopkins, Gerald, BR-CC	49	161	25	44	59	5	2	2	11	6	1	21	1	28	10	.273
Gattis, James, Vic	73	284	35	77	114	14	1	7	46	1	4	12	1	26	5	.271
Thurman, Mike, Seg	12	37	4	10	15	1	2	0	6	0	1	8	0	6	3	.270
Uhlaender, Theodore, RGV*	25	89	15	24	34	2	1	2	13	1	0	11	0	6	2	.270
Gregory, Gaylord, RGV*	68	234	37	63	73	8	1	0	36	1	4	42	2	25	3	.269
Kennemur, Paul, BR	21	41	6	11	15	1	0	1	5	0	1	11	0	9	0	.268
Bratson, James, CC*	75	266	48	71	115	12	4	8	35	1	2	41	0	51	4	.267
Mitchell, G. Hunt, Bee†	28	75	16	20	25	3	1	0	7	0	0	22	0	7	8	.267
Barefoot, Jeffrey, RGV	19	60	7	16	20	1	0	1	11	0	2	12	0	5	3	.267
Kertes, John, Vic	17	60	6	16	20	4	0	0	10	0	3	4	1	8	1	.267
Wallace, Rhoderick, Vic*	73	260	44	69	102	13	4	4	32	0	4	43	0	31	10	.265
Miller, Mickey, BR	37	147	27	39	48	7	1	0	16	2	1	16	3	3	0	.265
Flores, Bobby, Seg.	20	79	8	21	26	3	1	0	8	1	1	1	9	2	.266
Brockway, Ricky, RGV	70	260	70	68	102	10	3	6	30	5	4	56	3	37	28	.262
Ryan, Patrick, Vic	49	166	25	43	53	6	2	0	25	3	3	26	1	3	2	.259
Thomas, Paul, RGV	33	116	22	30	43	4	0	3	20	0	0	18	2	7	1	.259
Obal, David, BR	62	221	30	57	69	9	0	1	23	2	2	33	1	21	1	.258
LaFerrara, Stephen, Seg	51	171	18	44	54	7	0	1	14	5	1	16	2	22	5	.257
Stephenson, Ed, BR	52	187	38	48	87	9	3	8	37	4	4	26	2	20	2	.257
Sebek, Craig, CC	50	168	33	43	57	7	2	1	20	4	1	31	1	24	5	.256
Manderino, Michael, Bee	79	301	62	77	86	7	1	0	20	4	4	45	0	17	13	.256
Lewis, Bryan, Bee	2	4	1	1	1	0	0	0	2	2	1	0	0	1	0	.250
Wilmer, Morris, Bee	41	123	8	29	29	0	0	0	14	1	1	12	2	16	4	.236
Serna, Julian, CC-RGV	50	193	25	45	59	5	0	3	24	5	1	5	0	15	5	.233
Young, Albie, Seg	34	126	22	29	31	0	1	0	8	2	0	13	0	10	18	.230
Cannuci, Philip, Bee	27	98	17	22	26	4	0	0	13	0	1	18	1	9	2	.224
Houston, Donald, RGV	56	189	22	42	54	4	4	0	22	5	1	29	0	52	2	.222
Del Aquila, Vince, Seg	5	18	0	4	4	0	0	0	1	0	0	1	0	0	0	.222
Jones, Ricky, CC	4	18	3	4	5	1	0	0	0	1	0	3	0	2	0	.222
Giammaresi, Anthony, Bee	20	77	12	17	20	3	0	0	7	2	2	14	0	14	4	.221
Daniel, William, RGV*	41	127	20	28	37	6	0	1	15	2	2	33	1	22	2	.220
Harrison, John, Vic†	17	59	16	13	16	1	1	0	7	3	0	10	1	2	7	.220
Clay, Bill, BR	18	50	6	11	13	2	0	0	7	1	0	17	0	9	0	.220
Slaughter, James, Vic	39	105	16	23	27	1	0	1	16	2	4	23	1	13	0	.219
Peterson, Michael, Seg*	55	206	26	45	53	6	1	0	18	1	2	16	1	7	10	.218

Player and Club	G.	AB.	R.	H.	TB.	2B.	3B.	HR.	RBI.	SH.	SF.	BB.	HP.	SO.	SB.	Pct.
Visosky, Mark, Seg*	20	69	5	15	18	1	1	0	5	0	1	6	0	16	0	.217
Greene, Steven, Bee	20	61	8	13	22	2	2	1	7	0	0	16	2	18	0	.213
Cox, Robby, BR	30	94	12	20	25	1	2	0	14	1	0	19	0	8	1	.213
Kirk, Kevin, Bee	50	166	15	35	46	5	0	2	15	0	3	22	1	25	4	.211
Englishbey, Stephen, Bee*	45	153	20	32	55	13	2	2	12	0	1	35	0	20	0	.209
Snyder, Vernon, Seg	19	24	0	5	5	0	0	0	1	0	0	0	0	9	0	.208
Hart, John, RGV	16	63	11	13	19	0	0	2	12	1	1	9	0	22	1	.206
Diering, Robert, Bee	21	73	6	15	22	4	0	1	8	0	0	7	0	13	0	.205
Stinson, James, Bee†	41	78	10	16	21	3	1	0	14	0	1	16	0	15	1	.205
Hill, Perry, RGV	57	180	25	36	49	7	0	2	18	6	0	32	2	49	3	.200
Jones, Alvin, Seg	14	25	6	5	6	1	0	0	2	0	0	7	0	5	2	.200
Ehrig, Robert, Vic	5	15	2	3	3	0	0	0	2	0	1	3	0	6	0	.200
Sapp, Carl, CC	15	5	1	1	1	0	0	0	0	0	0	0	0	0	0	.200
Buckley, Larry, BR	27	109	10	21	29	3	1	1	12	0	0	5	1	27	2	.193
Darst, Gary, Seg	8	26	1	5	6	1	0	0	1	1	0	4	0	8	0	.192
Maynard, Royce, RGV	28	99	15	19	25	3	0	1	20	3	3	11	1	17	8	.192
Marino, David, Bee	17	47	8	9	13	1	0	1	3	1	0	3	0	5	1	.191
Weaver, Ricky, RGV	15	44	2	8	9	1	0	0	2	0	0	3	1	3	0	.182
Mershon, Bob, Seg	8	28	3	5	5	0	0	0	5	1	1	9	0	5	1	.179
Polaski, Robert, Seg	24	75	4	13	15	2	0	0	4	2	2	12	0	10	4	.173
Calhoun, Gary, BR	15	52	8	9	10	1	0	0	1	1	0	11	1	8	1	.173
Williams, Ronald, Seg	38	117	7	20	26	2	2	0	11	5	1	14	1	29	0	.171
Craft, Gerry, Vic	12	36	3	6	9	1	1	0	0	0	0	5	0	9	0	.167
Hemby, Leslie, Bee	29	78	10	13	27	2	0	4	12	2	1	20	1	21	3	.167
Mahon, Robert, BR	8	25	1	4	4	0	0	0	0	0	1	0	2	1	0	.160
Harmon, Ralph, Bee	19	52	4	8	8	0	0	0	6	0	1	11	0	9	0	.154
Marco, Jim, Seg	17	34	1	5	5	0	0	0	5	0	0	2	1	7	0	.147
Smith, Felix, BR	5	14	1	2	2	0	0	0	1	0	0	1	1	6	1	.143
Douglas, Fred, Seg	11	36	2	5	5	0	0	0	2	1	1	3	0	6	1	.139
Carp, Steven, Bee	11	8	1	1	1	0	0	0	0	0	0	1	0	0	0	.125
McGlade, Michael, Bee	11	25	1	3	4	1	0	0	1	0	0	5	0	5	0	.120
Vaden, Donald, Bee	7	23	1	2	3	1	0	0	4	0	1	4	0	5	0	.087
Cavaletto, Gary, Bee	15	35	6	2	2	0	0	0	2	0	0	15	0	15	0	.057
Hatfield, Robbie, Seg	6	22	3	1	4	0	0	1	4	1	0	1	0	5	0	.045
Bendick, James, Bee	10	27	2	0	0	0	0	0	1	0	0	7	0	9	0	.000
Fleming, B. William, Vic	19	6	0	0	0	0	0	0	0	1	0	0	0	2	0	.000
Brown, Perry, Bee	2	4	0	0	0	0	0	0	0	0	0	0	0	0	0	.000
Owens, Maddison, CC	20	4	0	0	0	0	0	0	0	0	0	0	0	0	0	.000
Kalmus, L. Joseph, Bee	28	2	0	0	0	0	0	0	0	0	0	0	0	2	0	.000
Mudano, Mario, Bee*	14	2	0	0	0	0	0	0	0	0	0	0	0	0	0	.000
Moore, Henry, Vic*	11	2	0	0	0	0	0	0	0	0	0	0	0	1	0	.000
Garrison, Steven, Vic*	7	1	1	0	0	0	0	0	0	0	0	0	0	0	0	.000
Saunders, Kenneth, RGV	13	1	0	0	0	0	0	0	0	0	0	0	1	0	0	.000
Brewer, Donald, BR	10	1	0	0	0	0	0	0	0	0	0	0	0	0	0	.000
Hirschy, Fran, CC	16	1	0	0	0	0	0	0	0	0	0	0	0	0	0	.000

The following pitchers had no plate appearances primarily through use of designated hitters, listed alphabetically by club, games in parentheses:

BATON ROUGE—Baltz, W. Nicholas (11); Brooks, Michael (6); Brown, Thomas (9); Coleman, Gary (2); Grunsky, Gary (12); Leach, Terry (2); Palmer, Ken (7); Pottier, Miles (8).

BEEVILLE—Franklin, David (16); Goff, Steve (3); Hayes, Rick (7); Holm, David (3); Krivda, Louis (15); Lundsford, David (3); Pifer, Griffin (10); Rusk, Michael (4).

CORPUS CHRISTI—Harrison, Ray (12); Kay, Jeffery (8); Kwasny, Joseph (21); Mazzone, Leo (13); Pointer, Steve (10).

RIO GRANDE VALLEY—Antor, Gregory (11); Edquist, Ron (13); Graham, Laconia (5); Hughes, Stephen (18); Jackson, Turner (4); Klein, Stephen (2); Longoria, Ernesto (7); Smith, Bob (7); Trinidad, Jesse (8).

SEGUIN—Bancroft, Charles (6); Joyce, Edward (17); Kanas, Joseph (11); Nickerson, Drew (7); Salyer, Ronald (21); Waldraven, Randy (15); Weiler, Tony (4).

VICTORIA—Fletcher, C. Scott (3); Francis, Phillip (2); Joyce, Timothy (3); McLaughlin, Byron (9); Prichard, Glenn (4); Ross, Brad (5); Roth, Robert (15); Slivinski, Frank (12).

GRAND-SLAM HOME RUNS—Capehart, Hatfield, Hemby, Lemmons, Serna, 1 each.

AWARDED FIRST BASE ON INTERFERENCE—Pagnotta (Ryan), Rainey (Gregory).

CLUB FIELDING

Club	G.	PO.	A.	E.	DP.	PB.	Pct.	Club	G.	PO.	A.	E.	DP.	PB.	Pct.
Rio Grande Val	72	1775	698	114	42	8	.956	Baton Rouge	70	1572	442	103	51	5	.951
Seguin	75	1810	754	122	55	24	.955	Corpus Christi	77	1891	647	142	69	15	.947
Victoria	78	1826	620	123	65	7	.952	Beeville	86	1858	882	171	43	31	.941

INDIVIDUAL FIELDING

FIRST BASEMEN

*Throws lefthanded.

Player and Club	G.	PO.	A.	E.	DP.	Pct.
Weaver, RGV	15	96	4	1	1	.990
Daniel, RGV*	41	361	18	4	8	.990
WALLACE, VIC*	73	489	36	6	30	.989
LaFerrera, Seg	10	83	5	1	1	.989
Wells, Beeville	81	429	30	6	30	.987
Bratsen, CC*	75	586	32	8	53	.987
Cole, BR	49	222	11	4	12	.983
Gregory, RGV	13	115	13	3	7	.977
Jacobs, Seg	41	325	22	10	21	.972

(Fewer Than Ten Games)

Player and Club	G.	PO.	A.	E.	DP.	Pct.
Peterson, Seg	8	65	3	0	4	1.000
Benson, BR	7	29	1	0	3	1.000
Delgado, Bee	2	10	1	0	1	1.000
Capehart, CC	1	9	0	0	1	1.000
Cox, BR	1	10	1	0	1	1.000
Mershon, Seg	8	74	5	1	6	.988
Seid, Seg	3	21	1	2	1	.917
Houston, RGV	3	30	2	4	0	.889

SECOND BASEMEN

Player and Club	G.	PO.	A.	E.	DP.	Pct.
Torres, Vic	52	96	98	5	3	.975
HILL, RGV	57	113	134	9	13	.965
Fornash, Seg	70	172	146	13	24	.961
Hiller, CC	71	155	184	17	38	.952
Miller, BR	37	36	58	6	2	.940
Manderino, Bee	30	59	99	10	18	.940
Wallace, BR	11	60	56	8	11	.935
Greene, Vic	10	23	33	4	4	.933
Serna, CC-RGV	26	40	36	6	7	.927
Buckner, Bee	33	77	94	14	5	.924

(Fewer Than Ten Games)

Player and Club	G.	PO.	A.	E.	DP.	Pct.
Bryan, Bee	2	4	6	0	2	1.000
Visosky, Seg	1	3	3	0	0	1.000
Harrison, Vic	9	19	22	4	3	.911
Ryan, Vic	1	3	1	1	0	.800
Holoubek, Vic	3	1	5	2	0	.750

THIRD BASEMEN

Player and Club	G.	PO.	A.	E.	DP.	Pct.
Wallace, BR	50	28	32	2	2	.968
BUCKNER, Bee	55	50	70	6	9	.952
Barefoot, RGV	17	19	29	3	3	.941
Sebek, CC	35	32	52	7	9	.923
Pompa, RGV	25	26	46	6	4	.923
Serna, RGV	16	22	21	4	0	.915
Polaski, Seg	24	12	35	5	0	.904
Mitchell, Seg	23	29	32	7	2	.897
Thomas, RGV	14	11	21	4	3	.889
Pagnotta, CC	15	17	30	6	3	.887
Gattis, Vic	69	67	101	23	5	.880
Visosky, Seg	14	28	29	9	1	.864
Kirk, Bee	20	15	14	5	4	.853
Keenum, BR	10	7	12	4	1	.826
Lair, CC	23	16	16	7	2	.821
Clay, BR	14	15	19	8	0	.810
Williams, Seg	13	1	10	4	1	.733
Del Aquila, Seg	18	3	7	5	0	.667

(Fewer Than Ten Games)

Player and Club	G.	PO.	A.	E.	DP.	Pct.
Cannucci, Bee	4	6	6	0	0	1.000
Darst, Seg	4	2	13	0	2	1.000
Kennemur, BR	4	0	4	0	0	1.000
Young, Seg	1	0	2	0	0	1.000
Riddell, Seg	4	4	3	1	1	.875
Hatfield, Seg	6	4	14	3	1	.857
Manderino, Bee	3	6	10	3	0	.842
Harmon, Bee	5	0	5	2	0	.714
Marino, Vic	2	0	3	2	0	.600
Ornest, Vic	3	0	1	1	0	.500

SHORTSTOPS

Player and Club	G.	PO.	A.	E.	DP.	Pct.
Manderino, Bee	45	53	82	7	4	.951
Williams, Seg	25	39	49	6	5	.936
HOLOUBEK, Vic	67	114	156	19	18	.934
Brockway, RGV	70	123	220	25	14	.932
Sebek, CC	14	20	32	4	7	.929
Flores, Seg	20	42	81	10	7	.925
Taylor, BR	32	34	40	6	4	.925
Pagnotta, CC	44	66	151	19	18	.919
Thurman, Seg	13	22	35	5	4	.919
Kirk, Beeville	10	16	18	5	3	.872
Hopkins, BR-CC	49	79	121	31	22	.866
Giammaresi, Bee	20	37	53	14	10	.865

(Fewer Than Ten Games)

Player and Club	G.	PO.	A.	E.	DP.	Pct.
Marino, Bee	9	13	23	1	3	.857
Darst, Seg	4	6	18	1	2	.960
Kennum, BR	3	9	4	1	0	.929
Visosky, Seg	2	8	1	1	0	.900
Hiller, CC	1	3	3	1	1	.857
Harrison, Vic	7	12	23	6	3	.854
Daniels, Seg	2	1	6	2	0	.778

OUTFIELDERS

Player and Club	G.	PO.	A.	E.	DP.	Pct.
Fogg, Baton Rouge	19	28	4	0	2	1.000
Calhoun, Baton R	15	22	2	0	0	1.000
Englishbey, Bee	20	15	1	0	1	1.000
Leja, Beeville*	14	3	5	0	0	1.000
Bonitto, RGV	53	99	6	1	0	.991
McLISH, RGV	71	187	9	3	2	.985
Peterson, Seg*	44	98	4	2	2	.981
Lair, CC	17	39	10	1	0	.980
Rainey, CC	54	130	9	3	3	.979
Uhlaender, RGV*	25	44	0	1	0	.978

OUTFIELDERS—Continued

Player and Club	G.	PO.	A.	E.	DP.	Pct.
Lemmons, Bee*	65	122	6	3	0	.977
Young, Seguin	22	36	3	1	0	.975
Greene, Vic	66	109	3	3	1	.974
Moore, Vic	67	96	9	3	3	.972
Lawrence, Seg	63	99	5	3	0	.972
Stevenson, BR	52	57	2	2	0	.967
Capehart, CC	68	93	10	4	3	.963
Hill, RGV	34	42	6	2	0	.960
James, Victoria	75	108	3	5	1	.957
Krizmanich, CC	64	73	12	4	1	.955
Osofsky, Beeville	73	104	10	6	0	.950
Kertes, Victoria	17	17	1	1	0	.947
Allen, BR	42	33	2	2	0	.946
Morris, Beeville	33	40	0	3	0	.930
Buckley, BR	27	49	2	4	1	.927
Register, Seguin	51	68	6	6	0	.925
Jacobs, Sequin	13	20	3	2	0	.920
Cavaletto, Bee	10	22	1	2	0	.920
Greene, Bee	20	26	4	3	0	.909
Cox, BR	29	13	1	2	0	.875
Maynard, RGV	28	39	1	9	0	.816

(Fewer Than Ten Games)

Player and Club	G.	PO.	A.	E.	DP.	Pct.
Jones, Seg	8	4	0	0	0	1.000
Craft, Vic	5	8	0	0	0	1.000
Jones, CC	4	4	1	0	0	1.000
Carp, Beeville	3	2	1	0	0	1.000
Vaden, Beeville	8	9	0	0	0	1.000
Gesquiere, RGV	1	1	0	0	0	1.000
Dunlap, BR	3	7	2	0	0	1.000
Buckner, Bee	4	6	0	0	0	1.000
Gattis, Vic	1	2	0	0	0	1.000
Visosky, Seg	2	1	1	0	0	1.000
Thomas, RGV	8	6	3	1	0	.900
Pompa, RGV	6	7	1	1	0	.889
Smith, BR	5	9	0	2	0	.818
Douglas, Seg	6	3	1	1	0	.800
Ryan, Vic	4	3	1	1	0	.800
Kennemur, BR	4	7	0	2	0	.778
Cole, BR	4	0	2	1	0	.667
Lollis, CC	1	1	0	1	0	.500
Brown, BR	2	1	0	1	0	.500

CATCHERS

Player and Club	G.	PO.	A.	E.	DP.	PB.	Pct.
OBAL, BR	62	183	20	3	3	5	.985
Ryan, Vic	31	101	15	2	0	1	.983
Laferrara, Seg	39	128	33	3	3	10	.982
Sinovich, CC.	64	298	37	13	0	14	.963
Slaughter, Vic	43	99	17	5	2	5	.959
Houston, RGV	27	61	3	3	0	4	.955
Cannucci, Bee	18	54	9	3	0	4	.955
Gregory, RGV	45	65	31	6	0	5	.941
Seid, Seguin	23	50	14	5	1	5	.928
Hemby, Bee	29	52	18	6	0	6	.921
Diering, Bee	21	27	9	5	3	5	.878

(Fewer Than Ten Games)

Player and Club	G.	PO.	A.	E.	DP.	PB.	Pct.
Davis, Bee	8	9	0	0		4	1.000
Hughes, Seg	5	28	4	0		0	1.000
McGlade, Bee	4	7	2	0		0	1.000
Marco, Seg	5	5	2	0		5	1.000
Osofsky, Bee	4	3	1	0		0	1.000
Ehrig, Vic	3	10	1	0		5	1.000
Lollis, CC	8	57	12	2	1	1	.972
Lair, CC	5	27	2	1	0	0	.967
Harmon, Bee	5	21	6	4	0	1	.871
Kirk, Beeville	5	13	4	4	0	8	.810
Delgado, Bee	1	1	3	1	0	0	.800

PITCHERS

Player and Club	G.	PO.	A.	E.	DP.	Pct.
FLEMING, Vic	19	8	14	0	0	1.000
Saunders, RGV	23	9	9	0	2	1.000
Brown, BR	13	11	6	0	0	1.000
Moore, Vic*	18	7	10	0	3	1.000
Snyder, Seguin	15	7	10	0	0	1.000
Stinson, Bee*	12	2	13	0	0	1.000
Hughes, RGV	20	9	3	0	0	1.000
Grunsky, BR	17	6	6	0	0	1.000
Palmer, BR	10	2	8	0	1	1.000
Kalmas, Bee	28	0	9	0	1	1.000
Pointer, BR-CC*	14	2	2	0	0	1.000
Slivinski, Vic	13	2	2	0	0	1.000
Marco, Seguin	11	2	1	0	1	1.000
Salyer, Seguin*	21	30	31	1	5	.984
Baltz, BR	14	10	27	1	2	.974
Kwasny, CC	35	10	19	1	0	.967
Antor, RGV	11	6	16	1	0	.957
Mazzone, CC*	14	8	9	1	0	.944
Kanas, Seguin	11	6	10	1	0	.941
Hirschy, CC	16	14	15	2	1	.935
Joyce, Seguin*	17	15	25	3	1	.930
McLaughlin, Vic*	15	4	8	1	0	.923
Hart, RGV	12	12	12	2	0	.923
Edquist, RGV	16	12	12	2	0	.923
Franklin, Bee	18	3	20	2	1	.920
Mudano, Bee*	14	8	16	3	0	.889
Owens, CC	20	6	22	4	0	.875
Roth, Vic	20	4	3	1	0	.875
Walraven, Seg	15	5	12	3	1	.850
Sapp, CC	15	3	17	4	1	.833
Pifer, Beeville*	13	3	7	2	2	.833
Krivda, Beeville	17	13	10	5	0	.821
Harrison, CC	10	1	3	1	0	.800
Gesquiere, RGV	19	10	4	4	0	.778

(Fewer Than Ten Games)

Player and Club	G.	PO.	A.	E.	DP.	Pct.
Kay, CC*	9	1	4	0	0	1.000
Brooks, BR	8	0	8	0	1	1.000
Longoria, RGV	8	3	2	0	0	1.000
Bancroft, Seg	7	0	2	0	0	1.000
Smith, RGV	7	2	2	0	0	1.000
Hayes, Bee	7	3	3	0	0	1.000
Brewer, BR	6	3	5	0	0	1.000
Osofsky, Bee	5	0	1	0	0	1.000
Garrison, Vic	5	0	3	0	0	1.000
Brownlee, CC	5	0	1	0	0	1.000
Leach, BR	5	0	3	0	0	1.000
Rusk, Beeville	4	3	2	0	0	1.000
Weiler, Seg	4	2	2	0	0	1.000
Neimeyer, Vic	4	0	1	0	0	1.000

PITCHERS—Continued

Player and Club	G.	PO.	A.	E.	DP.	Pct.	Player and Club	G.	PO.	A.	E.	DP.	Pct.
Kennemur, BR	3	0	6	0	0	1.000	Trinidad, RGV	8	6	11	1	1	.944
Goff, Beeville	3	1	3	0	1	1.000	Benson, BR	7	2	11	1	2	.929
Pottier, BR	3	1	1	0	0	1.000	Nickerson, Seg	7	5	5	1	0	.909
Lundsford, Bee	3	1	0	0	0	1.000	Farrow, Seg*	9	1	18	2	0	.905
Fletcher, Vic	3	1	2	0	0	1.000	Ross, Vic	7	5	2	1	0	.875
Rainey, CC	2	0	1	0	0	1.000	Graham, RGV	6	1	4	1	0	.833
Coleman, BR	2	1	1	0	1	1.000	Carp, Beeville	6	2	2	1	0	.800
Francis, Vic	2	1	0	0	0	1.000	Prichard, Vic	4	3	1	2	0	.667

NOTE—Fielding averages are incomplete.

PITCHERS' RECORDS
(Leading Qualifiers for Earned-Run Average Leadership—64 or More Innings)

*Throws lefthanded.

Pitcher—Club	G.	GS.	CG.	ShO.	W.	L.	Sv.	Pct.	IP.	H.	R.	ER.	HR.	BB.	Int. BB.	HB.	SO.	WP.	ERA.
T. Brown, B. Rouge	13	13	8	3	9	1	0	.900	101	82	34	17	2	22	3	0	80	2	1.51
McLaughlin, Vic*	15	14	11	1	10	4	0	.714	115	104	48	39	5	46	1	5	74	3	3.05
Stinson, Beeville*	17	5	4	0	7	2	3	.778	79	54	33	27	8	33	0	1	52	1	3.08
Baltz, Baton Rouge	14	11	10	0	7	6	0	.538	106	101	60	38	4	38	2	2	51	2	3.23
Salyer, Seguin	21	16	12	0	8	9	2	.471	130	137	68	49	6	33	0	3	54	4	3.39
Palmer, Baton Rouge	10	8	5	0	6	2	0	.750	73	66	35	28	5	24	0	0	38	1	3.45
Hart, Rio Grande Valley	16	14	13	2	8	6	0	.571	132	117	60	52	4	70	1	0	70	5	3.55
Saunders, Rio G. Valley	23	4	4	0	5	1	1	.833	92	96	48	37	7	33	0	2	22	4	3.62
Kwasny, Corpus Christi	31	3	3	1	9	5	7	.643	87	91	62	36	3	40	3	4	51	4	3.72
Farrow, Seguin*	10	9	2	0	2	4	0	.333	71	54	33	29	3	58	0	3	55	0	3.68

Departmental Leaders: G—Kwasny, 31; GS—H. Moore, 17; CG—Hart, 13; ShO—T. Brown, 9; W—McLaughlin, 10; L—Krivda, 10; Sv—Kwasny, 7; Pct—T. Brown, .900; IP—H. Moore, 139; H—H. Moore, 156; R—Owens, 91; ER—Owens, 70; HR—Leach, 12; BB—Owens, 102; IBB—Fleming, Krivda, 6; HB—Krivda, McLaughlin, 5; SO—Owens, 113; WP—Owens, 17.

(All Pitchers—Listed According to Earned-Run Average)

Pitcher—Club	G.	GS.	CG.	ShO.	W.	L.	Sv.	Pct.	IP.	H.	R.	ER.	HR.	BB.	Int. BB.	HB.	SO.	WP.	ERA.
Kennemur, BR	6	2	0	0	2	1	0	.667	28	24	7	4	1	11	1	0	19	1	1.29
T. Brown, BR	13	13	8	3	9	1	0	.900	101	82	34	17	2	22	3	0	80	2	1.51
Pointer, BR-CC	14	9	4	0	5	2	2	.714	63	52	24	15	2	31	0	2	53	3	2.14
Kay, CC*	9	3	0	0	2	0	0	1.000	29	37	9	7	0	19	0	0	16	2	2.17
Trinidad, RGV	8	7	3	0	4	1	0	.800	56	51	19	14	3	11	0	1	32	1	2.25
Snyder, Seg	19	1	1	0	5	1	0	.833	56	55	23	15	1	20	0	0	19	2	2.41
Brooks, BR	8	5	1	1	3	2	0	.600	51	49	19	15	0	35	0	0	23	0	2.65
Benson, BR	7	7	6	0	3	4	0	.429	61	59	25	18	2	12	0	1	43	1	2.66
Grunsky, BR	17	2	0	0	3	3	2	.500	49	35	22	16	1	22	1	0	16	1	2.94
McLaughlin, Vic*	15	14	11	1	10	4	0	.714	115	104	48	39	5	46	1	5	74	3	3.05
Stinson, Bee*	17	5	4	0	7	2	3	.778	79	54	33	27	8	33	0	1	52	1	3.08
Baltz, BR	14	11	10	0	7	6	0	.538	106	101	60	38	4	38	2	2	51	2	3.23
Marco, Seg	11	1	1	0	0	1	0	.000	24	21	12	9	0	14	1	0	4	0	3.38
Salyer, Seg	21	16	12	0	8	9	2	.471	130	137	68	49	6	33	0	3	54	4	3.39
Palmer, BR	10	8	5	0	6	2	0	.750	73	66	35	28	5	24	0	0	38	1	3.45
Brownlee, CC	5	0	0	0	1	1	0	.500	13	16	7	5	1	3	0	0	4	0	3.46
Ross, Vic	7	3	2	0	2	1	0	.667	18	21	9	7	3	9	1	0	4	0	3.50
Hart, RGV	16	14	13	2	8	6	0	.571	132	117	60	52	4	70	1	0	70	5	3.55
Saunders, RGV	23	4	4	0	5	1	1	.833	92	96	48	37	7	33	0	2	22	4	3.62
Farrow, Seg*	10	9	2	0	2	4	0	.333	71	54	33	29	3	58	0	3	55	0	3.68
Kwasny, CC	31	3	3	1	9	5	7	.643	87	91	62	36	3	40	3	4	51	4	3.72
Mazzone CC*	14	9	4	0	7	2	1	.778	99	64	47	4	58	0	1	67	1	3.73
Roth, Vic	20	0	0	0	0	2	3	.000	36	39	22	15	1	23	4	0	29	3	3.75
Fleming, Vic	19	13	7	0	7	7	0	.500	126	123	74	53	7	66	6	4	63	7	3.79
Pifer, Bee*	13	9	3	0	2	7	1	.222	62	92	57	27	2	24	0	0	23	4	3.92
H. Moore, Vic*	18	17	9	1	8	8	0	.500	139	156	84	61	6	73	2	3	82	8	3.95
Franklin, Bee	18	14	10	0	6	8	0	.429	114	121	79	52	2	45	1	2	57	5	4.11
Krivda, Bee	17	11	5	1	4	10	0	.286	123	144	83	57	2	77	6	5	54	7	4.17
Pottier, BR	3	3	1	0	0	3	0	.000	25	27	16	12	2	9	2	2	15	0	4.32
Gesquiere, RGV	18	10	6	0	4	6	1	.400	96	90	64	47	4	58	0	1	48	7	4.41
Slivinski, Vic	13	8	6	0	9	2	0	.818	83	82	44	41	6	22	2	1	44	1	4.45
Nickerson, Seg	7	2	1	0	1	4	0	.200	30	32	23	15	0	19	1	1	22	4	4.50
Sapp, CC	15	14	6	1	9	4	0	.692	120	145	70	60	5	46	0	1	63	3	4.50
Bancroft, Seg	7	2	0	0	1	2	1	.333	18	17	11	9	2	12	0	1	5	2	4.50
Lundsford, Bee	3	0	0	0	1	2	0	.333	6	9	3	3	0	8	0	0	2	0	4.50
Clay, BR	1	0	0	0	0	0	0	.000	2	2	1	1	0	0	0	0	1	0	4.50

Pitcher–Club	G.	GS.	CG.	ShO.	W.	L.	Sv.	Pct.	IP.	H.	R.	ER.	HR.	BB.	Int. BB.	HB.	SO.	WP.	ERA.
Mudano, Bee*	14	10	2	0	7	4	0	.636	81	105	62	41	4	40	0	0	30	7	4.56
Antor, RGV	11	8	4	0	3	6	0	.333	80	81	57	41	4	38	0	1	20	5	4.61
Hirschy, CC	16	14	6	0	7	7	0	.500	112	136	68	58	6	42	1	4	63	7	4.66
Brewer, BR	6	1	0	0	1	1	0	.500	13	18	8	7	0	6	1	0	8	1	4.85
Weiler, Seg	4	3	1	0	1	0	0	1.000	22	18	16	12	0	25	0	2	18	1	4.91
Owens, CC	20	16	8	0	8	5	0	.615	128	112	91	70	3	102	1	3	113	17	4.92
Kanas, Seg	11	3	1	0	2	3	1	.400	42	43	36	23	1	32	0	2	24	6	4.93
Carp, Bee	6	1	0	0	0	1	0	.000	16	11	17	9	0	27	1	1	7	3	5.06
Leja, Bee*	14	1	0	0	2	2	1	.500	49	64	37	28	2	4	0	3	24	1	5.14
Kalmus, Bee	28	1	0	0	2	3	1	.400	63	55	45	38	2	56	0	3	38	8	5.43
Edquist, RGV	16	13	5	0	3	9	0	.333	26	24	21	16	0	18	0	0	5	0	5.54
Neimeyer, Vic	4	1	0	0	0	2	0	.000	13	8	9	8	0	14	0	0	10	1	5.54
Francis, Vic	2	2	0	0	1	1	0	.500	8	12	6	5	0	3	0	0	6	0	5.63
Longoria, RGV	8	0	0	0	0	0	0	.000	20	22	15	13	2	20	0	0	10	0	5.85
Hughes, RGV	20	2	0	0	1	3	4	.250	46	50	44	30	6	29	0	0	42	7	5.87
Peterson, Seg*	1	0	0	0	0	0	0	.000	6	7	5	4	1	4	0	0	5	0	6.00
Leach, BR	5	1	1	0	2	0	0	1.000	19	43	21	13	12	14	0	0	15	1	6.16
Fletcher, Vic	3	3	0	0	1	1	0	.500	10	12	11	7	2	7	1	0	2	0	6.30
Walraven, Seg	15	11	3	0	3	8	0	.273	86	94	79	61	4	89	1	2	35	9	6.38
Rusk, Bee	4	2	1	0	1	1	0	.500	19	24	18	14	0	25	2	1	10	2	6.63
Smith, RGV	7	5	1	0	2	5	0	.286	31	32	35	24	3	32	0	2	11	3	6.97
Graham, RGV	6	5	2	0	2	3	0	.400	34	54	30	27	3	13	0	0	21	0	7.15
Rainey, CC	2	0	0	0	0	0	0	.000	5	8	4	4	0	0	0	0	0	0	7.20
Goff, Bee	3	2	0	0	0	2	0	.000	15	21	15	13	0	9	0	1	10	2	7.80
Prichard, Vic	4	3	0	0	1	1	0	.500	16	23	20	14	0	18	0	0	8	3	7.88
Holm, Bee	3	0	0	0	0	1	0	.000	9	13	11	8	1	4	0	0	1	1	8.00
Hayes, Bee	7	5	1	0	1	3	0	.250	31	45	36	29	3	21	2	0	10	3	8.42
Coleman, BR	2	1	0	0	0	1	0	.000	3	6	3	3	0	3	0	0	3	0	9.00
Joyce, Vic	2	0	0	0	1	0	0	1.000	3	2	4	3	0	5	0	0	3	0	9.00
Osofsky, Bee	3	2	0	0	0	1	0	.000	11	15	16	13	1	11	0	3	6	0	10.64
Garrison, Vic	5	0	0	0	0	1	1	.000	8	11	14	12	2	13	0	0	5	3	13.50
Klein, RGV	2	0	0	0	0	1	0	.000	1	1	6	6	0	6	0	1	1	0	18.00

COMBINATION SHUTOUTS: Fletcher-Roth, Victoria; Walraven-Hughes, Seguin.

NO-HITTERS: Smith, Rio Grande Valley, defeated Beeville 12-1, June 6 (seven innings).

BALKS: Salyer, 4; Mudano, 3; Baltz, Kennemur, Stinson, 2 each; Trinidad, Farrow, Palmer, Clay, Antor, Weiler, Kanas, Neimeyer, Osofsky, Joyce, Longoria, 1 each.

NOTE: No club pitching figures available.

Mexican Center League

CLASS A

CHAMPIONSHIP WINNERS IN PREVIOUS YEARS

1960—Salamanca .... .582	1967—Leon .... .604	1972—Ebano .... .692
1961—Aguascalientes .... .567	1968—Saltillo .... .648	Aguascalientes* .... .703
1962—Fresnillo .... .588	1969—San Luis Potosi* .... .705	1973—Zacatecas† .... .721
1963—Guanajuato .... .627	Zacatecas .... .667	Ebano .... .657
1964—Leon .... .630	1970—Ciudad Madero .... .632	1974—Durango† .... .693
1965—San Luis Potosi .... .633	Ciudad Madero .... .655	Ciudad Valles .... .513
1966—Guanajuato* .... .701	1971—Ebano† .... .704	1975—Uriangato‡ .... .797
San Luis Potosi .... .750	San Luis Potosi .... .625	

*Won split-season playoff.
†League divided into Gulf and Center divisions; won playoff.
‡Declared champion when playoffs were not completed.

STANDING OF CLUBS AT CLOSE OF SEASON, JUNE 27

Club	L.M.	Gto.	Vic.	Acam.	Zac.	Fre.	W.	L.	T.	Pct.	G.B.
Lagos de Moreno (Mexico Tigers)	..	6	13	6	7	15	47	20	1	.701	......
Guanajuato (Aguas/Durango)	3	..	12	12	3	4	34	33	2	.507	13
Ciudad Victoria (Monterrey)............	5	8	..	6	6	7	32	35	0	.478	15
Acambaro (Tampico)	4	8	3	..	11	6	32	36	1	.471	15½
Zacatecas (Union Laguna)	3	6	4	9	..	8	30	37	1	.448	17
Fresnillo (Mexico Reds).................	5	5	3	3	10	..	26	40	3	.394	20½

Farm clubs of Mexican League teams as shown in parentheses.

Playoff—None.

Regular-Season Attendance—Acambaro, 7,749; Fresnillo, 25,326; Guanajuato, 7,426; Lagos de Moreno, 9,288; Ciudad Victoria, 7,097; Zacatecas, 11,300. Total, 68,186. No playoffs. No all-star game.

Managers: Acambaro—Roberto Castellon; Fresnillo—Mario Pelaez, Armando Ortiz; Guanajuato—Hugo Rios, Hector Rodriguez; Lagos de Moreno—Domingo Rivera; Victoria—Leo Rodriguez; Zacatecas—Felipe Hernandez, Manolo Fortes.

All-Star Team: 1B—Valle, Guanajuato; 2B—Robles, Guanajuato; 3B—Zamora, Lagos de Moreno; SS—V. Lopez, Victoria; OF—Guzman, Lagos de Moreno; M. Chavarria, Zacatecas; Rodriguez, Lagos de Moreno; C—Heras, Lagos de Moreno; P—Munguia, Lagos de Moreno; Casas, Acambaro.

(Compiled by Antonio Silva Vidaurry, League Statistician, Mexico, D. F.)

CLUB BATTING

Club	G.	AB.	R.	OR.	H.	TB.	2B.	3B.	HR.	RBI.	SH.	SF.	BB.	Int. BB.	HP.	SO.	SB.	CS.	LOB.	Pct.
La de Moreno....	68	2137	413	216	656	968	103	25	53	371	39	26	259	24	39	254	75	42	429	.307
Zacatecas	68	2107	302	341	624	832	88	18	28	294	44	21	165	13	24	257	48	30	447	.296
Guanajuato	69	2236	322	313	655	923	112	30	32	303	26	21	200	9	23	329	39	29	530	.293
Acambaro	69	2136	314	336	603	774	95	23	10	292	48	24	192	12	28	297	54	33	461	.282
Fresnillo	69	2117	303	403	577	762	71	24	22	274	30	22	220	10	46	324	50	47	481	.273
Ciudad Victoria	67	2069	289	334	541	714	68	21	21	269	32	26	209	11	17	346	87	53	437	.261

INDIVIDUAL BATTING

(Leading Qualifiers for Batting Championship—189 or More Plate Appearances)

*Bats lefthanded. †Switch-hitter.

Player and Club	G.	AB.	R.	H.	TB.	2B.	3B.	HR.	RBI.	SH.	SF.	BB.	HP.	SO.	SB.	CS.	Pct.
Guzman, Ubaldo, Lagos de M........	68	235	55	88	126	14	3	6	42	11	1	32	3	19	30	4	.374
Robles, Rigoberto, Guan	69	277	49	101	137	16	1	6	42	5	2	17	3	17	9	4	.365
Rodriguez, Jaime, LM	62	216	53	76	120	17	3	7	32	3	3	30	2	24	5	5	.352
Chavarria, Miguel, Zac	63	218	42	76	95	12	2	1	19	5	1	21	4	33	9	3	.349
Zamora, Roberto, LM	68	233	42	81	114	9	6	4	52	4	4	27	3	20	5	4	.348
Heras, Roberto, Lagos de M	62	210	38	72	102	14	5	2	41	1	4	31	6	24	5	4	.343
Villagomez, David, Fre	62	215	41	72	128	11	0	15	63	1	4	20	0	18	6	2	.335
Contreras, Juan V., Zac...............	66	231	50	77	116	10	4	7	38	2	2	22	3	22	6	2	.333
Villela, Jesus, Guanajuato...........	69	266	39	87	122	16	2	5	26	5	2	20	0	38	8	8	.327
Guzman, Ramiro, Acambaro*	58	193	38	62	91	8	9	1	31	4	1	18	4	14	6	3	.321
Arredondo, Eulogio, LM	66	240	45	77	112	12	4	5	41	3	1	14	6	16	6	7	.321

Departmental Leaders: G—Acosta, Barrera, Montiel, Robles, Roman, Romo, Valle, Villela, 69; AB—Robles, 277; R—U. Guzman, 55; H—Robles, 101; TB—Robles, 137; 2B—J. Rodriguez, 17; 3B—R. Guzman, Valle, 9; HR—Heras, 15; RBI—Barrera, Heras, 63; SH—U. Guzman, 11; SF—Barrera, Castro, Iniguez, Ornelas, 5; BB—Figueroa, Ornelas, 40; HP—Pacheco, 14; SO—Acosta, 79; SB—U. Guzman, 30; CS—Clayton, 13.

(All Players—Listed Alphabetically)

Player and Club	G.	AB.	R.	H.	TB.	2B.	3B.	HR.	RBI.	SH.	SF.	BB.	HP.	SO.	SB.	CS.	Pct.
Acosta, Leonardo, Fre	69	232	38	48	80	8	3	6	31	0	2	30	8	79	4	2	.207
Aguilar, Roberto J., Acam	58	157	20	43	51	6	1	0	14	3	2	22	0	15	6	3	.274
Alvarez, Jose Luis, Acam	68	221	31	61	66	5	0	0	24	6	2	21	2	34	2	6	.276
Anaya, Jesus, Guan	50	192	31	60	85	12	2	3	35	3	1	13	4	22	3	0	.313
Arredondo, Eulogio, LM	66	240	45	77	112	12	4	5	41	3	1	14	6	16	6	7	.321
Avila, Javier, Acam	35	79	7	17	23	3	0	1	11	1	2	8	1	21	0	0	.215
Banuelos, Ramiro, LM	68	221	29	51	62	5	3	0	29	6	2	19	1	23	2	1	.231
Barrera, Nelson, Fre	69	245	36	78	125	13	2	10	63	0	5	22	5	21	5	6	.318
Beltran, Martin, Zac	15	26	6	7	7	0	0	0	6	0	0	2	1	6	1	0	.269
Bernal, Othon, C Vic	47	171	17	45	75	7	1	7	39	1	4	8	0	39	1	3	.263
Blancas, Guadalupe, Acam	11	27	1	3	3	0	0	0	2	0	0	1	0	5	0	1	.111
Camargo, Julian, C Vic	67	232	26	60	78	12	0	2	23	5	1	18	1	26	4	8	.259
Cardona, Arturo, Zac	26	63	5	13	16	1	1	0	2	1	0	1	0	14	4	0	.206
Carreno, Luis Alb., Guan	16	55	2	13	16	0	0	1	4	0	0	3	0	10	1	0	.236
Castellon, Roberto, Acam	45	142	21	55	77	16	3	0	27	1	3	13	2	9	0	1	.387
Castro, Alberto, Zac	39	130	15	33	46	4	3	1	20	4	5	8	0	10	6	1	.254
Chavarria, Miguel, Zac	63	218	42	76	95	12	2	1	19	5	1	21	4	33	9	3	.349
Chavarria, Roberto, Zac	33	95	8	23	28	2	0	1	12	4	1	8	0	11	4	1	.242
Cifuentes, Jose, Zac	1	5	0	1	1	0	0	0	0	0	0	0	0	0	0	0	.200
Clayton, Leonardo, C Vic*	66	239	52	70	99	10	5	3	27	6	1	37	0	31	26	13	.293
Cobos, Jose, Fre	1	4	0	0	0	0	0	0	0	0	0	0	0	1	0	0	.000
Contreras, Jesus, Fre	9	25	5	6	7	1	0	0	1	3	0	0	0	6	1	1	.240
Contreras, Juan V., Zac	66	231	50	77	116	10	4	7	38	2	2	22	3	22	6	2	.333
Contreras, Mario, Guan	5	15	2	3	3	0	0	0	1	0	0	1	3	1	0	0	.200
Del Bosque, Manuel, Guan	31	80	10	13	24	5	0	2	11	0	1	11	2	23	1	0	.163
Escalante, Isaias, Guan	5	10	2	4	5	1	0	0	1	0	0	3	0	3	0	0	.400
Esqueda, Carlos, Zac	60	196	21	53	73	7	2	3	34	6	2	13	2	26	3	6	.270
Esquer, Marco Ant., C Vic	33	66	7	21	26	0	1	1	16	1	2	9	2	14	2	1	.318
Figueroa, Roman, LM	66	230	52	64	90	11	3	3	29	3	3	40	2	21	9	7	.278
Flores, Ignacio, C Vic	54	200	33	54	65	6	1	1	22	3	2	9	3	23	4	3	.270
Gallegos, Candelario, C Vic	4	8	1	0	0	0	0	0	0	0	0	0	0	4	0	0	.000
Garcia, Arturo, Acam	33	104	15	29	35	3	0	1	22	1	2	2	2	16	0	2	.279
Gonzalez, Adalberto, Acam	47	127	17	35	43	4	2	0	16	2	1	17	3	32	4	1	.276
Guzman, Horacio, Acam	68	241	39	59	93	14	4	4	28	3	1	15	4	46	7	5	.245
Guzman, Ramiro, Acam*	58	193	38	62	91	8	9	1	31	4	1	18	4	14	6	3	.321
Guzman, Thomas, Acam†	50	145	18	39	50	7	2	0	23	1	4	12	3	7	3	1	.269
Guzman, Ubaldo, LM	68	235	55	88	126	14	3	6	42	11	1	32	3	19	30	4	.374
Heras, Roberto, LM	62	215	41	72	128	11	0	15	63	1	4	20	0	18	6	2	.335
Hermosillo, Carlos F., Acam	54	166	26	44	65	12	0	3	20	3	1	26	1	28	4	5	.265
Hurtado, Antonio, Acam	57	193	20	57	63	4	1	0	33	7	1	5	3	29	5	1	.295
Ibarra, Carlos, Fre	7	18	0	5	9	2	1	0	3	0	0	0	0	4	0	1	.278
Iniguez, Roberto, Zac	64	199	35	63	101	13	2	7	37	3	5	36	3	21	5	2	.317
Jimenez, Fco. Javier, Acam	46	135	20	39	43	2	1	0	14	6	0	6	0	11	5	2	.289
Limon, Jose Antonio, LM	2	4	1	2	2	0	0	0	1	0	0	1	1	0	0	0	.500
Lizarraga, Raul, Acam	25	91	14	25	30	5	0	0	12	5	2	4	2	14	2	1	.275
Lopez, Raul, C Vic	67	224	21	51	60	9	0	0	25	3	2	19	3	32	4	7	.228
Lopez, Vicente, C Vic	65	202	37	52	75	8	3	3	15	4	1	29	0	48	15	5	.257
Lozano, Jesus, Zac	42	116	12	32	38	3	0	1	9	2	1	7	5	21	2	2	.276
Luna, Jose Luis, C Vic	15	55	2	9	10	1	0	0	1	0	0	1	0	16	0	0	.164
Madrigal, Raciel, Fre	4	7	0	0	0	0	0	0	0	0	0	0	0	4	0	0	.000
Mariscal, German, Guan	35	113	18	39	51	8	2	0	14	4	1	13	0	15	0	1	.345
Martinez, Antonio, LM*	57	189	30	40	51	9	1	0	18	2	0	30	5	48	3	3	.212
Martinez, Hector, Fre	36	99	7	17	20	3	0	0	10	0	1	5	0	46	1	2	.172
Martinez, Juan H., C Vic	28	98	19	33	44	6	1	1	24	1	3	8	1	16	4	1	.337
Miranda, Jaime, Fre	65	206	23	55	67	5	2	1	21	5	3	19	3	30	7	3	.267
Molina, Jose Ma., Guan	48	158	23	45	77	9	1	7	30	1	1	17	4	38	0	3	.285
Mondragon, David F., LM	1	2	0	1	1	0	0	0	1	0	0	0	0	0	0	0	.500
Montiel, Julio, Fre	69	229	31	62	70	4	2	0	25	5	3	26	7	10	12	5	.271
Morales, Ramon, Guan	9	29	1	3	3	0	0	0	0	0	0	0	0	7	0	1	.103
Moreno, Refugio, Acam	27	60	14	19	21	2	0	0	3	3	0	10	1	12	8	1	.317
Munguia, Ramon, LM	1	2	0	0	0	0	0	0	0	0	0	0	0	1	0	0	.000
Munoz, Francisco, Fre	36	96	9	23	24	1	0	0	10	4	1	7	5	22	1	4	.240
Munoz, Hector, Guan	12	37	7	12	14	2	0	0	4	0	1	5	1	4	1	1	.324
Murillo, Mario, LM	35	95	16	29	43	6	1	2	18	1	3	13	2	16	4	1	.305
Muro, Miguel, Zac	31	97	10	23	28	2	0	1	9	0	0	6	2	11	2	0	.237
Nava, Mario, Zac	13	45	5	11	16	5	0	0	8	1	0	3	1	5	0	0	.244
Navarrete, Aaron, Zac	38	137	24	34	40	2	2	0	12	3	0	3	0	18	2	2	.248
Nolasco, Juan, LM	22	61	8	19	19	0	0	0	10	1	2	6	0	9	1	2	.311

Player and Club	G.	AB.	R.	H.	TB.	2B.	3B.	HR.	RBI.	SH.	SF.	BB.	HP.	SO.	SB.	CS.	Pct.
Oliva, Ernesto, Zac	8	11	2	4	5	1	0	0	1	0	1	0	0	2	0	0	.364
Ornelas, Jesus, C Vic	65	184	21	33	42	2	2	1	25	5	5	40	1	54	10	4	.179
Ortiz, Armando, Fre	33	98	20	35	46	6	1	1	19	1	0	16	2	8	5	4	.357
Pacheco, Claudio, LM	61	194	41	56	100	9	1	11	35	4	3	28	14	38	4	6	.289
Pereda, Pablo, Fre	5	6	1	0	0	0	0	0	0	0	0	1	0	1	0	0	.000
Perez, Alfredo, Zac	43	144	24	49	68	11	1	2	26	2	0	15	2	12	0	6	.340
Perez, Joel, Guan	25	96	8	29	45	9	2	1	15	0	1	6	0	9	1	0	.302
Pineda, Juan Jose, Guan	20	67	10	14	20	2	2	0	6	0	2	14	0	3	2	2	.209
Podres, Guillermo, Fre	2	3	0	0	0	0	0	0	0	0	0	0	0	0	0	0	.000
Prior, Trinidad, Guan	2	5	0	0	0	0	0	0	0	0	0	0	0	2	0	0	.000
Ramirez, Armando, Guan	41	116	17	35	46	4	2	1	22	1	2	17	1	24	1	1	.302
Reynoso, Jesus, Fre	4	4	0	0	0	0	0	0	0	1	0	0	0	1	0	0	.000
Rios, Carlos, Guan	22	87	14	23	39	2	4	2	15	1	2	4	0	7	1	0	.264
Robles, Rigoberto, Guan	69	277	49	101	137	16	1	6	42	5	2	17	3	17	9	4	.365
Rodriguez, Israel, Guan	40	99	19	18	23	3	1	0	10	1	1	25	1	35	2	1	.182
Rodriguez, Jaime, LM	62	216	53	76	120	17	3	7	32	3	3	30	2	24	5	5	.352
Rojas, Olegario, Zac	3	8	1	3	3	0	0	0	2	0	0	0	0	0	0	0	.375
Roman, Dagoberto, Fre*	69	269	43	81	105	6	6	2	21	0	1	23	2	31	4	7	.301
Romo, Jesus, Fre	69	241	44	64	74	6	2	0	20	8	1	30	7	24	3	6	.266
Sanchez, Juan, Zac	49	143	20	55	75	8	4	4	28	4	2	16	1	17	1	1	.385
Sanchez, Mariano, C Vic	30	91	11	21	32	3	4	0	11	1	2	10	2	17	3	2	.231
Sauceda, Ramiro, C Vic	19	45	6	11	11	0	0	0	4	0	0	9	0	7	1	0	.244
Solis, Guillermo, Acam	2	2	1	1	1	0	0	0	1	0	0	1	0	0	0	0	.500
Soto, Gregorio, Guan	32	107	11	27	31	1	0	1	8	1	1	7	2	18	4	1	.252
Torres, Eduardo, Zac	66	233	22	67	76	7	1	0	31	7	1	10	0	28	3	4	.288
Torres B., Jesus, Fre	43	125	8	31	33	2	0	0	10	2	1	10	1	12	2	2	.248
Torres, Nemesio, C Vic	65	254	36	81	97	4	3	2	37	2	3	12	4	19	13	6	.319
Urias, Eladio, Acam	28	51	12	15	19	4	0	0	11	2	2	11	0	4	2	0	.294
Urias, Juan, Acam	2	2	0	0	0	0	0	0	0	0	0	0	0	0	0	0	.000
Valle, Olegario, Guan	69	249	29	74	107	9	9	2	32	0	1	13	1	35	3	6	.297
Velarde, Juan Roman, Guan	52	178	30	55	75	13	2	1	27	4	2	12	3	16	1	0	.309
Villagomez, David, Fre	62	210	38	72	102	14	5	2	41	1	4	31	6	24	5	4	.343
Villela, Jesus, Guan	69	266	39	87	122	16	2	5	26	5	2	20	0	38	8	8	.327
Zamora, Roberto, LM	68	233	42	81	114	9	6	4	52	4	4	27	3	20	5	4	.348

The following pitchers had no plate appearances primarily through use of designated hitters, listed alphabetically by club, games in parentheses:

ACAMBARO—Avalos, Santiago (10); Casas, Arturo (17); Gutierrez, J. Luis (13); Lagunes, Arturo (2); Lopez, Norberto, (15); Moreno, Antonio (8); Moreno, Geronimo (17); Olivares, Hector (3).

FRESNILLO—Ayon, Tomas, (12); Castillo, Alberto (8); Diaz, Gerardo (14); Guerrero, Felipe (1); Mendoza, Isidro (15); Romero, Francisco (6).

GUANAJUATO—Avila, Manuel (15); Cervantes, Antonio (14); Cervantes, Lauro (15); Contreras, Mauricio (2); Galata, Raul (6); Gastelum, Facundo (8); Herrera, Juan (1); Marin, Jose (13); Unate, Jesus (1); Valdez, Jesus (3); Valdez, Jorge (15); Vargas, Fidel (3); Vargas, Sergio (10); Vazquez, Homero (21).

LAGOS DE MORENO—Esparza, Jesus (13); Garcia, Felipe (8); Garcia, Valentin (6); Pina, Javier R. (21); Ruiz, Miguel (14).

CIUDAD VICTORIA—Acuna, Eleazar (13); Esquer, Mercedes (14); Guadiana, Roberto (2); Martinez, Gabriel (21); Nieblas, Armando (3); Perez, Candelario (22); Raga, Reyes, (1); Tafoya, Daniel (17).

ZACATECAS—Beltran, Margarito (13); Berumen, Jose (2); Camarena, Luis (13); Felix, Victor (3); Flores, Jesus (14); Ibarra, Camilo (16); Mena, Jorge (1); Pena, Manuel (4); Robles, Manuel (12); Torres F., Jesus (11); Valdez, Humberto (13).

GRAND-SLAM HOME RUNS—Heras, 2; Barrera, N. Torres, Zamora, 1 each.

AWARDED FIRST BASE ON INTERFERENCE—None.

CLUB FIELDING

Club	G.	PO.	A.	E.	DP.	PB.	Pct.	Club	G.	PO.	A.	E.	DP.	PB.	Pct.
Lagos de Moreno	68	1674	732	95	58	20	.962	Ciudad Victoria	67	1623	736	120	53	48	.952
Zacatecas	68	1602	704	115	46	23	.952	Guanajuato	69	1656	751	125	53	35	.951
Acambaro	69	1650	769	122	60	43	.952	Fresnillo	69	1650	736	131	48	48	.948

Triple Play—Fresnillo.

INDIVIDUAL FIELDING

*Throws lefthanded.

FIRST BASEMEN

Player and Club	G.	PO.	A.	E.	DP.	Pct.	Player and Club	G.	PO.	A.	E.	DP.	Pct.
Pacheco, Lagos de M	22	198	9	1	15	.995	Villagomez, Fre	32	286	5	7	19	.977
Perez, Zac	34	243	15	3	20	.989	Camargo, C.Vic	15	106	14	3	9	.976
Barrera, Fre	10	74	4	1	3	.987	Hermosillo, Acam	39	343	20	10	28	.973
T. Guzman, Acam	30	254	14	5	22	.982	Muro, Zac	27	194	14	6	11	.972
Bernal, C.Vic	36	306	8	6	26	.981	R. Lopez, C.Vic	18	125	9	5	10	.964
VALLE, Guan	69	509	34	11	43	.980	Martinez, Lagos de M	45	351	11	16	33	.958
Torres B., Fre	14	89	4	2	8	.979							

FIRST BASEMEN—Continued

(Fewer Than Ten Games)

Player and Club	G.	PO.	A.	E.	DP.	Pct.	Player and Club	G.	PO.	A.	E.	DP.	Pct.
Castro, Zac	6	40	6	0	3	1.000	E. Urias, Acam	2	4	0	0	1	1.000
Heras, Lagos de M	3	17	0	0	2	1.000	Martin Beltran, Zac	5	36	2	1	1	.974
Iniguez, Zac	2	15	1	0	1	1.000	Ortiz, Fre	7	65	4	2	1	.972
M. A. Esquer, C.Vic	1	10	1	0	0	1.000	H. Martinez, Fre	9	63	2	4	7	.942
Molina, Guan	1	6	1	0	1	1.000							

Triple Play—H. Martinez.

SECOND BASEMEN

Player and Club	G.	PO.	A.	E.	DP.	Pct.	Player and Club	G.	PO.	A.	E.	DP.	Pct.
Ortiz, Fre	20	53	33	3	7	.966	Romo, Fre	40	86	82	10	16	.944
Perez, Guan	11	19	28	2	6	.959	Arredondo, Lagos de M ..	66	141	151	19	38	.939
ALVAREZ, Acam	68	160	145	13	34	.959	Navarrete, Zac	39	84	70	11	16	.933
Robles, Guan	56	163	128	15	29	.951	Iniguez, Zac	18	40	42	6	9	.932
Torres, C.Vic	60	148	157	16	34	.950	R. Chavarria, Zac	12	24	24	4	5	.923

(Fewer Than Ten Games)

Player and Club	G.	PO.	A.	E.	DP.	Pct.	Player and Club	G.	PO.	A.	E.	DP.	Pct.
R. Moreno, Acam	2	2	0	0	0	1.000	Contreras, Fre	9	14	12	5	2	.839
Sanchez, C.Vic	7	14	23	2	5	.949	Rojas, Zac	2	2	8	2	3	.833
Rodriguez, Lagos de M ..	3	7	5	2	2	.857	Munoz, Guan	3	4	5	3	1	.750

Triple Play—Romo.

SHORTSTOPS

Player and Club	G.	PO.	A.	E.	DP.	Pct.	Player and Club	G.	PO.	A.	E.	DP.	Pct.
R. Chavarria, Zac	18	28	38	3	6	.957	Romo, Fre	29	56	79	13	12	.912
Rios, Guan	13	28	27	3	5	.948	Anaya, Guan	46	75	111	18	14	.912
Montiel, Fre	40	68	136	13	14	.940	Nava, Zac	13	23	28	5	5	.911
BANUELOS, LM	68	101	186	21	28	.932	Lizarraga, Acam	25	31	85	12	10	.906
E. Torres, Zac	18	37	53	8	3	.918	V. Lopez, C.Vic	65	108	176	30	26	.904
Jimenez, Acam	42	75	109	17	17	.915	Esqueda, Zac	14	16	34	6	7	.893

(Fewer Than Ten Games)

Player and Club	G.	PO.	A.	E.	DP.	Pct.	Player and Club	G.	PO.	A.	E.	DP.	Pct.
Castellon, Acam	4	6	11	0	2	1.000	Iniguez, Zac	6	12	14	2	3	.929
Carreno, Guan	2	4	5	0	0	1.000	Velarde, Guan	2	3	3	2	1	.750
R. Lopez, C.Vic	0	4	0	0	0	1.000	Solis, Acam	2	4	2	2	1	.750
Perez, Guan	8	18	28	3	6	.939	Camargo, C.Vic	2	1	6	3	0	.700

THIRD BASEMEN

Player and Club	G.	PO.	A.	E.	DP.	Pct.	Player and Club	G.	PO.	A.	E.	DP.	Pct.
Esqueda, Zac	46	66	139	11	9	.949	R. Moreno, Acam	23	20	52	7	5	.911
FLORES, Fre	54	83	129	13	17	.942	Montiel, Fre	29	27	84	11	7	.910
Zamora, Lagos de M	68	64	188	18	16	.933	Miranda, Fre	37	39	96	15	7	.900
Pineda, Guan	13	17	41	5	3	.921	Contreras, Zac	11	11	21	5	3	.865
Gonzalez, Acam	26	12	75	8	4	.916	Garcia, Acam	30	31	69	16	5	.862
Robles, Guan	10	15	27	4	2	.913	Velarde, Guan	28	33	64	16	9	.858

(Fewer Than Ten Games)

Player and Club	G.	PO.	A.	E.	DP.	Pct.	Player and Club	G.	PO.	A.	E.	DP.	Pct.
Anaya, Guan	6	7	10	0	2	1.000	Barrera, Fre	3	3	4	1	1	.875
Carreno, Guan	5	3	17	1	1	.952	R. Chavarria, Zac	6	8	8	3	1	.842
Avila, Acam	3	7	3	1	3	.909	Perez, Guan	8	11	14	5	3	.833
Torres, C.Vic	7	12	12	3	1	.889	Sanchez, C.Vic	8	7	10	4	1	.810
Castro, Zac	6	8	14	3	3	.880							

Triple Play—Miranda.

OUTFIELDERS

Player and Club	G.	PO.	A.	E.	DP.	Pct.	Player and Club	G.	PO.	A.	E.	DP.	Pct.
M. CHAVARRIA, Zac	63	131	9	0	2	1.000	Clayton, C.Vic*	66	140	9	4	2	.974
Lozano, Zac	37	55	0	0	0	1.000	Villagomez, Fre	21	29	1	1	0	.968
Sanchez, C.Vic	24	39	2	0	1	1.000	Ornelas, C.Vic	65	112	7	4	1	.967
Gonzalez, Acam	18	31	2	0	0	1.000	J. Martinez, C.Vic	28	53	5	2	1	.967
Perez, Zac	12	25	1	0	0	1.000	E. Torres, Zac	49	99	8	4	1	.964
Miranda, Fre	12	17	2	0	2	1.000	Rodriguez, Guan	33	50	3	2	2	.964
Pacheco, Lagos de M	16	15	1	0	0	1.000	Villela, Guan	69	139	14	6	5	.962
Avila, Acam	10	12	1	0	0	1.000	Acosta, Fre	69	122	9	6	1	.956
Guzman, Lagos de M...	68	128	10	1	1	.993	R. Guzman, Acam	57	92	11	5	3	.954
Hurtado, Acam	57	99	5	1	0	.990	Roman, Fre	69	167	15	9	6	.953
H. Guzman, Acam	65	128	12	3	2	.979	Rodriguez, Lagos de M ..	56	76	3	4	0	.952
Figueroa, Lagos de M	65	118	8	3	2	.977	Mariscal, Guan	31	36	2	2	0	.950

OUTFIELDERS—Continued

Player and Club	G.	PO.	A.	E.	DP.	Pct.
Velarde, Guan	13	18	1	1	0	.950
Cardona, Zac	22	32	1	2	0	.943
Munoz, Fre	33	48	1	3	0	.942
Soto, Guan	32	55	3	4	1	.935
Iniguez, Zac	16	29	0	2	0	.935
R. Lopez, C.Vic	24	39	2	3	0	.932
Contreras, Zac	13	6	1	1	0	.875
Molina, Guan	13	13	0	2	0	.867

(Fewer Than Ten Games)

Player and Club	G.	PO.	A.	E.	DP.	Pct.
Pineda, Guan	7	12	0	0	0	1.000
E. Urias, Acam	6	7	0	0	0	1.000
Escalante, Guan	4	5	0	0	0	1.000
T. Guzman, Acam	7	4	0	0	0	1.000
Morales, Guan	7	14	0	1	0	.933
Barrera, Fre	5	7	1	1	0	.889

CATCHERS

Player and Club	G.	PO.	A.	E.	DP.	PB.	Pct.
Nolasco, Lagos de M	16	74	7	0	0		1.000
Ramirez, Guan	27	142	29	3	1	11	.983
Del Bosque, Guan	16	102	12	2	1	8	.983
Martinez, Fre	20	92	14	2	3	16	.981
HERAS, Lagos de M.	58	366	47	8	2	16	.981
Molina, Guan	24	125	42	4	4	15	.977
Barrera, Fre	52	219	42	7	7	14	.974
Castro, Zac	27	124	24	5	3	7	.967
Aguilar, Acam	57	235	46	10	4	33	.966
Sanchez, Zac	43	189	34	8	1	16	.965
M. A. Esquer, C.Vic	16	64	18	3	1	8	.965
Camargo, C.Vic	49	208	50	10	4	35	.963

(Fewer Than Ten Games)

Player and Club	G.	PO.	A.	E.	DP.	PB.	Pct.
Prior, Guan	2	10	0	0	0		1.000
Cobos, Fre	1	1	0	0	0	2	1.000
Blancas, Acam	9	46	5	1	2	7	.981
Luna, C.Vic	7	25	5	1	0	5	.968
Avila, Acam	8	25	11	2	0	3	.947

PITCHERS

Player and Club	G.	PO.	A.	E.	DP.	Pct.
PINA, Lagos de M	21	3	26	0	1	1.000
Munguia, Lagos de M	18	1	20	0	1	1.000
Sauceda, C.Vic	18	3	17	0	1	1.000
Ruiz, Lagos de M	14	4	15	0	2	1.000
Perez, C.Vic	22	2	13	0	0	1.000
Esparza, Lagos de M	13	2	13	0	0	1.000
F. Mondragon, LM*	14	1	12	0	0	1.000
G. Moreno, Acam	17	3	9	0	1	1.000
Ayon, Fre	12	1	7	0	1	1.000
Avila, Guan	15	1	4	0	0	1.000
S. Vargas, Guan	10	2	1	0	0	1.000
Vazquez, Guan	21	6	23	1	1	.967
Torres B., Fre	15	4	16	1	1	.952
Jorge Valdez, Guan	15	2	14	1	1	.941
Camarena, Zac	13	3	12	1	2	.938
Reynoso, Fre	11	3	12	1	0	.938
Torres F., Zac	11	5	9	1	0	.933
Ibarra, Fre	17	5	23	2	1	.933
G. Martinez, C.Vic	21	5	23	2	0	.933
Limon, Lagos de M	14	4	10	1	1	.533
Flores, Zac	14	4	10	1	0	.933
Casas, Acam	17	5	8	1	0	.929
Diaz, Fre	14	1	12	1	2	.929
Gutierrez, Acam	13	3	10	1	0	.929
J. Urias, Acam	19	2	22	2	2	.923
Mart. Beltran, Zac	14	4	20	2	1	.923
Lopez, Acam	15	4	17	2	2	.913
Marg. Beltran, Zac	16	6	14	2	1	.909
Ibarra, Zac	16	0	10	1	0	.909
Solis, Acam	16	3	16	2	2	.905
Tafoya, C.Vic	17	4	15	2	1	.905
L. Cervantes, Guan	13	2	7	1	0	.900
Acuna, C.Vic	15	3	15	2	2	.900
Mer. Esquer, C.Vic	14	6	17	3	3	.885
Mendoza, Fre	15	7	16	3	1	.885
Avalos, Acam	13	1	5	1	0	.857
Valdez, Zac	13	0	16	3	1	.842
Marin, Guan*	14	2	12	3	1	.824
A. Cervantes, Guan	14	2	12	3	1	.824
Pereda, Fre	18	2	12	3	1	.824
Madrigal, Fre	14	1	8	2	0	.818
Robles, Zac	12	1	4	2	0	.714

(Fewer Than Ten Games)

Player and Club	G.	PO.	A.	E.	DP.	Pct.
Gastelum, Guan	8	0	8	0	1	1.000
Jesus Valdez, Guan	3	2	5	0	1	1.000
V. Garcia, Lagos de M	6	2	5	0	0	1.000
Galata, Guan	6	2	4	0	0	1.000
A. Moreno, Acam	8	0	5	0	0	1.000
Felix, Zac	3	1	2	0	0	1.000
F. Garcia, Lagos de M	8	1	5	1	0	.857
Oliva, Zac	8	0	6	2	1	.750
Cifuentes, Zac	6	0	3	1	0	.750

NOTE: No compilation made of fielders who had no chances.

CLUB PITCHING

Club	G.	CG.	ShO.	Sv.	IP.	H.	R.	ER.	HR.	BB.	Int. BB.	HB.	SO.	WP.	Bk.	ERA.
Lagos de Moreno	68	40	6	4	558	514	216	137	29	185	3	32	411	22	3	2.21
Guanajuato	69	36	4	5	552	600	313	184	22	194	13	24	338	45	5	3.00
Zacatecas	68	31	5	2	534	638	341	196	23	188	13	25	279	35	2	3.30
Acambaro	69	32	3	3	550	588	306	206	21	228	16	30	279	43	10	3.37
Ciudad Victoria	67	35	5	6	541	619	334	217	28	245	15	35	255	38	2	3.61
Fresnillo	69	26	6	4	550	697	403	250	43	205	19	31	245	42	3	4.09

PITCHERS' RECORDS

(Leading Qualifiers for Earned-Run Average Leadership—56 or More Innings)

*Throws lefthanded.

Pitcher–Club	G	GS	CG	ShO	W	L	Sv	Pct.	IP	H	R	ER	HR	BB	Int. BB	HB	SO	WP	ERA
Munguia, LM	18	9	8	2	10	3	0	.769	86	65	18	10	2	30	1	2	70	1	1.05
Mart. Beltran, Zac	14	14	13	3	7	6	0	.538	97	91	30	16	1	19	3	1	66	8	1.48
Esparza, LM	13	9	5	1	7	3	1	.700	73	35	21	13	2	26	1	3	46	5	1.60
Marg. Beltran, Zac	13	12	9	1	6	5	0	.545	93	85	32	17	3	18	0	2	49	4	1.65
Jorge Valdez, Guan	15	10	7	1	3	4	0	.429	81	81	36	16	3	31	7	1	46	1	1.78
Limon, Lagos de M	14	13	8	0	9	2	0	.818	91	90	32	19	3	26	0	3	72	0	1.88
Pina, Lagos de M	21	15	10	1	9	5	2	.643	134	119	53	35	9	49	1	17	111	9	2.35
Casas, Acambaro	17	14	11	1	10	3	0	.769	105	93	43	28	4	25	3	9	66	7	2.40
Mer. Esquer, CVic	14	13	7	2	5	6	0	.455	90	87	38	24	3	36	2	4	37	6	2.40
A. Cervantes, Guan	14	11	9	2	6	4	1	.600	81	77	39	24	3	23	1	2	56	13	2.67

Departmental Leaders: G—Perez, 22; GS—G. Martinez, Pina, 15; CG—Martin Beltran, 13; ShO—Martin Beltran, Reynosa, 3; W—Casas, Munguia, Vazquez, 10; L—Ibarra (Fresnillo), 8; Sv—Perez, 4; Pct.—Limon, .818; IP—Pina, 134; H—G. Martinez, 148; R—G. Martinez, 81; ER—G. Martinez, 50; HR—Mendoza, 10; BB—Vazquez, 55; IBB—G. Martinez, Jorge Valdez, 7; HB—Pina, 17; SO—Pina, 111; WP—A. Cervantes, 13.

(All Pitchers—Listed Alphabetically)

Pitcher–Club	G	GS	CG	ShO	W	L	Sv	Pct.	IP	H	R	ER	HR	BB	Int. BB	HB	SO	WP	ERA
Acuna, CVic	13	5	1	0	3	1	0	.750	50	72	48	31	6	23	2	4	9	1	5.58
Avalos, Acam	10	1	0	0	1	2	0	.333	26	23	18	10	1	13	1	4	6	2	3.46
Ayon, Fre	12	8	1	0	1	7	0	.125	51	75	51	33	6	20	1	7	19	7	5.82
Avila, Guan	15	0	0	0	0	1	0	.000	33	52	36	21	4	7	0	0	16	5	5.73
Marg. Beltran, Zac	13	12	9	1	6	5	0	.545	93	85	32	17	3	18	0	2	49	4	1.65
Martin Beltran, Zac	14	14	13	3	7	6	0	.538	97	91	30	16	1	19	3	1	66	8	1.48
Bernal, CVic	4	2	2	1	2	0	0	1.000	16	13	6	2	1	5	0	1	10	3	1.13
Berumen, Zac	2	0	0	0	0	2	0	.000	3	6	4	3	0	1	0	1	1	2	9.00
Camarena, Zac	13	2	1	0	2	3	0	.400	32	59	40	18	2	13	1	2	10	4	5.06
Casas, Acam	17	14	11	1	10	3	0	.769	105	93	43	28	4	25	3	9	66	7	2.40
Castillo, Fre	8	0	0	0	1	1	0	.500	12	22	16	9	0	9	2	0	4	2	6.75
Castro, Zac	1	0	0	0	0	0	0	.000	2	4	2	1	1	0	0	0	1	0	4.50
A. Cervantes, Guan	14	11	9	2	6	4	1	.600	81	77	39	24	3	23	1	2	56	13	2.67
L. Cervantes, Guan	15	11	7	0	6	5	2	.545	82	93	39	27	6	23	0	2	66	8	2.96
Cifuentes, Zac	6	1	0	0	0	0	0	.000	11	16	16	11	2	7	2	1	7	0	9.00
Clayton, CVic	2	0	0	0	0	0	0	.000	1	1	6	3	0	5	0	1	0	0	27.00
Mau. Contreras, Guan	2	0	0	0	0	0	0	.000	5	5	3	2	0	5	0	0	1	0	3.60
Diaz, Fre	14	1	1	0	2	3	0	.400	46	41	21	8	1	14	1	1	14	2	1.57
Esparza, LM	13	9	5	1	7	3	1	.700	73	35	21	13	2	26	1	3	46	5	1.60
Mer. Esquer, CVic	14	13	7	2	5	6	0	.455	90	87	38	24	3	36	2	4	37	6	2.40
Felix, Zac	3	2	0	0	0	2	0	.000	5	16	12	7	2	2	0	0	6	0	12.60
Flores, Zac	14	9	1	0	2	2	1	.500	55	81	43	29	2	24	2	0	17	1	4.75
F. Garcia, LM	8	8	3	1	5	0	0	1.000	52	51	19	13	3	18	0	0	43	2	2.25
V. Garcia, LM	6	4	3	0	2	2	0	.500	35	37	11	9	2	6	0	2	22	0	2.31
Gastelum, Guan	8	3	0	0	0	1	0	.000	23	34	15	9	1	4	0	2	15	4	3.52
Guadiana, CVic	2	0	0	0	0	0	0	.000	2	3	4	3	0	2	0	0	2	0	13.50
Guerrero, Fre	1	0	0	0	0	0	0	.000	3	9	6	3	0	1	0	0	1	0	9.00
Gutierrez, Acam	13	12	1	0	2	5	0	.286	65	84	55	35	3	45	3	6	44	7	4.85
Herrera, Guan	1	1	0	0	0	1	0	.000	5	7	4	2	0	4	2	0	3	0	3.60
Ibarra, Fre	16	1	1	0	1	1	0	.500	47	57	33	13	2	14	1	2	35	4	2.49
Ibarra, Fre	17	14	7	1	5	8	1	.385	96	110	60	39	6	42	3	6	53	8	3.66
Lagunes, Acam	2	0	0	0	0	0	0	.000	3	5	3	2	0	4	0	0	1	0	6.00
Limon, LM	14	13	8	0	9	2	0	.818	91	90	32	19	3	26	0	3	72	0	1.88
Lopez, Acam	15	13	3	0	2	6	1	.250	87	88	59	37	4	50	0	7	49	10	3.83
Madrigal, Fre	14	7	1	0	1	4	0	.200	51	74	38	25	5	10	1	2	17	1	4.41
Marin, Guan*	13	13	6	0	3	7	0	.300	70	81	40	26	2	28	1	4	29	3	3.34
G. Martinez, CVic	21	15	8	0	5	7	1	.417	127	148	81	50	5	54	7	9	51	9	3.54
Mena, Zac	1	1	0	0	0	1	0	.000	1	1	3	1	0	2	0	0	0	0	9.00
Mendoza, Fre	15	12	6	1	6	5	0	.545	82	109	64	43	10	19	3	3	34	2	4.72
F. Mondragon, LM*	14	3	1	0	1	1	1	.500	30	39	17	9	1	9	0	1	16	3	2.70
A. Moreno, Acam	8	1	0	0	2	1	0	.667	28	32	17	9	0	15	1	1	11	4	2.89
G. Moreno, Acam	17	1	1	0	4	5	2	.444	42	45	22	13	0	13	2	1	19	2	2.79
Munguia, LM	18	9	8	2	10	3	0	.769	86	65	18	10	2	30	1	2	70	1	1.05
Murillo, LM	1	0	0	0	0	0	0	.000	2	1	0	0	0	1	0	0	2	0	0.00
Nieblas, CVic	3	3	2	1	2	0	0	1.000	13	9	4	4	0	7	0	0	20	0	1.57
Oliva, Zac	8	8	0	0	3	1	0	.750	40	41	26	18	0	42	0	6	25	6	4.05
Olivares, Acam	3	0	0	0	0	0	0	.000	4	3	3	2	2	4	1	0	1	1	4.50
Ornelas, CVic	2	0	0	0	0	0	0	.000	5	4	1	1	0	2	0	0	2	0	1.80
Pena, Zac	4	2	2	0	3	0	0	1.000	14	9	7	6	1	4	0	1	16	0	3.00
Pereda, Fre	18	9	4	1	4	4	1	.500	70	77	43	23	5	38	6	2	46	6	2.96
Perez, CVic	22	1	0	0	3	7	4	.300	51	65	44	31	2	34	2	7	23	3	5.47

Pitcher—Club	G.	GS.	CG.	ShO.	W.	L.	Sv.	Pct.	IP.	H.	R.	ER.	HR.	Int. BB.	BB.	HB.	SO.	WP.	ERA.
Pina, LM	21	15	10	1	9	5	2	.643	134	119	53	35	9	49	1	17	111	9	2.35
Podres, Fre	9	2	0	0	3	0	0	.000	22	35	21	14	0	11	1	1	6	4	5.73
Raga, CVic	1	1	0	0	1	0	0	.000	3	9	6	4	1	2	0	0	0	0	12.00
Reynoso, Fre	11	9	5	3	4	2	1	.667	55	62	29	19	3	9	1	2	32	1	3.11
Robles, Zac	12	3	0	0	2	4	0	.333	40	52	34	21	3	13	2	4	14	5	4.73
Romero, Fre	6	0	0	0	0	1	0	.000	11	17	7	4	2	2	0	0	3	0	3.27
Ruiz, LM	14	7	2	0	4	4	0	.500	55	77	45	29	7	20	0	4	29	2	4.75
Sauceda, CVic	18	13	8	1	5	7	0	.417	90	109	48	34	7	29	1	6	51	6	3.40
Solis, Acam	16	13	7	2	5	7	0	.417	83	88	52	33	2	16	0	1	35	5	3.58
Tafoya, CVic	17	14	7	0	7	6	1	.538	83	89	44	30	3	46	1	3	50	10	3.25
Torres B., Fre	15	7	1	0	2	2	1	.500	51	66	47	30	5	30	0	7	16	9	5.29
Torres F., Zac	11	9	4	0	2	5	0	.286	53	62	31	21	2	11	1	1	14	1	3.57
Unate, Guan	1	1	1	0	0	1	0	.000	8	2	1	0	0	1	0	1	10	0	0.00
J. Urias, Acam	19	14	9	0	6	7	0	.462	107	127	64	37	5	43	5	1	47	5	3.11
Valdez, Zac	13	2	0	0	2	5	1	.286	37	48	25	14	2	18	1	4	18	4	3.41
Jesus Valdez, Guan	3	3	2	0	1	2	0	.333	23	25	12	7	0	4	0	1	14	2	2.74
Jorge Valdez, Guan	15	10	7	1	3	4	0	.429	81	81	36	16	3	31	7	1	46	1	1.78
F. Vargas, Guan	3	2	0	0	2	0	0	.000	5	8	8	2	1	0	0	0	2	3	3.60
S. Vargas, Guan	10	0	0	0	2	0	1	1.000	29	31	13	7	2	4	0	3	15	0	2.17
Vazquez, Guan	21	12	4	0	10	4	2	.714	93	86	57	35	0	55	1	8	65	4	3.39

BALKS—Casas, 4; Lopez, 3; Ruiz, Jorge Valdez, 2 each; Diaz, Mer. Esquer, Felix, Flores, Gastelum, Ibarra (Fre), Marin, F. Mondragon, G. Moreno, Pereda, Sauceda, Solis, J. Urias, Vazquez, 1 each.

COMBINATION SHUTOUTS—Marin-Vazquez, Guanajuato; Esparza-V. Garcia, Lagos de Moreno; Oliva-Ibarra, Zacatecas.

NO-HIT GAMES—Reynoso, Fresnillo, defeated Ciudad Victoria, 2-0, May 8 (seven innings); Esparza, Lagos de Moreno, defeated Fresnillo, 7-0, May 16.

Mexican Pacific League

CLASS A

STANDINGS OF CLUBS AT CLOSE OF SEASON, JULY 25

Club	W.	L.	T.	Pct.	G.B.	Club	W.	L.	T.	Pct.	G.B.
Ciudad Obregon	28	22	0	.560	......	Guasave	26	24	0	.520	2
Navojoa	26	22	2	.542	1	Hermosillo	24	25	1	.490	3½
Los Mochis	27	23	0	.540	1	Guaymas	19	28	3	.404	7½
Mazatlan	27	23	0	.540	1	Guamuchil (Culiacan)	20	30	0	.400	8

Playoffs—Los Mochis defeated Mazatlan, two games to none; Ciudad Obregon defeated Navojoa, two games to one. Ciudad Obregon defeated Los Mochis, three games to two.

Regular-Season Attendance—Ciudad Oregon, 15,146; Guamuchil, 6,992; Guasave, 3,965; Guaymas, 3,847; Hermosillo, 4,420; Los Mochis, 3,500; Mazatlan, 2,311; Navojoa, 14,264. Total, 54,445. No playoff figures available. No all-star game.

(Compiled by Humberto Galaz V., League Statistician, Hermosillo, Sonora, Mexico)

CLUB BATTING

Club	G.	AB.	R.	H.	TB.	2B.	3B.	HR.	RBI.	SH.	SF.	BB.	Int. BB.	HP.	SO.	SB.	LOB.	Pct.
Los Mochis	50	1558	212	406	522	60	16	8	167	16	16	104	13	13	232	53	298	.261
Ciudad Obregon	50	1668	204	413	499	35	21	3	147	48	12	88	37	12	150	57	344	.248
Guasave	42	1247	170	297	372	32	11	7	131	39	10	108	13	8	182	81	246	.238
Guamuchil	46	1424	187	332	431	53	5	12	139	42	6	183	12	13	229	38	273	.233
Mazatlan	46	1436	205	334	444	37	14	15	141	27	10	108	7	19	195	47	294	.233
Navojoa	50	1604	173	369	434	31	11	4	125	24	14	113	27	27	256	118	289	.230
Guaymas	50	1638	160	362	430	35	15	1	119	24	12	137	28	20	262	67	366	.221
Hermosillo	50	1618	147	317	374	30	12	1	105	48	9	115	28	17	308	35	294	.196

INDIVIDUAL BATTING

(Leading Qualifiers for Batting Championship—135 or More Plate Appearances)

Player and Club	G.	AB.	R.	H.	TB.	2B.	3B.	HR.	RBI.	SH.	SF.	BB.	HP.	SO.	SB.	Pct.
Vega, Ricardo, L Mochis	45	158	29	57	75	11	2	1	22	0	2	4	2	20	14	.361
Valdez, Baltazar, Cd Obr	43	147	21	45	60	4	4	1	19	1	1	6	1	26	0	.306
Felix, Concepcion, L Mochis	50	166	19	50	68	8	2	2	21	2	2	9	2	13	5	.301
Valenzuela, Guillermo, L Mochis	43	150	25	45	54	3	0	2	20	1	2	8	0	29	5	.300
Pacheco, Miguel A., L Mochis	44	155	23	46	55	7	1	0	10	3	2	7	2	17	9	.297
Mares, Hilario, Cd Obr	50	183	27	54	69	5	5	0	15	2	0	6	0	20	4	.295
Rojas, Humberto, Cd Obr	48	176	18	51	56	3	1	0	20	7	1	9	1	18	10	.290
Villela, David, Mazatlan	42	156	19	45	46	1	0	0	11	4	0	7	3	10	9	.288
Arandas, Severo, Mazatlan	46	163	27	47	70	6	1	5	30	0	6	13	0	30	4	.288
Gonzalez, Ernesto, Guaymas	50	185	18	53	66	5	4	0	21	3	3	15	1	17	8	.286
Bobadilla, Manuel, Cd Obr	47	175	28	50	58	8	0	0	16	3	1	7	0	23	7	.286

Departmental Leaders: G—Alcantar, Felix, C. Flores, G. Flores, E. Gonzalez, Mares, L. Morales, Navarrete, Sotelo, Torres, 50; AB—G. Flores, Navarrete, 188; R—Ric Vega, 29; H—Ric Vega, 57; TB—Ric Vega, 75; 2B—Ric Vega, 11; 3B—Buelna, Mares, Torres, 5; HR—Noris, 6; RBI—Arandas, 30; SH—J. Garcia (Herm), Munoz, 8; SF—Arandas, 6; BB—E. Espinoza, 22; HP—L. Morales, 8; SO—Sergio Valenzuela, 50; SB—Villaflor, 28.

(All Players—Listed Alphabetically)

Player and Club	G.	AB.	R.	H.	TB.	2B.	3B.	HR.	RBI.	SH.	SF.	BB.	HP.	SO.	SB.	Pct.
Alcantar, Carlos, Herm	50	179	15	26	37	4	2	1	7	5	0	9	1	37	4	.145
Alvarez, Miguel, Guas	18	63	8	22	28	1	1	1	13	0	0	1	1	5	4	.349
Alvarez, Jose M., L Mochis	1	1	0	0	0	0	0	0	0	0	0	0	0	1	0	.000
Amescua, Fernando, Maz	36	113	11	27	30	1	1	0	6	2	1	5	1	12	1	.239
Arandas, Severo, Maz	46	163	27	47	70	6	1	5	30	0	6	13	0	30	4	.288
Arce, Alfredo, Guay	15	28	1	3	3	0	0	0	1	5	0	0	0	7	0	.107
Arce, Francisco, Guay	7	14	2	3	3	0	0	0	1	1	0	5	0	7	0	.214
Arias, Ernesto, Maz	43	137	24	31	33	2	0	0	5	5	1	10	3	17	4	.226
Arias, Jesus, Guas	9	27	3	5	8	0	0	1	5	0	0	5	0	9	1	.185
Armenta, Eliodoro, Guam	22	62	6	13	13	0	0	0	5	3	1	5	1	18	2	.210
Ayon, Jaime, Guam	18	55	5	11	11	0	0	0	5	1	0	10	0	4	2	.200
Baldenegro, Fdo., Guas	27	66	11	11	15	4	0	0	4	2	1	7	0	20	3	.167

Player and Club	G.	AB.	R.	H.	TB.	2B.	3B.	HR.	RBI.	SH.	SF.	BB.	HP.	SO.	SB.	Pct.
Barret, Francisco, Maz	46	145	23	31	36	5	0	0	11	2	2	18	3	20	10	.214
Beltran, Gregorio, Guam	43	119	20	31	42	5	0	2	13	1	0	12	0	19	4	.261
Benitez, Julio Cesar, Guam	34	96	9	15	19	4	0	0	5	2	0	8	1	23	1	.156
Bernal, Cosme, Guas	38	111	15	24	34	3	2	1	13	6	2	10	3	23	5	.216
Bojorquez, Guadalupe, Guam	16	58	14	18	24	1	1	1	11	3	0	10	0	10	4	.310
Borbon, Marcelo, Cd Obr	47	173	20	46	53	2	1	1	19	4	1	14	0	29	11	.266
Buelna, Santos, Cd Obr	31	135	18	36	50	4	5	0	16	3	2	2	0	15	3	.267
Bobadilla, Manuel, Cd Obr	31	175	28	50	58	8	0	0	16	3	1	7	0	23	7	.286
Cabanillas, Luis, Herm	37	116	17	25	28	3	0	0	6	3	0	8	2	36	3	.216
Camacho, Daniel, Maz	9	14	1	3	5	0	1	0	2	0	0	1	0	5	0	.214
Camacho, Jose M., L Mochis	7	13	0	1	1	0	0	0	0	1	0	0	0	4	0	.077
Camacho, Sergio, Guas	16	45	8	9	9	0	0	0	5	1	0	4	1	10	1	.200
Campos, Cecilio, Guas	36	124	18	31	34	5	0	0	8	3	0	10	0	11	7	.250
Campos, Macario, Guas	30	81	10	22	24	2	0	0	7	5	1	9	0	6	5	.272
Castillo, Javier, Guas	28	87	9	17	23	4	1	0	10	1	2	7	2	14	5	.195
Castro, Pablo, Guas	7	18	1	2	2	0	0	0	1	0	1	0	0	4	2	.111
Cecena, Alberto, L Mochis	5	6	2	2	2	0	0	0	3	0	0	3	0	1	0	.333
Cervantes, Jorge, Guam	5	19	0	0	0	0	0	0	0	0	0	1	0	5	0	.000
Chavez, Roberto, Cd Obr	31	89	7	19	20	1	0	0	9	4	2	1	1	9	1	.213
Chig, Luis Alfonso, L Mochis	26	72	10	16	19	1	1	0	6	3	0	5	1	11	3	.222
Cota, Angel, Nav	35	116	6	26	30	2	1	0	3	1	0	5	0	18	6	.224
Cota, Gumaro, Nav	19	30	2	5	5	0	0	0	2	0	1	8	0	8	0	.167
De la Cruz, Jorge, Herm	1	1	0	0	0	0	0	0	0	0	0	0	0	0	0	.000
Diaz, Enrique, Guam	4	6	2	2	2	0	0	0	1	0	1	0	0	2	0	.333
Diaz, Fernando, Maz	7	13	0	2	2	0	0	0	0	1	0	1	1	2	0	.154
Duran, Ubaldo, Guay	39	116	13	33	36	1	1	0	11	4	0	13	3	14	7	.284
Enriquez, Jorge, Cd Obr	1	1	0	0	0	0	0	0	0	0	0	0	0	1	0	.000
Espinoza, Ernesto, Guam	44	135	18	33	48	7	1	2	7	1	0	22	2	19	7	.244
Espinoza, Javier, Guas	1	1	0	0	0	0	0	0	0	0	0	0	0	0	1	.000
Estrada, Pablo, Guay	3	4	1	2	2	0	0	0	0	0	0	0	0	1	1	.500
Fabela, Arturo, Guam	7	57	4	6	7	1	0	0	2	2	0	7	0	6	1	.105
Felix, Concepcion, L Mochis	50	166	19	50	68	8	2	2	21	2	2	9	2	13	3	.301
Flores, Cesar, Nav	50	178	19	48	57	3	3	0	20	3	2	9	2	24	5	.270
Flores, Guillermo, Herm	50	188	17	40	47	1	3	0	13	5	0	14	0	26	8	.213
Gamez, Ramon, Guam	3	4	0	1	1	0	0	0	0	1	0	0	0	1	0	.250
Garcia, Jesus, Herm	47	155	13	33	37	2	1	0	11	8	0	11	1	21	6	.213
Garcia, Jesus, Maz	24	93	12	24	31	1	3	0	11	1	0	8	3	14	4	.258
Garcia, Manuel, Guay	13	47	3	12	14	2	0	0	4	0	0	3	0	7	1	.255
Garcia, Rogelio, L Mochis	1	4	1	0	0	0	0	0	0	0	0	0	0	0	0	.000
Gaxiola, Ramon, Guam	25	70	11	17	24	7	0	0	8	2	0	13	1	8	3	.243
Gonsalez, Armando, Nav	11	30	1	5	5	0	0	0	2	1	1	2	2	2	0	.167
Gonzalez, Ernesto, Guay	50	185	18	53	66	5	4	0	21	3	3	15	1	17	8	.286
Gonzalez, Gabino, Cd Obr	31	94	8	19	22	1	1	0	6	4	0	5	0	19	1	.202
Gonzalez, Rene, Guay	18	45	6	7	9	0	1	0	2	0	0	3	0	11	0	.156
Grijalva, Francisco, Herm	31	87	7	15	17	2	0	0	5	6	0	8	0	20	0	.172
Gutierrez, Francisco, Herm	4	6	1	1	1	0	0	0	0	0	0	2	1	1	0	.167
Gutierrez, Porfirio, Guas	1	2	0	0	0	0	0	0	0	0	0	0	0	0	0	.000
Heredia, Manuel, L Mochis	11	35	6	9	12	1	1	0	6	0	0	2	2	9	1	.257
Juarez, Francisco, Maz	42	137	21	36	52	2	4	2	17	4	1	16	1	19	2	.263
Kawtman, Federico, Guam	34	109	19	29	41	3	0	3	17	3	0	7	2	25	1	.266
Leal, Francisco, Herm	3	3	1	0	0	0	0	0	0	1	0	1	0	1	0	.000
Leal, Marcos, Guay	48	180	12	42	53	7	2	0	21	2	1	7	0	19	4	.233
Leon, Ernesto, Nav	39	126	20	26	29	3	0	0	5	1	1	12	2	18	5	.206
Leon, Fernando, Nav	5	11	2	2	2	0	0	0	0	0	0	0	0	2	0	.182
Lopez, Alejandro, Guam	2	5	1	2	2	1	0	0	0	0	0	0	0	3	2	.400
Lopez, Bernardo, Guas	8	28	4	7	9	2	0	0	1	0	0	2	0	3	2	.250
Lopez, Jesus Manuel, Cd Obr	23	68	13	18	19	1	0	0	2	1	0	9	2	10	1	.265
Lopez, Jose Manuel, L Mochis	5	14	2	4	4	0	0	0	0	1	0	2	0	4	1	.286
Lugo, Roberto, L Mochis	14	31	1	5	5	0	0	0	1	2	0	0	0	7	0	.161
Madero, Carlos, Herm	29	89	3	10	10	0	0	0	5	3	1	3	1	10	0	.112
Mares, Hilario, Cd Obr	50	183	27	54	69	5	5	0	15	2	0	6	0	20	4	.295
Martinez, Oscar, L Mochis	9	38	4	12	12	0	0	0	4	0	0	0	1	0	0	.316
Martinez, Ricardo, Nav	1	0	1	0	0	0	0	0	0	0	0	0	0	0	0	.000
Martinez, Ruben, Guam	39	134	23	38	50	9	0	1	14	4	2	11	0	9	1	.284
Mascareno, Francisco, Guam	16	30	1	5	5	0	0	0	5	0	0	6	0	4	0	.167
Mejia, Miguel Angel, Guam	19	56	8	17	23	4	1	0	6	3	0	7	3	11	7	.304
Meza, Juan Jesus, Guay	26	85	6	13	14	1	0	0	4	1	0	13	3	19	1	.153
Milanes, Luis Fdo., Nav	36	121	7	25	25	0	0	0	3	0	0	4	2	22	6	.207
Montoya, Javier, Guas	2	2	0	0	0	0	0	0	0	0	0	0	0	0	0	.000
Mora, Manuel, Guas	39	124	17	28	34	3	0	1	14	5	1	15	1	23	13	.226
Morales, Luis, Nav	50	167	19	35	46	2	0	3	14	7	2	6	8	45	13	.210
Morales, Pablo, Cd Obr	19	60	4	11	13	2	0	0	6	0	1	2	1	9	0	.183
Munoz, David, Cd Obr	26	64	5	13	14	1	0	0	3	8	0	4	1	14	1	.203
Murillo, Jaime, Guay	18	63	6	9	11	0	1	0	3	0	0	11	1	8	2	.143
Navarrete, Francisco, Cd Obr	50	188	27	49	58	3	3	0	12	7	1	18	2	36	16	.261

Player and Club	G.	AB.	R.	H.	TB.	2B.	3B.	HR.	RBI.	SH.	SF.	BB.	HP.	SO.	SB.	Pct.
Navarro, Jesus, Maz	35	105	15	29	36	3	2	0	12	2	0	7	0	8	2	.276
Noriega, Raul, Herm	25	86	3	17	18	1	0	0	11	4	1	2	0	14	2	.198
Noris, Oscar R., Maz	46	160	22	36	66	10	1	6	17	2	1	11	3	29	2	.225
Ornelas, Jose, Herm	5	17	1	2	2	0	0	0	2	0	1	2	0	8	0	.118
Osuna, Victor M., L Mochis	10	31	2	5	6	1	0	0	2	1	0	3	0	6	1	.161
Pacheco, Miguel A., L Mochis	44	155	23	46	55	7	1	0	10	3	2	7	2	17	9	.297
Palomares, Trancito, Maz	21	56	9	8	12	2	1	0	4	1	0	7	0	13	2	.143
Parra, Esteban, Guam	6	14	1	1	1	0	0	0	0	0	0	5	0	4	1	.071
Poom, Jose Luis, Nav	48	178	17	37	46	7	1	0	22	0	1	19	0	32	6	.208
Quijano, Oscar, L Mochis	34	101	17	23	26	3	0	0	4	1	0	15	1	23	3	.228
Quinones, Ventura, Guas	25	63	10	12	12	0	0	0	2	4	0	1	0	9	2	.190
Quintero, Guadalupe, L Mochis	10	26	3	5	6	1	0	0	2	0	0	2	0	9	0	.192
Quintero, Victor, L Mochis	47	163	20	42	58	8	4	0	26	2	2	13	1	9	8	.258
Reyes, Juan, L Mochis	47	155	23	42	61	8	1	3	19	1	1	6	1	24	0	.271
Reyes, Pedro, L Mochis	17	46	6	7	9	0	1	0	1	0	0	8	0	12	1	.152
Rivera, Adrian, L Mochis	34	92	9	16	23	5	1	0	15	0	3	9	0	17	0	.174
Rojas, Humberto, Cd Obr	48	176	18	51	56	3	1	0	20	7	1	9	1	18	10	.290
Rojo, Artemio, Guay	9	34	3	7	8	1	0	0	0	0	0	2	0	0	0	.206
Rojo, Miguel A., Guam	17	41	10	9	11	0	1	0	2	4	0	14	1	9	2	.220
Rosas, Arturo, Nav	6	15	1	0	0	0	0	0	0	0	0	1	0	2	0	.000
Ruiz, Jose Luis, Guam	23	69	6	12	13	1	0	0	4	1	0	5	1	12	1	.174
Saiz, Herminio, Guam	8	16	2	5	5	0	0	0	1	0	0	6	0	1	0	.313
Salas, Cesareo, Nav	49	179	22	41	46	3	1	0	15	2	1	16	3	32	22	.229
Salas, Javier, Nav	33	157	18	43	48	3	1	0	10	4	5	17	0	16	26	.274
Sambrano, Francisco, Guam	26	91	8	27	34	4	0	1	12	3	0	12	0	9	1	.297
Sanchez, Aureliano, Guam	16	61	7	20	26	3	0	1	12	0	1	6	1	7	1	.328
Sanchez, Mariano, Guam	12	42	5	15	17	2	0	1	3	2	1	6	0	1	0	.357
Sanchez, Victor, Guas	38	124	17	29	42	4	3	1	14	1	0	12	0	11	5	.234
Sandoval, Antonio, Guay	46	165	18	32	38	4	1	0	5	1	2	6	2	37	8	.194
Sepulveda, Hector, Nav	4	10	2	3	4	1	0	0	0	0	0	1	0	1	1	.300
Sotelo, Emilio, Nav	50	173	22	40	48	2	3	0	13	3	2	17	4	25	15	.231
Soto, Porfirio, Guam	6	14	0	2	2	0	0	0	1	1	0	3	1	5	0	.143
Tabardillo, Luis, Cd Obr	6	11	2	2	2	0	0	0	3	0	1	3	0	7	0	.182
Tanori, Porfirio, Herm	44	145	22	36	39	1	1	0	10	1	1	21	2	30	4	.248
Tellaeche, Jorge, Guay	43	136	17	36	38	2	0	0	12	3	0	13	1	9	3	.265
Tellez, Ricardo, Guay	47	170	13	34	46	6	3	0	17	1	4	15	1	25	2	.200
Tirado, Ricardo, Maz	24	78	8	17	24	2	1	0	10	3	1	2	1	16	6	.218
Torres, Raymundo, Herm	50	186	12	47	60	3	5	0	23	7	4	5	5	29	10	.253
Trigueros, Fermin, Guay	17	58	7	13	19	1	1	1	4	0	0	5	0	11	1	.224
Valenzuela, Alfonso, Maz	16	59	10	17	21	2	1	0	6	0	0	4	0	2	0	.288
Valenzuela, Guillermo, L Mochis	43	150	25	45	54	3	0	2	20	1	2	8	0	29	5	.300
Valenzuela, J. Antonio, Cd Obr	34	76	6	15	18	0	0	1	7	2	0	5	0	12	1	.197
Valenzuela, S. Luis, Herm	20	57	7	8	9	1	0	0	4	1	0	6	0	20	1	.140
Valenzuela, Sergio, Herm	49	170	20	32	44	8	2	0	10	2	2	15	0	50	5	.188
Valdes, Baltazar, Cd Obr	43	147	21	45	60	4	4	1	19	1	1	6	1	26	0	.306
Valdes, Rodolfo, L Mochis	39	109	14	24	28	2	1	0	7	2	0	10	0	15	5	.220
Valverde, Juan M., Guay	24	78	4	17	22	3	1	0	6	0	0	7	0	26	2	.218
Vazquez, Pablo, Herm	25	65	7	10	10	0	0	0	2	0	0	5	1	15	0	.154
Vega, Ramon, Guas	42	141	22	40	53	4	3	1	20	3	0	12	0	6	10	.284
Vega, Ricardo, L Mochis	45	158	29	57	75	11	2	1	22	2	0	4	2	20	14	.361
Velasquez, Miguel A., Guas	42	132	18	27	33	1	1	1	12	6	3	18	0	23	18	.205
Verdugo, Agustin, Guam	8	19	2	3	3	0	0	0	2	1	0	1	0	8	0	.158
Verdugo, Jesus, Guam	14	43	5	9	11	2	0	0	3	2	0	3	0	8	1	.209
Villaflor, Francisco, Guay	45	155	23	29	30	1	0	0	6	3	3	20	2	24	28	.187
Villanueva, Jaime, Guam	4	9	0	1	2	1	0	0	1	1	0	0	0	3	0	.111
Villela, David, Maz	42	156	19	45	46	1	0	0	11	4	0	7	3	10	9	.288
Zuniga, Rafael, Nav	31	112	16	32	40	5	0	1	14	3	0	5	5	14	12	.286

The following pitchers had no plate appearances primarily through use of designated-hitters, listed alphabetically by club, games in parentheses:

CIUDAD OBREGON—Alvares, Angel (14); Alvares, Guadalupe (3); Armenta, Alfonso (15); Leyva, Jesus (12); Sabardillo, Luis (3); Valenzuela, Daniel (11).

GUAMUCHIL—Angulo, Oscar (29); Bustamante, Francisco (4); Camacho, Daniel (13); Castro, Hector (4); Garcia, Rogelio (7); Leon, Sergio (3); Rubio, Jose (4); Sanudo, Acencion (7).

GUASAVE—Berrelleza, Fidel (4); Castillo, Fernando (8); Castro, Ignacio (2); Espinoza, Jesus (3); Lara, Jose Manuel (16); Longoria, Federico (8); Montoya, Jose E. (10).

GUAYMAS—Arredondo, Francisco (6); Fuerte, Heliodoro (13); Lagunas, Arturo (3); Meza, Rigoberto (18); Olea, Manuel (4).

HERMOSILLO—Martinez, Hector (12); Martinez, Jesus (12); Ortiz, Leonardo (4); Rodriguez, Jesus R. (7); Sonoki, Eligio (4); Vazquez, Andres (14); Vazquez, Celso (9); Villegas, Ramon (15).

LOS MOCHIS—Almada, Raymundo (16); Alvares, Leopoldo (5); Castro, Juan (14); Rodriguez, Ramon (4); Salinas, Alberto (12); Soto, Emeterio (15); Vidana, Alejandro (7).

MAZATLAN—Gonsalez, Francisco (12); Lucas, Patricio (8); Peraza, Vidal (9); Rodriguez, Francisco (1); Rodriguez, Ignacio (7); Rodriguez, Sergio (11); Torres, Juan Manuel (13).

NAVOJOA—Ayala, Mario (14); Balderrama, Miguel (10); Fuerte, Jose Luis (6); Ortega, Francisco Javier (13); Valdez, Alvaro (15).

GRAND-SLAM HOME RUNS—None listed.

AWARDED FIRST BASE ON INTERFERENCE—None listed.

CLUB FIELDING

Club	G.	PO.	A.	E.	DP.	PB.	Pct.	Club	G.	PO.	A.	E.	DP.	PB.	Pct.
Cuidad Obregon	50	1318	620	83	38	12	.959	Mazatlan	46	1104	545	99	21	4	.943
Navojoa	50	1314	592	89	24	8	.995	Guaymas	50	1299	571	117	34	23	.941
Hermosillo	50	1309	613	94	35	11	.953	Guasave	42	933	441	91	24	12	.938
Los Mochis	50	1306	606	108	27	10	.947	Guamuchil	46	1159	547	134	15	15	.927

Triple Plays—None.

INDIVIDUAL FIELDING

FIRST BASEMEN

Player and Club	G.	PO.	A.	E.	DP.	Pct.	Player and Club	G.	PO.	A.	E.	DP.	Pct.
Garcia, Guay	13	116	7	0	6	1.000	Noris, Mazatlan	46	390	26	10	15	.977
Valdez, Cd Obr	28	266	3	3	13	.989	Mora, Guasave	39	239	18	7	16	.973
POOM, Navojoa	38	362	34	5	13	.988	Soto, Guamuchil	3	24	2	1	0	.963
Zuniga, Navojoa	10	74	6	1	3	.987	Gaxiola, Guamuchil	20	161	12	7	7	.961
S. Valenzuela, H	49	475	52	8	27	.985	Sanchez, Guam	12	65	9	3	3	.961
Bobadilla, Co Obr	36	270	55	5	26	.985	Arias, Guasave	8	46	3	3	3	.942
Valenzuela, LM	42	396	19	9	12	.979	Mejia, Guamuchil	19	144	8	10	2	.938
Leal, Guaymas	50	306	29	8	19	.977							

SECOND BASEMEN

Player and Club	G.	PO.	A.	E.	DP.	Pct.	Player and Club	G.	PO.	A.	E.	DP.	Pct.
Gutierrez, Herm	3	4	6	0	1	1.000	Reyes, Los Mochis	17	40	35	5	6	.938
P. Vazquez, Herm	22	43	42	2	10	.977	Arias, Guamuchil	42	92	35	9	10	.934
Zuniga, Navojoa	7	14	18	1	1	.970	Quijano, L Mochis	33	99	76	13	14	.931
BORBON, Cd Obr	46	126	122	8	20	.969	Sandoval, Guay	44	114	94	16	17	.929
Ayon, Guamuchil	17	29	32	2	3	.968	Campos, Guasave	35	74	68	11	12	.928
Tanori, Herm	40	87	77	6	11	.965	Diaz, Mazatlan	4	11	8	2	0	.905
Flores, Navojoa	50	102	99	11	11	.948	Castro, Guasave	7	11	5	3	1	.842
Zanbrano, Guam	26	62	46	7	2	.939							

THIRD BASEMEN

Player and Club	G.	PO.	A.	E.	DP.	Pct.	Player and Club	G.	PO.	A.	E.	DP.	Pct.
Rosas, Navojoa	2	1	8	0	0	1.000	Gonsalez, Guas	46	58	110	21	4	.889
Parra, Guamuchil	5	11	18	2	1	.935	Valenzuela, Maz	13	18	38	7	3	.889
C. SALAS, Nav	49	64	140	17	5	.923	Sanchez, Guasave	38	37	78	15	3	.885
Felix, Los Mochis	50	44	144	16	10	.922	Cabanillas, Herm	5	9	18	4	2	.871
Mares, Cd Obr	46	63	131	18	11	.915	Garcia, Mazatlan	24	28	39	11	2	.859
Arandas, Cd Obr	26	21	60	8	3	.910	Favela, Guamuchil	14	18	29	9	0	.839
Kawtman, Guam	29	42	56	10	0	.907	Heredia, L Mochis	7	9	13	5	0	.815
Garcia, Herm	42	45	97	15	6	.904	Rojo, Guasave	10	11	22	8	1	.805
J. Meza, Guas	23	40	51	11	8	.892							

SHORTSTOPS

Player and Club	G.	PO.	A.	E.	DP.	Pct.	Player and Club	G.	PO.	A.	E.	DP.	Pct.
Rojo, Guamuchil	17	31	34	2	2	.970	Quintero, L Mochis	47	76	165	26	15	.903
FLORES, Herm	50	87	171	13	15	.952	Salas, Navojoa	43	59	128	20	8	.903
J. Valenzuela, Cd Obr	33	33	80	6	1	.950	Saiz, Guamuchil	7	18	19	4	1	.902
Villela, Mazatlan	41	68	120	15	13	.926	Quinones, Guasave	24	31	51	13	5	.863
Gonzalez, Cd Obr	29	41	74	10	11	.920	Ruiz, Guaymas	23	43	47	15	7	.857
M. Campos, Guasave	28	51	61	11	7	.911	Bojorquez, Guam	16	24	69	17	5	.845
A. Arce, Guaymas	13	14	37	5	4	.911	Osuna, Guamuchil	10	11	32	8	0	.843

OUTFIELDERS

Player and Club	G.	PO.	A.	E.	DP.	Pct.	Player and Club	G.	PO.	A.	E.	DP.	Pct.
E. Leon, Navojoa	23	57	4	0	1	1.000	Murillo, Guaymas	18	34	1	1	0	.972
Arandas, Mazatlan	20	39	3	0	3	1.000	Trigueros, Guaymas	16	30	1	1	0	.969
Tellez, Guaymas	24	36	2	0	0	1.000	Chig, Los Mochis	24	30	0	1	2	.968
Martinez, L Mochis	9	10	3	0	0	1.000	J. Reyes, L Mochis	35	78	3	3	8	.964
Tabardillo, Cd Obr	6	6	4	0	1	1.000	Juarez, Mazatlan	42	48	4	2	0	.963
Lopez, Guasave	8	4	5	0	0	1.000	Villaflor, Guaymas	44	71	2	3	1	.961
TORREZ, Hermosillo	50	138	12	2	1	.987	Pacheco, Los Mochis	44	63	6	3	1	.958
Velazquez, Guasave	41	91	9	2	0	.980	Sotelo, Navojoa	49	118	7	6	2	.954
Noriega, Hermosillo	35	43	1	1	1	.978	Alcantar, Hermosillo	50	75	8	4	1	.954

OUTFIELDERS—Continued

Player and Club	G.	PO.	A.	E.	DP.	Pct.
Valdez, Los Mochis	27	36	4	2	0	.952
Camacho, Guasave	13	17	2	1	0	.950
Vega, Los Mochis	40	53	3	3	0	.949
Navarrete, Cd Obr	50	68	4	4	2	.947
Buelna, Cd Obr	20	33	3	2	1	.947
Milanes, Navojoa	36	47	5	3	2	.945
Martinez, Guamuchil	37	65	2	4	0	.944
Morales, Navojoa	49	88	9	6	4	.942
Tirado, Mazatlan	23	40	6	3	1	.939
Rojas, Cd Obr	48	70	5	5	2	.938
Lopez, Cd Obr	22	27	3	2	0	.938
Verdugo, Guam	7	11	4	1	0	.938

Player and Club	G.	PO.	A.	E.	DP.	Pct.
Espinoza, Guam	40	52	5	4	2	.934
Morales, Cd Obr	13	12	2	1	0	.933
Beltran, Guamuchil	37	69	8	6	0	.928
Bernal, Guasave	34	42	5	4	1	.922
S. Valenzuela, Herm	19	34	0	3	0	.919
Baldenegro, Guas	25	30	3	3	1	.917
Cervantes, Guam	4	11	0	1	0	.917
Barret, Mazatlan	46	72	3	7	1	.915
Duran, Guaymas	31	42	3	5	1	.900
Alvarez, Guasave	7	9	0	1	0	.900
M. Sanchez, Guam	12	15	0	2	0	.882
Ornelas, Herm	1	2	0	1	0	.667

CATCHERS

Player and Club	G.	PO.	A.	E.	DP.	PB.	Pct.
Cecena, Los Mochis	2	7	2	0	0	1	1.000
Sepulveda, Nav	1	6	0	0	0	1	1.000
CHAVEZ, Cd Obr	32	159	19	1	0	5	.994
Valverde, Guaymas	21	115	33	1	5	13	.993
Gonsalez, Navojoa	10	66	13	1	0	4	.988
J. Castillo, Guas	8	58	13	1	2	2	.986
Lugo, Los Mochis	13	56	12	1	1	3	.986
Navarro, Maz	34	144	38	3	0	4	.984
A. Cota, Navojoa	34	205	30	4	4	5	.983
G. Cota, Navojoa	11	40	8	1	1	0	.980
Tellaeche, Guaymas	37	228	30	7	2	9	.974

Player and Club	G.	PO.	A.	E.	DP.	PB.	Pct.
Verdugo, Guam	12	48	10	2	0	0	.967
Vega, Guasave	38	229	70	11	4	8	.965
Palomares, Maz	18	69	8	3	0	1	.963
Madero, Herm	22	94	20	5	2	2	.958
Benitez, Guam	19	84	21	5	0	6	.955
Quintero, L Mochis	9	32	9	2	0	3	.953
Munoz, Cd Obr	28	129	28	8	0	5	.952
Armenta, Guam	20	83	16	6	3	2	.943
Rivera, L Mochis	35	145	35	11	1	3	.942
Grijalva, Herm	29	121	18	10	2	9	.933
Leal, Hermosillo	2	7	2	1	0	1	.900

PITCHERS

Player and Club	G.	PO.	A.	E.	DP.	Pct.
I. Rodriguez, Maz	6	2	9	0	2	1.000
S. Rodriguez, Maz	7	8	0	0	0	1.000
F. Rodriguez, Maz	1	0	1	0	0	1.000
Espinosa, Guasave	11	3	7	0	2	1.000
Castillo, Guasave	4	0	1	0	0	1.000
Longoria, Guasave	5	0	4	0	1	1.000
I. Castro, Guasave	2	0	1	0	0	1.000
Leon, Guamuchil	2	1	2	0	0	1.000
Castro, Guamuchil	4	0	3	0	0	1.000
CAMACHO, Guam	12	3	16	0	1	1.000
G. Alvarez, Co Obr	3	0	1	0	0	1.000
Martinez, Navojoa	15	2	10	0	0	1.000
C. Vazquez, Herm	7	0	5	0	0	1.000
Olea, Guaymas	4	4	11	0	0	1.000
Lagunas, Guaymas	2	0	2	0	1	1.000
L. Alvarez, L Mochis	5	0	2	0	0	1.000
Almada, L Mochis	12	3	12	0	0	1.000
Vidana, L Mochis	4	0	5	0	0	1.000
Mascareno, Guam	13	21	18	1	0	.975
R. Meza, Guaymas	14	6	18	1	2	.960
Castro, L Mochis	13	2	19	1	0	.955
Leyva, Cd Obr	10	2	17	1	0	.950
Estrada, Guaymas	16	20	25	3	3	.938
F. Leon, Navojoa	10	1	13	1	1	.933
Gonzalez, Maz	8	5	21	2	0	.929
Armenta, Cd Obr	13	6	19	2	2	.926
Gutierrez, Guasave	10	3	9	1	2	.923
F. Arce, Guaymas	13	3	9	1	0	.923
Ortega, Navojoa	10	1	10	1	0	.917
A. Alvarez, Cd Obr	13	4	18	2	2	.917
Salinas, Guamuchil	9	2	9	1	0	.917

Player and Club	G.	PO.	A.	E.	DP.	Pct.
Torres, Mazatlan	12	1	20	2	0	.913
Montoya, Guasave	9	0	9	1	0	.900
Gonsalez, Guaymas	17	25	16	5	0	.891
De la Cruz, Herm	14	5	27	4	1	.889
Camacho, L Mochis	15	8	20	4	0	.875
Lara, Guasave	14	3	11	2	0	.875
Garcia, Guamuchil	4	1	6	1	0	.875
Fuerte, Guaymas	12	4	9	2	3	.867
Sanudo, Guamuchil	7	2	11	2	0	.867
Amezcua, Maz	13	8	22	5	0	.857
Enriquez, Cd Obr	12	4	20	4	1	.857
D. Valenzuela, Co Obr	8	2	10	2	0	.857
Martinez, Herm	7	1	5	1	0	.857
Fuerte, Navojoa	6	4	12	3	0	.842
Soto, Los Mochis	14	1	9	2	0	.833
Balderrama, Nav	10	0	5	1	0	.833
Ayala, Navojoa	12	0	10	2	1	.833
Vasquez, Herm	12	2	8	2	0	.833
Ortiz, Hermosillo	3	2	3	1	0	.833
Valdez, Navojoa	14	0	14	3	1	.824
Martinez, Herm	10	1	8	2	0	.818
Villegas, Herm	14	7	18	6	1	.806
Lopez, Guamuchil	4	1	3	1	0	.800
Gamez, Guamuchil	7	0	15	4	0	.789
Rodriguez, Herm	5	0	7	2	0	.778
Arredondo, Guasave	6	1	6	2	0	.778
Peraza, Mazatlan	8	2	7	3	0	.750
Sonoqui, Herm	2	1	1	1	1	.667
Lucas, Mazatlan	5	0	2	1	0	.667
Bustamante, Guam	4	2	2	2	1	.667
Rodriguez, LM	3	0	2	1	0	.667

NOTE: Fielding averages are incomplete.

PITCHERS' RECORDS
(Leading Qualifiers for Earned-Run Average Leadership—40 or More Innings)

Pitcher—Club	G.	GS.	CG.	ShO.	W.	L.	Sv.	Pct.	IP.	H.	R.	ER.	HR.	BB.	Int. BB.	HB.	SO.	WP.	ERA.
Olea, Guaymas	4	4	4	1	4	0	1	1.000	42	21	9	3	0	7	1	3	26	0	0.64
Armenta, Cd Obregon	15	12	7	4	7	3	0	.700	94	67	24	11	0	14	7	4	62	1	1.05
A. Alvarez, Cd Obregon	14	12	7	3	6	6	1	.500	104	63	26	13	0	21	2	5	75	3	1.13
Mascareno, Guamuchil	9	8	4	1	4	3	0	.571	46	46	21	7	1	17	3	4	19	3	1.37
Peraza, Mazatlan	9	4	1	0	3	3	0	.500	42	39	20	7	0	8	0	1	13	0	1.50

Pitcher–Club	G	GS	CG	ShO	W	L	Sv	Pct.	IP	H	R	ER	HR	BB	Int. BB	HB	SO	WP	ERA.
H. Martinez, Hermosillo ..	12	5	1	0	4	3	1	.571	45	35	12	8	0	21	1	0	11	2	1.60
Camacho, Los Mochis	15	11	6	1	5	5	0	.500	82	70	35	16	1	25	2	1	51	10	1.76
F. Arce, Guaymas	13	2	1	0	1	2	0	.333	41	35	13	8	0	8	2	0	20	2	1.76
Villegas, Hermosillo	15	12	7	1	4	7	2	.364	99	73	40	20	0	13	8	5	44	0	1.82
Estrada, Guaymas	15	12	9	2	7	5	1	.583	107	79	37	22	1	34	4	8	112	12	1.85
Ayala, Navojoa.................	14	12	9	3	8	3	1	.727	102	87	27	21	2	14	8	1	92	7	1.85

Departmental Leaders: G–Martinez (Nav), Meza, 18; GS–Castro (LM), De la Cruz, 13; CG–Castro (LM), 10; ShO–Armenta, 4; W–Castro (LM), Lara, 9; L–Fuerte (Gs), R. Gonzalez, 8; Sv–Enriquez, Ortega, 3; Pct.–Longoria, .833; IP–Estrada, 107; H–Lara, 83; R–Fuerte (Gs), 53; ER–Fuerte (Gs), 38; HR–Lopez, Jose Montoya, 4; BB–Estrada, 34; IBB–Valdez, 10; HB–Estrada, 8; SO–Estrada, 112; WP–Estrada, 12.

(All Pitchers–Listed Alphabetically)

Pitcher–Club	G	GS	CG	ShO	W	L	Sv	Pct.	IP	H	R	ER	HR	BB	Int. BB	HB	SO	WP	ERA.
Almada, L.Mochis	16	11	6	0	6	5	0	.545	78	64	34	24	1	27	2	2	45	8	2.79
A. Alvarez, Cd.Obr..........	14	12	7	3	6	6	1	.500	104	63	26	13	0	21	2	5	75	3	1.13
G. Alvarez, Cd.Obr..........	3	2	0	0	1	0	0	1.000	10	10	6	3	0	4	1	0	5	0	2.70
J. Alvarez, L.Mochis........	2	1	0	0	0	1	0	.000	7	13	9	9	2	3	0	0	2	0	11.57
L. Alvarez, L.Mochis	5	0	0	0	1	0	0	1.000	24	21	13	5	2	6	1	1	15	2	1.88
Amezcua, Maz..................	14	11	8	1	7	4	0	.636	90	76	36	19	1	26	1	2	65	2	1.90
Angulo, Guam	2	1	0	0	1	0	0	.000	3	5	3	1	0	0	0	0	0	0	3.00
F. Arce, Guay	13	2	1	0	1	2	0	.333	41	35	13	8	0	8	2	0	20	2	1.76
Armenta, Cd.Obr	15	12	7	4	7	3	0	.700	94	67	24	11	0	14	7	4	62	1	1.05
Arredondo, Guay	6	6	1	0	0	3	0	.000	39	39	15	11	0	13	4	5	23	4	2.54
Ayala, Nav	14	12	9	3	8	3	1	.727	102	87	27	21	2	14	8	1	92	7	1.85
Balderrama, Nav	10	6	2	1	3	2	0	.600	34	27	11	5	0	13	4	1	36	1	1.32
Berrelleza, Guas	4	1	0	0	1	0	0	1.000	8	8	4	4	0	1	0	0	3	1	4.50
Bustamante, Guam	4	0	0	0	0	1	0	.000	15	17	18	8	2	5	1	0	9	3	4.80
Camacho, Guas	13	5	1	1	2	2	0	.500	52	46	33	15	3	14	1	0	25	5	2.60
Camacho, L.Mochis	15	11	6	1	5	5	0	.500	82	70	35	16	1	25	2	1	51	10	1.76
F. Castillo, Guas	8	4	0	0	0	3	0	.000	14	18	16	11	1	17	0	0	5	0	7.07
Castro, Guam	4	0	0	0	1	1	0	.500	9	6	3	1	0	2	0	1	0	0	1.00
I. Castro, Guas	2	2	0	0	0	1	0	.000	6	12	8	7	0	0	0	3	0	0	10.50
Castro, L.Mochis.............	14	13	10	1	9	2	0	.818	87	79	36	24	0	32	3	2	49	2	2.48
De la Cruz, Herm	14	13	6	0	4	6	0	.400	87	78	38	18	0	25	2	4	49	11	1.86
Enriquez, Cd.Obr	15	9	4	0	3	5	3	.375	81	62	28	21	1	27	5	3	47	4	2.33
J. Espinoza, Guas	11	3	2	0	0	4	0	.000	40	40	21	17	0	15	1	2	24	1	3.83
Espinoza, Guas	3	1	0	0	0	1	0	.000	10	5	4	2	0	8	0	2	7	0	1.80
Estrada, Guay	15	12	9	2	7	5	1	.583	107	79	37	22	1	34	4	8	112	12	1.85
Fuerte, Guay...................	13	9	4	0	2	8	0	.200	67	76	53	38	0	9	2	3	41	2	5.10
Fuerte, Nav	6	6	2	0	2	3	0	.400	44	44	20	15	0	12	4	2	32	6	3.07
Gamez, Guam	9	7	5	0	3	5	0	.375	50	40	23	16	1	16	1	1	32	4	2.88
Garcia, Guam	7	6	0	0	1	3	0	.250	40	43	25	20	0	7	1	3	17	0	4.50
Gonsalez, Maz	12	9	7	1	3	7	1	.300	65	57	23	18	2	18	0	0	31	6	2.49
R. Gonzalez, Guay	12	9	2	0	2	8	0	.200	59	45	32	18	1	30	3	1	32	7	2.75
Gutierrez, Guas	17	6	2	0	4	5	0	.444	67	62	35	25	0	19	2	3	35	4	3.36
Lagunas, Guay	3	2	0	0	0	1	0	.000	6	12	7	7	0	2	1	0	2	0	10.50
Lara, Guas	16	11	7	3	9	3	0	.750	76	83	36	27	1	19	2	4	64	5	3.20
F. Leon, Nav	10	8	0	0	3	4	0	.429	52	47	25	16	0	13	8	2	21	5	2.77
Leon, Guam	3	2	0	0	0	3	0	.000	9	15	11	11	1	3	1	0	3	0	11.00
Leyva, Cd.Obr	12	12	7	2	7	4	0	.636	86	58	23	20	0	23	4	3	62	2	2.09
Longoria, Guas	8	7	4	0	5	1	0	.833	53	41	21	14	0	15	1	3	34	2	2.38
Lopez, Guam	8	5	2	0	2	2	0	.500	43	47	24	15	4	5	1	1	17	3	3.14
Lucas, Maz	8	3	0	1	1	1	0	.500	14	17	10	8	0	16	0	1	2	3	5.14
H. Martinez, Herm	12	5	1	0	4	3	1	.571	45	35	12	8	0	21	1	0	11	2	1.60
J. Martinez, Herm	12	2	1	1	2	2	0	.500	34	42	23	14	0	12	1	3	9	4	3.71
Martinez, Nav	18	1	0	0	3	2	2	.600	51	51	23	21	0	6	7	1	16	3	3.71
Mascarfio, Guam	9	8	4	1	4	3	0	.571	46	46	21	7	1	17	3	4	19	3	1.37
R. Meza, Guay	18	4	2	0	3	1	1	.750	57	52	29	26	1	22	4	3	35	9	4.11
Ja. Montoya, Guas	6	4	2	0	2	1	0	.667	23	21	23	6	0	5	1	0	21	1	2.35
Jose Montoya, Guas	10	3	0	0	1	0	0	.000	24	32	13	11	4	10	0	1	20	1	4.13
Olea, Guay	4	4	4	1	4	0	0	1.000	42	21	9	3	0	7	1	3	26	0	0.64
Ortega, Nav	13	5	4	0	2	4	3	.333	54	35	15	14	0	3	5	0	30	3	2.33
Ortiz, Herm.....................	4	3	1	0	2	2	0	.500	22	11	4	4	0	11	1	1	14	2	1.64
Peraza, Maz....................	9	4	1	0	3	3	0	.500	42	39	20	7	0	8	0	1	13	0	1.50
F. Rodriguez, Maz	1	1	0	0	0	1	0	.000	6	5	4	4	1	2	0	0	1	0	6.00
I. Rodriguez, Maz	7	2	1	0	2	0	0	1.000	24	31	10	5	2	2	0	1	11	0	1.88
Rodriguez, Herm	7	7	3	2	3	3	0	.500	45	47	16	13	0	14	1	0	21	3	2.60
Rodriguez, L.Mochis	4	1	0	0	1	1	0	.500	14	19	11	11	0	8	1	0	12	1	7.07
S. Rodriguez, Maz	11	6	2	1	4	2	0	.667	48	39	20	15	0	13	1	0	11	2	2.81
Rubio, Guam	4	0	0	0	0	1	0	.000	5	10	7	3	2	0	0	0	1	5	5.40
Salinas, L.Mochis	12	3	1	0	4	0	0	1.000	41	40	21	12	1	12	0	1	16	4	2.63
Sanchez, Guas.................	1	0	0	0	0	1	0	.000	2	4	4	4	1	3	1	0	0	0	18.00

Pitcher—Club	G.	GS.	CG.	ShO.	W.	L.	Sv.	Pct.	IP.	H.	R.	ER.	HR.	BB.	Int. BB.	HB.	SO.	WP.	ERA.
Sanudo, Guam	7	4	2	0	2	3	0	.400	32	29	13	9	1	11	2	1	18	5	2.53
Sonoki, Herm	4	1	0	1	0	1	0	.000	13	14	11	6	0	6	0	1	5	0	4.15
Soto, L.Mochis	15	11	6	1	5	7	0	.417	78	63	40	20	0	32	6	3	43	10	2.31
Sabardillo, Cd.Obr	3	1	0	0	1	1	0	.500	13	9	5	3	0	2	0	2	3	0	2.08
Torres, Maz	13	8	4	1	5	3	0	.625	75	49	25	17	0	23	1	4	48	5	2.04
D. Valenzuela, Cd.Obr	11	2	1	0	2	3	1	.400	36	40	22	10	0	9	6	1	7	0	2.50
Valdez, Nav	15	12	4	1	5	4	0	.556	95	69	30	24	0	23	10	1	64	8	2.27
A. Vazquez, Herm	14	6	3	1	4	1	2	.800	70	64	18	15	0	18	1	2	27	1	1.93
C. Vazquez, Herm	9	0	0	0	1	0	2	1.000	25	16	4	0	0	14	1	1	20	1	0.00
Vidana, L.Mochis	7	1	0	0	0	2	0	.000	17	14	8	6	0	10	1	2	4	2	3.18
Villegas, Herm	15	12	7	1	4	7	2	.364	99	73	40	20	0	13	8	5	44	0	1.82

No balks, combination shutouts, nor no-hit games listed. No club pitching totals available.

MAJOR LEAGUE CENTRAL SCOUTING BUREAU

1200 Quail Street, Suite 270

Newport Beach, California 92660

Phone: 752-0712 (Area Code 714)

Midwest League

CLASS A

CHAMPIONSHIP WINNERS IN PREVIOUS YEARS

1947 – Belleville .... .667	1958 – Michigan City................. .623	1967 – Wisconsin Rapids.......... .685
Belleville .... .672	Waterloo z..................... .613	Appleton z..................... .587
1948 – West Frankfort*............ .708	1959 – Waterloo .... .613	1968 – Decatur .... .656
1949 – Centralia .... .627	Waterloo .... .613	Quad Cities z .... .648
Paducah (4th)†.......... .454	1960 – Waterloo .... .629	1969 – Appleton .... .648
1950 – Centralia‡ .... .675	Waterloo .... .677	Appleton .... .690
1951 – Paris§ .... .700	1961 – Waterloo .... .613	1970 – Quincy z .... .691
Danville (4th)† .... .432	Quincy z .... .594	Quad Cities .... .581
1952 – Danville x .... .685	1962 – Dubuque z................... .667	1971 – Appleton .... .642
Decatur (3rd)† .... .584	Waterloo .... .625	Quad Cities a .... .548
1953 – Decatur* .... .576	1963 – Clinton .... .710	1972 – Appleton .... .598
1954 – Decatur .... .587	Clinton .... .629	Danville a .... .584
Danville (2nd)‡ .... .528	1964 – Clinton .... .667	1973 – Wisconsin Rapids a .... .562
1955 – Dubuque* .... .587	Fox Cities z................... .667	Danville..................... .537
Dubuque .... .603	1965 – Burlington .... .667	1974 – Appleton .... .593
1956 – Paris y .... .656	Burlington .... .677	Danville a .... .517
1957 – Decatur y .... .683	1966 – Fox Cities z................... .689	1975 – Waterloo a................... .727
Clinton............................ .623	Cedar Rapids .... .762	Quad Cities .... .624

*Won championship and four-club playoff. †Won four-club playoff. ‡Playoff finals canceled because of bad weather. xWon first half of split-season and tied Paris for second-half title. yWon first-half title and four-team playoff. zWon split-season playoff. (NOTE – Known as Illinois State League in 1947-48 and Mississippi-Ohio Valley League from 1949 through 1955.)

aLeague divided into Northern and Southern divisions and played split-season. Playoff winner.

STANDING OF CLUBS AT CLOSE OF FIRST HALF, JUNE 20

NORTHERN DIVISION

Club	W.	L.	T.	Pct.	G.B.
Waterloo (Royals)	38	24	0	.613	......
Wisconsin Rapids (Twins)	35	29	0	.547	4
Dubuque (Astros)	31	31	0	.500	7
Wausau (Mets)	31	33	0	.484	8
Appleton (White Sox)	24	38	0	.387	14

SOUTHERN DIVISION

Club	W.	L.	T.	Pct.	G.B.
Cedar Rapids (Giants)	37	24	0	.607	......
Burlington (Brewers)	34	30	0	.531	4½
Quad Cities (Angels)	30	31	0	.492	7
Clinton (Co-op)	28	36	0	.438	10½
Danville (Dodgers)	22	34	0	.393	12½

STANDING OF CLUBS AT CLOSE OF SECOND HALF, AUGUST 26

NORTHERN DIVISION

Club	W.	L.	T.	Pct.	G.B.
Waterloo (Royals)	40	28	0	.588	......
Wisconsin Rapids (Twins)	32	34	0	.485	7
Appleton (White Sox)	32	36	0	.471	8
Dubuque (Astros)	28	40	0	.412	12
Wausau (Mets)	25	40	0	.385	13½

SOUTHERN DIVISION

Club	W.	L.	T.	Pct.	G.B.
Quad Cities (Angels)	42	28	0	.600	......
Cedar Rapids (Giants)	41	29	0	.586	1
Burlington (Brewers)	34	31	0	.523	5½
Clinton (Co-op)	31	34	0	.477	8½
Danville (Dodgers)	34	39	0	.466	9½

COMPOSITE STANDING OF CLUBS AT CLOSE OF SEASON, AUGUST 26

NORTHERN DIVISION

Club	Wat.	W.R.	Dub.	Wau.	Apl.	C.R.	Q.C.	Bur.	Cln.	Dan.	W.	L.	T.	Pct.	G.B.
Waterloo (Royals)		9	10	7	8	8	7	7	11	11	78	52	0	.600	......
Wisconsin Rapids (Twins)	5	....	11	9	12	6	4	4	7	9	67	63	0	.515	11
Dubuque (Astros)	4	3	....	12	9	5	6	6	7	7	59	71	0	.454	19
Wausau (Mets)	7	5	6	....	6	6	3	9	7	7	56	73	0	.434	21½
Appleton (White Sox)	6	6	5	8	....	3	10	6	4	8	56	74	0	.431	22

SOUTHERN DIVISION

Club	Wat.	W.R.	Dub.	Wau.	Apl.	C.R.	Q.C.	Bur.	Cln.	Dan.	W.	L.	T.	Pct.	G.B.
Cedar Rapids (Giants)	10	8	9	8	11	....	8	7	9	8	78	53	0	.595	......
Quad Cities (Angels)*	7	10	8	11	4	7	....	7	11	7	72	59	0	.550	6
Burlington (Brewers)	7	10	8	5	8	7	7	....	8	8	68	61	0	.527	9
Clinton (Co-op)	3	7	7	6	10	5	7	6	....	8	59	70	0	.457	18
Danville (Dodgers)	3	5	7	7	6	6	7	9	6	....	56	73	0	.434	21

Quad Cities represented Davenport and Bettendorf, Ia., and Moline and Rock Island, Ill.

Major league affiliations in parentheses.

Playoffs—(*) Defeated Cedar Rapids, first half leader in Southern Division, in one-game playoff to determine winner of second half (included in final team standings and all team and individual batting, fielding and pitching statistics). Also defeated Cedar Rapids for Southern Division championship. Waterloo (Northern Division Champion) defeated Quad Cities (Southern Division Champion) two games to none for League Championship.

Regular-Season Attendance—Appleton, 55,398; Burlington, 46,675; Cedar Rapids, 78,801; Clinton, 35,425; Danville, 28,325; Dubuque, 58,437; Quad Cities, 66,062; Waterloo, 56,390; Wausau, 57,797; Wisconsin Rapids, 57,816. Total, 541,425. All-Star Game, 1,481. Playoffs, 9,163.

Managers: Appleton—Jim Napier; Burlington—Matt Galante; Cedar Rapids—Francis (Salty) Parker; Clinton—Robert Hartsfield; Danville—Dick McLaughlin; Dubuque—Robert Cluck; Quad Cities—Larry (Moose) Stubing; Waterloo—John Sullivan; Wausau—Bill Monbouquette; Wisconsin Rapids—Harry Warner.

All-Star Team: 1B—Garcia, Waterloo; 2B—Lacy, Waterloo; 3B—Fischetti, Danville; SS—Doerr, Clinton; OF—Barrios, Cedar Rapids; Parker, Waterloo; Pisker, Dubuque; Monasterio, Wausau; C—Cato, Cedar Rapids; Bulling, Wisconsin Rapids; DH—Hill, Wisconsin Rapids; P—Johnson, Cedar Rapids; Hodges, Cedar Rapids; Manager—Parker, Cedar Rapids.

(Compiled by Howe News Bureau, Chicago, Ill.)

CLUB BATTING

Club	G.	AB.	R.	OR.	H.	TB.	2B.	3B.	HR.	RBI.	SH.	SF.	BB.	HP.	SO.	SB.	CS.	LOB.	Pct.
Waterloo	130	4167	711	545	1109	1598	164	26	91	622	38	42	677	39	32	739	95	32	1058	.2661
Dubuque	130	4278	619	743	1137	1624	197	40	70	537	61	35	548	32	28	751	74	44	1059	.2657
Cedar Rapids	131	4201	654	505	1100	1568	178	43	68	558	66	40	599	28	39	630	71	26	1027	.262
Quad Cities	131	4316	654	570	1130	1560	184	45	52	559	36	48	591	28	28	622	176	59	1035	.262
Wis. Rapids	130	4286	736	704	1111	1649	190	24	100	648	40	35	727	27	30	827	95	39	1057	.259
Danville	129	4144	596	692	1063	1459	169	43	47	469	29	33	513	31	42	695	310	108	884	.257
Clinton	129	4133	579	648	1050	1363	149	34	32	485	49	43	578	27	36	655	222	55	980	.254
Wausau	129	4235	549	660	1065	1455	137	20	71	472	21	27	488	15	46	792	162	46	994	.251
Burlington	129	4306	623	551	1063	1496	180	35	61	517	60	35	575	30	26	683	118	43	1006	.247
Appleton	130	4105	572	693	978	1348	137	46	47	461	47	34	583	15	32	822	271	111	914	.238

INDIVIDUAL BATTING

(Leading Qualifiers for Batting Championship—351 or More Plate Appearances)

*Bats lefthanded. †Switch-hitter.

Player and Club	G.	AB.	R.	H.	TB.	2B.	3B.	HR.	RBI.	SH.	SF.	BB.	HP.	SO.	SB.	CS.	Pct.
Pisker, Donald, Dubuque*	86	322	51	111	183	25	10	9	51	2	1	24	2	64	12	7	.345
Fischetti, Arthur, Dan†	125	452	76	144	205	24	8	7	60	4	2	60	8	35	63	19	.319
Bulling, Terry, WR	112	352	85	109	150	13	2	8	50	4	4	102	2	33	1	0	.310
Cato, Wayne, CR	107	354	49	109	159	16	5	8	63	3	3	30	7	29	5	2	.308
Bradley, Mark, Danville	119	381	73	117	160	19	3	6	47	2	3	95	12	72	54	9	.307
Gillen, Kevin, Waterloo*	99	326	57	96	148	16	6	8	55	2	3	47	3	50	5	4	.294
Cipot, Edwin, Wausau*	127	446	71	131	197	21	0	15	77	0	2	81	9	53	9	4	.294
Brewster, Richard, QC*	112	436	73	128	155	9	9	0	39	10	3	45	3	28	34	11	.294
Yurak, Jeffrey, CR†	113	334	57	98	144	20	1	8	57	2	2	56	8	65	3	0	.293
Garcia, Daniel R., Wat*	123	422	73	123	141	12	0	2	44	6	7	73	6	44	26	5	.291
Clark, Robert C., QC	129	477	82	139	204	19	8	10	77	2	4	52	3	88	25	8	.291

Departmental Leaders: G—Clark, deLeeuw, Ditto, Etchandy, Romero, 129; AB—S. Benson, 498; R—Hill, 112; H—Fischetti, 144; TB—Hill, 260; 2B—Hill, Monteau, 30; 3B—Pisker, 10; HR—Hill, 30; RBI—Hill, 103; SH—LaRocque, Woodbrey, 13; SF—Quirk, 10; BB—Bulling, 102; HP—Bradley, 12; SO—Trucks, 132; SB—Fischetti, 83; CS—DelVecchio, 25.

(All Players—Listed Alphabetically)

Player and Club	G.	AB.	R.	H.	TB.	2B.	3B.	HR.	RBI.	SH.	SF.	BB.	HP.	SO.	SB.	CS.	Pct.
Adams, Robert W., Dan	2	3	0	0	0	0	0	0	0	0	0	1	0	1	0	0	.000
Alvarez, Jose R., Dub	20	53	15	10	11	1	0	0	5	0	1	26	1	14	1	0	.189
Alvarez, Juan C., Dan	7	23	4	4	7	0	0	1	2	1	0	1	0	9	0	1	.174
Aman, Kevan, Wausau*	57	189	16	44	53	4	1	1	14	0	0	17	1	32	3	5	.233
Amico, Robert, Danville	52	157	16	38	46	2	0	2	17	0	3	15	1	22	7	3	.242
Anderson, Gregory, Bur	103	389	62	97	142	13	4	8	38	2	2	47	3	82	26	9	.249
Antone, Michael, WR*	51	167	27	34	45	8	0	1	24	0	2	32	1	31	9	1	.204
Ashline, Steven, Wausau	13	35	2	10	10	0	0	0	3	0	0	4	1	9	1	0	.286
Attardi, Gerald, Apl*	6	9	0	1	1	0	0	0	0	0	0	0	0	1	0	0	.111
Bacon, Mike, WR	12	16	2	2	5	0	0	1	2	1	1	2	0	6	0	0	.125
Barranca, German, Wat*	92	319	69	89	109	14	3	0	27	3	2	69	2	48	7	3	.279
Barrios, Jose, CR	86	293	38	83	117	12	2	6	36	5	3	34	4	48	2	3	.283
Barton, Kenneth, CR†	116	399	56	90	130	19	3	5	45	8	5	50	1	43	4	1	.226
Bauer, Phillip, Clinton	125	458	69	116	139	17	0	2	44	6	3	68	8	55	26	4	.253
Bedrosian, David, Wau	52	181	19	42	42	0	0	0	14	1	0	29	2	40	11	2	.232
Beene, Stephen, Waterloo	67	185	26	37	64	4	1	7	22	3	1	39	0	57	2	2	.200
Benson, Steve, WR	124	498	89	135	191	25	2	9	65	9	3	64	3	88	23	10	.271
Benton, Alfred, Wausau	120	431	43	105	145	14	1	8	63	0	7	48	8	78	6	5	.244

Player and Club	G.	AB.	R.	H.	TB.	2B.	3B.	HR.	RBI.	SH.	SF.	BB.	HP.	SO.	SB.	CS.	Pct.
Bochy, Bruce, Dubuque	30	103	9	25	32	4	0	1	8	1	0	12	0	11	1	0	.243
Bodie, Keith, Wausau	115	428	59	111	154	15	2	8	43	1	3	41	3	77	5	4	.259
Bolek, Kenneth, Clinton*	53	147	21	42	53	6	1	1	18	2	2	53	1	31	4	0	.286
Boyle, Gary, Quad Cities	2	0	1	0	0	0	0	0	0	0	0	0	0	0	0	0	.000
Boyne, Bryan, CR	88	305	48	72	87	6	0	3	35	4	1	54	3	28	6	4	.236
Bradbury, George, Wausau	25	69	6	7	10	1	1	0	3	2	0	10	1	18	0	1	.101
Bradley, Mark, Danville	119	381	73	117	160	19	3	6	47	2	3	95	12	72	54	9	.307
Breaux, John, WR	1	1	0	0	0	0	0	0	0	0	0	0	0	1	0	0	.000
Brewster, Richard, QC*	112	436	73	128	155	9	9	0	39	10	3	45	3	28	34	11	.294
Brodell, Donald, Dan	25	78	8	10	13	3	0	0	4	1	0	3	0	14	1	0	.128
Bulling, Terry, WR	112	352	85	109	150	13	2	8	50	4	4	102	2	33	1	0	.310
Byrd, Leland, Clinton	82	225	27	40	55	4	1	3	21	2	5	49	2	40	5	3	.178
Calufetti, Lawrence, Wau	57	183	26	45	66	9	0	4	24	0	0	30	0	33	2	0	.246
Castino, John, WR	65	252	42	72	109	15	2	6	41	1	2	40	3	44	4	4	.286
Cato, Wayne, CR	107	354	49	109	159	16	5	8	63	3	3	30	7	29	5	2	.308
Channel, Thomas, WR	107	291	40	66	89	12	1	3	41	5	3	50	1	109	7	3	.227
Chappas, Harry, Apl*	102	378	61	99	136	9	8	4	38	3	1	54	2	55	40	20	.262
Cipot, Edwin, Wausau*	127	446	71	131	197	21	0	15	77	0	2	81	9	53	9	4	.294
Clark, Robert C., QC	129	477	82	139	204	19	8	10	77	2	4	52	3	88	25	8	.291
Cliburn, Stanley, QC	76	262	39	80	110	15	0	5	44	1	4	34	2	33	5	1	.305
Cloherty, John, Dub*	5	17	3	6	6	0	0	0	1	0	0	1	0	6	0	0	.353
Coulter, E. Roy, Apl*	3	2	0	0	0	0	0	0	0	0	0	1	0	1	0	0	.000
Curbelo, Jorge, WR	15	36	1	9	10	1	0	0	5	1	0	4	0	5	0	0	.250
Danson, J. Roger, Bur	66	247	47	61	94	18	3	3	26	1	3	36	0	52	14	5	.247
Davis, George H., Cln*	25	81	12	16	16	0	0	0	7	0	0	6	3	19	1	0	.198
de la Cruz, Gerardo, Dan	69	248	32	71	95	14	5	0	33	2	3	7	3	26	11	7	.286
deLeeuw, Karel, Waterloo	129	485	88	126	207	22	1	19	88	0	2	69	1	109	8	3	.260
de los Santos, German, CR	78	256	44	69	112	17	1	8	35	1	2	19	1	53	0	0	.270
DelVecchio, James, Dan	112	415	66	99	113	6	4	0	24	4	3	66	4	69	57	25	.239
DeMerritt, Martin, Dub	1	2	0	1	2	1	0	0	2	0	0	0	0	0	0	0	.500
DiPietro, Alfred, 32 Cln-15 WR	47	140	11	33	38	5	0	0	18	2	2	17	1	30	0	0	.236
Ditto, Julian, Clinton	129	469	75	132	189	26	8	5	71	4	2	63	4	76	34	9	.281
Doerr, Timothy, Clinton	128	494	72	143	199	24	4	8	76	4	5	40	2	55	16	2	.289
Echols, Tony, Wausau	101	370	45	89	117	11	1	5	28	4	0	25	2	88	32	6	.241
Ellison, J. Jeffrey, Dub	38	110	22	35	45	5	1	1	16	4	1	36	1	8	1	2	.318
Encarnacion, Miguel, Bur	75	253	16	59	71	10	1	0	27	8	4	13	3	58	0	0	.233
Etchandy, Curtis, Apl	129	447	77	115	184	21	3	14	70	4	5	65	8	97	22	11	.257
Eubanks, Larry, Dubuque	47	159	22	47	77	7	1	7	31	1	2	12	0	19	0	0	.296
Evans, Freeman, Clinton†	125	492	95	141	166	15	5	0	32	6	1	71	3	55	79	18	.287
Ewing, William, QC	18	71	8	20	31	4	2	1	5	0	0	4	0	9	2	0	.282
Fermin, Pompilio, Cln	17	57	7	9	14	3	1	0	2	1	0	2	0	26	0	1	.158
Fischetti, Arthur, Dan†	125	452	76	144	205	24	8	7	60	4	2	60	8	35	83	19	.319
Flannery, John, QC	121	418	59	82	96	12	1	0	36	8	5	51	5	65	11	4	.196
Fletcher, Donald, Clnt	26	66	6	7	8	1	0	0	4	1	0	17	0	27	1	0	.106
Flores, Adalberto, Bur	65	215	23	48	64	4	3	2	31	2	2	11	1	42	3	0	.223
Franklin, Elliott, Bur*	21	76	16	20	25	0	1	1	11	0	0	12	0	18	2	3	.263
Gale, Richard, Waterloo	1	1	0	1	1	0	0	0	0	0	0	0	0	2	0	0	1.000
Garcia, Daniel R., Wat*	123	422	73	123	141	12	0	2	44	6	7	73	6	44	26	5	.291
Gaughran, Gregg, WR*	84	249	47	58	89	14	1	5	38	1	1	52	2	67	3	1	.233
Gillen, Kevin, Waterloo*	99	326	57	96	148	16	6	8	55	2	3	47	3	50	5	4	.294
Glabman, Barry, Dubuque	112	368	60	92	148	23	0	11	56	4	6	68	6	77	2	2	.250
Globig, David, Bur	1	1	0	0	0	0	0	0	0	0	0	0	0	0	0	0	.000
Gomez, Miguel, Danville	1	1	0	0	0	0	0	0	0	0	0	0	0	0	0	0	.000
Grimes, Steven, CR	119	378	52	90	127	20	4	3	45	4	7	70	1	68	13	6	.238
Gulden, Bradley, Dan*	103	334	42	95	128	20	2	3	51	4	3	43	2	35	12	9	.284
Hallgren, Robert, Dub*	36	85	13	18	27	1	1	2	10	3	1	16	0	21	3	0	.212
Hamann, Kenneth, Apl	57	215	24	68	90	10	3	2	39	2	2	18	2	20	7	2	.316
Handley, James, Apl	1	1	0	0	0	0	0	0	0	0	0	0	0	1	0	0	.000
Harper, Marshall, Apl	112	367	51	90	104	9	1	1	27	6	3	35	0	37	17	11	.245
Hasley, Michael, Dub*	2	3	1	1	1	0	0	0	0	0	0	0	0	0	0	0	.333
Hicks, Edward, Wausau	76	291	54	79	108	4	2	7	35	1	2	47	1	71	46	6	.271
Hill, Elmore, WR	128	486	112	132	260	30	4	30	103	0	5	80	4	92	1	1	.272
Holcomb, Donald, WR	3	8	3	2	3	1	0	0	1	0	0	2	0	3	0	0	.250
Hollifield, David, QC*	9	16	0	2	2	0	0	0	1	0	0	3	0	5	0	0	.125
Holmberg, Dennis, Bur*	93	288	48	86	144	18	2	12	62	7	4	48	2	47	0	0	.299
Hurdle, Clinton, Wat*	127	429	89	101	190	22	5	19	89	1	1	18	4	112	1	3	.235
Johnson, John H., CR*	2	2	0	0	0	0	0	0	0	0	0	0	0	2	0	0	.000
Jones, Bryan, Waterloo	11	39	8	9	15	0	0	2	19	0	1	10	0	8	2	0	.231
Jones, Sammie, Bur	97	346	42	89	145	12	7	10	56	3	1	38	8	46	12	1	.265
Kelly, Rafael, QC	27	76	4	14	20	3	0	1	6	1	0	6	0	21	0	2	.184
Kesses, Steven, Wausau	13	41	6	10	14	1	0	1	3	0	0	7	1	10	3	0	.244
Kline, Gregory, Clinton*	7	31	1	4	4	0	0	0	1	0	0	0	0	5	1	0	.129
Knicely, Alan, Dubuque	77	156	23	45	68	9	1	4	20	1	2	26	3	31	1	0	.288
Lacy, Steven, Waterloo*	117	389	43	111	126	15	0	0	47	8	6	55	3	41	10	3	.285
LaHonta, Kenneth, Dub*	108	330	39	80	98	11	2	1	22	7	2	42	1	76	12	5	.242

Player and Club	G.	AB.	R.	H.	TB.	2B.	3B.	HR.	RBI.	SH.	SF.	BB.	HP.	SO.	SB.	CS.	Pct.
Lansford, Carney, QC	121	418	87	120	191	19	5	14	86	2	6	72	3	70	26	7	.287
LaRocque, Gary, Bur*	114	452	86	127	154	16	4	1	38	13	4	54	1	42	27	7	.281
Laseter, Thomas, Wat	19	81	22	27	49	3	2	5	18	1	1	8	0	10	1	0	.333
Llodrat, Fernando, Wat	5	16	1	3	0	0	0	0	1	0	0	1	0	3	0	0	.188
Madden, Robert, Appleton	1	1	0	0	0	0	0	0	0	0	0	0	0	1	0	0	.000
Maddon, Joseph, QC	50	163	18	48	59	9	1	0	22	0	4	18	1	22	1	2	.294
Maldonado, Santiago, Dan	37	107	6	10	10	0	0	0	6	0	1	4	2	23	4	5	.093
Maropis, Peter, Appleton	123	428	65	98	114	8	4	0	26	10	0	57	1	94	63	14	.229
Martinson, Michael, QC	43	152	24	41	52	6	1	1	20	0	2	33	0	14	5	1	.270
McIver, Jeryl, Wausau	111	417	44	102	140	14	3	6	37	5	5	37	3	77	18	5	.245
Melendez, William, Dub	47	110	15	26	35	6	0	1	14	4	2	18	1	22	0	0	.236
Mendoza, Michael, Dub	1	1	1	1	1	0	0	0	0	0	0	0	0	0	0	0	1.000
Mercado, Candido, Apl	35	49	6	10	10	0	0	0	4	0	0	9	0	11	3	4	.204
Meyer, William, Danville	97	355	50	94	132	13	5	5	43	2	4	36	1	62	8	4	.265
Mills, James, Wausau	83	260	35	57	84	9	0	6	25	2	3	39	2	60	2	0	.219
Moffitt, G. Scott, QC	52	180	22	41	54	8	1	1	18	0	0	23	1	19	5	1	.228
Moline, Stanley, QC	1	0	0	0	0	0	0	0	0	0	0	0	1	0	0	0	.000
Monasterio, Juan, Wausau	122	487	61	140	191	15	6	8	66	3	2	25	2	57	10	7	.287
Monteau, R. Samuel, Bur†	121	455	78	125	188	30	0	11	63	3	5	59	3	79	3	0	.275
Moreta, Manuel, Waterloo	70	238	33	41	43	2	0	0	17	5	3	19	3	46	6	2	.172
Murray, Richard, CR	66	178	24	47	80	7	4	6	30	0	2	21	1	37	3	1	.264
Nerone, Philip, Appleton	49	141	17	27	47	7	5	1	14	1	0	23	3	36	2	2	.191
Nieves, Raul, Dubuque	34	103	15	27	36	4	1	1	18	1	1	15	0	12	2	2	.262
Olson, Dean, WR*	2	0	1	0	0	0	0	0	0	0	0	0	0	0	0	0	.000
Olszta, Edwin, Appleton	128	429	73	109	177	24	7	10	69	1	2	77	1	117	21	9	.254
Paciorek, Michael, Dan	52	174	28	41	63	5	1	5	27	0	3	30	1	54	8	4	.236
Palmer, Denzil, Clinton	46	149	17	31	42	2	3	1	13	0	2	17	1	31	3	1	.208
Parish, Jacky, 21 Dan-57 Cln	78	256	37	62	83	10	1	3	33	1	2	36	3	44	11	1	.242
Parker, Darrell, Wat†	75	299	55	94	140	14	4	8	50	2	3	23	3	45	7	1	.314
Pascarella, Andrew, Bur	38	137	12	26	43	8	0	3	16	3	1	7	2	36	0	0	.190
Pasillas, J. Andrew, Apl	15	15	0	1	1	0	0	0	0	0	0	2	0	2	0	0	.067
Passmore, W. Jason, Bur	2	0	1	0	0	0	0	0	0	0	0	1	0	0	0	0	.000
Patterson, W. O. Ricky, Wau	37	120	14	27	34	3	2	0	9	0	1	16	8	17	3	1	.225
Pechek, Wayne, CR*	57	176	32	47	58	5	3	0	20	2	1	30	1	24	7	0	.267
Phelps, Kenneth, Waterloo*	24	72	12	19	30	8	0	1	10	1	0	26	0	9	0	0	.264
Pisker, Donald, Dubuque*	86	322	51	111	183	25	10	9	51	2	1	24	2	64	12	7	.345
Pittman, John, WR	116	420	68	118	189	20	3	15	85	1	3	70	2	101	6	1	.281
Pittman, Joseph, Dubuque	109	442	68	123	160	19	6	2	34	10	1	36	1	59	17	8	.278
Prather, Billy, CR	26	76	9	17	24	4	0	1	7	2	2	11	1	18	1	0	.224
Price, Harris, Appleton*	27	71	6	20	25	2	0	1	11	1	2	8	1	10	1	2	.282
Pryor, James, CR	8	15	1	1	1	0	0	0	0	0	0	2	0	4	0	0	.067
Quirk, Eugene, Clinton*	123	451	63	131	163	22	2	2	69	8	10	66	3	40	22	8	.290
Raines, Levi, WR*	85	253	50	72	103	11	4	4	37	2	0	51	0	36	17	9	.285
Ramirez, Mario, Wausau	89	287	48	66	90	16	1	2	28	2	2	32	2	73	11	0	.230
Restin, Eric, Burlington	53	161	19	31	41	3	2	1	13	0	2	22	2	22	10	5	.193
Rex, Michael, CR	39	94	18	23	29	4	1	0	4	3	0	10	2	4	0	1	.245
Richards, David, Dan.	18	41	2	11	13	2	0	0	4	1	0	7	0	7	2	0	.268
Richartz, Scott, Apl	117	396	48	95	123	12	5	2	51	3	9	56	0	61	11	10	.240
Roberts, William, Dub	38	129	17	36	41	3	1	0	12	2	2	8	1	16	0	2	.279
Robles, Silvano, 29 Apl-25 Cln	54	168	27	34	46	3	3	1	21	2	2	23	0	39	5	2	.202
Roche, Timothy, Dan*	110	357	64	92	144	21	5	7	44	1	1	71	2	69	9	6	.258
Romero, Edgardo, Bur	129	462	58	101	129	23	1	1	32	7	1	57	0	37	7	3	.219
Rondon, Alberto, Dub†	88	233	22	32	50	7	1	3	17	3	0	39	2	82	5	4	.137
Rosario, Simon, Dubuque	110	384	57	105	128	13	5	0	49	5	3	14	2	64	8	2	.273
Ross, R. Charles, Bur*	89	282	32	68	86	11	2	1	38	2	1	64	1	35	0	0	.241
Rouse, Randy, Dubuque	28	76	9	17	19	2	0	0	2	1	0	11	0	6	0	0	.224
Santos, Edgardo, Dan	60	204	32	57	77	8	3	2	25	2	2	13	1	32	17	0	.279
Sasser, Donald, CR	120	389	56	102	149	13	8	6	62	5	4	61	0	46	8	3	.262
Schoenhaus, Edward, CR	100	312	43	81	99	12	3	0	39	9	5	44	1	30	8	0	.260
Schultz, Theodore, Apl†	38	103	6	16	21	3	1	0	9	1	0	24	0	20	2	2	.155
Silverio, Luis, Waterloo	122	463	75	126	194	20	3	14	82	1	5	57	2	87	13	3	.272
Slater, Robert, QC	25	101	19	30	42	8	2	0	9	1	2	17	0	14	6	3	.297
Slettvet, Douglas, QC	109	389	58	108	161	21	1	10	56	1	3	78	0	67	7	1	.278
Smith, Jeffrey, Dub*	110	373	55	106	169	28	4	9	64	5	3	43	3	51	1	3	.284
Smith, Michael, Apl*	74	209	11	43	63	7	2	3	22	0	2	12	4	53	5	3	.206
Smith, Ronald W., Bur	114	401	57	96	129	9	3	6	49	8	4	75	0	49	10	8	.239
Snider, Kelly, Danville*	36	113	10	30	39	6	0	1	15	3	1	9	1	17	1	3	.265
Sofield, Richard, WR*	104	340	43	81	112	11	4	4	55	3	5	55	1	84	6	4	.238
Stanfield, Kevin, WR*	1	0	0	0	0	0	0	0	0	0	0	1	0	0	0	0	.000
Starks, Robert, 14 QC-36 Cln*	50	160	15	31	47	2	4	2	22	0	2	23	2	43	3	3	.194
Tanks, Talmadge, Bur	65	151	26	29	41	5	2	1	17	1	1	31	0	37	4	2	.192
Tanner, Roy, Waterloo†	21	60	13	16	18	2	0	0	7	0	0	4	2	9	1	1	.267
Taylor, William, QC*	33	90	9	15	22	4	0	1	11	3	0	20	3	17	1	2	.167
Tebbetts, Steve, QC*	101	339	37	85	123	15	7	3	39	1	8	44	0	20	16	4	.251
Thomasson, Harold, Wat	107	343	47	90	120	10	1	6	46	5	7	57	3	60	6	2	.262

Player and Club	G.	AB.	R.	H.	TB.	2B.	3B.	HR.	RBI.	SH.	SF.	BB.	HP.	SO.	SB.	CS.	Pct.
Thompson, Fay, Dubuque*	104	341	53	95	156	18	2	13	57	3	2	56	1	77	1	3	.279
Thompson, Narciso, Dan	74	266	37	57	92	8	3	7	35	0	3	21	2	55	5	2	.214
Thon, Richard, QC	69	246	46	68	90	11	4	1	32	2	2	33	1	19	19	7	.276
Toman, Thomas, Appleton*	99	305	51	78	100	11	4	1	35	6	2	69	8	41	57	14	.256
Trucks, Phil, 11 Cln-93 Apl	104	313	36	57	85	8	1	6	24	6	4	35	2	132	12	3	.182
Tullish, William, CR*	6	14	1	3	4	1	0	0	0	1	0	3	0	1	0	0	.214
Twellman, Thomas, Dub	18	47	7	7	7	0	0	0	3	1	1	11	1	3	1	2	.149
Tyler, Michael, Dubuque*	89	286	34	76	105	8	3	5	39	3	2	30	1	26	5	1	.266
Vaughn, Michael, Clinton	1	3	0	0	0	0	0	0	1	0	0	1	0	3	0	0	.000
Vogel, Gregory, WR*	67	204	26	43	60	3	1	4	14	4	0	34	2	38	1	0	.211
Walbring, Lawrence, Cln*	39	122	10	25	32	5	1	0	4	1	0	14	0	16	5	1	.205
Ward, James, Appleton	38	99	15	25	31	3	0	1	9	1	0	16	1	17	3	2	.253
Washington, Lozando, CR	42	84	11	14	21	1	3	0	4	2	1	11	0	30	2	1	.167
Washington, Malvin, QC	21	79	15	21	31	4	3	0	10	0	1	13	1	26	7	1	.266
White, Myron, Danville*	108	365	40	77	101	13	4	1	29	2	1	23	2	77	27	11	.211
Whitehead, Steven, QC*	23	84	8	11	19	5	0	1	11	1	1	9	1	29	2	0	.131
Wilkins, Steve, CR*	66	216	52	63	113	11	3	11	40	2	1	44	4	38	1	1	.292
Willeford, Jerry, Dub*	19	45	6	15	19	2	1	0	6	0	2	4	1	6	1	1	.333
Wilson, Gary, Dubuque	3	0	1	0	0	0	0	0	0	0	0	0	0	0	0	0	.000
Wilson, Michael, Danville	2	2	1	1	1	0	0	0	0	0	0	0	0	1	0	0	.500
Wilson, Ward, Clinton	88	283	31	69	88	7	0	4	40	8	7	29	3	28	5	1	.244
Woodbrey, Mark, CR*	87	294	56	84	103	9	2	2	30	13	0	43	2	58	8	2	.286
Wright, Kenneth, QC	102	357	55	95	124	16	2	3	43	3	3	41	4	68	10	5	.266
Wurth, J. Leon, WR	50	189	29	40	52	6	0	2	28	1	1	32	1	39	3	1	.212
Yarborough, Donald, WR	2	1	0	0	0	0	0	0	0	0	0	0	0	1	0	0	.000
Yesenchak, Edward, Apl	31	77	12	18	25	4	0	1	3	2	1	9	0	15	2	2	.234
Young, Ernest, CR†	13	32	6	7	11	1	0	1	6	0	1	6	0	3	0	1	.219
Youngbauer, Jeffrey, WR*	125	485	66	127	168	17	0	8	53	7	3	55	6	42	14	4	.262
Yurak, Jeffrey, CR†	113	334	57	98	144	20	1	8	57	2	2	56	8	65	3	0	.293

The following pitchers had no plate appearances primarily through use of designated-hitters, listed alphabetically by club, games in parentheses:

APPLETON—Evans, Ricky (7); Farrell, Michael (37); Girkins, Kim (14); Howard, Fred (6); Joyce, Thomas (27); Kautzer, William (13); Lehman, William (49); Lukevics, Mitchell (22); Nored, Michael (9); Ramstack, Curtis (10); Seltzer, Randy (1); Sturgeon, William (10); Thoren, Richard (19).

BURLINGTON—Conn, Garry (35); Dempsey, J. Michael (25); Dick, William (26); Edge, Alvin (24); Edge, Claude (5); Ford, Richard (20); Frazier, George (20); Gaton, Francisco (11); Hannon, John (28); O'Keeffe, Richard (25); Pena, Abelino (2); Smith, David A. (26); Wrona, Ron (18).

CEDAR RAPIDS—Adams, Terry (7); Anderson, David (19); Barnicle, Theodore (24); Glinatsis, Michael (6); Halls, Gary (8); Hodges, Ronald A. (17); McKown, Steven (2); Mendoza, David (13); Peterson, Timothy (5); Roy, Patrick (28); Sherman, Steve (15); Watson, Steven (21); Wilson, Barney (19).

CLINTON—Bigusiak, Michael (16); Buford, Bobby (26); Burress, J. David (14); Elders, Michael (31); Garcia, Miguel (2); Getter, R. Kerry (6); Hunziker, Kent (24); Johnson, Joseph E. (3); King, Thomas F. (24); Reed, Steven (1); Uhey, Jackie (16); Vavruska, Paul (13); Wood, David (29).

DANVILLE—Evans, James (19); Heredia, Ubaldo (2); MacWhorter, Keith (13); Moreno, Cesar (29); Patterson, David (12); Repke, Frederick (10); Reyes, Jose (24); Scheller, Rodney (23); Stewart, David (4); Stoffle, Robert (23); Tennant, Michael (14); Townsend, Kenneth (5); Van DeCasteele, Michael (28).

DUBUQUE—Andersen, Edward (14); Aragon, Reinaldo (7); Clark, LeRoy (7); Cooper, M. Neal (23); Lauzerique, George (33); Lee, John N. (7); Miller, Richard L. (23); Perez, Martin (26); Pladson, Gordon (27).

QUAD CITIES—Beerbower, Dan (15); Botting, Ralph (9); Boyd, Robert (8); Brust, Gerard (45); Clear, Mark (30); Eddy, Steven (10); Ferris, Robert (6); Mercedes, Manuel (20); Mraz, Donald (22); Officer, James (6); Porter, Charles (13); Quigley, Jerry (30); Racanelli, John (13); Smith, Randy (6); Steck, David (22).

WATERLOO—Barr, Robert (26); Cvejdlik, Kent (22); Dubee, Richard (2); Eaton, Craig (7); Hrovat, Dale (12); Kainer, Ronald (12); Passalacqua, Francisco (5); Peterson, Jerry (27); Quisenberry, Daniel (34); Sempsrott, Edward (21); Smith, Ronald C. (21); Souza, K. Mark (36); Viebrock, Alan (22); Williams, Michael W. (16).

WAUSAU—Allen, Neil (6); Bardot, Gene (33); Barger, Robert (16); Brown, Randall S. (23); Cacciatore, Paul (6); Clark, Russell (14); Corrado, Gary (10); Darnell, R. Steven (14); Frankum, Randall (12); Hamner, J. Peter (12); Lunar, Luis (25); O'Neill, Theodore (24); Robinson, Martin (1); Seaman, Kim (15); Simon, Willie (3); Von Ohlen, David (9); Westfall, Frederick (28).

WISCONSIN RAPIDS—Benson, James (13); Border, Bob (10); Christensen, Steven (10); Field, Gregory (25); Franz, Robert (24); Hassell, E. Carroll (5); Jones, Ronald (12); McMakin, C. Wallace (22); McWilliams, Thomas (15); Petrowitz, Daniel (7); Rothrock, Brian (39); Serum, Gary (7); Tarin, Fernando (21); Wagner, Steven (22).

TWO CLUBS—Carlson, Thomas (13 Danville, 8 Clinton); Gonzalez, Juan (13 Danville, 16 Clinton); Mueller, Willard (17 Burlington, 12 Clinton).

GRAND-SLAM HOME RUNS—Hill, Hurdle, John Pittman, 2 each; Amico, Benton, Bulling, Calufetti, deLeeuw, Ditto, Etchandy, Gillen, Hamann, B. Jones, Lansford, Monasterio, Pisker, Joseph Pittman, Quirk, Thomasson, 1 each.

AWARDED FIRST BASE ON INTERFERENCE—White 7 (Benton 2, Bulling, Cato, Cliburn, Flores, Sasser); Monteau 3 (Benton, Gulden, Parish); Gaughran 2 (Gulden 2); Glabman 2 (Cato, Gulden); Trucks 2 (Maddon 2); S.

Benson (Cato); Echols (Gulden), Gulden (Cliburn), Maropis (Maddon), Parker (Tyler), Pascarella (Patterson), Schultz (Gulden), Tebbetts (Calufetti), F. Thompson (Cato), Youngbauer (Cato).

CLUB FIELDING

Club	G.	PO.	A.	E.	DP.	PB.	Pct.	Club	G.	PO.	A.	E.	DP.	PB.	Pct.
Burlington	129	3394	1457	201	109	10	.960	Clinton	129	3261	1420	253	110	29	.949
Waterloo	130	3227	1412	196	103	23	.959	Appleton	130	3287	1564	272	125	29	.947
Quad Cities	131	3344	1477	238	110	11	.953	Wausau	129	3254	1332	277	93	46	.943
Wisconsin Rap.	130	3346	1443	241	101	29	.952	Danville	129	3257	1374	282	105	41	.943
Cedar Rapids	131	3293	1395	240	101	30	.951	Dubuque	130	3258	1374	286	116	47	.942

Triple Play—Wausau.

INDIVIDUAL FIELDING
FIRST BASEMEN

*Throws lefthanded.

Player and Club	G.	PO.	A.	E.	DP.	Pct.	Player and Club	G.	PO.	A.	E.	DP.	Pct.
Schultz, Appleton	25	219	16	0	24	1.000	Toman, Appleton*	24	203	10	4	20	.982
Knicely, Dubuque	13	76	4	0	11	1.000	Tanks, Burlington*	51	488	30	10	38	.981
Monteau, Bur.	63	560	40	3	41	.995	Paciorek, Danville	50	439	24	9	39	.981
Hamann, Appleton	50	462	30	3	38	.994	Garcia, Waterloo*	99	861	63	21	61	.978
Holmberg, Bur.	22	152	10	1	16	.994	Thompson, Dubuque*	76	599	41	15	52	.977
Moffitt, Q.C.	14	123	12	1	12	.993	Cipot, Wausau*	58	463	40	12	35	.977
Snider, Danville*	34	244	11	2	22	.992	Pittman, W.R.	112	930	73	25	75	.976
Fischetti, Dan.	25	223	13	2	12	.992	Slettvet, Q.C.	104	957	44	25	69	.976
DITTO, Clinton	129	1231	62	18	98	.986	Smith, Appleton	36	258	24	7	25	.976
Mills, Wausau	73	593	35	9	48	.986	Rosario, Dubuque	45	300	22	10	31	.970
Phelps, Waterloo*	24	205	12	3	21	.986	Murray, C.R.	28	207	10	7	15	.969
Clark, Q.C.	13	111	9	2	6	.984	Rondon, Dubuque	12	88	3	3	3	.968
Sasser, C.R.	113	953	69	18	67	.983	Amico, Danville	11	85	6	4	12	.958
Meyer, Danville	15	113	4	2	7	.983	Antone, W.R.*	12	93	6	5	5	.952
Hill, W.R.	15	109	6	2	6	.983							

Triple Play—Mills.

(Fewer Than Ten Games)

Player and Club	G.	PO.	A.	E.	DP.	Pct.	Player and Club	G.	PO.	A.	E.	DP.	Pct.
Melendez, Dubuque	7	21	0	0	4	1.000	Ward, Appleton	6	50	2	1	4	.981
R. Smith, Bur.*	3	17	3	0	0	1.000	deLeeuw, Waterloo	4	36	1	1	2	.974
Bochy, Dubuque	2	7	0	0	0	1.000	Cliburn, Q.C.	5	22	0	1	2	.957
Yurak, C.R.	3	5	0	0	0	1.000	Tanner, Waterloo	7	60	2	3	6	.954
Pechek, C.R.*	1	3	0	0	0	1.000	Tyler, Dubuque	2	12	3	1	0	.938
Calufetti, Wausau	1	1	0	0	0	1.000	Benton, Wausau	3	25	1	2	2	.929

SECOND BASEMEN

Player and Club	G.	PO.	A.	E.	DP.	Pct.	Player and Club	G.	PO.	A.	E.	DP.	Pct.
Bradbury, Wausau	22	43	63	1	12	.991	Maropis, Appleton	121	301	366	40	88	.943
Pascarella, Bur.	38	86	106	4	15	.980	Bauer, Clinton	124	256	363	38	66	.942
de los Santos, C.R.	14	16	22	1	0	.974	Pittman, Dubuque	99	231	247	30	59	.941
LACY, Waterloo	114	207	309	18	56	.970	Brewster, Q.C.	68	123	206	21	20	.940
Fischetti, Dan.	27	64	63	4	10	.969	Maldonado, Dan.	16	44	28	5	6	.935
Flannery, Q.C.	36	74	98	6	21	.966	Ellison, Dubuque	16	28	28	4	5	.933
LaRocque, Bur.	69	173	201	16	41	.959	Raines, W.R.	30	52	67	9	16	.930
Slater, Q.C.	25	63	79	6	17	.959	McIver, Wausau	110	239	287	40	42	.929
Vogel, W.R.	66	147	160	14	36	.956	Smith, Dubuque	12	13	28	4	8	.911
DelVecchio, Dan.	87	210	228	22	40	.952	Franklin, Bur.	10	24	26	5	4	.909
Barton, C.R.	112	222	281	26	60	.951	Jones, Waterloo	11	25	30	6	6	.902
Wurth, W.R.	50	115	145	15	20	.945							

Triple Play—Bradbury.

(Fewer Than Ten Games)

Player and Club	G.	PO.	A.	E.	DP.	Pct.	Player and Club	G.	PO.	A.	E.	DP.	Pct.
Twellman, Dubuque	9	25	27	0	8	1.000	McMakin, WR	1	1	0	0	0	1.000
Woodbrey, CR	6	22	16	0	5	1.000	Schultz, Appleton	1	1	0	0	0	1.000
Whitehead, QC	6	18	16	0	4	1.000	Llodrat, Waterloo	5	10	5	1	2	.938
Evans, Clinton	3	4	14	0	2	1.000	Restin, Burlington	7	14	13	2	2	.931
Meyer, Danville	4	11	7	0	2	1.000	Richartz, Appleton	8	18	21	3	3	.929
Byrd, Clinton	1	6	4	0	1	1.000	Tanner, Waterloo	4	5	6	1	1	.917
Bedrosian, Wausau	2	5	4	0	1	1.000	Jones, Burlington	5	12	14	3	4	.897
Wright, QC	1	3	3	0	2	1.000	Rex, Cedar Rapids	3	6	8	2	1	.875
Holmberg, Bur	3	1	4	0	0	1.000	Nieves, Dubuque	3	3	4	1	1	.875
Rondon, Dubuque	1	1	2	0	0	1.000	Mercado, Appleton	6	7	16	4	1	.852
Glabman, Dubuque	1	1	1	0	0	1.000	Palmer, Clinton	1	1	1	1	0	.667
Tebbetts, QC*	1	0	2	0	0	1.000							

THIRD BASEMEN

Player and Club	G.	PO.	A.	E.	DP.	Pct.
THOMASSON, Wat	107	78	234	23	19	.931
Castino, WR	65	60	155	16	16	.931
Holmberg, Bur	54	44	105	12	8	.925
Etchandy, Apl	129	110	278	34	21	.919
Knicely, Dubuque	22	14	31	4	3	.918
Moffitt, QC	16	8	14	2	2	.917
Meyer, Danville	43	25	82	10	8	.915
Lansford, QC	111	115	213	34	20	.906
Bedrosian, Wausau	11	6	12	2	2	.900
Byrd, Clinton	67	60	124	21	13	.898
Sofield, WR	37	39	74	13	8	.897
Grimes, CR	113	90	250	40	13	.895
Bodie, Wausau	113	123	149	34	9	.889
DelVecchio, Dan	25	11	51	8	2	.886
Smith, Dubuque	71	51	119	23	15	.881
Palmer, Clinton	37	37	81	16	7	.881
Doerr, Clinton	24	24	57	11	3	.880
Encarnacion, Bur	75	47	133	25	8	.878
Fischetti, Dan	47	37	77	16	5	.877
de la Cruz, Dan	11	7	14	3	1	.875
Raines, WR	29	27	45	11	1	.867
Moreta, Waterloo	25	19	37	9	3	.862
Bacon, WR	11	10	8	3	0	.857
Roche, Danville	10	10	10	4	1	.833
de los Santos, CR	17	6	31	8	3	.822
Rouse, Dubuque	11	10	13	7	1	.767
Rondon, Dubuque	18	8	27	13	2	.729

(Fewer Than Ten Games)

Player and Club	G.	PO.	A.	E.	DP.	Pct.
Rex, Cedar Rapids	5	4	9	0	1	1.000
Robles, Clinton	3	3	3	0	0	1.000
Evans, Clinton	1	2	2	0	1	1.000
Mercado, Appleton	2	1	3	0	0	1.000
Schultz, Appleton	1	1	2	0	0	1.000
Adams, Danville	2	0	3	0	0	1.000
Rosario, Dubuque	1	0	2	0	0	1.000
Flores, Burlington	1	1	0	0	0	1.000
Hamann, Appleton	1	1	0	0	0	1.000
Twellman, Dubuque	9	8	21	1	2	.967
Ashline, Wausau	8	5	18	1	2	.958
Boyne, CR	3	6	5	1	0	.917
LaRocque, Bur	5	1	10	1	0	.917
Flannery, QC	8	6	14	2	0	.909
Bradbury, Wausau	3	2	8	1	0	.909
Glabman, Dubuque	4	2	8	1	0	.909
Franklin, Bur	4	4	5	1	0	.900
Pittman, Dubuque	5	4	8	2	0	.857
Nieves, Dubuque	4	1	5	1	0	.857
Eubanks, Burlington	1	2	0	1	0	.667
Whitehead, QC	1	0	2	1	0	.667
Wilson, Clinton	1	0	1	1	0	.500
Schoenhaus, CR	1	0	0	1	0	.000

SHORTSTOPS

Player and Club	G.	PO.	A.	E.	DP.	Pct.
Alvarez, Dubuque	19	19	75	5	7	.949
DOERR, Clinton	104	171	336	28	51	.948
Whitehead, QC	12	15	39	3	7	.947
Romero, Burlington	129	187	419	41	64	.937
Flannery, QC	60	109	186	22	33	.931
Glabman, Dubuque	101	174	296	41	63	.920
S. Benson, WR	124	207	336	50	50	.916
Moreta, Waterloo	43	62	113	16	22	.916
Barranca, Waterloo	88	117	265	37	37	.912
Chappas, Appleton	92	125	304	43	58	.909
Bedrosian, Wausau	40	58	111	17	19	.909
Boyne, CR	85	129	228	36	39	.908
de los Santos, CR	43	56	112	17	22	.908
Mercado, Appleton	21	23	42	7	5	.903
Thon, Quad Cities	61	96	193	32	26	.900
Bradley, Danville	118	196	343	62	55	.897
Ramirez, Wausau	89	145	253	46	31	.896
Richartz, Appleton	32	58	86	21	22	.873
Maldonado, Dan	12	14	31	7	6	.865
Rex, Cedar Rapids	13	17	26	8	3	.843
Fermin, Clinton	17	21	37	18	10	.763

Triple Play—Ramirez.

(Fewer Than Ten Games)

Player and Club	G.	PO.	A.	E.	DP.	Pct.
Raines, WR	7	13	13	0	3	1.000
DelVecchio, Dan	2	1	6	0	0	1.000
Meyer, Danville	2	4	1	0	0	1.000
Lansford, QC	1	0	1	0	0	1.000
LaRocque, Bur	1	0	1	0	0	1.000
Pittman, Dubuque	7	6	12	1	0	.947
Ashline, Wausau	5	5	12	1	2	.944
Nieves, Dubuque	4	2	10	2	0	.857
Rondon, Dubuque	8	5	12	3	3	.850
Palmer, Clinton	7	9	18	6	1	.818
Bauer, Clinton	1	2	4	2	1	.750
Lacy, Waterloo	4	2	4	2	0	.750
Byrd, Clinton	2	1	1	1	0	.667
Grimes, CR	2	1	3	3	0	.571

OUTFIELDERS

Player and Club	G.	PO.	A.	E.	DP.	Pct.
Laseter, Waterloo	19	28	4	0	1	1.000
Kelly, Quad Cities	21	27	2	0	0	1.000
Flannery, QC	12	24	1	0	0	1.000
Walbring, Clinton*	19	20	3	0	1	1.000
Taylor, QC	15	18	1	0	0	1.000
Jones, Burlington	63	89	8	1	1	.990
LaRocque, Bur	43	77	7	1	3	.988
Antone, WR*	40	60	8	1	1	.986
Wilkins, CR	64	107	8	2	2	.983
SILVERIO, Wat	119	270	9	6	2	.979
Bolek, Clinton*	53	84	6	2	1	.978
Cipot, Wausau*	43	41	4	1	1	.978
Nerone, Appleton	35	41	0	1	0	.976
Ewing, QC	16	37	3	1	1	.976
Barrios, CR	84	76	3	2	1	.975
Clark, QC	115	254	19	8	9	.972
Moffitt, QC	19	34	1	1	0	.972
Youngblauer, WR	125	255	10	8	1	.971
Danson, Bur	65	129	3	4	1	.971
Woodbrey, CR	80	156	4	5	2	.970
Hurdle, Waterloo	124	179	12	7	4	.965
Quirk, Clinton*	123	281	6	11	2	.963
Schoenhaus, CR	97	141	15	6	1	.963
Richartz, Apl	67	118	9	5	2	.962
deLeeuw, Waterloo	26	24	1	1	0	.962
Nieves, Dubuque	26	45	3	2	0	.960
Pecheck, CR*	55	88	5	4	1	.959
Wright, QC	98	117	9	6	1	.955
LaHonta, Dubuque*	102	158	6	8	1	.953
Aman, Wausau*	46	76	5	4	2	.953

OUTFIELDERS—Continued

Player and Club	G.	PO.	A.	E.	DP.	Pct.
Garcia, Waterloo*	24	40	1	2	0	.953
Echols, Wausau	101	202	9	11	1	.950
Roberts, Dubuque	38	72	2	4	0	.949
Anderson, Bur	82	137	9	8	2	.948
Evans, Clinton	122	218	11	13	1	.946
Parker, Waterloo	73	103	3	6	1	.946
Harper, Appleton	109	175	9	11	1	.944
Sofield, WR	67	122	12	8	3	.944
Tebbetts, QC*	93	140	8	9	3	.943
Thompson, Dan	63	109	7	7	0	.943
Fischetti, Dan	10	15	1	1	1	.941
Channel, WR	106	168	18	12	3	.939
Toman, Appleton*	57	89	3	6	1	.939
Olszta, Appleton	114	182	14	13	1	.938
Restin, Bur	40	81	1	6	0	.932
Ellison, Dubuque	20	26	1	2	0	.931
Santos, Danville	58	111	8	9	1	.930
Brodell, Danville	23	37	2	3	1	.929
R. Smith, Bur*	103	155	9	13	4	.927
Washington, CR	36	51	0	4	0	.927
Roche, Danville	80	123	10	11	1	.924
Smith, Dubuque	18	23	1	2	0	.923
Wilson, Clinton	10	11	1	1	0	.923
White, Danville*	105	225	11	20	2	.922
Hicks, Wausau	75	114	5	10	1	.922
Pisker, Dubuque*	64	99	8	9	2	.922
Rondon, Dubuque	47	56	3	5	1	.922
Monasterio, Wau	119	230	25	22	5	.921
Gaughran, WR	80	108	2	10	0	.917
Amico, Danville	23	19	1	2	0	.909
Hallgren, Dubuque	31	36	2	4	0	.905
de la Cruz, Dan	43	61	5	7	2	.904
Lansford, QC	11	15	1	2	0	.889
Eubanks, Dubuque	39	51	4	7	2	.887
Rosario, Dubuque	47	61	3	9	1	.877
Kesses, Wausau	12	13	1	2	0	.875
Murray, CR	11	6	1	1	0	.875
Robles, Apl-Cln	31	34	2	6	1	.857
Byrd, Clinton	10	5	1	1	0	.857
Washington, Cln	21	29	0	5	0	.853
Starks, QC-Cln*	34	42	3	9	1	.833

(Fewer Than Ten Games)

Player and Club	G.	PO.	A.	E.	DP.	Pct.
Maldonado, Dan	4	8	1	0	0	1.000
Hollifield, QC*	7	8	0	0	0	1.000
Glabman, Dubuque	5	3	1	0	0	1.000
Fletcher, Clinton	6	4	0	0	0	1.000
Parish, Danville	1	2	1	0	0	1.000
Gulden, Danville	3	2	1	0	0	1.000
Kline, Clinton*	3	3	0	0	0	1.000
Young, CR	3	3	0	0	0	1.000
Holmberg, Bur	7	3	0	0	0	1.000
Tanner, Waterloo	8	3	0	0	0	1.000
Cato, Cedar Rapids	3	2	0	0	0	1.000
Bradley, Danville	1	1	0	0	0	1.000
Tyler, Dubuque	1	0	1	0	0	1.000
Passmore, Bur	2	1	0	0	0	1.000
Schultz, Appleton	3	1	0	0	0	1.000
Yurak, CR	3	1	0	0	0	1.000
Tullish, CR	5	11	0	1	0	.917
Hill, WR	5	10	0	1	0	.909
Holcomb, WR	3	6	0	1	0	.857
Ward, Appleton	7	6	0	1	0	.857
Mercado, Appleton	3	3	0	1	0	.750
Rouse, Dubuque	3	5	0	2	0	.714
Hasley, Dubuque*	1	0	0	1	0	.000
Melendez, Dubuque	2	0	0	1	0	.000

CATCHERS

Player and Club	G.	PO.	A.	E.	DP.	PB.	Pct.
Melendez, Dub	29	125	7	1	2	8	.992
GILLEN, Wat	81	447	50	5	3	11	.990
Prather, CR	25	140	22	2	2	5	.988
Ross, Bur	84	540	57	9	11	6	.985
Young, CR	10	57	7	1	1	0	.985
Cliburn, QC	57	336	41	6	6	7	.984
Bulling, WR	111	623	105	17	10	23	.977
Parish, Dan-Cln	53	305	42	8	4	20	.977
Martinson, QC	41	244	27	7	2	4	.975
Cato, CR	100	587	49	17	4	24	.974
Bochy, Dubuque	26	158	25	5	3	1	.973
Price, Apl	14	92	15	3	2	1	.973
Tyler, Dubuque	79	486	71	16	5	32	.972
Beene, Waterloo	57	313	24	10	3	12	.971
Richards, Dan	17	78	22	3	2	3	.971
Flores, Bur	52	309	38	11	1	4	.969
Calufetti, Wau	17	104	12	4	1	2	.967
Wilson, Clinton	58	278	31	11	4	9	.966
Yesenchak, Apl	28	144	16	6	4	8	.964
Maddon, QC	38	165	25	8	1	0	.960
Trucks, Cln-Apl	104	549	104	31	8	22	.955
Benton, Wausau	89	527	69	28	6	36	.955
Curbelo, WR	13	70	9	4	1	2	.952
Patterson, Wau	26	154	31	10	3	8	.949
DiPietro, Cln-WR	42	206	27	13	6	10	.947
Gulden, Danville	96	519	89	39	8	25	.940
Pasillas, Apl	15	36	1	4	0	0	.902

(Fewer Than Ten Games)

Player and Club	G.	PO.	A.	E.	DP.	PB.	Pct.
Willeford, Dub	7	31	5	0	0	1	1.000
Pryor, CR	7	22	6	0	0	1	1.000
Roche, Danville	3	15	2	0	1	2	1.000
Yurak, CR	1	5	0	0	0	0	1.000
Smith, Dubuque	1	3	1	0	0	1	1.000
Rondon, Dubuque	1	1	0	0	0	0	1.000
Alvarez, Dan	7	45	7	1	0	3	.981
Sasser, CR	5	30	2	1	1	0	.970
Rouse, Dubuque	9	48	4	4	0	4	.929

PITCHERS

Player and Club	G.	PO.	A.	E.	DP.	Pct.
FIELD, WR	25	7	34	0	0	1.000
Rothrock, WR	39	10	20	0	0	1.000
Johnson, CR*	20	9	20	0	0	1.000
Gonzalez, Dan-Cln	29	8	19	0	0	1.000
Smith, Waterloo	21	7	19	0	0	1.000
Quisenberry, Wat	34	3	23	0	0	1.000
Joyce, Appleton*	27	4	21	0	1	1.000
Wood, Clinton	29	2	19	0	1	1.000
Mendoza, CR*	13	2	18	0	4	1.000
Patterson, Dan	12	5	13	0	0	1.000
Racanelli, QC	13	5	13	0	1	1.000
McWilliams, WR*	15	5	13	0	0	1.000
Hamner, Wausau	12	6	11	0	0	1.000
Uhey, Clinton	16	5	11	0	0	1.000

PITCHERS—Continued

Player and Club	G.	PO.	A.	E.	DP.	Pct.
Lauzerique, Dub.	33	5	8	0	1	1.000
Souza, Waterloo*	36	1	12	0	1	1.000
Christensen, WR	10	3	9	0	0	1.000
Frazier, Bur	20	3	9	0	1	1.000
MacWhorter, Dan	13	0	10	0	1	1.000
Breaux, WR	28	3	7	0	0	1.000
Wilson, CR	19	1	8	0	1	1.000
Franz, WR*	24	1	8	0	0	1.000
Ford, Burlington*	20	1	7	0	1	1.000
Carlson, Dan-Cln*	21	0	8	0	1	1.000
Hrovat, Waterloo	12	0	7	0	0	1.000
Tarin, WR	21	3	4	0	0	1.000
Peterson, Waterloo	27	3	4	0	1	1.000
Corrado, Wausau*	10	0	5	0	0	1.000
Sturgeon, Appleton	10	0	5	0	0	1.000
Border, WR	10	0	4	0	0	1.000
Frankum, Wausau	12	1	3	0	0	1.000
Gaton, Burlington	11	0	3	0	1	1.000
Barger, Wausau*	16	1	1	0	1	1.000
Ramstack, Appleton	10	0	1	0	0	1.000
Stoffle, Danville	23	10	29	1	3	.975
Wagner, WR	22	12	20	1	0	.970
Cvejdlik, Waterloo	22	9	20	1	1	.967
Kainer, Waterloo	12	7	20	1	2	.964
King, Clinton*	24	4	23	1	3	.964
Porter, QC	13	6	20	1	0	.963
Viebrock, Wat*	22	12	39	2	2	.962
Attardi, Appleton	31	8	40	2	4	.960
Roy, Cedar Rapids	27	6	18	1	0	.960
Westfall, Wausau	28	14	10	1	1	.960
Boyle, QC	35	11	36	2	1	.959
Eddy, Quad Cities	10	8	14	1	1	.957
Conn, Burlington	35	6	16	1	0	.957
Williams, Wat*	16	8	30	2	2	.950
DeMerritt, Dub.	35	3	16	1	3	.950
Tennant, Danville	14	4	14	1	0	.947
Moreno, Danville	29	4	14	1	1	.947
Brust, Quad Cities	45	4	14	1	1	.947
Clark, Wausau	14	7	26	2	2	.943
Pladson, Dubuque	27	13	20	2	0	.943
Hannon, Burlington	28	7	24	2	1	.939
O'Keeffe, Bur*	25	10	34	3	0	.936
Coulter, Appleton*	32	4	25	2	1	.935
Evans, Danville*	19	2	12	1	0	.933
Lehman, Appleton	49	7	7	1	1	.933
Dick, Burlington*	26	7	34	3	0	.932
O'Neill, Wausau	24	18	35	4	1	.930
Lukevics, Appleton	22	6	20	2	2	.929
Reyes, Danville	24	4	22	2	3	.929
Thoren, Appleton*	19	3	10	1	1	.929
Vavruska, Clinton	13	3	22	2	2	.926

Player and Club	G.	PO.	A.	E.	DP.	Pct.
Burress, Clinton	14	3	9	1	0	.923
Wrona, Burlington	18	3	9	1	0	.923
Quigley, QC	30	1	11	1	1	.923
Van DeCasteele, Dan	28	6	17	2	0	.920
Watson, CR	21	10	33	4	4	.915
Anderson, CR	19	9	22	3	0	.912
Brown, Wausau	23	5	25	3	1	.909
Bigusiak, Clinton	16	2	8	1	0	.909
Wilson, Dubuque	24	9	19	3	0	.903
Olson, WR*	26	12	34	5	0	.902
Knicely, Dubuque	24	8	19	3	0	.900
D. Smith, Bur	25	4	23	3	1	.900
Gomez, Danville*	10	3	6	1	0	.900
Sherman, CR*	15	0	9	1	0	.900
McMakin, WR	21	3	6	1	1	.900
Lunar, Wausau	25	8	27	4	1	.897
Clear, Quad Cities	30	5	21	3	1	.897
Hunziker, Clinton	24	9	41	6	4	.893
Gale, Waterloo	23	11	22	4	1	.892
Scheller, Danville	23	12	21	4	0	.892
Farrell, Appleton	37	8	24	4	2	.889
Jones, WR	12	9	7	2	2	.889
Andersen, Dubuque	14	3	5	1	0	.889
Kautzer, Appleton	13	6	25	4	2	.886
Buford, Clinton	26	9	22	4	1	.886
Hodges, CR	17	16	30	6	4	.885
Elders, Clinton	31	5	10	2	2	.882
Barnicle, CR*	24	4	25	4	0	.879
Perez, Dubuque	25	7	22	4	1	.879
Steck, Quad Cities	22	8	20	4	0	.875
A. Edge, Bur.	24	9	19	4	1	.875
Mueller, Bur-Clin.	29	2	12	2	0	.875
Bardot, Wausau	33	4	10	2	1	.875
Dempsey, Bur.	25	9	18	4	3	.871
Seaman, Wausau*	15	2	4	1	0	.857
Sempsrott, Wat*	21	6	16	4	1	.846
Vaughn, Clinton	13	4	7	2	0	.846
Mendoza, Dubuque	27	2	24	5	2	.839
Hasley, Dubuque*	31	3	16	4	0	.826
Mraz, Quad Cities	22	7	15	5	0	.815
Girkins, Appleton	14	6	2	2	0	.800
Repke, Danville*	10	0	4	1	0	.800
Darnell, Wausau*	14	1	3	1	1	.800
Stanfield, WR*	17	0	4	1	0	.800
Handley, Appleton	24	3	12	4	0	.789
Cooper, Dubuque	23	2	10	4	1	.750
Miller, Dubuque*	23	1	8	3	0	.750
Barr, Waterloo*	26	2	7	3	0	.750
J. Benson, WR	13	4	4	3	0	.727
Moline, QC	40	3	7	4	0	.714
Beerbower, QC	10	0	5	2	0	.714

(Fewer Than Ten Games)

Player and Club	G.	PO.	A.	E.	DP.	Pct.
Smith, QC*	6	0	12	0	0	1.000
Serum, WR	7	3	9	0	0	1.000
Allen, Wausau	6	4	7	0	1	1.000
Heredia, Danville	2	2	5	0	1	1.000
Lee, Dubuque	7	0	7	0	1	1.000
Eaton, Waterloo	7	3	4	0	0	1.000
Cacciatore, Wausau	6	2	4	0	0	1.000
Evans, Appleton	7	1	5	0	0	1.000
Johnson, Clinton	3	3	2	0	0	1.000
Von Ohlen, Wausau	9	1	4	0	0	1.000
Dubee, Waterloo	2	1	3	0	1	1.000
Hassell, WR	5	2	1	0	0	1.000
Petrowitz, WR*	7	1	2	0	0	1.000
Stewart, Danville	4	1	1	0	0	1.000
Getter, Clinton	6	0	2	0	0	1.000
Adams, CR	7	0	2	0	0	1.000
Garcia, Clinton	2	0	1	0	0	1.000
McKown, CR	2	0	1	0	0	1.000

Player and Club	G.	PO.	A.	E.	DP.	Pct.
Harper, Appleton	4	0	1	0	0	1.000
Clark, Dubuque	7	0	1	0	0	1.000
Glinatsis, CR	6	4	9	2	0	.867
Boyd, Quad Cities	8	2	9	2	1	.846
Botting, QC*	9	0	8	2	0	.800
Townsend, Dan.	5	2	5	2	2	.778
Officer, QC*	6	0	7	2	0	.778
Aragon, Dubuque	7	1	2	1	0	.750
Halls, CR	8	2	1	1	0	.750
Ferris, QC	6	3	1	2	0	.667
Mercedes, QC	4	1	1	1	0	.667
C. Edge, Bur.	5	0	2	1	0	.667
Howard, Appleton	6	1	1	1	0	.667
Nored, Appleton*	9	1	1	1	0	.667
Robinson, Wausau	1	1	0	1	0	.500
Madden, Appleton	5	1	0	1	0	.500
Passalacqua, Wat*	5	0	1	1	0	.500

The following players did not have any recorded accepted chances at the positions indicated; therefore, are not listed in the fielding averages for those particular positions: Davis, of; de los Santos, p; Pena*, p; T. Peterson, p; Reed, p; Seltzer*, p; Simon, p; Tyler, p; Yarborough, c; Youngbauer, p. Cloherty, Globig and M. Wilson appeared as designated-hitters, pinch-hitters and/or pinch-runners only.

CLUB PITCHING

Club	G.	CG.	ShO.	Sv.	IP.	H.	R.	ER.	HR.	BB.	Int. BB.	HB.	SO.	WP.	Bk.	ERA.
Cedar Rapids	131	56	16	9	1098	910	505	369	55	577	23	38	787	39	15	3.03
Quad Cities	131	33	6	21	1115	1056	570	411	45	543	17	32	674	39	9	3.32
Burlington	129	38	12	12	1131	1067	551	446	77	522	24	30	775	72	10	3.55
Waterloo	130	38	13	21	1076	970	545	431	80	457	21	36	718	54	13	3.61
Clinton	129	41	8	13	1087	1098	648	483	49	594	19	35	633	73	12	4.00
Wausau	129	45	4	15	1085	1061	660	492	82	655	35	33	745	80	18	4.08
Danville	129	47	5	14	1086	1120	674	515	53	632	6	30	693	83	8	4.27
Wisconsin Rapids	130	43	6	10	1115	1180	704	533	93	615	34	28	684	64	7	4.30
Appleton	130	20	9	18	1096	1160	693	532	41	597	41	54	703	60	7	4.37
Dubuque	130	33	4	17	1086	1184	743	575	64	687	52	23	804	75	9	4.77

PITCHERS' RECORDS

(Leading Qualifiers for Earned-Run Average Leadership—104 or More Innings)

*Throws lefthanded.

Pitcher—Club	G.	GS.	CG.	ShO.	W.	L.	Sv.	Pct.	IP.	H.	R.	ER.	HR.	BB.	Int. BB.	HB.	SO.	WP.	ERA.
Hodges, CR	17	17	12	6	14	2	0	.875	138	84	31	19	0	59	2	7	100	3	1.24
Boyle, QC	35	13	8	1	9	6	8	.600	144	125	38	29	4	35	2	2	69	2	1.81
Johnson, CR*	20	19	8	4	13	2	0	.867	131	93	42	28	7	50	0	2	94	3	1.92
Watson, CR	21	21	12	2	13	6	0	.684	159	131	57	47	4	72	3	8	86	7	2.66
O'Keeffe, Bur*	25	25	7	3	7	4	0	.636	166	143	75	53	12	95	0	4	113	5	2.87
Hunziker, Cln	24	22	10	2	12	10	1	.545	168	144	79	55	4	77	2	9	137	8	2.95
Steck, QC	22	17	5	1	14	2	0	.875	137	124	71	45	2	57	0	5	72	6	2.96
Lukevics, Apl	22	17	6	1	10	5	1	.667	126	104	51	42	3	33	3	6	91	2	3.00
Field, WR	25	21	13	0	10	7	0	.588	163	168	79	55	11	49	2	3	123	1	3.04
Cvejdlik, Wat	22	13	7	2	9	4	1	.692	120	100	53	43	7	59	4	4	82	4	3.23

Departmental Leaders: G—Lehman, 49; GS—Attardi, 27; CG—Field, Stoffle, 13; ShO—Hodges, 6; W—Hodges, Steck, 14; L—Joyce, Lunar, 15; Sv—Lehman, 13; Pct.—Hodges, Steck, .875; IP—Olson, 177; H—Attardi, 196; R—Scheller, 109; ER—Dempsey, 83; HR—O'Neill, 17; BB—Barnicle, 142; IBB—Farrell, Lehman, 8; HB—Lunar, MacWhorter, 11; SO—Barnicle, 160; WP—Lunar, 17.

(All Pitchers—Listed Alphabetically)

Pitcher—Club	G.	GS.	CG.	ShO.	W.	L.	Sv.	Pct.	IP.	H.	R.	ER.	HR.	BB.	Int. BB.	HB.	SO.	WP.	ERA.
Adams, CR	7	2	0	0	1	1	0	.500	16	17	10	10	1	17	0	0	14	2	5.63
Allen, Wausau	6	6	2	0	4	2	0	.667	48	51	27	20	4	20	0	1	34	1	3.75
Andersen, Dub	14	4	1	0	1	3	1	.250	39	40	31	25	2	24	2	0	34	3	5.77
Anderson, CR	19	16	5	0	5	9	0	.357	105	112	69	45	7	46	6	4	72	7	3.86
Aragon, Dubuque	7	1	0	0	1	0	1	1.000	14	10	10	8	0	18	1	1	11	2	5.14
Attardi, Apl*	31	27	6	1	10	11	0	.476	162	196	89	72	8	60	2	5	73	5	4.00
Bardot, Wausau	33	0	0	0	3	2	6	.600	61	48	28	26	6	35	2	0	45	4	3.84
Barger, Wausau*	16	0	0	0	2	2	3	.500	28	26	13	9	2	15	1	0	24	6	2.89
Barnicle, CR*	24	24	9	1	9	10	0	.474	163	132	94	73	12	142	1	4	160	6	4.03
Barr, Waterloo*	26	5	1	0	5	6	0	.455	62	65	51	43	6	38	1	5	45	2	6.24
Beerbower, QC	10	0	0	0	3	2	0	.600	19	19	7	4	0	11	0	1	16	0	1.89
J. Benson, WR	13	13	1	0	4	4	0	.500	73	78	57	52	15	42	1	3	50	2	6.41
Bigusiak, Cln	16	9	1	0	2	5	0	.286	67	79	56	35	7	44	2	1	32	3	4.70
Border, WR	10	0	0	0	1	1	0	.500	13	19	18	15	0	10	0	1	3	3	10.38
Botting, QC*	9	6	1	1	4	4	0	.500	45	39	23	20	2	28	0	1	38	2	4.00
Boyd, QC	8	8	1	0	3	4	0	.429	42	45	32	21	1	27	0	1	27	2	4.50
Boyle, QC	35	13	8	1	9	6	8	.600	144	125	38	29	4	35	2	2	69	2	1.81
Breaux, Wausau	28	0	0	0	5	4	1	.556	39	45	31	28	4	23	2	0	21	2	6.46
Brown, Wausau	23	23	8	0	7	14	0	.333	143	137	92	64	8	92	4	5	91	6	4.03
Brust, QC*	45	0	0	0	8	4	4	.667	72	55	28	22	2	31	3	0	44	1	2.75
Buford, Clinton	26	17	4	0	6	7	0	.462	133	133	74	62	6	75	2	4	54	10	4.20
Burress, Cln	14	7	0	0	2	3	0	.400	54	60	37	26	2	43	0	2	28	8	4.33
Cacciatore, Wau	6	6	0	0	0	4	0	.000	20	21	25	21	1	29	0	4	19	7	9.45
Carlson, 13 Dan-8 Cln*	21	2	0	0	2	1	0	.667	45	41	49	40	4	79	0	1	34	9	8.00
Christensen, WR	10	10	0	0	1	3	0	.250	52	53	37	27	6	41	4	2	23	1	4.67
Clark, Dubuque	7	0	0	0	0	1	0	1.000	9	12	8	6	0	14	0	0	8	3	6.00
Clark, Wausau	14	14	10	0	8	6	0	.571	103	97	46	29	5	46	1	2	73	4	2.53
Clear, QC	30	18	7	0	8	10	2	.444	144	135	84	63	5	111	5	6	109	8	3.94
Conn, Bur	35	0	0	0	6	1	4	.857	80	58	27	15	3	35	6	4	64	4	1.69
Cooper, Dubuque	23	10	2	0	7	7	0	.500	73	79	56	46	0	59	6	0	43	4	5.67
Corrado, Wau*	10	0	0	0	0	0	0	.000	16	28	17	11	3	5	1	0	9	1	6.19
Coulter, Apl*	32	15	2	0	7	10	1	.412	112	93	71	54	3	88	2	6	88	6	4.34
Cvejdlik, Wat	22	13	7	2	9	4	1	.692	120	100	53	43	7	59	4	4	82	4	3.23
Darnell, Wau*	14	0	0	0	3	0	4	1.000	31	39	21	15	2	20	7	0	13	1	4.35
de los Santos, CR	2	0	0	0	0	0	0	.000	2	1	0	0	0	0	0	1	1	0	0.00
DeMerritt, Dub	35	3	1	0	4	4	6	.500	79	87	54	48	7	46	7	0	75	6	5.47
Dempsey, Bur	25	24	9	1	8	12	0	.400	158	141	92	83	15	84	3	8	135	14	4.73
Dick, Bur*	26	25	9	3	10	11	0	.476	162	170	77	64	11	62	2	1	70	7	3.56

Pitcher–Club	G	GS	CG	ShO	W	L	Sv	Pct.	IP	H	R	ER	HR	BB	Int. BB	HB	SO	WP	ERA
Dubee, Waterloo	2	2	0	0	2	0	0	1.000	12	9	5	3	0	9	0	0	7	1	2.25
Eaton, Waterloo	7	7	2	0	3	3	0	.500	39	34	23	21	3	16	0	1	28	0	4.85
Eddy, QC	10	10	1	0	1	4	0	.200	60	64	37	18	0	33	2	3	29	1	2.70
A. Edge, Bur	24	15	1	0	2	7	0	.222	98	121	68	52	10	52	1	1	65	7	4.78
C. Edge, Bur	5	1	0	0	0	1	0	.000	10	11	5	2	0	7	1	0	12	2	1.80
Elders, Clinton	31	0	0	0	5	2	5	.714	57	37	9	1	0	10	0	1	43	1	0.16
Evans, Dan*	19	12	3	0	1	8	0	.111	75	75	53	52	5	80	0	0	46	7	6.24
Evans, Appleton	7	0	0	0	1	1	0	.500	20	17	14	7	1	12	1	1	13	2	3.15
Farrell, Apl	37	3	0	0	6	6	2	.500	103	103	58	40	4	50	8	4	55	9	3.50
Ferris, QC	6	6	0	0	1	0	0	1.000	19	17	7	7	0	9	0	0	7	1	3.32
Field, WR	25	21	13	0	10	7	0	.588	163	168	79	55	11	49	2	3	123	1	3.04
Ford, Bur*	20	4	0	0	6	2	0	.750	51	50	26	24	4	30	1	1	33	4	4.24
Frankum, Wausau	12	1	0	0	1	0	0	1.000	30	32	18	18	3	27	0	1	21	3	5.40
Franz, WR*.	24	0	0	0	2	1	1	.667	29	32	24	21	1	34	4	1	18	4	6.52
Frazier, Bur	20	0	0	0	7	2	2	.778	36	30	9	7	1	14	3	0	28	3	1.75
Gale, Waterloo	23	22	8	3	11	6	0	.647	148	118	64	57	14	76	3	3	88	10	3.47
Garcia, Clinton	2	0	0	0	0	0	0	.000	6	5	5	4	1	3	0	3	4	1	6.00
Gaton, Bur	11	0	0	0	1	0	0	1.000	18	25	11	10	1	9	1	1	10	3	5.00
Getter, Clinton	6	0	0	0	1	2	0	.333	11	15	16	10	0	11	0	4	11	0	8.18
Girkins, Apl	14	1	0	0	3	1	0	.750	32	32	18	16	0	25	3	4	30	2	4.50
Glinatsis, CR	6	6	0	0	4	0	0	.000	41	44	25	17	2	20	1	2	18	1	3.73
Gomez, Dan*	10	1	0	0	1	2	0	.333	34	25	20	11	0	26	0	2	26	2	2.91
Gonzalez, 13 Dan-16 Cln	29	12	4	0	3	9	3	.250	102	120	66	58	9	46	3	0	38	8	5.12
Halls, CR	8	0	0	0	0	0	0	1.000	17	25	15	13	1	6	0	0	10	0	6.88
Hamner, Wausau	12	2	1	0	3	2	0	.600	48	34	18	17	4	17	2	2	39	0	3.19
Handley, Apl	24	11	0	0	4	4	0	.500	84	117	62	48	3	52	5	6	60	5	5.14
Hannon, Bur	28	10	3	1	5	8	1	.385	111	112	60	50	7	36	2	3	70	7	4.05
Harper, Apl	4	0	0	0	0	0	0	.000	6	4	2	0	0	3	0	0	6	0	0.00
Hasley, Dub*	31	13	3	0	4	8	1	.333	97	123	72	50	6	44	4	0	63	4	4.64
Hassell, WR	5	0	0	0	0	0	0	.000	12	11	6	4	0	7	0	0	7	3	3.00
Heredia, Dan	2	2	1	0	1	0	0	1.000	13	11	3	2	0	6	0	0	3	2	1.38
Hodges, CR	17	17	12	6	14	2	0	.875	138	84	31	19	0	59	2	7	100	3	1.24
Howard, Apl	6	0	0	0	0	0	0	.000	13	17	10	7	1	6	0	0	4	4	4.85
Hrovat, Wat	12	0	0	0	2	1	0	.667	17	12	3	2	1	10	2	2	14	2	1.06
Hunziker, Cln	24	22	10	2	12	10	1	.545	168	144	79	55	4	77	2	9	137	8	2.95
Johnson, CR*	20	19	8	4	13	2	0	.867	131	93	42	28	7	50	0	2	94	3	1.92
Johnson, Cln	3	0	0	0	0	0	0	.000	8	13	16	10	0	12	1	0	7	2	11.25
Jones, WR	12	12	5	0	6	5	0	.545	82	86	50	29	8	37	4	3	47	0	3.18
Joyce, Apl*	27	24	3	1	6	15	0	.286	132	157	91	62	9	60	2	0	63	5	4.23
Kainer, Wat	12	11	2	0	5	2	1	.714	73	59	35	26	8	19	0	2	53	4	3.21
Kautzer, Apl	13	13	2	0	2	6	0	.250	77	84	58	44	3	44	3	3	37	3	5.14
King, Clinton*	24	22	7	0	6	12	0	.333	133	167	88	63	5	58	3	1	58	8	4.26
Knicely, Dub*	24	12	5	2	7	3	2	.700	107	100	58	47	9	62	0	1	87	7	3.95
Lauzerique, Dub	33	1	0	0	4	5	4	.444	59	55	33	27	7	32	5	3	54	6	4.12
Lee, Dubuque	7	2	1	1	2	1	0	.333	22	23	14	14	2	20	3	2	16	2	5.73
Lehman, Apl	49	0	0	0	4	4	13	.500	78	66	29	23	1	46	8	1	65	6	2.65
Lukevics, Apl	22	17	6	1	10	5	1	.667	126	104	51	42	3	33	3	6	91	2	3.00
Lunar, Wausau	25	25	12	2	7	15	0	.318	166	136	97	61	6	109	5	11	134	17	3.31
MacWhorter, Dan	13	13	2	0	1	7	0	.125	79	78	56	47	1	52	0	11	51	7	5.35
Madden, Apl	5	2	0	0	2	0	0	.000	17	17	19	17	1	18	0	3	19	2	9.00
McKown, CR	2	0	0	0	0	0	0	.000	5	3	1	0	2	0	0	1	0	4.50	
McMakin, WR	21	0	0	0	3	3	0	.500	40	43	30	23	4	32	0	3	20	6	5.18
McWilliams, WR*	15	15	2	0	5	3	0	.625	90	105	53	45	6	47	2	2	54	4	4.50
Mendoza, CR*.	13	11	6	2	8	3	0	.727	87	59	25	18	3	20	0	2	56	2	1.86
Mendoza, Dub	27	11	2	0	1	8	0	.111	98	111	76	53	3	75	6	2	79	13	4.87
Mercedes, QC	4	2	0	0	0	2	0	.000	13	12	12	6	1	10	1	1	9	2	4.15
Miller, Dub*	23	13	2	0	5	9	0	.357	86	108	58	39	3	41	3	1	72	4	4.08
Moline, CR	40	1	1	0	7	3	3	.700	86	69	35	24	2	48	4	1	51	3	2.51
Moreno, Dan	29	2	0	0	2	4	4	.333	65	61	45	33	3	54	0	6	66	13	4.57
Mraz, QC	22	19	3	1	8	6	0	.571	114	113	71	51	9	77	0	1	49	9	4.03
Mueller, 17 Bur-12 Cln	29	3	2	1	4	3	5	.571	72	58	20	14	2	28	2	0	40	7	1.75
Nored, Apl*	9	1	0	0	0	2	0	.000	16	21	34	29	2	36	0	2	10	2	16.31
Officer, QC*	6	4	0	0	1	2	0	.333	27	39	25	19	0	19	0	1	20	2	6.33
O'Keeffe, Bur*	25	25	7	3	7	4	0	.636	166	143	71	53	12	95	0	4	113	5	2.87
Olson, WR*	26	26	9	2	11	10	0	.524	177	146	93	70	5	136	1	6	133	14	3.56
O'Neill, Wausau	24	24	7	2	9	8	0	.529	167	160	85	68	17	80	2	3	96	14	3.66
Passalacqua, Wat	5	0	0	0	0	0	0	.000	8	8	5	5	0	6	0	1	1	1	4.50
Patterson, Dan	12	11	3	1	8	1	1	.889	75	83	27	14	3	17	2	2	54	3	1.68
Pena, Bur*	2	0	0	0	0	2	0	.000	1	3	2	2	1	3	1	0	3	1	18.00
Perez, Dubuque	25	19	5	1	7	6	0	.538	123	137	86	75	12	78	4	5	81	3	5.49
Peterson, Wat	27	1	0	0	3	1	3	.750	59	51	24	20	3	31	3	5	57	5	3.05
Peterson, CR	5	0	0	0	0	0	0	.000	6	5	6	1	1	3	0	0	1	1	9.00
Petrowitz, WR*.	7	0	0	0	0	0	0	.000	16	22	12	12	3	4	0	0	10	3	6.75
Pladson, Dub	27	17	1	0	7	4	1	.636	127	129	88	66	7	90	7	1	63	12	4.68
Porter, QC	13	13	5	0	5	4	0	.556	101	90	42	36	5	27	1	5	65	1	3.21

Pitcher—Club	G.	GS.	CG.	ShO.	W.	L.	Sv.	Pct.	IP.	H.	R.	ER.	HR.	BB.	Int. BB.	HB.	SO.	WP.	ERA.
Quigley, QC	30	4	1	0	2	5	4	.286	79	75	34	24	3	42	1	3	58	0	2.73
Quisenberry, Wat	34	0	0	0	2	1	11	.667	42	28	4	3	1	9	4	1	19	1	0.64
Racanelli, QC	13	6	1	0	4	3	2	.571	62	65	39	31	7	17	2	1	51	2	4.50
Ramstack, Apl	10	1	1	0	0	1	0	.000	19	18	21	20	0	17	0	4	10	1	9.47
Reed, Clinton	1	1	0	0	0	1	0	.000	4	4	5	5	1	2	0	0	3	0	11.25
Repke, Danville*	10	1	0	0	0	3	1	.000	24	35	30	25	3	21	0	0	15	3	9.38
Reyes, Danville	24	10	2	1	6	6	0	.500	91	100	58	37	5	41	1	5	41	3	3.66
Robinson, Wau	1	0	0	0	0	0	0	.000	6	6	6	5	1	4	0	1	3	3	7.50
Rothrock, WR	39	6	5	3	8	5	2	.615	100	90	45	29	10	33	3	2	46	4	2.61
Roy, CR	27	6	2	0	3	6	2	.333	71	71	54	39	6	33	3	2	63	0	4.94
Scheller, Dan	23	23	11	0	10	10	0	.500	166	174	109	80	5	106	0	0	98	13	4.34
Seaman, Wausau*	15	10	1	0	4	5	0	.444	52	58	39	32	5	42	5	1	34	5	5.54
Seltzer, Apl*	1	0	0	0	0	0	0	.000	1	2	2	0	1	0	0	0	0	0	18.00
Sempsrott, Wat*	21	20	6	2	8	5	0	.615	114	132	79	62	10	35	0	0	87	4	4.89
Serum, WR	7	7	2	0	1	4	0	.200	46	52	30	18	3	18	1	0	30	1	3.52
Sherman, CR*	15	7	1	0	2	4	1	.333	44	33	32	25	7	28	0	5	35	4	5.11
Simon, Wausau	3	0	0	0	0	0	0	.000	8	10	11	10	2	15	0	0	4	2	11.25
D. Smith, Bur	25	24	9	3	12	9	1	.571	158	142	81	75	12	64	0	5	117	6	4.27
Smith, QC*	6	5	0	0	1	1	0	.500	35	39	20	15	3	9	0	1	15	0	3.86
Smith, Waterloo	21	11	3	0	4	7	0	.364	98	97	53	36	4	29	0	4	50	5	3.31
Souza, Wat*	36	0	0	0	6	2	5	.750	57	45	22	18	4	31	3	2	64	9	2.84
Stanfield, WR*	17	0	0	0	3	1	6	.750	23	25	13	5	0	11	4	1	16	2	1.96
Steck, QC	22	17	5	1	14	2	0	.875	137	124	71	45	2	57	0	5	72	6	2.96
Stewart, Dan	4	3	0	0	0	2	0	.000	10	17	20	18	1	16	0	1	10	2	16.20
Stoffle, Dan	23	23	13	1	9	12	0	.429	162	183	88	67	9	50	1	0	89	4	3.72
Sturgeon, Apl	10	0	0	0	2	1	1	.667	18	26	17	11	1	7	1	2	11	1	5.50
Tarin, WR	21	1	0	0	2	1	0	.667	46	58	30	25	4	35	4	1	22	1	4.89
Tennant, Dan	14	14	7	0	5	6	0	.455	91	82	52	44	5	57	1	0	70	9	4.35
Thoren, Apl*	19	15	0	0	1	5	0	.167	81	87	47	38	1	39	3	7	68	5	4.22
Townsend, Dan	5	4	0	0	0	3	0	.000	20	32	23	15	2	11	0	1	10	2	6.75
Tyler, Dubuque	1	0	0	0	0	0	0	.000	1	1	1	0	0	0	0	0	1	0	0.00
Uhey, Clinton	16	16	5	2	6	5	0	.545	105	121	63	46	8	23	2	2	51	5	3.94
Van DeCasteele, Dan	28	1	1	0	7	5	7	.583	80	57	19	13	3	23	0	1	61	3	1.46
Vaughn, Cln	13	8	4	1	3	4	1	.429	73	68	41	32	5	35	3	3	48	4	3.95
Vavruska, Cln	13	13	7	0	8	5	0	.615	94	82	38	28	4	35	0	4	71	6	2.68
Viebrock, Wat*	22	22	5	2	11	8	0	.579	128	128	74	53	12	39	0	2	62	1	3.73
Von Ohlen, Wau	9	4	0	0	1	4	0	.200	31	42	27	16	1	21	2	0	18	1	4.65
Wagner, WR	22	19	6	1	5	11	0	.313	115	147	95	74	13	54	2	0	60	13	5.79
Watson, CR	21	21	12	2	13	6	0	.684	159	131	57	47	4	72	3	8	86	7	2.66
Westfall, Wau	28	13	4	0	4	8	2	.333	127	136	90	70	12	78	3	2	88	5	4.96
Williams, Wat*	16	16	4	1	7	6	0	.538	96	84	49	40	6	50	1	4	61	5	3.75
Wilson, CR	19	1	0	0	3	3	2	.500	31	29	7	4	1	12	1	2	19	0	1.16
Wilson, Dubuque	24	24	10	0	10	12	0	.455	151	169	99	71	6	84	4	7	117	6	4.23
Wood, Clinton	29	7	1	0	5	6	0	.455	85	86	66	55	1	102	2	1	44	9	5.82
Wrona, Bur	18	0	0	0	3	1	3	.750	46	30	11	4	0	13	1	2	37	3	0.78
Youngbauer, WR	1	0	0	0	0	0	0	.000	1	0	1	1	0	2	0	0	1	0	9.00

BALKS—Lunar, 6; Souza, 5; Barnicle, 4; Attardi, Hasley, Mendoza (CR), O'Neill, Roy, Sempsrott, Watson, Wrona, 3 each; J. Benson, Boyd, Cacciatore, Evans (Dan), Girkins, Hamner, Hunziker, Kainer, Mercedes, Mueller, Olson, Quigley, Vavruska, Westfall, 2 each; Andersen, Brown, Buford, Burress, Christensen, Clark (Wau), Clear, Coulter, Cvejdlik, Dempsey, Dick, Eddy, A. Edge, Ford, Franz, Gale, Glinatsis, Gonzalez, Handley, Hannon, Johnson (CR), Johnson (Cln), Lauzerique, MacWhorter, McMakin, Mendoza (Dub), Mraz, O'Keeffe, Perez, Peterson (Wat), Pladson, Schellar, Seaman, D. Smith, Stewart, Stoffle, Tennant, Townsend, Vaughn, Wilson (Dub), Wood, 1 each.

COMBINATION SHUTOUTS—Lukevics-Lehman 2, Coulter-Lehman-Joyce-Farrell, Handley-Lehman, Attardi-Lukevics, Attardi-Lehman, Appleton; Dempsey-Conn, Burlington; Watson-Wilson, Cedar Rapids; Vavruska-Elders 2, Clinton; Gonzalez-Van DeCasteele, MacWhorter-Patterson, Danville; Botting-Quigley-Brust, Ferris-Boyle, Quad Cities; Viebrock-Peterson-Souza, Kainer-Gale-Souza, Kainer-Peterson, Waterloo.

NO-HIT GAMES—Mraz, Quad Cities, defeated Wisconsin Rapids, 3-0, May 31 (seven innings); Barnicle, Cedar Rapids, defeated Dubuque, 5-0, June 29; Botting, Quad Cities, defeated Wausau, 3-0, July 26 (seven innings).

NY-Pennsylvania League

CLASS A

CHAMPIONSHIP WINNERS IN PREVIOUS YEARS

1939—Olean*	.631	1952—Hamilton	.659	1964—Auburn§	.622
1940—Olean*	.625	Jamestown (2nd)†	.643	1965—Binghamton	.677
1941—Jamestown	.618	1953—Jamestown*	.704	Binghamton	.607
Bradford (2nd)†	.549	1954—Corning*	.621	1966—Auburn x	.620
1942—Jamestown*	.672	1955—Hamilton	.656	Binghamton	.646
1943—Lockport	.591	1956—Wellsville*	.617	1967—Auburn	.667
Wellsville (3rd)†	.532	1957—Wellsville	.632	1968—Auburn	.645
1944—Lockport	.608	Erie (2nd)†	.598	Oneonta (2nd)*	.558
Jamestown (2nd)†	.565	1958—Wellsville	.556	1969—Oneonta	.662
1945—Batavia*	.677	Geneva (2nd)†	.548	1970—Auburn	.623
1946—Jamestown‡	.672	1959—Wellsville†	.635	1971—Oneonta	.662
Batavia‡	.672	1960—Erie	.643	1972—Niagara Falls	.686
1947—Jamestown*	.690	Wellsville (2nd)†.	.535	1973—Auburn	.667
1948—Lockport*	.603	1961—Geneva	.616	1974—Oneonta	.768
1949—Bradford*	.635	Olean (4th)†	.512	1975—Newark	.688
1950—Hornell	.653	1962—Jamestown	.580	Newark	.714
Olean (2nd)†	.568	Auburn (3rd)†	.521		
1951—Olean	.622	1963—Auburn	.585		
Hornell (3rd)†	.568	Batavia (3rd)†	.485		

*Won championship and four-club playoff. †Won four-club playoff. ‡Jamestown and Batavia declared co-champions; Batavia defeated Jamestown in final of four-club playoff. §Won championship and two-club playoff. xWon split-season playoff. (NOTE—Known as Pennsylvania-Ontario-New York League from 1939 through 1956.)

STANDING OF CLUBS AT CLOSE OF FIRST HALF, JULY 27

Club	W.	L.	T.	Pct.	G.B.	Club	W.	L.	T.	Pct.	G.B.
Elmira (Red Sox)	24	9	0	.727	......	Batavia (Indians)	15	18	0	.455	9
Newark (Brewers)	22	10	0	.688	1½	Auburn (Phillies)	11	21	0	.344	12½
Niagara Falls (Pirates)	17	17	0	.500	7½	Oneonta (Yankees)	10	24	0	.294	14½

STANDING OF CLUBS AT CLOSE OF SECOND HALF, AUGUST 31

Club	W.	L.	T.	Pct.	G.B.	Club	W.	L.	T.	Pct.	G.B.
Elmira (Red Sox)	26	11	0	.703	......	Batavia (Indians)	15	22	0	.405	11
Newark (Brewers)	24	14	0	.632	2½	Oneonta (Yankees)	14	22	0	.389	11½
Niagara Falls (Pirates)	18	17	0	.514	7	Auburn (Phillies)	13	24	0	.351	13

COMPOSITE STANDING OF CLUBS AT CLOSE OF SEASON, AUGUST 31

Club	Elm.	New.	N.F.	Bat.	Aub.	Ont.	W.	L.	T.	Pct.	G.B.
Elmira (Red Sox)	..	6	10	10	13	11	50	20	0	.714	......
Newark (Brewers)	8	..	8	9	11	10	46	24	0	.657	4
Niagara Falls (Pirates)	4	6	..	9	6	10	35	34	0	.507	14½
Batavia (Indians)	4	5	5	..	7	9	30	40	0	.429	20
Auburn (Phillies)	1	3	7	7	..	6	24	45	0	.348	25½
Oneonta (Yankees)	3	4	4	5	8	..	24	46	0	.343	26

Major league affiliations in parentheses.
Forfeited Game—Batavia forfeited to Elmira, August 18.
Playoff—None.

Regular-Season Attendance—Auburn, 35,352; Batavia, 40,716; Elmira, 45,045; Newark, 12,501; Niagara Falls, 45,687; Oneonta, 21,082. Total, 200,383. No playoff. No all-star game.

Managers—Auburn—Michael Compton; Batavia—Jack Cassini; Elmira—Richard (Dick) Berardino; Newark—Anton (Tony) Roig; Niagara Falls—Glenn Ezell; Oneonta—Ed Napoleon.

All-Star Team: 1B—Holle, Newark; 2B—Denton, Elmira; 3B—Walterhouse, Niagara Falls; SS—Pyka, Newark; Utility—Hogenstyn, Oneonta; OF—Ongarato, Elmira; Smith, Oneonta; Bonaparte, Auburn; D. Howard, Niagara Falls; Oppenheimer, Newark; C—Shoebridge, Newark; Thiel, Oneonta; P—Howard, Elmira; Kienzle, Niagara Falls; Sorensen, Newark; Teising, Batavia; Manager—Berardino, Elmira.

(Compiled by Howe News Bureau, Chicago, Ill.)

CLUB BATTING

Club	G.	AB.	R.	OR.	H.	TB.	2B.	3B.	HR.	RBI.	SH.	SF.	Int. BB.	HP.	SO.	SB.	CS.	LOB.	Pct.
Elmira	70	2234	431	303	614	833	84	18	33	368	54	22	416	19	12	313	88	20	604	.275
Newark	70	2311	433	324	618	887	89	21	46	352	19	25	369	14	24	442	67	23	577	.267
Oneonta	70	2251	339	403	564	757	72	26	23	265	21	20	375	15	32	466	44	30	604	.251
Niagara Falls	69	2277	350	362	557	755	68	23	28	291	43	20	404	23	25	425	83	30	598	.245
Auburn	69	2150	281	400	502	659	66	26	13	231	19	22	297	3	19	409	69	15	507	.233
Batavia	70	2107	346	388	488	659	67	19	22	263	45	24	400	18	25	416	125	39	524	.232

INDIVIDUAL BATTING

(Leading Qualifiers for Batting Championship–189 or More Plate Appearances)

*Bats lefthanded. †Switch-hitter.

Player and Club	G.	AB.	R.	H.	TB.	2B.	3B.	HR.	RBI.	SH.	SF.	BB.	HP.	SO.	SB.	CS.	Pct.
Smith, Garry, Ont	44	169	34	66	103	13	6	4	34	0	1	10	1	18	6	0	.391
Ongarato, Michael, Elm	62	226	38	81	106	11	1	4	40	2	0	20	1	23	7	0	.358
LaTorre, Gary, Elm	63	215	52	72	98	6	1	6	50	5	4	33	0	36	5	1	.335
Holle, Gary, New	69	245	70	81	162	16	4	19	77	1	1	52	6	44	8	2	.331
Walterhouse, Richard, NF*	69	258	46	79	104	9	2	4	42	4	3	48	2	23	18	5	.306
Steele, Carlton, Elm	62	201	53	61	67	4	1	0	31	11	1	53	2	17	30	2	.303
Honeycutt, Frederick, NF*	59	186	35	56	77	9	0	4	25	0	0	53	1	29	5	4	.301
Adams, W. Craig, Bat	59	213	37	64	88	6	6	2	36	1	0	35	2	44	21	8	.300
Oppenheimer, Jose, New	47	155	34	45	53	4	2	0	23	1	1	34	0	16	2	3	.290
Eshelman, Peter, Ont*	58	167	29	48	70	6	2	4	30	1	0	28	6	16	0	0	.287

Smith did not have the required number of plate appearances but when charged with 6 official at bats to reach the qualification plateau he thus becomes the leader with a .377 batting average. Under the provisions of Rule 10.23 (a), Smith, Oneonta, qualifies for the batting championship.

Departmental Leaders: G–Holle, Toups, Walterhouse, 69; AB–Walterhouse, 258; R–Holle, 70; H–Holle, Ongarato, 81; TB–Holle, 162; 2B–Holle, 16; 3B–Adams, Bonaparte, Smith, 6; HR–Holle, 19; RBI–Holle, 77; SH–Toups, 14; SF–Lloyd, 7; BB–Buszka, 76; HP–Toups, 7; SO–Dorville, 73; SB–Steele, 30; CS–Adams, 8.

(All Players–Listed Alphabetically)

Player and Club	G.	AB.	R.	H.	TB.	2B.	3B.	HR.	RBI.	SH.	SF.	BB.	HP.	SO.	SB.	CS.	Pct.
Adams, W. Craig, Bat	59	213	37	64	88	6	6	2	36	1	0	35	2	45	21	8	.300
Aguayo, Luis, Aub	51	197	27	49	62	9	2	0	23	0	1	12	1	17	7	1	.249
Angulo, Aquiles, Bat	1	3	0	1	1	0	0	0	0	0	0	1	0	1	0	1	.333
Arp, Ronnie, Bat	4	4	0	0	0	0	0	0	0	0	0	0	0	2	0	0	.000
Batchko, Mark, NF	25	73	3	13	14	1	0	0	6	3	1	16	1	22	0	0	.178
Bellony, Rodrigo, Ont*	38	126	20	35	44	5	2	0	13	0	0	39	2	24	0	4	.278
Bevington, Terry, Ont	2	3	0	0	0	0	0	0	0	0	0	0	0	1	0	0	.000
Boggs, Wade, Elm*	57	179	29	47	53	6	0	0	15	3	1	29	0	15	2	2	.263
Bonaparte, Elijah, Aub*	59	198	24	42	58	4	6	0	20	1	3	26	0	37	11	1	.212
Brown, John E., Bat*	38	132	25	25	44	5	1	4	26	1	4	39	1	29	17	5	.189
Brunswick, Thomas, Aub	26	66	6	10	10	0	0	0	3	1	1	5	2	12	1	2	.152
Buchan, William, Aub	24	58	11	10	11	1	0	0	6	0	0	20	0	16	0	0	.172
Bullard, Larkin, Bat	5	12	1	3	3	0	0	0	1	0	0	2	0	3	0	0	.250
Burke, Tom, NF	10	29	8	9	13	0	2	0	2	0	1	3	1	1	0	1	.310
Burkett, J. Mark, NF*	1	1	0	0	0	0	0	0	0	0	0	0	0	0	0	0	.000
Buszka, John, Bat*	67	203	46	41	47	6	0	0	16	5	3	76	2	25	17	1	.202
Cajide, Alberto, Bat	1	1	0	0	0	0	0	0	0	0	0	0	0	1	0	0	.000
Camacho, Anulfo, New*	5	14	4	4	6	0	1	0	1	0	0	5	0	4	2	0	.286
Carty, Jorge, NF	52	174	26	39	49	3	2	1	13	3	1	17	3	18	13	4	.224
Crawford, John, Ont*	59	181	23	42	54	4	1	2	25	0	1	41	3	63	6	5	.232
Curtis, Randall, Aub	42	111	10	31	33	2	0	0	13	1	1	16	0	14	2	0	.279
Denton, David, Elm	61	204	43	53	75	8	1	4	30	8	1	25	3	25	12	3	.260
Donovan, Gary, New	24	71	14	24	29	3	1	0	13	0	1	4	0	4	3	2	.338
Dorville, Francisco, Ont	52	164	13	25	38	3	2	2	15	0	0	13	3	73	0	2	.152
Doss, Dennis, Bat	3	7	0	2	2	0	0	0	0	0	0	0	0	2	0	0	.286
Edwards, John, Elm	18	51	9	13	21	2	0	2	16	2	2	15	0	6	1	0	.255
Eshelman, Peter, Ont*	58	167	29	48	70	6	2	4	30	1	0	28	6	16	0	0	.287
Estevez, Bernardo, Ont	57	198	40	50	55	3	1	0	11	4	0	47	3	22	11	7	.253
Faccinto, John, Elm	21	44	8	9	10	1	0	0	4	3	0	12	0	8	0	0	.205
Felt, William, Aub*	42	66	8	14	21	2	1	1	10	0	3	28	0	13	0	0	.212
Fischlin, Michael, Ont	14	55	13	14	17	3	0	0	5	0	1	8	1	6	3	1	.255
Fisher, Glenn, Elm	13	32	9	6	11	3	1	0	4	1	0	6	0	3	1	0	.188
Fleming, Steven, NF*	41	104	22	20	34	3	1	3	16	0	0	40	1	28	3	2	.192
Fowlkes, David, Bat*	54	152	20	38	49	6	1	1	15	1	0	33	0	21	3	2	.250
Franklin, Elliott, New*	39	154	27	40	56	7	0	3	25	1	1	15	1	33	5	1	.260
Gale, David, Aub*	23	81	15	26	30	2	1	0	8	0	0	6	1	11	4	1	.321
Gault, Raymond, Bat	2	1	0	0	0	0	0	0	0	0	0	1	0	1	0	0	.000
Gingerich, Gary, New	58	231	39	58	77	6	2	3	22	1	4	25	1	44	8	3	.251
Glass, Timothy, Bat	41	103	15	17	25	5	0	1	7	0	0	14	4	27	3	2	.165
Globig, David, New	24	76	9	16	24	3	1	1	8	2	2	2	2	18	2	0	.211
Gomez, Esteban, New	13	32	5	6	8	0	1	0	4	0	0	5	0	13	0	1	.188
Gonzalez, Eugenio Guzman, Aub	13	39	6	12	15	1	0		3	1	1	6	0	6	1	0	.308

Player and Club	G.	AB.	R.	H.	TB.	2B.	3B.	HR.	RBI.	SH.	SF.	BB.	HP.	SO.	SB.	CS.	Pct.
Greenhalgh, Jeffrey, NF*	24	61	11	7	11	1	0	1	5	1	0	26	2	25	2	2	.115
Hammock, Harvin, Aub	37	115	10	26	32	2	0	12	2	0	12	0	12	1	0	.226
Harmon, Larry, Bat	36	116	13	26	31	5	0	0	15	4	1	6	1	30	5	0	.224
Harrington, Ronald, Elm	52	154	26	39	63	13	1	3	29	2	4	34	1	22	0	1	.253
Harvey, M. Craig, Bat	27	40	10	9	14	2	0	1	2	1	1	11	0	10	0	0	.225
Hawkins, Brad, Elm*	29	77	13	20	22	2	0	0	8	2	0	20	0	7	7	1	.260
Hoffman, Glenn, Elm	60	191	29	52	72	7	2	3	34	5	2	23	2	9	2	1	.272
Hogestyn, Donald, Ont	39	131	24	40	61	9	3	2	23	2	1	29	2	27	0	0	.305
Holle, Gary, New	69	245	70	81	162	16	4	19	77	1	1	52	6	44	8	2	.331
Honeycutt, Frederick, NF*	59	186	35	56	77	9	0	4	25	0	0	53	1	29	5	4	.301
Howard, D. Richard, NF	62	193	34	52	71	7	3	2	31	3	2	53	0	41	6	2	.269
Hyman, Larry, Elm†	49	150	26	42	77	7	2	8	41	1	2	38	1	34	3	2	.280
Jacobs, Ronald, New	10	27	8	9	14	2	0	1	4	1	0	12	0	4	0	0	.333
Jeansonne, Kevin, Bat*	66	212	30	51	73	3	2	5	30	2	4	31	1	52	8	3	.241
Johnson, Jeffrey, Aub	8	12	0	0	0	0	0	0	0	0	0	0	0	5	0	0	.000
Jones, Joe Louis, Aub	64	224	37	59	78	11	1	2	27	0	2	26	0	49	3	1	.263
Kidd, John, Elm	13	38	10	5	8	1	1	0	4	1	0	9	0	7	0	0	.132
Lara, Cesar, Bat	12	31	5	4	4	0	0	0	1	2	0	5	0	7	0	1	.129
LaTorre, Gary, Elm	63	215	52	72	98	6	1	6	50	5	4	33	0	36	5	1	.335
Lebron, Jorge, Aub	43	129	20	32	42	7	0	1	13	4	1	33	2	25	1	2	.248
Leech, Allen, NF	41	138	20	27	34	4	0	1	12	4	3	21	4	37	3	0	.196
Lloyd, Benny, Ont	65	224	33	47	66	5	4	2	25	3	7	32	4	48	3	4	.210
Long, Robert E., NF	3	3	2	1	1	0	0	0	2	1	0	0	0	1	0	0	.333
Manning, Melvin, New	25	80	17	23	26	1	1	0	8	0	1	18	2	19	0	0	.288
Maria, Esteban, New	45	134	20	28	45	3	1	4	16	2	3	16	1	38	4	1	.209
Mattson, Ronald, Aub	6	22	1	7	9	2	0	0	4	0	1	1	0	4	0	0	.318
McCarron, Michael, Aub*	9	24	2	3	3	0	0	0	1	0	0	7	0	6	2	0	.125
McDougal, Ricky Dee, Aub	9	28	3	7	11	1	0	1	7	0	0	3	1	7	0	1	.250
McGlade, Michael, Bat	2	3	1	1	1	0	0	0	1	0	0	1	0	0	0	0	.333
Montgomery, Larry, New	1	3	0	1	1	0	0	0	0	0	0	1	0	1	0	0	.333
Monzon, Daniel, New	7	25	3	5	6	1	0	0	5	1	0	2	0	4	1	0	.200
Muriel, Arnaldo, Aub	43	154	19	45	62	8	3	1	20	1	2	12	1	14	4	2	.292
Narleski, Steven, Bat	1	2	0	1	1	0	0	0	1	0	0	0	0	0	0	0	.500
Nelson, Chester, New	34	120	8	29	38	3	0	2	18	0	2	11	2	32	0	1	.242
Nichols, T. Reid, Elm	23	53	8	18	19	1	0	0	9	0	2	11	1	9	2	2	.340
Ongarato, Michael, Elm	62	226	38	81	106	11	1	4	40	2	0	20	1	23	7	0	.358
Oppenheimer, Jose, New	47	155	34	45	53	4	2	0	23	1	1	34	0	16	2	3	.290
Ortiz, Christopher, Bat*	2	7	0	1	1	0	0	0	0	0	0	0	0	0	0	0	.143
Packer, Louis, Aub	46	129	21	25	34	3	3	0	7	4	3	17	3	38	7	0	.194
Partridge, Glenn, New*	34	124	22	38	41	3	0	0	12	1	2	19	0	17	8	2	.306
Pascarella, Andrew, New	22	81	18	19	28	4	1	1	14	2	1	13	1	17	1	0	.235
Passmore, W. Jason, New	24	73	12	12	15	3	0	0	2	0	0	16	2	19	1	0	.164
Perez, Benjamin, Ont	21	80	10	26	30	4	0	0	8	1	1	8	1	6	2	0	.325
Plantery, Mark, Ont	27	90	3	16	17	1	0	0	4	0	0	13	2	26	0	0	.178
Pozo, Melanio, Aub	28	98	15	22	27	3	1	0	10	1	1	13	1	12	5	1	.224
Preseren, Kenneth, Bat*	24	62	15	18	21	1	1	0	9	3	0	16	0	7	9	0	.290
Puryear, Nathaniel, Bat	2	3	0	0	0	0	0	0	0	0	0	0	0	3	0	0	.000
Pyka, Garry, New	43	181	38	49	57	6	1	0	11	3	1	18	2	22	8	2	.271
Rentas, Rosendo, Elm	17	42	7	8	8	0	0	0	3	0	0	6	0	5	0	0	.190
Rodriguez, Luis R., Aub	4	12	0	0	0	0	0	0	0	0	0	1	0	3	0	0	.000
Rogers, Darnell, Bat	3	6	0	0	0	0	0	0	0	0	0	0	0	3	0	0	.000
Roman, Noel, Elm	18	48	9	13	16	1	1	0	5	0	1	4	1	6	2	0	.271
Roman, Norberto, Aub†	47	143	24	38	62	4	1	6	25	2	0	24	2	36	8	1	.266
Rouse, Charles, NF*	55	215	25	52	63	5	3	0	20	1	0	28	1	43	8	2	.242
Rowe, Michael, Bat*	13	37	8	8	11	1	1	0	4	1	0	8	0	15	2	0	.216
Royster, Willie, NF	53	196	30	46	79	7	1	8	35	2	3	30	3	51	10	2	.235
Salazar, Luis, NF	42	151	18	36	50	3	4	1	17	5	4	7	2	26	7	2	.238
Sandoval, Jesus, Ont.*	32	83	11	16	20	2	1	0	7	1	1	17	0	36	1	0	.193
Santana, Simon, NF*	64	250	34	49	58	5	2	0	25	11	1	33	2	45	5	3	.196
Sauer, Jack, Elm	42	129	26	37	47	5	1	1	17	3	1	29	0	16	14	2	.287
Scaffidi, Philip, NF	33	83	12	23	25	0	1	0	12	4	0	11	1	11	1	0	.277
Shoebridge, Terence, New	56	172	36	44	71	9	0	6	33	0	2	52	1	34	3	1	.256
Smith, Garry, Ont	44	169	34	66	103	13	6	4	34	0	1	10	1	18	6	0	.391
Spence, John, Bat	2	2	0	0	0	0	0	0	0	0	0	0	0	1	0	0	.000
Spence, Samuel, Bat	1	2	0	0	0	0	0	0	0	1	0	0	0	1	0	0	.000
Steele, Carlton, Elm	62	201	53	61	67	4	1	0	31	11	1	53	2	17	30	2	.303
Tabler, Patrick, Ont	65	238	27	55	61	3	0	1	20	2	3	27	2	35	6	2	.231
Tanks, Talmadge, New	41	143	23	33	46	3	2	2	20	3	2	34	0	37	8	2	.231
Tasker, Paul, Bat	23	62	12	16	23	2	1	1	8	3	0	6	3	11	1	0	.258
Teising, John, Bat*	2	2	0	1	1	0	0	0	0	0	0	2	0	1	0	0	.500
Thiel, Mark, Ont	51	152	35	40	58	6	0	4	27	4	3	42	2	9	1	0	.263
Thomas, Luis, Ont	10	30	2	4	6	1	0	0	1	0	0	2	0	11	0	0	.133
Tomski, Jeffrey, Bat	29	70	11	15	21	3	0	1	9	0	0	16	0	18	1	0	.214
Toups, Frank, Bat	69	251	41	59	79	8	3	2	21	14	4	30	7	40	20	7	.235
Twogood, Mark, Elm	35	91	14	16	25	1	1	2	12	4	0	23	0	35	0	0	.176

Player and Club	G.	AB.	R.	H.	TB.	2B.	3B.	HR.	RBI.	SH.	SF.	BB.	HP.	SO.	SB.	CS.	Pct.
Tyson, Terry, Bat	61	202	25	49	59	8	1	0	26	2	2	29	1	31	13	4	.243
Vega, Jesus, New	45	169	25	53	83	12	3	4	36	0	1	15	3	22	3	2	.314
Verhelst, Edwing, Elm	17	38	5	4	5	1	0	0	2	1	0	2	0	10	0	0	.105
Vincent, Happy, Elm	22	43	6	13	20	3	2	0	7	0	1	13	0	10	0	1	.302
Virgil, Osvaldo, Aub	39	113	10	16	24	1	2	1	10	1	2	15	3	36	2	0	.142
Walker, Cleotha, Elm†	22	28	5	5	10	1	2	0	1	0	0	11	0	10	0	2	.179
Walterhouse, Richard, NF*	69	258	46	79	104	9	4	42	4	3	48	2	23	18	5	.306
Waters, Darnell, Ont	21	75	14	24	38	2	3	2	10	1	0	12	0	19	3	4	.320
Weismiller, Robert, NF	3	2	1	0	0	0	0	0	0	0	0	0	0	2	0	0	.000
Wilborn, Thaddeaus, Ont	28	85	8	16	19	3	0	0	4	2	1	7	0	26	2	1	.188
Wilder, Troy, Bat*	1	2	0	0	0	0	0	0	0	1	0	0	0	1	0	0	.000
Williams, Eddie Lee, Aub	44	131	12	28	35	3	2	0	9	0	0	16	2	37	10	2	.214
Wilson, Duane, Bat*	52	163	30	38	60	6	2	4	35	3	4	34	2	28	5	5	.233
Yandrick, Jerome, NF*	41	161	23	48	72	11	2	3	28	1	1	18	1	22	2	1	.298

The following pitchers had no plate appearances primarily through use of designated hitters, listed alphabetically by club, games in parentheses:

AUBURN—Burdette, Ricky (1); Davis, Charles (17); Kruzelock, Michael (15); Kuhn, Shawn (14); Lasek, James (14); Mack, Henry (13); Mattice, Gary (16); Morales, Jose M. (13); Nunn, Wallace (9); Watts, Brian (17); Welborn, Sammye (10); Whaley, R. Jarrell (12); Wilson, Lee (2); Wolff, Chris (2).

BATAVIA—Mitchell, William (6); Rodriguez, Julian (14); Smith, Reggie T. (11); Vaughn, Michael (3).

ELMIRA—Burtt, Dennis (8); Carlander, Paul (9); de Leon, Antonio (6); Fox, Jimmy L. (15); Howard, Michael S. (14); Hurst, Bruce (9); King, Jerome (3); Lopez, Carlos R. (11); Miller, Steven (10); Parks, Danny (14); Patrick, Ronny (8); Senneck, Steven (22); Schoppee, David (12); Serwon, Stephen (2); Smith, Douglas (12); Tagliarino, John (20); Trask, James (11).

NEWARK—Bannister, Timothy (13); Frazier, George (6); Fritch, Gary (14); Harryman, Jeffrey (16); Meagher, Bradley (12); Offermann, Thomas (15); Quinn, James (8); Quinones, Felipe (13); Quinones, Rene (17); Reyes, Rafael (1); Rodriguez, Jose A. (9); Roesch, John (7); Sorensen, Lary (13).

NIAGARA FALLS—Cain, Don (11); Howard, Mark (12); Kienzle, Laurence (18); Parke, James (13); Peterson, Eric (5); Prentice, Stephen (17); Rogers, J. David (14); Schwerman, Brian (7); Semerano, Robert (3).

ONEONTA—Atkins, Frederick (2); Carmarena, Rafael (10); Delgatti, Scott (13); Fisk, Donald (16); Gaube, Gerald (15); Laurent, Leonce (3); Lombardi, David (9); Palmer, D. Neil (7); Riggar, Calvin (13); Robles, Julio (13); Santana, Rafael (15); Softy, Mark (13); Williamson, Ronald (5).

GRAND SLAM HOME RUNS—Holle 2, Jeansonne, McDougal, Royster, Walterhouse, 1 each.

AWARDED FIRST BASE ON INTERFERENCE—Smith 2 (McDougal, Tomski), Buszka (Batchko), Eshelman (Tomski), Jones (Tomski), Steele (Tasker).

CLUB FIELDING

Club	G.	PO.	A.	E.	DP.	PB.	Pct.	Club	G.	PO.	A.	E.	DP.	PB.	Pct.
Newark	70	1780	730	119	70	15	.955	Batavia	70	1718	767	151	48	24	.943
Elmira	70	1758	678	124	53	16	.952	Niagara Falls	69	1822	735	169	47	19	.938
Auburn	69	1693	648	134	55	20	.946	Oneonta	70	1719	669	182	53	18	.929

Triple Play—Oneonta.

INDIVIDUAL FIELDING

FIRST BASEMEN

Player and Club	G.	PO.	A.	E.	DP.	Pct.	Player and Club	G.	PO.	A.	E.	DP.	Pct.
Vincent, Elmira	18	79	6	0	11	1.000	Felt, Oneonta	20	173	8	4	9	.978
Eshelman, Oneonta*	5	22	5	0	2	1.000	Muriel, Auburn	20	133	3	3	11	.978
Johnson, Auburn	2	8	0	0	1	1.000	Greenhalgh, NF	24	171	15	6	14	.969
Tanks, Newark*	1	5	1	0	0	1.000	Dorville, Oneonta	51	324	21	13	36	.964
Jeansonne, Batavia	1	6	1	0	0	1.000	Roman, Auburn	8	48	3	2	8	.962
LaTORRE, Elmira	63	506	44	6	38	.9892	Sandoval, Ont*	26	153	14	7	11	.960
Holle, Newark*	69	587	36	7	57	.9888	Rowe, Batavia*	6	48	2	4	0	.926
Gale, Auburn*	23	171	8	2	17	.989	Honeycutt, NF*	2	12	0	1	1	.923
Buszka, Batavia*	45	366	25	6	28	.985	Walterhouse, NF	1	10	0	1	1	.909
Wilson, Batavia	20	173	8	3	9	.984	Scaffidi, NF	6	35	7	7	2	.857
Yandrick, NF*	41	343	28	7	22	.981							

Triple Play—Dorville.

SECOND BASEMEN

Player and Club	G.	PO.	A.	E.	DP.	Pct.	Player and Club	G.	PO.	A.	E.	DP.	Pct.
Harmon, Batavia	2	3	2	0	1	1.000	Aguayo, Auburn	33	72	83	5	18	.969
Preseren, Batavia	2	3	1	0	0	1.000	DENTON, Elmira	61	118	150	9	30	.968
Roman, Elmira	2	1	3	0	0	1.000	Toups, Batavia	69	186	186	14	28	.964
Rogers, Batavia	1	1	1	0	0	1.000	Franklin, Newark	32	96	79	7	20	.962
Scaffidi, NF	1	1	0	0	0	1.000	Rouse, NF	55	141	130	13	27	.954
Pozo, Auburn	26	70	64	2	13	.985	Pascarella, Newark	18	47	48	5	11	.950
Pyka, Newark	7	18	17	1	3	.972	Estevez, Oneonta	15	41	35	4	11	.950

SECOND BASEMEN—Continued

Player and Club	G.	PO.	A.	E.	DP.	Pct.	Player and Club	G.	PO.	A.	E.	DP.	Pct.
Nichols, Elmira	5	7	9	1	2	.941	Perez, Oneonta	21	49	61	10	5	.917
Partridge, Newark	15	30	33	4	7	.940	Walker, Newark	11	9	18	3	4	.900
Walterhouse, NF	12	26	25	4	5	.927	Fisher, Elmira	3	5	4	1	3	.900
Gonzalez, Auburn	13	26	22	4	7	.923	Salazar, NF	1	2	1	1	0	.750
Bellony, Oneonta	37	79	75	14	17	.917							

THIRD BASEMEN

Player and Club	G.	PO.	A.	E.	DP.	Pct.	Player and Club	G.	PO.	A.	E.	DP.	Pct.
Bullard, Batavia	2	7	5	0	1	1.000	Hogestyn, Oneonta	24	23	40	8	4	.887
Roman, Elmira	2	5	0	0	0	1.000	Harmon, Batavia	15	15	23	5	1	.884
Felt, Auburn	1	2	0	0	0	1.000	Boggs, Elmira	57	36	75	16	5	.874
Donovan, Newark	11	10	16	1	2	.963	Nichols, Elmira	5	3	3	1	0	.857
Muriel, Auburn	21	9	44	4	3	.930	Faccinto, Elmira	21	11	24	6	2	.854
Waters, Oneonta	3	5	6	1	0	.917	Thomas, Oneonta	2	2	3	1	0	.833
GINGERICH, Newark	48	41	106	15	10	.907	D. Howard, NF	13	12	28	9	1	.816
Walterhouse, NF	55	59	115	18	7	.906	Aguayo, Auburn	10	6	16	5	2	.815
Tyson, Batavia	8	8	21	3	4	.906	Preseren, Batavia	4	2	5	2	0	.778
Monzon, Newark	7	5	14	2	1	.905	Franklin, Newark	1	0	3	1	0	.750
Tabler, Oneonta	41	32	70	11	4	.903	Vincent, Elmira	2	2	1	1	0	.750
Fowlkes, Batavia	47	36	81	13	7	.900	Cajide, Batavia	1	0	2	1	0	.667
Lebron, Auburn	39	34	64	11	12	.899	Estevez, Oneonta	2	1	0	1	0	.500
Partridge, Newark	6	7	17	3	0	.889							

Triple Play—Tabler

SHORTSTOPS

Player and Club	G.	PO.	A.	E.	DP.	Pct.	Player and Club	G.	PO.	A.	E.	DP.	Pct.
Rodriguez, Auburn	3	4	12	0	1	1.000	Preseren, Batavia	10	8	27	4	1	.897
Aguayo, Auburn	1	1	0	0	1	1.000	Estevez, Oneonta	41	76	97	20	18	.896
Honeycutt, NF*	1	1	0	0	0	1.000	Leech, NF	41	59	135	23	23	.894
TYSON, Batavia	54	83	175	15	30	.945	Curtis, Auburn	41	48	87	16	17	.894
Pyka, Newark	36	50	109	10	20	.941	Lara, Batavia	9	11	20	4	1	.886
Johnson, Auburn	4	6	9	1	4	.938	Salazar, NF	19	41	46	12	5	.879
Brunswick, Auburn	24	28	61	7	9	.927	Fisher, Elmira	10	15	23	6	3	.864
Hoffman, Elmira	59	71	139	17	18	.925	Hogestyn, Oneonta	16	25	36	10	5	.859
Fischlin, Oneonta	14	36	48	7	12	.923	Roman, Elmira	11	10	21	8	5	.795
Gingerich, Newark	9	22	28	5	8	.909	Mattson, Auburn	6	4	15	5	0	.792
Manning, Newark	25	46	68	12	11	.905	Thomas, Oneonta	4	5	5	5	0	.667
Scaffidi, NF	15	33	34	7	6	.905							

Triple Play—Estevez

OUTFIELDERS

Player and Club	G.	PO.	A.	E.	DP.	Pct.	Player and Club	G.	PO.	A.	E.	DP.	Pct.
Kidd, Elmira	11	20	2	0	0	1.000	Wilson, Batavia	18	17	0	1	0	.944
McCarron, Auburn	9	12	0	0	0	1.000	Jeansonne, Batavia*	63	73	10	5	5	.943
Sandoval, Oneonta*	2	6	0	0	0	1.000	Williams, Auburn	43	43	6	3	1	.942
Royster, NF	2	4	1	0	0	1.000	Ongarato, Elmira	60	97	5	7	0	.936
Camacho, Newark*	5	3	0	0	0	1.000	Harmon, Batavia	15	10	4	1	1	.933
Thiel, Oneonta	1	2	0	0	0	1.000	Carty, NF	49	81	5	7	1	.925
Passmore, Newark	24	54	0	1	0	.982	Adams, Batavia	58	95	9	9	1	.920
Maria, Newark	44	50	3	1	2	.981	Smith, Oneonta*	29	54	2	5	0	.918
Tabler, Oneonta	24	47	1	1	0	.980	Sauer, Elmira	37	54	1	5	0	.917
Hawkins, Elmira*	28	39	1	1	0	.976	Oppenheimer, New	40	61	0	6	0	.910
Packer, Auburn	46	126	6	5	0	.964	Roman, Auburn	30	62	6	7	3	.907
Wilborn, Oneonta	23	48	3	2	1	.962	D. Howard, NF	43	62	3	7	1	.903
Fleming, NF	35	46	1	2	0	.959	Crawford, Oneonta*	55	77	5	10	0	.891
STEELE, Elmira	60	108	6	5	1	.958	Brown, Batavia*	37	45	1	6	1	.885
Waters, Oneonta	18	41	2	2	0	.956	Salazar, NF	17	30	3	5	0	.868
Vega, Newark	41	80	5	4	2	.955	Hammock, Auburn	35	50	2	8	1	.867
Lloyd, Oneonta	63	117	5	6	0	.953	Twogood, Elmira	34	40	5	7	1	.865
Bonaparte, Auburn*	58	96	5	5	1	.953	Hyman, Elmira	4	6	0	1	0	.857
Santana, NF*	64	132	3	7	1	.951	Buszka, Batavia*	22	19	5	5	0	.828
Tanks, Newark*	40	75	3	4	0	.951	Gomez, Newark	5	4	0	1	0	.800
Globig, Newark	23	32	2	2	0	.944	Nichols, Elmira	2	1	0	1	0	.500
Burke, NF	8	16	1	1	0	.944							

CATCHERS

Player and Club	G.	PO.	A.	E.	DP.	PB.	Pct.	Player and Club	G.	PO.	A.	E.	DP.	PB.	Pct.
Edwards, Elm	11	72	8	0	1	0	1.000	HARRINGTON, Elm	46	270	26	5	2	5	.983
Fowlkes, Bat	5	11	1	0	1	2	1.000	Shoebridge, New	39	293	23	6	3	5	.981
McGlade, Bat	2	2	1	0	0	1	1.000	Jacobs, Newark	6	36	8	1	1	3	.978
Harvey, Bat	14	75	6	1	1	2	.988	Royster, NF	49	288	41	9	1	13	.973
Verhelst, Elm	16	70	5	1	1	5	.987	Virgil, Auburn	26	153	14	5	0	5	.971
Buchan, Auburn	14	66	4	1	0	7	.986	Nelson, Newark	29	175	16	6	1	7	.970

CATCHERS—Continued

Player and Club	G.	PO.	A.	E.	DP.	PB.	Pct.
Batchko, NF	22	153	10	5	1	5	.970
Thiel, Oneonta	45	242	43	10	3	7	.966
Jones, Auburn	26	171	23	7	5	7	.965
Glass, Batavia	31	146	4	6	0	6	.962
Tomski, Batavia	27	134	14	6	1	5	.961

Player and Club	G.	PO.	A.	E.	DP.	PB.	Pct.
McDougal, Aub	8	51	4	3	1	1	.948
Plantery, Ont	27	182	15	11	2	11	.947
Rentas, Elmira	16	74	10	5	1	6	.944
Tasker, Batavia	17	104	12	9	0	8	.928
Salazar, NF	1	0	0	1	0	1	.000

Triple Play—Thiel.

PITCHERS

Player and Club	G.	PO.	A.	E.	DP.	Pct.
HOWARD, Elmira	14	4	15	0	1	1.000
Montgomery, New	10	7	10	0	0	1.000
Parks, Elmira	14	4	12	0	0	1.000
Harryman, Newark*	16	3	12	0	1	1.000
Whaley, Auburn*	12	5	8	0	1	1.000
Doss, Batavia	12	5	8	0	1	1.000
Hurst, Elmira*	9	1	8	0	1	1.000
Fox, Elmira	15	3	6	0	0	1.000
Santana, Oneonta	15	2	6	0	1	1.000
Carlander, Elmira	9	2	5	0	0	1.000
Cain, NF	11	2	4	0	0	1.000
Kruzelock, Aub	15	0	6	0	0	1.000
Mattice, Auburn	16	1	5	0	0	1.000
Burtt, Elmira	8	2	3	0	0	1.000
Smith, Elmira	12	2	3	0	1	1.000
Tagliarino, Elm	20	1	4	0	0	1.000
F. Quinones, New	2	1	2	0	1	1.000
Serwon, Elmira	2	1	2	0	0	1.000
Watts, Auburn	17	1	2	0	0	1.000
Atkins, Oneonta	2	1	1	0	0	1.000
de Leon, Elmira	6	0	2	0	0	1.000
Burdette, Aub*	1	0	1	0	0	1.000
Reyes, Newark	2	0	1	0	0	1.000
Wilson, Auburn	2	0	1	0	0	1.000
Wolff, Auburn	5	0	1	0	0	1.000
Williamson, Ont	6	0	1	0	0	1.000
Mitchell, Bat*	6	0	1	0	1	1.000
Palmer, Oneonta*	7	0	1	0	1	1.000
Rodriguez, New*	9	1	0	0	0	1.000
Felt, Auburn	10	0	1	0	0	1.000
R. Quinones, New	17	5	19	1	1	.960
Teising, Batavia*	16	1	16	1	1	.944
Weismiller, NF	19	7	8	1	0	.938
Burkett, NF	19	2	12	1	0	.933
Long, NF	11	5	8	1	1	.929
Honeycutt, NF*	13	13	25	3	2	.927
Schwerman, NF	7	4	8	1	0	.923
Cajide, Bat	11	4	8	1	0	.923
Sorensen, New	13	7	15	2	1	.917
Prentice, NF	17	4	7	1	0	.917
Kuhn, Aub	14	6	14	2	0	.909
Rogers, NF	14	1	9	1	0	.909
S. Spence, Bat	10	5	12	2	0	.895

Player and Club	G.	PO.	A.	E.	DP.	Pct.
Meagher, New*	12	4	13	2	1	.895
Miller, Elm	10	3	5	1	0	.889
Bannister, New	13	5	10	2	0	.882
Morales, Aub	13	4	10	2	1	.875
Eshelman, Ont*	7	0	7	1	0	.875
Riggar, Ont*	13	4	22	4	1	.867
Schoppee, Elm	12	5	8	2	2	.867
Frazier, New	6	2	4	1	1	.857
Quinn, New	8	0	6	1	0	.857
Wilder, Bat*	9	0	6	1	0	.857
Harvey, Bat	13	0	6	1	0	.857
Gaube, Aub	15	1	5	1	0	.857
Arp, Batavia	16	3	18	4	0	.840
Delgatti, Ont	13	3	7	2	1	.833
M. Howard, NF	12	3	2	1	0	.833
Fritch, New	14	2	3	1	0	.833
Lasek, Aub	14	0	5	1	0	.833
Offermann, New*	15	6	8	3	0	.824
Narleski, Bat	18	3	6	2	1	.818
Mack, Aub	13	1	12	3	0	.813
Parke, NF	13	9	4	3	0	.813
Softy, Ont	13	4	9	3	1	.813
Bullard, Bat	17	2	11	3	0	.813
Kienzle, NF*	18	4	4	2	0	.800
Patrick, Elm*	8	0	4	1	1	.800
Fisk, Ont	16	7	8	4	1	.789
J. Spence, Bat	9	2	8	3	0	.769
Robles, Ont	13	4	11	5	0	.750
Davis, Aub	17	2	7	3	0	.750
Laurent, Ont	3	0	3	1	0	.750
Roesch, New*	7	0	3	1	1	.750
Lombardi, Ont	9	3	0	1	0	.750
Schneck, Elm	22	1	7	3	0	.727
Nunn, Aub	9	2	3	2	0	.714
Lopez, Elm	11	2	4	3	0	.667
Peterson, NF*	5	0	2	1	0	.667
Carmarena, Ont	10	0	2	1	0	.667
Gault, Bat	14	0	2	1	1	.667
Rodriguez, Bat	14	1	8	5	0	.643
Puryear, Bat	14	3	4	4	0	.636
Welborn, Aub	10	1	5	6	0	.500
Trask, Elm	11	0	1	1	0	.500

The following players do not have any recorded accepted chances at the positions indicated; therefore, are not listed in the fielding averages for those particular positions: King, p; Scaffidi, 3b; Semerano, p; R. Smith, p; Vaughn, p; Angulo, Bevington and Ortiz appeared as designated-hitters/pinch-hitters only.

CLUB PITCHING

Club	G.	CG.	ShO.	Sv.	IP.	H.	R.	ER.	HR.	BB.	Int. BB.	HB.	SO.	WP.	Bk.	ERA.
Elmira	70	4	7	15	586	487	303	218	21	360	20	20	462	41	4	3.35
Niagara Falls	69	18	2	10	607	604	362	245	21	299	8	21	411	48	1	3.63
Newark	70	25	9	12	593	556	324	243	30	346	6	19	384	45	6	3.69
Oneonta	70	25	1	7	573	585	403	282	24	382	28	20	381	33	3	4.43
Batavia	70	12	4	9	573	530	388	289	30	462	24	36	435	67	0	4.54
Auburn	69	12	3	8	564	581	400	324	39	412	6	21	398	50	4	5.17

PITCHERS' RECORDS

(Leading Qualifiers for Earned-Run Average Leadership—56 or More Innings)

*Throws lefthanded.

Pitcher—Club	G.	GS.	CG.	ShO.	W.	L.	Sv.	Pct.	IP.	H.	R.	ER.	HR.	BB.	Int. BB.	HB.	SO.	WP.	ERA.
Parks, Elm	14	11	4	2	6	3	0	.667	83	68	35	21	3	34	1	4	69	4	2.277
Sorensen, New	13	8	7	2	6	2	0	.750	75	58	22	19	2	27	0	3	65	1	2.280
S. Spence, Bat	10	9	3	0	3	2	1	.600	60	36	23	16	1	32	1	3	59	6	2.40

Pitcher–Club	G	GS	CG	ShO	W	L	Sv	Pct.	IP	H	R	ER	HR	BB	Int. BB	HB	SO	WP	ERA
Honeycutt, NF*	13	12	7	1	5	3	1	.625	97	91	36	28	5	20	0	4	98	2	2.60
Harryman, New*	16	10	2	1	5	3	0	.625	72	58	33	23	3	37	0	3	64	3	2.88
R. Quinones, New	17	8	4	1	6	5	2	.545	73	58	31	24	1	56	2	3	62	6	2.96
Montgomery, New	10	10	6	2	6	1	0	.857	75	80	29	25	2	25	1	0	23	4	3.00
Weismiller, NF	19	8	1	0	5	6	2	.455	65	66	40	25	1	19	1	1	60	4	3.46
Meagher, New*	12	10	4	0	6	4	0	.600	74	75	39	29	8	31	0	0	35	10	3.53
Fisk, Ont	16	11	5	0	4	6	0	.400	81	79	56	32	3	61	7	8	62	6	3.56

Departmental Leaders: G—Schneck, 22; GS—Kuhn, Mack, Parke, Rohles, 13; CG—Honeycutt, Sorensen, 7; ShO—Montgomery, Parks, Sorensen, 2; W—Howard (Elm), 8; L—Mack, 9; Sv—Schneck, 8; Pct.—Teising .875; IP—Honeycutt, 97; H—Robles, 105; R—Robles, 67; ER—Kuhn, 54; HR—Meagher, 8; BB—Mack, 67; IBB—Fisk, 7; HB—Gault, 12; SO—Honeycutt, 98; WP—Mack, Meagher, 10.

(All Pitchers–Listed Alphabetically)

Pitcher–Club	G	GS	CG	ShO	W	L	Sv	Pct.	IP	H	R	ER	HR	BB	Int. BB	HB	SO	WP	ERA
Arp, Bat	16	7	1	0	1	6	0	.143	57	56	36	24	2	41	3	3	28	8	3.79
Atkins, Ont	2	1	0	0	0	0	0	.000	5	0	2	2	0	8	0	0	4	1	3.60
Bannister, New	13	11	1	1	4	2	0	.667	57	58	45	30	5	36	0	2	30	4	4.74
Bullard, Bat	17	4	1	0	0	5	1	.000	50	45	27	15	3	29	1	2	26	3	2.70
Burdette, Aub*	1	1	0	0	0	0	0	.000	5	4	.3	1	1	3	0	0	1	0	1.80
Burkett, NF	19	1	0	0	0	3	2	.600	38	31	16	10	0	26	1	1	21	2	2.37
Burtt, Elm	8	5	0	0	3	2	0	1.000	44	22	7	6	0	20	1	0	34	2	1.23
Cain, NF	11	0	0	0	1	1	0	.500	21	13	9	6	0	4	0	1	13	3	2.57
Cajide, Bat	11	3	1	1	3	3	0	.500	26	15	14	12	1	24	2	2	23	7	4.15
Carlander, Elm	9	6	0	0	1	2	0	.500	32	32	21	21	0	25	1	1	20	2	5.91
Carmarena, Ont	10	0	0	0	1	0	0	1.000	26	28	17	12	0	16	2	2	14	2	4.15
Davis, Aub	17	1	0	0	0	1	1	.000	31	50	30	22	3	16	0	0	21	1	6.39
de Leon, Elm	6	0	0	0	0	1	0	.000	7	13	13	13	1	8	1	1	5	4	16.71
Delgatti, Ont	13	8	4	0	3	5	1	.375	70	65	43	29	1	43	4	0	56	3	3.73
Doss, Bat	12	7	0	0	1	3	0	.250	41	48	32	28	4	18	0	1	27	3	6.15
Eshelman, Ont*	7	2	0	0	1	2	1	.333	20	23	20	18	1	23	1	0	14	1	8.10
Felt, Aub	10	0	0	0	0	1	0	.000	18	17	12	9	0	16	1	2	14	0	4.50
Fisk, Ont	16	11	5	0	4	6	0	.400	81	79	56	32	3	61	7	8	62	6	3.56
Fox, Elm	15	0	0	0	2	0	1	1.000	29	26	14	7	1	13	0	3	19	5	2.17
Frazier, New	6	0	0	0	2	1	1	.667	15	11	3	3	0	4	0	0	17	3	1.80
Fritch, New	14	1	1	0	3	2	2	.600	26	32	28	15	2	21	3	2	13	5	5.19
Gaube, Ont	15	1	1	0	2	5	3	.286	28	26	17	11	1	22	2	0	23	1	3.54
Gault, Bat	14	3	0	0	3	3	0	.500	24	19	27	24	1	43	1	12	22	7	9.00
Harryman, New*	16	10	2	1	5	3	0	.625	72	58	33	23	3	37	0	3	64	3	2.88
Harvey, Bat	13	1	0	0	2	1	0	.667	33	36	25	17	1	25	2	1	23	4	4.64
Honeycutt, NF*	13	12	7	1	5	3	1	.625	97	91	36	28	5	20	0	4	98	2	2.60
M. Howard, NF	12	3	0	0	0	3	0	.000	29	30	13	9	0	21	1	0	16	0	2.79
Howard, Elm	14	12	0	0	8	2	1	.800	71	67	37	32	0	34	2	2	30	4	4.06
Hurst, Elm*	9	9	0	0	3	2	0	.600	42	25	18	14	2	38	0	0	40	5	3.00
Kienzle, NF*	18	6	3	0	4	2	2	.667	51	34	29	20	2	42	0	4	43	9	3.53
King, Elm	3	2	0	0	1	1	0	.500	8	6	8	7	0	10	0	1	10	1	7.88
Kruzelock, Aub	15	1	1	0	2	0	0	1.000	42	50	26	18	3	18	0	3	26	0	3.86
Kuhn, Aub	14	13	3	0	5	7	0	.417	85	102	59	54	7	47	0	1	44	4	5.72
Lasek, Aub	14	0	0	0	4	2	1	.667	28	17	9	5	0	14	2	1	25	4	1.61
Laurent, Ont	3	3	0	0	0	2	0	.000	9	15	9	2	1	11	0	2	3	3	8.10
Lombardi, Ont	9	1	0	0	1	1	1	.500	13	12	10	8	2	12	2	0	9	1	5.54
Long, NF	11	11	3	1	3	5	0	.375	68	74	44	31	1	35	1	1	32	6	4.10
Lopez, Elm	11	0	0	0	1	0	0	1.000	24	30	19	16	3	14	0	0	20	1	6.00
Mack, Aub	13	13	0	0	2	9	0	.182	54	54	49	44	6	67	0	2	44	10	7.33
Mattice, Aub	16	1	0	0	5	2	0	.000	32	38	31	22	2	19	0	2	14	3	6.19
Meagher, New*	12	10	4	0	6	4	0	.600	74	75	39	29	8	31	0	0	35	10	3.53
Miller, Elm	10	4	0	0	3	0	0	1.000	39	29	16	9	0	19	0	1	36	4	2.08
Mitchell, Bat*	6	0	0	0	0	0	0	.000	5	1	11	11	0	19	0	1	2	8	19.80
Montgomery, New	10	10	6	2	6	1	0	.857	75	80	29	25	2	25	1	0	23	4	3.00
Morales, Aub	13	12	4	1	2	8	0	.200	74	74	41	38	4	45	1	0	60	3	4.62
Narleski, Bat	18	1	0	0	2	1	4	.667	38	36	21	14	4	23	2	1	31	2	3.32
Nunn, Aub	9	2	1	0	1	1	0	.500	20	23	25	18	3	26	0	1	12	6	8.10
Offerman, New	15	3	1	1	4	1	1	.800	38	36	23	16	4	28	0	3	21	1	3.79
Palmer, Ont*	7	1	0	0	0	1	0	.000	10	12	12	6	1	15	0	0	9	5	5.40
Parke, NF	13	13	4	0	7	4	0	.636	84	100	65	42	2	42	2	2	40	5	4.50
Parks, Elm	14	11	4	2	6	3	0	.667	83	68	35	21	3	34	1	4	69	4	2.27
Patrick, Elm*	8	6	0	0	1	1	0	.500	19	16	13	10	2	11	2	8	16	0	6.16
Peterson, NF*	5	2	0	0	1	0	0	1.000	15	14	12	7	1	15	0	0	16	2	4.20
Prentice, NF	17	1	0	0	0	3	1	.000	46	55	38	27	5	20	0	3	32	3	5.28
Puryear, Bat	14	8	0	0	3	3	1	.500	52	44	42	31	0	60	1	2	38	6	5.37
Quinn, New	8	3	0	0	2	1	0	.667	24	24	19	16	1	31	0	0	13	1	6.00
F. Quinones, New	13	1	0	0	2	1	1	.667	34	34	22	19	2	15	0	1	22	3	5.03
R. Quinones, New	17	8	4	1	6	5	2	.545	73	58	31	24	1	56	2	3	62	6	2.96

Pitcher–Club	G	GS	CG	ShO	W	L	Sv	Pct.	IP	H	R	ER	HR	BB	Int. BB	HB	SO	WP	ERA
Reyes, New	1	0	0	0	0	0	0	.000	2	0	0	0	0	3	0	0	1	1	0.00
Riggar, Ont*	13	12	3	0	5	4	0	.556	79	73	45	34	3	48	1	2	57	4	3.87
Robles, Ont	13	13	5	0	2	7	0	.222	90	105	67	43	3	49	3	1	43	1	4.30
Rodriguez, New*	9	1	0	0	0	0	0	.000	13	14	10	10	0	9	0	0	8	0	6.92
Rodriguez, Bat	14	5	0	1	6	0	0	.143	37	45	38	29	5	42	6	1	25	5	7.05
Roesch, New*	7	4	0	0	1	0	0	.000	15	18	20	16	0	23	0	2	10	3	9.60
Rogers, NF	14	5	0	5	2	1	0	.714	55	50	32	17	2	28	1	2	22	9	2.78
Santana, Ont	15	5	2	1	3	5	1	.375	51	58	35	25	2	21	2	1	22	3	4.41
Schneck, Elm	22	1	0	0	3	2	8	.600	50	26	21	10	1	31	4	2	63	4	1.80
Schoppee, Elm	12	11	0	4	2	0	0	.667	51	44	28	19	3	33	2	0	33	1	3.35
Schwerman, NF	7	7	0	0	1	3	0	.250	36	41	24	19	2	22	0	2	15	4	4.75
Semerano, NF	3	0	0	0	0	0	0	.000	4	5	4	4	0	5	1	0	3	1	9.00
Serwon, Elm	2	1	0	0	0	0	0	.000	6	4	4	2	0	6	0	0	1	0	3.00
Smith, Elm	12	0	0	0	2	2	1	.500	20	20	9	6	1	21	2	1	18	1	2.70
Smith, Bat	11	0	0	0	1	0	2	1.000	16	11	3	2	0	9	2	0	15	2	1.13
Softy, Ont	13	12	5	0	2	7	0	.222	82	86	52	41	5	38	4	4	59	4	4.50
Sorensen, New	13	8	7	2	6	2	5	.750	75	58	22	19	2	27	0	3	65	1	2.280
J. Spence, Bat	9	4	0	0	3	0	0	.000	24	22	22	14	0	29	1	0	23	3	5.25
S. Spence, Bat	10	9	3	0	3	2	1	.600	60	36	23	16	1	32	1	3	59	6	2.40
Tagliarino, Elm	20	0	0	0	7	2	4	.778	39	31	19	10	3	16	3	0	40	1	2.31
Teising, Bat*	16	12	4	0	7	1	0	.875	70	79	48	38	4	40	2	5	55	0	4.89
Trask, Elm	11	2	0	2	0	0	1	1.000	22	25	18	12	3	17	1	1	16	2	4.91
Vaughn, Bat	3	0	0	0	1	0	0	1.000	6	5	4	4	2	4	0	1	5	1	6.00
Watts, Aub	17	2	0	1	3	3	3	.250	46	26	17	16	2	39	2	2	39	2	3.13
Weismiller, NF	19	8	1	0	5	6	2	.455	65	66	40	25	1	19	1	1	60	2	3.46
Welborn, Aub	10	1	1	3	4	0	0	.429	50	47	47	34	3	57	0	5	37	7	6.12
Whaley, Aub*	12	12	2	0	3	5	0	.375	69	65	44	37	5	40	0	1	53	9	4.83
Wilder, Bat*	9	6	2	1	2	2	0	.500	33	32	15	11	2	24	0	1	33	2	3.00
Williamson, Ont	5	0	0	0	0	1	0	.000	8	9	12	12	0	15	0	0	6	0	13.50
Wilson, Aub	2	1	0	0	0	0	0	.000	4	7	4	4	0	2	0	0	2	1	9.00
Wolff, Aub	2	0	0	0	0	0	0	.000	7	7	3	2	0	3	0	1	6	0	2.57

BALKS–R. Quinones, 3; F. Quinones, Schoppee, Whaley, 2 each; Carlander, Delgatti, Harryman, Lopez, Mack, Morales, Prentice, Santana, Softy, 1 each.

COMBINATION SHUTOUTS–Mack-Watts, Auburn; Teising-Vaughn-Bullard, Gault-S. Spence, Batavia; Burtt-Schneck, Burtt-Carlander, Howard-Schneck, Hurst-Smith, Miller-Fox, Elmira; Harryman-F. Quinones, Newark.

NO-HIT GAME–Kienzle, Niagara Falls, defeated Batavia, 4-1, July 30 (seven innings).

Northwest League

CLASS A

CHAMPIONSHIP WINNERS IN PREVIOUS YEARS

1901–Portland .675	1939–Wenatchee .601	1960–Yakima† .638
1902–Butte .608	Tacoma (2nd)† .533	Yakima .562
1903–Butte .578	1940–Spokane .587	1961–Lewiston* .621
1904–Boise .625	Tacoma (4th)† .500	Yakima .600
1905–Vancouver .586	1941–Spokane .669	1962–Wenatchee* .574
Everett* .667	1942–Vancouver .594	Tri-City .580
1906–Tacoma .600	1943-45–Did not operate.	1963–Lewiston .594
1907–Aberdeen .625	1946–Wenatchee .622	Yakima* .613
1908–Vancouver .578	1947–Vancouver .566	1964–Eugene .636
1909–Seattle .653	1948–Spokane .614	Yakima* .611
1910–Spokane .596	1949–Yakima .660	1965–Lewiston .667
1911–Vancouver .628	Vancouver (2nd)† .615	Tri-City* .681
1912–Seattle .600	1950–Yakima .613	1966–Tri-City .679
1913–Vancouver .600	1951–Spokane .655	1967–Medford .607
1914–Vancouver .632	1952–Victoria .631	1968–Tri-City .600
1915–Seattle .564	1953–Salem .635	1969–Rogue Valley .633
1916–Spokane .622	Spokane* .590	1970–Lewiston a .538
1917–Great Falls .592	1954–Vancouver* .636	Coos Bay-No. Bend .563
1918–Seattle .588	Lewiston .629	1971–Tri-City a .625
1919–Seattle .590	Eugene* .639	Bend .538
1920–Victoria .600	1955–Salem .646	1972–Lewiston a .675
1921–Yakima .710	Yakima .619	Walla Walla .513
Yakima .660	1956–Yakima .691	1973–Walla Walla b .638
1922–Calgary§ .600	Yakima .619	Portland .563
1923-36–Did not operate.	1957–Eugene .576	1974–Bellingham .619
1937–Wenatchee* .603	Wenatchee* .647	Eugene c .571
Tacoma* .627	1958–Lewiston .621	1975–Portland .545
1938–Yakima .583	Yakima* .594	Eugene d .684
Bellingham (2nd)† .511	1959–Salem .623	
	Yakima* .563	

*Won split-season playoff. †Won four-club playoff. §League disbanded June 18. aLeague divided into Northern and Southern divisions, declared champion under league rules. (NOTE–Known as Pacific Northwest League 1901-02, Pacific National League 1903-04, Northwestern League 1905-18, Pacific Coast International League 1919-22 and Western International League 1937-54.) bLeague divided into Eastern and Western divisions, declared champion under league rules. cLeague divided into Eastern and Western divisions; won two-team playoff. dLeague divided into Northern and Southern divisions; won two-team playoff.

STANDING OF CLUBS AT CLOSE OF SEASON, SEPTEMBER 4

NORTHERN DIVISION

Club	Port.	Sea.	G.H.	W.W.	Eug.	Boise	Bell.	W.	L.	T.	Pct.	G.B.
Portland (Independent)	..	5	6	8	7	7	7	40	32	0	.556	......
Seattle (Independent)	7	..	11	5	5	6	5	39	33	0	.542	1
Grays Harbor (Independent)	6	1	..	4	4	4	7	26	46	0	.361	14

SOUTHERN DIVISION

Club	Port.	Sea.	G.H.	W.W.	Eug.	Boise	Bell.	W.	L.	T.	Pct.	G.B.
Walla Walla (Padres)	4	7	8	..	9	10	8	46	26	0	.639	......
Eugene (Reds)	5	7	8	3	..	7	7	37	34	0	.521	8½
Boise (Athletics)	5	6	8	2	4	..	8	33	38	0	.465	12½
Bellingham (Dodgers)	5	7	5	4	5	4	..	30	42	0	.417	16

Grays Harbor club represented Aberdeen and Hoquiam, Washington.

Major league affiliations in parentheses.

Playoff–Walla Walla defeated Portland, two games to one.

Regular-Season Attendance–Bellingham, 23,225; Boise, 16,294; Eugene, 48,871; Grays Harbor, 28,842; Portland, 83,780; Seattle, 16,294; Walla Walla, 28,971. Total, 246,277. Playoffs–14,838. No all-star game.

Managers: Bellingham–Bill Berrier; Boise–Thomas Trebelhorn; Eugene–Gregory Riddoch; Grays Harbor–Carl Thompson, Sr.; Portland–Jack Spring; Seattle–Arthur Peterson; Walla Walla–Cliff Ditto.

All-Star Team: 1B–Kaage, Bellingham; 2B–Collette, Portland; 3B–O'Neill, Walla Walla; SS–Cervantes, Portland; OF–McNeely, Boise; Kraft, Seattle; Walker, Eugene; C–Wantz, Portland; DH–M. Rodriguez, Boise; P–Benson, Seattle; Brown, Eugene; Biggerstaff, Grays Harbor; Mura, Walla Walla; Joseph, Walla Walla; Lee, Walla Walla; Manager–Ditto, Walla Walla.

(Compiled by William J. Weiss, League Statistician, San Mateo, Calif.)

CLUB BATTING

Club	G.	AB.	R.	OR.	H.	TB.	2B.	3B.	HR.	RBI.	SH.	SF.	BB.	Int.	HP.	SO.	SB.	CS.	LOB.	Pct.
Boise	71	2311	497	535	682	1012	108	18	62	411	31	21	446	3	20	507	172	58	557	.295
Portland	72	2349	429	415	669	943	117	20	39	338	20	23	285	6	19	313	127	33	491	.285
Seattle	72	2279	355	320	608	738	76	9	12	288	36	26	362	5	17	370	82	27	567	.267
Eugene	71	2303	373	357	610	807	87	22	22	315	37	19	309	2	19	393	102	24	530	.265
Walla Walla	72	2370	396	312	624	920	90	19	56	346	40	18	325	9	34	477	75	27	570	.263
Bellingham	72	2349	373	433	595	791	72	14	32	302	13	17	359	7	28	551	117	37	566	.253
Grays Harbor	72	2297	329	380	551	719	99	9	17	277	30	24	363	4	20	432	42	19	572	.240

INDIVIDUAL BATTING

(Leading Qualifiers for Batting Championship—194 or More Plate Appearances)

*Bats lefthanded. †Switch-hitter.

Player and Club	G.	AB.	R.	H.	TB.	2B.	3B.	HR.	RBI.	SH.	SF.	BB.	HP.	SO.	SB.	CS.	Pct.
McNeely, Ronald, Boi*	40	159	46	64	77	10	0	1	30	4	2	23	1	12	18	10	.403
Perkins, Broderick, WW*	60	228	47	81	128	13	2	10	63	3	2	31	1	25	4	2	.355
Cervantes, Edward, Port	49	178	36	62	81	5	4	2	33	2	3	20	1	12	7	4	.348
Wilson, Michael, Bell	66	225	40	74	97	7	8	0	20	2	2	49	0	26	36	10	.329
Kraft, Robert, Sea*	72	233	50	73	88	10	1	1	44	4	2	72	1	31	25	8	.313
Collette, Steven, Port	72	265	52	83	110	12	3	3	33	3	3	34	0	33	14	6	.313
Edwards, Robert D., Port	69	237	31	73	98	16	0	3	45	1	3	29	3	18	12	1	.308
Wright, T. Barry, Boi	56	178	43	54	68	9	1	1	33	4	2	46	2	29	10	0	.303
Gilliam, Edward, Port	66	231	39	70	117	20	3	7	48	0	4	29	4	45	32	4	.303
Nichols, Alfred, Eug†	57	195	37	58	70	5	2	1	23	1	2	43	0	36	4	0	.297

(McNeely becomes league batting champion under provisions of Official Baseball Rule 10.23 (a), although falling five short of required 194 plate appearances. If five AB were added to his total of 159, his batting average of .390 would still lead league.)

Departmental Leaders: G—Attebery, Collette, Dixson, P. Gilmartin, Kraft, Thompson, 72; AB—Dixson, 284; R—Dixson, 63; H—Collette, 83; TB—Perkins, 128; 2B—Dixson, 22; 3B—Wilson, 8; HR—Rodriguez, 12; RBI—Perkins, 63; SH—C. Corcoran, Hallstrom, Kanikeberg, 7; SF—Deardorff, 7; BB—Kraft, 72; HP—O'Neill, 6; SO—Thompson, 75; SB—Wilson, 36; CS—A. Adams, McNeely, Wilson, 10.

(All Players—Listed Alphabetically)

Player and Club	G.	AB.	R.	H.	TB.	2B.	3B.	HR.	RBI.	SH.	SF.	BB.	HP.	SO.	SB.	CS.	Pct.
Adams, A. Dwight, WW†	53	196	37	56	77	5	2	2	25	1	0	27	2	39	19	10	.286
Adams, Robert W., Bell†	41	76	16	15	16	1	0	0	6	3	1	16	2	21	6	0	.197
Aiello, Paul, GH	9	24	0	5	5	0	0	0	3	2	1	2	0	2	0	0	.208
Alvarez, Juan, Bell	42	117	17	28	50	7	0	5	23	0	1	12	1	36	0	0	.239
Armstead, Vernon, Boi	28	40	6	4	5	1	0	0	4	0	0	12	1	20	4	0	.100
Attaway, Eric, Boi*	11	16	6	5	8	0	0	1	1	0	0	6	0	4	1	0	.313
Attebery, Russell, Sea	72	246	27	70	78	5	0	1	32	2	6	31	1	47	5	2	.285
Barnett, Ronnie, WW	3	10	2	2	6	1	0	1	3	1	0	3	0	7	0	0	.200
Bass, Richard, Boi	38	111	27	40	63	8	0	5	27	3	1	24	4	28	8	1	.360
Battey, Earl, WW	14	40	2	7	10	3	0	0	2	1	0	8	0	13	1	0	.175
Bennett, James, Boi*	43	133	26	43	66	9	1	4	21	1	2	16	1	33	10	2	.323
Beswick, James, WW†	42	112	13	24	34	2	1	2	8	1	1	16	1	43	6	1	.214
Billington, Michael, Boi	10	25	7	6	7	1	0	0	3	2	1	7	0	6	2	1	.240
Black, Lynn, WW	29	67	12	13	19	0	0	2	9	1	0	2	3	15	2	2	.194
Bonnell, Glenn, Eug	8	13	1	2	2	0	0	0	1	1	0	1	0	7	0	0	.154
Bowens, Ray, GH	66	242	31	57	65	5	0	1	13	1	2	22	2	40	4	1	.236
Brown, Scott E., Eug	16	3	0	1	2	1	0	0	0	0	0	0	0	3	0	0	.333
Bullas, Brian, Boi	1	1	0	0	0	0	0	0	0	0	0	0	0	1	0	0	.000
Bushong, Steven, GH*	17	16	1	4	4	0	0	0	0	0	0	2	0	4	0	0	.250
Carr, Donald, Eug	51	189	24	46	64	13	1	1	27	5	2	10	0	32	1	1	.243
Cervantes, Edward, Port	49	178	36	62	81	5	4	2	33	2	3	20	1	12	7	4	.348
Collette, Steven, Port	72	265	52	83	110	12	3	3	33	3	3	34	0	33	14	6	.313
Corcoran, Chad, GH†	70	259	50	70	92	9	2	3	27	7	3	40	2	39	20	4	.270
Corcoran, Patrick, Boi	65	240	53	71	119	11	2	11	41	0	2	39	1	43	14	4	.296
Costantine, Robert, Eug	71	248	35	71	90	9	2	2	38	3	1	39	3	42	5	2	.286
Dallas, Robert, GH	13	39	4	9	9	0	0	0	8	1	0	14	0	5	1	3	.231
Davis, Peter, GH	8	1	0	0	0	0	0	0	0	0	0	0	1	0	0	0	.000
Deal, Stephen, Eug*	8	15	3	3	3	0	0	0	1	1	1	4	0	5	0	0	.200
Deardorff, Craig, GH	67	237	43	69	102	17	2	4	53	1	7	44	2	32	0	1	.291
Derryberry, Timothy, WW*	41	139	22	39	55	7	0	3	21	2	1	17	0	21	1	1	.281
Dixson, Xavier, Sea*	72	284	63	81	112	22	3	1	45	2	1	39	1	37	11	4	.285
Dziemiela, Richard, Boi	40	125	35	40	58	9	0	3	15	4	0	28	0	21	2	2	.320
Edwards, Robert D., Port	69	237	31	73	98	16	0	3	45	1	3	29	3	18	12	1	.308
Eickenhorst, Randall, Eug	69	252	33	71	94	12	4	1	40	4	4	26	3	42	4	3	.282
Falkosky, David, Port	17	24	1	5	5	0	0	0	2	0	0	3	1	2	1	0	.208
Ferrara, Salvatore, Eug	8	7	0	3	3	0	0	0	1	0	0	0	0	2	0	0	.429
Foster, Douglas, Bell	59	187	27	48	59	2	0	3	24	0	1	24	2	36	7	2	.257
Garza, Joseph, Port	11	11	1	1	2	1	0	0	2	0	1	1	0	4	0	1	.091
Getz, R. William, Port*	22	49	8	9	10	1	0	0	6	0	0	6	0	2	0	1	.184
Giles, Jimmie, Bell	29	51	4	4	4	0	0	0	0	0	1	0	5	3	29	0	.078

Player and Club	G.	AB.	R.	H.	TB.	2B.	3B.	HR.	RBI.	SH.	SF.	BB.	HP.	SO.	SB.	CS.	Pct.
Gilliam, Edward, Port	66	231	39	70	117	20	3	7	48	0	4	29	4	45	32	4	.303
Gilmartin, Kevin, Sea*	18	26	6	2	3	1	0	0	1	0	0	9	0	9	0	1	.077
Gilmartin, Paul, Sea†	72	267	27	66	84	9	0	3	42	1	5	32	3	38	4	2	.247
Gorton, Tyler, Port.	51	142	32	42	53	8	0	1	13	1	1	28	2	4	5	1	.296
Grana, Anthony, Eug	16	1	0	0	0	0	0	0	0	0	0	0	0	1	0	0	.000
Guarino, John, Port	67	210	34	61	87	11	0	5	23	1	2	23	2	29	2	1	.290
Hallstrom, William, WW	62	191	39	51	64	4	0	3	19	7	1	48	4	20	15	5	.267
Harris, Wiley, Eug	43	163	31	47	58	6	1	1	29	4	1	14	0	20	5	1	.288
Henderson, Rickey, Boi	46	140	34	47	73	13	2	3	23	0	2	33	2	32	29	7	.336
Henley, Donald, Boi*	46	148	24	36	58	5	4	3	32	1	0	30	2	33	6	6	.243
Henry, Dan, Bell	69	241	30	62	82	9	1	3	37	1	2	29	5	54	7	3	.257
Hernandez, Juan, Bell	29	39	4	5	7	0	1	0	4	0	1	5	1	13	1	1	.128
Heuberger, Donald, Port	31	64	6	9	9	0	0	0	2	0	0	4	0	12	1	0	.141
Hicks, Joseph, WW	70	232	31	62	84	7	0	5	48	3	2	41	3	46	9	1	.267
Highfill, Billy, GH	8	32	2	1	1	0	0	0	1	0	0	1	0	10	0	0	.031
Holland, Clifton, Port*	59	156	28	42	57	9	0	2	14	1	0	10	1	12	11	2	.269
Hopper, Mark, Eug	69	241	36	68	85	11	3	0	36	4	1	23	1	13	16	4	.282
Hornacek, David, Boi	38	103	21	30	36	3	0	1	15	1	1	21	0	21	11	1	.291
Howard, Michael F., Bell	50	119	17	23	30	3	2	0	17	0	1	19	0	39	2	0	.193
Ilertsen, Dane, WW	46	131	20	37	59	8	1	4	18	1	1	17	4	26	0	0	.282
Ingraham, Patrick, Eug	43	119	22	33	38	3	1	0	15	1	0	18	3	31	12	3	.277
James, Ronald, WW	35	98	18	24	50	9	1	5	17	2	0	9	1	38	0	0	.245
Jensen, Christian, Boi	6	14	4	5	7	0	1	0	4	1	0	2	0	4	1	0	.357
Jones, Robert C., Eug	40	110	16	31	47	7	0	3	24	0	2	23	3	9	1	2	.282
Jones, Thomas, GH	71	261	34	60	73	5	1	2	25	3	3	19	1	38	3	1	.230
Jones, Timothy L., Bell	35	70	9	11	15	1	0	1	5	0	0	9	0	20	0	3	.157
Kaage, George, Bell*	69	257	40	72	107	11	0	8	56	0	1	37	4	52	4	2	.280
Kanikeberg, Kenneth, Sea*	69	239	28	60	72	5	2	1	23	7	0	20	3	36	3	0	.251
Kniss, John, Boi	39	102	22	20	28	2	0	2	12	2	0	16	1	21	7	2	.196
Kraft, Robert, Sea*	72	233	50	73	88	10	1	1	44	4	2	72	1	31	25	8	.313
Krenecki, Michael, GH	56	148	14	37	39	2	0	0	14	2	1	34	1	31	0	0	.250
Law, Rudy, Bell*	54	161	40	54	66	7	1	1	16	0	1	21	0	20	19	4	.335
Lee, Terry, Port*	7	19	3	5	9	2	1	0	3	0	0	4	0	4	1	0	.263
Le John, Donald, Bell*	36	95	16	24	26	2	0	0	11	0	0	20	2	26	6	2	.253
Loville, Darryl, Boi	18	56	9	15	18	0	0	1	7	0	0	12	0	7	4	0	.268
Malito, Steven, Boi†	11	35	5	10	12	2	0	0	1	1	0	9	0	6	2	3	.286
Malpas, Billy, GH†	46	150	30	39	55	13	0	1	21	0	1	43	4	14	3	4	.260
Markham, Harold, GH	9	24	2	5	6	1	0	0	1	0	0	2	0	6	0	0	.208
Martin, W. Anthony, Bell	16	4	1	1	1	0	0	0	0	0	0	1	1	0	0	0	.250
May, Kenneth, Sea*	49	155	28	42	46	4	0	0	18	4	1	22	3	23	4	1	.271
Mayberry, Carl, WW	3	3	0	0	0	0	0	0	0	1	0	2	0	3	0	0	.000
McClendon, Thomas, Eug	45	143	23	38	40	2	0	0	11	1	2	20	1	16	4	1	.266
McKinney, Kenneth, Boi†	7	19	2	2	3	1	0	0	4	0	2	4	0	5	1	1	.105
McNeely, Ronald, Boi*	40	159	46	64	77	10	0	1	30	4	2	23	1	12	18	10	.403
McPherson, George, Eug*	60	213	40	46	63	2	3	3	27	4	2	31	3	43	23	7	.216
Meily, Richard, Port*	53	141	31	36	60	10	1	4	25	2	1	36	0	27	3	2	.255
Melendez, Daniel, GH	15	50	6	7	10	3	0	0	2	0	1	5	1	16	0	0	.140
Merino, Phillip, 12 GH-6 Port.	18	11	1	2	3	1	0	0	1	0	0	0	0	5	0	0	.182
Merkley, Stephen, Port	23	27	11	6	7	1	0	0	4	0	0	5	0	9	5	1	.222
Miller, Danny, Sea†	59	206	44	61	78	7	2	3	23	4	3	42	0	37	19	6	.296
Miller, K. Randall, WW	40	130	16	30	54	7	1	5	25	2	0	12	2	37	0	1	.231
Miller, Mark J., Eug	43	128	9	21	25	4	0	0	10	3	1	12	1	41	0	0	.164
Minker, Allan, Boi	37	109	11	28	51	6	1	5	24	0	1	34	1	34	2	4	.257
Mobley, Jacky, GH*	38	125	25	35	41	3	0	1	9	6	0	23	0	30	3	1	.280
Moore, Charles A., Eug	17	6	0	1	1	0	0	0	1	0	0	0	0	3	0	0	.167
Moore, Ronald, GH	7	10	1	0	0	0	0	0	0	0	0	2	0	3	0	1	.000
Moore, Robert, Boi	19	11	2	4	5	1	0	0	1	0	0	0	0	4	2	0	.364
Morrow, Stacy, Eug*	21	5	1	1	1	0	0	0	2	2	0	1	0	2	0	0	.200
Muth, William, Port	8	22	1	3	6	0	0	1	3	2	0	0	0	9	0	0	.136
Necoechea, Steven, Boi*	30	102	24	32	59	8	2	5	29	0	1	14	0	21	7	1	.314
Nichols, Alfred, Eug†	57	195	37	58	70	5	2	1	23	1	2	43	0	36	4	0	.297
Nipert, Michael, Boi.	20	46	2	7	7	0	0	0	5	1	1	2	1	14	1	0	.152
O'Brien, Patrick, Boi*	11	0	2	0	0	0	0	0	0	0	0	0	0	0	0	0	.000
Olson, Tod, WW*	42	139	24	34	47	5	1	2	5	1	1	19	0	41	3	0	.245
O'Neill, Paul, WW	65	235	51	69	120	10	4	11	55	3	5	35	6	35	6	1	.294
Parma, Daniel, Port	59	202	36	56	79	8	6	1	28	0	4	15	1	29	13	5	.277
Perkins, Broderick, WW*	60	228	47	81	128	13	2	10	63	3	2	31	1	25	4	2	.355
Peters, Kendall, Sea	67	216	33	63	67	4	0	0	22	4	3	37	3	26	3	0	.292
Peterson, Brian, GH	26	9	0	3	3	0	0	0	0	0	0	1	0	4	0	0	.333
Peterson, Dennis, Sea†	1	2	0	0	0	0	0	0	0	0	0	0	0	1	0	0	.000
Peterson, Douglas, Sea†	68	254	33	64	81	9	1	2	41	4	2	32	2	46	1	2	.252
Rementer, Charles, Eug	29	76	21	19	20	1	0	0	6	2	0	17	0	11	1	0	.250
Robinson, Howard, Boi†	56	199	35	54	70	4	3	2	25	5	1	28	3	61	15	9	.271
Rodrigues, Kenneth, Boi	3	5	1	1	1	0	0	0	1	0	0	1	0	2	0	0	.200
Rodriguez, Michael, Boi	35	120	32	43	84	5	0	12	40	0	1	21	0	25	10	1	.358

Player and Club	G.	AB.	R.	H.	TB.	2B.	3B.	HR.	RBI.	SH.	SF.	BB.	HP.	SO.	SB.	CS.	Pct.
Rusteck, Richard, Port	15	1	0	0	0	0	0	0	0	0	0	0	0	0	0	0	.000
Ruzek, Donald, Bell	49	150	23	38	43	5	0	0	10	2	2	33	0	41	8	4	.253
Scala, Dominic, Boi	2	7	2	2	5	0	0	1	2	0	1	0	0	2	1	0	.286
Scioscia, Michael, Bell*	46	151	25	42	69	6	0	7	26	1	1	36	1	22	2	0	.278
Segrest, Walter, WW	13	30	2	5	5	0	0	0	2	1	1	2	2	12	0	0	.167
Sigman, S. Lee, Boi	13	48	10	16	21	0	1	1	11	0	0	8	0	11	2	1	.333
Simpson, William A., GH	52	175	17	40	62	9	2	3	30	2	2	20	3	37	2	1	.229
Smith, Steven, WW	50	186	33	54	64	6	2	0	12	5	2	11	2	7	2	1	.290
Spatz, Mark, WW	21	44	1	4	4	0	0	0	0	0	0	4	0	8	0	1	.091
Spaulding, Timothy, Boi	14	1	0	0	0	0	0	0	0	0	0	0	0	1	0	0	.000
Swoope, C. William, Bell	39	109	17	28	37	3	0	2	14	1	3	15	2	23	4	2	.257
Thomas, Reginald, Port	31	109	28	32	46	3	1	3	17	0	0	16	2	25	21	5	.294
Thompson, Thomas F., GH*	72	243	36	50	72	14	1	2	32	0	1	65	3	75	1	1	.206
Underwood, John, Eug	11	1	0	0	0	0	0	0	0	0	0	0	0	1	0	0	.000
Uremovich, Michael, GH*	57	211	24	50	66	14	1	0	34	3	2	21	1	28	5	1	.237
Venable, W. McKinley, Bell*	51	162	25	35	40	2	0	1	16	1	0	17	0	36	9	2	.216
Walker, Donald, Boi	8	18	6	3	3	0	0	0	1	0	0	9	0	6	2	2	.167
Walker, Duane, Eug*	46	172	41	49	100	11	5	10	24	0	0	26	1	33	26	0	.285
Walls, Gary, WW	8	26	5	6	9	0	0	1	6	1	0	5	1	7	0	0	.231
Wantz, Douglas, Port	58	196	31	55	85	9	0	7	29	1	0	8	2	33	3	0	.281
Washington, Donald, Bell	50	137	15	31	42	6	1	1	17	1	0	12	4	56	4	2	.226
Watson, Steven R., Sea†	48	147	17	26	29	3	0	0	10	4	1	25	0	38	7	3	.177
Wilber, Bruce, Port*	13	17	6	6	8	0	1	0	1	1	0	4	0	1	2	0	.353
Wilborn, W. Charles, WW	48	133	20	26	31	3	1	0	9	2	1	16	2	34	8	1	.195
Williams, Jimmie, Sea	17	0	0	0	0	0	0	0	0	0	0	1	0	0	0	0	.000
Wilson, Michael, Bell	66	225	47	74	97	7	8	0	20	2	2	49	0	26	36	10	.329
Woodard, Tommy, GH	8	4	1	1	1	0	0	0	0	0	0	0	0	1	0	0	.250
Wright, Harold, GH	11	30	8	8	10	2	0	0	4	0	0	3	0	9	0	0	.267
Wright, Jesse, Boi*	15	0	1	0	0	0	0	0	0	0	0	0	0	0	0	0	.000
Wright, T. Barry, Boi	56	178	43	54	68	9	1	1	33	4	2	46	2	29	10	0	.303
Yoshiwara, Jon, Port	30	44	13	12	13	1	0	0	8	1	1	10	0	3	2	1	.273

The following pitchers had no plate appearances primarily through use of designated hitters, listed alphabetically by club, games in parentheses:

BELLINGHAM—Albert, Jeffrey (14); Bain, Paul (15); Dorgan, Charles (14); Goulding, Richard (18); Keller, Joseph (7); Kryka, Mark (16); Lawson, Jack (7); Middleton, Dean (12); Peterson, James (21); Rodriguez, Miguel A (8); Schmidt, Eric (17); Stewart, David (25); Townsend, Kenneth (16).

BOISE—Eisinger, John (15); Fehrenkamp, Michael (17); Green, C. Randall (17); Little, Thomas (6); McKenzie, James (17); Meyl, Brian (9); Murphy, Guy (12); Patterson, Roderick (13); Schubert, Donald (13); Stolte, Steven (19); Walsh, Timothy (3); Ward, James D (1).

EUGENE—Berenyi, Bruce (12); Burress, J. David (10); Gosse, M. John (9); Groves, Lawrence (5); Harold, Robert (21); Howell, Jay (13); Mayer, Robert (5).

GRAYS HARBOR—Biggerstaff, Barry (19); Brannon, James (1); Hays, John (10); McKay, Jeff (7); Wasson, Gary (16); Wikel, Joseph (4).

PORTLAND—Blue, Lorenzo (14); Clawson, J. Curtis (7); Deck, Dennis E. (16); Emery, James (7); Guischer, Michael (13); Hagen, Stephen (3); Kay, Richard (3); Nelson, Robert (10); Rice, Richard (9); Trumbauer, Gary (2); Weber, James (5); Winkelbauer, Thomas (16).

SEATTLE—Barbisan, Vincent (22); Benson, George (14); Meyring, George (18); Sheehan, Terrence (11); Sloan, David (14); Stewart, C. David (17); Stillwell, Stephen (15).

WALLA WALLA—Bullock, Michael (8); Dupree, Bobby (9); French, Martin (6); Garner, Larry (4); Joseph, William (13); Keen, Daniel (12); Lee, Mark (28); Lucas, Gary (14); Maglio, Carl (11); Mura, Stephen (8); Schmidt, Jerry (12); Tellmann, Thomas (17).

GRAND-SLAM HOME RUNS—Alvarez, Bennett, Edwards, James, McNeely, Rodriguez, Swoope, Thomas, Walls, 1 each.

AWARDED FIRST BASE ON INTERFERENCE—Ilertsen (Peters), Timothy Jones (Attebery).

CLUB FIELDING

Club	G.	PO.	A.	E.	DP.	PB.	Pct.	Club	G.	PO.	A.	E.	DP.	PB.	Pct.
Seattle	72	1785	770	117	57	9	.956	Portland	72	1792	790	148	70	19	.946
Walla Walla	72	1854	905	129	83	18	.955	Bellingham	72	1813	770	169	61	37	.939
Eugene	71	1787	708	119	57	21	.954	Boise	71	1772	769	211	46	20	.923
Grays Harbor	72	1802	778	142	62	9	.948								

Triple Plays—None.

INDIVIDUAL FIELDING

FIRST BASEMEN

*Throws lefthanded.

Player and Club	G.	PO.	A.	E.	DP.	Pct.	Player and Club	G.	PO.	A.	E.	DP.	Pct.
P. GILMARTIN, Sea*	72	651	37	7	54	.990	Guarino, Port	60	477	41	10	46	.981
Costantine, Eug	70	572	39	7	52	.989	Kaage, Bell*	69	593	45	13	49	.980
Minker, Boi	36	268	30	4	19	.987	Thompson, GH	70	617	23	15	47	.977
Ilertsen, WW	15	112	10	2	13	.984	Corcoran, Boi	35	269	20	9	21	.970
Perkins, WW*	60	585	23	11	65	.982	Wilber, Port	10	46	2	2	5	.960

FIRST BASEMEN—Continued

(Fewer Than Ten Games)

Player and Club	G.	PO.	A.	E.	DP.	Pct.	Player and Club	G.	PO.	A.	E.	DP.	Pct.
Thomas, Port	5	32	3	0	3	1.000	Bass, Boi	1	2	0	0	0	1.000
Edwards, Port	3	19	3	0	1	1.000	Collette, Port	1	2	0	0	0	1.000
Holland, Port*	3	18	0	0	4	1.000	Jones, Bell	1	1	0	0	0	1.000
Mobley, GH*	3	16	2	0	1	1.000	T. B. Wright, Boi	1	1	0	0	0	1.000
Eickenhorst, Eug	4	16	0	0	2	1.000	Law, Bell*	2	15	1	2	4	.889
Rodriguez, Boi	3	13	0	0	2	1.000	Attaway, Boi*	9	36	0	6	0	.857
Beswick, WW	1	10	0	0	0	1.000	Henry, Bell	1	6	0	1	0	.857
Giles, Bell	2	8	0	0	0	1.000							

SECOND BASEMEN

Player and Club	G.	PO.	A.	E.	DP.	Pct.	Player and Club	G.	PO.	A.	E.	DP.	Pct.
Corcoran, GH	10	31	19	1	4	.980	Adams, Bell	25	33	35	5	9	.932
Malpas, GH	41	92	114	8	22	.963	Robinson, Boi	56	114	166	26	22	.915
Carr, Eug	44	88	117	8	19	.962	May, Sea	44	91	98	18	16	.913
Dallas, GH	13	37	36	3	7	.961	Olson, WW	35	86	114	20	30	.909
Watson, Sea	29	49	82	6	10	.956	Le John, Bell	32	39	71	12	9	.902
COLLETTE, Port	55	123	148	13	31	.954	Kniss, Boi	11	25	27	6	3	.897
Smith, WW	45	106	137	14	34	.946	Yoshiwara, Port	23	39	34	9	11	.890
Wilson, Bell	36	81	100	11	22	.943	Krenecki, GH	10	18	18	9	4	.800
McClendon, Eug	30	54	86	10	19	.933							

(Fewer Than Ten Games)

Player and Club	G.	PO.	A.	E.	DP.	Pct.	Player and Club	G.	PO.	A.	E.	DP.	Pct.
Hernandez, Bell	1	3	2	0	0	1.000	Jensen, Boi	5	8	11	3	2	.864
Muth, Port	1	2	0	0	0	1.000	Thomas, Port	8	13	21	6	8	.850
K. Gilmartin, Sea	5	14	12	1	2	.963	Gorton, Port	3	2	4	2	0	.750
McKinney, Boise	6	14	13	4	3	.871							

THIRD BASEMEN

Player and Club	G.	PO.	A.	E.	DP.	Pct.	Player and Club	G.	PO.	A.	E.	DP.	Pct.
DOUG PETERSON, S.	68	60	137	16	10	.925	Deardorff, GH	67	45	122	23	5	.879
O'Neill, WW	65	56	148	19	9	.915	Loville, Boi	16	13	34	7	4	.870
Eickenhorst, Eug	68	75	97	18	9	.905	Corcoran, Boi	11	7	14	4	0	.840
Henry, Bell	68	53	96	17	10	.898	Kniss, Boi	20	12	16	6	1	.824
Edwards, Port	64	62	113	24	14	.879	Hornacek, Boi	27	14	34	16	0	.750

(Fewer Than Ten Games)

Player and Club	G.	PO.	A.	E.	DP.	Pct.	Player and Club	G.	PO.	A.	E.	DP.	Pct.
Dziemiela, Boi	9	6	13	0	0	1.000	Watson, Sea	5	2	8	1	0	.909
Adams, Bell	7	2	5	0	0	1.000	Garza, Port	7	2	7	1	0	.900
Costantine, Eug	2	2	5	0	1	1.000	Wilson, Bell	4	2	6	1	0	.889
Hopper, Eug	1	3	3	0	1	1.000	Black, WW	3	0	8	1	0	.889
Carr, Eug	5	2	3	0	1	1.000	Thomas, Port	6	5	10	2	1	.882
Gorton, Port	4	0	3	0	1	1.000	Scala, Boi	2	1	4	1	0	.833
Hicks, WW	1	2	0	0	0	1.000	Giles, Bell	8	0	4	2	0	.667
Highfill, GH	4	6	5	1	0	.917	Walls, WW	1	0	2	2	1	.500
Rodriguez, Boi	6	3	7	1	0	.909	Bullas, Boi	1	0	0	1	0	.000
Battey, WW	5	2	8	1	0	.909	Melendez, GH	1	0	1	1	0	.000

SHORTSTOPS

Player and Club	G.	PO.	A.	E.	DP.	Pct.	Player and Club	G.	PO.	A.	E.	DP.	Pct.
SIMPSON, GH	48	85	142	13	28	.946	Miller, Sea	58	104	157	25	26	.913
Hallstrom, WW	59	76	211	17	44	.944	Watson, Sea	15	33	51	8	6	.913
Hopper, Eug	68	96	187	21	34	.931	Ruzek, Sea	49	59	137	19	19	.912
Wilson, Bell	14	31	31	5	6	.925	Hernandez, Bell	24	13	38	7	9	.879
Collette, Port	16	23	47	6	7	.921	Cervantes, Port	49	77	154	32	30	.878
Dziemiela, Boi	33	40	98	12	12	.920	Spatz, WW	17	17	26	6	8	.878
Sigman, Boi	13	21	36	5	7	.919	Jones, GH	21	25	60	12	10	.876

(Fewer Than Ten Games)

Player and Club	G.	PO.	A.	E.	DP.	Pct.	Player and Club	G.	PO.	A.	E.	DP.	Pct.
Malpas, GH	6	9	19	0	3	1.000	Corcoran, Boi	9	18	22	6	3	.870
K. Gilmartin, Sea	1	1	1	0	1	1.000	Adams, Bell	7	7	11	3	4	.857
Edwards, Port	2	0	1	0	0	1.000	Kniss, Boi	7	11	10	4	1	.840
McKinney, Boi	1	0	1	0	0	1.000	Muth, Port	7	13	14	7	5	.794
Walker, Boi	8	14	24	1	6	.974	Billington, Boi	8	10	16	7	0	.788
Lee, Port	6	12	13	1	5	.962	Bonnell, Eug	6	7	11	5	2	.783
Black, WW	9	7	15	2	3	.917							

OUTFIELDERS

Player and Club	G.	PO.	A.	E.	DP.	Pct.
Holland, Port*	40	58	2	0	0	1.000
Getz, Port*	13	12	2	0	0	1.000
Giles, Bell	16	8	1	0	0	1.000
Falkosky, Port	12	7	1	0	0	1.000
Howard, Bell	46	58	4	1	1	.984
DIXSON, Sea*	72	155	6	4	1	.976
Gorton, Port	45	79	3	2	1	.976
Bowens, GH	56	114	5	3	3	.975
Derryberry, WW	38	61	7	2	1	.971
Jones, GH	51	88	10	3	5	.970
Mobley, GH*	28	60	5	2	2	.970
McNeely, Boi	35	59	4	2	1	.969
Meily, Port	46	54	3	2	2	.966
Parma, Port	58	106	5	4	2	.965
Beswick, WW	39	44	2	2	0	.958
Wilborn, WW	43	40	4	2	0	.957
Law, Bell*	34	43	1	2	1	.957
Jones, Bell	25	18	4	1	0	.957
Hicks, WW	69	108	8	6	2	.951
Walker, Eug*	46	51	5	3	1	.949
Gilliam, Port	19	35	1	2	1	.947
Kraft, Sea*	72	97	4	6	0	.944
Washington, Bell	50	78	2	5	0	.941
Ingraham, Eug	39	61	3	4	0	.941
Merkley, Port	19	14	2	1	0	.941
Kanikeberg, Sea*	69	97	8	7	1	.938
Foster, Bell	56	61	6	5	2	.931
Malito, Boi*	11	27	0	2	0	.931
Henley, Boi*	33	37	3	3	0	.930
Corcoran, GH	59	83	8	7	1	.929
McPherson, Eug*	57	98	5	8	2	.928
Bass, Boi	36	47	2	4	0	.925
Nichols, Eug	37	45	4	5	0	.907
Henderson, Boi*	46	99	3	12	0	.895
Necoechea, Boi*	29	36	4	5	0	.889
Venable, Bell	50	58	4	8	0	.886
Bennett, Boi*	37	48	3	7	0	.879
Krenecki, GH	29	25	3	4	2	.875
Harris, Eug	42	50	4	8	0	.871
Adams, WW	42	30	2	5	0	.865
Armstead, Boi	22	12	3	4	1	.789

(Fewer Than Ten Games)

Player and Club	G.	PO.	A.	E.	DP.	Pct.
K. Gilmartin, Sea	9	12	1	0	1	1.000
Guarino, Port	4	10	0	0	0	1.000
Wilson, Bell	8	9	0	0	0	1.000
James, WW	3	2	0	0	0	1.000
Mayberry, WW	3	1	0	0	0	1.000
Corcoran, Boi	1	1	0	0	0	1.000
Thomas, Port	3	6	0	1	0	.857
Barnett, WW	3	4	1	1	0	.833
Hornacek, Boi	5	2	0	1	0	.667

CATCHERS

Player and Club	G.	PO.	A.	E.	DP.	PB.	Pct.
ATTEBERY, Sea	46	254	54	2	7	6	.994
Miller, WW	39	235	42	4	2	10	.986
Nipert, Boi	15	67	5	1	0	5	.986
James, WW	31	178	18	3	0	6	.985
Segrest, WW	12	58	6	1	1	2	.985
Rementer, Eug	28	175	13	3	0	9	.984
Miller, Eug	42	298	30	6	2	11	.982
Peters, Sea	27	140	24	3	1	3	.982
Wantz, Port	56	251	43	6	3	15	.980
Heuberger, Port	30	130	9	3	2	4	.979
Melendez, GH	10	61	9	2	0	2	.972
Alvarez, Bell	33	202	26	7	1	16	.970
Swoope, Bell	19	90	6	4	0	9	.960
T. B. Wright, Boi	50	281	47	15	3	9	.956
Rodriguez, Boi	18	102	10	6	1	6	.949
Uremovich, GH	56	327	57	21	10	5	.948
Scioscia, Bell	31	202	35	14	7	12	.944

(Fewer Than Ten Games)

Player and Club	G.	PO.	A.	E.	DP.	PB.	Pct.
Aiello, GH	6	35	4	0	1	1	1.000
Markham, GH	1	11	1	0	0	1	1.000
Jones, Bell	1	1	0	0	0	0	1.000
Deal, Eug	8	51	2	1	0	1	.981

PITCHERS

Player and Club	G.	PO.	A.	E.	DP.	Pct.
DECK, Port	16	7	25	0	1	1.000
Schmidt, WW	12	5	14	0	3	1.000
Wasson, GH*	16	1	17	0	0	1.000
Keen, WW*	12	3	12	0	3	1.000
Peterson, Bell	21	1	12	0	0	1.000
Sheehan, Sea	11	2	8	0	0	1.000
Stolte, Boi*	19	0	9	0	0	1.000
Townsend, Bell	16	3	5	0	0	1.000
Maglio, WW	11	4	3	0	0	1.000
Schubert, Boi	13	2	5	0	0	1.000
Rusteck, Port*	15	1	6	0	1	1.000
Grana, Eug	16	2	4	0	0	1.000
Morrow, Eug*	21	2	3	0	0	1.000
Middleton, Bell	12	2	2	0	0	1.000
Spaulding, Boi	14	1	1	0	0	1.000
Underwood, Eug	11	0	1	0	1	1.000
Bushong, GH*	13	6	21	1	0	.964
Moore, Eug	16	7	18	1	1	.962
Lucas, WW*	14	7	17	1	0	.960
Williams, Sea	17	6	13	1	1	.950
Tellmann, WW	17	4	14	1	0	.947
D. Stewart, Bell	24	5	12	1	1	.944
Stillwell, Sea*	15	4	10	1	0	.933
Joseph, WW*	13	0	14	1	1	.933
Howell, Eug	13	5	8	1	0	.929
Lee, WW	28	4	9	1	0	.929
Peterson, GH	24	3	10	1	0	.929
Patterson, Boi	13	2	11	1	1	.929
Winkelbauer, Port	16	7	18	2	1	.926
Nelson, Port*	10	3	9	1	0	.923
Benson, Sea	13	4	19	2	1	.920
Biggerstaff, GH*	19	3	29	3	0	.914
Blue, Port	14	11	9	2	1	.909
Eisinger, Boi	15	4	6	1	1	.909
J. Wright, Boi*	14	4	15	2	1	.905
Barbisan, Sea	22	3	6	1	2	.900
Kryka, Bell	16	3	6	1	0	.900
Burress, Eug	10	2	6	1	1	.889
Meyring, Sea	18	2	13	2	2	.882
Brown, Eug	16	4	18	3	1	.880
Bain, Bell	15	4	17	3	0	.875
Murphy, Boi	12	1	6	1	1	.875
Stewart, Sea*	17	4	9	2	1	.867
Schmidt, Bell*	17	1	5	1	1	.857
Hays, GH*	10	1	5	1	1	.857
Albert, Bell	14	6	16	4	2	.846
Holland, Port*	17	2	7	2	0	.818
Green, Boi	17	6	14	5	2	.800

PITCHERS—Continued

Player and Club	G.	PO.	A.	E.	DP.	Pct.
Harold, Eug	21	0	4	1	0	.800
Dorgan, Bell*	14	6	9	4	1	.789
Goulding, Bell	18	5	2	2	0	.778
Moore, Boi	14	3	4	2	0	.778
Merino, GH-Port	16	3	14	5	0	.773
Berenyi, Eug	12	1	9	3	0	.769

Player and Club	G.	PO.	A.	E.	DP.	Pct.
Fehrenkamp, Boi	17	2	4	2	0	.750
O'Brien, Boi*	10	2	4	2	1	.750
Guischer, Port	13	7	7	5	0	.737
Martin, Bell	14	2	6	3	0	.727
McKenzie, Boi	17	3	2	2	0	.714
Sloan, Sea	14	4	4	4	0	.667

(Fewer Than Ten Games)

Player and Club	G.	PO.	A.	E.	DP.	Pct.
Mura, WW	8	4	8	0	0	1.000
Ferrara, Eug	8	4	6	0	0	1.000
Dupree, Eug	9	3	4	0	0	1.000
Clawson, Port	7	2	4	0	0	1.000
Mobley, GH*	4	1	4	0	0	1.000
Getz, Port*	2	1	2	0	0	1.000
Weber, Port*	5	0	3	0	0	1.000
Groves, Eug	5	1	1	0	0	1.000
Emery, Port*	7	0	2	0	0	1.000
Rice, Port*	9	0	1	0	0	1.000
Garner, WW	4	0	1	0	0	1.000
Hagen, Port*	3	0	1	0	0	1.000
Walsh, Boi	3	0	1	0	0	1.000
Trumbauer, Port*	2	0	1	0	0	1.000

Player and Club	G.	PO.	A.	E.	DP.	Pct.
Gosse, Eug*	9	3	11	1	0	.933
Woodard, GH	6	0	14	1	0	.933
French, WW	6	1	15	2	1	.889
Meyl, Boi	9	4	3	1	0	.875
Davis, GH	8	1	3	1	0	.800
Little, Boi*	6	0	4	1	0	.800
Keller, Bell	7	1	2	1	0	.750
Mayer, Eug*	5	1	2	1	1	.750
Rodriguez, Bell	8	0	3	1	0	.750
McKay, GH	7	0	3	1	0	.750
Lawson, Bell	7	0	2	2	0	.500
Wikel, GH	4	0	1	1	0	.500
Bullock, WW	8	0	1	2	0	.333

The following players do not have any recorded accepted chances at the positions indicated; therefore, are not listed in the fielding averages for those particular positions: Attebery, 3b; Bonnell, 3b; Brannon, p; Bushong*, of; Collette, 3b; P. Corcoran, 2b; Falkosky, p; Garza, of; Heuberger, of; Kay, p; Krenecki, 3b; Markham, of; R. C. Moore, of-p; Ward, p; Wells, of; H. Wright, of; T. B. Wright, of. R. Jones and Dennis Peterson appeared as designated hitters/pinch-hitters only.

CLUB PITCHING

											Int.						
Club	G.	CG.	ShO.	Sv.	IP.	H.	R.	ER.	HR.	BB.	BB.	HB.	SO.	WP.	Bk.	ERA.
Walla Walla	72	26	8	10	618	591	312	223	34	280	7	19	458	42	5	3.25
Seattle	72	30	6	8	595	548	320	258	34	360	6	16	378	42	4	3.90
Eugene	71	23	5	6	596	567	357	274	32	379	5	25	510	43	4	4.14
Grays Harbor	72	38	5	0	601	652	380	297	22	325	2	27	411	32	3	4.45
Portland	72	28	4	6	597	638	415	301	37	337	9	19	369	50	4	4.54
Bellingham	72	13	4	11	604	590	433	322	17	444	2	20	478	89	6	4.80
Boise	71	9	1	13	591	753	535	392	59	324	6	30	441	76	5	5.97

PITCHERS' RECORDS
(Leading Qualifiers for Earned-Run Average Leadership—58 or More Innings)
*Throws lefthanded.

													Int.			
Pitcher—Club	G.	GS.	CG.	ShO.	W.	L.	Sv.	Pct.	IP.	H.	R.	ER.	HR.	BB.	BB.	HB.	SO.	WP.	ERA.
Mura, WW	8	7	4	1	7	0	0	1.000	59	41	14	9	1	18	0	0	68	5	1.37
Benson, Sea	13	12	9	3	9	2	0	.818	97	69	27	18	6	21	0	3	52	2	1.67
Brown, Eug	16	12	7	2	6	5	0	.545	102	77	42	29	2	62	0	2	84	1	2.56
Albert, Bell	14	14	8	3	8	3	0	.727	102	87	42	32	3	22	0	2	92	2	2.82
Joseph, WW*	13	13	5	2	6	4	0	.600	82	91	46	26	5	28	0	5	46	2	2.85
Keen, WW*	12	12	3	1	6	3	0	.667	71	62	29	23	6	35	0	4	54	5	2.92
Howell, Eug	13	12	5	2	5	4	0	.556	73	65	30	24	7	34	0	1	79	2	2.96
C. Moore, Eug	16	14	7	1	6	5	1	.545	99	93	43	34	3	44	1	2	68	5	3.09
Lucas, WW*	14	12	5	2	7	3	0	.700	93	91	40	32	6	30	0	2	49	0	3.10
Tellmann, WW	17	7	2	0	3	4	3	.429	69	56	37	25	1	33	3	2	46	4	3.26

Departmental Leaders: G—Lee, 28; GS—Biggerstaff, 17; CG—Biggerstaff, 15; ShO—Albert, Benson, Biggerstaff, 3; W—Winkelbauer, 10; L—Peterson (GH), 9; Sv—Lee, O'Brien, 5; Pct.—Mura, 1.000; IP—Biggerstaff, 144; H—Biggerstaff, 138; R—Biggerstaff, 77; ER—Biggerstaff, 55; HR—Wright, 15; BB—Meyring, 75; IBB—Lee, 4; HB—Merino, Meyring, 8; SO—Biggerstaff, 123; WP—Meyring, 16.

(All Pitchers—Listed Alphabetically)

													Int.			
Pitcher—Club	G.	GS.	CG.	ShO.	W.	L.	Sv.	Pct.	IP.	H.	R.	ER.	HR.	BB.	BB.	HB.	SO.	WP.	ERA.
Albert, Bell	14	14	8	3	8	3	0	.727	102	87	42	32	3	22	0	2	92	2	2.82
Bain, Bell	15	12	4	0	4	6	0	.400	77	80	55	35	0	59	0	0	42	11	4.09
Barbisan, Sea	22	1	0	0	6	4	2	.600	49	47	29	19	1	46	2	0	46	9	3.49
Benson, Sea	13	12	9	3	9	2	0	.818	97	69	27	18	6	21	0	3	52	2	1.67
Berenyi, Eug	12	11	0	0	3	1	0	.750	49	50	37	26	1	55	0	0	39	12	4.78
Biggerstaff, GH*	19	17	15	3	9	7	0	.563	144	138	77	55	7	58	0	6	123	2	3.44
Blue, Port	14	13	2	0	6	6	0	.500	76	80	51	34	2	42	0	2	40	6	4.03
Brannon, GH	1	0	0	0	0	1	0	.000	⅓	0	2	1	0	2	0	0	0	0	27.00

Pitcher–Club	G.	GS.	CG.	ShO.	W.	L.	Sv.	Pct.	IP.	H.	R.	ER.	HR.	BB.	Int. BB.	HB.	SO.	WP.	ERA.
Brown, Eug	16	12	7	2	6	5	0	.545	102	77	42	29	2	62	0	2	84	1	2.56
Bullock, WW	8	0	0	0	2	0	2	1.000	14	11	7	2	0	7	0	2	12	1	1.29
Burress, Eug	10	2	0	0	0	2	0	.000	24	31	20	16	5	19	0	2	18	2	6.00
Bushong, GH*	13	13	9	1	7	5	0	.583	94	90	48	36	5	47	1	4	59	5	3.45
Clawson, Port	7	0	0	0	1	0	1	1.000	14	18	16	15	2	9	0	3	10	2	9.64
Davis, GH	8	4	1	0	0	4	0	.000	27	37	16	12	0	20	0	2	12	3	4.00
Deck, Port	16	15	9	2	9	5	0	.643	124	129	66	49	8	33	2	3	106	7	3.56
Dorgan, Bell*	14	13	0	0	2	7	0	.222	70	64	53	41	2	71	0	2	59	9	5.27
Dupree, WW	9	2	0	0	2	1	0	.667	25	40	22	20	4	10	0	0	21	6	7.20
Eisinger, Boi	15	9	2	0	3	5	2	.375	56	69	49	40	9	34	1	2	40	9	6.43
Emery, Port*	7	3	0	0	0	2	1	.000	22	33	25	19	5	22	0	1	14	1	7.77
Falkosky, Port	1	0	0	0	0	0	0	.000	1	1	0	0	0	0	0	0	0	0	0.00
Fehrenkamp, Boi	17	4	1	0	5	1	2	.833	57	62	34	28	5	29	1	4	57	8	4.42
Ferrara, Eug	8	8	0	0	1	5	0	.167	34	51	46	40	2	32	0	4	37	5	10.59
French, WW	6	6	5	0	4	2	0	.667	48	36	16	12	3	9	0	2	31	2	2.25
Garner, WW	4	1	0	0	0	0	0	.000	8	10	6	6	1	10	0	0	7	1	6.75
Getz, Port*	2	0	0	0	0	0	0	.000	1	0	3	3	0	6	0	0	0	0	27.00
Gosse, Eug*	9	6	3	0	3	3	0	.500	46	51	25	19	2	19	0	2	40	4	3.72
Goulding, Bell	18	4	0	0	4	6	1	.400	48	53	34	18	1	24	0	0	46	5	3.38
Grana, Eug	16	0	0	0	0	4	0	1.000	25	21	18	10	2	11	0	1	15	1	3.60
Green, Boi	17	14	3	1	5	5	0	.500	79	112	71	47	5	28	0	3	40	9	5.35
Groves, Eug	5	0	0	0	1	0	0	.000	5	6	9	7	1	7	0	2	6	3	12.60
Guischer, Port	13	8	4	1	4	3	0	.571	65	64	41	29	2	22	1	1	52	5	4.02
Hagen, Port*	3	2	0	0	0	1	0	.000	5	11	12	12	0	6	0	0	1	3	21.60
Harold, Eug	21	1	0	0	2	5	3	.286	46	47	37	31	2	41	2	2	36	5	6.07
Hays, GH*	10	4	2	0	2	2	0	.500	41	69	34	31	3	16	0	2	24	4	6.80
Holland, Port*	17	5	4	1	4	3	1	.571	52	40	21	11	2	21	1	2	25	3	1.90
Howell, Eug	13	12	5	2	5	4	0	.556	73	65	30	24	7	34	0	1	79	2	2.96
Joseph, WW*	13	13	5	2	6	4	0	.600	82	91	46	26	5	28	0	5	46	2	2.85
Kay, Port	3	1	0	0	0	0	0	.000	6	14	10	7	2	3	1	1	2	0	10.50
Keen, WW	12	12	3	1	6	3	0	.667	71	62	29	23	6	35	0	4	54	5	2.92
Keller, Bell	7	5	0	0	0	1	0	.000	25	24	15	11	0	17	1	2	12	4	3.96
Kryka, Bell	16	3	0	0	1	3	1	.250	29	36	31	20	0	24	0	0	20	9	6.21
Lawson, Bell	7	1	0	0	0	0	0	.000	9	11	13	7	0	13	0	1	6	1	7.00
Lee, WW	28	0	0	0	5	3	5	.625	54	46	25	18	1	34	4	1	49	6	3.00
Little, Boi*	6	1	0	0	0	1	0	.000	9	16	11	6	0	5	1	1	4	1	6.00
Lucas, WW*	14	12	5	2	7	3	0	.700	93	91	40	32	6	30	0	2	49	0	3.10
Maglio, WW	11	3	0	0	1	1	0	.500	29	32	21	16	1	32	0	0	17	6	4.97
Martin, Bell	14	10	1	0	5	1	1	.833	60	51	45	39	2	48	0	5	47	12	5.85
Mayer, Eug*	5	2	1	0	3	0	0	1.000	18	11	6	5	2	5	0	1	15	0	2.50
McKay, GH	7	2	0	0	0	2	0	.000	17	20	20	15	2	14	0	1	11	0	7.94
McKenzie, Boi	17	1	0	0	2	1	0	.667	30	46	43	33	3	31	1	2	28	10	9.90
Merino, 10 GH-6 Port	16	12	4	0	5	6	0	.455	78	60	51	44	3	70	0	8	78	8	5.08
Meyl, Boi	9	8	0	0	2	5	1	.286	39	52	34	19	4	8	0	1	30	1	4.38
Meyring, Sea	18	7	3	2	5	3	2	.625	84	72	41	34	4	75	1	8	72	16	3.64
Middleton, Bell	12	1	0	0	2	2	0	.500	18	22	14	11	2	18	0	0	15	5	5.50
Mobley, GH*	4	2	0	0	0	1	0	.000	13	16	13	11	0	12	0	1	6	1	7.62
Moore, Eug	16	14	7	1	6	5	1	.545	99	93	43	34	3	44	1	2	68	5	3.09
Moore, Boi	14	1	0	0	0	0	0	.000	22	23	23	13	0	18	0	1	20	3	5.32
Moore, GH	1	0	0	0	0	0	0	.000	1	0	0	0	0	0	0	0	0	0	0.00
Morrow, Eug*	21	3	0	0	3	3	1	.500	61	50	34	23	2	42	2	4	64	3	3.39
Mura, WW	8	7	4	1	7	0	0	1.000	59	41	14	9	1	18	0	0	68	5	1.37
Murphy, Boi	12	9	0	0	2	3	0	.400	43	61	42	29	5	23	0	1	26	8	6.07
Nelson, Port*	10	3	2	0	0	2	0	.000	45	55	29	23	3	18	2	0	13	0	4.60
O'Brien, Boi*	10	2	0	0	2	0	5	1.000	35	21	17	12	0	18	0	3	34	3	3.09
Patterson, Boi	13	5	1	0	5	1	0	.833	42	46	35	31	4	28	0	0	30	2	6.64
Peterson, GH	24	3	2	0	2	9	0	.182	81	91	49	42	0	32	0	5	42	1	4.67
Peterson, Bell	21	1	0	0	2	5	4	.286	44	39	32	26	1	33	0	3	29	5	5.32
Rice, Port*	9	1	0	0	0	1	1	.000	8	16	12	10	1	4	0	0	7	1	11.25
Rodriguez, Bell	8	1	0	0	0	1	0	.000	10	12	10	7	3	9	0	1	8	1	5.25
Rusteck, Port*	15	0	0	0	3	0	2	1.000	34	37	21	10	0	25	2	1	15	3	2.65
E. Schmidt, Bell*	17	0	0	0	1	0	0	.000	29	29	37	29	1	35	0	1	30	6	9.00
J. Schmidt, WW	12	9	2	1	3	5	0	.375	67	75	44	34	5	34	0	1	58	4	4.57
Schubert, Boi	13	2	0	0	1	3	2	.250	32	47	37	28	5	24	1	3	25	7	7.88
Sheehan, Sea	11	7	1	1	1	3	1	.250	41	35	28	26	3	31	0	1	31	3	5.71
Sloan, Sea	14	14	4	0	3	6	0	.333	79	82	56	47	3	65	0	3	52	5	5.35
Spaulding, Boi	14	2	0	0	0	3	0	.000	34	50	34	28	1	14	0	3	18	7	7.41
Stewart, Sea*	17	0	0	0	3	2	3	.600	41	29	16	13	6	31	1	0	27	4	3.29
Stewart, Bell	24	2	0	0	1	1	1	.500	50	47	35	28	1	58	0	0	53	15	5.04
Stillwell, Sea*	15	15	5	0	4	5	0	.444	86	88	59	47	5	55	1	0	26	2	4.92
Stolte, Boi*	19	1	0	0	3	3	1	.500	31	44	39	28	2	31	0	1	24	3	8.13
Tellmann, WW	17	7	2	0	3	4	0	.429	69	56	39	25	5	23	3	2	46	4	3.26
Townsend, Bell	16	5	0	0	1	4	2	.200	32	35	17	15	1	13	1	3	19	4	4.22
Trumbauer, Port*	2	2	0	0	0	1	0	.000	2	2	13	12	0	14	0	2	0	2	54.00

Pitcher—Club	G.	GS.	CG.	ShO.	W.	L.	Sv.	Pct.	IP.	H.	R.	ER.	HR.	BB.	Int. BB.	HB.	SO.	WP	ERA.
Underwood, Eug	11	0	0	0	1	0	1	1.000	12	14	10	10	1	8	0	2	9	0	7.50
Walsh, Boi	3	0	0	0	0	1	0	.000	3	5	5	3	1	6	0	0	0	0	9.00
Ward, Boi	1	0	0	0	0	0	0	.000	2	2	1	1	0	1	0	0	0	0	4.50
Wasson, GH*	16	14	5	1	3	8	0	.273	91	119	63	46	5	50	0	0	51	5	4.55
Weber, Port*	5	0	0	0	1	1	0	.500	12	12	13	12	0	21	0	2	5	5	9.00
Wikel, GH	4	0	0	0	0	1	0	.000	14	12	8	7	0	11	1	0	12	3	4.50
Williams, Sea	17	16	8	0	8	8	0	.500	119	126	64	52	6	36	1	1	72	1	3.93
Winkelbauer, Port	16	15	7	0	10	5	0	.667	104	105	60	45	5	60	0	0	53	7	3.89
Woodard, GH	6	5	0	0	0	2	0	.000	25	25	21	18	0	24	0	0	19	5	6.48
J. Wright, Boi*	14	12	2	0	3	6	0	.333	78	97	60	46	15	26	1	6	65	5	5.31

BALKS—Dorgan, Stillwell, 4 each; Dupree, Green, Guischer, Lee, Sheehan, 2 each; Bain, Brown, Burress, Bushong, Hays, Holland, Howell, Mayer, Merino (GH), Meyring, Moore (Boise), Nelson, Schmidt (WW), Schubert, Stewart (Sea), Stewart (Bell), Williams, J. Wright, 1 each.

COMBINATION SHUTOUTS—Townsend-Martin, Bellingham; Joseph-Lee, Walla Walla.

NO-HIT GAMES—Biggerstaff, Grays Harbor, defeated Bellingham, 8-0, July 11; Guischer, Portland, defeated Boise, 7-0, July 11 (seven innings).

Western Carolinas League

CLASS A

CHAMPIONSHIP WINNERS IN PREVIOUS YEARS

1948 – Lincolnton* .... .627	1962 – Statesville .... .563	1969 – Greenwood‡ .... .587
1949 – Newton-Conover............ .667	Statesville .... .700	Shelby .... .565
Ruth'ford Co. (2nd)† .... .627	1963 – Greenville† .... .576	1970 – Greenville .... .576
1950 – Newton-Conover............ .627	Salisbury .... .631	Greenville .... .619
Lenoir (2nd)† .... .626	1964 – Rock Hill .... .672	1971 – Greenwood .... .631
1951 – Morganton .... .645	Salisbury‡ .... .631	Greenwood .... .759
Shelby (2nd)† .... .604	1965 – Salisbury .... .641	1972 – Spartanburg‡ .... .788
1952 – Lincolnton .... .649	Rock Hill‡ .... .603	Greenville .... .652
Shelby (2nd)† .... .645	1966 – Spartanburg .... .682	1973 – Spartanburg‡ .... .646
1953-59 – League inactive.	Spartanburg .... .767	Gastonia .... .619
1960 – Lexington .... .707	1967 – Spartanburg .... .730	1974 – Gastonia .... .606
Salisbury (2nd)† .... .650	Spartanburg .... .567	Gastonia .... .672
1961 – Salisbury .... .627	1968 – Spartanburg‡ .... .597	1975 – Spartanburg .... .543
Shelby (4th)† .... .481	Greenwood‡ .... .597	Spartanburg .... .614

*Won championship and four-club playoff. †Won four-club playoff. ‡Won split-season playoff. (NOTE – Known as Western Carolina League from 1948 through 1962.)

STANDING OF CLUBS AT CLOSE OF FIRST HALF, JUNE 24

Club	W.	L.	T.	Pct.	G.B.	Club	W.	L.	T.	Pct.	G.B.
Asheville (Rangers)...............	37	31	0	.544	......	Spartanburg (Phillies)	33	36	0	.478	4½
Greenwood (Braves)	33	36	0	.478	4½	Charleston (Pirates)	30	39	0	.435	7½

STANDING OF CLUBS AT CLOSE OF SECOND HALF, SEPTEMBER 2

Club	W.	L.	T.	Pct.	G.B.	Club	W.	L.	T.	Pct.	G.B.
Greenwood (Braves)...............	42	28	0	.600	......	Charleston (Pirates)	29	41	0	.414	13
Asheville (Rangers)...............	39	31	0	.557	3	Spartanburg (Phillies)	26	44	0	.371	16

FINAL STANDING OF WESTERN CAROLINAS LEAGUE VS. CAROLINA LEAGUE

Club	W.	L.	T.	Pct.	G.B.	Club	W.	L.	T.	Pct.	G.B.
Winston-Salem (Red Sox)	12	4	0	.750	......	Spartanburg (Phillies)	8	8	0	.500	4
Salem (Pirates)	10	6	0	.625	2	Charleston (Pirates)	6	10	0	.375	6
Peninsula (Phillies)	9	6	0	.600	2½	Asheville (Rangers)	5	10	0	.333	6½
Lynchburg (Mets)	9	7	0	.563	3	Greenwood (Braves)	4	12	0	.250	8

COMPOSITE STANDING OF CLUBS AT CLOSE OF SEASON, SEPTEMBER 2

Club	Ash.	Gwd.	Cha.	Spa.	W.-S.	Pen.	Sal.	Lyn.	W.	L.	T.	Pct.	G.B.
Asheville (Rangers)	..	21	22	28	1	0	2	2	76	62	0	.551	......
Greenwood (Braves)	18	..	30	23	0	3	1	0	75	64	0	.540	1½
Charleston (Pirates)	18	14	..	21	1	1	2	2	59	80	0	.424	17½
Spartanburg (Phillies)	16	17	18	..	2	2	1	3	59	80	0	.424	17½
Winston-Salem (Red Sox)	3	4	3	2	..	25	23	20	80	57	0	.584	......
Peninsula (Phillies)	3	1	3	2	18	..	22	22	71	65	0	.522	8½
Salem (Pirates)	2	3	2	3	15	17	..	26	68	69	1	.496	12
Lynchburg (Mets)	2	4	2	1	20	17	18	..	64	75	0	.460	17

Major league affiliations in parentheses.

Playoffs – Greenwood defeated Asheville, three games to one.

Regular-Season Attendance – Asheville, 41,580; Charleston, 34,249; Greenwood, 26,380; Spartanburg, 32,008. Total, 134,217. No All-Star Game. Playoffs, 4,314.

Managers: Asheville – Wayne Terwilliger; Charleston – Michael Ryan; Greenwood – Gene Hassell; Spartanburg – Lee Elia.

All-Star Team: 1B – Putnam, Asheville; 2B – Moreno, Spartanburg; 3B – Berra, Charleston; SS – Norman, Charleston; OF – Whisenton, Greenwood; E. Miller, Asheville; Convertino, Spartanburg; Utility – Doherty, Greenwood; Busby, Charleston; C – Russell, Asheville; DH – DeBattista, Charleston; P – Free, Greenwood; L. Jones, Greenwood; Mirabella, Asheville; Arroyo, Spartanburg; Manager – Hassell, Greenwood.

(Compiled by Howe News Bureau, Chicago, Ill.)

CLUB BATTING

Club	G.	AB.	R.	OR.	H.	TB.	2B.	3B.	HR.	RBI.	SH.	SF.	BB.	Int. BB.	HP.	SO.	SB.	CS.	LOB.	Pct.
Charleston	139	4599	631	776	1231	1741	195	30	85	548	44	28	491	34	44	744	105	51	1042	.268
Asheville	138	4505	822	696	1190	1704	192	29	88	679	38	57	732	35	75	788	256	59	1057	.264
Greenwood	139	4541	694	672	1193	1616	182	29	61	596	36	40	611	36	43	770	157	45	1084	.263
Spartanburg	139	4645	643	726	1203	1676	209	27	70	545	33	38	487	22	29	770	87	52	991	.259

INDIVIDUAL BATTING

(Leading Qualifiers for Batting Championship–378 or More Plate Appearances)

*Bats lefthanded. †Switch-hitter.

Player and Club	G.	AB.	R.	H.	TB.	2B.	3B.	HR.	RBI.	SH.	SF.	BB.	HP.	SO.	SB.	CS.	Pct.
Putnam, Patrick, Ash*	138	538	100	194	305	33	3	24	142	0	12	76	6	44	8	4	.361
Doherty, James, Greenwood	132	471	71	154	175	11	5	0	57	3	3	72	3	38	14	4	.327
Linares, Rufino, Greenwood	109	389	57	127	164	20	4	3	54	2	6	35	1	56	11	3	.326
Convertino, Philip, Spar*	129	454	64	139	208	33	3	10	72	5	6	55	5	62	8	6	.306
DeBattista, Daniel, Char	127	493	81	150	203	19	5	8	67	2	2	40	5	50	13	8	.304
Berra, Dale, Charleston	139	527	78	157	243	28	5	16	89	1	8	41	1	98	7	6	.298
Busby, James, Charleston*	128	446	65	128	181	23	3	8	54	2	3	50	3	40	25	11	.287
Robbins, W. Vaughn, Char*	137	502	58	143	206	28	1	11	77	5	5	85	4	72	2	1	.285
Moreno, Jose, Spartanburg	135	523	88	148	191	19	3	6	46	6	1	37	2	63	19	7	.283
Norman, Nelson, Char	128	544	88	151	174	15	1	2	48	4	2	27	2	42	8	3	.278

Departmental Leaders: G–Berra, 139; AB–Norman, 544; R–Washington, 106; H–Putnam, 194; TB–Putnam, 305; 2B–Convertino, Putnam, 33; 3B–Whisenton, 10; HR–Putnam, 24; RBI–Putnam, 142; SH–McDonald, A. Ryan, 9; SF–Putnam, 12; BB–Washington, 101; HP–E. Miller, 24; SO–Rein, 144; SB–E. Miller, 65; CS–Washington, 14.

(All Players–Listed Alphabetically)

Player and Club	G.	AB.	R.	H.	TB.	2B.	3B.	HR.	RBI.	SH.	SF.	BB.	HP.	SO.	SB.	CS.	Pct.
Adams, M. Brent, Spar	1	1	1	0	0	0	0	0	0	0	0	0	0	1	0	0	.000
Aguayo, Luis, Spartanburg	3	11	0	1	1	0	0	0	0	0	0	1	0	1	0	0	.091
Aranzamendi, Jorge, Gwd	8	17	4	6	8	2	0	0	2	0	0	1	0	1	1	0	.353
Baker, Richard, Charleston	9	26	4	8	12	1	0	1	2	1	0	2	2	5	0	0	.308
Ban, George, Greenwood	48	141	20	32	40	5	0	1	9	2	1	21	3	23	0	0	.227
Benedict, Bruce, Greenwood	21	54	7	13	17	1	0	1	10	2	1	7	1	6	1	0	.241
Berger, Kenneth, Spar*	120	433	67	108	141	16	1	5	32	4	1	51	2	77	18	7	.249
Berra, Dale, Charleston	139	527	78	157	243	28	5	16	89	1	8	41	1	98	7	6	.298
Brady, James, Charleston	103	337	44	84	126	17	2	7	39	6	0	58	3	77	17	1	.249
Brookens, Timothy, Ash	59	197	35	41	70	6	4	5	28	0	2	22	0	66	15	3	.208
Bucci, Michael, Asheville	20	69	16	14	27	2	1	3	16	1	1	19	1	11	6	1	.203
Busby, James, Charleston*	128	446	65	128	181	23	3	8	54	2	3	50	3	40	25	11	.287
Carty, Jorge, Charleston	21	63	9	12	16	2	1	0	6	0	0	5	0	13	1	1	.190
Charbonneau, Joseph, Spar.	43	121	20	36	51	3	0	4	18	0	1	9	2	25	1	1	.298
Clark, Bryan, Charleston*	1	1	0	1	1	0	0	0	0	0	0	1	0	0	0	0	1.000
Connolly, Kevin, Gwd*	72	230	20	54	74	11	0	3	21	5	2	22	0	21	1	0	.235
Convertino, Philip, Spar*	129	454	64	139	208	33	3	10	72	5	6	55	5	62	8	6	.306
Cooper, Gary N., Gwd*	129	459	97	109	131	17	1	1	29	3	3	79	7	121	39	10	.237
Cotes, Eugenio, Char	13	42	5	7	13	3	0	1	2	0	0	8	0	16	0	0	.167
Couch, Richard, Ash*	1	1	0	0	0	0	0	0	0	0	0	0	0	0	0	0	.000
DeBattista, Daniel, Char	127	493	81	150	203	19	5	8	67	2	2	40	5	50	13	8	.304
DelCarmen, Manuel, Spar.	36	138	19	35	43	6	1	0	16	0	0	10	0	21	1	1	.254
DeMeo, Robert, Spartanburg	31	100	9	20	24	1	0	1	12	2	3	10	1	17	1	0	.200
Doherty, James, Greenwood	132	471	71	154	175	11	5	0	57	3	3	72	3	38	14	4	.327
Edrington, Heyward, Char	2	1	0	0	0	0	0	0	0	0	0	0	0	0	0	0	.000
Fletcher, Donald, Greenwood†	15	21	3	7	8	1	0	0	4	0	0	4	0	8	0	0	.333
Fornash, Eugene, Greenwood	14	53	9	15	16	1	0	0	9	0	1	13	0	12	2	0	.283
Fulton, Gary, Charleston*	3	4	1	0	0	0	0	0	0	0	0	7	0	3	0	0	.000
Gaines, Jerald, Asheville	83	235	46	65	79	8	0	2	28	1	3	31	2	42	29	5	.277
Givler, Robert, Spar†	116	371	50	95	140	19	7	4	43	2	2	63	2	60	2	4	.256
Green, Richard B., Gwd†	138	526	74	142	203	29	1	10	81	1	3	52	2	67	2	2	.270
Hawkins, Dennis, Spar	9	20	4	3	3	0	0	0	0	1	0	2	1	6	0	0	.150
Howard, Mark, Charleston	5	2	0	0	0	0	0	0	0	0	0	0	0	0	0	0	.000
Hubbard, Glenn, Greenwood	33	126	26	40	62	8	1	4	21	0	1	17	2	26	4	1	.317
Hudson, Richard, Char	1	2	0	0	0	0	0	0	0	0	0	0	0	1	0	0	.000
Isaac, Joseph, Charleston	1	1	0	0	0	0	0	0	0	0	0	0	0	0	0	0	.000
Isales, Orlando, Spar	121	439	47	111	136	19	0	2	47	1	5	28	6	57	9	6	.253
Jones, Alvin, Greenwood*	38	117	20	21	31	2	1	2	9	0	0	15	1	35	4	0	.179
Jones, Joe Louis, Spar	14	46	6	11	15	1	0	1	9	0	0	3	0	10	0	1	.239
Keller, Charles, Gwd	21	81	14	24	45	6	0	5	29	0	2	10	0	16	0	0	.296
Kruzelock, Steven, Spar	66	232	31	53	79	14	0	4	28	0	3	30	0	46	0	0	.228
Linares, Rufino, Greenwood	109	389	57	127	164	20	4	3	54	2	6	35	1	56	11	3	.326
Lisi, Riccardo, Asheville	126	473	73	127	207	24	4	16	75	0	10	54	17	67	24	3	.268

Player and Club	G.	AB.	R.	H.	TB.	2B.	3B.	HR.	RBI.	SH.	SF.	BB.	HP.	SO.	SB.	CS.	Pct.
Lucy, Frank, Spartanburg	49	166	23	51	77	12	1	4	27	1	1	14	0	28	0	1	.307
Macha, Michael, Greenwood	92	303	34	75	109	7	0	9	52	2	2	41	2	56	3	3	.248
Mattson, Ronald, Spar	59	224	30	42	50	6	1	0	8	4	1	19	0	32	4	1	.188
Mazur, Robert, Charleston	1	1	1	0	0	0	0	0	0	0	0	0	0	0	0	0	.000
McDonald, Jerry, Char*	124	475	70	115	150	13	5	4	30	9	2	73	8	34	24	10	.242
Meistickle, Kevin, Gwd	1	1	0	0	0	0	0	0	0	0	0	0	0	0	0	0	.000
Miller, Edward, Asheville†	116	443	100	117	140	14	3	1	39	4	3	69	24	93	65	13	.264
Miller, Mark D., Ash†	76	223	34	60	79	11	1	2	41	5	2	41	1	35	2	0	.269
Moreno, Jose, Spartanburg	135	523	88	148	191	19	3	6	46	6	1	37	2	63	19	7	.283
Nickerson, James, Spar	1	1	0	0	0	0	0	0	0	0	0	0	0	0	0	0	.000
Norman, Nelson, Char	128	544	88	151	174	15	1	2	48	4	2	27	2	42	8	3	.278
O'Brien, Kenneth, Spar	73	219	31	58	72	9	1	1	21	2	2	37	1	37	4	2	.265
Olson, Larry, Charleston	56	165	16	31	46	4	1	3	13	1	0	22	2	48	1	2	.188
Ortiz, Leonardo, Char	43	144	15	40	62	6	2	4	19	3	1	5	2	29	0	1	.278
Pena, Antonio, Charleston	14	49	4	11	16	2	0	1	8	0	0	4	2	7	0	0	.224
Pinkerton, C. Wayne, Ash†	59	197	31	43	51	5	0	1	21	2	3	26	3	48	10	1	.218
Popovich, Nicholas, Spar	39	116	19	32	39	4	0	1	14	1	1	12	0	20	0	1	.276
Purvis, Glenn, Asheville	114	343	65	78	110	8	3	6	37	4	2	81	4	110	17	2	.227
Putnam, Patrick, Ash*	138	538	100	194	305	33	3	24	142	0	12	76	6	44	8	4	.361
Rein, Frederick, Char	125	428	57	112	186	17	3	17	70	2	4	44	4	144	5	3	.262
Reyes, Louis, Spartanburg	127	457	54	108	171	22	4	11	53	2	6	48	1	91	6	4	.236
Reynolds, Michael, Gwd*	100	282	48	54	66	5	2	1	29	2	3	57	3	52	13	1	.191
Reynolds, Randall, Ash	58	173	24	36	57	7	1	4	21	1	0	8	2	35	7	2	.208
Rivera, David, Asheville	41	151	24	30	47	6	1	3	19	1	1	12	1	32	7	0	.199
Robbins, W. Vaughn, Char*	137	502	58	143	206	28	1	11	77	5	5	85	4	72	2	1	.285
Robinson, Don, Charleston	1	0	0	0	0	0	0	0	0	0	0	1	0	0	0	0	.000
Rodriguez, Gregorio, Char	7	23	2	7	8	1	0	0	3	1	0	2	0	2	0	1	.304
Russell, Joseph, Ash	115	393	66	93	138	19	1	8	46	5	4	65	6	42	11	1	.237
Ryan, Albert, Greenwood	106	370	58	95	133	20	3	4	50	9	3	59	8	42	28	13	.257
Ryan, Michael, Charleston	3	12	0	2	2	0	0	0	0	0	0	0	0	2	0	0	.167
Sanchez, Orlando, Spar*	122	445	61	118	185	18	5	13	81	0	3	43	4	90	12	9	.265
Schwartz, Dennis, Char	2	5	0	1	1	0	0	0	0	0	0	0	0	3	0	0	.200
Stevens, David, Greenwood	6	25	3	6	8	2	0	0	6	0	1	2	2	0	0	0	.240
Stewart, Joseph, Asheville	119	393	65	109	164	26	1	9	70	3	7	90	5	87	18	8	.277
Stone, William, Asheville	65	189	34	54	63	6	0	1	21	6	1	37	2	22	5	2	.286
Ventura, Candido, Char	48	135	18	34	43	6	0	1	10	3	0	4	1	21	1	1	.252
Walker, Thomas, Spar	41	129	19	34	50	7	0	3	18	2	2	15	2	26	2	1	.264
Washington, LaRue, Ash	132	488	106	129	167	17	6	3	75	5	6	101	1	52	32	14	.264
Wessinger, James, Gwd	1	1	0	0	0	0	0	0	0	0	0	0	0	1	0	0	.000
Westlake, Thomas, Gwd*	10	23	4	7	7	0	0	0	2	1	0	6	0	3	1	0	.304
Whisenton, Larry, Gwd*	111	420	67	112	178	22	10	8	67	0	4	59	0	70	23	5	.267
Wick, R. Michael, Char	27	96	8	21	31	7	0	1	6	3	0	7	4	26	1	1	.219
Woods, Jeffrey, Char*	25	76	7	16	21	3	1	0	5	1	1	4	1	11	0	1	.211
Young, Donald, Greenwood	130	432	58	100	141	12	1	9	55	4	4	40	8	116	10	3	.231

The following pitchers had no plate appearances primarily through use of designated hitters, listed alphabetically by club, games in parentheses):

ASHEVILLE—Arrington, Michael (59); Carroll, Robert (17); Darwin, Danny (16); Glowzenski, Leonard (22); Griffin, Michael (11); Kelly, Harold (24); McCarthy, David (36); McMurray, Randall (5); Mirabella, Paul (22); Moock, Patrick (15); Patten, William (4); Scott, Jeffrey (3); Smith, Ward (17); Soroko, Mark (15); Tidwell, Danny (23); Watson, Phillip (7).

CHARLESTON—Burkett, J. Mark (5); Frye, Vincent (4); Jakubowski, Stanley (23); Leduc, Jean-Pierre (2); Martin, Ricky (31); Pinkus, Jeffrey (23); Presser, Donald (21); Reavis, Dean (20); Rivas, Martin (1); Seabol, Russell (2); Stadnika, Robert (7); Summers, Harry (14); Tapia, Mark (6); Vasquez, Rafael (4); Williams, Albert (26).

GREENWOOD—Amancio, Ramon (2); Breiby, David (15); Costello, Timothy (26); Free, William (25); Harlee, William (11); Harper, Terry (2); Jones, Lamar (44); King, William (14); Mahler, Richard (31); Matula, Richard (3); McWilliams, Larry (8); Morogiello, Daniel (8); Phillips, G. William (25); Pratt, Louis (4); Rios, Wilfredo (10); Stein, Gary (6); Theiss, Duane (36); Titus, Vincent (27).

SPARTANBURG—Arroyo, Carlos (37); Botelho, Derek (20); Bradford, Gregory (15); Burdette, Ricky (11); Dockins, Rodney (46); Downs, David (11); Gale, Keith (26); LaPointe, Raymond (24); Lasek, James (3); Noles, Dickie (24); Taylor, Jack (11); Welborn, Sammye (9); Wolff, Chris (21).

GRAND-SLAM HOME RUNS—Putnam, 2; Keller, Moreno, Young, 1 each.

AWARDED FIRST BASE ON INTERFERENCE—Berra (Ban).

CLUB FIELDING

Club	G.	PO.	A.	E.	DP.	PB.	Pct.	Club	G.	PO.	A.	E.	DP.	PB.	Pct.
Asheville	138	3559	1497	222	128	17	.958	Charleston	139	3499	1452	224	115	47	.957
Spartanburg	139	3566	1505	227	102	31	.957	Greenwood	139	3498	1355	234	124	21	.954

Triple Play—Asheville.

INDIVIDUAL FIELDING

FIRST BASEMAN

*Throws lefthanded.

Player and Club	G.	PO.	A.	E.	DP.	Pct.
PUTNAM, Asheville	131	1108	93	9	99	.993
O'Brien, Spar	12	86	8	1	6	.989
Kruzelock, Spar	63	594	26	8	42	.987

Triple Play—Putnam.

Player and Club	G.	PO.	A.	E.	DP.	Pct.
Robbins, Charleston	137	1129	101	19	97	.985
Green, Greenwood	138	1156	77	31	105	.975
Sanchez, Spar	70	620	26	17	35	.974

(Fewer Than Ten Games)

Player and Club	G.	PO.	A.	E.	DP.	Pct.
Fornash, Greenwood	1	9	0	0	0	1.000
Linares, Greenwood	1	6	2	0	2	1.000
DeMeo, Spartanburg	1	8	0	0	0	1.000
Lucy, Spartanburg	1	4	1	0	1	1.000

Player and Club	G.	PO.	A.	E.	DP.	Pct.
Lisi, Asheville	6	55	2	1	1	.983
Brookens, Asheville	6	42	5	1	7	.979
DeBattista, Char	4	22	1	1	1	.958

SECOND BASEMEN

Player and Club	G.	PO.	A.	E.	DP.	Pct.
Woods, Charleston	21	35	43	0	8	1.000
Stone, Asheville	38	61	86	1	13	.993
Reynolds, Greenwood	15	20	21	1	2	.976
M. Miller, Ash	37	88	102	5	31	.974
Ventura, Charleston	17	39	43	3	9	.965
Ryan, Greenwood	92	187	215	16	47	.962

Triple Play—Washington.

Player and Club	G.	PO.	A.	E.	DP.	Pct.
Hubbard, Greenwood	31	62	83	6	19	.960
BRADY, Charleston	102	225	278	24	59	.954
Moreno, Spartanburg	134	311	391	36	73	.951
Washington, Ash	75	150	221	20	37	.949
Fornash, Greenwood	12	28	26	6	5	.900

(Fewer Than Ten Games)

Player and Club	G.	PO.	A.	E.	DP.	Pct.
Rodriguez, Char	7	11	13	2	3	.923
Mattson, Spartanburg	2	2	5	1	1	.875

Player and Club	G.	PO.	A.	E.	DP.	Pct.
DelCarmen, Spar	2	2	5	1	0	.875
Aguayo, Spartanburg	3	5	2	1	0	.875

THIRD BASEMEN

Player and Club	G.	PO.	A.	E.	DP.	Pct.
M. Miller, Ash	24	16	31	1	1	.979
REYES, Spartanburg	124	131	256	21	19	.949
Washington, Ash	38	42	69	9	6	.925
Reynolds, Greenwood	84	68	147	21	20	.911

Player and Club	G.	PO.	A.	E.	DP.	Pct.
Berra, Charleston	139	129	269	41	27	.907
Lisi, Asheville	82	72	142	25	15	.895
O'Brien, Spar	20	15	42	8	3	.877
Macha, Greenwood	62	54	100	34	10	.819

(Fewer Than Ten Games)

Player and Club	G.	PO.	A.	E.	DP.	Pct.
Aranzamendi, Gwd	5	4	10	0	1	1.000
Gaines, Asheville	2	1	2	0	1	1.000

Player and Club	G.	PO.	A.	E.	DP.	Pct.
Ryan, Greenwood	4	3	11	1	1	.933
Westlake, Greenwood	3	8	2	1	1	.909

SHORTSTOPS

Player and Club	G.	PO.	A.	E.	DP.	Pct.
Popovich, Spar	38	50	119	5	10	.971
M. Miller, Ash	10	12	15	1	3	.964
DOHERTY, Greenwood	132	223	329	35	71	.940
Norman, Charleston	128	193	381	39	50	.936
Brookens, Ash	22	27	67	7	7	.931
Ventura, Char	14	20	18	3	2	.927

Triple Play—Pinkerton.

Player and Club	G.	PO.	A.	E.	DP.	Pct.
Mattson, Spar	58	97	162	23	27	.918
Gaines, Asheville	59	92	136	21	26	.916
Pinkerton, Ash	59	105	198	29	39	.913
O'Brien, Spar	14	13	38	7	4	.879
DelCarmen, Spar	34	38	118	22	17	.876

(Fewer Than Ten Games)

Player and Club	G.	PO.	A.	E.	DP.	Pct.
Edrington, Char	2	1	2	0	0	1.000
Aranzamendi, Gwd	3	1	2	0	0	1.000
Brady, Charleston	1	1	0	0	0	1.000

Player and Club	G.	PO.	A.	E.	DP.	Pct.
Ryan, Greenwood	7	5	21	3	1	.897
Reynolds, Gwd	2	1	6	1	1	.875
Wessinger, Gwd	1	1	2	1	0	.750

OUTFIELDERS

Player and Club	G.	PO.	A.	E.	DP.	Pct.
Charboneau, Spar	40	67	3	0	0	1.000
Brookens, Ash	25	38	3	0	1	1.000
WHISENTON, Gwd*	111	173	10	3	1	.984
Linares, Greenwood	25	46	2	1	0	.980
Givler, Spartanburg	48	84	4	2	0	.978
Berger, Spar*	113	236	12	6	4	.976
McDonald, Char	124	285	8	9	3	.970
Busby, Charleston*	128	249	18	9	4	.967
Young, Greenwood	127	313	10	12	4	.964
Convertino, Spar	122	199	15	8	3	.964
Macha, Greenwood	28	48	3	2	1	.962

Triple Play—Purvis.

Player and Club	G.	PO.	A.	E.	DP.	Pct.
Stewart, Asheville	119	187	9	8	6	.961
E. Miller, Ash	116	299	18	14	4	.958
Cooper, Greenwood	128	208	17	11	5	.953
Purvis, Asheville	114	203	18	12	4	.948
Ventura, Charleston	12	16	2	1	0	.947
Rein, Charleston	122	200	8	15	5	.933
Bucci, Asheville	16	26	1	2	1	.931
Isales, Spartanburg	112	202	19	21	1	.913
Carty, Charleston	17	15	3	2	0	.900
Cotes, Charleston	12	22	0	4	0	.846
Rivera, Asheville	27	20	4	7	0	.774

OUTFIELDERS—Continued

(Fewer Than Ten Games)

Player and Club	G.	PO.	A.	E.	DP.	Pct.
Olson, Charleston	6	11	0	0	0	1.000
Hawkins, Spartanburg	9	8	0	0	0	1.000
Fulton, Charleston*	3	5	1	0	1	1.000
Reynolds, Asheville	4	4	0	0	0	1.000
DeBattista, Char	2	3	0	0	0	1.000
Russell, Asheville	3	3	0	0	0	1.000

Player and Club	G.	PO.	A.	E.	DP.	Pct.
Reyes, Spartanburg	1	1	0	0	0	1.000
Fletcher, Greenwood	8	9	2	1	1	.917
A. Jones, Greenwood	8	11	0	1	0	.917
Gaines, Asheville	9	5	0	1	0	.833
Brady, Charleston	1	0	0	1	0	.000

CATCHERS

Player and Club	G.	PO.	A.	E.	DP.	PB.	Pct.
CONNOLLY, Gwd	70	354	50	4	3	12	.990
Wick, Charleston	27	194	13	3	3	8	.986
Lucy, Spartanburg	39	180	27	3	2	10	.986
Reynolds, Ash	29	133	12	2	5	6	.986
DeMeo, Spartanburg	28	127	20	3	2	4	.980
Walker, Spar	39	230	28	7	4	10	.974
Sanchez, Spar	32	183	8	5	1	7	.974

Player and Club	G.	PO.	A.	E.	DP.	PB.	Pct.
Pena, Charleston	14	64	7	2	1	3	.973
Russell, Ash	110	638	83	21	12	7	.972
Olson, Charleston	47	244	32	8	7	15	.972
Ortiz, Charleston	43	240	27	10	4	8	.964
Putnam, Asheville	12	48	4	2	3	4	.963
Ban, Greenwood	47	267	28	12	5	5	.961
Benedict, Gwd	20	93	12	5	3	2	.955

Triple Play—Russell.

(Fewer Than Ten Games)

Player and Club	G.	PO.	A.	E.	DP.	PB.	Pct.
Keller, Greenwood	8	47	2	0	0	1	1.000
Stevens, Gwd	6	35	7	0	0	1	1.000
DeBattista, Char	5	17	3	0	0	6	1.000

Player and Club	G.	PO.	A.	E.	DP.	PB.	Pct.
Baker, Charleston	9	46	4	1	2	7	.980
Jones, Spartanburg	6	21	2	2	0	0	.920

PITCHERS

Player and Club	G.	PO.	A.	E.	DP.	Pct.
ARRINGTON, Ash	59	6	16	0	1	1.000
Titus, Greenwood*	27	5	13	0	0	1.000
Martin, Charleston*	31	4	11	0	0	1.000
Schwartz, Charleston	16	6	6	0	0	1.000
Jakubowski, Char	23	4	7	0	1	1.000
Bradford, Spar*	15	2	8	0	1	1.000
Breiby, Greenwood	15	3	6	0	1	1.000
Adams, Spartanburg	22	2	7	0	0	1.000
Williams, Charleston	26	1	8	0	0	1.000
Moock, Asheville	15	3	5	0	1	1.000
Smith, Asheville*	17	0	8	0	1	1.000
Summers, Charleston	14	3	4	0	0	1.000
Taylor, Spartanburg	11	0	6	0	0	1.000
Wolff, Spartanburg	21	0	4	0	0	1.000
Tidwell, Charleston	23	13	30	1	2	.977
Botelho, Spartanburg	20	6	21	1	0	.964
Theiss, Greenwood	36	9	13	1	2	.957
Glowzenski, Ash	22	7	14	1	0	.955
LaPointe, Spartanburg	24	4	16	1	1	.952
Kelly, Asheville	24	17	16	2	1	.943
Meistick, Gwd	30	3	13	1	0	.941
Presser, Charleston	21	10	33	3	4	.935
Free, Greenwood	25	6	23	2	1	.935
Gale, Spartanburg	26	7	20	2	3	.931
Nickerson, Spar	35	6	20	2	3	.929

Player and Club	G.	PO.	A.	E.	DP.	Pct.
Isaac, Charleston	10	7	6	1	0	.929
L. Jones, Greenwood	44	4	9	1	2	.929
Robinson, Charleston	25	16	27	4	0	.915
Soroko, Asheville	15	10	20	3	2	.909
Phillips, Greenwood	25	7	21	3	1	.903
Mazur, Charleston	24	14	32	5	2	.902
Griffin, Asheville	11	7	2	1	0	.900
Arroyo, Spartanburg*	37	1	8	1	0	.900
Dockins, Spartanburg	46	6	11	2	0	.895
Noles, Spartanburg	24	11	30	5	0	.891
Burdette, Spar*	11	2	6	1	0	.889
Clark, Charleston*	22	3	12	2	1	.882
Mirabella, Asheville*	22	6	23	4	0	.879
Carroll, Asheville	17	6	8	2	0	.875
Costello, Greenwood*	26	5	9	2	2	.875
King, Greenwood	14	3	4	1	0	.875
Hudson, Charleston	10	3	3	1	0	.857
Downs, Spartanburg	11	1	5	1	0	.857
Reavis, Charleston	20	0	5	1	1	.833
Mahler, Greenwood	31	5	18	5	1	.821
Darwin, Asheville	16	3	14	4	2	.810
Rios, Greenwood*	10	0	8	2	1	.800
Pinkus, Charleston	23	11	12	7	0	.767
McCarthy, Asheville*	36	1	9	4	1	.714
Harlee, Greenwood*	11	0	1	2	0	.333

(Fewer Than Ten Games)

Player and Club	G.	PO.	A.	E.	DP.	Pct.
Stadnika, Charleston	7	2	5	0	0	1.000
Watson, Asheville	7	1	3	0	0	1.000
Scott, Asheville	3	1	2	0	0	1.000
Leduc, Charleston	2	1	1	0	0	1.000
Howard, Charleston	5	1	1	0	1	1.000
Tapia, Charleston	6	1	1	0	0	1.000
O'Brien, Spartanburg	1	1	0	0	0	1.000
Harper, Greenwood	2	1	0	0	0	1.000
Couch, Asheville*	4	0	1	0	0	1.000
Patten, Asheville*	4	0	1	0	0	1.000

Player and Club	G.	PO.	A.	E.	DP.	Pct.
McWilliams, Gwd*	8	4	12	1	0	.941
McMurray, Asheville	5	2	4	1	0	.857
Welborn, Spartanburg	9	2	4	1	0	.857
Stein, Greenwood	6	3	5	2	2	.800
Morogiello, Gwd*	8	3	3	2	0	.750
Burkett, Charleston	5	1	2	1	0	.750
Lasek, Spartanburg	3	0	2	2	0	.500
Frye, Charleston*	4	0	1	1	0	.500
Seabol, Charleston	2	0	0	1	0	.000

The following pitchers do not have any recorded accepted chances; therefore, are not listed in the fielding averages at that position: Amancio, DeMeo, Matula, Pratt*, Rivas, Vasquez. M. Ryan appeared as a designated hitter only.

CLUB PITCHING

Club	G.	CG.	ShO.	Sv.	IP.	H.	R.	ER.	HR.	BB.	Int. BB.	HB.	SO.	WP.	Bk.	ERA.
Greenwood	139	19	7	26	1166	1169	672	523	70	576	18	46	741	66	20	4.04
Asheville	138	43	9	24	1186	1294	696	575	79	512	28	29	769	78	34	4.36
Spartanburg	139	34	3	21	1189	1269	726	583	90	529	62	61	676	90	19	4.41
Charleston	139	41	8	13	1166	1147	776	636	78	700	27	57	756	139	26	4.91

PITCHERS' RECORDS
(Leading Qualifiers for Earned-Run Average Leadership–112 or More Innings)
*Throws lefthanded.

Pitcher–Club	G.	GS.	CG.	ShO.	W.	L.	Sv.	Pct.	IP.	H.	R.	ER.	HR.	BB.	Int. BB.	HB.	SO.	WP.	ERA.
Kelly, Asheville	24	24	10	4	13	8	0	.619	170	179	79	57	8	40	3	2	105	10	3.02
Robinson, Char.	25	24	11	1	12	9	0	.571	172	146	79	62	12	64	2	7	132	12	3.24
Free, Greenwood	25	25	5	1	12	8	0	.600	157	128	78	60	9	81	1	7	125	10	3.44
Botelho, Spa	20	19	9	0	9	9	0	.500	134	120	69	54	6	49	1	6	90	5	3.63
Glowzenski, Ash	22	22	7	2	10	8	0	.556	131	131	68	56	6	56	1	3	65	9	3.85
Mirabella, Ash*	22	22	7	0	10	7	0	.588	149	149	77	66	8	69	0	2	136	10	3.99
Mazur, Charleston	24	24	7	0	10	10	0	.500	167	158	88	74	6	111	2	8	89	13	3.99
Phillips, Gwd	25	19	5	2	5	12	1	.294	137	154	80	63	9	40	0	6	73	2	4.14
LaPointe, Spa	24	16	3	1	8	9	1	.471	121	130	68	56	5	46	6	3	61	3	4.17
Gale, Spartanburg	26	26	6	1	8	10	0	.444	164	176	91	78	13	51	5	5	75	6	4.28

Departmental Leaders: G–Arrington, 59; GS–Gale, 26; CG–Robinson, 11; ShO–Kelly, 4; W–Kelly, 13; L–Noles, 16; Sv–Arrington, 18; Pct.–L. Jones, .733; IP–Robinson, 172; H–Kelly, 179; R–Noles, 110; ER–Noles, 90; HR–Gale, Noles, 13; BB–Mazur, 111; IBB–Dockins, 10; HB–Noles, 13; SO–Mirabella, 136; WP–Clark, 31.

(All Pitchers–Listed Alphabetically)

Pitcher–Club	G.	GS.	CG.	ShO.	W.	L.	Sv.	Pct.	IP.	H.	R.	ER.	HR.	BB.	Int. BB.	HB.	SO.	WP.	ERA.
Adams, Spartanburg	22	0	0	0	1	4	1	.200	38	38	21	15	2	36	9	3	17	3	3.55
Amancio, Greenwood	2	0	0	0	0	0	0	.000	3	6	5	1	1	2	0	0	2	3	3.00
Arrington, Spa	59	0	0	0	7	9	18	.438	100	112	46	44	8	44	3	0	73	6	3.96
Arroyo, Spa*	37	8	1	0	7	4	3	.636	102	102	40	30	6	28	5	2	58	7	2.65
Botelho, Spa	20	19	9	0	9	9	0	.500	134	120	69	54	6	49	1	6	90	5	3.63
Bradford, Spa*	15	15	5	1	6	3	0	.667	100	88	45	36	11	43	2	4	50	4	3.24
Breiby, Greenwood	15	5	0	0	1	2	0	.333	50	60	41	31	5	28	0	2	24	4	5.58
Burdette, Spa*	11	11	1	0	3	5	0	.375	56	82	45	40	6	24	0	1	23	6	6.43
Burkett, Charleston	5	0	0	0	0	0	0	.000	11	10	19	14	0	20	0	1	10	6	11.45
Carroll, Asheville	17	5	1	0	3	3	1	.500	54	70	43	31	4	30	2	1	30	3	5.17
Clark, Charleston*	22	19	3	1	1	13	0	.071	103	97	87	70	1	104	1	3	79	31	6.12
Costello, Gwd*	26	23	0	0	6	9	0	.400	109	129	72	58	5	48	0	0	81	6	4.79
Couch, Asheville*	4	1	0	0	1	0	0	.000	4	12	11	9	0	3	0	0	2	1	20.25
Darwin, Asheville	16	16	6	1	6	3	0	.667	102	96	54	41	8	48	0	8	76	8	3.62
DeMeo, Spartanburg	1	0	0	0	0	0	0	.000	2	4	1	1	0	1	0	0	1	0	4.50
Dockins, Spa	46	0	0	0	6	2	14	.750	66	65	31	18	0	34	10	3	49	17	2.45
Downs, Spartanburg	11	10	0	0	1	6	0	.143	46	75	57	48	12	13	0	3	8	1	9.39
Free, Greenwood	25	25	5	1	12	8	0	.600	157	128	78	60	9	81	1	7	125	10	3.44
Frye, Charleston*	4	0	0	0	1	0	0	1.000	9	12	5	5	0	6	0	0	7	4	5.00
Gale, Spartanburg	26	26	6	1	8	10	0	.444	164	176	91	78	13	51	5	5	75	6	4.28
Glowzenski, Ash	22	22	7	2	10	8	0	.556	131	131	68	56	6	56	1	3	65	9	3.85
Griffin, Asheville	11	11	3	0	6	3	0	.667	65	71	36	35	3	25	1	5	26	4	4.85
Harlee, Greenwood*	11	6	0	0	0	2	0	.000	27	28	38	34	1	49	0	2	14	2	11.33
Harper, Greenwood	2	2	0	0	1	1	0	.500	8	9	10	10	3	7	0	0	4	0	11.25
Howard, Charleston	5	1	0	0	0	0	0	.000	16	16	15	15	2	8	0	1	8	0	8.44
Hudson, Charleston	10	0	0	0	2	0	0	1.000	21	30	28	15	2	10	1	0	16	8	6.43
Isaac, Charleston	10	5	1	0	0	4	0	.000	43	45	33	26	4	27	1	0	27	6	5.44
Jakubowski, Char.	23	0	0	0	2	3	3	.400	38	37	24	21	3	19	4	3	46	2	4.97
L. Jones, Gwd	44	0	0	0	11	4	10	.733	83	69	40	32	5	33	5	9	65	3	3.47
Kelly, Asheville	24	24	10	4	13	8	0	.619	170	179	79	57	8	40	3	2	105	10	3.02
King, Greenwood	14	7	1	0	1	3	0	.250	38	42	33	21	3	31	0	3	23	8	4.97
LaPointe, Spa	24	16	3	1	8	9	1	.471	121	130	68	56	5	46	6	3	61	3	4.17
Lasek, Spartanburg	3	2	0	0	0	1	0	.000	8	11	8	4	1	3	0	0	3	3	4.50
Leduc, Charleston	2	1	0	0	0	1	0	.000	6	7	3	3	1	1	0	0	1	1	4.50
Mahler, Greenwood	31	6	1	1	6	6	2	.500	105	96	49	34	5	49	1	2	68	7	2.91
Martin, Charleston*	31	6	3	2	5	6	2	.455	75	88	55	43	7	45	3	4	39	3	5.16
Matula, Greenwood	3	0	0	0	1	0	0	1.000	6	10	5	5	2	0	0	0	8	0	7.50
Mazur, Charleston	24	24	7	0	10	10	0	.500	167	158	88	74	6	111	2	8	89	13	3.99
McCarthy, Ash*	36	2	0	0	3	3	3	.500	72	77	52	40	4	47	4	1	52	7	5.00
McMurray, Ash	5	3	0	0	1	0	0	1.000	33	34	19	13	1	7	1	0	24	1	3.55
McWilliams, Gwd*	8	8	1	0	2	2	0	.500	48	40	19	14	3	13	1	3	44	3	2.63
Meistickle, Gwd	30	1	0	0	6	4	3	.600	108	93	50	35	4	48	2	2	75	3	2.92
Mirabella, Ash*	22	22	7	0	10	7	0	.588	149	149	77	66	8	69	0	2	136	10	3.99
Moock, Asheville	15	0	0	0	1	1	0	.500	33	52	32	30	5	13	3	0	26	2	8.18
Morogiello, Gwd*	8	8	1	0	4	1	0	.800	41	41	18	15	2	23	0	2	24	0	3.29

Pitcher–Club	G.	GS.	CG.	ShO.	W.	L.	Sv.	Pct.	IP.	H.	R.	ER.	HR.	BB.	Int. BB.	HB.	SO.	WP.	ERA.
Nickerson, Spa	35	1	1	0	2	4	1	.333	117	123	64	58	10	62	8	3	76	4	4.46
Noles, Spartanburg	24	24	7	0	4	16	0	.200	137	166	110	90	13	65	6	13	95	17	5.91
O'Brien, Spa	1	0	0	0	0	1	0	.000	5	2	0	0	0	2	0	1	2	0	0.00
Patten, Asheville*	4	0	0	0	0	0	0	.000	5	9	8	6	0	3	0	0	4	0	10.80
Phillips, Gwd	25	19	5	2	5	12	1	.294	137	154	80	63	9	40	0	6	73	2	4.14
Pinkus, Charleston	23	23	6	1	9	7	0	.563	135	125	86	66	10	65	2	10	68	16	4.40
Pratt, Greenwood*	4	1	0	0	0	0	0	.000	9	10	4	4	0	7	0	1	11	2	4.00
Presser, Charleston	21	19	7	1	5	8	0	.385	130	136	77	71	12	70	2	9	67	11	4.92
Reavis, Charleston	20	0	0	0	1	2	6	.333	28	28	16	11	2	11	1	2	15	3	3.54
Rios, Greenwood*	10	4	0	0	1	4	1	.200	27	37	19	17	2	12	0	2	10	2	5.67
Rivas, Charleston	1	0	0	0	0	0	0	.000	4	2	0	0	0	1	0	0	7	1	0.00
Robinson, Char	25	24	11	1	12	9	0	.571	172	146	79	62	12	64	2	7	132	12	3.24
Schwartz, Char	16	6	2	0	3	7	0	.300	60	59	42	36	6	37	3	4	35	5	5.40
Scott, Asheville	3	0	0	0	0	0	0	.000	5	5	3	3	0	5	1	1	4	1	5.40
Seabol, Charleston	2	0	0	0	0	0	0	.000	4	9	8	8	1	9	0	1	3	1	18.00
Smith, Asheville*	17	2	0	0	1	2	1	.333	31	40	31	24	6	20	2	0	29	1	6.97
Soroko, Asheville	15	15	0	8	5	5	0	.615	95	96	47	39	5	36	1	3	49	4	3.69
Stadnika, Char	7	7	0	0	0	2	0	.000	31	30	32	24	5	26	0	0	17	3	6.97
Stein, Greenwood	6	6	1	1	1	2	0	.333	30	32	23	15	2	16	0	2	16	1	4.50
Summers, Char	14	0	0	0	2	4	0	.333	26	30	31	26	0	30	2	2	18	5	9.00
Tapia, Charleston	6	1	0	0	0	1	0	.000	20	24	18	18	1	12	0	0	10	3	8.10
Taylor, Spartanburg	11	0	0	0	2	2	0	.500	27	26	13	6	0	7	2	1	21	2	2.00
Theiss, Greenwood	36	1	1	0	8	1	9	.889	83	68	24	21	4	43	6	2	46	5	2.28
Tidwell, Asheville	23	15	4	1	7	7	0	.500	125	143	78	70	10	60	5	3	50	9	5.04
Titus, Greenwood*	27	17	3	1	9	3	0	.750	98	117	64	53	5	46	2	1	28	6	4.87
Vasquez, Charleston	4	3	1	1	2	2	0	.500	22	19	5	4	1	2	0	1	13	0	1.64
Watson, Asheville	7	0	0	0	0	1	0	.000	13	18	12	11	3	6	1	0	18	2	7.62
Welborn, Spa	9	7	1	0	1	2	0	.333	33	23	32	25	2	44	2	8	28	3	6.82
Williams, Char	26	0	0	0	4	1	2	.800	46	39	25	24	2	22	3	1	49	5	4.70
Wolff, Spartanburg	21	0	0	0	1	3	1	.250	33	38	31	24	3	21	6	5	19	9	6.55

BALKS—Darwin, Mirabella, Pinkus, 5 each; McCarthy, Noles, Soroko, 4 each; Burdette, Carroll, Harlee, Mahler, Martin, Nickerson, Robinson, Stadnika, Tapia, Titus, Welborn, Williams, 3 each; Adams, Arrington, Arroyo, Costello, Free, Gale, Glowzenski, Kelly, Moock, Stein, Tidwell, Watson, 2 each; Breiby, Clark, Hudson, Jakubowski, L. Jones, Mazur, McMurray, McWilliams, Morogiello, Presser, Rios, Summers, 1 each.

COMBINATION SHUTOUTS—Glowzenski-Arrington, Asheville; Robinson-Martin-Jakubowski, Charleston; Costello-Theiss, Greenwood.

NO-HIT GAMES—None.

Appalachian League

ROOKIE CLASSIFICATION

CHAMPIONSHIP WINNERS IN PREVIOUS YEARS

1921 – Greenville	.608	1944 – Kingsport‡	.575	1961 – Middlesboro	.591
Johnson City*	.627	1945 – Kingsport‡	.670	1962 – Bluefield	.671
1922 – Bristol	.557	1946 – New River‡	.675	1963 – Bluefield	.652
1923 – Knoxville	.635	1947 – Pulaski	.648	1964 – Johnson City	.662
1924 – Knoxville*	.642	New River (3rd)†	.516	1965 – Salem	.614
Bristol	.607	1948 – Pulaski‡	.680	1966 – Marion	.623
1925 – Greenville	.667	1949 – Bluefield‡	.721	1967 – Bluefield	.627
1926-36 – Did not operate.		1950 – Bluefield	.600	1968 – Marion	.583
1937 – Elizabethton	.559	Bluefield z	.745	1969 – Pulaski a	.576
Pennington Gap*	.580	1951 – Kingsport‡	.659	Johnson City	.544
1938 – Elizabethton	.664	1952 – Johnson City	.595	1970 – Bluefield	.638
Greenville (3rd)†	.571	Welch (3rd)†	.509	1971 – Bluefield a	.609
1939 – Elizabethton‡	.597	1953 – Welch*	.705	Kingsport	.559
1940 – Johnson City§	.726	Johnson City	.672	1972 – Bristol a	.588
Elizabethton	.750	1954 – Bluefield‡	.619	Covington	.586
1941 – Johnson City	.614	1955 – Salem**	.689	1973 – Kingsport	.757
Elizabethton*	.661	1956 – Did not operate.		1974 – Bristol a	.754
1942 – Bristol	.667	1957 – Bluefield	.701	Bluefield	.536
Bristol x	.660	1958 – Johnson City	.662	1975 – Marion	.515
1943 – Bristol	.755	1959 – Morristown	.603	Johnson City a	.603
Bristol y	.617	1960 – Wytheville	.614		

*Won split-season playoff. †Won four-team playoff. ‡Won championship and four-team playoff. §Johnson City, first-half winner, won playoff involving six clubs. xWon both halves and defeated second-place Elizabethton in playoff. yWon both halves, but Erwin won four-team playoff. zWon both halves, but Bristol won two-club playoff. **Salem and Johnson City declared playoff co-champions when weather forced cancellation of final series. aLeague was divided into Northern, Southern divisions; declared league champion, based on highest won-lost percentage.

STANDING OF CLUBS AT CLOSE OF SEASON, AUGUST 31

SOUTHERN DIVISION

Club	J.C.	Bris.	Eliz.	Kpt.	Blu.	Cov.	Pul.	Mar.	W.	L.	T.	Pct.	G.B.
Johnson City (Cardinals)	....	7	10	5	6	8	7	7	50	20	0	.714	......
Bristol (Tigers)	3	....	6	5	4	3	7	7	35	32	0	.522	13½
Elizabethton (Twins)	0	4	....	9	4	4	3	3	27	43	0	.386	23
Kingsport (Braves)	5	2	1	....	3	5	4	5	25	42	0	.373	23½

NORTHERN DIVISION

Club	J.C.	Bris.	Eliz.	Kpt.	Blu.	Cov.	Pul.	Mar.	W.	L.	T.	Pct.	G.B.
Bluefield (Orioles)	4	6	6	7	....	7	5	7	42	28	0	.600	......
Covington (Astros)	2	7	6	5	3	....	7	8	38	32	0	.543	4
Pulaski (Co-op)	3	3	7	6	5	3	....	5	32	38	0	.457	10
Marion (Mets)	3	3	7	5	3	2	5	....	28	42	0	.400	14

Johnson City declared league champion on basis of highest won-lost percentage.
NOTE: Forfeited game. Pulaski forfeited to Marion, August 30.
Major league affiliations in parentheses.

Playoff—None.

Managers: Bluefield—Ben Hines; Bristol—Joe Lewis; Covington—Julio Linares; Elizabethton—Fred Waters; Johnson City—Carlton (Buzzy) Keller; Kingsport—Bobby Dews; Marion—Thomas Egan; Pulaski—Art Mazmanian.

Regular-Season Attendance—Bluefield, 28,487; Bristol, 32,409; Covington, 17,400; Elizabethton, 17,051; Johnson City, 37,569; Kingsport, 23,742; Marion, 7,198; Pulaski, 10,430. Total, 177,286. No all-star game. No playoff.

All-Star Team: 1B—Skaalen, Bluefield; 2B—Witt, Johnson City; 3B—Klimas, Covington; SS—Trammell, Bristol; Smith, Bluefield; OF—Corey, Bluefield; V. Thomas, Bluefield; Bowman, Johnson City; C—Baldwin, Covington; P—C. Thomas, Bluefield; Olmsted, Johnson City; Miscik, Covington. Manager—Keller, Johnson City.

(Compiled by Howe News Bureau, Chicago, Ill.)

CLUB BATTING

Club	G.	AB.	R.	OR.	H.	TB.	2B.	3B.	HR.	RBI.	SH.	SF.	BB.	Int. BB.	HP.	SO.	SB.	CS.	LOB.	Pct.
Johnson City	70	2248	344	218	620	872	81	30	37	287	30	26	256	7	17	349	105	48	490	.276
Bluefield	70	2352	362	294	638	934	94	20	54	305	41	26	258	15	12	455	72	51	504	.271
Covington	70	2379	319	303	581	800	89	17	32	273	10	18	267	11	18	464	46	40	524	.244
Marion	70	2166	285	320	522	748	76	21	36	228	17	14	255	10	12	447	58	36	473	.241
Kingsport	67	2157	255	291	502	669	77	15	20	211	27	17	255	8	20	415	49	25	483	.233
Pulaski	70	2229	286	350	515	692	84	21	17	208	17	23	324	12	16	448	103	19	510	.231
Elizabethton	70	2294	283	349	506	662	65	14	21	217	7	16	306	5	21	475	57	9	512	.221
Bristol	67	2019	235	244	434	584	61	16	19	194	17	5	296	9	17	452	67	33	440	.215

INDIVIDUAL BATTING
(Leading Qualifiers for Batting Championship—189 or More Plate Appearances)
*Bats lefthanded. †Switch-hitter.

Player and Club	G.	AB.	R.	H.	TB.	2B.	3B.	HR.	RBI.	SH.	SF.	BB.	HP.	SO.	SB.	CS.	Pct.
Corey, Mark, Bluefield	70	285	62	114	191	10	8	17	59	0	2	25	0	57	14	8	.400
Penniall, David, Johnson C	45	171	33	65	105	14	4	6	32	1	4	19	0	19	10	2	.380
Witt, Harold, Johnson City	66	224	44	77	129	10	3	12	40	7	2	31	5	50	12	3	.344
Thomas, Vernon, Bluefield	70	259	40	82	137	19	3	10	39	3	1	27	2	64	7	5	.317
Klimas, Phillip, Covington	70	247	48	73	118	18	3	7	47	0	4	53	2	50	3	1	.296
Smith, James L., Bluefield	70	262	46	76	107	14	1	5	35	7	8	31	1	47	7	4	.290
Bowman, William, Johnson C*	58	201	32	58	94	7	7	5	34	0	0	21	1	35	7	2	.289
Warren, Charles, Marion*	62	205	34	59	84	7	6	2	20	1	2	25	1	33	6	2	.288
Baldwin, Reginald, Covington	63	245	37	70	112	8	2	10	54	1	2	8	1	17	2	3	.286
Fisher, Curtis, Marion	65	201	31	57	91	11	1	7	33	0	3	35	1	35	4	0	.284

Departmental Leaders: G—Corey, A. Davis, Klimas, Pankovits, K. Paris, Skaalen, J. Smith, V. Thomas, 70; AB—Corey, 285; R—Corey, 62; H—Corey, 114; TB—Corey, 191; 2B—V. Thomas, 19; 3B—Corey, 8; HR—Corey, 17; RBI—Corey, 59; SH—A. Davis, 8; SF—Skaalen, J. Smith, 8; BB—Klimas, 53; HP—Ennis, 6; SO—Thurberg, 69; SB—Spain, 22; CS—Mota, 13.

(All Players—Listed Alphabetically)

Player and Club	G.	AB.	R.	H.	TB.	2B.	3B.	HR.	RBI.	SH.	SF.	BB.	HP.	SO.	SB.	CS.	Pct.
Adolphus, Maximo, Bluefield	8	25	3	6	6	0	0	0	0	0	0	2	0	7	0	0	.240
Albright, Gary, Bluefield	6	11	2	2	2	0	0	0	3	1	1	1	0	4	0	0	.182
Alfaro, Juan, Pulaski	27	82	9	23	28	5	0	0	9	2	1	13	0	0	2	0	.280
Allen, Warren, Elizabethton	54	184	28	42	48	2	2	0	14	0	1	27	3	23	1	1	.228
Angulo, Aquiles, Covington	22	68	4	10	11	1	0	0	4	0	0	2	0	17	3	3	.147
Armer, Richter, Marion	27	76	10	16	29	2	1	3	8	0	0	4	0	17	3	3	.211
Ashline, Steven, Marion	11	35	7	7	9	0	1	0	5	1	1	4	2	2	3	1	.200
Ashlock, Howard, 11 Blu-14 Pul*	25	31	2	2	2	0	0	0	2	0	0	2	0	13	0	0	.065
Bacon, Mike, Elizabethton	30	103	6	28	32	4	0	0	17	0	2	11	1	19	0	1	.272
Bagley, James, Kingsport	60	210	28	42	58	6	5	0	18	2	2	11	0	24	7	2	.200
Bailey, Matthew, Kingsport	58	179	27	38	48	8	1	0	14	5	2	34	2	36	1	2	.212
Baker, Curtis, Marion	29	91	7	20	24	4	0	0	5	2	0	7	1	15	2	2	.220
Baker, James A., Marion*	46	139	16	33	47	5	3	1	13	0	0	17	1	41	1	6	.237
Baldwin, Reginald, Covington	63	245	37	70	112	8	2	10	54	1	2	8	1	17	2	3	.286
Ballard, Glenn, Pulaski	40	100	13	16	21	1	2	0	7	1	1	20	0	13	2	0	.160
Beltre, Sergio, Marion	25	67	7	12	19	2	1	1	5	2	0	4	0	16	2	1	.179
Benedict, Bruce, Kingsport	17	63	10	18	19	1	0	0	4	1	0	10	1	5	0	1	.286
Benevento, Peter, Pulaski*	38	71	11	16	17	1	0	0	2	2	0	15	0	22	11	2	.225
Blakeley, Gordon, Bristol	67	221	27	56	72	9	2	1	31	0	2	41	3	39	1	1	.253
Blankmeyer, Edward, Pul*	10	20	3	3	6	3	0	0	5	1	2	5	0	3	0	0	.150
Bowman, William, Johnson C*	58	201	32	58	94	7	7	5	34	0	0	21	1	35	7	2	.289
Boyer, Raymond, Kingsport	24	82	11	21	24	3	0	0	11	0	1	10	2	8	4	0	.256
Brasher, Robert, Kingsport*	62	227	19	62	91	9	1	6	32	3	0	13	1	35	4	2	.273
Breivogel, Richard, Bri*	1	1	0	0	0	0	0	0	0	0	0	1	0	1	0	0	.000
Brigham, James, Bristol*	55	194	24	40	45	3	1	0	11	1	0	24	0	42	15	2	.206
Brock, Dale, Johnson City*	66	237	42	65	80	9	3	0	23	6	2	40	1	25	13	6	.274
Brooks, David A., Covington	1	0	0	0	0	0	0	0	0	0	0	1	0	0	0	0	.000
Bryant, Dwight, Kingsport	54	182	27	44	54	3	2	1	14	2	0	20	3	49	14	3	.242
Bryant, Robert, Marion*	7	21	4	9	15	1	1	1	7	0	0	4	0	3	0	0	.429
Cardwell, Elmer, Marion	47	148	17	35	50	4	1	3	18	0	0	24	0	31	5	1	.236
Carter, Gregory, Bristol	32	107	14	24	44	8	0	4	16	0	0	16	0	31	5	3	.224
Carty, Landre, Kingsport	2	4	0	1	1	0	0	0	0	0	0	0	0	0	0	0	.250
Castleberry, Robert, Bri	41	104	6	19	22	1	1	0	3	3	0	5	1	30	0	2	.183
Catanese, Paul, Eliz	35	110	12	26	28	2	0	0	6	0	2	10	0	34	2	3	.236
Chapman, Kevin, Marion	62	219	33	59	76	7	2	2	15	1	2	22	3	22	12	5	.269
Christian, Steven, Eliz	39	99	10	20	21	1	0	0	10	0	2	4	0	17	3	0	.202
Cias, Darryll, Bluefield	38	131	8	24	30	4	1	0	10	2	1	8	0	29	0	2	.183
Cloherty, John, Covington*	45	130	24	34	46	3	3	1	17	0	1	32	1	26	1	1	.262
Comoletti, Glenn, Johnson C*	1	1	0	0	0	0	0	0	0	0	0	0	0	0	0	0	.000

Player and Club	G.	AB.	R.	H.	TB.	2B.	3B.	HR.	RBI.	SH.	SF.	BB.	HP.	SO.	SB.	CS.	Pct.
Corey, Mark, Bluefield	70	285	62	114	191	10	8	17	59	0	2	25	0	57	14	8	.400
Curbelo, Jorge, Elizabethton	31	95	10	20	23	3	0	0	8	1	1	8	0	10	0	0	.211
Dalton, Richard, Eliz	67	258	24	52	60	8	0	0	16	0	0	25	1	23	4	1	.202
Darichuk, Greg, Bristol*	45	128	11	26	36	4	0	2	19	0	1	11	3	21	1	1	.203
Davis, Andrew, Bluefield†	70	269	55	62	76	6	1	2	11	8	0	44	1	42	14	7	.230
Davis, George H., Bristol*	43	137	21	40	55	7	1	2	29	1	1	26	4	29	6	4	.292
Davis, Jody, Marion	50	164	20	38	60	5	1	5	19	0	1	13	0	32	0	2	.232
de la Cruz, Miguelito, Pul	22	30	5	7	7	0	0	0	2	0	0	4	0	10	0	0	.233
Diaz, Vicente, Bristol	33	108	16	23	32	6	0	1	10	1	0	8	0	17	5	2	.213
Diering, Charles, Johnson C	55	191	23	47	65	5	5	1	18	2	3	20	1	33	6	9	.246
Douglas, Lawrence, Bristol	8	11	0	0	0	0	0	0	0	0	0	2	0	4	0	1	.000
Douglas, Stephen, Eliz	3	10	0	1	1	0	0	0	0	0	0	0	0	3	0	0	.100
Ennis, Jerry, Elizabethton	63	215	31	44	55	9	1	0	23	1	2	48	6	45	12	0	.205
Ferrer, Gabriel, Marion*	1	3	1	0	0	0	0	0	0	0	0	1	0	1	0	0	.000
Fisher, Curtis, Marion	65	201	31	57	91	11	1	7	33	0	3	35	1	35	4	0	.284
Forbes, Andres, Kingsport	3	7	1	2	2	0	0	0	0	0	0	4	0	1	1	0	.286
Frandsen, Allan, Pulaski*	38	95	13	25	29	2	1	0	8	1	1	17	0	18	4	2	.263
Fuentes, Frank, Johnson City	4	10	1	2	2	0	0	0	0	0	0	0	0	4	0	0	.200
Funderburk, Mark, Eliz	61	225	25	53	89	7	4	7	33	0	0	21	1	63	1	0	.236
Gardner, Charles, Covington	36	118	9	23	24	1	0	0	7	0	0	8	0	17	3	2	.195
Gomez, Carlos, Marion	20	35	8	7	8	1	0	0	0	0	0	8	0	16	2	0	.200
Grant, Robert, Marion	31	65	5	14	14	0	0	0	7	0	1	18	1	8	2	1	.215
Graser, Dennis, Eliz*	33	108	21	25	38	5	1	2	17	0	2	36	1	23	0	0	.231
Greenstein, Stuart, Marion	30	102	16	30	40	4	0	2	13	1	0	7	0	18	4	1	.294
Gustave, Michael, Eliz*	57	179	22	39	46	3	2	0	14	3	1	14	1	25	9	0	.218
Hakala, Keith, Bristol	48	147	17	31	45	4	2	2	15	3	0	23	1	22	2	3	.211
Hallgren, Robert, Covington*	55	214	29	50	72	11	1	3	19	0	1	16	2	37	2	3	.234
Hernandez, Gabriel, Bristol*	26	66	5	11	16	0	1	1	2	0	0	4	3	30	0	0	.167
Hicks, Joseph W., Kingsport	30	103	9	26	34	3	1	1	10	1	0	8	0	25	4	0	.252
Hogan, Jeffrey, Bristol*	1	1	1	0	0	0	0	0	0	0	0	0	0	0	1	0	.000
Holcomb, Donald, Eliz	11	35	2	4	4	0	0	0	0	0	0	2	0	9	0	0	.114
Hubbard, Glenn, Kingsport	37	136	29	40	54	8	0	2	15	2	3	18	1	16	2	3	.294
Huddleston, Eldgre, Kpt*	61	202	16	46	61	7	4	0	16	3	1	20	2	48	5	6	.228
Hudson, Aaron, Kingsport	41	111	10	13	26	4	0	3	14	1	0	21	2	46	0	2	.117
Hunsaker, Frank, Johnson C	30	89	11	29	35	3	0	1	16	1	1	14	1	6	1	0	.326
Ithier, Michael, Pulaski*	34	93	7	19	28	2	2	1	5	0	1	9	1	27	0	2	.204
Janney, Barry, Pulaski	67	255	30	70	106	9	3	7	33	2	3	13	3	63	6	0	.275
Jaskowski, John, Pulaski	38	88	9	17	24	4	0	1	12	0	0	12	1	24	1	0	.193
Johnson, Jerry D., Johnson C	49	155	15	34	46	4	1	2	9	1	0	10	0	33	2	1	.219
Johnson, Randall, Bluefield	29	109	15	21	30	4	1	1	13	3	0	14	1	19	2	3	.193
Johnson, Scott D., Bristol	35	101	7	15	18	3	0	0	7	1	0	17	1	22	3	2	.149
Keller, Charles, Kingsport	41	152	20	55	88	15	0	6	25	0	1	25	2	21	1	1	.362
Kennedy, Kevin, Bluefield	21	81	9	22	29	4	0	1	10	2	0	10	0	9	1	0	.272
King, Luis, Covington†	5	4	0	2	3	1	0	0	0	0	0	0	0	1	0	0	.500
Klimas, Phillip, Covington	70	247	48	73	118	18	3	7	47	0	4	53	2	50	3	1	.296
Kopatich, Richard, Bristol	7	7	0	1	1	0	0	0	0	0	0	3	0	3	0	0	.143
LaFountain, James, Eliz	60	199	24	45	81	9	0	9	30	0	2	32	2	43	1	0	.226
Lamb, Randolph, Covington	38	126	15	33	39	6	0	0	12	4	3	21	0	18	3	1	.262
Lane, Frederick, Covington	3	6	0	1	1	0	0	0	0	0	0	0	0	2	0	0	.167
Leader, Ramon, Covington*	48	159	7	40	45	5	0	0	17	1	0	6	0	31	5	5	.252
Martinez, Herman, Bluefield	4	16	2	3	5	0	1	0	0	0	0	0	0	6	2	0	.188
Martinson, Evon, 13 Pul-49 Blu	62	202	21	53	65	2	2	2	25	6	3	21	0	28	2	3	.262
McCann, Thomas, Covington	4	5	0	1	2	1	0	0	0	0	0	1	0	4	0	0	.200
McComb, Mitchell, Bluefield	27	50	4	10	11	1	0	0	2	1	0	3	2	15	1	1	.200
McDougal, Ricky, Pulaski	29	97	10	24	27	3	0	0	10	0	3	9	0	14	3	1	.247
Minier, Roberto, Pulaski	54	165	20	40	72	12	1	6	22	0	1	25	0	50	1	0	.242
Mitchell, G. Hunt, Pul†	13	38	5	4	4	0	0	0	0	0	0	10	0	5	4	0	.105
Montejano, Richard, JC.	1	0	0	0	0	0	0	0	0	1	0	0	0	0	0	0	.000
Morales, Lester, Marion	24	73	10	18	22	4	0	0	5	2	0	4	0	16	0	1	.247
Mota, Jose, Covington†	57	230	30	56	64	4	2	0	11	3	1	25	4	40	7	13	.243
Murphy, James, Marion	19	58	6	14	24	4	0	2	6	1	0	6	0	17	1	0	.241
Murray, E. Leon, Bluefield†	3	3	0	1	1	0	0	0	0	0	0	0	0	0	0	0	.333
Nelson, Erik, Pulaski*	37	55	9	13	13	0	0	0	4	0	1	19	0	6	2	0	.236
Niffenegger, James, Pulaski	61	195	40	39	62	9	7	0	18	1	3	50	1	38	8	1	.200
Nolan, Roger, Johnson City	38	120	11	36	41	3	1	0	17	2	1	14	1	20	10	5	.300
Northrup, John, Bristol	5	15	5	8	9	1	0	0	2	0	0	4	0	1	0	0	.533
Olivares, Ramon, Bluefield	3	7	1	1	4	0	0	1	1	0	0	1	0	4	0	0	.143
Ornest, Michael, Pulaski*	5	9	1	2	2	0	0	0	1	0	0	2	0	3	0	0	.222
Pankovits, James, Covington	70	275	50	68	96	9	2	5	31	1	4	34	2	49	3	4	.247
Pappageorgas, Robert, Marion	54	183	18	45	66	10	1	3	23	5	2	13	1	23	1	7	.246
Paris, Bret, Johnson City†	45	143	26	32	46	4	2	2	16	3	0	17	0	26	6	4	.224
Paris, Kelly, Johnson City†	70	247	40	68	96	7	3	5	30	1	5	37	2	28	20	8	.275
Penniall, David, Johnson C	45	171	33	65	105	14	4	6	32	1	4	19	0	19	10	2	.380
Perez, Hector, Covington	15	22	2	2	3	1	0	0	4	0	0	1	0	10	0	0	.091
Plante, Gerald, Pulaski	37	82	12	12	22	3	2	1	7	0	0	14	1	26	7	1	.146

Player and Club	G.	AB.	R.	H.	TB.	2B.	3B.	HR.	RBI.	SH.	SF.	BB.	HP.	SO.	SB.	CS.	Pct.
Polanco, Rodrigo, Kingsport	1	1	0	0	0	0	0	0	0	0	0	0	0	0	0	0	.000
Pritchett, Dennis, Johnson C	13	29	2	6	8	2	0	0	2	0	0	3	1	7	0	1	.207
Rajsich, Gary, Covington*	66	244	33	54	86	8	3	6	27	0	0	27	3	61	13	2	.221
Rinden, Ronnie, Pulaski*	51	145	19	30	33	1	1	0	10	2	2	28	2	33	21	2	.207
Rios, Yamil, Bluefield	11	11	1	1	2	1	0	0	0	1	0	3	0	5	0	1	.091
Rivera, Carlos, Pulaski	34	98	9	18	21	3	0	0	10	0	0	10	3	20	6	2	.184
Roberge, Bertrand, Cov	2	3	1	1	1	0	0	0	0	0	0	1	0	0	0	0	.333
Roberts, William, Covington	9	22	3	9	12	3	0	0	3	0	0	3	0	0	0	1	.409
Romero, John, Bristol	45	167	15	29	41	2	2	2	13	1	1	15	0	25	6	2	.174
Roof, Eugene, Johnson C†	53	174	21	39	49	4	0	2	28	4	4	10	3	29	2	1	.224
Sabino, Manuel, Kingsport	11	29	3	6	7	1	0	0	0	0	0	2	1	14	0	0	.207
Sampson, Steven, Eliz	7	20	2	5	5	0	0	0	2	0	0	3	0	3	0	0	.250
Seoanee, Isaac, Kingsport	50	167	14	31	34	3	0	0	16	2	2	26	0	22	0	0	.186
Silva, Jorge, Bluefield	7	9	1	2	3	1	0	0	2	1	0	0	0	2	0	0	.222
Skaalen, James, Bluefield	70	263	48	73	118	15	0	10	54	2	8	37	1	35	6	5	.278
Smith, David S., Covington	1	2	0	0	0	0	0	0	0	0	0	0	0	1	0	0	.000
Smith, James L., Bluefield	70	262	46	76	107	14	1	5	35	7	8	31	1	47	7	4	.290
Spain, Daniel, Eliz*	60	230	40	65	79	10	2	0	13	1	1	31	4	46	22	2	.283
Spies, Gary, Elizabethton	17	43	4	6	7	1	0	0	3	0	0	7	0	15	0	0	.140
Stewart, William, Kingsport	34	97	5	13	14	1	0	0	5	1	0	4	0	32	0	1	.134
Suggs, Alvin, Marion*	7	18	4	4	4	0	0	0	3	0	1	2	0	4	4	0	.222
Switzer, William, Bristol	3	6	0	1	1	0	0	0	0	0	0	1	0	3	0	0	.167
Thomas, Clint, Bluefield	1	3	0	0	0	0	0	0	0	0	0	1	0	0	0	0	.000
Thomas, Lynd, Bluefield*	51	125	21	24	38	6	1	2	13	2	0	19	2	33	4	1	.192
Thomas, Randall, Johnson C	40	158	31	43	54	6	1	1	10	1	2	11	1	16	14	6	.272
Thomas, Tonus, Marion	18	53	6	8	11	0	0	1	3	0	0	5	1	21	2	0	.151
Thomas, Vernon, Bluefield	70	259	40	82	137	19	3	10	39	3	1	27	2	64	7	5	.317
Thurberg, Thomas, Marion	57	169	13	31	48	4	2	3	18	0	1	28	0	69	2	3	.183
Torres, Jose Perez, Pulaski	51	164	19	58	75	14	0	1	15	1	2	8	4	11	3	0	.354
Trammell, Alan, Bristol	41	140	27	38	44	2	2	0	7	3	0	26	0	20	8	6	.271
Tryon, Donald, Elizabethton	24	58	8	13	14	1	0	0	4	1	0	3	0	17	1	0	.224
Valdez, R. Rafael, Johnson C	10	40	4	6	6	0	0	0	5	0	0	2	0	7	1	0	.150
Vaughn, Stephen, Bristol	51	149	16	30	38	2	3	0	7	1	0	26	1	45	13	3	.201
Warren, Charles, Marion*	62	205	34	59	84	7	6	2	20	1	2	25	1	33	6	2	.288
Weinkofsky, Charles, Bristol	47	145	17	33	49	7	0	3	17	1	0	25	0	36	1	1	.228
Wessinger, James, Kingsport	66	215	27	44	54	5	1	1	17	4	5	29	3	32	6	2	.205
White, Vincent, Pulaski	49	152	19	38	42	4	0	0	10	2	0	16	0	25	20	4	.250
Wiedenbauer, Thomas, Cov	55	193	21	40	50	8	1	0	14	0	1	17	0	53	2	0	.207
Wiencek, Gary, Bristol	26	70	6	9	16	2	1	1	5	0	0	18	0	31	0	0	.129
Williams, Antonio, Cov	13	23	2	2	3	1	0	0	2	0	1	1	1	12	0	2	.087
Williams, Dallas, Bluefield*	69	256	26	69	88	8	1	3	30	3	3	12	2	51	12	11	.270
Willeford, Jerry, Cov*	17	51	4	12	12	0	0	0	4	0	0	9	2	12	1	1	.235
Wilson, James, Elizabethton	16	48	6	9	14	0	1	1	5	0	0	7	1	23	0	0	.188
Witt, Harold, Johnson City	66	224	44	77	129	10	3	12	40	7	2	31	5	50	12	3	.344
Wolf, Richard, Marion	15	18	1	2	3	0	0	0	0	0	0	4	0	0	0	0	.111
Wylie, Anthony, Marion	4	13	1	3	3	0	0	0	1	0	1	0	2	2	0	0	.231
Yarborough, Donald, Eliz	25	75	8	9	17	1	2	2	0	0		16	0	34	1	1	.120
Zaya, Felipe, Johnson City	18	59	8	13	16	3	0	0	7	0	2	7	0	10	1	0	.220
Zentgraf, Anthony, Pulaski	44	134	17	31	42	7	2	0	13	1	1	19	0	23	2	2	.231

The following pitchers had no plate appearances primarily through use of designated hitters, listed alphabetically by club, games in parentheses:

BLUEFIELD—Allegrezza, Craig (24); Diekmann, Arthur (2); Fedoris, Steven (2); Kelly, Timothy (29); Lindal, Michael (12); Luna, Darwin (5); Neimeyer, Jack (5); Rohena, Wilberto (9); Torrez, Pete (19); Vallejos, Juan (2); Vasquez, Aquilino (8).

BRISTOL—Bell, Tyrone (4); Black, Gregory (3); Bradley, Scott (10); Burns, Michael (13); Corr, Larry (14); Felker, Kurt (2); Grafton, Garry (8); Halstead, David (11); Hayes, Melvin (6); Henderson, Thomas (13); McLaughlin, Joseph (2); Meyers, Kenneth (9); Petry, Daniel (14); Rivera, Jorge (6); Thomas, Donald E. (10); Weaver, Roger (13); Zimmerman, Dennis (17).

COVINGTON—Andersen, Edward (11); Aponte, Carmen (7); Aragon, Reinaldo (11); Bannister, Floyd (3); Corness, D. Wayne (9); Green, Larry (15); Jackson, Douglas (5); Miscik, Dennis (13); Ploucher, George (16); Salas, Roberto P. (5); Steen, Thomas (12).

ELIZABETHTON—Altman, John (9); Barstad, Eric (11); Border, Bob (18); Dobberstein, Bruce (2); Dobbs, Gary (10); Felton, Terry (14); Franz, Robert (8); Hypes, Steven (12); Ingram, David (12); Jones, John T. (4); Luedtke, Edward (13); Parrott, Stephen (11); Petrowitz, Daniel (5); Serum, Gary (6); Stanfield, Kevin (9); Tomasiak, Mark (12); Williams, Brett (9).

JOHNSON CITY—Arthur, James (11); Bugden, Gerald (3); Cruz, Victor (12); Grassano, Kenneth (8); Gray, Terry (13); Jacob, Terrence (8); Littlefield, John (14); Martinez, Nicolas (10); Morrissey, Kevin (13); Olmsted, Alan (14); Propst, James (11); Schopp, William (2).

KINGSPORT—Amancio, Ramon (12); Breiby, David (1); Bruno, Fernando (1); Chiti, H. Dominic (12); Culbreth, Jeffrey (16); Duncan, Dwight (1); Guzenski, Gordon (15); Marietta, Dean (13); Matula, Richard (20); Morogiello, Daniel (5); Pettaway, Felix (9); Pratt, Louis (9); Sams, Andre (5); Scruggs, Audrey (2); Tonkin, Wyatt (15).

MARION—Allen, Neil (6); Biehl, David (7); Cacciatore, Paul (10); Coppol, Carmen (25); Corrado, Gary (3); Grote, Robert (12); Joseph, Gilbert (16); Mitchell, Michael (9); Owen, David (19); Pearson, Donald (13); Robinson, Martin (2); Rodriguez (L), Juan (6); Rodriguez, Richard (14); Simon, Willie (3); Tanner, Michael (12); Von Ohlen, David (5).

PULASKI—Bordley, Arthur (14); Espinoza, Patrico (14); Ferrell, Kent (4); Fletcher, C. Scott (2); Garcia, Bartolome (15); Javie, Steven (7); Johnson, Philip (13); Long, Michael (3); Noonan, John (12); Pensiero, Russell (11); Presley, William (16); Rosario, Jose (9); Talerico, Amedeo (5).

TWO CLUBS—Welch, Robert (6 Pulaski-4 Bluefield).

GRAND-SLAM HOME RUNS—G. Davis, Greenstein, Pankovits, Skaalen, 1 each.

AWARDED FIRST BASE ON INTERFERENCE—L. Thomas 2 (J. Davis, S. Johnson); Catanese (J. Johnson), S. Johnson (Cloherty), Stewart (J. Davis).

CLUB FIELDING

Club	G.	PO.	A.	E.	DP.	PB.	Pct.	Club	G.	PO.	A.	E.	DP.	PB.	Pct.
Johnson City	70	1787	751	87	64	10	.967	Elizabethton	70	1837	717	122	55	22	.954
Bluefield	70	1844	681	103	45	12	.961	Marion	70	1706	708	127	45	7	.950
Kingsport	67	1709	738	107	53	19	.958	Covington	70	1850	878	148	73	19	.949
Bristol	67	1689	745	107	54	18	.958	Pulaski	70	1794	648	150	28	16	.942

Triple Play—Kingsport.

INDIVIDUAL FIELDING
FIRST BASEMEN

*Throws lefthanded.

Player and Club	G.	PO.	A.	E.	DP.	Pct.	Player and Club	G.	PO.	A.	E.	DP.	Pct.
Jaskowski, Pulaski	32	186	12	0	7	1.000	Fisher, Marion*	63	505	24	8	34	.985
Frandsen, Pulaski*	9	69	0	0	5	1.000	Keller, Kingsport	36	346	20	6	28	.984
Cloherty, Covington	4	33	3	0	3	1.000	Darichuk, Bristol*	40	351	13	6	21	.984
Wylie, Marion	3	31	2	0	1	1.000	LaFountain, Eliz	7	63	0	1	6	.984
Lamb, Covington	1	11	1	0	3	1.000	Graser, Eliz	25	226	12	4	18	.983
L. Thomas, Blue*	1	7	2	0	0	1.000	Rajsich, Covington*	66	649	75	14	58	.981
Ithier, Pulaski*	1	4	0	0	0	1.000	Murphy, Marion	6	39	1	1	2	.976
Bagley, Kingsport	1	2	1	0	0	1.000	Minier, Pulaski	43	353	12	10	11	.973
White, Pulaski	1	2	0	0	0	1.000	Weinkofsky, Bristol	31	249	11	8	20	.970
Bacon, Elizabethton	15	145	8	1	9	.994	Christian, Eliz	24	186	11	9	17	.956
SKAALEN, Bluefield	69	583	42	5	36	.992	Brasher, Kingsport*	6	48	2	3	3	.943
K. Paris, Johnson C	70	621	43	7	57	.990	Wiencek, Bristol	2	12	0	1	1	.923
Stewart, Kingsport	26	196	8	3	17	.986	Ashlock, Pulaski*	1	10	0	1	0	.909

Triple Play—Stewart.

SECOND BASEMEN

Player and Club	G.	PO.	A.	E.	DP.	Pct.	Player and Club	G.	PO.	A.	E.	DP.	Pct.
Niffenegger, Pul	3	4	3	0	1	1.000	Davis, Bluefield	69	159	175	19	23	.946
Allen, Elizabethton	5	2	4	0	2	1.000	Tryon, Elizabethton	7	17	16	2	3	.943
Johnson, Bluefield	1	1	1	0	0	1.000	Witt, Johnson City	62	130	162	18	42	.942
McComb, Bluefield	3	2	0	0	0	1.000	B. Paris, Johnson C	10	23	18	3	1	.932
King, Covington	1	1	0	0	0	1.000	Ashline, Marion	2	5	8	1	2	.929
Lamb, Covington	1	1	0	0	0	1.000	Gomez, Marion	13	14	21	3	3	.921
Hubbard, Kingsport	37	96	122	1	25	.995	Mitchell, Pulaski	6	13	10	2	0	.920
CHAPMAN, Marion	61	138	164	8	24	.974	Zentgraf, Pulaski	38	59	83	13	10	.916
Ennis, Elizabethton	63	172	157	10	42	.971	Benevento, Pulaski	30	29	34	6	4	.913
Hakala, Bristol	47	100	140	8	16	.968	Forbes, Kingsport	2	5	3	1	0	.889
Romero, Bristol	16	41	40	3	14	.964	Douglas, Bristol	7	10	10	3	3	.870
Pankovits, Cov	70	165	212	18	47	.954	Blankmeyer, Pulaski	6	9	15	7	0	.774
Hicks, Kingsport	28	71	77	8	17	.949							

THIRD BASEMEN

Player and Club	G.	PO.	A.	E.	DP.	Pct.	Player and Club	G.	PO.	A.	E.	DP.	Pct.
Wolf, Marion	2	5	2	0	1	1.000	Johnson, Bluefield	27	21	46	6	4	.918
Zentgraf, Pulaski	3	1	4	0	0	1.000	Bailey, Kingsport	57	52	109	15	6	.915
Wessinger, Kingsport	1	2	2	0	0	1.000	Cardwell, Marion	42	29	64	9	5	.912
Benevento, Pulaski	2	1	2	0	0	1.000	Diering, Johnson C	11	8	26	4	4	.895
Gomez, Marion	1	0	1	0	0	1.000	Hudson, Kingsport	17	14	33	6	4	.887
Huddleston, Kingsport	1	0	1	0	0	1.000	B. Paris, Johnson C	13	7	22	4	4	.879
Hakala, Bristol	2	0	1	0	0	1.000	Bacon, Elizabethton	12	5	22	4	0	.871
DALTON, Eliz	47	43	96	6	7	.959	Cias, Bluefield	38	22	65	15	3	.853
C. Baker, Marion	18	12	33	3	3	.938	Tryon, Elizabethton	11	9	16	5	2	.833
Murphy, Marion	12	11	19	2	1	.938	Holcomb, Eliz	7	10	14	6	3	.800
Janney, Pulaski	66	71	145	16	7	.931	McComb, Bluefield	7	4	8	3	0	.800
Klimas, Covington	70	72	178	21	18	.923	Ornest, Pulaski	1	0	3	1	0	.750
Blakeley, Bristol	67	51	127	15	11	.922	Hicks, Kingsport	1	0	2	1	0	.667
Roof, Johnson City	50	35	103	12	11	.920	Torres, Pulaski	1	0	2	1	0	.667

SHORTSTOPS

Player and Club	G.	PO.	A.	E.	DP.	Pct.	Player and Club	G.	PO.	A.	E.	DP.	Pct.
Lane, Covington	3	5	6	0	1	1.000	Alfaro, Pulaski	12	20	16	3	5	.923
Bailey, Kingsport	1	2	1	0	1	1.000	Allen, Elizabethton	50	75	145	19	24	.921
Diering, Johnson C	1	0	2	0	0	1.000	Wessinger, Kingsport	65	98	203	26	39	.920
Wiencek, Bristol	1	1	1	0	0	1.000	Gardner, Covington	36	50	130	16	26	.918
Wolf, Marion	1	1	1	0	0	1.000	Dalton, Elizabethton	22	28	61	8	5	.918
Carty, Kingsport	2	2	0	0	0	1.000	Zaya, Johnson City	12	10	34	4	6	.917
Thomas, Johnson C	40	55	135	7	22	.964	C. Baker, Marion	10	10	14	3	0	.889
B. Paris, Johnson C	18	20	50	3	6	.959	Lamb, Covington	36	51	87	21	16	.868
SMITH, Bluefield	69	101	206	14	24	.956	Niffenegger, Pul	56	69	133	32	9	.863
Ashline, Marion	8	11	29	2	5	.952	Mitchell, Pulaski	7	10	17	6	1	.818
Romero, Bristol	27	30	83	7	9	.942	Torres, Pulaski	1	6	3	2	1	.818
Trammell, Bristol	41	59	131	12	18	.941	Christian, Eliz	1	1	3	1	0	.800
Pappageorgas, Mar	54	77	168	17	27	.935	McComb, Bluefield	2	1	2	2	0	.600

Triple Play—Wessinger.

OUTFIELDERS

Player and Club	G.	PO.	A.	E.	DP.	Pct.	Player and Club	G.	PO.	A.	E.	DP.	Pct.
Davis, Bristol	43	54	2	0	1	1.000	Funderburk, Eliz	61	82	8	4	1	.957
Torres, Pulaski	32	46	3	0	0	1.000	Warren, Marion*	62	81	3	4	0	.955
Boyer, Kingsport	24	35	2	0	0	1.000	Beltre, Marion	24	39	1	2	0	.952
Wiencek, Bristol	20	30	1	0	1	1.000	Diering, Johnson C	41	69	6	4	2	.949
Brasher, Kingsport*	18	18	0	0	0	1.000	Gustave, Eliz	50	82	7	5	0	.947
Angulo, Covington	15	14	0	0	0	1.000	Greenstein, Marion	16	30	4	2	0	.944
B. Paris, Johnson C	3	9	0	0	0	1.000	Frandsen, Pulaski*	26	32	2	2	1	.944
Roberts, Covington	7	5	2	0	0	1.000	Vaughn, Bristol	50	96	2	6	0	.942
Northrup, Bristol	4	5	1	0	0	1.000	Valdez, Johnson C	8	15	0	1	0	.938
Ferrer, Marion*	1	2	1	0	0	1.000	Bagley, Kingsport	56	127	7	9	2	.937
Roberge, Covington	1	3	0	0	0	1.000	Thurberg, Marion	57	94	8	7	3	.936
Silva, Bluefield	4	3	0	0	0	1.000	Armer, Marion	24	27	1	2	0	.933
Murray, Bluefield	1	2	0	0	0	1.000	Thomas, Marion	15	14	0	1	0	.933
Rios, Bluefield	6	2	0	0	0	1.000	Rivera, Pulaski	33	63	1	5	1	.928
Martinson, Pulaski	1	1	0	0	0	1.000	Huddleston, Kpt	55	70	2	6	0	.923
Holcomb, Eliz	2	1	0	0	0	1.000	McDougal, Pulaski	7	9	2	1	0	.917
RINDEN, Pulaski	50	94	5	1	0	.990	Wiedenbauer, Cov	55	70	6	7	1	.916
Bowman, Johnson C*	44	55	4	1	1	.983	V. Thomas, Blu	70	110	8	11	1	.915
Brock, Johnson C*	66	127	5	3	0	.978	Leader, Covington*	35	50	4	6	2	.900
Plante, Pulaski	33	37	3	1	0	.976	Suggs, Marion*	7	8	1	1	0	.900
Hallgren, Covington	53	69	2	2	1	.973	Brigham, Bristol*	55	60	2	7	0	.899
Nolan, Johnson City	26	34	2	1	1	.973	Catanese, Eliz	29	27	7	4	0	.895
Corey, Bluefield	69	97	5	3	1	.971	Kopatich, Bristol	4	7	1	1	0	.889
Spain, Elizabethton	59	142	8	5	0	.968	Minier, Pulaski	3	7	0	1	0	.875
Castleberry, Bri*	40	56	4	2	0	.968	Nelson, Pulaski*	22	26	4	5	1	.857
J. Baker, Marion	16	28	2	1	0	.968	Ashlock, Pulaski*	3	6	0	1	0	.857
Wilson, Eliz	13	26	1	1	0	.964	Bryant, Marion	6	10	0	2	0	.833
Penniall, Johnson C	26	24	1	1	0	.962	Bacon, Elizabethton	3	5	0	1	0	.833
Williams, Bluefield*	69	161	11	7	2	.961	Morales, Marion	17	12	2	3	0	.824
Hudson, Kingsport	17	23	1	1	0	.960	Perez, Covington	8	4	0	1	0	.800
Mota, Covington	57	109	5	5	3	.958	Ithier, Pulaski*	2	3	0	1	0	.750
Bryant, Kingsport	42	65	3	3	1	.958	Roof, Johnson City	1	0	0	1	0	.000
White, Pulaski	48	85	5	4	0	.957							

Triple Play—Boyer.

CATCHERS

Player and Club	G.	PO.	A.	E.	DP.	PB.	Pct.	Player and Club	G.	PO.	A.	E.	DP.	PB.	Pct.
Pritchett, JC	10	46	2	0	0	0	1.000	Martinson, Pul-Blu	61	441	39	9	8	16	.982
de la Cruz, Pul	15	31	3	0	0	1	1.000	Curbelo, Eliz	31	196	18	4	2	6	.982
Sampson, Eliz	4	25	2	0	0	1	1.000	Diaz, Bristol	32	211	35	5	5	8	.980
Wolf, Marion	4	14	1	0	0	0	1.000	Hunsaker, J C	21	141	7	3	0	3	.980
Carter, Bristol	2	3	1	0	0	0	1.000	Grant, Marion	28	143	18	4	3	1	.976
Jaskowski, Pul	3	3	1	0	0	0	1.000	Benedict, Kpt	17	98	25	3	0	5	.976
LaFountain, Eliz	1	3	0	0	0	0	1.000	Johnson, Bristol	33	225	23	7	4	10	.973
Adolphus, Blu	1	2	0	0	0	0	1.000	Spies, Eliz	17	88	14	3	1	7	.971
Albright, Blu	1	1	0	0	0	0	1.000	Baldwin, Covington	51	303	43	12	4	10	.966
Ornest, Pulaski	1	1	0	0	0	0	1.000	Cloherty, Covington	17	100	8	4	0	8	.964
SEOANEE, Kpt	48	291	29	2	0	13	.994	Ballard, Pulaski	40	238	24	10	1	7	.963
Johnson, J C	49	336	26	3	2	7	.992	Davis, Marion	47	290	30	13	3	6	.961
McDougal, Pulaski	20	125	17	2	0	3	.986	Wiencek, Bristol	4	12	3	1	0	0	.938
Kennedy, Bluefield	21	160	15	3	1	1	.984	Willeford, Cov	6	41	2	4	1	1	.915
Yarborough, Eliz	24	159	18	3	2	8	.983	Sabino, Kingsport	3	16	0	2	0	1	.889

PITCHERS

Player and Club	G.	PO.	A.	E.	DP.	Pct.
TORREZ, Bluefield*	19	4	18	0	1	1.000
Gray, Johnson City	13	4	17	0	1	1.000
Parrott, Elizabethton	11	3	16	0	1	1.000
Miscik, Covington*	13	1	16	0	1	1.000
Corr, Bristol	14	2	14	0	0	1.000
C. Thomas, Bluefield	16	6	10	0	0	1.000
Cruz, Johnson City	12	3	11	0	1	1.000
Roberge, Covington	14	5	9	0	1	1.000
Kelly, Bluefield	29	2	12	0	0	1.000
Corness, Covington	9	1	12	0	1	1.000
Marietta, Kingsport	13	4	9	0	0	1.000
Javie, Pulaski	7	1	11	0	0	1.000
Tonkin, Kingsport	15	2	9	0	1	1.000
Culbreth, Kingsport	16	2	9	0	0	1.000
Johnson, Pulaski	13	2	8	0	1	1.000
Andersen, Covington	11	5	4	0	0	1.000
Tanner, Marion	12	1	8	0	0	1.000
Henderson, Bristol	13	0	9	0	1	1.000
Pratt, Kingsport*	9	2	6	0	0	1.000
Littlefield, J C	14	3	5	0	0	1.000
Aponte, Covington	7	3	4	0	1	1.000
Lindal, Bluefield*	12	3	4	0	0	1.000
Grafton, Bristol	8	2	4	0	0	1.000
Meyers, Bristol	9	2	4	0	0	1.000
Martinez, Johnson C	10	1	5	0	0	1.000
Tomasiak, Eliz	12	2	4	0	0	1.000
Comoletti, Johnson C*	14	1	5	0	1	1.000
Vallejos, Bluefield	2	3	1	0	0	1.000
McComb, Bluefield	4	0	4	0	0	1.000
Luna, Bluefield	5	2	2	0	0	1.000
Hypes, Elizabethton	12	1	3	0	0	1.000
Fedoris, Bluefield	2	1	2	0	0	1.000
Morogiello, Kpt*	5	0	3	0	0	1.000
Rivera, Bristol	6	0	3	0	0	1.000
Rohena, Bluefield*	9	0	3	0	0	1.000
Robinson, Marion	2	0	2	0	0	1.000
Bugden, Johnson City*	3	0	2	0	0	1.000
Sams, Kingsport	5	0	2	0	0	1.000
Talerico, Pulaski	5	0	2	0	0	1.000
Von Ohlen, Marion*	5	0	2	0	0	1.000
Halstead, Bristol	11	1	1	0	0	1.000
Duncan, Kingsport	1	0	1	0	0	1.000
Dobberstein, Eliz	2	0	1	0	0	1.000
McLaughlin, Bristol	2	0	1	0	0	1.000
Schopp, Johnson City	2	0	1	0	0	1.000
Bell, Bristol*	4	0	1	0	0	1.000
Ferrell, Pulaski	4	0	1	0	0	1.000
Neimeyer, Bluefield	5	1	0	0	0	1.000
Serum, Elizabethton	6	0	1	0	0	1.000
Mitchell, Marion*	9	0	1	0	0	1.000
Polanco, Kingsport	9	0	1	0	0	1.000
Olmsted, Johnson C*	14	3	26	1	0	.967
Petry, Bristol	14	4	19	1	0	.958
Chiti, Kingsport*	12	5	15	1	1	.952
Pensiero, Pulaski	11	2	17	1	0	.950
Grassano, Johnson C	8	2	13	1	0	.938
Aragon, Covington	11	8	16	2	1	.923
Felton, Elizabethton	14	5	7	1	0	.923
Welch, Pulaski-Blu	10	2	9	1	0	.917
Zimmerman, Bristol*	17	2	9	1	0	.917
Grote, Marion	12	1	20	2	0	.913
Dobbs, Elizabethton*	10	2	8	1	0	.909
Propst, Johnson City	11	3	7	1	0	.909
Matula, Kingsport	20	2	14	2	0	.889
Smith, Covington	15	8	23	4	2	.886
Jacob, Johnson City	8	1	6	1	1	.875
Green, Covington	15	3	10	2	1	.867
Bordley, Pulaski*	14	1	5	1	0	.857
Presley, Pulaski	16	0	6	1	2	.857
Burns, Bristol	13	4	13	3	1	.850
Amancio, Kingsport	12	4	7	2	0	.846
R. Rodriguez, Marion	14	5	6	2	0	.846
Allegrezza, Bluefield	24	2	9	2	0	.846
Espinoza, Pulaski	14	5	10	3	1	.833
Joseph, Marion	16	2	8	2	0	.833
Border, Elizabethton	18	1	9	2	0	.833
Thomas, Bristol	10	1	4	1	0	.833
Steen, Covington	12	7	17	5	1	.828
Weaver, Bristol	13	5	25	7	1	.811
Ingram, Elizabethton	12	2	6	2	0	.800
Allen, Marion	6	0	4	1	0	.800
Noonan, Kingsport	12	1	6	2	0	.778
Biehl, Marion*	7	2	8	3	0	.769
Pearson, Marion	13	9	7	5	0	.762
Guzenski, Kingsport	15	3	6	3	1	.750
Franz, Elizabethton*	8	3	3	2	0	.750
Wolf, Marion	8	2	4	2	0	.750
Morrissey, Johnson C	13	2	4	2	0	.750
Ploucher, Covington*	16	1	5	2	0	.750
Bannister, Cov*	3	2	1	1	0	.750
Simon, Marion	3	1	2	1	0	.750
Jackson, Covington	5	0	3	1	1	.750
Stanfield, Eliz*	9	0	3	1	1	.750
Montejano, Johnson C	10	0	3	1	0	.750
Owen, Marion*	19	0	3	1	0	.750
Cacciatore, Marion	10	2	11	6	0	.684
Pettaway, Kingsport	9	4	2	3	0	.667
Rosario, Pulaski*	9	0	6	3	0	.667
Coppol, Marion	25	1	5	3	0	.667
Bradley, Bristol*	10	1	3	2	1	.667
Luedtke, Eliz*	13	1	1	1	0	.667
Barstad, Eliz*	11	0	5	3	0	.625
Ashlock, Blu-Pulaski*	13	1	4	3	0	.625
Vasquez, Bluefield	8	1	3	3	0	.571
Altman, Elizabethton	9	0	2	2	0	.500
Diekmann, Bluefield	2	1	0	1	0	.500
Long, Pulaski	3	0	0	1	0	.000
Jones, Elizabethton*	4	0	0	1	0	.000

The following players do not have any recorded accepted chances at the positions indicated; therefore, are not listed in the fielding averages for those particular positions: Arthur*, p; Black, p; Breiby, p; Brooks, p; Bruno, p; Corrado*, p; Felker, p; Fletcher, p; Fuentes, c; Garcia, p; Hayes, p; Hernandez*, 1b; Olivares, of; Petrowitz*, p; Rinden, p; J. Rodriguez, p; Salas, p; Scruggs, p; B. Williams, p; Wilson*, p.

Breivogel, S. Douglas, Hogan, H. Martinez, McCann, Switzer, and A. Williams appeared as pinch-hitters/designated-hitters and/or pinch-runners only.

CLUB PITCHING

Club	G.	CG.	ShO.	Sv.	IP.	H.	R.	ER.	HR.	BB.	Int. BB.	HB.	SO.	WP.	Bk.	ERA.
Johnson City	70	26	11	8	596	462	218	167	28	256	2	13	493	26	5	2.52
Bristol	67	22	7	9	563	445	244	194	26	272	10	12	423	38	2	3.10
Covington	70	27	9	10	617	579	303	222	21	266	8	19	423	30	1	3.24
Bluefield	70	18	5	14	615	584	294	246	33	274	1	22	496	34	8	3.60
Kingsport	67	13	5	8	570	553	291	243	38	272	13	14	373	38	4	3.84
Pulaski	70	23	6	6	598	559	350	257	26	287	6	16	444	38	8	3.87
Marion	70	12	5	12	569	553	320	259	35	259	13	18	410	28	3	4.10
Elizabethton	70	12	1	5	612	583	349	280	29	331	24	19	443	49	1	4.12

PITCHERS' RECORDS
(Leading Qualifiers for Earned-Run Average Leadership—56 or More Innings)

*Throws lefthanded.

Pitcher–Club	G.	GS.	CG.	ShO.	W.	L.	Sv.	Pct.	IP.	H.	R.	ER.	HR.	BB.	Int. BB.	HB.	SO.	WP.	ERA.
Weaver, Bristol	13	11	4	1	6	2	0	.750	82	53	22	13	1	21	1	0	67	2	1.43
Olmsted, JC*	14	13	7	2	8	3	0	.727	90	55	22	15	2	27	0	1	79	1	1.50
Johnson, Pulaski	13	11	6	2	7	2	1	.778	92	48	24	18	0	43	0	3	101	3	1.76
Cruz, Johnson City	12	11	5	3	6	3	0	.667	80	57	23	18	6	23	0	3	100	1	2.03
C. Thomas, Blu.	16	14	8	0	11	4	0	.733	115	101	37	28	7	33	0	3	93	1	2.19
Green, Covington	15	7	3	1	5	2	3	.714	60	45	20	15	0	32	1	6	36	5	2.25
Steen, Covington	12	11	4	1	6	2	0	.750	83	100	33	21	1	11	0	1	31	0	2.28
Kelly, Bluefield	29	1	1	1	9	2	7	.818	80	59	23	21	2	24	1	4	90	3	2.36
Allegrezza, Blu	24	2	2	2	5	4	5	.556	74	56	25	20	1	32	0	2	75	4	2.43
Smith, Covington	15	12	6	1	5	5	2	.500	97	80	40	29	1	28	1	1	71	3	2.69

Departmental Leaders: G–Kelly, 29; GS–Torrez, 15; CG– C. Thomas, 8; ShO–Cruz, 3; W–C. Thomas, 11; L–Chiti, 9; Sv–Coppol, Kelly, 7; Pct–Gray, .889; IP–Torrez, 123; H–Torrez, 110; R–Espinoza, 56; ER–Noonan. 45; HR–Torrez, 9; BB–Petry, 56; IBB–Coppol, Stanfield, 4; HB–Green, 6; SO–Torrez, 102; WP–Amancio, 10.

(All Pitchers—Listed Alphabetically)

Pitcher–Club	G.	GS.	CG.	ShO.	W.	L.	Sv.	Pct.	IP.	H.	R.	ER.	HR.	BB.	Int. BB.	HB.	SO.	WP.	ERA.
Allegrezza, Blu	24	2	2	2	5	4	5	.556	74	56	25	20	1	32	0	2	75	4	2.43
Allen, Marion	6	4	2	1	2	0	1	1.000	33	23	8	7	1	6	1	0	29	1	1.91
Altman, Elizabethton	9	4	0	0	2	1	0	.667	26	16	10	7	0	13	0	0	13	2	2.42
Amancio, Kingsport	12	12	2	1	4	4	0	.500	69	54	37	34	7	34	0	2	47	10	4.43
Andersen, Covington	11	5	2	0	4	5	0	.444	38	44	30	26	1	22	1	2	22	0	6.16
Aponte, Covington	7	0	0	0	0	0	0	.000	12	14	9	7	4	2	1	2	8	0	5.25
Aragon, Covington	11	11	6	1	7	4	0	.636	85	66	39	28	4	54	0	2	38	6	2.96
Arthur, Johnson C*	1	0	0	0	0	0	0	.000	1	0	0	0	0	1	0	0	1	0	0.00
Ashlock, 5 Blu-8 Pul*	13	2	0	0	2	0	0	.000	33	37	24	19	1	18	0	0	16	1	5.18
Bannister, Cov*	3	2	0	0	0	0	1	.000	13	3	0	0	0	2	0	0	27	0	0.00
Barstad, Eliz*	11	5	0	0	3	4	0	.429	41	34	30	27	5	25	0	3	41	6	5.93
Bell, Bristol*	4	0	0	0	0	0	0	.000	4	9	10	10	2	7	0	0	8	2	22.50
Biehl, Marion*	7	5	0	0	3	0	0	.000	21	26	20	13	1	16	0	3	17	1	5.57
Black, Bristol	3	0	0	0	0	1	0	.000	2	1	3	3	0	2	0	0	0	0	13.50
Border, Eliz	18	1	1	0	2	0	1	1.000	49	51	20	9	3	16	1	4	28	3	1.65
Bordley, Pulaski*	14	2	0	0	3	1	0	.750	45	60	35	29	3	21	0	2	26	6	5.80
Bradley, Bristol*	10	7	2	1	2	5	0	.286	35	22	20	12	2	21	0	3	15	4	3.09
Breiby, Kingsport	1	0	0	0	0	0	0	......	0	2	2	2	0	1	1	0	0	1	......
Brooks, Covington	1	0	0	0	0	0	0	.000	2	5	2	2	1	1	0	0	1	0	9.00
Bruno, Kingsport	1	0	0	0	0	0	0	.000	2	0	0	0	0	0	0	0	2	0	0.00
Bugden, Johnson C*	3	0	0	0	0	0	0	.000	6	4	0	0	0	2	0	0	1	0	0.00
Burns, Bristol	13	12	6	0	7	3	0	.700	81	55	27	25	2	52	1	3	79	4	2.78
Cacciatore, Marion	10	10	0	0	3	6	0	.333	46	37	23	17	0	44	0	4	33	2	3.33
Chiti, Kingsport*	12	11	2	0	1	9	0	.100	64	68	39	26	6	31	3	0	40	3	3.66
Comoletti, JC*	14	2	0	0	3	1	2	.750	49	42	23	16	1	24	1	1	42	0	2.94
Coppol, Marion	25	1	0	0	6	1	7	.857	43	34	19	12	3	12	4	0	21	5	2.51
Corness, Covington	9	7	0	0	1	6	0	.143	43	49	35	28	2	28	0	2	17	4	5.86
Corr, Bristol	14	13	6	2	5	7	0	.417	88	84	36	33	6	25	1	2	67	3	3.38
Corrado, Marion*	3	0	0	0	0	0	1	1.000	9	7	3	3	0	3	0	0	4	2	1.80
Cruz, Johnson City	12	11	5	3	6	3	0	.667	80	57	23	18	6	23	0	3	100	1	2.03
Culbreth, Kpt	16	1	1	0	2	1	1	.667	58	53	29	28	2	21	2	3	28	1	4.34
Diekmann, Blu	2	0	0	0	0	0	0	.000	2	5	6	6	0	5	0	0	2	0	27.00
Dobberstein, Eliz	2	1	0	0	0	0	0	.000	5	6	4	4	0	5	1	0	4	1	7.20
Dobbs, Eliz*	10	4	2	0	3	3	1	.500	39	36	20	18	2	18	2	0	28	2	4.15
Duncan, Kingsport	1	0	0	0	0	0	1	.000	2	1	0	0	0	2	0	0	3	0	0.00
Espinoza, Pulaski	14	14	5	1	6	5	0	.545	101	102	56	42	3	35	1	2	70	4	3.74
Fedoris, Bluefield	2	1	0	0	0	1	0	.000	4	11	9	8	0	2	0	0	1	0	18.00
Felker, Bristol	2	0	0	0	0	0	0	.000	1	1	0	0	0	1	0	0	0	0	0.00
Felton, Eliz	14	12	2	0	2	6	0	.250	87	89	54	37	6	27	3	4	91	6	3.83
Ferrell, Pulaski	4	0	0	0	0	0	0	.000	10	12	11	9	0	13	0	2	7	4	8.10
Fletcher, Pulaski	2	0	0	0	0	1	0	.000	3	4	2	2	0	0	0	0	2	1	6.00
Franz, Eliz*	8	4	0	0	2	4	0	.333	29	26	19	13	2	23	0	0	22	3	4.03
Garcia, Pulaski	14	0	0	0	0	1	0	.000	28	31	19	17	2	18	2	2	15	0	5.46
Grafton, Bristol	8	0	0	0	3	1	2	.750	19	8	5	2	0	7	1	1	19	1	0.95
Grassano, Johnson C	8	7	2	0	4	0		1.000	36	31	15	12	0	21	0	2	26	5	3.00
Gray, Johnson City	13	12	5	2	8	1	0	.889	82	59	31	26	3	35	0	2	56	1	2.85
Green, Covington	15	7	3	1	5	2	3	.714	60	45	20	15	0	32	1	6	36	5	2.25
Grote, Marion	12	11	3	1	2	8	0	.200	71	63	32	30	8	20	0	2	62	1	3.80
Guzenski, Kpt	15	11	3	0	2	8	0	.200	64	68	44	37	7	38	1	3	36	6	5.20
Halstead, Bristol	11	1	1	0	3	1	2	.750	22	14	6	5	1	15	0	0	17	3	2.05
Hayes, Bristol	6	0	0	0	0	1	0	.000	8	11	8	8	1	9	0	0	5	4	9.00

Pitcher–Club	G	GS	CG	ShO	W	L	Sv	Pct.	IP	H	R	ER	HR	BB	Int. BB	HB	SO	WP	ERA
Henderson, Bristol	13	0	0	0	2	0	2	1.000	30	31	13	13	0	8	2	1	18	1	3.90
Hypes, Elizabethton	12	6	1	0	0	6	1	.000	44	38	26	23	2	23	1	0	28	3	4.70
Ingram, Eliz	12	7	0	0	0	1	1	.000	43	31	29	26	1	47	3	2	36	6	5.44
Jackson, Covington	5	0	0	0	0	0	0	.000	10	7	11	6	0	12	0	1	7	2	5.40
Jacob, Johnson City	8	1	1	1	2	0	1	1.000	33	24	10	8	4	9	0	0	25	0	2.18
Javie, Pulaski	7	7	2	0	1	5	0	.167	36	34	28	17	2	15	0	0	38	2	4.25
Johnson, Pulaski	13	11	6	2	7	2	1	.778	92	48	24	18	0	43	0	3	101	3	1.76
Jones, Eliz*	4	1	0	0	0	1	0	.000	6	10	11	10	0	13	1	0	0	2	15.00
Joseph, Marion	16	1	1	0	0	4	1	.000	38	28	22	15	5	17	1	1	31	2	3.55
Kelly, Bluefield	29	1	1	1	9	2	7	.818	80	59	23	21	2	24	1	4	90	3	2.36
Lindal, Bluefield*	12	10	1	0	3	5	0	.375	52	50	41	32	3	51	0	3	47	7	5.54
Littlefield, JC	14	2	2	1	6	3	3	.667	44	37	10	7	0	6	1	0	24	1	1.43
Long, Pulaski	3	0	0	0	0	0	0	.000	2	2	3	2	0	3	0	0	2	1	9.00
Luedtke, Eliz*	13	6	1	0	4	3	0	.571	53	53	27	24	1	18	1	1	20	1	4.08
Luna, Bluefield	5	3	0	0	1	1	0	.500	19	26	13	10	3	9	0	0	12	2	4.74
Marietta, Kingsport	13	13	4	0	4	4	0	.500	85	86	35	28	7	23	0	1	45	3	2.96
Martinez, JC	10	0	0	0	1	1	1	.500	21	15	11	7	0	15	0	2	17	1	3.00
Matula, Kingsport	20	0	0	0	3	5	6	.375	48	49	18	14	0	14	1	1	31	2	2.63
McComb, Bluefield	4	2	0	0	0	1	0	.000	14	17	6	6	0	6	0	0	11	2	3.86
McLaughlin, Bri	2	0	0	0	0	0	1	.000	2	3	2	2	0	1	0	0	0	0	9.00
Meyers, Bristol	9	0	0	0	1	2	0	.333	22	16	7	4	2	1	0	2	11	0	1.64
Miscik, Covington*	13	13	4	0	5	4	0	.556	89	95	41	33	5	34	0	0	89	4	3.34
Mitchell, Marion*	9	2	0	0	1	3	0	.250	17	27	26	23	4	13	0	0	17	4	12.18
Montejano, Johnson C	10	3	0	0	0	1	0	.000	30	28	18	16	2	22	0	0	20	3	4.80
Morogiello, Kpt*	5	5	0	0	1	2	0	.333	25	28	11	9	1	5	0	1	26	1	3.24
Morrissey, JC	13	9	3	2	6	2	1	.750	69	66	25	25	8	31	0	1	41	3	3.26
Neimeyer, Bluefield	5	5	0	0	1	1	0	.500	18	17	15	12	1	12	0	0	9	1	6.00
Noonan, Bluefield	12	12	2	0	3	7	0	.300	83	84	55	45	4	48	1	1	57	5	4.88
Olmsted, JC*	14	13	7	2	8	3	0	.727	90	55	22	15	2	27	0	1	79	1	1.50
Owen, Marion*	19	4	0	0	1	2	0	.333	47	61	32	26	3	17	0	2	26	0	4.98
Parrott, Eliz	11	9	4	0	1	5	0	.167	66	76	38	34	7	35	1	2	37	5	4.64
Pearson, Marion	13	12	5	0	6	4	0	.600	87	88	47	37	3	28	1	0	62	2	3.83
Pensiero, Pulaski	11	11	7	0	5	4	0	.556	74	63	33	24	6	25	1	0	41	4	2.92
Petrowitz, Eliz*	5	0	0	0	2	2	0	.500	10	12	7	2	0	8	2	0	5	0	1.80
Petry, Bristol	14	14	1	1	2	3	0	.400	79	54	42	33	4	56	3	0	51	9	3.76
Pettaway, Kingsport	9	7	0	0	1	4	0	.200	31	32	24	22	0	32	0	1	15	5	6.39
Ploucher, Cov*	16	2	2	1	3	2	3	.600	44	36	21	13	1	26	2	1	34	4	2.66
Palanco, Kingsport	9	1	1	1	3	0	0	1.000	34	34	17	15	4	13	2	1	32	3	3.97
Pratt, Kingsport*	9	5	0	0	3	2	0	.600	46	38	13	12	1	30	2	0	26	1	2.35
Presley, Pulaski	16	3	1	1	5	3	5	.625	47	39	14	8	2	16	0	0	51	0	1.53
Propst, Johnson C	11	8	1	0	5	4	0	.556	46	35	25	14	1	27	0	1	51	8	2.74
Rinden, Pulaski	1	0	0	0	0	0	0	.000	5	4	3	3	0	3	1	0	3	1	5.40
Rivera, Bristol	6	1	0	0	1	1	0	.500	17	17	10	8	3	10	0	0	10	1	4.24
Roberge, Covington	14	0	0	0	2	2	1	.500	36	33	21	13	1	12	2	1	40	2	3.25
Robinson, Marion	2	1	0	0	1	0	0	1.000	8	6	3	3	0	9	0	1	7	0	3.38
J. Rodriguez, Mar.	6	0	0	0	0	0	0	.000	9	13	11	11	1	3	0	0	6	0	11.00
R. Rodriguez, Mar	14	7	0	0	0	5	0	.000	40	45	35	27	2	33	3	1	29	5	6.08
Rohena, Bluefield*	9	7	0	0	2	3	0	.400	35	47	27	25	3	22	0	3	19	2	6.43
Rosario, Pulaski*	9	4	0	0	1	3	0	.250	27	33	26	22	0	23	0	2	13	3	7.33
Salas, Covington	4	0	0	0	0	0	0	.000	4	2	1	1	0	2	0	0	2	0	2.25
Sams, Kingsport	5	0	0	0	0	1	0	.000	13	12	5	5	1	10	0	1	12	0	3.46
Schopp, Johnson C	2	2	0	0	1	1	0	.500	10	9	5	3	1	13	0	0	10	2	2.70
Scruggs, Johnson C	2	0	0	0	0	0	0	.000	2	0	0	0	0	0	0	0	1	0	0.00
Serum, Elizabethton	6	3	0	0	1	2	0	.333	32	24	11	9	0	10	1	0	24	2	2.53
Simon, Marion	3	3	0	0	1	1	0	.500	18	18	5	4	0	5	0	0	14	0	2.00
Smith, Covington	15	12	6	1	5	5	2	.500	97	80	40	29	1	28	1	1	71	3	2.69
Stanfield, Eliz*	9	0	0	0	2	3	1	.400	21	23	7	6	0	8	4	0	19	0	2.57
Steen, Covington	12	11	4	1	6	2	0	.750	83	100	33	21	1	11	0	1	31	0	2.28
Talerico, Pulaski	5	0	0	0	0	1	0	.000	6	6	4	4	1	7	0	0	4	3	6.00
Tanner, Marion	12	1	0	0	0	2	0	.000	23	25	14	13	3	13	1	1	10	2	5.09
C. Thomas, Blu	16	14	8	0	11	4	0	.733	115	101	37	28	7	33	0	3	93	1	2.19
Thomas, Bristol	10	2	0	0	0	3	0	.000	26	23	14	10	1	12	0	0	20	4	3.46
Tomasiak, Eliz	12	7	1	0	3	1	0	.750	50	43	25	22	1	26	0	3	40	3	3.96
Tonkin, Kingsport	15	1	0	0	1	2	0	.333	28	28	17	11	2	18	1	0	29	2	3.54
Torrez, Bluefield*	19	15	6	1	9	2	2	.818	123	110	51	42	9	45	0	4	102	3	3.07
Vallejos, Bluefield	2	1	0	0	1	0	0	.000	7	8	6	5	1	3	0	0	2	0	6.43
Vasquez, Bluefield	8	4	0	0	1	0	1	1.000	33	28	6	5	0	11	0	2	15	3	1.36
Von Ohlen, Marion*	5	1	1	0	1	0	0	1.000	20	11	5	3	0	6	0	2	12	1	1.35
Weaver, Bristol	13	11	4	1	6	2	0	.750	82	53	22	13	1	21	1	0	67	2	1.43
Welch, 6 Pul-4 Blu	10	8	0	0	1	4	0	.200	42	49	33	22	5	18	0	3	18	3	4.71
Williams, Eliz	6	0	0	0	0	1	0	.000	11	14	9	7	0	11	3	0	5	3	5.73
Wilson, Eliz	2	0	0	0	0	0	0	.000	3	3	2	2	0	5	0	0	2	1	9.00
Wolf, Marion	8	6	0	0	2	2	0	.500	42	39	17	17	1	14	2	1	30	0	3.64
Zimmerman, Bristol*	17	6	2	0	3	2	2	.600	46	43	19	13	1	24	1	0	36	0	2.54

BALKS—Torrez, 4; Espinoza, Morrissey, Noonan, Owen, Rosario, 2 each; Amancio, Aragon, Ashlock, Barstad, Chiti, Cruz, Grassano, Gray, Grote, Kelly, Pensiero, Petry, Polanco, Pratt, C. Thomas, Thomas (Bri), Vallejos, Welch, 1 each.

COMBINATION SHUTOUTS—Rohena-Kelly, Bluefield; Weaver-McLaughlin, Zimmerman-Grafton, Bristol; Steen-Smith, Smith-Bannister, Bannister-Anderson, Green-Ploucher, Covington; Hypes-Franz, Elizabethton; Marietta-Matula, Guzenski-Culbreth, Pratt-Matula, Kingsport; Cacciatore-Owen, Cacciatore-Joseph, Cacciatore-Coppol, Marion; Noonan-Presley, Pulaski.

NO-HIT GAME—Jacob, Johnson City, defeated Elizabethton, 7-0, August 28 (seven innings).

Gulf Coast League

ROOKIE CLASSIFICATION

CHAMPIONSHIP WINNERS IN PREVIOUS YEARS

1964—Sarasota Braves .... .610
1965—Bradenton Astros .... .632
1966—New York A.L. .... .667
1967—Kansas City .... .614
1968—Oakland...................... .650

1969—Montreal .... .585
1970—Chicago A.L................. .600
1971—Kansas City .... .755
1972—Chicago N.L. a .... .651
     Kansas City a .... .651

1973—Texas .... .732
1974—Chicago N.L.................. .702
1975—Texas .... .774

(Note—Known as Sarasota Rookie League in 1964 and Florida Rookie League in 1965.) aDeclared co-champions; no playoff.

STANDING OF CLUBS AT CLOSE OF SEASON, AUGUST 27

Club	Tex.	Chi. N.L.	K.C.	St.L.	Chi. A.L.	Atl.	Pitt.	W.	L.	T.	Pct.	G.B.
Texas	..	6	7	6	5	7	7	38	16	0	.704	......
Chicago-NL............................	3	..	6	5	6	7	9	36	17	1	.679	1½
Kansas City............................	2	3	..	6	5	5	8	29	25	0	.537	9
St. Louis	3	3	4	..	5	6	6	27	24	1	.529	9½
Chicago-AL............................	4	3	3	4	..	3	6	23	30	0	.434	14½
Atlanta....................................	2	2	4	2	6	..	5	21	32	0	.396	16½
Pittsburgh	2	0	1	2	2	4	..	11	41	0	.212	26

Texas declared league champion on basis of highest won-lost percentage.
Club names indicate major league connections.

Playoff—None. Games played at Bradenton and Sarasota, Fla.

Regular Season Attendance—No paid attendance.

Managers: Atlanta—Chuck Goggin, Pedro Gonzalez, co-managers; Chicago AL—Joe Jones; Chicago NL—Walt Dixon; Kansas City—Jose Martinez; Pittsburgh—Elwood (Woody) Huyke; St. Louis—Dave Ricketts; Texas— Joe Klein.

All-Star Team: 1B—Phelps, K.C.; Jennings, Tex.; 2B—Sample, Tex.; Stevens, K.C.; 3B—Cotes, Pitts.; Zaya, St.L.; SS—Davis, Chi. NL; McCann, K.C.; OF—Hoscheidt, K.C.; Jemison, Tex.; Martin, Chi. NL; Long, Atl.; Rivera, Tex.; **Rackley, Chi. NL;** C—Evers, Chi. NL; Gaudet, K.C.; P—Clark, Chi. NL; Tulacz, Chi. AL; Couch, Tex.; **Searage, St.L.; England, Chi. NL;** Finch, Tex.; Gullette, Atl.; Howard, Chi. AL; Manager—Klein, Tex.

(Compiled by Howe News Bureau, Chicago, Ill.)

CLUB BATTING

Club	G.	AB.	R.	OR.	H.	TB.	2B.	3B.	HR.	RBI.	SH.	SF.	Int. BB.	BB.	HP.	SO.	SB.	CS.	LOB.	Pct.
Chicago-NL	54	1728	285	218	434	556	55	17	11	228	30	21	245	14	17	228	99	22	419	.251
Kansas City	54	1737	283	237	428	581	55	31	12	239	13	21	313	9	21	290	91	24	463	.246
St. Louis	52	1618	242	212	397	506	55	21	4	201	10	10	235	7	18	305	68	26	381	.245
Texas	54	1712	279	187	413	545	45	27	11	229	29	23	306	12	21	315	116	25	431	.241
Atlanta	53	1625	216	287	377	483	56	19	4	184	19	11	291	3	13	268	62	19	441	.232
Chicago-AL	53	1722	230	238	385	475	47	14	5	177	18	16	233	8	12	278	60	22	399	.224
Pittsburgh	52	1570	154	310	339	439	43	18	7	125	5	17	155	2	9	376	123	40	289	.216

INDIVIDUAL BATTING

(Leading Qualifiers for Batting Championship—146 or More Plate Appearances)

*Bats lefthanded.   †Switch-hitter.

Player and Club	G.	AB.	R.	H.	TB.	2B.	3B.	HR.	RBI.	SH.	SF.	BB.	HP.	SO.	SB.	CS.	Pct.
Sample, William, Texas......	45	152	35	58	86	7	9	1	33	3	3	39	2	14	27	3	.382
Long, David, Atlanta*....................	40	142	25	48	68	10	5	0	28	0	3	28	0	17	10	2	.338
Martin, Jared, Chicago-NL*.........	44	143	35	48	58	8	1	0	15	3	1	24	3	11	15	5	.336
Hoscheidt, John, Kansas City.........	50	184	35	59	81	5	7	1	30	1	2	18	2	18	14	3	.321
Cotes, Eugenio, Pittsburgh	42	141	21	42	60	7	4	1	16	0	3	15	2	26	24	2	.298
McCann, Francis, Kansas City........	47	164	29	46	63	4	5	1	24	0	5	24	2	35	20	1	.280
Jemison, Gregory, Texas*............	50	166	40	45	59	3	4	1	17	5	0	36	3	24	32	7	.271
Davis, Steven, Chicago-NL	52	160	28	43	62	4	3	3	26	7	2	24	2	10	14	3	.269
Mabee, Victor, Texas	43	145	21	38	45	2	1	1	26	2	2	22	1	31	9	0	.262
Evers, William, Chicago-NL...........	43	142	21	37	54	9	1	2	31	0	2	32	0	14	1	0	.261

Departmental Leaders: G—Davis, Hill, 52; AB—Hill, 210; R—Jemison, 40; H—Hoscheidt, 59; TB—Sample, 86;

2B—Lee, Long, 10; 3B—Sample, 9; HR—Rivera, Vosejpka, 4; RBI—Rivera, 40; SH—Davis, 7; SF—McCann, Rackley, Riley, 5; BB—Lee, 46; HP—Close, Jemison, Martin, McCracken, Robinson, Rokosz, Simpson, Stevens, Takacs, Tessler, 3; SO—Torres, 50; SB—Jemison, 32; CS—Stevens, 8.

(All Players—Listed Alphabetically)

Player and Club	G.	AB.	R.	H.	TB.	2B.	3B.	HR.	RBI.	SH.	SF.	BB.	HP.	SO.	SB.	CS.	Pct.
Alcala, Ruben, Kansas City	9	17	1	3	4	1	0	0	2	0	0	3	1	4	0	0	.176
Araujo, Francisco, Chi-NL	18	47	4	11	11	0	0	0	3	0	0	1	0	14	0	0	.234
Baez, Ramon, St. Louis	12	34	7	9	11	0	1	0	4	0	0	0	0	2	2	0	.265
Beardon, David, Atlanta	8	17	1	3	3	0	0	0	1	0	1	4	0	2	1	0	.176
Benoit, David, St. Louis	36	92	15	15	20	3	1	0	14	4	1	32	2	29	7	2	.163
Bertolotti, Fulvio, StL	14	47	7	8	9	1	0	0	5	0	0	3	0	7	1	0	.170
Boyer, Raymond, Atlanta	19	62	10	15	17	2	0	0	5	0	1	11	1	4	1	0	.242
Bright, Thomas, Chicago-AL	50	185	17	41	54	7	0	2	29	0	3	16	1	45	3	3	.222
Brockenbury, James, Atlanta*	50	172	18	41	50	3	0	2	29	1	2	20	1	10	1	0	.238
Bumstead, Mark, St. Louis	47	159	27	39	46	5	1	0	17	0	3	32	2	21	2	1	.245
Burroughs, David, Kan City	5	8	0	1	1	0	0	0	0	0	0	0	0	0	0	0	.125
Buscher, Bernard, Kan City	13	25	4	5	5	0	0	0	1	0	0	1	1	2	0	0	.200
Capowski, James, Texas	26	82	10	22	27	1	2	0	13	1	1	7	1	19	0	0	.268
Burroughs, David, Kan City.	5	8	0	1	1	0	0	0	0	0	0	0	0	0	0	0	.125
Carter, Larry, Chicago-NL	42	137	21	32	39	5	1	0	12	3	0	11	2	15	15	2	.234
Carty, Landre, Atlanta	40	120	15	26	30	4	0	0	9	1	0	18	0	16	4	1	.217
Castro, Samuel, Pittsburgh	1	1	0	0	0	0	0	0	0	0	0	0	0	1	0	0	.000
Close, Thomas, Kansas City	30	68	7	8	8	0	0	0	5	1	0	21	3	17	0	1	.118
Colbern, Michael, Chicago-AL	26	103	7	25	36	3	4	0	16	0	1	7	1	13	1	0	.243
Concepcion, Onix, Kan City	18	47	13	11	14	3	0	0	4	1	0	13	0	12	3	0	.234
Cotes, Eugenio, Pittsburgh	42	141	21	42	60	7	4	1	16	0	3	15	2	26	24	2	.298
Davis, Steven, Chicago-NL	52	160	28	43	62	4	3	3	26	7	2	24	2	10	14	3	.269
DiMatteo, George, Chicago-NL	47	118	22	29	36	2	1	1	14	0	3	26	0	19	8	2	.246
Dotson, J. Eugene, St. Louis	35	101	12	29	46	8	3	1	21	1	0	21	1	29	5	2	.287
Durbin, Richard, St. Louis	16	35	7	7	11	2	1	0	4	1	0	7	1	10	0	0	.200
Durham, Leon, St. Louis*	44	156	25	35	54	3	5	2	18	0	0	14	1	33	7	0	.224
Edrington, Heyward, 8 Atl-23 Pitt.	31	100	8	23	35	4	4	0	2	1	0	10	0	25	6	0	.230
Elliott, Clay, Atlanta	34	114	12	22	25	3	0	0	10	4	1	11	2	31	0	1	.193
Elter, Leo, Chicago-AL	29	97	8	17	21	4	0	0	8	0	1	20	1	16	1	0	.175
Evans, Marvin, 2 Atl-12 Pitt*	14	36	2	8	11	1	1	0	3	0	0	6	0	10	3	1	.222
Evers, William, Chicago-NL	43	142	21	37	54	9	1	2	31	0	2	32	0	14	1	0	.261
Ferrer, Miguel, Atlanta	21	51	12	12	16	4	0	0	6	3	0	6	2	5	2	0	.235
Finch, Willie, Atlanta*	1	1	0	0	0	0	0	0	0	0	0	0	0	0	0	0	.000
Forbes, Andres, Atlanta	44	143	14	34	38	0	2	0	13	1	1	17	2	13	2	2	.238
Fuentes, Frank, St. Louis	9	21	6	8	12	0	2	0	1	0	0	2	0	1	0	0	.381
Fulton, Gary, Pittsburgh*	37	88	12	19	24	3	1	0	2	0	0	32	2	32	23	2	.216
Gabella, James, Chicago-AL	29	95	11	13	15	2	0	0	2	3	0	9	1	13	2	3	.137
Garcia, Manuel A., Chi-NL	11	22	1	5	5	0	0	0	1	0	0	0	0	4	1	0	.227
Gaudet, James, Kansas City	30	101	17	35	46	9	1	0	15	0	1	11	0	8	0	2	.347
Gentile, Gene, Pittsburgh*	28	82	7	14	17	0	0	1	5	0	1	7	1	19	4	4	.171
Given, K. Theodore, StL	34	119	21	31	34	3	0	0	16	0	1	16	1	22	13	1	.261
Godard, M. Eric, Chi-NL*	21	39	8	8	14	2	2	0	4	1	0	8	0	10	1	0	.205
Goodrich, George, Pitt	47	162	21	40	51	4	2	1	11	0	2	23	1	41	25	5	.247
Graven, Timothy, Atlanta*	1	2	0	0	0	0	0	0	0	0	0	0	1	0	0	0	.000
Gray, Lorenzo, Chicago-AL	42	151	19	35	38	3	0	0	7	2	2	23	1	25	4	2	.232
Greenaway, David, Chi-AL	42	129	14	31	35	2	1	0	16	2	3	22	1	16	2	3	.240
Harper, Terry, Atlanta	51	185	21	48	69	6	6	1	37	2	1	24	0	23	6	4	.259
Harrison, Robert J., StL*	1	2	0	0	0	0	0	0	0	0	0	1	0	1	0	0	.000
Hernandez, Jose, 1 Atl-31 Pitt	32	100	5	14	15	1	0	0	4	0	0	2	1	33	6	2	.140
Hester, Tom, Kansas City*	29	63	11	16	24	3	1	1	9	0	0	17	1	8	7	1	.254
Hicks, Joseph W., Atlanta	17	59	6	10	13	1	1	0	2	0	0	8	1	11	5	1	.169
Hill, Anthony, Chicago-AL	52	210	38	46	51	1	2	0	20	1	1	24	1	41	14	1	.219
Hodgson, Gordon, Chicago-NL	16	33	5	4	5	1	0	0	5	0	1	1	1	12	0	0	.121
Hoscheidt, John, Kansas City	50	184	35	59	81	5	7	1	30	1	2	18	2	18	14	3	.321
Hudson, Jack, Kansas City	11	19	0	2	3	1	0	0	0	0	0	0	0	4	0	0	.105
Hunsaker, Frank, St. Louis	21	71	7	23	29	6	0	0	9	0	0	13	0	10	0	1	.324
Imhoff, Michael, Atlanta*	17	54	9	12	13	1	0	0	2	0	0	17	0	18	1	0	.222
Jaccar, Michael, Texas‡	36	96	14	22	24	2	0	0	8	1	2	24	0	10	9	2	.229
Jark, LaVerne, Chicago-NL*	37	120	12	32	38	4	1	0	8	5	0	10	1	3	9	1	.267
Jemison, Gregory, Texas*	50	166	40	45	59	3	4	1	17	5	0	36	3	24	32	7	.271
Jennings, James, Texas*	39	110	18	26	29	1	1	0	9	2	2	32	0	22	3	1	.236
Johnson, Bryan, Chicago-NL*	17	37	6	7	7	0	0	0	2	1	0	8	0	4	0	0	.189
Keatley, Gregory, Chicago-NL	10	44	12	14	26	3	0	3	18	0	1	3	0	10	1	0	.318
Keck, Paul, St. Louis	25	54	14	7	7	0	0	0	4	1	0	23	0	17	5	3	.130
Krattli, J. Thomas, Kan C*	50	165	19	30	37	3	2	0	13	0	0	30	0	35	2	0	.182
Lee, William S., Atlanta*	46	127	11	23	35	10	1	0	14	2	0	46	1	41	0	2	.181
Lewis, Alphonso, Texas	30	69	20	17	22	2	0	1	4	3	1	15	0	7	5	2	.246
Llodrat, Fernando, Kan City	40	100	15	21	25	0	2	0	9	0	1	17	0	11	4	2	.210
Long, David, Atlanta‡	40	142	25	48	68	10	5	0	28	0	3	28	0	17	10	2	.338
Lucas, Reggie, Atlanta	26	66	6	8	11	1	1	0	4	1	0	4	0	21	1	2	.121

Player and Club	G.	AB.	R.	H.	TB.	2B.	3B.	HR.	RBI.	SH.	SF.	BB.	HP.	SO.	SB.	CS.	Pct.
Mabee, Victor, Texas	43	145	21	38	45	2	1	1	26	2	2	22	1	31	9	0	.262
Madden, Robert, Chicago-AL	2	0	1	0	0	0	0	0	0	0	0	0	0	0	0	0	.000
Marsalan, Frank, St. Louis	12	24	0	1	1	0	0	0	0	0	0	1	1	10	0	0	.042
Martin, Jared, Chicago-NL*	44	143	35	48	58	8	1	0	15	3	1	24	3	11	15	5	.336
Martindale, Denzel, StL	9	39	4	8	10	2	0	0	3	0	0	3	0	2	1	2	.205
Martinez, Epifanio, StL*	34	108	16	29	34	3	1	0	10	1	0	9	1	11	10	2	.269
McCann, Francis, Kansas City	47	164	29	46	63	4	5	1	24	0	5	24	2	35	20	1	.280
McCracken, Douglas, Chi-NL*	23	57	10	14	15	1	0	0	6	0	0	3	3	6	4	0	.246
Mendez, Victor, Kansas City	9	16	1	1	2	1	0	0	3	0	0	1	0	3	0	0	.063
Mercedes, Hector, Pittsburgh	15	25	2	5	7	2	0	0	1	1	0	1	0	6	0	0	.200
Messer, Tony, Chicago-NL	11	17	1	4	4	0	0	0	2	0	1	5	0	5	0	0	.235
Mohr, Edward, Chicago-NL	21	41	8	9	13	1	0	1	6	1	0	9	0	13	1	2	.220
Morton, Jerry, Chicago-AL*	31	78	10	20	24	2	1	0	6	2	1	15	0	20	3	3	.256
Mota, Cornelio, 2 Atl-9 Pitt	11	35	1	8	8	0	0	0	5	0	1	1	0	10	1	3	.229
Newman, Bert, Chicago-NL	38	118	20	36	43	3	2	0	15	3	0	13	0	7	15	4	.305
Palmer, Denzil, Chicago-NL	1	0	0	0	0	0	0	0	0	0	0	1	0	0	0	0	.000
Parmenter, William, Chi-AL	37	117	16	31	38	5	1	0	8	2	1	20	0	22	9	0	.265
Pasillas, J. Andrew, Chi-AL	12	46	7	12	15	3	0	0	6	1	0	5	1	2	0	0	.261
Pena, Antonio, 2 Atl-31 Pitt	33	110	10	23	32	2	2	1	11	1	0	4	0	17	5	2	.209
Penniall, David, St. Louis	6	22	8	9	15	1	1	1	8	0	0	6	1	3	4	1	.409
Peoples, Charles, Chicago-NL	24	72	11	17	20	3	0	0	7	0	2	4	1	11	0	1	.236
Perez (M), Francisco, Pitt*	16	45	7	8	8	0	0	0	0	0	0	4	0	23	4	3	.178
Pergantis, Donald, Atlanta	1	1	0	0	0	0	0	0	0	0	0	0	0	0	0	0	.000
Peterson, D. Scott, Texas	32	94	10	22	29	4	0	1	18	4	2	16	0	19	0	1	.234
Phelps, Kenneth, Kan City*	28	98	20	29	50	6	3	3	28	0	2	28	2	9	0	0	.296
Pierce, Walter, St. Louis	27	82	5	19	22	1	1	0	9	1	1	9	2	19	1	2	.232
Rackley, Steven, Chicago-NL*	46	126	20	32	43	5	3	0	27	1	5	24	1	16	9	2	.254
Renfroe, George, Pittsburgh	39	122	6	23	28	2	0	1	16	0	4	10	0	9	4	1	.189
Rieger, Karl, St. Louis*	2	5	1	1	1	0	0	0	0	0	0	0	0	1	1	0	.200
Riley, Timothy, Kansas City	43	126	16	30	41	6	1	1	27	0	5	10	0	24	1	1	.238
Rivera, David, Texas	51	204	28	53	84	9	5	4	40	0	4	10	2	39	8	1	.260
Robinson, David, Texas*	31	90	16	20	29	3	0	2	14	2	0	17	3	28	10	1	.222
Rock, Robert, Pittsburgh	1	0	0	0	0	0	0	0	1	0	0	1	0	0	0	0	.000
Rodriguez, Gregorio, Pitt	48	172	19	38	41	1	0	0	12	0	0	14	0	32	10	5	.221
Rodriguez, Juan A., Kan City	40	147	31	35	37	2	0	0	13	1	2	15	2	23	25	2	.238
Rokosz, Keith, Chicago-AL*	50	184	25	38	47	9	0	0	25	2	1	28	3	15	3	2	.207
Romero, Joseph, Chicago-NL	44	144	18	29	34	1	2	0	11	1	3	15	1	15	1	0	.201
Roof, Eugene, St. Louis‡	5	21	0	5	5	0	0	0	2	0	1	0	0	3	0	0	.238
Rothwell, D. Joseph, Kan C	12	31	5	6	16	1	3	1	5	1	0	2	0	9	1	0	.194
Sample, William, Texas	45	152	35	58	86	7	9	1	33	3	3	39	2	14	27	3	.382
Seibert, Kurt, Chicago-NL†	10	26	10	7	7	0	0	0	3	1	0	11	0	5	4	0	.269
Seoanee, Isaac, Atlanta	12	46	3	9	9	0	0	0	4	0	1	1	0	3	0	0	.196
Serrano, Martin, Kansas City	24	73	12	25	26	1	0	0	9	2	0	11	2	3	3	3	.342
Simpson, William, Texas*	44	154	17	20	22	0	1	0	14	1	2	17	3	40	5	2	.130
Smith, Kenneth, Atlanta*	32	94	24	24	32	3	1	1	12	1	0	41	0	16	9	1	.255
Spicer, Leonard, Pittsburgh*	37	112	13	28	35	7	0	0	10	1	3	14	1	26	8	3	.250
Steuber, Eugene, Chicago-AL	33	111	20	26	39	3	2	2	14	1	0	25	0	21	4	0	.234
Stevens, Paul, Kansas City†	45	137	27	32	42	3	0	1	15	5	3	44	3	15	11	8	.234
Sutherland, Leonardo, Chi-AL*	51	199	34	48	60	3	3	1	18	2	2	27	1	25	13	4	.241
Swanson, Ronald, St. Louis	11	27	2	7	7	0	0	0	3	0	0	2	0	8	1	1	.259
Takacs, John, Texas*	42	125	16	26	35	3	0	0	13	1	2	22	3	13	3	2	.208
Tessler, Ronald, Atlanta	40	118	25	28	36	6	1	0	6	3	0	29	3	27	17	3	.237
Thompson, Joseph, Chicago-NL	24	60	7	9	14	2	0	1	9	2	0	7	0	15	0	0	.150
Toothman, Jeffrey, StL*	41	152	18	37	46	7	1	0	17	0	1	6	1	26	1	2	.243
Torres, Alfredo, Pittsburgh	47	161	17	35	55	6	4	2	17	0	3	10	1	50	1	4	.217
Valdez, R. Rafael, St. Louis	24	81	13	21	27	4	1	0	12	0	1	11	2	17	4	3	.259
Velasco, Daniel, Pittsburgh	11	30	0	1	1	0	0	0	2	0	0	1	0	12	0	0	.033
Velasco, Roy, Pittsburgh*	27	99	7	23	28	5	0	0	9	1	0	6	0	13	2	5	.232
Vosejpka, Darrell, Kan City	45	148	20	33	56	5	3	4	27	1	0	35	2	48	0	0	.223
Wilkerson, Wayne, Texas	23	81	16	17	20	1	1	0	6	2	2	15	1	12	1	1	.210
Williams, Glenn, Texas	32	87	12	18	26	5	0	1	7	1	0	28	2	22	3	2	.207
Winslow, Daniel, St. Louis	31	88	15	27	32	5	0	0	12	1	0	14	1	8	1	1	.307
Yesenchak, Edward, Chi-AL	6	18	2	2	2	0	0	0	2	0	0	3	0	4	1	1	.111
Zaya, Felipe, St. Louis	26	78	12	22	27	1	2	0	12	0	1	10	1	15	2	2	.282
Zilonis, Peter, Texas	21	55	6	9	11	2	0	0	7	1	0	6	0	15	1	0	.164

The following pitchers had no plate appearances primarily through use of designated hitters, listed alphabetically by club, games in parentheses.

ATLANTA—Brezeal, Ronald (7); Bruno, Fernando (16); Cowley, Joe (5); Cranford, William (10); Gullette, L. Leon (11); Harmon, John (2); Livingstone, Stuart (9); Royer, David (6); Utley, Chad (11); Wilkerson, J. Kenny (10).

CHICAGO-AL—Bishop, Brett (9); Evans, Ricky (11); Howard, Fred (14); Lamon, Martin (9); Martin, John M. (12); Nored, Michael (8); Seltzer, Randy (12); Soth, Paul (14); Trout, Steven (9); Tulacz, Michael (11).

CHICAGO-NL—Barreto, Miguel (11); Brown, Daniel (12); Brown, Peter (1); Clark, Robert A. (12); England, Daniel (13); Espina, Early (5); Herendeen, Richard (9); Lowe, Donald (11); McClure, Richard (14); Powell, Raymond (9); Reiter, John (10); Segelke, Herman (8).

KANSAS CITY—Cowan, Edward (8); Dubee, Richard (8); Eaton, Craig (5); Gowen, Timmy (7); Greene, Henry (13); Grzybek, Benjamin (6); Lizarraga, Robert (6); Passalacqua, Francisco (16); Prince, Raymond (11); Pulido, Philip (11); Sebastian, John (8); Simmons, Brad (6); Winters, David (11).

PITTSBURGH—Abreu, Marcial (12); Cruz, Arcadio (10); Martinez, Christian (10); Perez, Pascual (10); Rivas, Martin (11); Shackelford, Pat (8); Smith, James C. (7); Tello, Ramon (4); Valera, Salvador (6); Vasquez, Rafael (9).

ST. LOUIS—Arthur, James (6); Clark, Christopher (7); Dennard, Anthony (6); Figueroa, Fernando (2); Fulgham, John (12); Guerrero, Federico (9); Jacob, Terrence (4); Kirchenwitz, Arno (10); Lamer, Donald (8); Littlefield, John (3); Meza, Billy (6); Pantoja, Raul (8); Schopp, William (12).

TEXAS—Allard, Brian (13); Bianchi, Steven (14); Comer, Steven (9); Couch, Richard (9); Davis, Ted (7); Finch, Steven (10); Keenan, Kerry (8); Kiser, Orvin (7); Moock, Patrick (13); Roddy, Phillip (9); Watson, Phillip (12); Williamson, Michael (8).

TWO CLUBS—Fedoroko, John (1 Chicago-AL, 3 St. Louis) (4); Jorn, David (1 Chicago-AL, 8 St. Louis) (9); Leduc, Jean-Pierre (1 Atlanta, 8 Pittsburgh) (9); Searage, Raymond (1 Chicago-AL, 10 St. Louis) (11); Williams, Raymond (1 Chicago-AL, 8 St. Louis) (9).

GRAND-SLAM HOME RUNS—Bright, Davis, Renfroe, 1 each.

AWARDED FIRST BASE ON INTERFERENCE—None.

CLUB FIELDING

Club	G.	PO.	A.	E.	DP.	PB.	Pct.	Club	G.	PO.	A.	E.	DP.	PB.	Pct.
Kansas City	54	1363	612	82	45	12	.960	St. Louis	52	1273	567	109	47	11	.944
Texas	54	1414	648	89	44	16	.959	Atlanta	53	1284	537	124	39	12	.936
Chicago-NL	54	1364	567	95	45	8	.953	Pittsburgh	52	1269	483	150	37	15	.921
Chicago-AL	53	1363	568	111	37	20	.946								

INDIVIDUAL FIELDING

*Throws lefthanded.

FIRST BASEMEN

Player and Club	G.	PO.	A.	E.	DP.	Pct.	Player and Club	G.	PO.	A.	E.	DP.	Pct.
Phelps, Kansas City*	19	166	16	2	13	.989	Vosejpka, Kansas City	36	325	16	8	26	.977
Romero, Chicago-NL*	27	213	9	3	22	.987	Robinson, Texas	18	157	14	4	5	.977
Takacs, Texas	14	118	6	2	13	.984	Thompson, Chicago-NL	23	157	8	5	12	.971
GREENAWAY, Chi-AL	40	319	26	6	19	.983	Godard, Chicago-NL	21	87	7	3	4	.969
Lee, Atlanta	46	360	18	7	31	.982	R. Velasco, Pitt*	27	186	20	7	10	.967
Jennings, Texas*	31	256	15	6	21	.978	Durham, St. Louis*	33	283	4	10	25	.966
Toothman, St. Louis*	22	166	11	4	18	.978	Morton, Chicago-AL*	17	114	5	7	9	.944

(Fewer Than Ten Games)

Player and Club	G.	PO.	A.	E.	DP.	Pct.	Player and Club	G.	PO.	A.	E.	DP.	Pct.
Harper, Atlanta	3	17	1	0	0	1.000	Torres, Pittsburgh	5	35	8	2	6	.956
Brockenbury, Atlanta	2	13	2	0	1	1.000	Smith, Atlanta	6	39	2	2	5	.953
Mabee, Texas	1	4	1	0	0	1.000	Mota, Pittsburgh	3	31	0	2	3	.939
Long, Atlanta*	1	2	0	0	0	1.000	Rieger, St. Louis*	2	11	1	1	0	.923
Renfroe, Pittsburgh	8	57	6	2	6	.969	Evans, Pittsburgh	2	5	0	3	1	.625
Pena, Pittsburgh	9	60	7	3	4	.957							

SECOND BASEMEN

Player and Club	G.	PO.	A.	E.	DP.	Pct.	Player and Club	G.	PO.	A.	E.	DP.	Pct.
Benoit, St. Louis	10	16	19	0	4	1.000	Rodriguez, Pitt	48	119	100	11	26	.952
Lucas, Atlanta	11	18	20	1	8	.974	Forbes, Atlanta	44	101	99	10	21	.952
STEVENS, Kansas City	43	86	118	6	21	.971	Hill, Chicago-AL	27	88	67	8	16	.951
Jark, Chicago-NL	32	69	62	4	18	.970	Jaccar, Texas	19	46	57	6	18	.945
Sample, Texas	38	81	113	8	16	.960	Newman, Chicago-NL	23	54	59	7	16	.942
Gabella, Chicago-AL	26	46	74	5	4	.960	Bumstead, St. Louis	38	86	115	16	26	.926
Serrano, Kansas City	13	31	36	3	7	.957							

(Fewer Than Ten Games)

Player and Club	G.	PO.	A.	E.	DP.	Pct.	Player and Club	G.	PO.	A.	E.	DP.	Pct.
Llodrat, Kansas City	7	3	14	0	3	1.000	Cardenas, Chicago-NL	1	2	0	0	0	1.000
Capowski, Texas	2	2	10	0	1	1.000	Martindale, St. Louis	4	14	17	1	2	.969
Carter, Chicago-NL	4	7	3	0	0	1.000	Hernandez, Pitt	7	16	9	1	2	.962
Roof, St. Louis	1	2	3	0	0	1.000	Hicks, Atlanta	2	9	3	1	2	.923

THIRD BASEMEN

Player and Club	G.	PO.	A.	E.	DP.	Pct.	Player and Club	G.	PO.	A.	E.	DP.	Pct.
Wilkerson, Texas	16	10	33	1	3	.977	COTES, Pittsburgh	42	50	70	17	6	.876
Zaya, St. Louis	13	12	28	2	3	.952	Elter, Chicago-AL	29	24	49	12	4	.859
Takacs, Texas	27	27	42	4	5	.945	Gray, Chicago-AL	24	11	40	10	2	.836
Llodrat, Kansas City	32	26	49	5	7	.938	Elliott, Atlanta	31	22	63	17	8	.833
Riley, Kansas City	27	21	55	9	8	.894	Pierce, St. Louis	25	17	43	12	6	.833
Carter, Chicago-NL	30	23	53	9	4	.894	Cardenas, Chicago-NL	11	7	15	6	0	.786
Hicks, Atlanta	12	2	28	4	1	.882	Hodgson, Chicago-NL	12	6	13	10	0	.655

THIRD BASEMEN—Continued
(Fewer Than Ten Games)

Player and Club	G.	PO.	A.	E.	DP.	Pct.
Garcia, Chicago-NL	5	7	6	0	0	1.000
Given, St. Louis	5	1	9	0	0	1.000
Bumstead, St. Louis	2	0	5	0	1	1.000
Pena, Atlanta	2	1	4	0	1	1.000
Hernandez, Pitt	1	0	3	0	0	1.000
Jaccar, Texas	9	8	14	1	1	.957
McCann, Kansas City	3	1	9	1	0	.909
Alcala, Kansas City	9	12	14	3	1	.897
Harper, Atlanta	4	2	6	1	1	.889
Edrington, Pitt	9	9	23	6	3	.842
Lucas, Atlanta	9	8	18	6	2	.813
Zilonis, Texas	8	5	16	5	1	.808
Fuentes, St. Louis	6	2	17	5	0	.792
Newman, Chicago-NL	8	0	7	3	0	.700
Mercedes, Pitt	4	6	3	4	0	.692
Messer, Chicago-NL	6	2	6	4	0	.667
Martindale, St. Louis	1	1	1	1	0	.667
Hill, Chicago-AL	1	1	0	1	0	.500
Roof, St. Louis	1	0	1	2	0	.333

SHORTSTOPS

Player and Club	G.	PO.	A.	E.	DP.	Pct.
Serrano, Kansas City	10	6	29	0	3	1.000
DAVIS, Chicago-NL	49	76	158	4	27	.983
McCann, Kansas City	35	54	88	7	11	.953
Capowski, Texas	24	34	72	7	10	.938
Zaya, St. Louis	11	22	36	4	7	.935
Mabee, Texas	33	45	112	15	13	.913
Parmenter, Chi-AL	37	48	99	17	13	.896
Hill, Chicago-AL	14	28	36	8	4	.889
Concepcion, Kan City	14	16	40	8	9	.875
Benoit, St. Louis	26	50	77	20	19	.864
Carty, Atlanta	40	38	92	30	12	.813
Goodrich, Pittsburgh	44	45	87	39	14	.772

(Fewer Than Ten Games)

Player and Club	G.	PO.	A.	E.	DP.	Pct.
Roof, St. Louis	3	4	11	0	2	1.000
Palmer, Chicago-NL	1	3	1	0	0	1.000
Pierce, St. Louis	1	1	3	0	0	1.000
Carter, Chicago-NL	2	2	2	0	2	1.000
Zilonis, Texas	2	1	3	0	0	1.000
Williams, Texas	1	1	1	0	0	1.000
Messer, Chicago-NL	1	0	1	0	0	1.000
Bumstead, St. Louis	7	5	23	1	3	.966
Gray, Chicago-AL	6	10	13	2	3	.920
Seibert, Chicago-NL	7	8	20	3	3	.903
Elliott, Atlanta	8	10	18	3	3	.903
Martindale, St. Louis	4	5	13	2	2	.900
Hernandez, Atl-Pitt	9	8	17	4	3	.862
Garcia, Chicago-NL	4	3	7	2	1	.833
Mendez, Kansas City	5	7	3	2	1	.833
Edrington, Pitt-Atl	9	15	28	10	2	.811
Lucas, Atlanta	4	8	9	4	2	.810

OUTFIELDERS

Player and Club	G.	PO.	A.	E.	DP.	Pct.
JEMISON, Texas	45	66	2	0	0	1.000
Keck, St. Louis	24	36	0	0	0	1.000
Edrington, Pitt	13	27	7	0	3	1.000
Hester, Kansas City*	28	30	1	0	0	1.000
Williams, Texas	20	26	3	0	0	1.000
Hernandez, Pitt	14	24	2	0	0	1.000
Romero, Chicago-NL	17	23	2	0	0	1.000
Toothman, St. Louis*	21	22	3	0	0	1.000
Imhoff, Atlanta	13	19	0	0	0	1.000
Morton, Chicago-AL*	11	6	1	0	0	1.000
Buscher, Kansas City	11	5	1	0	0	1.000
Hoscheidt, Kan City	50	92	8	1	0	.990
Rackley, Chicago-NL	38	67	2	1	1	.986
Given, St. Louis	30	56	0	1	0	.982
Rokosz, Chicago-AL*	48	47	2	1	1	.980
Tessler, Atlanta	25	41	2	1	0	.977
Martin, Chicago-NL*	44	98	6	3	3	.972
Boyer, Atlanta	16	34	1	1	0	.972
Martinez, St. Louis*	25	31	3	1	0	.971
F. Perez, Pittsburgh	16	29	0	1	0	.967
Rivera, Texas	48	78	5	3	1	.965
Simpson, Texas	44	75	6	3	1	.964
Krattli, Kansas City	50	69	11	3	2	.964
Fulton, Pittsburgh*	37	73	3	3	1	.962
Smith, Atlanta	26	39	4	2	0	.956
Rodriguez, Kan City	40	81	3	4	2	.955
Bright, Chicago-AL	49	92	8	5	3	.952
Spicer, Pittsburgh*	35	77	3	4	1	.952
Mohr, Chicago-NL	20	20	0	1	0	.952
Long, Atlanta*	37	76	2	4	0	.951
DiMatteo, Chicago-NL	46	57	1	3	1	.951
McCracken, Chi-NL	18	18	1	1	1	.950
Dotson, St. Louis	35	53	2	3	1	.948
Gentile, Pittsburgh*	28	57	7	4	1	.941
Sutherland, Chi-AL*	51	95	6	7	3	.935
Harper, Atlanta	48	68	1	5	0	.932
Araujo, Chicago-NL	18	23	1	2	0	.923
Baez, St. Louis	10	18	1	2	0	.905
Evans, Atlanta-Pitt	10	11	2	2	0	.867

(Fewer Than Ten Games)

Player and Club	G.	PO.	A.	E.	DP.	Pct.
Swanson, St. Louis	9	11	0	0	0	1.000
Penniall, St. Louis	3	7	0	0	0	1.000
Rothwell, Kan City	8	6	1	0	0	1.000
Goodrich, Pittsburgh	1	4	0	0	0	1.000
Carter, Chicago-NL	3	3	0	0	0	1.000
Seibert, Chicago-NL	3	0	2	0	0	1.000
Castro, Pittsburgh	1	1	0	0	0	1.000
Hicks, Atlanta	1	1	0	0	0	1.000
Mota, Atlanta	1	1	0	0	0	1.000
Johnson, Chicago-NL	2	1	0	0	0	1.000
Pena, Pittsburgh	9	19	0	1	0	.950
Valdez, St. Louis	9	7	1	1	0	.889
Durham, St. Louis*	9	13	1	2	0	.875
Mercedes, Pittsburgh	5	5	1	2	0	.750
Robinson, Texas	9	5	1	2	0	.750
Wilkerson, Texas	7	7	0	5	0	.583
Gray, Chicago-AL	2	1	0	1	0	.500

CATCHERS

Player and Club	G.	PO.	A.	E.	DP.	PB.	Pct.
Hunsaker, St. Louis ..	11	55	9	0	0	1	1.000
Johnson, Kan City	10	47	6	0	0	2	1.000
Hudson, Kan City	11	29	5	0	0	1	1.000
STEUBER, Chi-AL..	27	197	17	2	0	11	.991
Lewis, Texas	27	133	7	2	0	8	.986
Winslow, St. Louis	25	113	16	2	1	4	.985
Peterson, Texas	32	197	25	4	2	8	.982
Ferrer, Atlanta	18	103	9	2	2	9	.982
Close, Kansas City	28	133	13	3	4	9	.980
Evers, Chicago-NL	22	113	17	4	2	1	.970
Peoples, Chi-NL	23	110	15	4	1	5	.969
Durbin, St. Louis	11	57	6	2	1	3	.969
Colbern, Chi-AL	18	142	15	6	3	8	.963
Gaudet, Kan City	27	119	21	9	1	2	.940
Torres, Pittsburgh	28	156	24	12	1	10	.938
Brockenbury, Atl	30	114	19	9	1	0	.937
Renfroe, Pitt	16	67	18	8	0	3	.914

(Fewer Than Ten Games)

Player and Club	G.	PO.	A.	E.	DP.	PB.	Pct.
Pasillas, Chi-AL	9	65	9	0	1	1	1.000
Seoanee, Atlanta	9	57	3	0	0	2	1.000
Beardon, Atlanta	6	43	4	0	0	1	1.000
Keatley, Chi-NL	7	37	7	0	1	0	1.000
Pena, Pittsburgh	7	28	3	0	0	1	1.000
D. Velasco, Pitt	5	16	1	0	0	0	1.000
Burroughs, Kan C	4	12	1	0	0	1	1.000
Mota, Pittsburgh	3	9	1	0	0	1	1.000
Hodgson, Chi-NL	1	3	0	0	0	0	1.000
Swanson, St. Louis	1	2	1	0	0	0	1.000
Zilonis, Texas	1	2	1	0	0	0	1.000
Rothwell, Kan City	1	1	0	0	0	0	1.000
Bertolotti, StL	8	49	4	1	1	1	.981
Marsalan, St. Louis	9	28	3	1	0	1	.965
Yesenchak, Chi-AL	1	8	1	1	0	0	.900
Fuentes, St. Louis	3	4	1	1	0	1	.833

PITCHERS

Player and Club	G.	PO.	A.	E.	DP.	Pct.
GRAVEN, Atlanta*	13	5	17	0	0	1.000
Howard, Chicago-AL	14	2	16	0	0	1.000
Evans, Chicago-AL	11	4	12	0	3	1.000
P. Perez, Pittsburgh	10	8	6	0	0	1.000
Seltzer, Chicago-AL*	12	4	7	0	0	1.000
Prince, Kansas City	11	4	6	0	0	1.000
Soth, Chicago-AL	14	3	7	0	0	1.000
Kirchenwitz, StL	10	1	8	0	2	1.000
Clark, Chicago-NL*	12	1	8	0	0	1.000
Cruz, Pittsburgh	11	2	5	0	0	1.000
Pulido, Kansas City	11	1	6	0	0	1.000
Bruno, Atlanta	16	1	6	0	0	1.000
Passalacqua, Kan City ..	16	3	4	0	0	1.000
Martinez, Pittsburgh	10	3	3	0	0	1.000
Barreto, Chicago-NL	11	0	4	0	0	1.000
Schopp, St. Louis	12	1	3	0	0	1.000
McClure, Chicago-NL	14	0	4	0	0	1.000
Utley, Atlanta	11	1	2	0	0	1.000
Finch, Texas	10	3	11	1	0	.933
Gullette, Atlanta	11	3	9	1	0	.923
Bianchi, Texas	14	11	11	2	0	.917
England, Chicago-NL	13	5	23	3	2	.903
Searage, Chi-AL-StL*	11	0	8	1	0	.889
Cranford, Atlanta*	10	0	6	1	0	.857
Abreu, Pittsburgh	12	3	3	1	0	.857
Martin, Chicago-AL	12	1	10	2	0	.846
Allard, Texas	13	2	9	2	0	.846
Reiter, Chicago-NL	10	3	7	2	0	.833
D. Brown, Chi-NL*	12	0	5	1	0	.833
Moock, Texas	13	0	5	1	0	.833
Tulacz, Chicago-AL*	11	2	12	3	0	.824
Lowe, Chicago-NL	11	3	9	3	0	.800
Finch, Atlanta*	11	1	3	1	1	.800
Fulgham, St. Louis	12	3	9	3	0	.750
Madden, Chicago-AL	13	3	9	4	0	.750
Winters, Kansas City	11	4	1	2	0	.714
Watson, Texas	11	0	2	1	0	.667
Greene, Kansas City*	13	1	1	1	0	.667
Wilkerson, Atlanta	10	0	1	1	0	.500
Rivas, Pittsburgh	11	1	0	1	0	.500

(Fewer Than Ten Games)

Player and Club	G.	PO.	A.	E.	DP.	Pct.
Comer, Texas	9	4	13	0	0	1.000
Vasquez, Pittsburgh	9	5	12	0	0	1.000
Roddy, Texas	9	4	12	0	0	1.000
Livingstone, Atlanta	9	4	11	0	1	1.000
Jorn, Chi AL-StL	9	1	13	0	1	1.000
Brezeal, Atlanta*	7	2	10	0	0	1.000
Gowen, Kansas City*	7	0	8	0	0	1.000
Rock, Pittsburgh	9	2	5	0	0	1.000
Meza, St. Louis	6	1	5	0	0	1.000
Simmons, Kan City*	6	1	5	0	0	1.000
Williams, Chi AL-StL	9	0	6	0	1	1.000
Tello, Pittsburgh*	4	1	4	0	0	1.000
Nored, Chicago-AL*	8	1	4	0	1	1.000
Pantoja, St. Louis*	8	0	5	0	0	1.000
Lamon, Chicago-AL	9	1	4	0	0	1.000
Pergantis, St. Louis	7	2	1	0	0	1.000
Lizarraga, Kan City	6	0	2	0	0	1.000
Clark, St. Louis	7	0	2	0	0	1.000
Guerrero, St. Louis	9	1	1	0	0	1.000
Powell, Chicago-NL*	9	0	2	0	0	1.000
Renfroe, Pittsburgh	1	0	1	0	0	1.000
Figueroa, St. Louis	2	0	1	0	0	1.000
Mercedes, Pittsburgh	1	0	1	0	0	1.000
Kiser, Texas	7	1	0	0	0	1.000
Couch, Texas*	9	1	13	1	1	.933
Leduc, Atlanta-Pitt	9	4	8	1	0	.923
Royer, Atlanta	5	3	8	1	1	.917
Dubee, Kansas City	8	3	8	1	0	.917
Harrison, St. Louis	6	2	8	1	0	.909
Eaton, Kansas City	5	3	6	1	0	.900
Grzybek, Kansas City	6	0	8	1	1	.889
Sebastian, Kan City	8	6	2	1	1	.889
Trout, Chicago-AL*	9	0	15	2	1	.882
Keenan, Texas	8	3	11	2	0	.875
Shackelford, Pitt	8	2	8	2	0	.833
Herendeen, Chi-NL*	9	2	3	1	0	.833
Dennard, St. Louis	6	2	6	2	0	.800
Segelke, Chicago-NL	8	3	5	2	0	.800
Cowley, Atlanta	5	0	4	1	2	.800
Williamson, Texas	8	1	3	1	0	.800
Valera, Pittsburgh	6	3	3	2	0	.750
Arthur, St. Louis*	6	0	3	1	0	.750
Smith, Pittsburgh	7	2	4	3	0	.667
Lamer, St. Louis	8	1	3	2	0	.667
Bishop, Chicago-AL	9	0	2	1	0	.667
Espina, Pittsburgh	5	1	0	1	0	.500

The following pitchers had no recorded accepted chances; therefore are not listed in the fielding averages for that position: P. Brown*, Davis, Fedoroko, Harmon, Jacob, Littlefield, D. Velasco.

CLUB PITCHING

Club	G.	CG.	ShO.	Sv.	IP.	H.	R.	ER.	HR.	BB.	Int. BB.	HB.	SO.	WP.	Bk.	ERA.
Texas	54	14	6	13	471	372	187	134	4	220	4	14	302	27	4	2.56
Chicago-NL	54	12	9	9	455	380	218	167	12	263	7	16	291	24	2	3.30
St. Louis	52	8	4	12	424	391	212	168	5	236	8	16	285	35	4	3.57
Chicago-AL	53	6	3	7	454	392	238	180	4	312	5	18	391	36	0	3.57
Kansas City	54	9	5	3	454	395	237	185	13	232	8	16	259	47	0	3.67
Atlanta	53	15	5	5	428	411	287	205	9	243	20	10	292	21	8	4.31
Pittsburgh	52	12	2	4	423	432	310	227	7	272	3	21	240	28	8	4.83

PITCHERS' RECORDS

(Leading Qualifiers for Earned-Run Average Leadership–43 or More Innings)

*Throws lefthanded.

Pitcher–Club	G.	GS.	CG.	ShO.	W.	L.	Sv.	Pct.	IP.	H.	R.	ER.	HR.	BB.	Int. BB.	HB.	SO.	WP.	ERA.
Comer, Texas	9	8	5	2	7	2	0	.778	60	35	9	6	0	18	1	0	40	1	0.90
Roddy, Texas	9	4	1	0	2	0	0	1.000	47	27	14	7	0	25	1	0	24	5	1.34
Clark, Chi-NL*	12	11	1	1	5	0	0	1.000	71	57	24	12	1	40	0	4	59	3	1.52
Livingstone, Atl	9	9	6	1	3	5	0	.375	70	43	22	13	0	11	2	1	35	0	1.67
England, Chi-NL	13	13	5	1	10	3	0	.769	96	66	25	18	1	38	0	2	63	6	1.69
Bianchi, Texas	14	5	2	0	6	3	2	.667	60	42	16	12	0	19	1	3	42	0	1.80
Howard, Chi-AL	14	8	4	1	4	5	1	.444	67	51	28	14	1	37	1	1	76	1	1.88
Prince, Kan City	11	11	1	1	4	0	0	1.000	68	42	18	15	0	32	0	3	32	1	1.99
Soth, Chicago-AL	14	4	0	0	3	2	1	.600	43	30	11	10	1	13	0	0	37	1	2.09
Kirchenwitz, StL	10	7	1	0	5	1	1	.833	50	47	16	12	1	11	2	3	20	1	2.16

Departmental Leaders: G–Bruno, Passalacqua, 16; GS–England, Graven, 13; CG–Livingstone, 6; ShO–Comer, Reiter, 2; W–England, 10; L–Cruz, Graven, 8; Sv–Moock, 5; Pct.–Clark (Chi-NL), 1.000; IP–England, 96; H–Graven, 87; R–Graven, 44; ER–Graven, 39; HR–Cranford, Passalacqua, Powell, 3; BB–Madden, 51; IBB–Bruno, 4; HB–Madden, 7; SO–Howard, 76; WP–Pulido, 13.

(All Pitchers–Listed Alphabetically)

Pitcher–Club	G.	GS.	CG.	ShO.	W.	L.	Sv.	Pct.	IP.	H.	R.	ER.	HR.	BB.	Int. BB.	HB.	SO.	WP.	ERA.
Abreu, Pittsburgh	12	0	0	0	0	0	1	.000	23	22	16	11	0	19	0	1	14	4	4.30
Allard, Texas	13	9	3	1	5	1	1	.833	68	46	25	18	1	33	0	2	35	7	2.38
Arthur, StL*	6	0	0	0	2	0	0	.000	9	7	4	4	1	10	0	0	7	0	4.00
Barreto, Chi-NL	11	1	0	0	0	4	0	.000	22	32	21	17	0	10	0	2	17	4	6.95
Bianchi, Texas	14	5	2	0	6	3	2	.667	60	42	16	12	0	19	1	3	42	0	1.80
Bishop, Chi-AL	9	0	0	0	2	2	1	.500	22	21	11	9	0	12	1	0	17	1	3.68
Brezeal, Atlanta*	7	1	0	0	1	1	0	.500	24	24	17	12	2	14	1	1	16	0	4.50
D. Brown, Chi-NL*	12	0	0	0	1	0	3	1.000	28	24	12	10	1	12	1	1	15	1	3.21
P. Brown, Chi-NL*	1	0	0	0	0	0	0	.000	0	3	4	3	0	0	0	0	0	0	....
Bruno, Atlanta	16	0	0	0	2	3	3	.400	27	18	12	8	0	15	4	0	17	4	2.67
Clark, St. Louis	7	1	0	0	1	1	1	.500	16	17	19	17	1	15	1	0	11	2	9.56
Clark, Chi-NL*	12	12	1	1	5	0	0	1.000	71	57	24	12	1	40	0	4	59	3	1.52
Comer, Texas	9	8	5	2	7	2	0	.778	60	35	9	6	0	18	1	0	40	1	0.90
Couch, Texas*	9	6	0	0	3	3	0	.500	42	40	19	12	0	22	0	0	13	2	2.57
Cowan, Kan City	8	5	1	1	4	2	0	.667	33	31	13	11	0	16	0	3	20	3	3.00
Cowley, Atlanta	5	3	0	0	0	4	0	.000	13	17	16	13	0	16	0	2	12	3	9.00
Cranford, Atlanta*	10	7	0	0	1	3	0	.250	42	47	38	29	3	33	3	3	31	3	6.21
Cruz, Pittsburgh	10	10	2	0	2	8	0	.200	59	53	35	26	1	42	0	6	34	1	3.97
Davis, Texas	7	6	0	0	0	1	0	.000	20	33	25	20	0	18	0	1	6	1	9.00
Dennard, StL	6	3	0	0	3	1	1	.750	22	20	14	9	0	16	1	0	17	2	3.68
Dubee, Kan City	8	8	2	0	4	1	0	.800	57	46	25	20	1	22	0	2	26	4	3.16
Eaton, Kan City	5	4	0	0	3	2	0	.600	29	22	9	6	2	9	0	0	22	0	1.86
England, Chi-NL	13	13	5	1	10	3	0	.769	96	66	25	18	1	38	0	2	63	6	1.69
Espina, Chi-NL	5	0	0	0	1	0	1	1.000	9	13	10	10	0	9	1	0	9	0	10.13
Evans, Chicago-AL	11	2	0	0	0	1	1	.000	37	43	29	22	0	26	0	2	22	8	5.35
Fedoroko, 1 Ch AL-3 StL	4	1	0	0	0	0	0	.000	8	8	3	3	0	13	0	1	8	0	3.38
Figueroa, StL	2	1	0	0	0	0	0	.000	3	4	3	3	0	6	0	1	3	1	9.00
Finch, Texas	10	9	1	0	4	1	0	.800	59	41	21	17	1	36	0	2	53	2	2.59
Finch, Atlanta*	11	0	0	0	0	0	1	.000	21	27	21	11	0	14	3	1	14	2	4.71
Fulgham, StL	12	7	3	1	3	3	1	.500	56	54	29	21	0	22	2	1	41	5	3.38
Gowen, Kan City*	7	5	1	1	1	5	0	.167	32	33	26	19	2	17	2	0	13	4	5.34
Graven, Atlanta*	13	13	4	0	5	8	0	.385	82	87	44	39	1	20	2	0	56	2	4.28
Greene, Kan City*	13	7	2	0	3	2	0	.600	58	44	25	24	1	35	1	3	47	3	3.72
Grzybek, Kan City	6	3	1	0	2	1	0	.667	33	31	24	19	2	10	0	3	14	1	4.32
Guerrero, St. Louis	9	0	0	0	1	0	0	1.000	16	12	1	1	1	11	0	2	14	1	0.56
Gullette, Atlanta	11	11	4	1	7	3	0	.700	73	61	34	29	1	28	1	1	49	2	3.58
Harmon, Atlanta	2	1	0	0	1	1	0	.500	7	8	5	3	0	6	0	0	4	0	3.86

Pitcher–Club	G	GS	CG	ShO	W	L	Sv	Pct.	IP	H	R	ER	HR	BB	Int. BB	HB	SO	WP	ERA
Harrison, StL	6	6	2	0	3	1	0	.750	36	37	14	12	0	10	0	1	16	1	3.00
Herendeen, Chi-NL*	9	1	0	0	2	3	1	.400	27	21	19	12	2	17	0	0	21	0	4.00
Howard, Chi-Atl	14	8	4	1	4	5	1	.444	67	51	28	14	1	37	1	1	76	1	1.88
Jacob, St. Louis	4	0	0	0	0	0	2	.000	6	8	1	1	0	2	0	0	8	0	1.50
Jorn, 1 Chi AL-8 StL	9	7	1	0	3	4	0	.429	43	45	28	20	0	23	0	1	17	5	4.19
Keenan, Texas	8	4	2	0	4	1	0	.800	36	33	9	8	0	9	1	1	24	2	2.00
Kirchenwitz, StL	10	7	1	0	5	1	1	.833	50	47	16	12	1	11	2	3	20	1	2.16
Kiser, Texas	7	0	0	0	1	2	1	.333	9	12	5	5	0	1	0	0	8	0	5.00
Lamer, St. Louis	8	2	0	0	3	2	1	.600	25	14	9	6	0	12	0	3	17	6	2.16
Lamon, Chicago-AL	9	1	0	0	1	1	0	.000	15	17	10	10	0	11	0	1	8	1	6.00
Leduc, 1 Atl-8 Pitt	9	6	3	0	1	5	0	.167	49	58	28	20	0	15	3	0	40	3	3.67
Littlefield, StL	3	0	0	0	1	0	0	1.000	7	5	3	2	0	3	0	0	10	1	2.57
Livingstone, Atl	9	9	6	1	3	5	0	.375	70	43	22	13	0	11	2	1	35	0	1.67
Lizarraga, Kan C	6	0	0	0	0	0	0	.000	12	17	10	9	0	8	1	0	9	1	6.75
Lowe, Chicago-NL	11	9	0	0	3	3	0	.500	53	42	41	36	1	50	0	5	31	7	6.11
Madden, Chi-AL	13	6	0	0	1	6	1	.143	53	36	25	17	1	51	0	7	41	5	2.89
Martin, Chi-AL	12	5	0	0	4	4	0	.500	39	45	27	25	0	29	0	0	31	3	5.77
Martinez, Pitt	10	0	0	0	2	0	0	.000	24	21	17	12	0	19	0	1	12	1	4.50
McClure, Chi-NL	14	0	0	0	0	0	0	.000	10	10	13	12	1	13	0	1	3	2	10.80
Mercedes, Pitt	4	0	0	0	0	0	0	1.000	21	27	11	10	0	12	0	0	13	0	4.29
Meza, St. Louis	6	2	0	0	2	1	5	.667	19	22	18	10	1	6	0	2	13	2	4.74
Moock, Texas	13	0	0	0	2	1	5	.000	26	27	19	19	0	35	1	1	23	6	6.58
Nored, Chi-AL*	8	3	0	0	1	0		.000	20	21	18	13	0	14	1	1	11	1	5.85
Pantoja, StL*	8	3	0	0	2	3	1	.400	30	35	20	15	3	15	2	3	8	2	4.50
Passalacqua, KC	16	10	2	0	2	5	0	.286	56	51	41	29	0	35	0	4	34	2	4.66
P. Perez, Pitt	10	2	0	0	2	0		.000	15	11	15	10	0	10	1	1	9	1	5.50
Pergantis, Atl	7	2	1	0	0	2	0	1.000	20	9	9	3		13	2	0	6	0	4.05
Powell, Chi-NL*	9	1	0	0	2	0		1.000	9	9	3	2	0	9	0	3	10	0	2.00
Prince, Kan City	11	11	1	1	4	0	0	1.000	68	42	18	15	0	32	0	3	32	1	1.99
Pulido, Kan City	11	3	0	0	1	4	0	.200	31	27	19	19	1	29	0	0	21	13	5.52
Reiter, Chi-NL	10	9	4	2	6	2	0	.750	59	47	23	18	0	36	0	3	31	0	2.75
Renfroe, Pitt	1	0	0	0	0	0	0	.000	2	0	0	0	0	2	0	0	0	0	0.00
Rivas, Pittsburgh	11	0	0	0	1	1	2	.500	20	18	6	4	0	10	1	0	10	0	1.80
Rock, Pittsburgh	9	6	0	0	0	4	1	.000	34	37	30	23	0	33	0	4	30	3	6.09
Roddy, Texas	9	4	1	0	2	0		1.000	47	37	14	7	0	25	1	0	24	5	1.34
Royer, Atlanta	5	5	0	0	2	0		.000	16	20	26	16	1	30	0	0	15	5	9.00
Schopp, Atlanta	12	4	0	0	0	3	0	.000	21	15	9	7	0	21	0	2	21	5	3.00
Searage, 1 ChAL-10 StL*	8	5	0	1	3	4		.250	32	24	17	15	1	22	1	0	31	2	4.22
Sebastian, Kan C	8	4	0	0	2	2	0	.500	30	36	19	15	2	8	0	0	17	3	4.50
Segelke, Chi-NL	8	8	2	0	3	2	0	.600	45	33	16	11	1	26	0	1	31	3	2.20
Seltzer, Chi-AL*	12	7	2	0	4	4	1	.500	50	57	30	26	1	32	0	1	46	1	4.68
Shackelford, Pitt	8	8	2	0	1	6	0	.143	47	49	28	24	1	31	1	1	8	5	4.60
Simmons, Kan C*	6	4	1	1	1	3	2	.250	28	30	15	12	0	8	0	0	13	1	3.86
Smith, Pittsburgh	7	4	1	1	1	5	0	.167	27	30	28	21	2	19	0	3	21	3	7.00
Soth, Chicago-AL	14	4	0	0	3	2	1	.600	43	30	11	10	1	13	0	0	37	1	2.09
Tello, Pittsburgh*	4	0	0	0	0	0	0	.000	10	15	11	11	1	3	0	0	7	0	9.90
Trout, Chicago-AL*	9	8	0	0	1	3	0	.250	38	28	18	11	0	29	1	1	35	6	2.61
Tulacz, Chi-AL*	11	7	0	0	4	0	0	1.000	54	38	18	13	0	29	0	2	51	1	2.17
Utley, Atlanta	11	0	0	0	1	0	1	1.000	18	27	23	12	0	18	1	0	14	2	6.00
Valera, Pittsburgh	6	0	0	0	0	0	0	.000	14	19	19	11	1	16	0	0	3	3	7.07
Vasquez, Pitt	1	0	0	0	0	0	0	.000	1	3	3	3	0	0	0	1	1	1	27.00
D. Velasco, Pitt	9	9	2	0	3	5	0	.375	53	56	35	20	0	14	0	0	30	0	3.40
Watson, Texas	12	0	0	0	0	0	3	1.000	22	21	10	4	0	15	0	0	20	0	1.64
Wilkerson, Atlanta	10	0	0	0	0	0	0	.000	12	12	14	10	1	18	0	0	13	0	7.50
Williams, 1 Chi AL-8 StL	9	5	1	0	1	2	0	.333	41	37	17	16	0	22	0	0	30	4	3.51
Williamson, Texas	8	3	0	0	3	1	1	.750	30	26	16	15	1	18	0	3	24	2	4.50
Winters, Kan City	11	0	0	0	2	0	0	1.000	21	8	11	8	1	21	1	0	17	8	3.43

BALKS—Abreu, Brezeal, Gullette, Martinez, Rivas, Royer, Seltzer, Vasquez, 2 each; Allard, Bruno, Clark (StL), Comer, Davis, Fulgham, Graven, McClure, Meza, Powell, Roddy, Schopp, Tulacz, 1 each.

COMBINATION SHUTOUTS—Trout-Tulacz, Tulacz-Howard, Chicago-AL; Segelke-McClure 2, Lowe-McClure, Clark-Barreto, England-Herendeen, Chicago-NL; Eaton-Pulido-Passalacqua, Prince-Grzybek, Kansas City; Vasquez-Rivas, Pittsburgh; Dennard-Clark, Searage-Arthur-Lamer, Kirchenwitz-Guerrero, St. Louis; Couch-Kiser, Bianchi-Watson, Keenan-Williamson, Texas.

NO-HIT GAMES—Livingstone, Atlanta, defeated Pittsburgh, 6-0, August 21; Prince, Kansas City, defeated Atlanta, 1-0, August 27.

Pioneer League

ROOKIE CLASSIFICATION

CHAMPIONSHIP WINNERS IN PREVIOUS YEARS

1939—Twin Falls* .... .581	1951—Salt Lake City .... .618	1961—Boise .... .638
1940—Salt Lake City .... .608	Great Falls (3rd)* .... .559	Great Falls* .... .571
Ogden (4th)* .... .492	1952—Pocatello .... .595	1962—Boise§ .... .565
1941—Boise .... .623	Idaho Falls (2nd)* ...... .573	Billings† .... .706
Ogden (2nd)* .... .598	1953—Ogden .... .679	1963—Idaho Falls .... .702
1942—Pocatello† .... .690	Salt Lake C. (4th)* ...... .527	Magic Valley† .... .643
Boise .... .683	1954—Salt Lake City .... .595	1964—Treasure Valley .... .615
1943-44-45—Did not operate.	Great Falls (4th)* .... .530	1965—Treasure Valley .... .530
1946—Twin Falls‡ .... .585	1955—Boise .... .588	1966—Ogden .... .591
Salt Lake City† .... .585	Magic Valley (4th)* ...... .489	1967—Ogden .... .621
1947—Salt Lake City .... .618	1956—Boise .... .561	1968—Ogden .... .609
Twin Falls† .... .600	1957—Salt Lake City .... .650	1969—Ogden .... .620
1948—Pocatello .... .611	Billings† .... .582	1970—Idaho Falls .... .629
Twin Falls (2nd)* .... .595	1958—Great Falls .... .582	1971—Idaho Falls .... .643
1949—Twin Falls.................... .624	Boise† .... .615	1972—Billings§ .... .694
Pocatello (3rd)* .... .595	1959—Boise .... .633	1973—Billings .... .629
1950—Pocatello .... .635	Billings (2nd)* .... .523	1974—Idaho Falls .... .569
Billings (3rd)* .... .571	1960—Boise† .... .686	1975—Great Falls .... .577
	Idaho Falls .... .650	

*Won four-club playoff. †Won split-season playoff. ‡Ended first half in tie with Salt Lake City and won one-game playoff. §Ended first-half in tie with Billings and Great Falls and won playoff.

STANDING OF CLUBS AT CLOSE OF SEASON, AUGUST 31

Club	G.F.	Bil.	I.F.	Leth.	W.	L.	T.	Pct.	G.B.
Great Falls (Giants)	....	12	15	14	41	30	0	.577	......
Billings (Reds)	11	....	12	13	36	35	0	.507	5
Idaho Falls (Angels)	9	12	....	15	36	36	0	.500	5½
Lethbridge (Expos)	10	11	9	....	30	42	0	.417	11½

Major league affiliations in parentheses.

Playoff—None.

Regular-Season Attendance—Billings, 34,673; Great Falls, 34,439; Idaho Falls, 18,769; Lethbridge, 19,200. Total, 107,081. No playoff. No all-star game.

Managers: Billings—James Hoff; Great Falls—Ernest Rodriguez; Idaho Falls—Larry Himes; Lethbridge—Walt Hriniak.

All-Star Team: 1B—Lyons, Idaho Falls; 2B—Strain, Great Falls; 3B—Scoras, Lethbridge; SS—Hendrickson, Idaho Falls; OF—Sylvester, Great Falls; Milner, Billings; Herring, Billings; C—Simunic, Lethbridge; P—Adams, Idaho Falls; Dawley, Billings; Johnson, Great Falls. Manager—Larry Himes, Idaho Falls.

(Compiled by William J. Weiss, League Statistician, San Mateo, Calif.)

CLUB BATTING

Club	G.	AB.	R.	OR.	H.	TB.	2B.	3B.	HR.	RBI.	SH.	SF.	Int. BB.	BB.	HP.	SO.	SB.	CS.	LOB.	Pct.
Lethbridge	72	2466	449	434	700	1007	108	41	39	372	19	29	320	12	23	459	68	29	571	.284
Idaho Falls	72	2366	437	462	668	888	86	43	16	345	35	29	350	21	19	413	107	53	518	.282
Great Falls	71	2392	430	350	639	879	110	26	29	359	26	25	355	12	17	437	120	39	575	.267
Billings	71	2269	354	424	565	752	88	15	23	280	23	32	349	12	18	477	97	34	532	.249

INDIVIDUAL BATTING

(Leading Qualifiers for Batting Championship—194 or More Plate Appearances)

*Bats lefthanded. †Switch-hitter.

Player and Club	G.	AB.	R.	H.	TB.	2B.	3B.	HR.	RBI.	SH.	SF.	BB.	HP.	SO.	SB.	CS.	Pct.
Scoras, John, Lethbridge	71	273	62	101	169	17	6	13	63	1	5	38	1	45	7	2	.370
Hendrickson, Craig, Idaho F	60	228	50	79	98	11	4	0	33	1	3	22	4	21	14	6	.346
Strain, Joseph, Great Falls	71	282	63	94	124	13	7	1	50	1	3	44	0	17	32	1	.333
Lyons, Donald, Idaho Falls*	65	239	48	78	105	9	9	0	47	3	4	36	2	13	11	5	.326
Wood, W. Christopher, Leth	66	269	55	86	129	17	10	2	37	1	3	20	4	31	13	4	.320
Brouhard, Mark, Idaho Falls	69	255	43	80	122	5	8	7	57	0	4	29	3	55	7	5	.314
Taylor, Goodrum, Idaho F*	58	192	56	58	73	7	4	0	21	3	1	50	0	44	13	9	.302
Sohns, Thomas, Billings*	71	263	41	77	101	10	1	4	39	2	3	33	1	21	12	4	.293
Newby, Kevin, Lethbridge*	70	277	49	81	103	12	5	0	33	2	7	46	1	49	17	11	.292
Young, William, Great Falls	61	219	35	64	81	14	0	1	28	2	1	31	3	21	2	0	.292

Departmental Leaders: G—Scoras, Sohns, Strain, 71; AB—Walker, 290; R—Sylvester, 66; H—Scoras, 101; TB—Scoras, 169; 2B—Scoras, Wood, 17; 3B—Wood, 10; HR—Scoras, 13; RBI—Scoras, 63; SH—Hollifield, 7; SF—Herring, Newby, 7; BB—Sylvester, 69; HP—Hendrickson, Knose, Kopp, Wardlow, Wood, 4; SO—Paige, 68; SB—Strain, 32; CS—Newby, 11.

(All Players—Listed Alphabetically)

Player and Club	G.	AB.	R.	H.	TB.	2B.	3B.	HR.	RBI.	SH.	SF.	BB.	HP.	SO.	SB.	CS.	Pct.
Alicea, Gilberto, Billings	28	64	9	12	16	1	0	1	3	0	0	4	1	20	2	0	.188
Bishop, Michael, Idaho F	68	231	45	67	102	8	9	3	40	3	4	45	2	50	2	1	.290
Bonnell, Glenn, Billings	8	16	3	4	5	1	0	0	1	1	0	1	0	3	0	1	.250
Brenly, Robert, Great Falls	25	86	16	27	37	5	1	1	17	0	0	12	0	9	1	1	.314
Brouhard, Mark, Idaho Falls	69	255	43	80	122	5	8	7	57	0	4	29	3	55	7	5	.314
Brown, Jimmy, Idaho Falls	5	8	1	1	1	0	0	0	1	0	0	1	0	1	0	0	.125
Brown, Stephen, Lethbridge	41	132	16	36	43	5	1	0	13	0	1	15	0	24	3	0	.273
Carballo, Pablo, Lethbridge	21	38	2	4	4	0	0	0	2	1	0	5	1	16	0	1	.105
Cipolla, Mitchell, Leth	47	150	28	42	59	8	0	3	25	2	0	32	2	41	2	2	.280
Da Costa, David, Idaho F	31	76	12	16	22	2	2	0	14	2	2	12	0	25	4	0	.211
Deal, Stephen, Billings*	9	15	1	2	2	0	0	0	1	0	0	2	0	4	1	0	.133
Dimino, Thomas, Billings	39	124	14	25	33	4	2	0	10	2	3	15	2	34	7	2	.202
Douglas, William, Idaho F	30	93	14	22	30	3	1	1	13	2	1	5	0	23	2	2	.237
Ferrell, Richard, Great F	62	223	35	59	93	13	3	5	44	2	3	20	1	29	2	1	.265
Fleury, Denis, Lethbridge	21	65	10	19	37	3	3	3	15	0	0	8	1	15	0	0	.292
Goldetsky, Lawrence, Leth	70	241	50	66	94	12	5	2	32	5	1	43	3	36	8	4	.274
Gooch, Kenneth, Idaho Falls	59	194	31	45	53	5	0	1	21	5	3	25	1	30	5	5	.232
Green, Doyle, Lethbridge	26	1	0	0	0	0	0	0	0	0	0	0	0	0	0	0	.000
Harmon, Willie, Great Falls	2	1	0	0	0	0	0	0	0	0	0	0	0	0	0	0	.000
Held, Daniel, Great Falls	49	166	20	39	53	11	0	1	26	2	3	19	0	32	1	3	.235
Hendrickson, Craig, Idaho F	60	228	50	79	98	11	4	0	33	1	3	22	4	21	14	6	.346
Herring, Paul, Billings	70	254	32	72	106	14	1	6	47	1	7	25	2	34	8	3	.283
Hollifield, David, Idaho F*	68	221	29	64	78	10	2	0	22	7	3	30	1	22	8	5	.290
Householder, Paul, Billings	50	149	23	38	51	3	2	2	19	1	0	23	0	33	9	3	.255
Jackson, Gregory, Billings	61	218	25	60	71	5	3	0	25	1	3	24	1	24	1	0	.275
Jensen, Kevin, Billings†	50	150	25	40	58	15	0	1	18	0	1	23	0	45	2	2	.267
Jones, Donny, Idaho Falls	67	217	29	47	63	9	2	1	16	6	3	19	1	49	11	3	.217
Knose, Mark, Lethbridge	25	70	15	18	27	4	1	1	11	1	3	8	4	25	2	0	.257
Kopp, Kevin, Idaho Falls	56	195	34	44	65	6	3	3	23	3	2	15	4	47	1	1	.226
Kopsky, Michael, Billings	61	173	25	37	51	6	1	2	15	2	2	28	0	62	1	2	.214
Kuecker, Mark, Great Falls	51	191	25	51	58	3	2	0	23	6	2	12	1	21	10	8	.267
LaFave, Robert, Idaho Falls	12	39	3	11	12	1	0	0	6	1	1	4	0	12	0	1	.282
Law, Randy, Billings	29	63	16	15	17	0	1	0	11	2	3	23	0	12	7	2	.238
Lyons, Donald, Idaho Falls*	65	239	48	78	105	9	9	0	47	3	4	36	2	13	11	5	.326
McQuay, Louis, Billings	4	2	1	0	0	0	0	0	0	0	0	1	0	1	0	0	.000
Meade, J. Scott, Billings	46	138	27	37	51	5	0	3	17	1	3	36	1	34	8	3	.268
Mercedes, Manuel, Idaho F	12	0	0	0	0	0	0	0	0	0	0	0	0	0	0	1	.000
Milner, Eddie, Billings*	67	231	51	59	85	14	3	2	27	5	2	49	3	23	17	5	.255
Moffitt, G. Scott, Idaho F	12	46	14	19	29	7	0	1	8	0	1	9	1	4	5	1	.413
Moore, David, Idaho Falls	58	192	28	42	47	3	1	0	32	0	1	32	3	40	7	5	.219
Newby, Kevin, Lethbridge*	70	277	49	81	103	12	5	0	33	2	7	46	1	49	17	11	.292
Norko, Thomas, Billings	29	67	15	18	22	1	0	1	7	3	0	15	1	27	5	0	.269
O'Donnell, Jeffrey, Great F	8	16	1	1	1	0	0	0	0	0	0	4	0	8	0	0	.063
Paige, Mark, Great Falls	52	201	23	39	57	6	6	0	17	2	1	12	0	68	9	6	.194
Parsons, Casey, Great F*	19	77	23	26	31	5	0	0	14	0	1	17	1	3	11	4	.338
Perez, Julio, Lethbridge†	34	127	22	47	60	6	2	1	26	0	2	13	0	3	4	0	.370
Pimentel, Carlos, Billings	38	97	9	18	21	3	0	0	11	0	3	11	1	20	2	2	.186
Pryor, James, Great Falls	10	29	3	10	13	1	1	0	2	0	0	4	0	3	0	0	.345
Rex, Michael, Great Falls	4	17	3	6	9	1	1	0	4	1	0	0	0	2	1	0	.353
Robie, Daniel, Bil†	43	115	18	25	27	2	0	0	12	1	1	10	1	34	4	1	.217
Rodriguez, Miguel, Billings	4	12	1	4	5	1	0	0	1	0	0	2	0	16	0	0	.158
Sanchez, Rafael, Lethbridge	14	38	4	6	8	0	1	0	5	0	0	10	0	21	3	2	.198
Schwartz, David, Great F	36	91	14	18	23	2	0	1	11	2	0	10	0	23	1	2	.198
Shourds, F. Jeffrey, G F	32	90	12	23	31	8	0	0	7	1	0	11	1	30	1	1	.256
Simunic, Douglas, Leth	68	242	42	59	100	9	1	10	51	0	3	47	2	48	1	1	.244
Slater, Robert, Idaho Falls	38	134	34	39	53	6	1	2	13	2	0	32	1	25	18	4	.291
Sohns, Thomas, Billings*	71	263	41	77	101	10	1	4	39	2	3	33	1	21	12	4	.293
Strain, Joseph, Great Falls	71	282	63	94	124	13	7	1	50	1	3	44	0	17	32	1	.333
Stumpff, Steven, Great F*	54	138	24	38	46	3	1	1	24	0	4	42	2	15	1	0	.275
Sylvester, John, Great F	63	202	66	56	100	12	1	10	42	1	1	69	2	43	16	5	.277
Taylor, Goodrum, Idaho F*	58	192	56	58	73	7	4	0	21	3	1	50	0	44	13	9	.302
Tremba, Michael, Lethbridge	28	61	14	13	18	2	0	1	7	0	0	6	0	23	1	0	.213
Walker, John, Lethbridge	68	290	46	78	91	7	3	0	29	3	2	21	0	40	9	3	.269
Wardlow, Michael, Great F	53	195	36	55	78	11	0	4	34	3	6	20	4	62	9	2	.282
Washington, Lozando, G F	55	172	31	33	44	2	3	1	16	1	0	28	2	53	22	6	.192
Welch, Alfred, Billings	39	95	8	20	28	3	1	1	14	1	1	17	3	31	6	2	.211
Wolever, Marti, Billings	20	19	10	2	2	0	0	0	0	0	0	3	0	4	13	4	.105
Wood, W. Christopher, Leth	66	269	55	86	129	17	10	2	37	1	3	20	4	31	13	4	.320
Young, William, Great Falls	61	219	35	64	81	14	0	1	28	2	1	31	2	21	2	0	.292

The following pitchers had no plate appearances primarily through use of designated hitters, listed alphabetically by club, games in parentheses:

BILLINGS—Adams, R. Lee (13); Binkley, Randall (13); Breitenbach, Mark (11); Dawley, William (13); Frakes, Lawrence (21); Gosse, M. John (6); Hillas, John (1); Kelly, William (13); King, Mark (13); Lear, Rickey (4); Marquis, Jean (1); Meyer, Gregory (11); Niewczyk, James (3); Odum, Michael (18); Ortiz, J. Antonio (6); Stryker, Ronald (18); Syers, Clarence (3).

GREAT FALLS—Adams, Terry (14), Cosio, Raymundo (12); Glinatsis, Michael (4); Halls, Gary (7); Harper, Jonathan (17); Hartwig, Daniel (10); Johnson, Arthur (9); McKown, Steven (6); Mendoza, David (1); Myers, David (4); Pearce, Steven (8); Peterson, Timothy (13); Redd, Charles (12); Sherman, Steven (1); Snyder, Eric (10); Steen, Rick (10).

IDAHO FALLS—Adams, Richard (14); Ball, Jim (13); Boyd, Robert (10); Comstock, Keith (15); Eddy, Steven (11); Hanson, David (2); Johnson, Gregory (14); Lettrich, Stephen (9); Ruppenthal, Barry (7); Schrom, Kenneth (16); Sentlinger, Rick (6); Thomas, Lee (11); Wolfe, Jeffrey (16).

LETHBRIDGE—Bidigare, Mark (10); Brooks, Michael L. (11); Goodwin, Douglas (4); Hemm, K. Warren (21); James, Robert (3); Lindell, Richard (11); O'Connor, Jack (5); Palmer, David (13); Roberts, Carlton (12); Sullivan, Michael (11); Watkins, Robert (11); Weatherford, Robert (10).

GRAND-SLAM HOME RUNS—Cipolla, Ferrell, Fleury, Held, Simunic, 1 each.

AWARDED FIRST BASE ON INTERFERENCE—Brenly 2 (Jones 2), Cipolla (Ferrell), Hollifield (Norko).

CLUB FIELDING

Club	G.	PO.	A.	E.	DP.	PB.	Pct.	Club	G.	PO.	A.	E.	DP.	PB.	Pct.
Great Falls	71	1825	776	136	70	27	.950	Idaho Falls	72	1845	756	184	55	32	.934
Lethbridge	72	1828	821	142	64	10	.949	Billings	71	1808	708	186	50	35	.931

Triple Plays—None.

INDIVIDUAL FIELDING
FIRST BASEMEN

*Throws lefthanded.

Player and Club	G.	PO.	A.	E.	DP.	Pct.	Player and Club	G.	PO.	A.	E.	DP.	Pct.
LYONS, Idaho Falls*	65	541	37	5	39	.991	Stumpff, Great Falls*	52	371	27	7	38	.983
Held, Great Falls	24	172	6	2	17	.989	Fleury, Lethbridge*	21	148	13	3	11	.982
Young, Great Falls	14	79	10	1	13	.989	Jackson, Billings*	61	500	22	10	41	.981
Kopp, Lethbridge	55	475	33	9	42	.983	Jensen, Billings	16	87	3	2	4	.978

(Fewer Than Ten Games)

Player and Club	G.	PO.	A.	E.	DP.	Pct.	Player and Club	G.	PO.	A.	E.	DP.	Pct.
Schwartz, Great Falls	2	5	0	0	1	1.000	Bishop, Idaho Falls	9	46	2	2	9	.960
LaFave, Idaho Falls	1	3	0	0	1	1.000	Brouhard, Idaho Falls	1	1	1	1	0	.667

SECOND BASEMEN

Player and Club	G.	PO.	A.	E.	DP.	Pct.	Player and Club	G.	PO.	A.	E.	DP.	Pct.
STRAIN, Great Falls	71	152	194	17	49	.9531	Sohns, Billings	71	160	146	23	33	.930
Goldetsky, Lethbridge	70	199	182	19	47	.9525	Moore, Idaho Falls	41	96	86	16	18	.919
Slater, Idaho Falls	34	78	62	8	16	.946							

(Fewer Than Ten Games)

Player and Club	G.	PO.	A.	E.	DP.	Pct.	Player and Club	G.	PO.	A.	E.	DP.	Pct.
Harmon, Great Falls	1	1	1	0	1	1.000	Washington, Great F.	3	4	4	1	0	.889
Pimentel, Billings	1	1	1	0	0	1.000	Taylor, Idaho Falls	3	6	5	2	1	.846
Sanchez, Lethbridge	1	0	1	0	0	1.000	Robie, Billings	5	2	1	3	0	.500
Perez, Lethbridge	2	5	4	1	0	.900	McQuay, Billings	2	1	0	1	0	.500

THIRD BASEMEN

Player and Club	G.	PO.	A.	E.	DP.	Pct.	Player and Club	G.	PO.	A.	E.	DP.	Pct.
Perez, Lethbridge	32	29	65	7	6	.931	Moffitt, Idaho Falls	10	6	20	4	1	.867
Brenly, Great Falls	15	10	16	2	5	.929	Wardlow, Great Falls	30	22	53	14	6	.843
Young, Great Falls	36	33	66	8	5	.925	Bishop, Idaho Falls	29	25	54	16	4	.832
KOPSKY, Billings	60	51	114	23	13	.878	Moore, Idaho Falls	16	11	21	7	0	.821
Scoras, Lethbridge	31	28	63	13	5	.875	Robie, Billings	12	7	20	7	0	.794
Taylor, Idaho Falls	18	15	33	7	2	.873							

(Fewer Than Ten Games)

Player and Club	G.	PO.	A.	E.	DP.	Pct.	Player and Club	G.	PO.	A.	E.	DP.	Pct.
Held, Great Falls	2	3	2	0	0	1.000	Law, Billings	6	0	5	1	1	.833
Welch, Billings	1	0	1	0	0	1.000	Householder, Billings	2	2	3	2	0	.714
Carballo, Lethbridge	9	5	9	1	0	.933	Slater, Idaho Falls	5	1	6	3	1	.700
Sanchez, Lethbridge	5	7	7	1	0	.933	Pimentel, Billings	2	2	2	2	0	.667

SHORTSTOPS

Player and Club	G.	PO.	A.	E.	DP.	Pct.	Player and Club	G.	PO.	A.	E.	DP.	Pct.
KUECKER, Great Falls	51	68	166	19	35	.925	Taylor, Idaho Falls	15	18	39	7	2	.891
Walker, Lethbridge	68	95	212	26	36	.922	Robie, Billings	23	26	53	10	9	.888
Hendrickson, Idaho F.	60	95	193	31	31	.903	Law, Billings	16	18	46	11	7	.853
Dimino, Billings	38	40	108	17	10	.897	Wardlow, Great Falls	17	24	39	12	7	.840

SHORTSTOPS—Continued

(Fewer Than Ten Games)

Player and Club	G.	PO.	A.	E.	DP.	Pct.	Player and Club	G.	PO.	A.	E.	DP.	Pct.
Strain, Great Falls	2	1	3	0	0	1.000	Bonnell, Billings	5	7	12	3	1	.864
Bishop, Idaho Falls	1	2	2	0	0	1.000	Sanchez, Lethbridge	8	0	19	5	0	.792
Sohns, Billings	1	0	1	0	0	1.000	Moore, Idaho Falls	2	1	2	4	0	.429
Rex, Great Falls	4	4	15	2	1	.905							

OUTFIELDERS

Player and Club	G.	PO.	A.	E.	DP.	Pct.	Player and Club	G.	PO.	A.	E.	DP.	Pct.
Tremba, Lethbridge	26	26	2	0	0	1.000	Hollifield, Idaho F.*	68	130	6	7	0	.951
Scoras, Lethbridge	21	15	3	0	0	1.000	Gooch, Idaho Falls	57	94	3	5	1	.951
Taylor, Idaho Falls	18	15	0	0	0	1.000	Householder, Billings	46	72	5	4	0	.951
Wolever, Billings	11	13	0	0	0	1.000	Bishop, Idaho Falls	29	34	4	2	1	.950
WOOD, Lethbridge	65	146	5	3	0	.981	Brenly, Great Falls	11	13	5	1	0	.947
Parsons, Great Falls	19	50	3	1	0	.981	Shourds, Great Falls	28	47	3	3	0	.943
Newby, Lethbridge	66	107	6	3	0	.974	Herring, Billings	67	105	8	8	0	.934
Knose, Lethbridge	23	34	2	1	0	.973	Brouhard, Idaho Falls	24	45	1	4	0	.920
Paige, Great Falls	51	99	6	3	0	.972	Welch, Billings	29	32	4	4	0	.900
Washington, Great F.	49	83	3	3	1	.966	Pimentel, Billings	14	17	0	3	0	.850
Sylvester, Great F.	38	74	8	3	0	.965	Brown, Lethbridge	24	14	1	3	0	.833
Schwartz, Great F.	30	49	2	2	0	.962	Douglas, Idaho Falls	16	9	1	2	0	.833
Milner, Billings*	67	149	12	7	1	.958	LaFave, Idaho Falls	11	13	1	4	0	.778

(Fewer Than Ten Games)

Player and Club	G.	PO.	A.	E.	DP.	Pct.	Player and Club	G.	PO.	A.	E.	DP.	Pct.
Jones, Idaho Falls	3	4	0	0	0	1.000	Held, Great Falls	7	6	0	1	0	.857
Moffitt, Idaho Falls	3	3	0	0	0	1.000	Wardlow, Great Falls	2	5	0	1	0	.833
Brown, Idaho Falls	3	2	0	0	0	1.000	Carballo, Lethbridge	6	5	1	2	0	.750
Da Costa, Idaho Falls	3	1	0	0	0	1.000	Rodriguez, Billings	3	1	0	1	0	.500

CATCHERS

Player and Club	G.	PO.	A.	E.	DP.	PB.	Pct.	Player and Club	G.	PO.	A.	E.	DP.	PB.	Pct.
Meade, Billings	28	189	24	6	2	12	.973	Alicea, Billings	24	133	14	7	0	5	.955
Da Costa, Idaho F.	22	80	13	3	1	9	.969	Norko, Billings	24	114	7	6	0	13	.953
SIMUNIC, Leth.	60	379	56	15	1	5	.967	Jones, Idaho Falls	65	438	55	25	2	23	.952
Ferrell, Great F.	61	338	48	14	3	20	.965								

(Fewer Than Ten Games)

Player and Club	G.	PO.	A.	E.	DP.	PB.	Pct.	Player and Club	G.	PO.	A.	E.	DP.	PB.	Pct.
Jensen, Billings	6	23	5	0	0	3	1.000	Cipolla, Lethbridge	9	60	9	3	1	4	.958
Deal, Billings	7	25	2	0	0	2	1.000	Pryor, Great Falls	6	30	3	2	0	4	.943
Brown, Lethbridge	2	8	1	0	0	0	1.000	Held, Great Falls	4	21	2	1	0	0	.920
O'Donnell, Great F.	8	26	1	1	0	3	.964	Scoras, Lethbridge	3	7	1	1	0	1	.889

PITCHERS

Player and Club	G.	PO.	A.	E.	DP.	Pct.	Player and Club	G.	PO.	A.	E.	DP.	Pct.
ODUM, Billings*	18	4	14	0	0	1.000	Adams, Billings	13	1	6	1	0	.875
Breitenbach, Billings	11	4	7	0	1	1.000	Boyd, Idaho Falls	10	1	6	1	0	.875
Adams, Great Falls	14	4	5	0	0	1.000	Mercedes, Idaho F.	11	5	12	3	0	.850
Comstock, Idaho F.*	15	0	6	0	0	1.000	Hemm, Lethbridge*	21	5	17	4	2	.846
Harper, Great Falls	17	1	4	0	0	1.000	Meyer, Billings*	11	4	6	2	1	.833
Steen, Great Falls	10	0	4	0	0	1.000	Bidigare, Leth.*	10	1	4	1	0	.833
Thomas, Idaho Falls*	11	0	2	0	0	1.000	Wolfe, Idaho Falls	16	2	7	2	0	.813
Peterson, Great F.	13	7	12	1	2	.950	Kelly, Billings	13	4	9	3	1	.813
Roberts, Lethbridge*	12	1	17	1	1	.947	Schrom, Idaho Falls	16	2	6	2	2	.800
Frakes, Billings	21	2	12	1	0	.933	Binkley, Billings*	13	2	2	1	0	.800
Brooks, Lethbridge	11	3	23	2	1	.929	Lindell, Lethbridge	11	6	12	5	2	.783
Ball, Idaho Falls	13	3	9	1	0	.923	Hartwig, Great Falls	10	2	5	2	0	.778
Cosio, Great Falls	12	2	10	1	2	.923	Watkins, Lethbridge	11	2	8	3	0	.769
Sullivan, Lethbridge	11	6	15	2	2	.913	Palmer, Lethbridge	13	4	12	5	2	.762
Adams, Idaho Falls	14	4	17	2	1	.913	Dawley, Billings	10	0	3	1	0	.750
Redd, Great Falls*	12	0	10	1	0	.909	Snyder, Great Falls	10	1	12	5	0	.722
King, Billings	13	2	7	1	1	.900	Weatherford, Leth.	10	3	1	2	0	.667
Johnson, Idaho Falls	14	5	17	3	0	.880	Green, Lethbridge	25	3	3	5	1	.545
Eddy, Idaho Falls	11	4	17	3	1	.875	Stryker, Billings	18	1	5	5	1	

(Fewer Than Ten Games)

Player and Club	G.	PO.	A.	E.	DP.	Pct.	Player and Club	G.	PO.	A.	E.	DP.	Pct.
Johnson, Great Falls	9	4	6	0	0	1.000	Goodwin, Lethbridge	4	1	3	0	0	1.000
Myers, Great Falls	4	1	6	0	0	1.000	Syers, Billings	5	1	1	0	0	1.000
Sentlinger, Idaho F.	6	0	7	0	0	1.000	Sherman, Great F.*	1	0	2	0	0	1.000
O'Connor, Leth.*	5	1	3	0	1	1.000	Ruppenthal, Idaho F.	7	1	0	0	0	1.000

PITCHERS—Continued

Player and Club	G.	PO.	A.	E.	DP.	Pct.		Player and Club	G.	PO.	A.	E.	DP.	Pct.
Niewczyk, Billings*	3	1	0	0	0	1.000		Pearce, Great Falls	8	4	5	2	1	.818
Brown, Idaho Falls	2	1	0	0	0	1.000		Gosse, Billings*	6	0	2	1	0	.667
Mendoza, Great F.*	1	0	1	0	1	1.000		Lear, Billings	4	0	2	1	0	.667
Glinatsis, Great F.	4	4	6	1	0	.909		Ortiz, Billings*	6	0	2	2	0	.500
Halls, Great Falls	7	2	4	1	0	.857		James, Lethbridge	3	0	1	1	0	.500
Lettrich, Idaho F.	9	2	3	1	0	.833		Hanson, Idaho Falls	2	0	0	1	0	.000

The following players do not have any recorded accepted chances at the positions indicated; therefore, are not listed in the fielding averages for those particular positions: Alicea, 1b; Bonnell, 2b; Cipolla, of; Hillas, p; Jensen, of-p; Kuecker, 2b; Marquis, p; McKown, p; Wardlow, p.

CLUB PITCHING

Club	G.	CG.	ShO.	Sv.	IP.	H.	R.	ER.	HR.	BB.	Int. BB.	HB.	SO.	WP.	Bk.	ERA.
Great Falls	71	22	5	6	608	609	350	257	23	294	24	16	385	56	12	3.80
Billings	71	11	2	13	603	612	424	282	33	315	5	10	460	62	9	4.21
Lethbridge	72	19	1	11	609	688	434	333	22	361	9	23	437	41	8	4.92
Idaho Falls	72	18	2	15	615	663	462	345	24	404	19	28	504	74	9	5.05

PITCHERS' RECORDS

(Leading Qualifiers for Earned-Run Average Leadership—58 or More Innings)

*Throws lefthanded.

Pitcher—Club	G.	GS.	CG.	ShO.	W.	L.	Sv.	Pct.	IP.	H.	R.	ER.	HR.	BB.	Int. BB.	HB.	SO.	WP.	ERA.
Frakes, Billings	21	0	0	8	0	7	1.000	59	37	15	10	2	17	2	0	50	3	1.53
A. Johnson, GF	9	8	5	2	7	0	0	1.000	68	51	22	14	2	23	2	0	40	3	1.85
Dawley, Billings	13	12	3	0	6	4	0	.600	78	62	42	24	1	37	0	1	80	5	2.77
Eddy, Idaho Falls	11	10	4	0	4	4	0	.500	79	63	38	25	3	37	1	1	54	11	2.85
Lindell, Leth	11	11	4	0	4	5	0	.444	83	89	43	30	4	22	1	3	66	4	3.25
Adams, Idaho Falls	14	11	5	0	6	4	0	.600	82	90	47	30	0	31	2	2	78	8	3.29
Hartwig, Great F	10	9	2	1	4	4	0	.500	67	75	38	26	1	25	3	1	42	3	3.49
Stryker, Billings	18	5	2	0	1	3	1	.250	59	69	42	23	3	23	1	1	42	4	3.51
Hemm, Lethbridge*	21	6	3	0	4	3	3	.571	84	93	56	35	2	33	1	2	67	4	3.75
Peterson, Great F	13	10	4	1	4	5	0	.444	71	77	48	31	4	29	2	1	36	9	3.93

Departmental Leaders: G—Green, 25; GS—G. Johnson, 14; CG—Brooks, 6; ShO—A. Johnson, 2; W—Ball, Frakes, 8; L—King, 8; Sv—Frakes, 7; Pct.—Frakes, A. Johnson, 1.000; IP—G. Johnson, 91; H—Cosio, 101; R—King, 63; ER—G. Johnson, 46; HR—G. Johnson, Palmer, 6; BB—Ball, Roberts, 60; IBB—Comstock, 4; HB—Sullivan, 5; SO—G. Johnson, 84; WP—Adams (Billings), 15.

(All Pitchers—Listed Alphabetically)

Pitcher—Club	G.	GS.	CG.	ShO.	W.	L.	Sv.	Pct.	IP.	H.	R.	ER.	HR.	BB.	Int. BB.	HB.	SO.	WP.	ERA.
Adams, Idaho Falls	14	11	5	0	6	4	0	.600	82	90	47	30	0	31	2	2	78	8	3.29
Adams, Billings	13	0	0	0	4	0	0	.000	24	28	45	29	1	40	0	2	18	15	10.88
Adams, Great Falls	14	1	0	0	0	1	0	1.000	38	34	27	21	1	20	2	3	31	4	4.97
Ball, Idaho Falls	13	12	3	0	8	5	0	.615	73	75	54	42	1	60	2	4	41	9	5.18
Bidigare, Leth*	10	0	0	0	0	1	0	.000	19	17	14	9	0	23	0	3	17	2	4.26
Binkley, Billings*	13	3	0	0	2	1	1	.667	36	37	21	12	4	24	0	0	23	2	3.00
Boyd, Idaho Falls	10	10	2	0	4	1	0	.800	49	47	34	26	2	30	0	4	42	3	4.78
Breitenbach, Bil	11	7	0	0	1	1	0	.500	34	42	35	33	3	31	0	2	24	1	8.74
Brooks, Lethbridge	11	11	6	0	6	2	0	.750	86	96	54	40	4	41	0	1	46	4	4.19
Brown, Idaho Falls	2	0	0	0	0	0	0	.000	2	1	0	0	0	2	0	0	4	0	0.00
Comstock, Idaho F*	15	2	0	0	1	4	5	.200	37	33	18	16	1	32	4	0	45	2	3.89
Cosio, Great Falls	12	12	5	1	5	4	0	.556	85	101	49	39	3	39	2	1	46	7	4.13
Dawley, Billings	13	12	3	0	6	4	0	.600	78	62	42	24	1	37	0	1	80	5	2.77
Eddy, Idaho Falls	11	10	4	0	4	4	0	.500	79	63	38	25	3	37	1	1	54	11	2.85
Frakes, Billings	21	0	0	0	8	0	7	1.000	59	37	15	10	2	17	2	0	50	3	1.53
Glinatsis, Great F	4	4	1	0	4	0	0	1.000	32	26	15	10	0	18	3	3	18	2	2.81
Goodwin, Leth	4	1	0	0	0	0	0	.000	15	20	14	12	0	11	0	1	6	3	7.20
Gosse, Billings*	6	2	0	0	0	1	0	.000	18	29	20	7	1	6	0	0	16	2	3.50
Green, Lethbridge	25	0	0	0	4	4	6	.500	34	34	15	11	0	18	1	0	22	1	2.91
Halls, Great Falls	7	2	0	0	3	3	0	.500	40	37	15	12	3	11	3	3	27	1	2.70
Hanson, Idaho F	2	0	0	0	0	0	0	.000	4	5	6	4	0	4	0	0	1	2	9.00
Harper, Great F	17	1	0	0	3	4	4	.429	29	27	17	16	2	19	3	0	29	1	4.97
Hartwig, Great F	10	9	2	1	4	4	0	.500	67	75	38	26	1	25	3	1	42	3	3.49
Hemm, Lethbridge*	21	6	3	0	4	3	3	.571	84	93	56	35	2	33	1	2	67	4	3.75
Hillas, Billings	1	0	0	0	0	0	0	.000	1	3	2	0	0	0	0	2	...		...
James, Lethbridge	3	0	0	0	1	0	0	.000	8	7	8	4	0	9	0	0	11	1	4.50
Jensen, Billings	1	0	0	0	0	0	0	.000	6	7	4	0	0	1	0	0	1	0	0.00
A. Johnson, GF	9	8	5	2	7	0	0	1.000	68	51	22	14	2	23	2	0	40	3	1.85
G. Johnson, IF	14	14	3	1	6	3	0	.667	91	99	59	46	6	55	1	4	84	4	4.55
Kelly, Billings	13	13	4	0	6	4	0	.600	88	97	49	41	4	22	0	1	62	3	4.19

Pitcher–Club	G	GS	CG	ShO	W	L	Sv	Pct	IP	H	R	ER	HR	BB	Int. BB	HB	SO	WP	ERA
King, Billings	13	11	2	1	3	8	0	.273	65	69	63	38	4	38	1	1	41	13	5.26
Lear, Billings	4	0	0	0	0	1	0	.000	10	14	9	7	1	6	0	0	6	1	6.30
Lettrich, Idaho F	9	1	0	0	0	0	0	1.000	16	31	36	35	0	27	0	0	14	6	19.69
Lindell, Leth	11	11	4	0	4	5	0	.444	83	89	43	30	4	22	1	3	66	4	3.25
Marquis, Billings	1	0	0	0	0	0	0	.000	1	2	3	3	0	3	0	0	1	0	27.00
McKown, Great F	6	1	0	0	0	0	0	.000	12	18	11	9	2	9	0	0	5	3	6.75
Mendoza, Great F*	1	1	0	0	0	0	0	.000	5	7	1	1	0	3	0	0	5	0	1.80
Mercedes, Idaho F	11	5	0	0	4	3	1	.571	50	59	39	36	5	33	2	3	33	10	6.48
Meyer, Billings*	11	9	0	3	3	4	0	.429	46	48	35	26	2	32	0	0	31	6	5.09
Myers, Great Falls	4	4	2	0	4	0	0	1.000	34	26	13	11	1	18	0	3	27	3	2.91
Niewczyk, Bil*	3	0	0	0	1	1	0	.500	5	4	1	1	1	2	0	0	5	1	1.80
O'Connor, Leth*	5	4	0	0	2	3	0	.400	21	22	16	15	0	20	0	1	17	3	6.43
Odum, Billings*	18	1	0	0	4	1	3	.800	47	35	15	7	2	17	1	1	46	2	1.34
Ortiz, Leth*	6	0	0	0	0	0	0	.000	15	14	7	5	2	4	0	1	7	0	3.00
Palmer, Lethbridge	13	3	0	0	0	5	0	.000	45	58	49	36	6	28	2	4	44	1	7.20
Pearce, Great F	8	6	0	0	1	1	0	.500	30	25	28	17	1	32	0	0	18	6	5.10
Peterson, Great F	13	10	4	1	1	4	0	.200	45	58	34	28	2	22	3	0	31	4	5.60
Redd, Great Falls*	12	7	1	0	1	1	0	.500	77	83	48	41	1	60	0	1	46	11	4.79
Roberts, Leth*	12	12	2	1	5	5	0	.500	9	22	29	17	2	15	0	3	6	4	17.00
Ruppenthal, Ida F	7	1	0	0	1	5	5	.167	48	42	31	20	0	32	2	4	46	3	3.75
Schrom, Idaho F	16	4	1	0	1	0	5	1.000	18	14	11	5	0	12	2	0	16	4	2.50
Sentlinger, Ida F	6	0	0	0	1	0	0	1.000	5	5	2	2	0	4	0	0	6	0	3.60
Sherman, Great F*	1	1	0	0	1	4	1	.200	17	19	19	12	1	15	1	1	11	8	6.35
Snyder, Great F	10	2	1	0	3	1	1	.750	30	23	11	8	0	6	0	0	12	2	2.40
Steen, Great Falls	10	2	1	0	1	3	1	.250	59	69	42	23	3	23	1	1	42	4	3.51
Stryker, Billings	18	5	2	0	3	6	0	.333	74	84	50	41	2	48	1	5	61	3	4.99
Sullivan, Leth	11	4	0	0	0	3	0	.000	17	23	19	13	1	10	0	0	7	2	6.88
Syers, Billings*	5	5	0	0	0	3	0	.000	18	27	14	12	0	10	0	0	18	3	6.00
Thomas, Idaho F*	11	0	0	0	1	0	0	1.000	1	0	0	0	0	1	0	0	1	0	0.00
Wardlow, Great F	1	0	0	0	0	0	0	.000	2	3	2	2	0	2	0	0	0	0	9.00
Watkins, Leth	11	2	0	0	0	5	2	.000	23	36	19	16	1	16	2	0	20	2	6.26
Weatherford, Leth	10	8	0	0	2	5	0	.286	41	49	48	43	2	32	1	3	14	2	9.44
Wolfe, Idaho Falls	16	2	0	0	1	4	3	.200	40	55	46	30	4	24	3	3	22	5	6.75

BALKS—Redd, 4; Dawley, Hemm, King, 3 each; Adams (Billings), Brooks, Comstock, Hartwig, Roberts, Snyder, 2 each; Boyd, Breitenbach, Halls, Hanson, Harper, G. Johnson, Mercedes, Palmer, Pearce, Peterson, Ruppenthal, Thomas, Wolfe, 1 each.

COMBINATION SHUTOUTS—King-Breitenbach, Billings; Mercedes-Comstock, Idaho Falls.

NO-HIT GAMES—None.

Index to Minor League Clubs, Cities

Index to Contents

AMERICAN LEAGUE

NATIONAL LEAGUE

1976 Game Scores

1976 Game Scores

NATIONAL ASSOCIATION (MINOR LEAGUE) AVERAGES